SELWYN'S LAW OF EMPLOYMENT

SELWYN'S
LAW OF
EMPLOYMENT

Eighteenth Edition

ASTRA EMIR

MA (Oxon), LLM (Lond), Barrister-at-Law

OXFORD
UNIVERSITY PRESS

OXFORD
UNIVERSITY PRESS

Great Clarendon Street, Oxford, OX2 6DP,
United Kingdom

Oxford University Press is a department of the University of Oxford.
It furthers the University's objective of excellence in research, scholarship,
and education by publishing worldwide. Oxford is a registered trade mark of
Oxford University Press in the UK and in certain other countries

Fifteenth edition 2008
Sixteenth edition 2010
Seventeenth edition 2012

Impression: 1

Published in the United States of America by Oxford University Press
198 Madison Avenue, New York, NY 10016, United States of America

British Library Cataloguing in Publication Data
Data available

Library of Congress Control Number: 2014933489

ISBN 978–0–19–968155–6

Printed in Italy by L.E.G.O. S.p.A.

Preface

Since 1976, the aim of this book has been to set out employment law in a manner that is clear, readable and up-to-date. It is known for its ease of use and neutrality, dealing with employers and employees equally, and is aimed at all who have to advise on the subject, and in particular lawyers, students and human resources personnel.

The past few months have seen extensive changes in the employment law field. Some of the most far-reaching have been made by the Enterprise and Regulatory Reform Act 2014, such as the introduction of ACAS early conciliation when bringing a claim in the employment tribunal and the renaming of compromise agreements as settlement agreements (Chapter 20), employee shareholders as a new form of employment status (Chapter 2), various changes to the whistleblowing legislation (Chapter 10), the removal of third party harassment and abolition of the discrimination questionnaire procedure (Chapter 4) and changes to the Health and Safety at Work Act 1974 removing the right of civil action against employers for breach of statutory duty other than where such a right is specifically provided for (Chapter 11). Changes have also been made to employment tribunal procedure, by the implementation of The Employment Tribunals (Constitution and Rules of Procedure) Regulations 2013 and The Employment Appeal Tribunal (Amendment) Rules 2013), and also changes made by the new costs regime in such tribunals (Chapter 20). Further reforms have been made to TUPE by the Collective Redundancies and Transfer of Undertakings (Protection of Employment) (Amendment) Regulations 2014 (Chapter 9), the consultation period for redundancies (Chapter 18), parental leave and flexible working (Chapter 6), the introduction of the Health at Work Assessment and Advisory Service (HWAS) (Chapter 1) and the renaming of the Criminal Records Bureau to Disclosure and Barring Service (Chapter 4). Expected future changes relate to the proposed new Children Act and changes to the parental and paternity leave systems (which may come into force in 2015), and the power to order mandatory equal pay audits (expected late 2014). The text has, of course, also been generally updated, with up-to-date case law and legislation. In addition, there is a revised and extended index, designed to make the text easier to use.

The figures for statutory payments, a week's pay, etc. are up to date as of April 2014. The latest figures will be found on the Online Resource Centre at www.oxfordtextbooks.co.uk/orc/selwyn18e/. This is updated at least twice a year, in a handy chapter-by-chapter format, and has the latest cases and legislation to complement the text.

I would like to thank all at Oxford University Press for their work on this book. I would also in particular like to thank Judith Selwyn for her kindness and support and, as always, my family.

Astra Emir

For Hannah, Bibi, Simon, and Jasmine (MJM)

Contents

Table of Statutes   xx

Table of Statutory Instruments   xxix

Table of European Legislation   xxxiii

Table of International Treaties and Conventions   xxxiv

Table of Cases   xxxv

1   The Institutions of Employment Law   1

Advisory, Conciliation and Arbitration Service   1
    A.   Advice   1
    B.   Conciliation   2
    C.   Arbitration   3
    D.   Enquiries   4
    E.   Codes of Practice   5

Certification Officer (TULR(C)A, s 254)   5

Central Arbitration Committee   6

Employment Appeal Tribunal (Employment Tribunals Act 1996, ss 20–37)   6

Employment tribunals   8
    A.   Territorial jurisdiction   11
    B.   Legal aid   13
    C.   Claims for breach of contract   13
    D.   Mediation   14

Industrial training boards   15

Equality and Human Rights Commission   15

Health and Safety Executive   16

Health and Work Advisory and Assessment Service   16

Low Pay Commission   17

The role of the government   17

Codes of practice   17

Supreme Court   18

The impact of the European Union   18
    A.   Treaty of Rome   18
    B.   Treaty of Lisbon   18
    C.   Expansion of the EU   19
    D.   EU institutions   19

European Union law   20
    A.   Articles of the Treaty   20
    B.   Directives   21
    C.   Recommendations   27
    D.   Decisions of the Court of Justice of the European Union   27

Human Rights Act 1998   28

2 The Nature of a Contract of Employment — 35

Parties to a contract of employment — 35
  A. Employers — 36
  B. Directors — 37
  C. Business consultants — 39
  D. Partners — 39
  E. Workers — 40
  F. Employees — 41
  G. Employee shareholders — 42

Distinction between employees and self-employed persons — 43
  A. Contract of service — 43
  B. Why the distinction is important — 49

Other categories of parties to a contract of employment — 51
  A. Office holders — 51
  B. Ministers of religion — 52
  C. Crown employees — 53
  D. Armed forces — 54
  E. Health service employees — 54
  F. Police — 54
  G. Those employees with special legal status — 55
  H. Temporary employees — 56
  I. Part-time workers — 56
  J. Probationary employees — 59
  K. Trainees — 60
  L. Civil partnerships — 60
  M. Apprentices — 61
  N. Those under the age of 18 — 61
  O. Domestic servants — 63
  P. Foreign employees — 63
  Q. Posted workers — 65
  R. Working abroad — 65
  S. Offshore employment — 66
  T. Retainers — 66
  U. Fixed-term contracts — 67
  V. Secondment of employees — 70
  W. Agency workers — 72
  X. Casual workers and global contracts — 77
  Y. National security (ERA, s 193) — 78

3 The Formation of a Contract of Employment — 79

The contract of employment — 79

Terms and conditions — 83
  A. Interpretation of terms — 84
  B. Express terms — 85
  C. Implied terms — 86
  D. Statutory terms — 91
  E. Collective agreements — 91
  F. Custom as a source of employment terms — 99
  G. Works/staff rules — 101

Other aspects of the contract of employment   103
  A. Disciplinary and grievance procedures   103
  B. Job description   104
  C. Variation of contractual terms   104
  D. Written particulars of the contract of employment   108
  E. Itemised pay statement (Employment Rights Act 1996, ss 8–10)   110
  F. Holidays   111
  G. Occupational pension schemes   111

4 Equality in Employment   113

Introduction   113
  A. Repeals and revocations   114

Key concepts   114
  A. Protected characteristics (ss 4–12, 18)   114
  B. Prohibited conduct (ss 13–27)   115

Prohibited conduct   115
  A. Direct discrimination (s 13)   115
  B. Motive for direct discrimination   116
  C. Indirect discrimination (s 19)   118
  D. Comparators (s 23)   118
  E. Discriminator's characteristics (s 24)   119
  F. Harassment (s 26)   120
  G. Victimisation (s 27)   121

Discrimination in employment   122
  A. Discrimination and victimisation in employment: s 39(1)–(4)   122
  B. Occupational requirements (Sch 9)   124
  C. Employer harassment (s 40)   124

Protected characteristics/prohibited conduct   125
  A. Age   125
  B. Disability   128
  C. Gender reassignment   136
  D. Marriage and civil partnership   136
  E. Pregnancy and maternity   137
  F. Race   139
  G. Religion or belief   142
  H. Sex   144
  I.   Sexual orientation   148

Common provisions   149
  A. Application of the Act   149
  B. Lawful discrimination (Sch 22)   150
  C. Illegal contracts   150
  D. Relationships that have ended (s 108)   150
  E. Liability of employers (s 109)   150
  F. Instructing, causing or inducing discrimination (s 111)   151
  G. Aiding contraventions (s 112)   152
  H. Positive action; recruitment and promotion (s 159)   152
  I.   Discriminatory advertisements   152
  J. Job advertisements   153
  K. Conduct giving rise to separate proceedings (s 140)   153

L. Unenforceable terms (s 142)   153
M. Restriction on contracting out (s 144)   153
N. Void and unenforceable terms (s 145)   154
O. National security (s 192)   154
P. Death of a claimant   154
Q. Other provisions   154

Submitting a complaint   154
A. Jurisdiction (s 120)   154
B. Time limits (s 123)   155
C. Burden of proof (s 136)   156
D. Transfer of proceedings (s 140)   156
E. Remedies (s 124)   157
F. Interest on awards (s 139)   158

Enforcement by the Commission: Equality Act 2006   158

Other protected groups   159
A. Rehabilitated persons   159
B. Access to criminal records   161
C. Unfair recruitment (TULR(C)A, s 137)   162
D. Employment of women   162
E. Employment of young persons   163
F. Adult workers   163

5 **Equal Pay**   164
Equality of terms (Equality Act ss 64–79)   165
Sex equality clause (s 66)   167
Equal work (s 65)   168
A. Like work (s 65)   168
B. Work rated as equivalent (s 65(4))   170
C. Work of equal value (s 65(6))   171
Defence of material factor (s 69)   172
Sex discrimination in relation to contractual pay (s 71)   174
Maternity equality clause (s 73)   174
Pay structures etc   175
Discussions about pay (s 77)   175
Gender pay gap information (s 78)   175
Equal pay audit   175
Jurisdiction (s 127)   175
Burden of proof (s 136)   176
Time limits (s 129)   176
Remedies (s 132)   176
Death of a claimant   177
Backdating awards   177

6 **Family Friendly Rights**   178
Maternity rights   178
A. Time off work for antenatal care (ERA, ss 55–57)   178

    B.   Risk assessment and suspension on maternity grounds   179
    C.   Maternity leave (ERA, ss 71–74, Maternity and Parental
          Leave etc Regulations 1999 as amended)   181
    D.   Remedies   187
    E.   Statutory Maternity Pay (SMP)   189
    F.   Maternity Allowance (Social Security Contributions and Benefits Act 1992)   190

Adoption leave (Paternity and Adoption Leave Regulations 2002)   190
    A.   Reasonable contact   191
    B.   Work during the adoption leave period   191
    C.   Returning to work after adoption leave   191
    D.   Remedies   192
    E.   Statutory adoption pay (SAP)   192

**Parental leave (Maternity and Parental Leave Regulations 1999–2001,
regs 13–21)**   192

Paternity rights and adoption leave   194
    A.   Paternity leave (Paternity and Adoption Leave Regulations 2002, as amended)   194
    B.   Statutory paternity pay (SPP)   195
    C.   Additional paternity leave   196

To care for dependants (ERA, s 57A)   198

Flexible working arrangements (ERA, ss 80F–80I)   199
    A.   Application for flexible working   200

Future proposals   202

7 Employment Protection   203

Guarantee payments (ERA, ss 28–35)   203

Suspension on medical grounds (ERA, ss 64–65)   204

Time off work   205
    A.   For public duties (ERA, s 50)   205
    B.   For occupational pension scheme trustees (ERA, s 58)   207
    C.   For employee representatives (ERA, s 61)   207
    D.   For young person for study or training (ERA, s 63A)   208
    E.   Time off for study or training (ERA, s 63D)   208
    F.   Other time off work   210

Statutory sick pay (SSP)   210
    A.   How the scheme works   210
    B.   Qualifying conditions   211
    C.   Exclusions from entitlement   212
    D.   Enforcement   212
    E.   Self-certification of illness   213

Working Time Regulations 1998 (as amended)   213
    A.   The regulations   213
    B.   The main provisions   214
    C.   Exclusions   220
    D.   Enforcement   222
    E.   Sunday trading   225
    F.   Christmas shopping   226
    G.   Jury service (Juries Act 1974)   226
    H.   Armed Forces Reserves   227

I.	Access to medical reports	228
J.	Rights in insolvency (Insolvency Act 1986, s 386, Sch 6)	228
K.	Payments from the National Insurance Fund (ERA, ss 182–189)	229
L.	Post-employment detriment	230

8 Protection of Wages 231

General restrictions on unauthorised deductions
and payments (ERA, ss 13, 15) 232
A.	Statutory deduction	232
B.	Contractual authorisation	232
C.	Written consent	233

What are 'wages'? (ERA, s 27(1)) 234

What are not 'wages'? (ERA, s 27(2)) 235

What is a deduction? (ERA, s 13(3)) 236

Excepted deductions and excepted payments (ERA, ss 14, 16) 237

Deductions and payments in retail employment (ERA, ss 17–18) 239

Complaints to an employment tribunal (ERA, s 23) 240

National minimum wage 240
A.	Who qualifies for the national minimum wage	241
B.	Calculating the hourly rate (reg 14)	241
C.	Enforcement by the worker	243
D.	Enforcement by the state	244
E.	Offences (ERA, ss 31–33)	245

9 Transfer of Undertakings 246

Background 246

Who is covered by the regulations? 247
A.	Transfer of an undertaking or business	248
B.	Transfer of part of a business	249
C.	Service provision change (reg 3(1)(b))	250
D.	Transfers within public administration (reg 3(5))	252
E.	Employees who work outside the United Kingdom (reg 3(4))	252

The mechanics of the transfer 252

The effect of the transfer 253
A.	Contracts of employment (reg 4)	253
B.	Statutory rights	255
C.	Other benefits	255
D.	Variation of the contract of employment (reg 4(4))	257
E.	Insolvency rights (reg 8)	258
F.	Permitted variations in insolvency proceedings (reg 9)	258

Dismissal on transfers (reg 7) 259
A.	ETO reason (regs 4, 7)	260

Refusing a transfer (reg 4(7)) 261

Employee liability information (regs 11–12) 262

Remedy for failure to notify employee liability information (reg 12) 263

Other matters 264
A.	Collective agreements (reg 5)	264

B. Trade union recognition (reg 6) 264
C. Consultation on transfers (reg 13) 264
D. Election of employee representatives (reg 14) 265
E. Failure to inform or consult (reg 15) 265

10 Performance of the Contract of Employment 267
Personal nature of the contract 267
Implied duties of the employer 269
A. Implied duty of trust and confidence 269
B. Duty to provide work 271
C. Duty to pay wages or other remuneration when there is no work 272
D. Payment of bonuses, etc 273
E. Duty of confidentiality 275
F. Duty to indemnify 276
G. Duty to insure 276
H. References 277
I. The right to privacy 279
J. Duty to ensure the employee's safety 280
Implied obligations of the employee 280
A. Duty of faithful service 280
B. Duty to obey lawful and reasonable orders 282
C. Duty to use skill and care 284
D. Secret bribes and commissions 285
E. Confidential information 285
F. Public interest disclosures (ERA, ss 43A–43K) 287
G. Patents, inventions and copyright 290
H. 'Moonlighting' 291
I. Duty of disclosure 292
J. The volcano effect 293
Employer's vicarious liability 294
Harassment and bullying 296

11 Health and Safety at Work 299
Health and Safety at Work etc. Act 1974 299
A. Background to the legislation 299
B. Enforcement of the Act 300
C. Statutory duties on health, safety and welfare 304
D. Health and safety regulations (s 15 and Sch 3) 314
E. The impact of European law 315
F. Codes of practice (s 16) 318
G. Penalties (s 33) 318
H. Burden of proof 319
I. Corporate manslaughter 320
Compensation for injuries at work 321
A. The extent of the duty owed 321
B. Duty to unborn children 324
C. Personal nature of the duty 325
D. The threefold nature of the duty 326
E. Breach of statutory duty 329

F.   Defences to an action for personal injuries   332
G.   Limitation of actions (Limitation Act 1980)   335

12 Disciplinary, Dismissal and Grievance Procedures   336

Disciplinary procedures   336
A.   Procedures in operation   336
B.   Types of disciplinary and grievance procedures   339
C.   Drawing up procedures   340
D.   Composition of procedural bodies   341
E.   Right to be accompanied: Employment Relations Act 1999, ss 10–15   344
F.   Appeal procedures   346

Disciplinary rules   348
A.   General rules   350
B.   Specific rules   350
C.   Special rules   351

Disciplinary powers   351
A.   Fines and deductions   352
B.   Suspension without pay for misconduct   352
C.   Precautionary suspension   353
D.   Warnings   355
E.   Reprimand   358
F.   Demotion   359
G.   Transfer   359
H.   Alternative employment   359
I.   Other sanctions   360
J.   Non-employment situations   360

13 Continuous Employment   361

Continuity of employment   361

Counting and computing continuity (ERA, ss 210–219)   362

Preserving continuity (s 212)   363
A.   Incapable of work because of sickness or injury (s 212(3)(a))   364
B.   Absent from work on account of a temporary cessation of work (s 212(3)(b)) 365
C.   Absent by arrangement or custom (s 212(3)(c))   367

Re-employment after unfair dismissal (s 219)   368

Weeks which do not count towards continuity (ss 215–217)   369
A.   Periods spent working abroad (s 215(1))   369
B.   Strikes and lock-outs (s 216)   369
C.   Military service (s 217)   370

Change of employer (s 218)   370

The effect of the continuity rules   371

Continuity table   372

14 Normal Working Hours and a Week's Pay   374

Normal working hours   374
A.   Employment Rights Act, ss 221–229   374
B.   Contractual provisions   374

A week's pay   375
   A. Quantifying a week's pay   376
   B. Capping a week's pay (ERA, s 227)   377
   C. The calculation date (ERA, ss 225–226)   377

15 Rights in Notice   379
Notice to be given by the employer   379
   A. Giving notice   380
   B. Taxation of payments   381
   C. Pay in lieu of notice   381
   D. Rights during the notice period (ERA, ss 88–91)   382
   E. Contractual rights during notice   384
   F. Dispensing with notice   384
   G. Notice and time limits   385
   H. Notice pay on insolvency (ERA, ss 182–186)   386
Notice to be given by the employee   387
Employer's remedies   387
Employee's remedies   388

16 Wrongful Dismissal   389
Background   389
Wrongful dismissal   390
Collateral contracts   392
Summary dismissal   392
Employment law remedies   394
   A. Common law remedies   394
   B. Public law remedies   399

17 Unfair Dismissal   401
Exclusions   401
What is a dismissal? (ERA, s 95)   403
   A. Employer termination   403
   B. Fixed-term contract expires   406
   C. Completion of a limited-term contract   406
   D. Constructive dismissal   406
Termination of the contract   413
   A. Resignation   413
   B. Constructive resignation   414
   C. Implied resignation   415
   D. Frustration of the contract   415
   E. Consensual termination   417
Fair and unfair dismissal (ERA, s 98)   418
   A. Is it fair?   418
   B. Reasons for the dismissal   422
   C. Dismissal for asserting a statutory right (ERA, s 104) 441
   D. Other dismissals   442
   E. National security   443

Written reasons for dismissal (ERA, s 92)   443
  A. Adequacy of the statement   443
  B. Written reasons for dismissal on grounds of maternity or
     adoption (ERA, s 92(4), (4A))   444

Interim relief (ERA, ss 128–132)   444

Remedies for unfair dismissal   444
  A. Reinstatement and re-engagement orders (ERA, s 113)   444
  B. Compensation (ss 117–127A)   447
  C. Compensatory award (ERA, s 123)   449
  D. Reducing the compensatory award (ERA, s 123(4), (6))   455
  E. Order of adjustments to compensation awards   459
  F. Additional award (ERA, s 117)   459
  G. Interest on awards   460
  H. Recoupment of job-seekers' allowance   460

18 Redundancy   461

Provisions of the Employment Rights Act 1996   461
  A. Persons covered by the Act   461
  B. What is dismissal? (s 136)   462
  C. Dismissal for reason of redundancy (s 139)   463
  D. Transferred redundancy   466
  E. Presumption of redundancy   467
  F. Renewal or re-engagement (ERA, s 138)   467
  G. Offer of suitable alternative employment (s 141)   468
  H. Laying off and short-time working (s 147)   469
  I. Time off to look for work (ERA, s 52)   470

Fair/unfair redundancy dismissals   470
  A. Guidelines for good industrial relations practice   470
  B. Handling redundancies   471
  C. Unfair selection for redundancy (ERA, s 105)   475
  D. Dismissal during the period of notice (s 140)   476

Excluded classes of employees   476

Claims for redundancy payments   477

Payments by the Secretary of State (ERA, ss 166–170)   477

Consultation on redundancies (TULR(C)A, ss 188–192)   478
  A. EC Directive on Collective Redundancies   478
  B. Who, and when to consult   478

What is an establishment?   480

The consultation provisions   480
  A. Disclosures required by the employer   482
  B. Special circumstances   482
  C. Protective award (TULR(C)A, s 189)   483

Notification of mass redundancies to the minister (TULR(C)A, s 193)   485

19 Duties of Ex-employees   486

Employees who are about to leave their employment   486

Garden leave   488

Employees who have left their employment 489
   A. Springboard injunctions 492
Post-employment restraints 492
   A. Trade secrets and confidential information 493
   B. Existing customers and connections 494
   C. Working for competitors 496
   D. Enticing existing employees 497
   E. Reasonableness of the covenant 497
   F. Interpreting a covenant in restraint of trade 499
   G. Breach of contract by the employer 500
   H. Restrictive covenants and transfers 501
   I. Remedies for breach of contract 501
Training agreements 503

20 Practice and Procedure 504

Making a claim to an employment tribunal 504
   A. Time limits for enforcing Community rights 508
   B. Effective date of termination (s 97) 509
   C. Restrictions on contracting out (ERA, s 203) 511
Employment tribunal procedure 515
   A. Submitting a claim 515
   B. Tribunal fees 516
   C. Employer's response 516
   D. Initial consideration of claim and response 517
   E. Preliminary hearings 517
   F. Case management 518
   G. The final hearing 521
   H. Allegations of bias 525
   I. Financial remedies 526
   J. Reconsideration of judgment 527
   K. Costs 528
   L. Preparation time order 529
   M. Wasted costs order 529
   N. Death of the employer or employee 530
   O. Appeals 530
   P. Reviews by the Employment Appeal Tribunal 534
   Q. Vexatious litigants (Employment Tribunals Act 1996, s 33) 534
   R. Further appeals 534

21 Individual Trade Union Rights 535

Rights vis-à-vis a trade union 535
   A. Right not to be excluded from any trade union (TULR(C)A, s 174) 535
   B. Right not to be unjustifiably disciplined (TULR(C)A, ss 64–65) 536
   C. Complaints of unjustifiable discipline (TULR(C)A, ss 66–67) 538
   D. Right to resign from a trade union (TULR(C)A, s 69) 538
   E. Right not to be expelled from the union (TULR(C)A, s 174) 539
   F. Remedies for wrongful exclusion or expulsion (TULR(C)A, ss 175–176) 539
   G. Right of access to the courts (TULR(C)A, s 63) 539
   H. Right to a ballot before industrial action (TULR(C)A, s 62) 540
   I. Other individual rights 540

Rights vis-à-vis an employer 540
  A. Access to employment (TULR(C)A, s 137) 541
  B. Inducements relating to union membership or activities (TULR(C)A, s 145A) 544
  C. Action short of dismissal (TULR(C)A, s 146, as amended) 544
  D. Detriment and dismissal in statutory recognition cases (TULR(C)A, Sch A1) 547
  E. Time off work for trade union duties (TULR(C)A, s 168) 548
  F. Time off work for trade union activities (TULR(C)A, s 170) 549
  G. Time off work for trade union learning representatives (TULR(C)A, s 168A) 549
  H. Check-off arrangements (TULR(C)A, s 68) 550
  I. Deductions for the political fund of the union (s 86) 550
  J. Dismissal on the ground of trade union membership or non-membership,
     or trade union activities (TULR(C)A, s 152) 551
  K. Dismissal in connection with industrial action (TULR(C)A, ss 237–239) 552
  L. Dismissal due to industrial pressure (ERA, s 107) 557
  M. Selection for dismissal on grounds of redundancy (TULR(C)A, s 153) 558
  N. Compensations for dismissals (TULR(C)A, ss 155–158) 558
  O. Interim relief for dismissed trade unionists or non-unionists (TULR(C)A, ss 161–166) 558

22 The Law Relating to Trade Unions 560
What constitutes a trade union? 560
  A. Definition of a trade union (TULR(C)A, s 1) 560
  B. Listing of trade unions (TULR(C)A, s 2) 561
  C. Certification of trade unions (TULR(C)A, s 6) 561
  D. Register of members (s 24) 564
Rules of a trade union 565
  A. Disciplinary action 566
  B. Conduct of union affairs 568
  C. Copy of the rules (s 27) 569
Executive committee (TULR(C)A, s 46) 569
  A. Election of candidates (TULR(C)A, s 47) 570
  B. Election addresses (TULR(C)A, s 48) 570
  C. Independent scrutineer (ss 49, 75, 100A, 226B) 571
  D. Remedies (s 54) 572
Accounts, records, etc (TULR(C)A, s 28) 572
  A. Right to inspect accounts (ss 29–31) 572
Offences (ss 45–45C) 573
  A. Indemnifying unlawful conduct (s 15) 573
  B. Remedies against trustees (s 16) 574
Political fund and political objects (TULR(C)A, ss 71–74) 574
  A. Complaints over political fund ballots (TULR(C)A, ss 79–81) 575
Breach of union rules (ss 108A–108B) 576
Amalgamation and transfers (ss 97–105) 576
Employers' associations 577
  A. Definition of employers' association (TULR(C)A, s 122) 577
  B. Listing of employers' associations (TULR(C)A, s 123) 577

23 Law Relating to Industrial Relations 578
Trade union recognition 578
  A. Voluntary recognition 578

B.	Statutory recognition (TULR(C)A, Sch A1)	579
C.	Employers' training policies (TULR(C)A, s 70B)	580

Collective bargaining (TULR(C)A, Sch A1, para 94) — 581
A.	Disclosure of information (TULR(C)A, s 181)	581
B.	Legal liabilities and legal proceedings	582

Statutory protections — 584
A.	'Trade dispute' (TULR(C)A, s 244)	585
B.	'In contemplation of'	587
C.	'In furtherance of'	587

Statutory protection and loss of immunities — 588
A.	The provisions of TULR(C)A, s 219	588
B.	Loss of immunities	589
C.	Immunity of trade unions (TULR(C)A, s 20)	596
D.	The effect of the Act	597

Amount of damages (TULR(C)A, s 22) — 597

Injunctions and interdicts (TULR(C)A, s 221) — 598
A.	Injunctive relief (TULR(C)A, s 20(6))	598
B.	Industrial action affecting an individual (s 235A)	599
C.	Industrial action and European law	599

Legal effect of collective agreements (TULR(C)A, ss 178–179) — 600

Peaceful picketing (TULR(C)A, s 220) — 601
A.	Sit-in	603

Union recognition — 604
A.	Union or non-union members only contracts (TULR(C)A, s 144)	604
B.	Prohibition on union recognition requirements (TULR(C)A, s 186)	604
C.	Refusal to deal on union exclusion grounds (TULR(C)A, s 187)	604

Criminal liabilities — 605
A.	Public Order Act 1986	606
B.	Intentional harassment	606

European Works Councils — 606
A.	Time off work for members of a European Works Council (regs 25–27)	608
B.	Protection from detriment and dismissal (regs 28–33)	608
C.	Information and Consultation of Employees Regulations 2004	609
D.	Pre-existing agreements (regs 8–9)	609
E.	Negotiated agreements (reg 7)	610
F.	Statutory default provisions (reg 18)	611
G.	Enforcement (reg 22)	612

Appendices — 613

Appendix A Monetary awards (as at 1 February 2014) — 614

Appendix B Statutory Redundancy Pay Calculation Table — 616

Index — 619

Table of Statutes

Access to Medical Reports Act 1988 . . . 7.128
Adoption and Children Act 2002 . . . 6.84
Agricultural Wages Act 1948 . . . 8.39
Agricultural Wages (Scotland) Act 1949 . . . 8.39
Apportionment Act 1870 . . . 8.10
   s 2 . . . 10.100
Apprenticeship, Skills, Children and Learning Act
   2009 . . . 2.105, 7.29
Arbitration Act 1996 . . . 1.13
Attachment of Earnings Act 1971 . . . 8.5

Bribery Act 2010 . . . 10.68
   s 1 . . . 10.68
   s 2 . . . 10.68
   s 6 . . . 10.68
   s 7 . . . 10.68

Child Support Act 1991 . . . 8.5
Children Act 1989
   s 3 . . . 6.84
Children (Scotland) Act 1995
   s 1(3) . . . 6.84
Children and Young Persons Act 1933 . . . 2.110
Children and Young Persons Act 1963 . . . 2.110
Children and Young Persons (Scotland) Act 1937
   . . . 2.110
Christmas Day and New Year's Day Trading
   (Scotland) Act 2007 . . . 7.119
Christmas Day (Trading) Act 2004 . . . 7.119
Civil Evidence Act 1968
   s 11 . . . 11.31
Civil Jurisdiction and Judgments
   Act 1982 . . . 2.121
Civil Partnership Act 2004 . . . 2.102, 4.123, 4.124
Companies Act 2006
   s 188 . . . 2.10
   s 228 . . . 2.10, 2.11
Compensation Act 2006 . . . 11.143
Congenital Disabilities (Civil Liability) Act 1976
   . . . 11.114
Constitutional Reform Act 2005 . . . 1.60
Consumer Protection Act 1987
   Sch 3 . . . 11.7
Contempt of Court Act 1981
   s 19 . . . 1.24
Continental Shelf Act 1964 . . . 11.3, 17.4
Contract (Applicable Law) Act 1990 . . . 2.121
Copyright, Designs and Patents Act 1988 . . .
   10.90
   s 11 . . . 10.90
Corporate Manslaughter and Corporate
   Homicide Act 2007 . . . 11.99, 11.101
Criminal Justice and Public Order Act 1994

   s 126 . . . 17.4
   s 126(1) . . . 2.73
   s 127 . . . 23.123
   s 154 . . . 23.130

Data Protection Act 1998 . . . 10.26, 10.27
Disability Discrimination Act 1995 . . . 1.93, 4.8,
   4.16, 4.102
Dock Work Act 1989 . . . 2.76

Education Act 1918
   s 14 . . . 2.110
Education Act 1996
   s 559 . . . 2.110
Education Reform Act 1988
   s 203 . . . 2.76
Education (Work Experience) Act 1973
   s 1 . . . 2.111
Employers' Liability Act 1880 . . . 2.106
Employers' Liability (Compulsory Insurance)
   Act 1969 . . . 11.123
Employers' Liability (Defective Equipment)
   Act 1969 . . . 11.123
Employment Act 1980 . . . 23.76
Employment Act 1982 . . . 23.30
Employment Act 1989
   s 1 . . . 4.257
   ss 1–7 . . . 4.8
   s 4 . . . 4.256
   s 9 . . . 4.8, 4.255
   s 11 . . . 17.148
   Sch 1 . . . 4.256
Employment Act 2002 . . . 3.116, 6.130, 14.11
   s 38 . . . 3.122, 17.237
Employment Act 2008 . . . 21.3
Employment Agencies Act 1973 . . . 1.28
Employment Protection Act 1975 . . . 1.1, 1.6,
   16.2, 22.5, 23.3
   s 99 . . . 18.69
Employment Protection (Consolidation) Act
   1978 . . . 16.2
Employment Relations Act 1999 . . . 1.19, 1.28,
   14.11, 23.5
   s 10 . . . 12.23
   Sch 8 . . . 2.68
Employment Relations Act 2004 . . . 21.49, 23.48
Employment Rights Act 1996 . . . 1.28, 1.90, 2.67,
   2.68, 2.71, 2.73, 2.125, 2.142, 2.172, 3.56, 4.67,
   4.211, 4.214, 4.232, 4.242, 6.2, 7.1, 8.22, 8.46,
   9.61, 10.20, 10.37, 14.1, 14.2, 16.2, 16.6, 17.4,
   17.4, 17.20, 18.2
   Pt II . . . 2.24, 8.3, 8.33
   Pt IVA . . . 2.24

Pt V ... 7.139
Pt X ... 21.63
s 1 ... 2.120, 3.52, 3.62, 3.63, 3.93, 3.112, 3.114, 3.116, 3.119, 3.120, 3.122, 3.125, 13.9, 13.43
ss 1–10 ... 1.84
s 1(1) ... 3.112
s 1(2) ... 3.112
s 1(4)(e) ... 15.2
s 1(4)(k) ... 2.120
s 3 ... 3.115, 3.116
s 3(1) ... 3.114
s 4(1) ... 3.117, 3.122
s 7A ... 3.116
s 7B ... 3.116
ss 8–10 ... 3.123
s 10 ... 12.26, 12.32
s 11 ... 1.25, 3.122, 12.32
s 12 ... 12.33
s 13 ... 3.35, 8.4, 8.17, 8.18, 8.23, 8.27, 12.31, 17.169, 18.37
ss 13–15 ... 10.101
ss 13–17 ... 8.31
ss 13–27 ... 2.28, 8.3
s 13(1) ... 15.35
s 13(3) ... 8.18, 8.21
s 13(4) ... 8.21
s 14 ... 8.23
s 14(1)(a) ... 8.23
s 14(1)(b) ... 8.23
s 14(2) ... 8.23
s 14(3) ... 8.23
s 14(4) ... 8.23
s 14(5) ... 8.23
s 14(6) ... 8.23
s 15 ... 8.4, 12.31
s 16 ... 8.23
s 17 ... 8.24, 8.27
s 17(4) ... 8.26
s 18 ... 8.24, 8.27, 12.57
s 19 ... 8.26
s 19(1) ... 15.28
s 20 ... 8.28
s 20(1) ... 8.31
s 21(1) ... 8.31
s 23 ... 1.25, 8.31, 8.48, 12.58, 21.56
s 25 ... 8.48
s 27(1) ... 8.13
s 27(2) ... 8.17
s 28 ... 7.2, 7.3, 7.133, 8.46
ss 28–35 ... 7.2
s 29 ... 13.43
s 30 ... 14.13
s 31 ... 7.4, 14.12
ss 31–33 ... 8.57
s 34 ... 1.25
s 35 ... 20.37
ss 36–43 ... 7.110
s 43A ... 23.153
ss 43A–43K ... 2.28
ss 43A–43L ... 10.74
s 43B ... 10.76

ss 43C–43H ... 10.79
s 43J ... 10.85
s 43K ... 2.24, 10.74
s 43M ... 7.120
s 44 ... 11.63, 11.64
s 45 ... 7.116
s 45A ... 7.106
s 47C ... 6.16, 6.50, 6.92
s 50 ... 7.13, 7.15, 7.18
ss 50–63 ... 15.10, 15.17
s 52 ... 7.133, 13.43, 14.13, 15.20, 18.38
s 54 ... 14.12
s 55 ... 7.133, 14.13
ss 55–57 ... 6.3
s 56 ... 6.5
s 57 ... 6.5
s 57(5) ... 6.8
s 57A ... 6.122
s 57A(1)(c) ... 6.124
s 58 ... 7.20
s 61 ... 7.23, 18.73
s 62 ... 14.13
s 63A ... 7.26, 7.28, 14.13
s 63D ... 2.32, 7.29, 7.33, 7.34, 7.37, 7.41, 17.81
s 63(I) ... 7.40
s 64 ... 7.133, 14.13
ss 64–65 ... 7.7
s 64(2) ... 17.4
s 65 ... 13.43
s 65(1) ... 7.10
s 65(3) ... 7.9
s 66 ... 6.13, 6.14, 7.133, 14.13
s 67 ... 6.12, 6.15, 6.16
s 68 ... 6.17
s 70 ... 1.25
s 71 ... 6.30
ss 71–74 ... 6.19
s 72 ... 6.20
s 72(1) ... 6.20
s 80 ... 6.91
s 80F ... 2.32, 14.13
s 80F–80I ... 6.129, 6.130
ss 86–90 ... 7.134
ss 86–91 ... 2.136
s 86(1) ... 15.4, 15.16
s 86(2) ... 15.31
s 86(3) ... 15.14
s 86(4) ... 2.141
s 87(4) ... 15.16
s 88 ... 15.21
ss 88–89 ... 15.17, 15.18
ss 88–90 ... 15.19
ss 88–91 ... 15.16, 15.17
s 88(1)(a) ... 15.17
s 88(1)(b) ... 15.17
s 88(1)(c) ... 15.17
s 88(1)(cc) ... 6.30, 6.33
s 88(1)(d) ... 15.17
s 89(1) ... 15.17
s 89(2) ... 15.17
s 89(3) ... 15.17

s 91 ... 15.17, 15.18
s 92 ... 13.43, 17.176, 17.178, 17.179, 17.180, 20.32
s 92(4) ... 6.55, 17.182
s 92(4A) ... 6.55, 17.182
s 92(7) ... 15.28
s 93 ... 17.181
s 93(3) ... 17.181
s 94 ... 2.32, 17.3, 20.32, 20.44
ss 94–107 ... 17.1
s 94(4) ... 6.77
s 95 ... 17.5
s 95(1) ... 3.103
s 95(1)(c) ... 17.57
s 95(2) ... 15.9
s 97(1) ... 20.29
s 97(2) ... 15.28, 17.4, 20.29, 20.32
s 97(4) ... 15.28, 20.34
s 98 ... 12.19, 17.73
s 98(1)–(3) ... 17.78
s 98(4) ... 17.74, 17.78, 17.92, 18.25
s 98B ... 7.120
s 99 ... 6.40, 6.45, 6.50, 6.52, 6.92, 17.81, 18.58
s 100 ... 11.66, 11.67, 17.81, 17.198, 17.203, 18.61
s 100(1)(a)–(b) ... 17.183, 17.196
s 100(1)(d) ... 11.66
s 101 ... 7.115, 17.81, 18.61
s 101A ... 7.61, 7.107, 17.81, 17.198, 18.61
s 101A(1)(d) ... 17.183, 17.196
s 102 ... 17.81, 17.198, 18.61
s 102(1) ... 17.183, 17.196
s 103 ... 17.81, 17.183, 17.196, 17.198, 18.61
s 103A ... 17.81, 17.183, 17.203, 18.61
s 104 ... 17.81, 17.165, 17.166, 17.169, 17.171, 18.61
s 104A ... 17.81, 18.61
s 104B ... 17.81, 17.81, 18.61
s 104C ... 17.81
s 105 ... 17.81
s 105(4A) ... 7.107
s 105(7) ... 17.167
s 106 ... 2.78, 6.53, 17.160
s 107 ... 21.118
s 108 ... 2.32, 13.93
s 108(1) ... 15.28
s 108(4) ... 17.82
s 110 ... 13.29, 22.16
s 111 ... 1.25
s 111(2) ... 20.32
s 111(3) ... 15.29, 17.13, 20.26, 20.30
s 111A ... 20.37
s 113 ... 17.185
ss 117–127A ... 17.192
s 119(1) ... 20.32
s 120 ... 17.198
s 121(a) ... 17.195
s 121(b) ... 17.195
s 122(3) ... 17.198
s 123 ... 17.201
s 123(1) ... 17.201

s 123(4) ... 17.237
s 123(6) ... 17.228, 17.237
s 123(7) ... 17.237
s 124(1A) ... 17.203
s 124(3) ... 17.240
s 128 ... 1.25
ss 128–130 ... 11.69
s 128(1)(b) ... 10.83
s 131 ... 1.25
s 132 ... 1.25, 4.40
s 133(1) ... 13.10
s 135 ... 2.32, 4.69, 6.52
s 136 ... 18.5
s 136(1)(b) ... 18.17
s 136(3) ... 13.10
s 138 ... 2.8, 17.195, 18.24, 18.26
ss 138–141 ... 3.105
s 138(1) ... 2.142
s 138(2)-(6) ... 2.142
s 138(3) ... 18.25
s 139 ... 18.11, 18.100
s 139(1) ... 2.8
s 139(1)(a) ... 18.14
s 140 ... 18.62, 18.63
s 141 ... 2.8, 2.142, 6.40, 6.45, 18.28
s 143 ... 18.63
s 145(3)(b) ... 13.10
s 145(5) ... 13.10
s 145(7) ... 13.10
s 146 ... 2.8
s 147 ... 10.20, 18.33
s 153 ... 13.10
s 155 ... 13.93
s 157 ... 18.64
s 159 ... 18.64
s 160 ... 18.64
s 161 ... 18.64
s 163 ... 1.25
s 163(2) ... 18.11, 18.23
s 164 ... 20.1
s 165 ... 18.66
s 166 ... 2.18
ss 166–167 ... 13.42
ss 166–170 ... 9.43, 18.67
s 170 ... 1.25
s 174 ... 13.10
s 175 ... 2.112
s 176(1) ... 13.10
s 182 ... 2.18, 2.155
ss 182–186 ... 15.30
ss 182–189 ... 7.134
ss 182–190 ... 9.43
s 183 ... 7.134, 15.30
s 184 ... 7.134
s 186 ... 14.11, 14.14
s 188 ... 1.25, 2.13
s 189 ... 7.134
ss 191–192 ... 2.23
s 193 ... 2.175
s 194 ... 2.69
s 195 ... 2.69

s 196 . . . 1.31
s 197(3) . . . 18.64
s 199(7) . . . 17.4
s 199(8) . . . 17.4
s 200 . . . 17.4
s 201 . . . 2.124
s 203 . . . 17.69, 17.70, 20.35
s 203(1) . . . 20.31
s 203(2)(e) . . . 1.9
s 203(3) . . . 13.29
s 203(3A) . . . 22.16
s 203(3B) . . . 2.8
s 205A . . . 2.31
s 205A(2) . . . 2.32
s 205A(5) . . . 2.31
s 205A(6) . . . 2.34
s 205A(7) . . . 2.34
s 205A(10) . . . 2.32
s 206 . . . 20.114
s 206(4) . . . 1.25
ss 210–219 . . . 2.137, 13.1
ss 210–219 . . . 13.4
s 210(3) . . . 13.4
s 210(4) . . . 13.4
s 210(5) . . . 2.141, 13.8
s 211(3) . . . 13.9
s 212 . . . 2.8, 2.42, 13.13
s 212(1) . . . 13.14, 13.37
s 212(2) . . . 13.15
s 212(3) . . . 2.137, 7.126
s 212(3)(a) . . . 13.16, 17.100
s 212(3)(b) . . . 13.18, 13.20
s 212(3)(c) . . . 13.2, 13.24, 13.27, 13.28, 13.31,
  15.25, 17.65
s 214 . . . 13.42
s 215(1) . . . 2.122, 13.34
s 215(2) . . . 13.33
s 215(3)(c) . . . 2.151
s 215(4) . . . 2.122
s 216 . . . 13.35
s 216(1) . . . 13.37
s 216(2) . . . 13.35
s 216(3) . . . 13.37
s 217 . . . 13.38
s 218 . . . 13.39, 13.41, 18.3
s 218(2) . . . 9.35, 13.40
s 218(3) . . . 13.40
s 218(4) . . . 13.40, 20.115
s 218(5) . . . 13.40
s 218(6) . . . 2.8, 13.40
s 218(7) . . . 13.40
s 218(7)–(10) . . . 2.6
s 218(8) . . . 13.40
s 219 . . . 13.29
ss 220–224 . . . 3.122
ss 220–229 . . . 7.28
ss 221–224 . . . 7.73
ss 221–229 . . . 14.1
s 221(2) . . . 14.7, 14.7
s 221(3) . . . 14.8
s 222 . . . 14.9

s 223 . . . 14.8
s 224 . . . 14.10
s 225 . . . 3.76
ss 225–226 . . . 14.13
s 227 . . . 14.11, 18.93
s 227(3) . . . 15.28, 20.32
s 229 . . . 14.8
s 230 . . . 2.23, 2.28, 2.99, 8.3
s 230(3) . . . 10.74
s 231 . . . 2.5, 13.40
s 234 . . . 7.28, 14.3
s 235(4) . . . 21.97
Sch 2, para 14(1) . . . 13.7
Sch 5 . . . 3.122
Employment Rights (Dispute Resolution) Act
  1998 . . . 17.4
Employment Tribunals Act 1996 . . . 1.24
  s 3 . . . 8.3
  s 4 . . . 1.25
  s 10 . . . 2.175
  s 18 . . . 1.7, 1.10, 13.29
  s 18(1) . . . 20.37
  s 18A . . . 1.8
  s 18B . . . 1.8
  ss 20–37 . . . 1.20
  s 21 . . . 1.21
  s 28(2) . . . 1.22
  s 28(3) . . . 1.22
  s 33 . . . 20.132
Employment of Women, Young Persons, and
  Children Act 1920
  ss 1–3 . . . 2.110
Enterprise and Regulatory Reform Act
  2013 . . . 1.22, 4.57, 10.82, 10.84, 11.130
  ss 7–9 . . . 1.8
  s 13 . . . 17.82
  ss 17–20 . . . 10.74
  s 69 . . . 11.130
  s 98 . . . 5.57
Equal Pay Act 1970 . . . 1.76, 4.6, 4.8, 5.5, 5.19,
  5.34
  s 1(6) . . . 2.8
Equality Act 2006 . . . 1.28, 1.48, 2.32, 4.235
  Pt 2 . . . 4.8
  Pt 4 . . . 4.8
  s 20 . . . 4.236
  s 21 . . . 4.236
  s 22 . . . 4.236
  s 24A . . . 4.235
  s 25 . . . 4.8
  s 26 . . . 4.8
  s 33 . . . 4.8
  s 43 . . . 4.8
  ss 71–72 . . . 4.235
  s 73 . . . 4.235
  s 81 . . . 4.8
  Sch 3 . . . 4.8
Equality Act 2010 *see generally* Chapter 4, . . . 1.28,
  1.35, 1.77, 1.93, 1.94, 2.26, 2.68, 2.71, 2.74, 2.81,
  2.102, 2.115, 2.125, 3.56, 5.34, 7.53, 10.37, 10.109,
  10.114, 17.104, 17.116, 17.144, 20.9, 20.37, 21.32

Pt 1 . . . 4.107
Pt 5 . . . 4.3, 4.217
Pt 8 . . . 4.3
Pt 9 . . . 4.3
Pt 10 . . . 4.3
Pt 11 . . . 4.3
ss 4–12 . . . 4.10
s 6 . . . 4.80
s 7 . . . 4.120
s 13 . . . 4.15, 4.16, 4.18, 4.28, 4.31, 4.45, 4.121,
    4.131, 4.160, 4.167, 4.180, 4.185, 4.235, 5.52
ss 13–25 . . . 4.44
ss 13–27 . . . 4.12
s 13(2) . . . 4.62
s 14 . . . 4.150
s 15 . . . 4.75, 4.99, 4.100, 4.235
s 16 . . . 4.235
s 18 . . . 4.10, 4.18, 4.134, 4.139, 4.235
s 18(5) . . . 4.137
s 19 . . . 4.23, 4.28, 4.66, 4.101, 4.121, 4.125,
    4.138, 4.148, 4.150, 4.161, 4.171, 4.186,
    4.229, 4.235
s 20 . . . 4.28, 4.112
ss 20–21 . . . 4.75
s 20(7) . . . 4.113
s 23 . . . 4.150
s 24 . . . 4.31
s 26 . . . 4.32, 4.44, 4.57, 4.66, 4.101, 4.121,
    4.151, 4.162, 4.186, 10.113
s 26(1) . . . 4.126, 4.138
s 26(2) . . . 4.126
s 26(3) . . . 4.126
s 27 . . . 4.44, 4.66, 4.101, 4.121, 4.125, 4.138,
    4.151, 4.162, 4.182, 4.186, 5.55
s 37 . . . 4.183
s 39 . . . 4.44, 4.66, 4.101, 4.102, 4.121, 4.125,
    4.138, 4.151, 4.162, 4.164, 4.177, 4.180,
    4.186, 4.189, 4.201, 4.203, 4.207, 4.208, 4.217
ss 39–40 . . . 4.44
s 39(1) . . . 4.45
s 39(1)–(4) . . . 4.45
s 39(1)(a) . . . 4.53, 4.108, 4.163
s 39(1)(c) . . . 4.53, 4.108, 4.163
s 39(2) . . . 4.48
s 39(2)(b) . . . 4.53, 4.163
s 39(2)(c) . . . 4.53, 4.163
s 39(6) . . . 10.24
s 40 . . . 4.32, 4.44, 4.55, 4.66, 4.101, 4.121,
    4.125, 4.138, 4.151, 4.162, 4.182, 4.186,
    10.113
s 41 . . . 4.216
s 42 . . . 4.216
s 44 . . . 4.216
s 47 . . . 4.216
s 48 . . . 4.216
s 49 . . . 4.216
ss 49–50 . . . 4.75
s 50 . . . 4.216
s 53 . . . 4.216
s 55 . . . 4.216
s 57 . . . 4.216

s 58 . . . 4.216
s 60 . . . 4.107, 4.109, 4.110, 4.213, 4.222
s 60(3) . . . 4.108
s 60(5) . . . 4.108
s 61 . . . 4.216
ss 64–70 . . . 5.6
ss 64–79 . . . 4.18, 4.180, 4.217, 5.5
s 64(2) . . . 5.12
s 65 . . . 5.22, 5.23
s 65(4) . . . 5.31
s 66 . . . 4.239, 5.15
s 69 . . . 5.43
s 69(3) . . . 5.47
s 71 . . . 5.52
s 73 . . . 5.53
s 77 . . . 5.55
s 78 . . . 5.56
s 79 . . . 5.6
s 80 . . . 5.3
s 83 . . . 4.191
s 108 . . . 4.196, 4.201, 4.203, 4.217
s 108(1) . . . 4.235
s 109 . . . 4.198, 4.199
s 110 . . . 4.199
s 111 . . . 4.201, 4.202, 4.203, 4.209, 4.217, 4.226
s 112 . . . 4.201, 4.203, 4.217, 4.249
s 113 . . . 4.250
s 113(6) . . . 4.228
s 115 . . . 4.251
s 119 . . . 4.227
s 120 . . . 4.211, 4.217, 4.218, 4.227
s 120(8) . . . 4.107
s 123 . . . 4.218, 4.232
s 124 . . . 4.227, 4.232
s 125 . . . 4.213
s 127 . . . 5.58
s 129 . . . 5.60
s 131 . . . 5.37
s 132 . . . 5.63
s 135 . . . 20.76
s 136 . . . 4.222, 5.59
s 136(2) . . . 4.108
s 139 . . . 4.233
s 139A . . . 5.57
s 140 . . . 4.209, 4.226
s 141 . . . 4.211
s 142 . . . 4.210
s 144 . . . 4.211
s 145 . . . 4.212
s 146 . . . 4.212
s 158 . . . 22.22
s 159 . . . 4.109, 4.204
s 192 . . . 4.213
Sch 1 . . . 4.75, 4.80
Sch 7 . . . 5.21
Sch 8 . . . 4.75, 4.112
Sch 9 . . . 4.67, 4.72, 4.75, 4.122, 4.152, 4.163,
    4.183, 4.189
    Pt 2 . . . 4.216
    para 1 . . . 4.53
    para 10 . . . 4.68

para 13 . . . 4.69
Sch 22 . . . 4.194
Sch 23 . . . 4.184
European Communities Act 1972
s 2 . . . 1.60, 20.22

Factories Act 1961 . . . 11.1, 11.70, 11.78
s 1 . . . 11.21
s 13 . . . 11.17
s 14 . . . 11.133
Sch 5 . . . 4.256, 6.20

Gender Recognition Act 2004 . . . 4.119
Growth and Infrastructure Act 2013
s 31 . . . 2.31

Health and Safety at Work etc. Act 1974 . . . 1.28,
1.52, 2.60, 2.61, 2.74, 2.100, 2.153, 7.101,
10.73, 10.117, 11.1, 11.2, 11.3, 11.7, 11.76,
17.148
s 2 . . . 11.34, 22.17
ss 2–7 . . . 11.89
ss 2–8 . . . 11.130
ss 2–9 . . . 11.31, 11.71
s 2(3) . . . 11.36
s 2(4) . . . 11.38
s 2(6) . . . 11.38, 11.40
s 2(7) . . . 11.38
s 3 . . . 11.49
s 4 . . . 11.50, 11.55
s 6 . . . 11.7, 11.51, 11.57
s 6(7) . . . 11.58
s 6(8) . . . 11.51
s 7 . . . 11.60
s 8 . . . 11.61
s 9 . . . 11.62
s 15 . . . 11.70
s 16 . . . 6.14, 7.7
s 21 . . . 11.11
s 22 . . . 11.12
s 24 . . . 11.14
s 25 . . . 11.26
s 26 . . . 11.29
s 28(8) . . . 11.30
s 33 . . . 11.92
s 36 . . . 11.94
s 37 . . . 11.92, 11.93
s 40 . . . 1.107, 11.32, 11.97, 11.98
s 42 . . . 11.27
s 47 . . . 11.31, 11.130
s 50 . . . 11.71
s 53 . . . 11.58
Sch 1 . . . 11.70
Sch 3 . . . 11.70
Health and Safety (Offences)
Act 2008 . . . 11.96
Highways Act 1959 . . . 23.110
Hours of Employment (Conventions) Act
1936 . . . 4.259
Human Rights Act 1998 . . . 1.13, 1.104, 1.106,
1.107, 10.44, 17.144, 22.25

Immigration, Asylum and Nationality Act 2006
s 15 . . . 2.115
s 21 . . . 2.115
Income Tax (Earnings and Pensions) Act
2003 . . . 15.11
ss 401–404 . . . 16.29
Industrial Relations Act 1971 . . . 10.3, 16.2,
21.16, 22.3, 22.5, 23.28
Industrial Training Act 1982 . . . 1.28, 1.46
Insolvency Act 1986 . . . 18.67
s 386 . . . 7.133
Sch 6 . . . 7.133

Juries Act 1974 . . . 7.120

Law Reform (Contributory Negligence) Act
1945 . . . 11.147
Law Reform (Miscellaneous Provisions) Act
1934 . . . 4.215, 5.65, 20.117
Legal Aid, Sentencing and Punishment of
Offenders Act 2012 . . . 1.39
Legislative and Regulatory Reform
Act 2006 . . . 11.74
Limitation Act 1980 . . . 1.74, 11.151
s 33 . . . 20.12
Limited Liability Partnerships Act 2000
s 4(4) . . . 2.17

Mines and Quarries Act 1954 . . . 4.259
s 124 . . . 2.110

National Health Service and Community Care
Act 1990
s 6 . . . 13.40
s 60 . . . 2.72
National Minimum Wage Act 1998 . . . 1.28, 1.56,
2.24, 2.61, 2.125, 3.56, 8.35, 8.37, 8.38, 17.200
s 1 . . . 8.35
s 2 . . . 8.35
s 9 . . . 8.45
s 10 . . . 8.45
s 11 . . . 1.25, 8.45
s 19 . . . 1.25
s 22 . . . 1.25
s 54 . . . 8.37

Offices, Shops and Railway Premises Act 1963 . . .
11.1, 11.70, 11.78, 11.132
Official Secrets Acts . . . 10.78

Partnership Act 1890
s 1 . . . 2.17
s 3 . . . 2.17
Patents Act 1977 . . . 10.86, 10.89, 10.90
s 39 . . . 10.86
s 40 . . . 10.86, 10.87
Pension Schemes Act 1993 . . . 1.28, 1.77, 22.17
s 126 . . . 1.25
Pensions Act 1995 . . . 1.77, 1.80
Pensions Act 2004 . . . 9.2
s 257 . . . 9.41

Police Act 1996
  ss 84–85 . . . 2.75
Police Act 1997 . . . 4.248, 4.253
  ss 112–127 . . . 3.4
Police (Health and Safety) Act 1997 . . . 2.74, 11.3
Prescription and Limitations (Scotland)
  Act . . . 11.151
Protection from Harassment Act 1997 . . . 4.60,
  10.109, 10.114
  s 1 . . . 10.110
  s 2 . . . 10.111
Public Health Act 1936
  s 205 . . . 4.256, 6.20
Public Interest Disclosure Act 1998 . . . 10.74,
  10.75
Public Order Act 1936 . . . 23.128
Public Order Act 1986 . . . 23.128
  s 1 . . . 23.128
  s 2 . . . 23.128
  s 3 . . . 23.128
  s 4 . . . 23.128
  s 5 . . . 23.128

Race Relations Act 1976 . . . 1.94, 2.99, 4.8
  s 4 . . . 2.99
  s 78 . . . 2.99
Redundancy Payments Act 1965 . . . 10.20, 18.1
Registration Services Act 1953 . . . 2.63
Regulation of Investigatory Powers Act
  2000 . . . 10.46, 10.47
Rehabilitation of Offenders Act 1974 . . . 4.241,
  4.246, 4.247, 4.250
  s 4(3)(b) . . . 4.242
Reserve Forces Act 1996 . . . 7.127
Reserve Forces (Safeguard of Employment) Act
  1985 . . . 7.121, 13.38
Restrictive Trade Practices Act 1956 . . . 19.18
Road Traffic Act 1974
  s 84 . . . 17.147
Road Traffic Act 1988 . . . 10.33

Safeguarding of Vulnerable Groups Act
  2006 . . . 3.4
Sale of Goods Act 1979 . . . 11.59
Schools Standard Framework Act 1998
  s 124A . . . 4.165
Serious Organised Crime and Police Act 2005
  s 158 . . . 2.74
Sex Discrimination Act 1975 . . . 1.93, 2.67, 4.8
  s 82(1) . . . 2.67
Sex Discrimination Act 1986 . . . 4.8
  s 7 . . . 4.257
Shops (Early Closing Days) Act 1965 . . . 4.259
Smoking (Health and Social Care) (Scotland) Act
  2005 . . . 11.87
Social Security Act 1989 . . . 1.81
Social Security Contributions and Benefits Act
  1992 . . . 2.58
  ss 151–163 . . . 7.43
  s 164 . . . 13.43
  s 171ZA(1) . . . 13.43

  s 171ZL(1) . . . 13.43
State Immunity Act 1978 . . . 1.107, 17.4
Sunday Trading Act 1994 . . . 7.110
  Sch 1, para 3 . . . 7.119
Sunday Working (Scotland) Act 2003 . . . 7.110

Trade Disputes Act 1906 . . . 23.79
Trade Union Act 1871 . . . 22.25, 23.1
  s 14 . . . 23.79
Trade Union and Labour Relations Act
  1974 . . . 1.6, 1.18, 16.2
Trade Union and Labour Relations
  (Consolidation) Act 1992 . . . 1.21, 1.28, 1.30,
  1.107, 2.24, 2.61, 2.68, 2.73, 2.125, 2.172,
  17.166, 18.2, 21.1, 22.1, 23.28
  s 1 . . . 22.2
  s 2 . . . 1.18, 22.5
  s 5 . . . 22.7
  s 5(a) . . . 22.12
  s 5(b) . . . 22.12
  s 6 . . . 1.18, 22.7
  s 10 . . . 22.4
  s 11 . . . 22.25
  s 15 . . . 22.63
  s 16 . . . 22.65
  s 20 . . . 23.92
  s 20(4) . . . 23.81
  s 20(6) . . . 23.92
  s 21 . . . 21.100, 23.82
  s 22 . . . 23.86
  s 24 . . . 22.19, 22.21
  s 24A . . . 22.20, 22.21
  s 25 . . . 22.21
  s 26 . . . 22.21
  s 27 . . . 22.39, 22.62
  s 28 . . . 22.56, 22.62
  s 29 . . . 22.62
  ss 29–31 . . . 22.58
  s 30 . . . 22.59
  s 31 . . . 22.60
  s 32 . . . 22.62
  ss 32–42 . . . 22.56
  s 32A . . . 22.57, 22.62
  ss 33–37 . . . 22.62
  s 37B . . . 22.61
  ss 38–42 . . . 22.62
  ss 45–45C . . . 22.62
  s 46 . . . 22.40
  s 47 . . . 22.45
  s 48 . . . 22.46, 22.47
  s 49 . . . 22.48
  s 51A . . . 22.51
  s 52 . . . 22.53
  s 52(4) . . . 22.54
  s 54 . . . 22.37, 22.55
  s 55 . . . 22.55
  s 56 . . . 22.55
  s 62 . . . 21.24, 21.24, 21.25, 23.47
  s 62(7) . . . 21.25
  s 62(8) . . . 21.24
  s 64 . . . 21.9, 21.12, 21.14

s 65 . . . 21.2, 21.9
ss 66–67 . . . 21.13
s 67 . . . 14.11
s 68 . . . 21.56, 21.79, 21.81
s 68(9) . . . 21.80
s 68A . . . 1.25
s 69 . . . 21.16
s 70B . . . 23.13, 23.13
s 71 . . . 22.75
ss 71–74 . . . 22.67
s 72A . . . 22.75
s 75 . . . 22.48
s 77 . . . 22.68
s 78(4) . . . 22.54
ss 79–81 . . . 22.76
s 86 . . . 21.83
s 87 . . . 1.25, 2.68, 21.84
ss 97–105 . . . 22.81
s 100 . . . 22.81
s 100A . . . 22.48
s 100E(6) . . . 22.54
s 103 . . . 22.83
s 105(7C) . . . 21.113
ss 108A–108B . . . 22.78
s 117 . . . 22.3
s 119 . . . 21.62
s 122 . . . 22.84
s 123 . . . 22.86
s 124(1) . . . 21.62
s 137 . . . 4.254, 21.28, 21.31, 21.34, 21.35
ss 137–143 . . . 1.30
s 137(3) . . . 21.32
s 137(4) . . . 21.33
s 138 . . . 21.34
s 138(3) . . . 21.34
ss 139–142 . . . 21.37
s 144 . . . 23.117, 23.119
s 145A . . . 2.175, 21.46, 21.48, 21.49, 21.85
ss 145A–151 . . . 1.30
s 145B . . . 2.175, 21.47, 21.48, 21.49, 21.85
s 146 . . . 2.175, 21.50, 21.52, 21.65
s 146(1) . . . 21.51, 22.16
s 149(2) . . . 21.60
s 150 . . . 21.58
s 152 . . . 17.196, 21.65, 21.85
s 152(1) . . . 21.89, 22.16
ss 152(1)–153 . . . 21.87
s 153 . . . 18.61, 21.120
s 154 . . . 17.81, 21.86
s 155 . . . 17.198, 17.231
ss 155–158 . . . 21.121
s 157 . . . 17.198
s 160 . . . 21.119, 21.128
s 161 . . . 1.25, 22.16
ss 161–166 . . . 11.69, 17.183, 21.122
s 162(3) . . . 21.128
s 165 . . . 1.25
s 166 . . . 1.25
s 168 . . . 7.133, 21.66, 21.71
ss 168–170 . . . 15.17, 22.17
ss 168–173 . . . 1.30, 12.30

s 168A . . . 21.74, 21.77, 21.78
s 170 . . . 21.72
s 174 . . . 21.2, 21.3, 21.5, 21.10, 21.12, 21.17,
    22.23
s 174(1) . . . 1.107, 21.3
s 174(4A) . . . 21.2, 21.3
s 174(4C) . . . 21.3
s 176 . . . 14.11
s 177 . . . 21.4, 21.17
s 178 . . . 21.68, 23.4, 23.14, 23.99
s 179 . . . 23.99, 23.100, 23.101
s 180 . . . 3.79, 22.16, 23.102
s 181 . . . 22.17, 23.15
s 182(1) . . . 2.8
s 183 . . . 1.19
s 184 . . . 2.68
s 186 . . . 18.91, 23.78, 23.120
ss 186–187 . . . 23.122
ss 186–190 . . . 15.10
s 187 . . . 23.121
s 188 . . . 9.78, 18.45, 18.69, 18.70, 18.71, 18.77,
    18.91, 22.17
ss 188–194 . . . 1.78, 2.68
s 188(1A) . . . 18.88
s 188(2) . . . 18.80
s 188(4) . . . 18.86
s 188(5) . . . 18.90
s 188A . . . 18.70, 18.72
s 189 . . . 7.133, 7.134, 18.91, 18.92
s 192 . . . 1.25
ss 193–194 . . . 1.30
s 193(7) . . . 18.89, 18.101
s 194(1) . . . 18.102
s 195 . . . 18.100
s 198A . . . 18.75
s 199 . . . 1.15
ss 201–202 . . . 1.17
s 203 . . . 1.59
s 207 . . . 1.16
s 207A . . . 17.220
s 210 . . . 1.5
s 210A . . . 1.5
s 211 . . . 1.7
s 212 . . . 1.13, 1.19
s 212A . . . 1.13, 4.211, 17.4, 20.37
s 213 . . . 1.4
s 214 . . . 1.14
s 218 . . . 1.6
s 219 . . . 2.70, 21.94, 21.95, 21.112, 21.113,
    23.41, 23.46, 23.68, 23.71, 23.72, 23.75,
    23.78, 23.79, 23.85, 23.87, 23.112, 23.116,
    23.119, 23.122, 23.127
s 219(1) . . . 23.41
s 219(2) . . . 23.43
s 219(3) . . . 23.112
s 220 . . . 23.77, 23.105, 23.109, 23.113
s 220(4) . . . 23.77, 23.106
s 221 . . . 23.90
s 221(2) . . . 23.91
s 222 . . . 21.111, 23.71
ss 222–235 . . . 21.95

s 222(3) . . . 23.119
s 223 . . . 21.111, 23.72
s 224 . . . 21.111, 23.73
s 224(2) . . . 23.74
s 224(6) . . . 2.22, 23.76
s 225 . . . 21.111, 23.78, 23.122
s 226 . . . 23.49, 23.95
ss 226–234 . . . 21.111
ss 226–234A . . . 23.47
ss 226–235 . . . 23.48
s 226(3) . . . 23.54
s 226A . . . 23.69, 23.87
s 226A(2)(c)(ii) . . . 23.50
s 226A(3A) . . . 23.49
s 226B . . . 22.48
s 226C . . . 22.49
s 227(1) . . . 23.52, 23.87
s 228 . . . 23.54
s 228(2) . . . 23.54
s 228(3) . . . 23.54
s 228A . . . 23.55, 23.54
ss 229–231A . . . 23.57
s 229(3) . . . 23.59
s 230(2) . . . 23.53, 23.59, 23.61
s 231 . . . 23.63
s 231A . . . 23.64, 23.69
s 232 . . . 23.56
s 232(3) . . . 23.56
s 232A . . . 23.52, 23.53
s 232B . . . 23.52, 23.53
ss 233–234 . . . 23.66
s 233(3) . . . 23.66
s 234A . . . 21.111, 23.69, 23.87
s 234A(3)(a)(ii) . . . 23.68
s 234A(7B) . . . 23.70
s 235 . . . 2.22
s 235A . . . 23.47, 23.95
s 236 . . . 10.7, 15.32, 23.93
s 237 . . . 21.92, 21.96, 21.100, 21.116
ss 237–239 . . . 21.90
s 237(1A) . . . 21.116
s 238 . . . 21.96, 21.103, 21.108, 21.110, 21.116
s 238(1)(a) . . . 21.91, 21.97
s 238(1)(b) . . . 21.101, 23.47
s 238(2) . . . 21.93, 21.94, 21.111
s 238(2)(b) . . . 21.101
s 238A . . . 17.81, 21.96, 21.111, 21.112, 21.113,
     21.115, 23.47, 21.95

s 238A(6) . . . 21.112
s 240 . . . 23.124
s 241 . . . 23.124, 23.125, 23.126
s 241(1) . . . 23.111
s 241(1)(a) . . . 23.126
s 244 . . . 1.6, 23.29
s 244(1)(a) . . . 23.30
s 244(4) . . . 23.33
s 247 . . . 1.1
s 248 . . . 1.1
s 251A . . . 1.1
s 254 . . . 1.18
ss 255–258 . . . 1.18
ss 256A–256AA . . . 1.18
s 277 . . . 2.69
s 287 . . . 2.124
s 288 . . . 18.96
s 295 . . . 2.28
s 296 . . . 2.21
Sch A1 . . . 17.81, 21.61, 21.65, 23.5, 23.6,
     23.13, 23.14
Pt 1 . . . 23.7, 23.14
Pt II . . . 23.8, 23.14
Pt III . . . 23.11, 23.14
Pt IV . . . 23.12
Pt V . . . 23.12
Pt VI . . . 23.12
Pt VII . . . 23.12
para 35 . . . 23.9
para 94 . . . 23.14
para 94(2) . . . 23.14
para 156 . . . 21.61
para 161 . . . 17.183
para 172 . . . 23.5
Sch 2A . . . 17.223
Trade Union Reform and Employment Rights Act
     1993 . . . 18.69
Transport Act 1968 . . . 4.259
Truck Act 1831 . . . 8.1
Truck Act 1896 . . . 8.2

Unfair Contract Terms Act 1977 . . . 11.146
     s 2 . . . 3.33, 11.146

Wages Act 1986 . . . 8.1, 8.2, 8.3
Work and Families Act 2006 . . . 1.28

Table of Statutory Instruments

ACAS (Flexible Working) Arbitration Scheme (Great Britain) Order 2004 . . . 1.13

Act of Sederunt (Interest in Sheriff Court Decrees or Extracts) 1975 . . . 17.243

Additional Paternity Leave (Adoption from Overseas) Regulations 2010 . . . 1.28, 6.111

Additional Paternity Leave Regulations 2010 . . . 1.28, 6.103
  reg 4 . . . 13.43

Agency Workers Regulations 2010 . . . 1.28, 1.96, 2.163, 13.43
  reg 5 . . . 2.164, 2.169, 2.170, 2.171
  reg 7(3) . . . 2.168
  reg 7(8) . . . 2.167
  reg 9 . . . 2.168, 2.171
  reg 12 . . . 2.166, 2.170, 2.171
  reg 13 . . . 2.166, 2.170, 2.171
  reg 14 . . . 2.169
  reg 15 . . . 2.172
  reg 17 . . . 2.171
  reg 17(2) . . . 2.171

Children (Performance) (Amendment) (Wales) Regulations 2007 . . . 2.110

Children (Performances) Regulations 1968 . . . 2.110

Children (Protection at Work) Regulations 1998–2000 . . . 2.110

Civil Partnership Act 2004 (Amendments to Subordinate Legislation) Order 2005 . . . 2.102, 4.123

Collective Redundancies and Transfer of Undertakings (Protection of Employment) (Amendment) Regulations 1995 . . . 9.2, 18.70

Collective Redundancies and Transfer of Undertakings (Protection of Employment) (Amendment) Regulations 2014 . . . 9.4, 9.18, 9.54, 9.80
  reg 8 . . . 9.56

Companies (Cross-Border Mergers) Regulations 2007 . . . 1.28, 7.24, 17.81, 22.17

Conduct of Employment Agencies and Employment Businesses Regulations 2003–2010 . . . 2.152

Construction (Design and Management) Regulations 2007 . . . 2.4

Construction (Health and Welfare) Regulations 1966 . . . 2.56
  reg 5 . . . 11.149

Continuity of Employment Regulations 1996 . . . 13.32

Control of Lead at Work Regulations 2002 . . . 5.21, 7.7, 7.9

Control of Substances Hazardous to Health Regulations 2002 . . . 7.7

Court Funds Rules 1987 . . . 17.243

Deregulation (Deduction from Pay of Union Subscriptions) Order 1998 . . . 21.79

Disability Discrimination Act 1995 (Amendment) Regulations 2003 . . . 1.93

Disability Discrimination (Blind and Partially Sighted Persons) Regulations 2003 . . . 4.84

Disability Discrimination (Employment) Regulations 1996 . . . 4.104

Ecclesiastical Offices (Terms of Service) Regulations 2009 . . . 2.67

Employee Study and Training (Procedural Requirements) Regulations 2010 . . . 7.33
  reg 3 . . . 7.34

Employers' Health and Safety Policy Statements (Exception) Regulations 1975 . . . 11.36

Employers' Liability (Compulsory Insurance) Regulations 1998 . . . 10.34

Employment Appeal Tribunal Rules 1993 . . . 1.22
  rr 13–17 . . . 1.22
  r 23 . . . 1.22
  r 23A . . . 1.22

Employment Equality (Age) Regulations 2006 . . . 1.28, 1.93, 4.8, 14.11, 17.197, 17.197, 18.61
  reg 32 . . . 4.72, 18.51
  reg 33 . . . 4.73
  Sch 6 . . . 4.67

Employment Equality (Religion or Belief) Regulations 2003 . . . 1.93, 4.8

Employment Equality (Repeal of Retirement Age Provisions) Regulations 2011 . . . 4.67

Employment Equality (Sexual Orientation) Regulations 2003 . . . 1.93, 1.107, 4.8

Employment Protection (Continuity of Employment of National Health Service Employees) (Modification) Order 1996 . . . 13.40

Employment Protection (Continuity of Employment) Regulations 1996 . . . 13.29, 13.43, 17.191
  reg 4 . . . 13.43

Employment Protection (Offshore Employment) Order 1976 . . . 17.4

Employment Protection (Recoupment of Jobseekers' Allowance and Income Support) Regulations 1996 . . . 17.244

Employment Relations Act 1999 (Blacklists) Regulations 2010 . . . 1.28, 17.81, 21.39
  reg 3 . . . 21.40, 21.41, 21.42, 21.44, 21.45

Employment Relations (Offshore Employment)
    Order 2000 . . . 1.28
Employment Tribunals Awards (Enforcement in
    case of Death) Regulations 1976 . . . 20.116
Employment Tribunals (Constitution and Rules
    of Procedure) Regulations 2004 . . . 1.28
    Sch 1 r 54(2) . . . 20.74
    Sch 2 . . . 2.176, 20.56
    Sch 4 . . . 11.22
    Sch 6 . . . 5.39
Employment Tribunals (Constitution and Rules
    of Procedure) Regulations 2013 . . . 1.29, 9.37,
    20.59
    Sch 1 . . . 20.46
    r 2 . . . 20.46
    r 27 . . . 20.54
    r 28 . . . 20.54
    r 29 . . . 20.73
    r 46 . . . 20.46
    r 70 . . . 20.101
    Sch 2 . . . 20.46
    Sch 3 . . . 1.47, 20.46
Employment Tribunals and the Employment
    Appeal Tribunal Fees Order 2013 . . . 20.51
Employment Tribunals Extension of Jurisdiction
    (England and Wales) Order 1994 . . . 1.25,
    1.28, 1.40, 1.43, 3.5, 6.54, 8.3, 8.16, 8.23, 8.34,
    15.6, 15.37, 16.19
Employment Tribunals Extension of Jurisdiction
    (Scotland) Order 1994 . . . 1.25, 1.40, 1.43, 3.5,
    6.54, 8.3, 8.16, 8.23, 8.34, 15.6, 15.37, 16.19
Employment Tribunals (Interest on Awards
    in Discrimination Cases) Regulations
    1996 . . . 4.233, 4.234, 17.242, 20.100
Employment Tribunals (Interest) Order
    1990 . . . 17.242, 20.99
Equal Pay (Amendment) Regulations
    1983 . . . 1.76
Equal Pay (Complaints to Employment
    Tribunals) (Armed Forces) Regulations
    1997 . . . 2.71
Equality Act 2010 (Disability) Regulations
    2010 . . . 4.79, 4.83
European Cooperative Society (Involvement of
    Employees) Regulations 2006 . . . 7.24, 17.81
European Public Limited Liability Company
    (Employee Involvement) (Great Britain)
    Regulations 2009 . . . 1.19, 1.21, 1.28, 7.24
European Public Limited-Liability Company
    (Employee Involvement) (Great Britain)
    Regulations 2009 . . . 17.81, 22.17

Fixed-Term Employees (Prevention of Less
    Favourable Treatment) Regulations 2002 . . . 1.28,
    1.91, 2.128, 2.130, 2.131, 17.19, 18.61, 20.37, 22.16
    reg 6 . . . 17.81
    reg 8 . . . 13.43
Flexible Working (Eligibility, Complaints and
    Remedies) Regulations 2002 . . . 1.28, 2.61,
    2.102, 6.130
    reg 3 . . . 13.43

Flexible Working (Procedural Requirements)
    Regulations 2002 . . . 1.28, 2.61, 6.130, 7.33, 14.11

Government Officers (Political Restrictions)
    Regulations 1990 . . . 1.107

Health and Safety (Consultation with Employees)
    Regulations 1996 . . . 1.28, 11.45, 11.46, 11.48
Health and Safety (Display Screen Equipment)
    Regulations . . . 11.78, 11.86
Health and Safety (Enforcing Authority)
    Regulations 1998 . . . 11.9
Health and Safety Enquiries (Procedure)
    Regulations 1975 . . . 1.54
Health and Safety (Fees) Regulations
    2012 . . . 11.14
Health and Safety (Training for Employment)
    Regulations 1990 . . . 2.100, 11.2

Immigration (Restrictions on Employment)
    Order 2004 . . . 2.115
Industrial Training Levy (Construction Board)
    Order 2009 . . . 1.47
Industrial Tribunals (Interest) Order
    1990 . . . 1.28
Information and Consultation of Employees
    Regulations 2004 . . . 1.28, 1.95, 7.24, 18.82,
    22.17, 23.142
    reg 2 . . . 23.143
    reg 4(3) . . . 23.144
    reg 7 . . . 23.146
    regs 8–9 . . . 23.145
    reg 18 . . . 23.151
    reg 21 . . . 23.148
    reg 22 . . . 23.156
Information and Consultation Regulations
    2004 . . . 1.19, 1.21
Insolvency of Employer (Excluded Classes)
    Regulations 1983 . . . 7.135
Ionising Radiations Regulations 1999 . . . 5.21, 7.7

Legislative Reform (Health and Safety Executive)
    Order 2008 . . . 1.51

Management of Health and Safety at Work
    Regulations 1999 . . . 1.87, 2.109, 2.153, 2.172,
    4.258, 6.9, 7.64, 10.117, 11.40, 11.78, 11.80,
    11.132, 11.136
    reg 3 . . . 11.139
    reg 6 . . . 11.139
    reg 6(1) . . . 11.46
    reg 7(1)(b) . . . 11.46
    reg 8 . . . 11.139
    reg 10 . . . 11.139
    reg 14 . . . 11.139
    reg 16 . . . 4.50, 6.10, 6.16, 11.139
Manual Handling Operations Regulations
    1992 . . . 11.78, 11.85
    Sch 1 . . . 11.85
Maternity (Compulsory Leave) Regulations
    1994 . . . 4.256

Maternity and Parental Leave etc
  Regulations 1999 . . . 1.28, 6.19, 6.21,
  17.81, 18.61, 22.16
  reg 10 . . . 6.38, 6.40, 6.45, 6.54
  reg 12A . . . 6.35, 6.36
  reg 13 . . . 13.43
  regs 13–21 . . . 6.82
  reg 13(1A) . . . 6.83
  reg 16(3) . . . 6.12
  reg 17 . . . 6.33
  reg 18(1) . . . 6.38
  reg 18(2) . . . 6.44
  reg 18(4) . . . 6.40
  reg 18A(1) . . . 6.38
  reg 18A(2) . . . 6.44
  reg 19 . . . 6.8, 6.24, 6.54
  regs 19(2)–20(3) . . . 6.48
  reg 20 . . . 6.24, 6.50, 6.54
  reg 20(1)(b) . . . 6.40
  reg 20(2) . . . 6.45
  Sch 1 . . . 6.90
  Sch 2 . . . 6.90
  para 8 . . . 6.87

National Minimum Wage Regulations 1999 . . .
  1.28, 8.38
  reg 13(2) . . . 2.8
  reg 14 . . . 8.40
  reg 15(1A) . . . 8.44

Occupational Pension Schemes (Disclosure of
  Information) Regulations 1986 . . . 3.126
Occupational and Personal Pension Schemes
  (Consultation with Employees) Regulations
  2006 . . . 1.28

Parental Leave (EU Directive) Regulations
  2013 . . . 6.130
Part-time Workers (Prevention of Less
  Favourable Treatment) Regulations
  2000 . . . 1.28, 1.89, 2.24, 2.61, 2.80, 2.81,
  17.81, 18.61, 20.37
  reg 5 . . . 2.88
  reg 6 . . . 2.89
  reg 7 . . . 2.92
  reg 17 . . . 2.66
Paternity and Adoption Leave Regulations
  2002 . . . 1.28, 2.102, 6.67, 6.93
  reg 4 . . . 13.43
Personal Protective Equipment at Work
  Regulations 1992 . . . 11.62, 11.78, 11.83
  reg 7 . . . 11.138
Police (Health and Safety) Regulations
  1999 . . . 2.74, 11.3
Provision and Use of Work Equipment
  Regulations 1998 . . . 11.78, 11.82, 11.149
  reg 5 . . . 11.149
  reg 6 . . . 11.133
  reg 20 . . . 11.149
Public Interest Disclosure (Prescribed Persons)
  Order 1999 . . . 10.80

Race Relations (Complaints to Employment
  Tribunals) (Armed Forces) Regulations
  1997 . . . 2.71
Race Relations (Prescribed Public Bodies)
  Regulations 1994 . . . 4.147
Redundancy Payments (Continuity of
  Employment in Local Government etc)
  (Modification) Order 1999 . . . 13.40
  Sch 1 . . . 13.40
Redundancy Payments (Local Government)
  (Modification) Order 1983 . . . 2.6
Redundancy Payments (National Health Service)
  (Modification) Order 1993 . . . 13.40
Regulation of Investigatory Powers (Interception
  of Communications: Code of Practice) Order
  2002 . . . 10.47
Rehabilitation of Offenders Act 1974 (Exceptions)
  Orders 1975 . . . 4.247
Right to Time Off for Study or Training
  Regulations 2001 . . . 1.28, 7.26
Right to Time Off for Study or Training
  (Scotland) Regulations 1999 . . . 7.26
Road Transport (Working Time) Regulations
  2005 . . . 7.56

Safety Representatives and Safety Committee
  Regulations 1977 . . . 1.28, 2.172, 11.39, 11.44,
  11.48
Sex Discrimination (Complaints to Employment
  Tribunals) (Armed Forces) Regulations
  1997 . . . 2.71
Sex Discrimination and Equal Pay (Remedies)
  Regulations 1993 . . . 5.66
Sex Discrimination (Indirect Discrimination and
  Burden of Proof) Regulations 2001 . . . 1.92
Smoke-Free (Penalties and Enforcement)
  Regulations 2006 . . . 11.87
Statutory Maternity Pay (General) Regulations
  1986 . . . 2.102, 6.56, 7.134
  reg 21(7) . . . 6.63
Statutory Sick Pay (General) Regulations
  1982 . . . 7.43
Statutory Sick Pay Percentage Threshold Order
  1995 . . . 7.45
Suspension from Work (on Maternity Grounds)
  Order 1994 . . . 1.28, 6.14

Telecommunications (Lawful Business Practice)
  (Interception of Communications) Regulations
  2000 . . . 1.107, 10.47
Time off Work for Study or Training Regulations
  2010 . . . 1.28, 7.26
Trade Union Ballots and Elections (Independent
  Scrutineers' Qualifications) Orders
  1988-2010 . . . 22.48
Trade Union Recognition (Method of Collective
  Bargaining) Order 2000 . . . 23.7, 23.104
Transfer of Employment (Pensions Protection)
  Regulations 2005 . . . 9.2, 9.41
Transfer of Undertaking (Protection of
  Employment) Regulations 1981 . . . 18.69

Transfer of Undertakings (Protection of
    Employment) Regulations 2006 ... 1.28, 1.79,
    2.61, 2.149, 2.172, 9.2, 9.4, 9.13, 9.31, 9.61, 9.63,
    10.2, 13.41, 13.42, 14.11, 17.166, 18.68, 18.84,
    22.17
reg 2(1) ... 9.5
reg 3(1)(a) ... 9.6
reg 3(1)(b) ... 9.14, 9.21
reg 3(2) ... 9.6
reg 3(4) ... 9.24
reg 3(5) ... 9.23, 9.28
reg 4 ... 9.30, 9.32, 9.35, 9.37, 9.56
reg 4(1) ... 9.39
reg 4(2) ... 9.60
reg 4(2)(b) ... 9.32
reg 4(3) ... 9.34
reg 4(4) ... 9.44, 9.46
reg 4(5) ... 9.44, 9.45, 9.58
reg 4(5B) ... 9.47
reg 4(6) ... 9.30
reg 4(7) ... 9.63
reg 4(9) ... 9.65
reg 4(10) ... 9.67
reg 4A ... 9.37
reg 5 ... 9.73
reg 5(1) ... 13.40
reg 5(2)(b) ... 9.32
reg 5(a) ... 9.68
reg 6 ... 9.74
reg 7 ... 9.54, 9.56
reg 7(1) ... 9.69
reg 7(2) ... 9.54, 9.55, 9.57, 9.58
reg 7(6) ... 9.62
reg 8 ... 9.48, 9.49
reg 8(7) ... 9.50
reg 9 ... 9.52, 9.53
reg 10 ... 9.41
reg 10(3) ... 9.41
reg 11 ... 9.68, 9.72
reg 12 ... 9.68, 9.70, 9.72
reg 13 ... 9.75, 9.78
reg 13(2)(b) ... 9.76
reg 13(5) ... 9.76
reg 13A ... 9.80
reg 14 ... 9.81
reg 15 ... 9.82
reg 15(10) ... 1.25
reg 17 ... 9.39
Transnational Information and Consultation
    of Employees (Amendment) Regulations
    2010 ... 23.132
Transnational Information and Consultation of
    Employees Regulations 1999 ... 1.19, 1.21,
    1.28, 1.86, 7.24, 17.81, 18.61, 22.17, 23.132
reg 6 ... 23.133

reg 7 ... 23.140
reg 8 ... 23.133
regs 11–17 ... 23.134
reg 17 ... 23.135
regs 25–27 ... 23.138
regs 28–33 ... 23.139

Unfair Dismissal and Statement of Reasons for
    Dismissal (Variation of Qualifying Period)
    Order 2012 ... 13.43

Working Time (Amendment) Regulations
    2007 ... 7.73
Working Time Regulations 1998 ... 1.28, 1.86,
    1.87, 2.24, 2.73, 2.108, 2.109, 3.52, 3.125, 4.258,
    4.259, 6.33, 7.54, 7.57, 7.99, 7.102, 11.138, 14.3,
    17.166, 17.169, 17.183, 22.16
reg 2 ... 7.63
reg 2(1) ... 2.25, 7.55
reg 4 ... 7.92, 7.94, 7.97
reg 4(1) ... 7.108
reg 4(2) ... 7.109
reg 5 ... 7.58
reg 5A ... 7.62, 7.92
reg 6 ... 7.63, 7.92, 7.94, 7.96, 7.97
reg 6A ... 7.62
reg 7 ... 7.62, 7.92
reg 8 ... 7.68, 7.92
reg 9 ... 7.69
reg 10 ... 7.70, 7.94, 7.96, 7.97, 7.103
reg 11 ... 7.66, 7.71, 7.94, 7.96, 7.97, 7.103
reg 12 ... 7.72, 7.94, 7.96, 7.97, 7.103
reg 13 ... 7.73, 7.103, 15.36
reg 14 ... 7.103
reg 14(3) ... 7.79
reg 16 ... 7.103
reg 18 ... 7.91
reg 20 ... 7.93
reg 21 ... 7.58, 7.95
reg 23 ... 7.97
reg 23(b) ... 7.58
reg 24 ... 7.96
regs 25–27A ... 7.98
reg 28 ... 7.99
reg 29 ... 7.101, 7.109
regs 30 ... 7.89, 7.109
reg 35(1) ... 7.79
Sch 1 ... 7.75
Sch 2 ... 7.98
Sch 3 ... 7.101
Workplace (Health, Safety and Welfare)
    Regulations 1992 ... 3.51, 4.18, 11.78, 11.81
reg 12 ... 11.132
reg 25(4) ... 6.13

Table of European Legislation

PRIMARY

Charter of Fundamental Rights of the European Union . . . 1.63, 1.107
EU Convention on Mutual Assistance in Criminal Matters . . . 10.46
Maastricht Treaty . . . 1.64
Treaty of Amsterdam . . . 1.62
Treaty on European Union . . . 1.64
Treaty on the Functioning of the European Union . . . 1.64, 1.72
    Art 45 . . . 1.72
    Art 157 . . . 1.64, 1.72, 5.1, 5.9, 5.10
    Art 234 . . . 1.101
Treaty of Lisbon . . . 1.63, 1.64, 1.67, 1.69, 1.107
Treaty of Rome . . . 1.62, 1.64, 1.71, 1.102
    Art 43 . . . 23.97
    Art 45 . . . 1.72
    Art 119 . . . 1.72
    Art 137 . . . 11.77
    Art 139 . . . 1.85
    Art 141 . . . 1.61, 1.64, 1.74, 2.66, 5.1, 11.41

SECONDARY

Directive 75/117/EEC (Equal Pay) . . . 1.76, 5.1
Directive 75/129/EEC (Collective Redundancies) . . . 1.78
    Art 1(1)(ii) . . . 18.77
    Art 2 . . . 18.69
Directive 76/207/EEC (Equal Treatment) . . . 1.77
Directive 77/187/EEC (Acquired Rights) . . . 1.79, 9.2, 9.7, 9.8, 9.10
Directive 79/7/EEC (Equal Treatment in Social Security Matters) . . . 1.80
Directive 80/987/EEC (Employers' Insolvency) . . . 1.74, 1.84
Directive 86/378/EEC (Equal Treatment in Occupational Social Security Schemes) . . . 1.81
Directive 86/613/EEC (Equal Treatment for Self-employed) . . . 1.82
Directive 89/391/EEC (Framework) . . . 11.33, 11.45
    Art 5(1) . . . 11.33
    Art 5(4) . . . 11.33

Directive 90/393/EEC (Carcinogens at Work) Annex I . . . 6.11
Directive 90/679/EEC (Biological Agents) . . . 6.11
Directive 92/85/EEC (Pregnant Workers) . . . 6.16, 6.51
    Annexes I–II . . . 6.10
Directive 93/104/EEC (Working Time) . . . 1.85, 7.54, 7.84, 7.88, 7.106
Directive 94/33/EC (Young Workers) . . . 1.87, 2.110, 7.54
Directive 94/45/EC (European Works Councils) . . . 1.86, 23.132
Directive 95/46/EC (Data Protection) . . . 10.26
Directive 96/34/EC (Parental Leave) . . . 1.88, 1.97
Directive 96/71/EC (Posted Workers) . . . 1.31, 1.38, 1.90, 2.118
Directive 97/66/EC (Telecommunications Data Protection) . . . 1.107, 10.47
Directive 97/80/EC (Burden of Proof) . . . 1.92
Directive 97/81/EC (Part-time Work) . . . 1.89, 2.80
Directive 98/59/EC . . . 1.78, 11.77
Directive 99/70/EC (Fixed-term Workers) . . . 1.73, 1.91, 2.128
Directive 2000/43/EC (Equal Treatment between Persons Irrespective of Racial or Ethnic Origins) . . . 1.94
Directive 2000/78/EC (Equal Treatment in Employment and Occupation) . . . 1.93, 4.16, 4.62, 4.63
Directive 2000/79/EC (Aviation) . . . 7.54
Directive 2001/23/EC . . . 1.79
Directive 2002/14/EC (Information and Consultation) . . . 1.95, 23.142
Directive 2003/88/EC . . . 1.85
Directive 2006/54/EC (Equal Treatment) . . . 1.98, 1.103, 4.128, 4.132, 4.255, 6.50, 6.51, 20.24, 20.96
Directive 2008/104/EC (Agency workers) . . . 1.96
Directive 2009/38/EC . . . 1.86, 23.132
Directive 2010/18/EU (Parental Leave) . . . 1.88, 1.97
Regulation (EC) 593/2008 (Rome I) . . . 1.38
Regulation (EC) 864/2007 (Rome II) . . . 1.38

Table of International Treaties and Conventions

European Convention on Human Rights . . . 1.39, 1.104, 1.105, 1.106, 10.44, 23.2
Art 4 . . . 1.107
Art 6 . . . 1.22, 1.107, 2.177, 11.97, 12.26, 12.27, 20.94
Art 6(1) . . . 12.26
Art 6(3) . . . 12.26
Art 8 . . . 1.105, 1.107, 10.43, 10.45, 12.54, 17.144, 20.74
Art 8(2) . . . 1.107
Art 9 . . . 1.107, 2.67, 4.155
Art 10 . . . 1.107, 10.83, 17.144
Art 11 . . . 1.107, 21.3, 22.25, 23.69
Universal Declaration of Human Rights . . . 10.16

Table of Cases

102 Social Club and Institute v Bickerton [1977] ICR 911, 12 ITR 442 (EAT) . . . 2.62

A v B [2003] IRLR 405; [2003] All ER (D) 184 (May) (EAT) . . . 12.3
A v B [2010] IRLR 844 . . . 12.4, 20.8, 20.57
A & B Marcusfield v Melhuish [1977] IRLR 484 (EAT) . . . 14.4
AB v CD [2001] IRLR 808; [2001] All ER (D) 354 (May) . . . 22.44, 22.45
AB v Ministry of Defence [2010] ICR 54 . . . 2.178
ABC News International v Gizbert (EAT) 22 August 2006 . . . 2.47
AEI Cables Ltd v McLay [1980] IRLR 84 (Ct of Sess) . . . 17.130
A-G v Blake [1997] Ch 84; [1996] 3 All ER 903; [1996] 3 WLR 741; [1996] FSR 727; [1996] EMLR 382; revsd [1998] Ch 439; [1998] 1 All ER 833; [1998] 2 WLR 805; [1998] EMLR 309; [1998] 04 LS Gaz R 33; [1998] NLJR 15; 142 Sol Jo LB 35 (CA); aff'd on other grounds [2001] 1 AC 268; [2000] 2 All ER (Comm) 487; [2000] EMLR 949; [2000] NLJR 1230; [2000] 32LS Gaz R 37; 144 Sol Jo LB 242; [2001] 1 LRC 260; [2000] IP & T 1261; [2000] All ER (D) 1074 (HL) . . . 10.57
A-G v Guardian Newspapers (No 2) [1990] 1 AC 109; [1988] 3 All ER 545; [1988] 2 WLR 805; aff'd [1990] 1 AC 109; [1988] 3 All ER 545; [1988] 2 WLR 805; 132 Sol Jo 566; [1988] NLJR 47 (CA); aff'd [1990] 1 AC 109; [1988] 3 All ER 545; [1988] 3 WLR 776; [1988] NJLR 296; [1988] LRC (Const) 938 (HL) . . . 10.69, 10.71
A-G v Wheen [2000] IRLR 461; [2000] All ER (D) 767 (EAT); aff'd [2001] IRLR 91; [2000] All ER (D) 2186 (CA) . . . 20.132
A-G's Reference (No 1 of 1983) [1985] QB 182; [1984] 3 All ER 369; [1984] 3 WLR 686; 79 Cr App R 288; [1984] Crim LR 570; 128 Sol Jo 596; [1984] LS Gaz R 2458 (CA) . . . 10.57
A-G's Reference (No 1 of 1983) [1985] QB 182; [1984] 3 All ER 369; [1984] 3 WLR 686; 79 Cr App R 288; [1984] Crim LR 570; 128 Sol Jo 596; [1984] LS Gaz R 2458 (CA) . . . 10.57
AJ Dunning & Sons (Shopfitters) Ltd v Jacomb [1973] ICR 448; [1973] IRLR 206; 15 KIR 9; 8 ITR 453 (NIRC) . . . 12.82, 17.86
ALM Medical Services Ltd v Bladon, EAT/709/00; EAT/967/00 (EAT); [2001] EWCA Civ 1183 (CA); [2002] EWCA Civ 1085; [2002] Emp LR 1054; [2002] ICR 1444; [2002] IRLR 807 (CA) . . . 20.65

ASLEF v UK (Application 11002/05) [2007] IRLR 361; 22 BHRC 140; (2007) 45 EHRR 34 (ECtHR) . . . 1.107
ASLEF v United Kingdom [2007] IRLR 361; (2007) 45 EHRR 34; 22 BHRC 140; (2007) *Times* 9 March . . . 21.3
AUEW v Cooper Plastics, IDS Brief 90 . . . 18.88
AUEW v Sefton Engineering [1976] IRLR 318 . . . 23.4
A Links & Co Ltd v Rose [1991] IRLR 353 (Ct of Sess) . . . 17.94
A Simpson & Son (Motors) v Reid [1983] IRLR 401 (EAT) . . . 18.41
Abadeh v British Telecommunications plc [2001] ICR 156; [2001] IRLR 23; [2001] Emp LR 440 . . . 4.82
Abbey National plc v Formoso [1999] IRLR 222 . . . 4.50, 12.22
Abercrombie v AGA Rangemaster Ltd [2013] EWCA Civ 1148 . . . 7.3
Aberdeen City Council v McNeill [2010] IRLR 374 . . . 17.39
Aberdeen Steak House Group v Ibrahim [1988] ICR 550; [1988] IRLR 420; [1988] NLJR 151 (EAT) . . . 20.80
Abrahams v Performing Rights Society [1995] ICR 1028; [1995] IRLR 486; (1995) *Times* 5 June; (1995) *Independent* 25 May . . . 15.15, 15.24, 16.7
Abrahamsson and Anderson v Fogelqvist [2000] ECR I-5539; [2002] ICR 932; [2000] IRLR 732 . . . 4.204
Adams v Charles Zub Associates Ltd [1978] IRLR 551 (EAT) . . . 17.23
Adams v John Wright & Sons (Blackwall) Ltd [1972] ICR 463; 7 ITR 191 (NIRC) . . . 14.8
Adamson v B & L Cleaning Services Ltd [1995] IRLR 193 (EAT) . . . 10.54, 19.4
Adda International Ltd v Curcio [1976] 3 All ER 620; [1976] ICR 407; [1976] IRLR 425 (EAT) . . . 17.203
Addis v Gramophone Co Ltd [1909] AC 488; 78 LJKB 1122; [1908-10] All ER Rep 1; 101 LT 466 (HL) . . . 10.21, 16.23, 16.25
Addison v London Philharmonic Orchestra Ltd [1981] ICR 261 . . . 2.4
Adeneler v Ellinikos Organismos Galaktos (C-212/04) [2006] ECR I-6057; [2006] IRLR 716; [2006] 3 CMLR 30; [2007] All ER (EC) 82 (ECJ) . . . 1.74
Aderemi v London & South East Railway UKEAT/0316/12/KN . . . 4.93

Adin v Sedco Forex International Resources Ltd [1997] IRLR 280 (Ct of Sess) . . . 3.31

Adlam v Salisbury and Wells Theological College [1985] ICR 786 (EAT) . . . 21.59

Adsett v K & L Steelfounders and Engineers Ltd [1953] 1 All ER 97n; [1953] 1 WLR 137; 51 LGR 99; 97 Sol Jo 49; aff'd [1953] 2 All ER 320; [1953] 1 WLR 773; 51 LGR 418; 97 Sol Jo 419 (CA) . . . 11.134

Affleck v Newcastle Mind [1999] ICR 852; [1999] IRLR 405 (EAT) . . . 2.4

Ahmad v United Kingdom (Application 8160/78) (1981) 4 EHRR 126 (EComHR) . . . 1.107

Ahmed v National Car Parks Ltd, IDS Brief 149 . . . 17.4

Ahmet v Trusthouse Forte Catering Ltd (unreported) . . . 2.54

Ahmad v United Kingdom (Application 8160/78) (1981) 4 EHRR 126 (EComHR) . . . 1.107

Ahmed v National Car Parks Ltd, IDS Brief 149 . . . 17.4

Ahmet v Trusthouse Forte Catering Ltd (unreported) . . . 2.54

Ahmed v National Car Parks Ltd, IDS Brief 149 . . . 17.4

Ahmet v Trusthouse Forte Catering Ltd (unreported) . . . 2.54

Ainsworth v Glass Tubes and Components [1977] ICR 347; [1977] IRLR 74 . . . 5.13

Ainsworth v Inland Revenue Commissioners [2009] UKHL 31; [2009] 4 All ER 1205; [2009] ICR 985; [2009] IRLR 677; (2009) Times 15 June . . . 7.89, 8.21

Airbus UK v Webb, EAT/0453/06 (EAT); [2008] EWCA Civ 49 (CA) . . . 12.79

Airfix Footwear Ltd v Cope [1978] ICR 1210; [1978] IRLR 396; 13 ITR 513 (EAT) . . . 2.49

Airlie v Edinburgh District Council [1996] IRLR 516 (EAT) . . . 3.65, 3.73

Akinosun (on behalf of General & Health Workers Union) v The Certification Officer UKEAT/0180/13/RN . . . 22.15

Akintola v Capita Symonds Ltd [2010] EWCA Civ 405 . . . 20.75

Aklagaren v Fransson (C-617/10) . . . 1.107, 17.4

Al-Malki v Reyes UKEAT/0403/12/GE . . . 1.107

Alabaster v Woolwich Bank [2005] EWCA Civ 508; [2005] 2 CMLR 19; [2005] Eu LR 824; [2005] ICR 1246; [2005] IRLR 576; (2005) Times 27 May . . . 6.63

Albion Automotive Ltd v Walker [2002] EWCA Civ 946 . . . 3.80

Albion Shipping Agency v Arnold [1982] ICR 22; [1981] IRLR 525 . . . 5.45

Alboni v Ind Coope Retail [1998] IRLR 131 (CA) . . . 20.25

Albron Catering BV v FNV Bondgenoten (C-242/09) [2011] IRLR 76; [2011] ICR 373 . . . 9.11

Alcan Extrusions v Yates [1996] IRLR 327 (EAT) . . . 3.103, 17.12

Alemo-Herron & Ors v Parkwood Leisure Ltd (C-426/11) . . . 9.37

Alexander v Home Office [1988] IRLR 190 (CA) . . . 20.97

Alexander v Midland Bank plc [2000] ICR 464; [1999] IRLR 723 . . . 11.120

Alexander v Standard Telephones and Cables plc [1990] ICR 291; [1990] IRLR 55 . . . 3.59, 3.63

Alexander v Standard Telephones and Cables plc [1990] ICR 464; [1990] IRLR 723 (CA) . . . 10.2, 16.6

Ali v Christian Salvesen Food Services Ltd [1996] ICR 1; [1995] IRLR 624 (EAT); revsd [1997] 1 All ER 721; [1997] ICR 25; [1997] IRLR 17; 140 Sol Jo LB 231, sub nom Salvesen (Christian) Food Services Ltd v Ali [1996] 41 LS Gaz R 29 (CA) . . . 3.55

Alidair Ltd v Taylor [1977] ICR 446; [1976] IRLR 420; 12 ITR 21 (EAT); aff'd [1978] ICR 445, sub nom Taylor v Alidair Ltd [1978] IRLR 82; 13 ITR 180; 121 Sol Jo 758 (CA) . . . 17.92

Allen Janes LLP v Johal [2006] EWHC 286 (Ch); [2006] ICR 742; [2006] IRLR 599 (Ch) . . . 19.47

Allen v National Australia Group Europe Ltd [2004] IRLR 847 (EAT) . . . 2.127

Allen v Stirling District Council [1994] ICR 434; [1994] IRLR 208 (EAT); revsd [1995] ICR 1082, sub nom Stirling District Council v Allen [1995] IRLR 301; 1995 SLT 1255 (Ct of Sess) . . . 9.60

Alliance Paper Group plc v Prestwich [1996] IRLR 25 . . . 19.42

Allonby v Accrington and Rossendale College [2005] All ER (EC) 289; [2004] ECR I-873; [2004] 1 CMLR 35; [2004] ICR 1328; [2004] IRLR 224; [2004] OPLR 83; [2004] Pens LR 199 . . . 4.191, 5.7

Allwood v William Hill Ltd [1974] IRLR 258 . . . 18.43

Alomo Group (Europe) Ltd v Tucker, EAT/994/01 (EAT) . . . 9.36

American Cyanamid Co v Ethicon Ltd [1974] FSR 312 (CA); revsd [1975] AC 396; [1975] 1 All ER 504; [1975] 2 WLR 316; [1975] FSR 101; [1975] RPC 513; 119 Sol Jo 136 (HL) . . . 10.6, 16.30, 19.62

Amicus v GBS Tooling Ltd [2005] IRLR 683 (EAT) . . . 18.95

Amicus v Macmillan Publishers Ltd [2007] IRLR 885, (2007) 151 SJLB 1058 (EAT) . . . 23.157

Amnesty International v Ahmed [2009] ICR 1450; [2009] IRLR 884; (2009) 159 NLJ 1400; (2009) Times 6 October . . . 4.144, 4.168, 17.48

Anandarajah v Lord Chancellor's Department [1984] IRLR 131 (EAT) . . . 17.77, 20.97

Anderson v Dalkeith Engineering Ltd [1985] ICR 66; [1984] IRLR 429 (EAT) . . . 9.57

Anderson v Newham College of Further
Education [2002] EWCA Civ 505; [2003] ICR
212; [2002] All ER (D) 381 (Mar) . . . 11.148

Anderson v Pringle of Scotland Ltd [1998] IRLR
64; 1998 SLT 754 (OH) . . . 3.63

Angestelltenbetriebsrat der Wiener v Wiener
[1999] ECR I-2865; [1999] 2 CMLR 1173;
[2000] ICR 1134; [1999] IRLR 804; (1999)
Times 20 May . . . 5.27

Anglia Television v Reed [1972] 1 QB 60; [1971]
3 WLR 528; [1971] 3 All ER 690; (1971) 115 SJ
723 . . . 10.52

Annandale Engineering v Samson [1994] IRLR
59 (EAT) . . . 3.13

Anton Piller KG v Manufacturing Processes Ltd
[1976] Ch 55; [1976] 2 WLR 162; [1976] 1
All ER 779; [1976] FSR 129; [1976] RPC 719;
(1975) 120 SJ 63 (CA) . . . 19.65

Anyanwu v South Bank Students' Union (2003)
Times 5 December . . . 4.203, 17.59

Aon Ltd v JLT Reinsurance Brokers Ltd [2010]
IRLR 600; [2009] EWHC 3448 (QB) . . . 20.63

Aparau v Iceland Frozen Foods Ltd (No 2) [1996]
IRLR 119 (EAT); revsd [2000] 1 All ER 228;
[2000] IRLR 196; [1999] 45 LS Gaz R 31
(CA) . . . 20.128

Apelogun-Gabriels v London Borough of
Lambeth [2001] EWCA Civ 1853; [2002] ICR
713; [2002] IRLR 116 . . . 4.158, 20.12

Appleyard v FM Smith (Hull) Ltd [1972] IRLR
19 . . . 17.147

Argent v Minister of Social Security [1968]
3 All ER 208; [1968] 1 WLR 1749; 112 Sol
Jo 801 . . . 2.49

Armour v Skeen [1977] IRLR 310; 1977 JC 15;
1977 SLT 71 . . . 11.93

Armstrong v British Coal Corpn (1996) Times
6 December (CA) . . . 11.120

Armstrong v Newcastle NHS Foundation Trust
[2006] IRLR 124 . . . 5.45

Armstrong Whitworth Rolls Ltd v Mustard
[1971] 1 All ER 598; 9 KIR 279; 6 ITR 79 (DC)
. . . 3.109, 14.2

Arthur Guinness Son & Co (Great Britain) Ltd v
Green [1989] ICR 241; [1989] IRLR 288 (EAT)
. . . 17.215, 20.87

Arthur White (Contractors) Ltd v Tarmac Civil
Engineering Ltd [1967] 3 All ER 586; [1967] 1
WLR 1508; 111 Sol Jo 831 (HL) . . . 2.146

Ashford v Association of Scientific, Technical
and Management Staffs [1973] ICR 296
(NIRC) . . . 21.16

Asociación Nacional de Grandes Empresas de
Distribución (ANGED) (C-78/11) . . . 7.86

Aspden v Webbs Poultry and Meat
Group (Holdings) Ltd [1996] IRLR 521 . . . 3.2,
3.31

Assamoi v Spirit Pub Company UKEAT/0050/11
. . . 17.24, 17.34

Associated British Ports v Palmer [1993] ICR 101;
[1993] IRLR 63; [1992] 42 LS Gaz R 39 (EAT);

revsd [1994] ICR 97; [1993] IRLR 336; [1993]
26 LS Gaz R 37; 137 Sol Jo LB 134 (CA); revsd
[1995] 2 AC 454; [1995] 2 All ER 100; [1995]
2 WLR 354; [1995] ICR 406; [1995] IRLR 258;
[1995] 17 LS Gaz R 48; [1995] NLJR 417 (HL)
. . . 21.31

Associated British Ports v Transport and
General Workers' Union [1989] IRLR 291;
on appeal [1989] 3 All ER 796; [1989] 1 WLR
939; [1989] ICR 557; [1989] IRLR 305 (CA);
revsd [1989] 3 All ER 822; [1989] 1 WLR 939;
[1989] ICR 557; [1989] IRLR 399 (HL) . . .
23.45

Associated Dairies Ltd v Hartley [1979] IRLR 171
. . . 11.20

Associated Foreign Exchange Ltd v International
Foreign Exchange (UK) Ltd [2010] EWHC
1178 (Ch); [2010] IRLR 964 . . . 19.40,
19.45

Associated Newspapers Ltd v Wilson [1992]
ICR 681; [1992] IRLR 440; [1992] 33 LS
Gaz R 35 (EAT); [1994] ICR 97; sub nom
Wilson v Associated Newspapers Ltd [1993]
IRLR 336 (CA); revsd sub nom Associated
Newspapers Ltd v Wilson [1995] 2 AC NLJR
417 (HL) . . . 21.31

Associated Society of Locomotive Engineers and
Firemen v Brady [2006] IRLR 576 (EAT) . . .
17.124

Association of HSD (Hatfield) Employees v
Certification Officer [1978] ICR 21; [1977]
IRLR 261 (EAT) . . . 22.12

Association of Pattern Makers and Allied
Craftsmen v Kirvin Ltd [1978] IRLR 318, 13
ITR 446 . . . 18.88

Association of Scientific, Technical and
Managerial Staffs v Hawker Siddeley Aviation
[1977] IRLR 418 . . . 18.96

Astbury v Gist, EAT/0619/06/DA, EAT/0446/04/
LA . . . 2.159, 2.160

Astley v Celtec Ltd (C-478/03) (2005) Times
9 June . . . 2.149, 9.29

Athinaiki Chartopoiia AE v Panagiotidis (C-
270/05) [2007] IRLR 284 (ECJ) . . . 18.77

Atkin v Enfield Hospital Management Committee
[1975] IRLR 217; 119 Sol Jo 575 (CA) . . .
17.138

Atkins v Coyle Personnel plc [2008]
IRLR 420 . . . 6.100

Attwood v Lamont [1920] 3 KB 571 . . . 19.33

Auguste Noel Ltd v Curtis [1990] ICR 604; [1990]
IRLR 326 (EAT) . . . 12.74

Autoclenz v Belcher [2011] UKSC 41 . . . 2.2,
2.156

Avon County Council v Haywood-Hicks [1978]
ICR 646; [1978] IRLR 118; (1978) 13 ITR 208
. . . 20.7

Avonmouth Construction Co Ltd v Shipway
[1979] IRLR 14 (EAT) . . . 18.43

Aylott v Stockton-on-Tees Borough Council
[2010] IRLR 994 (CA) . . . 4.82

Aziz v Bethnal Green City Challenge Co Ltd
  [2000] IRLR 111 (CA) . . . 20.119
Aziz v Trinity Street Taxis Ltd [1986] IRLR 435
  (EAT) aff'd [1989] QB 463; [1988] 2 All ER
  860; [1988] 3 WLR 79; [1988] ICR 534; [1988]
  IRLR 204; 132 Sol Jo 898; [1988] 26 LS Gaz R
  42 (CA) . . . 4.41
Azmi v Kirklees Metropolitan Borough Council
  [2007] ICR 1154; [2007] IRLR 484; [2007] ELR
  339; (2007) *Times* 17 April . . . 4.160, 4.161

B v BBA [2005] ICR 1530 . . . 2.175
BBC Scotland v Souster 2001 SC 458; [2001]
  IRLR 150; 2000 GWD 40-1490 . . . 4.140
BBC v Beckett [1983] IRLR 43 (EAT) . . . 12.86,
  17.40
BBC v Hearn [1978] 1 All ER 111; [1997] 1 WLR
  1004; [1977] ICR 685; [1977] IRLR 273; 121
  Sol Jo 374 (CA) . . . 23.35
BCCI SA v Ali (No 3) [2001] UKHL 8; [2002] 1
  AC 251; [2001] 1 All ER 961; [2001] 2 WLR
  735; [2001] ICR 337; [2001] IRLR 292; 151 NLJ
  351; 145 Sol Jo LB 67; [2001] All ER (D) 06
  (Mar) . . . 3.47, 10.12, 20.37
BG Gale Ltd v Gilbert [1978] ICR 1149; [1978]
  IRLR 453; 13 ITR 547 (EAT) . . . 17.50
BG plc v O'Brien [2002] ICR 721; (2002) IRLR
  444 . . . 3.48
BP plc v Elstone [2010] IRLR 558 . . . 10.74
BS v Dundee City Council [2013] CSIH 91 . . . 17.93
BSG Property Services v Tuck [1996] IRLR 134
  (EAT) . . . 9.8
BSM (1257) Ltd v Secretary of State for Social
  Services [1978] ICR 894 . . . 2.54
Bache v Essex County Council [2000] 2 All ER
  847; [2000] IRLR 251; [2000] 05 LS Gaz R 33;
  [2000] NLJR 99 (CA) . . . 20.70
Bacica v Muir [2006] IRLR 35 . . . 2.45
Badeck v Hessischer [2000] All ER (EC) 289;
  (2001) CMLR 79 . . . 4.204
Baggs v Fudge, 1400114/05/ET . . . 4.155
Bahl v Law Society [2004] EWCA Civ 1070;
  [2004] IRLR 799; (2004) 154 NLJ 1292; (2004)
  148 SJLB 976; (2004) *Times* 7 October . . . 4.22,
  4.223
Bainbridge v Circuit Foil UK Ltd [1997] ICR 541;
  [1997] IRLR 305 (CA) . . . 3.31
Baker v Superite Tools Ltd [1982] ICR 69 (EAT)
  . . . 1.23
Balfour Beatty Power Networks Ltd v Wilcox
  [2006] IRLR 258 (EAT); aff'd [2006] EWCA
  Civ 1240; [2007] IRLR 63 (CA) . . . 20.133
Balfour Kilpatrick Ltd v Acheson [2003] IRLR 683;
  [2003] All ER (D) 15 (Apr) (EAT) . . . 11.66
Balston Ltd v Headline Filters Ltd [1987] FSR
  330; [1990] FSR 385 . . . 19.3
Baluba v Waltham Forest College (2007) ICR
  1026; (2007) IRLR 346 . . . 10.77
Bamgbose v Royal Star and Garter Home (EAT)
  841/95 . . . 2.114, 3.16

Bamsey v Albion Engineering Ltd [2003] ICR
  1224; [2003] All ER (D) 424 (Mar) (EAT);
  aff'd *sub nom* Bamsey v Albion Engineering
  Ltd [2004] EWCA Civ 359; 148 Sol Jo LB 389;
  [2004] All ER (D) 482 (Mar) . . . 7.85, 14.3
Banking Insurance and Finance Union v Barclays
  Bank plc [1987] ICR 495 . . . 9.9
Banks v Ablex Ltd [2005] EWCA Civ 173; [2005]
  ICR 819; [2005] IRLR 357; (2005) 149 SJLB
  269; (2005) *Times* 21 March . . . 10.116
Barber v Guardian Royal Exchange Assurance
  Group [1991] 1 QB 344; [1991] 2 WLR 72;
  [1990] 2 All ER 660; [1990] ECR I-1889; [1990]
  2 CMLR 513; [1990] ICR 616; [1990] IRLR
  240; [1990] 1 PLR 103; (1990) 140 NLJ 925;
  (1990) *Times* 18 May; (1990) *Independent* 23
  May; (1990) *Financial Times* 25 May; (1990)
  Guardian 12 July . . . 5.2, 5.17, 5.41
Barber v Guardian Royal Exchange Assurance
  Group (C-262/88) [1991] 1 QB 344; [1990]
  2 All ER 660; [1991] 2 WLR 72; [1990] ECR
  I-1889; [1990] 2 CMLR 513; [1990] ICR 616;
  [1990] IRLR 240; [1990] NJLR 925 (ECJ) . . .
  1.81, 1.103
Barber v RJB Mining (UK) Ltd [1999] 2 CMLR
  833; [1999] ICR 679; [1999] IRLR 308; 143 Sol
  Jo LB 141; [1999] All ER (D) 244 . . . 7.108
Barber v Somerset County Council [2002] EWCA
  Civ 76; [2002] 2 All ER 1; [2002] IRLR 263; 68
  BMLR 115; [2002] All ER (D) 53 (Feb); revsd
  [2004] UKHL 13; [2004] 2 All ER 385; [2004]
  1 WLR 1089; 148 Sol Jo LB 419; [2004] All ER
  (D) 07 9 (Apr) . . . 11.108
Barber v Staffordshire County Council [1996] 2
  All ER 748; [1996] IRLR 209; [1996] 06 LS Gaz
  R 26; *sub nom* Staffordshire County Council v
  Barber [1996] ICR 379 (CA) . . . 20.23
Barclays Bank plc v James [1990] ICR 333; [1990]
  IRLR 90 . . . 5.7
Barclays Bank plc v Kapur [1991] 2 AC 355;
  [1991] 2 WLR 401; [1991] 1 All ER 646; [1991]
  ICR 208; [1991] IRLR 136; (1991) *Times* 25
  January; (1991) *Independent* 6 February;
  (1991) *Financial Times* 30 January; (1991)
  Guardian 31 January; (1991) *Daily Telegraph*
  7 February . . . 4.145, 4.223, 20.11
Barcock v Brighton Corpn [1949] 1 KB 339;
  [1949] 1 All ER 251; 47 LGR 253; 93 Sol Jo 119;
  65 TLR 90 . . . 11.125
Barke v SEETEC Business Technology Centre
  [2005] EWCA Civ 578; [2005] WLR (D) 46
  (CA) . . . 20.128
Barking and Dagenham London Borough
  Council v Oguoko [2000] IRLR 179
  (EAT) . . . 20.88
Barley v Amey Roadstone Corpn Ltd [1977] ICR
  546; [1977] IRLR 299; 11 ITR 283 (EAT) . . .
  18.50
Barnes v Gilmartin Associates (EAT) 825/97 . . .
  17.154, 18.16

Barratt Developments (Bradford) Ltd v UCATT [1978] ICR 319; [1977] IRLR 403; 12 ITR 478 (EAT) . . . 18.76

Barretts & Baird (Wholesale) Ltd v Institution of Professional Civil Servants [1987] IRLR 3; [1988] NLJR 357 . . . 23.45

Barry v Midland Bank [1999] 1 WLR 1465; [1999] 3 All ER 974; [1999] ICR 859; [1999] IRLR 581; (1999) 96(31) LSG 36; (1999) 149 NLJ 1253; (1999) 143 SJLB 221; (1999) *Times* 23 July; (1999) *Independent* 25 October . . . 5.19

Barry v Midland Bank plc [1997] ICR 192 (EAT); aff'd [1998] 1 All ER 805; [1999] ICR 319; [1998] IRLR 138 (CA); aff'd [1999] 3 All ER 974; [1999] 1 WLR 1465; [1999] ICR 859; [1999] IRLR 581; [1999] 31 LS Gaz R 36; [1999] NLJR 1253; 143 Sol Jo LB 221 (HL) . . . 2.91

Bartholomew v London Borough of Hackney [1999] IRLR 246 (CA) . . . 10.36

Barthorpe v Exeter Diocesan Board of Finance Ltd [1979] ICR 900; 123 Sol Jo 585 (EAT) . . . 2.62

Basnett v J & A Jackson Ltd [1976] ICR 63; [1976] IRLR 154 . . . 16.23, 16.24

Bass Leisure Ltd v Thomas [1994] IRLR 104 (EAT) . . . 18.14

Bass Taverns Ltd v Burgess [1995] IRLR 596 (CA) . . . 21.85

Bateman v Asda Stores Ltd [2010] IRLR 370 . . . 3.87, 17.12

Batisha v Say [1977] IRLIB; [1977] IRLR 6 . . . 4.47, 4.177

Batty v Melillo [2008] EWHC 1924 (QB); [2008] IRLR 760 . . . 15.33

Bauman v Hulton Press Ltd [1952] 2 All ER 1121 . . . 10.17

Bavin v NHS Trust Pensions Agency [1999] ICR 1192; [1999] OPLR 285 . . . 4.124

Baxter v Limb Group of Companies [1994] IRLR 572 (CA) . . . 18.11, 21.103

Baynton v South West Trains Ltd [2005] ICR 1730 . . . 20.8

Beanstalk Shelving Ltd v Horn [1980] ICR 273 (EAT) . . . 20.13, 20.14

Beasley v National Grid [1980] ICR 273 (EAT) . . . 20.13

Beaverbrook Newspapers Ltd v Keys [1978] ICR 582; [1978] IRLR 34 (CA) . . . 23.39

Bebbington v Palmer (t/a Sturry News) (EAT, 23 February 2010) . . . 2.41

Beckett Investment Management Group Ltd v Hall [2007] EWHC 241 (QB); revsd [2007] EWCA Civ 613; [2007] IRLR 793; (2007) 151 SJLB 891; [2007] ICR 1539 . . . 19.49, 19.55

Bell v Lever Bros Ltd [1932] AC 161; 101 LJKB 129; 37 Com Cas 98; [1931] All ER Rep 1; 76 Sol Jo 50; 146 LT 258; 48 TLR 133 (HL) . . . 10.94, 10.95

Beloff v Pressdram [1973] 1 All ER 241; [1973] FSR 33; [1973] RPC 765 . . . 2.37

Bendall v Paine and Betteridge [1973] IRLR 44 . . . 12.81

Bengey v North Devon District Council [1977] ICR 15; 11 ITR 211 (EAT) . . . 20.13

Benkharbouche v Embassy of the Republic of Sudan UKEAT/0401/12/GE . . . 1.107

Benkharbouche v Sudan UKEAT/0401/12/GE, UKEAT/0020/13/GE . . . 17.4

Bennett v Governing Body of Pennoweth School (EAT, 22 July 2008) . . . 20.121

Benson v Secretary of State for Trade and Industry [2003] ICR 1082; [2003] All ER (D) 113 (EAT) . . . 7.134

Bentley Engineering Co Ltd v Crown and Miller [1976] ICR 225; [1976] IRLR 146; 11 ITR 50 (DC) . . . 2.8, 13.20

Bentley Engineering Co Ltd v Mistry [1979] ICR 47; [1978] IRLR 437 (EAT) . . . 12.5

Benton v Sanderson Kayser Ltd [1988] ICR 313; [1988] IRLR 235; [1988] 8 LS Gaz R 35 (EAT); revsd [1989] ICR 136; [1989] IRLR 19 (CA) . . . 18.27

Bents Brewery Co Ltd v Hogan [1945] 2 All ER 570 . . . 10.69, 19.69, 23.37

Berkeley Garage Ltd v Edmunds [1975] ICR 228; [1975] IRLR 124; 10 ITR 70; 110 Sol Jo 460 (DC) . . . 20.101

Bernadone v Pall Mall Services Group Ltd [1999] IRLR 617; aff'd [2000] 3 All ER 544; [2000] Lloyd's Rep IR 665; [2000] IRLR 487 (CA) . . . 9.30, 9.39

Berriman v Delabole Slate Ltd [1984] ICR 636; [1984] IRLR 394 (EAT); aff'd [1985] ICR 546, *sub nom* Delabole Slate Ltd v Berriman [1985] IRLR 305 (CA) . . . 9.58

Berry v Ravensbourne National Health Service Trust [1993] ICR 871 . . . 20.10

Berry v Stone Manganese and Marine Ltd [1972] 1 Lloyd's Rep 182; 12 KIR 13; 115 Sol Jo 966 . . . 11.128

Berwick Salmon Fisheries Co Ltd v Rutherford [1991] IRLR 203 (EAT) . . . 13.21

Betts v Brintel Helicopters [1997] 2 All ER 840; [1997] ICR 792; [1997] IRLR 361; [1997] NLJR 561, *sub nom* Betts v Brintel Helicopters Ltd and KLM ERA Helicopters (UK) Ltd [1998] 2 CMLR 22 (CA) . . . 9.10

Bevan Ashford v Malin [1995] ICR 453; [1995] IRLR 360 (EAT) . . . 12.77

Bevan Harris Ltd v Gair [1981] IRLR 520 (EAT) . . . 12.85, 17.87

Beveridge v KLM UK Ltd [2000] IRLR 765 (EAT) . . . 10.19

Bex v Securicor Transport Ltd [1972] IRLR 68 . . . 3.108

Biffa Waste Services Ltd v Maschinenfabric GmbH [2009] QB 725; [2008] EWCA 6 . . . 10.103

Biggs v Somerset County Council [1995] [1995] ICR 811; [1995] IRLR 452 (EAT); aff'd [1996] 2 All ER 734; [1996] 2 CMLR 292; [1996] ICR 364; [1996] IRLR 203; [1996] 06 LS Gaz R 27; [1996] NJLR 174; 140 Sol Jo LB 59 (CA) . . . 1.28, 1.103, 20.22, 20.24

Bigham v GKN Kwikform Ltd [1992] ICR 113; [1992] IRLR 4 (EAT) . . . 21.106

Bilka-Kaufhaus v Weber von Hartz [1986] ECR 1607; [1986] 2 CMLR 701; [1987] ICR 110; [1986] IRLR 317 . . . 4.174

Birch and Humber v University of Liverpool [1985] ICR 470; [1985] IRLR 165; 129 Sol Jo 245 (CA) . . . 18.7

Birch v Liverpool University [1985] ICR 470; [1985] IRLR 165; 129 Sol Jo 245 (CA) . . . 17.68

Bird v British Celanese Ltd [1945] KB 336; [1945] 1 All ER 488; 43 LGR 199; 109 JP 170; 114 LJKB 184; 172 LT 260; 61 TLR 316 (CA) . . . 12.60

Birds Eye Walls Ltd v Harrison [1985] ICR 278; [1985] IRLR 47 (EAT) . . . 20.69

Birmingham City Council v Abdulla [2012] UKSC 47 . . . 5.62

Birmingham District Council v Beyer [1978] 1 All ER 910; [1977] IRLR 211; 8 BLR 83 (EAT) . . . 21.30, 21.85

Blackburn with Darwen Borough Council v Stanley [2005] All ER (D) 135 (May) . . . 17.43

Blackburn v Chief Constable of West Midlands Police [2008] EWCA Civ 1208; [2009] IRLR 135; (2008) 105(44) LSG 20; (2008) 158 NLJ 1603 . . . 5.29, 5.45

Blackman v Post Office [1974] ICR 151; [1974] IRLR 46 (NIRC) . . . 17.117

Blair v Lochaber District Council [1995] IRLR 135 (Ct of Sess) . . . 16.37

Blake v Berkel Auto Scales Co Ltd [1974] IRLR 272 . . . 3.91

Blake v Galloway [2004] EWCA Civ 814; [2004] 1 WLR 2844 . . . 11.129

Bleuse v MBT Transport Ltd [2008] ICR 488; [2008] IRLR 264 . . . 1.37, 4.217

Bliss v South East Thames Regional Health Authority [1987] ICR 700; [1985] IRLR 308 (CA) . . . 16.6

Blockleys plc v Miller [1992] ICR 749; [1992] 34 LS Gaz R 39 (EAT) . . . 20.130

Bloomfield v Springfield Hosiery Finishing Co Ltd [1972] 1 All ER 609; [1972] 1 WLR 386; [1972] ICR 91; 12 KIR 175; 7 ITR 89; 116 Sol Jo 141 (NIRC) . . . 13.35

Blower v CEGB (unreported) . . . 21.70

Blue Chip Trading Ltd v Helbaw [2009] IRLR 128 . . . 3.9

Blue Circle Staff Association v Certification Officer [1977] 2 All ER 145; [1977] 1 WLR 239; [1977] ICR 224; [1977] IRLR 20; 121 Sol Jo 52 (EAT) . . . 22.11

Blundell v St Andrew's Catholic Primary School [2007] ICR 1451; [2007] IRLR 652 . . . 6.43

Blyth v Scottish Liberal Club [1983] IRLR 245; 1983 SLT 260 (Ct of Sess) . . . 16.9

Boardman v Copeland Borough Council [2001] EWCA Civ 888; [2001] All ER (D) 99 (Jun) . . . 16.25

Bolton Roadways Ltd v Edwards [1987] IRLR 392 (EAT) . . . 13.36

Bolton School v Evans [2006] IRLR 500; [2006] ELR 255 (EAT); aff'd [2006] EWCA Civ 1653 [2007] ICR 641; [2007] IRLR 140; (2006) 103(46) LSG 30; (2006) 150 SJLB 1532 (CA) . . . 10.82

Bolwell v Redcliffe Homes Ltd [1999] IRLR 485; [1999] All ER (D) 33 (CA) . . . 9.1

Bonner v H Gilbert Ltd [1989] IRLR 475 (EAT) . . . 18.62

Bonser v RJB Mining (UK) Ltd [2004] IRLR 164 (CA) . . . 11.136

Bonsor v Musicians' Union [1954] Ch 479; [1954] 1 All ER 822; 98 Sol Jo 248 (CA); revsd [1956] AC 104; [1955] 3 All ER 518; [1955] 3 WLR 788; 99 Sol Jo 814 (HL) . . . 22.33

Boorman v Allmakes Ltd [1995] ICR 842; [1995] IRLR 553 (CA) . . . 17.198

Booth v United States of America [1999] IRLR 16; 611 IRLB 9 (EAT) . . . 2.137, 13.2

Boots Co plc v Lees-Collier [1986] ICR 728; [1986] IRLR 485 (EAT) . . . 17.187

Borders Regional Council v Maule [1993] IRLR 199 (EAT) . . . 7.19

Boston Deep Sea Fishing and Ice Co v Ansell (1888) 39 Ch D 339; [1886–90] All ER Rep 65; 59 LT 345 (CA) . . . 10.66

Botzen v Rotterdamsche Droogdok Maatschappij (186/83) [1985] ECR 519; [1986] 2 CMLR 50 (ECJ) . . . 9.12, 9.13

Bouchaala v Trusthouse Forte Hotels Ltd [1980] ICR 721; [1980] IRLR 382 (EAT) . . . 17.164

Boulting v Association of Cinematograph, Television and Allied Technicians [1963] 2 QB 606; [1963] 1 All ER 716; [1963] 2 WLR 529; 107 Sol Jo 133 (CA) . . . 21.5, 22.22

Bournemouth University Higher Education Corporation v Buckland [2010] EWCA Civ 121; [2010] ICR 908 . . . 17.23

Bowater Containers Ltd v McCormack [1980] IRLR 50 (EAT) . . . 3.104

Bowater plc v Charlwood [1991] ICR 798; [1991] IRLR 340 (EAT) . . . 20.71

Bowler v Lovegrove [1921] 1 Ch 642; 90 LJ Ch 356; 65 Sol Jo 397; 124 LT 695; 37 TLR 424 . . . 19.33

Boxfoldia Ltd v National Graphical Association [1988] ICR 752; [1988] IRLR 383 . . . 23.87

Boychuk v Symons Holdings Ltd [1977] IRLR 395 (EAT) . . . 17.138

Boyd v Renfrewshire Council 2008 SCLR 578; 2008 GWD 20-333 . . . 12.22

Boyo v Lambeth London Borough Council [1994] ICR 727; [1995] IRLR 50 (CA) . . . 3.96, 16.16

Brace v Calder [1895] 2 QB 253 . . . 16.26

Bracebridge Engineering Ltd v Darby [1990] IRLR 3 (EAT) . . . 4.34

Bradford v Robinson Rentals Ltd [1967] 1 All ER 267; [1967] 1 WLR 337, 1 KIR 486; 111 Sol Jo 33 . . . 11.122

Bradley v Opperman Gears [1975] IRLR 13 . . . 10.13

Bradshaw v Rugby Portland Cement Co Ltd [1972] IRLR 46 . . . 17.140

Braithwaite v Electrical Electronics and Telecommunications Union [1969] 2 All ER 859; 6 KIR 169; 113 Sol Jo 305 (CA) . . . 22.30

Brandeaux (Advisers) UK Ltd v Chadwick [2011] IRLR 224; [2010] EWHC 3241 (QB) . . . 10.54

Brasserie du Pêcheur SA v Germany (C-46/93) [1996] QB 404; [1996] 2 WLR 506; [1996] ECR I-1029; [1996] All ER (EC) 301; [1996] 1 CMLR 889; [1996] IRLR 267 (ECJ); apl'd [1998] 1 CMLR 1353; [1997] TLR 482; [1997] Eu LR 475; [1998] 1 All ER 736n (DC); aff'd [1998] 3 CMLR 192; [1998] NPC 68; [1998] TLR 261; [1998] Eu LR 456; [1999] 2 All ER 640n (CA); aff'd [2000] 1 AC 524; [1999] 4 All ER 906; [1999] 3 WLR 1062; [1999] 3 CMLR 597; [1999] 43 LS Gaz R 32 (HL) . . . 1.74

Brassington v Cauldon Wholesale Ltd [1978] ICR 405; [1977] IRLR 479 (EAT) . . . 21.60

Breach v Epsylon Industries Ltd [1976] ICR 316; [1976] IRLR 180 (EAT) . . . 10.17

Brennan and Ging v Ellward (Lancs) Ltd [1974] IRLR 153 (NIRC) . . . 21.53

Brennan v C Lindley & Co Ltd [1974] IRLR 153 (NIRC) . . . 15.8

Brennan v J H Dewhurst Ltd [1984] ICR 52; [1983] IRLR 357 . . . 4.46

Brewer & Sons v Dunston (unreported) . . . 11.17

Bridgen v Lancashire County Council [1987] IRLR 58 (CA) . . . 17.26

Briggs v Imperial Chemical Industries Ltd (1968) 5 KIR 492; 3 ITR 276; 112 Sol Jo 541 (DC) . . . 3.93

Briggs v North Eastern Education and Library Board [1990] IRLR 181 . . . 4.174

Briggs v Oates [1991] 1 All ER 407; [1990] ICR 473; [1990] IRLR 472; (1990) 140 NLJ 208 (ChD) . . . 19.57

Brink's Global Services Inc v Igrox Ltd [2011] IRLR 343 . . . 10.104

Bristol Channel Ship Repairers Ltd v O'Keefe [1977] 2 All ER 258; [1978] ICR 691; [1977] IRLR 13 (EAT) . . . 18.51

British Aerospace plc v Green [1995] ICR 1006; [1995] IRLR 433 (CA) . . . 18.42, 20.63

British Aircraft Corpn v Austin [1978] IRLR 332 (EAT) . . . 17.27

British Airways (European Operations at Gatwick) Ltd v Moore and Botterill [2000] 2 CMLR 343; [2000] ICR 678; [2000] IRLR 296 (EAT) . . . 6.15

British Airways plc v Mak [2011] EWCA Civ 184 . . . 4.192

British Airways plc v Unite (No 1) [2010] IRLR 423; [2009] EWHC 3541 (QB) . . . 23.52

British Airways plc v Unite (No 2) [2010] EWCA Civ 669; [2010] IRLR 80 . . . 23.63, 23.69

British Coal Corpn v Cheesbrough [1988] ICR 60, sub nom National Coal Board v Cheesbrough and Secretary of State for Employment [1988] IRLR 351 (CA); revsd sub nom British Coal Corpn v Cheesbrough [1988] ICR 769; [1988] IRLR 351 (CA); aff'd [1990] 2 AC 256; [1990] 1 All ER 641; [1990] 2 WLR 407; [1990] ICR 317; [1990] IRLR 148; 134 Sol Jo 661; [1990] 11 LS Gaz R 39 (HL) . . . 14.4

British Coal Corpn v Keeble [1997] IRLR 336 (EAT) . . . 20.9, 20.24

British Coal Corpn v Smith [1996] 3 All ER 97; [1996] ICR 515; [1996] IRLR 399; (1996) 93(25) LSG 28; (1996) 140 SJLB 134; (1996) Times 23 May; (1996) Independent 13 June . . . 5.7

British Gas plc v McCarrick [1991] IRLR 305 (CA) . . . 17.128

British Guiana Credit Corpn v Da Silva [1965] 1 WLR 248; 109 Sol Jo 30 (PC) . . . 16.21

British Home Stores v Burchell [1980] ICR 303n; [1978] IRLR 379; 13 ITR 560 (EAT) . . . 12.5, 17.126

British Industrial Plastics Ltd v Ferguson [1938] 4 All ER 504; 56 RPC 271; 82 Sol Jo 970; 160 LT 95 (CA); aff'd [1940] 1 All ER 479; 58 RPC 1; 162 LT 313 (HL) . . . 19.69

British Labour Pump Co Ltd v Byrne [1979] ICR 347; [1979] IRLR 94 (EAT) . . . 17.218

British Leyland (UK) Ltd v Ashraf [1978] ICR 979; [1978] IRLR 330; 13 ITR 500 (EAT) . . . 17.69

British Leyland (UK) Ltd v Swift [1981] IRLR 91 (CA) . . . 17.78

British Nursing Association v Inland Revenue (National Minimum Wage Compliance Team) [2001] IRLR 659; [2001] All ER (D) 59 (Aug) (EAT); aff'd [2002] EWCA Civ 494; [2003] ICR 19; [2002] IRLR 480; [2002] All ER (D) 419 (Mar) . . . 2.126, 8.43, 8.44

British Railways Board v Jackson [1994] IRLR 235 (CA) . . . 17.79, 17.133

British Telecommunications plc v Sheridan [1990] IRLR 27 (CA) . . . 20.122

British Telecommunications plc v Ticehurst [1992] ICR 383; [1992] 15 LS Gaz R 32; 136 Sol Jo LB 96, sub nom Ticehurst and Thompson v British Telecommunications plc [1992] IRLR 219 (CA) . . . 10.64

British Transport Commission v Gourley [1956] AC 185; [1955] 3 All ER 796; [1956] 2 WLR 41; [1955] 2 Lloyd's Rep 475; 34 ATC 305; 49 R & IT 11; [1955] TR 303; 100 Sol Jo 12 (HL) . . . 16.29

British United Shoe Machinery Co Ltd v Clarke [1978] ICR 70; [1977] IRLR 297; 12 ITR 473 (EAT) . . . 17.199, 18.44

Brito-Babapulle v Ealing Hospital NHS Trust UKEAT/0358/12/BA . . . 17.124

Britool Ltd v Roberts [1993] IRLR 481 (EAT) . . . 21.85

Broadbent v Crisp [1974] 1 All ER 1052; [1974] ICR 248; 16 KIR 168; [1974] ITR 147 NIRC . . . 2.28

Broaders v Kalkare Property Maintenance Ltd [1990] IRLR 421 (EAT) . . . 3.14

Brock v Minerva Dental Ltd [2007] ICR 917 . . . 13.32

Bromsgrove Casting and Machining Ltd v Martin [1977] 3 All ER 487; [1977] ICR 417; 12 ITR 177 (EAT) . . . 2.16

Brookes v Borough Care Services [1998] ICR 1198; [1998] IRLR 636 (EAT) . . . 9.28

Brookes v Olyslager OMS (UK) Ltd [1988] IRLR 590; 601 IRLB 6 (CA) . . . 19.20

Brooks v Ladbroke Lucky Seven Entertainment [1977] IRLIB . . . 4.244

Brooks (W) & Son v Skinner [1984] IRLR 379 . . . 12.41

Broome v DPP [1974] AC 587; [1974] 1 All ER 314; [1974] 2 WLR 58; [1974] ICR 84; [1974] IRLR 26; [1974] Crim LR 311; 118 Sol Jo 50 (HL) . . . 23.110

Broomsgrove v Eagle Alexander Ltd [1981] IRLR 127 (EAT) . . . 17.177

Brophy v Bradfield & Co Ltd [1955] 3 All ER 286; [1955] 1 WLR 1148; 53 LGR 665; 99 Sol Jo 778 (CA) . . . 11.144

Brown v Rentokil Ltd [1998] All ER (EC) 791; [1998] ECR I-4185; [1998] 2 CMLR 1049; [1998] CEC 829; [1998] ICR 790; [1998] IRLR 445; [1998] 2 FLR 649; [1999] 1 FCR 49; (1999) 48 BMLR 126; [1998] Fam Law 597; (1998) Times 2 July . . . 4.132

Brown v Rolls-Royce (1971) Ltd (1977) 12 ITR 382 (EAT) . . . 11.141

Brown v Southall and Knight [1980] ICR 617; [1980] IRLR 130 (EAT) . . . 15.7, 17.5

Brown v Stockton-on-Tees Borough Council [1986] ICR 842; [1986] IRLR 432; (1986) 83 LSG 3746; (1986) 136 NLJ 892 (EAT); aff'd [1987] ICR 897; [1987] IRLR 230 (CA); rev [1989] AC 20; [1988] 2 WLR 935; [1988] 2 All ER 129; [1988] ICR 410; [1988] IRLR 263; 86 LGR 561; (1988) 85(19) LSG 41; (1988) 138 NLJ Rep 117; (1988) 132 SJ 624 (HL) . . . 18.58

Browning v Crumlin Valley Collieries [1926] 1 KB 522; 24 LGR 302; 90 JP 201; 95 LJKB 711; [1926] All ER Rep 132; 134 LT 603; 42 TLR 323 . . . 10.19

Bruce v Wiggins Teape (Stationery) Ltd [1994] IRLR 536 (EAT) . . . 8.14, 8.18

Buchanan-Smith v Scheicher & Co International Ltd [1996] ICR 613; [1996] IRLR 547 (EAT) . . . 9.13

Buckland v Bournemouth University [2010] EWCA Civ 121; [2010] IRLR 445; (2010) Times 3 May . . . 17.34

Buckley v National Union of General and Municipal Workers [1967] 3 All ER 767; 112 Sol Jo 292 . . . 22.35

Budgen & Co v Thomas [1976] ICR 344; [1976] IRLR 174 (EAT) . . . 12.8

Bull & Bull v Hall & Preddy [2013] UKSC 73 . . . 4.157

Bullimore v Pothecary Witham Weld Solicitors (No 2) [2011] IRLR 18 . . . 10.37

Bullock v Alice Ottley School [1993] ICR 138; [1992] IRLR 564; 91 LGR 32; (1992) Times 7 November; (1992) Independent 11 November . . . 4.28

Bunce v Postworth Ltd (t/a Skyblue) [2005] EWCA Civ 490; [2005] IRLR 557 . . . 2.154, 2.161

Bunning v GT Bunning & Sons Ltd, EAT/0136/03 . . . 6.10

Burdett-Coutts v Hertfordshire County Council [1984] IRLR 91 . . . 16.32

Burgess v O'Brien (1966) 1 KIR 99; 1 ITR 164 . . . 18.4

Burke v Royal Liverpool University Hospital NHS Trust [1997] ICR 730 (EAT) . . . 3.72

Burns v Consignia plc (No 2) [2004] IRLR 425; [2004] ICR 1103 . . . 20.128

Burns v Ideal Timber Products [1975] IRLR 19; 10 ITR 14 . . . 17.135

Burns v Santander UK plc [2011] IRLR 639 . . . 8.12, 10.100

Burrett v West Birmingham Health Authority [1994] IRLR7 (EAT) . . . 4.21, 4.176

Burrow Down Support Services Ltd v Rossiter [2008] ICR 1172 . . . 8.44

Burrows v Ace Caravan Co (Hull) Ltd [1972] IRLR 4 . . . 10.13

Burton Allton and Johnson Ltd v Peck [1975] ICR 193; [1975] IRLR 87 (DC) . . . 17.68, 18.7

Burton Group Ltd v Smith [1977] IRLR 351 (EAT) . . . 3.60

Burton v Boneham & Turner Ltd, IDS Supp 15 . . . 17.99

Business Seating (Renovations) Ltd v Broad [1989] ICR 729 . . . 19.51, 19.52

Byrne Brothers (Formwork) Ltd v Baird [2002] ICR 667; [2001] All ER (D) 321 (Nov) (EAT); [2002] IRLR 96; [2002] Emp LR 567 . . . 4.191, 7.55

Byrne v Birmingham City Council 85 LGR 729; [1987] ICR 519; [1987] IRLR 191 (CA) . . . 13.19

Byrne v BOC Ltd [1992] IRLR 505 (EAT) . . . 12.9

Byrnell v British Telecommunications plc, IDS Brief 774 (EAT) . . . 20.39

CF Capital plc v Willoughby [2011] IRLR 985; [2011] EWCA Civ 1115 . . . 15.8

CLECE SA v Valor (C-463/09) [2011] IRLR 251; [2011] 2 CMLR 30 . . . 9.8

Cadbury Ltd v Doddington [1977] ICR 982 (EAT) . . . 17.199

Cadman v Health and Safety Executive [2007] All ER (EC) 1; [2006] ECR I-9583; [2007] 1 CMLR 16; [2007] CEC 318; [2006] ICR 1623; [2006] IRLR 969; (2006) *Times* 6 October . . . 5.44

Cadoux v Central Regional Council [1986] IRLR 131; 1986 SLT 117 (Ct of Sess) . . . 3.19, 3.66, 3.86

Cairns v Burnside Shoe Repairs Ltd (1966) 2 KIR 23; 2 ITR 75 . . . 18.62

Cairns v Visteon Ltd [2007] ICR 616; [2007] IRLR 175 . . . 2.158

Calder v James Finlay Corpn Ltd [1989] ICR 157 . . . 4.219

Caledonian Mining Co Ltd v Bassett and Steel [1987] ICR 425; [1987] IRLR 165 (EAT) . . . 17.10

Cambridge & District Co-operative Society Ltd v Ruse [1993] IRLR 156 (EAT) . . . 18.30

Cambridge & Peterborough Foundation NHS Trust v Crouchman [2009] ICR 1306 . . . 20.3

Camden Exhibition and Display Ltd v Lynott [1966] 1 QB 555 . . . 3.62

Camden and Islington Community Services NHS Trust v Kennedy [1996] IRLR 381 (EAT) . . . 20.16

Camelot Group plc v Centaur Communications Ltd [1999] QB 124; [1998] 1 All ER 251; [1998] 2 WLR 379; [1998] IRLR 80; [1998] EMLR 1; [1997] 43 LS Gaz R 30; [1997] NLJR 1618; 142 Sol Jo LB 19 (CA) . . . 10.72

Campbell v Dunoon and Cowal Housing Association Ltd [2000] IRLR 461; [2000] All ER (D) 767 (EAT); aff'd [2001] IRLR 91; [2000] All ER (D) 2186 (CA) . . . 20.133

Campbell v Frisbee [2002] EWHC 328 (Ch); [2002] EMLR 656; [2002] All ER (D) 211 (Mar); revsd [2002] EWCA Civ 1374; [2003] ICR 141; [2003] EMLR 76; [2003] IP & T 86; 146 Sol Jo LB 233; [2002] All ER (D) 178 (Oct) . . . 19.57

Canadian Pacific Rly Co v Lockhart [1942] AC 591; [1942] 2 All ER 464; 111 LJPC 113; 167 LT 231 (PC) . . . 10.106

Canadian Pacific Steamships Ltd v Bryers [1958] AC 485; [1957] 3 All ER 572; [1957] 3 WLR 993; [1957] 2 Lloyd's Rep 387; 101 Sol Jo 957 (HL) . . . 11.132

Canniffe v East Riding of Yorkshire Council [2000] IRLR 555 . . . 4.198

Cannon v Barnsley Metropolitan Borough Council [1992] 2 CMLR 795; [1992] ICR 698; [1992] IRLR 474 (EAT) . . . 1.102

Cantor Fitzgerald International v Callaghan [1999] 2 All ER 411; [1999] ICR 639; [1999] IRLR 234 (CA) . . . 3.35, 19.35

Cantor Fitzgerald International v Horkulak [2004] IRLR 942 (CA) . . . 10.23

Cantor Fitzgerald (UK) Ltd v Wallace [1992] IRLR 215 . . . 19.57

Capek v Lincolnshire County Council [2000] IRLR 590; [2000] All ER (D) 749 (CA) . . . 8.3

Capita Hartshead Ltd v Byard UKEAT/0445/11/RN . . . 18.51

Capital Foods Retail Ltd v Corrigan [1993] IRLR 430 (EAT) . . . 20.16

Capper Pass Ltd v Lawton [1977] QB 852; [1977] 2 WLR 26; [1977] 2 All ER 11; [1977] ICR 83; [1976] IRLR 366; (1976) 11 ITR 316; (1976) 120 SJ 768 . . . 5.23

Carl v University of Sheffield [2009] 3 CMLR 21; [2009] ICR 1286; [2009] IRLR 616 . . . 2.85

Carmichael v National Power plc [1998] ICR 1167; [1998] IRLR 301; [1998] 19 LS Gaz R 23; 142 Sol Jo LB 140; 593 IRLB 12 CA; revsd [1999] 4 All ER 897; [1999] 1 WLR 2042; [1999] ICR 1226; [2000] IRLR 43; [1999] 46 LS Gaz R 38; 143 Sol Jo LB 281; 632 IRLB 18 (HL) . . . 2.54, 2.174

Carr v Alexander Russell Ltd [1979] ICR 469n; [1976] IRLR 220 (Ct of Sess) . . . 17.121

Carrington v Therm-A-Stor Ltd [1982] ICR 8 (EAT); revsd [1983] 1 All ER 796; [1983] 1 WLR 138; [1983] ICR 208, *sub nom* Therm A Stor Ltd v Atkins [1983] IRLR 78; 126 Sol Jo 856 (CA) . . . 21.83

Carry All Motors Ltd v Pennington [1980] ICR 806; [1980] IRLR 455 (EAT) . . . 18.16

Carter v Credit Change Ltd [1979] ICR 908; [1979] IRLR 309 (EAT); revsd [1980] 1 All ER 252; [1979] ICR 908; [1979] IRLR 361; 123 Sol Jo 604 (CA) . . . 16.28, 20.71

Cartwright v G Clancey Ltd [1983] ICR 552; [1983] IRLR 355 (EAT) . . . 7.4

Cassidy v Ministry of Health [1951] 2 KB 343; [1951] 1 All ER 574; 95 Sol Jo 253; [1951] 1 TLR 539 (CA) . . . 2.59

Casson Beckman & Partners v Papi [1991] BCLC 299; [1991] BCC 68 (CA) . . . 3.54

Castledine v Rothwell Engineering Ltd [1973] IRLR 99 . . . 10.40, 17.74

Catamaran Cruisers v Williams [1994] IRLR 386 (EAT) . . . 3.107, 17.155

Caterpillar Logistics Services (UK) Ltd v de Crean [2012] EWCA Civ 156 . . . 19.5

Catherine Haigh Harlequin Hair Design v Seed [1990] IRLR 175 (EAT) . . . 17.180

Cavendish Munro Professional Risks Management v Geduld [2010] ICR 325; [2010] IRLR 38 . . . 10.82

Cavil v Barratt Homes Ltd [2003] All ER (D) 06 (Jul) (EAT) . . . 7.55

Central and North West London NHS Foundation Trust v Abimbola (EAT 3 April 2009) . . . 17.187, 17.189

Centrum voor gelijkheid van kansen v Firma
    Feryn [2008] All ER (EC) 1127; [2008] ECR
    I-5187; [2008] 3 CMLR 22; [2008] CEC 1032;
    [2008] ICR 1390; [2008] IRLR 732; (2008)
    Times 16 July . . . 4.16, 4.46, 4.205
Century Insurance Co Ltd v Northern Ireland
    Road Transport Board [1942] AC 509; [1942]
    1 All ER 491; 111 LJPC 138; 167 LT 404 (HL)
    . . . 10.106
Cerberus Software Ltd v Rowley [2000] ICR 35;
    [1999] IRLR 690 (EAT); revsd *sub nom* Rowley
    v Cerberus Software Ltd [2001] EWCA Civ 78;
    [2001] ICR 376; [2001] IRLR 160; [2001] All
    ER (D) 80 (Jan) . . . 15.15
Chacon Navas v Eurest Colectividades SA [2007]
    All ER (EC) 59; [2006] ECR I-6467; [2006]
    3 CMLR 40; [2007] ICR 1; [2006] IRLR 706;
    (2006) *Times* 9 August . . . 17.104
Chakki v United Yeast Co Ltd [1982] 2 All ER
    446; [1982] ICR 140 (EAT) . . . 17.67
Challinor v Taylor [1972] ICR 129; 7 ITR 104; 116
    Sol Jo 141 (NIRC) . . . 2.29, 18.4
Chan v London Borough of Hackney [1997] ICR
    1014 (EAT) . . . 17.208
Chant v Aquaboats Ltd [1978] 3 All ER 102;
    [1978] ICR 643 (EAT) . . . 21.85
Chaplin v Leslie Frewin (Publishers) Ltd [1966]
    Ch 71; [1965] 3 All ER 764; [1966] 2 WLR 40;
    109 Sol Jo 871 (CA) . . . 2.107
Chapman v Aberdeen Construction Group Ltd
    [1991] IRLR 505; 1993 SLT 1205 (Ct of Sess)
    . . . 16.23
Chapman v Goonvean and Rostowrack China
    Clay Co [1973] 1 All ER 218; [1972] 1 WLR
    1634; [1973] ICR 50 8 ITR 77; 116 Sol Jo 967
    (NIRC); aff'd [1973] 2 All ER 1063; [1973] 1
    WLR 678; [1973] ICR 310; 14 KIR 382; 9 ITR
    379; 117 Sol Jo 416 (CA) . . . 18.16
Chappell v Times Newspapers Ltd [1975] 2 All
    ER 233; [1975] 1 WLR 482; [1975] ICR 145;
    [1975] IRLR 90; 119 Sol Jo 82 (CA) . . . 10.2
Chapple v Electrical Trades Union [1961] 3 All ER
    612; [1961] 1 WLR 1290; 105 Sol Jo 723 . . . 22.30
Charlton v Forrest Printing Ink Co Ltd [1978]
    IRLR 559; 122 Sol Jo 730; revsd [1980] IRLR
    331 (CA) . . . 11.125
Chattopadhyay v Headmaster of Holloway School
    [1982] ICR 132; [1981] IRLR 487 . . . 4.224
Cheall v Vauxhall Motors Ltd [1979] IRLR
    253 . . . 21.60
Cheeseman v Brewer Contracts Ltd [2001] IRLR
    144 . . . 9.14
Chelsea Football Club and Athletic Co Ltd v
    Heath [1981] ICR 323; [1981] IRLR 73 (EAT)
    . . . 17.199
Chequepoint UK Ltd v Radwan (unreported,
    15 September 2000) . . . 10.22
Chesham Shipping Ltd v Rowe [1977] IRLR 391
    (EAT) . . . 17.17
Chief Constable of Avon and Somerset v Chew
    [2001] All ER (D) 101 (Sep) (EAT) . . . 6.129

Chief Constable of Bedfordshire Constabulary v
    Graham [2002] IRLR 239; [2002] Emp LR 752
    . . . 4.181
Chief Constable of Dumfries & Galloway v Adams
    [2009] ICR 1034; [2009] IRLR 612 . . . 4.98
Chief Constable of Lincolnshire Police v Stubbs
    [1999] ICR 547; [1999] IRLR 81 . . . 4.58
Chief Constable of Lincolnshire Police v Weaver
    (EAT, 19 March 2008) . . . 4.117
Chief Constable of South Yorkshire Police v Jelic
    [2010] IRLR 744 (EAT) . . . 4.116, 4.117
Chief Constable of West Midlands Police v
    Blackburn [2008] EWCA Civ 1208; [2009]
    IRLR 135; (2008) 105(44) LSG 20; (2008) 158
    NLJ 1603 . . . 5.29, 5.45
Chief Constable of West Yorkshire v Khan [2000]
    ICR 1169; [2000] NLJR 308; [2000] All ER
    (D) 237 (CA); revsd [2001] UKHL 48; [2001]
    1 WLR 1947; [2001] ICR 1065; [2001] IRLR
    830; [2001] 42 LS Gaz R 37; 145 Sol Jo LB 230;
    [2001] All ER (D) 158 (Oct); *sub nom* Khan
    v Chief Constable of West Yorkshire Police
    [2001] 4 All ER 834 . . . 4.38, 10.37
Chief Constable of Yorkshire v A [2004] ICR 806
    . . . 4.119
Chiltern House Ltd v Chambers [1990] IRLR 88
    (EAT) . . . 8.23
Chipchase v British Titan Products Co Ltd
    [1956] 1 QB 545; [1956] 1 All ER 613; [1956]
    2 WLR 677; 54 LGR 212; 100 Sol Jo 186
    (CA) . . . 11.131
Chohan v Derby Law Centre [2004] IRLR 685
    . . . 20.12
Chondol v Liverpool City Council (EAT, 11
    February 2009) . . . 4.158
Chowles t/a Granary Pine v West (EAT, 8 January
    2009) . . . 20.52
Christie v Department for Constitutional Affairs
    [2007] ICR 1553 (EAT) . . . 2.94
Christie v Johnston Carmichael [2010] IRLR 1016
    . . . 15.21, 19.9
Christou and Ward v London Borough of
    Haringey [2013] EWCA Civ 178 . . . 12.11
Chubb Fire Security Ltd v Harper [1983] IRLR
    311 . . . 3.107
Church v West Lancashire NHS Trust [1998]
    ICR 423; [1998] IRLR 4; 588 IRLB 7 (EAT) . . .
    18.21, 20.53, 20.120
City and County of Swansea v Honey (EAT,
    7 November 2008) . . . 20.91, 20.94
City and East London FHS Authority v Durcan,
    EAT 721/96 . . . 2.53
City of Edinburgh District Council v Stephen
    [1977] IRLR 135 (EAT) . . . 17.130
City and Hackney Health Authority v National
    Union of Public Employees [1985] IRLR 252
    (CA) . . . 23.115
City of Newcastle upon Tyne v Allen [1995] CLY
    3664 . . . 5.66
Claridge v Daler Rowney Ltd [2008] ICR 1267;
    [2008] IRLR 672 . . . 17.36

Clark v BET plc [1997] IRLR 348 . . . 3.2, 10.22, 15.38

Clark v Civil Aviation Authority [1991] IRLR 412 (EAT) . . . 12.20, 17.80

Clark v Clark Construction Initiatives Ltd [2008] EWCA Civ 1446; [2009] ICR 718 . . . 2.15

Clark v Fahrenheit 451 (Communications) Ltd, EAT 591/99 . . . 15.3

Clark v NATSOPA (SOGAT '82) [1986] ICR 12; *sub nom* Clark v NATSOPA (SOGAT '82) [1985] IRLR 494 (EAT) . . . 21.7

Clark v Nomura International [2000] IRLR 766; 651 IRLB 17 . . . 10.22

Clark v Oxfordshire Health Authority [1998] IRLR 125; (1998) 41 BMLR 18 (CA) . . . 2.46, 2.174

Clarke v Arriva Kent Thameside Ltd [2001] All ER (D) 485 (Jul) (EAT) . . . 1.27

Clarke v Hampshire Electro-Plating Co Ltd [1992] ICR 312; [1991] IRLR 490; (1991) *Times* 1 October . . . 4.219, 20.11

Clarke v Hays Distribution Services Ltd (unreported) . . . 8.14

Clarke v Redcar and Cleveland Borough Council [2006] IRLR 324 . . . 1.10

Clarke v Trimoco Motor Group Ltd [1993] ICR 237; [1993] IRLR 148 (EAT) . . . 12.22

Clarks of Hove Ltd v Bakers' Union [1978] 2 All ER 15; [1978] 1 WLR 563; [1977] ICR 838; [1977] IRLR 264; 121 Sol Jo 528 (EAT); revsd [1979] 1 All ER 152; [1978] 1 WLR 1207; [1978] ICR 1076; 13 ITR 356; *sub nom* Bakers' Union v Clarks of Hove Ltd [1978] IRLR 366; 122 Sol Jo 643 (CA) . . . 18.76, 18.88

Clearsprings Management Ltd v Ankers (EAT, 24 February 2009) . . . 9.22

Clements v London and North-Western Rly Co [1894] 2 QB 482; 58 JP 818; 63 LJQB 837; 9 R 641; 42 WR 663; 38 Sol Jo 562; 70 LT 896; 10 TLR 539; [1891-4] All ER Rep Ext 1461 (CA) . . . 2.106

Cleveland Ambulance NHS Trust v Blane [1997] ICR 851; [1997] IRLR 332 (EAT) . . . 21.60

Cleveland County Council v Springett [1985] IRLR 131 (EAT) . . . 11.38

Clift v West Riding County Council (1964) *Times* 10 April . . . 3.77

Close v Steel Co of Wales Ltd [1960] 2 QB 299; [1960] 2 All ER 657; [1960] 3 WLR 401; 58 LGR 297 (CA); aff'd [1962] AC 367; [1961] 2 All ER 953; [1961] 3 WLR 319; 59 LGR 439; 105 Sol Jo 586 (HL) . . . 11.122

Clyde & Co LLP v Winkelhof [2012] EWCA Civ 1207 . . . 2.19

Clyde Pipeworks v Foster [1978] IRLR 313 (EAT) . . . 18.55

Coales v John Wood (Solicitors) & Co [1986] ICR 71; [1986] IRLR 129; [1986] LS Gaz R 117 (EAT) . . . 3.124

Coates v Modern Methods and Material Ltd [1983] QB 192; [1982] 3 All ER 946; [1982] 3 WLR 764; [1982] ICR 763; [1982] IRLR 318; 126 Sol Jo 577 (CA) . . . 13.36

Coca-Cola Enterprises Ltd v Shergill (EAT, 2 September 2002) . . . 4.97

Cochrane v A D Bly Construction Ltd, EAT/0243/05 . . . 2.47

Coddington v International Harvester Co of Great Britain Ltd (1969) 6 KIR 146; 113 Sol Jo 265 . . . 11.129

Cold Drawn Tubes Ltd v Middleton [1992] ICR 318; [1992] IRLR 160 (EAT) . . . 17.189

Cole v Fred Stacey Ltd [1974] IRLR 73; 9 ITR 11 . . . 3.8

Cole v Midland Display Ltd [1973] IRLR 62 (NIRC) . . . 3.28

Coleman v Attridge Law [2010] 1 CMLR 28; [2010] ICR 242; [2010] IRLR 10; (2009) 153(42) SJLB 28; (2009) *Times* 5 November . . . 4.16

Coleman v Magnet Joinery Ltd [1974] ICR 25; [1973] IRLR 361; 17 KIR 11; 9 ITR 74 (NIRC); aff'd [1975] ICR 46; [1974] IRLR 343; [1975] KILR 139 (CA) . . . 17.189

Colen v Cebrian (UK) Ltd [2003] EWCA Civ 1676; [2004] ICR 568; [2004] IRLR 210; (2004) 101(2) LSG 27; (2003) *Times* 27 November . . . 3.9

Collinson v BBC [1998] ICR 669; [1998] IRLR 238 (EAT) . . . 13.1

College of Ripon and York St John v Hobbs [2002] IRLR 185 . . . 4.82

Collidge v Freeport plc [2008] EWCA Civ 485; [2008] IRLR 697 . . . 20.41

Collier v Sunday Referee Publishing Co [1940] 2 KB 647; [1940] 4 All ER 234; 109 LJKB 974; 84 Sol Jo 538; 164 LT 10; 57 TLR 2 . . . 10.17, 16.6

Collins v John Ansell & Partners Ltd (unreported) . . . 9.54

Comerford v Swel Foods Ltd [1972] IRLR 17 . . . 10.65

Commercial Plastics Ltd v Vincent [1965] 1 QB 623; [1964] 3 All ER 546; [1964] 3 WLR 820; 108 Sol Jo 599 (CA) . . . 19.39, 19.44, 19.46

Commission of the European Communities v United Kingdom [2007] IRLR 720 . . . 11.33

Commission for Healthcare Audit and Inspection v Ward (EAT, 6 March 2008) . . . 18.31

Commission for Racial Equality v Amari Plastics [1982] QB 1194; [1982] 2 WLR 972; [1982] 2 All ER 499; [1982] ICR 304; [1982] Crim LR 152; (1982) 126 SJ 227 . . . 4.239

Commission for Racial Equality v Imperial Society for Teachers of Dancing [1983] ICR 473; [1983] IRLR 315 . . . 4.202

Commissioners for Revenue and Customs v Annabel's (Berkeley Square Ltd) [2009] EWCA Civ 361 . . . 8.41

Commotion Ltd v Rutty [2006] ICR 290 (EAT) . . . 6.136

Community Task Force v Rimmer [1986] ICR 491; [1986] IRLR 203; (1986) 83 LSG 968 . . . 6.45

Company's Application, Re A [1989] Ch 477;
[1989] 2 All ER 248; [1989] 3 WLR 265; [1989]
ICR 449; [1989] IRLR 477; [1989] BCLC 462;
133 Sol Jo 917 . . . 19.20

Conn v Sunderland City Council [2007] EWCA
Civ 1492; [2008] IRLR 324; (2007) *Times* 23
November . . . 10.111

Connex South Eastern Rly v National Union of
Rail, Maritime and Transport Workers [1999]
IRLR 249 (CA) . . . 23.42, 23.57

Connor v Halfords Ltd [1972] IRLR 109 . . . 10.61

Consignia plc v Sealy [2002] EWCA Civ 878;
[2002] 3 All ER 801; [2002] ICR 1193; [2002]
IRLR 624; [2002] All ER (D) 129 . . . 20.15

Consistent Group Ltd v Kalwak [2008] EWCA
Civ 430; [2008] IRLR 505 . . . 2.156, 2.160

Construction Industry Training Board v Leighton
[1978] 2 All ER 723; [1978] IRLR 60, *sub nom*
Leighton v Construction Industry Training
Board [1978] ICR 577 (EAT) . . . 3.120

Contract Bottling v Cave UKEAT/0525/12/
DM . . . 18.20

Converform (Darwen) Ltd v Bell [1981] IRLR
195 (EAT) . . . 17.96

Conway v George Wimpey & Co Ltd [1951] 1 All ER
56; 94 Sol Jo 823; [1951] TLR 215 (CA) . . .
10.104

Conway v Matthew, Wright & Nephew [1977]
IRLR 89 (EAT) . . . 12.66, 17.132

Conway v Wade (1908) 24 TLR 604; on appeal
[1908] 2 KB 844; 78 LJKB 14; 52 Sol Jo 748;
99 LT 634; 24 TLR 874 (CA); revsd [1909] AC
506; 78 LJKB 1025; [1908-10] All ER Rep 344;
53 Sol Jo 754; 101 LT 248; 25 TLR 779 (HL)
. . . 23.38

Cook v Thomas Linnell & Sons Ltd [1977] ICR
770; [1977] IRLR 132 (EAT) . . . 17.91

Cooner v P S Doal & Sons [1988] ICR 495; [1988]
IRLR 338 (EAT) . . . 14.5

Cooper v Weatherwise (Roofing and Walling) Ltd
[1993] ICR 81 (EAT) . . . 20.80

Coors Brewers Ltd v Adcock [2007] EWCA Civ
19; [2007] ICR 983; [2007] IRLR 440; (2007)
151 SJLB 160 . . . 8.33

Coote v Granada Hospitality Ltd [1998] IRLR 656
(ECJ) . . . 4.42, 10.37

Coppage & Anor v Safety Net Security Ltd [2013]
EWCA Civ 972 . . . 19.32

Coral Leisure Group Ltd v Barnett [1981]
ICR 503; [1981] IRLR 204; 125 Sol Jo 374
(EAT) . . . 3.17

Coral Squash Clubs Ltd v Matthews [1979] ICR
607; [1979] IRLR 390 (EAT) . . . 20.82

Corby v Morrison (t/a The Card Shop) [1980]
ICR 564; [1980] IRLR 218 (EAT) . . . 3.18

Cornelius v University College of Swansea [1987]
IRLR 141; 131 Sol Jo 359; [1987] LS Gaz R
1141 (CA) . . . 4.39

Corner v Buckinghamshire Country Council
(1978) 77 LGR 268; [1978] ICR 836; [1978]
IRLR 320; 13 ITR 421 (EAT) . . . 7.17

Cory Lighterage v Transport and General
Workers' Union [1973] 2 All ER 558; [1973] 1
WLR 792; [1973] ICR 339; [1973] IRLR 152; 14
KIR 479 (CA) . . . 3.19, 16.1, 23.33

Cotswold Developments Construction Ltd v
Williams [2006] IRLR 181 . . . 2.40

Coulson v Felixstowe Dock & Rly Co Ltd [1975]
IRLR 11 . . . 17.95

Council of the City of Sunderland v Brennan
[2012] EWCA Civ 413 . . . 5.45

Council of Civil Service Unions v Minister for the
Civil Service [1984] IRLR 309; revsd [1984]
IRLR 353 CA; aff'd *sub nom* Council of Civil
Service Unions v Minister for the Civil Service
[1985] AC 374; [1984] 3 All ER 935; [1984]
3 WLR 1174; [1985] ICR 14; 128 Sol Jo 837;
[1985] LS Gaz R 437, *sub nom* R v Secretary of
State for Foreign and Commonwealth Affairs
ex p Council of Civil Service Unions [1985]
IRLR 28 (HL) . . . 16.33

Council of Engineering Institutions v Maddison
[1977] ICR 30; [1976] IRLR 389; 11 ITR 272
(EAT) . . . 20.36

Courage Take Home Trade Ltd v Keys [1986] ICR
874; [1986] IRLR 427 (EAT) . . . 17.202

Courtaulds Northern Spinning Ltd v Moosa . . .
17.211, 17.213

Courtaulds Northern Spinning Ltd v Sibson [1984]
ICR 218; [1984] IRLR 43 (EAT) . . . 17.23

Courtaulds Northern Textiles v Andrew [1979]
IRLR 84 (EAT) . . . 2.4, 17.27

Coward v John Menzies (Holdings) Ltd [1977]
IRLR 428 (EAT) . . . 17.89

Cowell v Quilter Goodison Co Ltd [1989] IRLR
392 (CA) . . . 9.5

Cowen v Rentokil Initial Facility Service (UK)
Ltd (EAT, 6 March 2008) . . . 17.206

Cowley v Manson Timber Ltd [1994] ICR 252
(EAT); aff'd [1995] ICR 367; [1995] IRLR 153
(CA) . . . 17.185

Cox v Sun Alliance Life Ltd [2001] EWCA Civ
1010; [2001] IRLR 448; [2001] All ER (D) 108
(May) . . . 10.36

Coxall v Goodyear GB Ltd [2002] EWCA Civ
1010; [2003] 1 WLR 536; [2003] ICR 152;
[2002] IRLR 742; [2002] All ER (D) 303 (Jul)
. . . 11.119

Coyne v Home Office [2000] ICR 1443; [2000]
IRLR 838 . . . 4.50

Craigie v Haringey (EAT, 12 January 2007) . . .
2.159

Cranleigh Precision Engineering Ltd v Bryant
[1964] 3 All ER 289; [1965] 1 WLR 1293;
[1966] RPC 81; 109 Sol Jo 830 . . . 10.71

Crawford v Suffolk Mental Health Partnership
NHS Trust [2012] EWCA Civ 138 . . . 12.65

Crawford v Swinton Insurance Brokers Ltd [1990]
ICR 95; [1990] IRLR 42 (EAT) . . . 9.58

Credit Suisse Asset Management Ltd v Armstrong
[1996] ICR 882; [1996] IRLR 450; [1996] 23 LS
Gaz R 36; 140 Sol Jo LB 140 (CA) . . . 19.13

Credit Suisse First Boston (Europe) Ltd v Lister [1999] ICR 794; [1998] IRLR 700; [1998] 44 LS Gaz R 35; 142 Sol Jo LB 269 (CA) . . . 9.36

Credit Suisse v Padiachy [1998] 2 CMLR 1322; [1999] ICR 569; [1998] IRLR 504 . . . 9.36, 19.60

Cresswell v Board of Inland Revenue [1984] 2 All ER 713; [1984] ICR 508; [1984] IRLR 190; 128 Sol Jo 431 . . . 3.41

Crofter Hand Woven Harris Tweed Co v Veitch [1942] AC 435; [1942] 1 All ER 142; 111 LJPC 17; 166 LT 172; 58 TLR 125 (HL) . . . 23.24

Crofts v Cathay Pacific Airways Ltd [2005] IRLR 423 . . . 2.150

Cross v British Airways [2006] EWCA Civ 549; [2006] ICR 1239; [2006] IRLR 804; [2006] Pens LR 155; (2006) 103(21) LSG 24; (2006) *Times* 5 June; (2006) *Independent* 18 May . . . 4.174

Crossley v Faithful and Gould Holdings Ltd [2004] EWCA Civ 293; [2004] NLJR 653; [2004] All ER (D) 295 (Mar) . . . 3.40, 10.15

Crosville Motor Services Ltd v Ashfield [1986] IRLR 475 (EAT) . . . 21.85

Crosville Wales Ltd v Tracey [1993] IRLR 60 (EAT); revsd *sub nom* Tracey v Crosville Wales Ltd [1996] ICR 237; *sub nom* Crosville Wales Ltd v Tracey (No 2) [1996] IRLR 91 (CA); aff'd *sub nom* Tracey v Crosville Wales Ltd [1998] AC 167; [1997] 4 All ER 449; [1997] 3 WLR 800; [1997] ICR 862; [1997] 41 LS Gaz R 28; [1997] NLJR 1582, *sub nom* Crosville Wales Ltd v Tracey (No 2) [1997] IRLR 691 (HL) . . . 17.231, 21.109

Crowson Fabrics Ltd v Rider [2007] EWHC 2942 (Ch); [2008] IRLR 288; [2008] FSR 17 . . . 19.22

Cruickshank v VAW Motorcast Ltd [2002] ICR 729; [2002] IRLR 24 . . . 4.96

Crystal Palace FC (2000) Ltd v Kavanagh [2013] EWCA Civ 1410 . . . 9.51

Crystal Palace FC (2000) Ltd v Dowie [2007] EWHC 1392 (QB); [2007] IRLR 682 . . . 20.40

Cummings (or McWilliam) v Sir William Arrol Ltd 1961 SC 134; 1961 SLT 265 (Ct of Sess); aff'd *sub nom* Cummings (or McWilliams) v Sir William Arrol & Co Ltd [1962] 1 All ER 623; [1962] 1 WLR 295; 106 Sol Jo 218; 1962 SC 70; 1962 SLT 121 (HL) . . . 11.127

Curr v Marks & Spencer Ltd [2002] All ER (D) 76 (Mar) (EAT); revsd [2002] EWCA Civ 1852; [2003] ICR 443; [2003] IRLR 74; [2002] All ER (D) 205 (Dec) . . . 2.151, 13.27

Customer Systems Plc v Ranson [2011] EWHC 3304 . . . 10.55

Cuthbertson v AML Distributors [1975] IRLR 228 . . . 3.121

DJM International Ltd v Nicholas [1996] ICR 214; [1996] IRLR 76 (EAT) . . . 9.30, 9.32

DPP v Marshall [1998] ICR 518 (EAT) . . . 20.24

Da Costa v Optolis [1977] IRLR 178 (EAT) . . . 17.129

Da Silva v Composite Mouldings & Design Ltd [2009] ICR 416 . . . 13.23

Da'Bell v NSPCC [2010] IRLR 19 . . . 4.230

Dacas v Brook Street Bureau [2003] IRLR 190; [2003] All ER (D) 241 (Jan) (EAT); revsd [2004] EWCA Civ 217; [2004] All ER (D) 125 (Mar) . . . 2.154, 2.158, 2.159

Daleside Nursing Home Ltd v Mathew (EAT 18 February 2009) . . . 20.107

Daley v Allied Suppliers Ltd [1983] ICR 90; [1983] IRLR 14 (EAT) . . . 2.99

Dalgleish v Kew House Farm Ltd [1982] IRLR 251 (CA) . . . 2.98, 15.26

Dalgleish v Lothian and Borders Police Board [1991] IRLR 422; 1992 SLT 721 (Ct of Sess) . . . 10.25

Dalton v Burton's Gold Medal Biscuits Ltd [1974] IRLR 45 (NIRC) . . . 10.53, 12.44

Dansie v Commissioner of Police for Metropolis (EAT, 20 October 2009) . . . 4.21

Darby v GKN Screws and Fasteners Ltd [1986] ICR 1 . . . 11.112

Darr v LRC Products Ltd [1993] IRLR 257 (EAT) . . . 17.210, 17.241

Davenport v Taptonholme for the Elderly (unreported) . . . 17.162

Davidson v Pillay [1979] IRLR 275 . . . 3.18

Davie v New Merton Board Mills [1959] AC 604; [1959] 1 All ER 346; [1959] 2 WLR 331; 103 Sol Jo 177 . . . 11.123

Davies v Anglo Great Lakes Corpn [1973] IRLR 133 . . . 12.63

Davies v GKN Birwelco (Uskside) Ltd [1976] IRLR 82 . . . 12.16

Davies v Health and Safety Executive [2002] EWCA Crim 2949; [2003] IRLR 170; [2003] 09 LS Gaz R 27; [2003] JPN 142; 147 Sol Jo LB 29 [2002] All ER (D) 275 (Dec) . . . 1.107, 11.97

Davies v Hotpoint Ltd [1994] IRLR 538 (EAT) . . . 8.19

Davies v Neath Port Talbot County Borough Council [1999] ICR 1132; [1999] IRLR 769 (EAT); (1999) *Times* 26 October . . . 5.17, 11.41

Davies v Presbyterian Church of Wales [1986] 1 All ER 705; [1986] 1 WLR 323; [1986] ICR 280; [1986] IRLR 194; 130 Sol Jo 203 . . . 2.55

Davies v Richard Johnson & Nephew Ltd (1934) 78 Sol Jo 877; 51 TLR 115 . . . 3.45

Davies v Sandwell Metropolitan Borough Council [2013] EWCA Civ 135 . . . 12.75

Davis v New England College of Arundel [1977] ICR 6; 11 ITR 278 (EAT) . . . 2.51, 2.54

Davison v Kent Meters Ltd [1975] IRLR 145 . . . 17.85

Davy v Collins (Builders) Ltd [1974] IRLR 324 . . . 17.16

Dawkins v Department of the Environment [1993] ICR 517; [1993] IRLR 284; (1993) *Times* 4 February; (1993) *Independent* 12 February; (1993) *Guardian* 1 February . . . 4.140

Dawnay Day Ltd v de Braconier d'Alphen [1997] IRLR 285; aff'd [1998] ICR 1068; [1997] IRLR

442; [1997] 26 LS Gaz R 30; 141 Sol Jo LB 129
    (CA) . . . 19.42
Day v T Pickles Farms Ltd [1999] IRLR
    217 . . . 4.50, 6.10
Daynecourt Insurance Brokers Ltd v Iles [1978]
    IRLR 335 (EAT) . . . 17.177
De Francesco v Barnum 45 Ch D 430; 60 LJ Ch
    63; 39 WR 5; [1886–90] All ER Rep 414; 63 LT
    438; 6 TLR 463 . . . 2.106
De Grasse v Stockwell Tools Ltd [1992] IRLR 269
    (EAT) . . . 18.46
Deary v Mansion Hide Upholstery Ltd [1983]
    ICR 610; [1983] IRLR 195; 147 JP 311 . . . 11.23
Debaughn v Star Cinemas (London) Ltd
    (unreported) . . . 17.163
Deeley v British Rail Engineering Ltd [1980]
    IRLR 147 (CA) . . . 3.30
Defrenne v Sabena (43/75) [1981] 1 All ER 122;
    [1976] ECR 455; [1976] 2 CMLR 98; [1976]
    ICR 547 (ECJ) . . . 1.72, 20.22
Defrenne v Sabena [2000] ECR I-6155; [2002] 1
    CMLR 6; [2000] Pens LR 261 . . . 5.1
Degnan v Redcar Borough Council [2005]
    EWCA Civ6726; [2005] IRLR 615; [2005] ELR
    475 . . . 5.41
Dekker v Stichting Vormingscentrum voor Jong
    Volwassenen (VJV-Centrum) Plus (C-177/88)
    [1990] ECR I-3941; [1992] ICR 325; [1991]
    IRLR 27 (ECJ) . . . 1.74, 4.136
Del Monte Foods v Mundon [1980] ICR 694;
    [1980] IRLR 224 . . . 6.52
Delaney v Staples [1990] ICR 364; [1990] IRLR
    86; [1990] 10 LS Gaz R 35 (EAT); on appeal
    [1991] 2 QB 47; [1991] 1 All ER 609; [1991] 2
    WLR 627; [1991] ICR 331; [1991] IRLR 112
    (CA); aff'd [1992] 1 AC 687; [1992] 1 All ER
    944; [1992] 2 WLR 451; [1992] ICR 483; [1992]
    IRLR 191; [1992] 15 LS Gaz R 32; 136 Sol Jo LB
    91 (HL) . . . 8.16, 15.12
Demir v Turkey [2009] IRLR 766 (2009) 48
    EHRR 54 . . . 1.107, 23.98
Dench v Flynn & Partners [1998] IRLR 653 (CA)
    . . . 17.206, 17.211, 17.213, 17.234
Denco Ltd v Joinson [1992] 1 All ER 463; [1991]
    1 WLR 330; [1991] ICR 172; [1991] IRLR 63
    (EAT) . . . 17.138
Denmark Productions Ltd v Boscobel
    Productions Ltd [1969] 1 QB 699; [1968] 3
    All ER 513; [1968] 3 WLR 841; 112 Sol Jo 761
    (CA) . . . 2.107
Department of Constitutional Affairs v Jones
    [2007] EWCA Civ 894; [2008] IRLR 128 . . . 20.9
Department for Work and Pensions v Webby
    [2004] EWCA Civ 1745 (CA) . . . 2.133
Depledge v Pye Telecommunications Ltd [1981]
    ICR 82; [1980] IRLR 390 (EAT) . . . 21.73
Derby City Council v Marshall [1979] ICR 731;
    [1979] IRLR 261 (EAT) . . . 17.47
Devine v Designer Flowers Wholesale Florist
    Sundries Ltd [1993] IRLR 517 (EAT) . . .
    17.212

Devon Primary Care Trust v Readman [2013]
    EWCA Civ 1110 . . . 18.30
Devonald v Rosser & Sons [1906] 2 KB 728; 75
    LJKB 688; [1904-7] All ER Rep 988; 50 Sol
    Jo 616; 95 LT 232; 22 TLR 682 (CA) . . . 3.80,
    10.17, 10.19, 15.14
Dhaliwal v British Airways Board [1985] ICR 513
    (EAT) . . . 12.17
Dhatt v McDonalds Hamburgers Ltd [1988] ICR
    591 (EAT); aff'd [1991] 3 All ER 692; [1991] 1
    WLR 527; [1991] ICR 238; [1991] IRLR 130
    (CA) . . . 2.116, 4.146
Dickens v O2 plc [2008] EWCA Civ 1144 . . .
    11.107
Dickie v Cathay Pacific Airways Ltd [2005]
    EWCA Civ 599; [2005] ICR 1436; [2005] IRLR
    624; (2005) Times 31 May . . . 1.38
Dietman v London Borough of Brent [1987]
    IRLR 146 (CA) . . . 16.21, 16.31, 19.57
Diggins v Condor Marine [2009] EWCA Civ 1133;
    [2010] ICR 213; [2010] IRLR 119 . . . 1.32
Digital Equipment Co Ltd v Clements [1996] ICR
    829; [1996] IRLR 513 (EAT) . . . 17.237
Dines v Initial Healthcare Services Ltd [1995]
    ICR 11; [1994] IRLR 336 (CA) . . . 9.26
Diocese of Hallam Trustees v Connaughton
    [1996] 3 CMLR 93; [1996] ICR 860; [1996]
    IRLR 505; (1996) Times 11 June . . . 5.12
Diocese of Southwark v Coker [1996] ICR 896
    (EAT); aff'd [1998] ICR 140; [1997] 29 LS Gaz
    R 29; 141 Sol Jo LB 169 (CA) . . . 2.67
Discount Tobacco and Confectionery Ltd v
    Armitage [1990] IRLR 15; [1995] ICR 431
    (EAT) . . . 21.85
Discount Tobacco and Confectionery Ltd v
    Williamson [1993] ICR 371; [1993] IRLR 327
    (EAT) . . . 8.9, 8.27
Divine-Bortey v Brent London Borough
    Council [1998] ICR 886; [1998] IRLR 525;
    [1998] 22 LS Gaz R 29; 142 Sol Jo LB 152
    (CA) . . . 20.50
Dixon & Constanti v BBC [1978] QB 438;
    [1978] 2 All ER 465; [1978] 2 WLR 50; [1978]
    ICR 357; [1977] IRLR 337; 13 ITR 169; 121
    Sol Jo 632 (EAT); aff'd [1979] QB 546; [1979]
    2 All ER 112; [1979] 2 WLR 647; [1979]
    ICR 281; [1979] IRLR 114; 122 Sol Jo 713
    (CA) . . . 15.25
Dixon and Shaw v West Ella Developments Ltd
    [1978] ICR 856; [1978] IRLR 151; 13 ITR 235
    (EAT) . . . 21.55
Dixon v Stenor Ltd [1973] ICR 157; [1973] IRLR
    28; 8 ITR 141 (NIRC) . . . 20.26
Doble v Firestone Tyre and Rubber Co Ltd [1981]
    IRLR 300 (EAT) . . . 17.8
Docherty v Reddy [1977] ICR 365 (EAT) . . .
    20.83
Dolphin Drilling Personnel PTE Ltd v Winks
    (EAT (Scotland), 21 April 2009) . . . 1.33
Dominguez v Centre informatique du Centre
    Ouest Atlantique (C-282/10) . . . 7.88

Donald Cook v Carter [1977] IRLR 88 (EAT)
... 12.73

Donn v Greater London Council IDS Brief 65
... 20.86

Donn v Greater London Council, IDS Brief 65
... 2.96

Donnelly v Kelvin International Services [1992]
IRLR 496 (EAT) ... 13.16

Donoghue v Stevenson [1932] AC 562; 1932 SC
(HL) 31; 1932 SLT 317; [1932] WN 139 ...
11.123

Donovan v Invicta Airways Ltd [1969] 2 Lloyd's
Rep 413; [1970] 1 Lloyd's Rep 486 (CA) ...
10.10

Doughty v Rolls-Royce plc [1992] 1 CMLR 1045;
[1992] IRLR 126, *sub nom* Rolls-Royce plc v
Doughty [1992] ICR 538 (CA) ... 1.73

Dowden and Pook Ltd v Pook [1904] 1 KB 45; 73
LJKB 38; 52 WR 97; 48 Sol Jo 50; 89 LT 688; 20
TLR 39 (CA) ... 19.33

Down v Dudley Coles Long Ltd (unreported,
1969) ... 11.110

Doyle v Northumbria Probation Committee
[1991] 4 All ER 294; [1991] 1 WLR 1340;
[1992] ICR 121; [1991] NLJR 855 ... 16.36

Dr Sophie Redmond Stichting v Bartol (C-29/91)
[1992] ECR I-3189; [1994] 3 CMLR 265;
[1992] IRLR 366 (ECJ) ... 9.8

Drage v Governors of Greenford High School
[2000] ICR 899; [2000] IRLR 314; 144 Sol Jo
LB 165; [2000] All ER (D) 343 (CA) ... 20.27

Drakard & Sons Ltd v Wilton [1977] ICR 642 ..
. 20.102

Dresdner Kleinwort Ltd v Commerzbank AG v
Attrill [2013] EWCA Civ 394 ... 3.100

Drinkwater Sabey Ltd v Burnett [1995] ICR 328;
[1995] IRLR 238 (EAT) ... 20.17, 20.19

Driskel v Peninsula Business Services [2000]
IRLR 151 (EAT) ... 4.34

Dryden v Greater Glasgow Health Board [1992]
IRLR 469 (EAT) ... 3.90, 17.28

D'Souza v London Borough of Lambeth [2003]
ICR 867 ... 4.197

Duffy v Northampton Area Health Authority
(unreported) ... 12.39

Duffy v Yeomans and Partners Ltd [1993] ICR
862; [1993] IRLR 368 (EAT); aff'd [1995] ICR
1; [1994] IRLR 642 (CA) ... 18.49

Dugdale v Kraft Foods Ltd [1976] 1 WLR 1288;
[1977] 1 All ER 454; [1977] ICR 48; [1976]
IRLR 368; (1979) 11 ITR 309; (1976) SJ 780
... 5.28

Duke v Prospect Training Services Ltd [1988]
ICR 521; [1989] IRLR 196 (EAT) ... 20.118

Duncan v GEC Telecommunications Ltd [1976]
IRLR 3 ... 12.78

Duncan Webb Offset (Maidstone) Ltd v Cooper
[1995] IRLR 633 (EAT) ... 9.12, 9.13

Duncombe v Secretary of State for Children,
Schools and Families (No 2) [2011] UKSC 36
... 1.32

Dundon v GPT Ltd [1995] IRLR 403 (EAT) ...
21.89

Dunk v George Waller & Son Ltd [1970] 2 QB
163; [1970] 2 All ER 630; [1970] 2 WLR 1241;
114 Sol Jo 356 (CA) ... 2.103, 16.21

Dunlop Ltd v Farrell [1993] ICR 885 (EAT) ...
18.50

Dunlop Pneumatic Tyre Co Ltd v New Garage &
Motor Co [1915] AC 79; 83 LJKB 1574; [1914-
15] All ER Rep 739; 111 LT 862; 30 TLR 625
(HL) ... 15.35

Dunlop Tyres Ltd v Blow [2001] EWCA Civ 1032;
[2001] IRLR 629; [2001] All ER (D) 179 (Jun)
... 3.27, 3.80

Dunn v AAH Ltd [2009] EWHC 692 (QB);
[2010] IRLR 709 ... 16.11

Dunnachie v Kingston upon Hull City Council
[2004] EWCA Civ 84; [2004] 2 All ER 501;
[2004] NLJR 248; 148 Sol Jo LB 233; [2004] All
ER (D) 185 (Feb) ... 11.113, 16.5, 17.213

Duport Steels Ltd v Sirs [1980] ICR 112 (CA);
revsd [1980] 1 All ER 529; [1980] 1 WLR 142;
[1980] ICR 161; [1980] IRLR 116; 124 Sol Jo
133 (HL) ... 23.73

Duthie v Bath & North East Somerset Council
[2003] ICR 1405; [2003] 26 LS Gaz R 37;
[2003] All ER (D) 358 (Apr) (EAT) ... 11.41

Dutton & Clark Ltd v Daly [1985] ICR 780;
[1985] IRLR 363 (EAT) ... 17.27

Dutton v Hawker Siddeley Aviation Ltd [1978]
ICR 1057; [1978] IRLR 390 ... 18.39

Dwyer v Superguard Ltd (unreported) ... 3.101

Dynamex Friction Ltd v Amicus [2008] EWCA
Civ 381; [2009] ICR 511; [2008] IRLR 515;
(2008) 152(17) SJLB 31 ... 9.59

E Green & Son (Castings) Ltd v Association of
Scientific, Technical and Management Staffs
[1984] ICR 352; [1984] IRLR 135 (EAT) ... 2.9

EC Commission v United Kingdom (C-
382/92) [1994] ECR I-2435; [1995] 1 CMLR
345; [1994] ICR 664; [1994] IRLR 392
(ECJ) ... 1.101, 18.69

ECM (Vehicle Delivery Services) Ltd v Cox
[1998] ICR 631; [1998] IRLR 416; 596 IRLB
8 (EAT); aff'd [1999] 4 All ER 669; [2000] 1
CMLR 224; [1999] ICR 1162; [1999] IRLR 559;
[1999] All ER (D) 838 (CA) ... 9.8, 9.10

EDF Energy Powerlink v UK [2010] IRLR 114
... 23.69

EFTA Surveillance Authority v Kingdom of
Norway [2008] 1 CMLR 44 ... 4.204

Eagland v British Telecommunications plc [1990]
ICR 248; [1990] IRLR 328 (EAT); aff'd [1993]
ICR 644; [1992] IRLR 323 (CA) ... 3.121

East Berkshire Health Authority v Matadeen
[1992] ICR 723; [1992] IRLR 336; [1992] 29 LS
Gaz R 24 (EAT) ... 12.70, 20.123

East Lindsey District Council v Daubney [1977]
ICR 566; [1977] IRLR 181; 12 ITR 359 (EAT)
... 17.93

East Sussex County Council v Walker (1972) 7
ITR 280 (NIRC) . . . 17.9

Eastwood v Magnox Electric plc [2002] EWCA
Civ 463; [2003] ICR 520n; [2002] IRLR 447;
[2002] All ER (D) 366 (Mar) . . . 11.113, 16.5,
16.17, 16.25

Eaton Ltd v King [1995] IRLR 75 (EAT); revsd
sub nom King v Eaton Ltd [1996] IRLR 199;
[1997] SLT 654 (Ct of Sess) . . . 18.54

Eaton Ltd v Nuttall [1977] 1 WLR 549; [1977] 3
All ER 1131; [1977] ICR 272; [1977] IRLR 71;
(1977) 11 ITR 197; (1977) 121 SJ 353 . . . 5.30,
5.32

Ecclestone v National Union of Journalists [1999]
IRLR 166 . . . 22.45

Eclipse Blinds Ltd v Wright [1992] IRLR 133;
1992 SLT 664 (Ct of Sess) . . . 20.124

Edgar v Giorgine Inns Ltd (unreported) . . . 6.7

Edgell v Lloyd's Register of Shipping [1977] IRLR
463 . . . 6.43

Edinburgh Council v Brown [1999] IRLR 208
(EAT) . . . 3.63

Edmunds v Lawson [2000] IRLR 18 . . . 8.39

Edwards v Cardiff City Council [1979] IRLR 303
(EAT) . . . 21.104

Edwards v Chesterfield Royal Hospital NHS
Foundation Trust [2011] UKSC 58 . . . 16.3

Edwards v National Coal Board [1949] 1 KB 704;
[1949] 1 All ER 743; 93 Sol Jo 337; 65 TLR 430
(CA) . . . 11.135

Edwards v Surrey Police [1999] IRLR 456 (EAT)
. . . 20.33

Edwards v West Herts Group Hospital
Management Committee [1957] 1 All ER 541;
[1957] 1 WLR 415; 121 JP 212; 101 Sol Jo 190
(CA) . . . 3.51

Egg Stores (Stamford Hill) Ltd v Leibovici
[1977] ICR 260; [1976] IRLR 376; 11 ITR 289
(EAT) . . . 17.63, 17.93

Ekpe v Metropolitan Police Comr [2001] ICR
1084; [2001] IRLR 605; [2001] Emp LR 741
. . . 4.97

Electrical, Electronic Telecommunications and
Plumbing Union v Times Newspapers [1980]
QB 585; [1980] 1 All ER 1097; [1980] 3 WLR
98; 124 Sol Jo 31 . . . 22.4

Electrolux Ltd v Hutchinson [1977] ICR 252;
(1976) 12 ITR 40 . . . 5.18, 5.26

Elizabeth Claire Care Management v Francis
[2005] IRLR . . . 3.35, 8.21

Elliot v Richard Stump Ltd [1987] ICR 579;
[1987] IRLR 215; [1987] LS Gaz R 1142 (EAT)
. . . 18.27

Elliott Bros Ltd v Colverd [1979] IRLR 92 (EAT)
. . . 12.45

Elliott Turbomachinery v Bates [1981] ICR 218
(EAT) . . . 18.21

Elliott v Waldair (Construction) Ltd [1975] IRLR
104 . . . 17.7

Ely v YKK Fasteners (UK) Ltd [1993] IRLR 500
(CA) . . . 17.53, 17.161

Emmerson v IRC [1977] IRLR 458 . . . 7.17

Employment Tribunals (Constitution and
Rules of Procedure) Regulations 2013 . . .
20.59

Enderby v Frenchay Health Authority [2000]
ICR 612; [2000] IRLR 257; (2000) *Times*
29 February . . . 5.4, 5.64

Enessy Co SA v Minoprio [1978] IRLR 489 (EAT)
. . . 17.189

Enfield Technical Services v Payne [2008] EWCA
Civ 393; [2008] ICR 1423; [2008] IRLR 500;
(2008) *Times* 2 June . . . 3.12

English v Thomas Sanderson Blinds Ltd [2008]
EWCA Civ 1421; [2009] 2 All ER 468; [2009]
2 CMLR 18; [2009] ICR 543; [2009] IRLR 206;
(2009) 153(1) SJLB 31; (2009) *Times* 5 January
. . . 4.59, 4.188

Etam plc v Rowan [1989] IRLR 150 . . . 4.184

Euro Brokers Ltd v Rabey [1995] IRLR 206 . . .
19.10, 19.12

Evans v Elemeta Holdings Ltd [1982] ICR 323;
[1982] IRLR 143 (EAT) . . . 17.152

Evans v Malley Organisation Ltd [2002] All ER
(D) 93 (May) (EAT); revsd [2002] EWCA Civ
1834; [2003] ICR 432; [2003] IRLR 156; [2002]
All ER (D) 397 (Nov) . . . 7.85

Evans v National Union of Printing
Bookbinding and Paperworkers [1938] 4 All
ER 51 . . . 22.29

Evans v Permacell, EAT 0350/07 . . . 18.94

Evening Standard Co Ltd v Henderson [1987]
ICR 588; [1987] IRLR 64 (CA) . . . 15.21

Eversheds Legal Services Ltd v De Belin [2011]
IRLR 448 . . . 6.41

Evesham v North Hertfordshire Health Authority
[2000] ICR 612; [2000] IRLR 257; (2000) *Times*
29 February . . . 5.64

Eweida v British Airways [2010] EWCA Civ 80;
[2010] IRLR 322; (2010) 107(9) LSG 19; (2010)
Times 18 February . . . 4.30

Eweide, Ladele, Chaplin and Macfarlane v
UK (Applications nos 48420/10, 59842/10,
51671/10 and 36516/10) . . . 4.137

Examite Ltd v Whittaker [1977] IRLR 312 (CA)
. . . 23.36

Executors of Soutar v James Murray & Co
(Cupar) Ltd [2002] IRLR 22; [2002] All ER (D)
45 (Jan) . . . 20.117

Express Newspapers v Keys [1980] IRLR 247
. . . 23.35

Express and Star Ltd v Bunday [1987] ICR 58;
[1986] IRLR 477; [1986] LS Gaz R 3591 (EAT);
revsd [1988] ICR 379; [1987] IRLR 422 (CA)
. . . 21.97

Express and Star Ltd v National Graphical
Association [1985] IRLR 455; aff'd [1986] ICR
589; [1986] IRLR 222; [1986] LS Gaz R 2083
(CA) . . . 23.85

Ezsias v N Glamorgan NHS Trust,
EAT/0705/05; EAT/0612/05; aff'd [2007]
EWCA Civ 330; [2007] 4 All ER 940; [2007]

ICR 1126; [2007] IRLR 603; (2007) 104(12) LSG 34 . . . 20.56

F W Farnsworth Ltd v McCoid [1998] IRLR 362 (EAT); aff'd [1999] ICR 1047; [1999] IRLR 626; [1999] 16 LS Gaz R 35 (CA) . . . 21.51

FATA Ltd v Addison [1988] QB 280; [1987] 3 WLR 122; [1987] 2 All ER 784; [1987] ICR 805; [1987] IRLR 173; [1987] 1 FTLR 505; (1987) 84 LSG 1409 . . . 17.209

FC Gardner v Beresford [1978] IRLR 63 . . . 3.2, 3.43, 17.32

FC Shepherd & Co Ltd v Jerrom [1985] ICR 552; [1985] IRLR 275; [1985] LS Gaz R 2162 (EAT); revsd [1987] QB 301; [1986] 3 All ER 589; [1986] 3 WLR 801; [1986] ICR 802; [1986] IRLR 358; 130 Sol Jo 665 (CA) . . . 17.60, 17.66

FTATU v Lawrence Cabinet, IDS Brief 96 . . . 18.88

Faccenda Chicken Ltd v Fowler [1985] 1 All ER 724; [1985] FSR 105; [1984] ICR 589; [1984] IRLR 61; aff'd [1987] Ch 117; [1986] 1 All ER 617; [1986] 3 WLR 288; [1986] FSR 291; [1986] ICR 297; [1986] IRLR 69; 130 Sol Jo 573 (CA) . . . 19.14, 19.15

Facey v Midas Retail Security [2001] ICR 287; [2000] All ER (D) 1306 (EAT) . . . 20.126, 20.129

Fairfield Ltd v Skinner [1992] ICR 836; [1993] IRLR 4; [1992] LS Gaz R 39 (EAT) . . . 8.11

Falconer v ASLEF and NUR [1986] IRLR 331; [1986] BTLC 258 . . . 23.20

Famatina Development Corpn Ltd, Re [1914] 2 Ch 271; 83 LJ Ch 712; on appeal [1914] 2 Ch 271; 64 LJ Ch 48; 30 TLR 696 (CA) . . . 10.33

Faramus v Film Artistes' Association [1963] 2 QB 527; [1963] 1 All ER 636 (CA); on appeal [1964] AC 925; [1964] 1 All ER 25; [1964] 2 WLR 126; 108 Sol Jo 13 (HL) . . . 21.5, 22.22

Farmiloe v Lane Group plc [2004] PIQR P22 . . . 4.102, 4.194

Farnborough v Governors of Edinburgh College of Art [1974] IRLR 245 (NIRC) . . . 12.82

Farr v Hoveringham Gravels Ltd [1972] IRLR 104 . . . 17.149

Farrant v Woodroffe School [1998] ICR 184; [1998] IRLR 176 (EAT) . . . 3.26, 3.104, 10.63, 17.156

Fearnon v Smurfit Corrugated Cases Ltd [2008] NICA 45; [2009] IRLR 132 . . . 5.50

Fellowes & Son v Fisher [1976] QB 122; [1975] 2 All ER 829; [1975] 3 WLR 184; 119 Sol Jo 390 (CA) . . . 19.46

Fennelly v Connex South Eastern Ltd [2001] IRLR 390; [2000] All ER (D) 2233 (CA) . . . 10.105

Fentiman v Fluid Engineering Products Ltd [1991] ICR 570; [1991] IRLR 150 (EAT) . . . 17.207

Ferguson v Prestwick Circuits Ltd [1992] IRLR 266 (EAT) . . . 18.46

Ferodo Ltd v Barnes [1976] ICR 439; [1976] IRLR 302; ITR 177 (EAT) . . . 12.15, 12.16, 20.86

Financial Times v Bishop (EAT, 25 November 2003) . . . 1.33

Finch v Betabake (Anglia) Ltd [1977] IRLR 470 . . . 17.113

Finch v Telegraph Construction and Maintenance Co Ltd [1949] 1 All ER 452; 47 LGR 710; 93 Sol Jo 219; 65 TLR 153 . . . 11.126

Finnie v Top Hat Frozen Foods [1985] ICR 433; [1985] IRLR 365 (EAT) . . . 17.209

First Castle Electronics Ltd v West [1989] ICR 72 (EAT) . . . 20.71

First Leeds v Haigh [2008] IRLR 182 (EAT) . . . 3.40

Fisher v Hoopoe Finance Ltd (unreported) . . . 18.29

Fisscher v Voorhuis Hengelo BV . . . 20.20

Fitch v Dewes [1921] 2 AC 158; 90 LJ Ch 436; [1921] All ER Rep 13; 65 Sol Jo 626; 125 LT 744; 37 TLR 784 (HL) . . . 19.45

Fitton v City of Edinburgh Council (EAT (Scotland), 5 June 2008) . . . 2.144

Fitzgerald v Hall, Russell & Co Ltd [1970] AC 984; [1969] 3 All ER 1140; [1969] 3 WLR 868; [1969] 2 Lloyd's Rep 514; 7 KIR 263; 5 ITR 1; 1970 SC 1; 1970 SLT 37; 113 Sol Jo 899 (HL) . . . 13.18, 13.19

Fitzgerald v University of Kent at Canterbury [2003] All ER (D) 152 (May) (EAT); revsd [2004] EWCA Civ 143; 148 Sol Jo LB 237; [2004] All ER (D) 262 (Feb) . . . 20.31

Fitzpatrick v British Railways Board [1990] ICR 674 (EAT); revsd [1992] ICR 221; [1991] IRLR 376 (CA) . . . 21.30, 21.85

Flett v Matheson [2006] EWCA 53; [2005] ICR 1134; [2005] IRLR 412 . . . 2.101

Flynn v Torith Ltd [2003] All ER (D) 45 (Jan) . . . 2.25

Folami v Nigerline (UK) Ltd [1978] ICR 277 (EAT) . . . 2.11

Foley v Post Office [2001] 1 All ER 550; [2000] ICR 1283; [2000] IRLR 827, *sub nom* Post Office v Foley 652 IRLB 7 (CA) . . . 17.76

Foot v Eastern Counties Timber Co Ltd [1972] IRLR 83 . . . 17.149

Force One Utilities v Hatfield [2009] IRLR 45 . . . 20.56

Ford Motor Co Ltd v Hudson [1978] 3 All ER 23; [1978] ICR 482; [1978] IRLR 66 (EAT) . . . 21.118

Ford v Milthorn Toleman Ltd [1980] IRLR 30 (CA) . . . 17.47

Ford v Stakis Hotels and Inns Ltd [1987] ICR 943; [1988] IRLR 46; [1987] LS Gaz R 2192 (EAT) . . . 20.14

Ford v Warwickshire County Council [1976] ICR 225; [1976] IRLR 146; 11 ITR 50 (DC) . . . 13.20, 13.28

Ford v Weston (Chemists) Ltd (1977) 12 ITR 369 . . . 5.27

Forex Neptune (Overseas) Ltd v Miller [1987] ICR 170; (1987) 84 LSG 112 . . . 5.49

Forman Construction Ltd v Kelly [1977] IRLR 468 (EAT) . . . 18.45, 18.99

Forshaw v Archcraft Ltd [2006] ICR 70; [2005] IRLR 600 (EAT) . . . 17.152

Forster & Sons Ltd v Suggett (1918) 35 TLR 87 . . . 19.29

Forster v Cartwright Black [2004] ICR 1728 (EAT) . . . 6.124

Forsyth v Fry's Metals Ltd [1977] IRLR 243 . . . 21.127

Fosca Services (UK) Ltd v Birkett [1996] IRLR 325 (EAT) . . . 2.98, 15.40, 16.21

Foster v British Gas (C-188/89) [1991] 1 QB 405; [1990] 3 All ER 897; [1991] 2 WLR 258; [1990] ECR I-3313; [1990] 2 CMLR 833; [1991] ICR 84; [1990] IRLR 353 (ECJ) . . . 1.73, 1.74, 18.69

Foster v Scaffolding (GB) Ltd (1973) (342/73) IDS Brief 13 . . . 10.70

Foster Wheeler (London) Ltd v Jackson [1990] ICR 757; [1990] IRLR 412 (EAT) . . . 8.17

Fougère v Phoenix Motors [1977] 1 All ER 237; [1976] 1 WLR 1281; [1976] ICR 495; [1976] IRLR 259 11 ITR 181; 120 Sol Jo 603 (EAT) . . . 17.211, 17.224, 20.126

Fowler v Cammell Laird (Shipbuilders) Ltd [1973] IRLR 72 . . . 12.21

Fowler v Waltham Forest [2007] All ER (D) 126 . . . 4.117

Fox Maintenance Ltd v Jackson [1978] ICR 110; [1977] IRLR 306; 12 ITR 455 (EAT) . . . 15.28, 17.4

Frame v McKean & Graham Ltd [1974] IRLR 179 . . . 10.91, 12.49

Frames Snooker Centre v Boyce [1992] IRLR 472 (EAT) . . . 17.158

Framptons Ltd v Badger, EAT/0138/06 . . . 3.58

Francovich v Italy (C-6/90 and 9/90) [1991] ECR I-5357; [1993] 2 CMLR 66; [1995] ICR 722; [1992] IRLR 84 (ECJ) . . . 1.28, 1.74

Frank Wright & Co Ltd v Punch [1980] IRLR 217 (EAT) . . . 17.26, 17.35

Franks v Reuters Ltd [2002] All ER (D) 239 (Jun) (EAT); revsd [2003] EWCA Civ 417; [2003] ICR 1166; [2003] IRLR 423; [2003] 25 LS Gaz R 45; 147 Sol JO LB 474; [2003] All ER (D) 160 (Apr) . . . 2.158

Fraser v Hlmad Ltd [2006] EWCA Civ 738 . . . 1.44

Freeman v Sovereign Chicken Ltd [1991] ICR 853; [1991] IRLR 408 (EAT) . . . 20.37

French v Barclays Bank plc [1998] IRLR 646 (CA) . . . 3.22, 3.89

Friend v Institution of Professional Managers and Specialists [1999] IRLR 173 . . . 22.35

Frost v Chief Constable of South Yorkshire Police [1998] QB 254; [1997] 1 All ER 540; [1997] 3 WLR 1194; [1997] IRLR 173; 33 BMLR 108; [1996] NLJR 1651 (CA); revsd sub nom White v Chief Constable of South Yorkshire Police

[1999] 2 AC 455; [1999] 1 All ER 1; [1998] 3 WLR 1509; [1999] ICR 216; 45 BMLR 1; [1999] 02 LS Gaz R 28; [1998] NLJR 1844; [1999] 3 LRC 644, sub nom Frost v Chief Constable of South Yorkshire Police 143 Sol Jo LB 51 (HL) . . . 11.104

Fry v Foreign and Commonwealth Office [1997] ICR 512 (EAT) . . . 20.74

Fuß v Stadt Halle (No 2) (C-429/09) [2011] IRLR 176 (CJEU) . . . 7.104, 7.106

Fuller v Lloyds Bank plc [1991] IRLR 336 (EAT) . . . 12.22

Fuller v Stephanie Bowman (Sales) Ltd [1977] IRLR 87 . . . 18.32

Furness v Midland Bank plc (unreported 10 November 2002) . . . 11.135

Futty v D and D Brekkes Ltd [1974] IRLR 130 . . . 17.14

Fyfe v Scientific Furnishing Ltd [1989] ICR 648; [1989] IRLR 331 (EAT) . . . 17.226

Fytche v Wincanton Logistics plc [2003] EWCA Civ 874; [2003] ICR 1582; 147 Sol Jo LB 785; [2003] All ER (D) 334 (June) . . . 11.131, 11.138

G F Sharp & Co Ltd v McMillan [1998] IRLR 632 (EAT) . . . 13.24, 15.5, 17.65, 17.100

G v X School [2010] EWCA Civ 1; [2010] 2 All ER 555; [2010] IRLR 222; [2010] HRLR 13; [2010] BLGR 207; [2010] Med LR 45; (2010) Times 23 February . . . 1.107

G4S Justice Services (UK) Ltd v Anstey [2006] IRLR 588 (EAT) . . . 9.34

GF Sharp & Co Ltd v McMillan [1998] IRLR 632 (EAT) . . . 15.25

GFI Group Inc v Eaglestone [1994] IRLR 119 . . . 19.54, 19.63

GFI Holdings Ltd v Camm [2008] All ER (D) 74 . . . 20.71

GMB and AEEU v Campbell's UK Ltd (unreported) . . . 18.81

GMB v Allen [2007] IRLR 752; (2007) 104(33) LSG 26; (2007) 151 SJLB 1129 (EAT) . . . 22.38

GMB v Hamm, IDS Brief 682 . . . 21.18

GMB v Man Truck and Bus UK Ltd [2000] ICR 1101; [2000] IRLR 636 (EAT) . . . 18.100

GMB v Rankin and Harrison [1992] IRLR 514 (EAT) . . . 18.89

GPMU v Derry Print Ltd [2002] IRLR 380 . . . 2.9

GW Plowman & Sons Ltd v Ash [1964] 2 All ER 10; [1964] 1 WLR 568; 108 Sol Jo 216 (CA) . . . 19.32

Gadhok v Commonwealth Secretariat (1977) 12 ITR 440 (CA) . . . 17.4

Gale v Northern General Hospital NHS Trust [1994] IRLR 292 (CA) . . . 13.40

Gallacher v Department of Transport [1993] ICR 654 (EAT); aff'd [1994] ICR 967; [1994] IRLR 231 (CA) . . . 21.52

Gallagher v Post Office [1970] 3 All ER 712; 114 Sol Jo 736 . . . 3.78

Gallear v JF Watson & Son Ltd [1979] IRLR 306 (EAT) . . . 10.35

Gallop v Newport City Council [2013] EWCA Civ 1583 . . . 4.115

Galloway v Export Packing Services Ltd [1975] IRLR 306 . . . 18.66

Galt v Philp [1984] IRLR 156; 1984 SLT 28 . . . 23.126

Gardener v National Coal Board, EAT 375/82 . . . 13.31

Gardiner v London Borough of Merton [1981] QB 269; [1981] 2 WLR 232; [1981] ICR 186; [1980] IRLR 472; 79 LGR 374; (1981) 125 SJ 97; (1980) *Times* 26 November . . . 5.6

Gardiner v Newport County Borough Council [1974] IRLR 262 . . . 12.51, 17.140

Gardiner-Hill v Roland Berger Technics Ltd [1982] IRLR 498 (EAT) . . . 17.214, 17.224, 17.236

Garland v British Rail Engineering Ltd [1983] 2 AC 751; [1982] 2 WLR 918; [1981] 2 CMLR 542; [1982] ICR 420 (HL); ref'd 12/81 [1983] 2 AC 751; [1982] 2 All ER 402; [1982] 2 WLR 918; [1982] ECR 359; [1982] 1 CMLR 696; [1982] ICR 420; [1982] IRLR 111 (ECJ); apl'd [1983] 2 AC 751; [1982] 2 All ER 402; [1982] 2 WLR 918; [1982] 2 CMLR 174; [1982] ICR 420; [1982] IRLR 257; 126 Sol Jo 309 (HL) . . . 1.72, 5.2, 5.17

Garrard v AE Southey & Co and Standard Telephones and Cables Ltd [1952] 2 QB 174; [1952] 1 All ER 597; 96 Sol Jo 166; [1952] 1 TLR 630 . . . 2.148

Garrett v Lidl Ltd (EAT, 16 December 2009) . . . 4.117

Garricks (Caterers) Ltd v Nolan [1980] IRLR 259 (EAT) . . . 17.102

Garvey v J & J Maybank (Oldham) Ltd [1979] IRLR 408 . . . 7.3

Gascol Conversions Ltd v Mercer [1974] ICR 420; [1974] IRLR 155; [1975] KILR 149; 9 ITR 282; 118 Sol Jo 219 (CA) . . . 3.77, 3.81

Gate Gourmet London Ltd v TGWU [2005] EWHC 1889 (QB); [2005] IRLR 881 . . . 23.114

Gateway Hotels Ltd v Stewart [1988] IRLR 287 (EAT) . . . 9.57

Gemmell v Darngavil Brickworks Ltd (1967) 2 ITR 20 . . . 18.13

General Aviation Services (UK) Ltd v Transport and General Workers' Union [1974] ICR 35; [1973] IRLR 355 (NIRC); revsd [1975] ICR 276; 119 Sol Jo 589 (CA); on appeal [1985] ICR 615; [1976] IRLR 224 (HL) . . . 23.21

General Billposting Co Ltd v Atkinson [1908] 1 Ch 537; 77 LJ Ch 411; [1908-10] All ER Rep 619; 52 Sol Jo 240; 98 LT 482; 24 TLR 285 CA; aff'd [1909] AC 118; 78 LJ Ch 77; [1908-10] All ER Rep 619; 99 LT 943; 25 TLR 178 (HL) . . . 16.6, 19.56

General Cleaning Contractors Ltd v Christmas [1953] AC 180; [1952] 2 All ER 1110; [1953] 2 WLR 6; 51 LGR 109; 97 Sol Jo 7 (HL) . . . 11.35

General and Municipal Workers' Union v Certification Officer [1977] 1 All ER 771; [1977] ICR 183; 120 Sol Jo 736 (EAT) . . . 22.8

General and Municipal Workers' Union v Wailes Dove Bitumastic [1977] IRLR 45 . . . 18.90

Geys v Société Générale [2012] UKSC 63 . . . 16.6

Gibb v Maidstone & Tunbridge Wells NHS Trust [2010] IRLR 786; [2010] EWCA Civ 678 . . . 16.27, 20.42

Gibb v United Steel Companies Ltd [1957] 2 All ER 110; [1957] 1 WLR 668; 101 Sol Jo 393 . . . 2.37

Gibson v Ciro Cittero (unreported) . . . 9.57

Gibson v National Union of Dyers, Bleachers and Textile Workers (1972) 13 KIR 143; [1972] ITR 324 . . . 10.91

Gilbert v Goldstone Ltd [1977] 1 All ER 423; [1977] ICR 36; [1976] IRLR 257 (EAT) . . . 3.45

Gilbert v Kembridge Fibres Ltd [1984] ICR 188; [1984] IRLR 52 (EAT) . . . 1.10, 20.37

Gilham v Kent County Council (No 3) [1986] ICR 52; [1986] IRLR 56 (EAT) . . . 17.205

Gill v Cape Contracts Ltd [1985] IRLR 499 . . . 16.8

Gillespie v Northern Health and Service Board [1997] NI 190; [1997] Eu LR 566; [1997] IRLR 410 . . . 5.17

Gillespie v Northern Ireland Health and Social Services Board [1996] All ER (EC) 284; [1996] ECR I-475; [1996] 2 CMLR 969; [1996] ICR 498; [1996] IRLR 214; (1996) 31 BMLR 65; (1996) *Times* 22 February . . . 4.136

Gills v Wall's Meat Co Ltd, HSIB 22 . . . 17.148

Ging v Ellward Lancs Ltd [1991] ICR 222n; 13 ITR 265 (EAT) . . . 17.207

Giraud UK Ltd v Smith [2000] IRLR 763; 668 IDS Brief 7 (EAT) . . . 15.35

Gisda Cyf v Barratt [2010] UKSC 41 . . . 17.5, 20.31

Glasgow City Council v McNab [2007] IRLR 476 . . . 4.164

Glasgow v Independent Printing Co [1901] 2 IR 278; 34 ILTR 66 . . . 2.17

Gledhow Autoparts v Delaney [1965] 3 All ER 288; [1965] 1 WLR 1366; 109 Sol Jo 571 (CA) . . . 19.34

Glendale Managed Services v Graham [2003] EWCA Civ 773; [2003] IRLR 465; [2003] All ER (D) 225 (May) . . . 3.2, 3.68

Glitz v Watford Electric Co Ltd [1979] IRLR 89 (EAT) . . . 3.98

Global Plant Ltd v Secretary of State for Health and Social Security [1972] 1 QB 139; [1971] 3 All ER 385; [1971] 3 WLR 269; 115 Sol Jo 506 . . . 2.54

Gogay v Hertfordshire County Council [2000] IRLR 703; [2001] 1 FCR 455; [2000] Fam Law 883; [2000] All ER (D) 1057 (CA) . . . 12.67

Goodwin v Patent Office [1999] ICR 302; [1999] IRLR 4; [1999] Disc LR 104; (1998) *Times* 11 November . . . 4.96, 20.65

Gorfin v Distressed Gentlefolk's Aid Association [1973] IRLR 290 . . . 17.160

Goring v British Actors Equity Association [1987] IRLR 122 . . . 22.25

Gorris v Scott (1874) LR 9 Exch 12; 43 LJ Ex 92; 2 Asp MLC 282; 22 WR 575; 30 LT 431 . . . 11.138

Gough v County Sports (Wales) Ltd (unreported) . . . 6.7

Gouriet v Union of Post Office Workers [1977] QB 729; [1977] 1 All ER 696; [1977] 2 WLR 310; 121 Sol Jo 103 (CA); revsd [1978] AC 435; [1977] 3 All ER 70; [1977] 3 WLR 300; 141 JP 552; 121 Sol Jo 543 (HL) . . . 23.123

Government Communications Staff Federation v Certification Officer [1993] ICR 163; [1993] IRLR 260; [1993] 5 LS Gaz R 41 (EAT) . . . 22.14

Gozdzik v Chlidema Carpet Co, IDS Brief 163 . . . 17.89

Graham Oxley Tool Steels Ltd v Firth [1980] IRLR 135 (EAT) . . . 17.27

Graham v ABF Ltd [1986] IRLR 90 (EAT) . . . 18.46, 18.54

Graham v Co-operative Wholesale Society Ltd [1957] 1 All ER 654; [1957] 1 WLR 511; 55 LGR 137; 101 Sol Jo 267 . . . 11.142

Grainger Ltd v Nicholson [2010] 2 All ER 253; [2010] ICR 360; [2010] IRLR 4; (2009) 159 NLJ 1582; (2009) *Times* 11 November . . . 4.155

Grant v HM Land Registry [2011] EWCA Civ 769; [2011] IRLR 748 (CA) . . . 4.188

Grant v South-West Trains Ltd (C-249/96) [1998] ECR I-621; [1998] All ER (EC) 193; [1998] 1 CMLR 993; [1998] ICR 449; [1998] IRLR 206; [1998] 1 FCR 377; [1998] 1 FLR 839; [1998] Fam Law 392; 3 BHRC 578 (ECJ) . . . 3.21, 3.89

Gravil v Carroll [2008] EWCA Civ 689; [2008] ICR 1222; [2008] IRLR 829; (2008) 105(26) LSG 26; (2008) 158 NLJ 933; (2008) *Times* 22 July . . . 10.105

Gray v Burntisland Shipbuilding Co (1967) 2 ITR 255 . . . 13.28

Gray v C & P Pembroke Ltd (1972) (1350/72), IDS Brief 10 . . . 10.91, 17.143

Green v DB Group Services (UK) Ltd [2006] EWHC 1898 (QB); [2006] IRLR 764 . . . 10.115

Green v Wavertree Heating and Plumbing Co Ltd (unreported) . . . 9.11

Greenall Whitley plc v Carr [1985] ICR 451; [1985] IRLR 289 (EAT) . . . 12.34, 17.80

Greenhoff v Barnsley Metropolitan Borough Council [2006] ICR 1514 . . . 17.216

Greer v Sketchley Ltd [1979] FSR 197; [1979] IRLR 445 (CA) . . . 19.46

Greg May (Carpet Fitters and Contractors) Ltd v Dring [1990] ICR 188; [1990] IRLR 19 (EAT) . . . 8.15

Gregory v Ford [1951] 1 All ER 121 . . . 10.33

Gregory v Tudsbury Ltd [1982] IRLR 267 . . . 6.6

Grieg v Community Industry [1979] ICR 356; [1979] IRLR 158 . . . 4.168

Griffin v South West Water Services Ltd [1995] IRLR 15 . . . 18.69

Griffiths v Buckinghamshire County Council [1999] IRLR 208 (EAT) . . . 3.63

Griffiths v Vauxhall Motors Ltd [2003] EWCA Civ 412; [2003] All ER (D) 167 (Mar) . . . 11.136

Grimaldi v Fonds des Maladies Professionnelles (C-322/88) [1989] ECR 4407; [1991] 2 CMLR 265; [1990] IRLR 400 (ECJ) . . . 1.99

Grix v Munford Ltd (unreported) . . . 3.104

Group 4 Nightspeed Ltd v Gilbert [1997] IRLR 398; 574 IRLB 13 (EAT) . . . 8.32

Grundy (Teddington) Ltd v Willis [1976] ICR 323; [1976] IRLR 118; 11 ITR 26 . . . 17.76, 18.59

Grundy v British Airways plc [2007] EWCA Civ 1020; [2008] IRLR 74; (2007) 104(43) LSG 33; (2007) 151 SJLB 1401 . . . 5.10, 5.48

Gubala v Crompton Parkinson [1977] IRLR 10 . . . 4.175

Gunton v London Borough of Richmond [1981] Ch 448; [1980] 3 All ER 577; [1980] 3 WLR 714; 79 LGR 241; [1980] ICR 755; [1980] IRLR 321; 124 Sol Jo 792 (CA) . . . 3.96, 12.13, 16.3, 16.6, 16.6, 16.30

Gutridge v Sodexo Ltd [2009] EWCA Civ 729; [2009] ICR 1486; [2009] IRLR 721; (2009) 106(30) LSG 13; (2009) *Times* 6 October . . . 5.61

Guy v Delanair (Car Heater) Ltd [1975] IRLR 73 . . . 18.53

Gwynedd County Council v Jones [1986] ICR 833; (1986) 83 LSG 3836 . . . 4.140

H Campey & Sons Ltd v Bellwood [1987] ICR 311 (EAT) . . . 21.97

HM Prison Service v Johnson [2007] IRLR 951; (2007) 151 SJLB 1165 . . . 4.231

HM Prison Service v Salmon [2001] IRLR 425; [2001] Emp LR 1035 . . . 4.231

HSBC v Madden [2001] 1 All ER 550; [2000] ICR 1283; [2000] IRLR 827; 652 IRLB 7 (CA) . . . 17.78

Habib v Elkington & Co Ltd [1981] ICR 435; [1981] IRLR 344 (EAT) . . . 1.25

Hackney London Borough Council v Usher [1997] ICR 705 (EAT) . . . 20.85

Haddon v Van Den Bergh Foods Ltd [1999] ICR 1150; [1999] IRLR 672; 628 IRLB 3 (EAT) . . . 17.78

Hadjioannou v Coral Casinos Ltd [1981] IRLR 352 (EAT) . . . 12.46, 17.130

Hagen v ICI Chemicals plc [2002] IRLR 31; [2002] PLR 1; [2002] Lloyd's Rep PN 288; 683 IRLB 13; [2001] All ER (D) 273 (Oct) . . . 9.72

Hair Colour Consultants v Mena [1984] ICR 671; [1984] IRLR 386; [1984] LS Gaz R 2147 (EAT) . . . 2.7

Hairsine v Kingston upon Hull City Council [1992] ICR 212; [1992] IRLR 211 (EAT) . . . 21.70

Halford v Sharples [1992] ICR 146 (EAT); aff'd [1992] 3 All ER 624; [1992] 1 WLR 736; [1992] ICR 583 (CA) . . . 20.67

Halford v United Kingdom (Application 20605/92) (1997) 24 EHRR 523 [1997] IRLR 471; [1998] Crim LR 753; 94 LS Gaz R 24; 3 BHRC 31 (ECtHR) . . . 1.107, 10.45

Hall v Lodge (unreported) . . . 12.85

Hall v Lorimer [1992] 1 WLR 939; [1992] STC 599; 66 TC 349; [1992] ICR 739; [1992] 26 LS Gaz R 32; 136 Sol Jo LB 175; aff'd [1994] 1 All ER 250; [1994] 1 WLR 209; [1994] STC 23; 66 TC 349; [1994] ICR 218; [1994] IRLR 171; [1993] 45 LS Gaz R 45; 137 Sol Jo LB 256 (CA) . . . 2.54, 2.55

Hall v Woolston Hall Leisure Centre [2001] 1 WLR 225; [2000] 4 All ER 787; [2001] ICR 99; [2000] IRLR 578; (2000) 97(24) LSG 39; (2000) 150 NLJ 833; (2000) Times 31 May; (2000) Independent 8 June . . . 3.8, 3.11, 4.195

Hamblin v London Borough of Ealing [1975] IRLR 354 . . . 2.96

Hamilton v Argyll and Clyde Health Board [1993] IRLR 99 (EAT) . . . 17.134

Hamilton v Futura Floors Ltd [1990] IRLR 478 (OH) . . . 3.70

Hamilton v GMB (Northern Region) [2007] IRLR 391 . . . 20.92

Hammersmith London Borough Council v Ladejobi [1999] ICR 673 (EAT) . . . 20.118

Hancill v Marcon Engineering Ltd [1990] ICR 103, [1990] IRLR 51 (EAT) . . . 2.6

Hancock v Middleton [1982] ICR 416 (EAT) . . . 20.101

Handels-og v Dansk Arbejdsgiverforening [1990] ECR I-3979; [1992] ICR 332; [1991] IRLR 31; (1990) Times 20 December . . . 5.4

Handels-og-Kontorfuntionaererenes Forbund I Danmark v Dansk (acting for Danfloss) [1997] ECR I-2757; [1997] 2 CMLR 915; [1997] IRLR 643 . . . 5.44

Handelsog (acting on behalf of Larsson) v Dansk Handel & Service [1997] IRLR 643 . . . 4.136, 6.50

Hanks v Ace High Productions Ltd [1978] ICR 1155; [1979] IRLR 32; 13 ITR 524 (EAT) . . . 20.87

Hanley v Pease & Partners [1915] 1 KB 698, 79 JP 230, 84 LJKB 532, [1914-15] All ER Rep 984, 112 LT 823 . . . 12.63

Hannan v TNT-IPEC (UK) Ltd [1986] IRLR 165 (EAT) . . . 20.53

Hanover Insurance Brokers Ltd v Schapiro [1994] IRLR 82 (CA) . . . 19.41, 19.42

Hanson v Fashion Industries (Hartlepool) Ltd [1981] ICR 35; [1980] IRLR 393 (EAT) . . . 13.3, 13.35

Hardwick v Leeds Area Health Authority [1975] IRLR 319 . . . 3.81

Hardy v Polk (Leeds) Ltd [2005] ICR 557 (EAT) . . . 15.38, 17.226

Hardys & Hanson plc v Lax [2005] EWCA Civ 846; [2005] ICR 1565; [2005] IRLR 726;
(2005) 102(29) LSG 31; (2005) Times 26 July . . . 4.172

Harlow v Artemis International Corporation Ltd [2008] EWHC 1126 (QB); [2008] IRLR 629; (2008) 105(23) LSG 27 . . . 3.85

Harris (Ipswich) Ltd v Harrison [1978] ICR 1256; [1978] IRLR 382 (EAT) . . . 12.5

Harris and Russell Ltd v Slingsby [1973] 3 All ER 31; [1973] ICR 454; [1973] IRLR 221; 15 KIR 157; 8 ITR 433 (NIRC) . . . 15.8, 17.18, 19.2

Harris and Shepherd v Courage (Eastern) Ltd [1982] ICR 530; [1982] IRLR 509 (CA) . . . 12.5

Harris v Richard Lawson Autologistics Ltd [2002] EWCA Civ 442; [2002] ICR 765; [2002] IRLR 476; [2002] All ER (D) 214 (Mar) . . . 3.60, 3.102

Harrison v George Wimpey & Co Ltd (1972) 7 ITR 188 (NIRC) . . . 17.58

Harrison v Kent County Council [1995] ICR 434 (EAT) . . . 21.31

Harrow London Borough v Cunningham [1996] IRLR 256 (EAT) . . . 12.48

Hart v AR Marshall & Sons (Bulwell) Ltd [1978] 2 All ER 413; [1977] 1 WLR 1067; [1977] ICR 539; [1977] IRLR 51; 12 ITR 190; 121 Sol Jo 677 (EAT) . . . 17.64, 17.93

Hartlepool Borough Council v Dolphin [2009] IRLR 168; (2008) 152(38) SJLB 30 . . . 5.45

Hartlepool Borough Council v Llewellyn [2009] ICR 1426; [2009] IRLR 796; (2009) Times 9 July . . . 5.14

Hartley v Mayoh & Co [1953] 2 All ER 525; 117 JP 369; aff'd [1954] 1 QB 383; [1954] 1 All ER 375; [1954] 1 WLR 355; 52 LGR 165; 118 JP 178; 98 Sol Jo 107 (CA) . . . 11.131

Hartman v South Essex Mental Health and Community Care NHS Trust [2005] EWCA Civ 6 . . . 11.105

Harvard Securities plc v Younghusband [1990] IRLR 17 (EAT) . . . 17.179

Harvest Press Ltd v McCaffrey [1999] IRLR 778 (EAT) . . . 11.66

Harvey v Yankee Traveller Restaurant [1976] IRLR 35 . . . 17.8

Haseltine Lake & Co v Dowler [1981] ICR 222; [1981] IRLR 25 (EAT) . . . 17.31

Hasley v Fair Employment Agency [1989] IRLR 106 (NICA); [1988] 13 NIJB 63 . . . 2.6, 5.6

Haspell v Restron and Johnson Ltd [1976] IRLR 50 . . . 10.40

Hassan v Odeon Cinemas [1998] ICR 127 (EAT) . . . 12.70

Haughton v Hackney Borough Council (unreported) . . . 11.120

Hawkins v Atex Group Limited UKEAT/0302/11/2A . . . 4.124

Hawkins v Darken [2004] EWCA Civ 1755 . . . 4.191

Hawkins v Ian Ross (Castings) Ltd [1970] 1 All ER 180 . . . 11.117

Hawley v Luminar Leisure Ltd [2005] EWCA Civ 18 . . . 2.146, 10.108

Hayward v Cammell Laird Shipbuilders Ltd [1988] AC 894; [1988] 2 WLR 1134; [1988] 2 All ER 257; [1988] 2 CMLR 528; [1988] ICR 464; [1988] IRLR 257; (1988) 152 LG Rev 501; (1988) 138 NLJ Rep 133 . . . 5.40, 5.41

Hazell Offsets v Luckett [1977] IRLR 430 (EAT) . . . 21.118

Healey v Excel Logistics Ltd (unreported) . . . 11.66

Heath v Longman (Meat Salesmen) Ltd [1973] 2 All ER 1228; [1973] ICR 407; [1973] IRLR 214; 14 KIR 569; 8 ITR 427 (NIRC) . . . 21.108

Heatherwood & Wexham Park Hospitals NHS Trust v Kulubowila, EAT/0633/06 . . . 2.159

Heaton's Transport Ltd v Transport and General Workers' Union [1997] AC 15; [1972] 2 All ER 1214; [1972] 3 WLR 73; 14 KIR 1; 116 Sol Jo 484 CA; revsd [1973] AC 15; [1972] 3 All ER 101; [1972] 3 WLR 431; [1972] 1CR 308; [1972] IRLR 25; 14 KIR 48; 116 Sol Jo 598 (HL) . . . 3.82, 23.21

Hedger v Davy & Co Ltd [1974] IRLR 138 . . . 17.162

Hedley Byrne & Co Ltd v Heller & Partners Ltd [1962] 1 QB 396; [1961] 3 All ER 891; [1961] 3 WLR 1225; 105 Sol Jo 910 (CA); aff'd [1964] AC 465; [1963] 2 All ER 575; [1963] 3 WLR 101; [1963] 1 Lloyd's Rep 485; 107 Sol Jo 454 (HL) . . . 10.39

Heimann and another v Kaiser GmbH C-229/11, 230/11 ECJ . . . 7.85

Heinisch v Germany [2011] IRLR 922 . . . 10.83

Hellyer Bros Ltd v McLeod [1987] 1 WLR 728; [1987] ICR 526; 131 Sol Jo 805; [1987] LS Gaz R 1056, sub nom McLeod v Hellyer Bros Ltd [1987] IRLR 232, CA . . . 2.174

Hellyer Bros v Atkinson [1992] IRLR 540 (EAT); revsd [1994] IRLR 88 (CA) . . . 18.7

Helmet Integrated Systems Ltd v Tunnard [2006] FSR 41; PCC; aff'd [2006] EWCA Civ 1735; [2007] IRLR 126; [2007] FSR 16 . . . 10.56, 19.5

Help the Aged Housing Association (Scotland) Ltd v Vidler [1977] IRLR 104 (EAT) . . . 20.101

Hempell v W H Smith & Sons Ltd [1986] ICR 365; [1986] IRLR 95 (EAT) . . . 18.25

Henderson v Connect (South Tyneside) Ltd [2010] IRLR 466 . . . 17.162

Henderson v Wakefield Shirt Co Ltd [1997] PIQR P413 (CA) . . . 11.119

Hendrickson Europe Ltd v Pipe [2003] All ER (D) 280 (Apr) (EAT) . . . 2.91

Hendry v Scottish Liberal Club [1977] IRLR 5 . . . 4.242

Henke v Gemeinde Schierke (C-298/94) [1996] ECR I-4989; [1996] IRLR 710 . . . 9.28

Hennessy v Craigmyle & Co Ltd [1986] ICR 461; [1986] IRLR 300; 130 Sol Jo 633; [1986] LS Gaz R 2160 (CA) . . . 1.11

Henry v London General Transport Services Ltd [2000] All ER (D) 2049 (EAT); aff'd [2002]

EWCA Civ 488; [2002] IRLR 472; [2002] All ER (D) 322 (Mar) . . . 3.69, 3.83, 3.100

Hepworths Ltd v Comerford, unreported . . . 17.224

Herbert Clayton & Jack Waller Ltd v Oliver [1930] AC 209; 99 LJKB 165; [1930] All ER Rep 414; 74 Sol Jo 187; 142 LT 585; 46 TLR 230 (HL) . . . 10.17, 16.21

Herbert Morris Ltd v Saxelby [1915] 2 Ch 57; 84 LJ Ch 521; 59 Sol Jo 412; 112 LT 354; 31 TLR 370 (CA); on appeal [1916] 1 AC 688; 85 LJ Ch 210; [1916-17] All ER Rep 305; 60 Sol Jo 305; 114 LT 618; 32 TLR 297 (HL) . . . 19.21, 19.30, 19.45

Heron v Citilink-Nottingham [1993] IRLR 372 (EAT) . . . 18.48

Hewage v Grampian Health Board [2012] UKSC 37 . . . 4.29

Hewcastle Catering Ltd v Ahmed [1992] ICR 626; [1991] IRLR 473 (CA) . . . 3.15

Heyday Case see Incorporated Trustees of the National Council on Ageing Hibbins v Hester Way Neighbourhood Project [2009] 1 All ER 949; [2009] ICR 319; [2009] IRLR 198 . . . 10.74

High Court Lonmar Global Risks Ltd v West [2011] IRLR 138 . . . 10.94

High Table Ltd v Horst [1998] ICR 409; [1997] IRLR 513 (CA); sub nom Horst v High Table Ltd [1997] 28 LS Gaz R 25; 141 Sol Jo LB 161 . . . 18.14

High v British Railways Board [1979] IRLR 52 (EAT) . . . 12.87, 17.40

Higham v International Stores (unreported) . . . 12.53

Highland Fabricators Ltd v McLaughlin [1985] ICR 183; [1984] IRLR 482 (EAT) . . . 21.107

Hill v Archbold [1967] 2 QB 418; [1967] 1 All ER 1038; [1967] 2 WLR 1180; 111 Sol Jo 193; aff'd [1968] 1 QB 686; [1967] 3 All ER 110; [1967] 3 WLR 1218; 111 Sol Jo 543 (CA) . . . 22.36

Hill v CA Parsons & Co Ltd [1972] Ch 305; [1971] 3 All ER 1345; [1971] 3 WLR 995; 12 KIR 135; 115 Sol Jo 868 (CA) . . . 10.3, 10.4, 10.16, 15.3, 15.39

Hill v Chapell [2003] IRLR 19; [2002] All ER (D) 461 (May) (EAT) . . . 7.85

Hill v General Accident Fire and Life Insurance Co [1998] IRLR 641; 1999 SLT 1157; 1998 SCLR 1030; 609 IRLB 8 (OH) . . . 17.105, 18.58

Hillingdon London Borough Council v Thomas [2002] All ER (D) 202 (Sep) (EAT) . . . 17.138

Hillyer v St Bartholomew's Hospital [1909] 2 KB 820; 73 JP 501; 78 LJKB 958; 53 Sol Jo 714; 101 LT 368; 25 TLR 762 (CA) . . . 2.59

Hilton International Hotels (UK) Ltd v Protopapa [1990] IRLR 316 (EAT) . . . 17.27

Hilton v Shiner Ltd [2001] IRLR 727; [2001] All ER (D) 316 (May) (EAT) . . . 3.48, 10.11, 17.47

Hindle v Percival Boats Ltd [1969] 1 All ER 836; [1969] 1 WLR 174; 4 ITR 86; 113 Sol Jo 13 (CA) . . . 18.18

Hinton v University of London [2005] ICR 1260; [2005] EWCA Civ 532 (CA) . . . 20.38

Hitchcock v Post Office [1980] ICR 100 (EAT) . . . 2.38

Hivac Ltd v Park Royal Scientific Instruments Ltd [1946] Ch 169; [1946] 1 All ER 350; 115 LJ Ch 241; 90 Sol Jo 175; 174 LT 422; 62 TLR 231 (CA) . . . 10.92, 17.143, 19.69

Holden v Bradville Ltd [1985] IRLR 483 (EAT) . . . 18.45

Holis Metal Industries Ltd v GMB [2008] ICR 464; [2008] IRLR 187 (EAT) . . . 9.21, 9.79

Holland v Glendale Industries Ltd [1998] ICR 493 (EAT) . . . 17.21, 17.42

Holliday v National Telephone Co [1899] 2 QB 392; 68 LJQB 1016; 47 WR 658; [1895-99] All ER Rep 359; 81 LT 252; 15 TLR 483 (CA) . . . 10.103

Hollier v Plysu Ltd [1983] IRLR 260 (CA) . . . 17.233

Hollis & Co v Stocks [2000] IRLR 712 (CA) . . . 19.44, 19.53

Hollister v National Farmers' Union [1978] ICR 712; [1978] IRLR 161 (EAT); revsd [1979] ICR 542; [1979] IRLR 238 (CA) . . . 3.107, 17.163

Home Office v Ayres [1992] ICR 175; [1992] IRLR 59 (EAT) . . . 8.23

Home Office v Bailey [2005] IRLR 757 . . . 5.35

Home Office v Evans [2007] EWCA Civ 1089; [2008] IRLR 59; [2008] ICR 302 . . . 18.6, 18.14

Home Office v Holmes [1985] 1 WLR 71; [1984] 3 All ER 549; [1984] ICR 678; [1984] IRLR 299; (1984) 81 LSG 2463; (1984) 128 SJ 645 . . . 4.173

Home Office v Robinson [1982] ICR 31; [1981] IRLR 524 (EAT) . . . 2.73

Home Office v Tariq [2010] EWCA Civ 462; [2011] UKSC 35 . . . 2.177, 20.74

Homer v Chief Constable of West Yorkshire Police [2012] UKSC 16; [2010] EWCA Civ 419; (2010) 107(19) LSG 24 . . . 4.65

Hone v Six Continents Retail [2005] EWCA Civ 922 (CA) . . . 11.108

Honeywell Ltd v Scott, IDS Handbook . . . 5.44, 5.51

Hooper v British Railways Board [1988] IRLR 517 (CA) . . . 3.1, 3.25

Hopkins v National Union of Seamen [1985] ICR 268; [1985] IRLR 157 . . . 22.37

Horcal Ltd v Gatland [1983] IRLR 459; [1983] BCLC 60; 133 NLJ 1133; on appeal [1984] IRLR 288; [1984] BCLC 549 (CA) . . . 10.66

Horizon Holidays Ltd v Grassi [1987] ICR 851; [1987] IRLR 371 (EAT) . . . 17.210

Horkulak v Cantor Fitzgerald International [2003] EWHC 1918 (QB); [2003] IRLR 756; [2003] All ER (D) 542 (Jul) . . . 10.14

Horne v Lec Refrigeration Ltd [1965] 2 All ER 898 . . . 11.144

Horsley Smith and Sherry Ltd v Dutton [1977] ICR 594; [1977] IRLR 172; ITR 351 (EAT) . . . 17.179

Horton v Taplin Contracts Ltd [2002] EWCA Civ 1604; [2003] ICR 179; [2003] PIQR P180; [2003] BLR 74; [2003] 01 LS Gaz R 24; 146 Sol Jo LB 256; [2002] All ER (D) 122 (Nov) . . . 11.149

Hosnan v Al Baca Ltd (unreported) . . . 17.244

Hough v Leyland DAF Ltd [1991] ICR 696; [1991] IRLR 194 (EAT) . . . 18.78

Hovell v Ashford & St Peter's Hospital NHS Trust [2009] EWCA Civ 670; [2009] ICR 1545; [2009] IRLR 734; (2009) 106(29) LSG 17; (2009) Times 5 October . . . 5.38

Howard v Millrise Ltd [2005] ICR 435 (EAT) . . . 18.72

Howe v Gloucester and Severnside Co-operative Society [1975] IRLR 17 . . . 16.13

Howgate v Fane Acoustics [1981] IRLR 161 (EAT) . . . 12.40

Howlett Marine Services Ltd v Bowlam [2001] ICR 595; [2001] IRLR 201; [2000] All ER (D) 2494 (EAT) . . . 18.98

Howman & Son v Blyth [1983] ICR 416; [1983] IRLR 139 . . . 3.46

Hoyland v Asda Stores Ltd [2006] CSIH 21; 2006 SC 550; 2006 SLT 524; [2006] IRLR 468; 2006 GWD 14-263 . . . 6.29, 10.24

Huckerby v Elliott [1970] 1 All ER 189; 134 JP 175; 113 Sol Jo 1001 . . . 11.92

Hudson v George Harrison Ltd [2003] All ER (D) 381 (Mar) (EAT) . . . 18.30

Hudson v GMB [1990] IRLR 67 . . . 22.32

Hudson v Ridge Manufacturing Co Ltd [1957] 2 QB 348; [1957] 2 All ER 229; [1957] 2 WLR 948; 101 Sol Jo 409 . . . 11.129

Hughes v Alan Dick & Co Ltd [2008] EWHC 2695 (QB) . . . 1.33

Hulme v Ferranti Ltd [1918] 2 KB 426; 16 LGR 813; 87 LJKB 938; 62 Sol Jo 668; 118 LT 719; 34 TLR 500 (DC) . . . 10.20

Hunt v British Railways Board [1979] IRLR 379 (EAT) . . . 17.42

Hunter v Smith's Dock Co Ltd [1968] 2 All ER 81; [1968] 1 WLR 1865; [1968] ITR 198; 112 Sol Jo 963; [1968] 1 Lloyd's Rep 354 (DC) . . . 13.19

Huntley v Thornton [1957] 1 All ER 234; [1957] 1 WLR 321; 101 Sol Jo 171 . . . 23.38

Hussain v Acorn Independent College Ltd [2011] IRLR 463 . . . 13.20

Hussain v Elonex plc [1999] IRLR 420 (CA) . . . 12.22

Hussein v Mite Security Ltd, UKEAT/0342/08 . . . 20.127

Hussman Manufacturing Ltd v Weir [1998] IRLR 288 IRLB 5 (EAT) . . . 8.18

Hutchings v Coinseed Ltd [1998] IRLR 190 (CA) . . . 15.22

Hutchins v British Railways Board [1974] IRLR 303 . . . 12.22

Hutchinson v Enfield Rolling Mills Ltd [1981] IRLR 318 (EAT) . . . 17.111

Hutchinson v London and North Eastern Rly Co [1942] 1 KB 481, [1942] 1 All ER 330, 111

LJKB 369, 166 LT 228, 58 TLR 174, CA . . .
11.103
Hygia Professional Training v Cutter (2007) 151
SJLB 1297 . . . 20.127
Hyland v JH Barker (North West) Ltd [1985] ICR
861; [1985] IRLR 403 (EAT) . . . 3.16, 13.11
Hynd v Armstrong [2007] CSIH 16; 2007 SC 409;
2007 SLT 299; [2007] IRLR 338; 2007 GWD
8-145 . . . 9.55

ILEA v Gravett [1988] IRLR 497 (EAT) . . .
17.189
IMI Yorkshire Imperial Ltd v Olender [1982] ICR
69 (EAT) . . . 1.23
IRC v Bebb Travel plc [2002] 4 All ER 534; [2003]
ICR 201; [2002] IRLR 783; [2002] NLJR 1350;
[2002] All ER (D) 105 (Aug) (EAT); aff'd
[2003] EWCA Civ 563; [2003] 3All ER 546;
[2003] ICR 1271; [2003] NLJR 633; 147 Sol Jo
LB 505; [2002] All ER (D) 291 (Apr) . . . 8.51
IRC v St Hermans Estate Co Ltd [2002] IRLR 788;
[2002] All ER (D) 58 (Jul) (EAT) . . . 8.52
ITT Components (Europe) v Kolah [1977] ICR
740, [1977] IRLR 53 (EAT) . . . 14.2
Iceland Frozen Foods Ltd v Jones [1983] ICR 17;
[1982] IRLR 439 (EAT) . . . 17.78
Igbo v Johnson Matthey Chemicals Ltd [1986]
ICR 82; [1985] IRLR 189; [1985] LS Gaz 1011
(EAT), revsd [1986] ICR 505, [1986] 215, 130
Sol Jo 524, [1986] LS Gaz 2089 (CA) R . . .
17.69, 17.70
Impact v Ministry of Agriculture & Food [2009]
All ER (EC) 306; [2008] ECR I-2483; [2008] 2
CMLR 47; [2009] CEC 871; [2008] IRLR 552;
[2008] Pens LR 323 1.72 (EAT); revsd [1986]
ICR 505; [1986] IRLR 130; 215 Sol Jo 524;
[1986] LS Gaz R 2089 (CA) . . . 1.73
Incorporated Trustees of the National Council
on Ageing v Secretary of State for Business
Enterprise and Regulatory Reform [2009] All
ER (EC) 619; [2009] ECR I-1569; [2009] 3
CMLR 4; [2009] CEC 754; [2009] ICR 1080;
[2009] IRLR 373; [2009] Pens LR 115; (2009)
Times 5 March . . . 4.62
Independent Insurance Co Ltd v Aspinall [2011]
IRLR 716 . . . 18.92
Independent Research Services Ltd v Catterall
[1993] ICR 1 (EAT) . . . 20.67
Industrial Rubber Products v Gillon [1977] IRLR
389; 13 ITR 100 (EAT) . . . 17.25
Industrious Ltd v Horizon Recruitment Ltd IDS
Brief 774 (EAT) . . . 20.40
Ingham v ABC Contract Services Ltd
(unreported) . . . 19.42
Ingram v Foxon [1984] ICR 685; [1985] IRLR 5
(EAT) . . . 13.26
Initial Services Ltd v Putterill [1968] 1 QB 396;
[1967] 3 All ER 145; [1967] 3 WLR 1032; 2 KIR
863; 111 Sol Jo 541 (CA) . . . 19.18
Inner London Education Authority v Lloyd
[1981] IRLR 394 (CA) . . . 2.96

Insitu Cleaning Co Ltd v Heads [1995] IRLR 4
(EAT) . . . 4.34
Institute of Journalists v Daily Telegraph, IDS
Supp 22 . . . 23.15
Intel Corporation (UK) Ltd v Daw [2007] EWCA
Civ 70; [2007] 2 All ER 126; [2007] ICR 1318;
[2007] IRLR 355; (2007) 104(8) LSG 36; (2007)
157 NLJ 259; (2007) 151 SJLB 259 . . .
11.105
InterCity West Coast Ltd v National Union of Rail
Maritime and Transport Workers [1996] IRLR
583 (CA) . . . 23.54
International Computers v Kennedy [1981] IRLR
28 (EAT) . . . 18.8
International Consulting Services (UK) Ltd v
Hart [2000] IRLR 227 . . . 19.32
International Packaging Corpn (UK) Ltd v
Balfour [2003] IRLR 11; [2002] All ER (D) 146
(Nov) . . . 8.18, 18.37
International Sports Ltd v Thomson [1980] IRLR
340 (EAT) . . . 17.110
International Transport Workers' Federation
v Viking Line (C-438/05) [2008] All ER
(EC) 127; [2007] ECR I-10779; [2008] 1
CMLR 51; [2008] CEC 332; [2008] ICR 741;
[2008] IRLR 143; (2007) Times 14 December
(ECJ) . . . 23.97, 23.98
Irani v Southampton and South West Hampshire
Health Authority [1985] ICR 590; [1985] IRLR
203 . . . 10.4, 16.3
Ironmonger v Movefield Ltd [1988] IRLR
461 . . . 15.27
Iske v P & O European Ferries (Dover) Ltd [1997]
IRLR 401 (EAT) . . . 6.15
Item Software (UK) Ltd v Fassihi [2002] EWHC
3116 (Ch); [2003] IRLR 769; [2003] 2 BCLC
1; [2002] All ER (D) 62 (Dec) . . . 8.10, 10.94,
16.12, 16.24

J & S Bickley Ltd v Washer [1977] ICR 425; 12
ITR 137 (EAT) . . . 14.4
J & J Stern v Simpson [1983] IRLR 52
(EAT) . . . 17.17
J Sainsbury Ltd v Savage [1981] ICR 1; [1980]
IRLR 109 . . . 4.197, 12.38, 20.27
JA Mont (UK) Ltd v Mills [1993] FSR 577; [1993]
IRLR 172 (CA) . . . 19.10, 19.48
JN Dairies Ltd v Johal Dairies Ltd [2010] EWCA
Civ 348 . . . 19.2
JNJ Bricklaying Ltd v Stacey [2003] All ER (D) 96
(Jul) (EAT) . . . 7.55
Jack Allen (Sales and Service) Ltd v Smith [1999]
IRLR 19; 1999 SLT 820 (OH) . . . 19.15, 19.30
Jackson v Computershare Investor Services Ltd
[2007] EWCA Civ 1065; [2008] IRLR 70;
(2007) 104(44) LSG 32; (2007) 151 SJLB 1434;
[2008] ICR 341 . . . 9.39
James v Eastleigh Borough Council [1990] 2 AC
751; [1990] 3 WLR 55; [1990] 2 All ER 607;
[1990] ICR 554; [1990] IRLR 288; (1991) 155 L
Rev 205; (1990) 140 NLJ 926 . . . 4.19

James v Greenwich Council [2007] ICR 577; [2007] IRLR 168 (EAT); aff'd [2008] EWCA Civ 35, [2008] ICR 545, [2008] IRLR 302 . . . 2.159

James v Hepworth and Grandage Ltd [1968] 1 QB 94; [1967] 2 All ER 829; [1967] 3 WLR 178; 111 Sol Jo 232 (CA) . . . 11.117

James v Redcats (Brands) Ltd [2007] ICR 1006; [2007] IRLR 296 . . . 8.37

James v Waltham Holy Cross UDC [1973] ICR 398; [1978] IRLR 202; 14 KIR 576; 8 ITR 467 (NIRC) . . . 12.82

James W Cook & Co Ltd v Tipper [1990] ICR 716; [1990] IRLR 386; (1990) Times 31 May; (1990) Independent 28 May . . . 20.8

Janah v Libya UKEAT/0020/13/GE . . . 1.107

Janata Bank v Ahmed [1981] ICR 791; [1981] IRLR 457 (CA) . . . 10.65

Jarmain v E Pollard & Co Ltd (1967) 2 ITR 406 . . . 18.62

Jayes v IMI (Kynoch) Ltd [1985] ICR 155; [1984] LS Gaz R 3180 (CA) . . . 11.148

Jeffries v BP Tanker Co Ltd [1974] IRLR 260 . . . 3.91

Jenkins v Kingsgate (Clothing Productions) Ltd [1981] ICR 715; [1981] IRLR 388 (EAT) . . . 1.101

Jennings v Salford Community Service Agency [1981] ICR 399; [1981] IRLR 76 (EAT) . . . 13.4

Jennings v Westwood Engineering Ltd [1975] IRLR 245 . . . 2.58

Jeremiah v Ministry of Defence [1980] QB 87; [1979] 3 WLR 857; [1979] 3 All ER 833; [1980] ICR 13; [1979] IRLR 436; (1979) 123 SJ 735 . . . 4.48, 4.51

Jewell v Neptune Concrete Ltd [1975] IRLR 147 . . . 3.61, 10.20

Jiminez Melgar v Ayuntamiento de los Barrios (C-438/99) [2001] ECR I-6915; [2003] 3 CMLR 67; [2001] IRLR 848; [2001] All ER (D) 42 (Oct) (ECJ) . . . 6.51

Jiminez v Nelabrook Ltd, EAT 614/97 . . . 17.169

Jiminez v Southwark London Borough Council [2003] EWCA Civ 502; [2003] ICR 1176; [2003] IRLR 477; [2003] 23 LS Gaz R 37; 147 Sol Jo LB 476; [2003] All ER (D) 123 (Apr) . . . 20.95

John Brown Engineering Ltd v Brown [1997] IRLR 90 (EAT) . . . 18.57

John Lewis Partnership v Charman, UKEAT/0079/11/ZTT . . . 20.4

John Michael Design plc v Cooke [1987] 2 All ER 332; [1987] ICR 445; 131 Sol Jo 595; [1987] LS Gaz R 1492 (CA) . . . 19.64

John Summers & Sons Ltd v Frost [1955] AC 740; [1955] 1 All ER 870; [1955] 2 WLR 825; 53 LGR 32; 99 Sol Jo 257 (HL) . . . 11.133

John v Rees [1970] Ch 345; [1969] 2 All ER 274; [1969] 2 WLR 1294; 113 Sol Jo 487 . . . 12.3, 12.22

Johnson Matthey Metals v Harding [1978] IRLR 248; 13 ITR 407 (EAT) . . . 12.5

Johnson Matthey plc v Watters, EAT/0236/0237/0238/06 . . . 17.189

Johnson v Cross [1977] ICR 872 (EAT) . . . 18.35

Johnson v Nottinghamshire Combined Police Authority [1974] 1 All ER 1082; [1974] 1 WLR 358; [1974] ICR 170; [1974] IRLR 20; 9 ITR 164; 118 Sol Jo 166 (CA) . . . 18.16

Johnson v Ryan [2000] ICR 236 (EAT) . . . 2.65

Johnson v Tesco Stores Ltd [1976] IRLR 103 . . . 17.163

Johnson v Timber Tailors (Midlands) Ltd [1978] IRLR 146 . . . 4.224

Johnson v Unisys Ltd [1999] 1 All ER 854; [1999] ICR 809; [1999] IRLR 90 (CA); aff'd [2001] UKHL 13; [2003] 1 AC 518; [2001] 2 All ER 801; [2001] 2 WLR 1076; [2001] ICR 480; [2001] IRLR 279; [2001] All ER (D) 274 (Mar) . . . 3.48, 16.3, 16.25

Johnstone v Bloomsbury Health Authority [1992] QB 333; [1991] 2 All ER 293; [1991] 2 WLR 1362; [1991] ICR 269; [1991] IRLR 118; [1991] 22 Med LR 38 (CA) . . . 11.104

Jones v Associated Tunnelling Co Ltd [1981] IRLR 477 (EAT) . . . 3.45

Jones v British Rail Hovercraft Ltd [1974] IRLR 279 . . . 12.65

Jones v Burdett Coutts School [1997] ICR 390; 571 IRLB 9 (EAT); revsd [1999] ICR 38; [1998] IRLR 521; [1998] 18 LS Gaz R 32; 142 Sol Jo LB 142 (CA) . . . 18.25

Jones v DAS Legal Expenses Insurance Co Ltd [2003] EWCA Civ 1071; [2004] IRLR 218; 147 Sol Jo LB 932; [2003] All ER (D) 425 (Jul) . . . 1.22, 20.91

Jones v GEC Elliott Automation Ltd [1972] IRLR 111 . . . 12.82, 17.89

Jones v Gwent County Council [1992] IRLR 521 . . . 10.6, 16.16

Jones v Lee and Guilding (1980) 78 LGR 213; [1980] ICR 310; [1980] IRLR 67; 123 Sol Jo 785 (CA) . . . 3.96, 16.16

Jones v Lionite Specialities Ltd (1961) 105 Sol Jo 468; revsd 105 Sol Jo 1082 (CA) . . . 11.144

Jones v London Co-operative Society [1975] IRLR 110 . . . 12.43

Jones v R M Douglas Construction Ltd [1975] IRLR 175 . . . 12.90

Jones v Sirl & Son (Furnishers) Ltd [1997] IRLR 493 (EAT) . . . 17.43

Jones v Tower Boot Co Ltd [1997] 2 All ER 406; [1997] ICR 254; [1997] IRLR 168; (1997) 147 NLJ 60; (1996) Times 16 December; (1997) Independent 16 January . . . 4.56, 4.198

Jorgensen v Foreningen AF Speciallaeger Sygesikringens Forhandlingsudvalg [2000] ECR I-2447; [2002] 1 CMLR 40; [2000] IRLR 726 . . . 5.16

Joshua Wilson & Bros Ltd v Union of Shop, Distributive and Allied Workers [1978] 3 All

ER 4; [1978] ICR 614; [1978] IRLR 120; 13 ITR 229 (EAT) . . . 18.88

Judge v Crown Leisure Ltd [2005] EWCA Civ 571; [2005] IRLR 823 . . . 3.20

Junk v Wolfgang Kuhnell (C-188/03) IDS Brief 775 (ECJ) . . . 18.74

Jupiter General Insurance Co v Shroff [1937] 3 All ER 67 (PC) . . . 16.9

Jurkowska v Hlmad Ltd [2008] EWCA Civ 231; [2008] CP Rep 27; [2008] ICR 841; [2008] IRLR 430 . . . 20.119

Justfern Ltd v D'Ingerthorpe [1994] ICR 286; [1994] IRLR 164 (EAT) . . . 17.207

KHS AG v Schulte (C-214/10) [2011] ECR I-11757 . . . 7.87

Kalwak v Consistent Group Ltd [2007] IRLR 560 (EAT) . . . 2.48

Kapidia v London Borough of Lambeth [2000] IRLR 699 . . . 4.92

Kara v United Kingdom, unreported (ECtHR) . . . 1.107

Katsikas v Konstantinidis (C-132, 138 and 139/91) [1992] ECR I-6577; [1993] 1 CMLR 845; [1993] IRLR 179 (ECJ) . . . 9.63

Keane v Investigo (EAT, 11 December 2009) . . . 4.24, 4.52, 4.208

Keeley v Fosroc International Ltd [2006] EWCA Civ 1277; [2006] IRLR 961; (2006) LSG 33; (2006) 150 SJLB 1328 . . . 3.85, 3.88

Keen v Dymo Ltd [1977] IRLR 118 . . . 17.178

Keir and Williams v Hereford and Worcester County Council [1985] IRLR 505; (1985) 82 LSG 2823; (1985) Times 17 June . . . 16.32

Kelly & Chui v GE Healthcare Ltd [2009] EWHC 457 (Pat); (2009) 32(5) IPD 32036 . . . 10.87

Kelly v National Society of Operative Printers' Assistants (1915) 84 LJKB 2236; 59 Sol Jo 716; 113 LT 1055; 31 TLR 632 (CA) . . . 22.29

Kendrick v Aerduct Productions [1974] IRLR 322 . . . 17.14

Kenneth MacRae & Co Ltd v Dawson [1984] IRLR 5 (EAT) . . . 18.36

Kenny v Hampshire Constabulary [1999] ICR 27; [1999] IRLR 76; [1999] Disc LR 118; (1998) Times 22 October . . . 4.117

Kenny v Minister for Justice (C-427/11) . . . 5.45, 5.59

Kenny v Ministry of Defence (unreported) . . . 4.170

Kenny v South Manchester College [1993] ICR 934; [1993] IRLR 265 . . . 9.9

Kent County Council v Gilham [1985] ICR 227, sub nom Gilham v Kent County Council [1985] IRLR 16 (CA) . . . 17.79

Kent Free Press v National Geographical Association [1987] IRLR 267 . . . 23.85, 23.94

Kent Management Services Ltd v Butterfield [1992] ICR 272; [1992] IRLR 394 (EAT) . . . 8.14, 8.20, 10.21

Kerr v Lister & Co Ltd [1977] IRLR 259 . . . 5.29

Kerr v Nathan's Wastesavers Ltd (unreported) . . . 11.67

Kerr v Sweater Shop (Scotland) Ltd [1996] IRLR 424 (EAT) . . . 8.4, 8.7, 8.8, 8.14

Kerrigan v Rover Group Ltd (unreported) . . . 17.109

Kerry Foods Ltd v Lynch [2005] IRLR 680 . . . 17.41

Key2Law (Surrey) LLP v De'Antiquis [2011] EWCA Civ 1567 . . . 9.49, 9.50

Khan v Home Office (EAT, 14 February 2008) . . . 17.186

Khan v Vignette Europe Ltd (EAT, 14 January 2010) . . . 1.107

Khatri v Cooperative Centrale Raiffeisen-Boerenleenbank BA [2010] IRLR 715; [2010] EWCA 397 . . . 3.100

Kidd v AXA Equity and Law Life Assurance Society plc [2000] IRLR 301 . . . 10.36

Kimberley Group Housing Ltd v Hambley [2008] ICR 1030; [2008] IRLR 682 . . . 9.22

King v Motorway Tyres and Accessories Ltd [1975] IRLR 51 . . . 12.84

King v Webb's Poultry Products (Bradford) Ltd [1975] IRLR 135 . . . 17.14

Kirklees Metropolitan Council v Radecki [2009] EWCA Civ 298; [2009] ICR 1244; [2009] IRLR 555 . . . 17.10

Kirtruna SL v Red Elite Electrodomesticos SA [2008] ECR I-7907; [2009] 1 CMLR 14; [2009] CEC 407 . . . 9.8

Kleinwort Benson Ltd v Glasgow City Council (C-346/93) [1996] QB 57; [1995] 3 WLR 866; [1995] ECR I-615; [1995] All ER (EC) 514 (ECJ); re-heard [1996] QB 678; [1996] 2 All ER 257; [1996] 2 WLR 655 (CA); revsd [1999] 1 AC 153; [1997] 4 All ER 641; [1997] 3 WLR 923; [1997] NLJR 1617; 141 Sol Jo LB 237 (HL) . . . 1.106

Kleinwort Benson Ltd v Lincoln City Council [1999] 2 AC 349; [1998] 4 All ER 513; [1998] 3 WLR 1095; [1999] LGR 1; [1998] NLJR 1674; [1998] RVR 315; 142 Sol Jo LB 279; [1999] 3 LRC 219; [1998] All ER (D) 518 (HL) . . . 8.23

Knapton v EEC Card Clothing Ltd [2006] ICR 1084; [2006] IRLR 756 (EAT) . . . 17.216

Knight v A-G [1979] ICR 194; 123 Sol Jo 32 (EAT) . . . 2.62

Knowles v Fire Brigade Union [1996] 4 All ER 653; [1997] ICR 595; [1996] IRLR 617; [1996] 34 LS Gaz R 34; 140 Sol Jo LB 206 (CA) . . . 21.9

Knowsley Hospitals NHS Trust v Brownbill [2011] EWCA Civ 903 . . . 5.41

Knox v Down District Council [1981] IRLR 452 (NICA) . . . 3.61

Knulty v Eloc Electro Optick Communicatie BV [1979] ICR 823 . . . 1.34

Kopel v Safeway Stores plc [2003] IRLR 753; [2003] All ER (D) 05 (Sep) (EAT) . . . 20.108

Kores Manufacturing Co Ltd v Kolok Manufacturing Co Ltd [1957] 3 All ER 158; [1957] 1 WLR 1012; [1957] RPC 431; 101 Sol Jo 799; [1957] CLY 1285; aff'd [1959] Ch 108; [1958] 2 All ER 65; [1968] 2 WLR 858; [1958] RPC 200; 1958 SLT 221; [1958] JBL 306; 102 Sol Jo 362 (CA) . . . 19.43

Kovats v TFO Management LLP [2009] ICR 1140; (2009) 106(18) LSG 18 . . . 2.17

Kraft Foods Ltd v Fox [1978] ICR 311; [1977] IRLR 431 (EAT) . . . 12.79, 17.229

Kristapaitis v Thistle Seafood Ltd (EAT (Scotland), 29 October 2009) . . . 17.218

Kücükdeveci v Swedex GmbH & Co KG (C-555/07) . . . 1.107, 17.4

Kulkarni v Milton Keynes Hospital NHS Foundation Trust [2009] EWCA Civ 789; [2010] ICR 101; [2009] IRLR 829; [2009] LS Law Medical 465; (2009) 109 BMLR 133; (2009) *Times* 6 August . . . 1.107, 12.26, 12.28

Kwamin v Abbey National plc [2004] IRLR 516 (EAT) . . . 20.130

Kwik-Fit (GB) Ltd v Lineham [1992] ICR 183; [1992] IRLR 156; [1992] 4 LS Gaz R 31 (EAT) . . . 15.8, 17.51

Kynixa Ltd v Hynes [2008] EWHC 1495 (QB) . . . 19.22

L Lipton Ltd v Marlborough [1979] IRLR 179 (EAT) . . . 17.71

LIFFE Administration and Management v Pinkava [2006] EWHC 595 (Pat); aff'd [2007] EWCA Civ 217; [2007] Bus LR 1369; [2007] 4 All ER 981; [2007] ICR 1489; [2007] RPC 30 (CA) . . . 10.86

Labour Party v Oakley [1987] ICR 178; [1987] IRLR 79; [1987] LS Gaz R 189 (EAT); revsd [1988] ICR 403, *sub nom* Oakley v Labour Party [1988] IRLR 34 (CA) . . . 17.19

Ladbroke Racing Ltd v Arnott [1979] IRLR 192 (EAT); on appeal [1983] IRLR 154 (Ct of Sess) . . . 12.45, 17.133

Lake v Essex County Council (1979) 77 LGR 708; [1979] ICR 577; [1979] IRLR 241 (CA) . . . 3.41

Lambeth London Borough Council v Commission for Racial Equality [1990] ICR 768; [1990] IRLR 231 . . . 4.153

Lancashire Fires Ltd v SA Lyons & Co Ltd [1999] 30 LS Gaz R 28 (CA) . . . 10.70, 19.4, 19.17

Land Securities Trillium Ltd v Thornley [2005] IRLR 765 . . . 3.99

Land and Wilson v West Yorkshire Metropolitan County Council [1981] ICR 334; [1981] IRLR 87 (CA) . . . 3.111

Landeshauptstadt Kiel v Jaeger (C-151/02) [2003] 3 CMLR 493; [2003] IRLR 804; 75 BMLR 201; [2003] All ER (D) 72 (Sep) (ECJ) . . . 7.60, 7.91

Landsorganisationen I Danmark v Ny Molle Kro (287/86) [1987] ECR 5465; [1989] ICR 330; [1989] IRLR 37 (ECJ) . . . 9.25

Lane v Shire Roofing Co Ltd [1995] IRLR 493; [1995] PIQR P 417 (CA) . . . 2.58

Langley and Carter v Burlo [2006] 2 All ER 1104; [2006] ICR 850; [2006] IRLR 460 (EAT); aff'd [2006] EWCA Civ 1778; [2007] 2 All ER 462; [1007] ICR 390; [2007] IRLR 145; (2007) 104(2) LSG 30; (2007) 151 SJLB 61 (CA) . . . 17.209

Langston v AUEW [1974] 1 All ER 980; [1974] 1 WLR 185; [1974] ICR 180; [1974] IRLR 15; 16 KIR 139; 118 Sol Jo 97 (CA) . . . 10.16, 10.17

Langston v Cranfield University [1998] IRLR 172 (EAT) . . . 20.79

Lansing Linde Ltd v Kerr [1991] 1 All ER 418; [1991] 1 WLR 251; [1991] ICR 428; [1991] IRLR 80; [1990] NLJR 1458 (CA) . . . 19.15, 19.62

Lanton Leisure Ltd v White and Gibson [1987] IRLR 119, EAT . . . 17.4

Larkfield of Chepstow Ltd v Milne [1988] ICR 1; [1987] LS Gaz R 2530 (EAT) . . . 20.103

Larkin v Cambos Enterprises (Stretford) Ltd [1978] ICR 1247 (EAT) . . . 14.2

Lassman v De Vere University Arms Hotel [2003] ICR 44; [2002] All ER (D) 83 (Oct) (EAT) . . . 17.68, 18.7

Lassman v Secretary of State for Trade and Industry [1999] ICR 416; [1999] IRLR 413 (EAT); revsd *sub nom* Secretary of State for Trade and Industry v Lassman (Pan Graphics Industries Ltd, in receivership) [2000] ICR 1109; [2000] IRLR 411 (CA) . . . 18.68

Latimer v AEC Ltd [1952] 2 QB 701; [1952] 1 All ER 1302; 50 LGR 555; 96 Sol Jo 376; [1952] 1 TLR 1349 (CA); aff'd [1953] AC 643; [1953] 2 All ER 449; 51 LGR 457; 117 JP 387; 97 Sol Jo 486 (HL) . . . 11.141

Laughton and Hawley v Bapp Industrial Supplies Ltd [1986] ICR 634; [1986] IRLR 245 (EAT) . . . 16.12, 19.4

Laurie v Fairburn, IDS Brief 109 . . . 17.126

Laurie v Holloway [1994] ICR 32 (EAT) . . . 20.81

Lavarack v Woods of Colchester Ltd [1967] 1 QB 278; [1966] 3 All ER 683; [1966] 3 WLR 706; 1 KIR 312 110 Sol Jo 770 (CA) . . . 10.22, 16.23

Law Hospital NHS Trust v Rush 2002 SC 24; 2002 SLT 7; [2001] IRLR 611; 2001 GWD 21-810 . . . 4.96

Lawal v Northern Spirit Ltd [2002] ICR 486; [2002] IRLR 228; [2002] All ER (D) 36 (Jan) (EAT); aff'd [2002] EWCA Civ 1218; [2002] ICR 1507; [2002] IRLR 714; [2002] 46 LS Gaz R 33; [2002] All ER (D) 442 (Oct); revsd [2003] UKHL 35; [2004] 1 All ER 187; [2003] ICR 856; [2003] IRLR 538; [2003] 28 LS Gaz R 30; [2003] NJLR 1005; 147 Sol Jo LB 783; [2003] All ER (D) 255 (Jun) . . . 1.22, 1.107

Lawlor v Union of Post Office Workers [1965] Ch 712; [1965] 1 All ER 353; [1965] 2 WLR 579 . . . 22.31

Lawrence v Regent Office Care Ltd [2002] ECR I-7325; [2002] 3 CMLR 27; [2003] ICR 1092;

[2002] IRLR 822; [2002] Emp LR 1248; (2002) *Times* 10 October ... 5.7

Lazarus v Firestone Tyre and Rubber Co Ltd *Times*, 2 May 1963 ... 11.109

Leach v The Office of Communications (OFCOM) [2012] EWCA Civ 959 ... 17.164

Lee Ting Sang v Chung Chi-Keung [1990] 2 AC 374; [1990] 2 WLR 1173; [1990] ICR 409; [1990] IRLR 236; (1990) 87(13) LSG 43; (1990) 134 SJ 909 ... 2.55

Lee v GEC Plessey Telecommunications [1993] IRLR 383 ... 3.71

Lee v IPC Business Press Ltd [1984] ICR 306 (EAT) ... 17.205

Lee v Lee's Air Farming Ltd [1961] AC 12 ... 2.12

Lee v Nottinghamshire County Council [1979] ICR 818; [1979] IRLR 294; 123 Sol Jo 404 (EAT); revsd 78 LGR 568; [1980] ICR 635; [1980] IRLR 284 (CA) ... 18.17

Lee v Showmen's Guild [1952] 2 QB 329; [1952] 1 All ER 1175; 96 Sol Jo 296; [1952] 1 TLR 1115 (CA) ... 22.29

Lees v Arthur Greaves Ltd [1974] 2 All ER 393; [1974] ICR 501; [1974] IRLR 93; [1975] KIR 37; [1974] ITR 91 ... 15.9

Leicester University v A [1999] ICR 701; [1999] IRLR 352 (EAT) ... 20.57

Leicestershire County Council v Unison [2005] IRLR 920 (EAT) ... 18.78

Leighton v Michael [1995] ICR 1091; [1996] IRLR 67 (EAT) ... 3.8

Leisure Employment Services Ltd v HM Revenue and Customs [2007] EWCA Civ 92; [2007] ICR 1056; [2007] IRLR 450; (2007) *Times* 7 March ... 8.17, 8.42

Leisure Leagues UK Ltd v Maconnachie [2002] IRLR 600; [2002] All ER (D) 223 (Mar) (EAT) ... 7.85

Les Ambassadeurs Club v Bainda [1982] IRLR 5 (EAT) ... 17.213

Lesney Products & Co Ltd v Nolan [1977] ICR 235; [1977] IRLR 77; 12 ITR 6 (CA) ... 18.17

Lethaby v Horsman Andrew and Knill Ltd [1975] IRLR 119 ... 12.58

Letheby & Christopher Ltd v Bond [1988] ICR 480 (EAT) ... 13.25

Lewen v Denda (2000) IRLR 67; (2000) ICR 648 ... 5.2, 6.29, 10.24

Lewis Shops Group v Wiggins [1973] ICR 335; [1973] IRLR 205 (NIRC) ... 12.11, 17.139

Lewis v Motorworld Garages Ltd [1986] ICR 157; [1985] IRLR 465 (CA) ... 17.38, 17.44

Lewisham and Guys Mental Health NHS Trust v Andrews [1999] ICR 774; [1999] IRLR 407; [1999] Disc LR 143; (1999) *Times* 21 April ... 4.215

Lewisham and Guys Mental Health NHS Trust v Andrews [2000] 3 All ER 769; [2000] ICR 707; [2000] IRLR 320; (2000) 97(15) LSG 40; (2000) 144 SJLB 159; (2000) *Times* 28 March; (2000) *Independent* 29 March ... 5.65, 20.117

Leyland Vehicles Ltd v Reston [1981] ICR 403; [1981] IRLR 19 (EAT) ... 3.76, 15.23

Lightfoot v D & J Sporting Ltd [1996] IRLR 64 (EAT) ... 3.13

Lignacite Products Ltd v Krollman [1979] IRLR 22 (EAT) ... 18.62

Lincolnshire County Council v Hopper [2002] All ER (D) 401 (May) (EAT) ... 2.63

Lindsay v Fife Forge [1976] IRLR 47 ... 12.43

Linfood Cash and Carry Ltd v Thomson [1989] ICR 518; [1989] IRLR 235 (EAT) ... 12.6, 12.22

Lion Laboratories Ltd v Evans [1985] QB 526; [1984] 2 All ER 417; [1984] 3 WLR 539; 128 Sol Jo 533 (CA) ... 19.19

Lipkin Gorman v Karpnale Ltd [1992] 4 All ER 331; [1987] 1 WLR 987; [1986] FLR 271; [1987] BCLC 159; 131 Sol Jo 940; [1987] LS Gaz R 2272; [1986] NLJ Rep 659; on appeal [1992] 4 All ER 409; [1989] 1 WLR 1340; [1989] FLR 137; [1989] BCLC 756n; 134 Sol Jo 234; [1990] 4 LS Gaz R 40; [1989] NLJR 76 (CA); varied [1991] 2 AC 548; [1992] 4 All ER 512; [1991] 3 WLR 10; [1991] NLJR 815; 135 Sol Jo LB 36 (HL) ... 8.23

Lipscombe v Forestry Commission [2007] EWCA Civ 428 ... 20.121

Lister v Hesley Hall Ltd [2001] IRLR 390; [2000] All ER (D) 2233 (CA) ... 10.105

Lister v Romford Ice and Cold Storage Co Ltd [1957] AC 555; [1957] 1 All ER 125; [1957] 2 WLR 158; [1956] 2 Lloyd's Rep 505; 121 JP 98; 101 Sol Jo 106 (HL) ... 10.65

Litster v Forth Dry Dock and Engineering Co Ltd [1990] 1 AC 546; [1989] 1 All ER 1134; [1989] 2 WLR 634; [1989] ICR 341; [1989] IRLR 161; 133 Sol Jo 455; [1989] NLJR 400; 1989 SC (HL) 96 ... 9.3, 9.34, 9.57

Litster v M Thom & Sons Ltd [1975] IRLR 47 ... 17.117

Littlewoods Organisation Ltd v Egenti [1976] ICR 516; [1976] IRLR 334 (EAT) ... 17.86

Littlewoods Organisation Ltd v Harris [1978] 1 All ER 1026; [1977] 1 WLR 1472; 121 Sol Jo 727 (CA) ... 19.38

Liversidge v London Residuary Body (1989) 87 LGR 399; [1989] ICR 228; [1989] 5 LS Gaz R 41 (EAT) ... 13.40

Livingstone v Hepworth Refractories Ltd [1992] 3 CMLR 601; [1992] ICR 287; [1992] IRLR 63; [1992] 5 LS Gaz R 31 (EAT) ... 20.37

Lloyd v Grace, Smith & Co [1911] 2 KB 489; 80 LJKB 959; 104 LT 789; 27 TLR 409 (CA); revsd [1912] AC 716; 81 LJKB 1140; [1911-13] All ER Rep 51; 56 Sol Jo 723; 107 LT 531; 28 TLR 547 (HL) ... 10.107

Lloyd v Taylor Woodrow plc [1999] IRLR 782 (EAT) ... 18.56

Lloyds Bank Ltd v Secretary of State for Employment [1979] 2 All ER 573; [1979] 1 WLR 498; [1979] ICR 258; [1979] IRLR 41; 123 Sol Jo 47 (EAT) ... 13.25

Locabail Ltd v Bayfield Properties Ltd (1999)
Times 31 March; (1999) *Independent* 19 April
... 20.92

Lock International plc v Beswick [1989] 3 All ER
373; [1989] 1 WLR 1268; [1989] IRLR 481; 133
Sol Jo 1297; [1989] NLJR 644 ... 19.16, 19.65

Lock v Cardiff Rly Co [1998] IRLR 358; 599 IRLB
6 (EAT) ... 1.16, 12.11, 17.75

Lock v Connell Estate Agents [1994] ICR 983;
[1994] IRLR 444 (EAT) ... 17.199

Lockwood v Crawley Warren Group Ltd [2001]
Emp LR 322 ... 4.173

Lockwood v Department of Work and Pensions
[2013] EWCA Civ 1195 ... 4.72

Logabax Ltd v Titherley [1977] ICR 369; [1977]
IRLR 97; 12 ITR 158 (EAT) ... 17.21

Logan Salton v Durham County Council [1989]
IRLR 99 (EAT) ... 17.70

Logan v Celyn House Ltd UKEAT/0069/12/JOJ
... 17.38

Logan v Customs and Excise Comrs [2002] All
ER (D) 360 (May) (EAT); aff'd [2003] EWCA
Civ 1968; [2004] ICR 1; [2004] IRLR 63; [2003]
37 LS Gaz R 31; [2003] All ER (D) 388 (Jul)
... 20.85

London Ambulance Service NHS Trust v
Charlton [1992] ICR 773; [1992] IRLR 510
(EAT) ... 21.68

London Ambulance Service NHS Trust v Small
[2009] EWCA Civ 220; [2009] IRLR 563 ... 17.79

London Borough of Hackney v Sivanandan
[2011] IRLR 740 ... 4.200

London Borough of Tower Hamlets v Wooster
[2009] IRLR 980; [2010] BLGR 268 ... 4.66

London International College v Sen [1992] IRLR
292 ... 20.7

London Passenger Transport Board v Moscrop
[1942] AC 332; [1942] 1 All ER 97; 40 LGR 67;
106 JP 97; 111 LJ Ch 50; 166 LT 202; 58 TLR
120 (HL) ... 3.75

London and South of England Building Society
v Stone (1981) 261 Estates Gazette 463; revsd
[1983] 3 All ER 105; [1983] 1 WLR 1242; 127
Sol Jo 446; [1983] LS Gaz R 3048; 267 Estates
Gazette 69 (CA) ... 16.26

London Transport Executive v Clarke [1980] ICR
532 (EAT); revsd [1981] ICR 355; [1981] IRLR
166; Sol Jo 306 (CA) ... 3.36, 17.56, 17.59

London Underground Ltd v Edwards [1999]
ICR 494; [1998] IRLR 364; (1998) 95(26) LSG
32; (1998) 148 NLJ 905; (1998) 142 SJLB 182;
(1998) *Times* 1 June; (1998) *Independent* 5 June
... 4.173

London Underground Ltd v Ferenc-Batchelor
[2003] ICR 656; [2003] IRLR 252; [2003] All
ER (D) 252 (Mar) (EAT) ... 12.24

London Underground Ltd v Fitzgerald [1997]
ICR 271 (EAT) ... 15.25

London Underground Ltd v National Union of
Rail, Maritime and Transport Workers [1996]
ICR 170 (CA) ... 23.52

London University Ltd v National Union of
Railwaymen (unreported) ... 23.58

Lonmar Global Risks Ltd v West [2011] IRLR 138
(QBD) ... 19.56

Lord Advocate v De Rosa [1974] 2 All ER 849;
[1974] 1 WLR 946; [1974] ICR 480; [1974]
IRLR 215; 118 Sol Jo 479 (HL) ... 13.12

Lord Advocate v Scotsman Publications Ltd
1988 SLT 490 (Ct of Sess); aff'd *sub nom* Lord
Advocate v Scotsman Publications Ltd [1990]
1 AC 812; [1989] 2 All ER 852; [1989] 3 WLR
358; 1989 SC (HL) 122; 1989 SLT 705; [1989]
NLJR 971 ... 10.25

Lotus Cars Ltd v Sutcliffe [1982] IRLR 381 (CA)
... 14.3

Louies v Coventry Hood and Seating Co Ltd
[1990] ICR 54; [1990] IRLR 324 (EAT) ...
12.22

Lovie Ltd v Anderson [1999] IRLR 164 (EAT)
... 12.4

Lowndes v Specialist Heavy Engineering Ltd
[1977] ICR 1; [1976] IRLR 246; 8 BLR 76
(EAT) ... 10.65, 17.86

Luce v London Borough of Bexley (1990) 88 LGR
909; [1990] ICR 591; [1990] IRLR 422; [1990]
27 LS Gaz R 41 (EAT) ... 21.72

Luke v Stoke on Trent CC [2007] IRLR 305
(EAT); aff'd [2007] EWCA Civ 761; [2007]
IRLR 777; [2007] ICR 1678 ... 3.42, 3.104

Lumley v Gye (1853) 2 E & B 216; 22 LJQB 463;
17 Jur 827; 1 WR 432; [1843–60] All ER Rep
208 ... 23.20

Lunt v Merseyside TEC Ltd [1999] ICR 17; [1999]
IRLR 458 (EAT) ... 20.37, 20.38

Lyddon v Englefield Brickworks Ltd [2007] All
ER (D) 198 ... 7.84

Lynn v Rokeby School Board of Governor [2001]
Pens LR 273 ... 5.20

Lynock v Cereal Packaging Ltd [1988] ICR 670;
[1988] IRLR 510 (EAT) ... 17.107

Lyon v St James Press Ltd [1976] ICR 413; [1976]
IRLR 215 (EAT) ... 21.65

Lyons v Mitie [2010] ICR 628; [2010] IRLR 288
... 7.83

Lyritzis v Inmarsat (unreported) ... 2.127,
2.142

M & P Steelcraft Ltd v Ellis [2008] ICR 578;
[2008] IRLR 355 ... 3.7

M and S Drapers v Reynolds [1956] 3 All ER 814;
[1957] 1 WLR 9; 101 Sol Jo 44 (CA) ... 19.34

M and W Grazebrook Ltd v Wallens [1973] 2 All
ER 868; [1973] ICR 256; [1973] IRLR 139; 8
ITR 258 (NIRC) ... 20.43

M Young Legal Associates Ltd v Zahid Solicitors
[2006] EWCA Civ 613; [2006] 1 WLR 2562;
(2006) 103(22) LSG 26; [2006] NPC 57 ... 2.17

MBS Ltd v Calo [1983] ICR 459; [1983] IRLR 189
(EAT) ... 17.210

MG Rover Group Ltd v Kaur [2005] IRLR 40
(CA) ... 3.63

MSF v Refuge Assurance plc [2002] ICR 1365;
[2002] IRLR 324; [2002] All ER (D) 209 (Feb)
(EAT) . . . 18.71
Mabirizi v National Hospital for Nervous
Diseases [1990] ICR 281; [1990] IRLR 133
(EAT) . . . 17.240
McAdie v Royal Bank of Scotland [2007] EWCA
Civ 806; [2007] IRLR 895; (2007) 104(32) LSG
27; (2007) 157 NLJ 1355; (2007) 151 SJLB 1060
. . . 17.101
McAlwane v Boughton Estates [1973] 2 All ER
299; [1973] ICR 470 (NIRC) . . . 15.9, 18.10
McAndrew v Prestwick Circuits Ltd [1988] IRLR
514 (EAT); on appeal *sub nom* Prestwick
Circuits Ltd v McAndrew [1990] IRLR 191;
1990 SLT 654 (Ct of Sess) . . . 17.224
McArdle v Andmac Roofing Co [1967] 1 All ER
583; [1967] 1 WLR 356; 111 Sol Jo 37 (CA)
. . . 2.60
Macari v Celtic Football and Athletic Co Ltd
[1999] IRLR 787;2000 SLT 80; 2000 SCLR 209
. . . 10.62
Macarthys Ltd v Smith (129/79) [1978] 2 All
ER 746; [1978] 1 WLR 849; [1978] ICR 500;
[1978] IRLR 10; 122 Sol Jo 456 (EAT); on
appeal [1979] 3 All ER 325; [1979] 1 WLR
1189; [1979] 3 CMLR 44; [1979] ICR 785;
[1979] IRLR 316; 123 Sol Jo 603 (CA); refd
[1981] QB 180; [1981] 1 All ER 111; [1980] 3
[1980] ECR 1275; [1980] 2 CMLR 205; [1980]
ICR 929; [1980] 2 CMLR 217; [1980] ICR 672;
[1980] IRL 672; [1980] IRLR 210; 124 Sol Jo
808 (ECJ); apld [1981] QB 180; [1981] 1 All ER
111; [1980] 3 WLR [1981] QB 180; [1980] 3
WLR 929; [1981] 1 All ER 111; [1980] 2 CMLR
217; [1980] ICR 672; [1980] IRLR 210; (1980)
124 SJ 808 . . . 1.101, 5.11
McCabe v Cornwall County Council [2002]
EWCA Civ 1887; [2003] ICR 501; [2003] IRLR
87; [2003] 09 LS Gaz R 27; [2002] All ER (D)
294 . . . 16.25
McCaffrey v EE Jeavons & Co Ltd (1967) 2 ITR
636 (DC) . . . 18.6
McCall v Post Office IRLR LIB . . . 4.103
MacCartney v Oversley House Management
[2006] ICR 510; [2006] IRLR 514 . . . 7.72,
8.43
McClelland v Northern Ireland General Health
Services Board [1957] NI 100; [1957] 2 All ER
129; [1957] 1 WLR 594; LGR 281; Sol Jo 355
(HL) . . . 2.76, 16.6
McClintock v Department of Constitutional
Affairs [2008] IRLR 29; (2007) *Times*
5 December . . . 4.159
McClory v Post Office [1993] 1 All ER 457; [1992]
ICR 758; [1993] IRLR 159 . . . 3.51, 10.17,
12.69
McCormick v Horsepower Ltd [1980] ICR 278;
[1980] IRLR 182 (EAT); aff'd [1981] 2 All ER
746; [1981] 1 WLR 993; [1981] ICR 535; [1981]
IRLR 217; 125 Sol Jo 375 (CA) . . . 21.104

McCree v Tower Hamlets London Borough
Council (1992) 90 LGR 137; [1992] ICR 99;
[1992] IRLR 56 (EAT) . . . 8.5
MacCulloch v ICI plc [2008] ICR 1334; (2008)
IRLR 846 . . . 4.73
Macdonald v Advocate General for Scotland
[2003] ECR 937 . . . 4.57
MacDonald v Free Presbyterian Church of
Scotland [2010] CSOH 55; 2010 GWD
16-303 . . . 2.67
Macer v Abafast Ltd [1990] ICR 234; [1990] IRLR
137 (EAT) . . . 13.41
MacFarlane v Glasgow City Council [2001] IRLR
7 . . . 2.40, 2.44
McGhee v Transport and General Workers' Union
[1985] ICR 503; [1985] IRLR 198 (EAT) . . . 21.17
McGivney v Portman Mansions Management Ltd
. . . 17.103
McGowan v Scottish Water [2005] IRLR 167
(EAT) . . . 1.107
McGregor v Gibbings Amusements Ltd [1975]
ITR 64 . . . 20.101
Machine Tool Industry Research Association
v Simpson [1988] ICR 558; [1988] IRLR
212 . . . 20.10
MacKay Decorators (Perth) Ltd v Millar, EAT
782/98 . . . 12.85
McKindley v William Hill (Scotland) Ltd [1985]
IRLR 492 (EAT) . . . 18.25
McLaren v Home Office [1990] COD 257
(CA) . . . 16.35
MacLea v Essex Line Ltd (1933) Ll L Rep
254 . . . 3.67
McLean v Rainbow Homeloans Ltd [2007] IRLR
14 . . . 7.61
McLoughlin v Jones [2001] EWCA Civ 1743;
[2002] QB 1312; [2002] 2 WLR 1279; [2002]
PLQR P20; [2002] PNLR 21 . . . 20.133
McMaster v Manchester Airport plc [1998] IRLR
112; 593 IRLB 17 (EAT) . . . 17.5, 20.31
McMeecham v Secretary of State for Employment
[1995] ICR 444; [1995] IRLR 461 (EAT); aff'd
[1997] ICR 549; [1997] IRLR 353 (CA) . . .
2.154, 2.155
McMenemy v Capita Services [2006] IRLR 761;
(2006) 150 SJLB 665 (EAT) (SC); aff'd 2007
SC 492; 2007 SLT 428; [2007] IRLR 400; 2007
GWD 13-267 (IH, Ex Div) . . . 2.90
MacNeilgae v Arthur Roye Ltd [1976] IRLR 88
. . . 17.211
McPhail v Gibson [1977] ICR 42; [1976] IRLR
254 (EAT) . . . 17.229
McVitae v UNISON [1996] IRLR 33 . . . 22.28
McWilliam v Glasgow City Council [2011] IRLR
568 . . . 20.38
McWilliams v Sir William Arrol & Co Ltd 1961
SC 134; 1961 SLT 265 (Ct of Sess); aff'd *sub
nom* Cummings (or McWilliams) v Sir William
Arrol & Co Ltd [1962] 1 All ER 623; [1962]
1 WLR 295; 106 Sol Jo 218; 1962 SC 70; 1962
SLT 121 (HL) . . . 11.131, 11.137

Mailway (Southern) Ltd v Willsher [1978] ICR 511; [1978] IRLR 322; (1978) 122 SJ 79; (1977) *Times* 9 December . . . 7.3

Mainstream Properties Ltd v Young [2005] EWCA Civ 861; [2005] IRLR 964; (2005) 102(30) LSG 31 . . . 23.22

Mainwaring v Corus UK Ltd, EAT/53/07 . . . 17.111

Majrowski v St Thomas's NHS Trust [2006] UKHL 34; [2007] 1 AC 224; [2006] 3 WLR 125; [2006] 4 All ER 395; [2006] ICR 1199; [2006] IRLR 695; (2006) 91 BMLR 85; (2006) 156 NLJ 1173; (2006) 150 SJLB 986; (2006) *Times* 13 July; (2006) *Independent* 14 July . . . 10.111

Malcolm v London Borough of Lewisham [2008] UKHL 43; [2008] 1 AC 1399; [2008] 3 WLR 194; [2008] 4 All ER 525; [2008] IRLR 700; [2008] HLR 41; [2008] BLGR 549; (2008) 11 CCL Rep 573; (2008) 102 BMLR 170; [2008] 2 P & CR 18; [2008] L & TR 29; [2008] 26 EG 117 (CS); (2008) 105(26) LSG 23; (2008) 152(26) SJLB 29; [2008] NPC 76; (2008) *Times* 26 June . . . 4.3, 4.100

Malik v BCCI SA [1995] 3 All ER 545; [1996] ICR 406; [1995] IRLR 375; [1995] NLJR 593; CA; revsd [1998] AC 20; [1997] 3 All ER 1; [1997] 3 WLR 95; [1997] ICR 606; [1997] IRLR 462; [1997] 94 LS Gaz R 33; [1997] NLJR 917 (HL) . . . 3.47, 10.11, 16.25, 17.34

Mallone v BPB Industries Ltd [2001] All ER (D) 28 (Mar); aff'd [2002] EWCA Civ 126; [2002] ICR 1045; [2002] All ER (D) 242 (Feb) . . . 3.2, 10.21

Malone v British Airways plc [2011] IRLR 32; [2010] EWCA Civ 1225; [2011] ICR 125 . . . 3.63

Managers (Holborn) Ltd v Hohne [1977] IRLR 230; 12 ITR 379 (EAT) . . . 18.15

Mandla v Dowell Lee [1983] 2 AC 548; [1983] 2 WLR 620; [1983] 1 All ER 1062; [1983] ICR 385; [1983] IRLR 209; (1983) 127 SJ 242 . . . 4.140

Mangold v Helm [2006] All ER (EC) 383; [2005] ECR I-9981; [2006] 1 CMLR 43; [2006] CEC 372; [2006] IRLR 143 . . . 1.37

Manifold Industries Ltd v Sims [1991] ICR 504; [1991] IRLR 242 (EAT) . . . 13.36, 21.102

Manor House Healthcare v Hayes, EAT 1196/99 . . . 10.22

Marder v ITT Distributors Ltd [1976] IRLR 105 . . . 17.97

Maris v Rotherham Corpn [1974] 2 All ER 776; [1974] ICR 435; [1974] IRLR 147; 16 KIR 466; 9 ITR 288 (NIRC) . . . 17.232

Market Investigations Ltd v Minister of Social Security [1969] 2 QB 173; [1968] 3 All ER 732; [1969] 2 WLR 1; 112 Sol Jo 905 (EAT) . . . 2.49, 2.54

Marks & Spencer v Williams-Ryan [2005] ICR 1293 . . . 20.4

Marleasing SA v La Comercial Internacional de Alimentación (C-106/89) [1990] ECR I-4135;

[1992] 1 CMLR 305; [1993] BCC 421; 135 Sol Jo 15 (ECJ) . . . 1.74, 1.106

Marley Homecare v Dutton [1981] IRLR 380 (EAT) . . . 12.5

Marley Tile Co Ltd v Johnson [1982] IRLR 75 (CA) . . . 19.32

Marley Tile Co Ltd v Shaw [1978] ICR 828; [1978] IRLR 238; 13 ITR 257 (EAT); revsd [1980] ICR 72; [1980] IRLR 25; 123 Sol Jo 803 (CA) . . . 21.53, 21.55

Marley v Forward Trust Group Ltd [1986] ICR 115; [1986] IRLR 43 (EAT); revsd [1986] ICR 891; [1986] IRLR 369 (CA) . . . 3.66

Marriott v Oxford and District Co-operative Society (No 2) [1969] 1 All ER 471; [1969] 1 WLR 254; 6 KIR 479; 113 Sol Jo 34; revsd [1970] 1 QB 186; [1969] 3 All ER 1126 . . . 3.100, 18.6

Marsden v Fairey Stainless Ltd [1979] IRLR 103 (EAT) . . . 21.101

Marsh v Judge International, HSIB 15 . . . 17.138

Marshall (Cambridge) Ltd v Hamblin [1994] ICR 362; [1994] IRLR 260 (EAT) . . . 15.14

Marshall v Alexander Sloan & Co Ltd [1981] IRLR 264 . . . 3.46

Marshall v English Electric Co Ltd [1945] 1 All ER 653; 43 LGR 275; 109 JP 145; 89 Sol Jo 315; 173 LT 134; 61 TLR 379 (CA) . . . 12.63

Marshall v Gotham Co Ltd [1954] AC 360; [1954] 1 All ER 937; [1954] 2 WLR 812; 98 Sol Jo 268 (HL) . . . 11.32, 11.135

Marshall v Harland and Wolff Ltd [1972] 2 All ER 715; [1972] 1 WLR 899; [1972] ICR 101; [1972] IRLR 90; 7 ITR 150; 115 Sol Jo 484 (NIRC) . . . 17.61, 17.100, 18.9

Marshall v Industrial Systems and Control Ltd [1992] IRLR 294 (EAT) . . . 16.12, 19.6

Marshall v NM Financial Management Ltd [1995] 4 All ER 785; [1995] 1 WLR 1461; [1995] ICR 1042; [1996] IRLR 20; on appeal [1997] 1 WLR 1527; [1997] ICR 1065; [1997] IRLR 449 (CA) . . . 19.49

Marshall v Southampton and South West Hampshire Area Health Authority [1983] 2 AC 751; [1982] 2 WLR 918; [1981] 2 CMLR 542; [1982] ICR 420 (HL); refd 12/81 [1983] 2 AC 751; [1982] 2 All ER 402; [1982] 2 WLR 918; [1982] ECR 359; [1982] 1 CMLR 696; [1982] ICR 420; [1982] IRLR 111 (ECJ); apld [1983] 2 AC 751; [1982] 2 All ER 402; [1982] 2 WLR 918; [1982] 2 CMLR 174; [1982] ICR 420; [1982] IRLR 257; 126 Sol Jo 309 (HL) . . . 1.73

Martin v Glynwed Distribution Ltd [1983] ICR 511, *sub nom* Martin v MBS Fastenings (Glynwed) Distribution Ltd [1983] IRLR 198 (CA) . . . 17.9, 17.55

Martin v Scottish Transport and General Workers' Union [1952] 1 All ER 691; 96 Sol Jo 212; [1952] 1 TLR 677; 1952 SLT 224 (HL) . . . 22.22

Martin v Solus Schall [1979] IRLR 1
(EAT) . . . 3.34

Martin v South Bank University (C-4/01) [2004]
1 CMLR 472; [2004] IRLR 74; [2003] All ER
(D) 85 (Nov) (ECJ) . . . 9.42

Martin v Southern Health and Social Care Trust
[2010] IRLR 1048; [2010] NICA 31 . . . 7.72

Martin v Yeoman Aggregates Ltd [1983] ICR 314;
[1983] IRLR 49 (EAT) . . . 17.18

Martins v Marks & Spencer plc [1998] ICR 1005,
[1998] IRLR 326, (1998) *Times*, 15 January . . .
4.198, 20.65

Martland v Cooperative Insurance Ltd (EAT, 10
April 2008) . . . 17.154

Masiak v City Restaurants (UK) Ltd [1999] IRLR
780 (EAT) . . . 11.66

Mason v Provident Clothing and Supply Co Ltd
[1913] AC 724; 82 LJKB 1153; [1911-13] All
ER Rep 400; 57 Sol Jo 739; 109 LT 449; 29 TLR
727 (HL) . . . 19.44

Massey v Crown Life Insurance Co [1978] 2
All ER 576; [1978] 1 WLR 676; [1978] ICR
590; [1978] IRLR 31; 13 ITR 5; 121 Sol Jo 791
(CA) . . . 2.52

Massey v UNIFI [2007] EWCA Civ 800; [2007]
IRLR 902; (2007) 151 SJLB 1059; [2008] ICR
62 . . . 21.15

Mathewson v R B Wilson Dental Laboratory Ltd
[1988] IRLR 512 (EAT) . . . 17.142

Mathieson v WJ Noble [1972] IRLR 76 . . . 17.147

Matthews v Kent & Medway Towns Fire
Authority [2004] ICR 257; [2003] IRLR 732;
[2003] All ER (D) 90 (Aug) (EAT) . . . 2.86

Matuszowicz v Kingston-upon-Hull City Council
[2009] EWCA Civ 22; [2009] 3 All ER 685;
[2009] ICR 1170; [2009] IRLR 288 . . . 4.118

Maurice Graham Ltd v Brunswick (1974) 16 KIR
158; 118 Sol Jo 294 . . . 2.56

Mawson v Leadgate Engineering Ltd [1972] IRLR
105 . . . 20.82

Maxwell v Walter Howard Designs Ltd [1975]
IRLR 77 . . . 17.61

May Gurney Ltd v Adshead, EAT/0150/06 . . .
14.8

Mayr v Backerei und Konditorei Gerhard Flocker
OHG [2008] All ER (EC) 613; [2008] ECR
I-1017; [2008] 2 CMLR 27; [2008] CEC 549;
[2008] IRLR 387; [2008] 1 FLR 1242; [2008]
3 FCR 44; [2008] Fam Law 512; (2008) *Times*
12 March . . . 4.128, 6.4

Mba v Mayor & Burgesses of the London
Borough of Merton [2013] EWCA Civ
1562 . . . 4.156

Meade v Haringey London Borough Council
[1979] 2 All ER 1016; [1979] 1 WLR 637;
77 LGR 577; [1979] ICR 494; 123 Sol Jo 216
(CA) . . . 23.45

Meadows v Faithful Overalls Ltd [1977] IRLR
330 . . . 7.3

Mears v Safecar Security Ltd [1983] QB 54; [1982]
2 All ER 865; [1982] 3 WLR 366; [1982] ICR

626; [1982] IRLR 183; 126 Sol Jo 496; [1982] LS
Gaz R 921 (CA) . . . 3.38

Measham v AEEU [1994] IRLR 218 . . . 10.2

Meikle v McPhail [1983] IRLR 351 (EAT) . . .
9.57, 18.41

Meikle v Nottinghamshire County Council
[2005] ICR 1 . . . 17.38

Meister v Speech Design Carrier Systems GmbH
(C-415/10) (ECJ) . . . 4.46

Melhuish v Redbridge Citizens Advice Bureau
[2005] IRLR 419 (EAT) . . . 3.7

Melia v Magna Kansei Ltd [2006] ICR 410; [2005]
EWCA Civ 1547 (CA) . . . 17.213

Melon v Hector Powe Ltd [1980] IRLR 80 (Ct of
Sess); aff'd [1981] 1 All ER 313; [1981] ICR 43;
[1980] IRLR 477; 124 Sol Jo 827 (HL) . . .
13.40

Mennell v Newell & Wright (Transport
Contractors) Ltd [1996] ICR 607; [1996]
IRLR 384 (EAT); revsd [1997] ICR 1039;
[1997] IRLR 519; [1997] 33 LS Gaz R 26
(CA) . . . 17.169, 17.170

Mensah v East Hertfordshire NHS Trust [1998]
IRLR 531; [1998] All ER (D) 260 (CA) . . . 20.50

Mental Health Care (UK) Ltd v Biluan
UKEAT/0248/12/SM . . . 18.52

Menzies v Smith and McLaurin Ltd [1980] IRLR
180 (EAT) . . . 21.69

Mercury Communications Ltd v Scott-Garner
[1984] Ch 37; [1984] 1 All ER 179; [1983] 3
WLR 914; [1984] ICR 74; [1983] IRLR 485;
revsd [1984] Ch 37; [1984] 1 All ER 179;
[1983] 3 WLR 914; [1984] ICR 74; [1983] IRLR
494; 127 Sol Jo 764 (CA) . . . 23.30

Meridian Ltd v Gomersall [1977] ICR 597; [1977]
IRLR 425; 12 ITR 323 (EAT) . . . 12.44

Merino Gomez v Continental Industrias del
Caucho (C-342/01) [2004] 2 CMLR 38; [2004]
All ER (D) 350 (Mar) (ECJ) . . . 6.29

Mersey Docks and Harbour Board v Coggins &
Griffiths (Liverpool) Ltd [1947] AC 1; [1946]
2 All ER 345; 115 LJKB 465; 90 Sol Jo 466; 175
LT 270; 62 TLR 533 (HL) . . . 2.145

Merseyside and North Wales Electricity Board v
Taylor [1975] ICR 185; [1975] IRLR 60; 10 ITR
52; 119 Sol Jo 272 . . . 17.98

Messenger Newspapers Group Ltd v National
Graphical Association [1984] IRLR 397; aff'd
[1984] 1 All ER 293; [1984] ICR 345; 134 NLJ
257 (CA) . . . 23.27

Methven v Cow Industrial Polymers Ltd [1980]
ICR 463; [1980] IRLR 289; (1980) 124 SJ
374 . . . 5.49

Metrobus Ltd v UNITE [2009] EWCA Civ 829;
[2010] ICR 173; [2009] IRLR 851 . . . 1.107,
23.69

Metropolitan Police Comr v Harley . . . 20.33

Metropolitan Police Comr v Lowrey-Nesbitt
[1999] ICR 401 (EAT) . . . 2.73

Metropolitan Resources Ltd v Churchill Dulwich
Ltd [2009] ICR 1380; [2009] IRLR 700 . . . 9.14

Mezey v South West London & St George's Mental NHS Trust (No 1) [2007] EWCA Civ 106 ... 10.17, 12.68

Michael Peters Ltd v Farnfield [1995] IRLR 190 (EAT) ... 9.11

Micklefield v SAC Technology [1991] 1 All ER 275; [1990] 1 WLR 1002; [1990] IRLR 218; [1990] 28 LS Gaz R 43 ... 16.24

Mid-Staffordshire General Hospitals NHS Trust v Cambridge [2003] IRLR 566 ... 4.106

Middlebrook Mushrooms Ltd v Transport and General Workers' Union [1993] ICR 612; [1993] IRLR 232 (CA) ... 23.113

Middlesbrough Borough Council v Surtees [2008] EWCA Civ 885; [2009] ICR 133; [2008] IRLR 776 ... 5.49

Middlesbrough Borough Council v TGWU [2002] IRLR 332; [2001] All ER (D) 79 (May) (EAT) ... 18.81

Midland Plastics Ltd v Till [1983] ICR 118; [1983] IRLR 9; 126 Sol Jo 707 (EAT) ... 21.108

Mikkelson v Danmols Inventar A/S (105/84) [1985] ECR 2639; [1986] 1 CMLR 316 (ECJ) ... 9.5

Miles v Wakefield Metropolitan District Council 2 LGR 395; [1984] ICR 332; on appeal [1985] 1 All ER 905; [1985] 1 WLR 822; 83 LGR 335; [1985] ICR 363; [1985] IRLR 108; 129 Sol Jo 299; [1985] LS Gaz R 116 (CA); revsd [1987] AC 539; [1987] 1 All ER 1089; [1987] 2 WLR 795; 85 LGR 649; [1987] ICR 368; [1987] IRLR 193; 131 Sol Jo 408; [1987] LS Gaz R 1239; [1987] NLJ Rep 266 (HL) ... 2.64, 10.100

Millar v Inland Revenue Commissioners 2006 SC 155; 2005 SLT 1074; [2006] IRLR 112; 2005 GWD 32-615 ... 4.82

Millbrook Furnishing Industries Ltd v McIntosh [1981] IRLR 309 (EAT) ... 18.5

Miller Bros & FP Butler Ltd v Johnston [2002] ICR 744; [2002] IRLR 386; [2002] All ER (D) 220 (Mar); [2002] Emp LR 1088 (EAT) ... 1.40, 20.42

Miller v Hamworthy Engineering Ltd [1986] ICR 846; [1986] IRLR 461; [1986] LS Gaz R 1901 (CA) ... 3.102, 10.19, 16.32

Miller v Shanks & McEwan, IDS Handbook 12 ... 17.42

Mingeley v Pennock and Ivory [2004] EWCA Civ 328; [2004] ICR 727; [2004] IRLR 373; (2004) 101(11) LSG 33; (2004) Times 4 March ... 4.191

Mining Supplies (Longwall) Ltd v Baker [1988] ICR 676; [1988] IRLR 417 (EAT) ... 17.202, 18.50

Ministry of Defence v Hunt [1996] ICR 554; [1996] IRLR 139 (EAT) ... 20.98

Ministry of Justice v Prison Officers Association [2008] ICR 702 ... 1.107

Minter v Wellingborough Foundries Ltd [1981] IDS Brief 202 ... 17.138

Mirror Group Newspapers Ltd v Gunning [1986] 1 WLR 546; [1986] 1 All ER 385; [1986] ICR 145; [1986] IRLR 27; (1986) 136 NLJ 967; (1985) 130 SJ 242 ... 4.191

Mitchells Solicitors v Funkwerk Informations Technologies York Ltd [2008] PNLR 29 ... 20.106

Mitie Managed Services Ltd v French [2002] IRLR 512; [2002] All ER (D) 150 (Sep) (EAT) ... 9.39

Moberly v Commonwealth Hall (University of London) [1977] ICR 791; [1977] IRLR 176 ... 4.177

Mock v IRC [1999] IRLR 785 (EAT) ... 20.118

Monsanto plc v Transport and General Workers' Union [1987] 1 All ER 358; [1987] 1 WLR 617; [1987] ICR 269; [1986] IRLR 406; 131 Sol Jo 690; [1987] LS Gaz R 1572; [1986] NLJ Rep 917 (CA) ... 23.67

Montgomery v Johnson Underwood Ltd [2001] EWCA Civ 318; [2001] ICR 819; [2001] IRLR 269; [2001] Emp LR 405; (2001) 98(20) LSG 40; (2001) Times 16 March; (2001) Independent 7 May ... 2.40

Moody v Telefusion Ltd [1978] IRLR 311; 12 ITR 425 (EAT) ... 17.160

Moore v C & A Modes [1981] IRLR 71 (EAT) ... 17.142

Moore v Dupont Furniture Products [1982] ICR 84; [1982] IRLR 31; 126 Sol Jo, (HL) ... 1.10

Morgan v West Glamorgan County Council [1995] IRLR 68 (EAT) ... 8.5, 8.20, 8.21

Morganite Electrical Carbon Ltd v Donne [1988] ICR 18; [1987] IRLR 363 (EAT) ... 17.211

Morgans v Alpha Plus Security Ltd [2005] ICR 525 (EAT) ... 17.208

Morley v Heritage plc [1993] IRLR 400 (CA) ... 3.52

Morley's of Brixton Ltd v Minott [1982] ICR 444; [1982] IRLR 270 (EAT) ... 12.17, 17.127

Morris Angel & Son Ltd v Hollande [1993] 3 All ER 569; [1993] ICR 71; [1993] IRLR 400 (CA) ... 9.31, 9.36, 19.60

Morris v CW Martin & Sons Ltd [1966] 1 QB 716; [1965] 2 All ER 725; [1965] 3 WLR 276; [1965] 2 Lloyd's Rep 63; 109 Sol Jo 451 (CA) ... 10.107

Morris v London Iron and Steel Co Ltd [1986] ICR 629 (EAT); revsd [1988] QB 493; [1987] 2 All ER 496; [1987] 3 WLR 836; [1987] ICR 855; [1987] IRLR 182; 131 Sol Jo 1040; [1987] LS Gaz R 2274 (CA) ... 20.77

Morris v Scott [1976] IRLR 238 ... 4.50

Morris v Secretary of State for Employment [1985] ICR 522, [1985] IRLR 297 (EAT) ... 7.134

Morris v Walsh Western Electric UK Ltd [1997] IRLR 562 (EAT) ... 13.26, 13.31

Morrish v Henlys (Folkestone) Ltd [1973] 2 All ER 137; [1973] ICR 482; [1973] IRLR 61; 8 ITR 167 (NIRC) ... 10.59

Morrison v Amalgamated Transport and
General Workers' Union [1989] IRLR 361
(NICA) . . . 17.230

Morton Sundour Fabrics Ltd v Shaw (1966) 2 KIR
1; 2 ITR 84 (DC) . . . 15.1, 18.8

Mowlem Northern Ltd v Watson [1990] ICR 751;
[1990] IRLR 500 (EAT) . . . 15.8

Moyes v Hylton Castle Working Men's Social
Club [1986] IRLR 482 (EAT) . . . 12.9

Moyhing v Barts & London NHS Trust [2006]
IRLR 860 . . . 4.179

Mugford v Midland Bank plc [1997] ICR 399;
[1997] IRLR 208 (EAT) . . . 18.47

Muggridge and Slade v East Anglia Plastics Ltd
[1973] IRLR 163 . . . 17.152

Mukoro v European Bank for Reconstruction and
Development [1994] ICR 897 (EAT) . . . 17.4

Mullet v Brush Electrical Machines Ltd [1977]
ICR 829 (EAT) . . . 17.205

Munro v Allied Suppliers [1977] IRLIB . . . 4.47

Murco Petroleum Ltd v Forge [1987] ICR 282;
[1987] IRLR 50 (EAT) . . . 17.33

Murphy v A Birrell & Sons Ltd [1978] IRLR 458
(EAT) . . . 13.26

Murray v East Lothian Regional Council [1977]
CLY 972 . . . 5.45

Murray v Foyle Meats Ltd [1997] NI 429 (NICA);
aff'd [2000] 1 AC 51; [1999] 3 All ER 769;
[1999] 3 WLR 356; [1999] ICR 827; [1999]
IRLR 562; [1999] 31 LS Gaz R 36; 143 Sol Jo LB
214 (HL) . . . 18.20, 18.22

Murray v Leisureplay plc [2005] EWCA Civ 963;
[2005] IRLR 946 (CA) . . . 16.27

Murray v Murray (t/a Newholme Decorators)
EAT 750/93 . . . 13.18

Murray v Powertech (Scotland) Ltd [1992] IRLR
257 . . . 4.230

NAAFI v Varley (1976) *Times* 25 October . . . 5.45

NHS Leeds v Larner [2012] EWCA
Civ 1034 . . . 7.86

NHS Manchester v Fecitt [2011] EWCA Civ
1190 . . . 10.83

NRG Victory Reinsurance Ltd v Alexander
[1992] ICR 675 (EAT) . . . 20.45

NUGSAT v Albury Bros Ltd [1978] ICR 62;
[1977] IRLR 173; 12 ITR 413 (EAT); aff'd
[1979] ICR 84; [1978] IRLR 504; 122 Sol Jo 662
(CA) . . . 23.4

NUTGW v Charles Ingram & Co Ltd [1978] 1 All
ER 1271; [1977] ICR 530; [1977] IRLR 147; 12
ITR 285 (EAT) . . . 23.4

NWL Ltd v Nelson and Laughton [1979] 2 Lloyd's
Rep 317; [1979] ICR 755; [1979] IRLR 321;
123 Sol Jo 488 (CA); aff'd [1979] 3 All ER 614
[1979] 1 WLR 1294; [1980] 1 Lloyd's Rep 1;
[1979] ICR 867; [1979] IRLR 478; 123 Sol Jo
751 (HL) . . . 23.91

Nagarajan v London Regional Transport [1995]
ICR 520; [1994] IRLR 61 (EAT); aff'd *sub nom*
[1998] IRLR 73 (CA); revsd [2000] 1 AC 501;

[1999] 4 ALL ER 65; [1999] 3 WLR 425; [1999]
ICR 877; [1999] IRLR 572; [1999] 31 LS Gaz R
36; 143 Sol Jo LB 219 (HL) . . . 4.38

Nagle v Feilden [1966] 2 QB 633; [1966] 2 WLR
1027; [1966] 1 All ER 689; (1966) 110 Sol Jo
286 (CA) . . . 10.16, 21.5, 21.7, 22.22

Narich Pty Ltd v Payroll Tax Com [1984] ICR 286
(PC) . . . 2.37

National Coal Board v Galley [1958] 1 All ER 91;
[1958] 1 WLR 16; 102 Sol Jo 31 (CA) . . . 3.62

National Coal Board v National Union of
Mineworkers [1986] ICR 736; [1986] IRLR 439
. . . 3.59, 23.101

National Grid Co plc v Virdee [1992] IRLR 555
(EAT) . . . 20.61

National and Local Government Officers'
Association v Killorn [1991] ICR 1; [1990]
IRLR 464 (EAT) . . . 21.10

National Power plc v Young [2004] EWHC 2972
(QB); [2005] 2 Lloyd's Rep 46 . . . 5.60

National Union of Mineworkers (Yorkshire Area)
v Millward [1995] ICR 482; [1995] IRLR 411
(EAT) . . . 22.24

National Union of Public Employees v General
Cleaning Contractors [1976] IRLR 362 . . .
18.88

National Union of Rail, Maritime & Transport
Workers v Serco Ltd (t/a Serco Docklands)
[2011] EWCA Civ 226; [2011] IRLR 399;
[2011] ICR 848; [2011] 3 All ER 913 . . . 1.107,
23.69

National Union of Rail, Maritime and Transport
Workers v Midland Mainline Ltd [2001] EWCA
Civ 1206; [2001] IRLR 813; [2001] 38 LS Gaz R
37; [2001] All ER (D) 352 (Jul) . . . 23.52

National Union of Teachers v Avon County
Council (1978) 76 LGR 403; [1978] ICR 626;
[1978] IRLR 55 (EAT) . . . 18.79

National Vulcan Engineering Insurance Group v
Wade [1979] QB 132; [1978] 3 WLR 214; [1978]
3 All ER 121; [1978] ICR 800; [1978] IRLR 225;
(1978) 13 ITR 212; (1978) 122 SJ 470 . . . 5.46

Nationwide Building Society v Benn,
UKEAT/0273/09/JOJ . . . 9.56

Natt v Hillingdon Area Health Authority
(unreported) . . . 12.38

Naylor v Orton & Smith Ltd [1983] ICR 665;
[1983] IRLR 233 (EAT) . . . 23.42

Neale v Hereford and Worcester County Council
[1985] IRLR 281 (EAT); revsd [1986] ICR
471; *sub nom* Hereford and Worcester County
Council v Neale [1986] IRLR 168 (CA) . . . 20.122

Neary v Dean of Westminster [1999] IRLR 288
. . . 10.57

Nelson v BBC (No 2) [1980] ICR 110; [1979]
IRLR 346; 123 Sol Jo 552 (CA) . . . 17.228

Nelson and Woollett v Post Office [1978] IRLR
548 (EAT) . . . 3.111

Nerva v United Kingdom (Application 42295/98)
[2002] IRLR 815; 13 BHRC 246; [2002] All ER
(D) 137 (Sep) (ECtHR) . . . 8.14

Nethermere (St Neots) Ltd v Gardiner [1984]
ICR 612, *sub nom* Nethermere (St Neots)
Ltd v Taverna and Gardiner [1984] IRLR 240
(CA) . . . 2.54

Network Rail Infrastructures Ltd v Gammie (EAT
(Scotland), 6 March 2009) . . . 4.26, 4.172

New ISG Ltd v Vernon [2007] EWHC 2665 (Ch);
[2008] IRLR 115; [2008] ICR 319 . . . 9.64

New Southern Railway Ltd v Quinn [2006] ICR
761 (EAT); [2006] IRLR 266 . . . 6.12, 6.16

New Victoria Hospital v Ryan [1993] ICR 201;
[1993] IRLR 202; [1993] 5 LS Gaz R 41 (EAT)
. . . 20.68

Newalls Insulation Co Ltd v Blakeman [1976]
ICR 543; [1976] IRLR 303 (EAT) . . . 12.72

Newham London Borough Council v National
and Local Government Officers' Association
[1993] ICR 189; [1993] IRLR 83 (CA) . . . 23.66

Newham London Borough v Ward [1985] IRLR
509 (CA) . . . 20.28

Newland v Simons and Willer (Hairdressers)
Ltd [1981] ICR 521; [1981] IRLR 359
(EAT) . . . 3.18

Newlands v Howard & Co Ltd [1973] IRLR
9 . . . 16.13

Newman v Alarmco [1976] IRLR 45 . . . 17.138

News Group Newspapers Ltd v Society of
Graphical and Allied Trades 1982 [1986] ICR
716; [1986] IRLR 227; 130 Sol Jo 407; [1986] LS
Gaz R 1726 (CA) . . . 23.44, 23.111

Nicoll v Nocorrode Ltd [1981] ICR 348; [1981]
IRLR 163; (1981) *Times* 10 February . . .
13.8

Nicolson Highlandwear Ltd v Nicolson [2010]
IRLR 859 . . . 20.44

Noble v David Gold & Son (Holdings) Ltd [1980]
ICR 543; [1980] IRLR 253 . . . 5.25

Nokes v Doncaster Amalgamated Collieries
[1940] AC 1014; [1940] 3 All ER 549; 109
LJKB 865 85 Sol Jo 45; 163 LT 343; 56 TLR 988
(HL) . . . 9.1

Nolan v Dental Manufacturing Co Ltd [1958]
2 All ER 449; [1958] 1 WLR 936; 102 Sol Jo
619 . . . 11.128

Noorani v Merseyside TEC Ltd [1999] IRLR 184
(CA) . . . 1.29

Norbrook Laboratories Ltd v King [1982] IRLR
456; [1982] 2 NIJB; aff'd [1984] IRLR 200;
[1983] 14 NIJB (NIRC) . . . 23.115

Nordenfelt v Maxim Nordenfelt Ltd [1895] 1 QB
151; 64 LJQB 182; 2 Mans 20; 14 R 71; 71 LT
565; 11 TLR 26 (CA) . . . 19.44, 19.45

Norris v Brown & Root Ealing Technical Services
[2002] All ER (D) 413 (Oct) (EAT) . . . 9.45

Norris v Southampton City Council [1982] ICR
177; [1982] IRLR 141 (EAT) . . . 17.59

North Cumbria Acute Hospitals NHS Trust v
Potter [2009] IRLR 900 . . . 5.9

North Riding Garages Ltd v Butterwick [1967] 2
QB 56; [1967] 1 All ER 644; [1967] 2 WLR 571;
2 ITR 229; 111 Sol Jo 72 . . . 18.18

North v Dumfries and Galloway Council [2011]
IRLR 239; [2011] CSIH 2 . . . 5.8

North v Dumfries and Galloway Council
(Scotland) [2013] UKSC 45 . . . 5.8

North v Pavleigh Ltd [1977] IRLR 461 . . . 7.2

Northamptonshire County Council v Entwhistle
[2010] IRLR 740 (EAT) . . . 20.7

Northern Ireland Hotel and Catering College v
National Association of Teachers in Further
and Higher Education [1995] IRLR 83 (NICA)
. . . 18.72

Norton Tool Co Ltd v Tewson [1973] 1 All ER
183; [1973] 1 WLR 45; [1972] ICR 501; [1972]
IRLR 86; 117 Sol Jo 33 (NIRC) . . . 17.203,
17.213

Norwest Holst Group Administration Ltd v
Harrison [1984] IRLR 419 (EAT); aff'd [1985]
ICR 668; *sub nom* Harrison v Norwest Holst
Group Administration Ltd [1985] IRLR 240
(CA) . . . 17.46

Notcutt v Universal Equipment Co (London)
Ltd [1986] 3 All ER 582; [1986] 1 WLR 641;
[1986] ICR 414; [1986] IRLR 218; 130 Sol Jo
392; [1986] LS Gaz R 1314; [1986] NLJ Rep 393
(CA) . . . 17.60

Nothman v London Borough of Barnet [1978] 1
WLR 220; [1978] ICR 336; [1977] IRLR 398
(EAT); revsd [1978] 1 All ER 1243; [1978] 1
WLR 220; 76 LGR 617; [1978] ICR 336; [1978]
IRLR 489; 13 ITR 125; 121 Sol Jo 813 (CA);
aff'd [1979] 1 All ER 142; [1979] 1 WLR 67; 77
LGR 89; [1979] ICR 111; [1979] IRLR 35; 123
Sol Jo 64 (HL) . . . 17.189

Nottingham University v Fishel [2000] ICR 1462;
[2000] IRLR 471; [2000] ELR 385; [2001] RPC
367; [2000] All ER (D) 269 . . . 10.56, 10.93,
19.5, 19.68

Nova Plastics Ltd v Froggatt [1982] IRLR 146
(EAT) . . . 17.143

O'Murphy v Hewlett Packard Ltd [2002] IRLR
4; [2001] All ER (D) 91 (Sep) (EAT) . . . 2.36,
2.157

OCS Cleaning Scotland Ltd v Rudden, IDS Brief
644 . . . 9.10

OCS Group UK Ltd v Jones (EAT, 4 August 2009)
. . . 9.22

Oakland v Wellswood (Yorkshire) Ltd [2009]
EWCA Civ 1094; [2010] BCC 263; [2010]
IRLR 82 . . . 9.35, 9.53, 13.40

O'Brien v Ministry of Justice [2010] UKSC 34
. . . 2.66

O'Brien v Prudential Assurance Co [1979] IRLR
140 (EAT) . . . 17.151

O'Conner v Kontiki Travel, IDS Brief 98 . . .
4.184

Octavius Atkinson & Sons Ltd v Morris [1988]
ICR 880 (EAT); revsd [1989] ICR 431; [1989]
IRLR 158 (CA) . . . 16.15, 18.60

O'Dea v ISC Chemical Ltd [1996] ICR 222;
[1995] IRLR 599 (CA) . . . 21.88

Odeco (UK) Inc v Peacham [1979] ICR 823 ... 1.34

Office Angels Ltd v Rainer-Thomas [1991] IRLR 214 (CA) ... 19.36, 19.44, 19.47

O'Flynn v Airlinks the Airport Coach Co Ltd [2002] All ER (D) 05 (Jul) (EAT) ... 17.138

O'Grady v M Saper Ltd [1940] 2 KB 469; [1940] 3 All ER 527; 109 LJKB 785; 84 Sol Jo 501; 163 LT 165; 56 TLR 913 (CA) ... 3.38

O'Hanlon v Commissioners for HM Revenue and Customs [2007] ICR 1359; (2007) IRLR 404 ... 4.117

O'Kelly v Trusthouse Forte plc [1984] QB 90; [1983] 3 All ER 456; [1983] 3 WLR 605; [1983] ICR 728; [1983] IRLR 369; 127 Sol Jo 632; [1983] LS Gaz R 2367 (CA) ... 2.55

O'Laoire v Jackel International Ltd [1990] ICR 197; [1990] IRLR 70 (CA) ... 16.3, 16.28

Oliver v JP Malnick & Co [1983] 3 All ER 795; [1983] ICR 708; [1983] IRLR 456; 127 Sol Jo 646 (EAT) ... 2.99

Oliver v Sperry Vickers [1975] IRLR 358 ... 17.153

Omilaju v Waltham Forest London Borough Council [2004] EWCA Civ 1493; [2005] IRLR 35 (CA) ... 17.44

O'Neill v Governors of St Thomas More School [1997] ICR 33 4.135102 Social Club and Institute v Bickerton [1977] ICR 911 12 ITR 442 (EAT) ... 4.136

Onu v Akwiku UKEAT/0283/12/RN & UKEAT/0022/12/RN ... 4.42

Onyango v Berkeley Solicitors UKEAT/0407/12 ... 10.74

Optare Group Ltd v TGWU [2007] IRLR 931; (2007) 104(30) LSG 34 (EAT) ... 18.74

Optical Express Ltd v Williams [2007] IRLR 928; [2008] ICR 1 (EAT) ... 18.26

Optikinetics Ltd v Whooley [1999] ICR 984 (EAT) ... 17.199, 17.201

O'Reilly v Hotpoint Ltd (1969) 5 ITR 68; 113 Sol Jo 979 (DC) ... 17.100

Orthet Ltd v Vince-Cain [2005] ICR 374 (EAT) ... 17.225, 17.235

Osborne v Bill Taylor of Huyton Ltd [1982] ICR 168; [1982] IRLR 17 (DC) ... 11.36

Ottoman Bank v Chakarian [1930] AC 277; 99 LJPC 97; 142 LT 465 (PC) ... 10.59

Oudahar v Esporta Group Ltd [2011] IRLR 730, EAT ... 11.66

Owen v Crown House Engineering Ltd [1973] 3 All ER 618; [1973] ICR 511; [1973] IRLR 233; 16 KIR 67; [1973] ITR 539 ... 20.7

Oy Lukkene Ab v Liskojarvi (C-172/99) [2001] All ER (EC) 544; [2001] ECR I-745; [2001] 3 CMLR 37; [2002] ICR 155; [2001] IRLR 171; [2001] Emp LR 235 (ECJ) ... 9.10

P v National Association of Schoolmasters/Union of Women Teachers [2001] EWCA Civ 652; [2001] ICR 1241; [2001] IRLR 532; [2001] ELR 607; [2003] NLJR 350; [2001] All ER (D) 107 (May); aff'd [2003] UKHL 8; [2003] 2 AC 663; [2003] 1 All ER 993; [2003] 2 WLR 545; [2003] ICR ... 23.30, 23.53

P v Nottinghamshire County Council [1992] ICR 706; [1992] IRLR 362 (CA) ... 12.18, 12.88, 17.128

P v S (C-13/94) [1996] ECR I-2143; [1996] All ER (EC) 397; [1996] 2 CMLR 247; [1996] ICR 795; [1996] IRLR 347 ... 1.77

P v T Ltd [1997] 4 All ER 200; [1997] 1 WLR 1309; [1977] ICR 887 ... 12.7

P & O Trans European Ltd v Initial Transport Services Ltd [2003] IRLR 128; [2002] All ER (D) 116 (Nov) (EAT) ... 9.10

PSM International plc v Whitehouse [1999] 30 LS Gaz R 28 (CA) ... 10.70

Page v Freight Hire (Tank Haulage) Ltd [1981] 1 All ER 394; [1981] ICR 299; [1981] IRLR 13 ... 11.34

Paggetti v Cobb [2002] IRLR 861; [2002] All ER (D) 394 (Mar) (EAT) ... 14.5, 17.200

Pakenham-Walsh v Connell Residential [2006] EWCA Civ 90 ... 7.109

Palacios de la Villa v Cortefiel el Servicios SA [2008] All ER (EC) 249; [2007] ECR I-8531; [2008] 1 CMLR 16; [2009] ICR 1111; [2007] IRLR 989; [2007] Pens LR 411; (2007) Times 23 October ... 4.63

Palfrey v Transco plc [2004] IRLR 916 (EAT) ... 15.29, 20.25

Palmanor Ltd v Cedron [1978] ICR 1008; [1978] IRLR 303; 13 ITR 450 (EAT) ... 14.4, 17.27, 17.205

Palmer v Southend-on-Sea Borough Council [1984] 1 WLR 1129; [1984] 1 All ER 945; [1984] ICR 372; [1984] IRLR 119; (1984) 81 LSG 893; (1984) 134 NLJ 148; (1984) 128 SJ 262 ... 20.4

Palmer v Vauxhall Motors Ltd [1977] ICR 24 (EAT) ... 12.55, 17.138

Panesar v Nestle & Co Ltd [1980] ICR 144; [1980] IRLR 64 ... 4.149

Parade Park Hotel v Comrs of HM Revenue and Customs [2007] STC (SCD) 430; [2007] STI 1183 ... 2.46

Paris v Stepney Borough Council [1950] 1 KB 320; [1949] 2 All ER 843; 113 JP 507; 93 Sol Jo 710; 65 TLR 723 (CA); revsd [1951] AC 367; [1951] 1 All ER 42; 49 LGR 293; 115 JP 22; [1951] 1 TLR 25; 84 Ll L Rep 525; 94 Sol Jo 837 (HL) ... 11.109, 11.116

Park Cakes Ltd v Shumba [2013] EWCA Civ 974 ... 3.80

Parker v Clifford Dunn Ltd [1979] ICR 463; [1979] IRLR 56 (EAT) ... 17.122

Parker v Orr (1966) 1 KIR 513 ... 18.4

Parker v Westland Helicopters Ltd, IDS Supp 15 ... 17.99

Parkers Bakeries Ltd v Palmer [1977] IRLR 215; ITR 111 (EAT) ... 12.16, 17.138

Parkins v Sodexho Ltd [2002] IRLR 109; [2001] All ER (D) 377 (Jun) (EAT) . . . 10.76

Parr v Whitbread & Co plc [1990] ICR 427; [1990] IRLR 39 (EAT) . . . 17.157

Parry v Holst & Co (1968) 3 ITR 317 . . . 3.82, 3.110

Parsons & Co Ltd v McLoughlin [1978] IRLR 65 (EAT) . . . 17.138

Parsons v Albert J Parsons & Sons Ltd [1979] FSR 25; [1979] ICR 271; [1979] IRLR 117; 122 Sol Jo 812 (CA) . . . 2.11

Parsons v Bristol Street Motors (EAT, 28 February 2008) . . . 17.26

Parsons v Fisons Ltd (unreported) . . . 17.113

Parsons v LCC (1893) 9 TLR 619 . . . 12.91

Patel v Oldham Metropolitan Borough Council [2010] ICR 603; [2010] IRLR 280 . . . 4.88

Patel v RCMS Ltd [1999] IRLR 161 (EAT) . . . 1.41, 20.19

Paton Calvert & Co Ltd v Westerside [1979] IRLR 108 (EAT) . . . 18.30

Paul v East Surrey District Health Authority [1995] IRLR 305 30 BMLR 41 (CA) . . . 12.46, 17.131

Pay v Lancashire Probation Service [2004] ICR 187; [2004] IRLR 129; [2003] All ER (D) 468 (Oct) (EAT) . . . 17.144

Payne v Spook Erection Ltd [1984] IRLR 219 (EAT) . . . 10.60

Peace v City of Edinburgh Council [1999] IRLR 417; 1999 SLT 712 (OH) . . . 12.13

Peach Grey & Co v Sommers [1995] 2 All ER 513; [1995] ICR 549; [1995] IRLR 363; [1995] 13 LS Gaz R 31 . . . 1.24

Peake v Automotive Products [1977] QB 780; [1977] 2 WLR 751; [1977] ICR 480; [1977] IRLR 105; 12 ITR 259; 121 Sol Jo 222 (EAT); revsd [1978] 1 All ER 106; [1977] 3 WLR 853; [1977] ICR 968; 121 Sol Jo sub nom Automotive Products Ltd v Peake [1977] IRLR 365; 12 ITR 428 (CA) . . . 3.91

Pearce v University of Aston in Birmingham [1991] 2 All ER 461 (CA) . . . 2.76

Pearson v Kent County Council [1992] ICR 20; [1992] IRLR 110 (EAT); aff'd [1993] IRLR 165 (CA) . . . 13.17

Peixoto v British Telecommunications plc (EAT, 22 January 2008) . . . 20.62

Pel Ltd v Modgill [1980] IRLR 142 (EAT) . . . 4.18, 4.142

Pename Ltd v Paterson [1989] IRLR 195 (EAT) . . . 8.8

Pendragon plc v Jackson [1998] ICR 215; [1998] IRLR 17 (EAT) . . . 3.21

Pendragon plc v Jackson (No 2) . . . 10.22

Pengilly v North Devon Farmers Ltd [1973] IRLR 41 (EAT) . . . 10.61, 17.135

Pennington v Minister of Social Security (unreported) . . . 2.58

Pepper and Hope v Daish [1980] IRLR 13 (EAT) . . . 3.48, 17.35

Pepper v Webb [1969] 2 All ER 216; [1969] 1 WLR 514; 113 Sol Jo 186 (CA) . . . 10.58, 16.10

Perceval-Price v Department of Economic Development [2000] IRLR 380 (NICA) . . . 2.66

Percy v Church of Scotland Board of National Mission [2006] IRLR 195 (HL) . . . 2.66, 2.67

Pereda v Madrid Movilidad SA [2010] 1 CMLR 3; [2009] IRLR 959; (2009) 159 NLJ 1323; (2009) Times 8 October . . . 7.86

Perez v Mercury Display Ltd [1977] IRLIB . . . 18.87

Perkin v St George's Healthcare NHS Trust [2005] IRLR 934 . . . 17.159

Petch v Customs and Excise Comrs [1993] ICR 789; 137 Sol Jo LB 120 (CA) . . . 11.104, 11.120

Peter Carnie & Son Ltd v Paton [1979] IRLR 260 (EAT) . . . 17.40

Peter Simper & Co Ltd v Cooke [1986] IRLR 19 (EAT) . . . 20.129

Peterborough Regional College v Gidney, EAT 1270/97; 1270A/97 . . . 17.46

Petrie v MacFisheries Ltd [1940] 1 KB 258; [1939] 4 All ER 281; 38 LGR 44; 104 JP 40; 109 LJKB 263; 83 Sol Jo 959; 161 LT 408; 56 TLR 119 (CA) . . . 3.32

Pfeiffer v Deutsches Rotes Kreuz [2005] IRLR 137 . . . 7.58

Philip Hodges & Co v Crush (EAT) 1061/95 . . . 17.169

Phillips v Xtera Communications Ltd [2011] IRLR 724 . . . 18.72

Phoenix Partners Group LLP v Asoyag [2010] EWHC 846 (QB); [2010] IRLR 594 . . . 19.27

Photostatic Copiers (Southern) Ltd v Okuda [1995] IRLR 11 (EAT) . . . 20.127

Pickford v ICI plc [1997] ICR 566; [1996] IRLR 622; [1997] 8 Med LR 270; 140 Sol Jo LB 202 (CA); revsd [1998] 3 All ER 462; [1998] 1 WLR 1189; [1998] ICR 673; [1998] IRLR 435; [1998] 31 LS Gaz R 36; [1998] NJLR 978; 142 Sol Jo LB 198; [1998] All ER (D) 302 (HL) . . . 11.120

Pickstone v Freemans plc [1989] AC 66; [1988] 3 WLR 265; [1988] 2 All ER 803; [1988] 3 CMLR 221; [1988] ICR 697; [1988] IRLR 357; (1988) 138 NLJ Rep 193; (1988) Times 1 July; (1988) Independent 1 July; (1988) Financial Times 5 July; (1988) Guardian 1 July . . . 5.42

Piddington v Bates [1960] 3 All ER 660; [1961] 1 WLR 162; 105 Sol Jo 110 (DC) . . . 23.109

Piggott Bros & Co Ltd v Jackson [1992] ICR 85; [1991] IRLR 309 (CA) . . . 20.123

Pinkney v Sandpiper Drilling Ltd [1989] ICR 389; [1989] IRLR 425 (EAT) . . . 2.6

Piperdy v UEM Parker Glass, IDS Supplement . . . 4.224

Pirelli General Cable Works v Murray [1979] IRLR 190 (EAT) . . . 12.22

Pirie and Hunter v Crawford (unreported) . . . 12.62

Pitts v Revertex (unreported) . . . 12.41

Polentarutti v Autokraft Ltd [1991] ICR 757;
    [1991] IRLR 457 (EAT) . . . 17.230
Polkey v AE Dayton Services Ltd [1987] UKHL
    8 . . . 12.14, 17.218
Port of London v Payne [1993] ICR 30; [1992]
    IRLR 447; [1992] 31 LS Gaz R 35 (EAT);
    aff'd [1994] ICR ICR 555; [1994] IRLR 9
    (CA) . . . 17.190
Porter v National Union of Journalists [1979]
    IRLR 404 (CA); aff'd [1980] IRLR 404
    (HL) . . . 22.30
Post Office v Moore [1981] ICR 623
    (EAT) . . . 20.13
Post Office v Mughal [1977] ICR 763; [1977]
    IRLR 178; 12 ITR 130 (EAT) . . . 2.96
Post Office v Roberts [1980] IRLR 347
    (EAT) . . . 3.53
Post Office v Union of Communication Workers
    [1990] 3 All ER 199; [1990] 1 WLR 981; [1990]
    ICR 258; [1990] IRLR 143 (CA) . . . 23.57, 23.67
Post Office v Wilson [2000] IRLR 834
    (CA) . . . 17.114
Potter v Hunt Contracts Ltd [1992] ICR 337;
    [1992] IRLR 108 (EAT) . . . 8.8, 8.9, 8.32
Powell v London Borough of Brent [1988] ICR
    176; [1987] IRLR 466 (CA) . . . 10.5, 16.16, 16.30
Power v Greater Manchester Police Authority,
    EAT/0087/10 . . . 4.155
Power v Panasonic UK Ltd [2003] IRLR 151;
    (2003) 72 BMLR 1 . . . 4.83
Prater v Cornwall County Council [2006] EWCA
    Civ 102; [2006] 2 All ER 1013; [2006] ICR 731;
    [2006] IRLR 362; [2006] BLGR 479; (2006) 156
    NLJ 372; (2006) *Independent* 28 February . . . 2.42
Premier Motors (Medway) Ltd v Total Oil Great
    Britain Ltd [1984] 1 WLR 377; [1984] ICR 58;
    [1983] IRLR 471; 128 Sol Jo 151 (EAT) . . . 9.8,
    9.25
President of the Methodist Conference v Parfitt
    [1984] ICR 176 . . . 2.58, 2.67
President of the Methodist Conference v Preston
    [2013] UKSC 29 . . . 2.67
Presley v Llanelli Borough Council [1979] ICR
    419; [1979] IRLR 381 (EAT) . . . 20.34
Pressure Coolers Ltd v Molloy [2011] IRLR
    630 . . . 9.48
Prestige Group plc-, Re [1984] 1 WLR 335; [1984]
    ICR 473; [1984] IRLR 166; (1984) 81 LSG 134;
    (1984) 128 SJ 131 . . . 4.238
Printers and Finishers Ltd v Holloway [1964] 3
    All ER 731; [1965] 1 WLR 1; [1965] RPC 239;
    109 Sol Jo 47 . . . 10.70, 19.16
Prison Officers Association v Gough (EAT, 15
    December 2009) . . . 2.30
Prison Service v Bewley [2004] ICR 422; [2004]
    All ER (D) 22 (Mar) (EAT) . . . 7.97, 23.101
Procter v British Gypsum Ltd [1964] 3 All ER
    731; [1965] 1 WLR 1; [1965] RPC 239; 109 Sol
    Jo 47 . . . 17.134
Property Guards Ltd v Taylor and Kershaw [1982]
    IRLR 175 (EAT) . . . 4.243

Protectacoat Firthglow Ltd v Szilagyil [2009]
    EWCA Civ 98; [2009] ICR 835; [2009] IRLR
    365 . . . 2.2, 2.156
Provident Financial Group plc v Hayward [1989]
    3 All ER 298; [1989] ICR 160; [1989] IRLR 84
    (CA) . . . 10.17, 19.9, 19.12
Pruden v Cunard Ellerman Ltd [1993] IRLR
    317 . . . 20.6
Puglia v C James & Sons [1996] ICR 301; [1996]
    IRLR 70 (EAT) . . . 17.208
Purdy v Willowbrook International Ltd [1977]
    IRLR 388 . . . 7.3
Pyle v Cleeson Civil Engineering Ltd, IDS
    Handbook 12 . . . 18.55

Qua v John Ford Morrison (Solicitors) [2003]
    ICR 482; [2003] IRLR 184; [2003] NLJR 95;
    [2003] All ER (D) 29 (Jan) (EAT) . . .
    6.128
Qualcast (Wolverhampton) Ltd v Haynes [1959]
    AC 743; [1959] 2 All ER 38; [1959] 2 WLR 510;
    103 Sol Jo 310 (HL) . . . 11.128
Quinn v Calder Industrial Materials Ltd [1996]
    IRLR 126 (EAT) . . . 3.85
Quinn v Leathem [1901] AC 495; 65 JP 708; 70
    LJPC 76; 50 WR 139; [1900-3] All ER Rep
    1; 85 LT 289; 17 TLR 749; [1901] 2 IR 705
    (HL) . . . 23.23
Quinnen v Hovells [1984] ICR 525; [1984] IRLR
    227; (1984) 81 LSG 1438; (1984) 134 NLJ 360;
    (1984) 128 SJ 431 . . . 5.3

R v A-G for Northern Ireland, ex p Burns [1999]
    IRLR 315 . . . 7.63
R v Admiralty Board of the Defence Council, ex
    p Lustig-Prean [1996] QB 517; [1996] 2 WLR
    305; [1996] ICR 740, *sub nom* R v Ministry
    of Defence, ex p Smith [1996] 1 All ER 257;
    [1996] IRLR 100 (CA) . . . 1.105
R v Associated Octel [1994] 4 All ER 1051; [1995]
    ICR 281; [1994] IRLR 540; [1994] 36 LS Gaz R
    37; [1994] NLJR 1312; 138 Sol Jo LB 194 (CA);
    aff'd [1996] 4 All ER 846; [1996] 1 WLR 1543;
    [1996] ICR 972; [1997] IRLR 123; [1997] Crim
    LR 355; [1996] NLJR 1685 (HL) . . . 11.49
R v BBC ex p Lavelle [1983] 1 All ER 241; [1983]
    1 WLR 23; [1983] ICR 99; [1982] IRLR 404;
    126 Sol Jo 836 . . . 2.66, 16.30
R v Boal [1992] QB 591; [1992] 3 All ER 177;
    [1992] 2 WLR 890; 95 Cr App R 272; [1992]
    ICR 495; [1992] IRLR 420; 156 JP 617; [1992]
    BCLC 872; [1992] 21 LS Gaz R 26; 136 Sol Jo
    LB 100 (CA) . . . 11.93
R v British Coal Corpn, ex p Price [1993] ICR
    720; [1993] IRLR 104 . . . 18.85
R v Carr-Briant [1943] KB 607; [1943] 2 All ER
    156; 41 LGR 183; 29 Cr App R 76; 107 JP 167;
    112 LJKB 581; 169 LT 175; 59 TLR 300 (CCA)
    . . . 11.97
R v Chargot Ltd [2008] UKHL 73; [2009] 1 WLR
    1; [2009] 2 All ER 645; [2009] ICR 263; (2009)

153(1) SJLB 32; (2008) *Times* 16 December
... 11.98
R v Chief Constable of Merseyside Police [2001]
IRLR 442 ... 12.22
R v Chief Constable of Merseyside Police, ex p
Calveley [1986] QB 424; [1986] 1 All ER 257;
[1986] 2 WLR 144; 130 Sol Jo 53; [1986] LS
Gaz R 124 (CA) ... 16.20
R v Commission for Racial Equality, ex p
Westminster City Council [1985] ICR 827;
[1985] IRLR 426 ... 4.144
R v East Berkshire Health Authority, ex p Walsh
[1985] QB 152; [1984] 3 All ER 425; [1984] 3
WLR 818; [1984] ICR 743; [1984] IRLR 278;
128 Sol Jo 664; [1984] LS Gaz R 2223 (CA)
... 16.34
R v Governors of X School [2011] IRLR 756;
[2011] UKSC 30 ... 12.27, 12.28
R v Howe & Son (Engineers) Ltd [1999] 2 All ER
249; [1999] 2 Cr App R (S) 37; [1999] IRLR
434; 163 JP 359; [1999] Crim LR 238; [1998]
46 LS Gaz R 34; [1998] All ER (D) 552 (CA)
... 11.96
R v Leicestershire Fire Authority, ex p Thompson
(1979) 77 LGR 373; [1979] IRLR 166 (DC)
... 8.23
R v Lord Chancellor's Department, ex p Nangle
[1992] 1 All ER 897; [1991] ICR 743; [1991]
IRLR 343; [1991] COD 484 ... 2.68, 3.7
R v N Ltd [2008] EWCA Crim 1223; [2008] 1
WLR 2684; [2009] 1 Cr App R 3; (2008) *Times*
25 August ... 11.98
R v Secretary of State for Employment, ex p
Seymour-Smith and Perez [1994] IRLR 448
(DC); aff'd on other grounds [1996] All ER
(EC) 1; [1995] ICR 889; [1995] IRLR 464 CA;
revsd [1997] 2 All ER 273; [1997] 1 WLR 473;
[1997] 2 CMLR 904; [1997] ICR 371; [1997]
IRLR 315; 56 IRLB 15 (HL); refd *sub nom*
R v Secretary of State for Employment, ex p
Seymour-Smith (C-167/97) [1999] 2 AC 554;
[1999] 3 WLR 460; [1999] All ER (EC) 97;
[1999] 2 CMLR 273; [1999] ICR 447; [1999]
IRLR 253 (ECJ); apld *sub nom* R v Secretary
of State for Employment, ex p Seymour-
Smith (No 2) [2000] 1 All ER 857; [2000] 1
WLR 435; [2000] 1 CMLR 770; [2000] ICR
244; [2000] IRLR 263; [2000] 09 LS Gaz R 40
(HL) ... 1.71
R v Secretary of State for Transport, ex p
Factortame (C-48/93) [1996] QB 404; [1996]
2 WLR 506; [1996] ECR I-1029; [1996] All ER
(EC) 301; [1996] 1 CMLR 889; [1996] IRLR
267 (ECJ); apld [1998] 1 CMLR 1353; [1997]
TLR 482; [1997] Eu LR 475; [1998] 1 All ER
736n (DC); aff'd [1998] 3 CMLR 192; [1998]
NPC 68; [1998] TLR 261; [1998] Eu LR 456;
[1999] 2 All ER 640n (CA); aff'd [2000] 1 AC
524; [1999] 4 All ER 906; [1999] 3 WLR 1062;
[1999] 3 CMLR 597; [1999] 43 LS Gaz R 32
(HL) ... 1.71, 1.74

R v Secretary of State for Transport, ex p
Factortame (No 2) (C-213/89) [1991] 1 AC
603; [1990] 3 WLR 818; [1990] ECR I-2433;
[1990] 3 CMLR 1; [1990] 2 Lloyd's Rep 351;
[1990] 41 LS Gaz R 33; *sub nom* Factortame
Ltd v Secretary of State for Transport (No
2) [1991] 1 All ER 70; [1990] NLJR 927
(ECJ); apld *sub nom* R v Secretary of State for
Transport, ex p Factortame Ltd (No 2) [1991]
1 AC 603; [1990] 3 WLR 818; [1990] 3 CMLR
375; [1990] 2 Lloyd's Rep 365n; [1991] 1 Lloyd's
Rep 10; 134 Sol JO 1189; [1990] 41 LS Gaz R
36; [1990] MLJR 1457, *sub nom* Factortame
Ltd v Secretary of State for Transport (No 2)
[1991] 1 All ER 70 (HL) ... 1.74
R v Secretary of State for Education, ex p Prior
[1994] ICR 877; [1994] ELR 231 ... 12.19
R v Secretary of State for Employment, ex p
Equal Opportunities Commission [1993]
1 All ER 1022; [1993] 1 WLR 872; [1993] 1
CMLR 915; [1993] ICR 251; [1993] IRLR 10;
[1993] NLJR 332n (CA); on appeal [1995]
1 AC 1; [1994] 2 WLR 409; [1995] 1 CMLR
391; 92 LGR 360; [1994] IRLR 176; [1994]
18 LS Gaz R 43; NLJR 358, *sub nom* Equal
Opportunities Commission v Secretary of State
for Employment [1994] 1 All ER 910; [1994]
ICR 317 (HL) ... 20.22
R v Secretary of State for Employment, ex p
Equal Opportunities Commission [1993]
1 All ER 1022; [1993] 1 WLR 872; [1993] 1
CMLR 915; [1993] ICR 251; [1993] IRLR 10;
[1993] NLJR 332n (CA); on appeal [1995]
1 AC 1; [1994] 2 WLR 409; [1995] 1 CMLR
391; 92 LGR 360; [1994] IRLR 176; [1994]
18 LS Gaz R 43; NLJR 358, *sub nom* Equal
Opportunities Commission v Secretary of State
for Employment [1994] 1 All ER 910; [1994]
ICR 317 (HL) ... 1.71, 1.103, 2.81
R v Secretary of State, ex p Council of Civil
Service Unions ... 16.35
R v Secretary of State for the Home Department,
ex p Benwell [1985] QB 554; [1984] 3 All ER
854; [1984] 3 WLR 843; [1984] ICR 723; [1985]
IRLR 6; 128 Sol Jo 703 ... 16.3
R v Secretary of State for Trade and Industry, ex
p UNISON [1997] 1 CMLR 459; [1996] ICR
1003; [1996] IRLR 438 ... 11.45
R v Securities & Futures Authority Ltd, ex p
Fleurose [2002] IRLR 297 (CA) ... 1.107
R v Southampton Industrial Tribunal, ex p INS
News Group Ltd [1995] IRLR 247 ...
20.57
R v Swan Hunter Shipbuilders Ltd [1982] 1 All
ER 264; [1981] ICR 831; [1981] IRLR 403;
[1981] Crim LR 833; *sub nom* R v Swan Hunter
Shipbuilders Ltd and Telemeter Installations
Ltd, HMS Glasgow [1981] 2 Lloyd's Rep 605
(CA) ... 11.34, 11.49
R (E) v Jewish Free School [2010] IRLR 136;
(2010) 1 All ER 319 ... 4.140

R (Kwik-Fit (GB) Ltd) v Central Arbitration
   Committee [2002] EWHC 277 (Admin);
   [2002] All ER (D) 111 (Feb); revsd [2002]
   EWCA Civ 512; [2002] ICR 1212 [2002] IRLR
   395; [2002] All ER (D) 272 (Mar) . . .
   23.10
R (NUJ) v CAC [2005] IRLR 28 . . . 23.9
R (Puri) v Bradford Teaching Hospitals NHS
   Foundation Trust [2011] IRLR 582; [2011]
   EWHC 970 (Admin) . . . 12.19, 12.26
R (Reilly) v Secretary of State for Work and
   Pensions [2013] UKSC 68 . . . 1.107
R (Shoesmith) v OFSTED [2011] IRLR 679;
   [2011] EWCA Civ 642 . . . 12.22
RDF Media Group v Clements [2007] EWHC
   2892 (QB); [2008] IRLR 207 . . . 10.15
RF Hill Ltd v Mooney [1981] IRLR 258
   (EAT) . . . 17.23
RGB Resources plc v Rastogi [2004] All ER (D)
   258 (Apr) . . . 10.96
RJB Mining (UK) Ltd v National Union of
   Mineworkers [1997] IRLR 621 . . . 23.67
RMT v UK, formerly EDF Energy Powerlink v
   UK (Application 31045/10) [2010] IRLR 114
   . . . 1.107, 23.69
RNLI v Bushaway [2005] IRLR 674 (EAT) . . .
   2.79, 2.162, 13.8
RS Components Ltd v Irwin [1974] 1 All ER 41;
   [1973] ICR 535; [1973] IRLR 239 (NIRC) . . .
   3.94, 17.152, 19.25
Rai v Somerfield Stores Ltd [2004] IRLR 124
   (EAT) . . . 17.13, 20.30
RailTrack plc v Smallwood [2001] EWHC
   Admin 78; [2001] ICR 714; [2001] 09 LS Gaz
   R 40; 145 Sol Jo LB 52; [2001] All ER (D) 103
   (Jan) . . . 11.12
Rainey v Greater Glasgow Health Board [1987]
   AC 224; [1986] 3 WLR 1017; [1987] 1 All ER
   65; 1987 SC (HL) 1; 1987 SLT 146; [1987] 2
   CMLR 11; [1987] IR 129; [1987] IRLR 26;
   (1987) 84 LSG 188; (1986) 136 NLJ 1161;
   (1986) 130 SJ 954 . . . 5.45
Ramdoolar v Bycity Ltd [2005] ICR 368 (EAT)
   . . . 4.129, 6.52
Ranger v Brown [1978] 2 All ER 726; [1978] ICR
   603; 13 ITR 42 (EAT) . . . 2.112
Rank Nemo (DMS) Ltd v Coutinho [2009]
   EWCA Civ 454; [2009] ICR 1296; [2009] IRLR
   672; (2009) Times 8 June . . . 4.40
Rank Xerox (UK) Ltd v Goodchild [1979] IRLR
   185 (EAT) . . . 12.22
Ranson v Customer Systems PLC [2012] EWCA
   Civ 841 . . . 19.2, 19.5
Rao v Civil Aviation Authority [1992] ICR 503;
   [1992] IRLR 203 (EAT); on appeal [1994] ICR
   495; [1994] IRLR 240 (CA) . . . 17.189, 17.237
Rask and Christiensen v ISS Kantineservice A/S
   (C-209/91) [1992] ECR I-5755; [1993] IRLR
   133 (ECJ) . . . 9.9, 9.11
Rastegarnia v Richmond Design (unreported)
   . . . 3.8

Ratcliffe v Dorset County Council [1978] IRLR
   191 . . . 7.18
Ravat v Halliburton Manufacturing & Services
   Ltd [2012] UKSC 1, [2012] IRLR 315, SC
   . . . 1.32
Raymond v Sir Lindsay Parkinson Ltd [1974]
   IRLR 298 . . . 12.71
Raynor v Remploy Ltd [1973] IRLR 3 . . . 17.74
Rayware Ltd v Transport and General Workers'
   Union [1989] 3 All ER 583; [1989] 1 WLR 675;
   [1989] ICR 457; [1989] IRLR 134; [1989] 29 LS
   Gaz R 44 (CA) . . . 23.108
Readman v Devon PCT, UKEAT/0116/11/ZT
   . . . 18.30
Ready Mixed Concrete Ltd (South East) v
   Minister of Pensions and National Insurance
   [1968] 1 All ER 433; (1968) 2 QB 497 . . . 2.43,
   2.54
Red Bank Manufacturing Co Ltd v Meadows
   [1992] ICR 204; [1992] IRLR 209 (EAT) . . .
   20.129
Redbridge London Borough Council v Fishman
   (1978) 76 LGR 408; [1978] ICR 569; [1978]
   IRLR 69 (EAT) . . . 3.29
Redcar & Cleveland Borough Council v
   Bainbridge [2005] EWCA Civ 726; [2005]
   IRLR 504 . . . 1.28
Redcar and Cleveland Borough Council v
   Bainbridge [2008] EWCA Civ 885; [2009] ICR
   133; [2008] IRLR 776 . . . 5.34, 5.45, 5.47,
   5.66
Redrow Homes (Yorkshire) Ltd v Buckborough
   [2009] IRLR 34 . . . 2.156
Reed & Bull Information Systems Ltd v Stedman
   [1991] IRLR 299 (EAT) . . . 4.35
Refund Rentals Ltd v McDermott [1977] IRLR 59
   (EAT) . . . 17.132
Regent Security Services Ltd v Power [2007] 4
   All ER 354; [2007] ICR 970; [2007] IRLR 226
   (EAT); aff'd [2007] EWCA Civ 1188; [2008]
   IRLR 66; (2007) 104(47) LSG 26; [2008] ICR
   442 . . . 9.46
Reid v Galbraith's Stores 1970 SLT (Notes)
   83 . . . 11.132
Reid v Rush & Tompkins Group plc [1989] 3 All
   ER 228; [1990] 1 WLR 212; [1990] RTR 144;
   [1989] 2 Lloyd's Rep 167; [1990] ICR 61; [1989]
   IRLR 265 . . . 2.123, 3.52, 10.34
Reiss Engineering Co Ltd v Harris [1985] IRLR
   232 (EAT) . . . 10.86
Renfrewshire Council v Martin (EAT, 30 April
   2008) . . . 4.74
Retarded Children's Aid Society v Day [1978] 1
   WLR 763; [1978] ICR 437; [1978] IRLR 128;
   122 Sol Jo 385 (CA) . . . 17.139
Reuben v Brent London Borough Council [2000]
   ICR 102; [2000] IRLR 176 (EAT) . . . 20.128
Rex Stewart Jeffries Parker Ginsberg Ltd v Parker
   [1988] IRLR 483 (CA) . . . 19.51, 19.57
Reynolds v Cornwall County Council, EAT
   1189/95 . . . 8.5

Rhys-Harper v Relaxation Group plc [2003] UKHL 33; [2003] 4 All ER 1113; [2003] 2 CMLR 44; [2003] ICR 867; [2003] IRLR 484; (2003) 74 BMLR 109; (2003) 100(30) LSG 30; (2003) 147 SJLB 782; (2003) *Times* 23 June; (2003) *Independent* 24 June . . . 4.196, 7.139

Richard Read (Transport) Ltd v National Union of Mineworkers (South Wales Area) [1985] IRLR 67 . . . 23.84

Richards v Bulpitt & Sons Ltd [1975] IRLR 134 . . . 17.133

Richards v Highway Ironfounders (West Bromwich) Ltd [1955] 3 All ER 205; [1955] 1 WLR 1049; 53 LGR 641; 99 Sol Jo 580 (CA) . . . 11.134

Richards v National Union of Mineworkers [1981] IRLR 247 . . . 22.74

Richards v S and H E Fielding Ltd (1966) 1 KIR 365; 1 ITR 376 . . . 13.42

Richardson v City of Bradford Metropolitan Council [1975] IRLR 296 . . . 17.140

Richardson v U Mole Ltd [2005] IRLR 668 . . . 20.47

Richmond Adult Community College v McDougall [2008] EWCA Civ 4; [2008] ICR 431; [2008] IRLR 227; (2008) 105(4) LSG 23; (2008) 152(4) SJLB; (2008) *Times* 22 February . . . 4.85, 4.92

Richmond Pharmacology v Dhaliwal [2009] ICR 724; [2009] IRLR 336 . . . 4.36

Richmond Precision Engineering Ltd v Pearce [1985] IRLR 179 (EAT) . . . 3.107, 17.155

Ricketts v Torbay Council HSB No 326 . . . 11.132

Riddick v Thames Water Board Mills Ltd [1977] QB 881; [1977] 3 All ER 677; [1977] 3 WLR 63; 121 Sol Jo 274 (CA) . . . 20.64

Ridge v Baldwin [1963] 1 QB 539; [1961] 2 All ER 523; [1961] 2 WLR 1054; 59 LGR 327; JP 422; 105 Sol Jo 384; aff'd [1963] 1 QB 539; [1962] 1 All ER 834; [1962] 2 WLR 716; 60 LGR 229; JP 196; Sol Jo 111 CA; revsd [1964] AC 40; [1963] 2 All ER 66; [1963] 2 WLR 935; LGR 369; JP 295; Sol Jo 313 (HL) . . . 2.75, 16.1

Ridgeway v JP Morgan Chase National Bank, 2007 IDS Brief 835 . . . 10.21

Riezniece v Zemkopibas Ministrija (Case C-7/12) [2013] WLR (D) 247 . . . 6.45, 18.58

Rigby v Ferodo Ltd [1987] ICR 457; [1987] IRLR 61 CA; aff'd [1988] ICR 29; [1987] IRLR 516 (HL) . . . 3.102, 3.107, 16.6, 16.31, 16.32

Rigden-Murphy v Securicor Ltd [1976] IRLR 106 . . . 12.42

Riley-Williams v Argos Ltd [2003] All ER (D) 58 (Jul) (EAT) . . . 7.13

Riordan v War Office [1959] 3 All ER 552; [1959] 1 WLR 1046; 103 Sol Jo 921; aff'd [1960] 3 All ER 774n; [1961] 1 WLR 210 (CA) . . . 15.8

Road Transport Industry Training Board v Readers Garage Ltd (1969) 6 KIR 137; 113 Sol Jo 125 (DC) . . . 2.11

Robb v Green [1895] 2 QB 1, 59 JP 695, 64 LJQB 593, 44 WR 26, 39 Sol Jo 921, 72 LT 686, 11 TLR 330; aff'd [1895] 2 QB 315, 59 JP 695, 64 LJQB 593, 14 R 580, 44 WR 25, [1895-99] All ER Rep 1053, 39 Sol Jo 653, 73 LT 15, 11 TLR 517 (CA) . . . 19.4

Robb v Leon Motor Services [1977] IRLR 245; revsd [1978] ICR 506; [1978] IRLR 26 (EAT) . . . 21.54

Robb v London Borough of Hammersmith and Fulham [1991] ICR 514; [1991] IRLR 72 . . . 15.39

Robert Seligman Corpn v Baker [1983] ICR 770 (EAT) . . . 9.9

Robert Whiting Designs Ltd v Lamb [1978] ICR 89 (EAT) . . . 17.229

Roberts v Aegon UK Corporate Services Ltd [2009] EWCA Civ 932; [2010] ICR 596; [2009] IRLR 1042; (2009) 106(31) LSG 18 . . . 17.217

Roberts v Skelmersdale College [2002] All ER (D) 145 (Nov) (EAT); revsd [2003] EWCA Civ 954; [2003] ICR 1127; [2004] IRLR 69; [2003] All ER (D) 272 (Jun) . . . 20.85

Roberts v West Coast Trains Ltd [2004] EWCA Civ 900; [2005] ICR 254; [2004] IRLR 788; (2004) 101(28) LSG 33; (2004) *Times* 25 June . . . 13.32

Robertson v Bexley Community Centre [2002] All ER (D) 78 (Jul) (EAT); revsd [2003] EWCA Civ 576; [2003] IRLR 434; [2003] All ER (D) 151 (Mar) . . . 20.18

Robertson v Blackstone Franks Investment Management Ltd [1998] IRLR 376 (CA) . . . 8.14

Robertson v British Gas Corpn [1983] ICR 351 . . . 3.64

Robertson v Department for Environment, Food and Rural Affairs [2005] EWCA Civ 138; [2005] ICR 750; [2005] IRLR 363; (2005) 102(15) LSG 33; (2005) *Times* 2 March; (2005) *Independent* 24 February . . . 5.7

Robertson v Magnet Ltd (Retail Division) [1993] IRLR 512 (EAT) . . . 18.49

Robertson v Securicor Transport Ltd [1972] IRLR 70 . . . 17.9

Robinson v Crompton Parkinson Ltd [1978] ICR 401; [1978] IRLR 61 (EAT) . . . 3.43, 17.27

Robinson v Fairhill Medical Practice UKEAT/0313/12/JOJ . . . 20.31

Robinson v Flitwick Frames Ltd [1975] IRLR 261 . . . 10.63

Robinson v Post Office [2000] IRLR 804 . . . 20.7

Robinson v Tescom Corporation [2008] IRLR 408 . . . 3.106

Robinson v Ulster Carpet Mills Ltd [1991] IRLR 348 (NICA) . . . 18.56

Robinson-Steele v RD Retail Services Ltd (C-131/04) [2006] IRLR 386 (ECJ) . . . 7.84

Robson v Brian Mills [1977] IRLIB . . . 17.142

Rock Refrigeration Ltd v Jones [1997] 1 All ER 1; [1997] ICR 938; [1996] IRLR 675; [1996] 41 LS Gaz R 29; 140 Sol Jo LB 226 (CA) . . . 19.58

Rock-It Cargo Ltd v Green [1997] IRLR 581 (EAT) . . . 20.42

Rockfon A/S v Specialarbejderforbundet i Danmark . . . 18.77

Roger Bullivant Ltd v Ellis [1987] FSR 172; [1987] ICR 464; [1987] IRLR 491 (EAT) . . . 19.3

Rogers v Bodfari (Transport) Ltd [1973] ICR 325; [1973] IRLR 172; 14 KIR 532 (NIRC) . . . 20.2, 20.19

Rolls Royce Ltd v Walpole [1980] IRLR 343 (EAT) . . . 17.102

Rolls Royce plc v Riddle [2008] IRLR 873 . . . 20.56

Rolls Royce plc v Unite [2009] EWCA Civ 387; [2010] 1 WLR 318; [2010] ICR 1; [2009] IRLR 576; (2009) 106(21) LSG 15; (2009) 153(20) SJLB 38; (2009) Times 27 May . . . 4.72, 18.51

Rookes v Barnard [1963] 1 QB 623; [1961] 2 All ER 825; [1961] 3 WLR 438; 105 Sol Jo 530; revsd [1963] 1 QB 623; [1962] 2 All ER 579; [1962] 3 WLR 260; 106 Sol Jo 371 (CA); revsd in part [1964] AC 1129; [1964] 1 All ER 367; [1964] 2 WLR 269; [1964] 1 Lloyd's Rep 28; 108 Sol Jo 93 (HL) . . . 3.79, 23.25, 23.42

Rose v Plenty [1976] 1 All ER 97; [1976] 1 WLR 141; [1976] 1 Lloyd's Rep 263; [1975] ICR 430; [1976] IRLR 483; [2002] All ER (D) 143 (May) . . . 10.104

Rosenthal v Louis Butler Ltd [1972] IRLR 39 . . . 12.81

Ross v Aquascutum Ltd [1973] IRLR 107 . . . 16.10

Ross v Delrosa Caterers Ltd [1981] ICR 393 (EAT) . . . 13.42

Ross v Micro Focus Ltd (EAT, 18 November 2009) . . . 20.93

Rossiter v Pendragon plc [2001] ICR 1265; [2001] IRLR 256; [2001] All ER (D) 412 (Feb) (EAT); revsd in part [2002] EWCA Civ 745; [2002] ICR 1063; [2002] IRLR 483; [2002] All ER (D) 143 (May) . . . 9.65

Rothwell v Association of Professional, Executive and Computer Staff and the Trade Union Congress [1976] ICR 211; [1975] IRLR 375 . . . 21.6

Rowan v Machinery Installations (South Wales) Ltd [1981] ICR 386; [1981] IRLR 122 (EAT) . . . 13.42, 17.176

Rowe v Radio Rentals [1982] IRLR 177 . . . 12.36

Rowell v Hubbard Group Services [1995] IRLR 195 (EAT) . . . 18.48, 18.83

Rowstock Ltd v Jessemey UKEAT/0112/12 . . . 4.42

Roy v Kensington and Chelsea and Westminster Family Practitioner Committee [1989] 1 Med LR 10; on appeal [1990] 1 Med LR 328 CA; aff'd [1992] 1 AC 624; [1992] 1 All ER 705; [1992] 2 WLR 239 [1992] IRLR 233; 8 BMLR 9; [1992] 17 LS Gaz R 48; 136 Sol Jo LB 62 (HL) . . . 16.36

Royal Bank of Scotland v Harrison . . . 6.123

Royal Mail Group Ltd v Communication Workers Union [2009] EWCA Civ 1045; [2010] ICR 83; [2009] IRLR 1046; (2009) 106(41) LSG 20; (2009) Times 16 October . . . 18.85

Royal Mail Group Ltd v CWU [2009] EWCA Civ 1045; [2010] ICR 83; [2009] IRLR 1046; (2009) 106(41) LSG 20; (2009) Times 16 October . . . 9.76

Royal Ordnance plc v Pilkington [1988] ICR 606; [1988] IRLR 466 (EAT); revsd [1989] ICR 737; [1989] IRLR 489 (CA) . . . 13.40

Royal Society for the Protection of Birds v Croucher [1984] ICR 604; [1984] IRLR 425 (EAT) . . . 12.5

Rubenstein v McGloughlin (1995) Times 28 December (EAT) . . . 17.208

Rugamer v Sony Music Entertainments UK Ltd [2002] EWCA Civ 1074; [2002] ICR 1498; [2002] IRLR 711; [2002] Emp LR 1097; (2003) 71 BMLR 1; (2002) 99(38) LSG 33; (2002) 146 SJLB 201; (2002) Times 26 August . . . 4.82

Russell v Elmdon Freight Terminal Ltd [1989] ICR 629 (EAT) . . . 2.7, 20.127

Russell v Transocean International Resources Ltd [2011] UKSC 57 . . . 7.81

Rutherford v Seymour Pierce Ltd [2010] IRLR 606; [2010] EWHC 375 (QB) . . . 10.22

Rygaard v Stro Molle Akustik [1996] IRLR 51 (ECJ) . . . 9.8

S & U Stores Ltd v Wilkes [1974] 3 All ER 401; [1974] ICR 645; [1974] IRLR 283; [1975] KILR 117; 9 ITR 415 (NIRC) . . . 14.4, 17.205

SBJ Stephenson Ltd v Mandy [2000] IRLR 233 . . . 19.15, 19.30, 19.67

SC Brown Communications Ltd v Walker (unreported) . . . 12.22

SCA Packaging Ltd v Boyle [2009] UKHL 37; [2009] 4 All ER 1181; [2009] NI 317; [2009] ICR 1056; [2009] IRLR 746; (2009) 109 BMLR 53; (2009) 153(26) SJLB 27; (2009) Times 6 July . . . 4.86

SG & R Valuation Service Co v Boudrais [2008] EWHC 1340 (QB); [2008] IRLR 770 . . . 15.21, 19.7, 19.23

SH Muffett Ltd v Head [1987] ICR 1; [1986] IRLR 488; [1986] LS Gaz R 2653 (EAT) . . . 17.215

SIP Industrial Products Ltd v Swinn [1994] ICR 473; [1994] IRLR 323 (EAT) . . . 8.23

SW Strange Ltd v Mann [1965] 1 All ER 1069; [1965] 1 WLR 629; 109 Sol Jo 352 . . . 19.26

Saavedra v Aceground Ltd [1995] IRLR 198 . . . 8.14

Safeway Stores plc v Burrell [1997] ICR 523; [1997] IRLR 200; 567 IRLB 8 (EAT) . . . 18.19, 18.21, 18.22

Sagar v Ridehalgh [1930] 2 Ch 117; revsd [1931] 1 Ch 310; 29 LGR 421; 95 JP 42; 100 LJ Ch 220; [1930] All ER Rep 288; 144 LT 480; 47 TLR 189 (CA) . . . 3.80, 13.28

Sainsbury's Supermarkets Ltd v Hitt [2001] All ER (D) 344 (Dec) (EAT); revsd [2002] EWCA Civ

1588; [2003] ICR 111; [2003] IRLR 23; 146 Sol
Jo LB 238; [2002] All ER (D) 259 (Oct) . . . 12.10

St Anne's Board Mills Co Ltd v Brien [1973] ICR
444; [1973] IRLR 309 (NIRC) . . . 20.86

St Basil's Centre Ltd v McCrossan [1992] ICR 140;
[1991] IRLR 455 (EAT) . . . 20.14, 20.15

St Helen's Borough Council v Derbyshire [2007]
UKHL 16; [2007] 3 All ER 81; [2007] ICR
841; [2007] IRLR 540; (2007) 104(19) LSG
26; (2007) 157 NLJ 635; (2007) 151 SJLB 573;
(2007) Times 27 April . . . 4.41

St John of God (Care Services) Ltd v Brooks
[1992] ICR 715; [1992] IRLR 546; [1992] 29 LS
Gaz R 24 (EAT) . . . 17.150

St Matthias Church of England School v Crizzle
[1993] ICR 401; [1993] IRLR 472; (1993)
Times 26 February; (1993) Independent 4
March . . . 4.149

Sakar v West London Mental Health Trust [2010]
IRLR 508; [2010] EWCA Civ 289 (CA) . . . 12.2

Salford Royal NHS Foundation Trust v
Roldan [2010] IRLR 721; [2010] EWCA Civ
522 . . . 12.5

Salvation Army v Dewsbury . . . 13.9, 17.4

Salvesen v Simons [1994] ICR 409; [1994] IRLR
52 (EAT) . . . 3.12

Samways v Swan Hunter Shipbuilders Ltd [1975]
IRLR 190 . . . 3.83

Sanders v Ernest A Neale Ltd [1974] 3 All ER 327;
[1974] ICR 565; [1974] IRLR 236 (NIRC) . . .
18.11, 21.103

Sandhu v Jan de Rijk Transport Ltd [2007] EWCA
Civ 430; [2007] IRLR 519; (2007) 104(21) LSG
27; (2007) 151 SJLB 672; [2007] ICR 1137 . . .
17.50, 17.72

Santemera v Express Cargo Forwarding [2003]
IRLR 273; [2002] All ER (D) 379 (Nov)
(EAT) . . . 12.22

Sarker v South Tees Acute Hospitals NHS
Trust [1997] ICR 673; [1997] IRLR 328
(EAT) . . . 3.5, 15.6

Saunders v Richmond-upon-Thames London
Borough Council [1978] ICR 75; [1977] IRLR
362; (1977) 12 ITR 488 . . . 4.46

Savage v British India Steam Navigation Co
(1930) 46 TLR 294 . . . 16.13

Savage v Saxena [1998] ICR 357; [1998] IRLR 182
(EAT) . . . 17.208, 17.226

Savoia v Chiltern Herb Farms Ltd [1981] IRLR
65 (EAT); aff'd [1982] IRLR 166 (CA) . . . 17.47

Sayers v Cambridgeshire County Council [2006]
EWHC 2029 (QB); [2007] IRLR 29 . . . 7.109,
11.138

Scala Ballroom (Wolverhampton) Ltd v Ratcliffe
[1958] 3 All ER 220; [1958] 1 WLR 1057; 102
Sol Jo 758 (CA) . . . 23.24

Scally v Southern Health and Social Services
Board [1992] 1 AC 294; [1991] 4 All ER 563;
[1991] 3 WLR 778; [1991] ICR 771; [1991]
IRLR 522; 135 Sol Jo LB 172 (HL) . . . 3.39,
3.40

Scanfuture UK Ltd v Secretary of State for Trade
and Industry [2001] ICR 1096; [2001] IRLR
416; [2001] Emp LR 590 (EAT) . . . 1.107

Scarlett v Godfrey Abbott Group Ltd [1978] ICR
1106; [1978] IRLR 456; 13 ITR 519 (EAT)
. . . 13.16

Scarr v FW Goodyear & Sons Ltd [1975] IRLR
166 . . . 17.62

Schmidt v Spar-und Leihkasse der Früheren (C-
392/92) [1994] ECR I-1311; [1995] 2 CMLR
331; [1995] ICR 237; [1994] IRLR 302 (ECJ)
. . . 9.7, 9.15

Schulz-Hoff v Deutsche Rentenversicherung
Bund [2009] ICR 932 . . . 7.86

Schutz v Esso Petroleum [1999] ICR 1202 . . .
20.11

Science Research Council v Nassé [1978] ICR
777; [1978] IRLR 201; 122 Sol Jo 316 (EAT); on
appeal [1979] QB 144; [1978] 3 All ER 1196;
[1978] 3 WLR 754; [1978] ICR 1124; [1978]
IRLR 352; 122 Sol Jo 593 (CA); aff'd [1980]
AC 1028; [1979] 3 All ER 673; [1979] ICR 921;
[1979] IRLR 465; 123 Sol Jo 768 (HL) . . . 20.66

Scotch Premier Meat Ltd v Burns [2000] IRLR
639 (EAT) . . . 18.78

Scott Packing and Warehousing Co v Paterson
[1978] IRLR 166 (EAT) . . . 17.163

Scott v Commissioners of Inland Revenue [2004]
EWCA Civ 400; [2004] ICR 1410; [2004] IRLR
713; (2004) 148 SJLB 474; (2004) Times 19
April . . . 4.231, 20.63, 20.97

Scott v Pattison [1923] 2 KB 723; 92 LJKB 886;
129 LT 830; 39 TLR 557 (DC) . . . 3.84

Scottbridge Construction Ltd v Wright, 2003
SC 520; 2002 SLT 1356; [2003] IRLR 21; 2002
GWD 34-1150 . . . 8.43

Scottish Co-operative Wholesale Society Ltd v
Lloyd [1973] ICR 137; [1973] IRLR 93; 8 ITR
178 (NIRC) . . . 17.228

Scottish Coal Co Ltd v McCormack, IDS Brief
791 . . . 9.10

Scottish and Newcastle Breweries plc v
Halliday [1986] ICR 577; [1986] IRLR 291
(EAT) . . . 17.224

Scottish Special Housing Association v Cooke
[1979] IRLR 264 (EAT) . . . 17.122

Scotts Company (UK) Ltd v Budd [2004] ICR
299; [2003] IRLR 145; [2002] All ER (D) 58
(Nov) (EAT) . . . 6.30, 15.16

Scullard v Knowles and Southern Regional Council
[1996] ICR 399; [1996] IRLR 344 . . . 2.8, 5.6

Scully UK Ltd v Lee [1998] IRLR 259
(CA) . . . 19.34

Secretary of State for Employment v Globe Elastic
Thread Co Ltd [1978] QB 86; [1978] 1 All ER
987; [1977] 3 WLR 293; [1978] ICR 473; [1977]
IRLR 233; 12 ITR 402; 121 Sol Jo 407 (EAT);
aff'd [1979] QB 18; [1978] 3 All ER 954; [1978]
3 WLR 679; [1978] ICR 1041; [1978] IRLR 417;
13 ITR 540; 122 Sol Jo 661 (CA); revsd [1980]
AC 506; [1979] 2 All ER 1077; [1979] 3 WLR

143; [1979] ICR 706; [1979] IRLR 327; 123 Sol
Jo 504 (HL) . . . 13.3
Secretary of State for the Department of Business
Enterprise and Regulatory Reform v Neufeld
[2009] EWCA Civ 280; [2009] 3 All ER 790;
[2009] BCC 687; [2009] 2 BCLC 273; [2009]
ICR 1183; [2009] IRLR 475; [2009] BPIR 909;
(2009) 106(15) LSG 15; (2009) *Times* 10 April
. . . 2.13, 2.54, 18.4
Secretary of State for Employment v Associated
Society of Locomotive Engineers and Firemen
[1972] 2 QB 443; [1972] 2 All ER 853; [1972]
2 WLR 1362; [1972] ICR 7; 116 Sol Jo 333
(NIRC); aff'd *sub nom* Secretary of State
for Employment v Associated Society of
Locomotive Engineers and Firemen (No 2)
[1972] 2 QB 455; [1972] 2 All ER 949; [1972] 2
WLR 1370; [1972] ICR 19; 13 KIR 1; 116 Sol Jo
467 (CA) . . . 3.90, 10.49
Secretary of State for Employment v Banks [1983]
ICR 48 (EAT) . . . 20.13
Secretary of State for Employment v Crane [1988]
IRLR 238 (EAT) . . . 14.10
Secretary of State for Employment v Forde [1997]
ICR 231; [1997] IRLR 387 (EAT) . . . 2.18,
7.134
Secretary of State for Employment v John
Woodrow & Sons (Builders) Ltd [1983] ICR
582; [1983] IRLR 11 (EAT) . . . 14.5
Secretary of State for Employment v Mann [1996]
ICR 197; [1996] IRLR 4 (EAT); revsd [1997]
ICR 209 (CA); aff'd on other grounds *sub nom*
Mann v Secretary of State for Employment
[1999] ICR 898; [1999] All ER (D) 791 . . .
1.18, 1.74
Secretary of State for Employment v Newbold
[1981] IRLR 305 (EAT) . . . 2.7
Secretary of State for Employment v Wilson
[1978] 3 All ER 137; [1978] 1 WLR 568; [1978]
ICR 200; [1977] IRLR 483; 13 ITR 191; 121 Sol
Jo 791 (EAT) . . . 7.134, 15.30, 15.38
Secretary of State for Health v Rance [2007] IRLR
665; [2007] Pens LR 313 (EAT) . . . 20.121
Secretary of State for Justice v Mansfield,
EAT/0539/09/RN . . . 12.4, 12.5
Secretary of State for Scotland v Campbell [1992]
IRLR 263 (EAT) . . . 12.18
Secretary of State for Trade and Industry v Cook
[1997] 3 CMLR 1465; [1997] ICR 288; [1997]
IRLR 150; 562 IRLB 12 (EAT) . . . 9.64
Secretary of State for Trade and Industry v Lassman
[2000] ICR 1109; [2000] IRLR 411; (2000) *Times*
5 May; (2000) *Independent* 4 May . . .
13.42
Secretary of State for Trade and Industry v Slater
[2008] BCC 70; [2008] ICR 54; [2007] IRLR
928 . . . 9.49
Secretary of State for Trade and Industry v
Walden [2000] IRLR 168 (EAT) . . . 7.134
Securicor Guarding Ltd v R [1994] IRLR 633
(EAT) . . . 17.141

Securicor Ltd v Smith [1989] IRLR 356
(CA) . . . 12.47
Securiplan v Bademosi, IDS Brief 746 . . . 9.12
Security Facilities Division v Hayes [2001] IRLR
81 (CA) . . . 3.100
Sehmi v Gate Gourmet London Ltd [2009] IRLR
807 . . . 21.98
Selby and Tesse v Plessey Co Ltd [1972] IRLR
36 . . . 18.52
Seldon v Clarkson, Wright & Jakes [2010] IRLR
865; [2010] EWCA Civ 899; [2012] UKSC
16 . . . 4.67
Selfridges Ltd v Mali [1998] ICR 268; [1997]
IRLR 577 (EAT) . . . 17.240
Senior Heat Treatment Ltd v Bell [1997] IRLR
614 . . . 9.63
Serco Ltd v Lawson [2006] UKHL 3; [2006] 1
All ER 823; [2006] ICR 250; [2006] IRLR 289;
(2006) 103(6) LSG 36; (2006) 156 NLJ 184;
(2006) 150 SJLB 131; (2006) *Times* 27 January
. . . 1.32, 1.36, 2.150, 4.192, 4.217
Setiya v East Yorkshire Health Authority [1995]
IRLR 348 (EAT) . . . 1.103
Shamoon v Chief Constable of the Royal Ulster
Constabulary [2003] UKHL 11; [2003] 2 All
ER 26; [2003] NI 174; [2003] ICR 337; [2003]
IRLR 285; (2003) 147 SJLB 268; (2003) *Times* 4
March . . . 4.30, 4.169
Shanahan Engineering Ltd v UNITE (EAT, 22
February 2010) . . . 18.88
Sharma v Hindu Temple (unreported) . . . 2.114
Sharma v Manchester City Council [2008] ICR
623; (2008) IRLT 336 . . . 2.86
Sharma v West Yorkshire Passenger Transport
Executive [1977] IRLIB . . . 12.22
Shea v Marcos Fidelio, UKEAT/0159/11/
JOJ . . . 20.75
Sheffield Forgemasters International Ltd v Fox
[2009] ICR 333; [2009] IRLR 192 . . . 17.208
Sheffield v Oxford Controls Co Ltd [1979] ICR
396; [1979] IRLR 133 (EAT) . . . 17.50, 17.72,
20.36
Shell UK Ltd v Lostock Garage Ltd [1977] 1 All
ER 481; [1976] 1 WLR 1187; 120 Sol Jo 523
(CA) . . . 3.48
Shepherd v Firth Brown Ltd (unreported 17 April
1985) . . . 11.118
Shepherds Investments Ltd v Walters [2006]
EWHC 836 (Ch); [2007] 2 BCLC 202; [2007]
IRLR 110; [2007] FSR 15; (2006) 150 SJLB 536
. . . 10.56, 19.2, 19.5
Sheppard v National Coal Board (1966) 1 KIR
101; 1 ITR 177 . . . 18.29
Shillito v Van Leer (UK) Ltd [1997] IRLR 495
(EAT) . . . 11.65
Shipping Co Uniform Inc v International
Transport Workers' Federation [1985] 1 Lloyd's
Rep 173; [1985] ICR 245; [1985] IRLR 71
. . . 23.76
Shook v London Borough of Ealing [1986] ICR
314; [1986] IRLR 46 (EAT) . . . 16.3

Shortland v Chantrill [1975] IRLR 208 . . . 2.103

Shove v Downs Surgical plc [1984] 1 All ER 7; [1984] ICR 532; [1984] IRLR 17; 128 Sol Jo 221 . . . 16.22, 16.26

Shrewsbury & Telford Hospital NHS Trust v Lairikyengban [2010] ICR 66 . . . 3.10

Sillars v Charrington Fuels Ltd [1988] ICR 505; [1988] IRLR 180; [1988] 16 LS Gaz R 42 (EAT); aff'd [1989] ICR 475; [1989] IRLR 152 (CA) . . . 13.21

Silvey v Pendragon plc [2001] EWCA Civ 784; [2001] IRLR 685 . . . 16.23

Sim v Rotherham Metropolitan Borough Council [1987] Ch 216; [1986] 3 All ER 387; [1986] 3 WLR 851; 85 LGR 128; [1986] ICR 897; [1986] IRLR 391; 130 Sol Jo 839; [1986] LS Gaz R 3746 . . . 3.37, 3.50, 8.23, 10.50

Simmonds v Dowty Seals Ltd [1978] IRLR 211 (EAT) . . . 17.23

Simmonds v Milford Club UKEAT/0323/12/KN . . . 12.75

Simmons v Hoover Ltd [1975] IRLR 263; aff'd [1977] QB 284; [1977] 1 All ER 775; [1976] 3 WLR 901; [1977] ICR 61; [1976] IRLR 266; 10 ITR 234; 120 Sol Jo 540 (EAT) . . . 18.63

Simmons v Medway Welding Ltd [1973] ITR 373 (NIRC) . . . 20.101

Simon v Brimham Associates [1987] ICR 596; [1987] IRLR 307 . . . 4.146

Simpson v Endsleigh Insurance Services [2010] UKEAT/544/09; [2011] ICR 75 . . . 6.46

Simrad Ltd v Scott [1997] IRLR 147 (EAT) . . . 17.213, 17.235

Sinclair v Neighbour [1967] 2 QB 279; [1966] 3 All ER 988; [1967] 2 WLR 1; 110 Sol Jo 808 (CA) . . . 16.10

Sindicato de Médicos de Asistencia Pública (SIMAP) v Conselleria de Sanidad y Consumo de la Generalidad Valenciana [2001] All ER (EC) 609; [2000] ECR I-7963; [2001] 3 CMLR 42; [2001] ICR 1116; [2000] IRLR 845; (2000) Times 18 October . . . 7.60

Singh v British Steel Corpn [1974] IRLR 131 . . . 3.74, 3.75, 3.81

Singh v Lyons Maid Ltd [1975] IRLR 328 . . . 3.93

Sisley v Britannia Security Systems Ltd [1983] ICR 628; [1983] IRLR 404 . . . 4.184

Skiggs v South West Trains Ltd [2005] IRLR 459 . . . 12.2

Skillen v Eastwoods Froy Ltd (1966) 2 ITR . . . 14.4

Skyrail Oceanic Ltd v Coleman [1981] ICR 864; [1981] IRLR 398; (1981) Times 28 July . . . 4.20, 4.175

Slaughter v C Brewer & Sons Ltd [1990] ICR 730; [1990] IRLR 426 (EAT) . . . 17.229

Slaven v Thermo Engineers Ltd [1992] ICR 295 . . . 7.124

Small v Boots Co plc [2009] IRLR 328 . . . 3.88

Smith v Austin Lifts [1959] 1 All ER 81; [1959] 1 WLR 100; [1958] 2 Lloyd's Rep 583; 103 Sol Jo 73 (HL) . . . 11.109

Smith v Baker & Sons [1891] AC 325 . . . 11.145

Smith v Cherry Lewis Ltd [2005] IRLR 86 (EAT) . . . 18.95

Smith v Du Pont (UK) Ltd [1976] IRLR 107 . . . 17.138

Smith v Glasgow City District Council [1985] IRLR 79; [1985] SLT 138 (Ct of Sess); aff'd [1987] ICR 796; [1987] IRLR 326; [1987] SC (HL) 175; 1987 SLT 605 . . . 20.78, 20.82

Smith v Royal Alfred Merchant Seamen's Society, HSIB 9 . . . 17.106

Smith v Safeways plc [1996] ICR 868 [1996] IRLR 456 (CA) . . . 1.107, 4.21, 4.176, 4.181

Smith v Secretary of State for Trade and Industry [2000] ICR 69; [2000] IRLR 6 (EAT) . . . 1.107

Smith v United Kingdom (Applications 33985/96 and 33986/96) 29 EHRR 493; [1999] ECHR 33985/96 (ECtHR) . . . 1.105, 1.107

Smiths Industries Aerospace and Defence Systems v Rawlings [1996] IRLR 656 (EAT) . . . 11.68

Smoker v London Fire and Civil Defence Authority [1991] 2 AC 502; [1991] 2 WLR 422; [1990] IRLR 271; revsd [1991] IRLR 22 (CA); aff'd [1991] 2 AC 502; [1991] 2 All ER 449; [1991] 2 WLR 1052; [1991] ICR 449; [1991] IRLR 271 (HL) . . . 17.208

Snook v London and West Riding Investments [1967] 2 QB 786; [1967] 2 WLR 1020; [1967] 1 All ER 518; (1967) 111 SJ 71 . . . 2.14

Snoxell v Vauxhall Motors Ltd [1977] ICR 700 . . . 5.51

Sogbetun v Hackney London Borough [1998] ICR 1264; [1998] IRLR 676 (EAT) . . . 1.27

Solihull Metropolitan Borough Council v National Union of Teachers [1985] IRLR 211 . . . 23.85

Somerset County Council v Chamber UKEAT/0417/12/KN . . . 8.17

Somjee v United Kingdom (Application 42116/98) [2002] IRLR 886; [2002] All ER (D) 214 (Oct) (ECtHR) . . . 1.107

Sood Enterprises v Healy UKEATS/0015/12 . . . 7.86

Soros v Davison [1994] ICR 590; [1994] IRLR 264 (EAT) . . . 17.202

Sothern v Franks Charlesly & Co [1981] IRLR 278 (CA) . . . 17.15, 17.52

Sougrin v Haringey Health Authority [1992] ICR 650; [1992] IRLR 416; (1992) Times 8 June; (1992) Independent 2 July . . . 4.220

South East Sheffield Citizens Advice Bureau v Grayson (EAT) (unreported) . . . 3.7

South Surbiton Co-operative Society v Wilcox [1975] IRLR 292 . . . 11.19, 11.22

South West Launderettes Ltd v Laidler [1986] IRLR 68 (EAT); on appeal [1986] ICR 455; [1986] IRLR 305 (CA) . . . 2.7

Southwark London Borough v O'Brien [1996] IRLR 420 (EAT) . . . 8.17

Sovereign House Security Services Ltd v Savage [1989] IRLR 115 (CA) . . . 17.52

Spaceright Europe Ltd v Baillavoine [2012] IRLR 212 . . . 9.51

Spafax Ltd v Harrison [1980] IRLR 442 (CA) . . . 17.37, 17.40, 19.25

Spalding v Port of London Authority [1977] HSIB . . . 17.113

Spanlite Structures Ltd v Jarrett [1973] ICR 465; [1973] IRLR 280; 16 KIR 79; 8 ITR 511 (NIRC) . . . 2.5

Speciality Care plc v Pachela [1996] ICR 633; [1996] IRLR 248 (EAT) . . . 21.85

Spence v British Railways Board [2001] ICR 232; [2000] All ER (D) 1956 (EAT) . . . 17.4

Spence v Intype Libra Ltd (EAT, 27 April 2007) . . . 17.104

Spencer Jones v Timmens Freeman [1974] IRLR 325 . . . 3.82

Spencer v Gloucestershire County Council [1985] ICR 223 (EAT); revsd [1985] IRLR 393 (CA) . . . 18.30

Spencer v Paragon Wallpapers Ltd [1977] ICR 301; [1976] IRLR 373 (EAT) . . . 17.97

Spencer v Secretary of State for Work and Pensions [2008] EWCA Civ 750; [2009] QB 358; [2009] 2 WLR 593; [2009] 1 All ER 314; [2008] CP Rep 40; [2009] RTR 5; [2008] 3 CMLR 15; [2008] Eu LR 779; [2008] ICR 1359; [2008] IRLR 911; [2008] PIQR P21; (2008) 152(27) SJLB 31; (2008) Times 24 July . . . 1.74

Spijkers v Gebroeders Benedik Abattoir (24/85) [1986] ECR 1119; [1986] 2 CMLR 296 (ECJ) . . . 9.8

Spiller v Wallis Ltd [1973] IRLR 362 . . . 12.54

Spinpress Ltd v Turner [1986] ICR 433; [1986] NLJ Rep 892 (EAT) . . . 18.34

Spook Erection Ltd v Thackray [1984] IRLR 116; 1983 SLT 630 (Ct of Sess) . . . 20.122

Spring v Guardian Assurance plc . . . 10.35, 10.38

Spring v National Amalgamated Stevedores and Dockers' Society [1956] 2 All ER 221; [1956] 1 WLR 585; [1956] 1 Lloyd's Rep 331; 100 Sol Jo 401 . . . 22.27

Springboard Sunderland Trust v Robson [1992] ICR 554; [1992] IRLR 261 . . . 5.33

Squibb UK Staff Association v Certification Officer [1978] ICR 115; [1977] IRLR 355 (EAT); revsd [1979] 2 All ER 452; [1979] 1 WLR 523; [1979] ICR 235; [1979] IRLR 75; 123 Sol Jo 352 (CA) . . . 22.13

Stacey v Babcock Power Ltd [1986] QB 308; [1986] 2 WLR 207; [1986] ICR 221; [1986] IRLR 3; 130 Sol Jo 71 (EAT) . . . 17.80, 18.60

Stadt Lengerich v Helmig [1994] ECR I-5727; [1995] 2 CMLR 261; [1996] ICR 35; [1995] IRLR 216; (1995) Financial Times 10 January . . . 5.18

Staffordshire Sentinel Newspapers Ltd v Potter [2004] IRLR 752 . . . 2.44

Stallite Batteries Co Ltd v Appleton, HSLB 147 (EAT) . . . 7.9

Stanley Cole (Wainfleet) Ltd v Sheridan [2003] ICR 297; [2003] IRLR 52; [2002] All ER (D) 11 (Nov) (EAT); aff'd [2003] EWCA Civ 1046; [2003] 4 All ER 1181; [2003] ICR 1449; [2003] IRLR 885; [2003] 38 LS Gaz R 33; [2003] All ER (D) 446 (Jul) . . . 12.76

Stapp v Shaftesbury Society [1982] IRLR 326 (CA) . . . 16.24

Stark v Post Office [2000] All ER (D) 276 (CA) . . . 11.133

Stedman v United Kingdom (1997) 23 EHRR CD 168; [1997] EHRLR 545 . . . 1.107

Steere v Morris Bros, IDS Handbook . . . 4.178

Stein v Associated Dairies [1982] IRLR 447 . . . 12.83

Stekel v Ellice [1973] 1 WLR 191; [1973] 1 All ER 465; [1973] CLY 2472 . . . 2.17

Stenhouse Australia Ltd v Phillips [1974] AC 391; [1974] 1 All ER 117; [1974] 2 WLR 134; [1974] 1 Lloyd's Rep 1; 117 Sol Jo 875 (PC) . . . 19.15

Stevedoring & Haulage Services Ltd v Fuller [2001] EWCA Civ 651; [2001] IRLR 627; [2001] All ER (D) 106 (May) . . . 2.174, 3.54

Stevens v Bexley Health Authority [1989] ICR 224; [1989] IRLR 240 (EAT) . . . 1.102

Stevens v Bower [2004] ICR 1582; [2004] IRLR 957 (CA) . . . 13.40

Stevenson, Jordan and Harrison Ltd v MacDonald and Evans (1952) 69 RPC 10; [1952] 1 TLR 101 (CA) . . . 2.39

Stevenson v J M Skinner & Co (EAT, 6 March 2008) . . . 6.12

Stevenson v Teesside Bridge and Engineering Ltd [1971] 1 All ER 296; 10 KIR 53; 6 ITR 44; 114 Sol Jo 907 (DC) . . . 3.44

Stevenson v United Road Transport Union [1976] 3 All ER 29; aff'd [1977] 2 All ER 941; [1977] ICR 893 (CA) . . . 16.31

Stewart v Cleveland Guest (Engineering) Ltd [2004] EWCA Civ 1070; [2004] IRLR 799; (2004) 154 NLJ 1292; [2004] 148 SJLB 976; (2004) Times 7 October; [1994] ICR 535; [1994] IRLR 440 (EAT) . . . 4.21

Stokes v Guest, Keen and Nettlefold [1968] 1 WLR 1776; 5 KIR 401; 112 Sol Jo 821 . . . 11.108, 11.111

Storer v British Gas plc [2000] 2 All ER 440; [2000] 1 WLR 1237; [2000] ICR 603; [2000] IRLR 495 (CA) . . . 20.73

Storey v Allied Brewery (1976) 84 IRLB 9 . . . 17.153

Strathclyde Regional Council v Neil [1984] IRLR 11 (Sh Ct); aff'd sub nom Neil v Strathclyde Regional Council [1984] IRLR 14; 1983 SLT (Sh Ct) 89 . . . 19.70

Street v Derbyshire Unemployed Workers' Centre [2004] ICR 213; [2004] 02 LS Gaz R 29; [2003] All ER (D) 75 (Dec) (EAT) . . . 10.82

Stringer v HMRC [2009] All ER (EC) 906; [2009] ECR I-179; [2009] 2 CMLR 27; [2009] ICR 932; [2009] IRLR 214; (2009) *Times* 28 January ... 7.86, 7.88

Stuart Peters Ltd v Bell [2009] EWCA Civ 938; [2010] 1 WLR 10; [2010] 1 All ER 775; [2009] ICR 1556; [2009] IRLR 941; (2009) *Times* 7 October ... 17.230

Stuart v London City Airport UKEAT/0273/12/ BA ... 12.5, 17.123

Suffolk County Council v Secretary of State for the Environment (1983) 82 LGR 557; revsd 83 LGR 130; [1984] ICR 882; [1985] IRLR 24 (HL) ... 2.126

Sulemany v Habib Bank Ltd [1983] ICR 60 (EAT) ... 21.122

Sun Alliance & London Insurance Co v Dudman [1978] ICR 551; [1978] IRLR 169 ... 4.124

Sunley Turriff Holdings Ltd v Thomson [1995] IRLR 184 (EAT) ... 9.11

Superlux v Plaisted [1958] CLY 195; *Times* 12 December (CA) ... 10.65

Susie Radin Ltd v GMB [2003] All ER (D) 192 (Sep) (EAT); aff'd [2004] EWCA Civ 180; [2004] 2 All ER 279; 148 Sol Jo LB 266; [2004] All ER (D) 353 (Feb) ... 18.94

Sutcliffe & Eaton Ltd v Pinney [1977] IRLR 349 (EAT) ... 17.119, 17.147

Sutherland v Hatton [2002] EWCA Civ 76; [2002] 2 All ER 1; [2002] ICR 613; [2002] IRLR 263; 68 BMLR 115; [2002] All ER (D) 53 (Feb); revsd [2004] UKHL 13; [2004] 2 All ER 385; [2004] 1 WLR 1089; 148 Sol Jo LB 419; [2004] All ER (D) 07 (Apr) ... 11.105, 11.107, 11.119

Sutherland v Sonat Offshore (UK) Inc, EAT 186/93 ... 12.22

Sutton & Co Ltd v Davies (unreported) ... 11.17

Sutton and Gates Ltd v Boxall [1979] ICR 67; [1978] IRLR 486 (EAT) ... 17.86

Suzen v Zehnacker Gebaudereinigung GmbH (C-13/95) [1997] ECR I-1259; [1997] All ER (EC) 289; [1997] 1 CMLR 768; [1997] ICR 662; [1997] IRLR 255; [1997] EC 289 (ECJ) ... 9.10

Swainston v Hetton Victory Club Ltd [1983] 1 All ER 1179; [1983] ICR 341; [1983] IRLR 164; (1983) 127 SJ 171 ... 20.5

Sweeney v JS Henderson (Concessionaires) Ltd [1981] ICR 399; [1981] IRLR 76 (EAT) ... 13.5

Sweetin v Coral Racing [2006] IRLR 252 (EAT) ... 9.84

Swithland Motors plc v Clarke [1994] ICR 231; [1994] IRLR 275 ... 4.221

Sybron Corpn v Rochem Ltd [1984] Ch 112; [1983] 2 All ER 707; [1983] 3 WLR 713; [1983] ICR 801; [1983] IRLR 253; [1983] BCLC 43; 127 Sol Jo 391 (CA) ... 10.94

Sycamore v H Myer & Co Ltd [1976] IRLR 84 ... 17.153

Symbian Ltd v Christensen [2001] IRLR 77 (CA) ... 19.11

System Floors (UK) Ltd v Daniel [1982] ICR 54; [1981] IRLR 475 (EAT) ... 3.119, 13.9

T&GWU v Dyer [1977] IRLR 93; 12 ITR 113 (EAT) ... 23.4

T&GWU v Stanhope Engineering IRLR (LIB (121)) ... 23.4

TBA Industrial Products Ltd v Locke [1984] ICR 228; [1984] IRLR 48 (EAT) ... 17.209

TC Harrison (Newcastle-under-Lyme) Ltd v Ramsey [1976] IRLR 135 ... 11.21

TGWU v Brauer Coley [2007] ICR 226; [2007] IRLR 207 ... 18.92

TSB Bank plc v Harris [2000] IRLR 157 (EAT) ... 10.35

TSC Europe UK Ltd v Massey [1999] IRLR 22 ... 19.41

T & K Home Improvements Ltd v Skilton [2000] ICR 1162; [2000] IRLR 595; 645 IRLB 14 (CA) ... 15.24

T Lucas & Co Ltd v Mitchell [1972] 2 All ER 1035; [1972] 1 WLR 938; 116 Sol Jo 506; revsd [1974] Ch 129; [1972] 3 All ER 689; [1972] 3 WLR 934; 116 Sol Jo 711 (CA) ... 19.50

Talbot v Hugh H Fulton Ltd [1975] IRLR 52 ... 3.92

Tanner v DT Kean Ltd [1978] IRLR 110 (EAT) ... 17.17, 17.49, 17.50

Tapere v South London & Maudsley NHS Trust [2009] ICR 1563; [2009] IRLR 972 ... 9.66

Taplin v C Shippam Ltd [1978] ICR 1068 (EAT) ... 21.126

Tarmac Roadstone Holdings Ltd v Peacock [1973] 2 All ER 485; [1973] 1 WLR 594; [1973] ICR 273; [1973] IRLR 157; 14 KIR 277; 8 ITR 300; 117 Sol Jo 186 (CA) ... 14.3

Tasci v Pekalp of London Ltd [2001] ICR 633; [2000] All ER (D) 2157 (CA) ... 11.34

Taylor v Alidair Ltd [1978] ICR 445; [1978] IRLR 82; (1978) 13 ITR 180; (1977) 121 SJ 758 ... 16.13, 17.90

Taylor v Conveyancer Ltd [1972] IRLR 37 ... 18.53

Taylor v East Midlands Offender Employment [2000] IRLR 760 (EAT) ... 3.125

Taylor v Merseyside Electrics 2002 Ltd, EAT/0162/07 ... 17.111

Taylor v National Union of Mineworkers (Derbyshire Area) [1984] IRLR 440 ... 22.37

Taylor v National Union of Seamen [1967] 1 All ER 767; [1967] 1 WLR 532; [1966] 2 Lloyd's Rep 504; 111 Sol Jo 192 ... 22.31

Taylor v OCS Group Ltd [2006] EWCA Civ 702; [2006] ICR 1602; [2006] IRLR 613; (2006) 103(24) LSG 28; (2006) 150 SJLB 810; (2006) *Times* 12 July ... 4.105, 12.35

Taylor v Parsons Peebles Ltd [1981] IRLR 119 (EAT) ... 17.130

Taylor v Rover Co Ltd [1966] 2 All ER 181; [1966] 1 WLR 1491 ... 11.124

Taylor v Triumph Motors Ltd [1975] IRLR
    369 . . . 13.24
Taylor v XLN Telecom Ltd [2010] IRLR 499
    (EAT) . . . 4.230
Taylorplan Catering (Scotland) Ltd v McInally
    [1980] IRLR 53 (EAT) . . . 17.94
Tayside Regional Council v McIntosh (1978)
    76 LGR 408; [1978] ICR 569; [1978] IRLR 69
    (EAT) . . . 3.30, 17.118
Teinaz v London Borough of Wandsworth [2001]
    All ER (D) 497 (Nov) (EAT); aff'd [2002]
    EWCA Civ 1040; [2002] ICR 1471; [2002]
    IRLR 721; [2002] All ER (D) 238 (Jul) . . . 20.85
Tele-Danmark A/S v Handels (HK) per Brandt-
    Nielsen (C-109/00) [2001] ECR I-6993; [2001] All
    ER (EC) 941; [2002] 1 CMLR 105; [2001] IRLR
    853; [2001] All ER (D) 37 (Oct) (ECJ) . . . 6.51
Telephone Information Services Ltd v Wilkinson
    [1991] IRLR 148 (EAT) . . . 20.44
Temco Service Industries SA v Imzilyen (C-
    51/00) [2002] ECR I-969; [2004] 1 CMLR 877;
    [2002] IRLR 214; [2002] All ER (D) 199 (Jan)
    (ECJ) . . . 9.27
Terry v East Sussex County Council [1977] 1 All
    ER 567; 75 LGR 111; [1976] ICR 536; [1976]
    IRLR 332; 12 ITR 265 (EAT) . . . 17.19
Tesco (Holdings) Ltd v Hill [1977] IRLR 63 (EAT)
    . . . 12.3, 12.22
Tesco Stores Ltd v Pook [2004] IRLR 618
    (EAT) . . . 10.67, 10.95
Thames Television v Wallis [1979] IRLR 136
    (EAT) . . . 2.142
Thames Water Utilities v Reynolds [1996] IRLR
    186 (EAT) . . . 8.14
Thamesdown Borough Council v Turrell
    (unreported) . . . 17.189
Thomas and Betts Manufacturing Ltd v Harding
    [1978] IRLR 213 (EAT); aff'd [1980] IRLR 255
    (CA) . . . 18.44
Thomas Marshall (Exports) Ltd v Guinle [1979]
    Ch 227; [1978] 3 All ER 193; [1978] 3 WLR
    116; [1979] FSR 208; [1978] ICR 905; [1978]
    IRLR 174; 122 Sol Jo 295 . . . 15.25, 19.31
Thomas Scott & Sons (Bakers) Ltd v Allen [1983]
    IRLR 329 (CA) . . . 21.71
Thomas v Farr plc [2007] EWCA Civ 118; [2007]
    ICR 932; [2007] IRLR 419; (2007) 151 SJLB
    296 . . . 19.14
Thomas v General Industrial Cleaners Ltd
    (3964/72) IDS Supp 21 . . . 17.11
Thomas v National Union of Mineworkers (South
    Wales Area) [1986] Ch 20; [1985] 2 All ER 1;
    [1985] 2 WLR 1081; [1985] ICR 886; [1985]
    IRLR 136; 129 Sol Jo 416; [1985] LS Gaz R
    1938 . . . 23.111
Thompson v ASDA-MFI Group plc [1988] Ch
    241; [1988] 2 All ER 722; [1988] 2 WLR 1093;
    [1988] IRLR 340; 132 Sol Jo 497; [1988] 15 LS
    Gaz R 34 . . . 9.40
Thompson v Bristol Channel Ship Repairer and
    Engineers Ltd [1969] 1 Lloyd's Rep 407; 6

KIR 510; 4 ITR 262; 113 Sol Jo 382 (DC); aff'd
    [1971] 1 Lloyd's Rep 105; 8 KIR 687; 5 ITR 85;
    114 Sol Jo 167 (CA) . . . 13.22
Thompson v Tech Communications Ltd
    (unreported) . . . 8.14
Thomson v Alloa Motor Co Ltd [1983] IRLR 403
    (EAT) . . . 17.136
Thorn v Meggitt Engineering Ltd [1976] IRLR
    241 . . . 4.178
Throsby v Imperial College of Science and
    Technology [1978] QB 438; [1978] 2 All ER
    465; [1978] 2 WLR 50; [1978] ICR 357; 13
    ITR 169; 121 Sol Jo 632 (EAT); aff'd sub nom
    Dixon v BBC [1979] QB 546; [1979] 2 All ER
    112; [1979] 2 WLR 647; [1979] ICR 281; [1979]
    IRLR 114; 122 Sol Jo 713 (CA) . . . 2.30
Tice v Cartwright [1999] ICR 769 (EAT) . . . 2.7
Tiffin v Lester Aldridge LLP [2012] EWCA Civ
    35 . . . 2.17
Timeplan Education Group Ltd v National Union
    of Teachers [1997] IRLR 457 (CA) . . . 23.22
Times Newspapers v O'Reagan [1973] 3 All ER
    618; [1973] ICR 511; [1973] IRLR 233; 16 KIR
    67; [1973] ITR 539 . . . 20.7
Tirkey v Chandok, unreported, case number
    3400174/2013 . . . 4.141
Tithebarn Ltd v Hubbard, EAT 532/89 . . . 19.6
Toal v GB Oils Ltd UKEAT/0569/12/LA . . .
    12.23
Todd v British Midlands Airways Ltd [1978] ICR
    959 . . . 1.32
Tolson v Mixenden Community School [2003]
    IRLR 842; [2003] All ER (D) 312 (Oct)
    (EAT) . . . 17.48
Tom Findlay & Co Ltd v Devlin (EAT (Scotland)
    9 November 2007) . . . 15.9, 17.54
Tomlinson v Dick Evans U Drive Ltd [1978] ICR
    639; [1978] IRLR 77 (EAT) . . . 3.8, 14.4
Tomlinson v London, Midland and Scottish Rly
    Co [1944] 1 All ER 537 (CA) . . . 12.61
Torquay Hotel Co Ltd v Cousins [1969] 2 Ch
    106; [1968] 3 All ER 43; [1968] 3 WLR 540; 4
    KIR 635; 112 Sol Jo 688; aff'd [1969] 2 Ch 106;
    [1969] 1 All ER 522; [1969] 2 WLR 289; 6 KIR
    15; 113 Sol Jo 52 (CA) . . . 23.20
Tottenham Green Under Fives' Centre v Marshall
    [1991] ICR 320 . . . 4.153
Tower Hamlets Health Authority v Anthony
    [1989] ICR 656; [1989] IRLR 394 (CA) . . . 12.79
Tower Hamlets London Borough v Bull [2001]
    All ER (D) 209 (May) (EAT) . . . 17.102
Tower Hamlets v Balgobin [1987] ICR 829; [1987]
    IRLR 401; (1987) 84 LSG 2530 . . . 4.198
Tracey v Crosville Wales Ltd . . . 21.110
Tradition Securities SA v Fariad [2009] IRLR 354
    . . . 20.57
Transco plc v O'Brien [2001] IRLR; [2001] All ER
    (D) 169 (May) (EAT); aff'd sub nom O'Brien v
    Transco plc (formerly BG plc) [2002] EWCA
    Civ 379; [2002] ICR 721; [2002] IRLR 444;
    [2002] All ER (D) 80 (Mar) . . . 3.49, 10.10

Transport and General Workers' Union v Howard [1992] ICR 106; [1992] IRLR 170 (EAT) . . . 17.231

Transport and General Workers' Union v Ledbury Preserves (1928) Ltd [1986] ICR 855; [1986] IRLR 492 (EAT) . . . 18.79

Transport and General Workers' Union v Webber [1990] ICR 711; [1990] IRLR 462; [1990] 27 LS Gaz R 40 (EAT) . . . 21.10

Treganowan v Robert Knee & Co Ltd [1975] IRLR 112; aff'd [1975] ICR 405; [1975] IRLR 247; 10 ITR 121; 119 Sol Jo 490 . . . 16.3

Trimble v Supertravel Ltd [1982] ICR 440; [1982] IRLR 451 (EAT) . . . 20.104

Trotter v Grattan plc, IDS Brief 757 18 . . . 3.94

Troutbeck SA v White [2013] EWCA Civ 1171; [2013] IRLR 286 . . . 2.37

Trusthouse Forte Hotels Ltd v Murphy [1977] IRLR 186 (EAT) . . . 17.125

Tsangacos v Amalgamated Chemicals Ltd [1997] ICR 154; [1997] IRLR 4 (CA) . . . 9.33

Tsoukka v Potomac Restaurants Ltd (1968) 3 ITR 259 . . . 14.4

Tullett Prebon Group Ltd v Ghaleb El-Hajjali [2008] EWHC 1924 (QB); [2008] IRLR 760 . . . 3.6, 10.52, 15.33

Tullett Prebon v BGC Brokers [2011] EWCA 131 . . . 10.55

Turner v Commonwealth and British Minerals Ltd [2000] IRLR 114; [1999] All ER (D) 1097 (CA) . . . 19.27, 19.51

Turner v Goldsmith [1891] 1 QB 544; 60 LJQB 247; 39 WR 547; [1891-4] All ER Rep 384; 64 LT 301; 7 TLR 233 (CA) . . . 10.17

Turner v Pleasurama Casinos Ltd [1976] IRLR 151 . . . 12.52

Turner v Vesteric Ltd [1980] ICR 528; [1981] IRLR 23 (EAT) . . . 17.160

Tynan v Balmer [1967] 1 QB 91; [1966] 2 All ER 133; [1966] 2 WLR 1181; 110 Sol Jo 129 (DC) . . . 23.109

Tyne and Clyde Warehouses Ltd v Hamerton [1978] ICR 661; 13 ITR 66 (EAT) . . . 2.51, 2.54

UBAF Bank Ltd v Davis [1978] IRLR 442 (EAT) . . . 17.205

UBS Wealth Management (UK) Ltd v Vestra Wealth LLP [2008] EWHC 1974 (QB); [2008] IRLR 965; (2008) 105(37) LSG 21 . . . 19.23, 19.24

UCATT v Glasgow City Council [2009] IRLR 253 . . . 9.79

UK Coal Mining Ltd v National Union of Mineworkers [2008] ICR 163; [2008] IRLR 4; (2007) 151 SJLB 1400; (2007) Times 23 November . . . 18.82

UNISON v Westminster County Council [2001] EWCA Civ 443; [2001] LGR 378; [2001] ICR 1046; [2001] IRLR 524; [2001] 20 LS Gaz R 41; [2001] All ER (D) 250 (Mar) . . . 23.30

USA v Nolan [2010] EWCA Civ 1223 . . . 18.74

USDAW v Sketchley Ltd [1981] ICR 644; [1981] IRLR 291 (EAT) . . . 23.4

USDAW v UNITE the Union, UKEAT/0547/12/ KN UKEAT/0548/12 . . . 18.77

Ulsterbus Ltd v Henderson [1989] IRLR 251 (NICA) . . . 12.10

Unicorn Consultancy Services Ltd v Westbrook [2000] IRLR 80 (EAT) . . . 9.40

Union Cartage Co Ltd v Blunden [1977] ICR 420; [1977] IRLR 139 . . . 20.7

Union of Shop, Distributive and Allied Workers v Leancut Bacon Ltd [1981] IRLR 295 (EAT) . . . 18.88

Union Traffic Ltd v Transport and General Workers' Union [1989] ICR 98; [1989] IRLR 127 (CA) . . . 23.107

United Arab Emirates v Abdelghafar [1995] ICR 65; [1995] IRLR 243 . . . 20.119

United Bank Ltd v Akhtar [1989] IRLR 503 (EAT) . . . 3.2, 3.24, 17.29, 17.37

United Distillers v Conlin [1992] IRLR 503 (EAT); Conlin v United Distillers [1994] IRLR 169 (Ct of Sess) . . . 20.124

United Kingdom Atomic Energy Authority v Claydon [1974] ICR 128; [1974] IRLR 6 (NIRC) . . . 10.58, 18.14

United Kingdom v EU Council (C-84/94) [1996] ECR I-05755 . . . 1.85

United States of America v Nolan [2010] EWCA Civ 1223; [2011] IRLR 40 . . . 18.74

United Sterling Corpn v Felton [1973] FSR 409; [1974] IRLR 314; [1974] RPC 162 . . . 19.21

Universe Tankships v ITWF [1981] ICR 129; [1980] IRLR 239; varied [1980] 2 Lloyd's Rep 523; [1981] ICR 129; [1980] IRLR 363 CA; on appeal [1983] 1 AC 366; [1982] 2 All ER 67; [1982] 2 WLR 803; [1982] 1 Lloyd's Rep 537; [1982] ICR 262; [1982] IRLR 200; 126 Sol Jo 225 (HL) . . . 3.19, 23.100

University of Aston in Birmingham v Malik [1984] ICR 492; [1984] LS Gaz R 1438 (EAT) . . . 13.19

University College London Hospitals NHS Trust v UNISON [1999] ICR 204; [1999] IRLR 31; [1998] 41 LS Gaz R 45; 142 Sol Jo LB 270; [1998] All ER (D) 450 (CA) . . . 23.34

University of Nottingham v Eyett [1999] 2 All ER 437; [1999] 1 WLR 594; [1999] ICR 721; [1999] IRLR 87; [1999] ELR 141; [1999] 01 LS Gaz R 24; [1998] All ER (D) 584 . . . 10.15

University of Oxford v Humphreys [2000] 1 All ER 996; [2000] 1 CMLR 647; [2000] IRLR 183 (CA) . . . 9.65

University of Swansea v Cornelius [1988] ICR 735 (EAT) . . . 1.25

Unkles v Milanda Bread Co Ltd [1973] IRLR 76 . . . 12.64

Utopia (UK) Ltd v Wright [2007] EWHC 321 (QB) . . . 19.24

Vakante v Governing Body of Addey and Stanhope School [2004] ICR 279; [2003] All ER (D) 352 (Dec) (EAT) . . . 3.11

Van Duyn v Home Office (No 2) (C-41/74) [1975] Ch 358; [1975] 3 All ER 190; 2 WLR 760; [1974] ECR 1337; [1975] 1 CMLR 1; 119 Sol Jo 302 (ECJ) . . . 1.72

Vaughan v Weighpack Ltd [1974] ICR 261; [1974] IRLR 105; 16 KIR 233; 9 ITR 226 (NIRC) . . . 17.209

Veakins v Kier Islington Ltd [2009] EWCA Civ 1288; [2010] IRLR 132; (2010) Times 13 January . . . 10.112

Vento v Chief Constable of West Yorkshire Police (No 2) [2002] EWCA Civ 1871; [2003] ICR 318; [2003] IRLR 102; [2003] Po LR 171; (2003) 100(10) LSG 28; (2003) 147 SJLB 181; (2002) Times 27 December . . . 4.230

Vernon v Event Management Catering Ltd 2007, IDS Brief No 835 . . . 13.14

Vestergaard Frandsen v Bestnet Europe Ltd [2013] UKSC 31 . . . 10.71

Viasystems (Tyneside) Ltd v Thermal Transfers (Northern) Ltd [2005] EWCA Civ 1151 . . . 2.147

Vinnyey v Star Paper Mills [1965] 1 All ER 175 . . . 11.109, 11.128

Virdee v EEC Quarries Ltd [1978] IRLR 295 . . . 4.224

Visa International Services Association v Paul [2004] IRLR 42 . . . 6.46

Vokes Ltd v Bear [1974] ICR 1; [1973] IRLR 363; 15 KIR 302; 9 ITR 85 (NIRC) . . . 18.44

WA Goold (Pearmak) Ltd v McConnell [1995] IRLR 516 (EAT) . . . 3.51

WE Cox Toner (International) Ltd v Crook [1981] ICR 823; [1981] IRLR 443 (EAT) . . . 17.42

WHPT Housing Association Ltd v Secretary of State for Social Services [1981] ICR 737 . . . 2.54

WRN Ltd v Ayris [2008] EWHC 1080 (QB); [2008] IRLR 889; (2008) 152(23) SJLB 29 . . . 19.33

W Devis & Sons Ltd v Atkins [1976] 2 All ER 822; [1976] 1 WLR 393; [1976] ICR 196; [1976] IRLR 16; 11 ITR 15; 120 Sol Jo 62; on appeal [1977] AC 931; [1977] 2 All ER 321; [1977] 2 WLR 70; [1977] ICR 377; [1976] IRLR 428; 12 ITR 12; 121 Sol Jo 52 (CA); aff'd [1977] AC 931; [1977] 3 All ER 40; [1977] 3 WLR 214; 8 BLR 57; [1977] ICR 662; [1977] IRLR 314; 13 ITR 71; 121 Sol Jo 512 (HL) . . . 17.202, 17.219, 20.84

Wadcock v London Borough of Brent [1990] IRLR 223 . . . 10.2, 16.30

Waddington v Leicester Council for Voluntary Services [1977] 1 WLR 544; [1977] ICR 266; [1977] IRLR 32; (1976) 12 ITR 65; (1977) 121 SJ 84 . . . 5.45

Wadham Stringer Commercials (London) Ltd v Brown [1983] IRLR 46 (EAT) . . . 17.23

Wadley v Eager Electrical Ltd [1986] IRLR 93 (EAT) . . . 17.162

Wailes Dove Bitumastic v Woolcocks [1977] ICR 817; 12 ITR 420 (EAT) . . . 18.55

Wakeman v Quick Corpn [1999] IRLR 424 . . . 4.29, 4.150

Walker v Cotswold Chine Home School (1977) 12 ITR 342 (EAT) . . . 15.9

Walker v Josiah Wedgwood [1978] ICR 744; [1978] IRLR 105; 13 ITR 271 (EAT) . . . 17.27

Walker v Northumberland County Council [1995] 1 All ER 737; [1995] ICR 702; [1995] IRLR 35; [1995] ELR 231; [1994] NLJR 1659 . . . 11.120

Walker v Sita Information Networking Computing Ltd UKEAT/0097/12 . . . 4.94

Wallace Bogan & Co v Cove [1997] IRLR 453 (CA) . . . 19.21

Wallace v C A Roofing Services Ltd [1996] IRLR 435 . . . 2.103, 2.127

Walls Meat Co Ltd v Selby [1989] ICR 601 (CA) . . . 18.45

Walls Meat Co v Khan [1978] IRLR 499; [1979] ICR 52 . . . 20.5

Walmsley v UDEC Refrigeration Ltd [1972] IRLR 80 . . . 10.59

Walters v British Steel Corpn, IDS Brief 150 . . . 7.16

Walton Centre for Neurology NHS Trust v Bewley [2008] ICR 1047; [2008] IRLR 588; (2008) 152(23) SJLB 30 . . . 5.10, 5.12

Walton v Independent Living Organisation [2002] ICR 1406; [2002] All ER (D) 241 (Apr) (EAT); aff'd [2003] EWCA Civ 199; [2003] ICR 688; [2003] IRLR 469; 147 Sol Jo LB 266; [2003] All ER (D) 373 (Feb) . . . 8.44

Walton v TAC Construction Materials Ltd [1981] IRLR 357 (EAT) . . . 17.138

Waltons & Morse v Dorrington [1997] IRLR 488 (EAT) . . . 17.28

Wandsworth London Borough Council v D'Silva [1998] IRLR 193 (CA) . . . 3.21, 3.89

Wandsworth London Borough Council v National Association of Schoolmasters Union of Women Teachers 92 LGR 91; [1994] ICR 81; [1993] IRLR 344; [1994] ELR 170; [1993] NLJR 655n (CA) . . . 23.32

Wang v University of Keele [2011] IRLR 542 (EAT) . . . 15.28

Ward Evans Financial Services Ltd v Fox [2001] EWCA Civ 1243; [2002] IRLR 120; [2001] All ER (D) 415 (Jul) . . . 10.54

Ward v Bradford Corpn (1971) 70 LGR 27; 115 Sol Jo 606 (CA) . . . 12.36

Wardle v Credit Agricole Corporate and Investment Bank (Calyon) [2011] IRLR 604; [2011] EWCA Civ 545 . . . 17.211

Warner Bros Pictures Inc v Nelson [1937] 1 KB 209; [1936] 3 All ER 160; 106 LJKB 97; 80 Sol Jo 855; 155 LT 538; 53 TLR 14 . . . 10.1

Warner v Barbers Stores [1978] IRLR 109 (EAT) . . . 3.43

Washington Arts Association Ltd v Forster [1983] ICR 346 (EAT) ... 2.7

Waters v Metropolitan Police Comr [1995] ICR 510; [1995] IRLR 531 (EAT); aff'd [1997] ICR 1073; [1997] IRLR 589 CA; revsd [2004] 4 All ER 934; [2000] 1 WLR 1607; [2000] ICR 1064 (HL) ... 2.74

Watling & Co v Richardson [1978] ICR 1049; [1978] IRLR 255; (1979) 13 ITR 333 ... 18.51

Watson v University of Strathclyde [2011] IRLR 458 ... 12.19

Weakley v Amalgamated Union of Engineering Workers (1975) 125 NLJ 621 ... 22.36

Weathersfield Ltd v Sargent [1999] ICR 425; [1999] IRLR 94; [1999] Disc LR 290; (1999) 96(5) LSG 35; (1999) 143 SJLB 39; (1998) Times 31 December ... 4.201

Webb v Anglian Water Authority [1981] ICR 811; 125 Sol Jo 693; [1981] IRLR 494 (EAT) ... 20.126

Weight Watchers (UK) Ltd v HMRC (2011) FTC/57-59/2010 [2011] BTC 1895 ... 2.44

Wells v West Ltd [1979] IRLR 269 ... 12.81

Welton v Deluxe Retail (t/a Madhouse) UKEAT/0266/12/ZT ... 13.23

Werhof v Freeway Traffic Systems GmbH (C-499/04) [2006] ECR I-2397; [2006] 2 CMLR 44; [2006] CEC 653; [2006] IRLR 400 (ECJ) ... 9.73

Wessex Dairies v Smith [1935] 2 KB 80; 104 LJKB 484; [1935] All ER Rep 75; 153 LT 185; 51 TLR 439 (CA) ... 10.93

Wessex National Ltd v Long (1978) 13 ITR 413 (EAT) ... 13.22

West Kent College v Richardson [1999] ICR 511 (EAT) ... 17.80

West Midland Co-operative Society v Tipton [1986] AC 536; [1986] 1 All ER 513; [1986] 2 WLR 306; [1986] ICR 192; [1986] IRLR 112; 130 Sol Jo 143; [1986] LS Gaz R 780; [1986] NLJ Rep 163 (HL) ... 12.34

West Midlands Passenger Transport Executive v Singh [1988] 1 WLR 730; [1988] 2 All ER 873; [1988] ICR 614; [1988] IRLR 186; (1988) 132 SJ 933 ... 4.225

West Midlands Travel Ltd v Transport and General Workers' Union [1994] ICR 978; [1994] IRLR 578 (CA) ... 23.57

West v Kneels Ltd [1987] ICR 146; [1986] IRLR 430; [1986] LS Gaz R 2488 (EAT) ... 15.7, 17.4, 20.29

West v Secretary of State for Scotland [1992] IRLR 399; 1992 SC 385; 1992 SLT 636; 1992 SCLR 504 (Ct of Sess) ... 16.37

Western Excavating (ECC) Ltd v Sharp [1978] QB 761; [1978] 1 All ER 713; [1978] 2 WLR 344; [1978] ICR 221; [1978] IRLR 27; 121 Sol Jo 814 (CA) ... 17.22, 17.22, 17.32, 17.37

Westminster City Council v Cabaj [1996] ICR 960; [1996] IRLR 399 (CA) ... 12.19

Westminster City Council v Select Managements Ltd [1985] 1 All ER 897; [1985] 1 WLR 576; 83 LGR 409; [1985] ICR 353; 129 Sol Jo 221; [1985] 1 EGLR 245; [1985] LS Gaz R 1091, sub nom Select Managements Ltd v Westminster City Council [1985] IRLR 344 (CA) ... 11.50

Weston v University College Swansea [1975] IRLR 102; 10 ITR 60 ... 2.97

Westwood v Secretary of State for Employment [1982] ICR 534; [1982] IRLREAT; aff'd [1985] AC 20; [1983] 3 WLR 730; [1983] ICR 820; [1983] IRLR 419; 127 Sol Jo 731 (CA); revsd [1985] AC 20; [1984] 1 All ER 874; [1984] 2 WLR 418; [1985] ICR 209; [1984] IRLR 209; 128 Sol Jo 221; [1984] LS Gaz R 1443 (HL) ... 7.134, 15.30, 15.38

Wheeler v Patel [1987] ICR 631; [1987] IRLR 211; [1987] LS Gaz R 1240 (EAT) ... 9.57

Whelan v Richardson ... 17.207, 17.211

Whiffen v Milham Ford Girls' School [2001] EWCA Civ 385; [2001] LGR 309; [2001] ICR 1023; [2001] IRLR 468; [2001] All ER (D) 256 (Mar) ... 18.42

Whitaker v Milk Marketing Board [1973] IRLR 100 ... 17.74

Whitbread plc v Mills [1988] ICR 776; [1988] IRLR 501 (EAT) ... 12.35

Whitbread plc v Rees, EAT/1292-1293/97 ... 20.8

White v Chief Constable of South Yorkshire Police [1999] IRLR 110 ... 11.104

White v Holbrook Precision Castings Ltd [1985] IRLR 215 (CA) ... 11.118

White v Kuzych [1951] AC 585; [1951] 2 All ER 435; 95 Sol Jo 527; [1951] 2 TLR 277 (PC) ... 21.20

White v Pressed Steel Fisher [1980] IRLR 176 (EAT) ... 11.41

White v Reflecting Roadstuds Ltd [1991] ICR 733; [1991] IRLR 331 (EAT) ... 3.24, 17.37

White v University of Manchester [1976] ICR 419; [1976] IRLR 218; 11 ITR 143; 120 Sol Jo 503 (EAT) ... 20.63

Whitehouse v Charles Blatchford & Sons Ltd [1999] IRLR 492; [1999] All ER (D) 414 (CA) ... 9.57

Whitely v Marton Electrical Ltd [2003] ICR 495; [2003] IRLR 492; [1999] All ER (D) 370 (Nov) (EAT) ... 2.104

Whitlow v Alkanet Construction Ltd [1975] IRLR 321 ... 17.145

Whittaker v Minister of Pensions and National Insurance [1967] 1 QB 156; [1966] 3 All ER 631; [1966] 3 WLR 1090; 110 Sol Jo 924 ... 2.37, 2.39

Whittlestone v BJP Home Support Limited UKEAT/0128/13/BA ... 8.44

Whitwood Chemical Co v Hardman [1891] 2 Ch 416; 60 LJ ch 428; 39 WR 433; 64 LT 716; 7 TLR 325 (CA) ... 10.1

Wicks v Charles A Smethurst Ltd [1973] IRLR 327 . . . 10.59

Widdicombe v Longcombe Software Ltd [1998] ICR 710 (EAT) . . . 17.5

Wigan Borough Council v Davies [1979] ICR 411; [1979] IRLR 127 . . . 10.117

Wignall v British Gas Corpn [1984] ICR 716; [1984] IRLR 493 (EAT) . . . 21.73

Wilcox v HGS [1975] ICR 333, sub nom Wilcox v Humphreys and Glasgow Ltd [1975] IRLR 211; [1975] ITR 103; aff'd sub nom Wilcox v HGS [1976] ICR 306; [1976] IRLR 222; 11 ITR 43 (CA) . . . 17.138

Wilding v British Telecommunications plc [2001] All ER (D) 03 (Apr) (EAT); aff'd [2002] EWCA Civ 349; [2002] ICR 1079; [2002] IRLR 524; [2002] All ER (D) 278 (Mar) . . . 17.227

Wileman v Minilec Engineering Ltd [1988] ICR 318; [1988] IRLR 144 (EAT) . . . 4.36

Wilkes v Fortes (Sussex) Ltd, IRRR (EAT) . . . 17.112

Willcox v Hastings [1987] IRLR 298 (CA) . . . 18.23

Willerby Holiday Homes Ltd v Union of Construction Allied Trades and Technicians [2003] EWHC 2608 (QB); [2003] All ER (D) 93 (Nov) . . . 23.87

William Hill Organisation Ltd v Tucker [1999] ICR 291; [1998] IRLR 313; [1998] 20 LS Gaz R 33; 142 Sol Jo LB 140 (CA) . . . 10.17, 19.10

William Muir (Bond 9) Ltd v Lamb [1985] IRLR 95 (EAT) . . . 12.22, 17.224

Williams v British Airways plc (C-155/10) (ECJ) . . . 7.73

Williams v Compair Maxam Ltd [1982] ICR 156; [1982] IRLR 83 (EAT) . . . 18.40, 18.41

Williams v University of Nottingham [2007] IRLR 660 . . . 1.36

Williams v Watsons Luxury Coaches Ltd [1990] ICR 536; [1990] IRLR 164 (EAT) . . . 17.62, 17.63

Willow Oak Developments Ltd v Silverwood [2006] ICR 55; [2006] IRLR 28 (EAT); aff'd [2006] EWCA Civ 660; [2006] ICR 1552; [2006] IRLR 607; (2006) 103(23) LSG 29 (CA) . . . 19.59

Willy Scheidegger Swiss Typewriting School (London) Ltd v Minister of Social Security (1968) 5 KIR 65 . . . 2.54

Wilson v Health and Safety Executive [2009] EWCA Civ 1074; [2010] 1 CMLR 24; [2010] ICR 302; [2010] IRLR 59; (2009) 153(40) SJLB 36; (2009) Times 26 October . . . 5.44

Wilson v IDR Construction Ltd [1975] IRLR 260 . . . 10.63

Wilson v Racher [1974] ICR 428; [1974] IRLR 114; 16 KIR 212 (CA) . . . 16.9, 16.10

Wilson v St Helens BC [1996] ICR 711; [1996] IRLR 320; [1996] IRLR 541 (EAT); revsd [1997] 3 CMLR 1267; [1998] ICR 387; [1997] IRLR 505; [1997] 33 LS Gaz R 26; [1997] NLJR 1150 575 IRLB 12 (CA); revsd [1999] 2 AC 52; [1998] 4 All ER 609; [1998] 3 WLR 1070; [1999] 1 CMLR 918; [1999] LGR 255; [1998] ICR 1141; [1998] IRLR 706; [1998] All ER (D) 516 (HL) . . . 9.46, 9.60

Wilson v TB Steelworks, IDS Brief 150 . . . 4.143

Wilson v Underhill House School Ltd [1977] IRLR 475; 12 ITR 165 (EAT) . . . 17.149

Wilson v United Kingdom (Applications 30668/96, 30679/96 and 30678/96) [2002] IRLR 568; 13 BHRC 39; [2002] All ER (D) 35 (Jul) (ECtHR) . . . 1.107, 21.49

Wilsons & Clyde Coal Co Ltd v English [1938] AC 57; [1937] 3 All ER 628; 106 LJPC 117; 81 Sol Jo 700; 157 LT 406; 53 TLR 944 (HL) . . . 11.115

Wilton Ltd v Peebles (unreported) . . . 3.67

Wiltshire County Council v National Association of Teachers in Further and Higher Education and Guy (1978) 77 LGR 272; [1978] ICR 968; [1978] IRLR 301; 13 ITR 437; 122 Sol Jo 626 (EAT); aff'd 78 LGR 445; [1980] ICR 455; [1980] IRLR 198 (CA) . . . 2.127

Wiltshire Police Authority v Wynn [1981] QB 95; [1980] 3 WLR 445; LGR 591; [1980] ICR 649; 124 Sol Jo 463 . . . 2.73, 2.75, 2.99

Wiluszynski v London Borough of Tower Hamlets [1988] IRLR 154; on appeal 88 LGR 14; [1989] ICR 493; [1989] IRLR 259; 133 Sol Jo 628 (CA) . . . 8.23, 10.51

Wincanton Ltd v Cranny [2000] IRLR 716 (CA) . . . 19.48

Winterhalter Gastronom Ltd v Webb [1973] ICR 245; [1973] IRLR 120; 8 ITR 313 (NIRC) . . . 17.89

Wishart v National Association of Citizens' Advice Bureaux Ltd [1990] ICR 794; [1990] IRLR 393 (CA) . . . 3.3

Wishaw & District Housing Association v Moncrieff UKEATS/0066/08 . . . 17.45

Withers v Flackwell Health Football Supporters' Club [1981] IRLR 307 (EAT) . . . 2.50

Withers v General Theatre Corpn [1933] 2 KB 536; 102 LJKB 719; [1933] All ER Rep 385; 149 LT 487 (CA) . . . 16.21

Withers v Perry Chain Co Ltd [1961] 3 All ER 676; [1961] 1 WLR 1314; 59 LGR 496; 105 Sol Jo 648 (CA) . . . 11.109, 11.119

Witley and District Men's Club v MacKay [2001] IRLR 595; [2001] All ER (D) 31 (Jun) (EAT) . . . 7.79

Wolf v Stadt Frankfurt am Main [2010] IRLR 244 . . . 4.63

Wolstenholme v Refreshment Systems Ltd (t/a Northern Vending Services) [2004] All ER (D) 185 (Mar) (EAT) . . . 1.21

Wood Group Heavy Industrial Turbines Ltd v Crossan [1998] IRLR 680 (EAT) . . . 17.189

Wood v Coverage Care Ltd [1996] IRLR 264 (EAT) . . . 4.247

Wood v Cunard Line Ltd [1989] ICR 398; [1989] IRLR 431; [1989] LS Gaz R 42 (EAT); aff'd [1991] ICR 13; [1990] IRLR 281 (CA) . . . 17.4

Wood v William Ball Ltd [2000] ICR 277; [1999] IRLR 773 . . . 5.37

Wood v York City Council [1978] ICR 840; [1978] IRLR 228; 122 Sol Jo 192 (CA) . . . 13.1, 13.8

Woodcock v Cumbria Primary Care Trust [2012] EWCA Civ 330 . . . 4.67

Woodhouse v West North West Homes Leeds Limited UKEAT/0007/12 . . . 4.43

Woods v W M Car Services (Peterborough) Ltd [1981] ICR 666; [1981] IRLR 347 (EAT); aff'd [1982] ICR 693; [1982] IRLR 413; [1982] Com LR 208 (CA) . . . 17.47

Woodward v Abbey National [2005] ICR 1750 (EAT); rev [2006] EWCA Civ 822; [2006] 4 All ER 1209; [2006] ICR 1436; [2006] IRLR 677; (2006) 103(27) LSG 31; (2006) 150 SJLB 857 . . . 7.139

Working Links v Public and Commercial Services Union UKEAT/0305/12/RN . . . 23.4

Worringham v Lloyds Bank [1982] 1 WLR 841; [1982] 3 All ER 373; [1982] ICR 299; [1982] IRLR 74; (1982) 126 SJ 99; (1981) *Times* 18 December . . . 5.2, 5.17

Wrexham GC v Ingham UKEAT/0190/12/RN . . . 18.51

Wright v Dunlop Rubber Co (1971) 11 KIR 311; 115 Sol Jo 366 . . . 11.110

Wynnwith Engineering Co Ltd v Bennett [2002] IRLR 170 (EAT) . . . 9.9

X v EC Commission [1995] IRLR 320 . . . 4.105

X v Metropolitan Police Comr [2003] ICR 1031; [2003] IRLR 411; [2003] NLJR 719 (EAT) . . . 20.57

X v Mid-Sussex CAB [2012] UKSC 59 . . . 4.191

X v Y [2004] EWCA Civ 662; [2004] ICR 1634 (CA) . . . 1.107

XXX v YYY [2004] EWCA Civ 231; [2004] IRLR 137; [2004] All ER (D) 144 (Feb) . . . 20.74

Yeboah v Crofton [2002] EWCA Civ 794; [2002] IRLR 634; [2002] All ER (D) 512 (May) . . . 20.123

Yemm v British Steel plc [1994] IRLR 117 (EAT) . . . 8.14

Yetton v Eastwoods Froy Ltd [1966] 3 All ER 353; [1967] 1 WLR 104; 111 Sol Jo 32 . . . 16.26

Yewens v Noakes (1880) 6 QBD 530; 1 TC 260; 45 JP 8, 468; 50 LJQB 132; 28 WR 562; 44 LT 128 (CA) . . . 2.37

Yorkshire Blood Transfusions Service v Plaskitt [1994] ICR 74; (1993) *Times* 17 August . . . 5.45

Yorkshire Traction Co Ltd v Searby [2003] EWCA Civ 1856; 148 Sol Jo LB 61; [2003] All ER (D) 409 (Dec) . . . 11.150

Young & Woods Ltd v West [1980] IRLR 201 (CA) . . . 2.54

Young, James and Webster v United Kingdom (Applications 7601/76 and 7806/77) 4 EHRR 38; [1981] IRLR 408 (ECtHR) . . . 1.107

Young v Daniel Thwaites & Co Ltd [1977] ICR 877; 12 ITR 392 (EAT) . . . 9.25

Young's of Gosport Ltd v Kendell [1977] ICR 907; [1977] IRLR 433; 12 ITR 269 (EAT) . . . 17.212

Zarb and Samuels v British and Brazilian Produce Co (Sales) Ltd [1978] IRLR 78 (EAT) . . . 2.7

Zarczynska v Levy [1979] 1 WLR 125; [1979] 1 All ER 814; [1979] ICR 184; [1978] IRLR 532; (1978) 122 SJ 776 . . . 4.143

Zarkasi v Anindita [2011] UKEAT/0400 . . . 3.8

Zentralbetriebsrat der Landeskrankenhaüser Tirols (C-486/08) [2010] IRLR 631 . . . 7.76

1

The Institutions of Employment Law

Advisory, Conciliation and Arbitration Service

1.1 The Advisory, Conciliation and Arbitration Service (ACAS) was placed on a statutory basis by the Employment Protection Act 1975 and continued by virtue of the Trade Union and Labour Relations (Consolidation) Act 1992 (TULR(C)A, s 247). It is charged with the general duty of promoting the improvement of industrial relations. Its work is directed by a Council, which consists of a chairman and up to nine other members appointed by the Secretary of State. Three of these are to be appointed after consultations with employers' organisations, three after consultation with workers' organisations, and three 'neutral' (usually academic) appointments are usually made. Additionally up to three deputy chairmen may be appointed. The Secretary of State may appoint two further members of the Council, after consultation with both sides of industry. Currently, the Council has 12 members. The appointments will be initially for a period of five years, and may be renewed for a further period (TULR(C)A, s 248).

1.2 ACAS will appoint its own staff, including a secretary, and will also provide staff for the Certification Officer and the Central Arbitration Committee. Although it will perform its functions on behalf of the Crown, it shall not be subject to any directions from any minister as to the manner in which it is to exercise any of those functions. It is this complete independence from government control which is a distinguishing feature of ACAS. It will make an annual report on its activities and those of the Central Arbitration Committee to the Secretary of State, which will be laid before Parliament and published.

Whenever it thinks appropriate to do so, ACAS may charge a fee for its services, and also the Secretary of State may direct ACAS to charge fees, either at a full economic cost or a specified proportion or percentage of the economic cost. However, ACAS must notify the person concerned that a fee may or will be charged (TULR(C)A, s 251A).

1.3 The function of ACAS can be examined under the following headings:

A. **Advice**

1.4 ACAS may, on request or otherwise, give employers, employers' associations, workers and trade unions such advice as it thinks appropriate on matters connected with or likely to affect industrial relations. General advice on this topic may also be published (TULR(C)A, s 213). ACAS has produced a number of Advisory Booklets and Advice Leaflets on a wide range of topics with the aim of giving advice to employers and employees about employment rights generally.

B. **Conciliation**

1.5 Where a trade dispute exists or is apprehended, ACAS may offer its assistance to the parties, either on its own volition or at the request of any party, with a view to bringing about a settlement. This may be achieved by conciliation or other means, and by the appointment, if necessary, of someone outside ACAS whose assistance may be used. Due regard will be had to the desirability of encouraging the parties to use any appropriate agreed procedures (TULR(C)A, s 210).

If there is a dispute over union recognition, ACAS may be invited to use its conciliation role. At the request of both parties, it may hold a ballot of workers involved in the dispute, and/or ascertain the strength of union membership of such workers. However, any such request may be withdrawn by either side, whereupon ACAS shall cease to take any further steps in the matter (TULR(C)A, s 210A).

1.6 It should be noted that for conciliation purposes, the definition of 'trade dispute' is the old definition (based on the Employment Protection Act 1975), now contained in TULR(C)A, s 218, not the more restricted definition (based on the Trade Union and Labour Relations Act 1974) now contained in TULR(C)A, s 244. The effect is to give ACAS a wider conciliation brief.

1.7 Conciliation officers will also be appointed for the purpose of settling by conciliation certain matters which are, or could be, the subject of proceedings before an employment tribunal under any legislation, whenever passed (TULR(C)A, s 211), provided the relevant legislation so indicates (see Employment Tribunals Act 1996, s 18).

1.8 The Enterprise and Regulatory Reform Act (ERRA) 2013, ss 7–9 introduced a further type of individual pre-trial conciliation scheme from April 2014, by inserting ss 18A and 18B to the Employment Tribunals Act 1996. The aim of this 'Early Conciliation' scheme is to reduce the number of employment tribunal cases, and extending the former pre-claim conciliation system, which was very successful.

A person who wants to make an employment tribunal claim is therefore obliged to contact ACAS first, by submitting an 'Early Conciliation' form giving basic details. ACAS will then contact the claimant to obtain further details and offer conciliation. If this is accepted, then ACAS will take steps to resolve the matter within one month. If the matter is not resolved, or the parties refuse conciliation, then ACAS will issue a certificate to the claimant. The claimant will not be permitted to make a claim to the tribunal without this.

Submission of the Early Conciliation form will 'stop the clock' on the time limit on submitting a claim (see para 20.6), and the clock will restart when the certificate is issued by ACAS.

In practice, a large number of claims made to employment tribunals are disposed of as a result of the intervention of the conciliation officer. The majority of these will be settled on the basis of the employer making some financial payment to the claimant, and the rest will be withdrawn or a private settlement reached.

1.9 Anything communicated to the conciliation officer in connection with the performance of his functions shall not be admissible in evidence in any proceedings before the tribunal without the consent of the party who communicated it. So far as dismissals are concerned, he shall try to promote the re-engagement or reinstatement of the claimant by the employer or by a successor or associated employer on terms appearing to him to be equitable or, if this is not possible, to try to promote a settlement on the sum to be paid by way of compensation. Apart from certain specific instances (see para 20.45), it is not possible for a person to contract out of his statutory rights, and any agreement to this effect is generally void, but this rule does not apply to any agreement reached through the intervention of the conciliation officer, and any such settlement agreed between the parties will be legally binding (Employment Rights Act 1996 (ERA), s 203(2)(e)).

1.10 In *Clarke v Redcar and Cleveland Borough Council*,[1] the EAT restated the principles which guide the conciliation process.

(a) ACAS officers have no responsibility to see that the terms of the settlement are fair on the employee.

(b) The expression 'promote a settlement' requires a liberal construction which will enable the officer to take such action as is appropriate in the circumstances of the case.

(c) ACAS officers must never advise on the merits of the case being brought by the claimant.

The employment tribunal should only be concerned with whether the officer has purported to act under s 18 of ERA.

It is only when the officer has acted in bad faith or has adopted unfair methods when promoting a settlement that the agreement reached under s 18 of the Employment Tribunals Act can be set aside and not bar subsequent proceedings. Thus if the parties have reached an agreement, the conciliation officer should not get involved in the merits but merely record it on the appropriate form and obtain the parties' signatures (*Moore v Dupont Furniture Products*[2]). Indeed, an agreement reached orally between the parties under the auspices of the conciliation officer is equally binding (*Gilbert v Kembridge Fibres*[3]).

1.11 In *Hennessy v Craigmyle & Co Ltd*,[4] the claimant was told that he would be dismissed summarily but, provided he signed an agreement which had been prepared by the conciliation officer giving up his rights to bring a complaint before an employment tribunal, he would be treated as having been made redundant, and would be given certain monies. After taking legal advice, he signed the agreement, but subsequently brought a claim for unfair dismissal. He alleged that his consent had been obtained by economic duress, and hence was void. The argument was dismissed by the employment tribunal, the EAT and the Court of Appeal. Economic duress was a ground for avoiding an agreement only if the claimant's will was so overborne that his consent was vitiated because he had no real alternative. In this case there was such an alternative, for he could have refused to sign the agreement and taken his chance in the employment tribunal. In any case, whether economic duress exists is a question of fact for the employment tribunal to determine.

1.12 ACAS also has an enhanced helpline (08457 474747) and is available from 8.00am to 8.00pm weekdays and 9am to 1pm on Saturdays. Either employers or employees (or their representatives) may approach ACAS for assistance over a dispute that has not been resolved by the use of internal grievance or disciplinary procedures, in advance of any formal complaint. If this fails, the right to make a complaint to an employment tribunal is still available.

C. **Arbitration**

1.13 At the request of one or more parties to a trade dispute, but with the consent of all of them, ACAS may refer any matter to arbitration for settlement, either by a person appointed from outside ACAS, or by the Central Arbitration Committee. However, arbitration is not to be used unless the parties have exhausted agreed procedures for negotiation or the settlement of disputes, unless there is a special reason which justifies arbitration

---

[1] [2006] IRLR 324.   [2] [1982] ICR 84, [1982] IRLR 31, 126 Sol Jo, HL.
[3] [1984] ICR 188, [1984] IRLR 52, EAT.
[4] [1986] ICR 461, [1986] IRLR 300, 130 Sol Jo 633, [1986] LS Gaz R 2160, CA.

as an alternative to those procedures (TULR(C)A, s 212). With the consent of all the parties, ACAS may decide to publish the award. The Arbitration Act 1996 does not apply to any arbitration under this section, and thus the award is not capable of being legally enforced in a court of law.

In an effort to reduce the number of cases going to employment tribunals, and to avoid the intense legalism which is frequently found there, TULR(C)A, s 212A enabled ACAS to introduce an arbitration alternative, whereby claims for unfair dismissal (only) may, with the agreement of both parties, be heard in private by a single arbitrator. The scheme only operates when both sides have signed a COT3 or a compromise agreement (see para 20.49). The arbitrator will be appointed from a special panel of ACAS arbitrators, the actual hearing will be as informal as possible, and held in private at a convenient location. By agreeing to submit to ACAS arbitration, both parties waive their rights to raise any jurisdictional issues, eg whether time limits have been observed, whether there was or was not a dismissal, etc. A constructive dismissal case can only be heard if both parties agree that there was in fact a dismissal.

The parties will be invited to submit a written statement of their case in advance of the hearing, and will be expected to cooperate in the production of relevant documents. The arbitrator will adopt an inquisitorial approach, ie he will generally ask the questions and seek out the relevant facts, rather than leaving it to the parties to adopt the traditional adversarial approach to the case. Legal representation is not necessary. Strict legal principles and legal precedents will not be followed, but the arbitrator will take account of the general principles of fairness and good practice set out in the ACAS Code of Practice on 'Disciplinary and Grievance Procedures' and the ACAS Handbook 'Discipline at Work'. The arbitrator can make awards (which will be confidential to the parties and ACAS) identical to those which could be made by an employment tribunal (see Chapter 17). An award will generally be binding, and no appeal will be permitted, except where there is a point of EC law or the Human Rights Act 1998 is relevant, or where there is an allegation of serious irregularity.

The scheme will not be suitable for cases where there is a jurisdictional issue (eg was the applicant an employee, etc), where there are complex legal issues involved (eg was there a transfer of an undertaking), or where issues arising out of the implementation of EC law are concerned (eg Working Time Regulations, sex discrimination cases, etc). If issues other than unfair dismissal are revealed, these must be settled, withdrawn, or heard by an employment tribunal.

If the arbitrator recommends that the employee is re-engaged or reinstated, this order can be enforced, if necessary, by an employment tribunal. Continuity of employment will be preserved.

To date, the scheme has not been a success. Since it was introduced, very few applications have been received.

Full details of the scheme can be found in the ACAS Arbitration Scheme (Great Britain) Order 2004.

ACAS also has an arbitration scheme to deal with disputes over applications for flexible working (see para 6.129). The scheme is set out in the ACAS (Flexible Working) Arbitration Scheme (Great Britain) Order 2004 and can be used as a voluntary alternative to employment tribunal proceedings. It is claimed that the scheme will be confidential, informal, relatively fast and cost efficient. Again, the scheme has not proven to be popular.

D. Enquiries

1.14 ACAS may enquire into industrial relations generally, or in a particular industry, or in a particular undertaking. After taking into account the views of the parties, such findings may be published (TULR(C)A, s 214).

E. **Codes of Practice**

1.15 ACAS may issue Codes of Practice containing such practical guidance as it thinks fit for the purpose of promoting the improvement of industrial relations (TULR(C)A, s 199). Four Codes are currently in force, namely:

(a) Disciplinary and Grievance Procedures;

(b) Disclosure of Information to Trade Unions for Collective Bargaining Purposes;

(c) Time Off for Trade Union Duties and Activities;

(d) Settlement Agreements.

1.16 The codes are first prepared and published in draft form, and then ACAS shall consider any representations made about them (and if necessary modify them) before they are finally submitted to the Secretary of State. If he approves, he shall lay them before Parliament. If he does not approve, he will give reasons for withholding his approval. After completing the Parliamentary procedure, the code will be issued in the form of a draft by ACAS and will come into effect on a day appointed by the Secretary of State. A failure on the part of any person to observe a code shall not of itself make him liable to any proceedings, but in any proceedings before an employment tribunal or the Central Arbitration Committee the code will be admissible in evidence, and any relevant provision shall be taken into account in determining the issue (TULR(C)A, s 207) (see *Lock v Cardiff Rly Co*[5]).

1.17 A Code of Practice may be revised or revoked with the approval of the Secretary of State (TULR(C)A, ss 201–202).

Certification Officer (TULR(C)A, s 254)

1.18 The post of Certification Officer was originally created to take over certain administrative functions exercised in connection with trade unions, although nowadays he has wide powers of investigation and supervision over matters such as register of members, accounting records, elections, breaches of union rules, funds for political objects, and so on (see Chapter 22). He is appointed by the Secretary of State, and will make an annual report to him and also to ACAS. Although the staff of the Certification Officer is provided by ACAS, he is completely independent of that organisation.

Since TULRA 1974 (now TULR(C)A, s 2) the Certification Officer has kept a list of organisations which are trade unions and employers' associations within the legal definition. Since the Employment Protection Act 1975 (now TULR(C)A, s 6) he has issued certificates of independence to those trade unions which have applied, and meet the necessary criteria (see Chapter 22). He has issued a booklet entitled 'Guidance for trade unions wishing to apply for a certificate of independence'. He has taken custody of all documents held by his predecessors since 1871, and will keep these for public inspection, along with the list of trade unions and records of all applications for certificates of independence (TULR(C)A, ss 255–258). The Certification Officer has wide powers in respect of complaints by trade union members of alleged breaches of trade union law and trade union rules, and can make declarations and orders on a number of matters, which may be enforced in the same manner as an order of the courts (see Chapter 22). An appeal from his decisions may be made on a point of law to the Employment Appeal Tribunal.

[5] [1998] IRLR 358, 599 IRLB 6, EAT.

The Certification Officer may also strike out an application or complaint on the ground that it is scandalous, vexatious, has no reasonable prospect of success, or is otherwise misconceived, or refuse to entertain an application by a vexatious litigant (TULR(C)A, ss 256A–256AA).

Central Arbitration Committee

1.19 This body consists of a chairman (and 11 deputy chairmen) appointed by the Secretary of State (after consultation with ACAS) and other persons appointed from representatives of employers and workers who are experienced in industrial relations. The appointments may be for up to five years, and are renewable. The Central Arbitration Committee (CAC) will exercise its functions on behalf of the Crown, but will not be subject to directions of any kind from any ministers as to the manner in which those functions are to be exercised. CAC has a central role in the new statutory scheme for the recognition of trade unions, created by the Employment Relations Act 1999 (see Chapter 23). In performing its functions, CAC must have regard to the object of encouraging and promoting fair and efficient practices and arrangements in the workplace, although it will remain neutral on the issue of collective bargaining. CAC will continue to exercise its former statutory functions to adjudicate on claims relating to disclosure of information for collective bargaining purposes brought under TULR(C)A, s 183 (see para 23.15) and will also adjudicate on certain disputes arising out of the provisions of the Transnational Information and Consultation of Employees Regulations 1999 (see para 23.132), and the Information and Consultation Regulations 2004 (see para 23.142).

CAC also resolves disputes concerning the provision of information, consultation and participation arising from the European Public Limited-Liability Company (Employee Involvement) (Great Britain) Regulations 2009, and can act as a voluntary arbitration body following a reference from ACAS under TULR(C)A, s 212.

Employment Appeal Tribunal (Employment Tribunals Act 1996, ss 20–37)

1.20 This tribunal consists of judges of the High Court appointed by the Judicial Appointments Commission on the recommendation of the Lord Chancellor in England, and the Lord President of the Court of Session in Scotland, plus other members (appointed on the joint recommendations of the Lord Chancellor and the Secretary of State) who have special knowledge or experience of industrial relations as representatives of employers or of workers. The Employment Appeal Tribunal (the EAT) is a superior court of record, with a central office in London, but it may sit anywhere in the country, and one or more divisions of the EAT may sit at the same time. In practice, hearings take place either in London or Edinburgh.

1.21 The jurisdiction of the EAT is as follows:

(a) to hear appeals on points of law from decisions of employment tribunals under the various statutory provisions set out in s 21 of the Employment Tribunals Act 1996, which generally cover most, but not all, of the jurisdiction enjoyed by employment tribunals (see para 1.28). In particular, it should be noted that appeals against decisions of an employment tribunal relating to the issue of improvement notices and prohibition notices go to the Divisional Court. The reason is that a breach of these notices amounts to a criminal offence, and the EAT only has specific civil jurisdiction. There have been a few cases where the relevant statutory provision has inadvertently not been included in s 21 of the Employment Tribunals Act, with the result that the EAT lacked jurisdiction to hear an appeal: see eg *Wolstenholme v Refreshment Systems Ltd (t/a Northern Vending Services*[6]*)*;

(b) to hear appeals from the decisions of the Certification Officer on various matters arising out of the Trade Union and Labour Relations (Consolidation) Act 1992 (TULR(C)A, see Chapter 22);

(c) to hear appeals from the decisions of the Central Arbitration Committee arising from the Transnational Information and Consultation of Employees Regulations 1999, the Information and Consultation of Employees Regulations 2004 (see Chapter 23) and the European Public Limited-Liability Company (Employee Involvement) (Great Britain) Regulations 2009.

1.22 The procedure before the EAT is governed by the Employment Appeal Tribunal Rules 1993, which have been amended several times in order to align procedures with those followed by employment tribunals. Thus the overriding objective of the Rules is to enable the EAT to deal with cases justly, including, so far as practicable, ensuring that the parties are on equal footing, saving expense, dealing with cases in ways which are proportionate to the importance and complexity of the issues, and ensuring that cases are dealt with expeditiously and fairly. The Rules lay down the procedure to be followed when lodging an appeal, although if a judge or Registrar thinks that an appeal has no reasonable grounds of succeeding, or is an abuse of process, he can notify the appellant accordingly, and order that no further action be taken in the matter. Further details of the procedure before the EAT can be found in Practice Direction 2008, which supersedes all previous directions.

A party may appear before the EAT in person, or be represented by a solicitor, barrister, representative of a trade union or employers association, or any other person whom he desires to represent him. Costs will not normally be awarded by the EAT, although there is a power to make a costs order, if the proceedings brought by a party were unnecessary, improper or vexatious, or there has been unreasonable delay or other unreasonable conduct in bringing or conducting the proceedings. The EAT may make a costs order in favour of a litigant in person, and also make a wasted costs order against a party's representative if there has been improper, unreasonable or negligent acts on his part.

The ERRA 2013 amended section 28(2) and (3) of the Employment Tribunals Act 1996 so that from 25 June 2013 cases in the EAT are heard by a judge sitting alone except where he directs that they are to be heard by a judge and either two or four lay members. This reversed the previous position.

If a judge feels that there may be a conflict of interest because he (or a member of his family) have had some form of professional or personal connection with one of the parties, he should ensure that the full facts are placed before the parties, with an explanation. If there is a real chance of an objection, he should ascertain whether there is another judge who can hear the case (*Jones v DAS Legal Expenses Insurance Co Ltd*[7]). For example, there is an objection to an advocate appearing before the EAT if he is also a part-time judge in that tribunal, and such action is contrary to Art 6 of the Human Rights Convention as being a violation of the right to a fair hearing (*Lawal v Northern Spirit Ltd*[8]). A restriction on proceedings order may be made to prevent vexatious litigants wasting court time (rr 13–17), and a restricting reporting order may be made in cases where sexual misconduct is alleged (r 23) or disability discrimination (r 23A). It is an offence, punishable by a fine

[6] [2004] All ER (D) 185 (Mar), EAT.
[7] [2003] EWCA Civ 1071, [2004] IRLR 218, 147 Sol Jo LB 932, [2003] All ER (D) 425 (Jul).
[8] [2002] ICR 486, [2002] IRLR 228, [2002] All ER (D) 36 (Jan), EAT; aff'd [2002] EWCA Civ 1218, [2002] ICR 1507, [2002] IRLR 714, [2002] 46 LS Gaz R 33, [2002] All ER (D) 442 (Oct); revsd [2003] UKHL 35, [2004] 1 All ER 187, [2003] ICR 856, [2003] IRLR 538, [2003] 28 LS Gaz R 30, [2003] NJLR 1005, 147 Sol Jo LB 783, [2003] All ER (D) 255 (Jun).

not exceeding level 5 on the standard scale (currently £5,000) to act in contravention of such an order.

1.23 An appeal can only be entertained by the EAT if there is a genuine dispute between the parties (*IMI Yorkshire Imperial Ltd v Olender*[9]) and appeals should not be pursued with other ulterior motives (*Baker v Superite Tools Ltd*[10]). A further appeal will lie on a point of law to the Court of Appeal or, in Scotland, to the Court of Session, and a final appeal will lie to the Supreme Court (formerly the House of Lords). At any time, however, a tribunal or court can refer a case to the European Court of Justice in Luxembourg, if a question arises as to the application of European law (see para 1.71).

Employment tribunals

1.24 The constitutional basis for employment tribunals can be found in the Employment Tribunals Act 1996. An employment tribunal is an inferior court, exercising the judicial powers of the state for the purpose of the Contempt of Court Act 1981, s 19, and contempt of court proceedings may be brought if there is an attempt to pervert the course of justice or any other breach of the Act (*Peach Grey & Co v Sommers*[11]).

1.25 An employment tribunal generally consists of an employment judge and two lay members, although employment judges now have powers to sit alone more often. The employment judge can be either a barrister or solicitor, and may be full-time or part-time. The lay members, who are all part-time, are selected from a panel drawn up after consultation with representatives of employers' organisations and trade unions. There is also a self-nomination procedure, designed to attract women, ethnic minorities, and persons with disabilities. Where a hearing consists of a judge and two lay members, there will always be a representative from each side of industry, although an employment judge can sit with one lay member only if both parties to the dispute agree, or alone in unfair dismissal cases. Each member of the employment tribunal has an equal vote, and although decisions can be reached by a majority vote, in practice it appears that, despite the somewhat diverse backgrounds, 96% of all decisions reached are unanimous. In the remaining cases, the 'wingmen' are just as likely to unite in outvoting the employment judge as the latter is likely to have the support of one or the other member. In cases of sex discrimination, it is desirable to have one member of either sex, and in race discrimination cases, a member who has special experience of race relations, but there is no absolute legal requirement that an employment tribunal should be so composed (*Habib v Elkington & Co Ltd*[12]). An employment judge or member should not have any connection with any of the parties who appear before them (see para 20.91), nor with any of the witnesses (*University of Swansea v Cornelius*[13]). However, the fact that the employment judge or members know an advocate who appears before them should not cause any problem, unless there is a close relationship between them.

Although, generally speaking, an employment tribunal will consist of an employment judge and two members, in the following circumstances an employment judge may sit alone (Employment Tribunals Act, s 4). These are:

    (a) the following complaints made under TULR(C)A, ie s 68A (unauthorised or excessive deductions of trade union subscriptions), s 87 (unauthorised deduction of contribution to a political fund), ss 161, 165, 166 (application for interim relief etc), s 192 (failure by employer to pay a protective award);

---

[9] [1982] ICR 69, EAT.   [10] [1986] ICR 189, [1985] LS Gaz R 2906, EAT.
[11] [1995] 2 All ER 513, [1995] ICR 549, [1995] IRLR 363, [1995] 13 LS Gaz R 31.
[12] [1981] ICR 435, [1981] IRLR 344, EAT.   [13] [1988] ICR 735, EAT.

(b) a complaint under the Pension Schemes Act 1993, s 126;

(c) proceedings brought under the following provisions of the Employment Rights Act 1996, ie s 11 (failure to give written statement of terms and conditions), s 23 (unauthorised deductions from wages), s 34 (failure to make a guarantee payment), s 70 (failure to pay remuneration following suspension on medical grounds), s 111 (unfair dismissal), ss 128, 131, 132 (application for interim relief etc), s 163 (right to or amount of redundancy payment), s 170 (reference following an application to the Secretary of State for a redundancy payment), s 188 (rights of employee on employer's insolvency), s 206(4) (appointment of an appropriate person where there is no personal representative of a deceased employee);

(d) complaints brought under the Transfer of Undertakings (Protection of Employment) Regulations 2006, reg 15(10) (failure to pay compensation in pursuance of an order made following a failure to consult on a transfer);

(e) complaints made under the National Minimum Wage Act 1998, s 11 (failure to allow access to records), s 19 (appeal by an employer against an enforcement notice), s 22 (appeal against a penalty notice);

(f) proceedings brought under the provisions of the Employment Tribunals Extension of Jurisdiction (England and Wales) Order 1994 and Employment Tribunals Extension of Jurisdiction (Scotland) Order 1994 (breach of contract claims);

(g) proceedings in which the parties give their written consent to be heard by an employment judge alone;

(h) proceedings in which the person against whom they are brought does not contest the case;

(i) complaints relating to the non-payment of holiday pay;

(j) stage one of equal pay cases.

1.26 However, in any of the circumstances in para 1.25, the employment judge may at any stage decide to have the case heard by a full tribunal:

(a) where there is a likelihood of a dispute arising from the facts;

(b) where there is a likelihood of an issue of law arising;

(c) having taken into account the views of any of the parties;

where there are other proceedings which might be heard concurrently and which do not come within the above categories which enable an employment judge to sit alone.

1.27 If the employment judge decides to hear the case sitting alone, he is under a continuing duty to keep that decision under review. Thus, if it becomes evident that the parties intend to call a number of witnesses, this would be a clear indication that the claim should be heard by a full tribunal (*Clarke v Arriva Kent Thameside Ltd*[14]). Indeed, an employment judge should not sit alone, even if all the parties agree to him so doing, where there is a likelihood of a dispute on the facts (*Sogbetun v Hackney London Borough*[15]).

1.28 The main jurisdiction of employment tribunals is to deal with claims made under the following statutory provisions:

(a) Employment Agencies Act 1973;

(b) Health and Safety at Work etc Act 1974;

(c) Industrial Training Act 1982;

---

[14] [2001] All ER (D) 485 (Jul), EAT.   [15] [1998] ICR 1264, [1998] IRLR 676, EAT.

(d) Trade Union and Labour Relations (Consolidation) Act 1992;

(e) Pension Schemes Act 1993;

(f) Employment Rights Act 1996;

(g) National Minimum Wage Act 1998;

(h) Employment Relations Act 1999;

(i) Equality Act 2006;

(j) Work and Families Act 2006;

(k) Equality Act 2010.

Employment tribunals also have jurisdiction to deal with claims made under the following statutory instruments:

(a) Safety Representatives and Safety Committee Regulations 1977;

(b) Industrial Tribunals (Interest) Order 1990;

(c) Employment Tribunals Extension of Jurisdiction Order 1994;

(d) Suspension from Work (on Maternity Grounds) Order 1994;

(e) Health and Safety (Consultation with Employees) Regulations 1996;

(f) Working Time Regulations 1998;

(g) National Minimum Wage Regulations 1999;

(h) Maternity and Parental Leave etc Regulations 1999;

(i) Transnational Information and Consultation of Employees Regulations 1999;

(j) Part-time Workers (Prevention of Less Favourable Treatment) Regulations 2000;

(k) Employment Relations (Offshore Employment) Order 2000;

(l) Right to Time Off for Study or Training Regulations 2001;

(m) Fixed-Term Employees (Prevention of Less Favourable Treatment) Regulations 2002;

(n) Paternity and Adoption Leave Regulations 2002;

(o) Flexible Working (Eligibility, Complaints and Remedies) Regulations 2002;

(p) Flexible Working (Procedural Requirements) Regulations 2002;

(q) Employment Tribunals (Constitution and Rules of Procedure) Regulations 2004;

(r) Information and Consultation of Employees Regulations 2004;

(s) Transfer of Undertakings (Protection of Employment) Regulations 2006;

(t) Occupational and Personal Pension Schemes (Consultation with Employees) Regulations 2006;

(u) Employment Equality (Age) Regulations 2006;

(v) Companies (Cross Border Mergers) Regulations 2007;

(w) European Public Limited Liability Company (Employee Involvement) (Great Britain) Regulations 2009;

(x) Agency Workers Regulations 2010;

(y) Employment Relations Act 1999 (Blacklists) Regulations 2010;

(z) Time off Work for Study or Training Regulations 2010;

(aa) Additional Paternity Leave Regulations 2010;

(ab) Additional Paternity Leave (Adoption from Overseas) Regulations 2010.

Employment tribunals have jurisdiction to apply EC law to claims made under UK law, ie as laid down in specific UK legislation (eg Equality Act). But there is no jurisdiction to hear or determine 'free-standing' claims based on the Treaty of Rome or an EC Directive, outside the domestic statutory framework (*Biggs v Somerset County Council*[16]). Also, there is no jurisdiction to hear '*Francovich*' style claims (*Secretary of State for Employment v Mann*[17]). An employment tribunal does have a duty to apply EC law to the extent of disapplying an offending provision in UK legislation if it is inconsistent with EC law (see *Redcar & Cleveland Borough Council v Bainbridge*,[18] para 5.34).

1.29 The procedure before employment tribunals is governed by the Employment Tribunals (Constitution and Rules of Procedure) Regulations 2013. These regulations provide for the making and rejection of claims, appearance by respondents, case management, further particulars, witness attendance orders, pre-hearing review, procedure at the hearing, applications for review, award of costs, extension of time, joinder of parties, default judgments, electronic communications and other miscellaneous matters. Generally speaking the tribunal has a wide discretion in operating its procedures, and its decision can only be challenged on appeal where the discretion was wrongly exercised because of a mistake of law, a disregard of principle, a misapplication of the facts, or the tribunal took into account irrelevant matters or failed to take into account relevant matters, or where the decision was outside the generous ambit within which a reasonable disagreement is possible (*Noorani v Merseyside TEC Ltd*[19]) (see Chapter 20).

A. **Territorial jurisdiction**

1.30 The jurisdiction of employment tribunals is based on particular statutory provisions. Thus certain sections of TULR(C)A do not apply to employment where an employee works outside Great Britain, ie access to employment (ss 137–143), inducement and detriment (ss 145A-151), time off for trade union duties and activities (ss 168–173) and duty to notify Secretary of State of redundancies (ss 193–194).

1.31 The territorial jurisdiction of the Employment Rights Act was originally found in s 196, which excluded a number of claims where the employee ordinarily worked outside Great Britain, but the section was repealed in 1999 (in order to comply with the Posted Workers Directive) and not replaced. It thus fell to the courts to devise tests for determining the territorial jurisdiction in respect of various statutory claims which were brought.

1.32 The leading case on territorial jurisdiction is the House of Lords' decision in *Lawson v Serco Ltd*,[20] where it was held that claimants could be divided into three categories:

(a) *Standard cases.* The question to be asked here is, was the claimant working in Great Britain? The contract of employment will be a major factor, but attention must also be paid to what happens in practice.

(b) *Peripatetic employees.* Here, the factual 'base' test could be used, eg where the employee lived, was paying taxes and where his work was organised from (*Todd v*

[16] [1995] ICR 811, [1995] IRLR 452, EAT; aff'd [1996] 2 All ER 734, [1996] 2 CMLR 292, [1996] ICR 364, [1996] IRLR 203, [1996] 06 LS Gaz R 27, [1996] NJLR 174, 140 Sol Jo LB 59, CA.

[17] [1996] ICR 197, [1996] IRLR 4, EAT; revsd [1997] ICR 209, CA; aff'd on other grounds sub nom *Mann v Secretary of State for Employment* [1999] ICR 898, [1999] All ER (D) 791.

[18] [2005] EWCA Civ 726, [2005] IRLR 504.

[19] [1999] IRLR 184, CA.

[20] [2006] UKHL 3, [2006] 1 All ER 823, [2006] ICR 250, [2006] IRLR 289, (2006) 103(6) LSG 36, (2006) 156 NLJ 184, (2006) 150 SJLB 131, (2006) *Times*, 27 January.

British Midlands Airways Ltd[21]), where his duty begins and where it ends (*Diggins v Condor Marine*[22]). Where the employee is working is a question of fact for the tribunal: *Ravat v Halliburton Manufacturing & Services Ltd*[23] where the Supreme Court emphasised the need for a sufficiently close connection between the employment and Great Britain, stronger than with the country where the employee works.

(c) *Expatriate employees.* Generally, the employee must rely on the law where he is working, but there are two major exceptions, ie where an employee is posted abroad for the purpose of a business carried on in Great Britain, and an expatriate working in an extraterritorial enclave in a foreign country. Thus in *Lawson v Serco Ltd*[24] the claimant was employed by a British company to work as a security supervisor on Ascension Island, a British Overseas Dependency with no local population. It was held that the connection with the employment relationship and the United Kingdom was overwhelmingly strong, and the claimant was entitled to pursue his claim for unfair dismissal in this country. This was also the case in *Duncombe v Secretary of State for Children, Schools and Families*,[25] where teachers were employed by the Secretary of State for Children, Schools and Families to work in European Schools abroad. Their employment was held to have an overwhelmingly closer connection with Britain and with British employment law than with any other system of law.

1.33 However, there are bound to be difficult decisions to be made regarding an employee who works abroad for a British employer for the purpose of a business carried on in the UK, eg a sales representative, or a newspaper correspondent whose despatches are sent to different countries (*Financial Times v Bishop*[26]). The correct approach when considering the territorial scope of the right to claim is to consider the place of employment as being the major determining factor, and there is no room for using the 'substantial connection with Great Britain' approach. It is only in exceptional circumstances that the employment tribunal will have jurisdiction where the employee works wholly abroad (*Dolphin Drilling Personnel PTE Ltd v Winks*[27]). In *Hughes v Alan Dick & Co Ltd*[28] the claimant was employed by a British company to work in Nigeria. It was held that the employment tribunal had no jurisdiction to hear his claim for unfair dismissal. Although he was recruited in England, worked for a British firm for a business conducted in a foreign country, and was paid in sterling to a British bank account, all of his work was carried out in the context of a substantial business operation carried on in Nigeria, and the connection with that country was greater and stronger than that of the United Kingdom.

1.34 If the respondent is a company registered in Great Britain, it is resident here even though it carries on business elsewhere (*Odeco (UK) Inc v Peacham*[29]), and it may carry on a business in Great Britain even though it has no registered office here (*Knulty v Eloc Electro Optick Communicatie BV*[30]).

1.35 The Equality Act 2010 is also silent on the question of territorial jurisdiction (unlike many of the repealed regulations) apart from certain provisions relating to ships, hovercraft and offshore work, and such questions must be determined by the employment tribunals in accordance with the principles outlined.

[21] [1978] IRLR 370, (1978) ICR 959.   [22] [2009] EWCA Civ 1133, [2010] ICR 213, [2010] IRLR 119.
[23] [2012] UKSC 1, [2012] IRLR 315 SC.
[24] [2006] UKHL 3, [2006] 1 All ER 823, [2006] ICR 250, [2006] IRLR 289, (2006) 103(6) LSG 36, (2006) 156 NLJ 184, (2006) 150 SJLB 131, (2006) *Times*, 27 January.
[25] (No. 2) [2011] UKSC 36.   [26] Employment Appeal Tribunal, 25 November 2003.
[27] [2009] UKEAT 0049_08_2104.   [28] [2008] EWHC 2695, QB.
[29] [1979] ICR 823.   [30] [1979] ICR 827.

1.36 Whether the work is for the purpose of a business carried on in Great Britain is to be determined in the light of the jurisdictional rules outlined in *Lawson v Serco Ltd*,[31] because, although that case concerned the issue of unfair dismissal, it is likely that the principles outlined therein will also apply to the various anti-discrimination provisions (*Williams v University of Nottingham*[32]).

1.37 Where an employee raises a claim under UK law which is derived from EU law, it is the duty of an employment tribunal to give effect to the EU derived entitlement, even though the work is performed by a foreign national outside Great Britain. In *Bleuse v MBT Transport Ltd*[33] a German employee, who worked as a driver in Europe, but never worked in the United Kingdom, was able to make a claim for holiday pay against his British employer, because the Working Time Regulations were intended to implement an EC Directive. Since most anti-discrimination rights are so derived, it seems clear that the wider tests will apply to claims brought under the Equality Act. Thus in *Mangold v Helm*[34] it was held that non-discrimination is a fundamental principle of EU law, which can be relied upon against private individuals as well as the state. Thus workers in the private sector, as well as those in the public sector, will be able to claim even though their connection with Great Britain is somewhat tenuous.

1.38 Contractual entitlements are separate from statutory employment rights. The parties are free to agree the law applicable to their employment contracts, subject to international conventions, including Rome I and II Regulations, the Posting of Workers Directive and the Brussels I Regulation, which generally provide that the employment rights of the country with which the employment is closely connected shall apply. Breach of contract claims (eg under the Employment Tribunals Extension of Jurisdiction Order) shadow the jurisdiction of the civil courts (*Dickie v Cathay Pacific Airways Ltd*[35]).

B. Legal aid

1.39 Legal aid is not generally available in England and Wales, although there is provision in the Legal Aid, Sentencing and Punishment of Offenders Act 2012 where the lack of legal aid would breach an individual's rights under the European Convention on Human Rights, or to the provision of services under EU law. In Scotland the system is more generous, but it is still only granted if (a) the applicant is unable to fund or find alternative representation elsewhere, (b) the case is an arguable one, and (c) the case is too complex to allow the applicant to present it to a minimum standard of effectiveness.

C. Claims for breach of contract

1.40 Under the Employment Tribunals Extension of Jurisdiction (England and Wales) Order 1994, and the Employment Tribunals Extension of Jurisdiction (Scotland) Order 1994, employment tribunals have jurisdiction to hear claims for damages for breach of a contract of employment, or any other contract (subject to certain exceptions, see para 1.42) connected with employment, including a claim for a sum due under such a contract, and a claim for the recovery of a sum in pursuance of any enactment relating to the terms or performance of such a contract. The claim must be outstanding on the termination of the employee's employment, which is the moment in time when the employee ceases to work

---

[31] [2006] UKHL 3, [2006] 1 All ER 823, [2006] ICR 250, [2006] IRLR 289, (2006) 103(6) LSG 36, (2006) 156 NLJ 184, (2006) 150 SJLB 131, (2006) *Times*, 27 January.

[32] [2007] IRLR 660.   [33] [2008] ICR 488, [2008] IRLR 264.

[34] [2006] All ER (EC) 383, [2005] ECR I–9981, [2006] 1 CMLR 43, [2006] CEC 372, [2006] IRLR 143.

[35] [2005] EWCA Civ 599, [2005] ICR 1436, [2005] IRLR 624, (2005) *Times*, 31 May.

for the employer (*Miller Bros & FP Butler Ltd v Johnston*[36]), and the maximum award which can be made in respect of any number of claims is £25,000. The claim must be brought within three months from the effective date of termination of the contract of employment (or within three months from the last day when the employee worked in the employment which has been terminated) with the usual extension of time if it was not reasonably practicable to bring the claim within that time (see also para 20.2). There is no requirement that the employee should have been employed for any particular period of employment before bringing a claim under the Order.

1.41 Once an employee has lodged such a claim, the employer may lodge a counterclaim in respect of breach of contract by the employee, within six weeks (or, if not reasonably practicable to do so, within such further time as the employment tribunal considers to be reasonable). The counterclaim is not limited by the amount of the original claim, and may be continued irrespective of what happens to the original claim, as long as it has been presented before the employee's claim has been settled or withdrawn. Indeed, if the employee's breach of contract claim fails because it was not presented within the appropriate time limits, the employer's counterclaim, validly presented, can still proceed (*Patel v RCMS Ltd*[37]).

1.42 Neither the employee nor the employer can bring a claim or counterclaim in respect of:

(a) damages for personal injuries;

(b) breach of a term requiring the employer to provide living accommodation for the employee, or a term imposing an obligation on either of them in connection with the provision of living accommodation;

(c) a term relating to intellectual property;

(d) a term imposing an obligation of confidence;

(e) a term which is a covenant in restraint of trade.

1.43 One effect of the Order is to give an alternative route for claims (other than the exceptions in para 1.42) which would otherwise have to be brought in the county court, although it should be noted that there are a number of differences in the respective jurisdictions and procedures (see para 8.3). Another effect of the Order is to enable employment tribunals to deal with matters which hitherto were not within the scope of the Wages Act 1986 (now Employment Rights Act 1996, ss 13–22, see para 8.4), in particular claims for payments in lieu of notice, holiday pay, advances etc. Again, there are differences between the Order and the Act, and it will be necessary to scrutinise the nature of a claim very carefully in order to bring it under the appropriate heading.

1.44 If a claimant is successful in recovering £25,000 under the provisions of the Order, he cannot recover any excess of that amount by instituting subsequent High Court proceedings in respect of a wrongful dismissal claim (*Fraser v Hlmad Ltd*[38]).

D. **Mediation**

1.45 Judicial mediation is available as an alternative to employment tribunal proceedings. The mediator, who will be a tribunal judge trained in alternative dispute resolution, will try to assist the parties to resolve their dispute by mutual agreement. Cases which are suitable for judicial mediation will be identified at the sift stage or preliminary hearing, and if all parties agree to this course being adopted, mediation will take place in private, and the proceedings will be entirely confidential. ACAS also provides access to mediation.

---

[36] [2002] ICR 744, [2002] IRLR 386, [2002] All ER (D) 220 (Mar), EAT.
[37] [1999] IRLR 161, EAT.   [38] [2006] EWCA Civ 738.

Industrial training boards

1.46 The Industrial Training Act 1982 enables the minister to set up training boards in any industry in order to provide for industrial and commercial training of persons who are over school-leaving age. Only two such statutory boards are currently operating (construction and engineering).

1.47 To meet its expenses a board may impose a levy on employers in the industry, which is assessed by reference to a percentage of the payroll. For this purpose a board may require employers to furnish returns and information, and keep and produce records (eg, see Industrial Training Levy (Construction Board) Order 2009). An employer who has been assessed for a levy may appeal to an employment tribunal which may rescind or reduce or increase it as the tribunal determines (see Employment Tribunals (Constitution and Rules of Procedure) Regulations 2004, Sch 3).

Equality and Human Rights Commission

1.48 The Equality Act 2006 created a new institution, called the Equality and Human Rights Commission (EHRC), which took over the existing functions of the Equal Opportunities Commission, the Commission for Racial Equality, and the Disability Rights Commission, but with additional responsibilities and wider powers.
Basically, the EHRC has the fundamental duty to create a society in which:

(a) people's ability to achieve their potential is not limited by prejudice or discrimination;
(b) there is respect for and protection of each individual's human rights;
(c) there is respect for the dignity and worth of each individual;
(d) each individual has an equal opportunity to participate in society; and
(e) there is mutual respect between groups based on understanding and valuing of diversity and on shared respect for equality and human rights.

1.49 The EHRC has wider functions than its predecessors, and will draw up a strategic plan showing the activities to be undertaken in pursuance of its statutory powers. In addition to taking over the work of the existing Commissions, the EHRC will assume responsibility for promoting understanding of the importance of equality and diversity, and work towards the elimination of unlawful discrimination in the areas of race, sex, religion or belief, sexual orientation, sexual reassignment, age, disability, as well as the promotion of human rights. It will promote good relations between and within different groups, encourage good practice in the area of relations between different groups, and work towards the elimination of prejudice, and hatred of and hostility towards members of groups. It will monitor the effectiveness of equality and human rights enactments, give advice to the Government, and make recommendations. It will issue (and revise, where necessary) Codes of Practice, which must be approved in draft by the Secretary of State, and be subject to the negative approval parliamentary procedure.

1.50 The EHRC can make enquiries into matters relating to its duties in respect of equality and diversity, human rights, disabilities and groups. It can make grants and carry out investigations. If, following an investigation, it is satisfied that a person has committed an unlawful act, it can issue an unlawful act notice, which may be followed by requiring that person to prepare an action plan for the purpose of avoiding repetition or continuance of the unlawful act. As an alternative, the Commission may enter into a legally enforceable agreement whereby the person concerned undertakes not to commit (or prepare to commit) an unlawful act, and in return the Commission undertakes not to proceed with an investigation or issue an unlawful act notice.

Health and Safety Executive

1.51 The former Health and Safety Commission and the Health and Safety Executive were abolished by the Legislative Reform (Health and Safety Executive) Order 2008, and replaced by a new unitary organisation, called the Health and Safety Executive. This consists of 11 non-executive members appointed by the Secretary of State. Three members are appointed after consultation with employers' associations, three members are appointed after consultation with employees' associations, one member is appointed after consultation with organisations representing local authorities, and up to four members are appointed after consultation with professional bodies and devolved administrations. The new HSE appoints a chief executive. All the powers and functions of the old Commission and Executive have been transferred to the new organisation.

1.52 It shall be the duty of HSE to do such things and make such arrangements as it considers appropriate for the general purposes of the Health and Safety at Work Act 1974. In particular, HSE shall:

(a) assist and encourage persons concerned with matters relevant to those purposes to further those purposes;

(b) make arrangements as it considers appropriate for the carrying out of research and the publication of the results of research, and the provisions of training and information, and encourage research and the provision of training and information by others;

(c) make arrangements to provide information and advisory services to government departments, local authorities, employers, employees and their organisations, and other purposes concerned with matters relevant to the general purposes of the Act.

1.53 HSE will submit proposals to the Secretary of State, provide particulars of what it proposes to do for the purpose of carrying out its functions, ensure that its activities are in accordance with proposals approved by, and give effect to any directions issued by, the Secretary of State. However, the Secretary of State may not give directions with regard to the enforcement of the relevant statutory provisions in any particular case.

1.54 HSE may carry out an investigation or hold an enquiry into any matter, occurrence, or situation, in accordance with the Health and Safety Enquiries (Procedure) Regulations 1975. It will issue guidance to local authorities, and work with them to establish best practice and consistency in the enforcement of health and safety law. The enforcement powers of HSE and local authorities remain unchanged.

Health and Work Advisory and Assessment Service

1.55 This new service is being rolled out around the country during 2014, and aims to give employers of all sizes help with managing long-term sickness absence, although it is expected to be particularly helpful to small employers who have no access to occupational health services. It will provide free advice and support to employers who have employees who are off work for over four weeks. There are two elements to the service: a health and work telephone helpline and online support for employers, employees and GPs, and access to an occupational health assessment for employees on a period of sickness absence lasting four weeks or more. HWAS will also aim to produce a 'return to work plan' setting out any obstacles, recommended interventions and a timetable.

Low Pay Commission

1.56 This body, which consists of a chairman and eight other members appointed by the Secretary of State, was put on a statutory basis by the National Minimum Wage Act 1998, and is responsible for recommending to the Secretary of State the level of the national minimum wage. Before making regulations establishing the national minimum wage, the Secretary of State will refer the following matters to the LPC, ie:

what single hourly rate should be prescribed as the national minimum wage;

what shall be the pay reference period;

what methods should be used for determining the hourly rate at which a person is remunerated;

whether persons under the age of 26 should be excluded from the right to a national minimum wage, or be entitled to a different hourly rate;

whether any other persons should be excluded, and if so, what hourly rate should be prescribed.

The role of the government

1.57 The responsibility for employment law issues is shared by a number of government departments, including the Department for Business, Innovation and Skills, the Department for Transport, the Department for Communities and Local Government, the Department for Work and Pensions, and so forth, each headed by a Secretary of State. Within these departments, junior ministers deal with a wide range of issues, such as employment relations generally, employment tribunals, ACAS and CAC, health and safety, race, sex and disability issues, job action programmes, maternity, paternity and adoption matters, pensions, work permits, adult and youth training, and so on.

Codes of practice

1.58 Codes of practice may be issued by the Advisory, Conciliation and Arbitration Service, the Equality and Human Rights Commission, the Health and Safety Executive, and the Secretary of State. A failure by a person to comply with a provision in the code will not, by itself, render a person liable for criminal or civil proceedings, but in any such proceedings a relevant code shall be admissible in evidence, and be taken account of by a court or tribunal when determining any issue before it.

1.59 The Secretary of State has power to issue Codes of Practice (TULR(C)A, s 203), and codes have been issued on Picketing, Industrial Action Ballots and Notice to Employers, and Access to Workers during Recognition and Derecognition Ballots. It is of interest to note that whereas codes of practice which have been issued by ACAS and EHRC are admissible before employment tribunals, those issued by the Secretary of State are also admissible in the courts.

Supreme Court

1.60 The Constitutional Reform Act 2005 paved the way for the abolition of the House of Lords as the highest court of appeal, with its powers and functions being transferred to a new Supreme Court. Earlier decisions of the House of Lords will, of course, still be binding on lower courts and tribunals. The Supreme Court commenced functioning in October 2009.

The impact of the European Union

1.61 As from 1 January 1973, the United Kingdom became a member of the European Union, and by the European Communities Act 1972 (s 2) all obligations arising out of the various treaties which set up the EU are to be given legal effect in this country without further enactment. European law is thus of particular importance in the study of domestic employment law, for it will override domestic provisions. In order to understand European Union law, we must examine the treaties, the institutions and the nature of the legal rules which take effect.

A. Treaty of Rome

1.62 This Treaty was signed in 1957 by the original six founding states (France, West Germany, Italy, Belgium, the Netherlands and Luxembourg). The UK, Ireland and Denmark acceded to the Treaty in 1973, Greece in 1981, Spain and Portugal became full members in 1992 and Austria, Finland and Sweden joined in 1995. The original Treaty required unanimity between all the member states before laws could be passed, although subsequently a system of qualified majority voting has been introduced. So far as is relevant, Art 140 of the Treaty stated that one of the objects of the Community was to harmonise laws relating to 'employment, labour law and working conditions, basic and advanced training, social security, protection against occupational accidents and diseases, occupational hygiene, law of trade unions, and collective bargaining between workers and employers'. The Treaty of Amsterdam brought about a renumbering of the Articles of the Treaty of Rome.

B. Treaty of Lisbon

1.63 The Lisbon Treaty has now been ratified by all member states of the EU. Among other things, the Treaty will make the Charter on Fundamental Human Rights legally binding on EU institutions, but this only affects member states when they are implementing EU law. Additionally, the UK Government has secured an opt-out protocol, which means that no court or tribunal can find the laws or practices of the UK to be inconsistent with the fundamental rights and freedoms of the Charter.

1.64 The Lisbon Treaty renamed the Treaty of Rome as the Treaty on the Functioning of the European Union (TFEU) and the Maastricht Treaty as the Treaty on European Union (TEU). The co-decision legislative procedure has been rebranded as the ordinary legislative procedure, whereby the European Commission will propose legislation, which then has to be passed by the Council of Ministers and the European Parliament before it becomes law. Some of the Articles of the Treaty of Rome have been renumbered (eg Art 141 on equal pay is now Art 157). A new 'double majority' voting system will come into force in 2014, and it is proposed to reduce the number of EU commissioners.

C. **Expansion of the EU**

1.65 At the meeting in Maastricht in 1992, the EU adopted criteria for other states to become members of the Union. The conditions were stable institutions guaranteeing democracy, the rule of law, human rights, and respect for and protection of minorities, a functioning market economy and the ability to take on the obligations of political, economic and monetary union. As a result, a further 10 countries joined the European Union in 2004, ie Cyprus, Czech Republic, Estonia, Hungary, Latvia, Lithuania, Malta, Poland, Slovak Republic and Slovenia. Romania and Bulgaria joined in 2007, and Croatia in 2013, bringing the total membership of the EU to 28. Macedonia, Iceland, Montenegro, Turkey and Serbia are candidate countries which have applied to join.

D. **EU institutions**

Council of Ministers

1.66 This is the supreme policy-making body of the EU. Each meeting of the Council is attended by a minister from each member state. Usually, this will be the respective prime ministers or foreign secretaries, but sometimes, when specific detailed proposals are being discussed, the respective 'portfolio' ministers will attend. One member of the Council will hold the presidency for six months and then the position rotates. The Council is assisted by a Secretariat (comprising a staff of some 2,500) and preparatory work for the meetings is undertaken by frequent meetings of senior civil servants from the respective countries, known as the Committee of Permanent Representatives (Coreper).

The Commission

1.67 This is sometimes described as being the 'bureaucracy' of the Union, but perhaps a more accurate description would be the 'engine room'. At present there are 28 commissioners (although this number will be reduced by the Lisbon Treaty), plus a President. However, although appointed by their respective countries, commissioners are totally independent of them. Each commissioner has certain departmental responsibilities and is assisted by a cabinet and directorate general. Decisions are taken on a collegiate basis.

1.68 The Commission has the responsibility of initiating and drafting proposals for approval by the Council. It acts as a mediator between states, and as a 'watchdog' to ensure that EU rules are being observed. Indeed, if the Commission considers that a member state is failing to comply with an EU law, it can take enforcement action by referring the alleged breach to the European Court of Justice for a ruling (see para 1.70).

European Parliament

1.69 This body sits in Strasbourg and Brussels and currently consists of 766 members of the European Parliament (MEPs) elected directly from each member state. It can express an opinion to the Council of Ministers on proposals which emanate from the Commission, can submit questions to both institutions, and can, as a final sanction, dismiss the Commission on a vote of censure passed by a two-thirds majority. The Lisbon Treaty increased the involvement of the European Parliament through an extended co-decision process with the Council of Ministers.

Court of Justice of the European Communities

1.70 This Court sits in Luxembourg, and comprises 27 judges and eight advocates general. Appointments are made for six years. The Court gives rulings on the interpretation of European law, either on a reference from the Commission, at the request of the courts of a member state or on a claim brought by an individual person or corporation in a member state. Once it has given its ruling the matter is then referred back to the courts of the member state for compliance.

European Union law

1.71 For the purpose of this book, the law of the European Union consists of (a) Articles of the Treaty of Rome, (b) Directives passed by the Council of Ministers, (c) Recommendations, and (d) Decisions of the European Court of Justice. It must be borne in mind that any common law or statutory rule which is contrary to European law is void, and if there is any conflict between European law and UK law, the former is to be applied. Indeed, if, in any preliminary proceedings, it appears that the sole obstacle towards granting interim relief is a rule of national law which is in conflict with European law, that national law has to be set aside (*R v Secretary of State for Transport, ex p Factortame (No 2)*[39]). Further, the UK courts have now held that an organisation (*R v Secretary of State for Employment, ex p Equal Opportunities Commission*[40]) or a private individual (*R v Secretary of State for Employment, ex p Seymour-Smith and Perez*[41]) can bring an action for a declaration that UK law does not correctly implement EU law.

A. Articles of the Treaty

1.72 If an article of the Treaty on the Functioning of the European Union (TFEU) is clear, precise, unconditional, requires no further implementation, and does not give any discretion to member states, it is directly applicable and becomes an integral part of the law of member states (*Defrenne v Sabena*[42]). For example, Art 157 (formerly 119) of the Treaty provides 'Each Member State shall ensure and maintain the application of the principle that men and women should receive equal pay for equal work . . .'. This article has been invoked in a number of cases, and has been held to confer a distinct legal right on an individual, which can be enforced in national courts, in addition to any legal right conferred by national law (*Garland v British Rail Engineering Ltd*[43]). Similarly, Art 45 (formerly 48) of the Treaty on the Functioning of the European Union provides that member states shall ensure

---

[39] (C-213/89) [1991] 1 AC 603, [1990] 3 WLR 818, [1990] ECR I–2433, [1990] 3 CMLR 1, [1990] 2 Lloyd's Rep 351, 1990] NLJR 927, ECJ; apld sub nom *R v Secretary of State for Transport, ex p Factortame Ltd (No 2)* [1991] 1 All ER 70, [1990] NLJR 927, ECJ; apld sub nom *R v Secretary of State for Transport, ex p Factortame Ltd (No 2)* [1991] 1 AC 603, [1990] 3 WLR 818, [1990] 3 CMLR 375, [1990] 2 Lloyd's Rep 365n, [1991] 1 Lloyd's Rep 10, 134 Sol Jo 1189, [1990] 41 LS Gaz R 36, [1990] NLJR 1457, sub nom *Factortame Ltd v Secretary of State for Transport (No 2)* [1991] 1 All ER 70, HL.

[40] [1993] 1 All ER 1022, [1993] 1 WLR 872, [1993] 1 CMLR 915, [1993] ICR 251, [1993] IRLR 10, [1993] NLJR 332n, CA; on appeal [1995] 1 AC 1, [1994] 2 WLR 409, [1995] 1 CMLR 391, 92 LGR 360, [1994] IRLR 176, [1994] 18 LS Gaz R 43, NLJR 358, sub nom *Equal Opportunities Commission v Secretary of State for Employment* [1994] 1 All ER 910, [1994] ICR 317, HL.

[41] [1994] IRLR 448, DC; aff'd on other grounds [1996] All ER (EC) 1, [1995] ICR 889, [1995] IRLR 464, CA; revsd [1997] 2 All ER 273, [1997] 1 WLR 473, [1997] 2 CMLR 904, [1997] ICR 371, [1997] IRLR 315, 56 IRLB 15, HL; refd sub nom *R v Secretary of State for Employment, ex p Seymour-Smith*: C-167/97 [1999] 2 AC 554, [1999] 3 WLR 460, [1999] All ER (EC) 97, [1999] 2 CMLR 273, [1999] ICR 447, [1999] IRLR 253, ECJ; apld sub nom *R v Secretary of State for Employment, ex p Seymour-Smith (No 2)* [2000] 1 All ER 857, [2000] 1 WLR 435, [2000] 1 CMLR 770, [2000] ICR 244, [2000] IRLR 263, [2000] 09 LS Gaz R 40, HL.

[42] (C-43/75) [1981] 1 All ER 122, [1976] ECR 455, [1976] 2 CMLR 98, [1976] ICR 547, ECJ.

[43] [1983] 2 AC 751, [1982] 2 WLR 918, [1981] 2 CMLR 542, [1982] ICR 420, HL; refd 12/81 [1983] 2 AC 751, [1982] 2 All ER 402, [1982] 2 WLR 918, [1982] ECR 359, [1982] 1 CMLR 696, [1982] ICR 420, [1982] IRLR 111, ECJ; apld [1983] 2 AC 751, [1982] 2 All ER 402, [1982 2 WLR 918, [1982] 2 CMLR 174, [1982] ICR 420, [1982] IRLR 257, 126 Sol Jo 309, HL.

the free movement of workers within the Community without discrimination as regards employment, remuneration and other conditions of work and employment, and this too has a direct legal effect (*Van Duyn v Home Office (No 2)*[44]). Thus if a national of a member state wishes to obtain employment in the United Kingdom, he does not need a work permit, and he must be given equal access to social security benefits, holidays, equal pay, etc.

B. **Directives**

1.73 A Directive, passed by the Council of Ministers, is binding as to the result to be achieved, but the national authorities are given a choice of form and methods. However, as Directives are binding on member states, it is the duty of those states to implement them, and if the state fails to do so, an individual may seek to enforce the terms of the Directive against a state in its capacity as an employer (*Marshall v Southampton and South West Hampshire Area Health Authority*[45]). For this purpose, 'the state' includes any body which is an emanation of the state (eg a nationalised industry) or which provides a public service under the control of the state. In other words, a state cannot take advantage of its own failure to comply with European law (*Foster v British Gas*[46]).

In *Doughty v Rolls-Royce plc*,[47] the Court of Appeal laid down three criteria to be applied in considering whether or not any particular body is 'an emanation of the State', following principles laid down by the European Court in *Foster v British Gas*. These are:

whether the entity was made responsible, pursuant to a measure adopted by the state, for providing a public service;

whether the service it provided was under the control of the state; and

whether it possessed or claimed to exercise any special powers.

Thus, although Rolls Royce was 100% owned by the state, it was a commercial undertaking rather than a state body for the purpose of enforcing the provisions of a Directive.

For example, in *Impact v Ministry of Agriculture & Food*[48] the ECJ held that the non-discrimination provisions of the Fixed-Term Workers Directive (99/70/EC) were sufficiently 'clear, precise and unconditional' to have a direct effect, and can thus be enforced directly against a public authority irrespective of the provisions of national law. This would include, for example, pension entitlements that were discriminatory. However, the provisions that provide for the conversion of successive fixed-term contracts into permanent ones did not have a direct effect, although national law should be interpreted consistently with the Directive if this was possible.

1.74 In strict legal theory, a Directive is not enforceable against a non-state body or a private individual. Thus, if there are no national rules on a subject, it is not permissible to rely on the provisions of a Directive as the basis of a claim. However, the European Court of Justice has gone a great deal further in a number of cases. In *Dekker v Stichting*

[44] (C-41/74) [1975] Ch 358, [1975] 3 All ER 190, 2 WLR 760, [1974] ECR 1337, [1975] 1 CMLR 1, 119 Sol Jo 302, ECJ.

[45] [1983] 2 AC 751, [1982] 2 WLR 918, [1981] 2 CMLR 542, [1982] ICR 420, HL; refd 12/81 [1983] 2 AC 751, [1982] 2 All ER 402, [1982] 2 WLR 918, [1982] ECR 359, [1982] 1 CMLR 696, [1982] ICR 420, [1982] IRLR 111, ECJ; apld [1983] 2 AC 751, [1982] 2 All ER 402, [1982] 2 WLR 918, [1982] 2 CMLR 174, [1982] ICR 420, [1982] IRLR 257, 126 Sol Jo 309, HL.

[46] (C-188/89) [1991] 1 QB 405, [1990] 3 All ER 897, [1991] 2 WLR 258, [1990] ECR I-3313, [1990] 2 CMLR 833, [1991] ICR 84, [1990] IRLR 353, ECJ.

[47] [1992] 1 CMLR 1045, [1992] IRLR 126, sub nom *Rolls-Royce plc v Doughty* [1992] ICR 538, CA.

[48] [2009] All ER (EC) 306, [2008] ECR I-2483, [2008] 2 CMLR 47, [2009] CEC 871, [2008] IRLR 552, [2008] Pens LR 323.

Vormingscentrum voor Jong Volwassenen (VJV-Centrum) Plus,[49] it was held that it is permissible to rely on the provisions of a Directive in order to interpret national law, and in particular those provisions of national law which were designed to implement a Directive. Thus the European Court will interpret national law in the light of the language and aims of the Directive. In *Marleasing SA v La Comercial Internacional de Alimentación*,[50] the Court went still further. They stated: 'It follows from the obligation on member states to take all measures appropriate to ensure the performance of their obligation to achieve the results provided for in Directives, that in applying national law, whether it was a case of provisions prior to or subsequent to the Directive, the national court called on to interpret it was required to do so as far as possible in the light of the wording and purpose of the Directive in order to achieve the result sought by the Directive.'

Finally, in an historic decision, the European Court has stated that if a member state fails to take the necessary steps to achieve the results required by a Directive, an individual who suffers damage thereby may sue the state for the loss suffered which results from that failure. In *Francovich v Italy*,[51] the Italian Government had failed to implement EC Directive 80/987 on the protection of employees on an employer's insolvency. In consequence, an employee was unable to recover wages owed to him following his employer's insolvency, and he sued the Italian Government for compensation. It was held that his claim could succeed as long as three conditions were satisfied. These were that: (a) the result required by the Directive includes the conferring of rights for the benefit of individuals, (b) the contents of those rights may be determined by reference to the provisions of the Directive, and (c) there is a causal link between the breach of the obligation of the state and the damage suffered by the person affected.

Since these three conditions were met, the claim succeeded. However, the European Court appeared to suggest that a claim could be made not only when a member state fails to implement the terms of a Directive, but also when it incorrectly implements a Directive. Further, national courts are the appropriate forum for such claims, without the necessity of seeking a remedy in the European Court. However it should be noted that in *R v Secretary of State for Transport, ex p Factortame*,[52] the Advocate-General expressed the view that such liability would only arise if the breach was 'manifest and serious', which suggests that inadvertent or unwitting breaches of European law may not necessarily attract such a remedy.

A *Francovich* claim must be brought within the six-year period laid down in the Limitation Act 1980 (*Spencer v Secretary of State for Work and Pensions*[53]).

Thus, although Directives are addressed to member states, and can be enforced by intended beneficiaries against the state, there also appears to be an interesting remedy against a state which fails to implement or incorrectly implements a Directive by persons who suffer damage thereby.

It should be noted that '*Francovich*' style claims arising from an alleged failure by a state properly to implement a Directive must be brought in the High Court, not an employment tribunal (*Secretary of State for Employment v Mann*[54]). In *Brasserie du Pêcheur SA v*

[49] (C-177/88) [1990] ECR I–3941, [1992] ICR 325, [1991] IRLR 27, ECJ.

[50] (C-106/89) [1990] ECR I–4135, [1992] 1 CMLR 305, [1993] BCC 421, 135 Sol Jo 15, ECJ.

[51] (C-6/90 and 9/90) [1991] ECR I–5357, [1993] 2 CMLR 66, [1995] ICR 722, [1992] IRLR 84, ECJ.

[52] (C-48/93) [1996] QB 404, [1996] 2 WLR 506, [1996] ECR I–1029, [1996] All ER (EC) 301, [1996] 1 CMLR 889, [1996] IRLR 267, ECJ; apld [1998] 1 CMLR 1353, [1997] TLR 482, [1997] Eu LR 475, [1998] 1 All ER 736n, DC; aff'd [1998] 3 CMLR 192, [1998] NPC 68, [1998] TLR 261, [1998] Eu LR 456, [1999] 2 All ER 640n, CA; aff'd [2000] 1 AC 524, [1999] 4 All ER 906, [1999] 3 WLR 1062, [1999] 3 CMLR 597, [1999] 43 LS Gaz R 32, HL.

[53] [2008] EWCA Civ 750, [2009] QB 358, [2009] 2 WLR 593, [2009] 1 All ER 314, [2008] CP Rep 40, [2009] RTR 5, [2008] 3 CMLR 15, [2008] Eu LR 779, [2008] ICR 1359, [2008] IRLR 911, [2008] PIQR P21, (2008) 152(27) SJLB 31, (2008) *Times*, 24 July.

[54] n 17.

Germany,[55] the European Court of Justice gave guidance on the principles and approach to be adopted when national courts deal with *Francovich* type claims. The three issues considered were liability, damages and retrospection.

So far as liability was concerned, the Court stated that there was no difference in principle between those EU rights which were directly or indirectly applicable. Thus a right arising out of the Treaty (eg Art 141) or a right against a state body by a state employee (*Foster v British Gas*[56]) is to be treated in the same way as those rights which were indirectly applicable (*Marleasing SA v La Comercial Internacional de Alimentación*[57]). Further, the state was to be considered as a single entity, and thus it did not matter if the breach was attributable to the executive, the legislature or the judiciary.

If the EU rule confers a wide discretion (as do some Directives), it must be established that it was intended to confer rights on an individual. If so, the next question to answer is whether the breach was 'sufficiently serious' in that there was a manifest and serious disregard of the discretion. This is for the national courts to decide, taking into account the clarity and precision of the rule that has been breached, the measure of the discretion given to national authorities, whether the breach was voluntary or involuntary, whether any error of law was excusable or inexcusable, whether it was caused or contributed to by any position taken by an EU institution, and the general adoption or retention of national measures which are contrary to EU law. A breach will be sufficiently serious if it has continued despite a judgment finding that there has been a breach, or where there has been a previous legal ruling from the ECJ making it clear that there has been an infringement.

So far as damages are concerned, the Court stated that national rules must not make it impossible or extremely difficult for an individual to obtain reparation, and damages awarded must be commensurate with the loss suffered. The criteria should not be less favourable than those applicable to similar claims based on domestic law. However, a national court is entitled to enquire into the steps taken by a complainant to mitigate the loss, in particular having regard to available legal remedies.

Finally, so far as retrospection was concerned, the ECJ was of the opinion that the main issue was whether the breach was sufficiently serious. If it was, then there was no temporal limit on the effect of an ECJ judgment. However, claims could be subjected to substantive and procedural limitations imposed by national law, which could take into account principles of legal certainty by applying time limits on claims.

If a Directive is not capable of having direct effect, but is then subsequently transposed into domestic law, national courts are required to interpret the legislation in a manner which gives effect to the aims of the Directive, from the date that the period for transposition into national law has expired (*Adeneler v Ellinikos Organismos Galaktos*[58]).

1.75 Currently, there are a number of Directives in force which have a particular bearing on employment law, and which have been implemented by UK legislation.

Directive 75/117/EEC (Equal Pay)

1.76 This states that the principle of equal pay means, for the same work or for work to which equal value has been attributed, the elimination of all discrimination on grounds

---

[55] (C-46/93) [1996] QB 404, [1996] 2 WLR 506, [1996] ECR I–1029, [1996] All ER (EC) 301, [1996] 1 CMLR 889, [1996] IRLR 267, ECJ; apld [1998] 1 CMLR 1353, [1997] TLR 482, [1997] Eu LR 475, [1998] 1 All ER 736n, DC; aff'd [1998] 3 CMLR 192, [1998] NPC 68, [1998] TLR 261, [1998] Eu LR 456, [1999] 2 All ER 640n, CA; aff'd [2000] 1 AC 524, [1999] 4 All ER 906, [1999] 3 WLR 1062, [1999] 3 CMLR 597, [1999] 43 LS Gaz R 32, HL.

[56] n 46.

[57] (C-106/89) [1990] ECR I–4135, [1992] 1 CMLR 305, [1993] BCC 421, 135 Sol Jo 15, ECJ.

[58] (C-212/04) [2006] ECR I–6057, [2006] IRLR 716, [2006] 3 CMLR 30, [2006] EUECJ C-212/04, [2007] All ER (EC) 82, ECJ.

of sex with regard to all aspects and conditions of remuneration. Member states shall take the necessary measures to ensure that provisions appearing in collective agreements, wage scales, wage agreements or individual contracts of employment which are contrary to the principle of equal pay shall be declared null and void or may be amended. The Equal Pay Act 1970 and the Equal Pay (Amendment) Regulations 1983 implemented this Directive.

Directive 76/207/EEC (Equal Treatment)

1.77 This states that men and women shall be entitled to equal treatment as regards access to employment, including promotion, and also to vocational training and working conditions. There shall be no discrimination on grounds of sex, either directly or indirectly by reference to marital or family status. To comply with this Directive, reference may now be made to the Equality Act 2010. Equal access to occupational pension schemes is now provided for in the Pension Schemes Act 1993, and equal benefits will come within the provisions of the Pensions Act 1995. The dismissal of a transsexual for a reason relating to a sex change is precluded by the Directive (see *P v S* and para 4.119).[59]

Directive 75/129/EEC (Collective Redundancies)

1.78 This Directive requires employers to consult with workers' representatives before making collective redundancies, and also requires that prior notification be given to the competent public authorities. The provisions of TULR(C)A, ss 188–194 (as amended) are designed to meet this Directive. This Directive has been repealed and replaced by 98/59/EC.

Directive 77/187/EEC (Acquired Rights)

1.79 This Directive provides for the safeguarding of the rights of employees when their employment is transferred from one employer to another. The transferor and transferee are also required to consult with employees' representatives about the consequences of the transfer. The Transfer of Undertakings (Protection of Employment) Regulations 2006 implement the Directive. This Directive has been repealed and replaced by 2001/23/EC.

Directive 79/7/EEC (Equal Treatment in Social Security Matters)

1.80 This Directive requires that there should be no discrimination on grounds of sex (either directly or indirectly by reference to marital or family status) in the scope of social security schemes (ie sickness, invalidity, old age, occupational accidents and diseases, and unemployment benefits), the conditions of access thereto, contributions, the calculation of benefits (including benefits for spouses and dependants) and the duration of benefits. However, excluded from this Directive are benefits which arise from the determination of pensionable age. At the present time, women are permitted to receive the state pension at 60, whereas men receive it when they are 65 although the Pensions Act 1995 makes provisions for the progressive equalisation of state pensions at age 65 for both sexes, and this is permissible under the Directive. Other social security legislation has been passed to conform to its provisions.

Directive 86/378/EEC (Equal Treatment in Occupational Social Security Schemes)

1.81 This Directive requires that there shall be no discrimination between men and women in access to and benefits from occupational pension schemes. The Social Security Act 1989 was designed to implement the Directive, but further problems have arisen as a result of the decision in *Barber v Guardian Royal Exchange Assurance Group*.[60]

---

[59] (C-13/94) [1996] ECR I–2143, [1996] All ER (EC) 397, [1996] 2 CMLR 247, [1996] ICR 795, [1996] IRLR 347, [1997] 2 FCR 180, [1996] 2 FLR 347, [1996] Fam Law 609, ECJ.

[60] (C-262/88) [1991] 1 QB 344, [1990] 2 All ER 660, [1991] 2 WLR 72, [1990] ECR I–1889, [1990] 2 CMLR 513, [1990] ICR 616, [1990] IRLR 240, [1990] NJLR 925, ECJ.

Directive 86/613/EEC (Equal Treatment for Self-employed)

1.82 This Directive requires that the laws of member states relating to self-employment shall not contain any discriminatory provisions, that there shall be protection for self-employed persons and their wives during pregnancy and motherhood, and that discrimination does not arise from the establishing of businesses or other self-employed activities.

Directive 80/987/EEC (Employers' Insolvency)

1.83 This Directive requires member states to guarantee the payment of certain outstanding claims due to an employee when his employer becomes insolvent, subject to certain limits. The provisions of the Insolvency Act 1986 meet the terms of this Directive.

Directive 91/533/EEC (Proof of Employment Relationship)

1.84 This Directive requires employers to inform employees on the terms and conditions which apply to the employment relationship. It has been given effect by the Employment Rights Act, ss 1–10.

Directive 93/104/EEC (Working Time)

1.85 This Directive concerns aspects of the organisation of working time, with compulsory rest periods, holidays, and a maximum working week of 48 hours. This Directive was passed under the provisions of Art 139 of the Treaty of Rome, which permits health and safety matters to be passed by a qualified majority vote. The lawfulness of this Directive was challenged by the UK Government (*United Kingdom v EU Council*[61]) but the ECJ held that it was properly a health and safety matter, and in consequence, the Working Time Regulations 1998 were introduced. This Directive has been repealed and replaced by 2003/88/EC.

Directive 94/45/EC (European Works Councils)

1.86 This Directive requires works councils to be set up in Community-scale undertakings, ie an undertaking with at least 1,000 employees in a member state and at least 150 employees in at least two member states. The Transnational Information and Consultation of Employees Regulations 1999 implement this Directive. This Directive has been repealed and replaced by 2009/38/EC.

Directive 94/33/EC (Protection of Young People at Work)

1.87 This Directive has been implemented by various provisions, eg Management of Health and Safety at Work Regulations, Working Time Regulations etc.

Directive 96/34/EC (Parental Leave)

1.88 This Directive gave certain minimum rights in relation to parental leave, and time off to care for dependants. It has been repealed and replaced by Directive 2010/18/EU (see para 1.97).

Directive 97/81/EC (Part-time Work)

1.89 This Directive requires the removal of less favourable treatment in respect of part-time workers. It has been implemented by the Part-time Workers (Prevention of Less Favourable Treatment) Regulations 2000.

Directive 96/71/EC (Posted Workers)

1.90 This Directive requires that workers who move from one EC country to another are treated no less favourably than the employees of the host country. The Directive has been implemented by various provisions in the Employment Rights Act.

---

[61] (C-84/94) [1996] ECR I–05755.

Directive 99/70/EC (Fixed-term Workers)

1.91 This Directive applies the principle of non-discrimination to employees who are in fixed-term employment, and requires that action be taken to eliminate the abuse of successive fixed-term contracts. The Fixed Term Employees (Protection of Less Favourable Treatment) Regulations 2002 implement this Directive.

Directive 97/80/EC (Burden of Proof)

1.92 This Directive requires that if a person claims that s/he has suffered direct or indirect discrimination, it shall be for the respondent to prove that there has been no breach of the principle of equal treatment. The Directive has been implemented by the Sex Discrimination (Indirect Discrimination and Burden of Proof) Regulations 2001.

Directive 2000/78/EC (Equal Treatment in Employment and Occupation)

1.93 This Directive requires that there shall be no discrimination in employment on grounds of religion or belief, disability, age or sexual orientation. These matters are dealt with generally by the Sex Discrimination Act, Disability Discrimination Act, Employment Equality (Sexual Orientation) Regulations 2003, Employment Equality (Religion or Belief) Regulations 2003, Disability Discrimination Act 1995 (Amendment) Regulations 2003 and the Employment Equality (Age) Regulations 2006 all of which were replaced by the Equality Act 2010.

Directive 2000/43/EC (Equal Treatment between Persons Irrespective of Racial or Ethnic Origins)

1.94 This Directive requires that there shall be no direct or indirect discrimination based on racial or ethnic grounds. Its provisions are covered by the Race Relations Act (now the Equality Act).

Directive 2002/14/EC (Information and Consultation)

1.95 This Directive required employers of a certain size to give information about the conduct of the undertaking. It is implemented by the Information and Consultation of Employees Regulations 2004.

Directive 2008/104/EC (Agency Workers Directive)

1.96 This Directive requires that temporary agency workers shall be given equal treatment in comparison to permanent workers in the same undertaking doing the same job, as regards basic working conditions, such as pay, working hours, rest breaks, night work and holidays. However, there is no protection for unfair dismissal, notice periods or the right to a redundancy payment. The Government has opted to make use of a permitted derogation that will provide that the equal treatment rule will only apply after the agency worker has been employed at the same job for 12 calendar weeks. However, entitlement to certain rights, such as the right to receive information about job vacancies, will operate from the commencement of employment. The Agency Workers Regulations 2010 implement this Directive (see para 2.163).

Directive 2010/18/EU (Parental Leave)

1.97 This Directive replaced Directive 96/34/EC with effect from 8 March 2012. It states that men and women have an individual right to parental leave on the grounds of the birth or adoption of a child to enable them to take care of that child, for at least four months, until the child reaches the age of eight. The length of service qualification should be no more than one year. In addition, the right is in principle 'non-transferable' ie either a man or woman can take leave in respect of a child, but not both of them, and not alternatively, however the Directive allows member states to make the leave transferable so long as at least one of the months is not transferable.

The Directive leaves it to member states to decide the details of how the scheme for parental leave should be implemented, eg on a full-time or part-time basis, in a piecemeal way, or in the form of a time credit system. There is to be protection against dismissal for applying for or taking parental leave, and, at the end of the leave, workers will have the right to return to their old job, or to a similar or equivalent job.

It also requires states to provide that employers take measures to ensure that workers returning from such leave may request changes to their working hours and/or patterns for a set period of time, and for employers to consider such requests. States are also required to provide that workers are to be permitted to take time off work in the event of *force majeure* for urgent family reasons in cases of sickness or accident. This Directive has led to the provisions on parental and paternity leave, time off work to care for dependants, and the right to request flexible working (see Chapter 6 for family friendly legislation).

Other Directives

1.98 A number of other Directives relating to health and safety at work have also been passed by the Council of Ministers, and these are referred to in Chapter 11. In 2006 all seven measures dealing with the implementation of the principle of equal opportunities and equal treatment of men and women in matters of employment and occupation were consolidated into the Equal Treatment Directive 2006/54/EC with effect from August 2009.

C. **Recommendations**

1.99 A Recommendation made under Community law has no binding effect, and cannot be relied upon to enforce a legal right in a national court. However, in *Grimaldi v Fonds des Maladies Professionnelles,*[62] the European Court of Justice held that national courts are bound to take Recommendations into account when determining disputes which are referred to them, in particular when they clarify the interpretation of laws passed to implement them, or when they are designed to supplement binding Community measures.

1.100 Recommendations have been made on such topics as the employment of disabled persons, hours of work and holidays generally, flexible retirement, vocational training for women and sexual harassment.

D. **Decisions of the Court of Justice of the European Union**

1.101 The Court of Justice of the European Union has jurisdiction under Art 234 of the Treaty of the Functioning of the European Union to give rulings concerning the interpretation of the Treaty or Regulations or Directives made by the Council of Ministers. A member state may be taken to the Court by another state or by the European Commission (see *EC Commission v United Kingdom,*[63] para 18.69). A UK court may, but is not bound to, make a reference to the Court if it is necessary to enable a decision to be made (see *Macarthys Ltd v Smith,*[64] para 5.11). Once the Court has given its opinion, the matter is

---

[62] (C-322/88) [1989] ECR 4407, [1991] 2 CMLR 265, [1990] IRLR 400, ECJ.

[63] (C-382/92) [1994] ECR I–2435, [1995] 1 CMLR 345, [1994] ICR 664, [1994] IRLR 392, ECJ.

[64] (C-129/79) [1978] 2 All ER 746, [1978] 1 WLR 849, [1978] ICR 500, [1978] IRLR 10, 122 Sol Jo 456, EAT; on appeal [1979] 3 All ER 325, [1979] 1 WLR 1189, [1979] 3 CMLR 44, [1979] ICR 785, [1979] IRLR 316, 123 Sol Jo 603, CA; refd [1981] QB 180, [1981] 1 All ER 111, [1980] 3 WLR 929, [1980] ECR 1275, [1980] 2 CMLR 205, [1980] ICR 672, [1980] IRLR 210, 124 Sol Jo 808, ECJ; apld [1981] QB 180, [1981] 1 All ER 111, [1980] 3 WLR 929, [1980] 2 CMLR 217, [1980] ICR 672, [1980] IRLR 210, 124 Sol Jo 808, CA.

referred back to the national court for the application of the opinion to the facts of the case (see *Jenkins v Kingsgate (Clothing Productions) Ltd*[65]).

1.102 It should be noted that there are no specified time limits for bringing a claim under European law, as the provisions of the Treaty of Rome came into force upon accession (see *Stevens v Bexley Health Authority*[66]). Time will start to run against a state body from the day the state makes good its failure to comply with the objectives laid down in the Directive (*Cannon v Barnsley Metropolitan Borough Council*[67]). However, the European Court may, when giving a ruling, indicate that this shall only apply to claims lodged at the date of the ruling (*Barber v Guardian Royal Exchange*[68]).

1.103 If a person is seeking to enforce a private right which has come to light as a result of the interpretation of EC law by the European Court, national domestic procedures relating to time limits must be adhered to. Thus in *Biggs v Somerset County Council*[69] the applicant was a teacher who worked for 14 hours per week. She was dismissed in 1976 but, relying on the House of Lords' decision in *R v Secretary of State for Employment, ex p Equal Opportunities Commission*[70] (which held that the 'hours' requirement was discriminatory and contrary to the EC Equal Treatment Directive), brought a claim for unfair dismissal in 1994. It was held that her claim was out of time. She was not seeking to enforce a Community right (there is no EC right to be unfairly dismissed), and there is no separate procedure for bringing claims under EC law (see also *Setiya v East Yorkshire Health Authority*[71] and Chapter 20). (Note that in case law before 2011 the court was referred to as the ECJ, after that time it became CJEU.)

Human Rights Act 1998

1.104 In order to prevent a re-occurrence of the horrors and atrocities which took place before and during the Second World War, the European Convention for the Protection of Human Rights and Fundamental Freedoms was signed in 1950. Many European countries subsequently incorporated the Convention into their domestic law, but UK citizens who wished to assert a Convention right were forced to petition the European Court of Human Rights in Strasbourg. The UK Government would always give effect to any ruling from that court, but the Convention itself was not enforceable in UK courts.

1.105 Despite the financial and practical difficulties involved in pursuing a claim under the Convention, some notable decisions were given against the UK Government in circumstances where the ordinary legal system could not or would not provide a remedy. For example, in *R v Admiralty Board of the Defence Council, ex p Lustig-Prean*,[72] the Court of Appeal refused to interfere with a decision to discharge the applicant from the Royal Navy on the ground that he was a homosexual, and he thus brought proceedings in the European Court of Human Rights. That Court held (*Lustig-Prean v United Kingdom*[73]) that a decision to discharge homosexuals from the armed forces on grounds of their sexual orientation was a violation of their right to respect for their private lives, and thus was contrary to Art 8 of the Convention. The outcome was the lifting of the ban on homosexuals and lesbians joining or staying in the armed forces. A similar outcome was reached in three other cases (see *Smith v United Kingdom*[74]).

---

[65] [1981] ICR 715, [1981] IRLR 388, EAT.   [66] [1989] ICR 224, [1989] IRLR 240, EAT.
[67] [1992] 2 CMLR 795, [1992] ICR 698, [1992] IRLR 474, EAT.   [68] n 60.   [69] n 16.
[70] n 40.   [71] [1995] IRLR 348, EAT.
[72] [1996] QB 517, [1996] 2 WLR 305, [1996] ICR 740, sub nom *R v Ministry of Defence, ex p Smith* [1996] 1 All ER 257, [1996] IRLR 100, CA.
[73] (1999) 29 EHRR 548, 7 BHRC 65, ECtHR.
[74] (Applications 33985/96 and 33986/96) 29 EHRR 493, [1999] ECHR 33985/96, ECtHR.

1.106 The Human Rights Act 1998 is designed to give effect to the rights and freedoms guaranteed under the Convention, by effectively incorporating it into UK law. It came into force in October 2000 and its basic provisions may be summarised as follows:

A court or tribunal determining a question which has arisen in connection with a Convention right must take into account any judgment, decision, declaration or advisory opinion of the European Court of Human Rights. But although it is mandatory to take these into account, the court or tribunal is given a discretion whether to follow that decision etc (see *Kleinwort Benson Ltd v Glasgow City Council*[75]). It has long been recognised that the Convention is a 'living instrument', and a previous decision of the Court need not be followed if it is out of step with current practices and opinions, or if it is unpersuasive. Further, the Court itself developed the doctrine of 'the margin of appreciation' which recognised the relatively restrained scrutiny of national law.

So far as it is possible to do so, primary and subordinate legislation must be read and given effect in a way which is compatible with Convention rights. Thus, if a court or tribunal has a choice to interpret a statute in two ways, one of which is compatible with the Convention and one not, the former interpretation must prevail (see *Marleasing*, para 1.74). This obligation arises whenever the statutory provisions were passed. But if a statute has only one possible meaning, effect must be given to it accordingly.

If a court (not a tribunal) is satisfied that a provision in primary legislation is incompatible with a Convention right, it may make a declaration of incompatibility, although before doing so it must give the Crown notice of such intention, so as to enable the Crown to be joined as a party to the proceedings. Such a declaration does not affect the validity of the provision in question, nor is it binding on the parties to the proceedings but, once made, doubtless Parliament will consider taking steps to ensure compliance with the Convention.

It is unlawful for a public authority to act in a way which is incompatible with a Convention right. There is some uncertainty as to which bodies are 'public authorities', which will doubtless be the subject of case law, but courts and tribunals are certainly within the meaning of the term. A person aggrieved by such an act may bring proceedings in an appropriate legal venue, and certain remedies, including compensation, are available.

1.107 So far as the law of employment is concerned, there are a number of possible implications arising from the Act. An employee cannot lodge a claim in an employment tribunal based directly on a Convention right, but in any claim brought in a tribunal based on domestic law, the tribunal will take those rights into account, unless prohibited from so doing by domestic law. The Act is beginning to impact on employment law claims, but it should be borne in mind that some of the rights are hedged with qualifications. The following Articles of the Convention may well be relevant:

(a) *Article 4* states that 'no one shall be required to perform forced or compulsory labour'. In *R (on the application of Reilly and another) v Secretary of State for Work and Pensions*,[76] the Supreme Court held that making jobseeker's allowance (JSA) conditional on work or work-related activity does not constitute forced labour, as it was work forming part of 'normal civic obligations'. This is not the type of exploitative conduct at which Art 4 is aimed (although fault was found with the regulations for other reasons).

---

[75] (C-346/93) [1996] QB 57, [1995] 3 WLR 866, [1995] ECR I–615, [1995] All ER (EC) 514, ECJ; re-heard [1996] QB 678, [1996] 2 All ER 257, [1996] 2 WLR 655, CA; revsd [1999] 1 AC 153, [1997] 4 All ER 641, [1997] 3 WLR 923, [1997] NLJR 1617, 141 Sol Jo LB 237, HL.

[76] [2013] UKSC 68.

(b) *Article 6.* In the determination of a person's civil rights and obligations, everyone is entitled to a fair and public hearing within a reasonable time by an independent and impartial tribunal established by law. Thus in *Somjee v United Kingdom*[77] three claims before an employment tribunal and the Employment Appeal Tribunal took more than seven years to be resolved. The European Court held that this violated Art 6 of the Convention. If a person is charged with misconduct before a public body, this is a determination of his civil rights, and the protection in Art 6 applies. Thus he is entitled to have a fair hearing, ie to know in good time the nature of the charges, be given adequate time to prepare his case, to question witnesses, and to call evidence, etc (*R v Securities & Futures Authority Ltd, ex p Fleurose*[78]). The right does not apply indiscriminately, however. In *Al-Malki & Anor v Reyes & Anor*[79] the fact that the diplomatic immunity of the employer prevented an employee from bringing an action in an employment tribunal did not breach the employee's rights under Art 6 (but see *Kücükdeveci* and *Aklagaren* later in this section) This case may go to the Court of Appeal.

It was suggested in *Smith v Secretary of State for Trade and Industry*[80] that the independence of employment tribunals themselves was in doubt, because the Secretary of State exercised control over the appointment, tenure and pay of lay members, but subsequently changes were made in these matters which allayed the fears of any conflict of interest or lack of impartiality, and it has now been accepted that employment tribunals are impartial and independent within the meaning of Art 6 (*Scanfuture UK Ltd v Secretary of State for Trade and Industry*[81]). It has been held that there is an objection to an advocate appearing before the Employment Appeal Tribunal if he is also a part-time judge of that Tribunal, because there was a real possibility that lay members who had sat with him in that capacity might subconsciously be biased in favour of submissions made in his capacity as an advocate (*Lawal v Northern Spirit Ltd,* see para 1.22). On the other hand, s 40 of the Health and Safety at Work Act (see para 11.97), which reverses the burden of proof which would ordinarily apply in criminal proceedings, did not violate Art 6. Balancing the fundamental rights of the individual with the general interests of the community in ensuring health and safety at work, the reversal was justified as necessary and proportionate, and therefore compatible with the Convention (*Davies v Health and Safety Executive*[82]).

It is not a violation of Art 6 for an employer to refuse an employee the right of legal representation at a disciplinary hearing, even when the ultimate sanction is likely to be the loss of a job. But a different consideration will apply if the sanction could result in being deprived of an opportunity to practice his or her chosen career, or where some other serious consequence could result, eg being placed on the sex offenders register. In *G v X School*[83] a teacher was brought before a disciplinary body charged with an allegation of sexual misconduct with a 15-year-old student. If the allegations were established this could have adversely affected his whole career. It was held that although he was not facing a criminal charge, the serious nature of the

---

[77] (Application 42116/98) [2002] IRLR 886, [2002] All ER (D) 214 (Oct), ECtHR.

[78] [2002] IRLR 297, CA. [79] UKEAT/0403/12/GE.

[80] [2000] ICR 69, [2000] IRLR 6, EAT.

[81] [2001] ICR 1096, [2001] IRLR 416, [2001] Emp LR 590, EAT.

[82] [2002] EWCA Crim 2949, [2003] IRLR 170, [2003] 09 LS Gaz R 27, [2003] JPN 142, 147 Sol Jo LB 29, [2002] All ER (D) 275 (Dec).

[83] [2010] EWCA Civ 1, [2010] 2 All ER 555, [2010] IRLR 222, [2010] HRLR 13, [2010] BLGR 207, [2010] Med LR 45, (2010) *Times*, 23 February.

allegations and the severity of the consequences meant that he was entitled to have legal representation under Art 6 of the Convention. A similar view appears to have been taken in *Kulkarni v Milton Keynes Hospital NHS Foundation Trust*,[84] where a junior doctor was accused of inappropriately touching a female patient. It was stated obiter that if an adverse outcome of the case was so potentially damaging as to make it highly unlikely that he would be able to work in his chosen profession, then Art 6 requires that he be given the right to legal representation.

These decisions only affect public employers, who are required to act in a way compatible with Convention rights. Whether the principle can be extended to private employers has yet to be determined.

The Convention will not assist a claimant to pursue whims and fancies. In *Khan v Vignette Europe Ltd*[85] an employment tribunal refused to grant an adjournment mid-way through a hearing so that the claimant could experience a period of mental and spiritual purity during Ramadan. It was held that the decision did not violate his right to a fair trial under Art 6.

Where a fundamental principle of EU law is concerned, such as the right to a fair hearing, domestic courts must disapply a provision which stands in its way. In *Kücükdeveci v Swedex GmbH & Co KG*[86] and *Aklagaren v Fransson*[87] (see also para 17.4(f)) the ECJ confirmed that where a fundamental principle of EU law is concerned, such as the right to a fair hearing, domestic courts must disapply a provision which stands in its way. This was done in *Benkharbouche v Sudan*,[88] where the State Immunity Act 1978 prevented domestic workers employed by two embassies from bringing claims. The EAT held that its provisions were to be disapplied by the Charter of Fundamental Rights of the European Union in relation to discrimination and working time claims. Further claims of unfair dismissal and the minimum wage were not covered, as they did not derive from EU law. The EAT effectively held that as a result of the Lisbon Treaty, the EU charter was now directly applicable in the UK, and the tribunal was therefore bound to disapply UK law which conflicted with these principles even between private litigants. It is likely that this case will be appealed. This is a significant decision, which could mean that even where the ERA does not allow a statutory provision to be disapplied, EU law will require a tribunal to do so where it concerns EU law. This is likely to be appealed.

(c) *Article 8*. Everyone has the right to respect for his private and family life, his home and his correspondence. This right is subject to certain qualifications, ie when the interference is by a public authority in accordance with the law, and is necessary in a democratic society in the interests of national security, public safety or the economic well-being of the country, for the prevention of disorder or crime, for the protection of health or morals, or for the protection of rights and freedoms of others. In *McGowan v Scottish Water*[89] the employer obtained evidence through covert surveillance that the employee had been falsifying his time sheets. He claimed that he had been unfairly dismissed, arguing that his right to respect for his private life under Art 8 of the Convention had been breached. His claim was dismissed by the EAT. The interference with his rights was justified under Art 8(2), in that the

---

[84] [2009] EWCA Civ 789, [2010] ICR 101, [2009] IRLR 829, [2009] LS Law Medical 465, (2009) 109 BMLR 133, (2009) *Times*, 6 August.

[85] Employment Appeals Tribunal, 14 January 2010. [86] C-555/07. [87] Section 1.01.

[88] *Benkharbouche v Embassy of the Republic of Sudan* UKEAT/0401/12/GE; *Janah v Libya* UKEAT/0020/13/GE.

[89] [2005] IRLR 167, EAT.

employer's actions were 'in accordance with the law and necessary for the prevention of disorder or crime . . .'.

The right to respect for private life includes the right to privacy with respect to a person's sexual orientation. The European Court in *Smith v United Kingdom*[90] held that to discriminate against a person on grounds of his/her sexual orientation was a violation of Art 8 of the Convention, and this was transposed into UK law by the Employment Equality (Sexual Orientation) Regulations 2003 (see para 4.185).

An employee has a reasonable expectation of privacy in respect of private telephone calls. In *Halford v United Kingdom*[91] the employee was a senior police officer who alleged that her employer had tapped a private work telephone, in order to obtain details of a claim for sex discrimination she was pursuing. The European Court of Human Rights held that as she had not been given any prior indication that her telephone calls were liable to interception, there had been a breach of Art 8.

The right to privacy in respect of correspondence clearly includes unauthorised monitoring by employers of telephone calls, e-mail communications, and the use of the internet at the workplace. An employer must therefore seek to justify any such interference by relying on one of the qualifications mentioned earlier, or by notifying employees that such interception may take place at any time. The position is further clarified by the Telecommunications (Lawful Business Practice) (Interception of Communications) Regulations 2000, designed to ensure compliance with the Telecommunications Data Protection Directive (EC 97/66), which permits the interception and monitoring of telephone calls, e-mail communications etc, for certain specified purposes (see para 10.47). However, Art 8 of the Convention does not apply in respect of the commission of a criminal offence in a public place (*X v Y*[92]).

There are a number of other possibilities arising out of Art 8, including the lawfulness of mandatory medical examinations, confidentiality of medical reports, etc. It is unlikely that any remedy will exist in cases where an employee has given his consent to such action, or where there is a contractual power to do so, and the qualifications to Art 8 must always be borne in mind.

(d) *Article 9*. This Article provides for the right to freedom of thought, conscience and religion, but it is subject to the same qualifications as are found in Article 8, relating to the limitations imposed in the interests of national security, public safety, economic well-being of the country, preventing disorder or crime, protecting health and morals, and protecting the rights and freedoms of others. Thus in *Ahmad v United Kingdom*[93] the employers refused to permit a devout Muslim to take 45 minutes off work every Friday in order to pray at the local mosque. Instead, they offered to reduce his working hours from a five-day week to four and a half days. He refused this offer, arguing that he would suffer a loss of pay and benefits if he accepted, and resigned, claiming that he had been constructively dismissed. His claim was dismissed by an employment tribunal, and an appeal to the European Court of Human Rights was rejected. By offering to reduce his working hours to enable him to attend the local mosque in his own time the employers had not infringed his right to practise his religion. Similarly, in *Stedman v United Kingdom*[94] a woman's contract of employment required her to work on Sundays. She refused to do so, and was

---

[90] n 74.

[91] (Application 20605/92) (1997) 24 EHRR 523, [1997] IRLR 471, [1998] Crim LR 753, 94 LS Gaz R 24, 3 BHRC 31, ECtHR.

[92] [2004] EWCA Civ 662, [2004] ICR 1634, CA.

[93] (Application 8160/78) (1981) 4 EHRR 126, EComHR.

[94] (1997) 23 EHRR CD 168, [1997] EHRLR 545.

dismissed. She claimed that the dismissal was in breach of Art 9 of the Convention, but it was held that it was her refusal to comply with her contractual obligations, not her religious beliefs, which led to her dismissal.

(e) *Article 10.* This Article provides that everyone has the right to freedom of expression, including the freedom to hold opinions and receive and impart information and ideas without interference by a public authority. Again, the exercise of such freedoms may be limited by such formalities, conditions, restrictions or penalties as are prescribed by law, and are necessary in a democratic society, in the interests of national security, territorial integrity or public safety, for the prevention of disorder or crime, for the protection of health or morals, for the protection of the reputation of others, for preventing the disclosure of information received in confidence, or for maintaining the authority and impartiality of the judiciary.

Thus freedom of speech is covered by the Convention, but hedged with a number of well-recognised limitations. In *Ahmad v United Kingdom*, the Local Government Officers (Political Restrictions) Regulations 1990 restricted the political activities of certain categories of local government officials. The applicant, who was a solicitor employed by one local authority, wished to stand as a candidate in the local elections in another area, but was obliged to withdraw his candidature. He claimed that his rights to freedom of expression had been infringed, but the European Court of Human Rights dismissed his claim. The restrictions imposed were 'prescribed by law', and they pursued a legitimate aim of aiming to ensure effective political democracy at the local level. The Court also applied the doctrine of 'margin of appreciation', ie leaving it to the contracting state to assess whether pressing social needs existed. In this case, the regulations had been passed following a thorough enquiry, and were a valid response by the legislature.

It could be argued that a requirement to follow a particular dress code potentially violates the right to freedom of expression, although a rule which applies to both men and women, and is designed to enforce a common standard of conventionality is not discriminatory on grounds of sex (*Smith v Safeways plc*[95]) and rules which are unlikely to come within the scope of the Convention. In *Kara v United Kingdom*[96] the Commission of Human Rights dismissed a claim by a male transvestite who wore female clothing at work, holding that a requirement to wear appropriate clothing was in accordance with the law and appropriate.

(f) *Article 11.* This states that everyone has the right to freedom of assembly and to freedom of association with others, including the right to form and join trade unions (see *Wilson v United Kingdom,*[97] para 21.49) for the protection of their interests. Again, there are the usual qualifications to this right, and, in addition, the Convention permits the imposition of lawful restrictions on the exercise of these rights by members of the armed forces, the police, and the administration of the state.

Freedom of assembly and freedom of association also implies a freedom not to assemble or associate. In *Young, James and Webster v United Kingdom*[98] it was held that a requirement to join a trade union which did not exist when workers were first employed (with the threat of a dismissal if there was a failure to do so) amounted to an interference with freedom guaranteed under Art 11. It was wrong to compel someone to join an association contrary to their convictions. Also, the prohibition

---

[95] [1996] ICR 868, [1996] IRLR 456, CA.   [96] Unreported ECtHR.
[97] (Applications 30668/96, 30679/96 and 30678/96) [2002] IRLR 568, 13 BHRC 39, [2002] All ER (D) 35 (Jul), ECtHR.
[98] (Applications 7601/76 and 7806/77) 4 EHRR 38, [1981] IRLR 408, ECtHR.

of the right of a trade union to exclude a person from membership because he holds political views which were inimical to the trade union, contained in s 174(1) of TULR(C)A was held by the ECJ in *ASLEF v UK*[99] to violate Art 11 (see para 21.17).

Article 11 contains no express right to strike (*Ministry of Justice v Prison Officers Association*[100]), but in *Demir v Turkey*[101] the European Court of Human Rights ruled that the right to strike is a human right recognised and protected in international law, and may only be limited in strictly defined circumstances. In this case, the Turkish Government issued a general ban on strike action by civil servants when a Turkish trade union organised a national action day for the recognition of the right to collective bargaining in the public sector. It was held that there was breach of Art 11 of the Convention on Human Rights, because the action taken was in violation of the rights of employees to form trade unions and bargain collectively.

It has been held that the provisions of the Trade Union and Labour Relations (Consolidation) Act 1992, with its stringent provisions and limitations on strike and other industrial action offend against the Convention, because balloting, industrial action notices, etc are prescribed by law, and it could be argued that these rules are necessary in a democratic society (*Metrobus v UNITE*[102]). It has also been suggested that the restriction on the number of pickets contained in the Code of Practice on Picketing (see para 1.59) is capable of being challenged, on the ground that there is no such restriction on any other form of public demonstration. However, Codes of Practice are not law, and a violation does not automatically lead to a breach of the law.

[99] (Application 11002/05) [2007] IRLR 361, 22 BHRC 140, (2007) 45 EHRR 34, ECtHR.
[100] [2008] ICR 702.   [101] [2009] IRLR 766, (2009) 48 EHRR 54.
[102] [2009] EWCA Civ 829, [2010] ICR 173, [2009] IRLR 851.

2

The Nature of a Contract of Employment

Parties to a contract of employment

2.1 The complex form of modern industrial and commercial organisation enables people to work under a variety of legal arrangements which may be entirely satisfactory to all concerned, but which are difficult to rationalise into well-defined categories necessary for the purpose of legal analysis. Legal rights and responsibilities are frequently at the mercy of verbal distinctions, for modern terminology does not assist in the process of drawing precise lines between different economic relationships. The nineteenth-century concept of 'master and servant', though somewhat servile by today's standards, at least had the merit of elegant simplicity.

2.2 It is the task of the employment tribunal to establish the true relationship between the parties. If there is a contractual document, the answer will normally be found therein. However, if it is asserted that the document does not represent or describe the true relationship, the tribunal is entitled to consider not only the words of the written contract at its inception and, where appropriate, the subsequent conduct of the parties, but also whether the true relationship is in fact something different. If the document can be shown to be a sham it can be wholly disregarded. If the evidence establishes that the true relationship was, and intended to be, something different from what is described in the document, then it is the true relationship, with its essential terms of mutuality of obligation and the obligation of personal service, which define the contract (*Protectacoat Firthglow Ltd v Szilagyi;*[1] *Autoclenz v Belcher*[2]). It has to be asked what was the true agreement between the parties in all the circumstances of the case (of which the written agreement is only a part), and to examine all the relevant evidence, including how the parties conducted themselves in practice. The relative bargaining power of the parties must be also taken into account in deciding whether the terms of any written agreement in truth represent what was agreed (*Autoclenz v Belcher*).

2.3 It is undoubtedly true that the courts have generally taken policy considerations into account when trying to devise 'tests' for determining into which category a particular person will fall. The fact that there is an inadequate statutory definition, coupled with inconsistent legal decisions based on different criteria which are adopted in order to achieve a particular end result means that there is confusion and uncertainty in what is, after all, a fundamental feature of employment law. The modern trend is to widen the scope of the law by extending legal rights to 'workers', but the 'economic man' refuses to be placed in neat legal pigeon-holes.

---

[1] [2009] EWCA Civ 98, [2009] ICR 835, [2009] IRLR 365.
[2] [2011] UKSC 41.

A. Employers

2.4 In this book we shall be dealing mainly with the legal relationship which exists between the employer and his employees, and, to a limited extent, between the employer and his workers (see para 2.19 for the definition of 'worker'). These terms are bland enough to state, but give rise to considerable problems in practice. The employer is usually a readily identifiable entity, and may be defined as any person, partnership, corporate body or unincorporated association who (or which) employs one or more persons under a contract of employment, although this definition is not particularly helpful. In the building industry, for example, an 'employer' is the term used for someone who 'engages' a main contractor, whereas he ought properly to be described as 'the client' (eg, see Construction (Design and Management) Regulations 2007). Frequently, the 'acts' of the employer are in reality done by various levels of management, who are themselves employees, yet it is 'the employer' who will be called to account (eg *Courtaulds Northern Textiles v Andrew*[3]). If the employer is an unincorporated association, a person employed by it will be employed by the members of the management committee for the time being (*Affleck v Newcastle Mind*[4]). A co-operative, on the other hand, might be an association of self-employed persons (*Addison v London Philharmonic Orchestra Ltd*[5]).

Associated employer

2.5 Certain legal consequences may flow from the fact that an employer is part of a group of employers, provided the respective employers are 'associated employers' in the legal sense. ERA, s 231 states that two employers shall be treated as being associated if:

    (a) one is a company, of which the other (directly or indirectly) has control, or

    (b) both are companies of which a third person (directly or indirectly) has control (*Spanlite Structures Ltd v Jarrett*[6]).

2.6 Companies in this connection, means limited companies, not other forms of statutory bodies corporate (*Hasley v Fair Employment Agency*[7]). But the definition covers companies which are incorporated under foreign law (*Hancill v Marcon Engineering Ltd*[8]) and a partnership of companies (*Pinkney v Sandpiper Drilling Ltd*[9]). The hardship which would otherwise be caused to employees in the public sector who are not employed by companies as defined has been somewhat mitigated by special legislation covering local government employees (Redundancy Payments (Local Government) (Modification) Order 1983, and continuity has been preserved for teachers in schools run by local government authorities and health service employees (ERA, s 218(7)–(10) (see para 13.40).

2.7 'Control' is a legal, not factual concept, and is determined by the number of votes attached to shares which can exercise control of a company in general meeting (*Secretary of State for Employment v Newbold*[10]). De facto control, ie, how the company is run in practice, is not sufficient (*Washington Arts Association Ltd v Forster*[11]). A negative control, ie a 50% shareholding, is not sufficient (*Hair Colour Consultants v Mena*[12]). It has been suggested that control by a person may be exercised by a group of persons, provided that in fact they act as one (*Zarb and Samuels v British and Brazilian Produce Co (Sales) Ltd*[13]), but this point has been seriously doubted (*South West Launderettes Ltd v Laidler*[14]), and there are a

---

[3] [1979] IRLR 84, EAT.   [4] [1999] ICR 852, [1999] IRLR 405, EAT.   [5] [1981] ICR 261.
[6] [1973] ICR 465, [1973] IRLR 280, 16 KIR 79, 8 ITR 511, NIRC.   [7] [1989] IRLR 106, NICA.
[8] [1990] ICR 103, [1990] IRLR 51, EAT.   [9] [1989] ICR 389, [1989] IRLR 425, EAT.
[10] [1981] IRLR 305, EAT.   [11] [1983] ICR 346, EAT.
[12] [1984] ICR 671, [1984] IRLR 386, [1984] LS Gaz R 2147, EAT.   [13] [1978] IRLR 78, EAT.
[14] [1986] IRLR 68, EAT; on appeal [1986] ICR 455, [1986] IRLR 305, CA.

number of conflicting decisions on this point (compare *Russell v Elmdon Freight Terminal Ltd*[15] with *Tice v Cartwright*[16]).

2.8 There are a number of legislative provisions where the fact that two employers are associated employers in the legal sense is important (see, in particular, para 13.39).

(a) An employee who is taken into the employment of another employer, who, at the time of the change, is an associated employer, will find that his period of employment is continuous, and the change does not break continuity (ERA, s 218(6)). If there is a gap between the two employments, continuity may be preserved by the provision of ERA, s 212 (*Bentley Engineering Ltd v Crown and Miller*[17]), see para 13.20).

(b) The definition of redundancy contained in ERA, s 139(1) (see para 18.12) is extended so that the business of associated employers shall be treated as one business.

(c) An offer of re-engagement in redundancy situations, made under the ERA, ss 138 or 141, can be made by an employer or an associated employer (ERA, s 146).

(d) Independent advice given by a lawyer on a compromise agreement must not be given by a lawyer who is employed by or acting for the employer or an associated employer (ERA, s 203(3B)).

(e) The reference in TULR(C)A, s 182(1) to the disclosure of information for collective bargaining purposes (see para 23.15) exempts information communicated in confidence by an associated employer.

(f) An equal pay claim may be made if a comparator is employed by an associated employer (Equal Pay Act 1970, s 1(6), see *Scullard v Knowles*, para 5.6).[18]

(g) An employee may be able to count employment with an associated employer for the purpose of obtaining the higher rate national minimum wage (National Minimum Wage Regulations, reg 13(2)).

2.9 But if the statute does not refer to an associated employer, then clearly no duty is imposed. Thus, there is a requirement for an employer to consult on redundancies if 20 or more employees are to be made redundant at the same establishment; several associated employers can therefore each make 19 employees redundant without involving the duty to consult (*E Green & Son (Castings) Ltd v Association of Scientific, Technical and Management Staffs*[19]). Employees of associated employers cannot be aggregated to pass the threshold of 20 employees in order to create a bargaining unit for the purpose of statutory recognition procedures (*GPMU v Derry Print Ltd*[20]).

B. **Directors**

2.10 A person who is a director of a limited company is not an employee of that company by virtue of his directorship, but he will be an employee if he has a service contract with the company, which can be express or implied. Every company must keep a copy of every written service agreement, or a written memorandum of a service agreement which is not in writing (Companies Act 2006, s 228). As a director, he can be voted out of office at any time by a simple majority of shareholders' votes at a general meeting of the company, but as an employee he will have all the protections afforded either by his service agreement or the rules of modern employment law. However, a company may not give a director security

---

[15] [1989] ICR 629, EAT.   [16] [1999] ICR 769, EAT.
[17] [1976] ICR 225, [1976] IRLR 146, 11 ITR 50, DC.   [18] [1996] ICR 399, [1996] IRLR 344, EAT.
[19] [1984] ICR 352, [1984] IRLR 135, EAT.   [20] [2002] IRLR 380.

of employment for more than two years, unless the arrangement has been approved by a resolution of the company in general meeting (Companies Act 2006, s 188).

2.11 A service contract between a company and a director can be either express or implied. In the absence of a written agreement or memorandum, it must be ascertained if the person concerned worked as a director, and only occasionally worked in the capacity as an employee, or if he kept regular working hours, or worked full-time, and spent only short or insignificant periods on his duties as a director (*Folami v Nigerline (UK) Ltd*[21]). Thus, if remuneration is by way of director's fees, rather than by a salary, if tax and national insurance contributions are not paid on the remuneration, and if there is an absence of a service agreement as required by s 228 of the Companies Act, it is unlikely that a director will be regarded as an employee of the company (*Parsons v Albert J Parsons & Sons Ltd*[22]). It is also possible for the law to change a person's legal status in accordance with the circumstances. In *Road Transport Industry Training Board v Readers Garage Ltd,*[23] the question was whether an industrial training levy could be assessed on the earnings of a controlling director who also worked as an employee, and the court held that if there was a contract of service implied between him and the company, the employment tribunal must assess how much of his drawings from the company were in respect of that service, and assess the levy on that amount. Any sum he received in his capacity as a director would not be assessed for levy purposes.

2.12 In the past the courts had difficulty in deciding whether a controlling director of a company could also be regarded as an employee of the company. The 1961 decision of the Privy Council in *Lee v Lee's Air Farming Ltd*[24] was authority for the proposition that a limited company is a separate legal entity, distinct from the persons who control it and thus, in theory, there is no reason why a sole shareholder could not be regarded as an employee of the company. But this theory sat uncomfortably with modern employment law concepts of unfair dismissal and other employment rights, and the issue was complicated by a number of factors, including whether tax and national insurance was paid, the hours worked, whether holidays were taken, whether a written contract was in existence, whether guarantees and/or personal loans were given and so on. Thus, if a person was a sole shareholder of a company, how could he dismiss himself? In particular, in recent years the courts had been faced with a number of conflicting decisions dealing with claims made by company directors for redundancy payments following the liquidation of their company.

2.13 Clarification on this issue has now been given by the Court of Appeal in *Secretary of State for the Department of Business Enterprise and Regulatory Reform v Neufeld.*[25] Here, the claimant owned 90% of the shares in a company, and was also the managing director. When the company went into liquidation, he sought a redundancy payment from the Secretary of State under s 188 of ERA (see para 18.67). He argued that he was also an employee of the company, having worked as part of the sales team. The employment judge found against him, partly because the claimant had given personal guarantees in respect of the company's liabilities, had lent money to it, and had not taken his full holiday entitlement. The decision was reversed by the EAT, and the Court of Appeal dismissed an appeal by the Secretary of State. The court held that there is no reason why someone who is a shareholder and director of a company cannot also be an employee of the company. Similarly, there is no reason in principle why someone whose shareholding gives him total control of the company cannot be an employee. To determine what is ultimately a question of fact, the employment

---

[21] [1978] ICR 277, EAT.   [22] [1979] FSR 254, [1979] ICR 271, [1979] IRLR 117, 122 Sol Jo 812, CA.
[23] (1969) 6 KIR 137, 113 Sol Jo 125, DC.   [24] [1961] AC 12.
[25] [2009] EWCA Civ 280, [2009] 3 All ER 790, [2009] BCC 687, [2009] 2 BCLC 273, [2009] ICR 1183, [2009] IRLR 475, [2009] BPIR 909, (2009) 106(15) LSG 15, (2009) *Times,* 10 April.

tribunal must start by asking two questions, namely (a) whether the putative contract is in fact a sham, and (b) assuming it is genuine, whether it amounts to a contract of employment or is a contract for services.

2.14 It is likely that the putative contract will be a sham if it is a formal written contract of employment, or a board minute or memorandum purporting to create a contract of employment (presumably because it is unlikely that the director/majority shareholder will sign a contract with himself!). Thus the enquiry will investigate the circumstances in which the document was created. The same principle will apply if the alleged contract is an oral one (see *Snook v London and West Riding Investments*[26]).

2.15 If the contract is not a sham, then a number of considerations must be taken into account. Thus, the fact that the claimant is a majority shareholder, or indeed the sole shareholder is not normally relevant to the enquiry whether or not the claimed contract amounts to a contract of employment. Nor is the fact that he will have share capital invested in the company, or that he made loans to it, or personally guaranteed its obligations. The Court of Appeal broadly accepted the guidance set out in *Clark v Clark Construction Initiatives Ltd*[27] by Elias J. If the contract does not appear to be a sham, the burden of seeking to deny its effect lies upon the party making that assertion (in most cases this will be the Secretary of State). Thus, if the individual pays tax and insurance as an employee, works the hours and takes the stipulated holidays, it is likely that a genuine employment relationship exists.

C. **Business consultants**

2.16 A person who works in a consultancy or advisory capacity is capable of being an employee, depending on the legal and factual arrangements which are made. In *Bromsgrove Casting and Machining Ltd v Martin*,[28] the applicant was a managing director of a company. He ceased to hold office, but continued to work as a director and consultant. There was no provision as to the number of hours to be worked, and his salary was unchanged. He was then dismissed, and he brought a complaint of unfair dismissal. It was held that in his capacity as a consultant, he was retained, not employed. His employment only came into being when he was actually called upon to give advice. Therefore, the employment tribunal should have enquired into the number of hours he was normally required to give advice, to see whether or not his contract was for the requisite number of hours per week in order to qualify for protection from unfair dismissal (NB: this is no longer a prerequisite for such a claim, as there is no longer an hours threshold for claiming unfair dismissal).

D. **Partners**

2.17 'A partnership is the relation which subsists between persons carrying on a business in common with a view of profit' (Partnership Act 1890, s 1). There is no reference to the sharing of that profit. Thus a person may be a partner even though he does not share in the profit of the firm (*M Young Legal Associates Ltd v Zahid Solicitors*[29]). Even if he does share in some profit, there is no minimum threshold that has to be reached in relation to his rights either to profits or to his involvement in management before he can be regarded as a partner rather than an employee (*Tiffin v Lester Aldridge LLP*[30]).

[26] [1967] 2 QB 786, [1967] 2 WLR 1020, [1967] 1 All ER 518, (1967) 111 SJ 71.
[27] [2008] EWCA Civ 1446, [2009] ICR 718.
[28] [1977] 3 All ER 487, [1977] ICR 417, 12 ITR 177, EAT.
[29] [2006] EWCA Civ 613, [2006] 1 WLR 2562, (2006) 103(22) LSG 26, [2006] NPC 57.
[30] [2012] EWCA Civ 35.

A salaried partner may be (or may not, depending on the facts of the case) a partner, although it has been suggested that the term should be avoided, because it creates confusion (*Stekel v Ellice*[31]). A partner in a limited partnership is not an employee (*Kovats v TFO Management LLP*[32]) but a salaried partner can be an employee (Limited Liability Partnerships Act 2000, s 4(4)).

Architects and dentists frequently engage 'associates', and may make contractual arrangements which suit all concerned, but in law such persons, however designated, are probably employees. However, the contract of engagement may specify to the contrary. A junior partner, however, is a partner with (usually) a lesser share of the profits and/or a smaller say in the conduct of the partnership business. The modern vogue for co-partnership and profit-sharing schemes may well throw up further problems in the future, for although the mere fact of sharing profits is not evidence that a partnership exists (Partnership Act 1890, s 3), it could together with other relevant circumstances, lead to that conclusion (see *Glasgow v Independent Printing Co*[33]).

2.18 If an employee is employed by a partnership, which ceases to trade, he may be able to recover a redundancy payment from the National Insurance Fund if he can show that he has taken all reasonable steps to recover the payment (ERA, s 166). But in order to obtain arrears of pay, notice money, holiday pay and compensation for unfair dismissal under s 182 of ERA, he would have to show that the employer is insolvent, which means that each and every one of the partners must be adjudged bankrupt. As long as there is a partner who is solvent, it is from such a person that the employee must first seek payment (*Secretary of State for Trade and Industry v Forde*[34]).

E. **Workers**

2.19 Consider the term 'worker'. This can mean 'anyone who works for a living', and would thus include all from a managing director of a large public company to a machine operator in an engineering factory; a bookmaker's clerk on a race track to a surgeon in a hospital (but not a partner in an LLP – *Clyde & Co LLP v Winkelhof*[35]). Nowadays it is surely a mistake to use the term with a socio-economic undertone. On the other hand, the term 'workman' has, in the past, been given a more precise legal meaning, though it appears to be falling into legislative disuse as legal rights are given a wider scope.

2.20 Whatever the currently acceptable meanings of these terms may be, it is clear that the law can place within its ambit anyone it wishes. Thus there are two main definitions of the term 'worker' currently in use, with some minor variations in particular circumstances.

2.21 Section 296 of TULR(C)A provides that a worker is an individual who works or seeks to work:

   (a) under a contract of employment, or

   (b) under any other contract whereby he undertakes to do or perform personally any work or services for another party to the contract who is not a professional client of his, or

   (c) is in employment under or for the purposes of a government department (otherwise than as a member of the armed forces) in so far as such employment does not come within (a) or (b) above.

2.22 At the same time, ss 224(6) and 235 of the Act define a contract of employment, for the purpose of the secondary action provisions (see para 23.73) and the balloting provisions

---

[31] [1973] 1 WLR 191, [1973] 1 All ER 465, [1973] CLY 2472.
[32] [2009] ICR 1140, (2009) 106(18) LSG 18.   [33] [1901] 2 IR 278, 34 ILTR 66.
[34] [1997] ICR 231, [1997] IRLR 387, EAT.   [35] [2012] EWCA Civ 1207.

THE NATURE OF A CONTRACT OF EMPLOYMENT

(see para 23.47) as including a contract under which one person personally does work or performs services for another.

2.23 Section 230 of ERA defines the term worker in similar, but not identical terms, ie an individual who has entered into or works under (or worked under)

(a) a contract of employment, or

(b) any other contract whereby the individual undertakes to do or perform personally any work or services for another party to the contract whose status is not by virtue of the contract that of client or customer of any profession or business undertaking carried on by the individual.

(The reason the definition does not deal with Crown employment is because there are other specific provisions which take effect, ie ss 191–192).

But when the terms 'shop worker' or 'betting worker' are used in this Act (see Chapter 8) they refer to employees, not workers!

2.24 The Trade Union and Labour Relations (Consolidation) Act deals with the rights of workers and employees. Part II of the Employment Rights Act, which deals with deductions from wages etc (see Chapter 8) applies to workers, as do the protected disclosure provisions contained in Pt IVA of the Act (see Chapter 10), albeit with a somewhat extended definition of the term (see s 43K). The National Minimum Wage Act 1998, the Working Time Regulations 1998, and the Part-time Workers (Prevention of Less Favourable Treatment) Regulations 2000 all apply to workers. The result is that when the term 'worker' is used, certain employment rights are extended to cover a wider group of persons, in line with the trend in modern employment law.

2.25 A 'worker', for some purposes, may have rights which are identical to those enjoyed by an employee, even though he is clearly not an employee, and is self-employed. Thus in *Flynn v Torith Ltd*,[36] the applicant worked as a self-employed joiner on a building site. He claimed he was entitled to holiday pay under the Working Time Regulations. The EAT noted that the regulations applied to 'a worker', which is defined as being an individual who works under ' . . . any other contract . . . ' whereby the individual undertakes to do or perform personally any work or services for another party to the contract. . . .'. The phrase 'any other contract' in reg 2(1) in those regulations was wide ranging, and included persons who worked under a contract to provide services or perform work for another, other than under a contract of employment. The only exception to reg 2(1) is an individual carrying on a profession or business undertaking of which the other party was a client. Thus the claimant was entitled to holiday pay.

2.26 The Equality Act 2010 applies to anyone who is employed under a contract of service or of apprenticeship or a contract personally to execute any work or labour. Thus the Act applies to employees and self-employed persons.

2.27 Various groups of workers are excluded from some (but not all) legal rights for reasons of policy, eg mariners and share fishermen, and there are a few groups who are outside the protection of employment law altogether, eg office holders (see para 2.62). For clergymen, see para 2.67.

F. **Employees**

2.28 The term 'employee' is defined in ERA, s 230 as an individual who enters into or works under (or, where the employment has ceased, worked under) a contract of employment,

[36] [2003] All ER (D) 45 (Jan).

which is a contract of service or apprenticeship, whether express or implied, and (if it is express) whether oral or in writing. The definition in TULR(C)A, s 295 is similar. Since the term 'employee' is narrower than the term 'worker' it follows that most of the rights contained in ERA are limited to employees, apart from certain specific provisions, eg, ss 13–27 (see para 8.4) and ss 43A–43K, see para 10.74). Thus all employees are workers, but not all workers are employees (*Broadbent v Crisp*[37]).

2.29 An employee, though easy to define, is not so easy to describe, for the relationship between A (the employer) and B (the employee) is complicated by the fact that there is also a relationship between B and the state. It is possible that a person can be an employee for one purpose, but not an employee for another. Thus in *Challinor v Taylor*,[38] a taxi driver was the night driver of a cab which was used during the day by the owner. The latter paid for the fuel, insurance and maintenance of the car, and took 65% of the gross takings. He also paid the cost of the employer's contribution towards the driver's national insurance stamp. The driver, however, was assessed for income tax purposes as a self-employed person under Schedule D. The owner sold the taxi and the driver was thus redundant. It was held that he was not an employee, and therefore not entitled to a redundancy payment.

2.30 There is no reason in principle why an employee cannot have more than two employers, and, provided he is within the appropriate protection of the law, pursue his legal remedies against either of them (*Prison Officers Association v Gough*[39]). Indeed, it is possible for an employee to have two contracts of employment with the same employer, so that if he is dismissed from his employment under one contract, he may pursue his remedy whilst still leaving the other contract subsisting (*Throsby v Imperial College of Science and Technology*[40]).

G. **Employee shareholders**

2.31 The Growth and Infrastructure Act, section 31 introduced the new status of employee shareholder in September 2013, by inserting a new section 205A of the ERA 1996. There has to be an agreement between the employee and the employer (who has to be a company) that the former will become an employee shareholder, and the employee will issue shares worth at least £2,000 to the employee. (The first £2,000 of shares will be free of tax and National Insurance.) The company has to give the individual a written statement setting out his status as an employee shareholder, and the rights which attach to the shares. The rights relating to his status are set out in sub-section (5).

2.32 If an employee enters into this agreement, he will lose various employment rights. Section 205A(2) provides that an employee shareholder will not have:

(a) the right to make an application under section 63D (request to undertake study or training),

(b) the right to make an application under section 80F (request for flexible working),

(c) the right under section 94 not to be unfairly dismissed (except note that this does not apply in a section 108 Health and Safety case, as set out in sub-s (10), a dismissal which is automatically unfair, or one which would be a contravention of the Equality Act), or

(d) the right under section 135 to a redundancy payment.

---

[37] [1974] 1 All ER 1052, [1974] ICR 248, 16 KIR 168, [1974] ITR 147, NIRC.
[38] [1972] ICR 129, 7 ITR 104, 116 Sol Jo 141, NIRC.
[39] Employment Appeal Tribunal, 15 December 2009.
[40] [1978] QB 438, [1978] 2 All ER 465, [1978] 2 WLR 50, [1978] ICR 357, 13 ITR 169, 121 Sol Jo 632, EAT; aff'd sub nom *Dixon v BBC* [1979] QB 546, [1979] 2 All ER 112, [1979] 2 WLR 647, [1979] ICR 281, [1979] IRLR 114, 122 Sol Jo 713, CA.

2.33 An employee shareholder also has to give longer notice (16 weeks) to notify the employer of the intention to return to work during maternity/paternity/adoption leave period).

2.34 Before such an agreement can be valid, the employee shareholder has to have received advice from an independent adviser, and the employer has to pay the reasonable costs of that advice (sub-sections (6) and (7)). The employee also has seven days in which to change his mind (sub-section (6)).

2.35 An employee will be protected from being subjected to a detriment for refusing to accept an employee-shareholder contract.

Distinction between employees and self-employed persons

A. Contract of service

2.36 The basic division for our purposes is between those who are employed persons and those who are self-employed, and the distinction between these categories is that the employed person works under a contract *of* service, whereas the self-employed person works under a contract *for* services. Again, it is easy to state this distinction, but in practice it has proved difficult to draw it, and over the years the courts have developed a number of tests designed to produce a given result. Fundamentally, for the relationship of employer/ employee to exist, there must be a contract of employment, either express or implied. It follows that if there is no contract of any sort between the parties, there cannot be a contract of employment, and the fact that a worker is taxed as an employee under IR 35 or pays Class 1 national insurance contributions is irrelevant (*O'Murphy v Hewlett Packard Ltd*[41]).

Control test

2.37 An important criterion for determining whether or not the relationship of employer/ employee exists is the extent to which a person is under the direction and control of the other party with regard to the manner in which the work is done (*Narich Pty Ltd v Payroll Tax Comr*[42]). Indeed, in the nineteenth century control was regarded as the sole determining factor. Thus if the employer could tell the employee not only what to do, but how to do it, then a contract of service existed (*Yewens v Noakes*[43]). In modern conditions the application of such a test is clearly unreal. An employee may be highly skilled and qualified, and employed specifically because he has professional training and competence, so that the employer is frequently unable (as well as being unwilling) to instruct the employee as to how the work is to be done. Despite this difficulty, some modern decisions have added to the control test a refinement which looks for *the right to control* as being the determinant factor (*Gibb v United Steel Companies Ltd*[44]) or even the existence of the right to control, even though this is seldom if ever exercised in practice. It is clear that the greater the degree of control which is exercisable by the employer, the more likely it will be that the contract is one of service (*Whittaker v Minister of Pensions and National Insurance*)[45] but 'the greater the skill required for an employee's work the less significant is control in determining whether the employee is under a contract of service' (*Beloff v Pressdram*[46]). Ultimately, though, it is the contractual right to control which is important, not necessarily day-to-day

---

[41] [2002] IRLR 4, [2001] All ER (D) 91 (Sep), EAT.   [42] [1984] ICR 286, PC.
[43] (1880) 6 QBD 530, 1 TC 260, 45 JP 8, 468, 50 LJQB 132, 28 WR 562, 44 LT 128, CA.
[44] [1957] 2 All ER 110, [1957] 1 WLR 668, 101 Sol Jo 393.
[45] [1967] 1 QB 156, [1966] 3 All ER 631, [1966] 3 WLR 1090, 110 Sol Jo 924.
[46] [1973] 1 All ER 241, [1973] FSR 33, [1973] RPC 765.

control. In *Troutbeck SA v White & Anor*,[47] a couple were employed to look after a farm, and were left to decide for themselves how to go about running the farm. While there was a low level of control, it was not completely absent, and so there was an employment relationship.

2.38 But the exercise of a degree of control is not conclusive. In *Hitchcock v Post Office*,[48] the applicant ran a sub-post office as part of a shop he owned. Although the Post Office exercised control over many of its activities, it was held that this was because of the need to ensure financial control and security, rather than being a control over managerial functions. Consequently, the sub-post master was not an employee of the Post Office.

Organisational test

2.39 In *Stevenson, Jordan and Harrison Ltd v MacDonald and Evans*,[49] Denning LJ suggested a more up-to-date test. 'Under a contract of service', he said, 'a man is employed as part of the business and his work is done as an integral part of the business'. This 'organisational' test has certain advantages, particularly in relation to skilled employees who are 'integrated' into an enterprise, eg doctors, nurses etc, in respect of whom the control test is inappropriate. In *Whittaker v Minister of Pensions and National Insurance* a trapeze artiste broke her wrist as a result of a fall in her act. It was held that she was an integral part of the circus business and thus an employee for the purpose of claiming industrial injuries benefit.

Mutuality of obligations

2.40 Mutuality of obligations, together with the elements of control, are usually seen as essential pre-requisites for a contract of employment to exist, whether the claimant is a worker or an employee (*Montgomery v Johnson Underwood Ltd*[50]). There must also be an irreducible level of personal service (*MacFarlane v Glasgow City Council*[51]). The question to be decided is whether the claimant is a worker, or an employee, or a self-employed businessman. To answer this, there must be a finding on (a) whether there is one contract or a succession of short-term contracts, (b) if there is one contract did the employer undertake to provide a minimum amount of work, (c) was there such control as to turn the arrangement into a contract of employment, and (d) was the claimant obliged to do a minimum amount of work (*Cotswold Developments Construction Ltd v Williams*[52]).

2.41 There must be an obligation on the part of the employer to provide work, and an equal obligation upon the worker to do the work when offered. If these features are not present, it is likely that no contract of employment exists. Thus in *Bebbington v Palmer (t/a Sturry News)*[53] a 14-year-old schoolboy was engaged to work on a paper round. When he did not turn up for work, other arrangements were made. There was no written contract, he was only paid on the days he worked, and he received no sick pay or holiday pay. Following an argument with his mother about the time when he was required to work, the employer stopped his paper round. His claim for unfair dismissal was dismissed. The EAT held that there was a lack of mutuality of obligations which were the irreducible minimum of the existence of a contract of employment.

2.42 Thus if the employer can decline to offer work, or the worker can refuse to do the work when offered, it is likely that no contract of employment exists. However, mutuality can be inferred from how the contract operated in practice over a period of time. In *Prater*

---

[47] [2013] EWCA Civ 1171, [2013] IRLR 286.   [48] [1980] ICR 100, EAT.

[49] (1952) 69 RPC 10, [1952] 1 TLR 101, CA.

[50] [2001] EWCA Civ 318, [2001] ICR 819, [2001] IRLR 269, [2001] Emp LR 405, (2001) 98(20) LSG 40, (2001) *Times*, 16 March, (2001) *Independent*, 7 May.

[51] [2001] IRLR 7.   [52] [2006] IRLR 181.   [53] Employment Appeal Tribunal, 23 February 2010.

v Cornwall County Council[54] the claimant was employed as a home tutor to teach children who were unable to attend school. The council was under no obligation to offer to send pupils to the claimant, and equally she was under no obligation to accept pupils sent to her. In practice, she never refused offers over a period of ten years, during which time she had a succession of individual teaching contracts. It was held that mutuality of obligations existed, and although there were gaps between the individual contracts, she could rely on the provisions of s 212 of ERA (see Chapter 13), and her claim based on continuity of employment succeeded.

2.43 Mutuality of obligations also requires the essential element of personal service. Thus if a worker is permitted to provide a substitute to do the work, no contract of employment can exist. In *Ready Mixed Concrete (South East) Ltd v Ministry of Pensions and National Insurance,*[55] a firm dismissed all its drivers, sold all the lorries to them, and re-employed them under a contract which contained obligations capable of leading to the conclusion that they were either employees or self-employed workers. Thus, the drivers had to wear the company's uniform, place the lorries at the disposal of the firm for a certain number of hours, only use them for the company's business, obey the orders of the foreman, and sell the lorries back to the company at an agreed valuation. On the other hand, the drivers had to maintain the lorries at their own expense and pay all the running costs. A driver could own more than one lorry, and could engage a substitute driver. They paid their own national insurance contributions, had no set hours or meal breaks, and made their own decisions on how to drive the lorries and which routes to take. McKenna J held that there were three conditions necessary to establish whether a contract of employment existed. The first was that the employee agreed to provide his own labour and skill in the performance of a service for the employer, the second was that there must be some element of control exercisable by the employer, and the third was that the other terms of the contract must not be inconsistent with the existence of a contract of employment. The fact that the drivers could (and did) employ a substitute was clearly a crucial factor in determining that they were self-employed haulage contractors.

2.44 But the fact that a contract permits a person to have the limited ability to delegate performance to another person is not conclusive. In *MacFarlane v Glasgow City Council*[56] the claimant was a part-time lecturer. If he was unable to take a class he could arrange for someone else to do it for him, but that person had to be selected from a register held by the local authority, and sometimes it was the local authority which organised the replacement. It was held that the claimant was an employee. There is a distinction between obtaining a substitute because one is unable to do the work and a general power to delegate performance at will (*Staffordshire Sentinel Newspapers Ltd v Potter*[57]). If the right to substitute is fettered, there may well be an employment contract (*Weight Watchers (UK) Ltd and Others v HMRC*[58] – although this was not an employment law case).

2.45 The element of control is also a factor in determining whether mutuality of obligations exist. Thus if a claimant is genuinely running his own business, then again he cannot be an employee. In *Bacica v Muir*[59] the claimant had his own business accounts, was in receipt of an allowance for business overheads, and worked for others whenever he wished. On the facts, he was clearly a self-employed person.

2.46 The fact that there is no entitlement to sick pay is merely one of the indications that there is a lack of mutuality of obligations (*Clark v Oxfordshire Health Authority*[60]),

---

[54] [2006] EWCA Civ 102, [2006] 2 All ER 1013, [2006] ICR 731, [2006] IRLR 362, [2006] BLGR 479, (2006) 156 NLJ 372, (2006) *Independent*, 28 February.

[55] [1968] 1 All ER 433, (1968) 2 QB 497.   [56] [2001] IRLR 7.   [57] [2004] IRLR 752.

[58] (2011) FTC/57-59/2010 [2011] BTC 1895.   [59] [2006] IRLR 35.

[60] [1998] IRLR 125, (1998) 41 BMLR 18.

and a similar conclusion was reached in a case concerning the payment of income tax and national insurance contributions. In *Parade Park Hotel v Comrs of HM Revenue and Customs*[61] a worker carried out maintenance at a hotel. The hotel did not have to offer him work, and he was under no obligation to accept work. He provided his own tools and equipment, and paid his own national insurance stamps and income tax. It was held that he was self-employed.

2.47 If the contract is so drafted as to exclude a finding of employment relationship, it will normally be upheld. In *Cochrane v A D Bly Construction Ltd*[62] the claimant was given a written contract which contained a clause stating that the employer was not obliged to offer work, the claimant was not obliged to accept an offer of work. It was further stated that the parties did not wish to create or imply any mutuality of obligations whatsoever. It was held that the claimant was neither a worker nor an employee for the purpose of the Working Time Regulations. But in a similar situation that arose in *ABC News International v Gizbert*,[63] it was held that there was an implied obligation on the claimant to decide in good faith whether or not to accept or reject assignments, and mutuality could be implied into the arrangements.

2.48 If a clause in a contract is so unrealistic when compared with what happens in practice, the employment tribunals will ignore it altogether. Thus, the fact that the contract states that there is no obligation on the worker to do the work personally, or that he can provide a substitute, or can refuse to accept the work offered, or is described as a self-employed sub-contractor, etc, these clauses will be disregarded if they do not reflect the reality of the relationship between the parties (*Kalwak v Consistent Group Ltd*,[64] see para 2.156).

Entrepreneurial test

2.49 Sometimes the entrepreneurial test seems to be the dominating feature. The problem is looked at from a self-employed person's point of view, and the question asked 'Is he in business on his own?' Again, no exhaustive list of considerations can be formulated. Does he provide his own equipment? Does he hire his own helpers? Is there any degree of financial responsibility for investment or degree of risk? Does he undertake any other sort of commission, business or employment? Is there any opportunity to profit from sound management? These questions were raised in *Market Investigations Ltd v Minister of Social Security*,[65] where a company employed women on a part-time basis to do market research. They could work as they chose, but according to a set pattern. It was held that the women were employees, and not employed in business 'on their own'. The more unskilled and untrained a person is, the less likely it will be that the employment tribunal will hold that he is running his own business. In *Airfix Footwear Ltd v Cope*,[66] the applicant was a home-worker making heels for shoes manufactured by the respondent company. She was provided with the necessary equipment and material, and worked in accordance with instructions given to her. The EAT upheld a finding that she was an employee. On the other hand, in *Argent v Minister of Social Security*,[67] an actor taught drama on a part-time basis at a school. It was held that he was a self-employed lecturer.

2.50 In *Withers v Flackwell Health Football Supporters' Club*,[68] the EAT stated that difficult cases could be resolved by using industrial, rather than legal, terminology. Hence, the person could be asked a simple question, 'Are you your own boss?'

---

[61] [2007] STC (SCD) 430, [2007] STI 1183.   [62] EAT/0243/05.   [63] EAT, 22 August 2006.
[64] [2007] IRLR 560, EAT.
[65] [1969] 2 QB 173, [1968] 3 All ER 732, [1969] 2 WLR 1, 112 Sol Jo 905, EAT.
[66] [1978] ICR 1210, [1978] IRLR 396, 13 ITR 513, EAT.
[67] [1968] 3 All ER 208, [1968] 1 WLR 1749, 112 Sol Jo 801.   [68] [1981] IRLR 307, EAT.

2.51 This pragmatic approach was taken even further in *Davis v New England College of Arundel*,[69] where the claimant was engaged as a lecturer on a yearly renewable contract. He specifically asked to be treated as being self-employed as he wished to retain that status for income tax and national insurance purposes. He was not re-engaged, and claimed that he had been unfairly dismissed. It was held that to determine whether or not he was an employee, the matter had to be looked at objectively. His request to be treated as being self-employed, and the fact that the college so regarded him, did not alter the nature of the contractual relationship between him and his employer. In reality, he was an employee of the college, and hence he was entitled to bring a claim. It is the essence of the arrangement, rather than the form, which is the determinant factor (*Tyne and Clyde Warehouses Ltd v Hamerton*[70]).

2.52 The difficulties inherent in such cases can be seen in *Massey v Crown Life Insurance Co*,[71] where the claimant was an employee of the respondents. It was then agreed that he should be treated as being self-employed, and a new agreement to this effect was signed. Although his actual duties were identical, the claimant was taxed under Schedule D, and paid self-employed insurance. He was then dismissed, and claimed unfair dismissal. It was held that he was working under a contract for services. While the parties cannot alter the nature of their relationship by putting a different label on it, where the situation was in doubt, or was ambiguous, an agreement which stipulated the nature of the relationship affords strong evidence of what it is. In this case, there was a genuine attempt to change the legal situation to that of an independent contractor. There was no attempt to deceive the Revenue. It was a genuine agreement to enable the applicant to be treated as being self-employed. Consequently, he could not claim that his dismissal was unfair.

Multifactorial approach

2.53 The rule that no single factor can, by itself, be conclusive, is illustrated by the decision of the EAT in *City and East London FHS Authority v Durcan*.[72] The claimant ran his own dental practice on a self-employed basis. Once each week, he worked on a rota at a local hospital, providing emergency services. He was paid a fixed fee, made his own arrangements for tax and national insurance, and, if he was unable to attend, he had to make arrangements for a replacement. When the hospital trust sought to reduce the number of hours worked, he claimed that he had been constructively and unfairly dismissed. The respondents resisted the claim, arguing that he was self-employed. The EAT noted that the claimant used the hospital's premises, equipment and medicines, but, on the other hand, he was not subject to any form of control as to how the work was to be done. The fact that he had to provide a replacement if he was unable to attend was not fatal to the existence of an employment contract, because the replacement had to be on an approved list, and this was not inconsistent with the modern trend towards job-sharing. It was true that the claimant did not enjoy the usual benefits of employment status, including sick pay, holiday pay, and notice rights, nor did he have the right to pursue any grievance procedure or take advantage of any disciplinary procedure. He had to treat any patient who attended for treatment, but his remuneration was not dependent on the number of patients who attended, and thus there was no risk of profit or loss from his working activities. The label attached to the relationship was not determinative of the worker's legal status, although it could tip the balance if all the relevant factors were evenly balanced. Mutuality of obligation is an important factor, but again not conclusive. Nor was it relevant that he worked only for a limited number of hours each week, because since the removal of the eight hour per week

---

[69] [1977] ICR 6, 11 ITR 278, EAT.   [70] [1978] ICR 661, 13 ITR 66, EAT.
[71] [1978] 2 All ER 576, [1978] 1 WLR 676, [1978] ICR 590, [1978] IRLR 31, 13 ITR 5, 121 Sol Jo 791, CA.
[72] EAT 721/96.

qualification, employment tribunals will increasingly be called upon to determine the legal status of workers who only work for a few hours each week. Taking into account all the considerations, the EAT refused to disturb the decision of the employment tribunal that the claimant was an employee, and was therefore entitled to pursue his claim.

2.54 An employment tribunal should therefore take the following factors into account, and make its determination accordingly:

(a) the contractual provisions (*BSM (1257) Ltd v Secretary of State for Social Services*);[73] and whether or not those provisions do represent the true relationship between the parties (see *Secretary of State for the Department of Business Enterprise and Regulatory Reform v Neufeld*,[74] para 2.13);

(b) the degree of control exercised by the employer (*Global Plant Ltd v Secretary of State for Health and Social Security*);[75]

(c) the obligation on the employer to provide work (*Nethermere (St Neots) Ltd v Gardiner*);[76]

(d) the obligation on the employee to do the work (*Ahmet v Trusthouse Forte Catering Ltd*);[77]

(e) the duty of personal service (*Ready Mixed Concrete Ltd (South East) v Minister of Pensions and National Insurance*);[78]

(f) the provision of tools, equipment, instruments, etc (*Willy Scheidegger Swiss Typewriting School (London) Ltd v Minister of Social Security*);[79]

(g) the arrangements made for tax, national insurance, VAT, statutory sick pay (*Davis v New England College of Arundel*);[80]

(h) the opportunity to work for other employers (*WHPT Housing Association Ltd v Secretary of State for Social Services*);[81]

(i) other contractual provisions, including holiday pay, sick pay, notice, fees, expenses, etc (*Tyne and Clyde Warehouses Ltd v Hamerton*);[82]

(j) the degree of financial risk and the responsibility for investment and management (*Market Investigations Ltd v Minister of Social Security*);[83]

(k) whether the relationship of being self-employed is a genuine one, or whether there is an attempt to avoid modern protective legislation (*Young & Woods Ltd v West*);[84]

(l) the number of assignments, the duration of the engagement, and the risk of running bad debts (*Hall v Lorimer*);[85]

(m) the presence or absence of mutuality of the obligation to provide or do the work (*Carmichael v National Power plc*[86]).

---

[73] [1978] ICR 894.

[74] [2009] EWCA Civ 280, [2009] 3 All ER 790, [2009] BCC 687, [2009] 2 BCLC 273, [2009] ICR 1183, [2009] IRLR 475, [2009] BPIR 909, (2009) 106(15) LSG 15, (2009) *Times,* 10 April.

[75] [1972] 1 QB 139, [1971] 3 All ER 385, [1971] 3 WLR 269, 115 Sol Jo 506.

[76] [1984] ICR 612, sub nom *Nethermere (St Neots) Ltd v Taverna and Gardiner* [1984] IRLR 240, CA.

[77] Unreported.   [78] n 55.   [79] (1968) 5 KIR 65.   [80] n 69.

[81] [1981] ICR 737.   [82] n 70.   [83] n 65.   [84] [1980] IRLR 201, CA.

[85] [1992] 1 WLR 939, [1992] STC 599, 66 TC 349, [1992] ICR 739, [1992] 26 LS Gaz R 32, 136 Sol Jo LB 175; aff'd [1994] 1 All ER 250, [1994] 1 WLR 209, [1994] STC 23, 66 TC 349, [1994] ICR 218, [1994] IRLR 171, [1993] 45 LS Gaz R 45, 137 Sol Jo LB 256, CA.

[86] [1998] ICR 1167, [1998] IRLR 301, [1998] 19 LS Gaz R 23, 142 Sol Jo LB 140, 593 IRLB 12, CA; revsd [1999] 4 All ER 897, [1999] 1 WLR 2042, [1999] ICR 1226, [2000] IRLR 43, [1999] 46 LS Gaz R 38, 143 Sol Jo LB 281, 632 IRLB 18, HL.

2.55 No single factor, by itself, is conclusive, and all the relevant circumstances must be considered. As long as the employment tribunals take these into account, their decision is a question of fact, not law, and their findings (either way) cannot normally be challenged (*O'Kelly v Trusthouse Forte plc*,[87] and see *Hall v Lorimer*) unless they took a view on the facts which would not reasonably be sustained (*Lee Ting Sang v Chung Chi-Keung*[88]). However, if there is a written contract which determines the relationship between the parties, the interpretation of that contract is a question of law, which can be considered on appeal (*Davies v Presbyterian Church of Wales*[89]).

B. Why the distinction is important

2.56 In truth, before a clear and satisfactory answer can be given to the question 'Who is an employee?' we may well need to pose a second one, namely, 'For what purpose is the question being asked?' A part-time lecturer may well be a self-employed person for income tax purposes but an employee in relation to national insurance contributions, and he may well be an employed person (using the 'organisational test') if the issue was raised as to the vicarious liability of his employer for wrongful acts committed by him during the course of his work. The pragmatic approach adopted by the courts is to say that the matter is a question of fact, to be determined by the evidence in each case. For example, in *Maurice Graham Ltd v Brunswick*,[90] a company engaged self-employed bricklayers, who paid their own income tax and were responsible for their own national insurance contributions. The company was convicted of breaches of the Construction (Health and Welfare) Regulations 1966, and argued on appeal that those regulations only applied to 'employees', not independent contractors. It was held that though the outward arrangement gave the appearance of a worker being an independent contractor, this was not conclusive. The company controlled and supervised the men, and supplied them with the necessary equipment and materials, and the court refused to disturb the convictions.

2.57 There are a number of reasons for stressing the importance of this distinction between a contract of service and a contract for services, although recent decisions are tending to minimise this importance.

Tax reasons

2.58 Under the Social Security Contributions and Benefits Act 1992 an employer must pay secondary Class 1 contributions in respect of employed earners (the primary contribution being made on an earnings-related basis by the employed earner – which term includes an office holder). Self-employed earners pay a flat-rate Class 2 contribution, and in addition a Class 4 contribution based on the gains or profits derived which are chargeable to income tax (see *Lane v Shire Roofing Co Ltd*[91]). They must also complete their own self-assessment tax form. The employer does not need to deduct PAYE income tax in respect of his self-employed independent contractors, and he need not pay a levy for industrial training purposes. An independent sub-contractor may have to charge VAT on services supplied, which would not be so if he were an employee. But it must be stressed that it is the substance of the relationship which will count, not the form. Thus if a person is an employee in the legal sense, the employer's obligations will arise despite any artificial attempt or

[87] [1984] QB 90, [1983] 3 All ER 456, [1983] 3 WLR 605, [1983] ICR 728, [1983 IRLR 369, 127 Sol Jo 632, [1983] LS Gaz R 2367, CA.
[88] [1990] 2 AC 374, [1990] 2 WLR 1173, [1990] ICR 409, [1990] IRLR 236, (1990) 87(13) LSG 43, (1990) 134 SJ 909.
[89] [1986] 1 All ER 705, [1986] 1 WLR 323, [1986] ICR 280, [1986] IRLR 194, 130 Sol Jo 203, HL.
[90] (1974) 16 KIR 158, 118 Sol Jo 294, DC.   [91] [1995] IRLR 493, [1995] PIQR P 417, CA.

arrangements made to avoid such duties (*Pennington v Minister of Social Security*[92]). Nor does the fact that a person pays his own national insurance and is responsible for his own income tax payments necessarily mean that he is a self-employed person. In *Jennings v Westwood Engineering Ltd*[93] the applicant was offered employment. He was told that he could work at a lower rate of remuneration on PAYE, or at a higher rate, paying his own tax and insurance, and he chose the latter option. It was held that he was employed under a contract of employment nonetheless. Conversely, in *President of the Methodist Conference v Parfitt*[94] the fact that the applicant paid Class 1 national insurance and was taxed under Schedule E did not in itself make him an employee.

Liability issues

2.59 An employer will not normally be vicariously liable for the tortious acts (civil wrongs) committed by independent contractors (though there are certain exceptions to this rule) whereas he would be so liable for torts committed by his employees in the course of their employment which cause injury or damage to third parties (see Chapter 10). Two contrasting cases will illustrate this point. In *Hillyer v St Bartholomew's Hospital*,[95] the plaintiff selected a consultant who negligently performed an operation. It was held that the hospital was not liable, because the consultant was an independent contractor who was merely using the facilities of the hospital. On the other hand, in *Cassidy v Ministry of Health*,[96] a resident surgeon operated negligently on the plaintiff, and it was held that the hospital board, as the employer, was liable.

Health and safety issues

2.60 An employer owes a duty at common law to his employees to take reasonable care for their safety, whereas these duties do not normally apply with respect to his independent contractors, although again, there are exceptions. Thus in *McArdle v Andmac Roofing Co*,[97] the claimant worked for one of several subcontractors who were employed on converting a building at a holiday camp, who were all under the direction of Pontins (Contractors) Ltd. The latter had made no arrangements for safety precautions with the sub-contractors, and as a result, the claimant suffered severe injuries when he fell off a roof. It was held that the main contractors (Pontins) assumed the responsibility of co-ordinating the work, and were therefore under a duty to ensure that reasonable safety precautions were taken for all those who were working on the job, even though they were not the employers of those who were working. The duties owed by the employer to his employees under the Health and Safety at Work etc Act 1974 and regulations made under the Act are more extensive than those owed to independent contractors (see Chapter 11). In practice this may mean that a self-employed person who is injured whilst at work may be unable to claim any compensation from the employer, and additionally will be unable to claim industrial injuries benefit and/or sick pay.

Statutory rights

2.61 Many statutory rights apply only to employees, not to workers. For example, an employee is entitled to all the rights contained in the Employment Rights Act, including a written statement of terms of employment, itemised pay statement, maternity, paternity, parental and adoption rights, guarantee pay, medical suspension pay, time off work, unfair

---

[92] Unreported.   [93] [1975] IRLR 245.   [94] [1984] ICR 176.
[95] [1909] 2 KB 820, 73 JP 501, 78 LJKB 958, 53 Sol Jo 714, 101 LT 368, 25 TLR 762, CA.
[96] [1951] 2 KB 343, [1951] 1 All ER 574, 95 Sol Jo 253, [1951] 1 TLR 539, CA.
[97] [1967] 1 All ER 583, [1967] 1 WLR 356, 111 Sol Jo 37, CA.

dismissal, redundancy rights, etc. Despite the appellation, shop workers and betting workers are employees! The Flexible Working Regulations, Fixed-term Employees Regulations, Transfer of Undertaking Regulations, etc apply to employees, as does the Health and Safety at Work Act and many regulations issued thereunder. A court may be able to make an attachment of earnings order whereby an employer is obliged to make certain deductions from the earnings of an employee, which would not be possible if the person concerned was a (self-employed) worker. On the other hand, the protection of wages and the public interest disclosure provisions of ERA apply to workers (which includes employees), as do the Part-Time Workers Regulations, Working Time Regulations, the various pieces of discrimination legislation, the National Minimum Wage Act and parts of the Trade Union and Labour Relations (Consolidation) Act.

Other categories of parties to a contract of employment

A. Office holders

2.62 A special category of persons exists who are technically known as office holders. They are not employed by virtue of a contract of employment, and therefore have certain privileges attached to their position. A judge, for example, holds office during good behaviour and may only be dismissed on a resolution passed by both Houses of Parliament. A magistrate is also an office holder (*Knight v A-G*[98]). However, some office holders may also have a contract of employment, eg a stipendiary reader in the Church of England (*Barthorpe v Exeter Diocesan Board of Finance Ltd*[99]). In *102 Social Club and Institute v Bickerton*,[100] a club secretary was paid an honorarium of £225 per year. The EAT held that the employment tribunal should consider whether the money was paid by way of a salary for services rendered, or whether it was an honorarium for work done as a member of the club in his capacity as an office holder. In the former case only would he be regarded as being an employee.

2.63 In *Lincolnshire County Council v Hopper*,[101] the council appointed the claimant as a registrar. The council also paid her remuneration, determined her hours of work, and made provision for her pension. However, the Registration Services Act 1953 stated that a registrar holds office during the pleasure of the Registrar General. It was held that the claimant was an office holder, not an employee. The council did not have the power to dismiss the claimant, which is an essential element of an employment relationship.

2.64 Regular earnings received by an office holder are more akin to remuneration for work done than by way of honorarium for tenure of office. Thus his claim for the money is closely analogous to a claim for a salary due under a contract of employment. It follows that the office holder must be willing and able to render the services required of him, and that if he refuses to perform his duties (as a form of industrial action) his paymaster is entitled to withhold the relevant part of his remuneration (*Miles v Wakefield Metropolitan District Council*[102]).

[98] [1979] ICR 194, 123 Sol Jo 32, EAT.   [99] [1979] ICR 900, 123 Sol Jo 585, EAT.
[100] [1977] ICR 911, 12 ITR 442, EAT.   [101] [2002] All ER (D) 401 (May), EAT.
[102] 2 LGR 395, [1984] ICR 332; on appeal [1985] 1 All ER 905, [1985] 1 WLR 822, 83 LGR 335, [1985] ICR 363, [1985] IRLR 108, 129 Sol Jo 299, [1985] LS Gaz R 1166, CA; revsd [1987] AC 539, [1987] 1 All ER 1089, [1987] 2 WLR 795, 85 LGR 649, [1987] ICR 368, [1987] IRLR 193, 131 Sol Jo 408, [1987] LS Gaz R 1239, [1987] NLJ Rep 266, HL.

2.65 In *Johnson v Ryan*,[103] the EAT held that there were three categories of office holders, namely:

(a) an office holder whose rights and duties are defined by the office they hold, and not by any contract (such as a police officer);

(b) persons who have the title of office holder, but who are in reality employees with a contract of service; and

(c) workers who are both office holders and employees, such as company directors.

2.66 Indeed, there is a fourth category of office holder, namely a worker who is not necessarily an employee. In *Perceval-Price v Department of Economic Development*,[104] the Northern Ireland Court of Appeal held that full-time holders of judicial posts in tribunals were 'workers' for the purpose of Art 141 of the Treaty of Rome, and hence provisions in domestic law which provided that statutory officers were not to be regarded as employed under a contract of service had to be disapplied. Part-time judges (known as daily fee-paid judges) are also regarded by the Supreme Court as workers (*O'Brien v Ministry of Justice*[105]) and as such entitled to pro-rata pensions given to full-time judges under regulation 17 of the Part-time Workers (Prevention of Less Favourable Treatment) Regulations 2000.

So far as EU law is concerned, the criterion was the existence of an employment relationship, regardless of the legal nature of that relationship and its purpose.

There is little doubt that the categories of people who nowadays could properly be described as 'office holders' is declining, because formerly the offices in question were attached to incorporeal hereditaments, and many such titles are nowadays largely obsolete. In *R v BBC, ex p Lavelle*,[106] Woolf J commented: 'The distinctions which previously existed between pure cases of master and servant and cases where a person holds an office are no longer clear.'

A useful summary of the legal position of office holders can be found in *Percy v Church of Scotland Board of National Mission*.[107]

B. Ministers of religion

2.67 It had long been thought that ministers of religion had few (if any) employment rights, as they were not employed under a contract of employment, having regard to the spiritual nature of their work (*President of the Methodist Conference v Parfitt*[108]), or were office holders (*Diocese of Southwark v Coker*).[109] This type of simplistic reasoning was rejected by the House of Lords in *Percy v Church of Scotland Board of National Mission*, where the claimant was appointed as an ordained minister. It was alleged that she had an affair with a married elder of the parish. She was suspended from her duties, pending preparation for a disciplinary hearing and eventually resigned. She brought proceedings in an employment tribunal, alleging unfair dismissal sex discrimination, arguing that in similar circumstances the church would not have taken such action against a male minister. Her claim was dismissed by an employment tribunal, on the ground that having regard to the essentially religious nature of her duties she was not employed under a contract of employment as defined in the Employment Rights Act and the Sex Discrimination Act. The decision was upheld by the EAT and Court of Session, but the House of Lords found in her favour on the sex discrimination point.

It was held that there was an offer and acceptance of a church post for a specific period, with detailed provision for the claimant's duties, remuneration, travel expenses, holidays

[103] [2000] ICR 236, EAT.   [104] [2000] IRLR 380, NICA.   [105] [2013] UKSC 6.
[106] [1983] 1 All ER 241, [1983] 1 WLR 23, [1983] ICR 99, [1982] IRLR 404, 126 Sol Jo 836.
[107] [2006] IRLR 195, HL.   [108] n 94.
[109] [1996] ICR 896, EAT; aff'd [1998] ICR 140, [1997] 29 LS Gaz R 29, 141 Sol Jo LB 169, CA.

and accommodation. As such, there was clearly an intention to create legal relations. Further, the claimant was employed under a contract 'personally to execute any work or labour' as defined in s 82(1) of the Sex Discrimination Act, and hence her claim for sex discrimination could proceed.

It is important to note that although the claimant originally claimed unfair dismissal, this matter was not pursued on appeal to the House of Lords, and the decision only applies to those legislative provisions which define 'employment' in a manner similar to the then Sex Discrimination Act, s 82(1).

There is no presumption that a minister and a church do not intend to enter into legal relations, and an individual can be an employee as well as an office holder. The test of whether or not a minister of religion is an employee must be resolved by ascertaining whether the normal tests for employment are satisfied in relation to that particular church and that particular minister. The decision was upheld by the Court of Appeal, who made it clear, however, that the case is not authority for a general finding that ministers of religion are employees. In *President of the Methodist Conference v Preston*[110] the Supreme Court emphasised that one had to look at the manner in which a minister is engaged, and the rules governing his service. These both depend on the intentions of the parties, and the factual background, which includes the fundamentally spiritual purpose of a minister of religion. The correct approach is to examine the rules and practices of the particular church and any special arrangements made with the particular minister.

Tribunals will therefore need to analyse the facts carefully, and the answer will probably vary from church to church and religion to religion before reaching a conclusion. The existence of a religious dogma that was opposed to the existence of a contract of employment would be an important factor. An employment tribunal is entitled to have regard to the historic background and ethos of the religion concerned, in particular its independence from the state, and the fact that employment status would be inconsistent with the beliefs of the religion in question (*MacDonald v Free Presbyterian Church of Scotland*[111]).

Further, to impose a contract of employment on a religion that was doctrinally opposed to it would be a breach of Art 9 of the European Convention on Human Rights (freedom of religion).

Church of England clergy now enjoy a parallel regime of employment type rights, which cover such matters as stipend, accommodation, education, training, time off, capability and grievance procedures, etc. They also have the right to claim unfair dismissal before an employment tribunal (Ecclesiastical Offices (Terms of Service) Regulations 2009). However, existing case law will continue to apply to ministers of other religions.

C. **Crown employees**

2.68 The precise legal nature of the relationship between the Crown and civil servants has long been a moot point, but it now appears that since such arrangements have an intention to create legal relations, a contract of employment exists, enforceable by private law remedies (*R v Lord Chancellor's Department, ex p Nangle*[112]). The provisions of the Equality Act 2010 do apply to the Crown. Most of the provisions of the Employment Rights Act 1996 apply to Crown employees, except those relating to rights to minimum periods of notice, redundancy payments, Sunday working for shop and betting office workers, and rights on insolvency. There are restrictions on the disclosure of information based on grounds of national security, but a Minister can no longer exclude the rights of certain employments on that ground (Employment Relations Act 1999, Sch 8). The provisions

---

[110] Supreme Court [2013] UKSC 29.   [111] [2010] CSOH 55, 2010 GWD 16-303.
[112] [1992] 1 All ER 897, [1991] ICR 743, [1991] IRLR 343.

of TULR(C)A similarly apply, except the power of the court to make an order against an employer in respect of a failure to ensure that a check-off arrangement excludes a payment to the political fund of a trade union (s 87), failure to comply with a declaration of the Central Arbitration Committee requiring an employer to disclose information for collective bargaining purposes (s 184), and the procedure for consulting with trade unions on redundancies (ss 188–194).

2.69 Members of the staff of the House of Commons have been accorded the same statutory protection in most fields as that enjoyed by Crown employees by virtue of ERA, s 195, with the House of Commons Commission (or Mr Speaker) being the employer. Staff employed by the House of Lords also have a similar full range of protections, except in relation to time off work for public duties connected with political activities and other minor exceptions (see ERA, s 194 and TULR(C)A, s 277).

2.70 However, where a person holds any office or employment under the Crown, which does not constitute a contract of employment, those terms shall be deemed to be such a contract for the purpose of the law relating to the liability in tort of any person who commits an act which induces another to break a contract, or interferes with the performance of any contract (or induces the interference), or consists of a threat that a contract will be broken, or its performance interfered with. In other words, Crown servants will be deemed to have contracts of employment for the purpose of tort liability arising out of industrial action, unless the protections of TULR(C)A, s 219 apply.

D. Armed forces

2.71 Various provisions in the Employment Rights Act apply to members of the naval, military or air forces of the Crown. These include written particulars, antenatal care, suspension on medical and maternity grounds, rights to maternity leave of absence, written reasons for dismissal, and unfair dismissal. The Equality Act 2010 also applies, but nothing is to be rendered unlawful if it was done for the purpose of ensuring combat effectiveness. Although there is a general rule that a member of the Armed Forces should go through service redress procedures before complaining to an employment tribunal, this is no longer always so (see Race Relations (Complaints to Employment Tribunals) (Armed Forces) Regulations 1997, Equal Pay (Complaints to Employment Tribunals) (Armed Forces) Regulations 1997, and Sex Discrimination (Complaints to Employment Tribunals) (Armed Forces) Regulations 1997).

E. Health service employees

2.72 Employees of the National Health Service or Health Trusts have the full range of employment protection rights (now including the right to redundancy payments, see National Health Service and Community Care Act 1990, s 60).

F. Police

2.73 A person is employed in the police service if he serves as a member of any constabulary maintained by virtue of an enactment, or in any capacity by virtue of which he has the powers or privileges of a constable. This includes special constables, but not police cadets (*Wiltshire Police Authority v Wynn*[113]), nor prison officers, who are now 'workers' for the purpose of ERA and TULR(C)A (see Criminal Justice and Public Order Act 1994,

---

[113] [1981] QB 95, [1980] 3 WLR 445, 79 LGR 591, [1980] ICR 649, 124 Sol Jo 463, CA.

s 126(1)). Otherwise, policemen, even though they may be engaged under a contract of employment in the police service, have few employment law rights. Thus, they are not entitled to an itemised pay statement, guarantee pay, rights under the Working Time Regulations, protection for employee representatives, rights in protected disclosure cases, leave for domestic reasons, time off work for public duties, time off work as an employee representative, suspension from work on medical or maternity grounds, right to return to work after childbirth, written reasons for dismissal, and unfair dismissal (except in health and safety cases), even in respect of conduct which occurs when he is not exercising the privileges or powers of a constable (*Home Office v Robinson*[114]). Nor can they claim in respect of unlawful deductions from wages (*Metropolitan Police Comr v Lowrey-Nesbitt*[115]). A policeman does have the right to have written particulars of his terms and conditions of employment, minimum periods of notice, and redundancy pay.

2.74 A policeman is deemed to be employed by the chief constable or the police authority for the purpose of the Equality Act 2010 in respect of any act done by him, or the authority in relation to discrimination in employment, but not acts committed outside the course of employment (*Waters v Metropolitan Police Comr*[116]). The Police (Health and Safety) Act 1997 applies the provisions of the Health and Safety at Work etc Act 1974 (see Police (Health and Safety) Regulations 1999) to holders of the office of constable (ie police, including police cadets), even though they are not employed under a contract of employment. For this purpose, the Chief Officer shall be treated as a corporation sole or distinct juristica (Serious Organised Crime and Police Act 2005, s 158). The Police Federation is to be treated as a recognised trade union for the purpose of appointing and consultation with safety representatives.

2.75 A policeman cannot be dismissed without a proper hearing in accordance with the rules of natural justice (*Ridge v Baldwin*[117]) (see Police Act 1996, ss 84–85), and, in the event of wrongful dismissal, he has the right to be reinstated. Police cadets are persons training to become police officers, and are not employees (*Wiltshire Police Authority v Wynn*).

G. **Those employees with special legal status**

2.76 Over the years a number of different groups of employees had additionally acquired a special legal status which overrode the existence of their contracts of employment (see, eg *McClelland v Northern Ireland General Health Services Board*[118]), but 'status' relating to a person's occupation is now in decline, and in this sense it may be truly said that in employment law, 'there is a movement from status to contract'. Thus registered dock workers no longer enjoy the special protection which they had under the dock labour scheme (see Dock Work Act 1989), and tenure for all university staff appointed or promoted after 20 November 1987 has been abolished (Education Reform Act 1988, s 203). In respect of university academic staff appointed prior to that date, regard must be had to the terms of their appointment. If these state that dismissal is only possible for 'good cause' then it is not possible to dismiss for any other reason, eg redundancy (*Pearce v University of Aston in Birmingham*[119]).

---

[114] [1982] ICR 31, [1981] IRLR 524, EAT.   [115] [1999] ICR 401, EAT.
[116] [1995] ICR 510, [1995] IRLR 531, EAT; aff'd [1997] ICR 1073, [1997] IRLR 589, CA; revsd [2004] 4 All ER 934, [2000] 1 WLR 1607, [2000] ICR 1064, HL.
[117] [1963] 1 QB 539, [1961] 2 All ER 523, [1961] 2 WLR 1054, 59 LGR 327, 125 JP 422, 105 Sol Jo 384; aff'd [1963] 1 QB 539, [1962] 1 All ER 834, [1962] 2 WLR 716, 60 LGR 229, 126 JP 196, 106 Sol Jo 111, CA; revsd [1964] AC 40, [1963] 2 All ER 66, [1963] 2 WLR 935, 61 LGR 369, 127 JP 295, 107 Sol Jo 313, HL.
[118] [1957] NI 100, [1957] 2 All ER 129, [1957] 1 WLR 594, 55 LGR 281, 101 Sol Jo 355, HL.
[119] [1991] 2 All ER 461, CA.

2.77 On the other hand, there are many groups of workers who have special protections and advantages by virtue of their situation, including pregnant women, trade unionists, safety representatives etc, and in this respect, therefore, 'status' still retains a certain significance.

H. Temporary employees

2.78 A temporary employee has all the rights of any other employee as long as he has the appropriate length of service. An exception here is to be found in ERA, s 106, which states that if an employee is employed on a temporary basis in order to replace a woman who has been given maternity leave or adoption leave or to replace someone suspended on medical grounds, and the latter returns to work, the dismissal of the temporary employee will amount to some other substantial reason for the dismissal, but without prejudice to the rule that the employer must still show that he acted reasonably in dismissing the employee. It is essential that the employee has been informed in writing that the employment will be terminated when the absent employee returns to work. However, since it is unlikely that the temporary employee will have obtained the two-year qualifying period of employment, s 106 has little value. Also, Sir John Donaldson thought that the temporary nature of the employment could well amount to 'some other substantial reason' so as to justify a dismissal, though the employment tribunal would have to be convinced that the employer had acted reasonably in the circumstances.

2.79 If a temporary worker is taken on with the expectation that, assuming all goes well, s/he will be made a permanent employee, it is probable that a contract of employment will retrospectively be implied, so as to enable the employee to obtain continuity from the date when the engagement first began. This is so even though the original engagement was made on the clear understanding that no contract of employment came into existence (*Royal National Lifeboat Institution v Bushaway*[120]).

I. Part-time workers

2.80 The Part-time Workers (Prevention of Less Favourable Treatment) Regulations 2000 (as amended) are designed to implement EC Directive 97/81/EEC, and to ensure that part-time workers are to be treated no less favourably, in relation to terms and conditions of employment, than a comparable full-time worker whether or not the latter is on a permanent or fixed-term contract. However, less favourable treatment will not be unlawful if it is objectively justified.

2.81 Hitherto, any rights enjoyed by part-time workers were inextricably bound up with claims of sex discrimination, on the basis that since the majority of part-time workers were women, any less favourable treatment which occurred was because of their sex (eg *R v Secretary of State for Employment, ex p Equal Opportunities Commission*, see para 1.70). The Part-Time Workers (Prevention of Less Favourable Treatment) Regulations 2000 will undoubtedly go some way towards the elimination of such claims. But the regulations only apply to direct discrimination, which is capable of being justified, whereas the Equality Act 2010 applies to direct and indirect discrimination, and only the latter is capable of being justified. The part-time worker will always have to find a full-time comparator of either sex for the purpose of showing less favourable treatment, whereas under the Equality Act 2010, the search is for a person of the opposite sex.

---

[120] [2005] IRLR 674, EAT.

2.82 The regulations apply to 'workers', not just employees. A worker is an individual who has entered into or works under (or worked under):

(a) a contract of employment;

(b) any other contract, whether express or implied, whereby the individual undertakes to do or perform personally any work or services for another party to the contract whose status is not by virtue of the contract that of a client or customer of any profession or business undertaking carried on by the individual.

2.83 In other words, a worker is anyone who works for another person (not necessarily under a contract of employment) other than in a professional or business relationship. Only genuinely self-employed persons are excluded from the regulations.

2.84 A part-time worker is defined as one who is paid wholly or in part by reference to the time he works and, having regard to the custom and practice of the employer in relation to workers employed by the worker's employer under the same type of contract, is not identifiable as a full-time worker. Conversely, a full-time worker is a worker who is paid wholly or in part by reference to the time he works and, having regard to the custom and practice of the employer in relation to workers employed by the worker's employer under the same type of contract, is identifiable as a full-time worker.

2.85 In order to avoid being subjected to less favourable treatment, the part-time worker must be able to compare his treatment with that given to a full-time worker. This involves finding the comparator, not a hypothetical one (*Carl v University of Sheffield*[121]). A full-time worker will be comparable if:

(a) both workers are employed by the same employer under the same type of contract, and engaged in the same or broadly similar work, having regard, where relevant, to whether they have a similar level of qualifications, skills and experience, and

(b) the full-time worker works or is based at the same establishment as the part-time worker or, where there is no full-time worker working or based at that establishment, works or is based at a different establishment and satisfies the above requirements. A part-time worker, whether permanent or on a fixed-term contract, can compare himself with a full-time permanent worker or worker on a fixed-term contract.

2.86 In *Matthews v Kent & Medway Towns Fire Authority*,[122] the House of Lords held that part-time firefighters could compare themselves with whole-time firefighters. The term 'the same type of contract' should not be read in an over precise way, thus allowing employers to take part-timers outside the scope of the regulations by setting different terms for them. The fact that not all part-time workers are treated adversely does not mean that a claim for discrimination cannot be made by those who are treated less favourably, if being part-time was the reason for their adverse treatment (*Sharma v Manchester City Council*[123]).

2.87 A full-time worker who becomes a part-time worker can compare his treatment with the way he was treated when he was full-time. A worker who has had a period of absence (which cannot exceed more than 12 months) and then returns to work at the same job or to a job at the same level but with fewer hours can compare his treatment with the way he was treated prior to his absence.

---

[121] [2009] 3 CMLR 21, [2009] ICR 1286, [2009] IRLR 616.
[122] [2004] ICR 257, [2003] IRLR 732, [2003] All ER (D) 90 (Aug), EAT.
[123] [2008] ICR 623, (2008) IRLT 336.

2.88 A part-time worker has the right not to be treated by his employer less favourably than a full-time worker is treated, as regards the terms of his contract, or be subjected to any detriment by any act, or deliberate failure to act, of his employer (reg 5). However, this right only applies if the treatment is on the ground that the worker is a part-time worker, and cannot be justified on objective grounds. A pro rata principle must be applied unless it is inappropriate to do so. Thus, where a comparable full-time worker is entitled to receive pay or any other benefit, a part-time worker is entitled to receive not less than the proportion of that pay or benefit that the number of his weekly working hours bears to the number of weekly working hours of the comparable full-time worker.

2.89 If a part-time worker considers that he is receiving less favourable treatment than a full-time worker (bearing in mind the pro rata principle) he may request from his employer a written statement giving particulars of the reasons for the treatment. The employer shall provide the statement within 21 days, but if, in subsequent tribunal proceedings, the tribunal finds that the employer deliberately and without reasonable excuse omitted to provide the statement or finds that the written statement is evasive or equivocal, the tribunal may draw any inference which it considers to be just and equitable to draw, including an inference that the employer has infringed the right in question (reg 6).

2.90 An interesting point dealing with part-time workers arose in *McMenemy v Capita Services*,[124] where an employee claimed holiday pay in lieu of bank holidays that fell on a Monday, a day on which he did not work. It was held that he had not been discriminated against when compared with a full-time employee. He received no pay for bank holidays which fell on a Monday because he did not work on Mondays. A full-time worker who worked from (say) Tuesday to Saturday would have been treated in the same way.

2.91 It is thus clear that as a matter of principle, part-time workers must be paid the same rate of pay as comparable full-time workers. Contractual sick pay, maternity pay, access to pension schemes, access to training, holiday entitlement, etc must all be no less favourable, on a pro rata basis. Statutory rights, such as time off work (see Chapter 7) apply. Any different treatment, eg on redundancy selection, or severance payments, must be capable of being justified (*Barry v Midland Bank plc*[125]). Thus to select an employee for redundancy because of his part-time status is to treat the employee less favourably, and is likely to be an unfair dismissal (*Hendrickson Europe Ltd v Pipe*[126]). But if a part-time worker works overtime, he will not be entitled to any overtime premium which a full-time worker receives until he works the normal standard working hours of the full-time worker. Also, since a part-time worker is not required to pay national insurance contributions if his or her wages are below the lower earning limit, this may result in the exclusion from the right to receive statutory maternity pay, statutory adoption pay and statutory sick pay.

2.92 A worker has the right not to suffer a detriment because he brought proceedings under the regulations, or requested a written statement, or gave evidence or information in connection with such proceedings brought by any worker, or otherwise did anything under the regulations, or alleged that the employer had infringed the regulations, or refused to forgo a right conferred by the regulations, or because the employer believed that the worker has done or intends to do any of these things. It will also be an automatic unfair dismissal to dismiss an employee (but not a worker) on any of those grounds (reg 7).

---

[124] [2006] IRLR 761, (2006) 150 SJLB 665, EAT(SC); aff'd 2007 SC 492, 2007 SLT 428, [2007] IRLR 400, 2007 GWD 13–267, IH (Ex Div).
[125] [1997] ICR 192, EAT; aff'd [1998] 1 All ER 805, [1999] ICR 319, [1998] IRLR 138, CA; aff'd [1999] 3 All ER 974, [1999] 1 WLR 1465, [1999] ICR 859, [1999] IRLR 581, [1999] 31 LS Gaz R 36, [1999] NLJR 1253, 143 Sol Jo LB 221, HL.
[126] [2003] All ER (D) 280 (Apr), EAT.

2.93 A worker may lodge a complaint to an employment tribunal that his rights under the regulations have been violated (within the usual time limits: see Chapter 20). The burden will be on the employer to identify the grounds for any less favourable treatment or detriment. The tribunal can make the usual awards (declaration, compensation, and recommendation) but not compensation for injury to feelings. The claimant is under a duty to mitigate the loss, and the rules on contributory conduct apply.

2.94 The regulations provide that so far as the police are concerned, the holding of an office of constable or police cadet (otherwise than under a contract of employment) shall be treated as being employment under a contract of employment. The regulations also apply to Crown employment, members of the armed forces, staff of the House of Lords and House of Commons, but not, apparently, to an individual in his capacity as the holder of a judicial office if he is remunerated on a daily fee-paid basis (*Christie v Department for Constitutional Affairs*[127]).

2.95 A set of guidance notes has been issued to assist in compliance with the regulations. Basically, these suggest that, unless there is some objective justification, part-time workers should receive the same treatment as full-time comparable workers, when considering hourly rates of pay, contractual sick pay and maternity pay (applied pro rata), access to pensions schemes, training, holiday entitlement, contractual maternity and parental leave, career breaks, selection for redundancy, etc. Less favourable treatment may be objectively justified if he intended to achieve a legitimate objective, is necessary to achieve that objective, and it is an appropriate way of doing so.

J. Probationary employees

2.96 The essence of a probationary appointment is that the employer retains the right not to confirm the appointment after a specified period, particularly on the grounds of capability. The majority of the tribunal in *Donn v Greater London Council*[128] thought that the tests which are applied to a probationary employee are not necessarily the same as those which apply to a confirmed appointment, and a decision not to retain a probationer may be justified even though a similar decision made with respect to a fully established employee may not be justified. This view has been followed on a number of occasions (eg *Hamblin v London Borough of Ealing*[129]), for a probationary employee must know that he is on trial, and must therefore establish his suitability for the post. The employer, however, must give the employee a proper opportunity to prove himself, and give a warning if the required standards are not being met (*Post Office v Mughal*[130]). A probationary employee is still an employee, and is therefore entitled to have appropriate guidance and advice (*Inner London Education Authority v Lloyd*[131]).

2.97 Certainly, if the probationary period is less than two years, few problems will arise, but a longer probationary period could create difficulties. In *Weston v University College, Swansea*,[132] the applicant was appointed as a lecturer for the probationary period of three years. At the end of this time he was not placed on the permanent staff. It was held that he was entitled to pursue his complaint in respect of his alleged unfair dismissal, for his contract was not for a fixed term. The employer must still show that he acted reasonably in dismissing a probationer, and that the reason was within the statutory requirements, and it is submitted that if a different test is to be applied, the employer must show a valid reason why a probationary period of such a length of time is required in order to establish the suitability of the employee for the post in question.

[127] [2007] ICR 1553, EAT.   [128] IDS Brief 65.   [129] [1975] IRLR 354.
[130] [1977] ICR 763, [1977] IRLR 178, 12 ITR 130, EAT.
[131] [1981] IRLR 394, CA.   [132] [1975] IRLR 102, 10 ITR 60.

2.98 If an employee is told that his appointment is subject to a probationary period of a certain length of time, this does not give him a legal right to be employed for that length of time, and the employer may lawfully dismiss him before that period has expired (*Dalgleish v Kew House Farm Ltd*[133]) as long as he is given his correct contractual notice (*Fosca Services (UK) Ltd v Birkett*[134]).

K. **Trainees**

2.99 Section 230 of ERA defines a contract of employment as 'a contract of service or apprenticeship, whether express or implied, and (if it is express) whether it is oral or in writing'. It is clear, therefore, that a trainee can be employed under a contract of employment, and this includes, for example, an articled clerk employed by a solicitor (*Oliver v JP Malnick & Co*[135]). However, not all such trainees are so employed. In *Wiltshire Police Authority v Wynn* (see para 2.73), it was held that police cadets are not employees, but persons who are training to become policemen. During their training, even though they are being paid, they are not employed under a contract of employment. Similarly, in *Daley v Allied Suppliers Ltd*,[136] a young black girl was working on a Youth Opportunities scheme operated by the respondents. She alleged that she had been discriminated against on the ground of race, but it was held that the Race Relations Act was not applicable, as she was not a person employed within the meaning of s 4 and s 78 of the Act.

2.100 Indeed, the fact that young people on work experience courses are not employees has caused some concern, particularly in relation to their health and safety, for many of the duties owed by an employer are only owed to employees. Consequently the Health and Safety (Training for Employment) Regulations 1990 apply the provisions of the Health and Safety at Work etc. Act 1974 to youth trainees as if they were employees.

2.101 A youth training scheme is a tripartite relationship between the individual, the employer and the training provider. Generally, the employer agrees to employ the trainee for the term of the training, and although the training is provided by a third party, the employer has somewhat wider responsibilities to the trainee than to an ordinary employee. Such arrangements, generally referred to as 'Modern Apprenticeship Agreements', are capable of amounting to a traditional contract of apprenticeship, because they secure wages for the apprentice during the period of apprenticeship, they provide training to enable the apprentice to obtain skills and give status in the labour market on successful completion of the training (*Flett v Matheson*[137]).

L. **Civil partnerships**

2.102 A civil partnership is a relationship which has been entered into by two persons of the same sex which is formed when they register as civil partners under the provisions of the Civil Partnership Act 2004. So far as the law of employment is concerned, a civil partnership is to be treated in the same way and to the same extent as a married relationship. Hence, the provisions in the Equality Act 2010 prohibiting unlawful discrimination against married persons apply equally to persons who have formed a civil partnership. Provisions in the Paternity and Adoption Leave Regulations, Statutory Maternity Pay Regulations, Flexible Working (Eligibility etc) Regulations have also been amended to apply to persons

---

[133] [1982] IRLR 251, CA.   [134] [1996] IRLR 325, EAT.
[135] [1983] 3 All ER 795, [1983] ICR 708, [1983] IRLR 456, 127 Sol Jo 646, EAT.
[136] [1983] ICR 90, [1983] IRLR 14, EAT.
[137] [2006] EWCA 53, [2005] ICR 1134, [2005] IRLR 412.

who have entered into a civil partnership in the same manner as they apply to married persons (Civil Partnership Act 2004 (Amendments to Subordinate Legislation) Order 2005).

M. Apprentices

2.103 A contract of apprenticeship is an agreement whereby the apprentice binds himself to his employer in order to learn a trade, and the employer on his part agrees to teach and instruct him. The contract must be in writing, signed by the parties, and cannot be terminated by the employer except for grave misconduct (such as theft) or a refusal to attend to his duties. However, it appears that there is no longer any need for a formal apprenticeship agreement to be entered into; to give a statement of terms and conditions which described a person as an 'apprentice sheet metal worker' was sufficient to create a contract of apprenticeship in *Wallace v C A Roofing Services Ltd*,[138] and it was not possible to terminate that contract on grounds of redundancy. An apprentice who is wrongfully dismissed may claim by way of damages not only his immediate loss, but a sum representing the value of his loss of future prospects as a qualified person (*Dunk v George Waller & Son Ltd*[139]). Also, since an employer is, in one sense, *in loco parentis* to an apprentice, a certain latitude must be shown in respect of minor lapses in conduct. For example, in *Shortland v Chantrill*,[140] an apprentice was criticised by a managing director about his work, and he retorted 'You couldn't have done any fucking better'. For this, he was dismissed. It was held that the dismissal was unfair; one isolated step of impudence did not warrant the termination of an apprenticeship which had only ten months to run.

2.104 An apprentice is employed for the duration of the apprenticeship, and may not be dismissed until it expires (other than for good cause). An apprenticeship differs from a contract of employment in that it is not terminable on notice, and, if there are provisions in the agreement which are inconsistent with the employer's normal terms and conditions of employment, it is the apprenticeship agreement which must prevail. In particular, an employer cannot dismiss an apprentice for reason of redundancy (*Whitely v Marton Electrical Ltd*[141]).

2.105 The Apprenticeship, Skills, Children and Learning Act 2009 (which mainly applies to England and Wales) provides that a person completes an apprenticeship if the standard completion conditions are met, ie a recognised apprenticeship agreement in connection with an apprenticeship framework. The certifying authority will issue apprenticeship certificates on completion. The Act also makes apprenticeship agreements to be treated as a contract of employment, which will give an apprentice all the usual employment rights.

N. Those under the age of 18

Minors

2.106 A contract of employment entered into by a minor (ie a person under the age of 18) is a valid agreement provided that on the whole it is substantially for his benefit. Otherwise, it will be void. Even though the contract contains terms which are onerous or detrimental to his interests, one must look at the effect of the whole agreement. In *De Francesco v Barnum*,[142] a 14-year-old girl bound herself by an apprenticeship deed to the claimant in

[138] [1996] IRLR 435.
[139] [1970] 2 QB 163, [1970] 2 All ER 630, [1970] 2 WLR 1241, 114 Sol Jo 356, CA.
[140] [1975] IRLR 208.
[141] [2003] ICR 495, [2003] IRLR 492, [1999] All ER (D) 370 (Nov), EAT.
[142] 45 Ch D 430, 60 LJ Ch 63, 39 WR 5, [1886–90] All ER Rep 414, 63 LT 438, 6 TLR 463.

order to become a professional dancer. She agreed not to marry during this time, and to perform engagements only with the plaintiff's permission. The claimant was under no obligation to provide engagements, but when he did, the pay was somewhat ungenerous. It was held that the deed was void, for it was totally unreasonable, and was not in the interests of the girl. In contrast, we can consider *Clements v London and North-Western Rly Co*,[143] where a boy entered into the defendants' employment on terms which excluded his right to sue under the Employers' Liability Act 1880, in respect of injuries suffered during his employment. Instead, he was covered by the company's own insurance scheme, which had a wider range of protection, though the benefits were somewhat lower than the State scheme. It was held that on the whole the contract was to his advantage and was therefore binding.

2.107 Cases on this subject illustrate somewhat graphically the changing social scene. In *Denmark Productions Ltd v Boscobel Productions Ltd*,[144] a contract by four infant members of a pop group to employ a manager was held to be binding, and in *Chaplin v Leslie Frewin (Publishers) Ltd*,[145] the son of a famous film star contracted to assign to a firm of publishers a book containing his life story. This too, was held to be binding, as it conferred a financial benefit on him.

Young persons

2.108 A young person is any person who has not attained the age of 18, and therefore includes children of any age. This is not to be confused with a young worker (a term used, for example, in the Working Time Regulations 1998), which refers to a person who has attained the age of 15 but not the age of 18 and who is over compulsory school age.

2.109 Special protection is given to young persons by the Management of Health and Safety at Work Regulations 1999. Before employing a young person, the employer must make a risk assessment, taking into account his inexperience, lack of awareness of risks and immaturity, the fitting and layout of the workplace, exposure to physical, biological and chemical agents, the way work equipment is handled, the organisation of the processes, the extent to which health and safety training is provided, and the risks from certain dangerous processes. Employers must ensure that young persons are protected at work from any risks to their health and safety which are a consequence of their lack of experience, absence of awareness of risks and lack of maturity. Special provision has been made for young workers in the Working Time Regulations 1998 (see para 7.62).

Children

2.110 The Children (Protection at Work) Regulations 1998–2000 deal with the employment of children below the minimum school leaving age, and amend the provisions of the Children and Young Persons Acts 1933 and 1963 and the Children and Young Persons (Scotland) Act 1937, in order to implement the requirements of Directive 94/33/EC on the Protection of Young Persons at Work.

The general principle is that a child under the age of 14 may not be employed in any work, other than as an employee of his parent or guardian in light agricultural work or horticultural work on an occasional basis. However, children over the age of 13 may be employed in categories of light work specified in local authorities' byelaws. Light work is defined as being work which does not jeopardise a child's safety, health, development, attendance at school or participation in work experience. Children have the right to have

---

[143] [1894] 2 QB 482, 58 JP 818, 63 LJQB 837, 9 R 641, 42 WR 663, 38 Sol Jo 562, 70 LT 896, 10 TLR 539, [1891–4] All ER Rep Ext 1461, CA.

[144] [1969] 1 QB 699, [1968] 3 All ER 513, [1968] 3 WLR 841, 112 Sol Jo 761, CA.

[145] [1966] Ch 71, [1965] 3 All ER 764, [1966] 2 WLR 40, 109 Sol Jo 871, CA.

a two-week break from any employment in school holidays. Local authorities have the power to prohibit the employment of children who are employed in a manner which may be prejudicial to their health, or render them unfit to obtain the benefit of full-time education, and they may impose restrictions on such employment (Education Act 1996, s 559).

This legislation, together with the Children (Performances) Regulations 1968 (see also Children (Performance) (Amendment) (Wales) Regulations 2007) extends controls on the employment of children in performances, including sport, advertising and modelling. A licence may be obtained from any justice of the peace if it is proposed to take a child abroad for these purposes.

Further information about these rules can be obtained from the education welfare office of a local education authority. Local authorities have the power to prohibit the employment of children who are employed in a manner which may be prejudicial to their health, or render them unfit to obtain the benefit of full-time education, and they may also impose restrictions on such employment (Education Act 1996, s 559). A child may not be employed in an industrial undertaking or on a sea-going boat, unless the undertaking or boat is one in which only members of the child's family are employed (Employment of Women, Young Persons, and Children Act 1920, ss 1–3). A child may not be employed in a factory (Education Act 1918, s 14) nor employed underground in a mine, except for the purpose of receiving prescribed instruction (Mines and Quarries Act 1954, s 124). A child may not be required to lift, carry or move anything so heavy as to be likely to cause injury.

2.111 School children may be employed for work experience from the beginning of the school term preceding the start of the school year in which they become entitled to leave school (Education (Work Experience) Act 1973, s 1, as amended).

O. **Domestic servants**

2.112 A domestic servant is an employee, and provided she has the requisite periods of continuous employment, may claim appropriate statutory rights. She may claim redundancy payment, for employment in a private household is deemed to be a business like any other. However, this does not apply if she is a close relative of the employer (see para 18.64). Nor do the special rules relating to the transfer of a business apply, except where the head of the household dies, for here there may be a transfer to the new head of the household for redundancy purposes (see ERA, s 175 and *Ranger v Brown*[146]).

P. **Foreign employees**

2.113 A person who is not a national of a member state of the European Economic Area (ie European Union, Iceland, Liechtenstein and Norway), or who is not a Commonwealth citizen with the right of abode, must obtain the necessary permission to take up employment in the United Kingdom, otherwise the employment will be illegal. The Immigration Rules currently in force detail a number of different categories of workers who may be granted entry clearance to enter this country for specified periods of time, with or without work permits, and the conditions which will be attached thereto if they wish to take up employment. A new simplified points-based system of immigration control has been introduced, which will replace the previous categories of persons entitled to come from non-EU countries. There are now five tiers, ie Tier 1 highly skilled migrants, entrepreneurs and innovators, Tier 2 skilled workers with job offers to fill shortages in the labour market, Tier 3 unskilled temporary seasonal labour (this category has been suspended indefinitely,

---

[146] [1978] 2 All ER 726, [1978] ICR 603, 13 ITR 42, EAT.

as the United Kingdom expects to fill such jobs from EU workers), Tier 4 students, and Tier 5 temporary workers (eg working holiday-makers). A consideration of these matters is outside the scope of this book, but information can be obtained from the UK Border Agency.

2.114 The illegality of the employment has three potential consequences. In the first place, a person who is employed under an illegal contract cannot acquire any legal rights under that contract. Thus he will have few employment rights (*Sharma v Hindu Temple*,[147] but see para 3.8). Additionally, if the contract was legal at one time, periods when the contract became illegal will not count towards continuity of employment, and will also break continuity (*Bamgbose v Royal Star and Garter Home*[148]).

2.115 Second, the Immigration, Asylum and Nationality Act 2006, s 15 provides that the Secretary of State may apply for a penalty notice against a person who employs an adult who is subject to immigration control, and:

(a) who has not been granted leave to enter or remain in the United Kingdom, or

(b) whose leave to enter or remain has expired, or is invalid, or

(c) who is subject to a condition prohibiting employment.

The amount of the penalty notice will be prescribed by regulations, currently up to £10,000 if the employment was due to negligence. The employer may object to the penalty notice, and the Secretary of State may cancel, reduce, increase or confirm it. In the alternative, an appeal against the penalty notice may be made to a county court (or sheriff's court).

The Secretary of State will issue a Code of Practice, specifying the factors to be considered in determining the amount of the penalty notice. The Code will also give advice on how to avoid a penalty under s 15, or an offence under s 21, without contravening the Equality Act 2010.

Third, it is also a criminal offence knowingly to employ an adult who is subject to the immigration controls referred to earlier, an offence punishable on indictment with a maximum of two years' imprisonment, or a fine, or both, and on summary conviction to 12 months' imprisonment (six months in Scotland) or a fine, or both (s 21). Where an offence is committed by a body corporate, any director, manager, secretary or similar officer (or person purporting to act as such) will be jointly liable, if the offence was committed with his consent, or connivance, or attributable to any neglect on his part. The above offence does not apply if the employee was an asylum seeker who has been given written permission to work, or an asylum seeker who had permission to work before appealing against a refusal to grant asylum. It will be a defence for the employer to show that before the employment began, he was shown a document which related to the employee, and which was of a description specified in an order made by the Secretary of State. The documents which are acceptable are set out in the Immigration (Restrictions on Employment) Order 2004, and basically consist of secure documents, which are either a UK or EEA passport, national identity card or UK residence permit, or the originals of certain other documents which will confirm that the holder is entitled to take the employment in question. A copy of the document must be kept for the duration of the employment and for a further six months after it ends.

2.116 The purpose behind the legislation was to try to limit the number of foreign nationals working here illegally. However, the requirement that before permitting a person to commence employment, the employer must ask certain questions and seek confirmation of nationality or status raises issues of race discrimination (*Dhatt v McDonalds Hamburgers Ltd*[149]). The EHRC has issued guidelines for employers which contain a number of 'good practice recommendations'.

[147] Unreported.   [148] EAT 841/95.

[149] [1988] ICR 591, EAT; aff'd [1991] 3 All ER 692, [1991] 1 WLR 527, [1991] ICR 238, [1991] IRLR 130, CA.

2.117 If the employment of a foreign worker is perfectly legal, then he will have all the employment protection rights which are applicable to his case, in the same manner as a UK or EU national, apart from being able to obtain employment in certain official posts.

Q. **Posted workers**

2.118 A posted worker is a worker who is sent from one EU member state to another state on a temporary basis in order to carry out some work in that other state. EC Directive 96/71/EC is designed to ensure that employers do not acquire a competitive edge by paying workers less favourable terms and conditions than the worker would otherwise earn according to the laws and practices in that other member state. They can, however, retain any terms and conditions which are more favourable under their existing contracts. It was not necessary for the UK to pass specific legislation to implement the Directive, although various minor amendments were made to a number of statutes which had previously limited the application of employment rights to persons who ordinarily work in the United Kingdom. With the removal of those limits, posted workers have the full range of appropriate rights.

R. **Working abroad**

2.119 An employee may be required to work outside the United Kingdom either permanently or on a temporary basis. The requirement will stem from an express term of the contract of employment, or by virtue of an implied term, when it is 'obvious' from the nature of the job and/or the employer's business.

2.120 If the employee is required to work outside the United Kingdom for more than one month, then, in addition to the matters which need to be contained in the written statement of terms and conditions given under ERA, s 1, the statement must:

(a) state the period for which the employee is to work outside the United Kingdom;

(b) state the currency in which remuneration is to be paid;

(c) give details of any additional remuneration paid and/or any extra benefits provided by reason of the requirement to work outside the United Kingdom; and

(d) specify any terms and conditions relating to the employee's return to the United Kingdom (s 1(4)(k)).

These details must be provided before the employee leaves the United Kingdom.

2.121 The parties can decide for themselves whether the contract will be governed by UK law or by the law of another country, although this cannot deprive the employee of the right to claim under the laws of the country in which he works. Otherwise the Contract (Applicable Law) Act 1990 provides that the contract will be governed by the law of the country in which the employee habitually carries out his duties. If this cannot be ascertained with certainty, the law to be applied will be the law of the country in which the employer's business is situated. Further, the Civil Jurisdiction and Judgments Act 1982 provides that if the employer is domiciled in a member state of the European Union, he can be sued in the courts of that state or in the courts of the state where the employee habitually carries out his work.

2.122 Any period spent working abroad will count for the purpose of computing the period of continuous employment (ERA, s 215(1)), but will only count for redundancy purposes if national insurance contributions are made in respect of such periods (ERA, s 215(4)). However, weeks of overseas employment do not break continuity for redundancy purposes, but the start of any such period will be postponed by seven days for each week that does not thus count.

2.123 There is no implied term that an employer will provide personal accident insurance for the benefit of a person who is required to work abroad. Nor is the employer obliged to give specific advice on special risks, or to advise the employee to take out his own personal accident insurance (*Reid v Rush & Tompkins Group plc*,[150] and see para 10.34). Nor can a duty in tort be imposed to expand contractual duties.

S. Offshore employment

2.124 Offshore employment is defined as employment for the purposes of activities: (a) in the territorial waters of the United Kingdom; or (b) connected with the exploration of the seabed or subsoil, or the exploration of their natural resources, in the United Kingdom sector of the continental shelf; or (c) connected with the exploration or exploitation, in a foreign sector of the continental shelf, of a cross-boundary petroleum field and renewable energy zones (eg wind farms) (ERA, s 201; TULR(C)A, s 287).

2.125 Orders have been made extending the provisions of various employment legislation to offshore employment, including the Employment Rights Act 1996 (except time off work for public duties), Equality Act 2010, National Minimum Wage Act 1998 and Trade Union and Labour Relations (Consolidation) Act 1992. Employment in the Frigg Gas Field comes within the scope of the various Acts if the employer is a British company, or has a place of business in Great Britain from which the activities are directed.

T. Retainers

2.126 A person who is retained for employment is not an employee merely because he is 'on call' even though he is paid during that time. Employment involves work or other activity carried out for the employer. In *Suffolk County Council v Secretary of State for the Environment*,[151] it was held that a retained fireman, who was permanently on call, was not an employee, for a contractual obligation to remain on call within a prescribed area did not constitute employment. His hours of work only began when he was on duty following a call.

However, a different result was reached in *British Nursing Association v Inland Revenue (National Minimum Wage Compliance Team)*,[152] where the employers provided a 'bank' of nurses for emergency duties. A booking system operated a 24-hour service. During the day, nurses could be contacted at the employer's premises, but at night they had to be contacted at their homes. The National Minimum Wage Compliance Team took the view that those nurses engaged on the night shift were entitled to a minimum hourly rate for all hours they were on duty, but the employers argued that the nurses were not actually working during their shift. Although they were required to be available to take telephone calls, they could spend their shift doing other activities, such as watching television or reading, etc. It was held that the nurses were entitled to the national minimum wage for all the hours they were on duty. They had to hold themselves ready to answer the telephone, they could not pick and choose the times at which they had to answer the telephone, and there was a continuing obligation throughout the night to be available.

---

[150] [1989] 3 All ER 228, [1990] 1 WLR 212, [1990] RTR 144, [1989] 2 Lloyd's Rep 167, [1990] ICR 61, [1989] IRLR 265, CA.

[151] (1983) 82 LGR 557; revsd 83 LGR 130, [1984] ICR 882, [1985] IRLR 24, HL.

[152] [2001] IRLR 659, [2001] All ER (D) 59 (Aug), EAT; aff'd [2002] EWCA Civ 494, [2003] ICR 19, [2002] IRLR 480, [2002] All ER (D) 419 (Mar).

U. **Fixed-term contracts**

2.127 A fixed-term contract is a contract of employment for a specified period of time, ie, with a defined beginning and a defined end (*Wiltshire County Council v National Association of Teachers in Further and Higher Education and Guy*[153]). As a general rule, such a contract cannot be terminated before its expiry date except for gross misconduct or by mutual agreement (*Lyritzis v Inmarsat*[154]). However, a contract can still be for a fixed term if it contains within it a provision enabling either side to terminate it on giving notice before the term expires (*Allen v National Australia Group Europe Ltd*[155]). A contract of apprenticeship is a classic example of a fixed-term contract (*Wallace v CA Roofing Services Ltd,* para 2.103).

The Fixed-term Employees (Prevention of Less Favourable) Treatment Regulations 2002

2.128 These regulations implement the Fixed-term Workers Directive (1999/70/EC). The regulations apply to employees (not workers) and are designed to introduce the principle of non-discrimination between those working on fixed-term contracts and comparators who are permanent employees. The main beneficiaries of the regulations will be employees who are employed in order to cover for employees who are on statutory periods of absence (maternity leave, adoption leave, parental leave, etc), those employed in periods of peak demand, those who are employed on contracts to carry out specific tasks, eg setting up a database, teachers in higher education, senior staff employed in the health service, etc.

2.129 A fixed-term contract is defined as being a contract of employment that, under its provisions determining how it will terminate in the normal course, will terminate (a) on the expiry of a specific term, or (b) on the completion of a particular task, or (c) on the occurrence or non-occurrence of any specific event other than the attainment by the employee of any normal and bona fide retiring age.

2.130 The regulations do not apply to agency workers, or to those working under a contract of apprenticeship, or on government training schemes, or doing work experience not exceeding one year as part of a higher education course.

2.131 The regulations do not provide for permanent employees to have the right to compare themselves with fixed-term employees, and so it is possible to treat the latter more favourably than the former, provided, of course, that no other aspect of employment law is infringed, such as sex discrimination etc.

Terms not less favourable

2.132 A fixed-term employee has the right not to be treated by his employer less favourably than a comparable permanent employee with regard to the terms of the contract, including any period of service qualification relation to a particular condition of service, the opportunity to receive training, or the opportunity to secure permanent employment in the establishment. He will also have the right not to suffer any other detriment by any act (or deliberate failure to act) of his employer. However, this right only applies if the treatment in question is on the ground that the employee is a fixed-term employee, and the treatment is not justified on objective grounds. The comparable permanent employee must be employed by the same employer at the same establishment (other locations can be considered if there is no-one appropriate at the same establishment) and be an employee who is

---

[153] (1978) 77 LGR 272, [1978] ICR 968, [1978] IRLR 301, 13 ITR 437, 122 Sol Jo 626, EAT; aff'd 78 LGR 445, [1980] ICR 455, [1980] IRLR 198, CA.
[154] Unreported.   [155] [2004] IRLR 847, EAT.

engaged on the same or broadly similar work, having regard to whether they have a similar level of qualifications and skills. A hypothetical comparator will not suffice. An employee is not a comparable permanent employee if his employment has ceased.

2.133 Terms which must be no less favourable include pay and pensions. Where appropriate, a 'pro rata' principle is to be applied, which means that the fixed-term employee is entitled to such proportions of pay or other benefits as is reasonable bearing in mind the length of his contract of employment and the basis on which pay or other benefits is offered. An employee on a fixed-term contract of three months or less has the right to receive statutory sick pay, and, after one month's continuous employment is entitled to a week's notice if the contract is terminated, and also has the right to receive guarantee payment and payment on medical suspension. But the non-renewal of a fixed term contract does not, by itself, amount to less favourable treatment (*Department for Work and Pensions v Webby*[156]).

2.134 It is, however, possible to justify the unequal treatment on objective grounds. In order to be objectively justified, the unequal treatment should be aimed at achieving a legitimate business objective, be necessary to achieve that objective, and be an appropriate way of achieving it. If the treatment by an employer of a fixed-term employee is less favourable than the treatment meted out to a comparable permanent employee, it will amount to objective justification if, taken as a whole, the terms and conditions of a fixed-term employee are at least as favourable as those which apply to a comparable permanent employee. Thus it is permissible to take a 'package' approach, as opposed to a term-by-term approach (as in equal pay cases). Higher salaries, or more holidays, etc can compensate for the lack of other benefits such as pensions, provided that the package as a whole is equivalent to or better than that of a permanent employee.

2.135 A fixed-term employee has the right to be informed of any permanent suitable vacancies, and may bring a claim in respect of the employer's failure to do so within three months from the date on which other individuals, whether employees or not, were informed of the vacancy.

The four-year rule and other rights

2.136 Where there is a fixed-term contract or a succession of such contracts which result in the employee being employed for four years or more, the contract will be deemed to be a contract of indefinite duration (unless there is objective justification when the contract was made or renewed), and the minimum period of notice provisions of ERA, ss 86–91 will apply (see para 15.4). The employee also has the right to request a written statement from his employer either giving reasons why his contract remains fixed-term beyond the four-year limitation period, or confirming that it has become open-ended. It should be noted that a fixed-term contract does not become a permanent contract until it is renewed. If it is renewed before the four-year point, it will become permanent as soon as the four-year point is reached. If it is renewed after the four-year point, it became permanent on renewal.

2.137 To benefit from the four-year rule, the employee would need to show that he has been continuously employed within the meaning of ERA, ss 210–219 (see Chapter 13). In particular, if a week's absence from work is not covered by s 212(3) (see para 13.24) continuity of employment will be broken. Thus if there is a gap of more than one week between successive fixed-term contracts, such contracts cannot be turned into a permanent contract under the four-year rule. The situation revealed in *Booth v United States of America* (see para 13.2) remains unaffected.[157]

---

[156] [2004] EWCA Civ 1745, CA.   [157] [1999] IRLR 16, 611 IRLB 9, EAT.

2.138 The requirement which permits an employee to opt out of his right to receive a redundancy payment is repealed, although contracts which were in force prior to the commencement of the regulations are able to retain this waiver during their term (see para 18.64).

2.139 A fixed-term employee will have the right to request in writing from his employer a written statement giving particulars of the reasons for any less favourable treatment, and the employer must reply within 21 days of the request. An identical right exists for an employee who considers that his contract is one of indefinite duration under the four-year rule to make a similar request for confirmation that the contract is to be so regarded. There is no remedy if the employer fails to comply with either of these requests, but if, in proceedings before an employment tribunal to enforce the fixed-term employee's rights under the regulations, it is shown that the employer deliberately and without reasonable excuse omitted to provide the written statement, or that it was evasive or equivocal, the tribunal may draw an inference that the employer has infringed the right in question. If an employee considers that he is a permanent employee under the four-year rule, he may present an application to an employment tribunal for a declaration to that effect, but he cannot do so unless he has previously requested a statement from his employer, and the employer has failed to provide one. He must also still be employed by the employer.

2.140 An employee has the right not to suffer a detriment, or be dismissed, because he did an act under the regulations, and may also bring a claim alleging unequal treatment contrary to the regulations. The claim must be brought within three months of the alleged infringement, although the tribunal can consider a complaint which is out of time if it considers that it is just and equitable to do so. If the employment tribunal finds in his favour, it may make a declaration as to the rights of the complainant and the employer, award compensation, and make a recommendation that the employer takes steps to obviate or reduce the adverse effects complained of. The compensation award shall be that which the tribunal considers to be just and equitable, and may include the loss of benefits and reasonable expenses. However, if the claim is based on less favourable treatment, there can be no award in respect of injured feelings.

Continuity rules

2.141 In respect of a fixed-term contract of short duration, the normal continuity rules apply on renewal (see Chapter 13), including the statutory presumption in favour of continuity (ERA, s 210(5)). This may enable an employee whose employment was intended to be temporary to obtain various employment protection rights in appropriate circumstances. The normal rules about giving statutory notice do not apply when the contract period expires, except where an employee has been employed under a fixed-term contract of one month or less, and has actually been employed for three months or more (ERA, s 86(4)).

Expiry of the fixed term

2.142 If a fixed-term contract is not renewed on expiry, that will not amount to a dismissal at common law, because the contract has been terminated automatically by effluxion of time. However, non-renewal under the same contract will be a dismissal for the purpose of ERA. Whether the dismissal was fair or unfair will be determined by whether or not the employer can show that he acted reasonably in not renewing the contract. If the contract is terminated prior to the expiry of the fixed term, the employee will have the normal rights in respect of breach of contract (see Chapter 15), and the employer will be liable to pay the employee for the rest of the term, subject to the employee's duty to mitigate against his loss. He will also have the right to claim unfair dismissal, provided he has been employed for the requisite period of continuous employment. However, if the contract is terminated by mutual agreement, no dismissal has taken place (*Lyritzis v Inmarsat*), although a mutual acknowledgement that the contract will terminate on the fixed date will be a dismissal nonetheless (*Thames Television v Wallis*[158]). Nor will there be a dismissal for redundancy payment purposes if the employee is employed under a new contract which takes effect within four weeks of the expiry of the old (ERA, s 138(1)). A dismissal will take place if the new contract is substantially different from the old (ERA, s 138(2–6)), but the right to obtain a redundancy payment will be lost if the employee unreasonably refuses an offer on the same or different terms (ERA, s 141).

V. Secondment of employees

2.143 Occasionally, an employer will second an employee to another employer, either for a specific task or for a specific period of time. This arrangement can give rise to a number of legal problems, eg (a) which employer is to accept liability if the seconded employee injures a third party; (b) which employer will be liable if the employee suffers an injury; and (c) the status of the seconded employee during the period of secondment and after it has concluded.

2.144 In *Fitton v City of Edinburgh Council*[159] the claimant was employed in the council's education department. She was then seconded to ELLP, another corporate body that provided educational services. It was intended that the secondment would last for 12 months, but it was later agreed to be open-ended. The council agreed that if the secondment came to an end she would be guaranteed a comparable post. The council continued to pay her salary, but this was done on the basis of a financial arrangement with ELLP. The claimant did no work for the council, and the council could no longer require her to work for them. After working for ELLP for two years, she resigned her employment with them, and brought claims for constructive dismissal, sex discrimination and sexual harassment against the council. The EAT upheld the finding of an employment tribunal that she was not employed by the council during her open-ended secondment. The irreducible minimum requirements of mutuality of agreement and control were absent. The fact that the arrangement used the term 'secondment' was not, by itself, determinative of the matter, if the facts establish that the 'seconded employee' had, in practice, been transferred from one employer to another.

Liability if the seconded employee injures a third party

2.145 As a general principle, it can be stated that if a skilled employee, together with complex or valuable machinery, is loaned to another employer, the original employer will still be liable if the employee's actions cause injury or damage to a third party. For example, in *Mersey Docks and Harbour Board v Coggins & Griffiths (Liverpool) Ltd*,[160] the harbour board loaned a crane and driver to a firm of stevedores, the latter being responsible for paying the driver's wages. Because of the driver's negligence, there was an accident. It was held that the harbour board was the driver's employer for the purpose of being held vicariously liable for the driver's negligence, for they had failed to discharge the burden of showing that the driver was no longer their employee.

2.146 A contrary conclusion was reached in *Arthur White (Contractors) Ltd v Tarmac Civil Engineering Ltd*,[161] where a crane and driver were hired out. Under the contract, which was the standard form used in the plant hire industry, the driver was stated to be

---

[158] [1979] IRLR 136, EAT.   [159] Employment Appeal Tribunal (Scotland), 5 June 2008.
[160] [1947] AC 1, [1946] 2 All ER 345, 115 LJKB 465, 90 Sol Jo 466, 175 LT 270, 62 TLR 533, HL.
[161] [1967] 3 All ER 586, [1967] 1 WLR 1508, 111 Sol Jo 831, HL.

under the direction and control of the hirer, and for all purposes was to be regarded as the employee of the hirer. It was held that as between the main employer and the hirer, the latter was liable for the damage which resulted from an accident due to the driver's negligence. In other words, the two employers had, as between themselves, come to a contractual arrangement as to their respective legal liability (see also *Hawley v Luminar Leisure Ltd*,[162] para 10.108).

2.147 But dual vicarious liability is legally permissible. The idea that when an employee is seconded to work for another employer, liability for his negligent act must rest with one employer or the other is a notion with no intrinsic justification. The core question is, who is entitled, or indeed obliged, to give orders as to how the work should be done or not done? If there is evidence of some form of dual control, then it would not be impossible to hold that both employers should share liability equally (*Viasystems (Tyneside) Ltd v Thermal Transfers (Northern) Ltd*[163]).

Liability if the seconded employee injures himself

2.148 If the seconded employee is injured, there is a strong likelihood that it will be the temporary employer who will be responsible. In *Garrard v AE Southey & Co and Standard Telephones and Cables Ltd*,[164] the claimant was loaned by his employers (the first defendants) to the second defendants to carry out some electrical work. The foreman of the second defendants not only told the claimant what to do but also specifically controlled the way he was to do his work. The claimant was injured, and sued both employers for common law negligence. It was held that the temporary employer was liable, as they were his employer for the purpose of ensuring his safety at work. The court drew a distinction between those cases where a complicated piece of equipment and/or a skilled employee was loaned, and where an unskilled or semi-skilled workman is loaned on his own. In the former case, it may be easier to infer that the general employer does not intend to part with control over a complex and valuable piece of machinery, but if labour only is loaned, it is easier to infer the transfer of the rights of the general employer to the temporary employer.

Status of the seconded worker during, and after, the period of employment

2.149 A third problem concerns the status of the employee who has been seconded. Is he an employee of the original employer, or of the employer to whom he has been seconded? What are his continuity rights if either employer terminates the contract? Is there an impact on the employment contract by virtue of the Transfer of Undertakings (Protection of Employment) Regulations? What is his pension position during the period of secondment? Some of these questions were raised in *Astley v Celtec Ltd*,[165] but the answers given were somewhat inconclusive.

2.150 What is the position of an employee who has been seconded to work abroad? It is now established that an employee working in another country may, in some circumstances, be able to bring a claim under UK employment legislation (see *Serco Ltd v Lawson*, para 1.32), but the position of seconded employees is not clear. Two problems are apparent, namely (a) who will be the employer against whom a claim is to be made, and (b) will the UK employment tribunals have jurisdiction to deal with a claim made by an employee who once worked in the United Kingdom, but who is then seconded to work abroad? It is a truism to state that each case will have to be determined on its own facts, but the trend is toward permitting such actions wherever possible (eg, see *Crofts v Cathay Pacific Airways Ltd*[166]).

---

[162] [2005] EWCA Civ 18.   [163] [2005] EWCA Civ 1151.
[164] [1952] 2 QB 174, [1952] 1 All ER 597, 96 Sol Jo 166, [1952] 1 TLR 630.
[165] (C-478/03) (2005) *Times*, 9 June.   [166] [2005] IRLR 423.

2.151 An allied problem arises if an employee takes a 'career break'. If the employee is expected to resign, continuity of employment is likely to be broken (*Curr v Marks and Spencer Ltd*[167]), but if he is on some form of leave of absence, continuity will be preserved by virtue of ERA, s 212(3)(c) (see para 13.24).

W. Agency workers

Employment agency or employment business?

2.152 An employer may turn to an agency to provide him with staff for a specific purpose or definite or indefinite period of time. The Conduct of Employment Agencies and Employment Businesses Regulations 2003–2010 set out the minimum standards which govern the conduct of the private recruitment industry. Generally, such agencies must comply with the legislation on equal opportunities, equal pay, health and safety, national minimum wage, working time, etc. BIS has produced a Guidance Note clarifying various issues.

An employment agency undertakes to find work for a work seeker, and once the worker is suitably placed, the agency will drop out of the picture, having obtained a fee from the worker's employer for its services.

On the other hand, an employment business is an organisation which supplies workers to hirers, often on a temporary basis (the term 'worker' is used in a neutral sense). The worker will do work for the hirer, but as a general rule the employment relationship is with the employment business, and it is the business which pays the worker his wages. The terms of the contract between the employment business and the worker shall specify in writing whether the worker is employed by the employment business under a contract of service or apprenticeship, or a contract for services, and, in any case, other terms and conditions relating to remuneration, notice, annual leave, etc.

Status of agency workers

2.153 In practice, there are three different scenarios to consider when dealing with the status of agency workers. The first arises out of employment legislation, when it has to be determined whether or not the worker is legally an employee, for such issues as unfair dismissal, redundancy payments, and other rights that exist for employees. The second issue arises when prosecutions are considered under the Health and Safety at Work Act and associated regulations, which generally speaking only apply to employees, although under the Management of Health and Safety at Work Regulations 1999 an employer also owes duties to visiting workers and temporary workers. Thirdly, claims for injuries based on common law negligence or vicarious liability are sometimes treated by the courts in a more relaxed manner, as the real defendant is the insurance company, not the employer!

2.154 In view of some difficult and frequently irreconcilable decisions it is trite to observe that it all depends on the facts of each case. The courts and tribunals have to decide whether the worker is an employee of the employment business (*McMeecham v Secretary of State for Employment*[168]), an employee of the client end-user (*Dacas v Brook Street Bureau*[169]), or an employee of neither (*Bunce v Postworth Ltd*[170]).

---

[167] [2002] All ER (D) 76 (Mar), EAT; revsd [2002] EWCA Civ 1852, [2003] ICR 443, [2003] IRLR 74, [2002] All ER (D) 205 (Dec).

[168] [1995] ICR 444, [1995] IRLR 461, EAT; aff'd [1997] ICR 549, [1997] IRLR 353, CA.

[169] [2003] IRLR 190, [2003] All ER (D) 241 (Jan), EAT; revsd [2004] EWCA Civ 217, [2004] All ER (D) 125 (Mar).

[170] [2005] EWCA Civ 490, [2005] IRLR 557.

2.155 One has to start with the terms of the contract between the worker and the employment business, although the label put on the contract is only determinative of the relationship between the parties if, having considered all the relevant factors, there is still some doubt about the worker's true status. In *McMeecham v Secretary of State for Employment* the claimant worked for an employment business under a series of temporary contracts. The terms of his engagement specifically stated that he was self-employed, but he was paid on a weekly basis when he worked, and tax and national insurance contributions were deducted. The business became insolvent and the claimant sought to recover wages owed to him from the National Insurance Fund (under ERA, s 182). In allowing his claim, the Court of Appeal drew a distinction between the general terms of engagement which existed with the employment business and the specific engagements a worker undertakes. In respect of the latter a single engagement was capable of giving rise to a contract of employment, even though the worker might not be entitled to employee status under his general terms of engagement.

2.156 In *Consistent Group Ltd v Kalwak*[171] the EAT expressed the view that the fact that the contract provides for unrealistic possibilities will not alter the true nature of the relationship if this is different from what happens in reality, and this view was expressly endorsed in *Protectacoat Firthglow Ltd v Szilagyi*[172] and by the Supreme Court in *Autoclenz v Belcher*.[173] The employment tribunal should adopt a robust and sensible view in order to prevent the substance of the relationship from being undermined by form. Clauses that are designed to prevent the relationship from being that of employer/employee (with the consequent dilution of employment rights) will only be upheld if the documentation realistically reflects what might be expected to occur (*Redrow Homes (Yorkshire) Ltd v Buckborough*[174]). The decision in *Protectacoat* was strengthened in *Autoclenz Ltd v Belcher*,[175] where it was stressed that the proper approach is to consider whether the written terms reflect the true intentions of the parties. It is not enough to argue that a clause has never been activated, if it is genuine. Thus, provisions that state that the employer has no obligation to provide work, or that the worker is under no obligation to do the work, or that the worker could provide a substitute if necessary, are not conclusive of anything, if they do not represent the true intent of the parties.

2.157 In the absence of a formal contract between the parties, it is necessary to draw conclusions about the legal nature of their relationship from all the surrounding circumstances, including how they act in practice. Thus in *Hewlett Packard Ltd v O'Murphy*,[176] a computer specialist set up his own limited company which then contracted with an employment business, which in turn provided his services to the respondent company. Even though the arrangement lasted for some years, and the worker was under the respondent's control so far as performance and discipline were concerned, the strict legal position was that there was no contractual nexus between the worker and the respondents, and his claim for unfair dismissal failed. The existence of 'one too many contracts' (ie between the individual service company-agency-end-user) was fatal to the claim.

2.158 In a number of cases, the existence of a contract of employment between the worker and client has been implied (eg see *Dacas v Brook Street Bureau*) but this can only be done if there is strong evidence that the agency worker has been integrated into the end-user's

---

[171] [2008] EWCA Civ 430; [2008] IRLR 505 (note that the EAT view in this case was specifically approved by the SC in *Autoclenz v Belcher,* as opposed to the judgment of the CA in *Kalwak*).
[172] [2009] EWCA Civ 98, [2009] ICR 835, [2009] IRLR 365.
[173] [2011] UKSC 41.   [174] [2009] IRLR 34.
[175] [2009] EWCA Civ 1046, [2010] IRLR 70, (2009) *Times,* 16 October.
[176] [2002] IRLR 4, [2001] All ER (D) 91 (Sep), EAT.

organisation, and treated on a day-to-day basis in the same way as it treats its own employees (*Franks v Reuters Ltd*[177]). Thus if the agency worker has a contract of employment with the agency, this would negate the existence of a contract of employment with the end-user client, and there is thus no necessity to imply a contract of employment between them (*Cairns v Visteon Ltd*[178]).

2.159 Sometimes a more cautious approach to the status of agency workers appears to be taken. In *Craigie v Haringey*[179] the EAT held that there was no necessity to imply a contract of employment between an agency worker and an end-user, and *Dacas v Brook Street Bureau* was not followed on this point. Further, the mere fact that an employee looks like an employee of the end-user, acted like an employee, and was treated like an employee does not mean that tribunals should therefore imply a contract of employment (*Heatherwood & Wexham Park Hospitals NHS Trust v Kulubowila*;[180] see also *Astbury v Gist*[181]). In *James v Greenwich Council*,[182] the claimant provided her services to the council for five years. Her contract with the agency stated that she was employed under a contract for services, and that no employment relationship existed with either the agency or the client. The council did not pay her wages, but made a payment to the agency. She was not subject to the council's disciplinary or grievance procedure, was not entitled to sick pay or holiday pay, and, when absent from work, was replaced by another agency worker. When she was not allowed to return to work after a period of sickness absence, she claimed unfair dismissal against the council, arguing that in view of the length of time she had worked for them, an implied contract of employment had come into existence. Her claim was dismissed by the employment tribunal, the EAT and the Court of Appeal. The fact that the arrangement had existed for a considerable length of time did not, per se, give rise to an implied contract of employment, for it is only in cases of necessity that such a contract can be implied.

2.160 It would appear that employment tribunals nowadays are more likely to give preference to contractually expressed intentions over the manner in which the relationship with the agency worker has worked in practice (*Astbury v Gist*) unless the documentation is totally unrealistic (*Consistent Group Ltd v Kalwak*, para 2.156).

2.161 The presence or absence of mutuality is a significant factor to be considered. In *Bunce v Postworth Ltd (t/a Skyblue)*,[183] the claimant registered for work with Postworth, an employment business. The written agreement described the claimant as 'an associate', and stated that it was a contract for services and not intended to give rise to a contract of employment. Postworth were not obliged to obtain work for the claimant, and in turn the claimant was not obliged to accept work offered. When he accepted work, he was obliged to accept the directions, supervision and instructions of any person in the client organisation to whom he was responsible, and to conform to the client's normal hours of work, and rules and regulations. Postworth paid the claimant's wages and holiday pay, but not sick pay. Over a period of one year, the claimant accepted 142 assignments, most of which were with the same client. However, after complaints were received about the quality of his work, Postworth informed him that the arrangement was terminated. His claim for unfair dismissal was rejected by the employment tribunal, the EAT and the Court of Appeal. So far as Postworth were concerned, there was an absence of control. So far as the client was concerned, there was an absence of mutuality. For the claimant, it had been argued

---

[177] [2002] All ER (D) 239 (Jun), EAT; revsd [2003] EWCA Civ 417, [2003] ICR 1166, [2003] IRLR 423, [2003] 25 LS Gaz R 45, 147 Sol JO LB 474, [2003] All ER (D) 160 (Apr).
[178] [2007] ICR 616, [2007] IRLR 175.   [179] Employment Appeal Tribunal, 12 January 2007.
[180] EAT/0633/06.   [181] EAT/0619/06/DA, EAT/0446/04/LA.
[182] [2007] ICR 577, [2007] IRLR 168, EAT; aff'd [2008] EWCA Civ 35, [2008] ICR 545, [2008] IRLR 302.
[183] n 170.

that he had an 'umbrella' contract, which covered all the separate arrangements made with Postworth, but the argument was dismissed by the Court of Appeal, who pointed out that the very detailed provisions in the contract left no room for implying an overall contract. Further, the fact that the claimant worked for more than one end user was fatal to the 'umbrella contract' argument.

2.162 An employee who is supplied by an agency on a temporary appointment, and who is then taken on as a full-time employee has continuity of employment from the date his temporary appointment commenced (*RNLI v Bushaway*[184]).

Agency Workers Regulations 2010

2.163 The Agency Workers Regulations 2010 apply to workers supplied by temporary work agencies, ie agencies that introduce workers to hirers for temporary worker only. They do not apply to employment agencies, as these look for permanent employment for workers. An agency worker is defined as an individual who is supplied by a temporary work agency to work for and under the direction of a hirer. The agency worker can be employed by the agency or treated as a worker by the hirer, but genuinely self-employed persons are excluded. Workers who work through an 'umbrella company' (which is usually used to exploit tax loopholes) or who are engaged by an intermediary are within the scope of the regulations.

2.164 An agency worker is entitled to the same basic working conditions and employment conditions as he would have if he had been recruited by the hirer directly, with the same terms and conditions of employment that are ordinarily included in contracts of employees of the hirer, whether by collective agreement or otherwise (reg 5). The relevant terms and conditions are those enjoyed by comparable employees of the hirer. A comparable employee is one who is, together with the agency worker, working for and under the supervision and direction of the hirer, and engaged on broadly similar work, having regard to whether they have a similar level of qualifications and skills, and based at the same establishment.

2.165 The relevant terms and conditions that must be applied to the agency worker are terms and conditions relating to pay, duration of working time, night work, rest periods, rest breaks and annual leave. 'Pay' means any sum payable, including fees, bonus, commission, holiday pay or other emoluments referable to the employment, but excluding the monetary value of benefits in kind, occupational sick pay, maternity, paternity and adoption pay, redundancy payments, profit-sharing schemes, etc. Bonuses that relate to personal and individual performances are included, but not those linked to long-term organisational performance.

2.166 The agency worker is entitled to be treated no less favourably than a comparable worker in relation to collective facilities provided by the hirer (reg 12) These include canteen or other similar facilities, child care facilities, and transport services, although less favourable treatment can be justified on objective grounds. During the assignment, the agency worker is entitled to be informed by the hirer of any relevant vacant posts with the hirer, and must be given the same opportunity as a comparable worker to find permanent employment with the hirer (reg 13). These are known as 'day one' rights.

2.167 To qualify for equal treatment, however, an agency worker must be employed in the same role for 12 continuous calendar weeks (part of a week counts as a full week). If there is a break between assignments, there are a number of circumstances when the break can

---

[184] [2005] IRLR 674, EAT.

be ignored for the purpose of computing continuity, ie for any reason up to six weeks, for sickness or injury up to 26 weeks, and periods of absence due to maternity leave, paternity leave, jury service, and so on (see reg 7(8)). The 12-week period must be continuous, with the agency worker doing the same job with the same hirer. If there is a break during an assignment, continuity is only broken if the break is for six calendar weeks or more.

2.168 Continuity will also be broken if the worker is given a new role with substantially different duties (reg 7(3)). But the work or duties must be substantially different from those that made up the previous assignment, and the employment agency must inform the agency worker in writing of the type of work he will be required to do in the new role. Further, the agency worker will be deemed to have satisfied the 12-week qualifying period if he is otherwise prevented from doing so by the structure of assignments. This will arise when the agency worker has completed two or more assignments with a particular hirer, or has worked in two or more substantially different roles with the same hirer, and the most likely explanation for it is that the hirer (or the agency) intended to prevent the agency worker from being entitled to equal treatment (reg 9). If an employment tribunal decides that the hirer's motive for moving the agency worker to a different job, or otherwise breaking the 12-week period, is to prevent the agency worker from obtaining equal treatment, it may make an award that the agency worker is entitled to equal treatment from the date from which he would otherwise be entitled, and a further award of up to £5,000 in respect of the breach of the equal treatment rule.

2.169 Liability for a breach of reg 5 (para 2.164) lies with the temporary work agency to the extent that it is responsible for the breach, although not if the agency has taken reasonable steps to obtain relevant information from the hirer about basic working and employment conditions in force in the hirer and, having received such information, acted reasonably in determining what the agency worker's basic working and employment conditions should be at the end of the qualifying period until the agency worker ceases to be entitled to the rights in reg 5 (see reg 14). To the extent that the temporary work agency is not liable under reg 14, the hirer will be liable for a breach of reg 5 to the extent that it is responsible for the breach.

2.170 If an agency worker considers that the hirer or temporary work agency have infringed his reg 5 rights, he may make a written request to the temporary work agency for a written statement containing information relating to the treatment in question. The temporary work agency shall respond within 28 days, setting out the relevant information relating to basic working and employment conditions of the workers of the hirer, the factors the temporary work agency considered when determining the basic working conditions that applied to the agency worker. If no response has been received within 30 days, the agency worker may request the hirer to provide a written statement containing information relating to the relevant basic working and employment conditions of workers of the hirer. Also, if the agency worker considered that he has not been given access to collective facilities or amenities (reg 12), or information regarding vacant posts with the hirer (reg 13), he may request the hirer to provide a written statement containing information relating to the treatment in question. The hirer shall respond to such a request with relevant information within 28 days.

2.171 An agency worker who is an employee has the right not to be unfairly dismissed because he has brought proceedings under the regulations, or done a number of acts in connection with his rights. He has also the right not to suffer a detriment as a result of any act, or deliberate failure to act, by the temporary work agency or the hirer (reg 17). An application may be made to an employment tribunal that the temporary work agency or the hirer has infringed a right conferred on the agency worker by regs 5, 9, 12, 13, 17(2). If the employment tribunal finds the complaint well founded, it may make a declaration as to the rights of the complainant, order the respondent to pay compensation to him, and make a recommendation that the respondent takes action for the purpose of obviating or reducing the adverse effect on the complainant of any matter to which the complaint relates.

2.172 Consequential amendments have been made to a number of existing legislative provisions, including the Trade Union and Labour Relations (Consolidation) Act, Employment Rights Act, Safety Representative and Safety Committees Regulations, Management of Health and Safety at Work Regulations, Transfer of Undertakings (Protection of Employment) Regulations, and so on.

2.173 It is not possible to contract out of the provisions of these regulations (reg 15).

X. Casual workers and global contracts

2.174 There are some workers who are employed on short-term periodic contracts, with various breaks in between, whose status has been the subject of a number of judicial decisions. If the employer is under no obligation to provide work, and if the worker is under no obligation to accept an offer of work, a contract of employment cannot exist. This is so even though during actual periods of working, income tax and national insurance contributions are deducted, for administrative reasons (*Stevedoring & Haulage Services Ltd v Fuller*[185]). Attempts have been made to treat such workers as being employed under one 'global contract' but with very limited success. A global contract cannot exist unless there is an irreducible minimum of obligations to offer and accept work existing between the parties (*Clark v Oxfordshire Health Authority*[186]), and it cannot be brought into existence merely by counting together a number of individual contracts which may have subsisted over a period of time (*Hellyer Bros Ltd v McLeod*[187]). In particular, where the terms upon which casual work is offered and accepted expressly negate mutuality of obligations, eg if the employment is specifically stated to be for an 'ad hoc or casual basis' or 'as and when required', there can be no global or overarching contract. The courts will not invent an implied term which specifically overrides the express term (*Stevedoring & Haulage Services Ltd v Fuller*).

    In *Carmichael v National Power plc*,[188] the appellant was engaged as a guide at a power station. She was paid for the number of hours worked, and had tax and national insurance deducted. Her contract stated that she was employed 'on a casual and as required basis'. The Court of Appeal held that, on the facts of the case, there was an implied term that the employer would offer her a reasonable amount of work, and that if so offered, she would carry out a reasonable amount of work. Thus it was held that a contract of employment existed. However, the House of Lords disagreed, and held that she was not an employee. The absence of mutuality of obligation will frequently by determinative of the matter, for if a person is not obliged to offer work, and the other party is not obliged to accept the work when offered, there is an absence of the irreducible minimum of mutual obligation necessary to create a contract of employment (see para 2.40). It would therefore appear that the fact that a contract is repeated does not create a global contract of employment.

---

[185] [2001] EWCA Civ 651, [2001] IRLR 627, [2001] All ER (D) 106 (May).

[186] [1998] IRLR 125, 41 BMLR 18, CA.

[187] [1987] 1 WLR 728, [1987] ICR 526, 131 Sol Jo 805, [1987] LS Gaz R 1056, sub nom *McLeod v Hellyer Bros Ltd* [1987] IRLR 232, CA.

[188] n. 86.

Y. National security (ERA, s 193)

2.175 There is a special regime to deal with cases involving issues of national security. The provisions of ERA dealing with protected disclosures do not apply in relation to employment for the purposes of the security service, the secret intelligence service, or the Government Communication Headquarters. Otherwise Crown employees (including the security services) may present claims to an employment tribunal, but claims for unfair dismissal and for victimisation on grounds of trade union membership based on ss 145A. 145B and 146 of TULR(C)A must be dismissed if it is shown that the action taken was for the purpose of safeguarding national security (Employment Tribunals Act, s 10). But it is still necessary to prove that the action was taken for the purpose of safeguarding national security, and although the action may be analogous with 'some other substantial reason' the employment tribunal is still entitled to consider the fairness or otherwise of a decision to dismiss in unfair dismissal cases (*B v BBA*[189]).

2.176 In such cases, a specially convened employment tribunal will be convened, with special powers and procedures to ensure that secrecy and confidentiality are maintained. Proceedings (in whole or in part) will be held in private, the claimant and/or his representative may be excluded, and the disclosure of documents may be prohibited. If the claimant or his representatives are excluded, a special advocate may be appointed (Employment Tribunals (Constitution and Rules of Procedure) Regulations 2004, Sch 2).

2.177 An argument that these provisions were incompatible with Art 6 of the Human Rights Act was rejected in *Home Office v Tariq*,[190] where the 'closed material procedure' was upheld, but it was also ruled that the claimant must be provided with the allegations against him in sufficient detail to enable him to give effective instructions to the special advocate, so as to enable the latter to challenge the allegations effectively.

2.178 It should be noted that these procedures apply in respect of the all the statutory jurisdiction of employment tribunals, including discrimination cases. Guidance on the approach to be adopted by employment tribunals when considering national security cases was given in *AB v Ministry of Defence*.[191] There must be cogent justification, and a judicial assessment on whether the interests of national security are at stake. The risks to the security services or the armed forces must be weighed against the principle of open justice. It is for the employment tribunals to make a necessary assessment when national security is involved.

---

[189] [2005] ICR 1530.
[190] [2010] EWCA Civ 462, [2011] UKSC 35.
[191] [2010] ICR 54.

3

The Formation of a Contract of Employment

The contract of employment

3.1 A contract of employment can be entered into formally or informally. It can emerge as a result of interviews, negotiations, exchange of letters, or a casual conversation at the factory door. It can be made orally or in writing, although apprenticeship deeds and articles for merchant seamen by definition must be written. But essentially it is a contract like any other contract, and in principle subject to the general contractual rules of the common law. The normal canons of legal construction must be applied (*Hooper v British Railways Board*[1]).

3.2 However, traditional legal reasoning based on the law of contract does not always sit comfortably with the expansion of workers' rights which has occurred over the past few decades, partly because of the acknowledged inequality of bargaining power between the parties, but also because a contract of employment involves a continuing relationship, unlike most other forms of contracts which are generally single transactions. In the world of employment, the parties have to live together and work together over a period of time. There has to be an element of trust and confidence. If there are areas where strict adherence to contractual rights can produce inequitable results, traditional contract doctrines may be circumvented. Consequently, the courts have thus developed and expanded the doctrine of the implied term of trust and respect which is sometimes used to override strict contractual obligations, on the basis that the exercise of contractual powers by management is subject to that power being exercised reasonably and not in an unconscionable manner. Thus issues such as discretionary bonuses (*Clark v BET plc*[2]), non-contractual share options (*Mallone v BPB Industries Ltd*[3]), implementation of mobility clauses (*United Bank Ltd v Akhtar*[4]), payment of non-contractual national pay rates (*Glendale Managed Services v Graham*[5]), capricious or inequitable favouritism in non-contractual pay awards (*FC Gardner v Beresford*[6]) etc, are well outside traditional contractual doctrines. Equally, the exercise of strict contractual rights which have the effect of depriving an employee of valuable benefits may also be frustrated by the use of the implied term doctrine (*Aspden v Webbs Poultry*[7]), although more recently adherence to strict contractual principles can be noted. The law of contract, when applied to employment situations, is not static.

3.3 There must be an offer of employment, and an acceptance of that offer. In *Wishart v National Association of Citizens' Advice Bureaux Ltd*,[8] the claimant was offered a job 'subject to the receipt of satisfactory references'. The defendants received references from the claimant's existing employer which indicated that he had been absent from work through illness

---

[1] [1988] IRLR 517, CA.   [2] [1997] IRLR 348.
[3] [2001] All ER (D) 28 (Mar); aff'd [2002] EWCA Civ 126, [2002] ICR 1045, [2002] All ER (D) 242 (Feb).
[4] [1989] IRLR 503, EAT.
[5] [2003] EWCA Civ 773, [2003] IRLR 465, [2003] All ER (D) 225 (May).   [6] [1978] IRLR 63.
[7] [1996] IRLR 521.   [8] [1990] ICR 794, [1990] IRLR 393, CA.

for a considerable number of days, and consequently the offer was withdrawn. The claimant sought an interlocutory injunction to restrain the defendants from appointing anyone else to the post and requiring them to provide him with the job in question. The injunction was granted by a deputy High Court Judge, but on appeal the decision was reversed by the Court of Appeal. On the facts, there was a conditional offer of employment, and the only obligation on the defendants was to consider the references in good faith. Whether or not the references were satisfactory was a subjective matter. The Court of Appeal suggested that it was possible to make a conditional offer of employment subject to something which could be objectively determined, eg the passing of a medical examination, but that did not apply in this case.

3.4 Of interest in connection with 'job offers' is the scheme arising from the Police Act 1997, ss 112–127, whereby the Secretary of State may issue certificates on application which will detail an individual's criminal record, or the absence of any such record (see para 4.248). Thus an employer would be able to discover certain relevant information prior to offering employment. Enhanced criminal records covering applicants who apply for certain sensitive posts (care of children or working with vulnerable adults) are also available (Safeguarding of Vulnerable Groups Act 2006).

3.5 If an employer makes an offer of employment, which is accepted, and before the date of performance the employer withdraws the offer, the disappointed employee is entitled to damages for breach of contract. These will usually be assessed according to the loss suffered, ie the lawful notice the putative employee would have been entitled to receive had he commenced the employment, less any mitigation of the loss, unless there is a collateral contract (see para 16.8). Further, such a claim for lawful notice may be brought in the employment tribunal under the provisions of the Employment Tribunals Extension of Jurisdiction Order (see para 1.40) which permits employment tribunals to hear claims arising or outstanding 'on the termination of the employee's employment', even though, as in this case, the employment had not commenced! The phrase has to be construed as meaning 'on the termination of the employee's contract of employment' (*Sarker v South Tees Acute Hospitals NHS Trust*[9]).

3.6 Conversely, if the employer makes a job offer which contains a 'no show' clause (ie a clause which provides that the employee would pay a specified amount if he fails to take up the employment) the amount can be liquidated damages, and not a penalty. In *Tullett Prebon Group Ltd v Ghaleb El-Hajjali*[10] the defendant was a successful broker with recognised skills. He was invited to join the plaintiffs' firm, and was advised by solicitors throughout the negotiations. His attention was specifically drawn to the 'no show' clause, and informed that if he breached it he would be liable for a sum equal to 50% of his net basic salary plus 50% of the signing payment that the plaintiffs had agreed to pay him. He then changed his mind about taking up the employment, and he was sued for the sum of £293,000. It was held that the clause was not a penalty clause, but liquidated damages. The defendant had received expert legal advice throughout the negotiations, and was well aware that the plaintiffs would sue if he breached the 'no show' clause. The amount claimed was not extravagant or unconscionable when compared with the loss the plaintiffs had suffered.

3.7 In addition, there must be an intention to create legal relations (see *R v Lord Chancellor's Department, ex p Nangle*,[11] para 2.68). Although there may be an element of personal service, if the object of the relationship is not employment, but something else (eg training), there is an absence of an intention to create legal relationship (*M & P*

---

9 [1997] ICR 673, [1997] IRLR 328, EAT. 10 [2008] EWHC 1924 (QB), [2008] IRLR 760.
11 [1992] 1 All ER 897, [1991] ICR 743, [1991] IRLR 343, [1991] COD 484.

Steelcraft Ltd v Ellis). There must be consideration (but this doctrine does not apply in Scotland) and the absence of vitiating elements (mistake, misrepresentation, illegality, etc). The consideration for the contract is that the employee agrees to work for the employer in return for remuneration. Thus a person who does voluntary work cannot benefit from legal employment rights because he is not employed under a contract of employment (*Melhuish v Redbridge Citizens Advice Bureau*[12]), there being no consideration for his services (*South East Sheffield Citizens Advice Bureau v Grayson*[13]).

3.8 If an employee is seeking to rely on, or enforce, or found a claim on a contract of employment, that contract must not be tainted with illegality, for it is contrary to public policy to claim statutory protection in respect of an illegal contract, eg when seeking compensation for unfair dismissal or a redundancy payment. But if the protection or remedy sought does not involve relying on or enforcing the contract of employment, the illegality of that contract is not a bar to a claim. Thus, a person may claim sex or race discrimination even though the contract is prima facie illegal (*Leighton v Michael*[14] and see *Hall v Woolston Hall Leisure Ltd*, para 3.11), but if the contract is central to the claim, eg in unfair dismissal complaints, and is tainted with illegality, it will be unenforceable (*Zarkasi v Anindita & Anor*[15]). In *Cole v Fred Stacey Ltd*,[16] the employee was given an additional payment which was not taxed as income. He was subsequently made redundant, but it was held that he was not entitled to a redundancy payment, as the contract was illegal and unenforceable, being a contract to defraud the Revenue (see also *Tomlinson v Dick Evans U Drive Ltd*[17]). In *Rastegarnia v Richmond Design*,[18] the applicant (who came from Iran) had been granted a work permit for a specific job. Without obtaining permission from the Department of Employment he changed his job and went to work for the respondents. He was subsequently dismissed, but his claim for unfair dismissal was rejected. His employment was unlawful, and he could not obtain any legal rights thereunder.

3.9 If a contract is lawful when entered into, and is intended by the parties to be performed legally, the fact that some of the work carried out is tainted with illegality will not render the whole contract unenforceable (*Colen v Cebrian (UK) Ltd*[19]). Thus in *Blue Chip Trading Ltd v Helbawi*[20] a foreign student was subject to an immigration condition that prohibited him from working more than 20 hours a week during term time. He subsequently claimed that he had not been paid the national minimum wage. His employer contended that the contract was tainted with illegality, because in some weeks he had worked over 20 hours a week. It was held that the legal and illegal parts of his contract could be severed, and whilst he could not claim the national minimum wage for work done when he was in breach of the immigration condition, he could succeed in a claim for those hours worked when he was not in fact in breach.

3.10 The fact that a contract of employment is ultra vires the employer's power to enter into it does not render that contract void for all purposes, and an employee employed under an ultra vires contract can still bring a claim for unfair dismissal, because his rights are determined by statute (*Shrewsbury & Telford Hospital NHS Trust v Lairikyengban*[21]).

3.11 An asylum seeker who is working in breach of the immigration rules and who deceives his employer about his immigration status cannot enforce a contract which is consequently illegal, and the employment tribunal has no jurisdiction to hear a claim based on that illegal contract (*Vakante v Governing Body of Addey and Stanhope School*[22]). But if, on a complaint of unlawful discrimination, it is discovered that the contract of employment

[12] [2005] IRLR 419, EAT.   [13] Unreported, EAT.   [14] [1995] ICR 1091, [1996] IRLR 67, EAT.
[15] [2011] UKEAT/0400.   [16] [1974] IRLR 73, 9 ITR 11.   [17] [1978] ICR 639, [1978] IRLR 77, EAT.
[18] Unreported.   [19] [2003] EWCA Civ 1676, [2004] ICR 568, [2004] IRLR 210, (2004) 101(2) LSG 27, (2003); *The Times*, 27 November.   [20] [2009] IRLR 128.
[21] [2010] ICR 66.   [22] [2004] ICR 279, [2003] All ER (D) 352 (Dec), EAT.

is tainted with illegality, it is still possible for an employment tribunal to make an award in respect of injury to feelings, although no compensation can be awarded for loss of earnings, since that would offend against the principle that the court will not enforce an illegal contract (*Hall v Woolston Hall Leisure Centre Ltd*[23]).

3.12 In *Salvesen v Simons*,[24] it was held that if the terms of the contract are designed to avoid or postpone the payment of income tax then the contract is illegal, and it matters not that the parties are unaware of the illegality, but this decision has been doubted. The test for illegality is some form of misrepresentation or some deliberate attempt to conceal the true nature of the employment situation. A contract will not be rendered unlawful merely because the parties have wrongly labelled the relationship or entered into an agreement which deprives the Inland Revenue (now HMRC) of tax (*Enfield Technical Services v Payne*[25]).

3.13 The fact that the employer makes an occasional tax-free payment to the employee does not render the contract illegal for this is not part of the remuneration as defined in the contract of employment (*Annandale Engineering v Samson*[26]). Nor is a legitimate tax avoidance scheme unlawful, provided it is a proper method of reducing liability for tax and national insurance contributions, and has been (or would be) disclosed to the Inland Revenue (*Lightfoot v D & J Sporting Ltd*[27]).

3.14 A fraud or dishonesty against an employer by an employee, whilst it may be grounds for dismissal, does not make the contract inherently illegal so as to make it void ab initio (*Broaders v Kalkare Property Maintenance Ltd*[28]).

3.15 Nor will the contract be unenforceable for illegality if the employee does not receive any benefit from the illegality. In *Hewcastle Catering Ltd v Ahmed*,[29] the employers devised a scheme to avoid paying VAT, and gave certain instructions to the employees to facilitate the scheme. The employees did not receive any direct benefit. Following investigations by the Customs and Excise, the employers were prosecuted, and the employees were called as prosecution witnesses. They were subsequently dismissed, and claimed that the dismissals were unfair. The employers argued that the contracts of employment, being tainted with illegality, were unenforceable, but this claim was rejected by the employment tribunal, the EAT and the Court of Appeal. The employers had involved the employees in the fraud, but the employees did not benefit from it and were not essential parties to it. It would be contrary to public policy to deny the employees compensation when the employers had involved them in the fraud and dismissed them because they gave evidence in criminal proceedings taken against the employers.

3.16 For an employee to have certain statutory rights, he must be continuously employed under a legal contract of employment, and any period wherein the contract becomes illegal cannot be relied upon in counting towards that continuity. Thus a period of time prior to the illegality, when the contract was legal, is lost, and continuity can only be reckoned from the date when the contract became legal (*Hyland v J H Barker (North West) Ltd*[30]). As already noted (see para 2.114), periods of employment when a foreign national is working in breach of immigration rules will render the contract unenforceable for illegality (*Bamgbose v Royal Star and Garter Home*).

3.17 If the alleged illegality lies in the performance of the contract, then a distinction must be drawn between the cases where the contractual obligation is to do an act which

[23] [1998] ICR 651, EAT; revsd [2000] 4 All ER 787, [2001] 1 WLR 225, CA.
[24] [1994] ICR 409, [1994] IRLR 52, EAT.
[25] [2008] EWCA Civ 393, [2008] ICR 1423, [2008] IRLR 500, (2008) *Times*, 2 June.
[26] [1994] IRLR 59, EAT.   [27] [1996] IRLR 64, EAT.   [28] [1990] IRLR 421, EAT.
[29] [1992] ICR 626, [1991] IRLR 473, CA.   [30] [1985] ICR 861, [1985] IRLR 403, EAT.

is unlawful, and those where the obligations are capable of being performed lawfully, but which were in fact performed by unlawful means. In *Coral Leisure Group Ltd v Barnett*,[31] the claimant was dismissed from his post as a public relations executive. It was alleged that part of his duties was to keep rich punters happy by obtaining for them, among other things, the services of prostitutes. It was held that the fact that an immoral or unlawful act was committed during the course of the employment did not render the contract void, unless it was entered into with the object of doing that unlawful or immoral act, or the contract itself (as opposed to the mode of performance) was prohibited by law.

3.18 But the contract will only be void if the party seeking to enforce it was aware of the illegality. If it can be shown that the employee was not a party to the illegality, or did not know about it, he can still rely on the contract as an innocent party (*Davidson v Pillay*[32]). The test is not whether the employee ought to have known of the illegality, but whether he actually did know (*Corby v Morrison (t/a The Card Shop)*[33]). Thus if an employee is paid part of his wages in cash as a tax-free payment, the essential question to ask is, has the employee knowingly been a party to a deception on the Revenue (*Newland v Simons and Willer (Hairdressers) Ltd*[34])?

Terms and conditions

3.19 It is usual to speak of the 'terms and conditions of employment' which are part of every contract of employment, although no attempt ever appears to have been made to define or delineate this expression (but see *Cory Lighterage v Transport and General Workers' Union*[35] and *Universe Tankships v ITWF*[36]). It is submitted that the terms of the employment are bilateral, ie they are part of the agreement made between the employer and employee, whereas the conditions of employment are unilateral instructions which are laid down by the employer. The result is that a change in the terms can only be made by an express or implied agreement to that effect, whereas a condition can be changed by the employer unilaterally at any time (see *Cadoux v Central Regional Council*[37]) on giving reasonable notice.

3.20 For the terms of a contract of employment to apply, there must be certainty as to the commitment entered into. In *Judge v Crown Leisure Ltd*,[38] an employer made a promise to the claimant at a staff Christmas party that the employee would be put on roughly the same level of remuneration as other managers. This was held not to be legally enforceable. The words used were too vague to amount to a contractual commitment.

3.21 If an employer has a code of practice, or issues a policy statement, such documents do not necessarily constitute employment terms. In *Wandsworth London Borough Council v D'Silva*,[39] the local authority issued a code of practice on staff sickness, to which they proposed to make changes unilaterally. The employment tribunal and the EAT held that the relevant provisions of the code were contractually binding and the employers could not alter them unilaterally, but the decision was reversed by the Court of Appeal. The code

---

[31] [1981] ICR 503, [1981] IRLR 204, 125 Sol Jo 374, EAT.
[32] [1979] IRLR 275.   [33] [1980] ICR 564, [1980] IRLR 218, EAT.
[34] [1981] ICR 521, [1981] IRLR 359, EAT.
[35] [1973] 2 All ER 558, [1973] 1 WLR 792, [1973] ICR 339, [1973] IRLR 152, 14 KIR 479, CA.
[36] [1981] ICR 129, [1980] IRLR 239; varied [1980] 2 Lloyd's Rep 523, [1981] ICR 129, [1980] IRLR 363, CA; on appeal [1983] 1 AC 366, [1982] 2 All ER 67, [1982] 2 WLR 803, [1982] 1 Lloyd's Rep 537, [1982] ICR 262, [1982] IRLR 200, 126 Sol Jo 225, HL.   [37] [1986] IRLR 131, 1986 SLT 117, Ct of Sess.
[38] [2005] EWCA Civ 571, [2005] IRLR 823.   [39] [1998] IRLR 193, CA.

merely set out good practice which management intended to follow, but did not constitute contractual requirements. Similarly, an equal opportunities policy was a mere statement of policy in generalised terms, and did not give rise to contractual obligations (*Grant v South-West Trains Ltd*[40]). In *Pendragon plc v Jackson*,[41] the employer inserted a clause into a share option scheme which stated that the scheme was non-contractual. It was held that the employee had no legal entitlement to any benefits under the scheme. The employers had discharged the burden of proof to show that the scheme was not intended to create a legally binding contract.

3.22 But although a policy or practice set out in a staff manual may not be contractual, if it is relied upon by an employee, it cannot be changed unilaterally to his detriment, because that would be a breach of the implied term of trust and confidence (*French v Barclays Bank plc*[42]).

3.23 Terms of employment can be found in express or implied agreements, collective agreements, and various statutory provisions; conditions of employment are usually contained in works rules, disciplinary and grievance procedures and job descriptions. Care should be taken not to place a term or condition in the wrong category. For example, it may be a term of a contract that an employee shall be entitled to six weeks' holiday per year; it will be a condition that he shall take those holidays at particular times of the year. A term will specify the number of hours he shall work; a condition will instruct him as to when he shall work those hours. A term will specify his employment duties; a condition will lay down how he shall perform those duties. The fact of payment is a term; the mode of payment is a condition.

A. Interpretation of terms

3.24 Under the modern law of employment, contractual terms are subject to an overriding obligation of trust and respect. In *United Bank Ltd v Akhtar*,[43] the claimant was subject to a clause in his contract which required him to work anywhere in Great Britain. On 5 June he was informed that as from 8 June he would be required to transfer from Leeds to a branch in Birmingham. He requested that the transfer be delayed for three months, because of his wife's illness, and also the impending sale of his house. This request was refused. He then asked if he could take 24 days' leave due to him to enable him to sort out his affairs, and he offered to commence work in Birmingham on 10 July, but he received no reply to this request. His pay was then stopped as from 5 June, so he resigned, and claimed he had been constructively dismissed. His claim succeeded. There was an implied term in his contract that the employers would give reasonable notice if they wished to exercise their rights under the mobility clause (see *White v Reflecting Roadstuds Ltd*,[44] para 17.37).

3.25 Similarly, an employer may still be acting fairly even though he dismisses an employee in circumstances which amount to a breach of contract by the employer, for statutory rights and obligations exist concurrent with, but are sometimes different from, those which exist at common law (see *Hooper v British Railways Board*[45]).

3.26 In *Farrant v Woodroffe School*,[46] the claimant was employed as a laboratory technician at a school. Following a reorganisation of technical support services he was required to transfer from the science department where he worked and divide his time between other departments. He refused to accept the new job description and was dismissed. The dismissal was held to be fair. The employers had given him ample warning of the proposed change, had fully

---

[40] (C-249/96) [1998] ECR I-621, [1998] All ER (EC) 193, [1998] 1 CMLR 993, [1998] ICR 449, [1998] IRLR 206, [1998] 1 FCR 377, [1998] 1 FLR 839, [1998] Fam Law 392, 3 BHRC 578, ECJ.

[41] [1998] ICR 215, [1998] IRLR 17, EAT.   [42] [1998] IRLR 646, CA.   [43] n 4.

[44] [1991] ICR 733, [1991] IRLR 331, EAT.   [45] n 1.

[46] [1998] ICR 184, [1998] IRLR 176, EAT.

consulted with him, and thus had acted reasonably in the circumstances in dismissing him. The lawfulness of the instruction is not by itself determinative of the fairness of a dismissal.

3.27 Where the terms of a contract of employment are ambiguous, it is open to the courts to look at the practice adopted by the parties, and to attach considerable importance to it as indicating the proper interpretation of contractual terms (*Dunlop Tyres Ltd v Blows*[47]).

B. Express terms

3.28 At the conclusion of the negotiations the parties may have expressly stated the terms which form the basis of the contract. These terms may deal with wages, salaries, commissions, bonuses, hours of work, the nature of the duties, holidays, overtime, sick pay, pension schemes and so on. The task of the courts and tribunals is to interpret the meaning of such express terms in a manner consistent with industrial realism. Thus in *Cole v Midland Display Ltd*,[48] the employee was a manager employed on a 'staff' basis. He refused to do overtime without pay, and his subsequent dismissal was held to be fair. The essence of being employed as 'staff' meant that he was guaranteed his wages whether there was work or not, and during sickness. In return, 'staff' are apparently required to work reasonable overtime without pay if required to do so.

3.29 On the other hand, in *Redbridge London Borough Council v Fishman*,[49] the employee was appointed as a teacher in charge of a resource centre. Gradually, she was asked to teach more and more, and eventually dismissed when she refused. Her dismissal was held to be unfair. A headteacher could require teachers to do work other than that for which they were engaged, provided that such requests were reasonable. In this case, the teaching was ancillary to her main job, which was as a director of the resource centre. Consequently, the headmaster's instructions went beyond the strict contractual obligations of the employee, and were therefore unreasonable.

3.30 Although it may be permissible to refer to statements made in a job advertisement to ascertain the terms of a contract (*Tayside Regional Council v McIntosh*[50]), such statement cannot override the express terms. In *Deeley v British Rail Engineering Ltd*,[51] the employers advertised for a 'Sales Engineer (Export)'. The claimant applied for the job and was appointed, but his contract was for a 'Sales Engineer'. It was held that there were no grounds for implying the word 'Export' into his contract.

3.31 If there is an express term in the contract which permits an employee to have short-term or long-term sickness benefits, or there is in force a permanent health insurance scheme, the employer cannot bring these to an end by dismissing the employee (*Adin v Sedco Forex International Resources Ltd*[52]), and it is probable that there is also an implied term that the employer will not dismiss an employee who is off work sick while covered by such a scheme (*Aspden v Webbs Poultry and Meat Group (Holdings) Ltd*). If the employer has the right to terminate the scheme without prior notice, benefits under the scheme will continue until the employee is notified of the change (*Bainbridge v Circuit Foil UK Ltd*[53]).

3.32 An express term may be used to negate a liability. In *Petrie v MacFisheries Ltd*,[54] the employers posted a notice stating that half pay for sickness would be paid as an act of grace by the company to all employees with over six months' service. All the employees knew of

---

[47] [2001] EWCA Civ 1032, [2001] IRLR 629, [2001] All ER (D) 179 (Jun).   [48] [1973] IRLR 62, NIRC.
[49] (1978) 76 LGR 408, [1978] ICR 569, [1978] IRLR 69, EAT.   [50] [1982] IRLR 272, EAT.
[51] [1980] IRLR 147, CA.   [52] [1997] IRLR 280, Ct of Sess.   [53] [1997] ICR 541, [1997] IRLR 305, CA.
[54] [1940] 1 KB 258, [1939] 4 All ER 281, 38 LGR 44, 104 JP 40, 109 LJKB 263, 83 Sol Jo 959, 161 LT 408, 56 TLR 119, CA.

the position and the company acted on it consistently. It was held that the company was not bound to make payments when employees were off sick.

3.33 If an employer provides facilities for his employee's property (eg car parks, cloak-rooms, etc) he cannot restrict his liability for death or personal injury resulting from negligence, and he may only be able to restrict or exclude his liability for damage to the employee's property by a term in the contract which is reasonable in the circumstances (Unfair Contract Terms Act 1977, s 2).

3.34 If the employee is in breach of a contractual term this will be ground for dismissal. Equally, if the employer is in breach, the employee may accept the breach and bring a claim for constructive dismissal (see Chapter 17). In either event, the fairness or unfairness of the dismissal has to be determined in accordance with established legal principles, though clearly the breach of a contractual term must be regarded with greater seriousness than the breach of a non-contractual term. In *Martin v Solus Schall*,[55] the claimant signed a contract which included a clause stating 'you will be expected to work such overtime as is necessary to ensure continuity of service'. This was held to be a contractual obligation, and on the facts his dismissal for refusing to do overtime was fair.

3.35 Whether a breach by the employer of a term in a contract is so fundamental as to amount to a repudiatory breach will depend on the nature of the breach and the circumstances which gave rise to it. Thus, if there is a non-payment of agreed wages, or an interference by the employer with a salary package, a distinction must be drawn between the employer's failure to pay, or his delay in paying, and his deliberate refusal to do so. A unilateral reduction in pay diminishes the value of the employee's remuneration, and undermines the whole foundation of the contract of employment. But if the failure to pay is a result of temporary fault in the employer's technology, or a simple accounting error or mistake, or due to accident or illness etc, it would be open to the court to hold that the breach did not go to the root of the contract although this may amount to a 'deduction' under ERA, s 13 (see *Elizabeth Claire Care Management v Francis*,[56] para 8.21). A repeated or persistent failure or delay, or one which was unexplained, might lead the court to hold that the breach was indeed repudiatory (*Cantor Fitzgerald International v Callaghan*[57]).

3.36 At one time it was thought that a breach of contract by an employee amounted to a 'constructive resignation', but this view is now regarded as being incorrect (see *London Transport Executive v Clarke*,[58] para 17.56). The legal position is that the employer may 'accept' the breach or not, as he wishes. If he does accept the breach, he dismisses the employee, and the fairness of the dismissal must be justified in accordance with the usual principles (see Chapter 17).

3.37 A strike by an employee is a breach of contract, as is a refusal to perform contractual duties. Either of these events gives rise to legal consequences, including the right of the employer to deduct a sum of money from the wages or salary of the employee, calculated on a proportional basis (*Sim v Rotherham Metropolitan Borough Council*[59]).

C. Implied terms

3.38 Occasionally the courts and tribunals are prepared to imply a term into the contract in circumstances where the parties did not expressly insert a term to meet a particular

---

[55] [1979] IRLR 1, EAT.   [56] [2005] IRLR 858.
[57] [1999] 2 All ER 411, [1999] ICR 639, [1999] IRLR 234, CA.
[58] [1980] ICR 532, EAT; revsd [1981] ICR 355, [1981] IRLR 166, 125 Sol Jo 306, CA.
[59] [1987] Ch 216, [1986] 3 All ER 387, [1986] 3 WLR 851, 85 LGR 128, [1986] ICR 897, [1986] IRLR 391, 130 Sol Jo 839, [1986] LS Gaz R 3746.

contingency. The theory adopted was that the term in question was so obvious that the parties did not see the need to state it expressly. Clearly, a certain amount of judicial hindsight is required in order to imply a term after a dispute has arisen, and there is frequent room for disagreement on whether or not the court was correct in making its assumptions. However, in *Mears v Safecar Security Ltd*[60], the Court of Appeal held that the correct approach was to consider all the facts and circumstances before implying a term into the contract, including the way the parties had carried out the contract since it was formed. There is no presumption either way about an implied term. For example, in *O'Grady v M Saper Ltd*,[61] the employee claimed his wages for a period in which he had been off work through sickness. He had been away sick before, and had not received any wages. Indeed, he never asked for them nor expected them, until he saw an item in a newspaper which led him to believe that he might be able to claim. It was held that there was an implied term that he would not be paid.

3.39 The original justification for the implied term theory was the need to give business efficacy to the contract, but there is now a much wider approach, implying terms which are a necessary incident of a definable category of contractual relationship. In *Scally v Southern Health and Social Services Board*,[62] the claimant was a doctor, whose terms and conditions of employment were to be found in a statutory scheme. This scheme gave doctors the right to purchase added years of pension entitlement, but this valuable right had to be exercised within certain time limits. The claimant was never informed about the scheme, and so he failed to exercise his option to purchase the added years' pension. When he did discover the existence of the scheme, he was outside the time limits. He claimed that his employers had broken an implied term of the contract by failing to take reasonable steps to bring to his notice his right to enhance his pension entitlement by the purchase of added years. The House of Lords unanimously upheld his claim. It was noted that the terms of the contract had not been negotiated with the individual employee, but were negotiated with a representative body or otherwise incorporated by reference. The contract thus contained a valuable right for the employee, but this was contingent on him taking action to avail himself of the benefit. He could not be expected to do this unless the term was drawn to his attention. There was an implied term, therefore, that the employer could take reasonable steps to bring the provisions of the pension scheme to the employee's attention, so that he could enjoy its benefits if he so wished.

3.40 But there is no implied term in a contract of employment that an employer will take reasonable care for the economic well-being of an employee. In *Crossley v Faithful and Gould Holdings Ltd*,[63] a senior employee wished to resign his employment due to ill-health. His employer did not advise him that if he did so he would lose entitlements under a permanent health insurance scheme, and he claimed that there was an implied term that his employer should have warned him about the effect of his retirement on his entitlement to that benefit. The Court of Appeal dismissed his claim. The claimant was a senior employee who should have been familiar with the terms of the insurance scheme, and he also had access to expert advice. It would impose an unfair and unreasonable burden on employers to imply a term that they should assume responsibility for financial advice in relation to benefits accruing from employment. The Court of Appeal noted that in *Scally's* case the House of Lords set out three strict criteria which had to be satisfied before placing a duty on an employer to inform employees of contractual benefits, one of which was that the

---

[60] [1983] QB 54, [1982] 2 All ER 865, [1982] 3 WLR 366, [1982] ICR 626, [1982] IRLR 183, 126 Sol Jo 496, [1982] LS Gaz R 921, CA.

[61] [1940] 2 KB 469, [1940] 3 All ER 527, 109 LJKB 785, 84 Sol Jo 501, 163 LT 165, 56 TLR 913, CA.

[62] [1992] 1 AC 294, [1991] 4 All ER 563, [1991] 3 WLR 778, [1991] ICR 771, [1991] IRLR 522, 135 Sol Jo LB 172, HL.   [63] [2004] EWCA Civ 293, [2004] NLJR 653, [2004] All ER (D) 295 (Mar).

employee cannot reasonably be expected to be aware of the particular term. This criteria was not satisfied in the instant case But the EAT has held that there is an implied term that an employer will take reasonable steps to ascertain whether an employee is entitled to the benefit of an ill-health retirement scheme, and it could be an unfair dismissal if the employee is thereby deprived of the benefits under the scheme (*First Leeds v Haigh*[64]).

3.41 It is not possible to imply terms which are too vague or unpredictable to be given efficacy, or to which the parties would not have agreed had the matter been drawn to their attention (*Lake v Essex County Council*[65]). Thus, in *Cresswell v Board of Inland Revenue*,[66] staff employed by the Inland Revenue habitually carried out their tasks by dealing manually with files and records. The Inland Revenue introduced a programme of computerisation, and the claimant alleged that in so doing there was a breach of contract, arguing that there was an implied term that he could not be required to perform tasks or carry out functions in a manner other than that which they had habitually used by custom and practice. He sought a declaration that he could not be required to operate computerised systems. It was held that the employers were not in breach of the contract by requiring employees to use computer systems. An employee is expected to adapt himself to new methods and techniques introduced in the course of his employment. It is a question of fact whether the retraining involved the acquisition of such esoteric skills that it would not be reasonable to expect the employee to acquire them. Nowadays, it is not unusual to ask an employee to acquire basic skills such as retrieving information from a computer or feeding information into one. However, the employer must be expected to provide any necessary training for the acquisition of these skills.

3.42 If exceptional circumstances arise, there is an implied term that an employee can be asked to perform duties which are outside his strict contractual obligations. Thus in *Luke v Stoke on Trent CC*,[67] an employee claimed she had been bullied. After the matter was investigated, she was offered temporary redeployment, which involved her doing work which was outside her contractual obligations. When she refused to accept the temporary change, her employers stopped paying her wages. Her subsequent claim against her employer was dismissed. The work was suitable for her to perform, she would have suffered no disadvantage in terms of contractual benefits or status, and the change in her duties was a temporary matter, designed to meet an exceptional circumstance.

3.43 Legal decisions have established that there is an implied term that an employer will treat the employee with respect and trust, and will not treat an employee in an arbitrary or vindictive manner. Thus, falsely to accuse an employee of theft (*Robinson v Crompton Parkinson Ltd*[68]), unreasonably to deny an employee an increase in remuneration which had been granted to other employees (*FC Gardner Ltd v Beresford*[69]) and, in the case of a large firm, to refuse to give an employee time off work to deal with a domestic emergency (*Warner v Barbers Stores*[70]), have all been held to amount to conduct by the employer which could constitute a breach of the implied term that the employer should treat an employee fairly and reasonably.

3.44 It may be possible to imply a term by reference to the practices of the industry and/or the national agreements which are in force. For example, in *Stevenson v Teesside Bridge and Engineering Ltd*,[71] a steel erector's employment was governed by the national agreement for the time being in force in the industry. Although there was no express term in his contract

---

[64] [2008] IRLR 182, EAT.   [65] (1979) 77 LGR 708, [1979] ICR 577, [1979] IRLR 241, CA.
[66] [1984] 2 All ER 713, [1984] ICR 508, [1984] IRLR 190, 128 Sol Jo 431.
[67] [2007] IRLR 305, EAT; aff'd [2007] EWCA Civ 761, [2007] IRLR 777, [2007] ICR 1678.
[68] [1978] ICR 401, [1978] IRLR 61, EAT.   [69] n 6.   [70] [1978] IRLR 109, EAT.
[71] [1971] 1 All ER 296, 10 KIR 53, 6 ITR 44, 114 Sol Jo 907, DC.

stating that he was expected to work away from home, this was clearly envisaged, for the national agreement made provision for lodging allowances, travelling expenses, etc. The court held that there was an implied term in his contract that he could be sent anywhere to work, for it was recognised that in the construction steel industry, where sites are, by their very nature, scattered around the country, employees know that mobility is a feature of their employment.

3.45 There is an implied term that the employer will not prevent the employee from performing his contract of employment, or delay or hinder him so as to prevent him from earning his full remuneration, but the employer is entitled to take steps which may improve that performance, and to see that the work is done in a proper manner, for example, by engaging time and motion experts (*Davies v Richard Johnson & Nephew Ltd*[72]). If an employee is contractually obliged to do overtime without pay, there is an implied term that the requirements of overtime will always be reasonable, and would not be excessive (*Gilbert v Goldstone Ltd*[73]). On the other hand, if a contract of employment is silent on the actual place of work, it may be necessary to imply a term to give that contract business efficacy. In *Jones v Associated Tunnelling Co Ltd*,[74] it was held that there was an implied term that the employers were entitled to require the employee to work anywhere within a reasonable daily commuting distance from his home.

3.46 An implied term is sometimes used to give the contract business efficacy (or business common sense: see *Marshall v Alexander Sloan & Co Ltd*[75]). Thus if a contract provides for the payment of sick pay, but is silent on the period for which it is payable, there is an implied term that the obligation is for a reasonable period only (*Howman & Son v Blyth*[76]).

3.47 There is also an implied term that the employer will not conduct his business in a fraudulent and dishonest manner so as to cause damage to the employees' reputation and consequently place him at a disadvantage in the labour market (*Malik v BCCI SA*[77]). However, a claimant must be able to show that the failure to obtain fresh employment was because of the stigma (*BCCI SA v Ali (No 3)*[78]).

3.48 The original basis for the implied term theory was that it is the court's (or tribunal's) view about a provision that was 'obvious' where the contract was silent. In *Shell UK Ltd v Lostock Garage Ltd*,[79] Lord Denning suggested that if a contract of employment did not define the obligations of the parties, the courts (or tribunals) should ask what would be reasonable in the general run of such cases, and then say what the obligation shall be. This view was followed in *Pepper and Hope v Daish*,[80] see para 17.35) and appears to have general acceptance, even though there is a fundamental difference between importing into a contract an implied term which is 'obvious' and one which is 'reasonable'. The courts have gone on to express the view that there is an implied term that the employer will not conduct himself in a manner likely to destroy or seriously damage the relationship of confidence and trust between the employer and employee, and if the conduct has that effect, then the question of whether there has been a reasonable and proper cause for the behaviour must be considered. If such reasonable and proper cause could not be shown, the employer would be acting in a manner which no reasonable employer would adopt. Thus to offer a particular benefit to the entirety of one class of employees bar one is capable of being an act calculated to seriously damage or destroy the trust and confidence between the employer

---

[72] (1934) 78 Sol Jo 877, 51 TLR 115.   [73] [1977] 1 All ER 423, [1977] ICR 36, [1976] IRLR 257, EAT.
[74] [1981] IRLR 477, EAT.   [75] [1981] IRLR 264.   [76] [1983] ICR 416, [1983] IRLR 139.
[77] [1995] 3 All ER 545, [1996] ICR 406, [1995] IRLR 375, [1995] NLJR 593, CA; revsd [1998] AC 20, [1997] 3 All ER 1, [1997] 3 WLR 95, [1997] ICR 606, [1997] IRLR 462, [1997] 94 LS Gaz R 33, [1997] NLJR 917, HL.
[78] [2001] UKHL 8, [2002] 1 AC 251, [2001] 1 All ER 961, [2001] 2 WLR 735, [2001] ICR 337, [2001] IRLR 292, 151 NLJ 351, 145 Sol Jo LB 67, [2001] All ER (D) 06 (Mar).
[79] [1977] 1 All ER 481, [1976] 1 WLR 1187, 120 Sol Jo 523, CA.   [80] [1980] IRLR 13, EAT.

and that employee (*BG plc v O'Brien*[81]). If it is done without reasonable and proper cause, it would be a breach of the employer's obligation of fair dealing (*Johnson v Unisys Ltd*[82]). But if the employer had reasonable and proper cause to act in the manner he did, then even though there are adverse consequences to the employee, there is no breach of the implied duty of trust and confidence (*Hilton v Shiner Ltd*[83]).

3.49 The implied term of trust and respect is both positive and negative, in the sense that it may require the employer to do something, as opposed to refrain from doing something. Thus there can be a breach of the term if an employer decides not to offer an employee a new contract, or a variation of the old one. There is an obligation to treat employees in a fair and even-handed manner (*Transco plc v O'Brien*[84]).

3.50 The contracts of employment of professional employees do not always detail the contractual obligations, and these may be defined by reference to the nature of the profession, and the obligations incumbent on those who follow that profession (*Sim v Rotherham Metropolitan District Council*, see para 3.37).

3.51 There is no implied term that an employer will look after the employee's property (clothes, car, etc) which are left on the employer's premises (*Edwards v West Herts Group Hospital Management Committee*,[85] though there is an obligation under the Workplace (Health, Safety and Welfare) Regulations 1992 for employers to provide suitable and sufficient accommodation for clothing which is not worn during working hours, and if there is a statutory obligation to do something, a failure to comply with that requirement will amount to a breach of an implied term (*W A Goold (Pearmak) Ltd v McConnell*.[86] see para 11.81). Nor is there an implied term that an employee will be entitled to work overtime if the employer is not contractually obliged to provide overtime (*McClory v Post Office*[87]).

3.52 There is no implied term that the employer will provide personal accident insurance for the benefit of an employee who is required to work abroad, or that the employer should give specific advice on special risks, and advise the employee to take out personal accident insurance (see *Reid v Rush & Tompkins Group plc* (see para 10.34). Nor can a duty in tort be imposed to enlarge on contractual duties.

If there is no agreement on the matters which should be included in the written statement which has to be given to employees under the provisions of s 1 of the Employment Rights Act 1996, it is not be possible to rely on an implied term concerning matters which ought to be, but are not, set out in the statement (eg whether an employee is entitled to accrued holiday pay on a pro rata basis, see *Morley v Heritage plc*[88]), but see now Working Time Regulations, para 7.54).

3.53 It is clear that if an employer breaks an express term of the contract, the employee may 'accept' the breach, resign from his employment, and claim that he had been 'constructively' dismissed (see para 17.21). This is equally true in the case of a breach of an implied term, and in particular when the conduct of the employer amounts to a breach of the implied term of mutual trust and confidence which must exist between the parties (*Post Office v Roberts*[89]). These developments will be considered in detail in Chapter 17.

[81] [2002] ICR 721, (2002) IRLR 444.

[82] [1999] 1 All ER 854, [1999] ICR 809, [1999] IRLR 90, CA; aff'd [2001] UKHL 13, [2003] 1 AC 518, [2001] 2 All ER 801, [2001] 2 WLR 1076, [2001] ICR 480, [2001] IRLR 279, [2001] All ER (D) 274 (Mar).

[83] [2001] IRLR 727, [2001] All ER (D) 316 (May), EAT.

[84] [2001] IRLR, [2001] All ER (D) 169 (May), EAT; aff'd sub nom *O'Brien v Transco plc (formerly BG plc)* [2002] EWCA Civ 379, [2002] ICR 721, [2002] IRLR 444, [2002] All ER (D) 80 (Mar).

[85] [1957] 1 All ER 541, [1957] 1 WLR 415, 121 JP 212, 101 Sol Jo 190, CA.   [86] [1995] IRLR 516, EAT.

[87] [1993] 1 All ER 457, [1992] ICR 758, [1993] IRLR 159.   [88] [1993] IRLR 400, CA.

[89] [1980] IRLR 347, EAT.

3.54 A term can only be implied into a contract of employment if it would have existed at the time the contract was made. Thus, generally speaking, it is not possible to imply a term when there is a changed situation (*Casson Beckman & Partners v Papi*[90]). Nor can an implied term be used to override an express term, although it may be used as a means of qualifying or explaining an express term (*Stevedoring & Haulage Services Ltd v Fuller*, see para 2.174).

3.55 It is not possible to predict when the courts or tribunals will imply a term into a contract. Thus in *Ali v Christian Salvesen Food Services Ltd*,[91] individual contracts of employment were varied by a collective agreement. Certain topics had been omitted, and the employment tribunal refused to fill in the gaps. The decision was reversed by the EAT, using implied terms, but that decision was itself reversed by the Court of Appeal. If there were omissions in a collective agreement, the inference is that the topic was too complex or controversial for discussion or agreement, and it is not for the judiciary to speculate on what might have been agreed.

D. **Statutory terms**

3.56 Superimposed on all contracts of employment are a number of statutory terms. These are in addition to a considerable number of statutory 'rights' which have been created by various legislative provisions. Thus the Equality Act 2010 imports an equality clause into contracts of employment, minimum wages for appropriately qualified persons are guaranteed by the National Minimum Wage Act 1998 and various employment rights are contained in the Employment Rights Act 1996 and various regulations, etc. These statutory terms may be improved upon by agreement between the parties, but any attempt to oust them will be of no effect.

E. **Collective agreements**

Express incorporation of the terms of a collective agreement

3.57 A collective agreement is an agreement made between an employers' association, or a single employer, on the one hand, and a trade union on the other, which, as well as laying down the procedure which will govern the relationship between the signatories will also provide for the terms and conditions of employment of those covered by the agreement. There are currently about 7,000,000 employees who are members of trade unions, and many of these, but not all, will doubtless be covered by such agreements, as well as an unknown number of non-trade unionists in respect of whom their employer will apply the terms of a relevant collective agreement. There are, however, a number of different situations to consider. There can be a national or federation agreement, made between an employers' association and a trade union, on the conclusion of which the individual employers who are members of the association will start to apply its provisions to their employees. There is no rule of law which requires this, only the practice of industrial relations. The terms of the agreement will be binding in law on the individual employer and the employee if, and only if, they are expressly or impliedly incorporated into the individual contract of employment. The same rule applies to a local or plant agreement, which is usually made between a single employer and a trade union. Also, there are some employers who, though not members of the employers' association, voluntarily undertake to observe the terms of a negotiated agreement.

[90] [1991] BCLC 299, [1991] BCC 68, CA.

[91] [1996] ICR 1, [1995] IRLR 624, EAT; revsd [1997] 1 All ER 721, [1997] ICR 25, [1997] IRLR 17, 140 Sol Jo LB 231, sub nom *Salvesen (Christian) Food Services Ltd v Ali* [1996] 41 LS Gaz R 29, CA.

3.58 In *Framptons Ltd v Badger*[92] the EAT gave a useful summary of the effect of a collective agreement on the contract of employment, as follows:

(a) employees do not derive rights directly from the collective agreement. The parties to the agreement are the employer and the union, and the union does not act as agent for its members;

(b) there is a presumption that the collective agreement is not intended to be legally enforceable as between the parties. Nonetheless, the rights and obligations found in the collective agreement can bind the employer and employee by being incorporated into the individual's contract of employment;

(c) incorporation can operate expressly or by implication. In order to determine whether this has occurred, it is necessary to focus on the relationship between the employer and the employee, not the employer and the trade union;

(d) not all terms typically found in a collective agreement will be incorporated. The terms must be suitable to take effect as contractual terms. Some terms will not be suitable, because they are too vague or aspirational;

(e) the terms of a collective agreement may continue to operate and bind the parties to the individual contract even when the collective agreement is brought to an end, and even possibly when the employer has withdrawn recognition from the union;

(f) there is a strong presumption that the parties to the individual contract of employment will have intended that the terms shall continue to be derived from the collective agreement, even after that agreement has ceased to have effect, if the consequence of not doing so is that there would be no binding contractual terms at all.

3.59 Certain terms contained in a collective agreement govern the relationship between the trade union and the employer. Other terms are designed to benefit individual employees, and this becomes part of the contract of employment (*National Coal Board v National Union of Mineworkers*[93]). These latter terms are said to have a 'normative' effect. In *Alexander v Standard Telephones and Cables plc*,[94] the claimant was employed on the basis of the terms contained in a collective agreement. The agreement contained a redundancy procedure, which stated that LIFO ('last in, first out') would be the basis of selection in the event of compulsory redundancies. The company wished to select on the basis of skills and flexibility, and the claimant sought an injunction to prevent this. The application failed, but it was suggested that there was an arguable case that the terms of the collective agreement formed part of his contract of employment. Any remedy for breach of that contract would lie in an action for damages and the case was sent for trial on that basis (see para 3.63).

3.60 The authority of a trade union to enter into agreements which will be binding on its members vis-à-vis their employers stems either from express authority, implied authority, or by virtue of the law of agency. Express authority will normally arise when a trade union (or an authorised official) is asked or is invited to negotiate on a specific issue which affects its members. Implied authority arises when a union negotiates nationally or locally on matters which affect all members (eg wage increases), and usually be inferred from the conduct of the parties and the circumstances of the case. Under the law of agency, a union would need ostensible or apparent authority to negotiate with an employer or employers. The mere fact that an employee is also a member of a trade union does not necessarily mean that the union has that authority (*Burton Group Ltd v Smith*[95]), although nowadays the courts appear to be more willing to accept that a trade union official (or shop steward,

---

[92] EAT/0138/06.   [93] [1986] ICR 736, [1986] IRLR 439.   [94] [1990] ICR 291, [1990] IRLR 55.
[95] [1977] IRLR 351, EAT.

in appropriate circumstances) has apparent or ostensible authority to negotiate a revision of terms and conditions of employment (*Harris v Richard Lawson Autologistics Ltd*[96]).

3.61 The 'normative' terms of a collective agreement may be incorporated into the individual contract of employment by an express provision to this effect. For example, employment may be undertaken on the basis of 'union rates of pay', or 'union conditions'. It is at least arguable that the former term refers solely to the wages rates clauses in the collective agreement, whilst the latter term may be somewhat wider, and may include other provisions. In *Jewell v Neptune Concrete Ltd*[97] the employee's written particulars stated that his rate of wages was to be based on the national agreement. It was held that this did not, by itself, incorporate the working rule agreement's lay-off provisions into his contract of employment. Employees who work for public bodies are normally engaged on the basis of the appropriate scale laid down by the negotiating bodies and the only scope for individual bargaining may be on the precise point of entry into the scale for salary purposes. Thus in *Knox v Down District Council*[98] the Northern Ireland Court of Appeal were prepared to incorporate into the employee's contract of employment a car assisted purchase scheme which had been negotiated by the National Joint Council, the terms of which were expressly incorporated into his contract. In *National Coal Board v Galley*,[99] the defendant was employed on the basis of 'the national agreements for the time being in force'. These agreements required him to do a certain amount of overtime, and when he refused to do a Saturday morning shift it was held that he was in breach of his contract.

3.62 Frequently the terms of a collective agreement will be expressly incorporated into the individual contract by means of the statement given to the employee under ERA, s 1. In *Camden Exhibition and Display Ltd v Lynott*,[100] notices issued to the employees stated that their hours of work, wages, etc, would be in accordance with the working rule laid down by the National Joint Council for the industry. Rule 6 of this agreement stated that 'Overtime required to ensure the due and proper performance of contracts shall not be subject to restriction, but may be worked by mutual agreement and direct arrangement between the employer and operatives concerned.' Workmen who were dissatisfied with a wage award decided to cease overtime working. It was held that r 6 was a term of the contracts of employment of each employee. However, its effect was obscure. Lord Denning thought that it meant that the workmen would not collectively impose an overtime ban, but Russell LJ thought that the rule did not import into the contract of any individual an agreement not to limit overtime save for a reason special to himself.

3.63 To determine whether or not the terms of a collective agreement can be incorporated into an individual's contract of employment, regard must be had to the contractual intentions of the parties. In *Alexander v Standard Telephones and Cables plc*,[101] the claimant was given a statement of written particulars, issued under ERA, s 1. This stated that the basic terms and conditions of employment were in accordance with and subject to the provisions of a plant agreement negotiated by his employers and a trade union. One of the terms of the collective agreement provided that in the event of redundancy, selection will be on the basis of service with the employers. When the company wished to make a number of employees redundant, it was decided to retain employees whose skills and flexibility were best suited to the circumstances. The trade union insisted that selection should be on the basis of length of service. After negotiations broke down, the employers went ahead with their proposals, and the claimant was one of those dismissed. He sought an interlocutory injunction to

[96] [2002] EWCA Civ 442, [2002] ICR 765, [2002] IRLR 476, [2002] All ER (D) 214 (Mar).
[97] [1975] IRLR 147.   [98] [1981] IRLR 452, NICA.
[99] [1958] 1 All ER 91, [1958] 1 WLR 16, 102 Sol Jo 31, CA.
[100] [1966] 1 QB 555.   [101] n 94.

restrain the employers from terminating his employment without applying the principles of collective agreement, but this was refused. He also claimed damages for breach of contract, arguing that he would have continued in his employment until retiring age.

His claim for damages was dismissed. The only relevant document applicable to the claimant's employment was the written statement issued under ERA, s 1. This had to be construed in accordance with the relevant contractual principles. The statutory statement did not deal with redundancy matters, and therefore it did not incorporate the terms of the collective agreement into his contract of employment. The collective agreement itself, not being a contract, could be incorporated into the individual contract of employment if there was a cogent indication that this was intended. However, the clauses in question had to be considered in the context of a joint consultation scheme of a procedure agreement, and it was not sufficiently cogently worded to support the inference of incorporation into the individual contract of employment. In *Malone v British Airways plc*[102] it was held that the terms of a collective agreement which set out minimum cabin crew numbers for aircraft on long haul flights did not form part of the cabin staffs' employment contracts, and an application for an injunction to prevent the airline from reducing cabin crew numbers was refused. It had not been intended that the statement in the collective agreement would be incorporated and thus enforceable by individual employees.

A contrary view was taken by the Court of Session in *Anderson v Pringle of Scotland Ltd*,[103] where the claimant's terms and conditions of employment were in accordance with the agreement made between the employer and a trade union. This agreement contained, inter alia, a redundancy procedure which provided that selection for redundancy was on the basis of last in first out (LIFO). When the employers decided to make a large number of employees redundant, they decided not to follow that procedure, but to use a selective scheme. The claimant would not have been selected under LIFO because of his long service, but he was to be chosen for redundancy under the selective scheme. He sought an injunction to prevent the employers from selecting for redundancy on any basis other than LIFO. The court granted the injunction. It was decided that the relevant terms of the collective agreement made between the employers and the trade union had been incorporated into the contracts of employment of the individual employees. Further, although the injunction would appear to have the effect of enforcing the performance of a contract of employment – which is not normally permissible (see Chapter 10) – in this case there was no loss of trust or confidence in the employee, for the issues were the mechanics of dismissal rather than the principles of dismissal. While it might be difficult for the employer to abide by the LIFO selection system, it was not unfair to hold them to the agreement they had made (see also *Edinburgh Council v Brown*[104]).

The terms of the collective agreement must be suitable for incorporation into the individual contract of employment. In *Griffiths v Buckinghamshire County Council*[105] a redundancy procedure agreement negotiated between the employers and a trade union recommended that 12 months' notice should be given of impending redundancies. It was held that this was advisory in nature, and was a procedural, not a contractual obligation. Equally, a statement made in a collective agreement that the employer will not institute a compulsory redundancy programme is aspirational, and not intended to be incorporated into any individual's contract of employment (*MG Rover Group Ltd v Kaur*[106]).

3.64 Once the terms of a collective agreement are incorporated into the individual contract of employment, they are part of that contract, and cannot be unilaterally altered.

---

[102] [2011] IRLR 32, [2010] EWCA Civ 1225, [2011] ICR 125.
[103] [1998] IRLR 64, 1998 SLT 754, OH.   [104] [1999] IRLR 208, EAT.
[105] [1994] ICR 265.   [106] [2005] IRLR 40, CA.

In *Robertson v British Gas Corpn*[107] the employee was appointed as a gas meter reader/collector, his letter of appointment stating that an incentive bonus scheme would apply. The terms of this scheme were negotiated between the employers and a trade union. Subsequently the employers gave notice to the trade union to terminate the scheme, and no new scheme was negotiated. The employee brought an action for arrears of pay. It was held that the letter of appointment was a binding contract, which gave the right to an incentive bonus scheme. Although the collective agreement had no legal force as between the signatories, it was incorporated into the employee's contract, and the employers could not terminate the scheme unilaterally.

3.65 A different result was reached in *Airlie v Edinburgh District Council*,[108] where the employers entered into a collective agreement with trade unions representing workers in the direct labour organisation which contained, inter alia, a bonus scheme. The scheme was incorporated into the individual contract of employment, but a clause permitted the employers to alter it after consultation with the unions. When the department was making a loss, the employers wanted to alter the scheme. The unions agreed that alterations had to be made, but there was a failure to reach agreement. Nonetheless, the employers modified the scheme, which resulted in a reduction in the wages of the employees concerned. It was claimed that an unlawful deduction had been made from wages, but the claim was dismissed by an employment tribunal and the EAT. The employers had properly consulted the unions about the changes, but there was nothing in the scheme which required the agreement of either the employees or the trade unions concerned.

3.66 Indeed, the fact that the collective agreement contains a clause to the effect that its terms are binding in honour only does not affect the legal enforceability of those terms which are expressly or impliedly incorporated into the individual contract (*Marley v Forward Trust Group Ltd*[109]). However, a distinction must always be made between contractual terms, which are bilateral in effect, and rules, which are unilateral. The latter do not have a legally binding effect (*Cadoux v Central Regional Council*, see para 3.19).

Implied incorporation of the terms of a collective agreement

3.67 It is equally possible to incorporate the terms of a collective agreement into an individual contract of employment by implication. In certain types of employment it will be 'assumed' that employees are employed on the basis of union/management agreements. Thus, in *MacLea v Essex Line Ltd*,[110] the plaintiff took a job as a seaman, and the court implied into his contract the contents of an agreement made by the National Maritime Board, which was the negotiating forum for the industry. In *Wilton Ltd v Peebles*[111] employers had paid to their employees for 20 years the annual pay increases negotiated by a national agreement made between the trade unions and the employers' trade association, and the EAT confirmed that, despite the absence of any written terms of employment or oral agreement as to pay, there was an implied term that the wages of employees were to be those stipulated in the national agreement.

3.68 If a contract of employment (or the written particulars which evidence that contract) states that pay will 'normally be in accordance with' nationally negotiated rates, 'as adopted from time to time' or if there is collective agreement which has not been specifically incorporated into the individual contract, then there is an implied term that the employer will inform the employee if and when there is a departure from the normal situation. An

---

[107] [1983] ICR 351. [108] [1996] IRLR 516, EAT.
[109] [1986] ICR 115, [1986] IRLR 43, EAT; revsd [1986] ICR 891, [1986] IRLR 369, CA.
[110] (1933) Ll L Rep 254. [111] Unreported.

employee is entitled to assume that such national rates will be applied unless he is informed to the contrary (*Glendale Managed Services v Graham*, see para 3.2).

3.69 The terms of a collective agreement can also be incorporated into an individual's contract of employment by virtue of custom and practice, provided the custom and practice is reasonable, certain and notorious. In *Henry v London General Transport Services Ltd*,[112] the employers, in preparation for a management buy-out, entered into negotiations with a trade union over changes to the employees' terms and conditions of employment. These negotiations resulted in a framework agreement which set out new and less advantageous terms and conditions, including reduced rates of pay. After holding workplace meetings, the union informed the employer that the majority of the staff affected had consented to the new terms, and these were subsequently put into effect. A number of dissident employees brought claims in an employment tribunal alleging unlawful deductions from wages (see Chapter 8). It was held that the tradition of collective bargaining between the employer and the trade union was sufficient to enable fundamental changes to be made in the employees' contract of employment, by virtue of custom and practice.

3.70 If the employers are not members of the employers' association, there is little scope for the implied incorporation of the terms of an industry-wide collective agreement into the individual contract of employment. There would have to be strong evidence to indicate that the agreement had been so incorporated by way of custom and practice (*Hamilton v Futura Floors Ltd*[113]).

Changing the terms of a collective agreement

3.71 Terms which are incorporated into the contract of employment as a result of a collective agreement remain part of that contract until or unless they are changed either by agreement with the employees concerned or under a specific right contained in the contract. The trade union is not, per se, an agent of its members with authority unilaterally to negotiate a variation. Thus, in *Lee v GEC Plessey Telecommunications*,[114] the employers had reached an agreement with trade unions in 1985 which gave enhanced redundancy terms to its employees. In 1990 they purported to withdraw those terms, but, following objections from the unions, negotiations took place on revised terms. An agreement appeared to have been reached which enabled the employers to withdraw the enhanced redundancy payments and substitute less favourable terms, but this was on the basis that there would be no further redundancies in the future. However, redundancies were announced, and individual employees brought an action for a declaration that the attempt to vary the enhanced redundancy terms was ineffective. Their claim succeeded in the High Court. It was not necessary to give fresh consideration every time a new collective agreement was reached, for a continuation by the workforce in their employment was a value attributed to the employer. Although the employers could unilaterally determine the collective agreement, this would not be effective to change the terms contained in the individual contracts of employment. Nor were the trade unions acting as agents for their members when they attempted to negotiate the change. They were acting in a collective manner, not on behalf of each individual.

3.72 Another example is *Burke v Royal Liverpool University Hospital NHS Trust*,[115] where the claimant was employed as a domestic worker. Her terms and conditions of employment were regulated by a Whitley Council agreement. In order to assist the trust in submitting a competitive tender, the two recognised trade unions agreed to less favourable terms and conditions than those previously enjoyed. The tender was successful, the lower wage rates

[112] [2000] All ER (D) 2049, EAT; aff'd [2002] EWCA Civ 488, [2002] IRLR 472, [2002] All ER (D) 322 (Mar).
[113] [1990] IRLR 478, OH.   [114] [1993] IRLR 383.   [115] [1997] ICR 730, EAT.

were put into effect, but the claimant made a complaint under the protection of wages provisions of the ERA, claiming that an unlawful deduction had been made to her wages. An employment tribunal held that the agreement made between the unions and the trust constituted a collective agreement which has the effect of incorporating the new terms and conditions into the claimant's contract of employment. An appeal against this decision was dismissed. The claimant had signed the new contract, the consideration for her agreement to accept a reduction in her wages was the greater sense of security of employment, and the agreement was capable of being incorporated into her contract of employment.

3.73 If an agreement states that its terms can be changed after consultation, that does not require the agreement of the parties, and provided the consultation is carried out in good faith, changes can be made unilaterally (*Airlie v Edinburgh District Council*, para 3.65).

Collective agreements and non-unionists

3.74 Just as the terms of a collective agreement may be binding on a non-federated employer who assents to it, so also will those terms apply to a non-unionist if his contract of employment states so expressly. In the absence of such express incorporation, the collective agreement will not apply. In *Singh v British Steel Corpn*,[116] the employee's contract stated that he was to work a 15-shift system over a five-day week. He resigned from his trade union, and instructed his employers to cease paying the union subscription under a check-off agreement. The union then negotiated a new agreement with the employers which provided for a 21-shift system over a seven-day week, but the employee refused to agree to this, and was dismissed. It was held that there was nothing in his contract which permitted a change in the system of working, either by the employers unilaterally or by means of a collective agreement. The tribunal thought that while he was a member of the union he was bound by such agreements because it was his negotiating body, but when he left, he ceased to be bound. The union and the employers had no power to vary the terms of his agreement without his consent.

3.75 There is clearly less scope for the implied incorporation of the terms of a collective agreement into the contracts of employment of non-unionists. In *London Passenger Transport Board v Moscrop*[117] a collective agreement provided that on a disciplinary charge, an employee could take with him a trade union official. The claimant was a member of another union which had not been a party to the agreement, and he wished to be accompanied by an official of his own union. It was held that the terms of the agreement were not necessarily applicable to employees who were not members of the signatory union. In *Singh v British Steel Corpn* (para 3.74) it was equally held that there was no implied term of his contract that as a non-union member he would be bound by union agreements.

Backdating agreements

3.76 A further problem can arise when the terms of a collective agreement are backdated. As a general rule, it would seem that there is no implied term in a contract of employment that a wage award can be backdated, although this may come about by an express agreement to that effect. However, an express agreement cannot override the statutory position. In *Leyland Vehicles Ltd v Reston*[118] the claimant was made redundant in February, and received his redundancy payment calculated on the basis of the wages he was then receiving. In April a new wage agreement was negotiated with the union, and this was backdated to January. The claimant contended that his redundancy pay should be calculated so as

[116] [1974] IRLR 131.
[117] [1942] AC 332, [1942] 1 All ER 97, 40 LGR 67, 106 JP 97, 111 LJ Ch 50, 166 LT 202, 58 TLR 120, HL.
[118] [1981] ICR 403, [1981] IRLR 19, EAT.

to take account of the increase in his wage rate, but his claim was dismissed by the EAT. Section 225 of ERA refers to the amount of pay actually payable at the calculation date. It does not include increases made by agreement concluded after the employment has ended, even though the agreement provided for the backdating of the increase. The payment of a backdated wage increase to employees who have left the firm is usually a matter to be considered on an *ex gratia* basis.

Conflicting collective agreements

3.77 A difficulty sometimes arises when there is an overlap between the national agreement and a local agreement which covers the same or similar ground. In *Clift v West Riding County Council*[119] the claimant was paid less by virtue of a local agreement than he would have received on the basis of a national agreement. It was held that since the local agreement was later in time, its terms prevailed. But 'the latest agreement prevails' doctrine is not a rule of law, as *Gascol Conversions Ltd v Mercer*[120] demonstrates. Here, a national agreement provided that the working week should be 40 hours, and overtime worked as necessary. It also stated that if the national agreement was at variance with any local agreement, the national agreement was to prevail. A subsequent local agreement provided that the working week should be 54 hours. The employee was made redundant, and the question arose as to whether his redundancy payment was to be calculated on the basis of a normal working week of 40 hours or one of 54 hours. The Court of Appeal held that the employee was employed on the basis of the national agreement, and though it was at variance with the local agreement, its terms took precedence.

Which terms are employment terms?

3.78 Another difficulty is to determine which terms of a collective agreement are to be incorporated into the individual contract of employment. Clearly, there are many terms which are capable of such incorporation, such as wage rates, hours, overtime payments, travel allowances, and so on. Equally, there are other terms which govern the relationship which is to exist between the signatories, and have no relevance to the individual contract of employment. For example, in *Gallagher v Post Office*,[121] the defendants recognised two trade unions for negotiating purposes, and informed their employees that they were entitled to join either union. Recognition was then withdrawn from one union, and the claimant alleged that this constituted a breach of contract. It was held that there was no term, express or implied, that the Post Office should continue to recognise the union to which the claimant belonged. Any statement about recognition was purely informative, and not part of the contract of employment of any individual employee.

3.79 Some difficulty has been experienced in the past with the 'no strike' clause, or the procedural aspects of settling disputes. In *Rookes v Barnard*,[122] this clause was held to have been incorporated into the contracts of employment of the employees, but as the point was conceded rather than argued, the case adds little to our knowledge of the subject. A great deal may well turn on the precise wording of the agreement. Supposing this states 'the union will not call a strike until the procedure for settling the dispute is exhausted'. This is an obligation on the union, and is not part of the contracts of employment of the employees. Supposing the agreement states 'the employees will not go on strike until the procedure for settling the dispute is exhausted'. This term is clearly capable of being so

---

[119] (1964) *Times*, 16 July.
[120] [1974] ICR 420, [1974] IRLR 155, [1975] KILR 149, 9 ITR 282, 118 Sol Jo 219, CA.
[121] [1970] 3 All ER 712, 114 Sol Jo 736.
[122] [1963] 1 QB 623, [1961] 2 All ER 825, [1961] 3 WLR 438, 105 Sol Jo 530; revsd [1963] 1 QB 623, [1962] 2 All ER 579, [1962] 3 WLR 260, 106 Sol Jo 371, CA; revsd in part [1964] AC 1129, [1964] 1 All ER 367, [1964] 2 WLR 269, [1964] 1 Lloyd's Rep 28, 108 Sol Jo 93, HL.

incorporated. However, by TULR(C)A, s 180, the incorporation of such a clause will not be binding unless:

(a) the collective agreement is in writing;

(b) it expressly states that the terms are to be incorporated into the individual contract;

(c) a copy of the collective agreement is reasonably accessible to the employees concerned;

(d) the agreement is made by an independent trade union; and

(e) the individual contract of employment expressly or impliedly incorporates the terms of the collective agreement.

However, it must be borne in mind that a strike, whether in breach of a collective agreement or not, is always a breach of contract at common law, so that the effect of s 180 must be minimal.

F. Custom as a source of employment terms

3.80 It is sometimes argued that terms of employment can be found in those practices which are customary in a particular industry or local area, or even within a single firm (as in *Park Cakes Ltd v Shumba & Ors*[123] where the Court of Appeal held that enhanced redundancy payments paid over a period of time can become contractually binding through custom and practice). Support for this view can also be gleaned from the case of *Sagar v Ridehalgh*,[124] where a deduction from the wages of a cotton weaver for bad workmanship was upheld by virtue of the existence of a long-standing custom of the trade which, apparently, was well known. The general rule is that a custom must be reasonable, notorious and certain (*Devonald v Rosser & Sons*[125]). It must also not be contrary to law, and strictly proved. Custom can even override a policy statement where an employee benefit is described as being 'ex gratia' (*Albion Automotive Ltd v Walker*[126]), but an alleged custom cannot be in conflict with an express term of the contract (*Dunlop Tyres Ltd v Blow*[127]).

3.81 In *Hardwick v Leeds Area Health Authority*[128] the claimant was dismissed after exhausting her period of sick pay, which was an entitlement of two months on full pay and two months on half pay. This was in accordance with the normal practice of the Health Service. It was held that such an automatic rule, whereby an employee could be dismissed irrespective of the circumstances, was totally outmoded and unreasonable, and the dismissal was held to be unfair. In *Singh v British Steel Corpn* (para 3.74) the fact that the claimant had considered himself in the past to be bound by trade union agreements was not sufficient evidence to establish a custom to that effect. Moreover, in *Gascol Conversions v Mercer* (para 3.77) the court stated that if the parties had reduced the contract to writing, it is not permissible to say that they intended something else, and thus it would appear that a custom cannot override a written statement of the terms of employment.

3.82 This point has considerable implications when, as sometimes happens, an appeal is made to 'custom and practice' as a basis of employment terms. It is true that in *Heaton's Transport Ltd v Transport and General Workers' Union*[129] the House of Lords upheld custom and practice as being the basis of the authority of a shop steward to initiate action on behalf of a trade union, but this was a case where the union rule-book was silent on the point.

---

[123] [2013] EWCA Civ 974.   [124] [1930] 2 Ch 117; revsd [1931] 1 Ch 310, 29 LGR 421, 95 JP 42, 100 LJ Ch 220, [1930] All ER Rep 288, 144 LT 480, 47 TLR 189, CA.   [125] [1906] 2 KB 728.

[126] [2002] EWCA Civ 946.   [127] [2001] EWCA Civ 1032, [2001] IRLR 629.   [128] [1975] IRLR 319.

[129] [1997] AC 15, [1972] 2 All ER 1214, [1972] 3 WLR 73, 14 KIR 1, 116 Sol Jo 484, CA; revsd [1973] AC 15, [1972] 3 All ER 101, [1972] 3 WLR 431, [1972] ICR 308, [1972] IRLR 25, 14 KIR 48, 116 Sol Jo 598, HL.

However, it might be easier to argue that 'custom and practice' can override the terms of a collective agreement which has been incorporated into an employment contract (see *Parry v Holst & Co*,[130] para 3.110). It is also arguable that a 'custom' is different from a 'practice'. The former has a legal significance which the latter does not possess. In *Spencer Jones v Timmens Freeman*,[131] it was a 'common practice' in the hairdressing trade for shops to be open on Saturday afternoons, but this did not make it a custom.

3.83 Clear and compelling evidence is required to establish that a custom and practice exists (*Henry v London General Transport Services Ltd*[132]). In *Samways v Swan Hunter Shipbuilders Ltd*[133] the claimant, who was originally employed as a labourer, was appointed as a chargeman over a gang, and was given an additional £4 per week allowance. The company then informed him that owing to a reduction in production, it was necessary to withdraw the allowance, and he was offered employment as a labourer. It was held that this constituted a dismissal for reason of redundancy, as there was a reduction in the requirements of the company for chargemen. An argument by the company that by virtue of custom and practice chargemen's allowances were temporary payments for additional responsibility so long as this lasted was rejected by the tribunal, who thought that the 'allowance' was in fact remuneration. That other men had, in the past, reverted from the job of chargeman to their former positions was not sufficient to establish a custom, for their conduct could be explained on the ground that they wanted to keep their job with the firm, and it did not follow that they were contractually bound to do so.

3.84 It may be possible to claim sick pay if there is a local custom to this effect which can be proven to exist (*Scott v Pattison*[134]).

3.85 It is submitted that with the increasing formalisation of contracts of employment, the scope for custom and practice as a source of employment terms has decreased, and indeed there is very little by way of modern legal authorities which could indicate that 'custom and practice' have any relevance in modern employment law. For example, in *Quinn v Calder Industrial Materials Ltd*,[135] a policy document was issued to all member companies of a group holding company, which contained guidelines on additional redundancy payments. The document had not been formally communicated to the employees or their trade unions, although its terms were generally known. Indeed, enhanced redundancy payments based on the document had been made on four occasions, although a decision to do so had to be made by higher management on each such occasion. When the claimant was made redundant, he was not given any enhanced redundancy payment, and he contended that the employers were in breach of their contractual obligation. He argued that his entitlement to enhanced payments had been incorporated into his contract through custom and practice. His claim failed. Factors to be taken into account include whether management had drawn the attention of employees to the policy, whether it had been followed without exception for a substantial period, and whether employees had a genuine expectation that the terms of the policy would be applied to them. In the circumstances, it was not possible to infer that the policy document had achieved the status of a contractual obligation. But a different conclusion on somewhat similar facts was reached in *Harlow v Artemis International Corporation Ltd*,[136] where an additional ground for holding that an enhanced redundancy payment policy was contractual was that it was also part of the individual's contract of employment through 'custom and practice' (see *Keeley v Fosroc International Ltd*,[137] para 3.88).

---

[130] (1968) 3 ITR 317, DC.   [131] [1974] IRLR 325.   [132] n 112.   [133] [1975] IRLR 190.
[134] [1923] 2 KB 723, 92 LJKB 886, 129 LT 830, 39 TLR 557, DC.   [135] [1996] IRLR 126, EAT.
[136] [2008] EWHC 1126 (QB), [2008] IRLR 629, (2008) 105(23) LSG 27.
[137] [2006] EWCA Civ 1277, [2006] IRLR 961, (2006) LSG 33, (2006) 150 SJLB 1328.

G. **Works/staff rules**

3.86 Some employers issue booklets or post notices containing the rules of the workplace, and the legal significance of these is still being explored. Such rules can either be part of the contractual terms or unilaterally imposed instructions, a distinction which is important because in the former case, they can only be changed by mutual assent and agreement, whereas in the latter case, the employer may, at any time and on reasonable notice, change them (see *Cadoux v Central Regional Council*[138]) and substitute new instructions or impose new obligations, and a failure by the employee to obey would be a breach of his duty to follow all lawful and reasonable orders.

3.87 Thus in *Bateman v Asda Stores Ltd*[139] the firm's staff handbook contained details of pay and other conditions of employment, which were incorporated into the contracts of employment of all staff. One clause read: 'The Company reserve the right to review, revise, amend or replace the contents of this handbook, and introduce new policies from time to time reflecting the changing needs of the business . . .' It was proposed to bring in a new pay structure, which was implemented after due consultation. A number of staff brought claims alleging unlawful deduction of wages, breach of contract and unfair dismissal, but these were dismissed by an employment tribunal and the decision was upheld on appeal by the EAT. The changes were within the terms of the handbook, and were made in a manner that did not breach the implied term of trust and confidence.

3.88 The courts appear to be more willing to incorporate the terms of a company's handbook as part of the contract of employment by looking at the importance of the provision to the overall bargain, including the employee's remuneration package. For example, even though an enhanced redundancy package is expressed to be discretionary, it may be contractual if there is evidence that it has been consistently applied in the past, and it is proper for the court to enforce a discretionary power (*Keeley v Fosroc International Ltd*, para 3.85). In *Small v Boots Co plc*[140] a bonus scheme, which was stated in the staff handbook to be discretionary and not intended to be contractual, was nonetheless held to have a contractual effect. The term 'discretionary' may be attached to the decision whether or not to pay a bonus at all, or it may refer to the method of calculating the bonus, or it may refer to the amount of the bonus. All the relevant circumstances must be taken into account, including the invariable practice of making payments over many years.

3.89 But a code of practice to be invoked in cases of long-term sickness (*Wandsworth London Borough Council v D'Silva*, see para 3.21) and an equal opportunities policy (*Grant v South Western Trains Ltd*, para 3.21) were statements of policies in general terms, and not contractual documents (but see *French v Barclays Bank plc*, para 3.22).

3.90 The fact that a change in the company's rules bears hard on a particular individual does not justify an inference that the employer has acted in such a way as to repudiate the contract of employment. In *Dryden v Greater Glasgow Health Board*,[141] the claimant was a heavy smoker, and was accustomed to smoking cigarettes in areas of the hospital where she worked set aside for this purpose. The employers decided to ban smoking throughout the hospital and, after extensive consultations, imposed a smoking ban. The claimant decided that she could not continue to work without smoking, and resigned her employment. She claimed that she had been constructively dismissed. It was held that 'the right to smoke' was not a customary term nor an implied term of the contract, and the employers had not acted in such a way as to frustrate the employee's ability to perform her contract. In *Secretary of State for Employment v Associated Society of Locomotive Engineers and*

---

[138] n 37.   [139] [2010] IRLR 370.
[140] [2009] IRLR 328.   [141] [1992] IRLR 469, EAT.

Firemen,[142] railwaymen proposed to engage in a work-to-rule campaign. If the rule book, by which they were working, was a part of their contracts of employment, then, by adhering to it, albeit strictly, they could hardly be said to be breaking their contracts. However, one of the rules stated that employees should 'make every effort to facilitate the working of trains and prevent unavoidable delay', which would clearly prohibit any deliberate attempt to interpret the rules in such a way as to achieve disruption of services, and to that extent there was clearly a breach of contract on either view of their legal significance. But Lord Denning held that the rules were 'in no way terms of his (ie the individual railwayman's) contract of employment. They were only instructions to a man on how he was to do his work.' It will clearly be an implied term of his contract of employment that he will interpret those rules reasonably.

3.91 In *Peake v Automotive Products*[143] it was held that the contents of a rule book were non-contractual administrative arrangements for running the factory. If this view is correct, then works rules are non-negotiable instructions laid down by the employer. They may deal with all manner of subjects, including the method of performing the work, safety policy, disciplinary matters, concessions and privileges, and so on. A breach of the rules may lead to appropriate penalties. In *Blake v Berkel Auto Scales Co Ltd*[144] an employee was summarily dismissed for a serious breach of the company's rules, and the dismissal was held to be fair. Indeed, a rule may be enforced even though the employee is in no way blameworthy. In *Jeffries v BP Tanker Co Ltd*[145] the company had a rule that an employee with a history of cardiac disease should not be employed at sea as a radio officer, and an employee who had had two heart attacks was held to have been fairly dismissed, even though he had made an excellent recovery. The rule in this case was more in the nature of company policy.

3.92 But this does not mean that an employer can lay down rules and act on them in an autocratic manner, for the courts and tribunals will use the test of reasonableness to circumscribe management prerogatives. The rules must be clear and unambiguous; their contents must be made known to the employees, and reasonable in the circumstances. Thus in *Talbot v Hugh H Fulton Ltd*[146] an employee was dismissed for having long hair, contrary to the works rules. It was held that this would only be reasonable if there was a safety hazard, and if the exact length which was acceptable was made known. Presumably the rule should have applied to female employees as well, otherwise it would have been discriminatory. (For a further discussion of dress codes, see para 4.21.)

3.93 There may be circumstances when some aspects of the works rules can be regarded as contractual terms, despite their unilateral nature. In *Briggs v Imperial Chemical Industries Ltd*[147] the claimant was employed as a process worker at a cyanide plant. The employers decided to pull the plant down and build another one, and consequently he was asked to work elsewhere in the firm as a process worker. He refused and claimed that he was entitled to a redundancy payment. The Divisional Court dismissed his appeal from an employment tribunal finding that he was not entitled. His terms of employment were governed by the statement given under ERA, s 1 (see para 3.112), which stated that his pay would vary with the job he was performing, and clearly this contemplated that he could be transferred from one job to another. Also, he had been issued with a booklet containing the works rules of

---

[142] [1972] 2 QB 443, [1972] 2 All ER 853, [1972] 2 WLR 1362, [1972] ICR 7, 116 Sol Jo 333, NIRC; aff'd sub nom *Secretary of State for Employment v Associated Society of Locomotive Engineers and Firemen (No 2)* [1972] 2 QB 455, [1972] 2 All ER 949, [1972] 2 WLR 1370, [1972] ICR 19, 13 KIR 1, 116 Sol Jo 467, CA.
[143] [1977] QB 780, [1977] 2 WLR 751, [1977] ICR 480, [1977] IRLR 105, 12 ITR 259, 121 Sol Jo 222, EAT; revsd [1978] 1 All ER 106, [1977] 3 WLR 853, [1977] ICR 968, 121 Sol Jo sub nom *Automotive Products Ltd v Peake* [1977] IRLR 365, 12 ITR 428, CA.   [144] [1974] IRLR 272.
[145] [1974] IRLR 260.   [146] [1975] IRLR 52.   [147] (1968) 5 KIR 492, 3 ITR 276, 112 Sol Jo 541, DC.

the factory, r 17 of which stated 'You must accept the right of management to transfer you to another job with a higher or lower rate of pay, whether day work, night work or shift work.' The court held that r 17 was a term of his employment, but this is probably because there was some implied (if obscure) reference to the works rules in his contract of employment. It would seem to follow that if the contract makes express reference to the works rules as being part of the contract of employment, they will more readily be regarded as part of the contractual terms. In *Singh v Lyons Maid Ltd*[148] it was a requirement of the company that employees should not wear beards; this was in order to maintain the company's high standards of hygiene. The applicant knew of this rule, but nonetheless grew a beard in accordance with his religious beliefs. The dismissal was held to be fair. He had refused to obey a contractual term which the employers felt to be fundamental and which did not appear to be unreasonable.

3.94 At this stage it can only be said that the legal significance of the rules is a question of fact, to be determined by the circumstances of each case. For example, if the company's rule permits security guards to search employees before they leave the premises, will a refusal to be searched amount to a breach of an express term of the contract, or will it amount to a breach of the duty to obey a lawful (and reasonable) order? If a company does not have such a 'search' policy, but wishes to introduce one, can it be done unilaterally, or must the consent of each individual employee be obtained? Would a refusal to agree to be searched amount to 'some other substantial reason' for dismissal, by analogy with *R S Components Ltd v Irwin* (see Chapter 19[149])? In *Trotter v Grattan plc*,[150] the employer, with the support of trade unions, introduced a random body search policy, in order to minimise thefts from the premises. The claimant objected to the policy and resigned, claiming constructive dismissal. An employment tribunal held that this was a unilateral variation of the claimant's contract and amounted to a breach of the implied term of trust and confidence, entitling the claimant to resign. However, it went on to hold that the dismissal was for 'some other substantial reason', and in the circumstances, fair.

Other aspects of the contract of employment

A. Disciplinary and grievance procedures

3.95 It is generally a condition of the contract that the employment is subject to the disciplinary and grievance procedures which are in force from time to time. These procedures are unilateral in the sense that it is the employer's responsibility to draw them up, with the co-operation of the employees and/or any relevant trade union if possible, without such assistance if necessary. Some form of incorporation into the individual contract of such conditions is also desirable, especially if these procedures are contained in a collective agreement, for this will then avoid the problems of incorporation so far as non-unionists are concerned.

3.96 But if a disciplinary procedure is incorporated into the contract, it must be adhered to, and a failure may attract the usual legal remedies. In *Jones v Lee and Guilding*,[151] the claimant was dismissed from his post as headmaster of a Roman Catholic school after he had divorced his wife and remarried. His conditions of tenure stated that before any decision to dismiss a teacher was taken, the teacher had a right to be heard and to be represented before the local education authority. This procedure had not been followed, and the Court of Appeal granted an injunction restraining the school managers from purporting

---

[148] [1975] IRLR 328.   [149] [1974] 1 All ER 41, [1973] ICR 535, [1973] IRLR 239, NIRC.
[150] IDS Brief 757 18.   [151] (1980) 78 LGR 213, [1980] ICR 310, [1980] IRLR 67, 123 Sol Jo 785, CA.

to dismiss the claimant without a hearing being held by the local education authority. In *Gunton v London Borough of Richmond*[152] the claimant was given one month's notice of dismissal, though the disciplinary procedure, which was conceded to be part of his contract of employment, had not been fully implemented. The Court of Appeal held that his damages for wrongful dismissal should be limited to the loss he had suffered, which was assessed by reference to a reasonable period it would have taken the employer to implement the disciplinary procedure. (The decision was followed, albeit with some reluctance, by another division of the Court of Appeal: see *Boyo v Lambeth London Borough Council*).[153]

3.97 Disciplinary procedures, discussed in Chapter 12, are designed to ensure that the employee is given every possible opportunity to put right any conduct which is likely to be the subject of critical appraisal; to this extent, the object of the procedure is corrective rather than punitive. Grievance procedures are designed to ensure that the individual employee has a proper outlet for such complaints that he may have, so as to prevent an employee from nursing a grievance.

B. Job description

3.98 A modern practice is to draw up and give to an employee a job description document, detailing the nature of his duties. Again, this should be a unilateral document, and should be specific enough to identify the employee's tasks, yet general enough to enable variations to take place within the context of the contract. The ambit of contractual obligations is not the same as the ambit of the duties which an employee in fact performs. This is especially true in small firms, where greater flexibility is needed, and thus the former may be wider than the latter (*Glitz v Watford Electric Co Ltd*[154]). An employer may be able to change the job description provided the proposed work is still within the contractual obligations.

3.99 The fact that a job description contains a flexibility clause does not give the employer carte blanche to change the fundamental nature of the employee's work. Any job change without the employee's assent must be qualified by the requirement that the change must be reasonable, and within the scope of the employee's contract (*Land Securities Trillium Ltd v Thornley*[155]).

C. Variation of contractual terms

3.100 Any variation does, like any other express term, have to be certain. Thus an announcement made by an employer to all the workforce can amount to a variation if it is in sufficiently certain terms and there is an intention to create legal relations (*Dresdner Kleinwort Ltd v Commerzbank AG v Attrill*). [156]The terms of the contract of employment may only be varied with the consent of both parties, and there is no power which enables one side to act unilaterally, unless the contract unambiguously provides for a unilateral variation (*Security Facilities Division v Hayes*[157] and see para 3.108). It follows that a unilateral variation which is not accepted amounts to the repudiation of the contract. Thus if an employee is demoted, this will be repudiatory conduct by the employer, and a consequent resignation by the employee will be an acceptance of the repudiation and hence is, in law, a dismissal by the employer (see *Marriott v Oxford and District Co-operative Society (No 2)*[158]). But if, subsequent to the variation, the employee stays on with the firm

[152] [1981] Ch 448, [1980] 3 All ER 577, [1980] 3 WLR 714, 79 LGR 241, [1980] ICR 755, [1980] IRLR 321, 124 Sol Jo 792, CA.   [153] [1994] ICR 727, [1995] IRLR 50, CA.   [154] [1979] IRLR 89, EAT.
[155] [2005] IRLR 765.   [156] [2013] EWCA Civ 394.   [157] [2001] IRLR 81, CA.
[158] [1969] 1 All ER 471, [1969] 1 WLR 254, 6 KIR 479, 113 Sol Jo 34; revsd [1970] 1 QB 186, [1969] 3 All ER 1126, [1969] 3 WLR 984, 113 Sol Jo 655, CA.

for a considerable length of time, it is likely that he may be regarded as having accepted the change, and the modified contract will be in existence. Where an employee protests about the change, but continues with the employment, it is a question of fact in each case as to whether or not he has accepted it (albeit under protest). If an employee continues to work under revised terms and conditions, albeit under protest, for a considerable length of time, it will be extremely difficult to conclude other than that he has accepted the revised terms (*Henry v London General Transport Services Ltd*, para 3.69). In *Khatri v Cooperative Centrale Raiffeisen-Boerenleenbank BA*,[159] however, a trader did not sign a variation letter presented by the employer, and was not pressed to do so. He continued to work for the bank. It was held that nothing in his conduct implied his acceptance of the change. The employer had purported unilaterally to change the terms of the contract, but the fact that the employee continued to work did not automatically mean acceptance of changes which were disadvantageous to him.

3.101 The employer unilaterally varies the contract if he insists that the employee performs duties other than those contained in the contract, as in *Dwyer v Superguard Ltd*,[160] where the applicant was engaged as a telephonist-typist. Typing work declined, and she was under-employed. She was asked to take on other work, splitting invoices, but she refused and was dismissed. This was held to be unfair, for her contract could only be varied with her consent. However, such a situation could be dealt with in future cases either by stating in the contract an obligation 'to perform such other duties as may be assigned from time to time', or by declaring a redundancy situation and making an offer of alternative employment.

3.102 An employer has no right unilaterally to vary the terms of a contract of employment, eg by reducing wages or salaries (*Miller v Hamworthy Engineering Ltd*)[161], and if he does so, the employee is entitled to a common law remedy for the whole of the time the employer is in breach, and not merely for the period of notice which the employer could lawfully give to terminate the contract. In *Rigby v Ferodo Ltd*[162] the claimant's wages were £192 per week, and his contract of employment terminable by 12 weeks' notice. As a result of a financial crisis, the employers tried to get the trade unions to agree to wage reductions, but the unions refused to agree. The employers then unilaterally reduced the plaintiff's wages by £30 per week. The claimant continued to work at the lower rate, but issued a writ claiming damages for breach of contract. The House of Lords upheld his claim. The employers had unilaterally repudiated the contract, but the employee had not accepted that repudiation, and thus the contract had not been terminated by the reduction in wages. Thus the employee was entitled to damages for the breach of contract for the whole of the period of the breach, and not for the period after 12 weeks when the employers could have lawfully terminated the contract. Whether a shop steward has apparent or ostensible authority to negotiate changes in terms and conditions of employment is a question of mixed fact and law, to be resolved according to the facts of each case (*Harris v Richard Lawson Autologistics Ltd*, para 3.60).

3.103 An employee has been 'dismissed' for the purpose of ERA, s 95(1) even though he remains in employment! Thus in *Alcan Extrusions v Yates*[163] the employers wished to impose a new working pattern system, which had the effect of reducing the employees' earnings. After negotiations with trade unions had failed, the new pattern was unilaterally imposed. Employees sent a pro forma reply to the employers, stating that they would

---

[159] [2010] EWCA 397.   [160] Unreported.
[161] [1986] ICR 846, [1986] IRLR 461, [1986] LS Gaz R 1901, CA.
[162] [1987] ICR 457, [1987] IRLR 61, CA; aff'd [1988] ICR 29, [1987] IRLR 516, HL.
[163] [1996] IRLR 327, EAT.

work the new system under protest, reserving their rights to claim unfair dismissal and/ or redundancy payments. They subsequently lodged claims with an employment tribunal, who held that they had been dismissed. The decision was upheld by the EAT. Where an employer unilaterally imposes radically different terms of employment, that could amount to a dismissal if the changes constitute a very substantial departure from the old contract. In this case, the old contract had been removed, and a new, substantially inferior, contract had been substituted.

3.104 But a contract of employment cannot remain static over the years, and some element of change is inevitable. In strict law, a variation must be mutually agreed by both sides, but if an employee refuses to accept such a change, this does not mean that he can exercise a power of veto over any new proposal. Ultimately, the employer retains an equal right lawfully to terminate the contract. In *Grix v Munford Ltd*[164] the employee was dismissed when she refused to work a new shift system at a service station, which the employers had claimed was necessary on the grounds of efficiency and financial expediency. The employment tribunal, in holding that the dismissal was fair, gave some guidelines on the approach which employers should adopt in these circumstances. They should consult fully and properly with the employee, and they must give reasonable and due consideration to any objections or alternative suggestions. It is also necessary to prove that the change is necessary, and thus amounts to 'some other substantial reason' should a dismissal prove to be necessary. It is not necessarily unfair to dismiss an employee who refuses to obey an order which is outside the terms of his contract, for the test is focused on the reasonableness of the employer's actions, not whether the employer was in breach of the contract (*Farrant v Woodroffe School,* para 3.26; see also *Luke v Stoke on Trent CC,* para 3.42). In *Bowater Containers Ltd v McCormack,*[165] the claimant was a supervisor. After a reorganisation, it was decided that another small section should come under his supervision. He refused to take on these additional duties, as he maintained that he was not contractually obliged to do so. His dismissal was held to be unfair by the employment tribunal, but the decision was reversed by the EAT. The reason for the dismissal, ie consequent on the reorganisation, was some other substantial reason and, in the circumstances, the employers had acted reasonably.

3.105 It is possible to dismiss an employee (with proper notice) and then offer to rehire him on new terms and conditions. There are a number of variations with such a policy, all of which give rise to legal complications. The simplest situation arises if the reason for the dismissal was redundancy, for then the provisions of ss 138–141 of ERA will come into effect (see Chapter 18). If there is a TUPE situation the variation must be unconnected with the transfer, or an economic, technical or organisational reason entailing a change in the workforce, or a reason connected with a business rescue provision (see Chapter 9). A change in terms and conditions can be permitted by an express term in the contract (eg a flexibility or mobility clause), or when the change has been made by a collective agreement which has been incorporated expressly or impliedly into the employee's contract of employment.

3.106 If an employer wishes unilaterally to change the terms or nature of the contractual obligations, and the employee objects to the change, he has two choices; (a) he could refuse to work under the new terms, and, if the employer still insists on imposing them, he can resign and claim constructive dismissal, or (b) he can work under the new terms under protest, and sue for breach of contract. But if he agrees to work under the new terms until matters are resolved, a subsequent refusal to comply with them can constitute a refusal to obey a lawful order, for which he may be dismissed (*Robinson v Tescom Corporation*[166]).

---

[164] Unreported.   [165] [1980] IRLR 50, EAT.   [166] [2008] IRLR 408.

3.107 Thus if the employer wishes to vary the contract, and the employee refuses to accept the variation, the employer must give notice to terminate the contract (*Rigby v Ferodo Ltd*[167]). This will, of course, amount to a dismissal, and would normally give the employee a right to bring a claim for unfair dismissal. In such proceedings, the employment tribunal may make a finding as to the advantages to the employers of the proposed changes, and whether it was reasonable for them to implement them by terminating the contract and offering a new one. The question then becomes one of whether the employers acted reasonably in dismissing the employee for his refusal to enter into the new contract (*Chubb Fire Security Ltd v Harper*[168]). To answer this question, the nature of the new offer, the advantages to the employer, and the method of handling the situation, the incentives offered, etc all become relevant considerations (*Hollister v National Farmers' Union*[169]). The dismissal will be fair if the offer is one which a reasonable employer would make in the circumstances (*Richmond Precision Engineering Ltd v Pearce*[170]). The employment tribunal should not look solely at the advantages and disadvantages of the new contract from the employee's point of view, but should also consider and take into account the benefits to the employer in seeking to impose the change (*Catamaran Cruisers v Williams*[171]).

3.108 However, the express terms of the contract may permit substantial variations, and if this is so, the other party is bound to accept, whether he agrees in principle or not. The terms may expressly permit a change in the location of employment, or the duties of the employee, or any other relevant matter. In *Bex v Securicor Transport Ltd*[172] it was a condition of the employee's contract that the nature of his work could be changed by the company. When they appointed him to another position, which he regarded as a demotion, he resigned. It was held that as the employers were expressly entitled to require the employee to serve the company in any capacity, there had been no breach of contract by the employer, and consequently his resignation did not amount to a dismissal. He had the choice of carrying out his contract, or resigning.

3.109 An implied variation, accepted by both sides, may be inferred from the parties' conduct. In *Armstrong Whitworth Rolls v Mustard*,[173] when the employee was engaged, his hours were fixed by a national agreement, and he worked an eight-hour shift for five days per week. One of his workmates left, and he was asked to work 12-hour shifts for five days per week. This arrangement continued for seven years, and when he was eventually made redundant, it was held that his redundancy payment was to be based on a normal working week of 60 hours. Although there was no express mutual agreement to vary his hours, such agreement could clearly be inferred from the conduct of the parties.

3.110 A contract may also be varied by virtue of the terms of a collective agreement. In *Parry v Holst* (see para 3.82) the claimant's employment was expressly governed by the terms of the Working Rule Agreement of the Civil Engineering Construction Conciliation Board, Clause XD (f) of which provided that '[a]t the discretion of the employer, an operative may be transferred at any time during the period of his employment from one job to another'. The employee's work in South Wales came to an end, and his employers asked him to work in Somerset. He refused, and claimed a redundancy payment. It was held that he was not entitled. His employment was subject to the Working Rule Agreement, which provided for travelling and shift allowances, and there was nothing unusual about the employers' request. However, if the proposed transfer had been so unreasonable that it could be said to be outside the contemplation of the parties to the contract, then the literal

---

[167] [1988] ICR 29, [1987] IRLR 516.   [168] [1983] IRLR 311, EAT.
[169] [1978] ICR 712, [1978] IRLR 161, EAT; revsd [1979] ICR 542, [1979] IRLR 238, CA.
[170] [1985] IRLR 179, EAT.   [171] [1994] IRLR 386, EAT.   [172] [1972] IRLR 68.
[173] [1971] 1 All ER 598, 9 KIR 279, 6 ITR 79, DC.

application of Clause XD (f) would be precluded. Also, it was suggested that the Clause would not apply if there was a custom and practice of a particular company which would have the effect of varying the way the rule operated. None of these considerations applied in this case, and the application for a redundancy payment was rejected.

3.111 Where a variation of an existing contract is based on a change brought about by a revised collective agreement, the change will only be binding on individual employees if it is accepted by them, or if they were collectively represented at the time the change was agreed (*Land and Wilson v West Yorkshire Metropolitan County Council*[174]). Thus employees who are not union members, or who are members of another union, are not necessarily bound by the change. But if the collective agreement is expressly incorporated into the individual's contract, or if the union has authority to negotiate a change, the variation will bind (*Nelson and Woollett v Post Office*[175]).

D. Written particulars of the contract of employment

3.112 Section 1 of the Employment Rights Act 1996 provides that no later than two months after the commencement of employment, the employer shall give to the employee a written statement containing the following information:

(1) (a) the names of the employer and employee;

(b) the date when the employment began;

(c) the date on which the employee's period of continuous employment began, taking into account any employment with a previous employer which counts towards continuity;

(2) as at a specified date, not more than seven days before the statement is given:

(a) the scale or rate of remuneration, or the method of calculating remuneration;

(b) the intervals at which remuneration is paid;

(c) any terms and conditions relating to hours of work;

(d) any terms and conditions relating to:

(i) entitlement to holidays, including public holidays, and holiday pay (being sufficient to calculate the entitlement, including accrued holiday pay on the termination of employment);

(ii) incapacity for work due to sickness or injury, including any provision for sick pay;

(iii) pensions and pension schemes;

(e) the length of notice the employee is obliged to give, and entitled to receive to determine the employment;

(f) the title of the employee's job;

(g) if the employment is not intended to be permanent, the period for which it is expected to continue; if it is for a fixed term, the date when it is to end;

(h) either the place of work or, where the employee is required or permitted to work at various places, an indication of that, and of the address of the employer;

(i) any collective agreement which directly affects the terms and conditions of employment; where the employer is not a party to the agreement, the persons by whom they are made;

---

[174] [1981] ICR 334, [1981] IRLR 87, CA.   [175] [1978] IRLR 548, EAT.

(j) where the employee is required to work outside the United Kingdom for more than one month:

   (i) the period for which he is to work outside the United Kingdom;

   (ii) the currency in which remuneration is to be paid while so working;

   (iii) any additional remuneration payable to him, and any benefits to be provided by reason of his working abroad; and

   (iv) any terms and conditions relating to his return to the United Kingdom.

3.113 So far as the matters in para 3.112 are concerned, it should be noted that:

(a) if there are no particulars to be entered under any of these headings, that fact should be stated;

(b) the written statement may refer the employee to the provisions of some other document which he has a reasonable opportunity of reading in the course of his employment, or which is made reasonably accessible to him in some other way, in respect of sick pay and pension schemes;

(c) all the above particulars shall be given in one document (known as the principal statement) except terms and conditions relating to sickness, pensions, length of temporary or fixed-term contracts, collective agreements and details given to employees who are to work outside the United Kingdom. These terms may be contained in a separate document or documents;

(d) the statement shall be given to the employee notwithstanding that his employment has ended before the end of two months from its commencement.

3.114 In addition to the matters required to be given by s 1, s 3(1) requires that the statement shall include a note:

(a) specifying any disciplinary rules applicable to the employee or referring him to the provisions of a document which is reasonably accessible to him specifying such rules;

(b) specifying any procedure applicable to the taking of disciplinary decisions relating to the employee, or a decision to dismiss him, or referring to the provisions of a document which is reasonably accessible to him and which specifies such procedure;

(c) specifying (by description or otherwise) a person to whom the employee can apply if dissatisfied with any disciplinary decision relating to him, or any decision to dismiss him.

3.115 However, the s 3 requirements do not apply to rules, disciplinary decisions, decisions to dismiss, grievances or procedures relating to health and safety at work.

3.116 Sections 7A and 7B of ERA (inserted by the Employment Act 2002) provide that the employer meets his obligation under s 1 and s 3 if he provides a written contract of employment or letter of engagement which provides the s 1 and s 3 information (except sick pay, pension schemes, notice entitlement, periods of non-permanent employment, collective agreements and the details relating to work outside the United Kingdom).

3.117 If there is any change in the matters specified in the written particulars, the employer shall give, within one month of the change, the relevant particulars (s 4(1)).

3.118 It is not necessary to give written particulars to an employee if his employment lasts for less than one month.

3.119 It must be borne in mind that the statement given by virtue of s 1 is not necessarily a contract, and is not conclusive evidence of that contract (*System Floors (UK) Ltd* *v Daniel*[176]). But it certainly helps to establish what those contractual terms were, and a failure by an employer to provide such a statement may well lead an employment tribunal to draw adverse presumptions against that employer in subsequent litigation, should the terms of the contract be in dispute.

3.120 If an employer does not provide the written statement under s 1, or if it is incomplete, the employee can require a reference to be made to an employment tribunal to determine what particulars ought to be included in such a statement. But this power only extends to matters which should be in the statement in accordance with the above statutory requirements. The tribunal has no power to amend or rewrite a contract of employment merely because there is some misunderstanding about its meaning (*Construction Industry Training Board v Leighton*[177]).

3.121 An employment tribunal may only state those terms which have been agreed. They cannot remake the contract and insert terms which should have been agreed. 'Mandatory' terms can be determined by looking at all the evidence, including the express, implied and statutory terms. If there has been no agreement on the 'non-mandatory' terms, the employment tribunal should record this (*Eagland v British Telecommunications plc*[178]). There is no power to insert terms which have not been agreed. For example, in *Cuthbertson v AML Distributors*[179] a tribunal declined to state whether three months' notice was reasonable for a senior executive, because this was a common law concept that would have to be determined in the ordinary courts.

3.122 The Employment Act 2002, s 38 provides for various sanctions to be applied when an employer fails to give the written statement under ERA, s 1 or the statement of changes under s 4(1) in respect of proceedings brought relating to a claim by an employee under any jurisdiction listed in Sch 5 (see Chapter 12). If, in respect of such proceedings, the employment tribunal finds in favour of the employee, but makes no award in respect of the claim, and, at the time proceedings were begun the employer was in breach of his duty to give a written statement of employment particulars or particulars of change, the tribunal must make an award of the minimum amount of two weeks' pay, and may, if it considers it just and equitable in all the circumstances, award the maximum amount of four weeks' pay. Equally, if the employment tribunal does make an award in respect of the claim, it must increase the award by two or four weeks' pay. In either case, these awards need not be made if there are exceptional circumstances which would make the award or increase unjust or inequitable. It must be borne in mind that the Employment Act 2002, s 38, does not give employees a free-standing claim to compensation for incomplete or inaccurate written particulars. It only applies when a claim is being brought under one of the jurisdictions set out in Sch 5 to the Act (see Chapter 12). A reference under ERA, s 11 is not specified in Sch 5, and therefore does not, by itself, give rise to any claim for compensation.

The week's pay is calculated in accordance with ERA, ss 220–224 (see Chapter 14), with the statutory maximum to be applied.

E. Itemised pay statement (Employment Rights Act 1996, ss 8–10)

3.123 Every employee has the right to be given by his employer an itemised pay statement, giving particulars of the gross amount of wages or salary, the amount of any

---

[176] [1982] ICR 54, [1981] IRLR 475, EAT.
[177] [1978] 2 All ER 723, [1978] IRLR 60, sub nom *Leighton v Construction Industry Training Board* [1978] ICR 577, EAT.
[178] [1990] ICR 248, [1990] IRLR 328, EAT; aff'd [1993] ICR 644, [1992] IRLR 323, CA.
[179] [1975] IRLR 228.

variable or fixed deductions, and the purposes for which they are made, the net wages or salary payable and, where the net amount is paid in different ways, the amount and method of each part-payment. A pay statement need not contain separate particulars or fixed deductions as long as the aggregate amount of all deductions is stated, and the employer had given to the employee a standing statement of fixed deductions which contains all the relevant details. Such standing statement must be reissued every 12 months.

3.124 The right to have an itemised statement is not conditional upon an employee making a request for one (*Coales v John Wood (Solicitors) & Co*[180]). If an employer fails to give an itemised pay statement, the employee may require a reference to be made to an employment tribunal, to determine what particulars ought to be included in such a statement. But where the tribunal finds that the employer has failed to give an employee any itemised pay statement, or that it does not give the required particulars concerning deductions, the tribunal shall make a declaration to that effect (*Coales v John Wood & Co*) and, if there have been any unnotified deductions from the employee's pay within 13 weeks preceding the date of the application for the reference to the tribunal, then the tribunal may award that the employer shall pay to the employee the aggregate of the deductions made. However, no application for a tribunal reference can be made more than three months after the employment has ceased. The requirement to give an itemised pay statement does not apply to employees who work outside Great Britain, share fishermen or merchant seamen.

F. Holidays

3.125 It will be recalled (see para 3.112) that the written statement to be given to employees under ERA, s 1 shall include any terms and conditions relating to entitlement to holidays, including public holidays and holiday pay, the particulars being sufficient to enable the employee's entitlement to be precisely calculated, including any entitlement to accrued holiday pay on the termination of the employment. Under the provisions of the Working Time Regulations 1998, (as amended) workers are entitled to 28 days' holidays from April 2009 (see para 7.73). Other than the provisions contained in the contract (or the written statement if used as evidence of the contract), there is no legal entitlement to bank or public holidays, and these may be used to discharge the employer's liability under the Working Time Regulations. Under the regulations, accrued holiday pay is payable on termination of the employment, but if the worker's entitlement is in excess of the statutory entitlement, then on termination of employment there may be problems in calculating the contractual entitlement (*Taylor v East Midlands Offender Employment*[181]).

G. Occupational pension schemes

3.126 The Occupational Pension Schemes (Disclosure of Information) Regulations 1986 require an employer who runs an occupational pension scheme to disclose automatically certain information to members and beneficiaries, including details of the scheme, rights of leavers, amount of pension payable to a new pensioner, and options available to persons on the death of a member or beneficiary. Other information is to be disclosed on request, including trust deeds and rules, benefit statements, the trustees' annual report and the actuarial valuation report.

---

[180] [1986] ICR 71, [1986] IRLR 129, [1986] LS Gaz R 117, EAT.   [181] [2000] IRLR 760, EAT.

3.127 The persons entitled to this information include current members and deferred pensioners, prospective members and their spouses, and recognised independent trade unions (except that the latter are not entitled to benefit statements).

3.128 In October 2012, the auto-enrolment into a pension scheme for employees aged 22 or over and earning more than the tax threshold came into force. By September 2016, the scheme will apply to all employers, including new businesses and small employers with fewer than 50 employees. Employers without a pension scheme can use the National Employment Savings Trust (NEST), which is a government sponsored scheme. Employees who do not wish to take part have to opt out.

4

Equality in Employment

Introduction

4.1 The Equality Act 2010 is a major piece of legislation. It purports to harmonise all the law dealing with the prevention of discrimination and the promotion of equality in society. It consists of 218 sections and 28 schedules, and applies across all sectors of public life, including employment, services, public functions, premises, education, associations, public sector equality duty, transport, and so on.

4.2 The Act repeals or revokes most of the previous law on the subject, makes some amendments to case law, and purports to strengthen the law in certain areas. Somewhat unusually, each page of the Act is accompanied by explanatory notes, which are for guidance only, and not to be regarded as being an authoritative interpretation. Also unusually, much of the Act is written in plain English, in an attempt to simplify many of the complex concepts.

4.3 In this chapter, only those provisions of the Act that impact on employment law will be considered. These generally are to be found in Parts 5, 8, 9, 10 and 11 of the Act, together with provisions found in various schedules. Other than those instances where specific legal decisions have been replaced by the Act (eg the decision in *Malcolm v London Borough of Lewisham*[1]) most of the old case law will presumably still apply, until modified or interpreted in accordance with the new provisions. Thus, pre-2010 legal decisions are included in the following text, with the reservation that they must be used with care, more by way of example and illustration, and are not to be taken as being authoritative unless and until confirmed by subsequent legal decisions. It is expected that the higher courts will adopt a pro-active approach to the legislation, consistent with the policy objectives.

4.4 Because of the way in which anti-discrimination legislation has been enacted over the years, a number of variations have occurred in the legislative provisions, which, though minor, have tended to produce significant differences in the approach taken by the courts and tribunals in specific instances. One of the aims of the Equality Act is to ensure uniformity of approach across the board where possible.

4.5 The Act commences with the key concepts of equality, which are the protected characteristics and which are the main object of the Act's provisions. This is then followed by the prohibited conduct in respect of those characteristics, which are the anti-discrimination provisions. However, each of the protected characteristics must be examined separately, because not all the prohibited conduct will necessarily be applicable in each case.

---

[1] [2008] UKHL 43, [2008] 1 AC 1399, [2008] 3 WLR 194, [2008] 4 All ER 525, [2008] IRLR 700, [2008] HLR 41, [2008] BLGR 549, (2008) 11 CCL Rep 573, (2008) 102 BMLR 170, [2008] 2 P & CR 18, [2008] L & TR 29, [2008] 26 EG 117 (CS), (2008) 105(26) LSG 23, (2008) 152(26) SJLB 29, [2008] NPC 76, (2008) *Times*, 26 June.

4.6 The next section deals with the application of the prohibited conduct to the various protected characteristics in the field of employment, which is the major concern of this book. The Act then deals with equality of terms (formerly found in the Equal Pay Act 1970) followed by the relevant enforcement provisions. Finally, there are some miscellaneous provisions that are common to a number of the protected characteristics.

4.7 Provisions contained in the Act which deal with public sector duties, services, occupational pension schemes, local authorities, education, transport, taxis, railways etc will no doubt be the concern of other commentators.

A. Repeals and revocations

4.8 The following important legislative provisions have been repealed or revoked:

(a) Equal Pay Act 1970;

(b) Sex Discrimination Act 1975;

(c) Race Relations Act 1976;

(d) Sex Discrimination Act 1986;

(e) Employment Act 1989 ss 1–7, 9;

(f) Disability Discrimination Act 1995;

(g) Equality Act 2006 (ss 25, 26, 33, 43, 81, Part 2 and Part 4, and part of Sch 3);

(h) Employment Equality (Religion or Belief) Regulations 2003;

(i) Employment Equality (Sexual Orientation) Regulations 2003;

(j) Employment Equality (Age) Regulations 2006.

Key concepts

4.9 The key concepts of the Act are the protected characteristics and the prohibited conduct in relation to those characteristics.

A. Protected characteristics (ss 4–12, 18)

4.10 The protected characteristics are given in alphabetical order, as follows:

(1) age;

(2) disability;

(3) gender reassignment;

(4) marriage and civil partnership;

(5) pregnancy and maternity;

(6) race;

(7) religion or belief;

(8) sex;

(9) sexual orientation.

4.11 While these characteristics are based largely on definitions contained in the repealed legislation, certain modifications have been made to some of them.

B. **Prohibited conduct (ss 13–27)**

4.12 Subject to certain exceptions, the prohibited conduct in relation to the protected characteristics that has general applicability is as follows:

(a) direct discrimination;

(b) discrimination arising from disability;

(c) gender reassignment discrimination;

(d) pregnancy and maternity discrimination (work);

(e) indirect discrimination;

(f) duty to make adjustments;

(g) harassment;

(h) victimisation.

(There was originally a further type of prohibited conduct known as combined (or dual) discrimination, but the Government have indicated that this is unlikely to be brought into force.)

4.13 Again, while largely based on the repealed discrimination law, a number of modifications have been made, mainly with a view to harmonising and simplifying the application of the prohibited conduct to the protected characteristics.

Prohibited conduct

4.14 We can now examine the various types of prohibited conduct, noting, in particular, some of the changes made to the legislation by the Act.

A. **Direct discrimination (s 13)**

4.15 A person discriminates against another if, because of a protected characteristic, he treats that other less favourably than he treats or would treat others.

4.16 As well as the obvious type of direct discrimination, there are several subtle implications arising from the wording of s 13.

(a) *Associative discrimination.* The definition in s 13 does not refer to the protected characteristic of any particular person, and hence associative discrimination is clearly covered. This arises when a person is discriminated against because of his/her association with a person who has the protected characteristic. In *Coleman v Attridge Law*[2] the claimant claimed that she was subjected to unfair treatment because she had a disabled son who required care. Although there was nothing in the Disability Discrimination Act that dealt with this point, the European Court held that associative discrimination was within the scope of the Employment Equality Directive 2000/78. This finding is now confirmed by this wording.

(b) *Perceptive discrimination.* The Explanatory Notes suggest that discrimination can occur if a person treats another less favourably because it is believed that that other has a protected characteristic. For example, it would be perceptive discrimination if a person with a foreign sounding name applies for a job but is not appointed because the

---

[2] [2010] 1 CMLR 28, [2010] ICR 242, [2010] IRLR 10, (2009) 153(42) SJLB 28, (2009) *Times*, 5 November.

employer thinks that the applicant is from an African country. Perceptive discrimination does not apply to the protected characteristics of marriage and civil partnerships.

(c) *Deterred discrimination*. If an employer gives an indication that persons who have a particular protected characteristic would not be considered for the post, this can amount to an act of deterred direct discrimination. This is because of the inclusion of the words '*or would treat*'. It must be shown that the person with the characteristic genuinely intended to apply for the post, and was suitably qualified for it. Otherwise it cannot be said that the person suffered less favourable treatment. If the indication is contained in an advertisement, this could result in a case being brought by the Equality and Human Rights Commission, even though no identifiable person with the protected characteristic could be found (see *Centrum voor gelijkheid van kansen v Firma Feryn*[3] and para 4.205).

4.17 Less favourable treatment must be distinguished from unfavourable treatment. Less favourable treatment requires a comparator, unfavourable treatment does not.

4.18 Section 13 is subject to the following qualifications:

(a) If the protected characteristic is age, there is no discrimination if it can be shown that the treatment is a proportionate way of achieving a legitimate aim (see para 4.68).

(b) If the protected characteristic is disability, there is no discrimination if the person with the disability is treated or would be treated in a way that is permitted by the Act, and another person who does not have the disability is not treated in that way. Thus more favourable treatment of a disabled person is permitted.

(c) If the protected characteristic is marriage or civil partnership, there is discrimination only if the treatment is because a person is married or a civil partner. In other words, associative discrimination does not apply to this protected characteristic.

(d) If the protected characteristic is race, less favourable treatment includes segregation but not congregation, if this is the wish of those concerned (see *Pel Ltd v Modgill*[4]).

(e) If the protected characteristic is sex, less favourable treatment of a woman who is breast-feeding does not apply in work situations. It will be noted that under the Workplace (Health and Safety) Regulations 1992 suitable facilities must be provided for pregnant women and nursing mothers. On the other hand, if the person discriminated against is a man, no account is to be taken of special treatment afforded to a woman in connection with pregnancy or childbirth. Provisions in a contract relating to pay and contractual terms are excluded from s 13, because they are otherwise dealt with in sections 64–79, which replicate the equal pay provisions (see Chapter 5).

(f) For work-related pregnancy and maternity discrimination, the test is whether a woman has been treated unfavourably, not less favourably, reflecting the fact that there is no need for a woman in such circumstances to compare the treatment with that offered to a comparator, (see s 18, para 4.134).

B. **Motive for direct discrimination**

4.19 The test for determining whether or not an act was an act of direct discrimination is objective, not subjective. In other words, regard must be had to what was done, not the

---

[3] [2008] All ER (EC) 1127, [2008] ECR I–5187, [2008] 3 CMLR 22, [2008] CEC 1032, [2008] ICR 1390, [2008] IRLR 732, (2008) *Times*, 16 July.
[4] [1980] IRLR 142, EAT.

reasons or motives behind what was done. The question to be asked is 'was the person so treated because of the protected characteristic?' A benign motive, however laudable, can still be discriminatory. Thus in *James v Eastleigh Borough Council*,[5] Mr and Mrs James were both aged 61. The local authority adopted a policy whereby children under the age of three, and members of the public over pensionable age, were permitted free entry into the local swimming pool, whereas everyone else had to pay the 75p entrance fee. Mr James complained that he had been discriminated against because of his sex, as he was required to pay an entrance fee, whereas his wife was not. The House of Lords upheld his contention. The purity of the discriminator's subjective motive, intention or reason for discriminating cannot save the criterion applied from the objective taint of discrimination on grounds of sex. The reason why the local authority adopted this particular policy, ie to benefit state pensioners, cannot affect the fact that men were treated less favourably than women.

4.20 A person can discriminate directly even though he is unaware that he is doing so. It may happen as a result of an inbuilt social prejudice or as a result of making a stereotype assumption. In *Skyrail Oceanic Ltd v Coleman*[6] the claimant worked as a booking clerk in a travel agency. She then became engaged to a man who worked for a rival firm. The two employers discussed the matter amicably, as it appeared there could be the possibility of the leakage of confidential information. It was agreed that as the husband-to-be would be the breadwinner of the family, the wife would be dismissed. The Court of Appeal upheld her claim for unfair dismissal. An assumption that men are more likely to be the breadwinner of a family was an assumption based on sex, and a dismissal based on that assumption amounted to an act of sex discrimination.

4.21 But the treatment afforded must be less favourable, and the fact that it is different does not mean, per se, that it is less favourable. Nor does it depend on whether the claimant thinks that the treatment is less favourable, because the test is an objective one, not subjective. In *Smith v Safeways Stores*[7] a male assistant who worked in the delicatessen department of a supermarket was dismissed because his ponytail hairstyle breached the company's rule that hairstyles should not be unconventional, and should not be permitted to grow below collar length. The Court of Appeal held that a code governing the appearance of male and female employees, which laid down conventional standards, and was even-handed in its approach, was not discriminatory on grounds of sex. There is a distinction between discrimination between the sexes (which may be permissible) and discrimination against one or another of the sexes, which is forbidden by the Act. In other words, there is a difference between treating differently and treating less favourably. There is no discrimination where dress code compliance requirements apply equally between the sexes (*Dansie v Commissioner of Police for Metropolis*[8]). In *Burrett v West Birmingham Health Authority*[9] male and female nurses were required to wear a uniform. Female nurses wore a starched cap, which had no practical or hygienic purpose. The claimant thought that the wearing of this cap was demeaning and undignified, and when she refused to wear one she was transferred to another department where she had less opportunity to work overtime. She claimed that she had been unlawfully discriminated against, but her claim was dismissed. The fact that there was a different uniform for men and women did not constitute less favourable treatment. Nor was the fact that she felt that she was being treated less favourably relevant, for the test of direct discrimination is an objective one, for the employment tribunal to determine (see also *Stewart v Cleveland Guest (Engineering) Ltd*[10]).

---

[5] [1990] 2 AC 751, [1990] 3 WLR 55, [1990] 2 All ER 607, [1990] ICR 554, [1990] IRLR 288, (1991) 155 LG Rev 205, (1990) 140 NLJ 926.

[6] [1981] ICR 864, [1981] IRLR 398, (1981) *Times*, 28 July.   [7] [1996] ICR 868, (1996) IRLR 456.

[8] Employment Appeal Tribunal, 20 October 2009.   [9] [1994] IRLR7, EAT.

[10] [1994] ICR 535, [1994] IRLR 440 EAT.

4.22 Unreasonable behaviour, by itself, does not equate with unlawful discrimination. In *Bahl v Law Society*[11] it was stated that all discriminatory behaviour is unreasonable, but not all unreasonable behaviour is discriminatory. Similarly, all racial language is offensive, but not all offensive language is racist. The fact that the victim of such treatment is of a particular sex or racial group etc is not conclusive of the perpetrator's actions. True, the burden of proof may be on the perpetrator, and adverse conclusions may be drawn in the absence of a satisfactory explanation, but if the alleged hostile action has nothing to do with the relevant protected characteristic, no discrimination has occurred.

C. Indirect discrimination (s 19)

4.23 A person indirectly discriminates against another if:

(a) he applies a provision, criterion or practice which is discriminatory in relation to that other's protected characteristic;

(b) the provision, criterion or practice is applies to persons who do not share that characteristic and puts or would put persons who do share that characteristic at a particular disadvantage compared with persons who do not share it;

(c) it puts or would put an individual with that characteristic at a disadvantage; and

(d) it cannot be shown that it is a proportionate means of achieving a legitimate aim.

4.24 Thus the provision, criterion or practice can apply generally to persons with a protected characteristic, or to an individual who has that characteristic. Further, perceived discrimination is covered. For example, if there is a criterion that a job applicant should be able to work a night shift, a woman who is otherwise qualified but is unable to comply with the criterion because she has young children to care for would be able to claim that she has been indirectly discriminated against on grounds of sex. The employer would have to show that the criterion is a proportionate means of achieving a legitimate aim. However, the woman must be able to show that she was genuinely deterred from applying for the job because of the criterion (see *Keane v Investigo*, para 4.208).

4.25 An important distinction between direct and indirect discrimination is that so far as the former is concerned, there is no defence of justification, whereas indirect discrimination can be justified if it is a proportionate means of achieving a legitimate end.

4.26 When determining whether a provision, criterion or practice was indirectly discriminatory, the employment tribunal must strike an objective balance between the discriminatory effect of the provision and the reasonable needs of the business. There must be a real need for the provision, and it must be appropriate and reasonably necessary (*Network Rail Infrastructures Ltd v Gammie*[12]).

4.27 Indirect discrimination applies to all the protected characteristics except pregnancy and maternity.

D. Comparators (s 23)

4.28 For the purpose of s 13 (direct discrimination) s 19 (indirect discrimination) and s 20 (duty to make adjustments) on a comparison of cases there must be no material difference

---

[11] [2004] EWCA Civ 1070, [2004] IRLR 799, (2004) 154 NLJ 1292, (2004) 148 SJLB 976, (2004) *Times*, 7 October.

[12] Employment Appeal Tribunal, 6 March 2009.

between the circumstances relating to each case. In other words, the treatment of the claimant must be compared with that of an actual or hypothetical person who does not share the
same protected characteristics as the claimant, but whose circumstances are otherwise not
materially different. Thus if the claimant is eg blind, and applying for a job as a computer
operator, he is to be compared with a person who is not blind but who is applying for a job
as a computer operator. In *Bullock v Alice Ottley School*[13] the employers decided to establish
a common retiring age for all members of their staff, irrespective of sex. Teaching, administrative and domestic staff had to retire at the age of 60, whereas gardeners and maintenance
staff had to retire at 65. The claimant was required to retire at the age of 60, and she claimed
that she had been discriminated against on grounds of sex because all the gardening and
maintenance staff who stayed on until 65 were men. The Court of Appeal dismissed her
claim. The comparison between the two groups could not be made, because there were
special difficulties in recruiting gardening and maintenance staff that justified them having
a later retiring age. The relevant circumstances had to be those circumstances that were
relevant to the comparison.

4.29 Similarly, a comparison between persons of different racial groups must be such that
the relevant circumstances are the same or not materially different. In *Wakeman v Quick
Corpn*,[14] Japanese managers who worked for a financial institution, were paid more than
locally recruited managers. It was held that the higher rate of pay was attributed to their
status as secondees. As such, their circumstances were materially different from those of
the claimant, who was English, so no proper comparison could be made. Choosing a comparator is a question of fact and degree, and it is open to a tribunal to hold that the people
chosen were appropriate comparators, despite the fact the situations being compared were
not the same, if there is sufficient evidence they were comparable: *Hewage v Grampian
Health Board*.[15]

4.30 If there is no actual comparator, the employment tribunal must create a hypothetical
one, drawing a careful inference from all the available evidence (*Shamoon v Chief Constable
of the Royal Ulster Constabulary*[16]) but again the circumstances must not be materially different. In *Eweida v British Airways*[17] the claimant claimed that a requirement that she was
not permitted to wear a cross on her necklace outside her uniform constituted indirect
discrimination on grounds of her religion. She compared herself with a hypothetical Sikh,
who would be permitted to wear a Karra (steel bracelet), but the EAT (upheld by the Court
of Appeal) held that the circumstances were not the same. They said it was not a religious
requirement for a Christian to wear a cross, whereas wearing a Karra was such a religious
requirement for a Sikh. The European Court of Human Rights, however, found for Mrs
Eweida, as the cross was discreet.

E. **Discriminator's characteristics (s 24)**

4.31 So far as direct discrimination is concerned (s 13), it is irrelevant that the alleged
discriminator has the same protected characteristics as the person discriminated
against.

---

[13] [1993] ICR 138, [1992] IRLR 564, 91 LGR 32, (1992) *Times*, 7 November, (1992) *Independent*, 11
November.

[14] [1999] IRLR 424.   [15] [2012] UKSC 37.

[16] [2003] UKHL 11, [2003] 2 All ER 26, [2003] NI 174, [2003] ICR 337, [2003] IRLR 285, (2003) 147 SJLB
268, (2003) *Times*, 4 March.

[17] [2010] EWCA Civ 80, [2010] IRLR 322, (2010) 107(9) LSG 19, (2010) *Times*, 18 February.

F. **Harassment (s 26)**

4.32 The Act defines three types of harassment that are of general application, and a further definition of harassment which relates specifically to employment situations (see s 40, para 4.55).

(a) A person harasses another if he engages in unwanted conduct which has the purpose or effect of violating that other person's dignity, or creating an intimidating, hostile, degrading, humiliating or offensive environment for that person. Motivation is irrelevant. This type of harassment applies to all the protected characteristics apart from pregnancy and maternity, and marriage and civil partnership.

(b) A person harasses another if he engages in any form of unwanted verbal or non-verbal or physical conduct of a sexual nature that has the effect of violating a person's dignity, or creating an intimidating, hostile, degrading, humiliating or offensive environment for that other. This type of harassment applies to all the protected characteristics.

(c) The third type of harassment is where one or more persons engage in conduct of a sexual nature, or that is related to gender reassignment or sex, and has the purpose or effect of violating another person's dignity, or creating a hostile, degrading, humiliating or offensive environment, and because the person offended rejects or refuses to submit to the conduct, he is treated less favourably than he would have been had he not rejected or submitted to the conduct. Again, this type of harassment applies to all the protected characteristics.

4.33 In deciding whether the conduct has that effect, the perception of the person allegedly harassed must be taken into account, as well as the other circumstances of the case, and whether it was reasonable for the conduct to have that effect.

4.34 Conduct is 'unwanted' in the sense of being 'unwelcome' or 'uninvited' (*Insitu Cleaning Co Ltd v Heads*[18]). A single incident can give rise to harassment under this section (*Bracebridge Engineering Ltd v Darby*[19]). If the conduct is of a sexual nature, the fact that similar treatment is meted out to men as well as to women is irrelevant (*Driskel v Peninsula Business Services*[20]).

4.35 If an employer has reason to believe that sexual harassment is taking place, it is incumbent on him to investigate the matter, and to take some action, if necessary, without waiting for a formal complaint to be made. A failure to do so could well amount to a breach of the implied term of trust and confidence (*Reed & Bull Information Systems Ltd v Stedman*[21]).

4.36 In *Richmond Pharmacology v Dhaliwal*[22] the EAT warned against encouraging a climate of hypersensitivity in harassment cases, stating that not every case of racially slanted adverse comment or conduct may constitute a violation of a persons' dignity, and presumably the same approach would apply to allegations of sexual harassment. For example, if a woman's actions are themselves provocative, it can hardly be said that she has suffered an injury to her feelings (*Wileman v Minilec Engineering Ltd*[23]).

---

[18] [1995] IRLR 4, EAT.   [19] [1990] IRLR 3, EAT.   [20] [2000] IRLR 151, EAT.
[21] [1991] IRLR 299, EAT.   [22] [2009] ICR 724, [2009] IRLR 336.
[23] [1988] ICR 318, [1988] IRLR 144, EAT.

G. **Victimisation (s 27)**

4.37 A person victimises another on grounds of any of the protected characteristics if he subjects that person to a detriment because he:

(a) brings proceedings under the Act;

(b) gives evidence or information in connection with proceedings;

(c) does any other thing for the purpose of or in connection with the Act;

(d) makes an allegation that another person has contravened the Act.

4.38 All that is necessary is for the claimant to show that the alleged victimiser was motivated because the victim had done one of the protected acts. Subconscious motivation will suffice (*Nagarajan v London Regional Transport*[24]). Whether the actions of the employer constitute victimisation would depend on the perception of the employee who alleges victimisation, but the perception must be reasonable. In *Chief Constable of West Yorkshire v Khan*[25] a police officer made a complaint to an employment tribunal alleging that he had been the victim of race discrimination, in that his application for promotion had not been supported. Before the claim was heard he applied for promotion to another police force, who wrote to his present employers for a reference. The latter's chief constable refused to provide the reference because he feared that it would prejudice his own case before the impending tribunal hearing. The claimant brought a claim alleging he had been victimised, but the claim was dismissed. The refusal to provide a reference was not because the claimant had brought proceedings in the employment tribunal, but because the chief constable wished to preserve his legal position in relation to those proceedings.

4.39 However, the giving of false evidence or information or making a false allegation is not protected if the information or allegation is given or made in bad faith (*Cornelius v University College of Swansea*[26]).

4.40 A claim alleging victimisation may be brought against a former employer who refuses to pay an employment tribunal award if the reason for non-compliance was related to the fact that the ex-employee has brought tribunal proceedings (*Rank Nemo (DMS) Ltd v Coutinho*[27]) However, a victimisation claim cannot be brought in respect of a failure by the employer to comply with an order made by the employment tribunal for reinstatement or re-engagement, because the Employment Rights Act, s 132 provides its own remedy for that failure.

4.41 In order to establish that a person was victimised, it must be shown that s/he did one of the protected acts, and that s/he suffered a detriment for doing so (*Aziz v Trinity Street Taxis Ltd*[28]). If an employer makes an honest and reasonable attempt to compromise proceedings in a dispute with employees by trying to persuade them to settle those proceedings, this does not amount to victimisation, but great care needs to be taken in such

[24] [1995] ICR 520, [1994] IRLR 61, EAT, affd sub nom [1998] IRLR 73, CA, revsd [2000] 1 AC 501, [1999] 4 ALL ER 65, [1999] 3 WLR 425, [1999] ICR 877, [1999] IRLR 572, [1999] 31 LS Gaz R 36, 143 Sol Jo LB 219, HL.

[25] [2000] ICR 1169, [2000] NLJR 308, [2000] All ER (D) 237, CA, revsd [2001] UKHL 48, [2001] 1 WLR 1947, [2001] ICR 1065, [2001] IRLR 830, [2001] 42 LS Gaz R 37, 145 Sol Jo LB 230, [2001] All ER (D) 158 (Oct), sub nom *Khan v Chief Constable of West Yorkshire Police* [2001] 4 All ER 834.

[26] [1987] IRLR 141, 131 Sol Jo 359, [1987] LS Gaz R 1141, CA.

[27] [2009] EWCA Civ 454, [2009] ICR 1296, [2009] IRLR 672, (2009) *Times*, 8 June.

[28] [1986] IRLR 435, EAT, affd [1989] QB 463, [1988] 2 All ER 860, [1988] 3 WLR 79, [1988] ICR 534, [1988] IRLR 204, 132 Sol Jo 898, [1988] 26 LS Gaz R 42, CA.

circumstances. In *St Helen's Borough Council v Derbyshire*[29] the employer sent letters to a number of women employees warning them that if they continued to pursue an equal pay claim, and succeeded, a number of members of staff would have to be made redundant. It was held that this amounted to an attempt to bring undue pressure to settle or abandon the claim, and constituted victimisation. Had the letter been sent to legal advisors there would have been no problem. But the letters were sent not only to the claimants, but also to other workers who had in fact settled their own claims, and who would no doubt have expressed their anger or disapproval with the claimants' action. Thus the letter constituted a detriment by reason that the women in question had brought an equal pay claim.

4.42 A person may be victimised even though the employment relationship has ended, if the conduct in question would have contravened the Act had it occurred during that relationship (see para 4.196). The Equal Treatment Directive would be undermined if the employer was permitted to take discriminatory action after the employment had ceased (*Coote v Granada Hospitality Ltd*[30]). While it is not specifically mentioned in the Act, the Court of Appeal in *Jessemey v Rowstock*[31] confirmed that a claim can be brought. It seems to be an involuntary omission as it appears in the Explanatory Notes.

4.43 There is no requirement for a comparator in cases of victimisation (*Woodhouse v West North West Homes Leeds Limited* UKEAT/0007/12).

Discrimination in employment

4.44 Sections 39–40 draw into the employment field the various forms of prohibited conduct relating to discrimination that are contained in ss 13–25, harassment in section 26 and victimisation in s 27. Section 39 deals with discrimination and victimisation by the employer, and s 40 deals with harassment by the employer.

A. Discrimination and victimisation in employment: s 39(1)–(4)

4.45 An employer must not discriminate against or victimise a person with any of the protected characteristics (subject to the exceptions noted at para 4.53):

(a) in the arrangements he makes for deciding to whom to offer employment;

(b) as to the terms on which he offers employment. This does not apply with respect to the protected characteristics of sex or pregnancy or maternity, unless, were the employee to accept the offer, an equality clause or rule would apply, or unless the term was directly discriminatory, or a breach of s 13 (see para 4.15);

(c) by not offering employment (s 39(1)).

4.46 Discrimination against job applicants with a particular protected characteristic can take many forms. There can be associative discrimination, perceived discrimination and deterred discrimination (see para 4.16). Job advertisements can be discriminatory, even though no potential victim is identified (*Centrum voor gelijkheid van kansen v NV Firma Feryn*[32]) as they are part of 'the arrangements for deciding to whom to offer employment', as are questions asked at job interviews (*Saunders v Richmond-upon-Thames London Borough*

---

[29] [2007] UKHL 16, [2007] 3 All ER 81, [2007] ICR 841, [2007] IRLR 540, (2007) 104(19) LSG 26, (2007) 157 NLJ 635, (2007) 151 SJLB 573, (2007) *Times*, 27 April.
[30] [1998] IRLR 656 ECJ.   [31] [2014] EWCA Civ 185.
[32] [2008] ICR 1390, (2008) IRLR 732.

Council[33]) or statements made at the actual interview (*Brennan v J H Dewhurst Ltd*[34]). Note that there is no right for an unsuccessful job applicant to have disclosure about the successful one, however, the refusal to disclose such information may be a factor to be taken into account when making a decision about discrimination: *Meister v Speech Design Carrier Systems GmbH*.[35]

4.47 To refuse to offer employment to a woman because 'it is a man's job' (*Batisha v Say*[36]) or to refuse to offer a man a job because women would not work with him (*Munro v Allied Suppliers*[37]) is also discriminatory.

4.48 An employer must not discriminate against an employee of his who has the protected characteristic or victimise him/her:

(a) as to the terms of that employee's employment. As noted in para 4.18 this does not apply to terms which may be subject to an equality clause (see para 5.15). However, if there are minor differences in the terms of employment offered to men and women, these may be ignored under the de minimis rule (*Jeremiah v Ministry of Defence*[38]);

(b) in the way the employer affords (or does not afford) the employee access to opportunities for promotion, transfer or training, or for receiving any other benefit, facility or service. However, positive action may be encouraged (see para 4.204);

(c) by dismissing the employee;

(d) by subjecting the employee to any other detriment (s 39(2)).

4.49 A dismissal includes the non-renewal of a fixed-term contract, including a period expiring by reference to an event or circumstances (see para 17.19) (although it will not be a dismissal if immediately after the termination the employment is renewed on the same terms), and a constructive dismissal (see para 17.21).

4.50 A detriment can take many forms. Thus to dismiss a woman following a disciplinary hearing which she was unable to attend because of a pregnancy-related illness amounted to a detriment in *Abbey National plc v Formoso*.[39] A failure to carry out a risk assessment when employing women of child-bearing age, as required by reg 16 of the Management of Health and Safety at Work Regulations (see para 11.80) was to subject the claimant to a detriment in *Day v T Pickles Farms Ltd*,[40] as was a failure to investigate an allegation of sexual harassment in *Coyne v Home Office*.[41] To put women on short-time working in preference to men was held to subject women to a detriment in *Morris v Scott*.[42]

4.51 A detriment may exist even though the employee is compensated for it. In *Jeremiah v Ministry of Defence*[43] it was the practice of the employer not to require women to do certain dirty work as they did not wish to take showers afterwards. When men did the work, they received extra pay. It was held that the fact that the men received an additional payment for the work in question did not mean that a detriment had not been suffered. An employer cannot buy the right to discriminate.

4.52 But there is no detriment if the job application is not genuine, or if the applicant has no intention of accepting the job (see *Keane v Investigo*, para 4.208).

[33] [1978] ICR 75, [1977] IRLR 362, (1977) 12 ITR 488.   [34] [1984] ICR 52, [1983] IRLR 357.
[35] C-415/10 (ECJ).   [36] [1977] IRLIB, [1977] IRLR 6.   [37] [1977] IRLIB.
[38] [1980] QB 87, [1979] 3 WLR 857, [1979] 3 All ER 833, [1980] ICR 13, [1979] IRLR 436, (1979) 123 SJ 735.
[39] [1999] IRLR 222.   [40] [1999] IRLR 217.   [41] [2000] ICR 1443, [2000] IRLR 838.
[42] [1976] IRLR 238.   [43] See n 39.

B. Occupational requirements (Sch 9)

4.53 Schedule 9 (para 1) sets out exceptions to s 39(1)(a) (arrangements for offering employment), s 39(1)(c) (failure to offer employment), s 39(2(b) (opportunities for promotion etc), and s 39(2)(c) (dismissal), when applying a requirement to have a particular protected characteristic is, having regard to the nature or context of the work, an occupational requirement. The application of the requirement must be a proportionate means of achieving a legitimate aim, and the person to whom it is applied does not meet it (or the employer has reasonable grounds for not being satisfied that the person concerned does meet it). Particular occupational requirements for the protected characteristics are dealt with under their respective headings. Occupational requirements apply to direct and indirect discrimination, not to cases of harassment or victimisation.

4.54 There are also particular occupational requirements exceptions relating to the protected characteristics or sex, transsexuals, civil partners, and marriage, and when the employment is for the purpose of an organised religion.

C. Employer harassment (s 40)

4.55 An employer must not harass an employee of his, or an applicant for employment.

4.56 Anything done by a person in the course of his employment shall be treated as done by his employer as well as by him, whether or not the act was done with the employer's knowledge or approval. This is the effect of the doctrine of vicarious liability. Thus in *Jones v Tower Boot Co Ltd*[44] an employee was racially harassed at work, by having to suffer physical and verbal abuse from his fellow employees. It was argued for the employer that the acts were not committed in the course of employment because it was no part of their work to do such things, which were unauthorised and unconnected with anything they were employed to do. The Court of Appeal rejected the argument, and held the employer liable for race discrimination. The words 'in the course of his employment' were to be given a purposive construction.

4.57 The Enterprise and Regulatory Reform Act 2013 removed specific liability for third party harassment from 1 October 2013, and the law on this reverted to the position before the Equality Act. This was set out in *Pearce v Governing Body of Mayfield School; Macdonald v Advocate General for Scotland* [2003] ICR 937,[45] where the House of Lords stated that while an employer's failure to prevent third parties committing acts of harassment could amount to discrimination, this could only be the case if the steps were not taken because of the employee's protected characteristic. A claimant can also bring an action under the general harassment provisions of the Act (section 26, para 4.32) or claim that the employer's failure to take steps could amount to a fundamental breach, entitling the employee to resign and claim constructive dismissal (para 17.21).

4.58 If an act of harassment takes place at a social gathering of work colleagues, it is for the employment tribunal to consider whether the circumstances can be treated as an extension of the employment. Factors to consider include (a) whether the conduct took place on the employer's premises, (b) whether the persons were still on duty, (c) whether the gathering was organised by or on behalf of the employer, and (d) whether the incidents took place immediately after work. These matters are to be questions of fact to be determined

---

[44] [1997] 2 All ER 406, [1997] ICR 254, [1997] IRLR 168, (1997) 147 NLJ 60, (1996) *Times*, 16 December, (1997) *Independent*, 16 January.
[45] [2003] UKHL 34.

by the employment tribunal acting as an industrial jury (*Chief Constable of Lincolnshire v Stubbs*[46]).

4.59 It is the objective nature of the alleged harassment itself that is determinative, not the circumstances of the victim. Thus to subject a person to homophobic abuse, even though it is known to the harassers the victim was not a homosexual, can still amount to harassment. Such abuse is on grounds of sexual orientation, it amounts to unwanted conduct, has the effect of violating the victim's dignity or creating a degrading, humiliating or offensive environment, and should reasonably be considered to have that effect (*English v Thomas Sanderson Blinds Ltd*[47]).

4.60 A common law action for the tort of harassment may be brought under the provisions of the Protection from Harassment Act 1997 (see para 10.109), although it is expected that most cases will be brought under the provisions mentioned earlier.

Protected characteristics/prohibited conduct

4.61 The protected characteristics and the prohibited conduct can now be drawn together, with the emphasis on discrimination in employment generally.

A. Age

Direct discrimination; age (Equality Act, s 13(2))

4.62 A person discriminates against another if because of a person's age he treats that other less favourably than he treats others ('age' in this connection, refers not only to a person's age but also to persons in a particular age group, eg 41–50-year-old persons). Associative, perceived and deterred discrimination also apply. For example, it would amount to discrimination if an employer treats an employee less favourably because the employee is caring for an elderly relative. However, there is no discrimination on grounds of age if it can be shown that the treatment so accorded is a proportionate means of achieving a legitimate aim. In *Incorporated Trustees of the National Council on Aging v Secretary of State for Business, Enterprise and Regulatory Reform*[48] (the *Heyday* case) the European Court of Justice held that it was permissible for a state to derogate from the principle in EC Directive 2000/78/EC (Equal Treatment in Employment) that prohibits discrimination on grounds of age only in respect of measures that are justified by legitimate social objectives, including matters of employment policy, the labour market or vocational training. It is for national courts to decide whether legislation is consistent with such legitimate aims, and whether the means chosen are appropriate and necessary to achieve those aims.

4.63 A Spanish law that permitted compulsory retirement on the ground of age was held by the ECJ not to be in breach of the EC Equal Treatment Directive. The legislation was held to be an appropriate and necessary means of checking unemployment and encouraging recruitment. The discriminatory effect was objectively justified (*Palacios de la Villa v Cortefiel el Servicios SA*[49]). Similarly, in *Wolf v Stadt Frankfurt am Main*[50] the ECJ held

---

[46] [1999] ICR 547, [1999] IRLR 81.

[47] [2008] EWCA Civ 1421, [2009] 2 All ER 468, [2009] 2 CMLR 18, [2009] ICR 543, [2009] IRLR 206, (2009) 153(1) SJLB 31, (2009) *Times*, 5 January.

[48] [2009] All ER (EC) 619, [2009] ECR I–1569, [2009] 3 CMLR 4, [2009] CEC 754, [2009] ICR 1080, [2009] IRLR 373, [2009] Pens LR 115, (2009) *Times*, 5 March.

[49] [2008] All ER (EC) 249, [2007] ECR I–8531, [2008] 1 CMLR 16, [2009] ICR 1111, [2007] IRLR 989, [2007] Pens LR 411, (2007) *Times*, 23 October.

[50] [2010] IRLR 244.

that a requirement that applicants for jobs in the fire service should be under the age of 30 was held to be justifiable as a genuine and determining occupational requirement. It was noted that fire-fighting and rescue duties were only carried out by younger officers, and that recruitment at an older age would have the consequences that too large a number of firemen could not be assigned to the most physically demanding duties.

4.64 Also, as already noted, discrimination on grounds of age is permitted for benefits which relate to child-care of children. Thus, the provision of childcare facilities for children under a certain age is permissible, even though this could amount to associative discrimination in respect of an employee who has a child above that age.

Indirect discrimination (s 19)

4.65 The statutory definition of indirect discrimination has been noted in para 4.23. So far as its application to age is concerned, indirect discrimination is aimed at disguised age barriers. In *Homer v Chief Constable of West Yorkshire Police*,[51] it was a requirement for promotion that a post holder should have a law degree. The claimant, who was 61 years of age, could not comply with that requirement before he retired, and he claimed the requirement was indirectly discriminatory. His claim succeeded. The particular disadvantage suffered by the claimant stemmed from the fact that his working life would have come to an end before he could qualify, and thus was an inevitable result of age, and the requirement to obtain a law degree was therefore one which indirectly discriminated against him on grounds of age. The case was returned to the tribunal to consider justification.

4.66 The other anti-discrimination provisions of the Act apply to the protected characteristic of age, ie s 19 (indirect discrimination), s 26 (harassment), s 27 (victimisation) discrimination in employment (s 39) and harassment by employers of employees and job applicants (s 40). Thus in *London Borough of Tower Hamlets v Wooster*[52] a 49-year-old man was dismissed for reasons of redundancy. There was evidence that the employer's failure to deploy him was a desire to avoid his becoming entitled to an early retirement pension, and it was held that the claimant had suffered unlawful age discrimination.

Repeal of default retirement age

4.67 The Employment Equality (Repeal of Retirement Age Provisions) Regulations 2011[53] repealed the default retirement age that was previously set out in Sch 9 of the Equality Act 2010 and Sch 6 of the Employment Equality (Age) Regulations 2006. The regulations also removed retirement as a fair reason for dismissal from the Employment Rights Act 1996. Dismissal for retirement reasons therefore, if justified, will be deemed to be some other substantial reason (SOSR) (see Chapter 17).

The employer is not precluded from setting a retirement age, but he will have to have an objective justification in each case, by showing that the compulsory retirement is a proportionate means of achieving a legitimate aim. The Supreme Court in *Seldon v Clarkson, Wright & Jakes*[54] gave guidance on what might constitute objective justification, saying that aims must be related to a general public interest, and not just aims specific to the business in question. The employer in *Woodcock v Cumbria Primary Care Trust*[55] had dismissed the claimant prematurely on grounds of redundancy so as to avoid his eligibility for early retirement, thereby saving between £500,000 and £1 million. The court said the cost saving cannot of itself justify discrimination on the grounds of age. The question is whether the cost saving is a proportionate means of achieving the legitimate aim. Here, it was acceptable as the legitimate aim was the need to reorganise and make redundancies.

---

[51] [2012] UKSC 15.   [52] [2009] IRLR 980, [2010] BLGR 268.   [53] SI 2011/1069.
[54] [2010] IRLR 865, [2010] EWCA Civ 899, CA, [2012] UKSC 16, SC.   [55] [2012] EWCA Civ 330.

Long-service benefits (Equality Act, Sch 9, para 10)

4.68 The general principle is that it is lawful to use length of service as a criterion for the provision of an additional benefit, facility or service. However, if an employee feels that he is at a disadvantage because the employer has used this criterion in relation to another employee, the employer would have an absolute defence where the benefit in question was awarded in relation to service of five years or less. If the length of service exceeds five years, then the exception applies if the employer could show that the reason the criterion was used was to fulfil a business need of the undertaking, eg by encouraging loyalty or motivation, or rewarding the experience of some, or all of his workers. In other words, if an employee has been employed for less than five years, he is entitled to complain if he is not given a benefit based on long service whereas another employee has been given such a benefit. To resist such a complaint, the employer must show the 'business need' of encouraging loyalty, etc.

Enhanced redundancy payments (Equality Act, Sch 9, para 13)

4.69 It is permissible for an employer to make an enhanced redundancy payment in which there is an in-built age factor, provided certain conditions are met. These are:

(a) the employee must be redundant (within the meaning of ERA, s 135). Employees who have less than two years' service may also be given an enhanced redundancy payment, as well as employees who volunteer to take redundancy;

(b) the method of calculation must be the same for all employees who are made redundant;

(c) the calculation is based on the statutory multiplier, ie one and a half weeks' pay for each year of employment in which the employee was not below the age of 41, one week's pay for a year of employment in which he was not below the age of 22, and half a week's pay for each year of employment below the age of 22;

(d) no more than 20 years' service is to count.

4.70 The employer may make an enhanced redundancy payment that is in excess of the statutory cap used for a week's pay purpose, and may increase the multiplier used to calculate the payment for each year's employment by more than one.

4.71 Length of service as a criterion for redundancy selection is prima facie discriminatory against younger workers, although there is an exception in respect of service-related benefits where the service to be taken into account is five years or less.

4.72 However, the use by an employer of a length of service criterion within a selection matrix for redundancy is a proportionate means of achieving a legitimate aim of advancing an employment policy that achieved a peaceable process of redundancy selection agreed with the recognised trade unions. Giving credit for length of service in a redundancy selection policy was considered to be a benefit under reg 32 of the Employment Equality (Age) Regulations, (now Sch 9 of the Equality Act; see *Rolls Royce plc v Unite*[56]). In *Lockwood Department of Work and Pensions*[57] it was held that a voluntary redundancy scheme which provided enhanced benefits for older employees to reflect the comparative difficulty of loss of employment suffered by them was justified. It was a proportionate means to achieve the legitimate aim of producing a proportionate financial cushion for the older workers until alternative employment was found.

---

[56] [2009] EWCA Civ 387, [2010] 1 WLR 318, [2010] ICR 1, [2009] IRLR 576, (2009) 106(21) LSG 15, (2009) 153(20) SJLB 38, (2009) *Times*, 27 May.

[57] [2013] EWCA Civ 1195.

4.73 There will be a consequential knock-on effect on contractual redundancy schemes, which are generally more beneficial than the state scheme. These will have to be reconsidered in the light of the new law and suitably amended to remove any semblance of age discrimination other than that permitted. The employer would need to show that long service 'fulfils a business need', etc. Thus in *MacCulloch v ICI plc*[58] the employer operated an enhanced contractual redundancy payment scheme whereby payments were increased in accordance with age and length of service. However, because of its complexity, it did not come under the exception to the anti-discrimination provisions contained in reg 33 of the Employment Equality (Age) Regulations. The claimant, who was made redundant, complained that the scheme was discriminatory under reg 33 of the regulations. The employer sought to rely on the defence of justification, arguing that there were three legitimate aims, namely (a) encouraging loyalty, (b) helping older workers who are more vulnerable in the job market if they are made redundant, and (c) encouraging older workers to take redundancy, thus freeing up senior posts for younger workers, avoiding compulsory redundancies and making it easier to manage change. However, while the EAT accepted that the scheme had identified certain legitimate aims, the claim was remitted back to the employment tribunal for further evidence on whether the means adopted were proportionate to those aims, having regard to the significant detriment suffered by the claimant. It was pointed out that legitimate aims and proportionality are two separate issues, and both need to be addressed.

Exceptions

4.74 There are exceptions in respect of an act done in order to comply with a statutory requirement (*Renfrewshire Council v Martin*[59]), on grounds of national security, national minimum wage, and positive action (but not positive discrimination).

B. Disability

4.75 The provisions relating to disability can be found in the Equality Act 2010, ss 15, 20–21, 39–40, 60, and Schs 1, 8 and 9, together with regulations to be made. The appropriate Minister may issue guidance about matters to be taken into account.

Regulations

4.76 The Minister will make regulations that will make provision for:

(a) conditions of a prescribed description to be an impairment;
(b) prescribed circumstances in which an effect is to be treated as being, or as not being, long term;
(c) prescribed circumstances when a severe disfigurement is not to be treated as having a substantial adverse effect on a person's ability to carry out normal day-to-day activities;
(d) the effect of a prescribed description on the ability of a person to carry out normal day-to-day activities to be treated as being, or as not being, a substantial adverse effect.

4.77 Regulations will also be made making provision for:

(a) persons of prescribed descriptions to be treated as having disabilities (deemed disabilities);

[58] [2008] ICR 1334, (2008) IRLR 846.   [59] Employment Appeal Tribunal, 30 April 2008.

(b) circumstances in which a person who has a disability is to be treated as no longer having the disability;

(c) a condition of a prescribed description to be treated as being, or not being, progressive.

Guidance

4.78 The Minister may issue guidance (subject to Parliamentary approval), which may give examples of:

(a) the effect that it would, or would not, be reasonable, in relation to particular activities, to regard as substantial adverse effects;

(b) substantial adverse effects that it would, or would not, be reasonable to regard as long-term.

4.79 In determining whether a person is a disabled person, an adjudicating body (ie an employment tribunal) must take account of such guidance as it thinks is relevant. Current guidance is provided by the Equality Act 2010 (Disability) Regulations 2010.[60]

Definition of disability (s 6, Sch 1)

4.80 A person has a disability if he has a physical or mental impairment, which has a substantial and long-term adverse effect on his ability to carry out normal day-to-day activities. The fact that a person is disabled within the meaning of other legislation (eg for the purpose of disability living allowance) does not mean that he comes within the definition of disability within the meaning of the Act.

4.81 There are thus three elements to consider, namely (a) impairment (physical or mental), (b) substantial and long-term adverse effect, and (c) normal day-to-day activities. The text that follows includes the pre-2010 case law and various regulations on disability discrimination, which are likely to be replicated.

Physical or mental impairment

4.82 The physical impairment must be real, and not the result of functional overlay (ie where the symptoms are imaginary manifestations of an individual's psychological state: see *Rugamer v Sony Music Entertainments UK Ltd*[61]). But if there are physical symptoms, the existence or non-existence of a physical cause is irrelevant (*College of Ripon and York St John v Hobbs*[62]), because an impairment may exist without any physical or mental causation. In other words, a claimant needs to show an impairment; but not why the impairment exists, ie by reference to a particular physical or mental illness. But if there is a dispute as to the nature of the impairment it is for the claimant to prove that it is physical or mental in character (*Millar v Inland Revenue Commissioners*[63]). A medical adviser can express an opinion about diagnosis, prognosis and observation of day-to-day activities, but it is for the employment tribunal to determine whether or not a person is disabled, and not for them merely to adopt the opinion of the medical adviser (*Abadeh v British Telecommunications plc*[64]). Direct discrimination claims must be decided in accordance with the evidence, not 'stereotyping' on the basis of assumed characteristics, such as assumptions that a tribunal made about the claimant's particular mental illness rather than on the basis of up-to-date

---

[60] SI 2010/2128.

[61] [2002] EWCA Civ 1074, [2002] ICR 1498, [2002] IRLR 711, [2002] Emp LR 1097, (2003) 71 BMLR 1, (2002) 99(38) LSG 33, (2002) 146 SJLB 201, (2002) *Times*, 26 August.

[62] [2002] IRLR 185.   [63] 2006 SC 155, 2005 SLT 1074, [2006] IRLR 112, 2005 GWD 32–615.

[64] [2001] ICR 156, [2001] IRLR 23, [2001] Emp LR 440.

medical evidence about the effect of his illness on his ability to continue in the employment (*Aylott v Stockton-on-Tees Borough Council*).[65]

4.83 Addictions to alcohol, nicotine or other substances do not amount to an impairment for the purpose of the Act, although if there is a physical or mental impairment, the fact that it was caused by such addiction is not relevant (*Power v Panasonic UK Ltd*[66]). What matters is the impairment, not how it is caused. A tendency to pyromania, kleptomania, physical or sexual abuse, exhibitionism or voyeurism are not impairments. Seasonal allergic rhinitis (hay fever) is excluded, but not if it aggravates another condition. Also excluded are tattoos or the piercing of the body by objects for decorative or non-medical purposes (Equality Act 2010 (Disability) Regulations 2010).

4.84 Persons who suffer from certain progressive illnesses, eg, HIV infection, cancer and multiple sclerosis, will be deemed to be disabled from the point in time of diagnosis, although certain types of minor cancers, which respond to quick and effective treatment, may be excluded by regulations. The Disability Discrimination (Blind and Partially Sighted Persons) Regulations 2003 provided that anyone certified or registered blind or partially sighted is deemed to be disabled for the purpose of the Act, and will no longer be required to establish that being blind or partially sighted has a substantial adverse effect on day-to-day activities.

4.85 However, any impairment, whether physical or mental, which ceases to have a substantial effect on a person's ability to carry out normal day-to-day activities is to be treated as continuing to have that effect if it is likely to recur. The likelihood of recurrence is to be judged at the date of the actual discrimination, and the fact that a recurrence takes place subsequently cannot be taken into account by the employment tribunal (*Richmond Adult Community College v McDougall*[67]).

Substantial and long-term effects

4.86 The effect of an impairment is long term if it has lasted for 12 months, or is likely to last for at least 12 months, or is likely to last for the rest of a person's life.

4.87 An impairment that ceases to have a substantial adverse effect on day-to-day activities is to be treated as still having that effect 'if that effect is likely to recur'. The word 'likely' means 'could well happen' not the stricter test of 'more probable than not'. Thus if a person is not actually suffering from an underlying condition at a particular moment in time, but remains susceptible to it, s/he is disabled for the purpose of the legislation (*SCA Packaging Ltd v Boyle*[68]). In assessing the likelihood of an impairment recurring, an employment tribunal should only take into account the evidence that was available at the time of the alleged act complained of, and not events that occur after the alleged act but before the tribunal hearing (*Richmond Adult Community College v McDougall*[69]).

4.88 The effect of a condition or illness that is likely to develop from another illness or condition is to be taken into account when forming an assessment of whether the original illness or condition was likely to have lasted for at least 12 months (*Patel v Oldham Metropolitan Borough Council*[70]).

---

[65] [2010] IRLR 994, CA.   [66] [2003] IRLR 151, (2003) 72 BMLR 1.

[67] [2008] EWCA Civ 4, [2008] ICR 431, [2008] IRLR 227, (2008) 105(4) LSG 23, (2008) 152(4) SJLB 30, (2008) *Times*, 22 February.

[68] [2009] UKHL 37, [2009] 4 All ER 1181, [2009] NI 317, [2009] ICR 1056, [2009] IRLR 746, (2009) 109 BMLR 53, (2009) 153(26) SJLB 27, (2009) *Times*, 6 July.   [69] n 68.

[70] [2010] ICR 603, [2010] IRLR 280.

4.89 A severe disfigurement is to be treated as having a substantial adverse effect on a person's ability to carry out normal day-to-day activities, although regulations may exclude certain severe disfigurements, including those that were deliberately acquired.

4.90 An impairment is to be treated as having a substantial adverse effect on the ability of the person concerned to carry out normal day-to-day activities if:

(a) measures are being taken to treat or correct it, and

(b) but for those measures, the impairment would be likely to have such effect.

4.91 Measures, include medical treatment and the use of a prosthesis or other aid, but not, in relation to a person's sight, the extent to which the impairment is correctable by spectacles or contact lenses, or other prescribed measures.

4.92 When determining whether a disability had a substantial adverse effect, account must be taken of the 'deduced effect' ie the likely effect upon the person's capability if aid or treatment is withdrawn. Thus, if a person is suffering from anxiety, he can be assessed as if he was not receiving counselling sessions from a psychologist (*Kapidia v London Borough of Lambeth*[71]). Account cannot be taken of events that occur after the alleged discriminatory act in order to determine the likelihood of a recurrence of a disability, but the statute does not require a prophesy to be made (*McDougall v Richmond Adult Community Centre*[72]).

4.93 To assess whether or not an impairment has a substantial adverse effect, a tribunal should concentrate on what a claimant cannot do, or can only do with difficulty, and not on what he can do (*Aderemi v London & South East Railway*[73]). When considering what is a 'substantial' effect, unless a matter can be classified as 'trivial' or 'insubstantial' then it must be substantial (*Aderemi v London & South East Railway*).

4.94 It is no longer necessary for a mental impairment to arise from 'a clinically well recognised illness', and thus physical and mental illnesses are to be treated alike from a diagnostic point of view. But vague expressions, such as 'depression', 'anxiety', 'stress' or 'nervous debility' will not, by themselves, lead to a conclusion that the person is disabled. Many instances of such illnesses do not last for a long period, and thus would fail to meet the requirement that the impairment must have a substantial and long-term adverse effect. If they do, however, it would count as a disability. In *Walker v Sita Information Networking Computing Ltd*[74] a tribunal was wrong to say that an obese claimant was not disabled because there was no recognisable pathological or mental cause for his symptoms, but should rather have looked at what effect the impairments had on everyday life. The focus should therefore be on the effect of the person's symptoms rather than their cause. The EAT said that the obesity was not a disability itself, but could make it more likely that a claimant would be disabled.

Normal day-to-day activities

4.95 The Act has dropped the list requirement in earlier legislation, which stated that an impairment is to be taken as affecting normal day-to-day activities only if it affected a person with regard to mobility, manual dexterity, physical coordination, continence, ability to lift, carry or move everyday objects, speech, hearing, eyesight, memory or ability to concentrate, learn or understand, or perception of risks of physical danger. The view was taken that such limitations were no longer necessary.

4.96 Whether an impairment has a substantial effect on a person's ability to carry out normal day-to-day activities should not be judged by reference to whether he is able to carry

---

[71] [2000] IRLR 699, (2000) All ER (D) 785.   [72] See n 68.
[73] UKEAT/0316/12/KN.   [74] UKEAT/0097/12.

out his job (*Goodwin v Patent Office*[75]) but evidence as to how he carries out his duties at work can be relevant in assessing the employee's credibility, provided that the duties carried out can be regarded as being normal day-to-day activities (*Law Hospital NHS Trust v Rush*[76]). If the effect of the impairment fluctuates, and is exacerbated by conditions at work, then an employee's ability to perform normal day-to-day activities both while at work and while not at work is to be taken into account when assessing whether the impairment has a substantial and long-term adverse effect (*Cruickshank v VAW Motorcast Ltd*[77]).

4.97 The playing of games or sports does not constitute 'normal day-to-day activities', because such activities are only normal for a particular group of persons (*Coca-Cola Enterprises Ltd v Shergill*[78]). But it is normal for a woman to put rollers in her hair and apply make-up to her face (*Ekpe v Metropolitan Police Comr*[79]).

4.98 'Normal day-to-day activities' does not apply to specialist skills that are required for some employment situations, but can include activities that are to be found across a range of employment situations. In *Chief Constable of Dumfries & Galloway v Adams*[80] a police officer, who suffered from ME, had mobility problems when working on a night shift. As the work activity was 'normal' in the sense it applied to a range of different work situations (because there are a number of employees who work on night shifts), it was held that the employee was disabled within the meaning of the Act.

Discrimination arising from disability (s 15)

4.99 A person discriminates against a disabled person if:

(a) he treats him unfavourably because of something arising in consequence of the disabled person's disability; and

(b) it cannot be shown that the treatment is a proportionate means of achieving a legitimate aim.

4.100 The first part of this section reverses the decision in *London Borough of Lewisham v Malcolm*,[81] which required the treatment of a disabled person to be 'less favourable' when compared with the treatment afforded to a non-disabled person. Section 15 is dealing with unfavourable treatment, and thus a comparator is not required. If the treatment results in the disabled person suffering a detriment, this will amount to discrimination. Associative, perceived and deterred discrimination also apply. But there will be no discrimination if the alleged discriminator does not know, and could not reasonably be expected to know, that the person discriminated against has the disability.

4.101 The provisions of s 19 (indirect discrimination), s 26 (harassment), s 27 (victimisation), s 39 (discrimination in employment) and s 40 (harassment) apply in disability cases.

4.102 However, the treatment will not be unfavourable under s 39 if it is a proportionate way of achieving a legitimate aim. For example, the provisions designed to prevent discrimination on grounds of disability are subordinate to health and safety law. In *Farmiloe v Lane Group plc*[82] the claimant worked in a warehouse. He could not wear safety boots because he

---

[75] [1999] ICR 302, [1999] IRLR 4, [1999] Disc LR 104, (1998) *Times*, 11 November.

[76] 2002 SC 24, 2002 SLT 7, [2001] IRLR 611, 2001 GWD 21-810.   [77] [2002] ICR 729, [2002] IRLR 24.

[78] Employment Appeal Tribunal, 2 September 2002.

[79] [2001] ICR 1084, [2001] IRLR 605, [2001] Emp LR 741.   [80] [2009] ICR 1034, [2009] IRLR 612.

[81] [2008] UKHL 43, [2008] 1 AC 1399, [2008] 3 WLR 194, [2008] 4 All ER 525, [2008] IRLR 700, [2008] HLR 41, [2008] BLGR 549, (2008) 11 CCL Rep 573, (2008) 102 BMLR 170, [2008] 2 P & CR 18, [2008] L & TR 29, [2008] 26 EG 117 (CS), (2008) 105(26) LSG 23, (2008) 152(26) SJLB 29, [2008] NPC 76, (2008) *Times*, 26 June.

[82] [2004] PIQR P22.

suffered with psoriasis. A local authority health and safety officer required him to wear safety boots, and threatened enforcement action if he failed to do so. The employers approached various footwear manufacturers, but none could provide suitable safety footwear. As there was no other employment available for him, he was dismissed. It was held that even though he had been discriminated against because of his disability, the principles of health and safety law overrode the principles behind the Disability Discrimination Act. The employers had made an effort to provide a reasonable adjustment and, as there was none available, and no other suitable employment for him, the claimant was fairly dismissed.

4.103 So too in *McCall v Post Office*,[83] where the claimant, unknown to his employers, suffered from epilepsy. He was employed as a cleaner, but had several fits of short duration. The personnel department took medical advice, and were told that he should be employed in a 'no risk' area. Unfortunately, there was no suitable vacancy, and he was dismissed. It was held that the dismissal was fair. On medical advice the employee had to be moved to a safe area, but as there was none available, it was in his interests (and in the interests of other employees) that he be dismissed.

4.104 There is no discrimination if the person with the disability is treated in a way permitted by the Act, and another person who does not have the disability is not treated in that way. Thus more favourable treatment of a disabled person is permitted. On the other hand, discriminatory treatment will be justified if it arises from performance-related pay, eligibility for and contributions to occupational pension schemes, and permits for incapacitated persons under the agricultural wages legislation (see Disability Discrimination (Employment) Regulations 1996).

4.105 Further, there is nothing in the Act that prohibits an employer from requiring a job claimant to undergo a pre-recruitment medical examination and, if a person refuses such a request, there is no obligation to offer him employment (*X v EC Commission*,[84] but see s 60, para 4.107). If a disabled person is dismissed, it must be shown that the disability-related reason was present in the employer's mind when the decision to dismiss was taken (*Taylor v OCS Group Ltd*[85]).

4.106 Thus once a disability is revealed, it will be necessary to obtain a proper assessment of the disabling condition, the prognosis, the effect of the disability on the employee's (or job applicant's) ability to undertake duties, the effect of the physical features of the workplace, and the steps that might be taken to reduce or remove the disadvantages to which the disabled person would otherwise be subjected to (*Mid-Staffordshire General Hospitals NHS Trust v Cambridge*[86]).

Enquiries about disability and health (s 60)

4.107 A person to whom an application for work is made must not ask the job applicant about his health before offering him work or before including the job applicant in a pool of candidates from which selection for employment is to be made. A contravention of s 60 is enforceable as an unlawful act by the Commission under Part I of the Equality Act 2006 (see s 120(8)).

4.108 Asking about the health of a job applicant does not, by itself, mean that there is a contravention of a relevant disability provision (s 60(3)), but conduct in reliance on information given in response may be a contravention. If this does occur, and the job applicant

---

[83] IRLR LIB.   [84] [1995] IRLR 320.
[85] [2006] EWCA Civ 702, [2006] ICR 1602, [2006] IRLR 613, (2006) 103(24) LSG 28, (2006) 150 SJLB 810, (2006) *Times*, 12 July.
[86] [2003] IRLR 566.

is not progressed to the next stage or is not appointed to the post, and he brings a claim alleging discrimination to an employment tribunal, the burden of proof (in s 136(2)) will be on the employer to show that the reason did not contravene s 39(1)(a) (arrangements for employment) or s 39(1)(c) (failure to offer employment). In the absence of a satisfactory explanation, the employment tribunal can conclude that a contravention of the Act has occurred (s 60(5)).

4.109 However, s 60 does not prohibit an employer from asking questions for the purpose of:

(a) establishing whether the job applicant is able to comply with a requirement to undergo an assessment, designed to give an indication of the applicant's suitability for the work concerned, or whether there would be a duty on the employer to make reasonable adjustments in connection with the requirement to undergo an assessment;

(b) establishing whether the job applicant will be able to carry out a function that is intrinsic to the work;

(c) monitoring diversity in the range of persons applying to the employer for work;

(d) establishing whether the employer can take lawful positive action under s 159;

(e) if there is a work requirement to have a particular disability, ascertaining if the job applicant has that particular disability. The requirement must be an occupational requirement and its application must be a proportionate means of achieving a legitimate aim.

4.110 Section 60 does not apply to anything done for the purpose of vetting applicants for work for reasons of national security.

Occupational requirement

4.111 There is no contravention of the employment provisions relating to disability if having regard to the nature or context of the work a requirement to have or not to have a particular disability is an occupational requirement, the requirement is a proportionate means of achieving a legitimate aim, and the person concerned does not meet it.

Duty to make adjustments (s 20, Sch 8)

4.112 The duty to make reasonable adjustments comprises of three requirements:

(a) Where a provision, criterion or practice puts a disabled person at a substantial disadvantage in relation to a non-disabled person, the employer must take such steps as are reasonable to avoid the disadvantage.

(b) Reasonable steps must be taken to ensure that a disabled person is not disadvantaged because of a physical feature, which may be because of the design or construction of a building, the approach, exit from or access to a building, a fixture or fitting, or furniture, furnishings, materials, equipment or other chattel in or on the premises, or any other physical element or quality. The steps to be taken include removing the physical feature in question, or altering it, or providing a reasonable means of avoiding it.

(c) Reasonable steps must also be taken to provide auxiliary aids or an auxiliary service where necessary to avoid a disadvantage.

4.113 A person discriminates against a disabled person if he fails to comply with any of these three requirements. So far as the first or third requirements are concerned, if they relate to the provision of information, steps must be taken to ensure that the information is provided in an accessible format. Further, the person on whom the burden to make the adjustments is placed cannot require the disabled person to pay for the costs of the adjustments unless there is an express provision to the contrary (s 20(7)).

4.114 If the employer is under a binding obligation to obtain the consent of another person to make alteration to the premises he occupies, or to vary the terms of the tenancy, or to obtain the consent of another person to an alteration to common parts, it is always reasonable for him to have to take steps to obtain consent, but it is never reasonable for him to have to make the alteration before the consent is obtained.

4.115 The duty applies in respect of job applicants as well as employees. The employer is not subject to this duty if he does not know and could not reasonably be expected to know that the job applicant has a disability or that an employee is likely to be placed at the disadvantage mentioned in the three requirements listed at para 4.112. An employer cannot rely solely on an occupational health report when considering disability, but should ask specific practical questions (*Gallop v Newport City Council*[87]). An employment tribunal may substitute its own view for that of the employer when considering whether or not an adjustment is reasonable in the circumstances.

4.116 The Minister may make regulations dealing with, inter alia, whether a particular step could amount to a reasonable adjustment, what is, or what is not, a provision, criterion or practice, a physical feature, and things that are or are not to be treated as auxiliary aids. It is likely that the regulations will deal with making adjustments to the premises, allocating the disabled person's duties to another person, transferring him to fill an existing vacancy, altering working hours, assigning to him a different place of work, permitting him to be absent during working hours for rehabilitation, assessment and/or treatment, providing training, acquiring or modifying equipment, modifying instructions or reference manuals or procedures for assessment or testing, providing a reader or interpreter, supplying auxiliary aids, and so on. But these suggestions will be illustrative, not exhaustive (*Chief Constable of South Yorkshire Police v Jelic*[88]).

4.117 In considering whether an employer has made reasonable adjustments, the operational needs of the employer and the interests of other employees may be taken into account (*Chief Constable of Lincolnshire Police v Weaver*[89]), as well as the extent to which the adjustment would prevent the discriminatory effect. The nature of the activities, the size of the employer's undertaking, and the financial implications of the adjustment may also be a relevant consideration (*O'Hanlon v Commissioners for HM Revenue and Customs*[90]). Reasonable adjustments must be job related. The employer is not bound to provide personal carers or special facilities (eg a disabled toilet must be provided, but not assistance in going to the toilet (*Kenny v Hampshire Constabulary*[91]). It is not a reasonable adjustment to continue to pay full pay or enhanced sick pay (*O'Hanlon v HM Revenue and Customs*[92]) to an employee who is off work for a disability-related reason when other employees do not receive such treatment, because this would not help the employee to return to work (*Fowler v Waltham Forest*[93]). But it can be a reasonable adjustment to move a disabled employee to a different place of work within the organisation if this would best achieve the necessary aim (*Garrett v Lidl Ltd*[94]) or swapping the role of a disabled person with that of another employee (*Chief Constable of South Yorkshire Police v Jelic*[95]), if such steps would best achieve the necessary aim.

---

[87] [2013] EWCA Civ 1583.   [88] [2010] IRLR 744,, EAT.
[89] Employment Appeal Tribunal, 19 March 2008.   [90] [2007] ICR 1359, (2007) IRLR 404.
[91] [1999] ICR 27, [1999] IRLR 76, [1999] Disc LR 118, (1998) *Times*, 22 October.   [92] See n 90.
[93] [2007] All ER (D) 126.   [94] Employment Appeal Tribunal, 16 December 2009.   [95] See n 89.

4.118 An employer's failure to make a reasonable adjustment that is inadvertent, eg through lack of diligence or competence, is to be regarded as a decision to make a deliberate omission, and thus a failure for the purpose of the time limits that apply to a claimant. It is up to the employer to assert an intervening date that could be taken as being the date when the 'decision to make an omission' from which date time will run (*Matuszowicz v Kingston-upon-Hull City Council*[96]).

C. Gender reassignment

4.119 A person has the protected characteristic of gender reassignment if s/he is proposing to undergo, is undergoing or has undergone a process for the purpose of reassigning that person's sex by changing physiological or other attributes of sex. This definition includes transsexuals, and it is no longer necessary for a person to be under medical supervision for reassignment purposes. It should be noted that once a person has undergone gender reassignment and obtained formal recognition under the Gender Recognition Act 2004, that person is entitled to be treated in all respects as a person of the acquired gender (see *Chief Constable of Yorkshire v A*[97]).

Discrimination on grounds of gender reassignment (s 16)

4.120 If a person is undergoing treatment for gender reassignment (as defined in s 7), it will be discrimination if he is treated less favourably than he would be treated if he was absent from work because of sickness or injury, or for some other reason, and it would not be reasonable for him to be treated less favourably.

4.121 The anti-discrimination provisions of the Act apply, ie direct discrimination (s 13), indirect discrimination (s 19), harassment (s 26), victimisation (s 27), discrimination or victimisation in employment (s 39) and harassment by employers of employees and job applicants (s 40).

Occupational requirements (Sch 9)

4.122 There is no contravention of the employment provisions if having regard to the nature or context of the work a requirement not to be a transsexual person is an occupational requirement, the requirement is a proportionate means of achieving a legitimate aim, and the person concerned does not meet it.

D. Marriage and civil partnership

4.123 A civil partnership is a relationship that has been entered into by two persons of the same sex that has been registered under the Civil Partnership Act 2004, and for all intents and purposes is to be treated to the same extent as a legal marriage (Civil Partnership Act 2004 (Amendment to Subordinate Legislation) Order 2005, see para 2.102).

Direct discrimination (s 13)

4.124 A person discriminates against another person if because of the protected characteristic of marriage or civil partnership he treats that person less favourably than he would treat another person. It is permissible to discriminate against a single person of either sex, but not in favour of such a person, because that would amount to discrimination against a married person. Thus if a firm were to offer special preferential mortgage facilities to its staff, then if these are made available to married men, they must be made available to

---

[96] [2009] EWCA Civ 22, [2009] 3 All ER 685, [2009] ICR 1170, [2009] IRLR 288.
[97] [2004] ICR 806, (2004) IRLR 573, [2005] AC 51.

married women (*Sun Alliance & London Insurance Co v Dudman*[98]). But it is permissible to exclude a single person of either sex from the scheme, and to discriminate against married and unmarried couples (*Bavin v NHS Trust Pensions Agency*[99]) although this would not apply if the unmarried couple have registered under the Civil Partnership Act 2004. Associative discrimination only applies when the victim is married or a civil partner. Note that it has been held that if an employer treats a woman less favourably not because she is married per se, but because she is married to a particular man then this does not amount to discrimination (*Hawkins v Atex Group Limited*[100]).

4.125 The other anti-discrimination provisions of the Act apply, ie s 19 (indirect discrimination), s 27 (victimisation), s 39 (discrimination or victimisation in employment) and s 40 (harassment).

4.126 Note that harassment under sub-s (1) of s 26 (unwanted conduct) (para 4.32) does not apply to the relevant protected characteristic of marriage and civil partnership, but sub-ss (2) and (3) of s 26 (ie harassment of a sexual nature) do apply, because s 26(1) refers to a 'relevant protected characteristic' whereas sub-ss (2) and (3) do not appear to be so limited.

4.127 There are no occupational requirements exemption for the employment aspects of this protected characteristic other than for the purpose of organised religion (see para 4.164).

E. **Pregnancy and maternity**

4.128 A woman becomes pregnant from the date when she carries a fertilised egg inside her body. If she has had in vitro fertilisation, the earliest point at which pregnancy begins is the date the fertilised ova are implanted into the woman's uterus (*Mayr v Backerei und Konditorei Gerhard Flocker OHG*[101]) at least until the end of the protected period (*Sahota v Home Office*[102]). It has also been suggested that a woman who is an advanced stage of her IVF treatment prior to implantation is also protected from dismissal and/or detriment for that reason by virtue of the Equal Treatment Directive. The pregnancy ceases if she has a miscarriage or abortion, the baby is born prematurely, or she gives birth in the normal manner.

4.129 However, so far as the discrimination provisions are concerned, she will not have the protection from the prohibited conduct of pregnancy unless the employer knows she is pregnant, or unless there are symptoms from which the employer can reasonably suspect she is pregnant (*Ramdoolar v Bycity Ltd*[103]).

4.130 There are a number of other protective legislative provisions that apply to pregnant women and women who have given birth. These include time off work for ante-natal care, risk assessments, suspension on maternity grounds, facilities for breast-feeding, maternity leave, maternity pay, the right to return to work, and written reason for dismissal.

Direct discrimination (s 13)

4.131 A person discriminates against a woman if because of the protected characteristic of pregnancy or maternity he treats her less favourably than he would treat others. More favourable special treatment is, of course, permitted. As already noted, there is no prohibited conduct of indirect discrimination in relation to pregnancy and maternity, as s 18 (para 4.134) provides sufficient protection.

---

[98] [1978] ICR 551, [1978] IRLR 169.   [99] [1999] ICR 1192, [1999] OPLR 285.
[100] UKEAT/0302/11/2A.
[101] [2008] All ER (EC) 613, [2008] ECR I–1017, [2008] 2 CMLR 27, [2008] CEC 549, [2008] IRLR 387, [2008] 1 FLR 1242, [2008] 3 FCR 44, [2008] Fam Law 512, (2008) *Times*, 12 March.
[102] Employment Appeal Tribunal, 15 December 2009.   [103] [2005] ICR 368.

4.132 So if a rule applies equally to men and women, but adversely affected pregnant women, it will be discriminatory. Thus in *Brown v Rentokil Ltd*[104] the employer had a rule which stated that any employee who was absent from work because of sickness for more than 26 weeks would be dismissed. The claimant had a series of pregnancy related-illnesses, and was dismissed after 26 weeks' absence. The European Court held that it was contrary to the Equal Treatment Directive to dismiss a woman at any time for absence due to pregnancy or pregnancy-related illnesses, even though a man absent for that period would have been dismissed.

4.133 However, if the person discriminated against is a man, no account is to be taken of special treatment afforded to a woman in connection with pregnancy or childbirth.

Discrimination at work (s 18)

4.134 A person discriminates against a woman if, in the protected period in relation to a pregnancy of hers, he treats her unfavourably because of her pregnancy or because of an illness suffered by her because of her pregnancy. The protected period begins when the pregnancy begins, and ends:

(a) if she has the right to ordinary and additional maternity leave, at the end of the additional maternity leave period or when she returns to work after the pregnancy if earlier;

(b) if she does not have that right, at the end of two weeks beginning with the end of the pregnancy.

(As already noted, 'unfavourable treatment' in s 18 does not require a comparator).

4.135 A person discriminates against a woman if he treats her unfavourably because she is on compulsory maternity leave or she is exercising or seeking to exercise the right to ordinary or additional maternity leave.

4.136 There are three circumstances to consider:

(a) If a woman is pregnant and applies for or remains in employment, any unfavourable treatment because of her pregnancy would be discrimination. In *Dekker v Stichting Vormingcentrum*[105] a refusal to employ a pregnant woman because of adverse financial consequences that would be suffered by the employer was held by the ECJ to be an act of discrimination. An extreme situation arose in *O'Neill v Governors of St Thomas More School*,[106] where the claimant, who was unmarried, was employed to teach religion at a Roman Catholic school. She was expected to teach the ideologies and ethos of the Catholic faith to her pupils. She then announced that she was pregnant as a result of having an affair with a Roman Catholic priest who used to visit the school, and who was well known locally. She took maternity leave and then announced her intention to return to work. When the school governors refused to permit this she claimed she had been discriminated on grounds of pregnancy. Her claim was upheld by the EAT. The treatment complained of was because of pregnancy and maternity, and the factors that motivated the discriminator were irrelevant.

(b) During the appropriate maternity leave period, the fact that a woman receives different treatment does not necessarily become unlawful, if the treatment is lawful by

---

[104] [1998] All ER (EC) 791, [1998] ECR I–4185, [1998] 2 CMLR 1049, [1998] CEC 829, [1998] ICR 790, [1998] IRLR 445, [1998] 2 FLR 649, [1999] 1 FCR 49, (1999) 48 BMLR 126, [1998] Fam Law 597, (1998) *Times*, 2 July.
[105] [1990] ECR I–3941, [1992] ICR 325, [1991] IRLR 27, (1990) *Times*, 12 December.
[106] [1997] ICR 33, (1996) IRLR 372.

national legislation. Thus in *Gillespie v Northern Ireland Health and Social Services Board*[107] a woman argued that she was entitled to receive full pay during her maternity leave, arguing that it was because of her pregnancy that she was receiving the lower statutory maternity pay. It was held by the ECJ that it was for national legislatures to set the rates of maternity pay, provided this was not so low as to defeat the purpose of maternity leave.

(c) When her leave period ends her special protection ends, and unfavourable treatment will only be unlawful if a man would have been treated more favourably. Thus in *Handelsog (acting on behalf of Larsson) v Dansk Handel & Service*[108] a woman remained absent from work after the conclusion of her maternity leave because of an illness that was caused by her pregnancy. She was dismissed because of her absences, and claimed that she had been discriminated against. It was held by the European Court that, outside the period of maternity leave laid down by national law, a woman has no more protection than a man would have had in respect of absences caused through illness.

4.137 Where a woman is treated unfavourably because of her pregnancy or a pregnancy-related illness, and the decision to treat her in that was taken during the protected period but not implemented until after the end of that period, the treatment is still regarded as occurring during the protected period (s 18(5)).

4.138 The anti-discrimination provisions of the Act apply, ie s 27 (victimisation) discrimination or victimisation in employment (s 39) and harassment by employers of employees and job applicants (s 40). Note that the indirect discrimination provisions of s 19 and harassment under s 26(1) do not apply to the pregnancy and maternity characteristic.

Occupational requirement

4.139 There is no occupational requirement exclusion in respect of pregnancy and maternity, because of the operation of s 18 (see para 4.134). There is no indirect discrimination provision for this protected characteristic, and hence it is not possible to apply a provision, requirement or practice relating to pregnancy or maternity that could be an occupational requirement.

F. Race

4.140 Race includes colour, nationality, ethnic or national origins. A racial group can be made up of two or more different racial groups, eg 'black/British'. Nationality and national origins are separate concepts: the former refers to citizenship, whereas the latter term refers to historical and/geographical features that would at some point in time reveal the existence of a nation. Thus England and Scotland were once separate nations and it was unlawful to discriminate against a person because of his national origins from either country (*BBC Scotland v Souster*[109]). In *Gwynedd County Council v Jones*[110] it was accepted that Welshmen were a distinct ethnic group. The term 'ethnic' is wider than 'race'. In *Mandla v Dowell Lee*[111] it was held that an ethnic group must regard itself as a distinct community by virtue of certain characteristics, including a long shared history, a cultural tradition, and

---

[107] [1996] All ER (EC) 284, [1996] ECR I–475, [1996] 2 CMLR 969, [1996] ICR 498, [1996] IRLR 214, (1996) 31 BMLR 65, (1996) *Times*, 22 February.

[108] [1997] IRLR 643.   [109] 2001 SC 458, [2001] IRLR 150, 2000 GWD 40–1490.

[110] [1986] ICR 833, (1986) 83 LSG 3836.

[111] [1983] 2 AC 548, [1983] 2 WLR 620, [1983] 1 All ER 1062, [1983] ICR 385, [1983] IRLR 209, (1983) 127 SJ 242.

other factors that set them apart from others in the community. Thus Sikhs who are born in the United Kingdom still retain their ethnicity (*Mandla v Dowell Lee*[112]), as do gypsies (*Dawkins v Department of the Environment*[113]). Jews share the characteristics of being an ethnic group (*Seide v Gillette Industries*[114]) and a racial group and religious group (*R (E) v Jewish Free School*[115]).

4.141 The Act confers on a Minister a power to specify that 'caste' shall be an aspect of race, which would bring certain groups from the Indian sub-continent etc within the scope of the Act. It is expected that this could be done by 2015, although an employment tribunal in 2014 has held that caste is included in the definition of race (*Tirkey v Chandok*[116]).

Direct discrimination (s 13)

4.142 A person discriminates against another if because of the protected characteristic of race he treats that person less favourably than he treats others. Less favourable treatment includes segregation (*Pel Ltd v Modgill*[117]), but not congregation (if that is the wishes of all concerned). It is irrelevant that the alleged discriminator has the same religion or belief as the person discriminated against.

4.143 Associative discrimination (see para 4.16) has always been applied in race cases. In *Zarczynska v Levy*[118] a barmaid alleged she was dismissed for refusing to obey an order not to serve coloured persons in a pub, and the EAT held that even though she was personally not discriminated against on grounds of her race, she was entitled to pursue her claim. In *Wilson v TB Steelworks*[119] a white woman was on the point of being offered employment, but when she disclosed that her husband was black, the offer was withdrawn. It was held that this amounted to unlawful discrimination.

4.144 The motive for the discrimination is irrelevant. In *R v Commission for Racial Equality, ex p Westminster City Council*[120] a black man applied for a job as a refuse collector. He was given a temporary appointment, but this was later withdrawn, as it was feared that other workers would take industrial action if his employment was continued. It was held that the Commission for Racial Equality was entitled to issue a non-discrimination notice. For an employer to give in to such threats would frustrate the purpose of the legislation. In *Amnesty International v Ahmed*[121] the claimant was not offered promotion because it was feared that her ethnicity would compromise the employer's impartiality. It was held that the employer's motive, however benign, was irrelevant to establishing direct discrimination on grounds of race.

4.145 The fact that an employee suffers a sense of grievance does not by itself mean that he has been treated less favourably than others, and an employee who, for sound reasons, is treated differently but no less generously than others in a different racial group does not necessarily mean that he has suffered a detriment (*Barclays Bank Ltd v Kapur*[122]).

4.146 To adopt a screening policy, whereby members of a particular racial group are eliminated from consideration for employment is discrimination, even though the

---

[112] See n 111.

[113] [1993] ICR 517, [1993] IRLR 284, (1993) *Times*, 4 February, (1993) *Independent*, 12 February, (1993) *Guardian*, 1 February.

[114] [1980] IRLR 427.   [115] [2010] IRLR 136, (2010) 1 All ER 319.

[116] Unreported, case number 3400174/2013.   [117] [1980] IRLR 142.

[118] [1979] 1 WLR 125, [1979] 1 All ER 814, [1979] ICR 184, [1978] IRLR 532, (1978) 122 SJ 776.

[119] IDS Brief 150.   [120] [1985] ICR 827, [1985] IRLR 426.

[121] [2009] ICR 1450, [2009] IRLR 884, (2009) 159 NLJ 1400, (2009) *Times*, 6 October.

[122] [1991] 2 AC 355, [1991] 2 WLR 401, [1991] 1 All ER 646, [1991] ICR 208, [1991] IRLR 136, (1991) *Times*, 25 January, (1991) *Independent*, 6 February, (1991) *Financial Times*, 30 January, (1991) *Guardian*, 31 January, (1991) *Daily Telegraph*, 7 February.

discriminator is unaware of whether a particular job applicant is a member of that group (*Simon v Brimham Associates*[123]). However, it is permissible to request, as part of the employment arrangements, that the job applicant produces evidence of his right to work in the United Kingdom (*Dhatt v McDonald's Hamburgers Ltd*[124]).

4.147 Discrimination on grounds of birth, nationality, descent or residence is permitted for employment with certain civil service posts and other public bodies (the Race Relations (Prescribed Public Bodies) Regulations 1994 are likely to be replicated).

Indirect discrimination (s 19)

4.148 A person discriminates against a person who has the protected characteristic of race if he applies a provision, criterion or practice which is discriminatory of that person, puts him at a disadvantage, and cannot be shown to be a proportionate means of achieving a legitimate aim.

4.149 To determine whether or not the provision, criterion or practice is proportionate, the employment tribunal should decide (a) whether the objective was legitimate, (b) whether the means used to achieve that objective were reasonable, and (c) were those means justified when balanced between the discriminatory effect upon the claimant's racial group and the needs of those applying the provision, criterion or practice (*St Matthias Church of England School v Crizzle*[125]). In *Panesar v Nestle & Co Ltd*[126] a chocolate factory had a rule that prohibited employees wearing beards and long hair. This was indirectly discriminatory against the claimant, who was a Sikh, but the Court of Appeal held that the condition was justified in the interests of hygiene and safety.

4.150 Section 23 of the Act provides that on a comparison of cases for the purpose of ss 14 and 19 there must be no material difference between the circumstances relating to each case. In *Wakeman v Quick Corpn*,[127] Japanese managers, who were seconded from Japan to work in England, were paid more than locally recruited managers. It was held that the higher rate of pay was attributed to their status as secondees. As such their circumstances were materially different from those of the claimant, who was English, so no proper comparison could be made between them.

4.151 The other anti-discrimination provisions of the Act apply to the protected characteristic of race, ie s 26 (harassment), s 27 (victimisation), s 39 (discrimination and victimisation in employment) and s 40 (harassment by employers of employees and job applicants).

Occupational requirement (Sch 9)

4.152 There is no contravention of the employment provisions if having regard to the nature or context of the work a requirement to be or not to be of a particular race is an occupational requirement, the requirement is a proportionate means of achieving a legitimate aim, and the person concerned does not meet it.

4.153 It is possible that the provision of personal service promoting the welfare of a racial group may, in particular cases, amount to an occupational requirement on racial grounds (*Tottenham Green Under Fives' Centre v Marshall*[128]), but in *Lambeth London Borough Council v Commission for Racial Equality*[129] the Court of Appeal refused to uphold the decision of a local authority to confine applications for the vacant posts in their housing

---

[123] [1987] ICR 596, [1987] IRLR 307.
[124] [1991] 1 WLR 527, [1991] 3 All ER 692, [1991] ICR 238, [1991] IRLR 130, (1990) *Times*, 13 November.
[125] [1993] ICR 401, [1993] IRLR 472, (1993) *Times*, 26 February, (1993) *Independent*, 4 March.
[126] [1980] ICR 144, [1980] IRLR 64.   [127] [1999] IRLR 424.
[128] [1991] ICR 320, (1991) IRLR 162.   [129] [1990] ICR 768, [1990] IRLR 231.

benefits department to applicants from the Afro-Caribbean or Asian communities, because the jobs were basically managerial in nature, and did not involve the provision of personal services promoting the welfare of a particular racial group.

G. **Religion or belief**

4.154 Religion means any religion, and belief means any religious or philosophical belief. A lack of belief (eg atheism, humanism etc) is also covered. As well as the more obvious religions that are within the definition (Christianity, Judaism, Islamism, Hinduism, etc), it is thought that the provisions apply to other religions, such as Baha'i, Buddhism, Rastafarianism, Scientology, Zoroastrianism, etc.

4.155 Philosophical beliefs are more difficult to define. In *Grainger Ltd v Nicholson*[130] the EAT stated that a philosophical belief (a) must be genuinely held, (b) it must be a belief and not an opinion or viewpoint based on the present state of information available, (c) it must be a belief as to a weighty and substantial aspect of human life and behaviour, (d) it must attain a certain level of cogency, seriousness, cohesion, and importance, and (e) it must be worthy of respect in a democratic society, be not incompatible with human dignity and not in conflict with the fundamental rights of others. Thus the belief must be more than an opinion based on perceived logic or information. It is thought that political beliefs, such as communism, socialism etc are not within the protection of the Act (see *Baggs v Fudge*[131]), but it will be for the employment tribunal to draw parameters on what does or does not constitute philosophical beliefs. The Guidance to the Act states that Darwinism is not within the provisions, but this must be considered to be doubtful. In *Grainger plc v Nicholson*[132] it was held that a belief that climate change was man-made was, if genuinely held, a philosophical belief for the purpose of the Religion and Belief Regulations. It was further suggested that while support for a political party would not come within the regulations, belief based on a political philosophy, such as Marxism, communism etc could be. The EAT has also held that a belief in spirituality could be regarded as a religious belief (*Power v Greater Manchester Police Authority*[133]). The regulations would not protect a racist or homophobic political philosophy, because such beliefs would not be worthy of respect in a democratic society, and would therefore offend against Art 9 of the European Convention on Human Rights.

4.156 A person still has the protection of the Act where they have a sincere belief about something, even if it is not a core component of the particular faith – *Mba v The Mayor & Burgesses of the London Borough of Merton*.[134] On the facts of this case, however it was proportionate for Ms Mba to be required to work on a Sunday.

4.157 In some cases, there is a conflict between the religion of the employee, and the requirements of the employer. The European Court of Human Rights jointly heard the four cases of *Eweide, Ladele, Chaplin and Macfarlane v UK*,[135] all of whom were committed Christians. The court found in favour of Ms Eweida but not of the other applicants. In *Eweida*, an employee of BA was not permitted to wear a visible cross with her uniform. The domestic courts were found to have accorded too much weight to the employer's wish to project a certain image, and there was no evidence of any real encroachment on the interests of others. Ms Eweida's cross was discreet and cannot have detracted from her personal appearance. In the case of *Chaplin*, however, the court emphasised that the

[130] [2010] 2 All ER 253, [2010] ICR 360, [2010] IRLR 4, (2009) 159 NLJ 1582, (2009) *Times*, 11 November.
[131] 1400114/05/ET.   [132] n 130.   [133] EAT/0087/10.
[134] [2013] EWCA Civ 1562.   [135] (Application nos 48420/10, 59842/10, 51671/10 and 36516/10).

reason for asking her to remove the cross, namely the protection of health and safety on a hospital ward, was inherently of a greater magnitude than that which applied in respect of Ms Eweida. Moreover, this is a field where the domestic authorities must be allowed a wide margin of appreciation. The hospital managers were better placed to make decisions about clinical safety than a court. For *Ladele* (a registrar who refused to perform civil partnerships for homosexuals) and *Macfarlane* (a counsellor who did not want to treat gay couples) the aim pursued by the local authority, which was to secure the rights of others and provide a service without discrimination, was legitimate. The court generally allows the national authorities a wide margin of appreciation when it comes to striking a balance between competing Convention rights and here they did not exceed that margin (see also the non-employment case of *Bull & Bull v Hall & Preddy*[136] where the Supreme Court decided a similar point). Following this judgment, the Equality and Human Rights Commission provided further guidance on religion and equality in the workplace.

4.158 On a slightly different point, in *Apelogun-Gabriels v London Borough of Lambeth*[137] the claimant was a committed Christian who distributed quotations from the Bible that condemned homosexuality to his work colleagues. He was dismissed, and he claimed religious discrimination. It was held that his dismissal was because he distributed homophobic materials, and was not because of his religious beliefs. If an employee is seeking to promote a religion or belief contrary to instructions, his dismissal is not because of his religion or belief, but his actions in disobeying a lawful order from his employer (*Chondol v Liverpool City Council*[138]).

4.159 The employer must know or be aware of the religious or philosophical belief of the claimant, otherwise it cannot be claimed that there has been an act of discrimination. In *McClintock v Department of Constitutional Affairs*[139] it was held that it would be absurd if an employer was to be held liable for religious discrimination when the employee had not made known his religious beliefs.

Direct discrimination (s 13)

4.160 A person discriminates against another if because of the protected characteristic of religion or belief he treats that person less favourably than he treats others. It is irrelevant that the discriminator has the same religion or belief as the person discriminated against. It did not constitute direct discrimination on grounds of religion for a local authority to require a female Muslim teacher to remove her full face veil while teaching her class. Another woman teacher, whether Muslim or not, who wore a veil for a reason other than her religious belief would have received the same treatment from her employer and hence there was no direct discrimination (*Azmi v Kirklees Metropolitan Borough Council*[140]).

Indirect discrimination (s 19)

4.161 A person discriminates against a person who has the protected characteristic of religion or belief if he applies a provision, criterion or practice that is discriminatory of that person, puts him at a disadvantage, and cannot be shown to be a proportionate means of achieving a legitimate aim. In *Azmi v Kirklees Metropolitan Borough Council*[141] it was held that there was no indirect discrimination, as the requirement was a proportionate means of achieving a legitimate aim. It is possible that the application of a dress code that adversely affected persons of certain religions may amount to indirect discrimination that would have to be justified, depending on the circumstances.

---

[136] [2013] UKSC 73. [137] [2001] EWCA Civ 1853, [2002] ICR 713, [2002] IRLR 116.
[138] Employment Appeal Tribunal, 11 February 2009. [139] [2008] IRLR 29, (2007) *Times*, 5 December.
[140] [2007] ICR 1154, [2007] IRLR 484, [2007] ELR 339, (2007) *Times*, 17 April. [141] See n 140.

4.162 The other anti-discrimination provisions of the Act apply, ie s 26 (harassment), s 27 (victimisation), s 39 (discrimination and victimisation in employment) and s 40 (harassment by third parties).

Exception for occupational requirement (Equality Act, Sch 9)

4.163 Certain provisions of the Act do not apply if it can be shown that the employment is for the purposes of organised religion, the post is an occupational requirement, and the application of the requirement is a proportionate means of complying with the doctrines of that religion. The requirement must arise because of the nature or context of the work, and must engage the compliance principle, ie it is applied so as to comply with the doctrines of the religion, or the non-conflict principle, ie to avoid conflicting with the strongly held religious convictions of a significant number of the religion's followers and the person to whom the requirement is applied does not meet it. The exceptions are s 39(1)(a) (arrangements for determining employment), s 39(1)(c) (refusing to offer employment), s 39(2)(b) (access to promotion etc) and s 39(2)(c) (dismissal). The requirement can be to be of a particular sex, or not to be a transsexual person, or not to be married or a civil partner, or not to be married to, or a civil partner of, a person who has a living former spouse, or relating to the circumstances in which a marriage or civil partnership came to an end, or a requirement related to sexual orientation.

4.164 The exceptions apply for purposes of organised religion. There is also a general exception from the employment provisions where a person with an ethos based on religion does not contravene the provisions in s 39 by applying in relation to work a requirement to be of a particular religion or belief, and it can be shown that having regard to that ethos and to the nature of the work, it is an occupational requirement, the application of which is a proportionate means of achieving a legitimate aim, and the person to whom it is applied does not meet it. Thus the nature of the work may involve leading or assisting in the observance of liturgical or ritualistic practices of the religion, or promoting the doctrine of the religion. However, the application of the requirement to be of a particular religion must be a proportionate means of achieving a legitimate aim. In *Glasgow City Council v McNab*[142] an atheist teacher was not interviewed for the post of acting principal teacher of pastoral care at a local authority maintained school. The EAT upheld a decision that he had been discriminated against on grounds of his beliefs. The job of pastoral care did not require that the holder be a Roman Catholic, and it was not proportionate to apply such a requirement. Consequently the defence of occupational requirement failed.

4.165 However, under s 124A of the Schools Standard Framework Act 1998, designated independent schools are permitted to give preference in the appointment, promotion and remuneration of persons whose religious opinions are in accordance with the tenets of the school.

H. Sex

4.166 This refers to the biological state of being a man or a woman.

Direct discrimination (s 13)

4.167 A person discriminates against another if because of the protected characteristic of sex he treats that person less favourably than he treats others.

4.168 The motive for the discriminator's action is irrelevant. In *Grieg v Community Industry*[143] the claimant and another woman were appointed to two jobs, which involved

---

[142] [2007] IRLR 476.   [143] [1979] ICR 356, [1979] IRLR 158.

working with men. The other woman failed to turn up for work, and so the claimant was not allowed to start work, as in the past there had been problems with one woman working alone with men. It was held that this constituted direct discrimination; the motive of the employers was irrelevant. This is so even though the action taken was well-intentioned, and for the protection of an employee (see *Ahmed v Amnesty International*,[144] para 4.144).

4.169 To establish direct discrimination, an employment tribunal should first identify an actual comparator, and then compare the treatment of the claimant with that afforded to a person of the other sex. The actual comparator's situation should be, in all material respects, identical to the claimant's. Where there is no actual comparator, the employment tribunal must create a hypothetical comparator, which can be done by carefully drawing inferences from all the available evidence (*Shamoon v Chief Constable of the Royal Ulster Constabulary*[145]).

4.170 It will amount to discrimination if persons from one sex are given preferential treatment in terms of recruitment or promotion etc, in order to redress an imbalance of the sexes, but this does not prevent positive action in appropriate circumstances (see para 4.204). An employer does not unlawfully discriminate against a woman if he fails to treat her more favourably than a man (*Kenny v Ministry of Defence*[146]).

Indirect discrimination (s 19)

4.171 An employer discriminates against a person who has the protected characteristic of sex if he applies a provision, criterion or practice that is discriminatory of that person, puts him/her at a disadvantage, and cannot be shown to be a proportionate means of achieving a legitimate aim.

4.172 An important distinction between direct and indirect discrimination is that so far as direct discrimination is concerned, there is no defence of justification, whereas in indirect discrimination, justification may be raised as a defence if it is a proportionate means of achieving a legitimate end. It is for the employment tribunal to determine where the provision, criterion or practice at issue is reasonably necessary (*Hardys & Hanson plc v Lax*[147]). There must be a real need for the provision etc, and it must be appropriate and reasonably necessary (*Network Rail Infrastructures Ltd v Gammie*[148]).

4.173 Thus a provision that requires a woman to work overtime, or a refusal to permit her to return to work on a part-time basis (*Home Office v Holmes*[149]) or a refusal to permit her to work from home where this is feasible (*Lockwood v Crawley Warren Group Ltd*[150]) could all amount to a provision that puts her at a disadvantage (eg because of childminding difficulties) that would amount to indirect discrimination unless the provision etc is a proportionate means of achieving a legitimate aim. In *London Underground Ltd v Edwards*[151] the claimant was employed as a train driver, generally working from 8.00am until 4.00pm. As part of a cost-saving plan, the employer introduced a new system, which required her to commence work at 4.45am. As a single mother with a young child, she was not prepared to work the new system, and she resigned claiming indirect discrimination. The EAT held that the employment tribunal was entitled to

---

[144] See n 121.

[145] [2003] ICR 337, [2003] IRLR 285.

[146] Unreported.

[147] [2005] EWCA Civ 846, [2005] ICR 1565, [2005] IRLR 726, (2005) 102(29) LSG 31, (2005) *Times*, 26 July.

[148] Employment Appeal Tribunal (Scotland), 6 March 2009.

[149] [1985] 1 WLR 71, [1984] 3 All ER 549, [1984] ICR 678, [1984] IRLR 299, (1984) 81 LSG 2463, (1984) 128 SJ 645.

[150] [2001] Emp LR 322.

[151] [1999] ICR 494, [1998] IRLR 364, (1998) 95(26) LSG 32, (1998) 148 NLJ 905, (1998) 142 SJLB 182, (1998) *Times*, 1 June, (1998) *Independent*, 5 June.

take into account their common knowledge that a proportionately larger number of women had childcare responsibilities than men, and, having regard to her length of service (10 years) and the fact that the demands of her family would be less in the future, the employer should have made arrangements to accommodate her personal requirements.

4.174 But it is possible to show that the application of the provision is proportionate and that the aim is legitimate. In *Briggs v North Eastern Education and Library Board*[152] the Northern Ireland Court of Appeal took the view that a contractual provision that was imposed on a school teacher that she should assist in the taking of games outside school hours was a requirement which was justified irrespective of sex or age or marital status etc. A balance must be drawn between the discriminatory effect of the provision and the reasonable needs of the employer, objectively determined (see also *Bilka-Kaufhaus v Weber von Hartz*[153]). Further economic factors, such as cost, can be weighed in the balance in assessing proportionality (*Cross v British Airways*[154]).

4.175 A person may discriminate (directly or indirectly) even though he is unaware that he is doing so. This may happen because of an inbuilt prejudice or the making of a stereotype assumption that a man is the 'breadwinner' of the family (*Skyrail Oceanic v Coleman*[155]). In *Gubala v Crompton Parkinson*[156] the choice of dismissal in a redundancy situation lay between a man and a woman. The woman had longer overall service, but the employers took into account the fact that the man was 58 years old, and had a family to support and a mortgage to keep up. The woman was young, married, with a husband who was working, and she was therefore dismissed for reason of redundancy. It was held that this amounted to unlawful discrimination; the tribunal refused to accept the 'breadwinner' criteria as a basis for redundancy selection.

4.176 On the other hand, it does not depend on whether the recipient thinks that the treatment is less favourable, for the test is an objective one for the employment tribunal to determine (*Burrett v West Birmingham Health Authority*[157]). Thus it has been held that a code governing the appearance of male and female employees, which was even-handed in its approach, was not discriminatory on grounds of sex. There is a distinction between discrimination between the sexes (which may be permissible) and discrimination against one or another of the sexes, which is not permitted (*Smith v Safeway plc*[158]).

Discrimination in employment (s 39)

4.177 We have already noted (para 4.45) the general provisions dealing with the employment or non-employment of persons with a protected characteristic. Thus to refuse to employ a woman because 'it is a man's job' is an example of direct discrimination (*Batisha v Say*[159]), but if the unfavourable treatment has nothing to do with the sex of the person concerned, there is no direct discrimination (*Moberly v Commonwealth Hall (University of London)*[160]).

4.178 A comparison of the cases of persons of different sex must be such that the relevant circumstances in the one case are the same, or not materially different, in the other. Thus in *Thorn v Meggitt Engineering Ltd*[161] a woman was refused employment as a radial driller because she was neither tall enough not strong enough, and it was held that no

---

[152] [1990] IRLR 181.   [153] [1986] ECR 1607, [1986] 2 CMLR 701, [1987] ICR 110, [1986] IRLR 317.
[154] [2006] EWCA Civ 549, [2006] ICR 1239, [2006] IRLR 804, [2006] Pens LR 155, (2006) 103(21) LSG 24, (2006) *Times*, 5 June, (2006) *Independent*, 18 May.
[155] [1981] ICR 864, [1981] IRLR 398, (1981) *Times*, 28 July.   [156] [1977] IRLR 10.
[157] [1994] IRLR 7.   [158] See n 7.   [159] [1977] IRLIB, [1977] IRLR 6.
[160] [1977] ICR 791, [1977] IRLR 176.   [161] [1976] IRLR 241.

direct discrimination had occurred. The reason for the treatment meted out had nothing to do with that characteristic. In *Steere v Morris Bros*[162] a woman applied for a job as a heavy goods vehicle driver. When she was refused employment she claimed that she had been discriminated against. However, the employers were able to show that the reason she was not offered the job was because she lived too far away from the place of employment. The reason for her non-appointment had nothing to do with her sex, and no comparative person was involved.

4.179 Direct discrimination, however well intentioned, is not capable of being justified. In *Moyhing v Barts & London NHS Trust*[163] the claimant was a male student nurse who was required to be chaperoned when carrying out an electrocardiogram procedure on female patients. This was because it was inevitable that he would be touching the patient's breasts, and the policy was felt to be necessary in order to avoid the risks of claims of assault upon female patients and/or false accusations of assault against male nurses. The claimant claimed that this policy treated him as a second class person, and demonstrated a widespread assumption that female nurses were automatically suited to provide personal care and that it was inappropriate for male nurses to provide intimate care for female patients. The EAT agreed that the claimant had suffered a detriment. That there were good and objective reasons for the policy was no defence, because there was no legal basis for treating male and female nurses differently so as to cause a detriment.

4.180 Provisions in an offer of employment or in the terms of employment which relate to pay are excluded from ss 13 and 39, because these are otherwise dealt with in ss 64–79, which replicate the equal pay provisions.

4.181 There is clearly an overlap with the characteristic of sex, and marriage and pregnancy, which could give rise to dual discrimination claims. Thus to refuse to promote a woman because she is married to a work colleague would be indirect discrimination on grounds of sex as well as being direct and indirect discrimination on grounds of marital status (*Chief Constable of Bedfordshire Constabulary v Graham*[164]). On the other hand, a dress code that differentiates between the requirements for men and for women is not discriminatory on grounds of sex provided it is applied in an even-handed manner (*Smith v Safeways plc*[165]).

4.182 The provisions of s 27 (victimisation) and s 40 (harassment) apply to the protected characteristic of sex.

Occupational requirement (Sch 9)

4.183 There is no contravention of the employment provisions in s 37 if having regard to the nature or context of the work a requirement to be or not to be of a particular sex is an occupational requirement, the requirement is a proportionate means of achieving a legitimate aim, and the person concerned does not meet it.

4.184 The Guidance Notes state that the occupational requirement must be crucial to the post, and not merely one of several important factors. There is a heavy burden of proof on those who seek to rely on an occupational requirement. Examples of occupational requirements that may still apply are:

(a) the job calls for authentic male or female characteristics (eg in a play or film);

(b) there are considerations of decency or privacy (eg public changing rooms, see eg *Etam plc v Rowan*;[166] *Sisley v Britannia Security Systems Ltd*[167]);

---

[162] IDS Handbook.   [163] [2006] IRLR 860.   [164] [2002] IRLR 239, [2002] Emp LR 752.
[165] See n 7.   [166] [1989] IRLR 150.   [167] [1983] ICR 628, [1983] IRLR 404.

(c) the job involves living in a private home where a person of one sex might object to the presence of a person of the other sex;

(d) the job involves living in accommodation where there are no separate sleeping facilities (see Sch 23);

(e) the job needs to be held by a man because it is likely to be performed in a country whose laws or customs are such that the duties could not be performed by a woman (but see *O'Conner v Kontiki Travel*[168] for evidential requirements);

(f) there may be religious or strongly held cultural objections to the job being done by a person of one sex.

I. Sexual orientation

4.185 This means a person's sexual orientation to persons of the same sex (ie a homosexual or lesbian), persons of the opposite sex (ie a heterosexual), or persons of either sex (ie a bisexual). It does not cover particular sexual practices or fetishes, eg sado-masochism or paedophile activities etc.

4.186 The provisions on direct discrimination (s 13), indirect discrimination (s 19), harassment (s 26), victimisation (s 27), discrimination or victimisation in employment (s 39) and harassment by employer (s 40) apply.

4.187 Indirect discrimination may occur when a provision, criterion or practice is applied that puts a person of a particular sexual orientation at a disadvantage when compared with others. For example, to advertise a job as being suitable for a married couple would be indirectly discriminatory of homosexual partners, since they cannot legally marry. Technically speaking, a civil partnership is not a marriage, although in effect it is to be treated as such.

4.188 So far as harassment is concerned it is the objective nature of the alleged harassment itself that is determinative, not the circumstances of the victim. Thus to subject a person to homophobic abuse, even though it is known to the harassers the victim was not a homosexual, can still amount to harassment. Such abuse is on grounds of sexual orientation, it amounts to unwanted conduct, has the effect of violating the victim's dignity or creating a degrading, humiliating or offensive environment, and should reasonably be considered to have that effect (*English v Thomas Sanderson Blinds Ltd*[169]). To harass a person because of his/her association with another who has the protected characteristic is also covered. On the other hand, a gay employee who had disclosed his sexual orientation in a previous job could not complain of discrimination when the manager in his new job, without any discriminatory purpose, revealed his sexual orientation to colleagues against his wishes. He may have been upset that he could not release the information in his own way, but that did not constitute harassment (*Grant v HM Land Registry*).[170]

Occupational requirements (Sch 9)

4.189 So far as s 39 (discrimination in employment) is concerned, there may be two occupational requirements. The first is where the nature of the employment is such that a particular sexual orientation is a proportionate means of achieving a legitimate aim, and the person concerned does not meet that requirement. The second applies to employment for the purposes of an organised religion, and there is a requirement as to sexual orientation in

---

[168] IDS Brief no 98.

[169] [2008] EWCA Civ 1421, [2009] 2 All ER 468, [2009] 2 CMLR 18, [2009] ICR 543, [2009] IRLR 206, (2009) 153(1) SJLB 31, (2009) *Times*, 5 January.

[170] [2011] IRLR 748, CA, [2011] EWCA Civ 769.

order to comply with the doctrines of the religion, or to avoid conflicting with the religious convictions of a significant number of the religions followers. Again, there is a heavy burden of proof on those who seek to rely on this exception.

Common provisions

4.190 A number of provisions in the Equality Act are common to all of the protected characteristics.

A. **Application of the Act**

4.191 The employment provisions of the Equality Act apply in respect of persons who are employed. 'Employment' for the purpose of the Act means employment under a contract of service or apprenticeship or a contract personally to do work (s 83). Thus self-employed persons are included in the definition (see *Allonby v Accrington and Rossendale College*[171]), but not volunteer workers (*X v Mid-Sussex CAB*[172]). The dominant purpose of the contract must be to carry out the work personally. Personal responsibility is not, by itself, sufficient (*Mirror Group Newspapers Ltd v Gunning*[173]). Nor is an option to carry out the work personally (*Inland Revenue Commissioners v Post Office Ltd*[174]). There must be a personal obligation to perform the work or labour, and that performance must be the dominant purpose of the contract (*Mingeley v Pennock and Ivory*[175]). But the fact that a contract permits the provision of a substitute worker does not take that contract outside the provisions as long as the right to provide a replacement is limited in some way (*Byrne Brothers (Formwork) Ltd v Baird*[176]). A blanket right to provide a substitute is unlikely to meet the requirement of personal service (*Hawkins v Darken*[177]).

4.192 The Act is silent on territorial jurisdiction (unlike such provisions formerly found in the various anti-discrimination regulations) and it is left to the employment tribunals to determine whether the law applies in any particular case, which will depend on how close is the connection between the employment relationship and Great Britain. Certain principles can be gleaned from the decision in *Lawson v Serco Ltd*,[178] and other such cases (see para 1.32). In *British Airways plc v Mak*, a case decided on previous discrimination legislation, the Court of Appeal ruled that cabin crew based in Hong Kong and who worked on flights between there and London were to be regarded as doing their work 'partly in Great Britain', which meant that their employment was to be treated as being at an 'establishment' in Great Britain, even though they did not actually work at an 'establishment' at all.[179]

4.193 The Act also applies to Crown employment, employment as a relevant member of the staff of the House of Commons and House of Lords, and service in the armed forces.

---

[171] [2005] All ER (EC) 289, [2004] ECR I–873, [2004] 1 CMLR 35, [2004] ICR 1328, [2004] IRLR 224, [2004] OPLR 83, [2004] Pens LR 199.
[172] [2012] UKSC 59.
[173] [1986] 1 WLR 546, [1986] 1 All ER 385, [1986] ICR 145, [1986] IRLR 27, (1986) 136 NLJ 967, (1985) 130 SJ 242.
[174] [2003] ICR 546, (2003) IRLR 199.
[175] [2004] EWCA Civ 328, [2004] ICR 727, [2004] IRLR 373, (2004) 101(11) LSG 33, (2004) *Times*, 4 March.
[176] [2002] ICR 667, [2002] IRLR 96, [2002] Emp LR 567.   [177] [2004] EWCA Civ 1755.
[178] [2006] UKHL 3, [2006] 1 All ER 823, [2006] ICR 250, [2006] IRLR 289, (2006) 103(6) LSG 36, (2006) 156 NLJ 184, (2006) 150 SJLB 131, (2006) *Times*, 27 January.
[179] [2011] EWCA Civ 184.

Offshore workers (who work on oil and gas rigs, and renewable energy installations) will be covered by an order in council.

B. **Lawful discrimination (Sch 22)**

4.194 There is no discrimination of a person with the protected characteristics if action is taken to comply with an enactment. Thus, it is permissible to refuse to sell alcohol or cigarettes to a person under the age of 18, a disabled person may be fairly dismissed if it is necessary to comply with health or safety requirements (see *Farmiloe v Lane Group plc*,[180] para 4.102), special treatment may be given on grounds of pregnancy or maternity, health and safety legislation passed for the special protection of women, certain educational appointments may be restricted to persons of a particular religion, there are lawful restrictions on the appointment of foreign nationals to certain posts in the security and intelligence services, and so on.

C. **Illegal contracts**

4.195 The fact that a person is employed under a contract of employment that is tainted with illegality will not necessarily exclude the operation of the anti-discrimination provisions of the Act (*Hall v Woolston Hall Leisure Centre*[181]). If a claimant is seeking to enforce a contract of employment that is tainted with illegality, it will probably be unenforceable, but if the remedy sought does not involve relying on the illegal contract, eg a claim of race or sex discrimination, the illegality is no bar to the claim (see para 3.8).

D. **Relationships that have ended (s 108)**

4.196 A person must not discriminate against another if the discrimination arises out of or is closely connected to the relationship that used to exist between them, and the conduct is of a description that would have contravened the Act if it had occurred during the relationship. This provision may have implications, for example, in respect of a refusal to give a reference (see *Rhys-Harper v Relaxation Group plc*[182]). Similarly, a person must not harass another if the harassment arises out of and is closely connected to a relationship that used to exist between them and the conduct would have contravened the Act had it occurred during the relationship.

4.197 Discrimination and harassment that takes place during an appeal against a dismissal (when technically the employee is no longer employed, see *J Sainsbury Ltd v Savage*[183]) or in the giving of a reference (*D'Souza v London Borough of Lambeth*[184]) is thus actionable in respect of all of the protected characteristics.

E. **Liability of employers (s 109)**

4.198 Anything done by an employee in the course of his employment must be treated as also done by the employer, and it does not matter whether the thing is done with the employer's knowledge or approval. The phrase 'in the course of employment' has to be

---

[180] [2004] PIQR P22.

[181] [2001] 1 WLR 225, [2000] 4 All ER 787, [2001] ICR 99, [2000] IRLR 578, (2000) 97(24) LSG 39, (2000) 150 NLJ 833, (2000) *Times*, 31 May, (2000) *Independent*, 8 June.

[182] [2003] UKHL 33, [2003] 4 All ER 1113, [2003] 2 CMLR 44, [2003] ICR 867, [2003] IRLR 484, (2003) 74 BMLR 109, (2003) 100(30) LSG 30, (2003) 147 SJLB 782, (2003) *Times*, 23 June, (2003) *Independent*, 24 June.

[183] [1981] ICR 1, [1980] IRLR 109.   [184] [2003] ICR 867, (2003) IRLR 484.

construed by an employment tribunal in a layman's sense, as a question of fact (*Jones v Tower Boot Co Ltd*[185]). However, it will be a defence for the employer to show that he took all reasonable steps to prevent that person from doing the thing or from doing anything of that description. Thus if the employer can show, for example, that he had given proper training to his employees to prevent discrimination and harassment, published an equal opportunities policy and was unaware that unlawful acts were being done, he may be able to successfully raise the defence. For example, in *Tower Hamlets v Balgobin*[186] the EAT commented that it was difficult to see what steps could have been taken by an employer to prevent harassment from occurring. The employment tribunal must consider whether the employer took any steps at all to prevent an employee from committing an act of discrimination, and then consider what further steps could have been taken which were reasonably practicable (*Canniffe v East Ridings of Yorkshire Council*[187]). In *Martins v Marks & Spencer plc*,[188] the Court of Appeal considered the firm's equal opportunity policy, their compliance with the Code of Practice on selection procedures, criteria and interviewing, and the inclusion on the interviewing panel of a person with an interest in recruiting from ethnic minorities, and held that in the circumstances the employers had made out a defence.

4.199 But s 109 does not exonerate the individual employee from liability and proceedings may be taken against the latter for a contravention of the Act by virtue of s 110, although there would be no contravention if the employee relied on a statement by his employer that what he did was not a contravention of the Act and it was reasonable for him to rely on that statement.

4.200 A discrimination claim can therefore be made against the individual discriminator as well as the employer, and compensation can be awarded on the basis of joint and several liability (*London Borough of Hackney v Sivanandan*).[189]

F. Instructing, causing or inducing discrimination (s 111)

4.201 A person must not instruct, cause or induce (directly or indirectly) another person to do anything with respect to a third person that would contravene s 39 (discrimination in employment, see eg, para 4.45) or s 108 (relationships that have ended, see para 4.196) or s 112 (aiding a contravention, see para 4.203). A refusal to follow an instruction to discriminate on a prohibited ground was held to be unlawful discrimination in *Weathersfield Ltd v Sargent*.[190]

4.202 Proceeding for a contravention of s 111 may be brought by:

(a) the person to whom the instruction or inducement was given, if he is subjected to a detriment as a result of the instruction or inducement;

(b) the person against whom the instruction or inducement was directed if he suffers a detriment as a result of the instruction or inducement (even though the instruction is not carried out);

(c) the Equality and Human Rights Commission (see eg *Commission for Racial Equality v Imperial Society for Teachers of Dancing*[191]).

---

[185] [1997] IRLR 168, (1997) ICR 254.   [186] [1987] ICR 829, [1987] IRLR 401, (1987) 84 LSG 2530.
[187] [2000] IRLR 555.   [188] [1998] ICR 1005, [1998] IRLR 326, (1998) *Times*, 15 January.
[189] [2011] IRLR 740.
[190] [1999] ICR 425, [1999] IRLR 94, [1999] Disc LR 290, (1999) 96(5) LSG 35, (1999) 143 SJLB 39, (1998) *Times*, 31 December.
[191] [1983] ICR 473, [1983] IRLR 315.

G. Aiding contraventions (s 112)

4.203 A person must not knowingly help another person to do anything that contravenes s 39 (discrimination in employment, see eg para 4.47) or s 108 relationships that have ended, see para 4.196) or s 111 (instructing, causing or inducing discrimination, see earlier). The help must be substantial or productive, but not so insignificant as to be negligible (*Anyanwu v South Bank Students' Union*[192]). A general attitude of helpfulness by the alleged aider is not enough to establish liability (*Hallam v Avery*[193]). There is no contravention of s 112 if the person who is asked to help relies on a statement that the act for which the help is asked does not contravene the Act, and it is reasonable for him to do so.

H. Positive action; recruitment and promotion (s 159)

4.204 An employer is permitted to take the protected characteristics into consideration when deciding whether to recruit or promote persons with that characteristic because they are under-represented in the workforce. But such positive action will only apply when the candidates for recruitment or promotion are equally qualified (*Abrahamsson and Anderson v Fogelqvist*[194]). 'Qualification' does not refer to academic achievements, but work experience, skills, and other competences can be taken into consideration. The action in question must be a proportionate means of achieving the aims of overcoming any disadvantage associated with the characteristic or enabling such disadvantaged persons to participate in an activity. A target scheme for recruitment, selection and promotion is not precluded by EC law if the scheme does not ensure that persons with the protected characteristic were automatically and unconditionally offered preferential treatment over those who do not share that characteristic (*Badeck v Hessischer*[195]). Thus positive discrimination is unlawful but positive action may be encouraged (*EFTA Surveillance Authority v Kingdom of Norway*[196]). More favourable treatment of those with the protected characteristic is not permitted, other than as permitted by the Act (eg on grounds of pregnancy and maternity). It seems likely that s 159 will not be brought into force in the near future, and hence case law decided by the European Court will be more relevant to this topic.

I. Discriminatory advertisements

4.205 The European Court has ruled that a discriminatory advertisement was direct discrimination even though there is no identifiable complainant. In *Centrum voor gelijkheid van kansen v Firma Feryn*[197] the employer was a company that specialised in installing security gates. A director of the company publicly stated that he would not employ immigrants because of the reluctance of customers to give such persons access to their homes during installation work. It was held that this constituted race discrimination and gave rise to a presumption of the existence of a recruitment policy that is directly discriminatory. The burden of proof would then shift to the employer to show that the actual recruitment practice did not correspond with the statement made. However, it was open to member states to decide whether to pass legislation to enable an appropriate body to bring proceedings in such cases where there is no identifiable victim.

---

[192] (2003) *Times*, 5 December.

[193] [2001] UKHL 15, [2001] 1 WLR 655, [2001] ICR 408, [2001] IRLR 312, [2001] BLGR 278, (2001) 98(21) LSG 39, (2001) 145 SJLB 116, (2001) *Times*, 27 March.

[194] [2000] ECR I–5539, [2002] ICR 932, [2000] IRLR 732.

[195] [2000] All ER (EC) 289, (2001) CMLR 79.   [196] [2008] 1 CMLR 44.   [197] See n 3.

4.206 Proceedings in respect of discriminatory job advertisements may be brought by the Equality and Human Rights Commission (see para 4.235).

J. Job advertisements

4.207 Job advertisements must not fall foul of anti-discrimination legislation. It is also clear that the wording of s 39 means that the publishing of an advertisement is part of the arrangements a person makes 'for deciding to whom to offer employment'.

4.208 Thus to advertise for a 'young person', 'attractive female', or 'Afro-Asian ethnicity' etc would be contrary to the age, sex and race anti-discriminatory provisions respectively, and would fall within the scope of s 39. But a person would only be able to make a claim of such discrimination if s/he had a genuine intention of applying for the post, but was deterred from doing so by the nature of the advertisement. In *Keane v Investigo*[198] the claimant was an accountant in her early 50s. She applied for more than 20 jobs, which were advertised as being suitable for a recently qualified accountant, and when she was not offered interviews she brought claims of age discrimination. Several such claims were settled out of court, but the present employer decided to resist the claim. It was held that her job applications were not bona fide, and by being turned down for a job which she had no genuine intention of accepting she had not suffered a detriment, or been treated unfavourably, or put at a disadvantage.

K. Conduct giving rise to separate proceedings (s 140)

4.209 If two or more separate proceedings are brought under the Act, with at least one being for a contravention of s 111 (instructing, causing or inducing contraventions) a court may transfer proceedings to an employment tribunal, and an employment tribunal may transfer the proceedings to a court, and the jurisdiction of the court or tribunal is transferred accordingly.

L. Unenforceable terms (s 142)

4.210 A term of a contract is unenforceable against a person in so far as it constitutes, promotes or provides for treatment that is of a description prohibited by the Act. On an application by a person who has an interest in a contract, a county court (or sheriff's court) may make an order for an unenforceable term to be removed or modified.

M. Restriction on contracting out (s 144)

4.211 A term of a contract is unenforceable by a person in whose favour it would operate in so far as it purports to exclude or limit a provision of the Act. However, this does not apply to a contract that settles a claim in respect of which the employment tribunal has jurisdiction (see s 120) if the contract:

(a) is made with the assistance of a conciliation officer (see para 1.7); or

(b) is a qualifying compromise contract. A qualified compromise contract is one drawn up by an independent adviser, provided the conditions set out in s 141 of the Employment Rights Act are complied with (see para 20.47);

(c) is a contract settled as a result of an arbitration award made in accordance with the scheme set out in s 212A of the Trade Union and Labour Relations Act 1992 (see para 1.13).

---

[198] Employment Appeal Tribunal, 11 December 2009.

N. **Void and unenforceable terms (s 145)**

4.212 A term of a collective agreement is void in so far as it constitutes, promotes or provides for treatment of a description prohibited by the Act. A rule of an undertaking is unenforceable against a person in so far as it constitutes, promotes or provides for treatment of the person that is of a description prohibited by the Act. This includes a rule made by an employer for application to employees, persons who apply for employment and persons the employer considers for employment. An application to an employment tribunal may also be made for a declaration that a term in a collective agreement that may be discriminatory in the future be declared unenforceable (s 146). It is also not possible to contract out of provisions made under the Act (eg by regulations).

O. **National security (s 192)**

4.213 A person does not contravene the Act by doing, for the purpose of safeguarding national security, anything it is proportionate to do for that purpose. Section 60 (enquiries about disability and health) does not apply to anything done for the purpose of vetting applicants for work for reasons of national security. So far as remedies are concerned, any recommendation made in national security cases can only be made in respect of the complainant, not other persons (s 125).

4.214 Proceedings in cases that involve national security come within the provisions of the Employment Rights Act 1996 (see para 17.173).

P. **Death of a claimant**

4.215 A cause of action under the Equality Act can be continued after the death of the claimant by his personal representatives, under the provisions of the Law Reform (Miscellaneous Provisions) Act 1934 (*Lewisham and Guys Mental Health NHS Trust v Andrews*[199]).

Q. **Other provisions**

4.216 There are further provisions in Act that relate specifically to contract workers (s 41), police (s 42), partnerships (s 44), barristers (s 47), advocates (s 48), personal office holders (s 49), appointments to public offices (s 50), qualification bodies (s 53), employment service providers (s 55), trade organisations (s 57), official business of local authorities (s 58), and occupational pension schemes (s 61: but see Sch 9 Part 2 for exceptions).

Submitting a complaint

A. **Jurisdiction (s 120)**

4.217 An employment tribunal has jurisdiction to determine a complaint arising from Part V of the Act, which includes the work provisions contained in s 39 (discrimination in employment), s 40 (harassment), s 108 (relationships that have ended), s 111 (instructing and causing discrimination), s 112 (aiding a contravention) and ss 64–79 (equality of terms). A civil court may strike out a claim relating to a non-discrimination rule if it

---

[199] [1999] ICR 774, [1999] IRLR 407, [1999] Disc LR 143, (1999) *Times*, 21 April.

appears that this could more conveniently be determined by an employment tribunal, and may also refer a matter to the employment tribunal for determination. The territorial jurisdiction must be determined by employment tribunals in accordance with the principles set out in *Lawson v Serco Ltd*[200] and, since most of the anti-discrimination provisions have their origins in EU law, the decisions in *Bleuse v MBT Transport*[201] (see para 1.37).

B. Time limits (s 123)

4.218 Proceedings on a complaint within s 120 may not be brought after the end of a period of three months starting with the date of the act to which the complaint relates, or such other period as the employment tribunal thinks just and equitable.

4.219 Conduct that extended over a period of time is to be treated as done at the end of that period, and a failure to do a thing is to be treated as occurring when the person in question decided on it. Thus a claim based on continuing discrimination may be brought up to three months after the discrimination has ceased (*Calder v James Finlay Corpn Ltd*[202]). But a distinction must be made between an act of continuing discrimination and an act of discrimination that has continuing consequences. In the latter case, the time limit of three months will normally apply. In *Clarke v Hampshire Electro-Plating Co Ltd*[203] the claimant, who is black, saw an advertisement for a supervisory job with his present employers. On 25 April he saw his employer about the vacancy, but was told he would not be considered. On 4 September a white man was appointed to the job, and the claimant then submitted a claim, alleging he had been discriminated against on grounds of race. An employment tribunal held that his complaint was out of time, but if there was discrimination it dated from 25 April. On appeal the decision was reversed by the EAT. Time will start to run from the date the cause of action crystallised, not from when the claimant felt he had been discriminated against. The cause of action had not crystallised when his application for promotion was rejected, but from the date when the white man was appointed, and this provided the comparison that enabled him to believe that he had been discriminated against.

4.220 A somewhat different result was reached in *Sougrin v Haringey Health Authority*,[204] where the claimant, a black nurse, appealed internally against her employer's decision to place her in a certain salary grade. Her appeal was unsuccessful, although an appeal by a white colleague succeeded. Six months later she submitted her application to an employment tribunal, arguing that she had been discriminated on grounds of race, and that the discrimination was a continuing act. It was held by the Court of Appeal that she had not submitted her application within the statutory time limit. The decision to reject her appeal was a one-off act with continuing consequences that resulted in her being paid less than the white colleague. There was no suggestion that the employers had a policy to pay black nurses less than white nurses. Had there been evidence of such a policy, it would have been possible to argue that there was an act of continuing discrimination but, since there was no such evidence, her claim was out of time.

4.221 But if there is a deliberate omission to do something, time will run from the date when the discriminator was in a position to do that thing (*Swithland Motors plc v Clarke*[205]).

---

[200] [2006] UKHL 3, [2006] 1 All ER 823, [2006] ICR 250, [2006] IRLR 289, (2006) 103(6) LSG 36, (2006) 156 NLJ 184, (2006) 150 SJLB 131, (2006) *Times*, 27 January.

[201] [2008] ICR 488, [2008] IRLR 264.   [202] [1989] ICR 157.

[203] [1992] ICR 312, [1991] IRLR 490, (1991) *Times*, 1 October.

[204] [1992] ICR 650, [1992] IRLR 416, (1992) *Times*, 8 June, (1992) *Independent*, 2 July.

[205] [1994] ICR 231, [1994] IRLR 275.

C. **Burden of proof (s 136)**

4.222 If there are facts from which an employment tribunal could decide, in the absence of any other explanation, that a person has contravened a provision in the Act, the tribunal must hold that the contravention has occurred, unless the person shows that he did not contravene the provision. This reversal of proof now applies to all the protected characteristics. The reversal of the burden of proof also applies when making enquiries about disability and health (see s 60, para 4.107).

4.223 It will be recalled that unreasonable behaviour, by itself, does not equate with unlawful discriminatory behaviour. In *Law Society v Bahl*[206] it was stated that all unlawful discriminatory behaviour is always unreasonable, but not all unreasonable behaviour is necessarily unlawfully discriminatory. Similarly, all racist language is offensive, but not all offensive language is racist, and the fact that members of a racial group are treated differently does not, by itself, constitute unlawful discrimination. It must be shown that the treatment was less favourable on grounds of race (*Barclays Bank plc v Kapur*[207]). Equally, the fact that the recipient of the offensive treatment is a woman, or disabled, etc, says nothing about the perpetrators actions. Thus if A is dismissed, and A is a woman, it does not necessarily follow that A was dismissed because she is a woman! If B is black, and B suffers a detriment, it does not necessarily follow that B has suffered the detriment because he is black! If hostile action has nothing to do with the relevant protected characteristic, no unlawful discrimination has occurred.

4.224 The fact that the employer already employs persons of different protected characteristics is not conclusive (*Johnson v Timber Tailors (Midlands) Ltd*[208]) but it is a relevant consideration of evidential value (*Piperdy v UEM Parker Glass*[209]). If an employer's replies to a questionnaire sent by the EHRC are evasive, it could lead to an inference that discrimination took place (*Virdee v EEC Quarries Ltd*[210]). Evidence of events that took place subsequent to the alleged act of discrimination is admissible where it is logically probative of a relevant fact (*Chattopadhyay v Headmaster of Holloway School*[211]).

4.225 A claimant may be able to obtain the discovery of existing statistics showing the number of persons from groups with different protected characteristics who have applied for posts, been engaged, or promoted, for such evidence may have some probative value from which inferences of discriminatory practices may be drawn (*West Midlands Passenger Transport Executive v Singh*[212]). But an employment tribunal cannot order a respondent to produce details of the composition of the workforce where such evidence does not exist, for this is not 'discovery' of documents, nor 'particulars' of the grounds on which the claimants seek to rely.

D. **Transfer of proceedings (s 140)**

4.226 If there are two or more separate proceedings being brought under the Act, with at least one of them dealing with a contravention of s 111 (instructing, causing or inducing discrimination, see para 4.201) proceedings may be transferred to or from a county court (or sheriff's court) or an employment tribunal, and the court or tribunal shall have jurisdiction to deal with the proceedings so transferred.

[206] See n 11.
[207] [1991] 2 AC 355, [1991] 2 WLR 401, [1991] 1 All ER 646, [1991] ICR 208, [1991] IRLR 136, (1991) *Times*, 25 January, (1991) *Independent*, 6 February, (1991) *Financial Times*, 30 January, (1991) *Guardian*, 31 January, (1991) *Daily Telegraph*, 7 February.
[208] [1978] IRLR 146.   [209] IDS Supplement.   [210] [1978] IRLR 295.
[211] [1982] ICR 132, [1981] IRLR 487.
[212] [1988] 1 WLR 730, [1988] 2 All ER 873, [1988] ICR 614, [1988] IRLR 186, (1988) 132 SJ 933.

E. Remedies (s 124)

4.227 If there has been a contravention of a provision mentioned in s 120 (see para 4.217) the employment tribunal may make the following remedies:

(a) a declaration as to the rights of the complainant and respondent in relation to the matters to which the proceedings relate;

(b) order the respondent to pay compensation to the complainant. The amount of the award should correspond to the amount that would be awarded by a county court or sheriff under s 119, and generally speaking is equivalent to the amounts that would flow from claims in tort, including an award in respect of injured feelings;

(c) make an appropriate recommendation (but see para 4.228). This will be that within a specified period the respondent takes specified steps for the purpose of obviating or reducing the adverse effect of any matter to which the proceedings relate on the complainant or any other person. The Explanatory Notes suggest that this power could be used for the benefit of persons other than the claimant, eg other employees, or to make improvements in the employer's policies and/or procedures. If the respondent fails, without reasonable excuse, to comply with the appropriate recommendation so far as it relates to the claimant, the tribunal can make or increase the compensation award. However, the Act is silent on how, if at all, other persons who are not parties to the proceedings can enforce any such recommendation.

4.228 The power to make a recommendation does not apply to equal pay claims (s 113(6)). The Deregulation Bill is expected to repeal the employment tribunal's power to make recommendations in discrimination cases. It is not yet known when this will be in force.

4.229 If there has been a contravention of s 19 (indirect discrimination), and the employment tribunal is satisfied that the provision, criterion or practice was not applied with the intention of discriminating against the complainant, it must not make an award of compensation unless it first considers whether to make a declaration or a recommendation.

4.230 Damages may include an award for injury to feelings, which is fundamental to a claim based on discrimination (*Murray v Powertech (Scotland) Ltd*[213]). There can be an award for injury to feelings even where the claimant did not know about the motivation of the discriminator, as in *Taylor v XLN Telecom Ltd.*[214] A black employee who brought a grievance complaining of race discrimination was dismissed, ostensibly for poor performance. He suffered distress and psychiatric injury as a result of the dismissal, but did not know then that the dismissal was in part prompted by his grievance relating to discrimination. The EAT held that it was nonetheless an injury attributable to the discriminatory conduct.

The award will usually fall within three bands, depending on the frequency and nature of the wrongful act. The lower band will be between £500–6,000, the middle band will be between £6,000–18,000 and the top band will be between £18,000–30,000 (*Vento v Chief Constable of West Yorkshire Police (No 2)*,[215] as updated in *Da'Bell v NSPCC*[216]).

4.231 An award may also be made for psychiatric illness suffered as a result of sex discrimination and/or harassment (*HM Prison Service v Salmon*[217]).

There is currently no limit on the amount that can be awarded, which can include aggravated damages if the injury was inflicted by conduct that was high-handed, malicious,

---

[213] [1992] IRLR 257.   [214] [2010] IRLR 499, EAT.
[215] [2002] EWCA Civ 1871, [2003] ICR 318, [2003] IRLR 102, [2003] Po LR 171, (2003) 100(10) LSG 28, (2003) 147 SJLB 181, (2002) *Times*, 27 December.
[216] [2010] IRLR 19.   [217] [2001] IRLR 425, [2001] Emp LR 1035.

insulting or oppressive (*HM Prison Service v Johnson*[218]) and such damages should not be aggregated with or treated as part of the damages awarded for injury to feelings (*Scott v Commissioners of Inland Revenue*[219]), but see para 20.104.

4.232 It must be borne in mind that ss 123–124 (see paras 4.218, 4.227) apply only to complaints brought under the Equality Act, and there are some differences from the provisions that apply to complaints made under the Employment Rights Act, for which see Chapter 17.

F. Interest on awards (s 139)

4.233 Interest on the compensation element (but not on the award to injured feelings) may be awarded, both in respect of the period up to the date when the compensation was assessed and the period following the promulgation of the award (but not if the full amount is paid within 14 days): see Employment Tribunals (Interest on Awards in Discrimination Cases) Regulations 1996, as amended.

4.234 The minister may make regulations for enabling an employment tribunal to include interest on an amount awarded by it in proceedings under the Act. It is likely that the pattern laid down in the Employment Tribunals (Interest on Awards in Discrimination Cases) Regulations 1996 (no longer in force) will be followed.

Enforcement by the Commission: Equality Act 2006

4.235 The enforcement powers of the Equality and Human Rights Commission can be found in the Equality Act 2006 (as amended). The Commission may bring proceedings under that Act in respect of alleged violation of provisions in the Equality Act 2010 dealing with direct discrimination (s 13), discrimination arising from disability (s 15), gender reassignment disability (s 16), pregnancy and maternity discrimination (s 18), the application of a provision, criterion or practice that by virtue of s 19 of the 2010 Act amounts to indirect discrimination, enquiries about disability and health, and relationships that have ended (s 108(1)) in so far as these provisions relate to the prohibited conduct of the protected characteristics in the employment field. It is immaterial whether the Commission knows or suspects that a person has been affected by the unlawful act (Equality Act 2006, s 24A). The proceedings must commence within six months of the act complained of, and an injunction may be obtained from a county court or sheriff court to restrain a person from repeating the unlawful act at any time within five years of a non-discrimination notice (Equality Act 2006, ss 71–72). The Commission may also bring a preliminary action in an employment tribunal on behalf of a person, even though that person has not made a complaint, and the employment tribunal can make an order of rights or a recommendation that appropriate action be taken to obviate or reduce the adverse effect of the discrimination (Equality Act 2006, s 73).

4.236 The Commission has power to investigate whether an unlawful act has been committed (Equality Act 2006, s 20) and, if so, may issue a notice requiring the person to whom it is given to prepare an action plan for the purpose of avoiding repetition or continuation of the unlawful act. An appeal against the notice may be made to the employment tribunal or county court as appropriate (Equality Act 2006, ss 21–22). The Commission may also enter into an agreement with a person under which he undertakes not to commit unlawful acts of a specific kind, and to take (or refrain from taking) other specified action.

---

[218] [2007] IRLR 951, (2007) 151 SJLB 1165.
[219] [2004] EWCA Civ 400, [2004] ICR 1410, [2004] IRLR 713, (2004) 148 SJLB 474, (2004) *Times*, 19 April.

4.237 The Commission may also apply to the court for an injunction (or interdict in Scotland) to restrain a person from committing an unlawful act or requiring him to comply with his undertaking, for example regarding unlawful advertising or instructions or pressure to discriminate. The Commission may give assistance in legal proceedings, and costs and legal representation may also be given to individuals in appropriate cases. It may intervene in legal proceedings, and in order to assist a person in obtaining the necessary information, the Commission may issue a questionnaire that can be sent to the alleged discriminator.

4.238 The Commission may carry out formal investigations, either on its own initiative or at the request of the Secretary of State, with specific terms of reference, and notice will be given to the persons affected. If the investigation is confined to the activities of a named person, an opportunity must be given for them to make oral or written representations (*Re Prestige Group plc*[220]). A person may be required to furnish information, or to attend a hearing and given oral evidence on specified matters, and to produce relevant documents. If a person fails or refuses to comply, the Commission may apply to a county court (or sheriff's court) for an order requiring him to comply, and a failure to do so is punishable in like manner as neglecting a witness summons. To wilfully alter, suppress, conceal or destroy a document, or knowingly or recklessly to make a statement that is false in a material particular is an offence, punishable on summary conviction by a fine not exceeding level 5 on the standard scale.

4.239 If, in the course of its investigations, the Commission is satisfied that a person is committing an unlawful discriminatory act, or contravening an equality clause (s 66 of the 2010 Act) the Commission may issue a non-discriminatory notice. It must first inform the person of its intentions, specifying the ground, and give him an opportunity to make oral or written representations (*Re Prestige Group plc*[221]). An appeal may be lodged to an employment tribunal within six weeks against any requirement, and the tribunal may quash the requirement it thinks to be unreasonable, or substitute its own directions. On such appeal, it is open to the person against whom the order has been made to challenge any finding of fact relating to the order (*Commission for Racial Equality v Amari Plastics*[222]). A public register of non-discrimination notices shall be kept, and if at any time within five years of the notice becoming final it appears to the Commission that the discriminatory act has been or is likely to be repeated, the Commission may apply to the county court for an injunction to restrain the person from doing so.

4.240 New codes of practice specific to the Equality Act have also been issued by the Commission and replace those that were issued by the previous commissions.

Other protected groups

A. **Rehabilitated persons**

4.241 The Rehabilitation of Offenders Act 1974 seeks to ensure that if a person has made a genuine effort to rehabilitate into society after conviction for a serious criminal offence, he may be spared the indignity and embarrassment of subsequently having to disclose his

---

[220] [1984] 1 WLR 335, [1984] ICR 473, [1984] IRLR 166, (1984) 81 LSG 134, (1984) 128 SJ 131.

[221] See n 220.

[222] [1982] QB 1194, [1982] 2 WLR 972, [1982] 2 All ER 499, [1982] ICR 304, [1982] Crim LR 152, (1982) 126 SJ 227.

unsavoury past. Provided he does not commit a serious offence within the rehabilitation period, he may, at the end of that time, be regarded as a rehabilitated person, and his conviction will be treated as having been 'wiped off the slate'. The Act is somewhat complex, but the general rule is that the length of the rehabilitation period will depend on the age of the offender at the time of conviction, and the sentence given for the offence. Thus the period will vary from six months in the case when an absolute discharge was granted up to ten years in respect of a sentence of imprisonment of 30 months. A sentence of imprisonment of more than 30 months will never become 'spent'. Once a person has become 'rehabilitated' evidence of his previous conviction is not generally admissible, and he may not be asked about it or, if he is asked, he need not tell the truth, and may deny his previous conviction. The rehabilitation period runs from the date of the conviction, not from the expiry of the sentence.

4.242 So far as the law of employment is concerned, s 4(3)(b) of the Act provides that (subject to certain exceptions) a 'spent' conviction, or failure to disclose such, shall not be grounds for dismissing or excluding a person from any office, profession, occupation or employment, or for prejudicing him in any way in any occupation or employment. However, the limits of the section need to be noted. At common law, an employer has the right to please himself whether or not to employ someone and although to refuse to employ a rehabilitated person may be to 'exclude' him, the section provides no remedy for a person who may feel that he has been discriminated against. Equally, a refusal to promote a rehabilitated person may amount to prejudicing him in that employment, but again no remedy is provided. On the other hand, if an employee who was a rehabilitated person was dismissed, and the sole ground was the discovery of his past convictions, this would undoubtedly amount to an unfair dismissal if he was otherwise within the protection of the Employment Rights Act (see Chapter 17). In *Hendry v Scottish Liberal Club*,[223] one of the reasons why the claimant was dismissed was connected with the discovery that he had been convicted many years ago of possessing cannabis. This conviction was 'spent' within the meaning of the Act, and hence it was not a statutory reason for dismissal.

4.243 In *Property Guards Ltd v Taylor and Kershaw*[224] the two claimants were employed as security guards. On commencing their employment they signed a statement to the effect that they had never been guilty of a criminal offence. When the employers discovered that they had both been convicted of minor offences of dishonesty, they were dismissed. The EAT upheld the finding of the employment tribunal that the dismissals were unfair. In both cases the convictions were 'spent' within the meaning of the Act. They were entitled not to disclose their previous convictions.

4.244 If an employer subsequently discovers that the employee has had a previous conviction, he must make all necessary enquiries to ascertain whether or not the conviction is spent before he starts taking action. In *Brooks v Ladbroke Lucky Seven Entertainment*,[225] the claimant was dismissed when it was discovered that he had had a prior conviction. It was argued on behalf of the employer that the dismissal was necessary in view of the nature of their business (as a gambling club), and as they did not know that the conviction was spent, they were not acting unreasonably. It was held that the employer should have sought further information about the nature of the offence and the penalty imposed, and a failure to do so rendered the dismissal unfair.

---

[223] [1977] IRLR 5.
[224] [1982] IRLR 175, EAT.
[225] [1977] IRLIB.

4.245 The main rehabilitation periods are as follows:

Sentence	Rehabilitation period
Imprisonment or youth custody of more than 6 months and up to 2½ years	10 years
Imprisonment or youth custody not exceeding 6 months	7 years
Fine or community punishment order or community rehabilitation order or detention and training order	5 years
Conditional discharge, bind over, care order, or supervision order	One year, or until order expires, whichever is the longer
Absolute discharge	6 months

The Government is currently considering reform of these time limits, with a view to reducing the rehabilitation period.

4.246 Other sentences which come within the Act include orders for custody in a remand home, an approved school, an attendance order, and a hospital order. In respect of persons under the age of 18 at the time of conviction, the rehabilitation period is generally reduced by half. In the case of imprisonment, it is the period of sentence imposed by the court which counts (including a suspended sentence) not the actual time spent in prison. The rehabilitation period runs from the date of the conviction. A prison sentence (or youth custody sentence) of more than two and a half years is never 'spent'.

4.247 The Act does not apply to questions which are asked of a person in order to assess the suitability of a person for admission to the professions of medical practitioner, barrister, accountant, solicitor, dentist, dental hygienist or auxiliary, veterinary surgeon, nurse, mid-wife, ophthalmic or dispensing optician, pharmaceutical chemist, or a Scottish registered teacher. Such people must still tell the truth about their previous convictions. Nor can a person tell a lie if the questions are asked for the purpose of assessing his suitability for the following employments, namely, certain legal appointments and offices, certain employment connected with the punishment of offenders, constables, traffic wardens, probation officers, carers and employment with children, further education teachers, proprietors of independent schools, certain local government social workers, hospital workers, persons who work for building societies or who provide financial services, youth club leaders and employment with cadet forces. Certain other occupations are also excluded from the provisions of the Act (see the Rehabilitation of Offenders Act 1974 (Exceptions) Orders 1975 as amended), and see *Wood v Coverage Care Ltd*).[226]

B. **Access to criminal records**

4.248 Employers who wish to know whether or not an applicant for employment has or has not got a criminal record may be able to use the procedures set out in the Police Act 1997, which makes arrangements for access to criminal records for employment-related purposes. This Act enables a criminal record check to be made available by the Disclosure and Barring Service (formerly the Criminal Records Bureau) from computerised national criminal records, in response to an application by a person who is the subject of the check or by a registered organisation. For an annual fee of £13, an individual can obtain a DBS certificate which can be transferred from job to job. Employers can then carry out free 'update' searches with the permission of the employee. There are three types of certificates which are now available.

Criminal conviction certificate (s 112)

4.249 This certificate gives prescribed details of every conviction which is recorded in central police records. A 'conviction' for this purpose means a conviction within the meaning of the Rehabilitation of Offenders Act, other than a conviction which is spent. Alternatively, the certificate will record that there is no conviction. An employer cannot apply direct to the Criminal Records Agency for this certificate, but can request that the job applicant provides one as a prerequisite for employment.

Criminal record certificate (s 113)

4.250 This is a more detailed certificate, which will record every matter recorded in central police records, including a conviction which is spent under the Rehabilitation of Offenders Act. This certificate can be asked for by a person seeking employment in one of the occupations where a conviction under the Rehabilitation of Offenders Act must be disclosed, even though it would otherwise be spent. An application for this type of certificate will be made by the subject of the check, countersigned by a person who is listed in a register to be kept by the Secretary of State as being likely to employ persons in occupations which are excluded from that Act. It is likely that this certificate will be sought by persons who wish to be employed in a large number of occupations which are exempt from the 1974 Act, including the judiciary, police, Crown employment, probation officers, prison staff, professional groups generally, banking and financial services, carers/social workers, etc.

Enhanced criminal record certificate (s 115)

4.251 This certificate, as well as containing the information found in the criminal record certificate, may contain additional information provided by local police forces, including cautions and relevant non-conviction information. This certificate will be used when seeking employment caring for or being in sole charge of persons under the age of 18 or vulnerable adults, or being involved in training or supervising them. Again, the application will be made by the job applicant, and countersigned by the registered person.

4.252 It is an offence for members and staff of any registered body to make an unauthorised disclosure of any information provided in a criminal records check or enhanced criminal records check.

4.253 A code of practice on the operation of the provisions of the Police Act has been issued.

C. Unfair recruitment (TULR(C)A, s 137)

4.254 There are provisions in the Trade Union and Labour Relations (Consolidation) Act 1992 which protect a person from being refused employment on grounds of trade union membership or non-membership. These matters will be considered in Chapter 21.

D. Employment of women

4.255 Most of the statutory provisions passed for the protection of female employees have been repealed in so far as they enabled different treatment to be accorded to women. Thus women may now clean parts of machinery while in motion, they may work underground in mines, and perform a number of other tasks which were previously not open to them (see Employment Act 1989, s 9). This is in accordance with the Equal Treatment Directive (see para 1.76) and the desire of the Government to reduce the legislative and administrative burdens on industry.

4.256 However, a number of statutory provisions relating to the health and safety of women have been retained, particularly dealing with those risks associated with pregnancy, childbirth and other risks specifically affecting women (see para 6.9). Thus a woman may not work in a factory within four weeks of childbirth (Factories Act 1961, Sch 5, Public Health Act 1936, s 205), or in any employment within two weeks of childbirth (Maternity (Compulsory Leave) Regulations 1994). Women are prohibited from working in certain processes and activities involving lead products (including lead paint); there are limits on exposure to ionising radiations, and on working in an aircraft or at sea while pregnant (Employment Act 1989, s 4 and Sch 1). Indeed, it is lawful to discriminate against a woman in so far as it is necessary to comply with the restrictions mentioned in para 4.194.

4.257 Restrictions on hours of work (including overtime and night work) for women were abolished in the Sex Discrimination Act 1986 (s 7) but the position is now governed by the Employment Act 1989 (s 1) which effectively nullifies any statutory provision which produces a discrimination as regards access to employment and working conditions.

E. Employment of young persons

4.258 Legislative provisions dealing with the health and safety of young persons (defined as persons over compulsory school leaving age) can be found in the Management of Health and Safety at Work Regulations 1999 (see para 11.80), and restrictions on the hours of work of young workers can be found in the Working Time Regulations 1998 (see para 7.62).

F. Adult workers

4.259 The sole remaining legislation imposing restrictions on the hours of work of adult workers are (1) Mines and Quarries Act 1954 (underground miners), (2) Hours of Employment (Conventions) Act 1936 (sheet glass workers), (3) Shops (Early Closing Days) Act 1965 (shop assistants), and (4) Transport Act 1968 (vehicle drivers) and the Working Time Regulations (see para 7.58).

5

Equal Pay

5.1 Article 157 of the Treaty on the Functioning of the European Union (formerly Art 141 of the Treaty of Rome) provides that member states shall maintain the application of the principle that men and women shall receive equal pay for equal work. Directive 75/117/EEC (Equal Pay Directive) states that the principle of equal pay means for the same work or work to which equal value has been attributed. Article 157 has direct effect (*Defrenne v Sabena*[1]), and thus it is clear that the overriding views of the European Court, when interpreting Art 157 and the Directive, must be applied.

5.2 'Pay' is a very wide concept, and means 'the ordinary basic or minimum wage or salary, and any other consideration, whether in cash or in kind, which a worker receives, directly or indirectly, in respect of his employment from his employer' (*Barber v Guardian Royal Exchange*[2]). All sorts of benefits must be equalised, including Christmas bonuses (*Lewen v Denda*[3]), travel facilities (*Garland v British Rail Engineering Ltd*[4]) as well as remuneration provisions (*Worringham v Lloyds Bank*[5]).

5.3 The equal pay provisions apply to employment under a contract of employment, contract of apprenticeship, or contract to do work personally (s 80). Thus workers are within the scope of the provisions, as well as employees. In *Quinnen v Hovells*[6] the claimant was a self-employed salesman engaged by the respondents to demonstrate goods for sale in a department store. He complained that two female demonstrators who were employees of the respondents were receiving a higher rate of pay, and the EAT held that he was entitled to have his claim considered on its merits, for the definition of employment clearly covered self-employed persons.

5.4 In principle, the burden of proof lies upon a claimant to show that, on the balance of probabilities s/he is not receiving equal pay, but in *Handels-og v Dansk Arbejdsgiverforening*[7] (the 'Danfoss' case) the ECJ held that if a pay system manifestly produces inequalities of pay between the sexes, the burden of proof lies upon the employer to show that the criteria used that produces those inequalities are not discriminatory. Thus once there is a suspicion of discrimination in pay scales, the burden of proof shifts to the employer to justify pay differentials (*Enderby v Frenchay Health Authority*[8]).

---

[1] [2000] ECR I–6155, [2002] 1 CMLR 6, [2000] Pens LR 261.
[2] [1991] 1 QB 344, [1991] 2 WLR 72, [1990] 2 All ER 660, [1990] ECR I–1889, [1990] 2 CMLR 513, [1990] ICR 616, [1990] IRLR 240, [1990] 1 PLR 103, (1990) 140 NLJ 925, (1990) *Times*, 18 May, (1990) *Independent*, 23 May, (1990) *Financial Times*, 25 May, (1990) *Guardian*, 12 July.
[3] (2000) IRLR 67, (2000) ICR 648.
[4] [1983] 2 AC 751, [1982] 2 WLR 918, [1982] 2 CMLR 174, [1982] ICR 420, [1982] IRLR 257, (1982) 126 SJ 309.
[5] [1982] 1 WLR 841, [1982] 3 All ER 373, [1982] ICR 299, [1982] IRLR 74, (1982) 126 SJ 99, (1981) *Times*, 18 December.
[6] [1984] ICR 525, [1984] IRLR 227, (1984) 81 LSG 1438, (1984) 134 NLJ 360, (1984) 128 SJ 431.
[7] [1990] ECR I–3979, [1992] ICR 332, [1991] IRLR 31, (1990) *Times*, 20 December.
[8] [2000] ICR 612, [2000] IRLR 257, (2000) *Times*, 29 February.

Equality of terms (Equality Act, ss 64–79)

5.5 The Equal Pay Act 1970 has been repealed, and its provisions re-enacted in ss 64–79 of the Equality Act 2010. Many of the interpretive decisions from the 1970 Act are repeated in the following text, with the usual caveat that the interpretation of reforming legislation is never static.

5.6 The provisions of ss 64–70 apply when a person is employed on work that is equal to the work that is done by a comparator of the opposite sex. A person is a comparator if s/he is employed by the same employer or an associated employer (see para 2.5), and they both work at the same establishment (s 79). But this only applies if the employers concerned are 'companies'. Statutory agencies, whether or not they are under the control of the Government, are not associate employers (*Hasley v Fair Employment Agency*[9]), because there is a distinction between 'bodies corporate' and 'companies' (*Gardiner v London Borough of Merton*[10]), but it is possible that this limitation is incompatible with the requirements of EC law (*Scullard v Knowles and Southern Regional Council*[11]). If they are employed by the same employer or associated employer, but work at different establishments, they are comparators if common terms of employment apply at those establishments. If work is not done at the same establishment it is to be treated as being done at the establishment with which it has the closest connection (s 80).

5.7 A major problem is to determine whether terms and conditions are 'common' as between two establishments (*British Coal Corpn v Smith*[12]). Thus if terms and conditions are governed by the same collective agreement, they will be common (*Barclays Bank plc v James*[13]). Having a common employer is not the same thing as being 'in the same employment', or having pay and conditions attributed to a 'single source' (*Lawrence v Regent Office Care Ltd*[14]), because there must be a single source responsible for the difference in pay (*Allonby v Accrington and Rossendale College*[15]). Thus in *Robertson v Department for Environment, Food and Rural Affairs*[16] male civil servants sought equal pay with senior secretaries employed in a different government department. The claim failed. Although they were in common employment, responsibilities for terms and conditions of employment had been transferred to the individual government departments, and thus there was no single source of the pay structure.

5.8 If a claimant seeks to rely on a comparator who is employed at a different establishment, there must be a real possibility of the comparator doing the same or a broadly similar job. The claimant must then show that the terms and conditions on which s/he would be employed are broadly similar to those on which s/he is currently employed. In the case of *North v Dumfries and Galloway Council*,[17] female school workers, such as classroom

---

[9] [1989] IRLR 106, [1988] 13 NIJB 63.

[10] [1981] QB 269, [1981] 2 WLR 232, [1981] ICR 186, [1980] IRLR 472, 79 LGR 374, (1981) 125 SJ 97, (1980) *Times*, 26 November.

[11] [1996] ICR 399, [1996] IRLR 344.

[12] [1996] 3 All ER 97, [1996] ICR 515, [1996] IRLR 399, (1996) 93(25) LSG 28, (1996) 140 SJLB 134, (1996) *Times*, 23 May, (1996) *Independent*, 13 June.

[13] [1990] ICR 333, [1990] IRLR 90.

[14] [2002] ECR I-7325, [2002] 3 CMLR 27, [2003] ICR 1092, [2002] IRLR 822, [2002] Emp LR 1248, (2002) *Times*, 10 October.

[15] [2005] All ER (EC) 289, [2004] ECR I-873, [2004] 1 CMLR 35, [2004] ICR 1328, [2004] IRLR 224, [2004] OPLR 83, [2004] Pens LR 199.

[16] [2005] EWCA Civ 138, [2005] ICR 750, [2005] IRLR 363, (2005) 102(15) LSG 33, (2005) *Times*, 2 March, (2005) *Independent*, 24 February.

[17] [2011] IRLR 239, [2011] CSIH 2.

assistants, learning assistants and nursery nurses, sought to compare themselves with male manual workers employed as groundsmen, road workers, refuse drivers, refuse collectors and a leisure attendant. The comparators were employed by the same local authority, but at depots rather than schools. In *North and others v Dumfries and Galloway Council (Scotland)*,[18] the Supreme Court said that the question was: if the comparators were employed at the same establishment, would they be employed on the same or broadly similar terms and conditions to those applicable in their current place of work? The comparators sometimes did occasionally do work at schools, and when they did, there was no change in their terms and conditions, and so the female workers succeeded.

5.9 If a claim for equal pay is brought under Art 157 of the Treaty, the pay of the comparator must be attributable to a single source, but in cases where the claim was brought under the Equality Act, the single source was not required, provided the comparator was in the same employment (*North Cumbria Acute Hospitals NHS Trust v Potter*[19]).

5.10 An equality clause is only applicable when there is an actual comparator of the opposite sex. Thus a woman who believes that she is poorly paid has no remedy in the absence of a male comparator (see observations of Elias J in *Walton Centre for Neurology NHS Trust v Bewley*[20]). But it has been held that if there is sufficient statistical evidence to support the assertion that women, as a class, are paid less than men, an equal value claim may lie under the provisions of Art 157 of the Treaty, even in the absence of a male comparator (*Grundy v British Airways plc*[21]), and a claim for sex discrimination could also be made (s 71).

5.11 It is possible to use a former employee as a comparator. In *Macarthys Ltd v Smith*[22] a man was employed as a stock room manager, and was paid £60 per week. He left the job, and four months later the woman claimant was appointed as stockroom manageress, and was paid £50 per week. The European Court upheld her claim, holding that the principle of equal pay for equal work applied to the situation where a woman received less pay than a male predecessor, provided they were both doing the same or broadly similar work.

5.12 It had been held that a woman cannot claim equal pay with a man who succeeds her in her job, because to hold otherwise would have been an exercise in speculation as to what would have happened if they had been employed contemporaneously (*Walton Centre for Neurology NHS Trust v Bewley*[23]). However s 64(2) of the Equality Act now provides that the relevant type of work is not restricted to work that is done contemporaneously, thus opening the possibility of a claim may be made citing a successor as well as a predecessor a comparator (see *Diocese of Hallam Trustees v Connaughton*[24]).

5.13 A woman can choose the man with whom she wishes to be compared. Thus, if she is getting equal pay with some men, she can still seek equal pay with a man who is paid at a higher rate, if their work is the same or broadly similar or has an equal value (*Ainsworth v Glass Tubes and Components*[25]).

5.14 A 'piggyback' claim may be brought by a man by comparing himself with a woman who has succeeded in an equal pay claim against a higher paid male comparator. The claim may be brought contingently, ie even before the woman's right to equal pay has been

[18] [2013] UKSC 45.   [19] [2009] IRLR 900.
[20] [2008] ICR 1047, [2008] IRLR 588, (2008) 152(23) SJLB 30.
[21] [2007] EWCA Civ 1020, [2008] IRLR 74, (2007) 104(43) LSG 33, (2007) 151 SJLB 1401.
[22] [1981] QB 180, [1980] 3 WLR 929, [1981] 1 All ER 111, [1980] 2 CMLR 217, [1980] ICR 672, [1980] IRLR 210, (1980) 124 SJ 808.
[23] [2008] ICR 1047, [2008] IRLR 588, (2008) 152(23) SJLB 30.
[24] [1996] 3 CMLR 93, [1996] ICR 860, [1996] IRLR 505, (1996) *Times*, 11 June.
[25] [1977] ICR 347, [1977] IRLR 74.

established (*Hartlepool Borough Council v Llewellyn*[26]). If the woman's claim is successful and a tribunal award is made, the man is entitled to arrears of pay for the same period as the female comparator.

Sex equality clause (s 66)

5.15 A sex equality clause is to be treated as being included in the terms under which persons are employed. Thus, any term in a contract that is less favourable than that of a comparator of the opposite sex is to be modified so as to ensure that it is not less favourable, and similarly a term that contains a benefit in the contract of a comparator of the opposite sex is to be included. If the contract of employment does not contain any term equivalent to that enjoyed by the comparator, the equality clause operates to insert such a term.

5.16 When considering an equality clause, the correct approach is to look at the situation term by term, so that a claimant can succeed in relation to any one particular element of the employment terms. The package approach, whereby more favourable terms can be set off against less favourable terms, is wrong (*Jorgensen v Foreningen AF Speciallaeger Sygesikringens Forhandlingsudvalg*[27]).

5.17 The equality clause applies not only in respect of remuneration, but also other benefits and facilities that are part of the contract of employment. This includes holiday entitlement, cars, privileged access to sports facilities, fringe benefits that continue after the employment has ended, eg travel facilities granted to retired rail workers (*Garland v British Rail Engineering Ltd*[28]), contributions to a pension scheme (*Worringham v Lloyds Bank*[29]) allowances to compensate for loss of earnings whilst on a training course (*Davies v Neath Port Talbot County Borough Council*[30]), severance payments (*Barber v Guardian Royal Exchange Assurance Group*[31]) and so on. But men cannot complain because women have certain advantages because of pregnancy or maternity, and similarly, women cannot claim full pay whilst on maternity leave (*Gillespie v Northern Health and Service Board*[32]).

5.18 The equality clause is not designed to produce absolute parity in contractual terms. Thus, if there is a non-discriminatory reason for an additional element in a man's pay (eg a special allowance for working unsocial hours: see *Electrolux Ltd v Hutchinson*[33]), the equality clause will not operate. In *Stadt Lengerich v Helmig*[34] employees who worked beyond 'normal working time' were entitled to overtime payments. Normal working time was defined as full-time working. The claimants, who worked part-time, argued that this was discriminatory, because even though they worked beyond their normal working hours, they would not receive the overtime payment until their working hours exceeded the equivalent of the full-time employees' hours. The European Court held that there was no

---

[26] [2009] ICR 1426, [2009] IRLR 796, (2009) *Times*, 9 July.

[27] [2000] ECR I–2447, [2002] 1 CMLR 40, [2000] IRLR 726.

[28] [1983] 2 AC 751, [1982] 2 WLR 918, [1982] 2 CMLR 174, [1982] ICR 420, [1982] IRLR 257, (1982) 126 SJ 309.

[29] [1982] 1 WLR 841, [1982] 3 All ER 373, [1982] ICR 299, [1982] IRLR 74, (1982) 126 SJ 99, (1981) *Times*, 18 December.

[30] [1999] ICR 1132, [1999] IRLR 769, (1999) *Times*, 26 October.

[31] [1991] 1 QB 344, [1991] 2 WLR 72, [1990] 2 All ER 660, [1990] ECR I–1889, [1990] 2 CMLR 513, [1990] ICR 616, [1990] IRLR 240, [1990] 1 PLR 103, (1990) 140 NLJ 925, (1990) *Times*, 18 May, (1990) *Independent*, 23 May, (1990) *Financial Times*, 25 May, (1990) *Guardian*, 12 July.

[32] [1997] NI 190, [1997] Eu LR 566, [1997] IRLR 410.   [33] [1977] ICR 252, (1976) 12 ITR 40.

[34] [1994] ECR I–5727, [1995] 2 CMLR 261, [1996] ICR 35, [1995] IRLR 216, (1995) *Financial Times*, 10 January.

unequal pay as between full-time and part-time employees, because their overall pay was the same for the number of hours worked. A part-time employee who worked for 19 hours would have received the same pay as a full-time employee who worked the same number of hours.

5.19 If the same rule applies equally to men and women, and to both full-time and part-time employees, the fact that some women are less well off in consequence is irrelevant. In *Barry v Midland Bank*[35] a contractual redundancy scheme, which provided for severance pay to be based on final salary at the date of termination, did not breach the Equal Pay Act, even though part-time women received less under the scheme than full-time employees. Their final salary was less because they were working fewer hours, and the calculation of the severance scheme was made on the same basis as part-time male employees.

5.20 A part-time employee cannot use a full-time employee as a comparator in an equal pay claim, because it is the employment status, not gender, that creates the difference in treatment (*Lynn v Rokeby School Board of Governors*[36]).

5.21 Neither the sex equality clause nor a maternity equality clause (see para 5.53) apply in relation to terms of work affected by compliance with laws regulating the employment of women or the special treatment afforded to women in connection with pregnancy or childbirth (Sch 7). Thus if there is a pay differential resulting from the restrictions on employing women in certain processes, eg Control of Lead at Work Regulations 2002, Ionising Radiations Regulations 1999, etc, unequal pay is possible. Nor does it have any effect in relation to terms of work affording special treatment to women in connection with pregnancy or childbirth.

Equal work (s 65)

5.22 The work of an employee is equal to the work of another colleague if:

(a) it is like work

(b) it is rated as equivalent

(c) it is of equal value.

A. Like work (s 65)

5.23 Work is like work if it is the same or broadly similar and such differences as there are between their work are not of practical importance in relation to the terms of their work. It is thus necessary to have regard to the frequency with which the differences between their work occur in practice, and the nature and extent of the differences. In *Capper Pass Ltd v Lawton*[37] a woman worked as a cook in a company directors' dining room, providing lunches for between 10 and 20 persons. She sought equal pay with two assistant chefs who worked in the factory canteen, and who prepared 350 meals each day. Other differences were that she worked 40 hours per week and had no supervisor, whereas the men worked 45 hours per week and were under the supervision of a head chef. The EAT upheld a decision that she was entitled to equal pay with the male chefs. The work did not have to be

---

[35] [1999] 1 WLR 1465, [1999] 3 All ER 974, [1999] ICR 859, [1999] IRLR 581, (1999) 96(31) LSG 36, (1999) 149 NLJ 1253, (1999) 143 SJLB 221, (1999) *Times*, 23 July, (1999) *Independent*, 25 October.

[36] [2001] Pens LR 273.

[37] [1977] QB 852, [1977] 2 WLR 26, [1977] 2 All ER 11, [1977] ICR 83, [1976] IRLR 366, (1976) 11 ITR 316, (1976) 120 SJ 768.

the same; it was sufficient if it was broadly similar and the differences were not of practical importance. It would have been wrong to take a too pedantic approach, or to find they were not on like work because of insubstantial differences.

5.24 If there are differences in the work done, the employment tribunal must assess if it was reasonable to expect those differences to be reflected in wage settlements. Three such differences may be noted.

5.25 *(i) Different duties.* In *Noble v David Gold & Son (Holdings) Ltd*[38] men worked in a warehouse loading and unloading, whereas women did lighter work such as sorting and packing and labelling. The Court of Appeal agreed with the finding of the employment tribunal that women were not on like work. Nor was the work broadly similar, for the differences were of practical importance in relation to terms and conditions of employment.

5.26 If there is a difference in the contractual obligations, this may negate equal pay, but it must be ascertained what happens in practice, and whether some other form of payment could be made for the different contractual obligations. In *Electrolux Ltd v Hutchinson*[39] men and women were performing broadly similar work, but the men were graded at a higher rate. The employers argued that the men had different contractual obligations, such as accepting transfer to different work, working compulsory overtime, and working nights. The EAT upheld a decision that the women were entitled to equal pay. The question had to be asked, what happened in practice? If and when the men performed these additional obligations, the situation could be dealt with by paying additional premiums.

5.27 But if male employees received different training, and thus could be called upon to perform different duties, they are not employed on the same work as women (*Angestelltenbetriebsrat der Wiener v Wiener*[40]). In *Noble v David Gold & Son (Holdings) Ltd*[41] men worked in a warehouse loading and unloading, whereas women did lighter work such as sorting, packing and labelling. The Court of Appeal upheld a decision of the employment tribunal that the women were not on like work. Nor was the work broadly similar, for the differences were of practical importance in relation to terms and conditions of employment. Also, the mere fact that a woman carried out the duties of a man for a short period of time or as a deputy as a temporary measure does not entitle the woman to equal pay with that man, for basically their responsibilities are different (*Ford v Weston (Chemists) Ltd*[42]).

5.28 *(ii) Different hours.* In *Dugdale v Kraft Foods Ltd*[43] men and women worked on broadly similar work, but the men had to do a compulsory night shift, and a voluntary shift on Sunday mornings. It was held that the time at which the work is performed is by itself no bar to equal pay at the basic rate. The men could be compensated for these extra burdens by receiving a night shift payment or premium.

5.29 But this reasoning only applies when the difference in pay for hours worked applies only to men. If men and women work different hours to other employees, then the difference between the former and the latter has nothing to do with the sex of the employees, and thus basic rates can vary between the employees concerned (*Kerr v Lister & Co Ltd*[44]). Nor is there a breach of the equality clause if the employer makes a priority payment to employee who work on a rotating 24/7 shift pattern, even though women with

[38] [1980] ICR 543, [1980] IRLR 253.

[39] [1977] ICR 252, (1976) 12 ITR 40.

[40] [1999] ECR I–2865, [1999] 2 CMLR 1173, [2000] ICR 1134, [1999] IRLR 804, (1999) *Times*, 20 May.

[41] n 37.   [42] (1977) 12 ITR 369.

[43] [1976] 1 WLR 1288, [1977] 1 All ER 454, [1977] ICR 48, [1976] IRLR 368, (1979) 11 ITR 309, (1976) SJ 780.

[44] [1977] IRLR 259.

child-caring responsibilities are unable to work those hours (*Blackburn v Chief Constable of West Midlands Police*[45]).

5.30 *(iii) Different responsibilities.* In *Eaton Ltd v Nuttall*,[46] a man and a woman worked on like work, but the man received higher pay because his responsibilities were greater. He handled more expensive products, and consequently a mistake by him would have had more serious financial consequences. The EAT held that it was proper to take into account the additional responsibilities which the job entailed.

B. Work rated as equivalent (s 65(4))

5.31 Work is rated as equivalent if a job evaluation study gives equal value to the jobs in terms of the demands made, or would give equal value if the job evaluation was not made on a sex-specific system, ie a system that sets different values for men and women. A system is sex-specific if it sets values for men different from those it sets for women.

5.32 A woman's work will be considered to have been rated equivalent to that of a man if it has been given equal value under a properly conducted job evaluation scheme, in terms of the different demands made upon an employee, eg, effort, skill, decision making etc. Such a scheme must be gender neutral and capable of satisfying the test of being thorough in analysis and impartial in application (*Eaton Ltd v Nuttall*[47]). Once it is established that it is a genuine scheme it must be accepted by the parties and employment tribunal, for the latter cannot be an appeal court from a valid scheme.

5.33 It is irrelevant if there emerges a difference between men and women in the actual points scored under the scheme, if there is no difference in the allocation to a particular salary grade. In *Springboard Sunderland Trust v Robson*[48] the claimant was awarded 400 following a job evaluation, which was increased to 410 following an appeal. She claimed equal pay with a man who had been awarded 428 points. The relevant salary scales for the grade in question was 410–449 points. Thus, although the jobs were not rated as equivalent to her comparator, her claim succeeded, because what mattered was the grade that was allocated to her following the evaluation, rather than the values assigned to her under the evaluation.

5.34 An unusual case was *Redcar and Cleveland Borough Council v Bainbridge*,[49] where a job evaluation scheme graded men lower than women, but nonetheless the men received higher pay! Clearly the jobs were not, strictly speaking, rated as equivalent, but the Court of Appeal had no difficulty in finding that the principle of equal pay had been breached. Relying on European law, the court gave a purposive interpretation of the Equal Pay Act by adding words to it, so that it read 'A woman is to be regarded as employed on work rated as equivalent with that of any men if, but only if, her job and their job have been given an equal value *or her job has been given a higher* value.' Under the Equality Act, there is little doubt that such a finding would be a breach of the quality clause and amount to sex discrimination under s 39.

5.35 However, if a job evaluation scheme produced a small, albeit significant, difference between the claimant and her comparator, it cannot be said that the two jobs are rated as equivalent (*Home Office v Bailey*[50]).

---

[45] [2008] EWCA Civ 1208, [2009] IRLR 135, (2008) 105(44) LSG 20, (2008) 158 NLJ 1603.
[46] [1977] 1 WLR 549, [1977] 3 All ER 1131, [1977] ICR 272, [1977] IRLR 71, (1977) 11 ITR 197, (1977) 121 SJ 353.
[47] n 46.   [48] [1992] ICR 554, [1992] IRLR 261.
[49] [2008] EWCA Civ 885, [2009] ICR 133, [2008] IRLR 776.   [50] [2005] IRLR 757.

C. **Work of equal value (s 65(6))**

5.36 Work is of equal value if it is not like work nor work rated as equivalent, but equal in terms of the demands made by reference to such factors as effort, skill and decision-making.

5.37 Where a question arises as to whether one person's work is of equal value to another's, the tribunal may, before determining the question, require a member of the panel of independent experts (who is designated by ACAS for the purpose) to prepare a report on the question (s 131). If the requirement has not been withdrawn, the tribunal must not determine the question unless it has received the report. If no report is commissioned by the employment tribunal, the tribunal shall not determine the matter without giving the parties an opportunity to adduce their own evidence (*Wood v William Ball Ltd*[51]). If there has been a job evaluation study that results in different values being given, that conclusion must be accepted unless there are reasonable grounds for suspecting that the evaluation was based on a system that discriminated because of sex, or that it is otherwise unreliable, for example if it was out-of-date (Equality Act, s 131).

5.38 Work that is rated under a job evaluation scheme and work rated under an equal value assessment are two different exercises. The fact that jobs have been rated as equivalent in the job evaluation scheme does not set up a presumption that they were of equal value. Moreover, an equal value claim may not be brought if the claim could be brought under the provisions for like work or work rated as equivalent (*Hovell v Ashford & St Peter's Hospital NHS Trust*[52]).

5.39 The Employment Tribunals (Equal Value) Rules of Procedure, contained in the Employment Tribunals (Constitution and Rules of Procedure) Regulations 2004, Sch 6, set out an improved procedure for dealing with equal value claims. Such cases form a small proportion of cases that come before employment tribunals, but because of their complexity, sometimes involving large numbers of claimants, they take up a disproportionate amount of time. Employment tribunals have been given wide powers of case management, with timetables set out, depending on whether or not evidence is being given by an independent expert appointed by the tribunal. Standard directions require an early exchange of information, with particular reference to identifying the areas of disagreement. There are also special rules that apply if the parties appoint their own experts, including a requirement that those experts prepare a joint report on matters on which they agree and disagree. Annexed to the Rules of Procedure is a timetable, in the form of a flowchart which indicates that an equal value claim that does not involve an independent expert should be heard within 25 weeks, and a claim that does involve an independent expert should be heard within 37 weeks.

5.40 In *Hayward v Cammell Laird Shipbuilders Ltd*[53] the claimant, a canteen worker, was paid at a lower rate than certain skilled workers, but she enjoyed superior sickness benefits, paid meal breaks and extra holidays. An independent expert concluded that her work was of equal value to the male comparators, but an employment tribunal dismissed her claim, holding that the terms and conditions *as a whole* must be not less favourable. Thus although her cash pay was less than the comparators, her other terms and conditions, which were more favourable, had to be taken into consideration. However, the House of Lords upheld her claim, holding that the employment tribunal should have considered each individual

---

[51] [2000] ICR 277, [1999] IRLR 773.

[52] [2009] EWCA Civ 670, [2009] ICR 1545, [2009] IRLR 734, (2009) 106(29) LSG 17, (2009) *Times*, 5 October.

[53] [1988] AC 894, [1988] 2 WLR 1134, [1988] 2 All ER 257, [1988] 2 CMLR 528, [1988] ICR 464, [1988] IRLR 257, (1988) 152 LG Rev 501, (1988) 138 NLJ Rep 133.

term which was not less favourable, and did not require a holding that terms as a whole should be not less favourable.

5.41 But the 'term by term' approach, if taken literally, could result in an equal pay claim ending up with unequal pay, which would defeat the purpose of the legislation. In *Degnan v Redcar Borough Council*[54] the Court of Appeal avoided such result by stating that the 'term' in question must be the same subject-matter. Thus basic rates, bonuses and attendance allowance were all part of one 'term' on remuneration, thus preventing a female claimant from cherry-picking the most advantageous part of a remuneration package of a number of male employees. However in *Knowsley Hospitals NHS Trust v Brownbill*,[55] the Court of Appeal has made clear that *Degnan* turned on its own special facts and did not give rise to an exception to the principle in *Hayward*. Equal pay claimants were entitled to compare the distinct contractual terms in their contracts governing the rate of pay for working unsocial hours to a similar term in the contracts of their male comparators, even though the women, overall, received higher pay than the men. Basing equal pay claims on a term-by-term comparison follows *Barber v Guardian Royal Exchange Assurance Group*,[56] which emphasised the importance of transparency.

5.42 An equal value claim may be brought by a woman even though she works with men doing the same work and who are paid the same as she, as long as there is another man earning a higher wage with whom she wishes to be compared. In *Pickstone v Freemans plc*[57] the claimant was a warehouse operative, who worked alongside other male warehouse operatives, all of whom received the same pay. She brought an equal value claim, naming her comparator a male checker warehouse operative who was earning a higher rate. It was held that her claim succeeded. To hold otherwise would enable an unscrupulous employer to defeat equal value claims by ensuring that one man who worked alongside women was paid the same.

Defence of material factor (s 69)

5.43 The sex equality clause will not take effect if the employer shows that the difference between the terms of persons of the opposite sex is because of a material factor, reliance on which:

(a) does not involve treating an employee less favourably because of the employee's sex than the employer would treat another employee of the opposite sex, and

(b) is a proportionate means of achieving a legitimate aim.

5.44 Pre-2010 cases held that length of service is an appropriate method of achieving the legitimate aim of rewarding experience required, which enables a worker to perform his duties better (*Cadman v Health and Safety Executive*[58]), but since length of service tends to disadvantage women, because they generally work for shorter periods of time than men, an employer would have to produce good and convincing reasons if the pay scale is arguably

---

[54] [2005] EWCA Civ 726, [2005] IRLR 615, [2005] ELR 475.

[55] [2011] EWCA Civ 903.

[56] See nn 2, 31.

[57] [1989] AC 66, [1988] 3 WLR 265, [1988] 2 All ER 803, [1988] 3 CMLR 221, [1988] ICR 697, [1988] IRLR 357, (1988) 138 NLJ Rep 193, (1988) *Times*, 1 July, (1988) *Independent*, 1 July, (1988) *Financial Times*, 5 July, (1988) *Guardian*, 1 July.

[58] [2007] All ER (EC) 1, [2006] ECR I–9583, [2007] 1 CMLR 16, [2007] CEC 318, [2006] ICR 1623, [2006] IRLR 969, (2006) *Times*, 6 October.

too long. Long-service-based increments must be shown to reward greater skill or experience, or achieve other aims such as the retention of labour (*Wilson v Health and Safety Executive*[59]). True, it was stated in *Handels-og-Kontorfuntionaererernes Forbund I Danmark v Dansk (acting for Danfloss)*[60] that '[l]ength of service goes hand in hand with experience, and since experience generally enables the employee to perform his duties better, the employer is free to reward him without having to establish the importance it has in the performance of specific tasks entrusted to the employee', but in *Cadman* it was stated that if the employee provides evidence that raises 'serious doubts' as to whether the general rule applies in a particular case, the employer will still have to prove objective justification. Thus it is not sufficient merely to state the fact of long-service increments without some attempt to justify them (*Honeywell Ltd v Scott*[61]).

5.45 Other non-sex material factors could be additional responsibility allowances (*Waddington v Leicester Council for Voluntary Services*[62]), extra pay for academic qualifications (*Murray v East Lothian Regional Council*[63]), long-service increments, a genuine mistake in putting an employee in the wrong grade (*Yorkshire Blood Transfusions Service v Plaskitt*[64]), productivity bonuses (*Redcar and Cleveland Borough Council v Bainbridge*[65]), anti-social working hours (*Chief Constable of West Midlands Police v Blackburn*[66]), differences in the place where the work was being done (*NAAFI v Varley*[67]), and differences between day work and night work (*Kerr v Lister & Co Ltd*[68]). Economic factors, such as a change in the volume of work that reflects the profitability of the firm (*Albion Shipping Agency v Arnold*[69]) or the need to attract qualified staff of either sex may also amount to a material factor (*Rainey v Greater Glasgow Health Board*[70]). Incentive bonus schemes may amount to a material factor, but if they maintain a pay differential between male dominated groups they should be monitored to ensure that they do what they are supposed to do, otherwise they will not amount to a material factor (*Hartlepool Borough Council v Dolphin*[71]). In an indirect sex discrimination equal pay case where the claimant has established that the factor relied on has an adverse disparate impact on women, if the employer can establish that the reason for the difference in pay is not sex-tainted, then there is no need to objectively justify the difference (*Armstrong v Newcastle NHS Foundation Trust*[72]). The fact that benefits paid to men under productivity schemes that were not discriminatory when they were introduced was not a sufficient justification where there was no longer a link between actual productivity and the bonus (*Council of the City of Sunderland v Brennan*[73]). The fact that rates of pay were agreed by collective bargaining is a factor that can be taken into account, but cannot be the only basis of justification (*Kenny v Minister for Justice*[74]).

5.46 A grading scheme which operates according to skill, experience and ability, and which is genuine and which is applied irrespective of the sex of the workers is not rendered inoperative by the Act (*National Vulcan Engineering Insurance Group v Wade*[75]).

---

[59] [2009] EWCA Civ 1074, [2010] 1 CMLR 24, [2010] ICR 302, [2010] IRLR 59, (2009) 153(40) SJLB 36, (2009) *Times*, 26 October.

[60] [1997] ECR I–2757, [1997] 2 CMLR 915, [1997] IRLR 643.   [61] IDS Handbook.

[62] [1977] 1 WLR 544, [1977] ICR 266, [1977] IRLR 32, (1976) 12 ITR 65, (1977) 121 SJ 84.

[63] [1977] CLY 972.   [64] [1994] ICR 74, (1993) *Times*, 17 August.

[65] [2008] EWCA Civ 885, [2009] ICR 133, [2008] IRLR 776.   [66] n 45.

[67] (1976) *Times*, 25 October.   [68] [1977] IRLR 259.   [69] [1982] ICR 22, [1981] IRLR 525.

[70] [1987] AC 224, [1986] 3 WLR 1017, [1987] 1 All ER 65, 1987 SC (HL) 1, 1987 SLT 146, [1987] 2 CMLR 11, [1987] ICR 129, [1987] IRLR 26, (1987) 84 LSG 188, (1986) 136 NLJ 1161, (1986) 130 SJ 954.

[71] [2009] IRLR 168, (2008) 152(38) SJLB 30.   [72] [2006] IRLR 124.

[73] [2012] EWCA Civ 413.   [74] Case C-427/11.

[75] [1979] QB 132, [1978] 3 WLR 214, [1978] 3 All ER 121, [1978] ICR 800, [1978] IRLR 225, (1978) 13 ITR 212, (1978) 122 SJ 470.

5.47 Pay protection schemes that are only offered to employees who would suffer as a result of the implementation of a job evaluation study are unlawful if they perpetuate historical indirect sex discrimination. Phasing out pay discrimination by cushioning the blow of pay cuts can be a legitimate objective, but may not be objectively justified if no thought is given to mitigating the continuing discriminatory effect (*Redcar and Cleveland Borough Council v Bainbridge*[76]). The long-term objective of reducing inequality between a man's and woman's terms of work is always to be regarded as a legitimate aim (s 69(3)).

5.48 The fact that a pay protection scheme has been negotiated with a trade union is not a justification for discrimination. Negotiators should pay attention to the possibility that differentials may have an adverse disparate impact on employees of a particular gender (*British Airways plc v Grundy*[77]).

5.49 'Red circle' treatment, ie the protection of a person's wages because of a demotion, transfer or downgrade, etc is permissible (*Forex Neptune (Overseas) Ltd v Miller*[78]) but the employment tribunal must be satisfied that the reason for the red circling has nothing to do with the sex of the person concerned (*Methven v Cow Industrial Polymers Ltd*[79]). Thus if there is direct discrimination, the material factor defence can never apply, because objective justification is not possible. It is possible that indirect discrimination can be objectively justified as long as the employer can disprove the influence of sex as a factor (*Middlesbrough Borough Council v Surtees*[80]).

5.50 Red circling of a comparator for a good reason is still a material factor defence, but there is an obligation to try to diminish its effects over time (usually by not increasing the red-circled pay to allow others to catch up (*Fearnon v Smurfit Corrugated Cases Ltd*[81]).

5.51 The mere attaching of a label of 'red circling' will not, by itself, constitute a material factor (*Honeywell Ltd v Scott*), particularly if past discrimination has contributed to the unequal pay (*Snoxell v Vauxhall Motors Ltd*[82]).

Sex discrimination in relation to contractual pay (s 71)

5.52 There may be circumstances where the absence of a comparator makes it impossible for the equality clause to operate (eg because a woman has no male colleague doing equal work with whom to compare), but nonetheless there is evidence of direct discrimination on grounds of sex (eg where the employer states that he would pay the employee more if she was a man). In these circumstances a claim for direct discrimination may be made under s 13 of the Act in respect of contractual pay even in the absence of a comparator.

Maternity equality clause (s 73)

5.53 The terms of employment of a woman must include a maternity equality clause. This means that any pay increase she receives (or would have received were she not on maternity leave) is to be taken into account in the calculation of her maternity pay. Pay (including any bonus) must be paid to her at the time she would otherwise have received it had she not been on maternity leave. On her return to work following maternity leave she is entitled to any pay increase she would have received had she not been on maternity leave.

[76] nn 46, 65.   [77] n 21.   [78] [1987] ICR 170, (1987) 84 LSG 112.
[79] [1980] ICR 463, [1980] IRLR 289, (1980) 124 SJ 374.
[80] [2008] EWCA Civ 885, [2009] ICR 133, [2008] IRLR 776.
[81] [2008] NICA 45, [2009] IRLR 132.   [82] [1977] ICR 700.

Pay structures etc

5.54 Any discrimination that is sex-based must be eliminated from an employer's pay structure, employment conditions, and collective agreements. An individual who considers that the terms of a collective agreement could have effect as being contrary to the principle of equal treatment may present a claim to an employment tribunal. This applies to actual and potential employees. If the complaint is well founded, the employment tribunal will declare the term to be void.

Discussions about pay (s 77)

5.55 A term of a person's work that purports to prevent or restrict that person from disclosing or seeking to disclose information about the terms of his/her work is unenforceable against that person, as is a term that is designed to prevent a person from seeking such information from a colleague or a former colleague. A relevant pay discussion is a discussion with a colleague about pay, and which relates to whether there is a connection between pay and having (or not having) a particular protected characteristic, and a colleague includes a former colleague in relation to the work in question. The discussion must be about pay, because s 77 does not cover discussions about other terms and conditions of employment. Thus a confidentiality clause, which purports to restrict a person from disclosing or seeking to disclose pay (including bonuses) with either colleagues or others (including, for example, a trade union official), would be unenforceable, if it is made for the purpose of establishing a connection between pay and a protected characteristics. The taking of disciplinary action against a person for entering into such discussions amounts to victimisation under s 27 (para 4.37).

Gender pay gap information (s 78)

5.56 The minister may make regulations requiring private sector employers with at least 250 employees to publish information about the differences in pay between their male and female employees.

Equal pay audit

5.57 Section 98 of the Enterprise and Regulatory Reform Act 2013 amends the Equality Act by introducing a new section 139A, which allows for regulations to be made to extend the powers of employment tribunals to require employers to conduct an equal pay audit, if the tribunal finds that they have discriminated on pay.

Jurisdiction (s 127)

5.58 An employment tribunal has jurisdiction to determine a complaint that relates to a breach of an equality clause. As well as complaints brought by a worker, an employer can seek a declaration as to the rights of the parties in the event of a dispute as to the effect of an equality clause, and a court may refer a claim or counterclaim that could more conveniently be dealt with in the employment tribunal.

Burden of proof (s 136)

5.59 If there are facts from which the employment tribunal could decide, in the absence of any other explanation, that the employer has contravened the provision concerned, the complaint must be upheld, but not if the employer satisfies the employment tribunal that there was no such contravention. The burden is therefore on the employer (*Kenny v Minister for Justice*, see para 5.45). The questionnaire procedure is also applicable (see paras 4.224 and 4.237).

Time limits (s 129)

5.60 A claim for the breach of an equality clause must normally be brought either during the employment or within six months of the end of the employment. Time will run from when the claimant left the employment, not from the time when s/he left the actual job on which the claim was based (*National Power plc v Young*[83]). However, if there has been a deliberate concealment by the employer of relevant information, without knowledge of which the worker could not reasonably be expected to bring the proceedings, or if the worker has been under an incapacity, the time limit will be extended to the end of the period of six months from the date when the concealment was first discovered, or the incapacity ceased, as the case may be.

5.61 If an employee is transferred from one employer to another, in circumstances where the transfer is governed by TUPE (see Chapter 9) employment with the transferor and transferee does not constitute a single period of employment. Thus, retrospective claims in respect of the pre-transfer period against the old employer must be brought within six months of the transfer date (*Gutridge v Sodexo Ltd*[84]).

5.62 In *Birmingham City Council (Appellant) v Abdulla and others (Respondents)*,[85] an equal pay claim which was brought outside the six months permitted by the employment tribunal was brought as a breach of contract claim in the ordinary courts (as equal pay relates to an implied equality clause in every contract), which have a time limit of six years (five in Scotland). This was because the six-month time limit in the tribunal cannot be extended on the grounds that it is just and equitable, unlike other types of discrimination claims. The defendants applied to have the claim struck out as an abuse of process. This was rejected by the Supreme Court on the basis that the six-month limitation period set for employment tribunal claims had never been made extendable, which suggested that Parliament recognised the availability of an alternative claim process in the High Court. The claim could therefore be brought in the High Court under the longer limitation period.

Remedies (s 132)

5.63 If the tribunal finds that there has been a breach of the equality clause, it may:

   (a) make a declaration as to the rights of the parties;

   (b) order an award by way of arrears of pay to the complainant.

---

[83] [2004] EWHC 2972 (QB), [2005] 2 Lloyd's Rep 46.
[84] [2009] EWCA Civ 729, [2009] ICR 1486, [2009] IRLR 721, (2009) 106(30) LSG 13, (2009) *Times*, 6 October.
[85] [2012] UKSC 47.

5.64 The claim can only be in respect of the salary the comparator was receiving, ignoring any potential increments which could have been earned. In *Enderby v Frenchay Health Authority*[86] the claimant worked for a health authority for six years. She successfully made an equal value claim, using as her comparator a man who had only been employed for one year. She argued that she was entitled to the pay her comparator would have received had he been employed as long as she, ie to include the potential increments he would have had. The Court of Appeal held that she was entitled to receive the same pay as her comparator was currently receiving (see also *Evesham v North Hertfordshire Health Authority*[87]).

Death of a claimant

5.65 A cause of action under the Equality Act can be continued after the death of the claimant by his personal representatives, under the provisions of the Law Reform (Miscellaneous Provisions) Act 1934 (*Lewisham and Guys Mental Health NHS Trust v Andrews*[88]).

Backdating awards

5.66 In England and Wales, the award in respect of equal pay and equal value claims cannot be backdated more than six years from the time when proceedings were instituted, and in Scotland the award cannot be backdated more than five years from when proceedings were commenced. An award in respect of a job evaluation scheme can only be backdated to the date when the scheme came into force (*Bainbridge v Redcar and Cleveland Borough Council*[89]). An award of interest may be made, calculated in accordance with the provisions of the Sex Discrimination and Equal Pay (Remedies) Regulations 1993. No compensation for injured feelings may be awarded (*City of Newcastle upon Tyne v Allen*[90]).

---

[86] [2000] ICR 612, [2000] IRLR 257, (2000) *Times*, 29 February.
[87] [2000] ICR 612, [2000] IRLR 257, (2000) *Times*, 29 February.
[88] [2000] 3 All ER 769, [2000] ICR 707, [2000] IRLR 320, (2000) 97(15) LSG 40, (2000) 144 SJLB 159, (2000) *Times*, 28 March, (2000) *Independent*, 29 March.
[89] nn 49, 65, 76.
[90] [1995] CLY 3664.

6

Family Friendly Rights

6.1 In this chapter we shall consider various family friendly rights designed to assist employees with parental and child-care responsibilities. These are maternity rights generally, ordinary and additional maternity leave, ordinary and additional adoption leave, parental leave, paternity leave, caring for dependants and applications for flexible working. The relevant statutory provisions are based on the implementation of a number of EU Directives, and to that extent EU jurisprudence must be considered where appropriate.

6.2 For the purposes of the Employment Rights Act 1996, childbirth is defined as the birth of a living child or the birth of a child whether living or dead after 24 weeks of pregnancy. Certain rights to be considered also apply on the adoption of a child.

Maternity rights

A. **Time off work for antenatal care (ERA, ss 55–57)**

6.3 An employee who is pregnant, and who, on the advice of a registered medical practitioner, registered midwife or registered health visitor, has made an appointment to attend any place for the purpose of receiving antenatal care, shall have the right not to be unreasonably refused time off work during her working hours to enable her to keep that appointment. This right arises from the moment the woman commences her employment, and is irrespective of the number of hours or days worked (but see para 6.6) or whether or not she is a permanent or temporary employee. The size of the employer's undertaking is also irrelevant. The only women who do not enjoy this right are those who are not employed under a contract of employment, or who are share fisherwomen, or women employed as members of any constabulary.

6.4 If requested to do so, she must produce a certificate stating that she is pregnant. (A woman who has had in vitro fertilisation is pregnant from the time when the fertilised ovary is implanted in her uterus (*Mayr v Backerei und Konditorei Gerhard Flockner OHG*[1]).) She must produce some documentary evidence of the antenatal appointment (but not the first appointment).

6.5 She is entitled to be paid for the period of her absence at the appropriate hourly rate (calculated in accordance with the provisions of s 56). If she is refused time off work, or if she is not paid for the time off taken, she may make a complaint to an employment tribunal (within three months of the date of the appointment in question, or within such further time as the employment tribunal considers to be reasonable) that her employer has unreasonably refused to permit her to have time off work, or has failed to pay her the whole or part of the amount to which she claims she was entitled. If the employment tribunal

---

[1] [2008] All ER (EC) 613, [2008] ECR I–1017, [2008] 2 CMLR 27, [2008] CEC 549, [2008] IRLR 387, [2008] 1 FLR 1242, [2008] 3 FCR 44, [2008] Fam Law 512, (2008) *Times*, 12 March.

upholds her complaint, it will make a declaration to that effect, and also award her the amount of remuneration to which she is entitled (s 57).

6.6 It should be noted that the right is not to be unreasonably refused time off work. Thus it may be possible to argue that in particular circumstances it would be reasonable for the woman to make arrangements for antenatal care outside working hours (eg in the case of a woman who works part-time, or less than five days each week). Antenatal care is not defined in the Act, but undoubtedly includes antenatal relaxation classes and (possibly) classes in parentcraft, provided she attends on the advice of a medical practitioner etc (see *Gregory v Tudsbury Ltd*[2]).

6.7 An employer cannot defeat a woman's statutory rights by rearranging her working hours or requiring her to work additional hours to make up for time lost (*Edgar v Giorgine Inns Ltd*[3]). On the other hand, if a woman abuses the time off provisions, and takes additional time off work for activities which are not antenatal care, she will have no rights under the Act, and will be subject to the usual consequences which flow from disciplinary proceedings (*Gough v County Sports (Wales) Ltd*[4]).

6.8 If an employer refuses to pay a pregnant woman when she takes time off work for ante-natal care, then as well as bringing a claim under s 57(5) of ERA for the amount due, she may also claim that she has suffered a detriment under reg 19 of the Maternity and Parental Leave etc Regulations, for which compensation may be awarded, including an award in respect of injury to feelings.

B. Risk assessment and suspension on maternity grounds

6.9 Under the Management of Health and Safety at Work Regulations 1999 (see Chapter 11) every employer is required to carry out a risk assessment, designed to ensure the health and safety at work of new or expectant mothers, defined as employees who are pregnant, who have given birth within the preceding six months, or who are breastfeeding.

6.10 The first requirement is that where the workforce includes women of childbearing age, *and* the work is of a kind which could involve risk to the health or safety (because of pregnancy or maternity) to a new or expectant mother, or to that of her baby, from any processes or working conditions, or from physical, biological or chemical agents (including those set out in Annexes I and II of Directive 92/85/EEC) the employer shall carry out a risk assessment; see reg 16. It should be noted that the provisions of the Management of Health and Safety at Work Regulations now confer a right of action in civil proceedings (see para 11.72). Thus in *Day v T Pickles Farm Ltd* the EAT thought that the failure to carry out a risk assessment on a woman of childbearing age could amount to sex discrimination and may also amount to a repudiatory breach of contract by the employer entitling the employee to resign and claim she has been constructively dismissed (*Bunning v GT Bunning & Sons Ltd*[5]).

6.11 The physical agents referred to are those which are likely to cause foetal lesions or disrupt placental attachment, eg shocks, movement, ionising or non-ionising radiation, extremes of heat or cold, travel, mental or physical fatigue, etc. The biological agents include those set out in Directive 90/679/EEC (the Biological Agents Directive) in so far as it is known that these agents can endanger the health of a woman or her unborn child. The chemical agents include dangerous substances set out in Directive 90/393/EEC (Carcinogens at Work Directive), Annex I. Also included are certain industrial processes,

---

[2] [1982] IRLR 267.   [3] Unreported.   [4] Unreported.   [5] EAT/0136/03.

underground mining work, pressurised enclosures (eg underwater diving), work with certain viruses (unless immunised), lead and lead derivatives. After the risk assessment has been carried out, the employer must provide all female workers of childbearing age with comprehensible and relevant information of the risks to their health identified by the assessment, and also with details of the preventative and protective measures which need to be taken to comply with the relevant statutory provisions (see Chapter 11).

6.12 Once the employer is aware that a woman employee is pregnant, or is breastfeeding, a second risk assessment needs to be made in respect of that woman, to ascertain what measures need to be taken to avoid the risk to her health. These risks could be heavy lifting, prolonged standing, night work, early shift work, work-related stress, threats from customers, exposure to nauseating smells, working excessive hours, lack of rest breaks, and so on. If measures cannot be taken to avoid the risk, the employer must alter her working hours or, if this is not feasible or would not avoid the risk, she should be offered alternative employment or put on paid leave of absence (ERA s 67, and reg 16(3) of the Maternity etc Regulations). The risk assessment does not need to be in writing when relating to a particular individual, because it is the employer's 'thought process' which is relevant (*Stevenson v J M Skinner & Co*[6]) Avoiding the risk does not mean eliminating altogether. It means reducing the risk to the lowest acceptable level (*New Southern Railways Ltd v Quinn*[7]). It should be noted that an employer is not obliged to alter her working conditions or working hours, or to suspend her from work, unless she has informed him in writing that she is pregnant, or has given birth within the previous six months, or is breastfeeding.

6.13 Next, if a new or expectant mother works at night, and a certificate from a registered medical practitioner or registered midwife shows that it is necessary for her health or safety that she should not be at work for any period identified in the certificate, then the employer shall suspend her from work (subject to ERA, s 66 below). There is also a requirement under health and safety legislation for an employer to provide suitable rest facilities for a pregnant woman, or a woman who has given birth within the previous six months, or who is breastfeeding (Workplace (Health, Safety and Welfare) Regulations 1992, reg 25 (4)).

6.14 The maternity provisions stem from ERA, s 66 because the Management of Health and Safety at Work Regulations are specified as being the 'relevant statutory provision' for the purpose of that section (see Suspension from Work (on Maternity Grounds) Order 1994). Additionally a woman is entitled to be suspended from work on maternity grounds due to any recommendation contained in an approved code of practice issued by the Health and Safety Executive under the Health and Safety at Work etc Act 1974, s 16 (see Chapter 11).

Flowing from her right to be suspended on maternity grounds, a woman will have two further rights.

Alternative work (ERA, s 67)

6.15 Before suspending a woman on maternity grounds, the employer, if he has available suitable alternative work, shall offer it to her. The alternative work must be of a kind which is suitable for her, and appropriate in the circumstances (see *Iske v P & O European Ferries (Dover) Ltd*[8]). If the terms and conditions differ from her normal contract of employment, they must not be substantially less favourable (see *British Airways (European Operations at Gatwick) Ltd v Moore and Botterill*[9]). A failure to make such an offer entitles the woman to bring a complaint to an employment tribunal; within the usual time limits, which may

[6] Employment Appeal Tribunal, 6 March 2008.
[7] [2006] ICR 761, [2006] IRLR 266.   [8] [1997] IRLR 401, EAT.
[9] [2000] 2 CMLR 343, [2000] ICR 678, [2000] IRLR 296, EAT.

make an award of compensation as the employment tribunal considers to be just and equitable in all the circumstances.

She is not entitled to be paid, however, if the employer offers her suitable alternative work which she unreasonably refuses to do.

6.16 The Pregnant Workers Directive (92/85/EEC) contains an absolute and express prohibition on exposure to the listed risks. However, the Management Regulations, reg 16 requires that risks to the health of a pregnant woman shall be avoided, which means that if the risk cannot be eliminated in its entirety, it must be reduced to its lowest acceptable level. Thus, if it is decided to remove a pregnant woman from her present job because of a perceived health or safety risk, this can be a pointless exercise if the new job offer contains equally perceived risks. To use a hypothetical risk as an excuse to demote a woman from her job (with a consequential reduction in salary) can amount to a detriment contrary to ERA, s 47C, and a failure to offer alternative employment on terms not substantially less favourable is contrary to ERA, s 67. It may be discrimination on grounds of sex, and could give rise to a potential constructive dismissal claim (*New Southern Railway Ltd v Quinn*[10]).

Maternity suspension pay (ERA, s 68)

6.17 A woman who is suspended from work on maternity grounds is entitled to be paid a week's pay in respect of each week of suspension, reduced proportionately if the suspension is for less than a week. She is entitled to be paid her normal hourly rate of pay (ie the week's pay will be divided by the number of normal working hours). If her working hours vary from week to week they are to be averaged over the previous 12 working weeks. If she has not completed 12 weeks' service, an average shall be estimated from the agreed terms and conditions and from the work pattern of others in comparable jobs. A failure by the employer to pay the whole or any part of the remuneration due entitles the woman to bring a complaint to an employment tribunal, which, if it finds the complaint well founded, shall order the employer to pay the amount of remuneration due to her.

6.18 Finally, it should be noted that no period of continuous employment is required for a woman to have these rights (in contrast to the general right to be suspended on medical grounds – see para 7.10, where continuous employment of one month is required).

C. **Maternity leave (ERA, ss 71–74, Maternity and Parental Leave etc Regulations 1999 as amended)**

6.19 There are three periods of maternity leave:

(a) Compulsory maternity leave. This prevents a woman from working for the period of two weeks immediately following the date of childbirth.

(b) Ordinary maternity leave (OML). All pregnant women are entitled to take 26 weeks OML irrespective of their length of service, provided they satisfy the relevant conditions.

(c) Additional maternity leave (AML). All women are entitled to a further 26 weeks AML at the end of their OML, irrespective of their length of service.

(NB Entitlement to ordinary and additional maternity leave must not be confused with entitlement to Statutory Maternity Pay (SMP) or Maternity Allowance (MA), for which see paras 6.56 and 6.65.)

---

[10] [2006] ICR 761, EAT.

Compulsory maternity leave (ERA, s 72(1))

6.20 The taking of ordinary maternity leave or additional maternity leave is an option for women who are pregnant. It is not compulsory. It is not unknown for some women to want to return to work as soon as possible after the birth. To prevent this, ERA, s 72 provides that an employer shall not permit a woman to work within two weeks of childbirth. A contravention of this provision can lead to a fine of not exceeding Level 2 on the standard scale. Any prohibition arising under the Health and Safety at Work Act will also apply. Also it is an offence (punishable by a fine of up to Level 1 on the standard scale) to permit a woman to work in a factory within four weeks of childbirth (Public Health Act 1936, s 205; Factories Act 1961, Sch 5).

Ordinary maternity leave and additional maternity leave

6.21 The Maternity and Parental Leave etc Regulations 1999 were amended in 2008 so as to remove the distinction between ordinary and additional maternity leave and the distinction between ordinary and additional adoption leave. This means in effect that certain benefits, such as company cars, gym membership, health insurance etc, which used to apply only during ordinary maternity and ordinary adoption leave, will now apply throughout additional maternity and additional adoption leave. Seniority and personal length of service rights (eg pay increments) will continue throughout both periods. The only practical difference nowadays between ordinary and additional maternity leave and ordinary and additional adoption leave concerns the right to return to work and the non-accrual of pension rights during the unpaid part of additional leave. Terms and conditions relating to remuneration remain unaffected.

6.22 An employee (not a worker), who is appropriately qualified, is entitled to 26 weeks ordinary maternity leave and a further 26 weeks additional maternity. This is irrespective of her length of service or whether or not she is a temporary or permanent employee. The only exclusions are in respect of members of the armed forces, share fisherwomen and members of the constabulary. In order to qualify for maternity leave, the employee must notify her employer (in writing if he so requests) no later than the end of the 15th week before the expected week of confinement of:

(a) her pregnancy

(b) the expected week of childbirth, and

(c) the date on which she intends her ordinary maternity leave period to start. This may start any time from the beginning of the 11th week before the expected week of confinement.

6.23 If it is not reasonably practicable for her to give 15 weeks' notice of her intention to take maternity leave, she must do so as soon as is reasonably practicable. If the employer so requests, she must produce for inspection a certificate from a registered medical practitioner or a registered midwife stating the expected week of childbirth. If she wishes to vary the date of the commencement of her ordinary maternity leave, she must give at least 28 days' notice, or, if that is not reasonably practicable, as soon as is reasonably practicable.

6.24 On receipt of the notice, the employer must notify the employee, within 28 days, of the date on which her additional maternity leave will end. If he fails to do so, he will not be able to complain if she returns to work too early or too late, and the employee may have a remedy under regs 19–20 in respect of detriment or dismissal.

6.25 Maternity leave will start on either (a) the date she has notified to her employer as the date she intends it to start, or (b) the day which follows the first day after the beginning of the fourth week before the EWC on which she is absent from work wholly or partly because of her pregnancy, or (c) the day that follows the day on which childbirth occurs. She can vary the date on which she intends to start her maternity leave by giving her employer notice of the new date 28 days before the date originally specified, or 28 days before the date on which she intends her maternity leave to start or, if that is not reasonably practicable, then as soon as is reasonably practicable. However, the revised date cannot be earlier than the beginning of the 11th week before the EWC, and the notification must be in writing if the employer so requests.

6.26 However, there are two exceptions to the notification requirements. These are:

(a) if the maternity leave commences with the day which follows the first day after the beginning of the fourth week before the EWC on which she is absent from work wholly or partly because of pregnancy; or

(b) if her maternity leave commences with the day which follows the day on which childbirth occurs.

6.27 In both cases she must notify the employer as soon as is reasonably practicable (in writing if he so requests) that she will be absent from work because of pregnancy or because she has given birth, and the date on which either event took place.

Terms and conditions during ordinary maternity leave

6.28 An employee who takes maternity leave is entitled to the benefit of all the terms and conditions of employment which would have applied had she not been absent, whether or not they arise under her contract of employment. In other words, she is to be treated as if her contract of employment continues during her maternity leave. The only exception is that she is not entitled to terms and conditions relating to remuneration. Thus contractual and non-contractual benefits, other than sums which would have been payable by way of wages or salary, must be continued, eg life and medical insurance, private use of a company car, mortgage subsidies, etc. Whether profit-related pay, bonuses and commissions which arises after the commencement of maternity leave are payable will depend on the purpose for which and the terms under which these payments are to be made. The test is whether or not these can be defined as being 'wages or salary'.

6.29 A woman who takes maternity leave during a year when a bonus is payable must be paid the bonus for the periods when she is at work and for the fortnight of compulsory maternity leave. The general principle was laid down by the European Court in *Lewen v Denda*[11] that an employer is entitled to make a pro rata deduction for work done during the employee's absence on maternity leave (except when on compulsory maternity leave). Any such deduction does not amount to sex discrimination because of the exclusion that relates to the payment of money during such leave (*Hoyland v Asda Stores Ltd*[12]). The employee cannot take contractual annual leave during her maternity leave, as this would come under the remuneration exclusion. She will be entitled to take statutory paid annual leave during a period other than the period of her maternity leave, because maternity leave is not a holiday, and the time spent by a woman on maternity leave cannot count against her holiday entitlement. This means that her annual holiday entitlement must be taken either before the start of maternity leave or after its expiry (*Merino Gomez v Continental Industrias del Caucho*[13]), although it is not certain if this rule applies if the current holiday year has expired.

---

[11] [2000] IRLR 67, (2000) ICR 648.

[12] [2006] CSIH 21, 2006 SC 550, 2006 SLT 524, [2006] IRLR 468, 2006 GWD 14–263.

[13] (C-342/01) [2004] 2 CMLR 38, [2004] All ER (D) 350 (Mar), ECJ.

6.30 Similarly, a woman who gives in her notice during her absence on maternity leave (or who is given notice by her employer) is entitled to be paid for the statutory notice period (ERA, s 88(1)(cc)), although this will not apply to notice given by either party if the period of notice to be given by the employer under the contract is at least one week longer than the statutory notice period (*Scotts Company (UK) Ltd v Budd*[14]). However, she would not be entitled to contractual notice pay, as this would fall to be excluded under the definition of remuneration (ERA, s 71).

6.31 For her part, during the period of maternity leave, the employee is bound by any obligations which arise under her terms and conditions of employment. Thus, she is still an employee, and must abide by relevant contractual obligations, such as confidentiality, etc (see Chapter 10). Obviously, she is not required to turn up for work, as this would be inconsistent with her statutory right but she can agree to 'keeping in touch' days (see para 6.35).

Additional maternity leave

6.32 An employee who is entitled to ordinary maternity leave is entitled to a further period of six months additional maternity leave, which must commence immediately following the end of the period of ordinary maternity leave. The only distinction between the two types of leave is that during additional maternity leave, she will not be entitled to accrued pension rights during the latter part of additional maternity leave (ie for the last 13 weeks), and her right to return to work is slightly more restricted.

Terms and conditions during additional maternity leave (reg 17)

6.33 During the period of additional maternity leave, the employee is entitled to the benefit of the employer's implied obligation of trust and confidence. She is also entitled to any terms and conditions relating to notice on termination by her employer, compensation in the event of redundancy, and the benefit of any disciplinary or grievance procedures. For her part, she is bound by any terms and conditions relating to the giving of notice by her, non-disclosure of confidential information, the acceptance of gifts or other benefits from third parties, and her participation in any other business. However, statutory annual leave entitlement under the Working Time Regulations will continue to accrue, as will her right to statutory notice on dismissal (see s 88(1)(c), at para 6.30).

6.34 The period of additional maternity leave will count towards the period of continuous employment for the purpose of statutory employment rights, but not for the purpose of assessing contractual rights which depend on length of service, eg contractual leave provisions, annual increments, seniority rights, etc.

Reasonable contact (reg 12A)

6.35 The employer and employee may agree to make reasonable contact with each other from time to time during the maternity leave period, and this will not bring that period to an end. It is suggested that this can be for the purpose of discussing details of the return to work, communicating information, informing the employee of promotion opportunities, etc. Contact may be by any suitable means eg, telephone, email, personal visits, etc.

Work during maternity leave period (reg 12A)

6.36 An employee may carry out up to 10 days' work for her employer during the statutory leave period without bringing that period to an end. Work, which includes training, will count as a full day if it is done for part of a day. The type of work that the employee

---

[14] [2004] ICR 299, [2003] IRLR 145, [2002] All ER (D) 58 (Nov), EAT.

may carry out will be a matter for agreement between the parties, but it would normally be any activity which would ordinarily be classed as work under the woman's contract of employment. She is entitled to be paid on an agreed basis, and her entitlement to statutory maternity pay will not be affected. Any such work will not extend the total duration of the maternity leave period. However, no such work can be done within the two weeks following childbirth.

6.37 A woman who refuses to keep in touch or to work during her maternity leave period has protection from suffering a detriment or dismissal in consequence of that refusal.

Returning to work after ordinary maternity leave (regs 18(1), 18A(1), 10)

6.38 An employee who wishes to return to work after her ordinary maternity leave is entitled to return to the job in which she was employed before her absence, with seniority, pension and similar as they would have been had she not been absent, and on terms and conditions not less favourable than those that would have applied if she had not been absent. Her period of absence during ordinary maternity leave will count as continuous employment for the purpose of any rights or benefits that depend on an employee's length of service, eg service-related pay increments. A refusal to permit her to return to her old job may amount to a dismissal, which could be unfair, and may also amount to direct discrimination.

6.39 However, there are certain exceptions to this rule. The first arises where she has taken two or more consecutive periods of statutory leave, which include the ordinary leave period, and any period of additional maternity leave, or additional adoption leave, or any period of parental leave lasting more than four weeks. If it is not reasonably practicable for a reason other than redundancy for her to return to the same job then she is entitled to be offered another job that is suitable and appropriate for her to do in the circumstances.

6.40 The second exception arises where a redundancy situation arises during the maternity leave, and it is not practicable to continue to employ her under the existing contract. In this situation she is entitled to be offered any suitable alternative employment, on terms and conditions that are not substantially less favourable (reg 18(4), reg 10). The work must be suitable and appropriate, and its provisions as to the capacity and place in which she is to be employed, and other terms and conditions, are not substantially less favourable to her than if she had continued to be employed under the previous contract. The new contract must take effect immediately on the ending of the previous contract. If a suitable vacancy exists, and the employer fails to offer it to her, the dismissal will be automatically unfair under s 99 of ERA if the principle reason was redundancy (reg 20(l)(b)). However, if there is no such vacancy, her dismissal for reason of redundancy will be fair. If she unreasonably refuses the offer, her dismissal will be fair, and she may lose her entitlement to a redundancy payment (ERA, s 141). If she is made redundant, then in addition to her redundancy payment (if she qualifies), she will be entitled to her notice period, and a written statement of the reasons for her dismissal.

6.41 Where the respondent had to choose between a man and a woman on maternity leave when deciding whom to make redundant, it was not reasonably necessary to give the female comparator a maximum notional score. There were more proportionate means available to ensure she did not lose out in the redundancy exercise because of her maternity absence, otherwise there was a risk of sex discrimination against the male claimant (*Eversheds Legal Services Ltd v De Belin*[15]).

---

[15] [2011] IRLR 448.

6.42 Finally, she will not be entitled to return to her old job if she has indicated that she does not wish to do so (eg because she wishes to change her location of work, or to work different hours, etc). However, a failure by an employer to accommodate the changed situation may amount to sex discrimination.

6.43 The 'job' to which she is entitled to return means the nature of the work she was employed to do in accordance with her contract, ie the same job she was doing before she went on maternity leave, and the capacity and place where she was employed. If there have been changes during her absence, these will be irrelevant as long as the contractual obligations are the same (*Edgell v Lloyd's Register of Shipping*[16]). In *Blundell v St Andrew's Catholic Primary School*[17] the claimant was a primary school teacher. It was the policy of the school to rotate teachers every two years. The claimant taught the reception class when she went on maternity leave, but when she returned to work she was allocated year 2. She claimed she had not been allowed to return to work at the job at which she was employed before her absence. Her claim was dismissed. Taking into account the nature, capacity and location of the respective jobs, the statutory requirements were satisfied. She had been offered her old job as a primary school teacher.

Returning to work after additional maternity leave (regs 18(2), 18A(2))

6.44 The position is similar, but not identical, in the case of a return to work after additional maternity leave. She is entitled to return to her old job, with her seniority, pension and similar rights as they would have been had she not been absent from work, on terms and conditions not less favourable than those that would have applied had she not been absent. Her period of absence during additional maternity leave will count towards continuity of employment for the purpose of the various statutory rights. However, there are two exceptions to this rule. First, her pension rights under an employment-related benefits scheme will have been suspended during the period of unpaid maternity leave, so that such rights are preserved as if the two periods on either side of the unpaid maternity leave were continuous. Second, where it is not reasonably practicable, for a reason other than redundancy, for an employer to permit her to return to her old job after taking additional maternity leave, she is entitled to be offered another job that is both suitable and appropriate for her to do in the circumstances.

Redundancy during maternity leave (reg 10)

6.45 If it is not practicable for reason of redundancy for her employer to continue to employ her under her existing contract, the employee is entitled to be offered a suitable alternative vacancy, with the employer, his successor or an associated employer (reg 10). The new contract must take effect immediately on the ending of the old one. The work must be suitable and appropriate for her to do in the circumstances, and the capacity and place of employment and other terms and conditions must be not substantially less favourable that if she had continued to work under the old contract. If such a suitable vacancy exists, and the employer fails to offer it to her, the dismissal will be automatically unfair under ERA, s 99. A suitable vacancy exists even though the employer may not wish to fill it for economic reasons (*Community Task Force v Rimmer*[18]). However, if there is genuinely no such vacancy, she will be entitled to a redundancy payment, although if she unreasonably refuses the offer, she may lose her right to a redundancy payment (ERA, s 141). If the employer fails to observe the appropriate procedure for selecting employees for redundancy (consultation, proper notice, search for alternatives etc) she may claim unfair dismissal in the ordinary way, and possibly claim sex discrimination. When selecting for redundancy an employer

---

[16] [1977] IRLR 463.   [17] [2007] ICR 1451, [2007] IRLR 652.
[18] [1986] ICR 491, [1986] IRLR 203, (1986) 83 LSG 968.

cannot assess those who have been off work on parental leave on different criteria to those who have not been on leave – *Riezniece v Zemkopibas Ministrija*.[19] Obviously, if her selection was due to her pregnancy or the fact that she took maternity leave, this will again be automatically unfair (reg 20(2)).

6.46 It should be remembered that the employer's duty to offer alternative employment to a woman who has been on maternity leave is an absolute one, ie the offer must be in preference to any other employee who is similarly affected by the redundancy situation but who has not been absent on maternity leave. This applies even though the woman is actually on maternity leave at the time the redundancy situation arises. The work, however, only needs to be offered if it is suitable for her in the circumstances (*Simpson v Endsleigh Insurance Services*[20]). A failure to notify a woman who is on maternity leave that there is a suitable vacancy for which she could have applied is a fundamental breach of the implied term of trust and confidence, entitling her to resign and claim constructive dismissal (*Visa International Services Association v Paul*[21]).

6.47 There is no need for her to give notice to her employer of the date when she will be returning to work after maternity leave or additional maternity leave. It will be recalled (see para 6.24) that once the employer has received notice that she intends to take maternity leave or additional maternity leave, he must write to her within 28 days confirming the date on which she is due to return to work. However, if she wishes to return earlier, she must give at least eight weeks' notice of her intention to do so. If she returns to work without giving this notice, the employer is entitled to postpone her return to a date which will secure eight weeks' notice (but not beyond the 26-week period of maternity leave or the 52-week period of additional maternity leave). If she actually returns to work without giving the notice, she is not entitled to be paid her contractual remuneration.

6.48 The general rule is that once maternity leave or additional maternity leave comes to an end, the employee has no right to postpone her return to work any longer. There are, however, three circumstances when she may do so. First, if the employer has failed to notify the employee of the date when her leave would end, and she reasonably believes that the period has not ended (regs 19(2)–20(3)). Second, if she is sick at the end of her maternity leave, she is entitled to be treated in the same way as any other employee who is off work sick. Thus she will have an entitlement to sick pay, and, if the absence is likely to last a length of time, the usual procedure for dealing with the long-term sick employee should be adopted (see para 17.93). Third, she may postpone her return to work by adding on another leave period, eg annual holidays, parental leave etc.

6.49 If the employee fails to return to work after her leave entitlement has come to an end, she should be treated as an unauthorised absentee, and dealt with under the appropriate disciplinary procedure. If she wishes to return to work, but the employer refuses to permit her to do so, this will amount to an automatically unfair dismissal if the reason was because she had given birth or exercised her rights to take maternity leave or additional maternity leave.

D. **Remedies**

6.50 An employee is entitled not to be subjected to any detriment because she is pregnant, gave birth to a child, was suspended from work on maternity grounds, or took ordinary or additional maternity leave (ERA, s 47C). She will be deemed to have been automatically unfairly

---

[19] (Case C-7/12); [2013] WLR (D) 247.
[20] [2010] UKEAT/544/09, [2011] ICR 75. [21] [2004] IRLR 42.

dismissed if the reason for her dismissal was that she was pregnant, gave birth to a child, or took ordinary or additional maternity leave. It will also be unfair to select her for redundancy for any of these reasons (ERA, s 99, reg 20). According to the European Court of Justice it is not contrary to the Equal Treatment Directive to dismiss a woman after her maternity leave has come to an end because of absences due to a pregnancy-related illness, even though that illness first appeared during her pregnancy (*Handels-og v Dansk Handel*, see para 4.136).

6.51 The dismissal of a pregnant woman who is unable to complete a fixed-term contract is sex discrimination under the Equal Treatment Directive and Pregnant Workers Directive, even though the woman knew she was pregnant when she was recruited, did not tell her employer, and her presence at work is essential for the proper functioning of the employer's business (*Tele-Danmark A/S v Handels (HK) per Brandt-Nielsen*[22]). Equally, the non-renewal of a fixed-term contract on grounds of pregnancy is discrimination, although not if the reason for the non-renewal had nothing to do with the fact of pregnancy (*Jiminez Melgar v Ayuntamiento de los Barrios*[23]).

6.52 Of course, if the employer did not know that she was pregnant, and dismisses her for a reason unconnected with her pregnancy, she will not be able to claim that her dismissal was contrary to s 99 of ERA. An employer must know, or believe in the existence of an employee's pregnancy in order to be liable for automatically unfair dismissal (*Del Monte Foods v Mundon*[24] approved in *Ramdoolar v Bycity Ltd*[25]). Equally, if she is selected for redundancy, and the pregnancy or childbirth had nothing to do with her selection, then her right to a redundancy payment falls to be considered under s 135.

6.53 If an employer has engaged a temporary replacement to do the work of a woman who is absent because of pregnancy or childbirth, then, if he has informed him/her in writing that the employment will be terminated on the return to work of the latter, and the employer does in fact dismiss the temporary replacement in order to make room for the woman returning from maternity leave, the dismissal shall be regarded as being for some other substantial reason of a kind to justify the dismissal, but the employer must still show that he acted reasonably in treating that reason as a sufficient ground for dismissal (see Chapter 17). The same rule applies when a replacement is taken on when a woman is suspended on medical or maternity grounds (ERA, s 106).

6.54 An employee may exercise her contractual or statutory rights, whichever is the more favourable. Her remedy for a breach of her contractual rights (other than in respect of remuneration) is by way of a claim for breach of contract in the county court, or a breach of contract claim under the provisions of the Employment Tribunals Extension of Jurisdiction Order (see para 1.40) where the claim is outstanding on the termination of her employment. She may also claim that she has suffered a detriment contrary to reg 19, or claim unfair dismissal under reg 10 or reg 20.

6.55 Finally, a woman who is dismissed at any time while she is pregnant or after childbirth when the maternity leave period ends by reason of the dismissal is entitled to be given written reasons for her dismissal, without any request being made (see para 17.177). This rule will also apply if an employee is dismissed while absent from work during an ordinary or additional adoption leave period (see para 6.67). In both cases, no period of continuous employment is required (ERA, s 92(4), (4A)).

---

[22] (C-109/00) [2001] ECR I-6993, [2001] All ER (EC) 941, [2002] 1 CMLR 105, [2001] IRLR 853, [2001] All ER (D) 37 (Oct), ECJ.
[23] (C-438/99) [2001] ECR I-6915, [2003] 3 CMLR 67, [2001] IRLR 848, [2001] All ER (D) 42 (Oct), ECJ.
[24] [1980] ICR 694, [1980] IRLR 224.
[25] [2005] ICR 368, EAT.

E. **Statutory Maternity Pay (SMP)**

6.56 The Statutory Maternity Pay (General) Regulations 1986 (as amended) make provision for SMP to be paid by employers, and recouped by them from the national insurance contributions they pay to the Revenue. SMP is payable for a period of 39 weeks to employees who satisfy the conditions of eligibility.

6.57 The first qualification for SMP is that the woman must be an 'employed earner', ie whose earnings attract a liability for employer's Class 1 national insurance contributions. This concept is slightly wider than the definition of 'employee' generally used in employment law, and refers to a woman who is gainfully employed under a contract of service or an office holder whose earnings are chargeable to income tax under Schedule E. The result could well be that a woman may be regarded as self-employed for SMP purposes, and thus not entitled to this benefit (eg because no Class 1 contributions are being made) but an employee for the purpose of employment protection rights, and thus be able to benefit from the provisions relating to maternity leave and the right to return to work. A woman who is employed by a foreign organisation with no place of business in the United Kingdom will also not qualify for SMP, although women who work within the European Community are so entitled.

6.58 Second, she must have been continuously employed (not necessarily working) for a period of 26 weeks immediately before the 15th week before the expected week of confinement. There is no minimum number of hours' qualification, she does not need to be actually working as long as the contract of employment is in existence, and there are a number of provisions which help her to retain continuity where it would otherwise be broken.

6.59 Third, she must satisfy the earnings rule, ie her average earnings (including overtime and bonuses) must be at or above the lower earnings limit at which national insurance contributions are payable (£111 per week from April 2014. Note that all figures listed are reviewed annually). Average earnings are to be calculated over a period of eight weeks ending with the last pay day before the end of the qualifying week.

6.60 Fourth, she must produce a medical certificate stating the expected week of confinement, and give 28 days' notice to her employer of the date when she expects the liability for SMP to begin.

6.61 Finally, SMP is not payable for weeks when she is actually working, and there are additional exclusions in respect of women who are taken into legal custody or who go outside the European Economic Area, on the death of the employer, and if she changes her employer after her baby is born.

6.62 SMP is payable at two rates. For the first six weeks, SMP is earnings-related, ie 90% of the employee's average weekly earnings. The remaining 33 weeks are paid at the prescribed rate, or 90% of average earnings if this is less than the prescribed rate (currently £138.18). SMP is subject to tax and NI contributions, and any other lawful deductions (eg pension contributions, trade union subscriptions etc). Any contractual remuneration (eg contractual sick pay or maternity pay) can be offset.

6.63 If a woman is entitled to a pay increase before the start of her maternity leave, or would have been awarded such an increase had she not been absent on statutory maternity leave, this must be taken into account when calculating her entitlement to SMP. If, during the period of maternity leave she becomes entitled to a pay increase, the employer must recalculate her SMP entitlement accordingly (Statutory Maternity Pay (General) Regulations, reg 21(7)). If an existing employee feels that she has been denied such entitlement in the past, she has six years from the date of the ruling in *Alabaster v Woolwich Bank*[26] to request a recalculation of her payment.

6.64 There are a number of provisions dealing with special situations which may arise, and which may affect entitlement to SMP. These include the dismissal of a woman because she is pregnant, when the employer becomes insolvent, if she is detained in legal custody, or working during the maternity pay period etc.

F. Maternity Allowance (Social Security Contributions and Benefits Act 1992)

6.65 A woman who does not qualify for statutory maternity pay may be entitled to maternity allowance (MA) paid to her direct by the Department for Work and Pensions. She must show that:

(a) she is pregnant, and has reached the start of the 11th week prior to the expected week of confinement;

(b) she has been employed as an employed earner or self-employed earner for at least 26 weeks in the 66 weeks preceding the EWC. These weeks do not have to be continuous, nor do they have to be with the same employer;

(c) her average weekly earnings are not less than the maternity allowance threshold in any of the 13 weeks in the test period (currently £30 per week). Earnings from more than one job will count if necessary.

6.66 Maternity allowance is paid for a period of 39 weeks, at a weekly rate of 90% of average weekly earnings, or the prescribed rate (currently £138.18), whichever is the smaller sum. It is not payable to women who travel outside the European Economic Area, or who are in legal custody.

Adoption leave (Paternity and Adoption Leave Regulations 2002)

6.67 To qualify for ordinary adoption leave, the employee:

(a) must have been employed for a period of not less than 26 weeks ending with the week in which s/he was notified that a match with the child to be adopted had been made;

(b) provide evidence of his/her entitlement; and

(c) inform the employer of the date when the child is expected to be placed for adoption and the date on which the employee has chosen for the leave period to begin.

6.68 The employer, for his part, must inform the employee of the date when the leave period entitlement will end, taking into account any additional adoption leave period to which the employee will be entitled. There are special provisions dealing with the situation arising from the interruption or termination of the child's placement. The ordinary adoption leave period is 26 weeks.

6.69 An employee who takes ordinary adoption leave is also entitled to additional adoption leave, which will last for a period of 26 weeks beginning on the day after the last day of ordinary adoption leave.

[26] [2005] EWCA Civ 508, [2005] 2 CMLR 19, [2005] Eu LR 824, [2005] ICR 1246, [2005] IRLR 576, (2005) *Times*, 27 May.

6.70 An employee who takes ordinary and additional adoption leave has the same rights as those enjoyed by a woman taking ordinary and additional maternity leave. During the leave period, the employee is entitled to the benefit of the terms and conditions of employment that would have applied if s/he had not been absent, excluding terms relating to remuneration (but statutory adoption pay is payable if the employee qualifies for this). This could include contractual benefits, such as membership of a health club, use of mobile telephones and company car, etc. S/he is entitled to the benefit of the employer's implied obligation of trust and confidence, and any terms relating to termination, redundancy payments and disciplinary and grievance procedures, etc. For her/his part, the employee is bound by the obligations of good faith, the giving of notice, disclosure of confidential information, and the taking of other employment etc.

6.71 The whole period of adoption leave does not break continuity of employment and will count for continuity purposes and for the purpose of assessing entitlement to contractual rights, such as assessing seniority, pay increments etc, except that the additional adoption leave period does not count for accrued pension rights purposes.

6.72 There are proposed changes to allow adoptive parents time off work in order to meet the children that they are adopting, and put paid adoptive leave in line with that of biological parents.

A. **Reasonable contact**

6.73 The employer and employee may agree to make reasonable contact with each other from time to time during the adoption leave period, which will not affect the rights of either party. It is suggested that this could be for the purpose of discussing details of return to work, communicating information, informing the employee of promotion opportunities, etc. Contact may be by any suitable means, eg telephone, emails, personal visits etc.

B. **Work during the adoption leave period**

6.74 An employee may carry out up to 10 days work for the employer during the adoption leave period without bringing that period to an end. Work, which includes training, will count as a full day if it is done for part of a day. The type of work that the employee may carry out will be a matter for agreement between the parties, but it would normally be any activity that would ordinarily be classed as work under the employee's contract of employment. He/she will be entitled to be paid on an agreed basis, and entitlement to statutory maternity pay will not be affected. Any period of work will not extend the total duration of the adoption leave period.

C. **Returning to work after adoption leave**

6.75 An employee who returns to work after ordinary adoption leave is entitled to return to the same job, with seniority, pension rights and other terms and conditions that are not less favourable than if s/he had not been absent. No notice of return to work need be given (it will be recalled that the employer will have already specified the date for return to work). However, if the employee wishes to return to work on a date before the end of the adoption leave period, eight weeks' notice of the intention to return early must be given.

6.76 An employee who returns to work after the additional adoption leave period is entitled to return to the same job, on the same terms and conditions as if they had not been absent. However, if it is not reasonably practical for the employer to continue to employ the employee under the existing contract of employment, then, where there is a suitable and appropriate vacancy, the employee is entitled to be offered alternative employment with the employer (or the employer's successor or an associated employer).

6.77 If the employee unreasonably refuses that offer, the reasonableness of the employee's dismissal (or resignation) will be tested in the usual way under the provisions of ERA, s 94(4).

D. **Remedies**

6.78 An employee has the right not to be subjected to any detriment because s/he took adoption leave, and it will generally be an unfair dismissal to dismiss the employee because adoption leave was taken.

E. **Statutory adoption pay (SAP)**

6.79 To qualify for statutory adoption pay, the adopter must:

(a) have been in employed earner's employment for a continuous period of at least 26 weeks;

(b) have normal weekly earnings in the eight weeks ending with the week in which the adopter is notified of the match which are not less than the lower earnings limit for the payment of national insurance contributions;

(c) have elected to receive SAP (and not SPP).

6.80 The employee must give evidence of his/her entitlement to SAP, and there are provisions relating to disentitlement if the employee works for the employer or another employer during the SAP period, if the adopter is entitled to statutory sick pay, in legal custody, etc. SAP is payable for a continuous period of 26 weeks during ordinary adoption leave and for a further 13 weeks if additional adoption leave is taken, at a rate which is the lesser of 90% of the employee's normal weekly earnings or the prescribed rate (currently £138.18). Contractual remuneration can be offset.

Recoupment by employer

6.81 An employer who pays SMP, SPP or SAP is entitled to recover 92% of the amount paid out by deducting the amount from PAYE tax and national insurance contributions which they make to the Revenue every month. A 'small employer', ie one whose gross NI contributions payments (including employers and employees contributions) is £45,000 or less in the qualifying tax year is entitled to recover 100% of the payments made, and in addition can claim a compensation payment of 4.5% of the gross payments made.

Parental leave (Maternity and Parental Leave Regulations 1999–2001, regs 13–21)

6.82 An employee (man or woman) who has been continuously employed for one year, and has (or expects to have) parental responsibility for a child, is entitled to have parental leave for a period of up to 18 weeks. This changed from a 13-week entitlement in March 2013.

6.83 The qualifying period of one year's employment will be measured backwards from the date when the leave is to start. There are more favourable rules in respect of parents of disabled children, who will be entitled, in certain circumstances, to count service with a previous employer (see reg 13(1A)).

6.84 A person has responsibility for a child if s/he has parental responsibility within the meaning of s 3 of the Children Act 1989 (as amended by the Adoption and Children Act 2002) or s 1(3) of the Children (Scotland) Act 1995. A mother automatically acquires parental responsibility; a father will do so if he is married to the child's mother or (in the case of an unmarried father) if he registers the birth jointly with the mother. Parental responsibility may also be acquired by a court order or by a formal agreement with the child's mother. Thus guardians and adoptive parents qualify for parental leave, but not step-parents or foster parents. However, the right does not apply to members of the armed forces, share fishermen and members of the constabulary.

6.85 Parental leave may be taken as soon as the child is born or adopted, and the right will last until the child reaches the age of five, or, in the case of an adopted child, until five years from the date of adoption or until the child reaches the age of 18, whichever is the earlier date. If the child is in receipt of disability living allowance the right to parental leave is extended until the child reaches the age of 18.

6.86 Unlike paternity leave, maternity leave and adoption leave there is no requirement that parental leave shall be with pay, although other social security benefits may be available (income support, housing and council tax benefit etc) as appropriate.

6.87 An employee may only take up to four weeks' parental leave in any one year (Sch 2, para 8) in respect of any individual child. Leave may only be taken in weekly blocks; thus if an employee takes less than a week's leave it will count as one week out of his total 18-week entitlement (*South Central Trains Ltd v Rodway*[27]). However, if the child is in receipt of disability living allowance, greater flexibility is allowed, and leave may be taken on a daily basis, so that up to 20 individual days' leave may be taken in any one year.

6.88 During parental leave, the employee's terms and conditions of employment are the same as those which are applicable during additional maternity leave. The employee is entitled to the benefit of the employer's obligation of trust and confidence, and any terms and conditions relating to notice of termination, compensation in the event of redundancy, and disciplinary and grievance procedures. For his or her part, the employee is bound by the obligation of good faith, and any terms and conditions relating to the giving of notice of termination, the disclosure of confidential information, the acceptance of gifts or other benefits, and participation in any other business. A period of leave will count as continuous service for the purpose of statutory employment protection rights.

6.89 If the employee has taken up to four weeks' parental leave (whether or not this was added on to paternity leave, ordinary maternity leave or ordinary adoption leave) s/he is entitled to return to the job he/she was doing before the absence. If parental leave followed a period of additional maternity leave or additional adoption leave or was more than four weeks, s/he is entitled to return to the job s/he was doing before the absence unless it is not reasonably practicable for the employer to permit the employee to return to the job, in which case the employer must offer a job which is suitable and appropriate for him/her to do in the circumstances. The terms and conditions must be no less favourable than those which would have applied if the employee had not been absent.

[27] [2004] IRLR 777, IDS Brief 765 10, EAT.

6.90 The regulations give power to employers and employees to enter into agreements which provide for a certain flexibility, by means of a collective agreement or a workforce agreement which must be incorporated into the individual contract of employment (see Sch 1 to the regulations). In the absence of any such agreement, the default provisions of Sch 2 will apply. This states that the employee give at least 21 days' notice of the dates when leave is being taken, and the employer is entitled to request proof of entitlement. A father who wishes to take leave in respect of a child not yet born can give 21 days' notice of the expected week of confinement, and he may start his leave as soon as the baby is actually born, even if this is earlier or later than the anticipated date of birth. Adopted parents must also give 21 days' notice, although if this is not reasonably practicable, notice must be given as soon as is reasonably practicable. Except in relation to new fathers and adoptive parents, the employer may postpone the leave where he considers that the operation of the business would be unduly disrupted if the employee took the leave during the period in question, but the postponement cannot be for more than six months.

6.91 An employee may present a complaint to an employment tribunal that his employer has unreasonably postponed a period of parental leave, or has prevented him from taking such leave. If the employment tribunal find the complaint well founded, it shall make a declaration to that effect, and may award compensation to the employee, the amount being such as is considered to be just and equitable, having regard to the employer's behaviour and any loss suffered by the employee (ERA, s 80).

6.92 An employee has the right not to suffer a detriment because s/he took parental leave (ERA, s 47C) and it will be an automatically unfair dismissal to dismiss an employee because s/he took or sought to take parental leave (ERA, s 99).

Paternity rights and adoption leave

A. **Paternity leave (Paternity and Adoption Leave Regulations 2002, as amended)**

6.93 In addition to taking 13 weeks' unpaid parental leave (see para 6.82) a father is entitled to take one or two weeks' paternity leave on the birth or adoption of a child, with pay at the statutory rate. Although 'paternity' is a peculiarly male concept, there are several circumstances when a woman may take paternity leave. Thus, if the partner of the birth mother or adoptive mother is a woman, then she will be entitled to paternity leave if she is a woman who has, or who expects to have, the main responsibility for raising the child. Also, if, when a couple adopt a child, the adoptive father takes adoption leave, the adoptive mother is entitled to take paternity leave. And if two people of the same sex living together adopt a child, one may take adoption leave and the other may take paternity leave.

6.94 The rules relating to paternity leave cater for paternity on the birth of a child and paternity arising from adoption. So far as the former is concerned, the right to paternity leave applies to employees (not workers) who have been continuously employed for at least 26 weeks ending with the week immediately preceding the 14th week before the expected week of birth. The employee must be the father of the child, or the mother's husband, or partner. Whether he is or is not the father of the child, he must have or expect to have the responsibility for the upbringing of the child. A 'partner' is a person who lives with the mother in an enduring family relationship, whether of the same or different sex, but must not be a relative of the mother.

6.95 So far as adoption is concerned, paternity leave may be taken in respect of a child who is under the age of 18 (there are special provisions relating to children who are adopted from overseas). Again, the employee must have been employed for at least 26 weeks ending with the week in which the child's adopter is notified of having been matched with the child. The employee must be married to, or the partner of the adopter, and have the main responsibility for the upbringing of the child. Again, a partner is a person (whether of the same or different sex) who lives with the adopter in an enduring family relationship.

6.96 An employee who wishes to take paternity leave can choose to take either one week or two weeks' leave. He cannot take odd days or non-consecutive weeks (a week, in this connection, is a period of seven days). The leave cannot be taken before the child is born (or the child is placed with the adopter) and must be taken within 56 days of the birth or placement. The employee must give his employer notice of the date from when he will take his leave, and the length of absence. If the employer so requests, the employee must provide a signed declaration stating (a) that the purpose of the absence from work is to take care of the child or support the child's mother (or adopter), (b) that he is the father of the child (or the mother's husband or partner) and that he expects to have responsibility for the upbringing of the child.

6.97 There are further provisions dealing with the effect of premature birth, stillbirth or the death of the child's mother, and multiple births, when only one period of paternity leave may be taken.

6.98 An employee who is absent from work on paternity leave is entitled to the benefit of all of the terms and conditions of employment that would have applied if he had not been absent (excluding terms and conditions concerning remuneration), and is bound by any obligation under those terms except in so far as they are inconsistent with his right to take paternity leave. He is entitled to return from his leave to the job in which he was employed before his absence, on terms and conditions not less favourable than those which would have applied had he not been absent. If, however, s/he has taken paternity leave as well as additional maternity leave or additional adoption leave, the right to return is limited to the considerations which apply in respect of those latter leave periods (see paras 6.44, 6.76).

6.99 Otherwise, an employee is entitled not to be subjected to a detriment because s/he took paternity leave, and it will also be automatically unfair to dismiss a person because s/he took such leave.

6.100 In *Atkins v Coyle Personnel plc*,[28] an employee was dismissed while on paternity leave, because he had engaged in an angry exchange of emails and telephone conversations with his manager. It was held that his dismissal was not connected with the fact that he took paternity leave, but because of the heated argument with his manager. It may have been associated with paternity leave, but was not connected with it.

B. **Statutory paternity pay (SPP)**

6.101 Statutory paternity pay (SPP) is payable to an employee who satisfies the conditions of eligibility. These are:

(a) he must have been employed for a continuous period of 26 weeks ending with the week immediately preceding the 14th week before the expected week of the child's birth, or the week in which the adopter was notified of the match being made;

(b) his normal weekly earnings in the 8 weeks ending with the relevant week are not less than the lower earnings limit for the payment of NI contributions;

---

[28] [2008] IRLR 420.

(c) he gives at least 28 days' notice before the date from which he expects SPP or SAP to be paid (or, if that is not reasonably practicable, as soon as is reasonably practicable);

(d) he provides evidence of the child's birth, and provides a written declaration that he meets the conditions as to the relationship with the child's mother.

6.102 Currently, statutory paternity pay is payable for two weeks at a weekly rate of either 90% of average weekly earnings or the prescribed rate (currently £138.18), whichever is the lesser sum.

C. **Additional paternity leave**

6.103 The Additional Paternity Leave Regulations 2010 are designed to give mothers of new-born babies (or adoptees) the option of going back to work before the end of their maternity leave period, and enabling a mother to transfer to the father of the child the remaining period of leave. Eligible fathers are able to take up to 26 weeks additional paternity leave, which may be taken by the father during what would have been the remaining part of the mother's maternity leave period, once she has returned to work. The earliest start date will be 20 weeks after the child's birth or placement for adoption, and must be completed by the time of the child's first birthday (or one year after placement for adoption). Additional statutory paternity pay, and additional statutory adoption pay, is only payable during the mother's statutory maternity, maternity allowance or adoption pay period. Note that there are currently plans to allow 'shared' parental leave. This is expected to allow parents to be absent from work to care for a child for a maximum of 52 weeks. Those who are eligible can also receive up to 39 weeks of shared parental pay. Draft regulations are expected and the scheme is likely to come into force in April 2015.

Eligibility

6.104 Additional paternity leave is available to the father of the child, and to partners and civil partners of mothers and adopters. The father must have completed 26 weeks' continuous employment with his employer, and also have the main responsibility for the upbringing of the child, and be taking leave for the purpose of caring for the child.

6.105 To be eligible for additional paternity pay the father's earning must be at least equal to the lower earnings limit (currently £111 per week) during the eight weeks prior to the relevant week, ie the eight weeks ending with the 15th week before the baby is due or being matched for adoption. The relevant week is the same one as is used to calculate the entitlement to ordinary statutory paternity leave and pay, which means that if the father is entitled to the latter, there will be no need to recalculate entitlement for additional statutory paternity pay. The right to additional paternity leave is in addition to the current entitlement of two weeks' paid paternity leave after the birth of the child.

6.106 The mother must provide a written declaration confirming that the person making the application for additional paternity leave is the father of the child, and that to her knowledge he is the only person entitled to additional paternity leave in respect of the child.

6.107 If the father's employer so requests, the father must provide information about the mother's employer, which will enable to father's employer to check that the mother is entitled to maternity or adoption pay, and that she has returned to work.

6.108 A father seeking to take additional paternity leave must so inform his employer at least eight weeks before the leave period is to start, and the employer must confirm entitlement within four weeks. If the father wishes to change the date on which he is due to start leave, he must give his employer six weeks' notice. If less than six weeks notice is given, then if it is not reasonably practicable for the employer to accommodate the change, the employer can insist that the original start date stands, or is deferred until six weeks' notice has been given.

6.109 An employee returning from a single period of additional paternity leave lasting 26 weeks or less is entitled to return to the same job as he was employed in before his absence. However, if he has taken two or more subsequent consecutive periods of statutory leave, he will be entitled to return to the same job unless it is not reasonably practicable for him to do so, in which case he is entitled to be offered suitable alternative employment. The father has the same protection in the event of redundancy as the mother would have if she had taken maternity or adoption leave, and there is similar protection against detriment and dismissal. Also, the father will be covered by the 'keeping in touch' provisions that apply to a mother on maternity or adoption leave. Up to 13 weeks of additional paternity leave will be paid at the same rate as statutory maternity pay if leave is taken during the mother's 39-week maternity pay period.

It will be an offence if either the employer or employee makes a fraudulent claim.

6.110 The regulations apply to children whose expected week of birth began on or after 3 April 2011.

Additional Paternity Leave (Adoptions from Overseas) Regulations 2010

6.111 The Additional Paternity Leave (Adoptions from Overseas) Regulations 2010 confer an entitlement for employees adopting children from overseas to take additional paternity leave in the first year after the child enters Great Britain. The right is conferred on spouses or partners of either sex of adopters, or, where a child is adopted by two persons jointly, spouses or partners of either sex of the adopter who has elected to take adoption leave. Leave may be taken for a minimum of two weeks and a maximum of 26 weeks.

Entitlement

6.112 The employee:

(a) must have been continuously employed for a period of 26 weeks before the child enters Great Britain, and remains in such continuous employment until the week before the first week of the commencement of the additional paternity leave;

(b) be either married to or be the civil partner or partner of the adopter; and

(c) has, or expects to have, the main responsibility for the upbringing of the child.

6.113 The adopter must have taken adoption leave and be returning to work when the employee commences the additional paternity leave.

6.114 Not less than eight weeks before the start of the date chosen for the period of leave, the employee must give his/her employer a leave notice, specifying the date on which the adopter received official notification that the adoption has been approved. He must also sign a declaration, signed by him/her stating that the purpose of the period of leave will be to care for the child, and that s/he is either married to, or a civil partner of, or the partner of, the adopter, and that s/he has, or expects to have the main responsibility for the upbringing of the child.

6.115 The employee must also provide the employer with an adopter written declaration, stating the adopter's name and address, the date when the adopter intends to return to work, the adopter's national insurance number, a confirmation that the employee will have the main responsibility for the upbringing of the child, and giving the adopter's consent to the employer processing such of the information as is contained in the declaration.

6.116 Within 28 days of the employer receiving the employee's leave notice, the employee must give the employer (a) a copy of the official notification relating to the child (b) evidence of the date on which the child entered Great Britain, and the name and address of the adopter's employer (or if the adopter is self-employed, the business address).

6.117 After giving leave notice, the employee must give the employer written notice as soon as is reasonably practicable, if the employee is no longer married to, a civil partner of the adopter, or no longer has the main responsibility for the upbringing of the child, or if the adopter is no longer entitled to adoption leave of statutory adoption pay. If the employee does not give a withdrawal notice within six weeks of the start date specified in the leave notice, the employer may require the employee to take a period of leave, if it is not reasonably practical for the employer to accommodate the change in the employee's arrangements.

6.118 Where the employee gives leave notice to the employer, the employer shall, in writing, within 28 days, confirm the start and end dates of the employee's leave. The employee's additional paternity leave will start on the date of the employee's leave notice.

6.119 There are special provisions that deal with the possibility that the adopter dies within 12 months of the child's entry into Great Britain, and also dealing with the possibility that the child dies or ceases to live with the adopter.

6.120 The employee may carry out up to 10 days' work for the employer during the additional paternity leave period without bringing that period to an end. During the period of additional paternity leave the employee is entitled to the benefit of all the terms and conditions of employment that would have applied had the employee not been absent (other than remuneration) and is bound by any obligations arising from those terms and conditions.

6.121 Provisions relating to returning to work, redundancy or detriment and dismissal during additional paternity leave mirror those contained in the maternity leave regulations.

To care for dependants (ERA, s 57A)

6.122 An employee is entitled to be permitted by his employer to take a reasonable amount of time off work during the employee's working hours in order to take action which is necessary:

(a) to provide assistance on an occasion when a dependant falls ill, gives birth, or is injured or assaulted;

(b) to make arrangements for the provision of care for a dependant who is ill or injured;

(c) in consequence of the death of a dependant;

(d) because of an unexpected disruption or termination of arrangements for the care of a dependant; or

(e) to deal with an incident which involves the child of the employee and which occurs unexpectedly in a period during which an educational establishment which the child attends is responsible for him.

6.123 In *Royal Bank of Scotland v Harrison* the unavailability of a child minder was 'unexpected' and therefore it was 'necessary' for the employee to take a day off work, even though she had two weeks notice of the unavailability of the childminder. However, the longer the time available to make alternative arrangements, the less likely it will be that the employee can establish the necessity.

6.124 Time off work under s 57A(1)(c) in order to take action which is necessary in consequence of the death of a dependent does not include the right to have time off work to deal with the emotional effect of a bereavement (*Forster v Cartwright Black*).[29]

6.125 The employee must tell his employer the reason for the absence as soon as is reasonably practicable, and also inform him how long he expects to be absent.

6.126 A dependant is a spouse, child, parent, or person living in the same household as the employee, otherwise than by reason of his being an employee, tenant, lodger or boarder. Additionally, for the purpose of para 6.122(a) and (b), a dependant can also be any person who reasonably relies on the employee for assistance on an occasion when he falls ill or is injured or assaulted, or to make arrangements for the provision of care in the event of illness or injury. For the purpose of (d), a dependant can also include any person who reasonably relies on the employee to make arrangements for the provision of care.

6.127 There is no service qualification for the enjoyment of these rights, but equally there is no requirement on the employer to pay an employee who takes such time off work. Any such entitlement must depend on the terms of the contract of employment.

6.128 An employee may complain to an employment tribunal (within the usual time limits) that his employer has unreasonably refused to permit him to take time off work for any of the purposes referred to earlier, and, if the complaint is well founded, the tribunal will make a declaration, and may award compensation as it considers to be just and equitable. Also, an employee has the right not to suffer a detriment because he took such time off work, and it will be automatically unfair to dismiss an employee for taking time off work for the purposes referred to. In *Qua v John Ford Morrison (Solicitors)*[30] the EAT gave guidance on how time off work for dependants' leave should be properly exercised, and the tests to be applied in determining whether there has been an automatically unfair dismissal under s 57A where the principal reason for the dismissal was that the employee had taken time off work to look after a dependant.

Flexible working arrangements (ERA, ss 80F–80I)

6.129 In recent years there appears to have developed a greater interest in finding alternatives to conventional full-time and part-time employment, partly with a view to trying to avoid legal responsibilities (which has had a very limited success) but mainly due to the genuine need of employers and employees for new-style flexible working arrangements, which can, in certain circumstances, be commercially advantageous to both sides. Flexitime itself has had a long history, but new arrangements, such as job-sharing, performance contracts, zero hours contracts, annualised hours contracts, home-working, etc, are now being used with greater frequency. However, because statutory rules were not designed to deal with these arrangements, legal disputes arising out of them had to be dealt with by the use of a certain amount of judicial creativity (see *Chief Constable of Avon and Somerset v Chew*[31]).

6.130 The Employment Act 2002 gave a new right for an employee to request flexible working arrangements, by inserting new ss 80F–80I into the Employment Rights Act 1996. However, there is no actual right to work flexibly. The Act only lays down a procedure

---

[29] [2004] ICR 1728, EAT.
[30] [2003] ICR 482, [2003] IRLR 184, [2003] NLJR 95, [2003] All ER (D) 29 (Jan), EAT.
[31] [2001] All ER (D) 101 (Sep), EAT.

whereby an application for flexible working may be made to an employer, which must be considered fairly by him. A remedy may only arise on an application to an employment tribunal if it can be shown that the employer has failed to follow the statutory procedure, or has based his decision on incorrect facts. The relevant rules are laid down in the Flexible Working (Procedural Requirements) Regulations 2002, and the Flexible Working (Eligibility, Complaints and Remedies) Regulations 2002 (as amended). From 8 March 2013 the Parental Leave (EU Directive) Regulations extended the right to request flexible working to employed agency workers returning from maternity/paternity leave.

A. **Application for flexible working**

6.131 An application for flexible working may be made by a qualifying employee, ie s/he must have been continuously employed for a period of 26 weeks at the date the application is made.

(a) The application may be made in order to care for a child up to the age of 16, or 18 if the child is disabled. The employee must have (or expect to have) responsibility for the child's upbringing, and be either the mother, father, adopter, guardian or foster parent of the child, or who is married to or the partner of such a person. In addition to adopters who are matched by an adoption agency, other adopters, ie relatives, inter-country adoptions and others who adopt without using an agency may now make an application, as may private foster-carers and employees who hold a residence order.

(b) An application for flexible working may be made by an employee who is a carer, ie an employee who is (or expects to be) caring for an adult or child, who is married to or is the partner or civil partner of the employee, or who is a near relative of the employee (parent, parent-in-law, guardian, adoptive relative, adult child, sibling, uncle, aunt, grandparent, or step-relative) or who lives at the same address as the employee.

It is expected that the right to apply for flexible leave will be extended to all employees with the relevant qualifying service some time in 2014. Only one application may be made in any 12-month period, and if the application is accepted, the resultant change to terms and conditions will be permanent.

The application may relate to a change of:

(a) the hours the employee is required to work;

(b) the times the employee is required to work;

(c) the place where the employee is required to work;

(d) such other aspects of the employee's terms and conditions of employment as may be specified in regulations.

6.132 The application, which must be in writing, must specify the change applied for, the date from which the proposed change will be effective, explain what effect, if any, the change will have on the employer's business and how such effect may be dealt with.

6.133 If the employer agrees to the application, he will notify the employee of the contract variation agreed to, and the date from which the variation is to take effect. Otherwise, he must hold a meeting with the employee within 28 days to discuss the matter. The time and place of the meeting must be convenient to both parties. The employer must give notice of his decision within 14 days. If the application is accepted, it will operate as a variation of the terms and conditions of employment of the employee's contract, which will be binding until and unless there is a further agreed variation. If the application is refused the employer must state his reasons, and provide for a right of appeal, which must be heard within 14 days, and a decision given within a further 14 days. The employee has the right to be accompanied at the original hearing and the appeal hearing by a fellow employee, who may address the hearing and confer with the employee. The companion is entitled to take time off work with pay for this purpose, and there are the usual sanctions if the employer fails to permit a companion to attend the hearing or the appeal hearing.

6.134 The employer will be under no duty to consider the application where the employee notifies him that it has been withdrawn, or if the employee fails without reasonable cause to attend a meeting more than once, or refuses without reasonable cause to provide the employer with further information needed in order to assess whether the contract should be varied.

6.135 The employer may refuse the request only for one of the following reasons:

(a) the burden of additional costs;

(b) the detrimental effect on ability to meet customer demand;

(c) the inability to re-organise work among existing staff;

(d) the inability to recruit additional staff;

(e) the detrimental impact on quality;

(f) the detrimental impact on performance;

(g) the lack of work during the periods when the employee proposes to work;

(h) the planned structural changes;

(i) other grounds which the Secretary of State may specify from time to time.

6.136 If the employer and employee are unable to reach an amicable agreement on the application for flexible working, then, if both parties agree, resort may be had to the ACAS Arbitration Scheme (see para 1.13). By so doing, the employee waives the right to present a claim to an employment tribunal. The decision of the arbitrator will be final. Otherwise, the employee may make a claim to an employment tribunal, on the ground that the employer has failed to comply with the procedural requirements as set out in the regulations, or has rejected the application on a ground that is not one of the permitted reasons for refusal, or has based his decision to reject the application on incorrect facts. It should be noted that the tribunal's role is merely to verify whether the employer has followed the correct procedure and to examine any disputed facts. The tribunal does not have the power to question the commercial validity of the employer's decision, nor can it substitute its own judgment on the business reasons for those of the employer. But the tribunal is entitled to look at the ground asserted by the employer as the reason why he did not grant the application, and to ascertain if it was factually correct. This may involve an examination of the evidence as to the circumstances surrounding the application, the effect of granting it, whether there would be any potential disruption, and the attitude of customers and other members of staff (*Commotion Ltd v Rutty*[32]). If it finds the complaint to be well-founded, the tribunal must make a declaration, and may make an order requiring the employer to reconsider the application. An award of compensation may be made, of such amount as the tribunal thinks just and equitable, up to a maximum of eight weeks' pay (not capped). The employee may also bring a complaint if there is a breach of his right to be accompanied at the hearing

---

[32] [2006] ICR 290, EAT.

or the appeal hearing, for which the remedy is an award of compensation up to a maximum of two weeks' pay (subject to the statutory maximum).

6.137 There is the usual protection against an employee suffering a detriment because an application for flexible working was made, and it will be automatically unfair to dismiss an employee for a reason relating to any such application.

Future proposals

6.138 The Children and Families Bill is likely to be implemented in 2014. Among other things, it will bring in the system of shared parental leave between parents, allow prospective parents to take time off to attend antenatal appointments, and bring the leave and pay entitlements for adoptive parents more closely in line with those available to birth parents. There are also proposals to extend the right to request flexible working to all employees. The Government plans to remove the current statutory procedure for considering requests. In its place, employers will have a duty to consider all requests in a reasonable manner but will be able to refuse requests on business grounds.

7

Employment Protection

7.1 In this chapter we will consider a number of miscellaneous legal rights given to employees in the Employment Rights Act 1996 and other legislation. These are minimum standards which can be exceeded by agreement or negotiation, but they cannot be denied to an employee.

Guarantee payments (ERA, ss 28–35)

7.2 Provided an employee has been continuously employed for at least one month, the employer is bound to pay him a guarantee payment in respect of any whole day in which the employee is not provided with work because:

(a) there is a diminution in the requirements of the employer's business for work of the kind which the employee is employed to do, or

(b) any other occurrence affecting the normal working of the employer's business in relation to work of that kind.

In *North v Pavleigh Ltd*[1] the owner of a company closed his factory for Jewish holidays. The employment tribunal held that no guarantee payment could be claimed. Section 28 only applies to a diminution of work, or an 'occurrence', such as a power failure or national disaster. It was not intended to cover the religious habits of the proprietor.

7.3 A guarantee payment is not payable if the workless day occurs in consequence of a trade dispute involving any employee of the employer or of any associated employer. In *Garvey v J & J Maybank (Oldham) Ltd*[2] there was a national lorry drivers' strike, and pickets at the employer's entrance refused to let the firm's own lorries in or out. The employer ordered the firm's drivers (who were not involved in the strike) to cross picket lines, but they refused. As a result, there were insufficient supplies coming into the firm, and the claimant was laid off. It was held that he was not entitled to guarantee pay. The refusal of the drivers to cross the picket lines meant that the lay off occurred in consequence of a trade dispute. Nor is the employee entitled to the payment if the employer offers to provide alternative work which is suitable in all the circumstances (whether or not it is within the employee's contract) and he unreasonably refuses that offer (*Purdy v Willowbrook International Ltd*[3]). Employees who had agreed to a temporary reduction in their work were entitled to a guarantee payment under section 28 (*Abercrombie & Ors v AGA Rangemaster Ltd*[4]). The claimants agreed to work four days a week rather than five when market conditions deteriorated. The respondent refused to pay them guarantee payments for the fifth day. It was held that during the currency of the agreement Fridays were days on which they were normally contracted to work, and as no work was provided, they were entitled to guarantee payments.

The employee must also comply with reasonable requirements imposed by the employer with a view to ensuring that his services are available (*Meadows v Faithful Overalls Ltd*[5]).

---

[1] [1977] IRLR 461.   [2] [1979] IRLR 408.   [3] [1977] IRLR 388.
[4] [2013] EWCA Civ 1148.   [5] [1977] IRLR 330.

Guarantee pay is only payable in respect of days on which the employee would otherwise be required to be at work (*Mailway (Southern) Ltd v Willsher*[6]).

7.4 The employee is entitled to be paid at the guaranteed hourly rate (which is one week's pay divided by the number of normal working hours) for the number of normal working hours in respect of any whole day he is laid off. He is entitled to be paid for five working days in any period of three months, at a maximum prescribed daily rate (currently £25) (ERA, s 31). In other words, the present position is that an employee will be entitled to the prescribed daily rate for a maximum of 20 days in each year. If the employee already has a contractual right to remuneration in respect of a workless day (eg by means of a collective agreement, etc) then any payment made under that agreement will go towards discharging the employer's liability to make the statutory guarantee payment, and equally, the latter will go towards discharging the contractual liability. If there is a guaranteed week agreement in existence, then the contractual remuneration shall be apportioned rateably between the workless days, and the statutory minimum will be used to 'top up' as appropriate. However, workless days when a contractual payment is made are taken into account when calculating the number of days guarantee pay is payable in any period of three months (*Cartwright v G Clancey Ltd*[7]). It should be noted that if a contractual or statutory guarantee payment is being made, the employee is not entitled to apply for jobseekers' allowance.

7.5 If an employer fails or refuses to pay the whole or part of the guarantee payment, the employee may complain within three months to an employment tribunal. If they find the complaint well founded, they will order the employer to pay to the claimant the amount due to him.

7.6 If there is a collective agreement in force which already relates to guarantee payments, then all the parties thereto may apply to the appropriate Minister for an exemption order. This will be granted if he is satisfied that the statutory provisions should not apply to those employees, but the collective agreement must contain provisions for an aggrieved employee to take a dispute about non-payment of the guarantee payment either to arbitration (or other procedure) or to an employment tribunal. A number of such exemption orders have been granted.

Suspension on medical grounds (ERA, ss 64–65)

7.7 Provided an employee has been employed for not less than one month, he will be entitled to be paid remuneration if he is suspended from work in consequence of a requirement imposed by certain statutory provisions or a recommendation made in a code of practice issued or approved under s 16 of the Health and Safety at Work etc Act 1974 (see Chapter 11). The statutory provisions in question are (a) Control of Lead at Work Regulations 2002, (b) Ionising Radiations Regulations 1999, and (c) Control of Substances Hazardous to Health Regulations 2002. If a health risk occurs within the scope of these provisions, certain processes must be suspended, and the result now is that in these circumstances the affected employees will be entitled to be paid for a period of up to six months from the day when the suspension period begins. An employee is not entitled to be paid during the suspension period if he is incapable of work because of illness or injury, or if he unreasonably refuses alternative work offered to him by the employer (whether within the terms of his contract or not) or if he does not make himself available for work.

6 [1978] ICR 511, [1978] IRLR 322, (1978) 122 SJ 79, (1977) *Times*, 9 December.
7 [1983] ICR 552, [1983] IRLR 355, EAT.

7.8 An employee who is thus suspended on medical grounds is entitled to a week's pay in respect of each week the suspension lasts, and though the contractual right to remuneration is unaffected, the contractual and statutory remuneration can be set off against each other as appropriate. If the employer fails to pay the whole or any part of the employee's remuneration, the latter may present a complaint to the employment tribunal within three months, and if it finds the complaint well founded, it shall order the employer to pay to the employee the amount due to him.

7.9 It must be stressed that a medical suspension payment can only be claimed if the employee is fit for work. In *Stallite Batteries Co Ltd v Appleton*,[8] the claimant became ill after falling into a skip containing lead paste. In consequence, his blood lead level exceeded the limit laid down in the Control of Lead at Work Regulations 1998 but no medical suspension certificate was issued by the employment medical adviser. Nonetheless, the applicant's own doctor considered that he was not fit for work. The EAT held that he was not entitled to a medical suspension payment. He was not available for work due to sickness, and his claim was excluded by s 65(3) of the Act.

7.10 If an employee is dismissed for a reason which would otherwise amount to a medical suspension, he is only required to have been employed for one month (instead of one year) in order to present a claim for unfair dismissal (s 65(1)).

7.11 If the employer wishes to engage a temporary employee to take the place of the suspended employee, then, as long as he has informed the temporary employee in writing that the employment will be terminated when the suspension has ended, a dismissal of the temporary employee in order to allow the suspended employee to return to work will amount to 'some other substantial reason' for the dismissal (see Chapter 17), although the employer will still have to show that he acted reasonably.

7.12 For medical suspension from work on maternity grounds, see Chapter 6.

Time off work

A. **For public duties (ERA, s 50)**

7.13 An employer shall permit an employee of his who is a justice of the peace to take time off during his working hours for the purpose of performing any of the duties of his office (see *Riley-Williams v Argos Ltd*[9]).

7.14 An employer shall also permit an employee who is a member of certain specified bodies to take time off work during his working hours for the purpose of attending at a meeting of the body or its committees or sub-committees, and to do any other thing approved by the body for the purpose of discharging its functions. The specified bodies are:

   (a) a local authority (including the Common Council of the City of London, a National Parks Authority and the Broads Authority);

   (b) a statutory tribunal;

   (c) a police authority or police member of the National Criminal Intelligence Service;

   (d) a board of prison visitors or prison visiting committee;

   (e) a relevant health body (including a National Health Service trust, a health authority or health board);

---

[8] HSLB 147, EAT.   [9] [2003] All ER (D) 58 (Jul), EAT.

(f) a relevant education body (managing or governing body of an educational estab-
     lishment maintained by a local authority or (in Scotland) a school or college council
     or governing body of further education);

(g) the Environment Agency or the Scottish Environment Protection Agency;

(h) Service Authority for the National Criminal Intelligence Service or the National
     Crime Squad;

(i) Scottish Water or Water Customer Consultation Panel;

(j) General Teaching Council for England and for Wales.

7.15 There is no requirement that the employee be paid for taking time off work under
s 50. The amount of time off permitted for these purposes, the occasions on which and the
conditions subject to which time off may be taken are those that are reasonable in all the
circumstances, having regard in particular to:

(a) how much time off is required for the performance of the duties;

(b) how much time off the employee has had already in respect of trade union duties
     and activities; and

(c) the circumstances of the employer's business and the effect of the employee's absence
     on the running of that business.

7.16 In *Walters v British Steel Corpn*[10] the claimant was transferred to an essential job, and
it was difficult to release him for certain public duties. When he took the job, he had agreed
that his public duties would take second place. Consideration of safety required certain
minimum manning levels, and his colleagues refused to cover for him. It was held that he
was not entitled to time off work for public duties, as the circumstances of the employer's
business had to be taken into account.

7.17 In considering the amount of time off to be given under s 50, the needs of the employee
to perform his public duties adequately must be balanced carefully with the requirements
of the employer to have the work done. In *Emmerson v IRC*[11] the claimant was the leader of
the opposition party on Portsmouth Council. He had been given 18 days' leave (paid) each
year to perform his duties, but this was insufficient. His application for further unpaid leave
of absence was refused by his employers, as it was argued that he could not be spared from
his job. The employment tribunal thought that the problem could be overcome by appointing a deputy to give him some assistance, for in other areas there was more than one person
doing the same job as the claimant, who should not be put at a disadvantage because he was
extra-efficient. Since the claimant was prepared to use some of his own holidays for public
duties, the tribunal thought that he should be given a further 12 days' leave of absence
without pay. However, in *Corner v Buckinghamshire County Council*,[12] the EAT held that
the employment tribunal has no power to make any recommendations of this nature, or to
impose conditions.

7.18 Section 50 requires the employer to give time off work to the employee. Rearranging
hours of work, and swapping duties so that the same number of hours are worked is not
giving time off (*Ratcliffe v Dorset County Council*[13]).

7.19 It has been noted that there is no legal requirement that the employee be paid for
time off work under s 50. But if he is refused time off, he may present a complaint to an
employment tribunal within the usual period of three months from the date of refusal. The
employment tribunal must take account of all the relevant considerations (*Borders Regional*

---

[10] IDS Brief 150.   [11] [1977] IRLR 458.
[12] (1978) 77 LGR 268, [1978] ICR 836, [1978] IRLR 320, 13 ITR 421, EAT.   [13] [1978] IRLR 191.

Council v Maule[14]) including the employee's efforts to reorganise his commitments so as to produce a reasonable pattern of work, and if the complaint is upheld, the tribunal shall make a declaration, and may award compensation of such amount as it considers just and equitable, having regard to the employer's default and any loss sustained by the employee.

B. **For occupational pension scheme trustees (ERA, s 58)**

7.20 An employee who is a trustee of an occupational pension scheme is entitled to be given time off work, with pay during working hours for the purpose of:

(a) performing any of his duties as such a trustee; or

(b) undergoing training relevant to the performance of those duties.

7.21 The amount of time off which the employee is to be permitted to take, the purpose for which, the occasions on which and any conditions subject to which time off may be taken are those that are reasonable in all the circumstances, having regard to:

(a) how much time off is required for the performance of the duties as a trustee of the scheme and to undergo the relevant training; and

(b) the circumstances of the employer's business and the effect of the employee's absence on the running of that business.

7.22 The employee must be paid his normal remuneration, or his average hourly earnings, or a fair estimate of those earnings, for the time off work under these provisions. If the employer refuses to permit him to take time off work, or refuses to pay for time off work taken, a complaint may be made to an employment tribunal. If the complaint is upheld, the employment tribunal shall make a declaration to that effect, and make an award of compensation to the employee, as it thinks just and equitable.

C. **For employee representatives (ERA, s 61)**

7.23 An employee who is a representative of an independent trade union, or an elected employee representative (or candidate for election) has the right to be allowed reasonable time off work, with pay, for the purpose of performing his functions as such when the employer is required to consult on redundancies (see para 18.69) or on transfers of undertakings (see para 9.75). He is entitled to have access to the affected employees, and such accommodation and facilities as may be appropriate.

7.24 Time off work may also be claimed under the following statutory provisions:

(a) Transnational Information and Consultation of Employees Regulations 1999;

(b) European Public Limited Liability Company (Employer Involvement) (Great Britain) Regulations 2009;

(c) Information and Consultation of Employees Regulations 2004;

(d) Occupational and Personal Pension Schemes Regulations 2006;

(e) European Co-operative Society (Involvement of Employees) Regulations 2006;

(f) Companies (Cross-Border Mergers) Regulations 2007.

7.25 An employee representative has the right not to suffer a detriment because he performed any function or activity as such, and it will be an automatic unfair dismissal to dismiss him for the same reason.

---

[14] [1993] IRLR 199, EAT.

D. For young person for study or training (ERA, s 63A)

7.26 An employee who:

    (a) is aged 16 or 17,

    (b) is not in full time secondary or further education, and

    (c) has not attained certain minimum standards of education as set out in the Right to Time Off Work for Study or Training Regulations 2001 (and/or the Right to Time Off Work for Study or Training (Scotland) Regulations 1999),

is entitled to be permitted by his employer to take time off during the employee's working hours in order to undertake study or training leading to the relevant qualification, which is an external qualification the attainment of which would contribute to the attainment of one of the prescribed standards set out in the regulations, and would be likely to enhance the employee's employment prospects (whether with his employer or otherwise). If an employee is aged 18, but began such studies before attaining that age, he is entitled to continue until he ceases to be 18.

7.27 The amount of time off, the occasions on which, and any conditions subject to which time off may be taken are those that are reasonable in all the circumstances, having regard to:

    (a) the requirements of the employee's study or training, and

    (b) the circumstances of the employer's business and the effect of the employee's time off on the running of that business.

7.28 The employee is entitled to be paid whilst taking time off work for study or training purposes, at the appropriate hourly rate, calculated in accordance with the normal rules which define 'week's pay' and 'normal working hours' (see ERA, ss 220–229, 234, para 14.1). A complaint may be made to an employment tribunal, within the usual time limits, that the employer has unreasonably refused to permit the employee to have time off work as required by s 63A, or has failed to pay the whole or part of the remuneration due to him. If the complaint is upheld, the tribunal will make a declaration and award the remuneration due.

E. Time off for study or training (ERA, s 63D)

7.29 Section 63D of the Employment Rights Act (inserted by the Apprenticeships, Skills, Children and Learning Act 2009) creates a right for a qualifying employee to make a request for time off work in order to pursue a course of study or training, the purpose of which is to improve the employee's effectiveness in the employer's business and the performance of the employer's business.

7.30 The right to apply for time off for study or training applies to employees who work for firms that employ more than 250 employees. There is no requirement that the employer shall pay the employee while he is taking time off, nor is the employer required to pay for the training or study.

7.31 A qualifying employee must have been employed for a period of at least 26 weeks, and not be an agency worker or a person in respect of whom learning needs are already catered for (eg young persons).

7.32 The study or training may be undertaken on the employer's premises, or the employee's home, or elsewhere, and could be during or outside the employee's working hours, supervised by the employer or someone else, undertaken with or without supervision, within or outside the United Kingdom, and need not be intended to lead to an award of a qualification to the employee. More than one course of study or training may be included in one request, but the employee must not have made a request within the previous 12 months (although in certain circumstances a previous request made within that period may be ignored). There is no limit to the amount of time off an employee may request, or whether to course of study or training shall be full-time or part-time. These matters will fall to be taken into account when the employer considers the request.

7.33 The Employee Study and Training (Procedural Requirements) Regulations generally follow the Flexible Working Regulations, and lay down the procedures to be followed for the making and consideration of a request. The employee's application (known as a s 63D application) must:

(a) give the following details of the proposed course of study or training:

   (i) its subject-matter;

   (ii) where it would take place;

   (iii) who would provide or supervise it;

   (iv) what qualification (if any) it would lead to; and

(b) explain how the employee thinks the proposed study or training would improve:

   (i) the employee's effectiveness in the employer's business; and

   (ii) the performance of the employer's business.

Dealing with the request

7.34 When the employer receives the s 63D application from the employee, then, provided the employee has not submitted an earlier application within the previous 12 months (other than a request which has to be ignored: see reg 3) the employer must consider the application, and, within 28 days, hold a meeting with the employee to discuss the request, at a time and place convenient to both parties. The employee will have the right to be accompanied at the meeting by a companion, and the meeting may be delayed if the companion is not available.

7.35 The employer is entitled to seek further information about the proposed course of study or training, and if the employee refuses to supply this, the request may be taken as having been withdrawn. Otherwise, within 14 days of the meeting, the employer must give the employee a written notice of the decision, stating the grounds for the refusal with an explanation as to why those grounds apply. The application may be refused (in whole or in part) on a number of permissible grounds, which are:

(a) the proposed study or training would not improve:

   (i) the employee's effectiveness in the employer's business; or

   (ii) the performance of the employer's business;

(b) the burden of additional costs;

(c) the detrimental effect of ability to meet customer demand;

(d) the inability to reorganise work among existing staff;

(e) the inability to recruit additional staff;

(f) the detrimental impact on quality;

(g) the detrimental impact on performance;

(h) the insufficiency of work during the periods the employee proposes to work;

(i) planned structural changes;

(j) any other grounds specified by the Secretary of State in regulations.

7.36 The employee will have a right to appeal within 14 days against the refusal, and a meeting to consider the appeal must be held within 14 days, and the decision must be notified to the employee within 14 days. If the appeal is dismissed, the grounds on which the appeal was dismissed must be stated.

7.37 If the s 63D application is granted, the employer must give the employee notice of the decision, in writing, and dated. The notice must give details of the subject of the study or training, where and when it will take place, who will provide or supervise it, and what qualifications (if any) it will lead to. The notice must also make clear whether any remuneration will be paid for the time spent on study or training, whether there will be any changes in the employee's working hours in order to accommodate the study or training, and how tuition fees or other direct costs are to be met.

7.38 If the application is granted in part, or varied, the employer's notice must make clear the variation agreed to, and supported by written evidence of the employee's agreement to the variation.

7.39 For his part, the employee must inform the employer:

(a) if he fails to start the agreed study or training;

(b) if he fails to complete the agreed study or training;

(c) if he undertakes or proposes to undertake study or training that differs from the agreed study or training.

Complaints to employment tribunal (s 63(I))

7.40 An employee may present a complaint to an employment tribunal that the employer has failed to deal with the application in accordance with the regulations, or refused on a ground other than the permissible ones, or that the employer's decision to refuse the application is based on incorrect facts. The complaint must be brought within three months of the date when the employee was notified of the decision on the appeal, or the employer was in breach of the statutory provisions, or such further period as the employment tribunal considers reasonable. On such a complaint the employment tribunal may make an order requiring the employer to reconsider the application, or make an award of compensation to the employee as is thought to be just and equitable, not exceeding eight weeks pay (capped).

7.41 An employee has the right not to be subjected to a detriment because he made or proposed to make a s 63D application, and it would be an automatically unfair dismissal if the making of such an application was the reason for the dismissal.

F. Other time off work

7.42 Time off work may also be claimed in order to care for dependants (see para 6.122), for trade union duties and activities (see para 21.66) and for redundant employees to look for work (see para 18.38).

Statutory sick pay (SSP)

A. How the scheme works

7.43 Under the provisions of the Social Security Contributions and Benefits Act 1992, ss 151–163 and the Statutory Sick Pay (General) Regulations employers will be responsible for paying to their employees statutory sick pay in respect of the first 28 weeks of absence through sickness (currently £87.55 per week).

7.44 Originally, the whole amount of SSP paid out by employers could be recovered by means of deductions from national insurance contributions sent to the Revenue, and there was also in existence a small employer's relief. However, these regimes have now been abolished and replaced by a percentage threshold scheme (PTS) designed to help all employers if they have a large number of employees off sick at the same time.

7.45 Until April 2014, an employer could recover SSP paid in a tax month where it exceeded 13% of the employer's national insurance contributions liability in the same tax month. The excess amount of SSP paid was deducted from the national insurance contributions due in that month. This is no longer the case.

7.46 To understand the scheme, certain expressions must be defined:

(a) *A day of incapacity for work*

This is any day when an employee is incapable, by reasons of some specific disease or mental or bodily disablement, of doing work of a kind he might reasonably be expected to do.

(b) *A period of incapacity for work*

This means any period of four or more consecutive days, each of which is a day of incapacity for work in relation to the employee's contract of employment.

(c) *A period of entitlement*

This period starts with the first day of incapacity for work, and ends when either:

i.   the period of incapacity has ended, or

ii.   the entitlement to SSP has been used up, or

iii. the contract of employment is terminated, or

iv.   a woman who is pregnant becomes disqualified under the provisions of the Act.

(d) *Qualifying days*

These are days on which the employee is required by his contract of employment to be available for work.

B. Qualifying conditions

7.47 To qualify for SSP, three conditions must be satisfied, namely:

(a) the employee's day of incapacity for work must form part of the period of incapacity for work (ie four or more consecutive days);

(b) the day must be within the period of entitlement;

(c) the day must be a qualifying day.

If there are two periods of incapacity (for the same or different reasons) separated by not more than eight weeks, they will be treated as a single period of incapacity. This means that an employee will not have to requalify with another three 'waiting days'. Moreover, if an employee leaves his job and starts another one, his period of incapacity with his previous employer counts with his new one.

7.48 The entitlement to SSP is a flat-rate payment for a maximum period of 28 weeks in any one period of entitlement of three years or in any one tax year. Thereafter, the employee will be able to claim employment and support allowance. SSP is payable to all employees who meet the qualifying conditions and whose average weekly earnings are above the level at which national insurance contributions are payable.

7.49 The above provisions apply to part-time employees (provided they earn the requisite amounts) and there is no minimum service qualification. SSP will be deemed remuneration, and therefore subject to deductions in respect of tax and national insurance contributions. Married women and widows who pay reduced national insurance contributions will qualify for SSP even though they do not qualify for employment and support allowance. Note that agency workers are also entitled to SSP.

C. **Exclusions from entitlement**

7.50 The following employees are excluded from entitlement:

(a) employees who are incapacitated from work for less than four days;

(b) employees who earn less than the current lower earnings limit (£111 per week from April 2014) averaged over an eight-week period;

(c) pregnant women whose first day of sickness is within the disqualifying period (ie 18 weeks beginning with the eleventh week prior to the expected week of confinement), or who are receiving SMP or MA;

(d) employees who would be workless on the day when the period of entitlement would begin because of a trade dispute, unless they can prove that they did not take part in the strike or did not have a direct interest in it;

(e) employees who are sick on the day they are due to start new employment (employment and support allowance may be payable);

(f) employees whose first day of sickness is within eight weeks of a claim in respect of one of the following state benefits – employment and support allowance, invalidity pension, maternity allowance, or a previous entitlement to incapacity benefit or severe disablement allowance;

(g) employees who are in legal custody or who are outside the European Economic Area.

D. **Enforcement**

7.51 If an employee has not been paid SSP, he may refer the matter to HM Revenue and Customs. A decision made in the employee's favour can be enforced in the county court, should this be necessary. Certain questions may be referred directly to the Secretary of State for Work and Pensions for a decision, namely:

(a) whether a person is, or was, the employee or employer of another person;

(b) whether an employer is entitled to deduct SSP from his contribution payments;

(c) whether two or more contracts of employment, or two or more employers, shall be treated as one for SSP purposes.

7.52 Any agreement which purports to exclude, limit or modify an employee's entitlement to SSP shall be void, but this does not prevent an employer from operating a sick pay scheme which is more favourable than the statutory scheme. Contractual sick pay may discharge the employer's liability for SSP, and any SSP payment will discharge contractual liability for the relevant days.

E. **Self-certification of illness**

7.53 Doctors are required to issue fit notes after seven days of absence from work. Employees who need to self-certify four or more days' absence should fill in form SC2, which helps to determine if they are entitled to SSP. The form must be completed and signed by the employee, which amounts to a self-certification of absence through illness. If the illness lasts for a period longer than seven days, a Statement of Fitness for Work can be obtained from the doctor. The traditional sick note, issued by general practitioners, has been replaced by these 'fit notes' in which the GP will spell out the tasks the worker can perform. The fit note allows the doctor to advise one of two options:

(a) not fit for work: where the assessment of the employee is that he should refrain from work for a stated period of time.

(b) may be fit for work, where the assessment is of the employee's condition does not necessarily mean he cannot return to work; however, he may not be able to complete all of his normal duties or hours, or may need some support to help him undertake his normal duties.

The guidance in relation to fit notes emphasises the importance of assessing an individual's health in relation to work in general, and not just in relation to one specific role. The doctor may be able to advise on what 'reasonable adjustments' could be made, eg altered hours, changed duties, workplace adaptations, etc, although the fit note is qualified by the addition of 'if available, and with your employer's agreement'. Moreover, a doctor may not necessarily be familiar with the resources available to the employer, and there is likely to be considerable disagreement over what amounts to a reasonable adjustment in the circumstances, and whether a doctor is sufficiently well informed to make certain suggestions.

The fit note also has implications for employees who have been dismissed after a long-term absence caused by injury or illness. If the absence is due to a disability within the meaning of the Equality Act 2010, the employer must take appropriate steps or risk a finding of unfair dismissal. A GP's view, while not being conclusive, will contain more information about an individual's condition and functional ability, and the reasonableness of the dismissal may be open to challenge if there has been a failure to consider the suggested reasonable adjustments.

Working Time Regulations 1998 (as amended)

A. **The regulations**

7.54 These regulations came into force in October 1998 and are designed to implement the provisions of the Working Time Directive (93/104/EC) and the Young Workers Directive (94/33/EC). They were amended in 1999 and in 2003 to extend coverage to non-mobile transport workers in the sea, inland waterways and fishing sectors, all workers in the railway and offshore sectors, and all workers in the aviation industry who are not covered by the separate Aviation Directive (2000/79/EC) and to mobile workers in the road transport industry in 2005.

7.55 Generally, the regulations give a series of new rights to 'workers', a term which is wider than 'employees', and which also applies to a person working under a contract 'to do or perform personally any work or services for another party to the contract whose status is not by virtue of the contract that of a client or customer of any profession or business undertaking carried on by the individual' (reg 2(1)). This clearly covers casual, freelance and some self-employed workers, other than self-employed persons who are pursuing a professional or business activity on their own account. Thus in *Byrne Bros (Farmwork) Ltd v Baird*[15] the claimant was a self-employed worker employed under a sub-contractor's agreement. He was taxed under Schedule D. The employer was not obliged to provide work, and the claimant was not obliged to do the work personally, although he was paid on a time basis. He claimed holiday pay for the Christmas and New Year closure under the Working Time Regulations. An employment tribunal upheld his claim, and the EAT confirmed the decision. As a 'labour-only sub-contractor' he undertook personally to provide work or services, and he did not work as part of 'any profession or business undertaking'. Thus he was a worker within the meaning of the regulations (see also *Cavil v Barratt Homes Ltd*[16]). So too are bricklayers who work in gangs and who are paid by the employer directly to each gang member (*JNJ Bricklaying Ltd v Stacey*[17]).

7.56 The regulations do not apply to certain seafarers, sea fishermen and workers who work on inland waterways, each of whom have their own special sector provisions. Non-mobile workers in the transport industry are included, but mobile workers in that industry are covered by the Road Transport (Working Time) Regulations 2005. There is partial exclusion for mobile staff who work in civil aviation (again covered by sector-specific provisions), and activities of the armed forces and police or specific activities in connection with civil protection services which inevitably conflict with the regulations.

7.57 The main provisions of the Working Time Regulations 1998–2009 are as follows.

B. The main provisions

Regulation 4 (maximum weekly working time)

7.58 A worker's average working time for each seven-day period, including overtime, must not exceed 48 hours in any period of 17 weeks, although in certain circumstances (reg 21, special cases) the reference period can be 26 weeks, or 52 weeks if permitted by a collective agreement or workforce agreement (reg 23(b)). The regulation will not apply if the worker agrees in writing to working more than 48 hours each week (reg 5). The agreement may be for a specified or an indefinite period, but may be terminated by either side giving the appropriate notice of not less than seven days and not more than three months. For a worker to opt out of the 48-hour week, the consent must be expressly and freely given (*Pfeiffer v Deutsches Rotes Kreuz*[18]).

To calculate the average hours in any reference period, the formula to be applied is:

$$\frac{A + B}{C}$$

7.59 This requires some explanation. In any reference period, there will be days when the employee will not work, because of annual holidays, sick leave, maternity leave, etc. Clearly, to exclude those days from the calculation would distort the average hours worked. Therefore, those 'excluded days' must be added back in to the calculation. 'A' is the total number of hours worked during the reference period; 'B' is the total number of hours worked immediately after the reference period during the number of days equivalent to the number of excluded days. 'C' will be the number of weeks in the reference period. Thus the formula (A + B ÷ C) will give the average number of hours in

---

[15] [2002] ICR 667, [2001] All ER (D) 321 (Nov), EAT.   [16] [2003] All ER (D) 06 (Jul), EAT.
[17] [2003] All ER (D) 96 (Jul), EAT.   [18] [2005] IRLR 137.

the reference period, which will, in effect, be extended by the equivalent number of 'excluded' days.

7.60 If a relevant agreement is provided for successive 17-week reference periods, then each reference period will be self-contained, for the purpose of calculating average working hours. In the absence of any such agreement, the reference period will be a 'rolling' 17-week period, ie each week will be the start of a new 17-week reference period. If a worker is required to remain at his place of work, even though he is not actually working, this is working time for the purpose of the regulations (*Sindicato de Médicos de Asistencia Pública (SIMAP) v Conselleria de Sanidad y Consumo de la Generalidad Valenciana*[19]). However, if the worker is permitted to be away from his place of work when on call, and accordingly free to pursue other activities, the on-call time does not amount to working time until he is called upon by the employer to work. If a person is permitted to sleep while on call, the period of inactivity is still on-call time (*Landeshaupstadt Keil v Jaeger*[20]).

7.61 An employer cannot insist that a worker works hours of work in excess of the restrictions imposed by the Working Time Regulations, and a dismissal for refusing to do so is automatically unfair under s 101A of ERA. The one year's qualifying period of employment for unfair dismissal does not apply in these circumstances (*McLean v Rainbow Homeloans Ltd*[21]).

Regulations 5A, 6A, 7 (young worker)

7.62 The working time of a young worker (ie who has attained the age of 15 but not the age of 18 and who is over compulsory school leaving age) shall not exceed 8 hours per day or 40 hours per week. A young worker shall not work during the restricted period, which is between 10pm and 6am or 11pm and 7am. An employer shall not assign a young worker to work during the restricted period unless the employer has ensured that the young worker will have the opportunity of a free assessment of his health and capacities before he takes up the assignment, and thereafter at such regular intervals as may be appropriate in his case.

Regulation 6 (length of night work)

7.63 The normal hours of work for a night worker (defined in reg 2) shall not exceed eight in any 24-hour period, again, the average being assessed over a 17-week period (which can be fixed successive 17-week periods, as set out in a relevant agreement, or, failing such agreement, a 'rolling' 17-week period). In *R v A-G for Northern Ireland, ex p Burns*[22] the claimant worked a cycle of 15 shifts of eight hours' duration. During five of these, at least three hours of her working time fell between 11pm and 6am. It was held that she was a night worker within the meaning of reg 6. It was noted that the Directive defined a night worker as a person who works at night 'as a normal course', and this phrase was to be construed as meaning 'as a regular feature'.

7.64 An employer shall ensure that no night worker whose work involves special hazards or heavy physical or mental strain works for more than eight hours in any 24-hour period. The work shall be regarded as involving special hazards or physical or mental strain if it is identified as such in a collective agreement or a workforce agreement, or in a risk assessment carried out under the Management of Health and Safety at Work Regulations 1999. Further, a night worker will be entitled to a free health assessment before he takes up the assignment, with further such assessments at regular intervals. If a registered medical

[19] [2001] All ER (EC) 609, [2000] ECR I–7963, [2001] 3 CMLR 42, [2001] ICR 1116, [2000] IRLR 845, (2000) *Times*, 18 October.
[20] [2004] ICR 1528, (2004) All ER (EC) 604.   [21] [2007] IRLR 14.   [22] [1999] IRLR 315.

practitioner advises the employer that a worker employed by him is suffering from health problems connected with night work, then, if possible, the employer should transfer the worker to other work for which he is suited, and undertaken at times so that he ceases to be a night worker.

7.65 To calculate the average working hours of a night worker, the normal working hours during the reference period must be divided by the number of working days in that period. The formula is

$$A \div (B - C)$$

Again, an explanation is required.

7.66 From the number of 24-hour periods during the reference period ('B') must be deducted the number of hours (divided by 24 to equate days) which comprise or are included in the weekly rest periods, as provided for in reg 11 ('C'). The amount of the normal working hours during the reference period ('A') can thus be ascertained by dividing the normal working hours during the reference period by the number of working days in that period.

7.67 If a worker has worked for less than 17 weeks, the average will be calculated by reference to the period since the worker started to work for the employer.

Regulation 8 (pattern of work)

7.68 Where the pattern according to which the employer organises work is such as to put the health and safety of a worker employed by him at risk, in particular because the work is monotonous or the work-rate is predetermined, the employer shall ensure that the worker is given adequate rest breaks.

Regulation 9 (records)

7.69 An employer shall keep records of the maximum weekly working time, length of night working, and health assessments etc of night workers, in respect of each worker in relation to whom they apply, and keep such records for two years.

Regulation 10 (daily rest)

7.70 An adult worker is entitled to a rest period of not less than 11 consecutive hours in each 24-hour period during which he works for an employer, although a young worker is entitled to a rest period of 12 consecutive hours.

Regulation 11 (weekly rest periods)

7.71 A worker is entitled to an uninterrupted rest period of not less than 24 hours in each seven-day period during which he works for his employer, although this can be changed to two uninterrupted periods of 24 hours in each 14-day period, or one uninterrupted period of 48 hours in each 14-day period. A young worker is entitled to a rest period of not less than 48 hours in any seven-day period, although this can be altered in certain circumstances.

Regulation 12 (rest breaks)

7.72 Where a worker's daily working time is more than six hours, he is entitled to a rest break, which shall be for an uninterrupted period of 20 minutes (unless a collective agreement or workforce agreement specifies otherwise), to be spent away from the workstation. A young worker who works for more than four and a half hours shall be entitled to a rest break of at least 30 minutes, spent away from the workstation.

A rest break must have an ascertainable beginning and end. If a worker is 'on call' the fact that he can take a rest break is not sufficient if he is subject to instant recall whilst having a break (*McCartney v Oversley House Management*[23]). Rest breaks are not to be regarded as time spent on call if the worker is not to be interrupted save in exceptional circumstances, even if the break is taken on site. (*Martin v Southern Health and Social Care Trust*[24]).

Regulation 13 (annual leave entitlement)

7.73 Under the Working Time (Amendment) Regulations 2007 statutory minimum annual leave was increased to 5.6 weeks from April 2009 (ie 28 days) for a worker who works five days a week, pro rata for workers who work part time. Public holidays may be included in this entitlement, but there is no legal entitlement to take time off work on the actual public holidays. Further, employers who at present grant time off for public holidays do not have to provide workers with any additional leave. A worker is entitled to receive his normal weekly pay during these holidays, calculated in accordance with ss 221–224 of ERA. Normal weekly pay includes any usual supplements (such as flight supplements for airline pilots, *Williams v British Airways plc*).[25]

7.74 Entitlement to statutory holidays applies to all workers, not just those who are employees in the legal sense. Thus self-employed workers, casual employees, part-time employees, etc are all entitled to holidays with pay, the only exception being a person who is a client or customer of any profession or business undertaking. Agency workers are entitled to holiday pay from whichever of the agent or principal is responsible for paying the agency worker.

7.75 A holiday year may be fixed by a relevant agreement, which can be a workforce agreement that meets the requirements of Sch 1 of the Working Time Regulations, or is a collective agreement with a recognised trade union, or a written contract of employment. In the absence of any such agreement, the holiday year will run from October each year or, in respect of workers who commenced work after 1 October 1998, from their start date and each subsequent anniversary.

7.76 The European Court has held that if a full-time worker becomes a part-time worker during the course of a year, and has not taken his full entitlement to annual leave before he changes, the employer cannot reduce the right to annual leave that the worker has already accumulated during the period of full-time employment but has not been able to take while working full-time (*Zentralbetriebsrat der Landeskrankenhaüser Tirols*[26]).

7.77 If a worker leaves his employment having taken less holiday than his entitlement at the time of leaving, he is entitled to be paid in respect of the untaken holiday period. If he leaves his employment having taken more holidays than his legal entitlement the relevant agreement may provide for a deduction in pay in respect of the excess holiday period.

7.78 To ascertain how much leave is owed on termination, the formula to use is $(A \times B) - C$, where 'A' is the period of leave the worker is entitled to under the regulations, 'B' is the portion of the leave year which has expired prior to the effective date of termination, and 'C' is the period of leave already taken by the worker. If a relevant agreement so permits, a worker who has already taken holiday entitlement in excess of his statutory entitlement can be required to compensate the employer, either by way of a payment, or doing additional work.

7.79 Where the contract of employment is terminated during the course of a leave year, and the employee has not taken his leave entitlement, reg 14(3) provides that he shall

---

[23] IDS Brief 801.   [24] [2010] IRLR 1048, [2010] NICA 31.
[25] ECJ Case C-155/10.   [26] (C-486/08) [2010] IRLR 631.

receive a payment in lieu, which shall be such sum as is provided for in a relevant agreement, or, if there are no such provisions, the formula (A × B) – C (para 7.78) will apply. In *Witley and District Men's Club v MacKay*[27] the employee was dismissed for gross misconduct. A relevant collective agreement provided that in such circumstances accrued holiday pay would not be payable. When the employers refused to make any such payment, the employee claimed that there was a breach of the Working Time Regulations. His claim was upheld. The words 'such sum' in reg 14(3) did not mean 'no sum'. Thus an agreement which provided for no sum to be paid in respect of outstanding leave entitlement is void by virtue of reg 35(1), as an attempt to exclude or limit the operation of the regulations. This clearly leaves open the possibility of an agreement being upheld if it provides for a minimal or token sum to be paid.

7.80 It goes without saying that clauses sometimes found in existing employment contracts which specify that an employee dismissed for reason of gross misconduct shall not be entitled to accrued statutory holiday pay are no longer valid although this rule would not apply in respect of additional contractual entitlement.

7.81 An employer can insist that offshore employees who work two weeks on and two weeks off take their annual leave during the 26 weeks of onshore time (*Russell v Transocean International Resources Ltd*).[28]

7.82 The worker may give notice to the employer of the dates when he wishes to take his holidays, subject to the employer requiring the worker to take his holidays on particular dates. The worker must give twice the number of days' notice as days' leave he wishes to take. The employer can prevent the employee taking leave on a particular day by giving notice equivalent to the same number of days as the length of leave the employee wishes to take. However, the notice provisions are capable of being overridden by a relevant agreement, which may provide for longer (or shorter) periods of notice.

7.83 If an employee fails to comply with the notice requirements as set out in his contract of employment he will lose his entitlement to statutory leave. In *Lyons v Mitie*[29] the contract stated that applications for holidays must be made on a request form and submitted at least four weeks before the holiday was to begin. The employee failed to give the requisite notice, and it was held that he was no longer entitled. However, the EAT cautioned that if an employer applied their rules in such a way as to effectively defeat a worker's entitlement to annual leave, or if the employee was forced to apply for holiday late in the year because of illness, EU law may well require the employer to permit him to take leave despite the failure to give proper notice.

7.84 There are conflicting decisions on whether holiday pay must be paid at the time when the worker is taking the holiday, or whether it can properly be paid along with basic pay but in *Robinson-Steele v RD Retail Services Ltd*,[30] the ECJ held that in principle, rolled-up holiday pay is not permitted by the EC Directive. Workers who take statutory leave must be placed in the same financial position as they would be in if they were carrying on work. An arrangement whereby annual leave payments are staggered over the corresponding annual period of work is precluded by the Directive. In other words, the point in time when payment is made for annual leave must be so fixed as to ensure that the worker can take his holiday entitlement. However, if there are genuine rolled-up holiday payments, made transparently and comprehensibly, these may be offset against a worker's entitlement to payment when leave is finally taken. In other words, if the percentage of holiday pay

---

[27] [2001] IRLR 595, [2001] All ER (D) 31 (Jun), EAT.   [28] [2011] UKSC 57.
[29] [2010] ICR 628, [2010] IRLR 288.   [30] (C-131/04) [2006] IRLR 386, ECJ.

allocated is clearly identified in the contract and/or on the payslip, and it is made clear that it is a true addition to the contractual rate of pay, credit for such payments may be given (*Lyddon v Englefield Brickworks Ltd*[31]).

7.85 Accrued holiday pay is to be calculated on the basis of the number of working days in the year (ie 233 days per year), not on the basis of a calendar year of 365 days (*Leisure Leagues UK Ltd v Maconnachie*[32]). If holiday pay is based on working hours, only con-tractual hours – not overtime hours – count for the purpose of computing the amount of the worker's holiday pay (*Bamsey v Albion Engineering Ltd*[33]). A similar rule applies in respect of commissions payable (*Evans v Malley Organisation Ltd*[34]). The holiday pay of a worker on a zero-hours contract placed on short-time working can be calculated on a pro rata basis. The situation is analogous to that of the part-time worker, not of someone on long-term sick leave (*Heimann and another v Kaiser GmbH*[35]). If the employee leaves his employment, having taken more than his annual leave entitlement, the employer can only recover the overpayment if there is a contractual provision to this effect, ie in the contract of employment, a workforce agreement or a collective agreement which has been incorpo-rated into the individual contract (*Hill v Chapell*[36]).

7.86 A period of illness while on holiday does not count towards the minimum period of four weeks' annual paid leave. In *Pereda v Madrid Movilidad SA*[37] the claimant suffered an accident at work 14 days before the commencement of his allocated period of four weeks' annual leave. The injury lasted for six weeks, and he was thus unable to take his planned holiday. His request for an additional period of annual leave was refused. The ECJ held that there can be no derogation from the entitlement to paid annual leave. Thus if a worker decides not to take his annual leave during a period of illness, he must be granted a replace-ment holiday period to ensure that he is not deprived of his entitlement to rest, relaxation and leisure. This principle applies if the employee falls sick before or during the annual leave period *Asociación Nacional de Grandes Empresas de Distribución (ANGED)*.[38] In *Stringer v HMRC*[39] the ECJ held that a worker who is on long-term sick leave is entitled to any holiday that accrues during his sickness absence, which he can presumably take on his return to work. An employee on long-term sick leave who did not have an opportunity to take her annual leave because of her illness was entitled to have the holiday carried forward to the next leave year automatically without having to request it (*NHS Leeds v Larner*[40]). This, however, only applies to the four weeks' leave set out in the European Directive, and not the additional 1.6 weeks granted by UK law, unless the parties have agreed otherwise. *Sood Enterprises v Healy*.[41]

If the employee is dismissed while on sick leave he is entitled to pay in lieu on any untaken leave that accumulated during his sickness absence. Where a worker has been prevented from taking his annual leave due to sickness, he must be allowed to take that leave when he returns in the new leave year, or receive a payment on termination (*Schulz-Hoff v Deutsche Rentenversicherung Bund*[42]).

---

[31] [2007] All ER (D) 198, (2008) IRLR 198.   [32] [2002] IRLR 600, [2002] All ER (D) 223 (Mar), EAT.

[33] [2003] ICR 1224, [2003] All ER (D) 424 (Mar), EAT; aff'd sub nom *Bamsey v Albion Engineering Ltd* [2004] EWCA Civ 359, 148 Sol Jo LB 389, [2004] All ER (D) 482 (Mar).

[34] [2002] All ER (D) 93 (May), EAT; revsd [2002] EWCA Civ 1834, [2003] ICR 432, [2003] IRLR 156, [2002] All ER (D) 397 (Nov).

[35] C-229/11 and 230/11 ECJ.   [36] [2003] IRLR 19, [2002] All ER (D) 461 (May), EAT.

[37] [2010] 1 CMLR 3, [2009] IRLR 959, (2009) 159 NLJ 1323, (2009) *Times*, 8 October.

[38] Case C-78/11.

[39] [2009] All ER (EC) 906, [2009] ECR I–179, [2009] 2 CMLR 27, [2009] ICR 932, [2009] IRLR 214, (2009) *Times*, 28 January.

[40] [2012] EWCA Civ 1034, CA.   [41] UKEATS/0015/12.   [42] [2009] ICR 932, (2009) IRLR 214.

7.87 Annual leave accrued on sick leave cannot be carried over indefinitely. In *KHS AG v Schulte*[43] the Court of Justice of the European Union allowed it to be carried over up to 15 months. This creates some uncertainty with domestic law, which does not currently make provision for the carrying over of annual leave.

7.88 Note that the paid annual leave provisions in the Working Time Directive have direct effect. This means that cases such as *Stringer & others v HMRC* referred to earlier can be enforced directly by public sector workers (*Dominguez v Centre informatique du Centre Ouest Atlantique*[44]) without waiting for UK case law or legislation.

7.89 In *Ainsworth v Inland Revenue Commissioners*[45] the House of Lords ruled that a claim for non-payment of holiday pay may be brought under the unlawful deductions provisions of ss 13–23 of the Employment Rights Act. The significance of this ruling is that the time for bringing a complaint will run from the last date of a series of unlawful deductions, and not from the more restrictive three-month time limit as laid down in reg 30 of the Working Time Regulations.

C. **Exclusions**

7.90 There are a number of excluded sectors of employment and specified activities to which specific regulations do not apply, as follows.

Regulation 18

7.91 The regulations do not apply to certain seafarers, workers on sea-going fishing vessels, and workers on board certain ships and hovercrafts. These workers have their own sector-specific provisions. Non-mobile workers in road, sea and inland waterways transport (eg clerical and administrative workers) are covered by the regulations, but mobile workers have limited exclusions. If a doctor is on call, but required to remain at a hospital, then periods of inactivity – even sleeping – can constitute working time. The fact that the doctor is required to be present at the place of work determined by the employer, and be available to provide services immediately in cases of need, means that such hours must be regarded as being within the ambit of the performance of his duties (*Landeshauptstadt Kiel v Jaeger*[46]).

Regulation 19

7.92 Domestic servants in a private household are excluded from reg 4 (maximum weekly working time), reg 5A (young worker), reg 6 (length of night work), reg 6A (night work by young worker), reg 7 (health assessment for night workers), reg 8 (safe pattern of work).

Regulation 20

7.93 Workers who, on account of the specific characteristics of the activities engaged in, or where the duration of the working time cannot be measured or predetermined, or which can be determined by the worker himself. In particular:

(a) managing executives or other persons with autonomous decision-making powers;

(b) family workers;

(c) workers officiating at religious ceremonies in churches and religious communities.

---

[43] (Case C-214/10) [2011] EUEJC.   [44] (Case C-282/10).

[45] [2009] UKHL 31, [2009] 4 All ER 1205, [2009] ICR 985, [2009] IRLR 677, *Times*, June 15, 2009.

[46] (C-151/02) [2003] 3 CMLR 493, [2003] IRLR 804, 75 BMLR 201, [2003] All ER (D) 72 (Sep), ECJ.

7.94 The above workers are excluded from reg 4 (maximum weekly working time), reg 6 (length of night work), reg 10 (daily rest), reg 11 (weekly rest period) and reg 12 (rest breaks).

Regulation 21

7.95 There is a limited exclusion for the following group of workers:

(a) workers whose activities are such that their place of work and place of residence are distant from one another, or whose different places of work are distant from one another;

(b) where a worker is engaged in security and surveillance activities requiring a permanent presence in order to protect property and persons, particularly security guards and caretakers or security firms;

(c) workers whose activities involve the need for continuity or service or production, particularly –

  (i) services relating to the reception, treatment or care provided by hospitals or similar establishments (including the activities of doctors in training), residential institutions and prisons,

  (ii) work at docks or airports,

  (iii) press, radio, television, cinematographic production, postal and telecommunications services and civil protection services,

  (iv) gas, water and electricity production, transmission and distribution, household refuse collection and incineration,

  (v) industries in which work cannot be interrupted on technical grounds,

  (vi) research and development activities,

  (vii) agriculture,

  (viii) the carriage of passengers on regular urban transport services;

(d) where there is a foreseeable surge of activity, particularly in –

  (i) agriculture,

  (ii) tourism, and

  (iii) postal services;

(e) where the worker's activities are affected by –

  (i) an occurrence due to unusual and unforeseeable circumstances, beyond the control of the worker's employer, or

  (ii) exceptional events, the consequences of which could not have been avoided despite the exercise of all due care, or

  (iii) an accident or the imminent risk of an accident;

(f) workers in railway transport whose activities are intermittent, who work on trains and whose activities are to ensure continuity and regularity of traffic.

7.96 In respect of the above group of workers, the following regulations do not apply, namely, reg 6 (length of night work), reg 10 (daily rest periods), reg 11 (weekly rest periods) and reg 12 (rest breaks). However, if a worker is required to work during what would normally be a rest period, the employer shall allow him to have a compensatory period of rest, or, if this is not possible, afford him appropriate protection (reg 24).

Regulation 23

7.97 This regulation provides that a collective agreement or a workforce agreement may modify or exclude the following regulations in relation to particular workers, namely reg 6 (length of night work), reg 10 (daily rest), reg 11 (weekly rest period) and reg 12 (rest breaks, see *Prison Service v Bewley*[47]). So far as reg 4 (maximum weekly working time) is concerned, such agreement can substitute a different period over which the average can be worked out, not exceeding 52 weeks (in place of 17 weeks).

7.98 There are also a number of other limited exclusions in respect of shift workers, offshore workers, workers in the armed forces, and young workers affected by *force majeure* or when no adult worker is available (regs 25–27A). There are also special rules for agricultural workers (Sch 2).

D. **Enforcement**

7.99 The regulations can be enforced in three ways. First, inspectors from the Health and Safety Executive (or, in appropriate circumstances, enforcement officers of local authorities) are responsible for the enforcement of the following relevant requirements (see reg 28), namely:

(a) the duty of an employer to take all reasonable steps to ensure that the provisions relating to the 48-hour week have been complied with, and also to keep up-to-date records of workers who are subject to an opting out agreement;

(b) the duty of an employer to take all reasonable steps to ensure that a young worker's working time does not exceed 8 hours per day and 40 hours in any week;

(c) the duty of an employer to take all reasonable steps to ensure that a night worker's normal hours of work do not exceed an average of eight hours in each 24 hours;

(d) the duty of an employer to ensure that no night worker whose work involves special hazards or heavy physical or mental strain works for more than eight hours in any 24-hour period;

(e) the duty of an employer to ensure that a young worker does not work between 10pm and 6am (or 11pm and 7am);

(f) the duty of an employer to provide a free health assessment for a night worker and for a young worker who works at night, and for the health assessment to be repeated at regular intervals;

(g) the duty of the employer to provide adequate rest breaks when the work is monotonous;

(h) the duty of the employer to keep adequate records, and to retain them for two years;

(i) where a young worker is permitted under the regulations to work at night, the duty of the employer to ensure that he is supervised by an adult worker, and be allowed a compensatory period of rest;

(j) where the application of the regulations to special cases or shift workers is excluded, the duty of the employer to ensure an equivalent compensatory period of rest;

(k) where certain mobile workers are excluded from the regulations, the duty of the employer to ensure adequate rest.

[47] [2004] ICR 422, [2004] All ER (D) 22 (Mar), EAT.

7.100 It may be noted that although the above provisions are generally enforced by health and safety inspectors, it is the duty of the Civil Aviation Authority to enforce the provisions in respect of relevant civil aviation workers, the Maritime and Coastguard Agency in respect of mobile workers in inland waterways and lake transport, and the Vehicle and Operator Services Agency in respect of relevant road transport workers.

7.101 The powers of inspectors to enforce the regulations are identical to those possessed by inspectors under the Health and Safety at Work Act (see para 11.10), as are the offences which may be committed by a person who obstructs, inhibits, gives false information, etc, while the inspector is exercising his powers (see reg 29 and Sch 3).

7.102 In respect of the matters just referred to, an employer may be prosecuted in the magistrates' courts, where a fine of up to £5,000 may be imposed, or an unlimited fine imposed in the Crown Court. Enforcement officers may also issue an Improvement Notice, requiring the employer to rectify matters specified therein, in order to ensure compliance with the statutory requirements, and a failure to comply with such notice can lead to a fine of up to £20,000, and/or six months' imprisonment in the magistrates' court, or an unlimited fine and/or up to two years' imprisonment in the Crown Court. Enforcement of Working Time Regulations by HSE is on a reactive basis, ie a worker must first make a complaint to the authority.

7.103 The second way in which the regulations can be enforced is by way of a complaint by a worker to an employment tribunal, alleging that the employer has failed to comply with any of the following provisions:

(a) the daily rest periods for adult or young workers (reg 10);

(b) the weekly rest periods for adult or young workers (reg 11);

(c) rest break periods for adult or young workers (reg 12);

(d) entitlement to annual leave (reg 13);

(e) entitlement to equivalent compensatory rest, where the provisions of regs 10, 11 and 12 have been excluded or modified;

(f) entitlement to compensatory rest where the provisions of regs 10 and 11 have been excluded in respect of young workers serving in the armed forces, or where the *force majeure* exemption applies;

(g) the duty of the employer to pay a worker's statutory annual leave pay, or pay for leave outstanding on the termination of employment (regs 14, 16);

(h) mobile workers, where regs 10, 11 or 12 have been excluded;

(i) young workers who are not permitted to take compensatory rest periods.

7.104 Although the regulations currently allow only the HSE to bring proceedings in respect of working time limits, as a result of the European Court of Justice decision in *Fuß v Stadt Halle (No. 2)*[48] those working for a public employer will be able to rely on the Working Time Directive and bring actions themselves in the employment tribunal for such breaches. It remains to be seen if this will be extended to other workers.

7.105 A complaint to an employment tribunal must be brought within three months from the date on which it is alleged that the exercise of the right should have been permitted, or, in the case of holiday pay, from the date when the payment should have been made, although the employment tribunal may extend the period if it was not reasonably practicable to bring the complaint earlier. If the complaint is well founded, the employment

[48] (Case C-429/09) [2011] IRLR 176, CJEU.

tribunal may make a declaration, and may award compensation of such amount as the tribunal consider to be just and equitable, having regard to the employer's default in refusing to permit the worker to exercise the right in question, and any loss sustained by the worker attributable to that default. In the case of holiday pay, the amount due will be awarded.

7.106 A worker will also have the right (ERA, s 45A) not to be subjected to any detriment because:

(a) he refused to comply with a requirement that the employer imposed which would be in contravention of the regulations;

(b) he refused to forgo a right conferred by the regulations;

(c) he failed to sign a workforce agreement or an individual agreement opting out of the regulations;

(d) he performed any functions or activities as a workforce representative, or as a candidate in an election for workforce representatives;

(e) he brought proceedings against the employer to enforce a right conferred by the regulations;

(f) he alleged that the employer had infringed a right conferred by the regulations.

The European Court of Justice has held that a detriment was suffered in the case of *Fuß v Stadt Halle*.[49] Here, a fire officer was timetabled to work an average of 54 hours per week. He asked his employers not to exceed the 48-hour limit in the Working Time Directive. The response of the employer was to transfer him to an office post with fewer hours, but also with lower pay, as his hours were no longer unsocial. The Court regarded the treatment as victimisation which deprived of all substance his right to a maximum 48-hour week and the fact that the Directive was intended to protect his safety and health.

7.107 An employee (not a worker) also has the right not to be unfairly dismissed for any of the above reasons (ERA, s 101A), and also the right not to be unfairly selected for redundancy (ERA, s 105(4A)). Again, the complaint must be brought within three months from the date of the act complained of, with the usual extension of time if it was not reasonably practicable to bring the complaint earlier. If the complaint is upheld, the employment tribunal will make a declaration, and may make an award of compensation, on just and equitable principles. If the employee was unfairly dismissed, no qualifying period of employment is required, interim relief may be available (see para 17.183), and the minimum basic award, as well as an additional award (of between 26 and 52 weeks' pay), may be made as appropriate.

7.108 The third way of enforcing the regulations is to seek an appropriate remedy for breach of contract of employment. In *Barber v RJB Mining (UK) Ltd*[50] pit deputies, although contractually obliged to work for 42 hours a week, regularly worked a considerable amount of overtime, in excess of 48 hours. They were asked to sign an agreement opting out of their rights under the regulations, but refused, and they sought from the court a declaration to the effect that they need not work at all until such time as their average working hours fell below the limit specified in reg 4(1). The High Court granted the declaration. It was held that it was clearly the intention of Parliament that their contract of employment should be read so as to provide that an employee should work no more than 48 hours a week during the relevant reference period. Thus reg 4(1) created a free-standing right which took effect as a contractual term in the contracts of employment of the pit deputies.

---

[49] (Case C-243/09) [2010] IRLR 1080.
[50] [1999] 2 CMLR 833, [1999] ICR 679, [1999] IRLR 308, 143 Sol Jo LB 141, [1999] All ER (D) 244.

7.109 The mere fact that an employee works in excess of the 48-hour limit imposed by reg 4(2) does not, by itself, give rise to a claim for breach of statutory duty (see Chapter 11). The regulations themselves provide for specific methods of enforcement, ie by way of a criminal offence under reg 29 and a complaint to an employment tribunal under reg 30 (*Sayers v Cambridgeshire County Council*[51]). Whether a claim at common law in respect of work-related stress caused by working long hours would succeed will depend on whether the illness suffered was reasonably foreseeable (*Pakenham-Walsh v Connell Residential*[52]).

E. Sunday trading

7.110 The Sunday Trading Act 1994 was passed to reform the law relating to the circumstances when shops may be open on Sundays, and, at the same time, gave certain protections to employees who did not wish to work on Sundays. Identical provisions apply to betting workers, who work at a track for a bookmaker, or who work in a licensed betting shop. The relevant law is now set out in ERA, ss 36–43 (see also Sunday Working (Scotland) Act 2003).

7.111 If an employee is a 'protected shop worker' or an 'opted-out shop worker' he may refuse to work on Sundays. Any agreement or provision in the contract of employment will be unenforceable in so far as it requires him to work on Sundays. Further, a dismissal because an employee refuses to do Sunday work will be automatically unfair.

7.112 An employee will be a protected shop worker if:

- he was in employment as a shop worker on the day the Act came into force (26 August 1994);
- he was not employed to work only on Sunday;
- he has been continuously employed since the Act came into force and the date he complains of dismissal, detrimental treatment or attempts by the employer to require him to work on Sundays under his contract of employment; and
- he has been a shop worker throughout that period of continuous employment.

A person is also a protected shop worker if he cannot be required to work on Sundays under his contract of employment, whether this was entered into before or after the Act came into force.

7.113 An employee will be an opted-out shop worker if:

- under his contract he may be required to work on Sundays; but
- he is not employed to work only on Sundays; and
- he has given his employer an opting-out notice stating that he objects to working on Sundays.

In these circumstances, the opted-out shop worker will obtain the statutory protections after three months from when the opting-out notice was served. However, an employer has a duty to provide any employee who could potentially be an opted-out shop worker with a statement in the prescribed form explaining his rights to become an opted-out shop worker (within two months from the commencement of the employment) and if the employer fails to do this, the three-month period referred to is reduced to one month.

7.114 A protected shop worker and an opted-out shop worker may decide to give his employer an 'opting-in notice' indicating that he wishes to work on Sundays or does not

---

[51] [2006] EWHC 2029 (QB), [2007] IRLR 29.   [52] [2006] EWCA Civ 90.

object to working on Sundays, in which case he will lose his status, provided he expressly agrees to work on Sundays or a particular Sunday. It would seem that any such agreement can be verbal or in writing.

7.115 It will be an automatic unfair dismissal:

(a) to dismiss an employee who is a protected or opted-out shop worker for refusing or threatening to refuse to work on Sundays;

(b) to dismiss an employee for giving or proposing to give an opting-out notice;

(c) to select a person for redundancy because he refused to work on Sundays, or because he is a protected or opted-out shop worker;

(d) to dismiss an employee because he has asserted his rights under the Act (ERA, s 101).

However, it should be noted that an opted-out shop worker has no protection until the expiry of the three-month notice period (see para 7.113).

7.116 An employer cannot subject a person to a detriment because he is a protected or opted-out shop worker on the ground that he refuses to work on Sundays or because he has given an opting-out notice. However, an employer can offer financial or other inducements to such workers if they are prepared to work on Sundays, and those who are not so prepared are not thereby deemed to be suffering from a detriment (ERA, s 45).

7.117 An employee who has protected status will not lose that status by agreeing to work on a Sunday, provided he has not given an opting-in notice. However, an opted-out employee will lose his status once he gives an opting-in notice, although presumably he can regain that status by giving a further notice.

7.118 Finally, it should be noted that there is no requirement of a period of continuous employment, or a minimum number of hours worked, for a worker to obtain rights under the Act.

F. Christmas shopping

7.119 The Christmas Day (Trading) Act 2004 prohibits a large shop from opening on Christmas Day for the serving of retail customers, but this does not apply to shops of a kind mentioned in the Sunday Trading Act 1994, Sch 1, para 3 (shops selling intoxicating liquor, motor or cycle supplies, pharmacies, petrol stations, etc). Also prohibited is the loading or unloading of goods except with the consent of local authorities. A large shop is one which has a relevant floor area exceeding 280 square metres (see also Christmas Day and New Year's Day Trading (Scotland) Act 2007).

G. Jury service (Juries Act 1974)

7.120 An employee who is summoned to attend for jury service must be given time off work for that purpose, unless he is within one of the excused categories, or unless he has been excused service on application to the appropriate authority or the court. Failure to attend without reasonable cause may result in a fine being imposed of up to £1,000. A juror is entitled to claim travel and subsistence allowances, and payment for financial loss at prescribed rates. An employee has the right not to be subjected to any detriment because he has been summoned for jury service (including a coroner's jury), but a failure to pay remuneration during such absence is not a detriment unless he is entitled to be paid under his contract of employment (ERA, s 43M). It will also be automatically unfair to dismiss an employee if the reason was his attendance at jury service, but this will not apply if the employer can show that the employee's absence was likely to cause substantial injury to the employer's undertaking, the employee knew of this, and the employee unreasonably refused to apply for an excusal form or deferral of the obligation to attend (ERA, s 98B).

H. **Armed Forces Reserves**

7.121 Reservists who are called up to serve in the armed forces (including those who volunteer for such service) have their civil employment rights protected by the Reserve Forces (Safeguard of Employment) Act 1985. When the military service comes to an end, an employer must re-employ the employee:

(a) in the occupation in which he was last employed before the full-time service, on terms and conditions not less favourable than those which would have been applicable had he not undertaken full-time service, or

(b) if reinstatement is not reasonable and practicable, the employee must be offered the most favourable occupation, and on the most favourable terms and conditions which are reasonable and practicable in his case.

7.122 The employee must apply for reinstatement in writing, before the end of the third Monday after the full-time service has ceased, unless he was prevented from making it within that time by illness or other reasonable cause. The employer must be notified of a date (not more than three weeks) when the employee will be available for employment.

7.123 If the employer has already filled the vacancy, he cannot claim that it was not reasonably practicable to reinstate the reservist because he would have to dismiss that other person, and in practice it should be made clear to the replacement that the appointment may be for a temporary period.

7.124 A person who claims that his rights under the Act have been infringed may make an application to a reinstatement committee (see *Slaven v Thermo Engineers Ltd*[53]). They may order the employer to reinstate the employee, or make an award of compensation of between 13 and 52 weeks' pay, depending on his length of service prior to being called up. A further appeal will lie to an umpire. It is a criminal offence to fail to comply with an order of the reinstatement committee or the umpire.

7.125 If an employee is dismissed before the commencement of military service, and the reason is the call-up, then, in addition to a claim being made for unfair dismissal, the employer again faces the prospect of being prosecuted for a criminal offence.

7.126 Once the employee returns to his employment, his employment will be deemed to be continuous. The period of absence will not count towards continuity, but will not break it. However, if the employee received permission from the employer to go, he will be absent from work by arrangement or agreement, and the period of absence will count under the provisions of ERA, s 212(3) (see para 13.24).

7.127 The Reserve Forces Act 1996 makes provisions which would enable a reservist to be called out for a period of up to nine months, with the consent of his employer, and for employees to enter into employee agreements with registered employers specifying the maximum liability to service of the employee as a special member, events which will terminate that liability, and other terms relating to the obligations of a special member.

---

[53] [1992] ICR 295.

I. Access to medical reports

7.128 The Access to Medical Reports Act 1988 gives an employee the right to refuse permission to his employer who is seeking a medical report on the employee, the right to see any such report before it is supplied to the employer, and the right to correct any errors contained in the report.

7.129 A medical report is defined as being a report relating to the physical or mental health of an individual which has been prepared by the medical practitioner who is responsible for the clinical care of the individual. This would normally be the employee's own doctor or specialist consultant. Thus the Act does not apply to examinations and reports made by a company's own medical advisers, or a specialist report made on an ad hoc basis.

7.130 If an employer wishes to obtain a medical report from the employee's own doctor (or specialist), he must inform the employee, in writing, that he intends to make such an application, inform the employee of his rights under the Act, and obtain the employee's consent. If the employee refuses to give his consent, that is the end of the matter, and the employer may take any other steps he deems necessary, having regard to the refusal. Alternatively, the employee may agree to the application being made, but may insist on seeing the report before it is sent to the employer. He may then refuse consent to it being sent to the employer, or request the doctor to make amendments to the report which the employee considers to be incorrect or misleading. If the doctor refuses to do this, the employee may request the doctor to attach to the report a written statement from the employee, setting out his views in respect of any part of the report which the doctor declines to amend.

7.131 A doctor is not obliged to show to an employee any part of a medical report if he is of the opinion that the disclosure would cause serious harm to the employee's physical or mental health, or would indicate the doctor's intentions with regard to another person. Also, the doctor would not give access to any part of a medical report if this would reveal information about another person (unless that person consents).

7.132 An employee is entitled to access to a medical report which has been supplied for employment purposes any time within the preceding six months.

J. Rights in insolvency (Insolvency Act 1986, s 386, Sch 6)

7.133 If an employer becomes insolvent (through bankruptcy or liquidation) certain preferential debts are paid in priority to others. These include:

    (a) up to four months' wages, up to £800 (Insolvency Act 1986, Sch 6);

    (b) accrued holiday pay;

    (c) any guarantee pay due under ERA, s 28;

    (d) remuneration payable on medical suspension under ERA, s 64, or suspension on maternity grounds under ERA, s 66;

    (e) any payment due for time off work for trade union duties (TULR(C)A, s 168), or time off to look for work (ERA, s 52) or time off for antenatal care (ERA, s 55);

    (f) remuneration due under a protective award (TULR(C)A, s 189);

    (g) holiday pay, contractual sick pay and statutory sick pay, and statutory maternity pay;

    (h) employer contributions to occupational pensions schemes and state scheme premiums.

The maximum sum which can be treated as a preferential debt is £800.

K. **Payments from the National Insurance Fund (ERA, ss 182–189)**

7.134 Certain monies due to an employee as a result of the employer's insolvency may be paid by the Secretary of State out of the National Insurance Fund (see *Secretary of State for Employment v Forde*, para 2.18). He must be satisfied that the employer is insolvent (ie bankrupt, or, if a company, being wound up or in receivership, ERA, s 183), that the employee was entitled to be paid the whole or part of the monies due, that the employee has not received payment as a preferred creditor, and that the debt was incurred prior to the employer becoming insolvent. The debts are (see s 184):

(a) any arrears of pay for a period not exceeding eight weeks. This also includes any guarantee pay, remuneration or suspension on medical grounds and maternity grounds, payment for time off work for trade union duties, and the protective award (TULR(C)A, s 189);

(b) any minimum period of notice as computed by ERA, ss 86–90 (see Chapter 15). The rights of the employee to claim against the Secretary of State are no greater than those he has against the employer. In *Secretary of State for Employment v Wilson*[54] the employee was dismissed without notice, but he obtained employment immediately. His former employers went into liquidation, and he claimed four weeks' notice from the Secretary of State. It was held that he was not entitled. He was under a duty as against his former employers to mitigate against his loss, and having done so, he would have had no claim against them. Consequently, he had no claim against the Minister. But the employee is not obliged to bring into account any social security benefits received (*Westwood v Secretary of State for Employment*[55]);

(c) any holiday pay due in the preceding 12 months (but not exceeding six weeks' pay);

(d) any basic award compensation for unfair dismissal (but not a compensatory or higher award);

(e) any reasonable sum by way of reimbursement of the whole or part of a premium paid by an apprentice or articled clerk;

(f) any of the priority debts mentioned earlier (para 7.133) which have not been satisfied as preferential debts in bankruptcy or liquidation, for a period not exceeding in the aggregate eight weeks;

(g) statutory maternity pay (Statutory Maternity Pay (General) Regulations 1986).

It is important to note that not all debts owed by an employer to his employees are covered by the insolvency provisions of s 184, but only those which fall within the ambit of the statutory provision (*Benson v Secretary of State for Trade and Industry*[56]).

Section 183 of ERA specifies the circumstances when a company can be regarded as being insolvent, namely (a) a winding-up or administration order, (b) the appointment of a receiver or manager, or (c) a voluntary arrangement has been approved under the Insolvency Act. The burden is on the applicant to show that one of these events has taken place. The fact that a company has ceased trading, or that it is unable to pay its debts when due, or has been dissolved, does not necessarily mean that it is insolvent within the meaning of s 183 (*Secretary of State for Trade and Industry v Walden*[57]).

---

[54] [1978] 3 All ER 137, [1978] 1 WLR 568, [1978] ICR 200, [1977] IRLR 483, 13 ITR 191, 121 Sol Jo 791, EAT.

[55] [1982] ICR 534, [1982] IRLREAT; aff'd [1985] AC 20, [1983] 3 WLR 730, [1983] ICR 820, [1983] IRLR 419, 127 Sol Jo 731, CA; revsd [1985] AC 20, [1984] 1 All ER 874, [1984] 2 WLR 418, [1985] ICR 209, [1984] IRLR 209, 128 Sol Jo 221, [1984] LS Gaz R 1443, HL.

[56] [2003] ICR 1082, [2003] All ER (D) 113, EAT.   [57] [2000] IRLR 168, EAT.

There is a maximum liability on the Insolvency Service of (currently) £464 per week in respect of any debt which is referable to a period of time (with a proportionate reduction for periods of less than a week). The Secretary of State is entitled to deduct tax and national insurance contributions (*Morris v Secretary of State for Employment*[58]). The person who is in charge of the winding up must provide the Secretary of State with a statement of the amount of the debt which is owed to the employee, although this is not essential if more than six months have elapsed since an application by the employee was made, and there appears to be a further delay, in which case the Secretary of State has a discretion to make the payment. The Act also provides that the Secretary of State may make payment out of the Fund in respect of any unpaid contributions which an insolvent employer has failed to make to an occupational pension scheme.

7.135 By the Insolvency of Employer (Excluded Classes) Regulations 1983, the right to claim payments on insolvency is extended to employees who, under their contracts of employment, ordinarily work in a member state of the European Community.

7.136 If the Secretary of State fails to make any of these payments, a complaint may be made to an employment tribunal within three months from his refusal (or within such further time as is reasonable). If the tribunal thinks that the payment ought to be made, it shall make a declaration to that effect, and state the amounts which the Secretary of State ought to pay.

7.137 On making the payment, the Secretary of State becomes subrogated to the rights of the employee (or pension fund) as a preferential creditor in the insolvency.

7.138 For claiming unpaid redundancy payments from the Insolvency Service, see para 18.67.

L. Post-employment detriment

7.139 We have seen that discrimination law applies to post-employment situations (see paras 4.44 and 4.198). The same rule applies to a detriment which is suffered after the termination of employment in respect of all the rights contained in Part V of ERA (ie jury service, health and safety cases, Sunday working, working time, occupational pension trustees, employee representatives, time off for study leave for family reasons, tax credits, flexible working). Even though those sections deal with the rights of an employee, they also apply to an ex-employee who can allege a breach of his rights. In *Woodward v Abbey National*[59] the claimant claimed that her former employer had refused to provide her with a suitable reference because she had made a protected disclosure under the whistle-blowing provisions of ERA. It was held that her claim could proceed. Thus if an employer provides an unfavourable reference or takes other steps to prevent an ex-employee from obtaining suitable employment, a claim by the ex-employee may well succeed if the reason for that action was because the employee sought to exercise a right under the various provisions of Pt V of ERA, as well as the various discrimination statutes (*Rhys-Harper v Relaxation Group plc*, para 4.196).

---

[58] [1985] ICR 522, [1985] IRLR 297, EAT.
[59] [2005] ICR 1750, EAT; rev [2006] EWCA Civ 822, [2006] 4 All ER 1209, [2006] ICR 1436, [2006] IRLR 677, (2006) 103(27) LSG 31, (2006) 150 SJLB 857.

8

Protection of Wages

8.1 Under the provisions of the Truck Act 1831 the wages of manual workers had to be paid in current coin of the realm. That Act (together with a number of similar legislative provisions) was repealed by the Wages Act 1986, and cashless pay was made lawful for all employees. The actual mode of payment of wages is a matter for agreement between employer and employee.

8.2 A further object of the Wages Act was to prevent an employer from making a deduction from a worker's wages, or requiring the worker to make a payment to the employer (except in specifically defined circumstances), and to give added protection to workers employed in retail trade. In consequence, the provisions of the Truck Act 1896 relating to fines and deductions were also repealed.

8.3 The Wages Act itself was repealed and re-enacted in ss 13–27 of the Employment Rights Act 1996 (ERA) and it is to this Act that reference will be made. Some confusion sometimes arises because of the provisions of the Employment Tribunals Extension of Jurisdiction Order (ETEJO, see para 1.40) made under what is now s 3 of the Employment Tribunals Act 1996, which gives jurisdiction to employment tribunals to deal with breach of contract claims. However, there are several important differences which need to be noted, as follows:

(a) Claims under ETEJO can only be brought in respect of matters outstanding on the termination of employment, whereas ERA claims are made in respect of unlawful deductions and payments made during the existence of the contract of employment (*Capek v Lincolnshire County Council*[1]).

(b) Claims under ETEJO can only be made by employees, whereas under Pt 2 of ERA claims can be made by 'workers', a category which is somewhat wider (see s 230 and para 2.19).

(c) Under ETEJO an employer can bring a counterclaim, but this not possible under ERA, and if an employer wishes to make some sort of 'set-off' claim, he must pursue it through the normal court machinery.

(d) A claim under ETEJO is essentially a common law claim for breach of contract, and is thus subject to the usual rules relating to mitigation of loss, whereas an ERA claim is a claim for a specific sum protected by statute, and the full sum must be awarded.

[1] [2000] IRLR 590, [2000] All ER (D) 749, CA.

General restrictions on unauthorised deductions and payments (ERA, ss 13, 15)

8.4 An employer must not make any deductions from the wages of any worker employed by him, nor receive any payment from him, unless:

(a) the deduction or payment is required to be made or is authorised by a statutory provision; or

(b) the deduction or payment is authorised by a relevant provision in a worker's contract of employment. This can be a written term in the contract of which the employer has given a copy prior to the making of the deduction, or a term of the contract (express or implied, and if express, orally or in writing), the existence and effect of which the employer has notified to the worker in writing. Thus in *Kerr v Sweater Shop (Scotland) Ltd*[2] it was held that the display of a notice by the employer, changing the company's rules so that a person dismissed for gross misconduct would not be paid accrued holiday pay, did not comply with the Act. The Act requires that the term must be 'notified to the worker'; this means that there must be a written notification given individually to each worker, eg by a statement inserted in the wage packet. The display of a notice was not sufficient to discharge the employer's obligation;

(c) the worker has signified in advance in writing his agreement to the deduction or payment.

These three categories need to be explored further.

A. Statutory deduction

8.5 The most usual type of deductions to be made under this heading will be income tax and national insurance contributions. Other examples include a deduction from earnings order made under the Child Support Act 1991 (whether or not the worker was correctly liable under that order: see *Reynolds v Cornwall County Council*[3]), and an attachment of earnings order made by an appropriate court to secure payments of a maintenance order, judgment debts, fines, costs, compensation, forfeiture of recognisances, and legal aid contribution order, under the Attachment of Earnings Act 1971. But the statutory provision in question must specifically authorise the deduction or require it to be made (see *McCree v Tower Hamlets London Borough Council*[4]); an employer cannot seek to rely on a statute which does not confer a power on an employer to do an act in consequence of which the alleged deduction is made (see *Morgan v West Glamorgan County Council*[5]).

B. Contractual authorisation

8.6 The relevant provision in a worker's contract of employment must be contained in a written document, a copy of which has been given to the worker before the employer makes the deduction, or be a contractual term (whether express or implied, and, if express, whether oral or in writing) whose effect and existence has been notified to the employee in writing before the deduction is made.

8.7 It will be noted that the power to make the deduction need not be in the actual contract. It is sufficient if the employer has notified the worker in writing of the term. Thus

[2] [1996] IRLR 424, EAT.　　[3] EAT 1189/95.
[4] (1992) 90 LGR 137, [1992] ICR 99, [1992] IRLR 56, EAT.　　[5] [1995] IRLR 68, EAT.

an implied term, or an oral term, will suffice, provided that the notification is given to the worker individually. The mere display of a notice on a notice board will not suffice (see *Kerr v Sweater Shop (Scotland) Ltd*; para 8.4).

C. **Written consent**

8.8 A deduction is permissible if the worker gives his written consent in advance. This provision is designed to cover those circumstances where there is no contractual term as such, but which are collateral to that contract. For example, an agreement to repay a loan made to purchase a season travel ticket, or the forfeiture of a week's pay from an employee who leaves without giving proper notice (see *Pename Ltd v Paterson*[6]) will be valid, provided the appropriate prior written notification is given, and the worker consents to it, either expressly or impliedly, ie by continuing to work once the term has been validly brought to his attention (see *Kerr v Sweater Shop (Scotland) Ltd*, para 8.4). But the agreement must indicate with sufficient clarity the source from which the deductions are to be made, ie the worker's wages, and that the worker authorises the deduction from that source. Otherwise, all that may exist is an agreement to repay a loan, not an agreement which authorises a deduction from wages. Thus in *Potter v Hunt Contracts Ltd*[7] the employer agreed to pay for the cost of an HGV driving course, on the understanding that the employee would repay some or all of the cost on leaving his employment. An agreement was drawn up requiring the employee to repay the fee incurred on a diminishing basis if he left the employment within two years. In fact, he left after one month, when most of the loan was still outstanding, and as this amount was more than the wages due to him on departure, he was not given any final wages. It was held that the deduction was unlawful. The loan agreement did not indicate that the repayment of the loan was to be made by way of deduction from wages.

8.9 It must further be noted that the worker's authority for the making of the deduction must not relate to anything that has happened before that authority was given. In other words, deductions must not have a retrospective effect, even if they are made with the worker's agreement. Thus a variation of a contract, or a worker's written consent, can only relate to future happenings (s 13(5), (6)). This is to prevent pressure being placed on a worker to agree or consent to deduction (*Discount Tobacco and Confectionery Ltd v Williamson*[8]).

8.10 The contractual provisions or written agreement which authorise the deductions must be clear and unambiguous, for the mere fact that the worker owes the employer money does not entitle the latter to make a deduction. Employment tribunals can be very astute in striking down terms and agreements which contain ambiguities, the benefit of the doubt being given to the worker (see *Potter v Hunt Contracts Ltd*, para 8.8). An employee's claim for part-payment of wages outstanding at the date of dismissal is not defeated by the fact that the dismissal was for reason of gross misconduct. The Apportionment Act 1870 applies when a contract of employment is terminated during the payment period, unless there is something in the contract of employment to the contrary (*Item Software (UK) Ltd v Fassihi*[9]).

8.11 Even if the employer does have the right to make a deduction, he must still show that the deduction is in fact justified. Thus in *Fairfield Ltd v Skinner*[10] a van driver was given a document indicating that the employer would charge the employee for private calls made from the van telephone, charge for private mileage, and that the employee would be liable for any excess insurance arising from damage caused to the vehicle. When the employee was

---

[6] [1989] IRLR 195, EAT.   [7] [1992] ICR 337, [1992] IRLR 108, EAT.
[8] [1993] ICR 371, [1993] IRLR 327, EAT.
[9] [2002] EWHC 3116 (Ch), [2003] IRLR 769, [2003] 2 BCLC 1, [2002] All ER (D) 62 (Dec).
[10] [1992] ICR 836, [1993] IRLR 4, [1992] LS Gaz R 39, EAT.

dismissed, a sum of £305 was withheld from his final pay packet. The employee brought a claim under the Act, arguing that the deduction was unlawful. The employer responded by claiming that half of the amount deducted represented damage caused to the van whilst being used privately, and the remainder was a provisional deduction for private mileage and telephone calls made. An employment tribunal found that the employee had carried out repairs to the van at his own expense, and that there was no evidence as to how the deduction for private mileage and telephone calls had been calculated. Thus the deduction was unlawful. The decision was upheld by the EAT. The fact that an employer had the right to make a deduction did not mean that he can make a deduction, if in fact the deduction is not justified on the facts of the case, and, if there was a dispute on those facts, it was for the employment tribunal to resolve the matter.

8.12 An employer is permitted to make deductions where a worker is ready and willing to perform his contract, but is remanded in custody as a result of his own actions. Such a remand is avoidable, and so the employee is not entitled to his contractual pay (*Burns v Santander UK plc*[11]).

What are 'wages'? (ERA, s 27(1))

8.13 The term 'wages' is defined as any sum payable to the worker by his employer in connection with his employment. These include:

(a) any fee, bonus, commission, holiday pay or other emolument referable to the employment, whether payable under his contract or otherwise;

(b) statutory sick pay, statutory maternity, paternity and adoption pay, guarantee pay, medical and maternity suspension pay, and payments for statutory time off work;

(c) payment made pursuant to a reinstatement or re-engagement order, interim relief order and protective award.

8.14 It will be noted that the definition is very wide. It includes overtime pay (*Bruce v Wiggins Teape (Stationery) Ltd*[12]), shift payments (*Yemm v British Steel plc*[13]) guaranteed monthly payments paid as a retainer (*Thompson v Tech Communications Ltd*),[14] long-service awards (*Clarke v Hays Distribution Services Ltd*[15]), holiday pay (*Thames Water Utilities v Reynolds*[16]) and accrued holiday pay (*Kerr v Sweater Shop (Scotland) Ltd,* para 8.4), commission not payable until after the employment has been terminated (*Robertson v Blackstone Franks Investment Management Ltd*[17]) and so on. A service charge added to a customer's bill in a restaurant (see *Saavedra a v Aceground Ltd*),[18] or a tip added to that bill when it is paid by cheque or credit card (see *Nerva v United Kingdom*[19]) is part of an employee's wages, although it is not part of the minimum wage (see para 8.41), and while the actual distribution of these monies among different employees may be allocated by the employer on a specified or discretionary basis (in accordance with the contracts of employment of his staff) he cannot appropriate part of the charge to himself, for, in doing so, he is making an unlawful deduction within the meaning of the Act. In *Kent Management Services Ltd v Butterfield*,[20] a discretionary bonus, expressed to be ex gratia, was held to

---

[11] [2011] IRLR 639.   [12] [1994] IRLR 536, EAT.   [13] [1994] IRLR 117, EAT.
[14] Unreported.   [15] Unreported.   [16] [1996] IRLR 186, EAT.
[17] [1998] IRLR 376, CA.   [18] [1995] IRLR 198.
[19] [2002] IRLR 815, 13 BHRC 246, [2002] All ER (D) 137 (Sep), ECtHR.
[20] [1992] ICR 272, [1992] IRLR 394, EAT.

be part of the employee's wages, although it was suggested obiter that if such payment was intended to be non-contractual and discretionary, and payable only on the employee achieving a satisfactory performance, words to that effect in the contract could well take the payment outside the Act.

8.15 Accrued holiday pay is 'wages' which an employee is entitled to receive unless there is an express term in the contract negating this right. For example, in *Greg May (Carpet Fitters and Contractors) Ltd v Dring*,[21] the employee's contract stated that on the termination of his employment he would be entitled to accrued holiday pay. However, this would not be paid if he was dismissed through gross misconduct. The employers dismissed the employee for what they claimed to be gross misconduct, and refused to pay him the accrued holiday pay. The employee complained to an employment tribunal that the employers had made an unlawful deduction. It was held that whether or not the sum 'was properly payable' was for the employment tribunal to investigate. On the facts, the employee had not been guilty of 'gross misconduct', and hence the accrued holiday pay was properly payable.

8.16 However, a payment in lieu of notice is not 'wages' under the Act, because it constitutes 'damages' for breach of contract, and is paid not in connection with the employment but in connection with its termination. In *Delaney v Staples*[22] the House of Lords held that payments made under a 'garden leave' dismissal (see para 15.12) constituted wages, but other situations where a payment in lieu of wages is made or promised were not within the Act, because the essential characteristic of wages was consideration for work done under a subsisting contract of employment. Thus a payment made in respect of a period after the contract has terminated cannot be wages. The matter now is perhaps academic, since the passing of the Employment Tribunals Extension of Jurisdiction Order (see para 1.40), except perhaps for a highly paid employee whose notice rights exceed the limits laid down in that Order.

What are not 'wages'? (ERA, s 27(2))

8.17 The following payments are excluded from the provisions of the Act:

(a) a payment made by way of an advance under an agreement for a loan or by way of an advance of wages, although s 13 (see para 8.4) will still apply to any deduction an employer may make from a worker's wages in order to recover that advance;

(b) any payment in respect of expenses incurred by the worker in carrying out his employment. It does not matter if there is an element of profit in those expenses, it is still excluded from the Act, for any such payment does not cease to be expenses merely because the employer is generous (*Southwark London Borough v O'Brien*[23]);

(c) any payment by way of a pension (including pension contributions – *Somerset County Council v Chambers*[24]), allowance or gratuity in connection with the worker's retirement or as compensation for loss of office. As noted at para 8.16, a payment in lieu of notice is not within the Act (*Foster Wheeler (London) Ltd v Jackson*[25]);

(d) any payment referable to a worker's redundancy, whether statutory or not;

(e) any payment made to a worker otherwise than in capacity as a worker;

---

[21] [1990] ICR 188, [1990] IRLR 19, EAT.

[22] [1990] ICR 364, [1990] IRLR 86, [1990] 10 LS Gaz R 35, EAT; on appeal [1991] 2 QB 47, [1991] 1 All ER 609, [1991] 2 WLR 627, [1991] ICR 331, [1991] IRLR 112, CA; aff'd [1992] 1 AC 687, [1992] 1 All ER 944, [1992] 2 WLR 451, [1992] ICR 483, [1992] IRLR 191, [1992] 15 LS Gaz R 32, 136 Sol Jo LB 91, HL.

[23] [1996] IRLR 420, EAT.   [24] UKEAT/0417/12/KN   [25] [1990] ICR 757, [1990] IRLR 412, EAT.

(f) any benefits in kind are not wages, except a voucher, stamp or similar document which is capable of being exchanged for money, goods or services (whether on its own or together with any other such document). Thus luncheon vouchers are wages within the Act, but other benefits, such as free meals, accommodation, discounts, etc, are not. In *Leisure Employment Services v HMRC*[26] it was held that a deduction from wages of £3 per week in respect of a payment for gas and electricity was part of the provision of living accommodation, and that since the deduction was for the employer's benefit, could not be counted towards the employees' wages.

What is a deduction? (ERA, s 13(3))

8.18 Where the total amount of wages paid on any occasion by an employer to a worker employed by him is less than the total amount of the wages properly payable (after lawful deductions), the amount of the deficiency shall be treated as a deduction made by the employer from the worker's wages on that occasion. Thus a reduction in wages amounts to a deduction. In *Bruce v Wiggins Teape* the employers agreed to pay enhanced overtime rates to employees who worked on a rolling night shift. It was subsequently decided (without the agreement of the employees or their trade union) to withdraw the enhanced payment. An employment tribunal held that the Act dealt with deductions from pay, not with reductions, but this was reversed by the EAT. The wages properly payable included the enhanced overtime rate, which the employers could not terminate unilaterally. Thus the deductions were unauthorised and therefore unlawful. If an employer reduced the hours of work of his employees without their consent, and pays them for the reduced working hours only, this can amount to an unlawful deduction from wages (*International Packaging Corpn (UK) Ltd v Balfour*[27]). But if the employer has lawful contractual authority to transfer an employee from one shift to another, with a resultant loss of a shift premium allowance, there is no unauthorised deduction from wages within the meaning of s 13 (*Hussman Manufacturing Ltd v Weir*[28]).

8.19 If a collective agreement, the terms of which are incorporated into the individual contracts of employment of employees, expressly provides for a reduction in rates of pay (eg when there is short-time working) such a deduction would not constitute a breach of the Act, although there would be a breach if the deduction could only be made with the approval of the employees and the trade union, and such approval was not obtained. It follows that if rates of pay are contained in a collective agreement which has been incorporated into the individual contracts of employment, these can only be changed in accordance with the terms of that agreement, not unilaterally by the employer (*Davies v Hotpoint Ltd*[29]).

8.20 If there is no power in the contract of employment to demote an employee, then to do so and consequently reduce his salary would be an unlawful deduction under the Act (*Morgan v West Glamorgan County Council*, see para 8.5). It will be recalled (see para 8.14) that in *Kent Management Services Ltd v Butterfield* the EAT held that even discretionary bonuses could constitute wages properly payable, if it was in the contemplation of the parties that outstanding commissions would be paid on termination of employment.

8.21 A failure to pay wages on time can amount to a deduction from wages (*Elizabeth Claire Care Management Ltd v Francis*, see para 3.35). However, s 13(4) provides that a deficiency in wages, attributable to an error affecting the computation by an employer of the gross wages due to the employee, is not an unlawful deduction for the purpose of s 13(3). In other words, an

[26] [2007] EWCA Civ 92, [2007] IRLR 450, [2007] ICR 1056.
[27] [2003] IRLR 11, [2002] All ER (D) 146 (Nov).
[28] [1998] IRLR 288, 599 IRLB 5, EAT.   [29] [1994] IRLR 538, EAT.

arithmetical mistake is not an unlawful deduction, although a mistaken belief that certain monies ought not to be paid is a deduction (*Morgan v West Glamorgan County Council*, para 8.20).

8.22 Applications for holiday pay must be brought as a claim for unlawful deductions of wages under ERA, see *Ainsworth v Inland Revenue Commissioners*, para 7.89.

Excepted deductions and excepted payments (ERA, ss 14, 16)

8.23 The following deductions and payments, whether lawfully or unlawfully made, are not within the scope of the protection of wages provisions. The employee's remedy, if any, would be to sue for breach of contract in the county court (unless the employment tribunal has jurisdiction to deal with the case under the provisions of the Extension of Jurisdiction Order, see para 1.40).

(a) A deduction or payment for the purpose of reimbursing the employer in respect of an overpayment of wages (s 14(1)(a)), or an overpayment of expenses incurred by the worker in carrying out his employment (s 14(1)(b)), made to the employee for any reason. In *SIP Industrial Products Ltd v Swinn*[30] an employer withheld part of an employee's wages as a reimbursement in respect of expenses which had been fraudulently claimed. An employment tribunal took the view that this deduction was not permitted by s 14(1)(b), because what the employee had done amounted to theft, and therefore had nothing to do with expenses incurred in the course of his employment. However, the EAT held that overpaid expenses made 'for any reason' were recoverable by the employer without being in breach of the Act.

   If the worker disputes that there has been an overpayment, or claims that he is not required to repay the overpayment, this matter must be resolved in the ordinary courts, under the general law relating to mistake. It is now settled that there is no difference between a mistake of law and a mistake of fact (*Kleinwort Benson Ltd v Lincoln City Council*[31]). All such overpayments are recoverable by the employer, except that he may not be able so to recover if:

   (i) he made a representation of fact which led the employee to believe that he was entitled to treat the money overpaid as his own, and

   (ii) the employee, bone fide and without notice of the mistake, consequently changed his position (eg by spending the money), and

   (iii) the overpayment was not caused by the fault of the employee.

   The general principles to be applied in such circumstances stem from the law of restitution (see *Lipkin Gorman v Karpnale Ltd*[32]).

(b) A deduction made in consequence of any disciplinary proceedings held by virtue of a statutory provision (s 14(2)). This provision probably refers to disciplinary proceedings held by the police or fire service (see *Chiltern House Ltd v Chambers*[33]).

[30] [1994] ICR 473, [1994] IRLR 323, EAT.

[31] [1999] 2 AC 349, [1998] 4 All ER 513, [1998] 3 WLR 1095, [1999] LGR 1, [1998] NLJR 1674, [1998] RVR 315, 142 Sol Jo LB 279, [1999] 3 LRC 219, [1998] All ER (D) 518, HL.

[32] [1992] 4 All ER 331, [1987] 1 WLR 987, [1986] FLR 271, [1987] BCLC 159, 131 Sol Jo 940, [1987] LS Gaz R 2272, [1986] NLJ Rep 659; on appeal [1992] 4 All ER 409, [1989] 1 WLR 1340, [1989] FLR 137, [1989] BCLC 756n, 134 Sol Jo 234, [1990] 4 LS Gaz R 40, [1989] NLJR 76, CA; varied [1991] 2 AC 548, [1992] 4 All ER 512, [1991] 3 WLR 10, [1991] NLJR 815, 135 Sol Jo LB 36, HL.

[33] [1990] IRLR 88, EAT.

Such proceedings, however, may be the subject of judicial review (*R v Leicestershire Fire Authority, ex p Thompson*[34]).

(c) A deduction made in consequence of a requirement imposed on an employer by a statutory provision to pay the money over to a public body, if the deduction is made in accordance with the relevant determination of that body (s 14(3)). This is not quite the same as the lawful deductions which can be made under s 13 (see para 8.4), and would cover a case where a public body (eg local authority) has power to require an employer to deduct a sum from the worker's wages and pay that sum to the authority in question.

(d) A deduction which is paid to a third party at the employee's request (s 14(4)). There must be a relevant provision in the contract, to which the employee has signified his consent in writing, or otherwise with the prior agreement or consent of the worker in writing. This exclusion would cover, for example, the check-off system, whereby an employer deducts trade union subscriptions from the worker's wages, and pays the money to the trade union (see Chapter 21).

(e) A deduction which is made by the employer because the worker has taken part in a strike or other industrial action (s 14(5), and see *Sim v Rotherham Metropolitan Borough Council*, paras 3.37 and 3.50). Thus, if the employee is not performing any of his duties the employer may deduct an amount which represents a fair proportion of his salary (*Miles v Wakefield Metropolitan District Council*, para 2.64). If the employee alleges that the employer has deducted more than a fair proportion, his remedy is to bring an action in the county court, not in the employment tribunal. In *Sunderland Polytechnic v Evans*[35] an employee took part in a half-day strike. The employer deducted a full day's salary from her monthly pay, and she complained that an unlawful deduction had been made from her wages. On her behalf, it was argued that s 14(5) only applied to a 'lawful' deduction, ie in respect of the half day she was on strike, and therefore the deduction of a full day's pay was not protected by s 14(5). The employment tribunal held that they had jurisdiction to determine if the deduction was indeed lawful, but this decision was reversed by the EAT. In an unusual move, the EAT decided to look at *Hansard*, and it was noted that in both the House of Commons and the House of Lords, Government ministers were quite clear in their views that if a worker believed that a deduction was not contractually authorised, the remedy would have to be an action in the county court, not in the employment tribunal. Thus, if the amount of the deduction is in dispute, the matter must be settled in the county court. A decision of the EAT to the contrary (*Home Office v Ayres*[36]) was disapproved.

More difficult, perhaps, is the situation where the employee is taking part in 'other industrial action', eg by working his full contractual hours, but only performing part of his contractual duties during those hours (eg by way of protest). In such circumstances, the employer will be entitled to deduct part of the employee's wages, based on his assessment of the amount of time when the employee is not working properly (*Wiluszynski v London Borough of Tower Hamlets*[37]).

(f) A deduction made with the prior agreement of the worker to satisfy an order made by a court or tribunal requiring the payment of any amount to the employer (s 14(6)).

---

[34] (1979) 77 LGR 373, [1979] IRLR 166, DC.
[35] [1993] ICR 392, [1993] IRLR 196, EAT.   [36] [1992] ICR 175, [1992] IRLR 59, EAT.
[37] [1988] IRLR 154; on appeal 88 LGR 14, [1989] ICR 493, [1989] IRLR 259, 133 Sol Jo 628, CA.

Deductions and payments in retail employment (ERA, ss 17–18)

8.24 Special rules apply for the protection of persons who are engaged in retail employment, which is defined as:

    (a) the carrying out of retail transactions, ie the sale or supply of goods or services (including financial services); or

    (b) the collection by the worker of amounts payable in connection with retail transactions carried out by other persons, or other individuals in their personal capacities.

8.25 The definition covers a wide range of activities, including shop assistants, bus drivers, bank cashiers, insurance agents, petrol pump attendants, credit collectors etc.

8.26 The Act permits an employer to make deductions or require payments from the wages of such retail workers in respect of cash shortages and/or stock deficiencies which arise in the course of retail employment. These include shortages or deficiencies arising from dishonest, negligent or other conduct by the employee, or any other event in respect of which he has a contractual liability. Nor is it relevant that the amount of the deduction or payment does not reflect the actual amount of the shortage or deficiency (s 17(4)). But an employer cannot evade the provisions of the Act by defining wages by reference to cash shortages or deficiencies, for in such circumstances the gross wages are to be treated as being the amount they would have been but for the shortage or deficiency (s 19).

8.27 Under ss 17–18 of the Act, it is permissible to make a deduction (or require a payment) in respect of cash shortages or stock deficiencies subject to two conditions. First, the requirements of s 13 (see para 8.4) must be met, ie an appropriate contractual agreement enabling the deductions (or payments) to be made. This contractual arrangement must have been agreed to before the happening of the event which was the cause of the purported deduction, because, as we have seen (see para 8.9) the Act is designed to prevent pressure being put on the employee to agree to the deduction (*Discount Tobacco and Confectionery v Williamson*, see para 8.9). Second, the deduction (or demand for payment) must not exceed 10% of the gross wages payable on the day in question (see s 18). If the shortage or deficiency is greater than the sum to be deducted or demanded the employer may continue to deduct or demand the balance on subsequent pay days, provided that on each occasion the deduction or demand does not exceed 10% of the gross wages payable.

8.28 If the employer wishes to make a demand for payment, he must do so in writing (on one of the worker's pay days) and notify him (again in writing) of the total liability, prior to receiving any payment (s 20).

8.29 Generally, the deduction or demand must be made within 12 months from the date when the employer discovers the cash shortage or stock deficiency, except:

    (a) if the deduction is one of a series of deductions in respect of the same shortage or deficiency in which case the 12-month period applied from the first deduction or demand of the series, or

    (b) if the employer ought reasonably to have discovered the cash shortage or stock deficiency earlier, the 12-month period will run from the date when he ought to have discovered it, not from when he actually did so.

8.30 However, once the employment comes to an end, there is no limit on the amount which the employer may deduct or demand.

Complaints to an employment tribunal (ERA, s 23)

8.31 A worker may complain to an employment tribunal that his employer has:

(a) made a deduction or received a payment in contravention of ss 13–17;

(b) made a deduction which is outside the limit of 12 months as required by s 20(3);

(c) received a payment in respect of a cash shortage or stock deficiency without notifying the worker in writing of his total liability, or without making the demand in the prescribed manner as required by s 20(1);

(d) made a deduction or received a payment in excess of the limit of 10% of the gross pay on a particular day as permitted by s 21(1).

8.32 The complaint must be made within three months from the time when the deduction was made or the payment received by the employer, with the usual extension of time if the employment tribunal is satisfied that it was not reasonably practicable to present a claim earlier. The three-month period runs from the date when contractually the wages were due to be paid, not when they were actually paid (*Group 4 Nightspeed Ltd v Gilbert*[38]). If the complaint is well founded, the employment tribunal shall make a declaration to that effect, and order the employer to reimburse the worker the amount of any unauthorised deductions made or payments received plus any additional financial loss sustained by the worker. It should be noted that there is no limit to the amount which the employment tribunal can order to be repaid. Further, if there is an unlawful deduction or payment, which the employment tribunal orders to be repaid, the employer will lose all rights to it, and may not seek to recover that which could lawfully be claimed from the employee by bringing an action at common law (*Potter v Hunt Contracts*, see paras 8.8 and 8.10).

8.33 A claim under the provisions of Pt 2 of ERA in respect of an unlawful deduction from wages must be in respect of a specific and identifiable sum. In *Coors Brewers Ltd v Adcock*[39] the claimants claimed an amount which they alleged was due to them under a bonus scheme. It was held that the employment tribunal was not the correct forum for such proceedings. A claim for unliquidated damages must be brought in the county court.

8.34 Finally, an ex-employee may bring a claim under the Extension of Jurisdiction Order, provided the amount does not exceed £25,000, and the money is outstanding on the termination of employment.

National minimum wage

8.35 Under the provisions of the National Minimum Wage Act 1998 workers are entitled to be remunerated in any pay reference period at a rate which is not less than the national minimum wage (s 1). The actual hourly rate will be determined in regulations made by the Secretary of State after receiving a recommendation from the Low Pay Commission, but he may not differentiate between different areas of the country, different sectors of employment, undertakings of different sizes, persons of different ages (except, in certain circumstances those under the age of 26) or persons of different occupations (s 2). There is no qualifying period of employment required, and no exclusion for small businesses.

[38] [1997] IRLR 398, 574 IRLB 13, EAT.
[39] [2007] EWCA Civ 19, [2007] ICR 983, [2007] IRLR 440, (2007) 151 SJLB 160.

8.36 The Department for Business Innovation and Skills has produced a lengthy 'Guidance' booklet which, although not legally binding, gives guidance to employers and workers, and is a powerful aid to understanding and implementing the regulations.

A. Who qualifies for the national minimum wage

8.37 The Act applies to a worker who works:

(a) under a contract of employment; or

(b) any other contract whereby the individual undertakes to do work personally, other than as a client or customer of any professions or business undertaking (s 54).

In other words, only the genuinely self-employed are excluded. Thus employees, agency workers, homeworkers etc are within the Act's provisions. In tribunal or court proceedings, the presumption is that an individual is qualified for the national minimum wage unless the employer can rebut that presumption by proving to the contrary. A review of 'worker status' was given by the EAT in *James v Redcats (Brands) Ltd*.[40]

8.38 The Act does not apply to share fishermen, voluntary workers, certain resident workers in religious communities, prisoners and serving members of the Armed Forces. Also excluded by the National Minimum Wages Regulations 1999 are:

(a) certain workers in schemes funded by the European Social Fund, on government-funded training schemes, work experience or temporary work schemes or schemes to help the unemployed to find work (who are not employed by the employer for whom they work under the scheme);

(b) undergraduates on sandwich course placements, trainee teachers on placement;

(c) homeless persons taking part in certain schemes under which they are provided with shelter and other benefits in return for work;

(d) au pairs, nannies, and companions who are treated as a member of the employer's family;

(e) members of the employer's family who live at home and participate in running the family business.

8.39 It has been held that pupil barristers are not engaged under a contract of apprenticeship, and therefore do not qualify for the national minimum wage (*Edmunds v Lawson*[41]). Agricultural workers covered by agriculture wages councils are entitled at least to the amount of the national minimum wage (Agricultural Wages Act 1948, Agricultural Wages (Scotland) Act 1949). Offshore workers are covered by the regulations.

B. Calculating the hourly rate (reg 14)

8.40 In order to determine whether or not a worker is being paid the national minimum wage it is necessary to determine his hourly rate. This is done by dividing the total remuneration received for the relevant pay period by the number of hours worked in that period. The pay reference period is a month. Certain deductions from wages can be ignored, ie repayment of loans, contractual repayments, advance of wages, accidental overpayments, and share purchases. Lump sums paid upon retirement, suggestion schemes awards, loans, redundancy payments and benefits in kind (other than accommodation) are not taken into

[40] [2007] ICR 1006, [2007] IRLR 296.　　[41] [2000] IRLR 18.

account for the purpose of calculating total remuneration. Nor are premium payments for overtime or shift work.

8.41 In *Commissioners for Revenue and Customs v Annabel's (Berkeley Square Ltd)*[42] the Court of Appeal confirmed that tips distributed through a 'tronc' system do not count towards the national minimum wage.

8.42 If an employer provides a worker with free accommodation, he is credited with making an additional payment to the worker of (currently) £4.91 per day in the pay reference period for which the accommodation is provided (see *Leisure Employment Services Ltd v HM Revenue and Customs*[43]).

8.43 The hours that count for the purpose of calculating the rate of the national minimum wage depend on the type of work the worker is doing. There are four types of work, namely:

(a) *a time worker*, who is paid according to set or varying number of hours, or periods of time worked. In *British Nursing Association v Inland Revenue*[44] a worker was required to answer the telephone from home during a shift period. It was held that the worker was on time work throughout the whole of the shift period, and not just during the periods when she was actually answering the telephone. So too a nightwatchman was engaged in time work throughout the whole of his shift, even during periods when he was asleep, He was 'on call throughout the entire period' (*Scottbridge Construction Ltd v Wright*[45]);

(b) *a salaried-hours worker*, who is paid for a predetermined number of minimum hours a year, and is contractually entitled to an annual salary for those hours worked in equal instalments. The fact that additional payments may be made for any overtime working, or that a bonus may be payable, does not prevent the contract being one for salaried hours (see, eg *MacCartney v Oversley House Management*[46]);

(c) *an output worker*, who is paid in accordance with each piece of work produced, or task performed (sometimes referred to as piece work); and

(d) *unmeasured work*, where the worker is paid a set amount for a task or for working a certain length of time, and which is not time work, salaried hours work or output work. This is work where the worker has no specific hours, and/or is required to work when needed or when work is available.

8.44 The hourly rate is payable for any period during which the worker is at the employer's disposal and carrying out his duties and activities (*British Nursing Association v Inland Revenue*; see para 8.43). It is payable for all times when a worker is required to be at the place of work and available for work, even though there may not be work available. But if a worker is permitted to use sleeping facilities at or near his place of work, only time when he is awake for the purpose of working will count (reg 15(1A)). In *Walton v Independent Living Organisation*[47] a carer lived on her client's premises for 24 hours each day. She was responsible for the client's washing, ironing, shopping, preparation of meals and medication but, when not performing services for the client, she could do what she wanted. Her daily rate of pay was £31.40, and she claimed that this did not equate with the national minimum wage

[42] [2009] EWCA Civ 361.
[43] [2007] EWCA Civ 92, [2007] ICR 1056, [2007] IRLR 450, (2007) *Times*, 7 March.
[44] [2002] EWCA Civ 494, [2003] ICR 19, [2002] IRLR 480, [2002] Emp LR 668.
[45] 2003 SC 520, 2002 SLT 1356, [2003] IRLR 21, 2002 GWD 34-1150.
[46] [2006] ICR 510, [2006] IRLR 514.
[47] [2002] ICR 1406, [2002] All ER (D) 241 (Apr), EAT; aff'd [2003] EWCA Civ 199, [2003] ICR 688, [2003] IRLR 469, 147 Sol Jo LB 266, [2003] All ER (D) 373 (Feb).

of (then) £3.60 per hour. Her claim failed. She was carrying out unmeasured work, not time work. The exclusion from the minimum wage legislation set out in reg 15(1A) relating to employees who are required to sleep in does not apply to those who can be required to work during the time they would otherwise be asleep. The exclusion only applies to those who are available for work, not to those who are actually working – *Burrow Down Support Services Ltd v Rossiter*.[48] This was followed in *Whittlestone v BJP Home Support Limited*,[49] where it was held that travelling time is time work, except where incidental to the duties being carried out. Where specific hours at a particular place are required, upon the pain of discipline if they are not spent at that place, and the worker is at the disposal of the employer during that period, it will normally constitute time work, even if the worker is sleeping. Terms such as 'on call' and 'core hours' can be misleading.

8.45 Every employer will be obliged to keep records (s 9), and if a worker believes that is being remunerated at a rate which is less than the national minimum wage, he may require his employer to produce those records, and the worker may inspect and examine them, accompanied by any other person he thinks fit. The worker must first give notice to his employer (a 'production notice'), and the employer must produce the records at the worker's place of work or any other place at which it is reasonable for the worker to attend and inspect the relevant records (s 10). If an employer fails to produce the relevant records, or fails to allow the worker to inspect them, or fails to allow the worker to be accompanied by someone, the worker may make a complaint to an employment tribunal, who, if they find the complaint to be well founded, will make a declaration to that effect, and make an award to the worker of a sum equal to 80 times the hourly amount of the national minimum wage (s 11).

C. **Enforcement by the worker**

8.46 A worker who believes that he is being paid less than the national minimum wage may bring a claim in an employment tribunal or a county court, seeking the additional remuneration, either as a claim for unlawful deduction from wages under the Employment Rights Act (see para 8.4), or as a claim for breach of contract. On such a claim, the burden of proof is reversed, ie it will be presumed that the worker was not getting the national minimum wage until the contrary is proved by the employer (s 28).

8.47 There is also a new formula for calculating arrears of the national minimum wage, which takes account of the length of time since the underpayment occurred and the current rates. This is (A/R1) x R2 where

A is the amount of underpayment for the pay reference period

R1 is the worker's national minimum rate which applied at the time of the underpayment

R2 is the worker's current national minimum wage

In essence, this means that the worker is entitled to be paid as additional remuneration, the greater of:

(a) the shortfall between the amount paid and the amount which should have been paid under the national minimum wage applicable at the time of the underpayment, and

(b) the sum payable if the rate of the national minimum wage applying at the time of the arrears being determined had been applicable throughout the relevant period.

---

[48] [2008] ICR 1172.   [49] UKEAT/0128/13/BA.

8.48 Further, employees have the right not to suffer a detriment or be dismissed (no qualifying period of employment being required) or victimised because they brought or became involved in proceedings relating to the enforcement of the national minimum wage (ss 23 and 25).

D. Enforcement by the state

8.49 The responsibility for ensuring compliance with the national minimum wage lies with HM Revenue and Customs (HMRC). Officers from this department can visit employers to check if the employer is paying the national minimum wage to workers. The officers can question workers and remove copies of records.

8.50 If the officer believes that an employer has failed to pay the national minimum wage to a worker, he may serve a notice of underpayment. This will require the employer to repay arrears to each named worker and pay a financial penalty to HMRC. The penalty is 50% of the total underpayment with a minimum penalty of £100, and a maximum penalty of £5,000. If the employer complies with the notice within 14 days of it being served there will be a discount of 50%.

8.51 In *IRC v Bebb Travel plc*[50] it was held that the Revenue had no power to serve enforcement notices in respect of workers who, although they were paid less than the prescribed amount in the past, had left the employment in question before the enforcement notices had been issued. However, this ruling was altered by the National Minimum Wage (Enforcement Notices) Act 2003 so as to enable enforcement officers to issue notices requiring employers to make good arrears of the national minimum wage to former workers who at any time within six years prior to the issue of the notice qualified for the minimum wage. The failure to comply with an enforcement notice is a criminal offence with daily financial penalties for failing to comply, and it is irrelevant that the employer is unable to comply with the notice because the worker in question has disappeared! The employer may appeal against the notice within four weeks to an employment tribunal. The employment tribunal will dismiss the appeal unless it is established that the facts were such that the officer had no reason to serve the notice, or that no sum was due to the worker, or that the amount specified as being due is incorrect.

8.52 If the amount specified in the notice is found to be incorrect, the employment tribunal has a duty to insert the correct figure. If the evidence is unsatisfactory, the tribunal must do the best it can on the material available (*IRC v St Hermans Estate Co Ltd*[51]).

8.53 An officer may withdraw an underpayment notice, and/or replace it with another. He may also withdraw and/or replace a penalty notice if the facts are such that the officer concerned had no reason to serve the notice, or the calculation of the penalty was incorrect.

8.54 If an employer does not comply with the notice of underpayment, the enforcement officer can present a claim to an employment tribunal or the county court (or sheriff's court) on behalf of the worker.

8.55 The employer can appeal to an employment tribunal against the notice of underpayment on the ground that:

(a) at the date set out in the notice no arrears were owing;

[50] [2002] 4 All ER 534, [2003] ICR 201, [2002] IRLR 783, [2002] NLJR 1350, [2002] All ER (D) 105 (Aug), EAT; aff'd [2003] EWCA Civ 563, [2003] 3 All ER 546, [2003] ICR 1271, [2003] NLJR 633, 147 Sol Jo LB 505, [2002] All ER (D) 291 (Apr).

[51] [2002] IRLR 788, [2002] All ER (D) 58 (Jul), EAT.

(b) the amount specified in the notice is incorrect; or

(c) the amount specified in the penalty is incorrect.

8.56 A successful appeal will result in the notice being rescinded or rectified.

E. Offences (ERA, ss 31–33)

8.57 It is an offence to:

(a) refuse or wilfully neglect to remunerate a worker for any pay period at a rate which is at least equal to the national minimum wage;

(b) fail to keep or preserve records;

(c) make false entries in records;

(d) produce or furnish any record or information which he knows to be false;

(e) intentionally delay or obstruct an inspector, or refuse or neglect to answer any question or produce any document when required to do so.

8.58 If the offence committed by a body corporate is proved to have been committed with the consent or connivance of an officer of that body, or attributable to any neglect on his behalf, then he, as well as the body corporate, shall be guilty of an offence and liable to be proceeded against and punished accordingly.

8.59 A person guilty of an offence shall be liable on conviction to a fine not exceeding level 5 on the standard scale (currently £5,000). This is expected to increase to £20,000 in 2014.

8.60 From October 2013 the national minimum wage was increased, as follows:

(a) adult rate (workers aged 21 and over) £6.31 per hour;

(b) development rate (18–20 year olds) £5.03 per hour;

(c) development rate (16–17 year olds) £3.72 per hour.

8.61 Apprentices under the age of 19, or between the ages of 19–26 in the first year of their apprenticeship, are entitled to a minimum wage of £2.68 per hour.

8.62 The rate for accommodation offset will increase to £34.37 per week (£4.91 per day). This is reviewed annually.

9

Transfer of Undertakings

Background

9.1 At common law, a contract of employment was a personal contract between the employer and employee; when that relationship ceased, the contract of employment came to an end. Thus if a business was sold, the purchaser had the right to choose who he wished to employ, and the employee had the right to choose for whom he worked. Indeed, '…the right to choose for himself whom he would serve…constituted the main difference between a servant and a serf' (*Nokes v Doncaster Amalgamated Collieries*[1]). Thus the sale or transfer of any business resulted in the termination of any existing contract of employment because at common law an employee's contract of employment cannot be transferred to another employer without his consent (*Bolwell v Redcliffe Homes Ltd*[2]).

9.2 This position was altered by the Transfer of Undertaking (Protection of Employment) Regulations 1981 (familiarly referred to as 'TUPE'), designed to give effect to the Acquired Rights Directive (77/187/EEC). These regulations generally tried to put the transferee employer in the same position as the transferor, so that the rights and obligations contained in the contract of employment made between the transferor are passed to the transferee. Various changes to these regulations were made by the Collective Redundancies and Transfer of Undertakings (Protection of Employment) (Amendment) Regulations 1995–1999, the Pensions Act 2004, and the Transfer of Employment (Pensions Protection) Regulations 2005.

9.3 However, the application of the regulations gave rise to a number of legal and practical problems, and was not helped by a series of irreconcilable decisions from the European Court of Justice and UK courts. Difficult factual questions arose on such issues as what a transfer is, what an undertaking is, whether statutory as well as contractual rights were transferred, pension rights, and so on. The House of Lords gave its approval to the adoption of a 'purposive approach' to the regulations, which went far beyond the traditional strict and literal application of recognised canons of construction, in order that, as far as possible, the rights of employees could be safeguarded (*see Litster v Forth Dry Dock and Engineering Co Ltd*[3]). Despite this novel approach, and the fact that the regulations were amended on several occasions, a number of outstanding issues remained unresolved.

9.4 After a lengthy consultation period, the Government introduced the Transfer of Undertakings (Protection of Employment) Regulations 2006. As well as seeking to clarify a number of small matters, the regulations were designed to deal with the thorny issues raised by 'service provision changes', deal with certain matters arising from transfer-related

---

[1] [1940] AC 1014, [1940] 3 All ER 549, 109 LJKB 865, 85 Sol Jo 45, 163 LT 343, 56 TLR 988, HL.
[2] [1999] IRLR 485, [1999] All ER (D) 33, CA.
[3] [1990] 1 AC 546, [1989] 1 All ER 1134, [1989] 2 WLR 634, [1989] ICR 341, [1989] IRLR 161, 133 Sol Jo 455, [1989] NLJR 400, 1989 SC (HL) 96.

dismissals and changes to terms and conditions of employment, require the transferor to notify the transferee of the identities of the employees to be transferred, as well as all rights and liabilities that will pass with the transfer, and provide for a certain amount of flexibility in cases where the transferor is insolvent and a 'rescue bid' is mounted. But these regulations still retained the same convoluted jargon as their predecessor, and there was also concern by employers that the regulations 'gold-plated' the European Directive by being more generous. Since then, the regulations have been amended by the Collective Redundancies and Transfer of Undertakings (Protection of Employment) (Amendment) Regulations 2014, in relation to transfers taking place from 31 January 2014.

Who is covered by the regulations?

9.5 The regulations apply to an 'employee', defined as 'any individual who works for another person, whether under a contract of service or apprenticeship or otherwise' (reg 2(1)). This definition is somewhat wider than the one used in the Employment Rights Act, and may, for example, include agency supplied employees, casual employees, and so on. *In Mikkelson v Danmols Inventar A/S*[4] the European Court of Justice held that the meaning of the term was for the national courts to decide. However, the definition does not include persons who work under a contract for services. In *Cowell v Quilter Goodison Co Ltd*[5] the claimant was an equity partner in a firm of stockbrokers. The firm was then taken over by a limited company, which continued to employ the claimant as an employee. It was held that the claimant's service as an equity partner could not be counted for the purpose of establishing continuous employment, because he was not an 'employee' at the time of the transfer.

9.6 The regulations apply to a transfer of an undertaking, business or part of an undertaking or business situated immediately before the transfer in the United Kingdom to another employer, where there is a transfer of an economic entity which retains its identity (reg 3(1) (a)). An 'economic entity' is an organised grouping of resources which has the objective of pursuing an economic activity, whether or not that activity is central or ancillary (reg 3(2)). The transferee will not necessarily take over the contracts of employment of those employees who are only temporarily assigned to the organised grouping, and it will be a question of fact and degree whether an employee is or is not so assigned, depending on such factors as the length of time he has been in the group, the work he does in the group, whether or not he is reassigned to other work, and so on.

9.7 However, 'an organised grouping of employees' can, in some circumstances, constitute one person, eg, if the cleaning of business premises is carried out by a single person. Thus in *Schmidt v Spar- und Leihkasse der Früheren*[6] the claimant was the sole cleaner at a branch of a bank. The bank transferred cleaning duties to a contracting firm, who dismissed the claimant when she refused to accept new terms which she considered to be inferior to those previously enjoyed. The ECJ held that (1) the fact that there was no transfer of tangible assets was not decisive in determining whether there was a transfer for the purpose of EC Directive 77/187/EEC; (2) the decisive factor was whether the business retained its identity; (3) the fact that the activity was ancillary to the main activity carried on did not exclude the operation of the Directive; and (4) the fact that the activity was carried on by a single person also did not exclude the operation of the Directive.

---

[4] (105/84) [1985] ECR 2639, [1986] 1 CMLR 316, ECJ.
[5] [1989] IRLR 392, CA.
[6] (C-392/92) [1994] ECR I–1311, [1995] 2 CMLR 331, [1995] ICR 237, [1994] IRLR 302, ECJ.

A. **Transfer of an undertaking or business**

9.8 The European Court has held that it is for the national court to consider all the factual circumstances and assess whether they are characteristic of a transfer of an undertaking within the meaning of the Directive. Thus the undertaking or business transferred must be a stable economic entity, which retains identity after the transfer, but it need not be a profit-making entity (*Dr Sophie Redmond Stichting v Bartol*[7]). The business or undertaking must be transferred 'as a going concern' (*Spijkers v Gebroeders Benedik Abattoir*[8]), and thus the mere transfer of assets does not come under the regulations (*Premier Motors (Medway) Ltd v Total Oil Great Britain Ltd*[9]). The sale of equipment is not within the scope of the regulations, unless some other part of a business is transferred (*ECM (Vehicle Delivery Service) Ltd v Cox*[10]). A building contract for a single project was not treated as an undertaking, because there has to be 'a stable economic entity' (*Rygaard v Stro Molle Akustik*[11]), but this decision appears to rely heavily in the fact that it was an activity under a one-off short term contract (see *BSG Property Services v Tuck*[12]). There is no transfer in a situation in which a municipal authority which had contracted out the cleaning of its premises to a private company but then decided to terminate its contract with that company and to undertake those cleaning services itself, by hiring new staff for that purpose (*CLECE SA v Valor*[13]). If an undertaking is transferred, the Directive cannot be used to preserve the lease of commercial premises entered into by the transferor with a third party, even though the termination of that lease is likely to entail the termination of the contracts of employment of the employees transferred. The Directive only applies to the transfer of employment relationship rights (*Kirtruna SL v Red Elite Electrodomesticos SA*[14]).

9.9 There must be the transfer of an identifiable business (*Banking Insurance and Finance Union v Barclays Bank plc*[15]) and the mere fact that staff are transferred from one status to another, eg by altering employees from direct staff to agency workers doing the same work is not a relevant transfer (*Wynnwith Engineering Co Ltd v Bennett*[16]). The decisive factor appears to be whether the business retains an identity, but it is also necessary to take into account the nature of the undertaking concerned, whether tangible assets were transferred, the value of intangible assets at the time of the transfer, whether or not the majority of employees were taken on by the new owner, whether customers or goodwill were transferred, the degree of similarity between the activities carried on before and after the transfer, and the period, if any during which those activities were suspended (*Rask and Christiensen v ISS Kantineservice A/S*[17]). A useful test is whether the essential business activity is carried on by the new owner (*Kenny v South Manchester College*[18]); conversely, if there is no transfer of goodwill a transfer may be outside the scope of the regulations (*Robert Seligman Corpn v Baker*[19]).

---

[7] (C-29/91) [1992] ECR I–3189, [1994] 3 CMLR 265, [1992] IRLR 366, ECJ.

[8] (24/85) [1986] ECR 1119, [1986] 2 CMLR 296, ECJ.

[9] [1984] 1 WLR 377, [1984] ICR 58, [1983] IRLR 471, 128 Sol Jo 151, EAT.

[10] [1998] ICR 631, [1998] IRLR 416, 596 IRLB 8, EAT; aff'd [1999] 4 All ER 669, [2000] 1 CMLR 224, [1999] ICR 1162, [1999] IRLR 559, [1999] All ER (D) 838, CA.

[11] [1996] IRLR 51, ECJ.   [12] [1996] IRLR 134, EAT.

[13] (Case C-463/09) [2011] IRLR 251, [2011] EUECJ C-463/09, [2011] 2 CMLR 30.

[14] [2008] ECR I–7907, [2009] 1 CMLR 14, [2009] CEC 407.   [15] [1987] ICR 495.

[16] [2002] IRLR 170, EAT.

[17] (C-209/91) [1992] ECR I–5755, [1993] IRLR 133, ECJ.

[18] [1993] ICR 934, [1993] IRLR 265.   [19] [1983] ICR 770, EAT.

9.10 Some confusion appears to stem from the decisions of the European Court in *Suzen v Zehnacker Gebaudereinigung GmbH*[20] and *Oy Lukkene Ab v Liskojarvi.*[21] In *Suzen* it was held that in the absence of a transfer of the workforce in a labour-intensive sector the EU Directive did not apply, and in *Oy Lukenne Ab* the same conclusion was reached in a case where there was an absence of an asset transfer in an asset-reliant sector. These decisions were discussed and distinguished in a series of cases (eg, *Betts v Brintel Helicopters,*[22] *ECM (Vehicles Delivery Services) Ltd v Cox,*[23] *OCS Cleaning Scotland Ltd v Rudden,*[24] etc), decisions which generated more heat than light. The issue was then considered in *Scottish Coal Co Ltd v McCormack,*[25] where a company took over mining operations without acquiring the outgoing company's plant or equipment. The Court of Session held that the two categories of 'labour intensive' and 'asset-reliant' were neither mutually exclusive nor exhaustively definitive. There is a range of intermediate possibilities, and the whole of the transaction, including the type of undertaking and the sector of activity in which it operates, must be looked at to see whether any particular factor is decisive. It appears that no single factor should be isolated, but a multi-factorial approach should be taken (*P & O Trans European Ltd v Initial Transport Services Ltd*[26]).

B. Transfer of part of a business

9.11 If part of a business is transferred, it is not necessary to show that it was a separate and self-contained business prior to the transfer. The part transferred has to be a recognisable and identifiable part of the business as a whole (*Green v Wavertree Heating and Plumbing Co Ltd*[27]), which means that ancillary activities, such as cleaning, catering, etc are within the scope of the regulations (*Rask v ISS*, see para 9.9). Problems sometime arise when an employee works for two or more companies in the same group, and one or more of those companies are transferred. In *Michael Peters Ltd v Farnfield,*[28] the claimant was the chief executive of Michael Peters Group Ltd, a holding company for 25 subsidiary companies. The group experienced financial difficulties, and receivers were appointed. Four of the subsidiary companies were then sold to another company, but the parent company was not a party to the sale. An employment tribunal held that all the companies formed a single economic unit, that part of the parent company had therefore been transferred, and the claimant was unfairly dismissed when he was taken on by the transferee. However, the EAT reversed the decision. It was inappropriate to apply the concept of 'single economic unit' and impermissible to pierce the veil of corporate personality. The business of the subsidiaries was not the business of the parent company. By contrast, in *Sunley Turriff Holdings Ltd v Thomson,*[29] the claimant was the company secretary and chief accountant of Lilley Construction Ltd and of Lilley Construction (Scotland) Ltd. The contract of employment was with the former company, although part of his work involved the latter. Both firms went into receivership, and the Scottish company was sold by the receiver to Sunley Turriff Holdings Ltd. It was held that the claimant's contract of employment was automatically transferred to the transferee, because he was part of the

[20] (C-13/95) [1997] ECR I–1259, [1997] All ER (EC) 289, [1997] 1 CMLR 768, [1997] ICR 662, [1997] IRLR 255, [1997] EC 289, ECJ.

[21] (C-172/99) [2001] All ER (EC) 544, [2001] ECR I–745, [2001] 3 CMLR 37, [2002] ICR 155, [2001] IRLR 171, [2001] Emp LR 235, ECJ.

[22] [1997] 2 All ER 840, [1997] ICR 792, [1997] IRLR 361, [1997] NLJR 561, sub nom *Betts v Brintel Helicopters Ltd and KLM ERA Helicopters (UK) Ltd* [1998] 2 CMLR 22, CA.

[23] [1998] ICR 631, [1998] IRLR 416, 596 IRLB 8, EAT; aff'd [1999] 4 All ER 669, [2000] 1 CMLR 224, [1999] ICR 1162, [1999] IRLR 559, [1999] All ER (D) 838, CA.

[24] IDS Brief 644.   [25] IDS Brief 791.   [26] [2003] IRLR 128, [2002] All ER (D) 116 (Nov), EAT.

[27] Unreported.   [28] [1995] IRLR 190, EAT.   [29] [1995] IRLR 184, EAT.

undertaking transferred. In *Albron Catering BV v FNV Bondgenoten*[30] an employee was employed by a service company within a corporate group and was then permanently assigned to another company within that group. The second company was later transferred. The European Court held that the latter company was the transferor, even though his contract was with the former, as the Directive is intended to protect employees in the event of a change of 'employer'.

9.12 Whether an employee is 'assigned' to an organised group is a question of fact in each case (*Botzen v Rotterdamsche Droogdok Maatschappij*[31]). Factors to be taken into account include the amount of time spent on a particular part of the business, the amount of value given to each part by the employee, the terms of the contract which detail the employee's duties, and how, if at all, the cost to the employer of the employee's services were allocated between the different parts of the employer's business (see *Duncan Web Offset (Maidstone) Ltd v Cooper*[32]). Further, if an employee works at a particular job on a temporary basis, he has not been 'assigned' to the organised group in question, and thus will be outside the scope of the regulations (*Securiplan v Bademosi*[33]).

9.13 What is his position if the employee performs services in part of the undertaking transferred, and also in part of the undertaking retained? The European Court of Justice in *Botzen v RDM* stated that the Directive protects those who are assigned to the transferred part, but this is not very helpful. Two theories are currently suggested by UK commentators. The first is to ascertain if the employee spends most of his activities in the department transferred, or for its benefit (the so-called 'location' theory). The second is to ascertain if the employee's post is part of the staffing structure of the department transferred (the so-called 'belonging' theory). The 'location' theory appears to have some support from the decision of the ECJ in *Botzen v RDM*, but the EAT in *Duncan Webb Offset (Maidstone) Ltd v Cooper* appears to have adopted the 'belonging' approach. The question as to whether or not the employee has been 'assigned' to the part transferred and the proportion of work he did for that part was to be determined on the facts by the employment tribunal. An employee does not have to work exclusively in the part of the undertaking transferred, and all the circumstances have to be taken into account (*Buchanan-Smith v Scheicher & Co International Ltd*[34]). It would appear that TUPE 2006 adopts the *Botzen* approach, ie assigned to an organised grouping.

C. Service provision change (reg 3(1)(b))

9.14 There has always been considerable uncertainty arising from 'outsourcing' or 'contracting out' of services, and the bringing back of services 'in house'. Typically, these will be labour intensive activities, such as cleaning services, catering, maintenance contracts, and so on. These situations are now covered by reg 3(1)(b). In *Metropolitan Resources Ltd v Churchill Dulwich Ltd*[35] it was held that the definition of 'service provision change', introduced in the 2006 version of TUPE, is to be viewed afresh, without reference to pre-2006 decisions on whether the old definition of relevant transfer (the economic entity approach) should be used. The modern test is to apply a pragmatic and common sense approach by going through the wording of reg 3(1)(b) carefully (*Cheeseman v Brewer Contracts Ltd*[36] not followed).

---

[30] (Case C-242/09) [2011] IRLR 76, [2011] ICR 373.
[31] (186/83) [1985] ECR 519, [1986] 2 CMLR 50, ECJ.
[32] [1995] IRLR 633, EAT.   [33] IDS Brief 746.
[34] [1996] ICR 613, [1996] IRLR 547, EAT.
[35] [2009] ICR 1380, [2009] IRLR 700.   [36] [2001] IRLR 144.

9.15 A service provision change can arise in one of three ways:

(a) activities which cease to be carried out by a person (a client) on his own behalf, and are carried out instead by another person on the client's behalf (a contractor). Normally, this would be a group of employees being transferred, but a single employee employed by the employer can be so transferred to the contractor if that employee's activities are transferred (see *Schmidt v Spar*, etc, para 9.7);

(b) activities cease to be carried out by a contractor on a client's behalf, and are carried out instead by another person (a subsequent contractor). This would occur, for example, as a result of competitive tendering;

(c) activities cease to be carried out by a contractor or a subsequent contractor on a client's behalf, and are carried out instead by the client on his own behalf. In other words, they are brought back 'in house'.

9.16 Generally, in any of these circumstances, there will have been a transfer within the meaning of the regulations.

Organised grouping

9.17 For a transfer to occur, there must be an organised grouping of employees which has as its principal purpose the carrying out of the activities concerned on behalf of the client. Thus if different employees are employed by a contractor to carry out an activity on behalf of a client, no transfer within the meaning of the regulations will take place if the client decides to use another contractor, because it would be unclear which employees should transfer. The group of employees is not an 'organised grouping'.

9.18 The 2014 regulations added that activities carried on after the change must be fundamentally the same as the activities carried out previously, to reflect the position taken in the case law. It is unlikely, however, that minor differences between the nature of the tasks would matter, so long as the activities are fundamentally the same.

One-off business tasks

9.19 If the client intends that the activities will, following the service provision change, be carried out by the transferee in connection with a single specific event or task, or a task of short-term duration, then no transfer will occur. Thus if a client engages a contractor to perform a 'one-off' business task, or a task which will only last for a short time, the regulations will not apply if the client subsequently engages another contractor to perform the task. There may be an organised grouping of staff on the project, but the one-off buying in of services, or services of short-term duration, will not bring the regulations into operation.

Procurement/supply of goods for client's use

9.20 No transfer will occur if the activities consist wholly or mainly of the procurement or supply of goods for the client's use. Thus if a client engages a contractor to supply food to the client's canteen, a reallocation of that contract will not come within the regulations, because the main activity will be the procurement or supply of goods (it will of course, be a different matter if the client engages a contractor to operate the canteen).

Outsourcing

9.21 There is no requirement in reg 3(1)(b) that the organised grouping of employees situated in Great Britain retain its identity after the purported transfer, and it would therefore appear that the closing down of a business (eg an in-house call centre) and its transfer to another country could well come within the regulations. As well as having implications for the transferred employees, the transfer would also give rise to the operation of the consultation provisions (*Holis Metal Industries Ltd v GMB*,[37] see para 9.79).

9.22 A service provision change may also occur if the activities are transferred to more than one transferee. In such circumstances liability for the transferred employees will pass to the company that took up the activities to which the employees had been assigned before the transfer (*Kimberley Group Housing Ltd v Hambley*[38]). In *OCS Group UK Ltd v Jones*[39] a catering contract was changed from a full canteen service, which supplied hot and cold food etc, to a reduced service selling pre-prepared sandwiches and salads. It was held that the new service was materially different from the old one, and it was held that no service provision change had taken place. Similarly, in *Clearsprings Management Ltd v Ankers*[40] the transferor's responsibilities were randomly distributed among three incoming contractors, and thus no single transferee could be identified as having taken over the activities formerly carried on by the transferor.

D. Transfers within public administration (reg 3(5))

9.23 A reorganisation of public administration, or the transfer of administrative functions between public administration (eg from central to local government, etc) will not be a relevant transfer for the purpose of the regulations. However, such transfers will come within a Governmental Statement of Practice, 'Staff transfers in the Public Sector' which guarantees TUPE-equivalent protection for employees who are transferred from one public sector body to another. But transfers from the public sector to the private sector are within the scope of the regulations in the same way as transfers between private sector employers.

E. Employees who work outside the United Kingdom (reg 3(4))

9.24 In principle, the regulations apply to an undertaking situated in the United Kingdom immediately before the transfer, or, if there is a change in a service provision, where the organised grouping of employees is situated in the United Kingdom immediately before the transfer. But if the transfer of the business or service provision is governed by the law of an overseas country, and the employment of persons so employed in the business or service provision are governed by the laws of that country, the regulations will still apply if the employees concerned are an organised group of employees and the undertaking itself is situated in the United Kingdom.

The mechanics of the transfer

9.25 A relevant transfer may take place in a number of ways. It can be by the sale of a business (but not the sale solely of assets), a merger of two or more companies, a change of a licensee or franchisee, changing contractors or the contracting out of services, the sale of a sole trader's business or of a partnership, and so on. As long as there is a change in the identity of the employer it does not matter if a formal legal transfer has not taken place (*Landsorganisationen I Danmark v Ny Molle Kro*[41]). Thus a transfer can take place on a grant, or the surrender and regranting of a lease (*Premier Motors (Medway) Ltd v Total Oil*

---

[37] [2008] ICR 464, [2008] IRLR 187, EAT.   [38] [2008] ICR 1030, [2008] IRLR 682.
[39] Employment Appeal Tribunal, 4 August 2009.   [40] Employment Appeal Tribunal, 24 February 2009.
[41] (Case C-287/86) [1987] ECR 5465, [1989] ICR 330, [1989] IRLR 37, ECJ.

GB Ltd, see para 9.8), because what matters is that there has been a change in the identity of the employer, not necessarily a change in the ownership of the business. In *Young v Daniel Thwaites & Co Ltd*[42] it was held that there was a relevant transfer when a change took place in the tenancy of a public house.

9.26 A transfer may be effected by two or more transactions, and the absence of a contractual link between the transferor and the transferee does not preclude the existence of a transfer. In other words, the business does not need to be transferred from the transferor to the transferee. In *Dines v Initial Healthcare Services Ltd*[43] the claimant was employed by a firm of cleaners to clean at a hospital. The hospital then went to competitive tendering, and awarded the cleaning contract to another firm. The claimant was dismissed by her original employers and offered new but less favourable terms by the transferee. It was held that the transfer had taken place in two stages, ie the handing back of the cleaning contract to the hospital and the subsequent transfer of the cleaning contract to the new contractors. Hence there had been a transfer of the cleaning services, and the regulations operated.

9.27 It is also irrelevant whether or not property passes from the transferor to the transferee. Thus a concession, or a permit to operate a licence, comes within the regulations. The absence of a contractual link between the transferor and the transferee does not preclude the existence of a transfer, because this can result in two or more successive contracts which are part of the web of contractual relations, albeit that the end result (ie the transfer of assets and activities) is somewhat indirectly achieved (*Temco Service Industries SA v Imzilyen*[44]).

9.28 There is no transfer if there is a take-over of shares, because the corporate personality of the company does not change (*Brookes v Borough Care Services*[45]). Nor is there a transfer within the scope of the regulations if there is a transfer of administrative functions between public authorities (reg 3(5), *Henke v Gemeinde Schierke*,[46] but see para 9.23).

9.29 The date when a transfer takes place is the date on which responsibility as employer for carrying on the business of the unit moves from the transferor to the transferee, and cannot be postponed to another date at the will of either party. Employment relationships existing at that date are deemed to be transferred on that date, subject only to the employee's objection to being transferred (*Celtec Ltd v Astley*[47]).

The effect of the transfer

A. **Contracts of employment (reg 4)**

9.30 A relevant transfer shall not operate so as to terminate the contract of employment of any person employed by the transferor and assigned to the organised grouping of resources or employees that is subject to the relevant transfer, but any such contract shall have effect after the transfer as if originally made between the person so employed and the transferee. On completion of the relevant transfer, all the transferor's rights, powers, duties and liabilities under or in connection with any such contract shall be transferred to the transferee, and any act or omission before the transfer is completed or in relation to the transferor in respect of that contract or person assigned to that organised grouping of resources or employees, shall be deemed to have been an act or omission of, or in relation to the transferee. Thus actual or potential claims which could be made against the transferor

---

[42] [1977] ICR 877, 12 ITR 392, EAT.   [43] [1995] ICR 11, [1994] IRLR 336, CA.
[44] (C-51/00) [2002] ECR I–969, [2004] 1 CMLR 877, [2002] IRLR 214, [2002] All ER (D) 199 (Jan), ECJ.
[45] [1998] ICR 1198, [1998] IRLR 636, EAT.   [46] (C-298/94) [1996] ECR I–4989, [1996] IRLR 710.
[47] (C-478/03) *Times*, 9 June 2005.

may be brought against the transferee, eg claims for discrimination (*DJM International Ltd v Nicholas*[48]), breach of contract, unfair dismissal, redundancy payments, etc even though these occurred before the transfer took place. Liability for an industrial accident which occurred before the transfer is also transferred, although the transferee could claim the benefit of any insurance policy belonging to the transferor which covered the accident (*Bernadone v Pall Mall Services Group Ltd*[49]). Clearly, it would make sense for the transferee to obtain an indemnity from the transferor against any such potential liabilities.

However, reg 4 does not transfer or otherwise affect the liability of any person to be prosecuted for, convicted of, or sentenced for, any offence (reg 4(6)).

9.31 This is the nub of the regulations, and constitutes a form of statutory novation of the contract of employment. The transferee 'steps into the shoes' of the transferor, and the contract of employment is continuous as from the date of the original contract of employment with the transferor. Rights and liabilities which existed under the original contract continue in favour of or against the transferee. For example, in *Morris Angel & Son Ltd v Hollande*[50] the defendant was the managing director of a company called Altolight Ltd. His service agreement provided that he would not seek business from any person with whom the company had done business within one year of the end of his employment. The company was then sold to the claimants, who sought to enforce the restrictive covenant. It was held that the effect of TUPE was to put the claimants in the place of the transferor company, and the covenant operated in favour of the claimants, who were the transferees.

9.32 Regulation 4 operates to include matters which were done by the transferor before the transfer, in respect of the employee transferred, even though the transferee is unaware of those matters. In *DJM International Ltd v Nicholas*[51] the claimant worked for a company for many years, but she was forced to retire when she reached the age of 60. Ten days later, she was re-engaged on a part-time basis, and two months after that, following a transfer of the undertaking, she commenced her employment with the respondent company. Five months later she was made redundant, and she brought a claim alleging that her previous employer (the transferor) had discriminated against her on grounds of sex when they terminated her employment at the age of 60 (although her claim was outside the normal three-month time limit, the employment tribunal exercised its discretion to extend the time limit). For the respondent it was argued that the contract of employment, in respect of which she was alleging sex discrimination, had been terminated before the transfer took place, and was not therefore transferred to the transferee. The EAT dismissed the argument, and upheld the claimant's right to pursue her claim. Regulation 5(2)(b) (now reg 4(2)(b)) is very wide, and applies not only to things done before the transfer in respect of the contract of employment, but also to anything done before the transfer in respect of a person's employment in that undertaking.

9.33 However, rights and liabilities are only transferred in respect of those employees who were 'employed immediately before the transfer'. In *Tsangacos v Amalgamated Chemicals Ltd*[52] the claimant lodged a claim for unfair dismissal and race discrimination in March 1995. In July 1995 the employer ceased trading, and all the staff, etc were transferred to another company. The claimant sought to join the latter employers as respondents to his claim, but this was refused by an employment tribunal chairman, and the decision was upheld on appeal. The rights and obligations of the transferor are only transferred in

---

[48] [1996] ICR 214, [1996] IRLR 76, EAT.
[49] [1999] IRLR 617; aff'd [2000] 3 All ER 544, [2000] Lloyd's Rep IR 665, [2000] IRLR 487, CA.
[50] [1993] 3 All ER 569, [1993] ICR 71, [1993] IRLR 400, CA.
[51] [1996] ICR 214, [1996] IRLR 76, EAT.   [52] [1997] ICR 154, [1997] IRLR 4, CA.

respect of those employees who were employed immediately before the transfer, and this clearly did not include the claimant.

9.34 The meaning of the phrase 'employed immediately before the transfer' gave rise to a number of difficulties in the past, although the matter was resolved by the House of Lords in *Litster v Forth Dry Dock & Engineering Co Ltd* (see para 9.3). The phrase includes not only those employees who were employed immediately before the transfer, but also those who would have been so employed had they not been unfairly dismissed because of the transfer, or a reason connected with the transfer that is not an economic, technical or organisational reason entailing a change in the workforce (reg 4(3)). In other words, dismissals unconnected with the transfer are to be ignored so far as the transferee is concerned, but obligations arising from dismissals which are connected with the transfer are transferred.

Thus in *G4S Justice Services (UK) Ltd v Anstey*[53] two employees were dismissed for gross misconduct. They lodged an internal appeal, but before the hearing the business was transferred to another company. The transferor then allowed the appeals against the dismissals, and ordered their reinstatement. The transferee, however, refused to reinstate them on the basis that they were not employed 'immediately before the transfer'. It was held that the successful appeal had expunged the dismissals, and the employees should be treated as being employed by the transferor right up to the date of the transfer, and thus the transferee was obliged to reinstate them.

9.35 As a general principle, if there has been a liquidation of assets on an insolvency, reg 4 can be disapplied, and no transfer of employees takes place. However, this may not be the end of the matter, because it is possible that s 218(2) of the Employment Rights Act comes into play (*Oakland v Wellswood (Yorkshire) Ltd*, see para 13.40).

B. **Statutory rights**

9.36 It is clear that contractual rights are thus transferred. Also transferred are statutory rights, such as claims for equal pay, maternity rights, etc as well as liability for a protective award (*Alomo Group (Europe) Ltd v Tucker*[54]). Restrictive covenants made by the employee with the transferor are also transferred, although these may need to be re-assessed in the light of the changed situation (*Morris Angel & Son Ltd v Hollande*, para 9.31). But a non-competition clause agreed by the transferred employee will not be enforced if it occurred by reason of the transfer (*Credit Suisse v Padiachy*[55]) because an employee cannot waive rights under the contract which he had with the transferor (*Credit Suisse First Boston (Europe) Ltd v Lister*[56]).

C. **Other benefits**

9.37 Where a contract incorporates provisions of a collective agreement, rights relating to such an agreement which come into force after the date of the transfer will not transfer under regulation 4 unless the transferee is a party to the collective bargaining (reg 4A). Terms which came into force before the transfer are still binding. This was inserted into section 4 by the 2013 regulations, and puts in statutory terms the CJEU decision in the case of *Alemo-Herron & Ors v Parkwood Leisure Ltd*,[57] where the claimant was employed by Lewisham Borough Council, with terms and conditions set out in a collective agreement made in the National Joint Council. He was subsequently transferred to the defendant

---

[53] [2006] IRLR 588, EAT.   [54] EAT/994/01, EAT.
[55] [1998] 2 CMLR 1322, [1999] ICR 569, [1998] IRLR 504.
[56] [1999] ICR 794, [1998] IRLR 700, [1998] 44 LS Gaz R 35, 142 Sol Jo LB 269, CA.   [57] C-426/11.

employer. After the transfer, the National Joint Council awarded pay increases, but the employer refused to implement the award, as it had not been a party to the agreement, and it was reached after the transfer had taken place. The European Court held that employees transferred under TUPE cannot after their transfer rely on collectively agreed terms and conditions where the transferee did not have the opportunity of participating in the negotiating process by which the agreement was made.

9.38 Transferees can renegotiate collectively agreed terms that do carry through one year after transfer, provided that overall the changes are no less favourable to the employee.

9.39 The question thus arises as to what other benefits are capable of being transferred, eg if the transferor employer has a permanent health insurance scheme or a profit sharing scheme which the transferee does not have. In *Mitie Managed Services Ltd v French*[58] it was impossible for the transferee to offer the transferred employees a contractual benefit, but the EAT held that they were entitled to participate in a scheme of substantial equivalence. In *Bernadone v Pall Mall Services Group* (para 9.30) the claimant suffered an accident at work in 1996. The following year the undertaking in which she was employed was transferred to a new employer. The claimant brought proceedings for damages against the transferor and the transferee. The transferor claimed that the liability had been transferred to the transferee, a claim which was upheld by the Court of Appeal. However, the court went further and held that the transferor's right to an indemnity under their employer's liability insurance policy was also transferred by reason of TUPE on the grounds that this was a right arising from or in connection with the employee's contract of employment (see reg 17). But this does not confer additional rights on the employee to improve his situation. In other words, reg 4(1) cannot be relied upon to give a transferred employee access to benefits other than those he was entitled to before the transfer (*Jackson v Computershare Investor Services Ltd*[59]).

9.40 Obligations under a share option scheme or profit sharing schemes are also transferred to the transferee (*Thompson v ASDA-MFI Group plc*[60]) which can bring about the odd result that the transferee will have to pay profit-related pay based on the employee's performance with the transferor (*Unicorn Consultancy Services Ltd v Westbrook*[61]).

9.41 Occupational pension schemes are not transferred under the regulations, either because they arise under legislation as opposed to contractual obligations, or because they were originally excluded from the Directive. That position remains basically unchanged (reg 10) and an employee whose contract of employment is so transferred is not entitled to bring a claim against the transferor for breach of contract or constructive dismissal arising out of a loss or reduction of his rights under such a scheme (reg 10(3)). However, under the Pensions Act 2004, s 257 if an employee is a member of an occupational pension scheme before the transfer, the transferee must ensure that the employee is eligible to become a member of a scheme operated by the transferee or a stakeholder arrangement. The specific requirements concerning the transferee's scheme are set out in the Transfer of Undertakings (Pension Protection) Regulations 2005. The minimum requirement is for the transferee to match the employee's contribution, up to 6% of salary, into a stakeholder pension, or offer an equivalent alternative. In the public sector, the Government will ensure the continuation of the policy set out in HM Treasury Note, 'A Fair Deal for Staff Pensions',

[58] [2002] IRLR 512, [2002] All ER (D) 150 (Sep), EAT.
[59] [2007] EWCA Civ 1065, [2008] IRLR 70, (2007) 104(44) LSG 32, (2007) 151 SJLB 1434, [2008] ICR 341.
[60] [1988] Ch 241, [1988] 2 All ER 722, [1988] 2 WLR 1093, [1988] IRLR 340, 132 Sol Jo 497, [1988] 15 LS Gaz R 34.
[61] [2000] IRLR 80, EAT.

which guarantees broadly comparable occupational entitlement when there is the transfer from the public to the private sector.

9.42 Early retirement benefits do not fall within the scope of the exclusion to be found in the Directive of terms relating to old age, invalidity or survivor's benefits, and therefore the transferee is obliged to offer early retirement benefits (including, where relevant, enhanced redundancy payments) which mirror those provided to the employees by the transferor (*Martin v South Bank University*[62]).

9.43 If there is a transfer following the insolvency of the transferor, any relevant debts owed to the relevant employees (ie those transferred to the transferee and those who were unfairly dismissed by reason of the transfer or for a non-ETO reason (see para 9.56) connected with the transfer) are not transferred to the transferee, but will be met by the Secretary of State. This is in line with the existing provisions which are found in ERA, ss 166–170 and ss 182–190 (see para 7.134).

D. Variation of the contract of employment (reg 4(4))

9.44 Any purported variation of the contract of employment shall be void if the reason for the variation is the transfer itself but it will not be void if it is for an economic, technical or organisational reason (ETO, see para 9.56) entailing changes in the workforce (reg 4(4)). Changes in the workforce include a change to the place of work. If there is a valid ETO reason, however, this provision enables an employer and employee to agree to a change in the terms of the contract (reg 4(5)), where the terms of the contract allow the employer to make the variation. In other words, an employer cannot unilaterally change the terms and conditions of employment of the employees transferred, but there are circumstances when the employer and employee can mutually agree to a variation of those terms, provided there is a genuine ETO reason.

9.45 Equally, a variation will be valid if it was for a reason unconnected with the transfer (reg 4(5)). In *Norris v Brown & Root Ealing Technical Services*[63] employees were offered new terms of employment some two years after a transfer took place. The reason was because the employer was having cash flow difficulties. It was held that the contractual variations were not transfer-connected reasons, but because the employer was having cash flow difficulties. The unexpected loss of a major order could also be an example of circumstances which would permit a variation, as it would be unconnected with the transfer.

9.46 Although reg 4(4) provides that any change in the terms of the contract made as a result of a transfer is void (see, for example, *Wilson v St Helens BC*[64]), this does not apply to changes which are for the benefit of the employee (*Regent Security Services Ltd v Power*[65]).

9.47 The above regulation does not apply to a variation to a term or condition in a collective agreement, provided the variation takes place more than one year after the date of the transfer, and the terms and conditions of the contract are not less favourable to the employee than they were before (reg 4(5B)). Obviously, this is for transfers that take place from 31 January 2014.

---

[62] (C-4/01) [2004] 1 CMLR 472, [2004] IRLR 74, [2003] All ER (D) 85 (Nov), ECJ.

[63] [2002] All ER (D) 413 (Oct), EAT.

[64] [1996] ICR 711, [1996] IRLR 320, [1996] IRLR 541, EAT; revsd [1997] 3 CMLR 1267, [1998] ICR 387, [1997] IRLR 505, [1997] 33 LS Gaz R 26, [1997] NLJR 1150, 575 IRLB 12, CA; revsd [1999] 2 AC 52, [1998] 4 All ER 609, [1998] 3 WLR 1070, [1999] 1 CMLR 918, [1999] LGR 255, [1998] ICR 1141, [1998] IRLR 706, [1998] All ER (D) 516, HL.

[65] [2007] 4 All ER 354, [2007] ICR 970, [2007] IRLR 226, EAT; aff'd [2007] EWCA Civ 1188, [2008] IRLR 66, (2007) 104(47) LSG 26, [2008] ICR 442.

E. Insolvency rights (reg 8)

9.48 If a company is put into liquidation or administration, which results in a transfer to which TUPE applies, employees who are dismissed can no longer claim against the transferor or transferee. Instead, they must seek payments from the national insurance fund. Further, when the transferor is in administration, its liability to pay certain debt to its employees (arrears of wages and holiday pay) does not transfer to the transferee, although the transferee will still be liable for any excess that the employees are owed above the statutory limits. Arrears that are above the statutory maximum will still transfer. Employees who are dismissed by the administrator for a reason connected with the transfer can claim arrears of wages and holiday pay up to the statutory limits from the national insurance fund. If there is an ETO reason for the dismissal, arrears of redundancy pay, wages, holiday pay and notice pay may also be claimed from the fund. (Where, however, an employee is unfairly and wrongfully dismissed by a transferee immediately following a TUPE transfer of an administration 'pre-pack', it is the transferee, rather than the Secretary of State, who is liable for the employee's basic award and notice pay (*Pressure Coolers Ltd v Molloy*[66]).)

9.49 Regulation 8 is part of the Government's pursuit of 'rescue culture' by providing that the transferee takes on an insolvent company free of those liabilities, which can now be met by the Secretary of State. However, the transfer of these liabilities to the Secretary of State does not apply if the insolvency proceedings have not been commenced at the time of the transfer (*Secretary of State for Trade and Industry v Slater,*[67] *Key2Law (Surrey) LLP v De'Antiquis*[68]).

9.50 In *Key2Law (Surrey) LLP v De'Antiquis*, the Court of Appeal (with whom the Supreme Court agreed) said that the primary objective of an administration appointment is the rescuing of the company as a going concern, and so companies in administration are not exempted from TUPE; therefore when a business is sold by an administrator, employees will transfer to the new employer and will be protected against transfer connected dismissals. Regulation 8(7) therefore does not apply in such cases.

9.51 However, a company administrator can make dismissals for an ETO reason and then sell the business without the purchaser being liable for TUPE if the reason for the dismissals was to enable the company to continue to trade. The case of *Crystal Palace FC Ltd v Kavanagh and others*[69] was distinguished from *Spaceright Europe Ltd v Baillavoine and another*.[70] In *Spaceright*, the court said for an ETO reason to be available there must be an intention to change the workforce and to continue to conduct the business, as distinct from the purpose of selling it. It is not available in the case of dismissing an employee to enable the administrators to make the business of the company a more attractive proposition to prospective transferees of a going concern. Here, the administrator dismissed the claimants in order to reduce the wage bill and keep the football club alive as a going concern, in the hope that there would be a sale in the future. (This is distinguished from *Spaceright*, where the reason was in order to make the business more attractive to the purchaser.)

F. Permitted variations in insolvency proceedings (reg 9)

9.52 It is permissible to vary the contracts of employment of the transferee's employees when the transferor is subject to insolvency proceedings, if the objective is to safeguard

---

[66] [2011] IRLR 630.   [67] [2008] BCC 70, [2008] ICR 54, [2007] IRLR 928.
[68] [2011] EWCA Civ 1567, CA.   [69] [2013] EWCA Civ 1410.   [70] [2012] IRLR 212.

employment opportunities by ensuring the survival of the undertaking which is the subject of the relevant transfer (this is to promote the 'rescue culture' in an attempt to facilitate employment prospects when an employer becomes insolvent). Two conditions must be present:

(a) The variation must be agreed between the transferee (or insolvency practitioner) and the appropriate representatives of the assigned employees. These will be either representatives of an independent trade union recognised by the employer, or, if there are no such representatives, employee representatives who have previously been appointed or elected who have authority to agree to the permitted variations on behalf of the employees, or employee representatives elected by assigned employees for the particular purpose.

(b) If the representation is by non-union representatives, the agreement recording the permitted variation must be in writing, the employer must give the affected employees copies of the text of the agreement, and such guidance as they might reasonably require in order to fully understand it. The agreement must then be signed by each of the representatives.

The permitted variation shall then take effect as a term or condition of the assigned employee's contract of employment in place of any term of condition it varies.

9.53 A problem may arise when a company is put into administration, because the administrator is generally appointed to carry on the business with a view to rescuing it. However, in *Oakland v Wellswood (Yorkshire) Ltd*[71] the employment tribunal found as a fact that the administrator was instituted with a view to the liquidation of the assets of the company. Thus the transfer was under the supervision of an insolvency practitioner, and reg 9 of TUPE applied.

Dismissal on transfers (reg 7)

9.54 Where, either before or after a relevant transfer, an employee of the transferor is dismissed, this will amount to an automatically unfair dismissal if the reason for the dismissal was the transfer, unless it is for an ETO reason. (Until the 2014 regulations, it was also automatically unfair if it was for a reason connected with the transfer, but that is no longer the case.) Regulation 7(2) provides that if the employee was dismissed for an economic, technical or organisational reason which entailed a change in the workforce of either the transferor or transferee, the reason for the dismissal will be treated as either being for redundancy (if that applies) or otherwise for a substantial reason of a kind such as to justify the dismissal of an employee holding that position (*Collins v John Ansell & Partners Ltd*[72]). Thus slimming down an overstaffed workforce so as to enable the transferee to continue to operate successfully would be an ETO reason, and it is then for the employer to show that he acted reasonably in treating that reason as a sufficient reason for the dismissal. If the reason shown is redundancy (and redundancy is the commonest of the ETO reasons), the employee will be able to claim a redundancy payment.

9.55 For the defence of reg 7(2) to apply, a transferor cannot plead that the transferee had an ETO reason, and the fact that the transferee had no need for the employee transferred is irrelevant. If in fact the employee is redundant in consequence of the transfer, a fair procedure for handling the situation must be followed (*Hynd v Armstrong*).

---

[71] [2009] EWCA Civ 1094, [2010] BCC 263, [2010] IRLR 82.   [72] Unreported.

A. **ETO reason (regs 4, 7)**

9.56 We have seen that it is permissible to vary the contracts of employment of transferred employees (with their agreement) and to dismiss transferred employees, if there is an economic, technical or organisational (ETO) reason which entails a change in the workforce (however this does not necessarily mean the entirety of the workforce (*Nationwide Building Society v Benn*[73])). An ETO reason includes a change in the place of work (reg 8, 2014 regulations). The phrase 'ETO' is not defined in the regulations, and is therefore the subject of interpretation by the courts and tribunals. In a Guide to the Regulations published by the DBIS, it is suggested that an economic reason would relate to the profitability or market performance of the transferee's business, a technical reason would relate to the nature of the equipment or production processes which the transferee operates, and an organisational reason would relate to the management or organisational structure of the transferee's business.

9.57 Potentially, 'economic, technical or organisational reasons' is a wide concept, but it is generally given a restricted meaning. In *Wheeler v Patel*,[74] the EAT held that an economic reason entailing a change in the workforce must relate to the conduct of the business concerned, so that the transferor's attempt to obtain a higher price for a sale by acceding to the demands of the transferee to dismiss the workforce does not constitute an economic reason. An earlier decision to the contrary (*Anderson v Dalkeith Engineering Ltd*[75]) has been disapproved (see *Gateway Hotels Ltd v Stewart*[76]). But a redundancy dismissal brought about solely to obtain a contract is an ETO reason, and is not analogous to a dismissal brought about solely to obtain a best price for the business (*Whitehouse v Charles Blatchford & Sons Ltd*[77]). If the transferee does not need the transferor's workforce, so that a redundancy situation is produced, this is within reg 7(2) (*Meikle v McPhail*[78]). If, on the transfer of the business, employees are dismissed for reason of redundancy without the transferor being contractually required to do so, this will be evidence of the unfairness of the dismissals (*Litster v Forth Dry Dock and Engineering Co Ltd*, see paras 9.3 and 9.34). Even when there is an ETO reason which results in redundancies, the employer concerned must still act fairly in treating that reason as a sufficient reason for the dismissal (*Gibson v Ciro Cittero*[79]). The standard way of dealing with redundancies must be followed, that is, fair selection procedures, search for alternatives, full consultation with the workforce and their representatives, etc.

9.58 The decision must be one made on the need to entail changes in the workforce. Generally, this could be a change in the number of employees employed, or a change in the functions of those employed. Thus if whole job contents have to be changed because of the transfer, this may constitute a change in the workforce (*Crawford v Swinton Insurance Brokers Ltd*[80]). If something else is sought to be changed (eg the pay of the employees who are transferred) the resultant dismissal does not come within reg 7(2), and the dismissal will be unfair (*Berriman v Delabole Slate Ltd*[81]). However, this does not prevent a mutually agreed variation for an ETO reason (see reg 4(5)).

9.59 In order to ascertain whether a dismissal was for economic reasons or a reason relating to the transfer, regard has to be paid to the thought processes of the person who took

---

    [73] UKEAT/0273/09/JOJ.   [74] [1987] ICR 631, [1987] IRLR 211, [1987] LS Gaz R 1240, EAT.
    [75] [1985] ICR 66, [1984] IRLR 429, EAT.   [76] [1988] IRLR 287, EAT.
    [77] [1999] IRLR 492, [1999] All ER (D) 414, CA.   [78] [1983] IRLR 351, EAT.
    [79] Unreported.   [80] [1990] ICR 95, [1990] IRLR 42, EAT.
    [81] [1984] ICR 636, [1984] IRLR 394, EAT; aff'd [1985] ICR 546, sub nom *Delabole Slate Ltd v Berriman* [1985] IRLR 305, CA.

the decision, which generally speaking will be the employer. In *Dynamex Friction Ltd v Amicus*[82] the managing director of a company realised that if he had to pay £2m by way of compensation to employees who had been unfairly dismissed, the company would be insolvent. He therefore placed the company in administration. The administrator decided to dismiss the employees because he had no money with which to pay them. There was no evidence to suggest that he dismissed the employees in order to have a better prospect of selling the business. Subsequently the administrator sold the business back to the managing director. It was held that the decision to dismiss was taken by the administrator, which was therefore an economic reason. There was no collusion between the administrator and the managing director, nor were the dismissals effected in order to escape the legitimate claims of the workforce.

9.60 If the employee is unfairly dismissed in connection with the transfer, his rights lie against the transferee, not the transferor. This is so even if the dismissal took place before the transfer, if the reason was connected with the transfer. Thus in *Allen v Stirling District Council*[83] the claimant was employed by the council's direct services department. Following competitive tendering, the work was awarded to an outside contractor. The claimant was dismissed by the council on 31 December, and the following day that outside contractor assumed responsibility for the service. The claimant brought a claim for unfair dismissal against the council, which failed. The Inner House of the Court of Session held that reg 4(2) was clear and unambiguous. All the transferor's duties and liabilities in connection with the contract of employment were transferred to the transferee. But a dismissed employee cannot compel the transferee to employ him, because the dismissal is not a legal nullity (*Wilson v St Helen's Borough Council*, see para 9.46).

9.61 If a dismissal takes place at the time of the transfer, but is for a reason unconnected with the transfer, none of the TUPE provisions apply, and the dismissal is to be tested under the usual provisions of ERA. For example, a dismissal which takes place following a disciplinary hearing would be unconnected with the transfer. So too would be the unexpected loss of a major order. A desire to harmonise terms and conditions of employment of the incoming employees with those of existing employees does not come within the ETO exception.

9.62 If an employee wishes to bring a complaint of unfair dismissal for a reason connected with the transfer under the provisions of TUPE, he is still required to meet the normal qualifying period of continuous employment of one year (reg 7(6)). If he wishes to claim a redundancy payment, he must be continuously employed for a period of two years.

Refusing a transfer (reg 4(7))

9.63 An employee is not bound to accept the transfer. He is free to choose for whom he will work, and cannot be compelled to work for an employer against his will. He can, at any time before the transfer, object to becoming an employee of the transferee. However, if he does so object, he will not be treated, for any purpose, as having been dismissed by the transferor (losing, for example, his right to a redundancy payment, see *Katsikas v Konstantinidis*[84]). There is no particular form of refusal, but it must be clear and unequivocal, and can be

---

[82] [2008] EWCA Civ 381, [2009] ICR 511, [2008] IRLR 515, (2008) 152(17) SJLB 31.
[83] [1994] ICR 434, [1994] IRLR 208, EAT; revsd [1995] ICR 1082, sub nom *Stirling District Council v Allen* [1995] IRLR 301, 1995 SLT 1255, Ct of Sess.
[84] (C-132, 138 and 139/91) [1992] ECR I–6577, [1993] 1 CMLR 845, [1993] IRLR 179, ECJ.

made to either the transferor or transferee. A protest in advance of the transfer will not by itself amount to an objection unless it is followed by an actual refusal to consent to the transfer. Thus, it has been held that to express a preference for a redundancy payment as opposed to a transfer was not enough to constitute an objection to the transfer (*Senior Heat Treatment Ltd v Bell*[85]). The employee has to specifically inform the transferor or transferee that he objects to the transfer.

9.64 There is no requirement that prior to the transfer the transferor must inform his employees of the identity of the transferee (*Secretary of State for Trade and Industry v Cook*),[86] although the new requirements on consultation (see para 9.75) in practice will mean that the identity of the transferee will be known. But if the employee does not know the identity of the transferee, and objects to being transferred as soon as he finds out, the objection will take effect retrospectively (*New ISG Ltd v Vernon*[87]).

9.65 An employee will be able to refuse to accept the transfer if it involves a substantial change in working conditions to his detriment. In these circumstances, reg 4(9) preserves the right of the employee to treat the contract of employment as having been terminated by the employer with notice (see *University of Oxford v Humphreys*[88]). What amounts to a substantial change is a matter to be determined in each individual case. Thus the loss of status, a requirement to relocate which is unacceptable, or a sound medical objection to working in new premises, etc could amount to being a substantial change in working conditions. Further, the employee may resign his employment, and claim that he was constructively dismissed, although for a successful claim he would have to show that the change in working conditions amounted to a repudiatory breach of contract by the employer. In *Rossiter v Pendragon plc*[89] the claimant was a car salesman. His employer operated a commission scheme which could be withdrawn or amended without notice. The business was then transferred to the respondent employer, who changed the commission scheme so that it was less beneficial to the claimant. Because of this, the claimant resigned and claimed he had been constructively dismissed. The Court of Appeal held that since there was no repudiation of the employment contract by the respondent employer, there was no liability for constructive dismissal.

9.66 The test for determining whether a substantial change to working conditions is to the detriment of the transferred employee is to look at the impact of the change from the employee's reasonable viewpoint, not by balancing the views of the employer and employee (*Tapere v South London & Maudsley NHS Trust*[90]).

9.67 Damages cannot be awarded against an employer in respect of his failure to pay wages to an employee in respect of a notice period which the employee has failed to work (reg 4(10)).

Employee liability information (regs 11–12)

9.68 The transferor shall notify the transferee of any employee liability information, ie information known to the transferor as to his rights, powers, duties and liabilities under

---

[85] [1997] IRLR 614.   [86] [1997] 3 CMLR 1465, [1997] ICR 288, [1997] IRLR 150, 562 IRLB 12, EAT.

[87] [2007] EWHC 2665 (Ch), [2008] IRLR 115, [2008] ICR 319.

[88] [2000] 1 All ER 996, [2000] 1 CMLR 647, [2000] IRLR 183, CA.

[89] [2001] ICR 1265, [2001] IRLR 256, [2001] All ER (D) 412 (Feb), EAT; revsd in part [2002] EWCA Civ 745, [2002] ICR 1063, [2002] IRLR 483, [2002] All ER (D) 143 (May).

[90] [2009] ICR 1563, [2009] IRLR 972.

or in connection with the contract of employment of any employee who is assigned to the organised grouping of resources that is the subject of the transfer. This will include:

(a) the identity and ages of employees to be transferred;

(b) the information contained in their statutory statement of particulars of employment;

(c) details or any formal disciplinary action or grievances raised in the previous two years;

(d) details of actual or potential legal action brought by the employees concerned in the previous two years or that the transferor has reasonable grounds to believe an employee may bring against the transferee arising out of the employee's employment with the transferor (ie, actual or potential claims); and

(e) information of any collective agreement which will have effect after the transfer in accordance with reg 5(a) (see para 9.73).

9.69 It must also include information about any employee who had been unfairly dismissed (in accordance with reg 7(1), see para 9.54) because of the transfer. Employee liability information shall contain information as at a specified date not more than 14 days before the date on which the information is notified to the transferee. The notification shall be in writing (or made available in a readily accessible form) and given not less than 28 days before the relevant transfer or, if special circumstances make this not reasonably practicable, then as soon as is reasonably practicable thereafter. The notification may be given in installments, and may come indirectly from a third party. If the specified information changes between the time when it has been provided and the time the transfer is completed, written notification must be given of those changes.

Remedy for failure to notify employee liability information (reg 12)

9.70 A transferee may present a claim to an employment tribunal that the transferor has failed to comply with the above provisions relating to employee liability information. The complaint must be made within three months of the relevant transfer (with an extension of time if it was not reasonably practicable to present the complaint within that period). If the employment tribunal finds the complaint to be well founded, it shall make a declaration to that effect, and may award compensation to the transferee to be paid by the transferor. The amount of compensation shall be such as the tribunal consider to be just and equitable, having regard to the loss suffered by the transferee, and the terms of the contract between the transferee and transferor under which the transferor may be liable to pay to the transferee in respect of any failure to notify the transferee of employee liability information.

9.71 The amount of compensation shall be not less than £500 per employee in respect of whom the transferor failed to comply with the provisions in reg 11, unless the tribunal considers it just and equitable to award a lesser sum. The transferee will be expected to take steps to mitigate against the loss suffered.

9.72 The purpose of regs 11–12 is to ensure that the transferee obtains full and accurate information about the rights and obligations which will be taken on, so that these can be honoured. At the same time, both the transferor and the transferee owe a duty of care to each other and to the affected employees not to negligently misrepresent the nature of various benefits which may or may not result from the transfer (*Hagen v ICI Chemicals plc*[91]).

---

[91] [2002] IRLR 31, [2002] PLR 1, [2002] Lloyd's Rep PN 288, 683 IRLB 13, [2001] All ER (D) 273 (Oct).

Other matters

A. Collective agreements (reg 5)

9.73 Where, at the time of the transfer, there exists a collective agreement made between the transferor with a recognised trade union in respect of employees to be transferred, then, in its application in relation to them, that agreement shall have effect as if made by or on behalf of the transferee with the trade union. Thus the rights of the transferred employees under existing collective agreements are protected, but the transfer does not bestow rights under any future collective agreement (*Werhof v Freeway Traffic Systems GmbH*[92]).

B. Trade union recognition (reg 6)

9.74 Where, before the transfer, an independent trade union is recognised by the transferor in respect of employees who are transferred, then, after the transfer, the union shall be deemed to have been recognised by the transferee to the same extent. However, this will only apply if, after the transfer, the transferred organised grouping of resources or employees maintains an identity distinct from the remainder of the transferee's undertaking. Any agreement for recognition may subsequently be varied or rescinded.

C. Consultation on transfers (reg 13)

9.75 On the transfer of an undertaking, it is clear that employees of the transferor and the transferee may be affected in some way. Regulation 13 provides that long enough before the relevant transfer to enable the employer of any affected employees to consult all persons who are appropriate representatives of any of the affected employees, the employer shall inform those representatives the fact that the relevant transfer is to take place, the date of the transfer, and the reasons for it, together with:

    (a) the legal, economic and social implications of the transfer for the affected employees;

    (b) the measures (if any) which he envisages he will take in relation to those employees; and

    (c) the measures (if any) which the transferor envisages the transferee will take in relation to the affected employees.

For this purpose, the transferee shall give to the transferor such information as will enable the transferor to perform his duty.

9.76 The information must be delivered to the appropriate representatives (reg 13(5)) and, if either employer envisages that he will take measures in respect of any employees affected by the transfer, he shall consult with the appropriate representatives with a view to seeking their agreement to the measures to be taken. The employer will consider any representations made by the appropriate representatives, reply to them and, if he rejects them, state his reasons. If there are special circumstances which render it not reasonably practicable for the employer to consult as required, he will take such steps towards performing that duty as are reasonably practicable in the circumstances. The language of reg 13(2)(b) obliges the employer to describe what he genuinely believes to be the legal, social and economic implications of the transfer, but he does not have to warrant that his belief is correct (*Royal Mail Group v CWU*[93]).

---

[92] (C-499/04) [2006] ECR I–2397, [2006] 2 CMLR 44, [2006] CEC 653, [2006] IRLR 400, ECJ.

[93] [2009] EWCA Civ 1045, [2010] ICR 83, [2009] IRLR 1046, (2009) 106(41) LSG 20, (2009) *Times*, 16 October.

9.77 The appropriate representatives are the representatives of a recognised independent trade union, or, in any other case, representatives appointed or elected by them for some other purpose (who have authority to receive such information and be consulted about the transfer) or employees' representatives elected for this specific purpose. The employer shall allow the appropriate representatives access to the affected employees and shall afford them such accommodation and other facilities as may be appropriate.

9.78 If the employer has invited the affected employees to elect representatives, and the invitation was issued long enough before the time when the employer is required to give the information as required under reg 13 to allow them to elect representatives by that time, the employer will have complied with the consultation provisions if he does consult as soon as is reasonably practicable after the election of the representatives. If the employees fail to elect representatives within a reasonable time after being invited to do so, the employer shall give the information to each of the affected employees. It should be noted that, unlike the provisions on consultation on redundancies (see TULR(C)A, s 188), there is no minimum number of employees who are affected before the duty to consult arises.

9.79 The obligation to consult applies even though the business concerned is transferred out of the United Kingdom and the European Community (*Holis Metal Industries Ltd v GMB*, see para 9.21). However, there is no obligation on a transferee employer to consult with a recognised trade union after a transfer has taken place regarding changes that it proposes to make in respect of employees who have been transferred to the new employer (*UCATT v Glasgow City Council*[94]).

9.80 The 2014 regulations insert reg 13A, allowing a micro-business (which is an employer with fewer than ten employees) to inform and consult directly with all affected employees in cases where there are no existing appropriate representatives.

D. Election of employee representatives (reg 14)

9.81 If there is no independent trade union recognised by the employer, the affected employees are entitled to elect their representatives, and reg 14 lays down detailed requirements for such elections. These must be fair, the number of representatives must be sufficient to represent the interests of all the affected employees, the candidates for employee representatives must be affected employees, voting must be secret, no affected employee shall be unreasonably excluded from standing in the election, and so on. Employees' representatives have the right not to suffer a detriment because they performed any function or activity (including standing for election) and have the right to reasonable time off work with pay, access to the affected employees, and to be provided with appropriate accommodation and facilities. It will be an unfair dismissal to dismiss an employee because he was an employee representative or candidate, or proposed to perform any functions or activities as such.

E. Failure to inform or consult (reg 15)

9.82 A complaint may be made to an employment tribunal in respect of a number of potential failures by the employer, as follows:

(a) if there is a failure to arrange for the election of employee representatives, by any employees who are affected employees;

(b) if there is any other failure relating to employee representatives, by the relevant employee representative;

[94] [2009] IRLR 253.

(c) if there is a failure relating to representatives of a trade union, by the trade union;

(d) in any other case, by any of the affected employees.

9.83 In respect of any such complaint, the employer may show that there were special circumstances which rendered it not reasonably practicable to perform the duty, and that he took all such steps towards its performance as were reasonably practicable in the circumstances.

9.84 If the complaint against the transferee is well founded, the employment tribunal shall make a declaration, and order appropriate compensation to be paid. If the complaint against the transferor is well founded, the employment tribunal shall make a declaration, and order the transferor to pay appropriate compensation. If the complaint is that the transferor failed to provide information about the measures which the transferee will take in connection with the transfer (and the transferor has given notice to the transferee that the latter will be made a party to the proceedings), the transferee may be ordered to pay appropriate compensation to the affected employees. The transferor and transferee shall be jointly and severally liable in respect of compensation payable. 'Appropriate compensation' means such sum not exceeding 13 weeks' pay, as the tribunal considers just and equitable having regard to the seriousness of the failure of the employer to comply with his duty. The maximum award of 13 weeks' pay should be made unless there are mitigating circumstances which would justify a reduction in the award (*Sweetin v Coral Racing*[95]).

9.85 The complaint must be presented to the employment tribunal within three months of the date when the relevant transfer is completed, or three months from the tribunal's order that a payment shall be made. There is a discretion to extend the presentation date for such further period as the tribunal thinks reasonable. An appeal against all tribunal decisions made under the regulations will lie to the EAT on a point of law.

---

[95] [2006] IRLR 252, EAT.

10

Performance of the Contract of Employment

Personal nature of the contract

10.1 A contract of employment is essentially one of personal service, which gives rise to duties and obligations on both sides, but the courts will not compel either side to carry out that contract by means of an order for specific performance or an injunction. In *Warner Bros Pictures Inc v Nelson*[1] a film actress agreed to work for the claimants, and not to work for any other film company. It was held that an injunction would be granted restraining her from breaking the negative stipulation, for while she could not work for a rival film company, there were presumably other ways in which she could earn her living. However, the injunction would not be granted if its effect would be to compel the performance of the contract. In *Whitwood Chemical Co v Hardman*[2] a manager agreed to devote the whole of his time to the company's business. He intended to work part-time for a rival company, and his employers sued for specific performance. It was held that the agreement was not enforceable, for while they could have obtained an injunction to restrain him from working for a competitor, the court would not compel him to work for the claimants.

10.2 By the same rule, the courts will not normally order an employer to continue to employ an employee (*Measham v AEEU*[3]), though there are cases where this had been done (see para 10.6) and in recent years the courts have been more willing to do so than hitherto (see the cases cited in *Wadcock v London Borough of Brent*[4]). There are also pressures on employers to offer reinstatement or re-engagement following employment tribunal proceedings (see Chapter 17) and a contract of employment may transfer from one employer to another when the Transfer of Undertakings (Protection of Employment) Regulations apply (see Chapter 9). But the rule generally remains. In *Chappell v Times Newspapers Ltd*,[5] members of a trade union were carrying on a disruptive campaign in support of a wage demand. The employers' association sent a telegram to the union stating that unless the campaign was called off, the members would be regarded as having broken their contracts of employment and thereby terminated their engagements. Several employees brought an action for an injunction to restrain their employers from terminating their contracts. It was held that, even on the assumption that the employers were acting in breach of contract, an injunction would not be granted, for to do so would be to compel specific performance by the employers. In particular, an injunction will not be granted if damages would be an adequate remedy for the alleged breach of contract (*Alexander v Standard Telephones and Cables plc*[6]).

---

[1] [1937] 1 KB 209, [1936] 3 All ER 160, 106 LJKB 97, 80 Sol Jo 855, 155 LT 538, 53 TLR 14.
[2] [1891] 2 Ch 416, 60 LJ Ch 428, 39 WR 433, 64 LT 716, 7 TLR 325, CA.
[3] [1994] IRLR 218.   [4] [1990] IRLR 223.
[5] [1975] 2 All ER 233, [1975] 1 WLR 482, [1975] ICR 145, [1975] IRLR 90, 119 Sol Jo 82, CA.
[6] [1990] ICR 464, [1990] IRLR 723, CA.

10.3 An exceptional case was *Hill v CA Parsons & Co Ltd*,[7] where, following the making of a closed shop agreement with a trade union, the employers wrote to the claimant giving him one month's notice of dismissal because of his failure to join the union. The court thought that the claimant, who was a senior engineer, was entitled to at least six months' notice, and granted an injunction restraining the employers from treating the notice as having terminated the contract. (The effect of this was to delay the dismissal until after the coming into effect of the Industrial Relations Act 1971, which would have protected the claimant from dismissal for non-membership of the union.) But the court conceded that there were special circumstances in the case which enabled them to grant the injunction. There was no loss of confidence between the employers and the claimant, for the employers were acting under union pressure, and therefore there was no difficulty in enforcing the continuance of the contract.

10.4 *Hill v CA Parsons & Co Ltd* was followed in *Irani v Southampton and South West Hampshire Health Authority*,[8] where the claimant was employed by the defendants as a part-time ophthalmologist. The claimant quarrelled with the consultant in charge of the clinic, and he was thus dismissed, although the defendants failed to operate the disputes procedure laid down in the Whitley Council Conditions of Service. The claimant was granted an injunction preventing the defendants from implementing the decision without invoking the disputes procedure. The court advanced three reasons. First, there was no lack of confidence in the claimant, for his professional competence was not in issue. Second, the claimant was seeking the protection of the disputes procedure which was incorporated into his contract. Third, damages would not be an adequate remedy. The balance of convenience lay in the granting of the injunction.

10.5 Whether the employee retains the confidence of the employer must be judged on the circumstances of the case, including the nature of the work, the people with whom the work is to be done, and the effect on the employer's operations if the injunction is granted. In *Powell v London Borough of Brent*,[9] the claimant was told that she had been selected for promotion. It was then thought that the selection may have been in breach of the council's equal opportunity code, and her promotion was rescinded and the post readvertised. The claimant brought an action for an injunction to restrain the council from treating her other than as being promoted. By the time the case came to court, she was able to show that she had worked in the senior post without any complaints about her work and there were no problems in her working relationships. It was held that the injunction would be granted. A bare assertion by her employers that there was a lack of confidence was not sufficient.

10.6 The normal remedy in such cases is for the employee who is being threatened with dismissal to seek an interlocutory injunction restraining the proposed dismissal until the trial of action. The court must then consider whether the balance of convenience requires such a course of action (see *American Cyanamid Co v Ethicon Ltd*[10]), leaving the substantial merits of the case to be argued subsequently at a full hearing. However, in *Jones v Gwent County Council*,[11] the court held that under the Rules of the Supreme Court a judge can give a final ruling on any question of law or construction of document without a full trial of action, and such ruling can finally determine the matter, subject to an appeal. In this case, the claimant had been subjected to two disciplinary hearings which ended in her favour. Nonetheless the council brought further disciplinary proceedings on the ground that her return to work would cause an irrevocable breakdown in relationships between management and staff. It

---

[7] [1972] Ch 305, [1971] 3 All ER 1345, [1971] 3 WLR 995, 12 KIR 135, 115 Sol Jo 868, CA.
[8] [1985] ICR 590, [1985] IRLR 203.   [9] [1988] ICR 176, [1987] IRLR 466, CA.
[10] [1974] FSR 312, CA; revsd [1975] AC 396, [1975] 1 All ER 504, [1975] 2 WLR 316, [1975] FSR 101, [1975] RPC 513, 119 Sol Jo 136, HL.
[11] [1992] IRLR 521.

was decided that she should be dismissed. It was held that a declaration could be made that her dismissal was not valid, and a permanent injunction was granted, restraining the council from dismissing her other than in accordance with the proper procedure as laid down in her terms of appointment, and unless proper grounds existed.

10.7 TULR(C)A, s 236 provides that no court shall compel an employee to work or attend at a place of work through the making of an order for specific performance, or an injunction. Thus an order cannot be granted, for example, to call off a strike.

Implied duties of the employer

10.8 We have seen (in Chapter 3) that there are a number of different ways by which the terms of a contract of employment may come into existence. We must now consider a number of duties and obligations which are imposed by law on both parties during the continuance of the performance of the contract. Some of these arise by virtue of the common law, but others arise out of the implications of legislative policy.

10.9 The distinction between those duties which are imposed by law and those which operate as an implied term of the contract is not at all clear. Prior to the massive explosion in employment law, which began in the 1960s, there were few legal authorities on the contractual nature of the employment relationship, and hence the courts were more ready to invent obligations as a necessary part of that relationship. In recent years there has been no dearth of legal authority arising from the contractual aspect, and hence rights have developed accordingly, whether as an express or implied term of the contract. But the more terms are expressly laid down, the less scope there is for implied terms to operate. Indeed, since an implied term cannot override an express term, and since express terms can exclude an implied term, the duties imposed by law begin to assume greater importance.

A. Implied duty of trust and confidence

10.10 Now that the age when management could 'hire and fire' at will has gone, it is possible to assert that the employer has a legal duty to treat his employees with due respect and consideration, mindful of their needs and problems, sympathetic to their difficulties. It is no longer possible to treat an employee as an expendable chattel, or as an object without feelings and emotions. This duty is implicit in a number of cases which will be considered in due course when dismissal or disciplinary policies are discussed, but it is particularly evident where the employer is alleged to have been carrying out provocative conduct. In *Donovan v Invicta Airways Ltd*[12] the employee resigned after what he considered to be a number of incidents where he thought the employer was being unfair, and claimed damages for breach of contract. In the circumstances it was held that such conduct, though irritating, was not substantial enough to amount to a breach, but it was stated that there was an implied duty that each of the parties to a contract of employment should treat the other with such a degree of consideration and courtesy as would enable the contract to be carried on. Thus it is a breach of the implied term of trust and confidence to single out an employee on capricious grounds and to refuse to offer him the same terms as are offered to the rest of the workforce (*Transco plc v O'Brien*, see para 3.49).

10.11 It will be recalled (see para 3.47) that in *Malik v BCCI SA* the House of Lords held that there was a duty on an employer to conduct his business so as not to damage an

[12] [1969] 2 Lloyd's Rep 413, [1970] 1 Lloyd's Rep 486, CA.

employee's future prospects in the labour market. While the *Malik* decision was probably decided on its own facts, it does raise a number of interesting possibilities, including, for example, the case of an employee who has been dismissed for misconduct alleging that his reputation has been damaged by a false accusation, and suing accordingly. In the words of Lord Nicholls: 'Employers must take care not to damage their employees' future employment prospects by harsh and oppressive behaviour or by any other form of conduct which is unacceptable today as falling below the standards set by the implied trust and confidence term.' But if the employer had reasonable and proper cause to act in the manner he did, then even though there are adverse consequences to the employee, there is no breach of the implied duty of trust and confidence (*Hilton v Shiner Ltd*, see para 17.47).

10.12 Although to carry on a business in a corrupt and dishonest manner is an example of a breach of the implied term of trust and confidence, if a former employee wishes to claim damages as a result, he must produce credible evidence that prospective employers rejected his applications for employment on such grounds (*Bank of Credit and Commerce International SA v Ali*, see para 3.47).

10.13 This duty arises at the outset of the employment, and continues during its performance right up to its termination. Employers will have to examine very closely their personnel and recruitment policies, for a mistake in selection or a failure to handle a problem in a proper manner could lead to an expensive action being brought in the future. For if an employer selects someone for a particular job, and that person does not have the necessary experience or capability for doing it, it is likely that the employer must accept some of the blame (*Bradley v Opperman Gears Ltd*[13]). As a result, many employers are now commencing employees on the basis of a probationary period in order to assess properly their capabilities. The employer also has an obligation to ensure that the employee is provided with an adequate job description, with objectives clearly mapped out, is provided with adequate facilities and support staff, and is properly trained and supervised where necessary. A failure by the employer to attend to these and allied matters may well mean that any shortcomings on the employee's part may not be entirely his own fault, and it could well be unfair to dismiss him in these circumstances (*Burrows v Ace Caravan Co (Hull) Ltd*[14]).

10.14 The frequent use of foul and abusive language by an employer can breach the implied duty of trust and confidence, entitling the employee to resign and claim constructive dismissal (*Horkulak v Cantor Fitzgerald International*[15]).

10.15 However, there are limits to the duty of trust and confidence. For example, in *University of Nottingham v Eyett*[16] it was held that the duty did not create a positive obligation on an employer to advise an employee that if he delayed taking retirement for another month, when he would have received a salary increase, his pension would have been correspondingly higher (see *Crossley v Faithful and Gould Holdings Ltd*, para 3.40). The implied duty is subject to the qualification that the employer must not act in such a way as to destroy or damage the trust and confidence which must otherwise exist between the parties without reasonable and proper cause. Thus if an employer, after a fair and full investigation, rejects a grievance raised by an employee, this will not give rise to a claim for constructive dismissal based on a breach of the implied term of trust and confidence. Equally, if the employee is himself in breach of the implied term, he cannot complain of his employer's breach (*RDF Media Group v Clements*[17]).

---

[13] [1975] IRLR 13.   [14] [1972] IRLR 4.

[15] [2003] EWHC 1918 (QB), [2003] IRLR 756, [2003] All ER (D) 542 (Jul).

[16] [1999] 2 All ER 437, [1999] 1 WLR 594, [1999] ICR 721, [1999] IRLR 87, [1999] ELR 141, [1999] 1 LS Gaz R 24, [1998] All ER (D) 584.

[17] [2007] EWHC 2892 (QB), [2008] IRLR 207.

B. Duty to provide work

10.16 The whole question of 'the right to work' is a confused one, principally because of the different meanings which may be given to the phrase. It may mean the right to work without a trade union membership card, as in *Hill v CA Parsons & Co Ltd* (paras 10.3 and 10.4), or the right not to be unreasonably discriminated against, as in *Nagle v Feilden*,[18] where the claimant argued that she had a right to obtain a licence to train horses despite the existence of an unwritten rule of the Jockey Club not to grant such licences to women. It can even mean the right to call on the state to provide jobs. In *Langston v AUEW*[19] the claimant objected to being compelled to join a trade union. The other employees threatened a strike, and so Chrysler suspended him from work for an indefinite period. He claimed that he had been denied the right to work, and in the Court of Appeal it was suggested that the courts would protect a man's right to work in appropriate circumstances, particularly if he was being denied job satisfaction. However, when the case was remitted to the National Industrial Relations Court, it was held that such documents as the Universal Declaration of Human Rights, para 9 of the 1971 Code of Practice, and other poetic allusions were considerations of public policy, rather than statements of contractual rights, and it was the contract which is the determining factor.

10.17 As a general rule, the employer is not under an obligation to provide work for his employee. As Asquith J said in *Collier v Sunday Referee Publishing Co*: 'Provided I pay my cook her wages regularly, she cannot complain if I choose to take any or all of my meals out'.[20] Indeed, there are many circumstances when the employer may find himself unable to provide work for his employees, for example, as a result of reorganisation, shortage of materials, lack of orders, due to a strike, etc, where the employer may prefer to keep his workforce together and pay them for doing nothing. However, there are certain special circumstances where the failure to provide work may result in the breach of a legal duty:

(a) If the failure to provide work can lead to a loss of reputation or publicity. In *Herbert Clayton and Jack Waller Ltd v Oliver*,[21] an actor was given a leading role in a musical comedy. He was subsequently offered a lesser role, but at the same salary. It was held that the employer was in breach of contract, because the nature of the work was as important as the salary to be paid.

(b) If the failure to provide work leads to a reduction in the employee's actual or potential earnings. Thus an employee is entitled to be given an opportunity to earn his commission (*Turner v Goldsmith*[22]) or to earn a reasonable sum if he is on piecework (*Devonald v Rosser & Sons*[23]). In *Bauman v Hulton Press Ltd*[24] it was held that the employers 'were bound to give the claimant a reasonable amount of work to enable him to earn that which the parties must be taken to have contemplated'. It was the lack of opportunity to earn premium payments for hours worked on night-shift and overtime which constituted the breach of contract by the employers in *Langston's* case (see para 10.16).

(c) There are dicta in *Langston's* case which suggest that if an employee needs practice in order to maintain or develop his skills in employment, the employer is under a duty

---

[18] [1966] 2 QB 633, [1966] 1 All ER 689, [1966] 2 WLR 1027, 110 Sol Jo 286, CA.
[19] [1974] 1 All ER 980, [1974] 1 WLR 185, [1974] ICR 180, [1974] IRLR 15, 16 KIR 139, 118 Sol Jo 97, CA.
[20] [1940] 2 KB 647, [1940] 4 All ER 234, 109 LJKB 974, 84 Sol Jo 538, 164 LT 10, 57 TLR 2.
[21] [1930] AC 209, 99 LJKB 165, [1930] All ER Rep 414, 74 Sol Jo 187, 142 LT 585, 46 TLR 230, HL.
[22] [1891] 1 QB 544, 60 LJQB 247, 39 WR 547, [1891–4] All ER Rep 384, 64 LT 301, 7 TLR 233, CA.
[23] [1906] 2 KB 728, 75 LJKB 688, [1904–7] All ER Rep 988, 50 Sol Jo 616, 95 LT 232, 22 TLR 682, CA.
[24] [1952] 2 All ER 1121.

to provide a reasonable amount of work for this purpose. This view has received further support from the 'garden leave' cases (see *Provident Financial Group plc v Hayward*,[25] para 19.9).

(d) Recent decisions seem to lean to the view that a failure to provide work may constitute a repudiation of the contract by the employer if it is possible to imply a term into the contract that the employer shall provide suitable work. This appears to be particularly true when the employee is appointed to a specific office. In *Breach v Epsylon Industries Ltd*,[26] the EAT thought that some of the earlier decisions on this subject were somewhat out of date and perhaps old fashioned in their approach. Consequently, in modern cases there may be facts which more readily lead to the conclusion that there is an implied term to the effect that there is an obligation to provide work. In *William Hill Organisation Ltd v Tucker*[27] it was stated in the Court of Appeal that times had moved on from the days when only musicians, actors etc were perceived as requiring regular exercise of their skills and public performances in order to keep up their reputation. All employees with specific skills are entitled to exercise those skills, even during notice periods, provided that there is work to be done (see para 19.10).

(e) If the contract of employment provides for suspension with pay pending the outcome of disciplinary enquiries, or criminal proceedings, there is no obligation on the employer to provide the employee with an opportunity to work overtime (*McClory v Post Office* (para 3.51), but see *Mezey v South West London & St George's Mental NHS Trust*, para 12.68).

C. Duty to pay wages or other remuneration when there is no work

10.18 The express terms of the contract will normally determine the amount of remuneration to be paid to the employee, but we must consider the situation where, because there is no work to do, the employee cannot earn his money. The question is, to what extent, if at all, does the employer undertake to pay the employee wages if the employer cannot provide work for the employee to do? To seek the answer, we must state the general rule, and then seek any modification which may exist by virtue of any express or implied terms of the contract of employment.

10.19 At common law an employee who is ready and willing to work is entitled to be paid wages, even though no work is available for him, unless there is a provision in the contract which enables the employer to withhold them (*Beveridge v KLM UK Ltd*[28]). Clearly, this is the position in respect of salaried staff (who are paid weekly or monthly: see *Miller v Hamworthy Engineering Ltd*, para 3.102), and there is no legal distinction between them and hourly-paid workers or piece-workers. An hourly-paid worker is entitled to be paid for the number of hours he makes himself available for work, not the number of hours the employers permit him to work, and a piece-worker, though paid for the work actually done, is entitled to expect that the employer will give him an opportunity to earn his wages. Because of this general common law rule, it was a comparatively simple matter to imply into the contract of an employee a term that he would be paid if there was no work. In *Devonald v Rosser & Sons* (see para 15.14) the plaintiff was a piece-worker. His employers closed down the factory, and gave him one month's notice. It was held that there

---

[25] [1989] 3 All ER 298, [1989] ICR 160, [1989] IRLR 84, CA.
[26] [1976] ICR 316, [1976] IRLR 180, EAT.
[27] [1999] ICR 291, [1998] IRLR 313, [1998] 20 LS Gaz R 33, 142 Sol Jo LB 140, CA.
[28] [2000] IRLR 765, EAT.

was an implied term in his contract that the employer would find him work to do, and he recovered damages based on his prior average earnings. An argument by the employers that there was a trade custom to the contrary was rejected by the court, because a custom has to be reasonable, certain and notorious. But if the failure to provide work was due to circumstances outside the control of the employer, different considerations could apply. In *Browning v Crumlin Valley Collieries*[29] a colliery had to close down because it was in a dangerous condition, through no fault of the employers. It was held that there was an implied term that the employers were not obliged to pay wages in these circumstances.

10.20 The common law rule, however, can be varied by an express or implied term to the contrary and, of course, a statutory provision will always override the rule. Thus if the contract states that there shall be no payment during a lay-off or in respect of short-time working, the employers will incur no obligation to pay at common law. In *Hulme v Ferranti Ltd*[30] the claimant was employed on terms that if there was no work, he would not be paid. He was laid off as a result of a strike involving other workers in the plant, and it was held that he was not entitled to be paid during that time. But the modern practice of concluding guarantee payment agreements lends greater credence to the view that the present law is that in respect of hourly or piece-workers, there is an implied term that they will not be paid during a lay-off or short-time working. For example, if an employer agrees to pay a minimum guarantee week to employees who have been employed by him for a certain period, those who do not qualify can scarcely be in a better position. The very existence of the guarantee payments rights in the Employment Rights Act 1996 (see Chapter 7) supports this view, for such rights would virtually be unnecessary if the common law rule was of general application. Nonetheless, a lay-off without pay is either a temporary suspension or a dismissal with the prospect of re-engagement, and the employer may only treat it as a suspension if there is an expressed or implied term in the contract giving him that right (*Jewell v Neptune Concrete Ltd*, para 3.61). In the absence of such a term the employee is entitled to treat the suspension as repudiatory conduct by the employer, and hence a dismissal. In appropriate circumstances (see Chapter 18) he may claim redundancy pay. Indeed, since there must be few contracts of employment which made provision for such eventuality, the Redundancy Payments Act 1965 was apparently based on the assumption that there was a general existence of an implied term that employees who are laid off or who are on short time are not entitled to be paid (see now ERA, s 147).

D. **Payment of bonuses, etc**

10.21 If a contract of employment contains an express term which provides for the payment of a bonus (or incentive scheme), problems may arise over interpretation, but not over entitlement. In the absence of any agreement, the courts will calculate or estimate what monies the employee would have received, and include that amount in the quantum of damages (*Addis v Gramophone Co Ltd*[31]). However, difficulties frequently arise when the bonus scheme purports to be discretionary, because, in the absence of clear and precise wording (see, eg *Kent Management Services Ltd v Butterfield*, paras 8.14 and 8.20), a legal obligation may nonetheless arise, as part of the implied duties of the employer. In *Mallone v BPB Industries plc* (see para 3.2) it was held that the directors of a company acted irrationally in cancelling mature share options, following the employee's dismissal for poor performance, even though the contract gave them an absolute discretion to reduce these

[29] [1926] 1 KB 522, 24 LGR 302, 90 JP 201, 95 LJKB 711, [1926] All ER Rep 132, 134 LT 603, 42 TLR 323.
[30] [1918] 2 KB 426, 16 LGR 813, 87 LJKB 938, 62 Sol Jo 668, 118 LT 719, 34 TLR 500, DC.
[31] [1909] AC 488, 78 LJKB 1122, [1908–10] All ER Rep 1, 101 LT 466, HL.

by an appropriate fraction. Thus, despite the fact that discretion is expressed to be absolute or unfettered, the courts are willing to impose limits on such management prerogatives, by implying a term that a discretion cannot be exercised in a manner which no reasonable employer would have done. But in *Ridgeway v JP Morgan Chase National Bank*[32] it was held that the employer did not act irrationally or perversely when it awarded an employee a 'nil bonus', even though a full performance review had not been carried out. The employee had lost a large sum of money in trading during the relevant period, and had done nothing in non-trading work to justify a bonus.

10.22 As a general principle, a dismissed employee cannot claim compensation for the loss of a benefit to which he is not contractually entitled (*Lavarack v Woods of Colchester Ltd*[33]), and if a bonus or other incentive scheme states that it is non-contractual the employer generally does not incur a legal binding obligation to make payments under the scheme (*Pendragon plc v Jackson (No 2)*, see para 3.21). But if there is a discretionary bonus scheme the terms of which have been notified to the employee, he will become entitled to it until he has been notified that the scheme has been changed or withdrawn (*Chequepoint UK Ltd v Radwan*[34]). There is no implied term in an employee's contract that a bonus would only be paid if the employee remained in employment or was not serving out a notice period at the date of the bonus payment (*Rutherford v Seymour Pierce Ltd*[35]). Even after a dismissal, anticipated discretionary bonus payments can be claimed on the basis that, although there was no obligation on the employer to pay, the court will assume that the discretion would have been exercised in good faith (*Clark v BET plc*, see para 3.2). Thus a refusal to make a non-contractual bonus payment will amount to a breach of contract if no reasonable employer would have exercised his discretion that way (*Clark v Nomura International*[36]). There is an implied duty on the employer to exercise his discretion in good faith, and not capriciously (*Manor House Healthcare v Hayes*[37]).

10.23 In an industry where there are high earnings and a competitive activity, a discretionary bonus scheme can be regarded as being part of the remuneration structure of the employers, and a contractual benefit to the employee, as opposed to being a mere declaration of the employer's right to pay a bonus if he so wishes. In such circumstances, the employee is entitled to a bona fide and rational exercise of the discretion by the employer in relation to the bonus scheme, and if the employer fails to do so, the employee is entitled to be compensated in respect of that failure (*Cantor Fitzgerald International v Horkulak*[38]).

10.24 A problem sometime arises as to whether or not a bonus (contractual or discretionary) should be paid to a woman who is on maternity leave. The general principle was laid down by the European Court in *Lewen v Denda*[39] that where a bonus is payable in respect of work done, an employer is entitled to make a pro rata reduction in respect of the period of absence during maternity leave. She is entitled to a contractual bonus for the periods when she is at work, and also in respect of the compulsory maternity leave period, but a pro rata deduction for periods when she is not at work did not amount to unlawful sex discrimination, because s 39(6) of the Equality Act excluded benefits that consisted of payments of money when the provision of those benefits was regulated by the woman's contract of employment (*Hoyland v Asda Stores Ltd*[40]).

---

[32] 2007 IDS Brief 835.
[33] [1967] 1 QB 278, [1966] 3 All ER 683, [1966] 3 WLR 706, 1 KIR 312, 110 Sol Jo 770, CA.
[34] Unreported, 15 September 2000.   [35] [2010] IRLR 606, [2010] EWHC 375 (QB).
[36] [2000] IRLR 766, 651 IRLB 17.   [37] EAT 1196/99.   [38] [2004] IRLR 942, CA.
[39] *Lewen v Dender* [2000] IRLR 67.
[40] [2006] CSIH 21, 2006 SC 550, 2006 SLT 524, [2006] IRLR 468, 2006 GWD 14–263.

E. **Duty of confidentiality**

10.25 Just as there is a duty on employees not to disclose confidential information about the employer's business (see para 10.69) so there is a similar duty on an employer not to disclose to third persons confidential information about the employee. This duty does not depend on any express or implied term of the contract (*Lord Advocate v Scotsman Publications Ltd*[41] per Lord Couldsfield). In *Dalgleish v Lothian and Borders Police Board*,[42] the employers held the names and addresses of all their employees. They were asked to provide this information to a local authority, for the purpose of discovering the identity of persons who had not paid the poll tax. The claimants sought an interim injunction restraining the employers from disclosing this information, which was granted. The information was not in the public domain, and was given by the employees to the employers for the purpose of the employment relationship, and for no other purpose. Hence it retained a characteristic of being confidential information, which could not be disclosed without the consent of the employees.

10.26 The EC Data Protection Directive (95/46/EC) requires member states to enact laws designed to protect the rights to privacy with respect to the processing of personal data. The Data Protection Act 1998 defined 'data' as information which is being processed by means of equipment operating automatically in response to instructions given for that purpose, or is recorded as part of a relevant filing system, or forms part of an accessible record (including health records). An employer who records such data must comply with the eight data principles, set out in the schedules to the Act, and if he fails to do so, he may have to compensate employees who suffer as a result. Further, before processing computer records containing personal data and certain other types of data, this must be included in a notification to the Information Commissioner.

10.27 Under the Data Protection Act 1998 workers have a right to have a copy of any information that an organisation has on them, and may apply to the court to obtain an order requiring a data controller to correct inaccurate information thereon, and seek compensation where damage or distress has been caused. The Act created the post of Information Commissioner, who has produced an Employment Practices Code which give guidance on how employment matters can be dealt with under the provisions of the Data Protection Act. The Code is in four parts, ie (a) Recruitment and Selection, (b) Employment Records, (c) Monitoring at Work, and (d) Information about Workers' Health. The Code itself is not legally binding, and any enforcement action has to be based on a breach of the Act. However, the relevant benchmarks would be cited by the Commissioner in such proceedings, and a disregard of those requirements is likely to mean that an employer does not comply with the Act.

10.28 Part 1 of the Code deals with advertising, applications and verifications, shortlisting and interviews of applications, pre-employment vetting, and retention of recruitment records.

10.29 Part 2 of the Code deals with procedures and penalties for storing personal data about employees and job applicants, as well as the processes for subject access requests.

10.30 Part 3 of the Code deals with monitoring at work. It covers the use of CCTV cameras, automatic checking software to monitor the use or misuse of e-mails, recording

---

[41] 1988 SLT 490, Ct of Sess; aff'd sub nom *Lord Advocate v Scotsman Publications Ltd* [1990] 1 AC 812, [1989] 2 All ER 852, [1989] 3 WLR 358, 1989 SC (HL) 122, 1989 SLT 705, [1989] NLJR 971.
[42] [1991] IRLR 422, 1992 SLT 721, Ct of Sess.

telephone calls, and videoing workers who are on sickness absence to ensure that they are not, in fact, malingering. Since a balance must be drawn between the worker's right to privacy and the employer's monitoring requirements, workers must be clearly informed of the purpose of those arrangements, and the employer must be satisfied that the particular arrangement is justified by the benefits which will ensure. The decision whether to monitor or not should be made by a senior member of staff, and it should be done with a minimum of intrusiveness, with spot checks and annual audits being preferred to continuous monitoring. All employees should, as far as possible, be treated equally.

10.31 Part 4 is entitled 'Information about workers' health' and covers such topics as occupational health schemes, medical examinations and testing, drug and alcohol testing, and genetic testing. Collecting and holding information about a worker's health may be intrusive, but may be done with a clear purpose and justified by real benefits.

F. Duty to indemnify

10.32 Any expenses reasonably incurred by the employee in the performance of his contract ought properly to be met by the employer. Normally, one would expect express agreement to this effect, for example, travelling or lodging allowances, but circumstances do arise when an employee spends his own money in pursuance of his employer's business, and it is submitted that he is entitled to be reimbursed. More difficult is the situation which arises when the employee commits a wrongful act. If this was done for the employer's business, and was authorised, or if the employee was acting under his employer's orders, then the employee is entitled to be indemnified for any personal loss he suffers.

10.33 For example, if an employer requires an employee to take out the firm's van, which has a defective tyre, and the employee is consequently fined, then it is reasonable to expect the employer to reimburse the amount, even though he may be prosecuted in addition. But if the work can be done in a lawful or unlawful manner, and the employee chose the latter option, the employer would not be required to reimburse such expenditure. For example, if the employee, in order to deliver some goods, parks illegally, then unless he was told to perform his work in this manner, he must bear any subsequent fine himself. In *Gregory v Ford*,[43] the claimant was injured due to the negligent driving of the defendant, whose employer did not have a valid third-party insurance policy as required by the Road Traffic Act 1988. It was held that there was an implied term of the contract that the employer would not require the employee to do an unlawful act, and therefore the employer should indemnify the employee in respect of the damages which were awarded to the claimant. In *Re Famatina Development Corpn Ltd*,[44] a consulting engineer employed by the company was asked to prepare a report on the conduct of the managing director. The latter brought an action for an alleged libel, which the engineer defended. It was held that he was entitled to be indemnified by the company for his costs in defending the action, for he had been requested by his directors to make the report, which was therefore in the course of his duties as an employee.

G. Duty to insure

10.34 In respect of work activities taking place within the United Kingdom, an employer is obliged to take out compulsory employers' liability insurance, for the benefit of his employees of at least £5m (Employers' Liability (Compulsory Insurance) Regulations 1998). However, an employer owes no duty in tort to any employee who is working abroad

---

[43] [1951] 1 All ER 121.
[44] [1914] 2 Ch 271, 83 LJ Ch 712; on appeal [1914] 2 Ch 271, 64 LJ Ch 48, 30 TLR 696, CA.

to take out appropriate insurance cover against special risks, or to advise the employee to take out his own cover. In *Reid v Rush & Tompkins Group plc* (see paras 2.123 and 3.52), the claimant worked for the defendants in Ethiopia. He received severe injuries in a road accident, which was the fault of the other driver, for whom the defendants were not responsible. The claimant was unable to obtain compensation from the other driver, as there is no third-party insurance in Ethiopia, and so he claimed damages from his employers. His statement of claim was struck out. An employer does not owe a duty to inform or advise on the potential danger of suffering economic loss in the form of uncompensated injuries.

H. **References**

10.35 In the absence of any express contractual obligation, the general rule is that an employer is under no legal duty to provide an employee or an ex-employee with a reference (*Gallear v JF Watson & Son Ltd*[45]) although in *Spring v Guardian Assurance plc* (see para 10.38) Lord Woolf suggested that there may be circumstances in which it is necessary to imply a term into a contract of employment that the employer would provide the employee with a reference, particularly in those areas of employment where it is normal practice to require a reference from a previous employer before employment is offered, eg in the financial services industry. An employer who does provide a reference about an existing employee who is seeking employment with another employer is under an obligation to ensure that it is fair and reasonable, and a failure to do so may amount to a breach of the implied duty of trust and confidence entitling the employee to resign and claim constructive dismissal. In *TSB Bank plc v Harris*[46] the employers sent a reference to a prospective employer about the employee which was factually true, but potentially misleading. Thus it stated that there were a number of complaints against her which were outstanding, but these complaints had never been drawn to her attention, and she had never had an opportunity to comment on them or to give her explanation. Her claim for constructive dismissal was upheld, even though she was considering leaving in any case. There is a difference between leaving without a job to go to and leaving in order to go to another job.

10.36 But although the duty is to provide a reference which is in substance fair, true and accurate, it does not have to be full and comprehensive in every case. In *Bartholomew v London Borough of Hackney*[47] the local authority commenced disciplinary proceedings against the claimant, in connection with alleged irregularities. Eventually, a settlement was reached whereby the claimant took voluntary severance, and the disciplinary action was terminated. Subsequently, in response to a request for a reference, the employers stated that at the time of leaving their employment, the claimant was under suspension, disciplinary action had been commenced, but this lapsed on the claimant's departure from the employment. The claimant claimed that the employers were in breach of their legal duty of care, because the reference, although factually correct, was unfair. The Court of Appeal dismissed his claim. Although the form of the reference might have been improved upon in some respects it was not unfair, inaccurate or false. The employers also owed a duty to the recipients of the reference not to be unfair or to mislead. The only duty on the employer is to take reasonable care not to give misleading information, not to make a selective provision of information, or make comments which could give rise to a false or misleading inference in the mind of the recipient (*Kidd v AXA Equity and Law Life Assurance Society plc*[48]). The employer should not, in a reference, deal with matters which have not been put to the

---

[45] [1979] IRLR 306, EAT.   [46] [2000] IRLR 157, EAT.
[47] [1999] IRLR 246, CA.   [48] [2000] IRLR 301.

ex-employee, and which he has not had a fair opportunity of rebutting following a proper investigation (*Cox v Sun Alliance Life Ltd*[49]).

10.37 While, as a general rule, there is no obligation on an employer to provide a reference for an ex-employee, the situation is different if the reason for the failure or refusal was an act of unlawful discrimination under the Equality Act 2010 or the whistle-blowing provisions of ERA (see para 10.74). The Equality Act now provides that it is unlawful to discriminate against a person by subjecting him/her to a detriment, where the discrimination arises out of or is closely connected with the relevant relationship. Thus, if the reason for a failure to provide a reference was because a woman had brought a claim alleging unfair maternity dismissal, this would be an act of unlawful discrimination (*Coote v Granada Hospitality Ltd*, see para 4.42). On the other hand if the refusal was based on other considerations, no victimisation has occurred (*Chief Constable of West Yorkshire v Khan*, see para 4.38). Where a an employer has victimised a former employee by giving her an adverse reference because she had previously brought discrimination proceedings against it, the employer can be liable for loss of earnings if a prospective job offer is withdrawn as a result of the reference. In *Bullimore v Pothecary Witham Weld Solicitors (No. 2)*,[50] in answer to a question about how the employment had ended, her manager referred not simply to the fact that she had resigned but also gratuitously to the fact that she had brought discrimination proceedings against the firm.

10.38 Several pitfalls can occur when providing a reference about an ex-employee to a prospective employer. First, a derogatory reference may expose the giver of the reference to an action for defamation. This may be defended on the ground that the statements made were true, or, if untrue, were made on an occasion when the law confers qualified privilege, and the statements were made without malice, in the sense of an improper motive. Next, the employer owes a duty of care to the ex-employee to ensure that the reference is not prepared carelessly or negligently, and will be consequently liable for damages in respect of any economic loss which flows from the negligent misstatement (*Spring v Guardian Assurance plc*, para 10.35). In this case, Lord Slynn suggested that the employers could avoid any liability by making it clear to the ex-employee that they will only provide a reference if he accepts that there will be a disclaimer of liability to him and to the recipient.

10.39 On the other hand, to give a commendatory reference about a prospective employee which is untrue, and which is relied upon by a subsequent employer to his detriment, may well lead to an action based on deceit or negligent misstatement, unless the reference is qualified by a disclaimer of responsibility (*Hedley Byrne & Co Ltd v Heller & Partners Ltd*[51]).

10.40 A further problem associated with the provision of a reference can arise in dismissal cases. In *Castledine v Rothwell Engineering Ltd*,[52] one of the reasons given by the employer for dismissing the firm's buyer was that he was incapable of performing his job adequately. The tribunal found this difficult to reconcile with the reference given by the employer, which stated that the employee 'had carried out his duties satisfactorily, often under difficult conditions'. Not surprisingly, the tribunal found that the employee had been unfairly dismissed! And in *Haspell v Restron and Johnson Ltd*[53] the respondents gave a reference which was laudatory of the claimant. It was held that they were estopped from relying on criticisms of her performance as a reason for her dismissal.

[49] [2001] EWCA Civ 1010, [2001] IRLR 448, [2001] All ER (D) 108 (May).
[50] [2011] IRLR 18.
[51] [1962] 1 QB 396, [1961] 3 All ER 891, [1961] 3 WLR 1225, 105 Sol Jo 910, CA; aff'd [1964] AC 465, [1963] 2 All ER 575, [1963] 3 WLR 101, [1963] 1 Lloyd's Rep 485, 107 Sol Jo 454, HL.
[52] [1973] IRLR 99.   [53] [1976] IRLR 50.

I. **The right to privacy**

10.41 There are many occasions during the performance of the contract of employment when an employer will be monitoring the employee's performance, as a matter of routine. The problem arises when such actions become intrusive into an employee's private life. For example, an employer may wish to monitor the employee's telephone calls, in order to assess performance, ensure that quality standards are met, that customer satisfaction is achieved, and provide a valuable record in the event of a subsequent dispute with customers or suppliers, etc. But what happens when the employee's telephone call is of a personal nature? Does this amount to an unwarranted infringement of his right to privacy?

10.42 The routine use of e-mail and the internet by employees during working hours will exacerbate the problem. The temptation for employees to use these facilities for their own purposes is ever-increasing, whether it be for booking holidays, purchasing goods for private use, playing games, or downloading pornography! The questions must be thus posed: can the employer (a) implement surveillance, (b) listen in and/or record such activities and (c) take disciplinary action in the event of suspected misuse? Clearly, a balance must be drawn between the employee's right to privacy on the one hand, and the legitimate interests of the employer in ensuring that the employee is doing his work properly, and not abusing facilities provided.

10.43 So far as the law is concerned, Art 8 of the European Convention on Human Rights provides:

(a) Everyone has the right to respect for his private and family life, his home and his correspondence.

(b) There shall be no interference by a public authority with the exercise of this right except such as is in accordance with the law and is necessary in a democratic society in the interests of national security, public safety or the economic well-being of the country, for the prevention of disorder or crime, for the protection of health or morals, or for the protection of the rights and freedoms of others.

10.44 It will be recalled (see para 1.104) that the Human Rights Act 1998 is designed to give effect to the provisions of the European Convention, and although this only applies to public authorities, the courts and tribunals use it as an aid in the decision-making process when dealing with the private employer.

10.45 The right to privacy was an issue in *Halford v United Kingdom* (see para 1.107), where the claimant, who was a senior police officer, alleged that she had been turned down for promotion because of her sex, and brought a claim of sex discrimination. She also alleged that her telephone calls at work and at home were being intercepted for the purpose of obtaining information to be used against her in the tribunal proceedings. The sex discrimination case was settled, but she brought further proceedings in the European Court of Human Rights, claiming that the interception of her telephone calls was an infringement of her right to privacy. Her claim succeeded. The Court held that telephone calls made from business premises may be covered by the notion of private life and correspondence within the meaning of Art 8 of the Convention. The Court refused to accept the notion that an employer could, without prior knowledge of the employee, monitor calls made by the employee on telephones provided by the employer.

10.46 The Regulation of Investigatory Powers Act 2000 makes it a criminal offence, without lawful authority, to intercept a communication in the course of its transmission by post or by a public or private telecommunication system. However, interceptions may be

lawful if the sender or intended recipient has consented to the interception, the intercep-
tor has a warrant (or, in certain circumstances, without a warrant, eg to comply with an
EU Convention on Mutual Assistance in Criminal Matters). Interception is also permitted
when done by the postal or telecommunications service provider for purposes connected
with the operations of the service.

10.47 There is no problem if the person making or receiving the communication consents
to its interception, but the Regulation of Investigatory Powers Act 2000 enables employees
to take legal action in tort against an employer whom they believe has unlawfully intercepted a telecommunication made to a third party on the employer's network. However,
such an interception is permissible under the Telecommunications (Lawful Business
Practice) (Interception of Communications) Regulations 2000, which were passed to give
effect to the EU Telecoms Data Protection Directive (97/66/EC). By virtue of these regulations, employers may legitimately monitor or record all telecommunications transmitted
over their systems, without the consent of the persons making those communications, for
the following purposes, namely, to establish the existence of facts, to ensure compliance
with regulatory or self-regulatory practices or procedures, for quality control purposes,
for the purpose of detection or prevention of crime, to ensure the effectiveness of their
telecommunications systems, or to check on whether the communications in question
were relevant to the employer's business. The Information Commissioner has produced
a Code of Practice on this topic (see Regulation of Investigatory Powers (Interception of
Communications: Code of Practice) Order 2002).

J. Duty to ensure the employee's safety

10.48 The law on compensation for injuries at work will be considered in Chapter 11.
Undoubtedly the most important aspect of the employer's duty which is implied by law is
the duty to take reasonable care to ensure the safety of his employees.

Implied obligations of the employee

A. Duty of faithful service

10.49 Since the relationship between the employer and employee is one of trust and
confidence the law implies into the contract of employment the term that every employee
shall serve his employer faithfully. This is a fundamental obligation, and any serious or
persistent course of conduct which is inconsistent with that obligation may well amount
to a breach of contract. Examples which readily spring to mind include persistent lateness,
incompetence, wilful neglect and theft of the employer's property. A strike, a go-slow, a
work-to-rule, a sit-in, being contrary to the fundamental nature of the contract – which
is to work in return for a reward – are also within this category, and an employee may
be dismissed for them (see Chapter 21). The employee undertakes to perform his duties
carefully and competently, with due regard for the interests of the employer. In *Secretary
of State for Employment v Associated Society of Locomotive Engineers and Firemen* (see
para 3.90) Roskill LJ thought that it was an implied term that each employee would
not, in obeying lawful instructions, seek to carry them out in a manner which had the
effect of disrupting the employer's business. Whether the 'implied term' theory can stand
up to analysis is another matter; all members of the Court of Appeal were prepared to
import some form of obligation of fidelity arising from the very nature of the contract of
employment.

10.50 In *Sim v Rotherham Metropolitan Borough Council* (para 3.50) it was held that the contractual obligations of a person employed in a professional capacity were those defined by the nature of his profession and the obligations incumbent on those who follow that profession.

10.51 If an employee fails to perform part of his duties, but indicates that he is prepared to perform the remainder, the employer may make it clear that he is not prepared to accept such partial performance, and may lawfully refuse to pay the employee the whole of the remuneration due (*Wiluszynski v London Borough of Tower Hamlets*, see para 8.23).

10.52 If the employee is in breach of contract, the employer may seek to recover expenditure incurred or wasted as a result of the breach. Thus in *Anglia Television Ltd v Reed* an actor agreed to play a leading role in a film. He subsequently repudiated the agreement and refused to perform. The company abandoned production of the film, and sued for the expenditure that had been wasted. It was held that both pre- and post-contractual expenditure was within the contemplation of the parties that would be wasted, and the company was entitled to recover their loss (see also *Tullett Prebon Group Ltd v Ghaleb El-Hajjali*, para 3.6).

10.53 A wrongful act which does not necessarily benefit the employee may still be a breach of fidelity if it is harmful to the employer's business. In *Dalton v Burton's Gold Medal Biscuits Ltd*[54] the employee was dismissed for falsifying the clock-card of a fellow employee, and this was held to be a fair dismissal. A more difficult situation arises if there is a conflict between the duty of fidelity on the one hand, and an obligation the employee owes by virtue of his membership of a professional organisation on the other. It is submitted that there is an implied term that the employer will not require an employee to act in a manner contrary to professional ethics, and that this would override the duty to the employer.

10.54 It is a breach of the employee's duty of faithful service to compete with the employer while he is still employed but it is not a breach if an employee indicates that he intends to take steps at some future date which will enable him to compete after the employment has ceased, in the absence of any restrictive covenant to that effect (see para 19.29). In other words, there is a distinction between an intention to set up in competition with the employer in the future, and competing with the employer while still employed. In *Adamson v B & L Cleaning Services Ltd*,[55] the employee was a foreman employed by a firm of cleaning contractors. The firm had a cleaning contract worth £60,000 per year. Tenders were invited for renewal, and the employee indicated that he had requested that his name be placed on the tender list. When the employers were informed of this, they asked him to sign an undertaking not to seek to obtain any contract for industrial cleaning while still in the firm's employment, but he refused to do so, and was dismissed. The dismissal was held to be fair. He was in breach of his duty of faithful service, which justified the termination of his employment. In *Ward Evans Financial Services Ltd v Fox*[56] the employee's contract of employment provided that he would act at all times in the best interests of his employer. He purchased an 'off the shelf' company, which did not commence trading until after his employment had ended, and he also informed existing clients about the new company. It was held that he had acted in breach of his duty of fidelity. It is a breach of the duty of fidelity for an employee to e-mail confidential company information to her personal e-mail account, even where it is done

---

[54] [1974] IRLR 45, NIRC.   [55] [1995] IRLR 193, EAT.
[56] [2001] EWCA Civ 1243, [2002] IRLR 120, [2001] All ER (D) 415 (Jul).

to protect her position in forthcoming litigation against the employer, and because of concerns about compliance in order to make a report to the regulator (*Brandeaux (Advisers) UK Ltd v Chadwick*).[57]

10.55 An employee who learns of confidential matters relating to competition from a prospective employer is not bound to pass the information to his existing employer, as he would then be in breach of confidence to the new employer. In *Customer Systems Plc v Ranson*,[58] the High Court followed *Tullett Prebon v BGC Brokers*[59] and said that a duty of fidelity to a current employer does not necessarily defeat the duty of confidence to a new employer.

10.56 As a general principle, an employee's duty of fidelity does not prevent him from competing with a former employer once he has left his employment, and the freedom to do so carries with it the freedom to prepare for future activities that the employee intends to pursue once he has left his employment (*Helmet Integrated Systems Ltd v Tunnard*[60]). But preparatory activities undertaken by directors or senior employees are more likely to constitute breaches of fidelity and fiduciary duties (*Shepherds Investment Ltd v Walters*[61]). In any particular case, it will be necessary to identify the particular duties undertaken by the employee and to ask whether, in all the circumstances, he has placed himself in a position where he must act solely in the interests of his employer (*Nottingham University v Fishel*[62]).

10.57 An employee must not make a secret profit out of his position of trust for his own benefit, without the knowledge or informed consent of the employer, and to do so will amount to a breach of contract which will justify summary dismissal (*Neary v Dean of Westminster*[63]). If the employee is in breach of a fiduciary obligation, then, if the normal remedies of damages or injunction are not sufficient, an action for an account of profits may be brought (*A-G v Blake*[64]). It is probable that this rule also applies to overpayments of wages or expenses received by the employee (see para 8.23). Indeed, it is possible to argue that if an employee knows that he has been overpaid, and deliberately keeps the money, or spends it after he realises that he has been overpaid, then he has committed a criminal offence (*A-G's Reference (No 1 of 1983)*[65]).

B. Duty to obey lawful and reasonable orders

10.58 The employee undertakes to obey all lawful and reasonable orders. In *United Kingdom Atomic Energy Authority v Claydon*,[66] the employee's contract required him to work anywhere in the United Kingdom. He refused to transfer to another base, and was dismissed. The order was clearly lawful and reasonable, for it was within the express terms of the contract. In

---

[57] [2011] IRLR 224, [2010] EWHC 3241 (QB).   [58] [2011] EWHC 3304.   [59] [2011] EWCA 131.
[60] [2006] FSR 41, PCC; aff'd [2006] EWCA Civ 1735, [2007] IRLR 126, [2007] FSR 16.
[61] [2006] EWHC 836 (Ch), [2007] 2 BCLC 202, [2007] IRLR 110, [2007] FSR 15, (2006) 150 SJLB 536.
[62] [2000] ICR 1462, [2000] IRLR 471, [2000] ELR 385, [2001] RPC 367, [2000] All ER (D) 269.
[63] [1999] IRLR 288.
[64] [1997] Ch 84, [1996] 3 All ER 903, [1996] 3 WLR 741, [1996] FSR 727, [1996] EMLR 382; revsd [1998] Ch 439, [1998] 1 All ER 833, [1998] 2 WLR 805, [1998] EMLR 309, [1998] 04 LS Gaz R 33, [1998] NLJR 15, 142 Sol Jo LB 35, CA; aff'd on other grounds [2001] 1 AC 268, [2000] 2 All ER (Comm) 487, [2000] EMLR 949, [2000] NLJR 1230, [2000] 32 LS Gaz R 37, 144 Sol Jo LB 242, [2001] 1 LRC 260, [2000] IP & T 1261, [2000] All ER (D) 1074, HL.
[65] [1985] QB 182, [1984] 3 All ER 369, [1984] 3 WLR 686, 79 Cr App Rep 288, [1984] Crim LR 570, 128 Sol Jo 596, [1984] LS Gaz R 2458, CA.
[66] [1974] ICR 128, [1974] IRLR 6, NIRC.

Pepper v Webb,[67] a gardener used some choice expletives accompanied by words which indicated that he had no intention of obeying his employer's instructions, and it was this refusal, rather than the language which accompanied it, which was held to be the breach of contract.

10.59 But if the employee can show that the order was unlawful, he need not obey it. In *Morrish v Henlys (Folkestone) Ltd*[68] the employee refused to falsify some records, and was dismissed. It was held that he was entitled to refuse to obey an unlawful order, and the dismissal was unfair. Whether an order is unreasonable may well be a question of fact in each case. In *Walmsley v UDEC Refrigeration Ltd*[69] the claimant was dismissed after refusing to work in Wexford in Eire on the grounds that it was a hotbed of IRA activity. He could not substantiate these allegations, and it was held that he had refused to obey a reasonable order. Had he been told to go to Belfast, a refusal may well have been justified, for this might involve a serious risk which was not contemplated at the time of the formation of the contract (*Wicks v Charles A Smethurst Ltd*[70]). An employee need not obey an order which would expose him to the risk of danger to life or liberty (*Ottoman Bank v Chakarian*[71]).

10.60 To determine whether or not an order is reasonable, principles of good industrial relations may be taken into account. Thus in *Payne v Spook Erection Ltd*,[72] a foreman was instructed to compile a merit table each week, listing the performance of 25 employees, and to send warning letters to those whose name appeared at the bottom of the list. As he did not see all the employees each week, he refused to operate the system, as he thought that it would be based largely on guesswork. He was told that unless he operated the system he would be dismissed, but he refused to comply. An employment tribunal, although they had little sympathy with the system, held the dismissal to be fair, but the decision was reversed by the EAT. In considering whether or not a decision of an employment tribunal was perverse, matters of good industrial relations could be considered. The weekly merit rating system was clearly unfair, and to dismiss the foreman for refusing to operate an unreasonable order was also unfair.

10.61 Difficulty is frequently caused by loose contractual expressions relating to overtime. If this is stated to be voluntary, then the employee is entitled to refuse. If it is stated to be worked by arrangement, then again, it becomes a matter for negotiation. But if it is clear that some overtime is to be worked, and the negotiations are merely about the details, the refusal may well be unreasonable, particularly if this is designed to bring improper pressure to bear on the employer (*Pengilly v North Devon Farmers Ltd*[73]). As we have seen (in Chapter 3) a refusal to accept a demotion or a change in contractual terms is not necessarily unreasonable, but refusal to obey instructions which are within the contract may be unreasonable. In *Connor v Halfords Ltd*[74] the employee was obliged to 'obey all orders and instructions received from the directors'. He was dismissed because he refused to go on a training course, and the dismissal was held to be fair.

10.62 An employee who refuses to obey a lawful and reasonable order, which was given in good faith and without any ulterior motive, is in repudiatory breach of contract, which the employer may accept by dismissing him without notice or pay in lieu of notice (*Macari v Celtic Football and Athletic Co Ltd*[75]).

---

[67] [1969] 2 All ER 216, [1969] 1 WLR 514, 113 Sol Jo 186, CA.
[68] [1973] 2 All ER 137, [1973] ICR 482, [1973] IRLR 61, 8 ITR 167, NIRC.   [69] [1972] IRLR 80.
[70] [1973] IRLR 327.   [71] [1930] AC 277, 99 LJPC 97, 142 LT 465, PC.
[72] [1984] IRLR 219, EAT.   [73] [1973] IRLR 41, EAT.   [74] [1972] IRLR 109.
[75] [1999] IRLR 787, 2000 SLT 80, 2000 SCLR 209.

10.63 However, it does not follow that an employee who refuses to obey a lawful order may automatically be dismissed, any more than it can be said that an employee cannot be dismissed if he refuses to obey an order which is outside his contractual obligations, for the strict legal rights are only relevant in considering the 'lawfulness' of the dismissal, but not its fairness. Two employment tribunal decisions will illustrate this point. In *Wilson v IDR Construction Ltd*[76] the claimant was contractually bound to move from site to site in accordance with management instructions. He was asked to move to a new site, but refused, as his wife was ill, and he was having difficulty with his car. Although his refusal to obey a lawful and reasonable order would have entitled the employers to dismiss him at common law, the tribunal held that this was not an invariable rule so far as unfair dismissal law was concerned. The employers should have given him a chance to explain his refusal, taken into account the genuineness of the reason, the fact that he had never refused to change sites before, and that his refusal related only to that one day. In the circumstances, the dismissal was held to be unfair. On the other hand, in *Robinson v Flitwick Frames Ltd*[77] the claimant was dismissed following his refusal to work overtime, although he was not contractually bound to do so. All the other employees in his section worked the necessary overtime, and the claimant gave no satisfactory explanation for his refusal. The tribunal held that his dismissal was for 'some other substantial reason' and that the employers had acted reasonably in the circumstances, for it would have caused considerable problems if the claimant had to be employed on terms different from the other employees (see also *Farrant v Woodroffe School*, paras 3.26 and 17.156).

10.64 If the employees are not prepared to give an undertaking that they will desist from future disruptive conduct, an employer may suspend them from work until they do so, and the employees, though willing to work, will not be entitled to remuneration for the period of suspension (*British Telecommunications plc v Ticehurst*[78]).

C. **Duty to use skill and care**

10.65 The employee undertakes to perform his work competently, using reasonable skill and care. This, of course, must be combined with the employer's duty to provide all necessary assistance, etc (see para 10.13), but if the employer has done all he can, then a dismissal for incompetence will usually be fair. Also, the employee undertakes to take proper care of the employer's property. In *Superlux v Plaisted*[79] the employee negligently allowed some of his employer's property to be stolen from a van, for which he was held responsible. On the other hand, a tribunal has held that an employee who negligently lost the company cat should receive some disciplinary action short of a dismissal! For a dismissal to be warranted, the act of negligence must be a serious one (*Comerford v Swel Foods Ltd*[80]) or a series of minor acts of neglect (*Lowndes v Specialist Heavy Engineering Ltd*,[81] para 17.86). It is an implied term of the contract of employment that an employee will exercise skill and care in the performance of his duties, and a breach of that term entitles the employer to claim damages in respect of the negligent performance of the contract. In *Janata Bank v Ahmed*,[82] the employee worked as a bank manager. It was alleged that he had been negligent in the way he carried out his duties, and after his dismissal, the bank issued a writ claiming £34,640 damages. The Court of Appeal upheld the claim. He had failed to exercise proper skill and

---

[76] [1975] IRLR 260.   [77] [1975] IRLR 261.

[78] [1992] ICR 383, [1992] 15 LS Gaz R 32, 136 Sol Jo LB 96, sub nom *Ticehurst and Thompson v British Telecommunications plc* [1992] IRLR 219, CA.

[79] [1958] CLY 195, *Times*, 12 December, CA.   [80] [1972] IRLR 17.

[81] [1977] ICR 1, [1976] IRLR 246, 8 BLR 76, EAT.   [82] [1981] ICR 791, [1981] IRLR 457, CA.

care, as implied by his contract. It is irrelevant that the cause of action arises in contract or in tort (see *Lister v Romford Ice and Cold Storage Co Ltd*[83]).

D. Secret bribes and commissions

10.66 The employee undertakes not to accept any secret bribes or commissions or gifts, or any reward in respect of his work other than from his employer. This rule applies even though the employee is in no way influenced by the favours he has received, for there is always the possibility that there will be a suspicion that his conduct has been influenced, or that it might be affected in the future. Tips, however, are a recognised method of being paid, and do not constitute a bribe which must be disclosed. An employee can only serve one employer, and it will be inconsistent with his obligation of faithful service to accept anything from another person in respect of things done within the performance of his work. In *Boston Deep Sea Fishing and Ice Co v Ansell*[84] the defendant was a managing director of the claimant company. He placed orders for supplies with other companies, from whom he received a commission. It was held that his dismissal was justified. It is a violation of the duty of honest and faithful service for an employee to have an interest in a firm which is transacting business with his employer without disclosing that interest, and on discovering the facts, the employer is entitled to dismiss the employee summarily (*Horcal Ltd v Gatland*[85]).

10.67 The employer may also take steps to recover the amount of the bribe from the employee, and refuse to pay certain benefits which may be due (see *Tesco Stores Ltd v Pook*,[86] para 10.95).

10.68 The rule is easy to state, but in practice it may be hard to apply, for there is no simple line between acts which are part of social or business intercourse and bribery. No one is going to quibble if a salesman offers a cigarette to the firm's buyer, or if two people go for a working lunch at a modest cafeteria. A hundred cigarettes or a slap-up lunch at an expensive restaurant may fall into a different category. Some firms may anticipate this problem by laying down the standards of conduct expected from those in a position of authority who may be affected by the rule. Employees may be warned not to accept gifts from suppliers, not to accept hospitality which might have a significant value, or to allow others to pay travel or hotel bills on their behalf.

(The issue of bribery has now been supplemented by legislation in the form of the Bribery Act 2010. While the details of the statute are outside the scope of this book, suffice it to say that it makes it a criminal offence for a person to bribe (s 1 active bribery) or receive a bribe (s 2 passive bribery). The Act has extraterritorial application, so that a bribe to a foreign public official can be prosecuted in the UK (s 6). It also makes it an offence for a commercial organisation to fail to prevent a bribe (s 7), but there is a defence if it can show that adequate procedures have been put in place to prevent bribery if these are necessary. Guidance on the Act can be found on the Justice website.)

E. Confidential information

10.69 There is a general rule that during the subsistence of the employment relationship, the employee must not disclose any confidential information about the employer's business

---

[83] [1957] AC 555, [1957] 1 All ER 125, [1957] 2 WLR 158, [1956] 2 Lloyd's Rep 505, 121 JP 98, 101 Sol Jo 106, HL.
[84] (1888) 39 Ch D 339, [1886–90] All ER Rep 65, 59 LT 345, CA.
[85] [1983] IRLR 459, [1983] BCLC 60, 133 NLJ 1133; on appeal [1984] IRLR 288, [1984] BCLC 549, CA.
[86] [2004] IRLR 618, EAT.

to an unauthorised person. To do so will amount to a breach of contract, and a third party who induces an employee to break his contract of employment in this way may also be sued (see *Bents Brewery Co Ltd v Hogan*,[87] para 23.37). To determine whether or not the information is indeed confidential, three requirements must be satisfied, namely:

(a) the information must have the necessary quality of confidence;

(b) the information must have been imparted to the employee in circumstances which import an obligation of confidence; and

(c) there must have been an unauthorised use of the information to the detriment of the employer (*A-G v Guardian Newspapers (No 2)*[88]).

10.70 The disclosure of information such as the profitability of the business, new models or designs, modes of operation, etc, could seriously harm the employer's business. Thus in *Foster v Scaffolding (GB) Ltd*[89] the employee gave confidential information to a rival company which was to the disadvantage of his employer, and he was held to have been fairly dismissed. The unauthorised disclosure of trade secrets would also fall within this rule (*Lancashire Fires Ltd v s A Lyons & Co Ltd*[90]), and indeed information may well be so highly confidential as to amount to a trade secret (*PSM International plc v Whitehouse*[91]). But an employee's skill and knowledge are his own possessions, and are not subject to any such restrictions (*Printers and Finishers Ltd v Holloway*[92]).

10.71 It has been held that the employee is not released from this obligation even when the information has been obtained or published by a third party (*Cranleigh Precision Engineering Ltd v Bryant*[93]) although it seems likely that in such circumstances the quality of confidence has been lost (*A-G v Guardian Newspapers (No 2)*, para 10.69). If, however an employee starts a new business with other employees who misuse confidential information without the first employee's knowledge, then she is not liable for that breach of confidence as she did not breach it (*Vestergaard Frandsen v Bestnet Europe Ltd*[94]).

10.72 If an employer discovers that an unidentifiable employee is leaking information to the press, he may be able to obtain a court order which will lead him to identify the person concerned (generally known as a 'whistleblower'). Clearly, there is a conflict between the public interest which requires that the press shall protect the identity of its sources and the right of an employer to identify a disloyal employee, particularly when it is likely that that employee may disclose other sensitive information. In *Camelot Group plc v Centaur Communications Ltd*[95] the Court of Appeal set out certain principles which should be applied in such cases, but stressed that the resolution of such conflicts will very much depend on the facts of each case, ie the nature of the information disclosed, whether there is an allegation of wrongdoing, whether the information would eventually be in the public domain, etc. The law does not enable the press to protect the identity of a whistleblower in all circumstances.

---

[87] [1945] 2 All ER 570.

[88] [1990] 1 AC 109, [1988] 3 All ER 545, [1988] 2 WLR 805; aff'd [1990] 1 AC 109, [1988] 3 All ER 545, [1988] 2 WLR 805, 132 Sol Jo 566, [1988] NLJR 47, CA; aff'd [1990] 1 AC 109, [1988] 3 All ER 545, [1988] 3 WLR 776, [1988] NJLR 296, [1988] LRC (Const) 938, HL.

[89] (1973) (342/73) IDS Brief 13.   [90] [1999] 30 LS Gaz R 28, CA.

[91] [1992] FSR 489, [1992] IRLR 279, CA.

[92] [1964] 3 All ER 731, [1965] 1 WLR 1, [1965] RPC 239, 109 Sol Jo 47.

[93] [1964] 3 All ER 289, [1965] 1 WLR 1293, [1966] RPC 81, 109 Sol Jo 830.

[94] [2013] UKSC 31.

[95] [1999] QB 124, [1998] 1 All ER 251, [1998] 2 WLR 379, [1998] IRLR 80, [1998] EMLR 1, [1997] 43 LS Gaz R 30, [1997] NLJR 1618, 142 Sol Jo LB 19, CA.

10.73 However, there are some important exceptions to the rule against the non-disclosure of confidential information. Thus the rule will not apply if the employee is obliged by law to disclose the information. For example, an employee is under a legal duty to give any necessary information to an inspector carrying out an examination or investigation under the Health and Safety at Work etc Act 1974 (see Chapter 11) and to produce any necessary books or documents.

F. Public interest disclosures (ERA, ss 43A–43K)

10.74 Under the provisions of the Public Interest Disclosure Act 1998 (as amended by ss 17–20 of the Enterprise and Regulatory Reform Act 2013), generally known as the 'Whistleblowers Act', or 'PIDA', which inserted ss 43A–43L into the Employment Rights Act, protection is given to a worker (a definition which is wider than that of 'employee', and indeed is wider than the definition of 'worker' contained in s 230(3), see ERA, s 43K), who makes a protected disclosure to a specified individual in prescribed circumstances. The primary aim of the Act is to encourage the resolution of concerns through proper workplace procedures, and has a more limited application to a worker who decides to go outside those procedures. The Act is not limited to cases where the disclosure relates to a wrongdoing or failure by the whistleblower's employer, but includes the disclosure made about the wrongdoing of any person or organisation (*Hibbins v Hester Way Neighbourhood Project*[96]) including a detriment suffered as a result of a disclosure made about the activities of a previous employer (*BP plc v Elstone*[97]; *Onyango v Berkeley Solicitors*[98]).

10.75 There are three conditions to be satisfied for the Act to apply, namely (i) there must be a qualifying disclosure, (ii) the qualifying disclosure must be a protected disclosure, and (iii) the worker must have been dismissed or suffered a detriment in consequence of the disclosure.

10.76 (i) A qualifying disclosure must be one of the six categories of subject matter specified in ERA, s 43B, namely, any disclosure of information which, in the reasonable belief of the worker making it, tends to show one or more of the following:

(a) that a criminal offence has been committed, is being committed or is likely to be committed;

(b) that a person has failed, is failing or is likely to fail to comply with any legal obligation to which he is subject (*Parkins v Sodexho Ltd*);[99]

(c) that a miscarriage of justice has occurred, is occurring or is likely to occur;

(d) that the health or safety of any individual has been, is being or is likely to be endangered;

(e) that the environment has been, is being or is likely to be damaged; or

(f) that information tending to show any matter falling within any one of the preceding paragraphs has been, is being or is likely to be deliberately concealed.

10.77 The standard to be used when considering the above categories is the subjective one, ie the worker does not have to prove the existence of any of the above state of affairs; he merely has to show that he had a reasonable belief that this was so. He does not have to prove that some offence has actually been committed (*Baluba v Waltham Forest College*[100]).

---

[96] [2009] 1 All ER 949, [2009] ICR 319, [2009] IRLR 198.   [97] [2010] IRLR 558.
[98] UKEAT/0407/12.   [99] [2002] IRLR 109, [2001] All ER (D) 377 (Jun), EAT.
[100] (2007) ICR 1026, (2007) IRLR 346.

Clearly, if he fails to show that he had grounds for his belief, it may well be that a tribunal would find that his belief was not reasonable.

10.78 A disclosure will not be a qualifying disclosure if the worker commits an offence by making it (eg in breach of the Official Secrets Acts), or if the information is covered by legal professional privilege. However, the substance of the disclosure can relate to matters which take place anywhere in the world.

10.79 (ii) A qualifying disclosure will be a protected disclosure if it is made in the reasonable belief of the worker making the disclosure, in the public interest, and is made in one of the six ways set out in the Act. In other words, the disclosure must be made through the appropriate channels, set out in ss 43C–43H. Four of these categories are to named persons, while the further two categories are subject to more stringent conditions. The disclosure does not actually have to be in the public interest – it is sufficient if the worker reasonably believes that it is so.

10.80 The disclosure must be made to one of the following persons:

(a) to his employer, or, where the worker reasonably believes that the relevant failure relates solely or mainly to the conduct of a person other than his employer, or any other matter for which a person other than the employer has legal responsibility, to that other person;

(b) in the course of obtaining legal advice (eg to a solicitor);

(c) where the worker's employer is an individual appointed under any enactment by a minister of the Crown, or a body any of whose members are so appointed, a disclosure made to a minister of the Crown;

(d) a disclosure to a prescribed person, and the worker reasonably believes that the relevant failure falls within the prescribed category, and the information disclosed, and any allegation made, is substantially true. The Public Interest Disclosure (Prescribed Persons) Order 1999 described the persons (and bodies) to which disclosure may be made for this purpose, and also described the matters in respect of which disclosure may be made. There are some 38 types of bodies so prescribed, including various regulatory bodies, local authorities, etc, and the matters which are the subject of a protected disclosure are generally those matters in which there is a serious public interest;

(e) in other cases, the worker must reasonably believe that the information disclosed, and any allegation contained in it, are substantially true, the disclosure is not made for personal gain, in the circumstances it was reasonable for him to make the disclosure, and it meets one of the following conditions, namely:

(i) that at the time he makes the disclosure, the worker reasonably believed that he would be subject to a detriment if he made the disclosure to his employer or to the prescribed person, or

(ii) where there is no person prescribed, the worker reasonably believes that evidence relating to the relevant failure will be concealed or destroyed if he makes the disclosure to his employer, or

(iii) the worker has previously made a disclosure to his employer or to a prescribed person of substantially the same information.

10.81 To decide whether or not it was reasonable for the worker to make the disclosure, the Act states that regard should be had to the identity of the person to whom the disclosure is made, the seriousness of the relevant failure, whether the failure is continuing or likely to occur in the future, whether the disclosure is made in breach of any duty of confidentiality owed by the employer to any other person, any action which the employer has taken which might reasonably be expected to have been taken as a result of a previous disclosure, and whether in making the disclosure to the employer the worker has complied with any procedure whose use by him was authorised by the employer;

(f) a disclosure will be protected if:

(i) the worker reasonably believes that the information disclosed, and any allegation made in it, are substantially true,

(ii) the disclosure is not made for personal gain,

(iii) the matter disclosed is of an exceptional serious nature, and

(iv) in all the circumstances, it was reasonable for the worker to make the disclosure.

10.82 A previous requirement for the disclosure to be made in good faith was removed by the ERRA 2013, although a tribunal has the power to reduce any compensation by up to 25% if it finds that a disclosure was made in bad faith. Thus when assessing compensation the whistleblower's motives for making the disclosure will be relevant. So, if he makes a disclosure because of some personal antagonism, or other improper motive, this will be evidence of a lack of good faith (*Street v Derbyshire Unemployed Workers' Centre*[101]). An employee is not protected by the whistleblowing provisions if he discloses information which he obtains by an illegal or wrongful act. In *Bolton School v Evans*[102] a teacher hacked into the school's computer system in order to demonstrate its poor security. When he was disciplined for doing so, he resigned and claimed constructive dismissal. His claim was rejected. The reason he was disciplined was not because he made a disclosure, but because he had committed an act of misconduct. There is also a distinction between giving information, which means conveying facts, and making allegations. The former comes within the whistleblowing provisions, the latter does not (*Cavendish Munro Professional Risks Management v Geduld*[103]).

10.83 (iii) A worker who makes a protected disclosure has the right not to suffer a detriment as a result of the disclosure. If he is an employee (but not a worker), he has the right not to be dismissed (or be made redundant) in consequence of the disclosure. Dismissal for whistleblowing can be a breach of the Article 10 right to freedom of expression (*Heinisch v Germany*[104]). It will also be automatically unfair to dismiss an employee because he made a protected disclosure covered by the Public Interest Disclosure Act (however the protected disclosure must be the sole or principal reason for the dismissal before it is deemed to be automatically unfair (*NHS Manchester v Fecitt*[105]). The two-year qualifying period of employment does not apply, and there is no ceiling on any compensation award. Interim relief is also available (ERA, s 128(1)(b)). If the worker is not an employee, he will have no right to complain of unfair dismissal, but if he is in fact dismissed, he can claim that this amounts to a detriment.

10.84 The ERRA introduced a vicarious liability on an employer for a detriment committed by co-workers, or an agent of the employer, on the worker who has made a protected disclosure. It is immaterial whether the detriment was done with the knowledge or approval of the employer. There is a defence for an employer who is able to show that it took all reasonable steps to prevent the detrimental treatment.

---

[101] (2007) ICR 1026, (2007) IRLR 346.

[102] [2006] IRLR 500, [2006] ELR 255, EAT; aff'd [2006] EWCA Civ 1653 [2007] ICR 641, [2007] IRLR 140, (2006) 103(46) LSG 30, (2006) 150 SJLB 1532, CA.

[103] [2010] ICR 325, [2010] IRLR 38.   [104] [2011] IRLR 922.   [105] [2011] EWCA Civ 1190.

10.85 Any agreement between the worker and his employer (including one which purports to settle legal proceedings) is void in so far as it precludes the worker from making a protected disclosure (s 43J).

G. Patents, inventions and copyright

10.86 The law relating to inventions made and patents taken out by employees was altered by the Patents Act 1977. According to s 39, an invention made by an employee shall belong to the employer if (a) it was made during the employee's normal duties, or if such duties were specifically assigned to him and in either case the circumstances were such that an invention might reasonably be expected to result from those duties, or (b) because of the employee's particular responsibilities, he has a special obligation to further the interests of the employer's undertaking (see *LIFFE Administration and Management v Pinkava*[106]). Any other invention made by an employee shall belong to him, notwithstanding any term to the contrary in the contract of employment (see *Reiss Engineering Co Ltd v Harris*[107]). Even if the invention belongs to the employer, the employee may apply to the Comptroller General of Patents (or Patents Court) for an award of compensation, which may be awarded if the patent is of outstanding benefit to the employer (having regard to the size and nature of the employer's undertaking) and it is just that compensation should be awarded. The amount of compensation should be a fair share of the benefit which the employer has derived, taking into account a number of factors, including (a) the nature of the employee's duties, his remuneration, etc, (b) the effort and skill provided by others, including any advice and assistance received from other employees, (c) the contribution made by the employer, whether by way of assisting in the manufacture, marketing, or other contribution, and, (d) whether the invention has resulted in an outstanding benefit to the employer (s 40).

10.87 In *Kelly & Chui v GE Healthcare Ltd*[108] (believed to be the first reported successful claim under s 40 of the Patents Act 1977) two research scientists were involved in the discovery of a compound, the patent of which was claimed by their employer, and which subsequently resulted in sales amounting to over £1bn. In a claim for 'just' compensation, the learned judge analysed the requirements of s 40, holding that 'outstanding benefit' meant something special, more than substantial or significant, and something more than one would normally expect to arise from the duties for which the employee is paid. The judge considered what the position of the company would have been had the patent not been granted, and compared this with the company's position with the benefit of the patent. In the circumstances of the case, the judge held that the patent had conferred an outstanding benefit, and made a 'just and fair' reward to the employees of £1m and £500,000 respectively.

10.88 If the invention belongs to the employee, he is free to dispose of it as he wishes. If he assigns his interest to his employer (whether by way of an assignment in the right to a patent, or a licensing arrangement, etc), then he is still entitled to apply for an award of statutory compensation, if he can show that the financial return he has received is inadequate in relation to the benefit derived from the patent by the employer, and it is just that compensation should be paid in addition to the benefit received from the relevant contractual arrangement between the parties. Such compensation will amount to a fair share of the benefit which the employer has derived from the assignment or licence, taking into account, inter alia: (a) any condition granted in respect of the licence or the patent, (b) the extent to which the invention was made jointly by the employee and any other person, and

[106] [2006] EWHC 595 (Pat), aff'd [2007] EWCA Civ 217, [2007] Bus LR 1369, [2007] 4 All ER 981, [2007] ICR 1489, [2007] RPC 30, CA.
[107] [1985] IRLR 232, EAT.   [108] [2009] EWHC 457 (Pat), (2009) 32(5) IPD 32036.

(c) the contribution made by the employer in the making, developing, manufacturing and marketing of the invention.

10.89 However, an award of compensation cannot be made if there is in force a relevant collective agreement which provides for payment of compensation for inventions made by employees. The collective agreement is only relevant if it is made by a trade union to which the employee belongs and by the employer, or an employers' association to which the employer belongs, which is in force at the time of the making of the invention. Non-unionists, therefore, may apply for compensation under the Act.

10.90 By the Copyright, Designs and Patents Act 1988, if the maker of a written work is employed under a contract of employment, the employer becomes the first owner of the copyright (s 11). This rule extends to literary, dramatic, musical or artistic works, but it is subject to any agreement to the contrary. There are no provisions in this Act for employee compensation on the lines of the Patents Act 1977.

H. 'Moonlighting'

10.91 The employee is obliged not to act in any manner which is inconsistent with his duty of fidelity. In *Gibson v National Union of Dyers, Bleachers and Textile Workers*[109] a full-time trade union official worked in a mill during his holidays. There was clearly a conflict of interests between his union position and his spare-time employment, and his dismissal was only held to be unfair because of the manner in which it was done. Indeed, the modern practice of 'moonlighting' whereby an employee undertakes spare-time work outside his employment hours can raise problems, particularly if the work is in competition with the employer's business. In *Gray v C & P Pembroke Ltd*[110] the employee agreed not to be engaged in any other business without the written consent of his employer. Contrary to this agreement, he took a part-time job with a rival employer. As well as being in breach of an express term of his contract, it was also a breach of fidelity, and his dismissal was held to be fair. On the other hand in *Frame v McKean & Graham Ltd*[111] the National Working Agreement for the Building Industry provided that no operative should undertake any jobbing work on his own account. This had never been enforced or referred to by the employer, and there was no mention of it in his contract of employment. The tribunal held that his dismissal for doing some work for a former customer of the firm was unfair, but the decision seems to rely heavily on the fact that the employer had, in the past, condoned his employees doing spare-time work, and even allowed them to purchase materials for this purpose.

10.92 In the absence of any contractual term, it appears that the employee may not work for a competitor in his spare time. In *Hivac Ltd v Park Royal Scientific Instruments Ltd*[112] an injunction was granted against the competitor restraining him from employing the claimant's employees who were making valves for him in their spare time. On the other hand, an employee cannot be restrained from working in a different business in his spare time which does not compete with his employer's business, provided, of course, that this does not interfere with his normal work.

10.93 An employee cannot undertake work for himself or for other persons during his working hours (*Wessex Dairies v Smith*[113]) nor can he use his employer's materials or equipment for his own purposes (ignoring matters which come within the *de minimis* rule).

---

[109] (1972) 13 KIR 143, [1972] ITR 324.   [110] (1972) (1350/72) IDS Brief 10.
[111] [1974] IRLR 179.
[112] [1946] Ch 169, [1946] 1 All ER 350, 115 LJ Ch 241, 90 Sol Jo 175, 174 LT 422, 62 TLR 231, CA.
[113] [1935] 2 KB 80, 104 LJKB 484, [1935] All ER Rep 75, 153 LT 185, 51 TLR 439, CA.

Thus if he uses the employer's facilities or equipment, or profits from work done by other employees under his supervision, this would amount to a breach of the duty of fidelity, and the employer would be entitled to an account of those profits (*University of Nottingham v Fishel*[114]).

I. Duty of disclosure

10.94 An employee is under no duty to disclose to his employer facts which are inimical to the employer (except in response to a direct question), nor to disclose his own misconduct (*Bell v Lever Bros Ltd*[115]), or that of another employee (*High Court Lonmar Global Risks Ltd v West*[116]). However, if the employee acts fraudulently or dishonestly, particularly when acting on the employer's behalf in circumstances when trust and confidence is being reposed in him, then he is under a duty to disclose his own misconduct, and may be sued by the employer for any loss suffered as a direct result of that misconduct (*Item Software (UK) Ltd v Fassihi*, see para 8.10). Also, he is under a duty to disclose the misconduct of his subordinates even if, by doing so, he incriminates himself. In *Sybron Corpn v Rochem Ltd*,[117] a man called Roques was the European manager for Gamblem Chemical Co (UK) Ltd. During his employment, payments were made on his behalf by the company into a pension scheme, and on his retirement he received a lump sum payment. It was then discovered that Roques, together with several subordinates, had been conspiring to set up in direct competition with Gamblem, and the company sought restitution of the pension payments, claiming that under the rules of the pension scheme, Roques could have been dismissed for gross misconduct, and the payments would not have been made. The Court of Appeal held that the company was entitled to have the money repaid. As a senior executive, Roques was under a duty to report the continuing misconduct of his subordinates, and for this breach of duty he could have been dismissed summarily. The money was therefore paid under a mistake of fact, since, had Gamblem known about the breach, they could have invoked the rules of the pension fund.

10.95 An employee who takes a bribe or receives a secret commission is in breach of his duty of fidelity. The employer can recover the amount from the employee. Further, the employer would be entitled to refuse to pay certain benefits to the employee who is consequently dismissed because of taking a bribe, because there is an implied term in the contract of employment that such a breach would disentitle the employee to receive such benefits (eg share options) (*Tesco Stores Ltd v Pook*, para 10.67). The effect of this case and *Rochem*, is to weaken the principle established in *Bell v Lever*.

10.96 A major problem will arise if an employee discovered a fraud or criminal offence being perpetrated within his employer's organisation. Should he report it and, if so, to whom? The police? The employer's lawyers? Senior management? Is there a duty of confidentiality which prevents reporting the fraud to persons outside the organisation, and is reporting a breach of confidence? Would the fear of job prospects being damaged be sufficient to amount to a defence in civil and/or criminal proceedings? Some answers to these questions were given in *RGB Resources plc v Rastogi*,[118] where a certified accountant

---

[114] [2000] ICR 1462, [2000] IRLR 471, [2000] ELR 385, [2001] RPC 367, [2000] All ER (D) 269.
[115] [1932] AC 161, 101 LJKB 129, 37 Com Cas 98, [1931] All ER Rep 1, 76 Sol Jo 50, 146 LT 258, 48 TLR 133, HL.
[116] [2011] IRLR 138.
[117] [1984] Ch 112, [1983] 2 All ER 707, [1983] 3 WLR 713, [1983] ICR 801, [1983] IRLR 253, [1983] BCLC 43, 127 Sol Jo 391, CA.
[118] [2004] All ER (D) 258 (Apr).

was employed as a financial controller. The chief executive officer of the company and two other senior employees were implicated in the misappropriation of hundreds of millions of pounds of loan capital, and the company's liquidator took action against the directors and the financial controller for recovery of the money. For the liquidator, it was argued that as a senior executive, the defendant was under a duty to make enquiries about suspicious conduct of the other directors, and should have taken steps to prevent dishonest activities. Further, he should have disclosed these irregularities both internally and externally, but had failed to do so. It was held that the liquidator was entitled to recovery from the defendant. A senior employee is under a duty to investigate wrongdoings and, where appropriate, to make a full disclosure to internal auditors, the board of directors, or, if necessary, the police or financial watchdog. The precise course of action will have to vary in each case, but the more senior the employee, the more serious the conduct in question, and the more serious the adverse effect on the employer's business is likely to be, the greater will be the duty to report and make a full disclosure to the proper person or authority.

10.97 The obligations of an employee who leaves the employment, or who is about to leave, will be considered in Chapter 19.

J. **The volcano effect**

10.98 The recent disruption caused to international air travel by the eruption of the Eyjafjallajökull volcano has raised a number of employment law issues. It is not possible to regard the situation as being unique, and it is likely that similar problems may arise out of other natural events, such as disruption caused by snow, blankets of fog, or possibly those arising from a human cause, eg a terrorist attack or a massive explosion similar to the one which occurred at Buncefield. These events give rise to questions as to the rights and obligations of the employee and employer.

10.99 The starting point will always be the express provisions found in the contract of employment. For example, if an employee is to be paid by the hour, then he will only be entitled to be paid for those hours when he attends work, and his inability to get to work, however caused, with generally be irrelevant. If he is paid weekly or monthly, then he will be entitled to be paid accordingly, as long as he is available for work. As well as contractual provisions, an employee could invoke custom and practice as a basis for his rights to be paid when absent from work.

10.100 Many employers will have terms that cover absences from work through illness, etc, and if there are problems arising, it is usually through the abuse of the system. For example, if the employee engages in hazardous activities outside working hours, eg rock climbing or violent sports, it is possible to reduce entitlement to sick pay in specified circumstances. But the general rule is that there is no implied term that an employee is entitled to pay whilst off work sick, even though the absence from work is not the fault of the employee. The employee must be able and willing to work, and if he is unable to attend work for a reason that is not covered by his contract, he loses his right to be paid for such absences. This will usually be done on a pro rata basis, based on the number of days lost in the calendar year (see Apportionment Act 1870, s 2, and *Miles v Wakefield Metropolitan District Council*[119]). In *Burns v Santander UK plc*[120] an employer was permitted to make deductions where a worker was ready and willing to perform his contract, but

---

[119] [1987] AC 539 [1987] 2 WLR 795 [1987] 1 All ER 1089 [1987] ICR 368 [1987] IRLR 193 [1987] 1 FTLR 533 85 LGR 649 (1987) 84 LSG 1239 (1987) 137 NLJ 266 (1987) 131 SJ 408.
[120] [2011] IRLR 639 (see also para 8.12).

was remanded in custody as a result of his own actions. The EAT held that such a remand was avoidable, and so the employee was not entitled to his contractual pay. (It is submitted that the question remains open what the situation would be if he was acquitted of the offence – would a court still find that he had disabled himself from work?)

10.101 This is also true of the 'volcano' effect, which arises when the employee is unable to get to work through no fault of his own, eg, because flights from foreign destinations are cancelled, or strikes prevent trains from running, or violent demonstrations affect departures from tourist resorts, and so on. If an employee fails to turn up for work in such circumstances, then, whilst an employer might take a sympathetic view of the reasons for the absence, the employee is not entitled to be paid, unless, of course, he has been able to do some work remotely. The problem for the employer will be that any deduction from wages must be in accordance with the provisions of ss 13–15 of the Employment Rights Act 1996 (see para 8.4); otherwise the employee may have a claim for unlawful deduction from wages.

Employer's vicarious liability

10.102 If an employee commits a wrongful (ie tortious) act in the course of his employment which causes injury or damage to a third party, the employee will, of course, be personally liable. In addition, however, the employer may be vicariously liable to compensate that third party. Two reasons are usually adduced for this principle. The first is that the employer, having initiated or created the situation where the employee has been in a position to cause the harm, should properly bear the loss; the second is the more practical reason that the employee will usually be unable to meet any substantial claim for damages, whereas the employer will normally have the financial resources to do so, or, at least, will be insured against such contingencies.

10.103 There are also a number of exceptional circumstances where an employer will be liable for the tortious acts of his independent contractors; for example, if he authorises the wrongful act, or where he has a responsibility to take care which cannot be delegated by employing someone else to do the work, eg if there is a hazardous task to be undertaken (see *Holliday v National Telephone Co*[121]). It is also true that in recent years the courts appear to be gradually extending this principle of legal liability, and to that extent the distinction between an independent contractor and an employee (discussed in Chapter 2) is becoming possibly less important than before. But the general rule remains as stated. It may be that a different principle applies if the activity of the sub-contractor damages property. In *Biffa Waste Services Ltd v Maschinenfabrik GmbH*[122] it was held that the principle that an employer is liable for the negligence of a sub-contractor should be applied as narrowly as possible, and only where the operations concerned would be hazardous whatever precautions were taken.

10.104 The major problem is to determine which acts are committed by the employee 'in the course of his employment', and there are a number of marginal situations which cause difficulty. It is clear that if the employer expressly authorises the wrongful act, he will be liable. Equally the employer will be liable if he authorises the act, and the employee performs it in a wrongful manner, for this is the very essence of the legal principle under discussion. If the employer expressly forbids the act, he may still be vicariously liable if it

---

[121] [1899] 2 QB 392, 68 LJQB 1016, 47 WR 658, [1895–99] All ER Rep 359, 81 LT 252, 15 TLR 483, CA.
[122] [2009] QB 725, [2008] EWCA 6.

can be shown that nonetheless the act was done in the scope of the employment, or for the purposes of the employer's business. In *Conway v George Wimpey & Co Ltd*[123] the employers issued instructions to their drivers that no person other than a fellow employee was permitted to ride as a passenger in their lorries. In breach of these instructions, a driver gave a lift to a non-employee, and the passenger was injured as a result of an accident. It was held that the employers were not liable, for the express prohibition had taken the act (of giving lifts) outside the scope of the employment. But in *Rose v Plenty*[124] the employers had made it clear that children were not allowed to travel on milk floats. In breach of this instruction, a milkman engaged a young boy to help him deliver and collect milk bottles, and as a result of negligent driving the boy was injured. The Court of Appeal held that the employers were nonetheless liable vicariously. The court distinguished cases like *Conway v George Wimpey & Co Ltd* on the ground that in the latter case, employees who disregarded instructions by giving lifts to unauthorised persons were acting outside the scope of their employment, because what they did was not for the purpose of the employers' business. In *Rose v Plenty*, the act (of giving a lift to an unauthorised person), although prohibited, was done for the purpose of the employers' business and hence was within the scope of the employment. Theft by an employee from the very container which he was instructed to fumigate was a risk reasonably incidental to the purpose for which he was employed, making it a sufficiently close connection between the employee's theft and the purpose of his employment (*Brink's Global Services Inc v Igrox Ltd*[125]).

10.105   The modern test is to concentrate on the closeness of the connection between the nature of the employment and the employee's wrongdoing (*Lister v Hesley Hall Ltd*). The idea of defining 'in the course of employment' by reference to an unauthorised or wrongful mode of doing an act authorised by the employer does not cope ideally with vicarious liability for intentional wrongdoing. Thus in *Fennelly v Connex South Eastern Ltd*[126] a ticket inspector assaulted a railway passenger following an argument. It was held that the act was committed in the course of employment. The courts should look at the job in general terms, and not divide each step and task performed into categories and ask whether each was authorised. The test for vicarious liability is whether the tort is so closely connected with the employment, ie that it is within what was authorised or expected of the employee, that it would be fair and just to hold the employer vicariously liable (*Gravil v Carroll*[127]).

10.106   If the employers permit the act, they cannot escape liability by prohibiting it from being done in a wrongful manner. In *Canadian Pacific Rly Co v Lockhart*,[128] the employers issued instructions that staff should not drive uninsured cars while on company business. One of their employees disregarded this prohibition, and through negligent driving, injured the claimant. The employers were held to be vicariously liable. It was not the driving which was prohibited, and the prohibition merely limited the way in which the employee was to do his work. The same principle applies if the employee negligently performs his duties. In *Century Insurance Co Ltd v Northern Ireland Road Transport Board*,[129] a driver of a petrol lorry, whilst transferring petrol from his lorry to an underground storage tank at a garage, struck a match in order to light a cigarette. He then threw the match on the floor, and an explosion ensued. It was held that the employers were liable. He was doing

[123] [1951] 1 All ER 56, 94 Sol Jo 823, [1951] TLR 215, CA.
[124] [1976] 1 All ER 97, [1976] 1 WLR 141, [1976] 1 Lloyd's Rep 263, [1975] ICR 430, [1976] IRLR 483, [2002] All ER (D) 143 (May).
[125] [2011] IRLR 343, [2010] EWCA Civ 1207.   [126] [2001] IRLR 390, [2000] All ER (D) 2233, CA.
[127] [2008] EWCA Civ 689, [2008] ICR 1222, [2008] IRLR 829, (2008) 105(26) LSG 26, (2008) 158 NLJ 933, (2008) *Times*, 22 July.
[128] [1942] AC 591, [1942] 2 All ER 464, 111 LJPC 113, 167 LT 231, PC.
[129] [1942] AC 509, [1942] 1 All ER 491, 111 LJPC 138, 167 LT 404, HL.

that which he was employed to do, namely, deliver petrol, although he was negligent in the manner in which he was performing his work.

10.107 The fact that the employee is seeking to obtain a personal gain will not necessarily take his acts outside the course of his employment. In *Lloyd v Grace, Smith & Co*[130] a managing clerk of a firm of solicitors induced the claimant, a client of the firm, to sign some documents, which transferred the claimant's properties to him. The firm was held liable, even though they stood to obtain no personal gain from the wrongful act. The clerk was merely performing the class of duties for which he was employed. This principle was taken further in *Morris v CW Martin & Sons Ltd*[131] where the claimant took a fur to a furrier for cleaning. This was stolen by an employee whose duty it was to do the work, and the employers were held liable.

10.108 For the purpose of vicarious liability, an employer may be a 'deemed temporary employer'. In *Hawley v Luminar Leisure Ltd* (see para 2.146) the claimant was visiting a nightclub when he was seriously injured by a doorman. The doorman was not employed by the nightclub, but by a security company to whom the nightclub had subcontracted its security. It was held that the nightclub exercised sufficient practical control over the doorman to make it the deemed temporary employer for the purpose of vicarious liability. The doorman was subject to the nightclub's code of conduct, was generally supervised by the nightclub manager, and given detailed instructions on where he should be stationed, who should be admitted, and what to do with troublesome customers.

Harassment and bullying

10.109 Statutory provisions relating to harassment are contained in the provisions of the Protection from Harassment Act 1997 and two sections of the Equality Act 2010. There is no statutory definition of bullying, but frequently such conduct will be associated with harassment, and there is a distinct overlap between the two concepts. Harassment, however, mainly occurs in relation to the protected characteristics, especially, but not limited to, sexual harassment, whereas bullying is indiscriminate, and can occur irrespective of a protected characteristic.

10.110 Civil liability for the tort of harassment is contained in s 1 of the Protection from Harassment Act 1997. The test is whether a reasonable person in possession of the same information would think that the course of conduct in question amounts to the harassment of another person. To amount to the statutory tort (a) the harassment must be intentional, (b) the alleged offender must have known or ought to have known that he was harassing another person if a reasonable person in possession of such information at the time of the alleged conduct would so regard it, (c) harassment includes alarming a person or causing distress, (d) there must be a course of conduct that involves harassment on at least two occasions, and (e) the same person must be the victim on each occasion.

10.111 It has been suggested that to determine whether harassment has occurred for the purpose of civil proceedings, the test is whether the gravity of the alleged misconduct would sustain criminal liability under s 2 of the Act (*Majrowski v St Thomas's NHS Trust*[132])

---

[130] [1911] 2 KB 489, 80 LJKB 959, 104 LT 789, 27 TLR 409, CA; revsd [1912] AC 716, 81 LJKB 1140, [1911–13] All ER Rep 51, 56 Sol Jo 723, 107 LT 531, 28 TLR 547, HL.

[131] [1966] 1 QB 716, [1965] 2 All ER 725, [1965] 3 WLR 276, [1965] 2 Lloyd's Rep 63, 109 Sol Jo 451, CA.

[132] [2006] UKHL 34, [2007] 1 AC 224, [2006] 3 WLR 125, [2006] 4 All ER 395, [2006] ICR 1199, [2006] IRLR 695, (2006) 91 BMLR 85, (2006) 156 NLJ 1173, (2006) 150 SJLB 986, (2006) *Times*, 13 July, (2006) *Independent*, 14 July.

but this is not essential, for the courts are well able to recognise the boundaries between conduct that was unattractive, even unreasonable, and conduct that was oppressive and unacceptable (*Conn v Sunderland City Council*[133]).

10.112 In *Veakins v Kier Islington Ltd*[134] a claim for damages for harassment succeeded, albeit the employer did not seek to challenge the employee's evidence, and did not dispute vicarious liability. The claimant's account of victimisation, and demoralisation, which reduced her to a state of clinical depression, crossed the line into conduct that was oppressive and unacceptable. The fact that a prosecutor would be reluctant to prosecute was not a conclusive factor, given the unchallenged evidence of the claimant. However, it was suggested that in the great majority of cases the remedy for high-handed or discriminatory conduct by or on behalf of an employer would be more fittingly in the employment tribunal.

10.113 As we have seen (see para 4.32) s 26 of the Equality Act provides that harassment is a prohibited conduct in a general sense, and in particular when it is harassment of a sexual nature. There is the further provision in s 40 of the Act, which is designed to prevent harassment by an employer towards his employees and towards job applicants, and harassment by a third party, where the employer fails to take steps as would be reasonably practicable to prevent the third party from doing so. However, the harassment must be known to the employer, and have occurred on at least two other occasions by the same or a different person.

10.114 There are some differences between liability for harassment under the Equality Act and a claim under the Protection from Harassment Act when an employer is faced with a claim based on vicarious liability. Under the latter Act, the statutory defence that the employer took all reasonable steps to prevent an employee from doing the act in question does not apply, and the only defence is whether it would be just and equitable to hold an employer vicariously liable. The limitation periods are not the same.

10.115 There is no statutory definition or judicial guidance on what bullying consists of. In its advisory leaflet 'Bullying and harassment at work' ACAS defines bullying as 'offensive, intimidating, malicious or insulting behaviour, an abuse or misuse of power through means intended to undermine, humiliate, denigrate or injure the recipient'. Signs of bullying may be overt or subtle. Examples include exclusion from meetings, being overloaded with work, persistent criticisms, the spreading of false or malicious rumours, being insulted, humiliated, as well as the threat of or infliction of physical force, and so on. For example, in *Green v DB Group Services (UK) Ltd*[135] the bullying levelled against the claimant consisted of withdrawing her name from circulation lists, withholding her post, laughing at her and making crude comments in her direction, thus interfering with her work with the purpose of undermining her. It was held that the bullying took place in the course of employment, and the employer was vicariously liable.

10.116 Whereas liability for harassment would normally be dealt with under the various statutory provisions outlined earlier, with claims being made to an employment tribunal, liability for bullying would be determined by the general principles which govern the duty of the employer to ensure the health, safety and welfare of his employees. Bullying can cause a number of illnesses associated with mental health and psychological problems, including stress, depression, panic attacks, anxiety, loss of confidence, and so on. The test is whether the employer knew, or ought to have known, of the existence of the state of affairs

---

[133] [2007] EWCA Civ 1492, [2008] IRLR 324, (2007) *Times*, 23 November.
[134] [2009] EWCA Civ 1288, [2010] IRLR 132, (2010) *Times*, 13 January.
[135] [2006] EWHC 1898 (QB), [2006] IRLR 764.

that gave rise to the illness, and whether the illness was itself reasonably foreseeable (*Banks v Ablex Ltd*[136]).

10.117 There is ample legal protection available. Under the Health and Safety at Work etc Act the employer has a duty to ensure, so far as is reasonably practicable, the health, safety and welfare of his employees, and, in particular, to maintain a working environment that is safe. Under the Management of Health and Safety at Work Regulations 1999, an employer must carry out an assessment of the risks to which employees are exposed whilst they are at work. The employer is also under a duty to maintain the relationship of trust and confidence, and to permit bullying to take place without taking steps to investigate or prevent it will undoubtedly seriously damage the relationship of trust and confidence that must exist between the parties. There is an implied term in the contract of employment that the employer would take such steps as were reasonable to support an employee without the latter being subjected to bullying or disruption from colleagues (*Wigan Borough Council v Davies*[137]). A failure to provide such support could give rise to a claim based on constructive dismissal.

---

[136] [2005] EWCA Civ 173, [2005] ICR 819, [2005] IRLR 357, (2005) 149 SJLB 269, (2005) *Times*, 21 March.
[137] [1979] ICR 411, [1979] IRLR 127.

11

Health and Safety at Work

Health and Safety at Work etc. Act 1974

A. **Background to the legislation**

11.1 As a result of the recommendations of the Robens Committee, the Health and Safety at Work etc Act 1974 was passed. In considering the then existing laws and practices relating to health and safety, the Committee came to a number of interesting conclusions. It found that in fact there was too much law, that much of it was unsatisfactory and unintelligible, and there was overlapping jurisdiction between those bodies whose task it was to enforce the law. The result of this was that there was a general feeling of apathy in the day-to-day implementation of safety rules, and little interest was shown in the subject. The Health and Safety at Work Act thus lays down the general legal obligations of all concerned in a single enactment, with the enforcement under the control of a unified administration. The old laws (Factories Act 1961, Offices, Shops and Railway Premises Act 1963, etc) were progressively repealed and replaced by regulations and approved codes of practice which are designed to maintain and improve the standards of health, safety and welfare. Two more recent reviews of the subject, by Lord Young in 2010 and Professor Löfstedt in 2011, have called for changes to the system, many of which have been accepted by the Government. It is expected that the amount of legislation related to health and safety will be reduced or consolidated in the coming years.

11.2 The 1974 Act applies to people, not to premises. It covers all employed persons (with the exception of domestic workers), wherever they work, and brought within the orbit of safety legislation an additional 7,000,000 employees who were hitherto outside the protection of statutory rules. In addition, the Health and Safety (Training for Employment) Regulations 1990 apply the provisions of the Act to trainees on government sponsored training schemes as if they were employees. The Act also applies to people who are not employees, in so far as they may be affected by activities which are being carried on in places of work. The proposed Deregulation Bill is expected to take away the liability of self-employed persons from health and safety legislation in low-risk occupations.

11.3 The Act applies to all employment situations, including (with appropriate modifications) to offshore installations and pipelines within UK territorial waters and areas designated under the Continental Shelf Act 1964, including construction work and diving activities. The Police (Health and Safety) Act 1997 applies the provisions of the Act to holders of the office of constable, even though they are not technically employees (Police (Health and Safety) Regulations 1999).

11.4 Next, it will be noted that obligations are placed on employers in their different capacities as manufacturers, suppliers, and importers of articles and substances to be used at work, to ensure that these can be used in safety and without risk to health. Health and safety has to be built into the design and manufacturing stages.

11.5 The emphasis of the Act is on criminal sanctions and enforcement of the law by new techniques, for the Act itself (unlike some of the regulations made under the Act) does not give rise to questions of civil liability. The inspectorate appears to be using their powers of prosecution at the rate of 1,000 per year, which is small compared with the number of offences revealed by inspections, for the emphasis is on co-operation rather than compulsion. In addition, however, the issuing of improvement and prohibition notices has been widely exercised, and these are proving to have very dramatic effects. Currently, about 13,000 such notices are issued each year.

11.6 Finally, there are a number of provisions designed to bring about a greater awareness by all concerned of the need to promote safety and health at work, and thus provide the impetus to the greater self-regulatory system which the Robens Committee thought to be desirable.

11.7 Some amendments to the Act have been made by the Consumer Protection Act 1987 (Sch 3). The Act now applies to fairground equipment and micro-organisms. Customs officers may detain articles and substances for the purpose of enabling enforcing officers to perform their duties, and s 6 of the Act (see para 11.51) was significantly improved.

11.8 We can examine the provisions of the Act under five headings.

B. Enforcement of the Act

11.9 The overall responsibility for supervising and administering the law on health and safety lies with the now unified Health and Safety Executive (see para 1.51), together with enforcement officers (usually designated Environmental Health Officers) of local authorities, to whom there has been a transfer of authority in respect of certain specified types of premises (Health and Safety (Enforcing Authority) Regulations 1998). Neither the Secretary of State nor the HSE can instruct an enforcement officer to enforce any particular provision or institute proceedings in any particular case.

Powers of inspectors

11.10 All enforcing authorities will appoint inspectors, who will have the following powers, for the purpose of giving effect to the relevant statutory provisions:

    (a) at any reasonable time, or, if there is a dangerous situation at any time, to enter premises;

    (b) to take with him a constable if he has reasonable cause to apprehend any serious obstruction in the execution of his duty;

    (c) to take with him any other authorised person and any equipment or materials required for any purpose for which the power of entry is being exercised;

    (d) to make such examination and investigation as may be necessary;

    (e) to direct that any premises shall be left undisturbed so long as is reasonably necessary for the purpose of examination or investigation;

    (f) to take such measures and photographs and make such recordings as he considers necessary;

    (g) to take samples of any articles or substances found in any premises and of the atmosphere in, or in the vicinity of, such premises. The Secretary of State may make regulations concerning the procedure to be adopted in such cases;

    (h) in the case of any article or substance likely to cause danger to health or safety, to cause it to be dismantled or subjected to any process or test, but not to damage or destroy it unless it is for the purpose of exercising his powers. If the person who has responsibilities in relation to those premises is present, and so requests, the inspector shall exercise this power in that person's presence, unless he considers that it would be prejudicial to the safety of the state to do so. In any case, before exercising these powers, he must consult with appropriate persons for the purpose of ascertaining what dangers, if any, there may be in doing what he proposes to do;

(i) in the case of any article or substance likely to cause danger to health or safety, to take possession of it, and detain it for so long as is necessary in order to examine it, to ensure it is not tampered with before he has completed his examination, and to ensure that it is available for use as evidence in any proceedings for an offence, or in respect of matters arising out of the issuing of an improvement notice or a prohibition notice. He must leave a notice giving particulars of the article or substance, stating that he has taken possession of it, and, if practicable to do so, leave a sample with a responsible person;

(j) if conducting an examination or investigation under (d) above, to require any person whom he has reasonable cause to believe to be able to give any information to answer such questions as the inspector thinks fit to ask, and to sign a declaration of the truth of his answers;

(k) to require the production of, inspect, and take copies of any entry in, any books or documents which are required to be kept, and any other book or document which it is necessary for him to see for the purpose of any examination or investigation under (d), above;

(l) to require any person to afford him such facilities and assistance within that person's control or responsibilities, as are necessary for him to exercise his powers;

(m) any other power which is necessary for the purpose of exercising any of the above powers.

Improvement notices (s 21)

11.11 If an inspector is of the opinion that a person is contravening one or more relevant statutory provisions, or has done so and the contravention is likely to be continued or repeated, he may serve on him an improvement notice, stating that opinion, specifying the relevant statutory provision, giving reasons why he is of that opinion, and requiring that person to remedy the contravention within such period as may be specified in the notice, but not less than 21 days (ie the period in which an appeal may be made – see later in the section).

Prohibition notices (s 22)

11.12 In respect of any activity covered by a relevant statutory provision, if the inspector thinks that those activities are carried on or are likely to be carried on so as to involve a risk of serious personal injury, the inspector may serve a prohibition notice. This will state his opinion, specify the provisions which give rise to that opinion, and direct that the activities to which the notice relates shall not be carried on by or under the control of that person on whom the notice was served unless the matters specified and any associated contravention are remedied. This direction takes effect at the end of the period specified in the notice or, if the notice so declares, immediately. Prohibition notices can be issued on persons, eg for a failure to wear protective eye shields. Activities are being carried on for the purpose of s 22 even though they are temporarily suspended (eg because of an accident). If there is a possibility that the activities may be resumed, the inspector is entitled to issue a prohibition notice requiring remedial action prior to the recommencement of those activities (*RailTrack plc v Smallwood*[1]).

---

[1] [2001] EWHC Admin 78, [2001] ICR 714, [2001] 09 LS Gaz R 40, 145 Sol Jo LB 52, [2001] All ER (D) 103 (Jan).

11.13 In the case of an improvement notice or a prohibition notice, the notice may (but need not) include directions as to the measure to be taken to remedy the contravention, which may be by reference to any approved code of practice or afford a choice between different ways of remedying the contravention. However, in respect of an improvement notice relating to a building, this cannot impose more onerous requirements than those imposed by the building regulations unless there is a statutory provision to the contrary. Also, if the notice relates to the means of escape in the event of fire, the inspector must engage in prior consultations with the fire authorities. Any improvement notice or a deferred prohibition notice may be withdrawn by the inspector before the expiry of 21 days, and may also be extended by the inspector at any time when an appeal is not pending.

11.14 From 1 October 2012, The Health and Safety (Fees) Regulations 2012 have allowed the HSE in most circumstances to recover their costs from employers who have been found to be in material breach of health and safety legislation. A material breach is where there has been a contravention that necessitates the issue of a notice in writing, such as an improvement or prohibition notice, or a prosecution. This is known as the 'fee for intervention' (FFI) cost recovery scheme and the hourly rate is £124. The FFI scheme only applies where the HSE is the enforcing authority.

Appeals against improvement or prohibition notices (s 24)

11.15 An appeal from the imposition of an improvement notice or a prohibition notice may be made to the employment tribunal, which can cancel or affirm it, or affirm it with such modifications as the tribunal thinks fit. For the purpose of hearing such appeals, the tribunal may include assessors specially appointed to sit with the regular members. Once an appeal has been lodged, this will suspend the operation of the improvement notice until such time as the appeal is disposed of or withdrawn; in the case of a prohibition notice, however, the lodging of an appeal will only suspend it if the tribunal so directs, and then only from the time it does so direct.

11.16 An appeal against an improvement notice or a prohibition notice can be made on a number of grounds.

11.17 First, it could be argued that there is no breach of a statutory duty. To determine this, a tribunal may refer to any relevant code of practice and guidance note. In *Sutton & Co Ltd v Davies*[2] the employers were in breach of s 13 of the Factories Act 1961 in not guarding transmission machinery. They appealed against an improvement notice, arguing that they had operated for 27 years without an accident. The appeal was dismissed, for the requirements of the Act are absolute. But in *Brewer & Sons v Dunston*[3] the inspector issued a prohibition notice on a machine. No accident had occurred in 18 years of use, and the tribunal held that there was no evidence to support the contention that there was risk of imminent danger. The distinction is that for an improvement notice, the sole issue is whether or not there has been a breach of a statutory provision, whereas a prohibition notice is concerned with whether there is a risk of serious personal injury.

11.18 Secondly, an appeal may be against the time limit imposed for remedying the defect, and there the tribunal may consider any serious embarrassment which may be caused to the company, and may take into account any history of recorded accidents at the firm. A company with a good record may well be given an extension of time so as to maintain production, so long as there is no immediate risk of danger or injury, and there is a willingness to make the appropriate modifications.

---

[2] Unreported.   [3] Unreported.

11.19 A third ground for appeal may be based on the absence of any risk or danger. In *South Surbiton Co-operative Society v Wilcox*,[4] a cracked washbasin was made the subject of an improvement notice. It was argued that the breach was trivial, there was little risk to health, and that there must be many employers who are similarly in breach and who have not been served with improvement notices. Nonetheless, the notice was confirmed by the tribunal. The requirements of the Act were absolute.

11.20 But in *Associated Dairies Ltd v Hartley*,[5] an improvement notice required the company to issue safety shoes free of charge to employees. In the previous year, one employee had been injured when the wheel of a truck ran over his foot. The company employed 1,000 employees, with a high turnover. Free footwear would have cost £20,000 in the first year. The tribunal held that the expense of providing protective footwear was disproportionate to the risk, and the notice was cancelled. In this case, the Act only required the employer to do that which was reasonably practicable.

11.21 A final ground for appeal may be based on the financial inability of the employer to comply with the order. Such an appeal is doomed from the start. In *TC Harrison (Newcastle-under-Lyme) Ltd v Ramsey*,[6] the company appealed against an improvement notice which required them to paint and clean the walls of the factory, in accordance with s 1 of the Factories Act 1961. It was stated that their financial position was precarious due to difficult trading conditions, but the employment tribunal had no hesitation in confirming the notice. To do otherwise would be to allow a firm to keep its charges low so as to undercut competitors, thus obtaining an unfair advantage over those who complied with the legal requirements. An employer cannot be relieved of his statutory duties because of financial difficulties.

11.22 Unlike other proceedings before employment tribunals, appeals against improvement and prohibition notices may result in an order for costs being made against the unsuccessful party. Such an order is entirely at the discretion of the tribunal, who may take into account the conduct of the party in failing to remedy the breach, and the hopelessness or otherwise of the appeal (see Employment Tribunals (Constitution and Rules of Procedure) Regulations 2004, Sch 4). In *South Surbiton Co-operative Society v Wilcox* (see para 11.19) no order for costs was made, as the tribunal considered that the breach was trivial.

11.23 A failure to observe the requirements of a prohibition or improvement notice is a criminal offence, and it is no defence in criminal proceedings to argue that the employer has done all that is reasonably practicable to comply. The proper forum in which to argue questions of practicability is the employment tribunal (*Deary v Mansion Hide Upholstery Ltd*[7]).

11.24 An appeal against a decision of an employment tribunal relating to a prohibition or improvement notice must be made to the Divisional Court. The reason is that the failure to comply with such notices is a criminal offence and the EAT, which would normally hear appeals from employment tribunals, is only concerned with civil matters.

Crown notices

11.25 Because there is a rule of law that the Queen cannot be prosecuted in her own courts, it is not possible to enforce prohibition and improvement notices against Crown organisations, even though they employ large numbers of employees in various government departments. Consequently, the HSE devised the Crown Notice, which will be issued when a prohibition or improvement notice would be appropriate. Such notices have only a

⁴ [1975] IRLR 292.   ⁵ [1979] IRLR 171.   ⁶ [1976] IRLR 135.
⁷ [1983] ICR 610, [1983] IRLR 195, 147 JP 311.

moral sanction, but are designed to draw attention to potential hazards, and, as copies are to be given to employees' representatives, will naturally attract publicity. A number of such notices are issued annually, requiring the same action from Crown employers as do prohibition and improvement notices issued to other employers. If there is a failure to comply, HSE can issue a censure notice, which is a formal recording that, but for Crown immunity, the evidence would have been sufficient to provide a realistic prospect of a conviction in the courts, and prosecution would have been in the public interest.

Power to deal with imminent danger (s 25)

11.26 If the inspector finds on any premises any article or substance which he has reasonable cause to believe is a cause of imminent danger of serious personal injury, he may seize it and cause it to be rendered harmless whether by destruction or otherwise. Before doing so, if it is practicable for him to do so, he will give a sample with an identifiable mark to a responsible person. Thereafter, he will prepare and sign a report giving particulars of the circumstances, and give a copy to a responsible person at those premises, and also to the owner.

Enforcement powers of the court (s 42)

11.27 Where a person is convicted of an offence under any relevant statutory provision, the court may, in addition to, or instead of, imposing any punishment, order him to take such steps as may be specified in the order to remedy the matters specified, within such time as may be fixed. Failure to do so may amount to contempt of court, but an application may be made for an extension of the time limit. During the period given to remedy matters, the person cannot be liable for a failure to observe the provisions. After that time, if he continues with the contravention, he can be sentenced to six months' imprisonment and/or fined up to £20,000 in the magistrates' courts, or up to two years' imprisonment and/or an unlimited fine in the Crown Court.

11.28 If a person is charged with an offence in connection with the acquisition of explosives, the court may order the article or substance in question to be forfeited and either destroyed or dealt with as the court so orders. However, such order cannot be made unless the court gives the owner or any other interested party an opportunity to be heard.

Other matters

11.29 By s 26, if an inspector exceeds his statutory powers the enforcing authority may nonetheless indemnify him against the costs, damages, or expenses incurred if it is satisfied that the inspector acted in the honest belief that the act complained of was within his powers.

11.30 By s 28(8) an inspector is empowered to give information to employed persons (or their representatives) if it is necessary to do so for the purpose of keeping them adequately informed about matters affecting their health, safety or welfare. This may be factual information about the premises or anything going on, or information about action he has taken or is proposing to take. If he does this, he must also give like information to the employer.

C. **Statutory duties on health, safety and welfare**

11.31 In general, there are three sets of guiding rules which will govern the operation of the law. The first of these is the general duties laid down in ss 2–9, and which must be observed by the specified persons. The second will be the regulations, which will supplement the law. The third will be the Codes of Practice, issued and approved from time to time. It must be borne in mind that a breach of the general duties laid down in ss 2–9 of the Act is a criminal offence, and does not give rise to civil proceedings (s 47), whereas a breach of the regulations will be actionable civilly if the regulations themselves provide for this. However, by the Civil Evidence Act 1968, s 11 any conviction for a criminal offence is admissible in civil proceedings as evidence that the person so convicted committed the offence, and therefore, a claimant may point to the conviction as being relevant to the issue of civil liability.

11.32 Some of the duties are absolute ones, which means that the person on whom the duty is placed must carry it out. Others are preceded by the words 'so far as is reasonably practicable'. This is a somewhat lesser standard. The employer must weigh, on the one hand, the time, trouble and expense, etc of meeting that duty against the risks involved and the nature of the obligation on the other hand. Also, the duty can only be performed against the background of current knowledge which the employer knows, or ought to know. However, in *Marshall v Gotham Co Ltd*[8] it was suggested that a precaution which was practicable would not lightly be held to be unreasonable. In other words, a duty or obligation must be performed or carried out unless it would be unreasonable to do so. Further, s 40 of the Act states that in any proceedings for a failure to comply with a duty or requirement, it will be for the accused to prove that it was not reasonably practicable to do more than was in fact done.

11.33 The fact that the duty on UK employers to ensure the health safety and welfare at work of all employees was imposed 'so far as is reasonably practicable' did not infringe the European Directive 89/391/EEC (*Commission of the European Communities v United Kingdom*[9]). The ECJ pointed out that Art 5(1) of the Directive does not impose no-fault liability for all accidents in the workplace. Article 5(4) provides that member states can exclude or limit the employer's responsibility where occurrences are due to unusual or unforeseeable circumstances, beyond the employer's control, or to exceptional events, the consequences of which could not be avoided despite the exercise of all due care.

Duties of the employer

Duties owed to his employees (s 2)

11.34 It shall be the duty of every employer to ensure, so far as is reasonably practicable, the health, safety and welfare at work of all his employees. In particular, the employer must:

(a) provide and maintain plant and systems of work that are, so far as is reasonably practicable, safe and without risks to health;

(b) make arrangements for ensuring, so far as is reasonably practicable, safety and absence of risks to health in connection with the use, handling, storage and transport of articles and substances (see *Page v Freight Hire (Tank Haulage) Ltd*[10]);

(c) ensure the provision of such information, instruction, training and supervision as is necessary to ensure, so far as is reasonably practicable, the health, safety and welfare at work of his employees. If an employee has a limited command of the English language, there is need for a greater degree of training, instruction and supervision (*Tasci v Pekalp of London Ltd*[11]). The employer must also give such information etc to his employees and to persons who are not his employees (eg to sub-contractors and their employees) if this is necessary to ensure the health and safety of the employees of the employer (*R v Swan Hunter Shipbuilders Ltd*[12]);

(d) so far as is reasonably practicable as regards any place of work under his control, ensure the maintenance of it in a condition that is safe and without risks to health,

---

[8] [1954] AC 360, [1954] 1 All ER 937, [1954] 2 WLR 812, 98 Sol Jo 268, HL.

[9] [2007] IRLR 720.   [10] [1981] 1 All ER 394, [1981] ICR 299, [1981] IRLR 13.

[11] [2001] ICR 633, [2000] All ER (D) 2157, CA.

[12] [1982] 1 All ER 264, [1981] ICR 831, [1981] IRLR 403, [1981] Crim LR 833, sub nom *R v Swan Hunter Shipbuilders Ltd and Telemeter Installations Ltd, HMS Glasgow* [1981] 2 Lloyd's Rep 605, CA.

and the maintenance of means of access and egress from it that are safe and without such risks;

(e) ensure the provision and maintenance of a working environment for his employees that is, so far as is reasonably practicable, safe, without risks to health, and adequate as regards facilities and arrangements for their welfare at work.

11.35 So far as these duties are concerned, it will be noted that they bear a strong resemblance to the common law duties of care (see para 11.103), spelt out, perhaps, in greater detail. An employer is only responsible for premises over which he has actual control, but that does not absolve him from the duty of ensuring a safe system of work on the premises of another (*General Cleaning Contractors Ltd v Christmas*[13]). The duty to provide a safe working environment would cover noise, fumes, heat, etc; welfare at work is not defined, but would presumably cover washing and toilet facilities, drinking water, and possibly eating arrangements.

Written safety policy (s 2(3))

11.36 Except for employers who employ fewer than five employees (see *Osborne v Bill Taylor of Huyton Ltd*[14] and Employers' Health and Safety Policy Statements (Exception) Regulations 1975) it shall be the duty of every employer to prepare and revise as often as is appropriate a written statement of his general policy with respect to the health and safety at work of all his employees, and the organisation and arrangements for the time being in force for carrying out that policy, and to bring this statement to the notice of all his employees. The Act does not give any guidance on the contents of this written statement, for the object of the exercise is for each employer to sit down and think about his own safety problems and work out the necessary solutions. Clearly, this would prove to be without value if the employer merely copied out a draft scheme drawn up by someone else.

11.37 It is suggested, however, that the safety policy should at least deal with the responsibility of all employees, including the board of directors, all levels of management, supervisors and operatives, inspection procedures, arrangements for dealing with special hazards, emergency arrangements, including fire drill, the provision and use of safety precautions generally, supervision, training, research and consultative arrangements. In drawing up the safety policy, it may be sound procedure to seek advice from the Commission, the Executive, employers' associations, and to consult with trade union representatives, but it must be stressed that the statement is not a joint consultative document, but one for which the employer has ultimate responsibility. The Act requires the statement to be brought to the notice of all employees, but no guidance is given on how this is to be done. It would clearly not be sufficient to place the statement on the notice board, and hope that work people will read it as they go past, and so the more formal channels of written communication should be used. If it is known that a particular employee does not read English, presumably some other way must be found of bringing it to his notice. The employer is obliged to revise the written statement as often as may be appropriate; it is suggested that the statement should be looked at at least once a year, in the light of practical experience of operating the safety policy, and taking into account any suggestions which might be received.

Safety representatives and safety committee (s 2(4), (6), (7))

11.38 A trade union which is recognised by an employer may appoint safety representatives from among the employees in respect of whom the union is recognised (*Cleveland County Council v Springett*[15]). The persons so appointed need not themselves be members of the union.

---

13 [1953] AC 180, [1952] 2 All ER 1110, [1953] 2 WLR 6, 51 LGR 109, 97 Sol Jo 7, HL.
14 [1982] ICR 168, [1982] IRLR 17, DC.   15 [1985] IRLR 131, EAT.

11.39 The legal requirements are contained in the Safety Representatives and Safety Committees Regulations 1977 (as amended) and a Code of Practice issued and approved by the former Health and Safety Commission. An independent trade union shall notify the employer in writing of the name of the safety representative, who shall hold the appointment until the union terminates it, or he ceases to be employed at the workplace, or resigns. So far as is reasonably practicable, he shall have been employed by that employer for the preceding two years, or have had at least two years' experience in similar employment.

11.40 An employer has a duty to consult with safety representatives over a wide range of issues, with a view to making and maintaining arrangements which will enable him and his employees to co-operate effectively in promoting and developing measures to ensure the health and safety at work of employees, and checking the effectiveness of those measures (s 2(6)). In particular, there shall be consultation about the introduction of measures which may substantially affect the health and safety of employees, the arrangements for appointing or nominating the safety assistant, the provision of health and safety information, the planning and organisation of health and safety training, and the health and safety consequences of the introduction of new technologies (Management of Health and Safety at Work Regulations 1999).

Additionally, the safety representative has the following functions:

(a) to investigate the potential hazards and dangerous occurrences at the workplace, and to examine the causes of accidents;

(b) to investigate complaints by any employee he represents relating to that employee's health, safety, or welfare at work;

(c) to make representations to the employer about these matters;

(d) to make representations to the employer on general matters affecting the health, safety and welfare at work of the employees at the workplace;

(e) to carry out inspections (see para 11.42);

(f) to represent employees in consultations with inspectors of the Health and Safety Executive;

(g) to receive information from the inspectors; and

(h) to attend meetings of safety committees in his capacity as safety representative.

11.41 In order to perform these functions adequately, the employer shall permit the safety representative to have time off work with pay during his working hours, and also for the purpose of undergoing training in aspects of those functions as may be reasonable in the circumstances (see *White v Pressed Steel Fisher*[16]). To determine what is reasonable in the circumstances, regard must be had to HSE's Code of Practice. Factors to be taken into account include the contents of the course and how it relates to the particular health and safety function of the employee, and whether the training would assist him in performing those functions. The test is whether the training is reasonable in all the circumstances, not whether it was necessary (*Duthie v Bath & North East Somerset Council*[17]). The safety representative is entitled to be paid his normal earnings or average hourly earnings. In *Davies v Neath Port Talbot County Borough Council*[18] it was held that a part-time employee, who went on a full-time health and safety training course, was entitled to be paid on the same basis as a full-time male counterpart. The training course was 'work' within the meaning of Art 141 of the Treaty of Rome, and therefore she was entitled to equal pay.

---

[16] [1980] IRLR 176, EAT.
[17] [2003] ICR 1405, [2003] 26 LS Gaz R 37, [2003] All ER (D) 358 (Apr), EAT.
[18] [1999] ICR 1132, [1999] IRLR 769, EAT.

11.42 Safety representatives are entitled to carry out an inspection of the workplace at least every three months (or more frequently with the employer's consent), and also further inspections if there has been some substantial change in the conditions of work (eg by the introduction of new working processes, or the coming to light of new information disclosing a potential hazard). Inspections may also be carried out after a notifiable accident has occurred or a notifiable disease contracted, for the purpose of determining the cause. The employer shall provide reasonable facilities and assistance, but he, or his representative, may be present during the inspection.

11.43 The employer shall establish a safety committee when at least two safety representatives make such a request. For this purpose, he shall consult with these representatives, and also those of any recognised trade unions. A notice must be posted stating the composition of the committee, which must be established within three months of the request being made.

11.44 A complaint may be made to an employment tribunal that the employer has failed to permit a safety representative to have time off work for these purposes, or has failed to pay for such time off. If the complaint is well founded, the tribunal shall make a declaration, and may make an award of compensation.

11.45 There was some doubt as to whether the Safety Representative and Safety Committee Regulations met the requirements of the 'Framework Directive' (89/391/EEC) because there was no means whereby employees in non-unionist firms could have a legal right to play their role in health and safety matters. Consequently, the Health and Safety (Consultation with Employees) Regulations 1996 were introduced. Under these regulations, an employer has two choices with respect to those employees who have no safety representative by virtue of the 1977 regulations. He can either consult with employees directly, or he can consult with one or more persons of any group of employees who were elected for the purposes of consultation, and who are referred to as 'representatives of employee safety'. There is no provision in the regulations as to how an employer shall organise any such elections, but apparently it is not necessary to have a statutory framework for this purpose (*R v Secretary of State for Trade and Industry, ex p UNISON*[19]).

11.46 Under the 1996 regulations, employers must consult with their employees, or their elected representatives of employee safety, in good time, on matters concerning their health and safety at work, and, in particular, with regard to:

(a) the introduction of any measures at the workplace which will substantially affect the health and safety of those employees;

(b) the employer's arrangements for appointing or nominating a competent person to assist him, as required by regs 6(1) and 7(1)(b) of the Management Regulations;

(c) any health and safety information he is required to provide to the employees under any relevant statutory provision;

(d) the planning and organisation of any health and safety training he is required to provide by virtue of any statutory provision; and

(e) the health and safety consequences for the employees of the introduction of new technologies into the workplace (including the planning thereof).

11.47 In such consultations, representatives of employee safety have the following functions:

(a) to make representations to the employer on potential hazards and dangerous occurrences at the workplace, which affect the employees represented;

---

[19] [1997] 1 CMLR 459, [1996] ICR 1003, [1996] IRLR 438.

(b) make representations to the employer on general matters affecting the health and safety of employees, in particular, on matters referred to in paras (a)–(e) (see para 11.46);

(c) represent the group of workers he represents in consultations at the workplace with health and safety inspectors.

11.48 If the employer consults with employees directly, he must make available to them such information as is necessary to enable the employees to participate fully and effectively in the consultation process. If the employer consults with representatives of employee safety, he must make available such information as is necessary to enable them to carry out their functions. But the rights and functions of employee representatives under the 1996 regulations are more limited than those which apply under the 1977 regulations. In particular, they have no right to carry out workplace inspections, attend meetings of a safety committee, inspect statutory health and safety documents, or investigate employees' complaints and notifiable accidents or dangerous occurrences. However, such matters are provided for in the guidance notes which have been issued. An employee safety representative has the right to be paid when carrying out his functions as such, or is being trained.

Duty owed to non-employees (s 3)

11.49 It shall be the duty of every employer, and every self-employed person, to conduct his undertakings in such a way as to ensure, so far as is reasonably practicable, that persons who are not his employees who may be affected thereby are not exposed to risks to their health or safety. This duty applies not only to persons who are lawfully on the employer's premises, for example, students in an educational establishment, but also persons who are outside those premises, but who may be affected by the activities in question. Thus if there is a potential hazard on the employer's premises, he must provide information not only to his own employees, but to visitors and the employees of a sub-contractor who may be working there (*R v Swan Hunter Shipbuilders Ltd*, para 11.34). The employer also has a duty to specialist contractors who come on to the employer's site for the purpose of carrying on activities in respect of the employer's undertaking (*R v Associated Octel*[20]).

Duties of controllers of premises (s 4)

11.50 Every person who has control of premises (not being domestic premises) must ensure, as far as it is reasonable for a person in his position to ensure, that so far as is reasonably practicable, all means of access thereto or egress therefrom, and plant and substance, in the premises, shall be safe and without risks to health in respect of persons who use those premises as a place of work (*Westminster City Council v Select Managements Ltd*[21]). A person who has, by virtue of a contract of tenancy, the obligation to maintain or repair those premises, or be responsible for the safety or absence of risks therein, shall be the person to be regarded as being in control.

Duties of manufacturers, etc (s 6 as amended)

11.51 A duty is imposed on any person who designs, manufacturers, imports or supplies any article for use at work or any article of fairground equipment:

(a) to ensure, as far as reasonably practicable, that the article is so designed and constructed that it will be safe and without risks to health at all times when it is being

---

[20] [1994] 4 All ER 1051, [1995] ICR 281, [1994] IRLR 540, [1994] 36 LS Gaz R 37, [1994] NLJR 1312, 138 Sol Jo LB 194, CA; aff'd [1996] 4 All ER 846, [1996] 1 WLR 1543, [1996] ICR 972, [1997] IRLR 123, [1997] Crim LR 355, [1996] NLJR 1685, HL.

[21] [1985] 1 All ER 897, [1985] 1 WLR 576, 83 LGR 409, [1985] ICR 353, 129 Sol Jo 221, [1985] 1 EGLR 245, [1985] LS Gaz R 1091, sub nom *Select Managements Ltd v Westminster City Council* [1985] IRLR 344, CA.

set, used, cleaned or maintained by a person at work. However, s 6(8) provides that where a person designs, manufactures, imports or supplies an article for use at work or an article of fairground equipment and does so for or to another on the basis of a written undertaking by that other that he will take specified steps to ensure, so far as is reasonably practicable, that the article will be safe and without risks to health at all the above-mentioned times, the undertaking will release the designer, manufacturer, importer or supplier (as the case may be) from this duty, to such an extent as is reasonable having regard to the terms of the undertaking. For example, if a person wishes to sell second-hand machinery, it might be advisable to extract a written undertaking from the purchaser to ensure its complete overhaul before putting it to use;

(b) to carry out or arrange for the carrying out of such testing and examination as may be necessary for the performance of the duty in (a). However, this does not require the repeating of any tests or examinations which may have been carried out by others, in so far as it is reasonable to rely on the results of those others' work;

(c) to take such steps as are necessary to secure that persons supplied by that person with the article are provided with adequate information about the use for which the article has been designed or has been tested, and about any conditions necessary to ensure that it will be safe and without risks to health at all times as are mentioned in (a), and also when it is being dismantled or disposed of;

(d) to take all such steps as are necessary to secure, so far as is reasonably practicable, that persons so supplied are provided with any revision of the information in (c) by reason of it becoming known that anything gives rise to a serious risk to health or safety.

11.52 Similar obligations are placed upon persons who design, manufacture, import or supply articles of fairground equipment used for or in connection with the entertainment of members of the public.

11.53 There is also a duty on designers and manufacturers (but not importers or suppliers) to carry out or arrange for the carrying out of any necessary research with a view to the discovery and, so far as is reasonably practicable, the elimination or minimisation of any risks to health or safety to which the design or article may give rise, but again, this does not require the repeating of any research already carried out, if it was reasonable to rely on the results.

11.54 It is the duty of any person who erects or installs any article for use at work, or any article of fairground equipment, to ensure, so far as is reasonably practicable, that nothing about the way in which the article is erected, or installed makes it unsafe or a risk to health, when it is being set, used, cleaned or maintained by a person at work.

11.55 A duty is imposed on any person who manufactures, imports or supplies any substance:

(a) to ensure, so far as is reasonably practicable, that the substance will be safe and without risks to health at all times when it is being used, handled, processed, stored or transported by a person at work or in premises to which s 4 (see para 11.50) applies;

(b) to carry out or arrange for the carrying out of such testing and examination as may be necessary for the performance of the above duty, but again this does not require the repeating of any tests or examinations which have been carried out by others, in so far as it is reasonable to rely on the results of those others' work;

(c) to take such steps as are necessary to secure that persons supplied by that person with the substance are provided with adequate information about any risks to health or safety to which the inherent properties of the substance may give rise, about the results of any relevant tests which have been carried out on or in connection with the substances, and about any conditions necessary to ensure that the substance will be safe and without risks to health at all such times as are mentioned above, and when it is being disposed of;

(d) to take such steps as are necessary to secure, so far as is reasonably practicable, that persons so supplied are provided with all such revisions of information as are necessary by reason of its becoming known that anything gives rise to a serious risk to health or safety.

11.56 A manufacturer of any substance is under a duty to carry out (or arrange for the carrying out of) any necessary research with a view to the discovery and, so far as is reasonably practicable, the elimination or minimisation of any risks to health or safety to which the substance may give rise, but he need not repeat any test, examination or research done by others in so far as it was reasonable for him to rely on the results thereof.

11.57 For the purposes of s 6, an absence of safety or a risk to health is to be disregarded in so far as it has arisen by an occurrence which could not be reasonably foreseen, and so far as the obligations placed on designers, manufacturers, importers and suppliers of articles and substances are concerned, regard may be had to any relevant information which has been provided by them to any person.

11.58 Section 6(7) provides that these duties only extend to things done in the course of a trade, business or undertaking (whether for profit or not), and to matters within a person's control. The definition of 'article for use at work' (see s 53) is 'any plant designed for use or operation (whether exclusively or not) by persons at work, and any articles designed for use as a component in any such plant', a definition which may be somewhat restrictive. A substance is defined as being 'any natural or artificial substance (including micro-organisms) whether in a solid or liquid form or in the form of gas or vapour'.

11.59 An interesting point arises concerning the effect on civil contracts of these provisions. Supposing, for example, an employer purchases a machine from a manufacturer, and this is delivered without safety instructions, or in an unguarded state. Could the employer reject the machine on the grounds that it was not fit for its purpose or not of satisfactory quality, contrary to the Sale of Goods Act 1979?

Duties of employees

Duties at work (s 7)

11.60 Every employee is under a duty while at work:

(a) to take reasonable care for the health and safety of himself and of others who may be affected by his acts or omissions at work; this could mean that an employee who failed or refused to wear or use safety precautions which are provided would be in breach of his legal duty;

(b) as regards any duty imposed on his employer or any other person, to co-operate with him so far as is necessary to enable that duty to be performed or complied with.

Duty not to interfere with safety provisions (s 8)

11.61 No persons shall intentionally or recklessly interfere with or misuse anything provided in the interest of health, safety or welfare in pursuance of any relevant statutory provisions. This duty is wider than the old law, which was directed against 'wilful' conduct, defined as perverse or deliberate action. Intentional or reckless conduct does not need to be wilful.

Duty not to charge (s 9)

11.62 An employer shall not charge any employee in respect of anything done or provided in pursuance of any relevant statutory provision (see Personal Protective Equipment at Work Regulations 1992, para 11.83).

Rights of employees

Right not to suffer a detriment in health and safety cases (ERA, s 44)

11.63 An employee is entitled not to be subjected to any detriment by an act or a failure to act by his employer on any of the following grounds:

(a) having been designated by the employer to carry out activities in connection with preventing or reducing risks to health and safety at work, he carried out (or proposed to carry out) those activities;

(b) being a safety representative or member of a safety committee, he performed (or proposed to perform) any functions as such or took part in consultations or in an election as an employee safety representative;

(c) if there is no safety representative or safety committee where he is, or, if there are, it is not reasonably practicable to raise such matters, he brought the employer's attention (by reasonable means) to circumstances connected with his work which he reasonably believed were harmful or potentially harmful to health or safety;

(d) in circumstances of danger which he reasonably believed to be serious and imminent and which he could not reasonably be expected to avert, he left, or proposed to leave, or, while the danger persisted, he refused to return to, his place of work or any dangerous part of his place of work;

(e) in circumstances of danger which he reasonably believed to be serious and imminent, he took, or proposed to take, appropriate steps to protect himself or other persons from the danger. This is to be judged by reference to all the circumstances, including his knowledge, and the facilities and advice available to him at the time. However, he will not have been subjected to a detriment if he was so negligent in the steps he took that the employer treated him as a reasonable employer would have done in those circumstances.

11.64 An employee who believes that he has suffered a detriment contrary to s 44 may bring a complaint before an employment tribunal within the usual time limits. If the complaint is upheld, the tribunal shall make a declaration to that effect, and also award compensation to the complainant, the amount being such as the tribunal considers to be just and equitable in all the circumstances. This will include any expenses incurred and take account of any benefits lost. The employee is expected to mitigate against his loss, and the compensation award can be reduced on the ground of contributory conduct (see para 17.228).

11.65 But if a safety representative acts in respect of matters which are not within the area of the workplace for which he is a representative, or acts outside the laid down procedure, or acts in bad faith, then it may be that he is not pursuing a genuine health and safety matter, but is pursuing a personal agenda in order to embarrass the employer. In such circumstances, he may be disciplined as appropriate (*Shillito v Van Leer (UK) Ltd*[22]).

Right not to be dismissed unfairly in certain circumstances involving health and safety cases (ERA, s 100)

11.66 It will be unfair to dismiss an employee because of any of the following circumstances arising out of health and safety matters:

[22] [1997] IRLR 495, EAT.

(a) having been designated by the employer to carry out activities in connection with preventing or reducing risks to health and safety at work, he carried out (or proposed to carry out) those activities. In *Healey v Excel Logistics Ltd*[23] a safety representative went to the site of another company in order to inspect an entry in that company's accident book concerning an accident which involved one of the employees he represented. His subsequent dismissal for doing so was held to be unfair, because his duties as a safety representative were not confined to incidents which took place on his employer's premises;

(b) being a safety representative or member of a safety committee he performed (or proposed to perform) any functions as such, or took part in consultations as an employee safety representative, or in an election of representatives of employee safety;

(c) if there is no safety representative or safety committee where he is, or, if there are, it is not reasonably practicable to raise such matters, he brought the employer's attention (by reasonable means) to circumstances connected with his work which he reasonably believed were harmful or potentially harmful to health or safety. In *Balfour Kilpatrick Ltd v Acheson*[24] it was held that the taking of industrial action was not, in the circumstances, reasonable means whereby employees may bring health and safety concerns to the employer's attention;

(d) in circumstances of danger which he reasonably believed to be serious and imminent and which he could not reasonably be expected to avert, he left, or proposed to leave, or, while the danger persisted, he refused to return to, his place of work or any dangerous part of his place of work. In *Harvest Press Ltd v McCaffrey*[25] an employee left work because he felt he was in danger of being injured due to the behaviour of another employee towards him, who had been abusive and aggressive. His dismissal for leaving work was held to be unfair, for s 100(1)(d) was not confined to circumstances of danger which arose from working methods or equipment;

(e) in circumstances of danger which he reasonably believed to be serious and imminent, he took, or proposed to take, appropriate steps to protect himself or other persons from the danger. This is to be judged by reference to all the circumstances, including his knowledge, and the facilities and advice available to him at the time. Where an employee has a reasonable belief in danger and takes appropriate action, the employer must take that belief seriously and cannot dismiss him or subject him to detriment simply because he disagrees whether there was in fact danger (*Oudahar v Esporta Group Ltd*[26]). The term 'other persons' includes members of the public, as well as fellow employees, so that a chef who was dismissed because he refused to cook food which he believed to be unfit for human consumption succeeded in a claim for unfair dismissal under s 100 (*Masiak v City Restaurants (UK) Ltd*[27]). However, his dismissal shall not be regarded as being unfair if he was so negligent in the steps he took that the employer treated him as a reasonable employer would have treated him in those circumstances.

11.67 It should be noted that if a dismissal is unfair by virtue of (a) or (b) in para 11.66, and the employer refuses to reinstate or re-engage the employee following a tribunal order, an additional award (see para 17.239) can be made. The test to be applied is not only whether the employee genuinely feared for his safety, but whether that fear was based on reasonable grounds. This is a question of fact, to be determined not only by the nature of the potential danger, but the steps which the employee could have taken to follow any

---

[23] Unreported.   [24] [2003] IRLR 683, [2003] All ER (D) 15 (Apr), EAT.
[25] [1999] IRLR 778, EAT.   [26] [2011] IRLR 730, EAT.   [27] [1999] IRLR 780, EAT.

procedures laid down by the employer which would militate against the danger (*Kerr v Nathan's Wastesavers Ltd*[28]). Otherwise, there is no limit on the amount of the compensation award if the dismissal (or selection for redundancy) was contrary to s 100.

11.68 However, when it comes to a dismissal on other grounds, the protection afforded to a safety representative is neutral. Like a shop steward, he has no specially privileged position, and thus may be selected for redundancy in accordance with the appropriate selection criteria (*Smiths Industries Aerospace and Defence Systems v Rawlings*[29]).

Interim relief in health and safety cases (ERA, ss 128–130)

11.69 If an employee is dismissed for an inadmissible reason because he has been designated to carry out health and safety activities, or is a safety representative or member of a safety committee (see para 11.38) and he proposed to carry out activities as such, he may apply for interim relief, within seven days following the effective date of termination of his employment. The procedure and remedies are similar to the interim relief provisions contained in TULR(C)A, ss 161–166 (see para 21.122).

D. Health and safety regulations (s 15 and Sch 3)

11.70 As has already been indicated, one of the main purposes of the Act was to replace the existing statutory provisions by regulations, and over a period of time, the 'old' law contained in the Factories Act 1961, Offices, Shops and Railway Premises Act 1963, and so forth (for a complete list, see column 3 in Sch 1 to the Act), was phased out, and replaced with a system of regulations and Codes of Practice which, in combination with the other provisions of the Act, were designed to maintain and improve the standards of health, safety and welfare. Regulations are of three general types; first, there are those which lay down standards to be applied in most or all employment situations, second, there are those which are designed to control a particular hazard which may exist in a particular industry, and third, there are those which refer to particular hazards or risks but which may be found in a number of different industries. The view appears to be held that the use of regulations as a device for laying down legal standards is a superior method to legislation, for regulations are simpler and more flexible; they can be altered more readily in accordance with experience and technological progress, and will be more manageable to those who have to implement them.

11.71 Regulations are to be made by the Secretary of State either as a result of proposals made to him by the HSE, or on his own initiative, but in the latter case he must consult with the HSE and any other appropriate bodies. If the HSE makes the proposals, it, too, must consult with the appropriate government departments and other bodies (s 50). Regulations may:

(a) repeal or modify any existing statutory provision;

(b) exclude or modify in relation to any specific class of case any of the provisions of ss 2–9 (paras 11.34–11.62) or any existing statutory provision;

(c) make a specific authority responsible for the enforcement of any relevant statutory provision;

(d) impose requirements by reference to the approval of the HSE or other specified body or person;

(e) provide that any reference in a regulation to a specific document shall include a reference to a revised version of that document;

---

[28] Unreported.   [29] [1996] IRLR 656, EAT.

(f) provide for exemptions from any requirement or prohibition;

(g) enable exemptions to be granted by a specified person or authority;

(h) specify the persons or class of persons who may be guilty of an offence;

(i) provide for specified defences either generally or in specified circumstances;

(j) exclude proceedings on indictment in relation to certain offences;

(k) restrict the punishment which may be imposed in respect of certain offences.

11.72 A breach of duty imposed by regulations is, of course, punishable as a criminal offence. Additionally, a breach may give rise to civil liability, if the regulations specifically provide for this.

11.73 A number of regulations have been passed since 1974 dealing with all aspects of health and safety law. Reference should be made to an established textbook on this topic.

11.74 The Legislative and Regulatory Reform Act 2006 sets out a simplified procedure for amending legislative provisions contained in Acts of Parliament or regulations passed thereunder. The Act enables a Minister of the Crown to introduce Orders before Parliament for the purpose of removing or reducing any burden which results from legislation. A burden can be a financial cost, an administrative inconvenience, an obstacle to efficiency or productivity or a sanction (criminal or otherwise) that affects the carrying on of any lawful activity. The purpose of the Order may also be to ensure that regulatory functions are carried out in a manner which is transparent, accountable, proportionate and consistent, and targeted only at cases in which action is needed. The Order may not create any new criminal offence, or impose abolish or vary any tax. Prior to making the Order, the Minister shall consult with representative interests, as appropriate.

11.75 This power enables the Minister to bypass the normal Parliamentary procedure for passing legislation by means of a statutory instrument. A draft Order must be laid before Parliament, together with an explanatory memorandum, and the Order will come into force as a result of its being approved by a negative or affirmative resolution Parliamentary procedure, as appropriate. A Better Regulation Commission advises the Government on actions which need to be taken in order to reduce unnecessary burdens.

11.76 The powers contained in the Act have been used to repeal a number of outdated health and safety regulations, and, more recently, were used to unify the Health and Safety Commission and Executive (see para 1.51).

E. The impact of European law

11.77 Article 137 of the Treaty of Rome provides that member states shall pay particular attention to encouraging improvements, especially to the working environment, as regards the health and safety of workers. Under this article, Directives may be adopted by the qualified majority voting system, and a considerable number of such Directives have been adopted. In particular, the 'Framework Directive' (98/391/EEC) and five 'Daughter Directives' have recently been given effect to by the so-called 'six-pack' regulations (see para 11.78). The general view taken by the HSC is that the European Directives did not involve any significant change in UK law, although they do require UK law to make explicit that which is generally regarded as being implicit. Legal standards on health and safety in the UK are very high, and it is not expected that the following of EU Directives will impose any onerous burdens on UK employers.

11.78 The so-called 'six pack' regulations came into force on 1 January 1993. These are (a) Management of Health and Safety at Work Regulations, (b) Personal Protective Equipment at Work Regulations, (c) Provision and Use of Work Equipment Regulations, (d) Workplace (Health, Safety and Welfare) Regulations, (e) Manual Handling Operations Regulations, and (f) Health and Safety (Display Screen Equipment) Regulations. Many previous regulations were revoked, and most of the existing protective legislation, found in the Factories Act 1961, Offices, Shops and Railway Premises Act 1963 etc, was repealed.

11.79 Fundamental to the law is the need to take proactive steps to ensure health and safety at work of employees and others. These will include risk assessment in certain specified situations, provision of information to all those who may be at risk, health surveillance, the use of safety advisers, co-operation between employers, the provision of approved equipment and personal protection equipment and so on. Employees have a duty to use the equipment etc provided in a proper manner, to report shortcomings in the employer's protection arrangements or which represent a serious and immediate danger to health and safety.

Management of Health and Safety at Work Regulations 1999 (as amended)

11.80 These regulations set out the principles of prevention which should be applied, require employers to make risk assessments (in particular when women of child-bearing age are employed (see para 6.9) and in respect of young persons, see para 2.108), provide employees with appropriate health surveillance, appoint safety advisers, establish emergency procedures, provide training and information to employees, and cooperate with other employers where the workplace is shared. Employees are required to use all machinery, equipment substances etc in accordance with any relevant training and instructions, and to inform the employer of any dangerous work situation or shortcomings in the health and safety arrangements.

Workplace (Health, Safety and Welfare) Regulations 1992

11.81 Workplaces are to be maintained in an efficient state, repaired and cleaned. There must be sufficient fresh or purified air, reasonable temperature, and heating must not produce injurious fumes. Lighting must be suitable and sufficient, there must be sufficient floor area, suitable seats provided if the work can be done seated, floors and traffic routes must be suitable, and windows, skylights and ventilators must be safe. Doors, gates, traffic routes and escalators must be constructed with safety in mind. There must be suitable and sufficient sanitary conveniences, washing facilities, and drinking water, and accommodation for clothes not worn during working hours and for changing clothes where necessary. Rest facilities must be provided, with suitable arrangements to protect non-smokers from discomfort from tobacco smoke, and suitable facilities for eating meals.

Provision and Use of Work Equipment Regulations 1998

11.82 Work equipment must be suitable, efficiently maintained, kept in good repair and conform to any legislation which implements any relevant EC Directive. Employees must be given adequate health and safety information, written instructions where appropriate, and be properly trained. Effective measures must be taken to prevent access to any dangerous parts of machinery, and measures must be taken to prevent or adequately control certain specified hazards. Starting and stopping controls (including emergency stop controls) must be provided and clearly marked. Work equipment must be stable, capable of being isolated from all its sources of energy, maintenance operations must be carried out while work equipment is shut down, and warning devices clearly visible, unambiguous, easily perceived and understood.

Personal Protective Equipment at Work Regulations 1992

11.83 Personal protective equipment (PPE) is all equipment intended to be worn or held by a person at work which protects him from risks to health or safety. PPE is not suitable unless it conforms to applicable EC standards.

11.84 Employers must provide suitable PPE, which must be compatible with other such equipment worn. There must be an assessment of the suitability, and PPE must be maintained in an efficient state, kept in good repair, and cleaned or replaced as appropriate. Employers must provide employees with information, instruction and training about risks PPE will avoid or limit, and ensure that it is properly used. Employees must use PPE in accordance with instructions and training given, and report any defect or loss.

Manual Handling Operations Regulations 1992

11.85 Every employer must, so far as is reasonably practicable, avoid the need for his employees to undertake manual handling operations which involve the risk of injury. If such operations cannot be avoided, the employer must carry out an assessment of the operations, and take appropriate steps to reduce the risk of injury, and provide employees with indications of the risk and the weight of the load. Schedule 1 to the regulations sets out a comprehensive list of questions to be asked and factors taken into account in order to avoid or minimise the risks from manual handling. Employees shall make proper use of any system of work provided.

Health and Safety (Display Screen Equipment) Regulations 1992

11.86 Employers are required to make an analysis of workstations for the purpose of assessing health and safety risks so as to reduce these to the lowest extent reasonably practicable. The activities of users must be planned, so as to ensure they have periodic breaks or changes in activities. If a user so requests, the employer must provide eye and eyesight testing, and provide special corrective appliances when needed. Adequate health and safety training must be given in the use of workstations, and information given about all aspects of health and safety relating to workstations.

No Smoking

11.87 The Smoke-Free (Penalties and Enforcement) Regulations 2006 came into force in England in July 2007. Similar provisions came into force in Wales and Northern Ireland in April 2007. These regulations provide that:

(a) all work premises shall be smoke free if enclosed or substantially enclosed. This is defined as meaning premises with a ceiling, unless more than 50% of the wall area is open to the outside;

(b) all occupiers of premises must display a prominent 'No Smoking' sign. The sign must be of at least A5 size, and contain the words 'No Smoking. It is against the law to smoke in these premises except in a designated room';

(c) company cars are deemed to be entirely non-smoking if they might be used by more than one person, except if it is a convertible car and the roof is open;

(d) an employer who fails to display a prominent 'No Smoking' sign may be fined a fixed penalty of £200. If he fails to take reasonable steps to prevent smoking he is liable to a fine of up to £2,500;

(e) an employee or a visitor who is caught smoking on work premises is liable to a fixed penalty of £50.

The Smoking (Health and Social Care) (Scotland) Act 2005 came into force in March 2006 in Scotland, and regulations made thereunder provide that all workplaces, as well as clubs, pubs, etc shall be free from tobacco smoke.

Other regulations

11.88 There are a considerable number of other regulations on health and safety matters which have been passed since 1974. The most important of these (and the date of the most recent version) deal with the following topics; first aid (1981), electricity (1989), safety signs and signals (1996), confined spaces (1997), lifting operations (1998), major accident hazards (1999), ionising radiations (1999), protection of children (2000), lead (2002), hazardous substances (2002), fire precautions (2005), noise at work (2005), work at height (2005), vibrations (2005), construction (2007), employers' liability compulsory insurance (2008), artificial optical radiation (2012), asbestos (2012), reporting of injuries, diseases and dangerous occurrences (2013) and so on. In addition, a number of regulations deal with specific industries and processes (railways, gas, transport, adventure activities, carriage of goods, offshore installations, compressed air, etc).

F. Codes of practice (s 16)

11.89 For the purpose of providing practical guidance with respect to the general duties imposed by ss 2–7 (paras 11.34–11.60), or by any regulation or any existing statutory provisions, the HSE may approve and issue codes of practice which are suitable for that purpose. The HSE may also approve other such suitable codes which are drawn up by other persons or organisations, and thus there is no reason why a private firm or employers' organisation should not draw up its own code and submit it for approval, should this be thought desirable. One might also expect approval to be given to the existing British Standards Institution's own codes. The HSE cannot approve a code without the consent of the Secretary of State, and prior to obtaining this, must consult with government departments and other appropriate bodies. The codes may be revised from time to time, and the HSE may, if necessary, withdraw its approval from a particular code.

11.90 A failure on the part of any person to observe the provisions contained in an approved code of practice shall not of itself render that person liable to any civil or criminal proceedings, but in any such criminal proceedings, if a person is alleged to have committed an offence concerning a matter in respect of which an approved code is in force, the provisions of that code shall be admissible in evidence, and a failure to observe it shall constitute proof of the breach of duty, or contravention of the regulation or statutory provision, unless the accused can satisfy the court that he complied with the requirements of the law in some other equally efficacious manner. The codes, therefore, will be the guides to good safety practice, and if a person follows the provisions of the codes, he cannot be successfully prosecuted for an offence. If he fails to follow the relevant code, he may be guilty of an offence unless he can show that he observed the specific legal requirement some other way.

11.91 The Act contains no guidance on the use of the codes in civil proceedings, but it is likely that a failure to observe any such provision as is contained therein may well constitute prima facie evidence of negligence, which can be rebutted by evidence to the contrary.

G. Penalties (s 33)

11.92 Any person or body corporate (eg a company) may be charged with and convicted of an offence under the Act, and punished accordingly. In addition, if an offence committed by a body corporate is proved to have been committed with the consent of, connivance of, or attributable to any neglect on the part of, any director, manager, secretary or other similar officer, then he, as well as the body corporate may be guilty of an offence, and liable to be proceeded against and punished accordingly (s 37) (see *Huckerby v Elliott*[30]).

11.93 In *Armour v Skeen*,[31] a senior local government official was prosecuted for failing to prepare and carry out a safety policy, for this neglect of duty ultimately led to breaches of safety provisions which resulted in the death of an employee. It was held that the official was guilty of an offence under s 37. He was in a senior position in his organisation, and was therefore responsible for the general safety policy in his department. But in *R v Boal*[32] the accused was an assistant manager in a bookshop. Following a visit by inspectors, he was prosecuted and convicted in respect of a number of offences. On appeal, it was held that criminal liability was to be imposed on persons in authority in the company who were the 'decision makers', with the power and responsibility to decide corporate policy. As the accused was an 'underling', his conviction was quashed.

11.94 Where the commission of an offence by a person is due to the default of another person, that other person may be proceeded against, whether or not proceedings are taken against the first mentioned person (s 36). No proceedings under the Act may be brought except by an inspector, or with the consent of the Director of Public Prosecutions (in Scotland, the Procurator Fiscal).

11.95 There is an anomaly, however, in that although Crown bodies (excluding health authorities) have the same obligations under the Act as other employers, they cannot be prosecuted, and it is not possible to issue improvement or prohibition notices against the Crown (see para 11.25). However, this rule does not prevent the prosecution of individual Crown employees.

11.96 The Health and Safety (Offences) Act 2008 applies to all offences committed on or after 17 January 2009. The Act increased the penalties for most health and safety offences to £20,000, and makes imprisonment, up to 12 months in the magistrates' courts, an option for an increased number of offences. Certain offences, hitherto triable in the magistrates' courts, may now be tried either summarily in the magistrates' court or on indictment in the Crown Court before a jury. If proceedings are brought on indictment, there is the possibility of an unlimited fine, and in certain specified cases, up to two years' imprisonment. In *R v Howe & Son (Engineers) Ltd*[33] the Court of Appeal gave guidance on how sentencing policies should be applied to convictions for health and safety offences.

H. **Burden of proof**

11.97 As a general rule, in criminal proceedings, it is for the prosecution to prove its case 'beyond reasonable doubt'. However, by the Health and Safety at Work Act, s 40, if the offence consists of a failure to comply with a duty or requirement to do something 'so far as is reasonably practicable', or to use 'the best practicable means', it shall be for the accused to prove that it was not reasonably practicable to do more than was in fact done, or that there were no better practicable means than were in fact used to satisfy the duty or requirement. When the burden of proof is thus placed on the accused, he may discharge that burden

---

[30] [1970] 1 All ER 189, 134 JP 175, 113 Sol Jo 1001.   [31] [1977] IRLR 310, 1977 JC 15, 1977 SLT 71.
[32] [1992] QB 591, [1992] 3 All ER 177, [1992] 2 WLR 890, 95 Cr App Rep 272, [1992] ICR 495, [1992] IRLR 420, 156 JP 617, [1992] BCLC 872, [1992] 21 LS Gaz R 26, 136 Sol Jo LB 100, CA.
[33] [1999] 2 All ER 249, [1999] 2 Cr App Rep (S) 37, [1999] IRLR 434, 163 JP 359, [1999] Crim LR 238, [1998] 46 LS Gaz R 34, [1998] All ER (D) 552, CA.

of proof on the balance of probabilities (*R v Carr-Briant*[34]). In *Davies v Health and Safety Executive* it was held that this reversal of the burden of proof did not violate Art 6 of the Convention on Human Rights (see para 1.107).

11.98 It is not necessary for the prosecution to identify a specific breach of duty by the defendant. It is sufficient to prove that there was a risk of injury arising from a state of affairs at work. The burden of proof then passes to the defendant under s 40 of the Act to prove that they had done all that was reasonably practicable to avoid the risk. Thus, if there has been no risk assessment, no training given, or no adequate safety precautions provided, it will be difficult for the accused to discharge that burden (*R v Chargot Ltd*[35]). But if the worker is injured because he has acted in a manner that a reasonable employer could not have foreseen, the employer cannot be successfully prosecuted, because the employee's action constitutes going 'on a frolic of his own' (*R v N Ltd*[36]).

I. Corporate manslaughter

11.99 The Corporate Manslaughter and Corporate Homicide Act 2007 created a new offence of corporate manslaughter in England, Wales and Northern Ireland, and corporate homicide in Scotland, which replaced the previous common law offence of manslaughter as it applied to organisations. The offence is committed when an organisation manages or organises its activities in such a way as to cause a person's death in a manner that amounts to a gross breach of duty of care. The way in which the senior managers, who play a significant role in the making of decisions about the whole or a substantial part of the organisation's activities, manage or organise its activities must be a substantial element in the breach. The breach will be gross if it falls far below what can reasonably be expected of the organisation in the circumstances.

11.100 A jury must consider such factors as (a) whether the organisation failed to comply with health and safety legislation, (b) the seriousness of the breach, (c) how much of a risk of death the breach posed. In addition, the jury may also take into account (a) the extent to which the evidence shows that there were attitudes, policies, systems or accepted practices within the organisation which were likely to have encouraged the failure, or to have produced tolerance of it, (b) any health and safety guidance that relates to the breach issued by an authority responsible for enforcing health and safety legislation, and (c) any other relevant matter.

11.101 A prosecution under the Act can only be undertaken by the Director of Public Prosecutions (in Scotland the Procurator Fiscal). If convicted, the court will impose a fine, and may also issue a remedial order requiring the organisation to take specified steps to remedy any relevant breach or any matter resulting from the breach that caused the death, or any health and safety deficiency in the organisation's policies or practices of which the relevant breach appears to be an indication. The court may also impose a publicity order, requiring the convicted organisation to publicise specific information about its failures.

11.102 The duty of care is owed (a) by an employer to his employees or other persons working for the organisation, (b) by an occupier of premises, (c) in connection with the supply of goods or services, construction or maintenance activities, using or keeping of plant etc, and (d) from a future date, to persons in custody.

---

[34] [1943] KB 607, [1943] 2 All ER 156, 41 LGR 183, 29 Cr App Rep 76, 107 JP 167, 112 LJKB 581, 169 LT 175, 59 TLR 300, CCA.

[35] [2008] UKHL 73, [2009] 1 WLR 1, [2009] 2 All ER 645, [2009] ICR 263, (2009) 153(1) SJLB 32, (2008) *Times*, 16 December.

[36] [2008] EWCA Crim 1223, [2008] 1 WLR 2684, [2009] 1 Cr App R 3, (2008) *Times*, 25 August.

Compensation for injuries at work

A. **The extent of the duty owed**

11.103 One of the prime duties of an employer is to ensure that his employees do not suffer an accident or injury while at work. There are a number of common law rules which determine the extent of that duty, and in addition there are certain statutory provisions designed to ensure the employee's safety which, if broken or not observed by the employer, may lead to an action for damages by an injured employee based on a breach of statutory duties, if a statutory instrument specifically provides for this.

Where a breach of statutory duty claim can be brought, the two actions are run together, so that an employee may succeed for breach of the common law duty and/or a breach of the statutory duty, though, of course, only one set of damages will be awarded. The purpose of the common law rules is to compensate for injuries incurred as a result of the employer's negligence; the object of the statute will be accident prevention enforced by criminal penalties, but with a potential liability for compensation as well. But as Goddard LJ said in *Hutchinson v London and North Eastern Rly Co*, 'The real incentive for the observance by employers of their statutory duties … is not their liability to substantial fines, but the possibility of heavy claims for damages.'[37] The whole question of compensation for injuries at work was reviewed by the Royal Commission on Civil Liability, but no significant changes were recommended in its report.

11.104 The duty owed by the employer is in respect of the employee's physical and mental health, including ill-health caused by overwork (*Johnstone v Bloomsbury Health Authority*[38]), psychiatric illness (*Frost v Chief Constable of South Yorkshire Police*[39]) and stress and anxiety caused thereby (*Walker v Northumberland County Council*[40]). But if the employers do not know of the risk, or if, having knowledge, they take such steps as are reasonable in the circumstances to minimise the risk, or provide appropriate healthcare, no liability arises (*Petch v Customs and Excise Comrs*[41]). A difficult case was *White v Chief Constable of South Yorkshire Police*,[42] where it was held that a policeman was not entitled to recover damages for psychiatric illness suffered as a result of assisting in the aftermath of the Hillsborough disaster, either as an employee or a rescuer.

11.105 Liability for psychiatric injury caused by stress at work is no different in principle from liability for physical injury. The test is whether the injury is a foreseeable breach of the employer's duty of care. It does not follow that, because a claimant suffers from stress at work, and that the employer was in some way in breach of a duty to allow that to occur, that the claimant is able to establish a claim in negligence (*Hartman v South Essex Mental Health and Community Care NHS Trust*[43]). As a result of a recent legal decision, the courts are likely to adopt a more cautious approach to claims for damages in respect of psychiatric injury caused by stress. In *Sutherland v Hatton*,[44] the Court of Appeal heard appeals

[37] [1942] 1 KB 481, [1942] 1 All ER 330, 111 LJKB 369, 166 LT 228, 58 TLR 174, CA.

[38] [1992] QB 333, [1991] 2 All ER 293, [1991] 2 WLR 1362, [1991] ICR 269, [1991] IRLR 118, [1991] 2 2 Med LR 38, CA.

[39] [1998] QB 254, [1997] 1 All ER 540, [1997] 3 WLR 1194, [1997] IRLR 173, 33 BMLR 108, [1996] NLJR 1651, CA; revsd sub nom *White v Chief Constable of South Yorkshire Police* [1999] 2 AC 455, [1999] 1 All ER 1, [1998] 3 WLR 1509, [1999] ICR 216, 45 BMLR 1, [1999] 02 LS Gaz R 28, [1998] NLJR 1844, [1999] 3 LRC 644, sub nom *Frost v Chief Constable of South Yorkshire Police* 143 Sol Jo LB 51, HL.

[40] [1995] 1 All ER 737, [1995] ICR 702, [1995] IRLR 35, [1995] ELR 231, [1994] NLJR 1659.

[41] [1993] ICR 789, 137 Sol Jo LB 120, CA.   [42] [1999] IRLR 110.   [43] [2005] EWCA Civ 6.

[44] [2002] EWCA Civ 76, [2002] 2 All ER 1, [2002] ICR 613, [2002] IRLR 263, 68 BMLR 115, [2002] All ER (D) 53 (Feb); revsd [2004] UKHL 13, [2004] 2 All ER 385, [2004] 1 WLR 1089, 148 Sol Jo LB 419, [2004] All ER (D) 07 (Apr).

by employers in four unconnected cases against awards of damages to employees who had stopped work because of stress-induced psychiatric illness. Three of the appeals were allowed, while the fourth was dismissed 'not without some hesitation'. The court laid down a number of practical propositions designed to help other courts deal with future claims. While conceding that it was the employer's duty to take reasonable steps to ensure the physical and mental health of his employees, it was held that in order for an employer to be liable, the stress-induced injury must be sufficiently foreseeable to be plain enough for any reasonable employer to realise that he should do something about it. The Court of Appeal stated that there were no occupations which are intrinsically dangerous to mental health, that employers are entitled to assume that employees can withstand the normal pressures of the job (unless they know of some particular problem or vulnerability), and that an employee who returns to work after being absent through sickness is implying that he is fit for work, and the employer is entitled to take that at its face value. To trigger a duty to take steps, the indications of impending harm to health arising from stress at work had to be plain enough for any reasonable employer to realise that he ought to do something about it, and the employer will only be liable if he fails to take reasonable steps, bearing in mind the magnitude of the risk, the gravity of the harm, the costs and practicability of preventing it, and the justification for running the risk. Thus it might be possible for the employer to suggest that the employee takes a sabbatical period of leave, or a transfer to other work, or a redistribution of the work, etc. Extra help may be provided, or a mentoring scheme introduced. But such assistance will depend very much on the employer's resources, and the interests of other employees at the workplace. The fact that an employer provides a counselling service for the benefit of employees who are suffering from stress-related illnesses does not, by itself, relieve the employer of the duty of care owed. Counselling services are not a panacea by which the duty of care can be discharged (*Intel Corporation (UK) Ltd v Daw*[45]).

11.106 The court went on to point out that it is not enough that the occupational stress has caused the harm. It must be shown that it was the employer's breach of duty to take reasonable care for the health of his employees that has caused or materially contributed to the harm. An employer can only reasonably be expected to take steps which are likely to do some good, and if the only reasonable steps an employer could take in order to remove the employee from a job which is causing stress is to demote the employee or dismiss him, and the employer will not be in breach of his duty for allowing a willing employee to continue in his job. If there is no alternative solution, it is for the employee to decide whether or not to continue in the job, and risk a breakdown in his health, or whether to leave the employment and look for work elsewhere. Finally, the consequence of the breach of duty may be only one of many stressful events which affected an employee's state of health, and the employer should only pay for that proportion of the harm which is attributable to his wrongdoing.

11.107 A somewhat different approach to stress at work claims was taken by the Court of Appeal in *Dickens v O2 plc*[46] where, although purporting to apply the guidelines in *Hatton*, it would seem that the requirements of reasonable foreseeability, breach of duty and causation are not as difficult for claimants to satisfy as the reading of *Hatton* may suggest. In this case it was held that a prior claim about stress should have alerted management to the existence of a potential problem, and steps should have been taken to have the affected employee examined by occupational health personnel. It was pointed out that the guidelines in *Hatton* must be taken in the context of the case, and not applied out of context to contort a case out of recognition.

---

[45] [2007] EWCA Civ 70, [2007] 2 All ER 126, [2007] ICR 1318, [2007] IRLR 355, (2007) 104(8) LSG 36, (2007) 157 NLJ 259, (2007) 151 SJLB 259.
[46] [2008] EWCA Civ 1144.

11.108 Thus an employer should always be alert to the problems likely to be suffered by a stressed employee. In *Barber v Somerset County Council*[47] the employee was the head of a department at a school. He had a very heavy workload, working between 60–70 hours per week. He was off work for three weeks suffering from 'overstressed/depression'. When he returned to work the school authorities were not very sympathetic towards him, and no steps were taken to improve the situation. The following term he found himself with the same or slightly heavier workload, and eventually left work altogether, suffering from moderate or severe depression. His claim for damages was upheld by the House of Lords. A prudent employer who knew that an employee had taken some time off work because of stress caused by work overload would have investigated the situation to see how the difficulties might be improved. If an employee works hours which are in excess of the 48-hour week, or in breach of the rest provisions, with the consequence that he suffers psychiatric injury caused by overwork, this can be taken into account when consideration is given to the foreseeability of the injury (*Hone v Six Continents Retail*[48]). While every case will turn on its own facts, the principles laid down in *Stokes v Guest, Keen and Nettlefold*[49] (see para 11.111) were approved, ie ' ... the overall test is still the conduct of a reasonable and prudent employer, taking positive thought for the safety of his workers in the light of what he knows or ought to know ... '.

11.109 The duty of the employer to take care is one aspect of the law of negligence which requires everyone to ensure that his activities do not cause injury or damage to another through an act of negligence. The standard of care which an employer must observe is, as Lord Oaksey pointed out in *Paris v Stepney Borough Council*, '[t]he care which an ordinary prudent employer would take in all the circumstances'.[50] The employer does *not* guarantee that an employee will not be injured; he only undertakes to take reasonable care, and he will only be liable if there is some lack of care on his part in failing to prevent something which was reasonably foreseeable. The employee, on his part, must be prepared to look after himself, and not expect to be able to blame the employer for every incident which takes place. In *Vinnyey v Star Paper Mills*,[51] the claimant was instructed by the foreman to clear and clean a floor area which had been made slippery by a viscous fluid. The foreman provided proper equipment and gave clear instructions. The claimant was injured when he slipped on the floor, and it was held that the employer was not liable, for there was no reasonably foreseeable risk in the performance of such a simple task. So too, in *Lazarus v Firestone Tyre and Rubber Co Ltd*,[52] where the claimant was knocked down in the general rush to get to the canteen. The court held that this was not the sort of behaviour which grown persons could be protected against. Such cases are in line with a number of judicial statements made in recent years deprecating 'any tendency to treat the relationship between employer and skilled workman as equivalent to that of nurse and imbecile child' (per Lord Simmons in *Smith v Austin Lifts*[53]), or that of 'schoolmaster and pupil' (per Devlin LJ in *Withers v Perry Chain Co Ltd*[54]).

11.110 Equally, if an employer does not know of the danger, and could not be expected to know in the light of current knowledge, or did not foresee the danger and could not be expected to foresee it, he will not be liable. In *Down v Dudley Coles Long Ltd*[55] an employee

[47] [2002] EWCA Civ 76, [2002] 2 All ER 1, [2002] IRLR 263, 68 BMLR 115, [2002] All ER (D) 53 (Feb); revsd [2004] UKHL 13, [2004] 2 All ER 385, [2004] 1 WLR 1089, 148 Sol Jo LB 419, [2004] All ER (D) 07 (Apr).
[48] [2005] EWCA Civ 922, CA.   [49] [1968] 1 WLR 1776, 5 KIR 401, 112 Sol Jo 821.
[50] [1950] 1 KB 320, [1949] 2 All ER 843, 113 JP 507, 93 Sol Jo 710, 65 TLR 723, CA; revsd [1951] AC 367, [1951] 1 All ER 42, 49 LGR 293, 115 JP 22, [1951] 1 TLR 25, 84 Ll L Rep 525, 94 Sol Jo 837, HL.
[51] [1965] 1 All ER 175.   [52] *Times*, 2 May 1963.
[53] [1959] 1 All ER 81, [1959] 1 WLR 100, [1958] 2 Lloyd's Rep 583, 103 Sol Jo 73, HL.
[54] [1961] 3 All ER 676, [1961] 1 WLR 1314, 59 LGR 496, 105 Sol Jo 648, CA.   [55] Unreported, 1969.

was partially deafened by the noise from a cartridge-assisted hammer gun. At the then state of medical knowledge (ie in 1964), a reasonable employer would not have known of the potential danger of using this particular piece of equipment without providing safety precautions, and hence the employer was not liable for the injury. But once the danger is discovered, he must take all reasonable steps to protect his employees from the conse-quences of risks which have hitherto been unforeseeable. In *Wright v Dunlop Rubber Co*,[56] the employers used an anti-oxidant known as Nonox S from 1940 onwards. The manu-facturers then discovered that the substance was capable of causing bladder cancer, and informed the defendants that all employees who had been exposed to it should be screened and tested. This was not done for some time, and thus the employers, as well as the manu-facturers, were held liable to the claimants.

11.111 The matter was summarised by Swanwick J in *Stokes v Guest, Keen and Nettlefold (Bolts and Nuts) Ltd* (see para 11.108).

(a) The employer must take positive steps to ensure the safety of his employees in the light of the knowledge which he has or ought to have.

(b) The employer is entitled to follow current recognised practice unless in the light of common sense or new knowledge this is clearly unsound.

(c) Where there is developing knowledge, he must keep reasonably abreast with it, and not be too slow in applying it.

(d) If he has greater than average knowledge of the risk, he must take more than average precautions.

(e) He must weigh up the risk (in terms of the likelihood of injury and possible conse-quences) against the effectiveness of the precautions needed to meet the risk, and the cost and inconvenience.

11.112 Applying these tests, if the employer falls below the standards of a reasonable and prudent employer, he will be negligent. On the other hand, if the employer takes all such steps as are reasonably practicable, he will not be liable at common law (*Darby v GKN Screws and Fasteners Ltd*[57]).

11.113 If, before his dismissal, an employee acquires a cause of action at common law (whether for breach of contract or breach of the duty to take reasonable care for the employee's health and safety) that cause of action remains unimpaired by the fact that the employee has brought a statutory unfair dismissal claim. Thus a claim for damages for psychiatric injury caused, for example, by a wrongful application of the contractual disci-plinary procedure may succeed (*Eastwood v Magnox Electric plc*[58]), even though there can be no award for psychiatric illness (or injury to feelings) caused by the manner of actual dismissal (*Dunnachie v Kingston upon Hull City Council*[59]).

B. Duty to unborn children

11.114 Under the Congenital Disabilities (Civil Liability) Act 1976, an employer may be liable to a child of an employee who is born disabled as a result of any breach of legal duty, whether imposed by statute or by common law, to the child's parent. The child may thus sue in respect of a pre-natal injury suffered, whether or not the parent suffered any injury, and

---

[56] (1971) 11 KIR 311, 115 Sol Jo 366.　　　[57] [1986] ICR 1.
[58] [2002] EWCA Civ 463, [2003] ICR 520n, [2002] IRLR 447, [2002] All ER (D) 366 (Mar).
[59] [2004] EWCA Civ 84, [2004] 2 All ER 501, [2004] NLJR 248, 148 Sol Jo LB 233, [2004] All ER (D) 185 (Feb).

whether or not the employer knew of the existence of the foetus. The right of the child to sue is contingent on the existence of a right for the parent to sue; in other words, the claim is as good as, but no better than, the claim of the parent. Any contributory negligence on the part of the parent may reduce the child's damages.

C. Personal nature of the duty

11.115 The duty of the employer is a personal one, in the sense that he cannot absolve himself by delegating the duty to someone else. In *Wilsons & Clyde Coal Co Ltd v English*,[60] the employer was compelled by law to employ a colliery agent who was responsible for mine safety; nonetheless, it was held that the employer was liable for an unsafe system of work in the mine. Thus it can never be a defence to argue that the employer has assigned the task of securing and maintaining safety precautions to a safety officer or other person.

11.116 Equally, the duty is owed to each employee as an individual, not to them all collectively. This means that one must take greater precautions when dealing, for example, with inexperienced employees, or with new and untrained employees or with young persons, etc, than one might do with more responsible staff. In *Paris v Stepney Borough Council* (see para 11.109) the claimant worked chipping away at rust and other superfluous rubbish which had accumulated underneath buses. Goggles were not provided for this work, for it was not customary to do so. The claimant only had one eye, and he was totally blinded when a splinter entered his good eye. It was held that the employers were liable. They should have foreseen that there was a risk of greater injury to the employee, and provided goggles for him, even though they may not have been under such a duty with respect to other employees.

11.117 Clearly, a higher standard of care must be shown to employees who lack a sufficient or adequate command of the English language, to ensure that they are properly trained and clearly instructed, so as not to cause injuries to themselves and to others. In *James v Hepworth and Grandage Ltd*[61] the employers put up large notices informing employees that they should wear spats for their personal protection. Unknown to them, the claimant could not read, and when he was injured he claimed damages from his employers. His claim failed. He had observed other workmen wearing spats, and the court concluded that his failure to make enquiries meant that even if he had been informed about the notice, he would not have worn them. But with the growth of foreign labour in UK factories, the problem is likely to cause growing concern, particularly as such labour tends to concentrate in the initial stages in those industries which have serious safety hazards. The responsibility of the safety officer, as the 'agent' of the employer, to ensure that the work can be done in safety is likely to be very onerous in practice (see *Hawkins v Ian Ross (Castings) Ltd*[62]).

11.118 An employer has a duty to warn an employee of risks to his health and safety where those risks are not common knowledge and cannot be guarded against by the taking of sensible precautions, and where that knowledge would affect the employee's decision to accept the work. But the employer does not guarantee absolutely the safety of the employee. In *White v Holbrook Precision Castings Ltd*[63] the claimant was employed as a grinder. He developed Reynaud's Disease (vibration white finger) and sued for damages. His claim was dismissed. The claimant knew of the risk when he accepted the employment, and the employers were merely aware that the disease could cause minor discomfort.

---

[60] [1938] AC 57, [1937] 3 All ER 628, 106 LJPC 117, 81 Sol Jo 700, 157 LT 406, 53 TLR 944, HL.
[61] [1968] 1 QB 94, [1967] 2 All ER 829, [1967] 3 WLR 178, 111 Sol Jo 232, CA.
[62] [1970] 1 All ER 180.   [63] [1985] IRLR 215, CA.

No precautions had ever been suggested or were viable. The claimant would still have taken the employment had he been specifically told of the risk. However, given the current state of medical and scientific knowledge, a different conclusion may well be reached nowadays (see *Shepherd v Firth Brown Ltd*[64]).

11.119 It has long been held that, as a general rule, there is no onus on an employer to remove an employee from unsafe work, the onus being on the employee to decide for himself whether to continue to take on the work (*Withers v Perry Chain Co Ltd* (see para 11.109), and *Henderson v Wakefield Shirt Co Ltd*[65]). Still less is there an obligation on the employer to dismiss the employee, if that was the only alternative. Indeed, in *Sutherland v Hatton* (see para 11.105) it was stated that if the only reasonable and effective step would have been to dismiss or demote the employee, the employer would not be in breach of his duty in allowing a willing employee to continue in the job. It is for the employee to decide whether or not to carry on in the employment and take the risk of a breakdown in his health. But there may well be cases where, despite the employee's desire to remain at work notwithstanding the risk he ran, the employer would be under a duty in law to dismiss him for his own good so as to protect him from physical danger (see *Coxall v Goodyear GB Ltd*[66]). In unfair dismissal proceedings, the employer would have to plead some other substantial reason, ie the common law duty. If disability discrimination proceedings were brought, the defence of reasonable adjustments would have to be raised.

11.120 Modern technologies and modern working methods inevitably bring about new and special problems, and legal decisions must be adapted from existing principles to meet the factual situations which arise. Thus claims have succeeded and failed in respect of repetitive strain injury or work related upper limb disorder (*Pickford v ICI plc*;[67] *Alexander v Midland Bank plc*[68]), vibration white finger (*Armstrong v British Coal Corpn*[69]), work induced stress (*Petch v Customs and Excise Comrs* (see para 11.104); *Walker v Northumberland County Council*, see para 11.104), acts of violence (*Haughton v Hackney Borough Council*[70]), breach of health and safety regulations (see para 11.70), and so on.

D. The threefold nature of the duty

11.121 Although there is only one single duty on an employer to take care, it is convenient to examine the nature of that duty under three sub-headings.

Safe plant and appliances

11.122 This means that all the equipment, tools, machinery, plant, etc, where the employee works shall be reasonably safe for work. In *Bradford v Robinson Rentals Ltd*,[71] a driver was required to drive an unheated van on a 400-mile journey during a bitterly cold spell of weather. It was held that the employer was liable when the driver suffered frostbite as a consequence. In *Close v Steel Co of Wales Ltd*,[72] it was suggested by Lord Goddard that if an employer knows that a machine has a tendency to throw out flying parts so as to constitute

---

[64] Unreported, 17 April 1985. [65] [1997] PIQR P413, CA.

[66] [2002] EWCA Civ 1010, [2003] 1 WLR 536, [2003] ICR 152, [2002] IRLR 742, [2002] All ER (D) 303 (Jul).

[67] [1997] ICR 566, [1996] IRLR 622, [1997] 8 Med LR 270, 140 Sol Jo LB 202, CA; revsd [1998] 3 All ER 462, [1998] 1 WLR 1189, [1998] ICR 673, [1998] IRLR 435, [1998] 31 LS Gaz R 36, [1998] NJLR 978, 142 Sol Jo LB 198, [1998] All ER (D) 302, HL.

[68] [2000] ICR 464, [1999] IRLR 723, CA. [69] (1996) *Times*, 6 December, CA. [70] Unreported.

[71] [1967] 1 All ER 267, [1967] 1 WLR 337, 1 KIR 486, 111 Sol Jo 33.

[72] [1960] 2 QB 299, [1960] 2 All ER 657, [1960] 3 WLR 401, 58 LGR 297, CA; aff'd [1962] AC 367, [1961] 2 All ER 953, [1961] 3 WLR 319, 59 LGR 439, 105 Sol Jo 586, HL.

a danger to the operative, this could well amount to common law negligence on the part of the employer if he fails to take reasonable precautions.

11.123 However, if an employer purchased tools or equipment from a reputable supplier, and has no knowledge of any defect in them, he will have performed his duty to take care, and will not be liable for negligence (see *Davie v New Merton Board Mills*[73]). This would not be so if the equipment was bought second-hand from, say, a scrapyard. If a remedy existed in *Davie's* case, it would be for the injured employee to sue the person responsible for the defect under the general law of negligence as propounded in the leading case of *Donoghue v Stevenson*,[74] but frequently this might prove to be difficult or impossible in practice. The employee might not be in a position to prove just who was negligent. It might be a firm of stevedores at the docks, a foreign manufacturer, and so on. In view of these problems, the law was changed with the passing of the Employers' Liability (Defective Equipment) Act 1969. This provides that if an employee suffers a personal injury in the course of his employment in consequence of a defect in equipment provided by his employers for the purpose of the employers' business, and the defect is attributable to the fault of a third party, the injury shall be deemed to be attributable to the negligence of the employer. Thus, should facts similar to *Davie's* case arise again, the employee would be able to sue his employer for the 'deemed' negligence, and the employer, for his part, would be able to recover the amount of damages paid from the third party whose fault it really was. At the same time, the Employers' Liability (Compulsory Insurance) Act 1969 was passed, to ensure that all employers had valid insurance cover to meet personal injuries claims from their employees.

11.124 If an employer is aware that there are defects in tools or equipment he has bought then he should withdraw them from circulation if he wishes to avoid liability. In *Taylor v Rover Co Ltd*[75] a batch of chisels had been badly hardened by the manufacturers. One had, in fact, shattered, without causing any injury, but the batch was still in use when another chisel shattered, injuring the claimant in his eye. The employers were held liable.

Safe system of work

11.125 Here we must consider all the factors which concern the manner in which the work is to be done. The layout, the systems laid down, the training and supervision, the provision of warnings, protective clothing, special instructions, and so forth, are all relevant. In *Barcock v Brighton Corpn*,[76] the claimant was employed at an electricity sub-station. A certain method of testing was in operation, which was unsafe, and in consequence the claimant was injured. The employers were held liable. But if the employer gives proper instructions which the employee fails to observe, the employer will not be liable for a subsequent injury. In *Charlton v Forrest Printing Ink Co Ltd*[77] a senior employee was required to collect the firm's wages of £1,500 each Friday from the bank. Because, several years earlier, there had been a wage snatch of the firm's payroll, the managing director had given instructions that the collection arrangements should be varied each week, for example, by using taxis instead of private cars, by going at different times and by different routes. Contrary to these instructions, in the course of time, a collecting pattern set in, and the employee suffered severe injuries when he was robbed in an attack. In the High Court, the judge found for the claimant arguing that the employers had been negligent in not employing a professional security

---

[73] [1959] AC 604, [1959] 1 All ER 346, [1959] 2 WLR 331, 103 Sol Jo 177, HL.
[74] [1932] AC 562, 1932 SC (HL) 31, 1932 SLT 317, [1932] WN 139.
[75] [1966] 2 All ER 181, [1966] 1 WLR 1491.
[76] [1949] 1 KB 339, [1949] 1 All ER 251, 47 LGR 253, 93 Sol Jo 119, 65 TLR 90.
[77] [1978] IRLR 559, 122 Sol Jo 730; revsd [1980] IRLR 331, CA.

firm, but this decision was reversed on appeal. The vast majority of firms of that size in that area made their own payroll collection, and hence the employers could not be said to be negligent in carrying on with that practice. Although there was a risk, they had taken reasonable steps to minimise or eliminate it. The Court of Appeal thought that the claimant's remedy would be through an application to the Criminal Injuries Compensation Board, which has funds for such contingencies.

11.126 If there are safety precautions laid down, the employee must be told what they are; if safety equipment is provided, it must be available for use. In *Finch v Telegraph Construction and Maintenance Co Ltd*[78] the claimant was employed as a grinder. Goggles had been provided, but he was not told where they were. The employers were held to be liable when he was injured by a flying piece of metal whilst doing his work.

11.127 But if the employer, though not providing the safety precautions, can show that even if he had provided them the employee would not have used them, he may escape liability. In *Cummings (or McWilliam) v Sir William Arrol Ltd*,[79] a steel erector fell from scaffolding and was killed. The employer had provided safety belts in the past, but these had not been used, and they had been taken away to be used on another site. It was held that even though the employer was negligent in not providing the safety belts, it was unlikely that the employee would have used them had they been available. Accordingly, the employer's negligence was not the cause of the death, since this would have occurred anyway.

11.128 The more dangerous the process, the greater the need for safety precautions. On the other hand, the employer cannot be expected to be held liable in respect of accidents which occur in simple situations, as *Vinnyey's* case (para 11.109) illustrates. A situation which gives rise to some legal difficulties is where the employer provides the safety precautions, but the employees fail or refuse to use them. Is the duty of the employer a merely passive one, to provide and do no more? Or is it an active one, to exhort, propagandise, instruct or even compel their use? It is submitted that the answer to these questions can be given in four propositions.

(a) If the risk is an obvious one, and the injury resulting from the failure to use the precautions is not likely to be serious, then the employer's duty is a passive one of merely providing the precautions, informing the employees and leaving it to them to decide for themselves whether or not to use them. In *Qualcast (Wolverhampton) Ltd v Haynes*,[80] an experienced workman was splashed by molten metal on his legs. Spats were available, but the employers did nothing to ensure that they were worn. The injury, though doubtless painful, was not of a serious nature, and the employers were held not liable.

(b) If the risk is that of a serious injury, then the duty of the employer is a higher one of doing all he can to ensure that the workmen will use the safety precautions which are provided. In *Nolan v Dental Manufacturing Co Ltd*[81] a toolsetter was injured when a chip flew off a grinding wheel. Because of the seriousness of the injury should such occur, it was held that the employer should have insisted that protective goggles were worn.

(c) If the risk is an insidious one, or one the seriousness of which the employee would not readily appreciate, then again, it is the duty of the employer to do all he can by

---

[78] [1949] 1 All ER 452, 47 LGR 710, 93 Sol Jo 219, 65 TLR 153.
[79] 1961 SC 134, 1961 SLT 265, Ct of Sess; aff'd sub nom *Cummings (or McWilliams) v Sir William Arrol & Co Ltd* [1962] 1 All ER 623, [1962] 1 WLR 295, 106 Sol Jo 218, 1962 SC 70, 1962 SLT 121, HL.
[80] [1959] AC 743, [1959] 2 All ER 38, [1959] 2 WLR 510, 103 Sol Jo 310, HL.
[81] [1958] 2 All ER 449, [1958] 1 WLR 936, 102 Sol Jo 619.

way of propaganda, constant reminders, exhortations, etc, to try to get the employ-ees to use the precautions. In *Berry v Stone Manganese and Marine Ltd*,[82] the claim-ant was working in an environment where the noise levels were dangerously high. Ear muffs had been provided, but no effort was made to ensure their use. It was held that as the workmen would not readily appreciate the dangers of injury to their hearing if they did not use the ear muffs, the employers were liable, as they had failed to take steps to impress on them the need to use the protective equipment.

(d) When the employer has done all he can do, when he has not only provided the pro-tection, but instructed on its use, advised on how to use it properly, pointed out the risks involved in a failure to use, and given constant reminders about its use, then he can do no more, and from that time he will be absolved from liability. Admittedly, this does not solve the problem, which is how to ensure that employees do their work safely. It is possible to make the use of safety equipment part of the contract of employment, or a provision in the works rules, and, it is submitted, a failure to observe these terms or instructions may, after due warning, enable the employer fairly to dismiss the employee. There appears to be no legal duty to do so in order to protect the employee from the physical consequences of his own folly.

Reasonably competent fellow employees

11.129 If an employer engages an incompetent person, whose actions injure another employee, the employer will be liable for failing to take reasonable care. In *Hudson v Ridge Manufacturing Co Ltd*[83] an employee who was known to be prone to committing practical jokes, carried one of his pranks too far, and injured a fellow employee. The employer was liable. The answer in these circumstances, is, after due warning, to dispense firmly with the services of such a person, for he is a menace to himself and to others. On the other hand, in *Coddington v International Harvester Co of Great Britain Ltd*,[84] for a joke, an employee, M, kicked a tin of burning thinners close to X, and another employee, Y, was scorched by the flames, and in the agony of the moment, kicked the tin away so that it enveloped the claim-ant in flames, causing him severe injuries. It was held that the defendants were not liable. There was nothing in M's previous conduct which suggested that he might endanger oth-ers, and his act was completely outside the scope of his employment. If a person is injured during horseplay, he would not be able to recover damages unless he could show that the injury was caused by a failure to take care which amounted to recklessness or a very high degree of carelessness, or that it was caused with intent to do harm (*Blake v Galloway*[85]).

E. **Breach of statutory duty**

11.130 The Health and Safety at Work Act 1974 specifically excludes the right to bring a civil action in respect of a breach of ss 2–8. In the past, however, an action could be brought for breach of statutory duty unless the particular regulations said otherwise. On 1 October 2013, section 69 of the Enterprise and Regulatory Reform Act came into force and amended section 47 of the Health and Safety at Work Act (HSA). The aim of the amendment was to 'remove the right of civil action against employers for breach of statutory duty in relation to certain health and safety legislation, other than where such a right is specifically provided for'. This reverses the previous position, and means that no civil claim can be brought for breach of statutory

---

[82] [1972] 1 Lloyd's Rep 182, 12 KIR 13, 115 Sol Jo 966.
[83] [1957] 2 QB 348, [1957] 2 All ER 229, [1957] 2 WLR 948, 101 Sol Jo 409.
[84] (1969) 6 KIR 146, 113 Sol Jo 265.
[85] [2004] EWCA Civ 814, [2004] 1 WLR 2844.

duty unless a regulation expressly provides for it. It effectively removes strict liability in most cases. The position therefore reverts in the majority of cases to that of the common law, where claimants will be required to prove the employer's negligence, and the courts will need to look at the employer's common law duties, such as the provision of safe plant and equipment, a safe place of work, properly qualified colleagues and a safe system of work.

The cases in this section were mainly decided before the ERRA came into force, and so should be read with that in mind – not all of the regulations mentioned would be actionable now, but they are referred to as illustrations of the point that they make.

Four elements

11.131 There are thus four elements of the tort of breach of statutory duty, namely, (a) that the defendant owed a duty to the claimant (*Hartley v Mayoh & Co*[86]), (b) that there was a failure to carry out that duty (*Chipchase v British Titan Products Co Ltd*[87]), (c) that the breach caused the damage (*McWilliams v Sir William Arrol & Co Ltd*, para 11.127), and (d) that the damage was the kind which the statute was designed to prevent (*Fytche v Wincanton Logistics plc*[88]). Claimants will generally bring such an action together with an action based on the tort of negligence, thus increasing the prospects of success, although, of course, only one amount of damages will be awarded. The main advantage in doing so is that, generally speaking, most statutory duties are absolute, ie a failure to perform the duty will inevitably mean that there has been a breach of that duty, whereas an action based on negligence is subject to various defences, eg reasonable foreseeability etc (see para 11.107).

(a) The defendant must have owed a duty to the claimant

11.132 Whether a duty is owed to a particular claimant is a question of construction. Thus, if a statutory provision is made for the benefit of a particular class off persons, only those in that class can take advantage of the statutory protection (*Canadian Pacific Steamships Ltd v Bryers*[89]). For example, the Management of Health and Safety at Work Regulations 1999 specify certain duties in relation generally to employees, and thus contract workers, agency workers, members of the public, etc are not so protected, and cannot sue for a breach of statutory duty by the employer. In *Ricketts v Torbay Council*[90] the claimant tripped on an uneven surface in a council car park. She sued for damages, arguing that the car park was a workplace, and under reg 12 of the Workplace (Health, Safety and Welfare) Regulations there was a requirement that every floor in a workplace and the surface of every traffic route shall be suitable for the purpose, and that floors and surfaces must be free from anything that may cause any person to slip, trip or fall. She argued that 'any person' meant any person who was lawfully there. Her claim was dismissed by the Court of Appeal. The regulations were designed to protect persons at work in the workplace. Similarly, in *Reid v Galbraith's Stores*[91] it was held that the provisions of the Offices, Shops and Railway Premises Act 1963 did not apply to a customer who was visiting the shop, as the Act was concerned with the protection of person who worked there.

(b) There was a failure to carry out that duty

11.133 An employer will be in breach of the duty if he fails to observe the relevant statutory provision. Thus, when s 14 of the Factories Act 1961 (now repealed) stated that '[e]very part of dangerous machinery shall be securely fenced' it imposed an absolute obligation to fence, and

[86] [1953] 2 All ER 525, 117 JP 369; aff'd [1954] 1 QB 383, [1954] 1 All ER 375, [1954] 1 WLR 355, 52 LGR 165, 118 JP 178, 98 Sol Jo 107, CA.

[87] [1956] 1 QB 545, [1956] 1 All ER 613, [1956] 2 WLR 677, 54 LGR 212, 100 Sol Jo 186, CA.

[88] [2003] EWCA Civ 874, [2003] ICR 1582, 147 Sol Jo LB 785, [2003] All ER (D) 334 (June).

[89] [1958] AC 485, [1957] 3 All ER 572, [1957] 3 WLR 993, [1957] 2 Lloyd's Rep 387, 101 Sol Jo 957, HL.

[90] HSB No 326.   [91] 1970 SLT (Notes) 83.

it was no defence for an employer to argue that it was impossible to fence the dangerous part and use the machine in question. The Act thus implicitly prohibited its use, and the factory occupier used the machine at his peril (*John Summers & Sons Ltd v Frost*[92]). Similarly, reg 6 of the Provision and Use of Work Equipment Regulations 1998 provides that every employer shall ensure that work equipment is maintained in an efficient state, in efficient working order and in good repair, and an employer was held liable when an employee was injured because the front brake on his delivery bicycle broke, even though the employer had no knowledge of the defect (*Stark v Post Office*[93]). The obligation imposed by the regulation was absolute.

11.134 On the other hand, if a statute or regulation imposed a duty to do something 'so far as is practicable' or 'to use the best practicable means', this is a high standard, but not an absolute one. Thus in *Richards v Highway Ironfounders (West Bromwich) Ltd*[94] it was not known at the time that an invisible dust could cause silicosis, and thus the employer could not be held liable for failing to insist that employees should wear masks. A defendant cannot be held liable for failing to use a precaution which was not then invented, or failing to protect against a danger which medical science had not yet identified (*Adsett v K & L Steelfounders and Engineers Ltd*[95]).

11.135 If a statutory provision requires that something should be done 'so far as is reasonably practicable' then again, different considerations apply. It is permissible to take into account on the one hand, the danger or hazard or risk of injury which may occur, and balance it against the cost, inconvenience time and trouble it would take to counter it. If the risk is insignificant in relation to the cost etc likely to be incurred, then it may not be reasonably practicable to take those steps (*Edwards v National Coal Board*[96]). Thus in *Marshall v Gotham & Co* (see para 11.32) the roof of a mine collapsed due to a rare geological fault, injuring a workman. The court held that the danger was a very rare one. The roof had been tested in the usual way, and any further precautions taken would not have afforded complete protection against the danger. In the circumstances, the employers had done all that was reasonable. Similarly, a failure on the part of an employer to note a trivial risk would not give rise to liability (*Furness v Midland Bank plc*[97]).

(c) The breach caused the damage

11.136 The breach of the duty must have been a cause of the damage. This is the causation rule. Clearly if the damage caused is physical, there are generally few problems. When the damage caused is psychological, it is a matter of construction and evidence as to whether the damage was foreseeable. Thus in order to succeed in a claim for damages for psychiatric illness caused by stress at work, it must be established not only that it was reasonably foreseeable that overwork would lead to stress, but that the failure to carry out a risk assessment or health surveillance would lead to a breakdown in the stressed employees' health (*Bonser v RJB Mining (UK) Ltd*[98]). If there is a failure to carry out a risk assessment as required by the Management of Health at Work Regulations (or other regulations which impose this requirement) it is a likely conclusion that that breach was in some way responsible for the accident or injury (*Griffiths v Vauxhall Motors Ltd*[99]).

---

[92] [1955] AC 740, [1955] 1 All ER 870, [1955] 2 WLR 825, 53 LGR 329, 99 Sol Jo 257, HL.
[93] [2000] All ER (D) 276, CA.
[94] [1955] 3 All ER 205, [1955] 1 WLR 1049, 53 LGR 641, 99 Sol Jo 580, CA.
[95] [1953] 1 All ER 97n, [1953] 1 WLR 137, 51 LGR 99, 97 Sol Jo 49; aff'd [1953] 2 All ER 320, [1953] 1 WLR 773, 51 LGR 418, 97 Sol Jo 419, CA.
[96] [1949] 1 KB 704, [1949] 1 All ER 743, 93 Sol Jo 337, 65 TLR 430, CA.
[97] Unreported, 10 November 2002.   [98] [2004] IRLR 164, CA.
[99] [2003] EWCA Civ 412, [2003] All ER (D) 167 (Mar).

11.137 But if the damage caused would have occurred even if the employer had complied with the statutory duty, there is no liability. In *McWilliams v Sir William Arrol & Co Ltd* (see paras 11.127 and 11.131), the employers provided safety belts on a site for the use of steel erectors, but as these were not being used by the employees, they were taken away to another site. A steel erector on the first site fell from scaffolding, and was killed. Although the employers were clearly in breach of their statutory duty to provide the safety belts, there was nothing to suggest that this employee, who had never used the belts before, would have worn them on the day he was killed. Thus the employers were held not liable for damages. The breach of the legal duty did not cause the damage, it would have occurred anyway.

(d) The damage was the kind the statute was designed to prevent

11.138 The harm done must be of a type which the legislation is designed to prevent (*Gorris v Scott*[100]). Thus in *Fytche v Wincanton Logistics plc* (see para 11.131) a driver was employed to collect milk from farms. He was provided with steel-capped safety boots, which were changed every six months. Water seeped through a tiny hole in one of his boots, and, because the weather was extremely cold, he contracted frostbite. He brought a claim under reg 7 of the Personal Protective Equipment Regulations, arguing that the boots were not in an efficient state or in good repair, as required by that regulation. His claim was dismissed by the House of Lords. The purpose of the safety boots was to protect against his feet being crushed by some heavy object while he was on the farms; it was not to prevent his feet from getting wet or cold. His only remedy would be an action for common law negligence, but as the judge found that there had been no breach of the duty of care (because the defect was not known to the employers, and could not have been discovered by reasonable care) his claim under this heading failed.

Similarly, it was not the intention of Parliament to enable an action for damages to be brought in respect of a breach of the Working Time Regulations, as these provide for their own remedies (*Sayers v Cambridgeshire County Council*, para 7.109).

11.139 So far as the Management of Health and Safety at Work Regulations are concerned, there are some specific provisions which are likely to be relevant in civil litigation, including reg 3 (risk assessment), reg 6 (health surveillance), reg 8 (provisions for serious and imminent danger), reg 10 (information for employees), reg 14 (duties of employees) and reg 16 (risk assessment for new or expectant mothers). All other regulations have specific requirements, a breach of which may, in appropriate circumstances, give rise to civil liability.

F. Defences to an action for personal injuries

11.140 An employer (in reality his insurance company) may be able to raise a number of defences to an action based on negligence or breach of statutory duties, as appropriate.

Denial of negligence

11.141 The employer may deny that he failed to take reasonable care, or claim that he did all that a reasonable employer would have done in the circumstances. In *Latimer v AEC Ltd*[101] a factory floor was made slippery owing to the interaction of water from an unprecedented rainfall with the oily surface of the floor. The management ordered sand and sawdust to be spread around, but there was not enough to cover the whole factory. The

---

[100] (1874) LR 9 Exch 125, 43 LJ Ex 92, 2 Asp MLC 282, 22 WR 575, 30 LT 431.
[101] [1952] 2 QB 701, [1952] 1 All ER 1302, 50 LGR 555, 96 Sol Jo 376, [1952] 1 TLR 1349, CA; aff'd [1953] AC 643, [1953] 2 All ER 449, 51 LGR 457, 117 JP 387, 97 Sol Jo 486, HL.

employee slipped on an untreated part and was injured. It was held that the employer had done all that a reasonable employer could have done, having regard to the nature of the risk. The only other alternative would have been to close down the factory, which would have been unreasonable in the circumstances. In *Brown v Rolls-Royce (1971) Ltd*[102] the claimant contracted dermatitis owing to the use of an industrial oil. The employers did not provide a barrier cream on the advice of their chief medical officer, who doubted its efficacy. It was again held that the employers were not liable, for they were entitled to rely on the skilled judgment of a competent adviser, and no more could be expected. Indeed, the medical officer had instituted his own preventative methods, as a result of which the incidence of dermatitis in the factory had decreased.

11.142 The duty of the non-specialist employer in these circumstances is somewhat different. After all, not every firm can be expected to employ their own medical officer. Nonetheless, they must pay attention to the current literature which is available to them, either through their employers' associations or other sources. In *Graham v Co-operative Wholesale Society Ltd*[103] the claimant worked in a furniture workshop where an electric sanding machine gave off a quantity of fine wood dust. This settled on his skin and caused dermatitis. No general precautions were taken against this, although the manager had received all the information which was commonly circulated in the trade. It was held that the employers had not been negligent. They did not know of the danger, nor ought they to have known. They had fulfilled their duty to take reasonable steps to keep their knowledge up to date.

11.143 Recent years have seen such an increase in negligence claims that many worthwhile activities (such as school outings etc) have been abandoned or restricted because of fears of potential litigation. To counter these fears, the Compensation Act 2006 provides that a court considering a claim in negligence or breach of statutory duty may, in determining whether the defendant should have taken particular steps to meet a standard of care (whether by taking precautions against a risk or otherwise), have regard to whether the requirement to take those steps might prevent a desirable activity from being undertaken at all, to a particular extent or in a particular way, or discourage persons from undertaking functions in connection with a desirable activity. Further, an apology or an offer of treatment or other redress shall not by itself amount to an admission of negligence or breach of statutory duty. The Act only applies to England and Wales.

The injury was the sole fault of the employee

11.144 If it can be shown that the accident or injury was solely due to the fault of the employee, the employer will not be liable. In *Jones v Lionite Specialities Ltd*[104] a foreman was addicted to a chemical vapour from a tank. One weekend he was found dead, having fallen into the tank. The employers were not liable. In *Brophy v Bradfield & Co Ltd*[105] a lorry driver was found dead inside a boiler house, having been overcome by the fumes. He had no reason to be there, and his employers had no reason to suspect his presence. Again, the employers were not liable. And in *Horne v Lec Refrigeration Ltd*,[106] a tool-setter had been trained to operate a machine, but was killed because of his failure to operate a safety drill. The employers were not liable, even though they were in breach of their statutory duty to ensure secure fencing.

---

[102] (1977) 12 ITR 382, EAT.   [103] [1957] 1 All ER 654, [1957] 1 WLR 511, 55 LGR 137, 101 Sol Jo 267.
[104] (1961) 105 Sol Jo 468; revsd 105 Sol Jo 1082, CA.
[105] [1955] 3 All ER 286, [1955] 1 WLR 1148, 53 LGR 665, 99 Sol Jo 778, CA.
[106] [1965] 2 All ER 898.

11.145 It used to be inferred that this defence was one of *volenti non fit injuria*, ie that a person consents to the risk of being injured. But the doctrine of consent rarely succeeds in employment cases. The fact that an employee knows that he runs the risk of being injured does not mean that he consents to that risk because of the employer's negligence (*Smith v Baker & Sons*[107]). The payment of 'danger money' to specialised employees (eg stunt artistes) may indicate that there is a special risk which cannot be guarded against, and to that extent consent may be raised; but even so, the real question to be asked is: was the employer negligent in the circumstances?

11.146 Moreover, the Unfair Contract Terms Act 1977 applies to those employment situations where the employer seeks to exclude his liability for injury to the employee by means of a prominently displayed notice or even a contract term. Section 2 of the Act states that a person cannot by reference to a contract term or to a notice exclude or restrict his liability for death or personal injury resulting from negligence. Thus an employer cannot escape his legal responsibility if he has been negligent.

Contributory negligence

11.147 This defence is based on the Law Reform (Contributory Negligence) Act 1945, which provides that if a person is injured, partly because of his own fault and partly due to the fault of another, damages shall be reduced to the extent the court thinks fit, having regard to the claimant's share in the responsibility for the damage. The defence is successfully raised in a number of cases. The employer will argue that even though he was negligent, so too was the injured employee, and a reduction in the amount of damages awarded will be the result. The actual percentage reduction made is scarcely based on scientific principles, and appeal courts may take a different view of the share of the blame to be apportioned.

11.148 Although in *Jayes v IMI (Kynoch) Ltd*[108] the Court of Appeal had held that there was no principle in law that rules out a finding of 100% contributory negligence, the case was disapproved by a more recent decision of the court in *Anderson v Newham College of Further Education*.[109] There is a distinction between arguing that a claimant is 100% contributorily negligent and arguing that an accident was entirely due to the fault of the claimant. Thus, if there has been a breach of a statutory duty by an employer it must be shown not only that the worker's breach of the same statutory duty was as great as that of the employer, but also that the employer did all he could to ensure compliance by the worker. If there is no breach of statutory duty by the employer, no question of contributory negligence arises (*Anderson v Newham College of Further Education*).

New intervening act

11.149 An employer will not be liable if the injury is caused by a new intervening act, ie by a person or event over which or whom the employer has no control. In *Horton v Taplin Contracts Ltd*[110] the claimant was standing on the platform of a scaffolding tower. A fellow worker, with whom he had previously had an altercation, deliberately pushed the tower over, and the claimant suffered serious injuries. He claimed damages from his employer, alleging a breach of the Provision and Use of Work Equipment Regulations, regs 5 and 20 (work equipment must be suitable for the purpose, and work equipment must be stabilised) as well as reg 5 of the Construction (Health Safety and Welfare) Regulations

---

[107] [1891] AC 325.   [108] [1985] ICR 155, [1984] LS Gaz R 3180, CA.

[109] [2002] EWCA Civ 505, [2003] ICR 212, [2002] All ER (D) 381 (Mar).

[110] [2002] EWCA Civ 1604, [2003] ICR 179, [2003] PIQR P180, [2003] BLR 74, [2003] 01 LS Gaz R 24, 146 Sol Jo LB 256, [2002] All ER (D) 122 (Nov).

(employers must keep the workplace safe for any person at work there). The claim failed. Under reg 5 of PUWER the suitability of work equipment was to be measured by taking into account those hazards which were reasonably foreseeable. The obligation to stabilise the equipment under reg 20 only arose when this was necessary for the purpose of health and safety, which introduced considerations of foreseeability. Finally, the scaffolding tower was a safe place of work; it only became unsafe as the result of the deliberate, violent and unpredictable act of a third party.

11.150 Similarly, in *Yorkshire Traction Co Ltd v Searby*,[111] a bus driver, while sitting in his driver's seat, was assaulted by a passenger. A county court judge held that the employers had been negligent in not inserting a screen to separate the driver from passengers, and thus there was a failure to provide work equipment which was 'suitable'. The decision was reversed by the Court of Appeal. In the first place, his trade union had strongly objected to the insertion of such screens, as these were considered to be a safety hazard. Indeed, some drivers had taken action to have the screens removed from their buses. It was further found that the risk of injury to bus drivers was very low. Thus the measure of the risk, the perceived disadvantages, and the attitude of the workforce was such that the failure by the employers to fit screens did not amount to negligence at common law. So far as a breach of statutory duty is concerned, the regulations do not require complete and absolute protection. In assessing the suitability of work equipment the test for liability involved a consideration of the degree of risk. Since the incidence of injury to drivers from passengers had been very low, it could not be said that the work equipment (ie the bus) was unsuitable.

G. Limitation of actions (Limitation Act 1980)

11.151 Any action in respect of negligence, nuisance or breach of statutory duty which has resulted in personal injury must be brought within three years from the date when the cause of action accrued, or from the date when the claimant had knowledge of the injury. 'Knowledge' in this connection, means when the injured person had knowledge that:

(a) the injury was significant;

(b) the injury was attributable wholly or partly to the act or omission which gave rise to the legal liability;

(c) the defendant was responsible;

(d) any other fact supporting the bringing of an action against the defendant.

A person's knowledge includes knowledge which he might reasonably be expected to acquire from facts which are observable by him, or from facts ascertainable by him with the help of medical or other expert advice which it is reasonable for him to seek. The Act does not apply in Scotland, where the Prescription and Limitations (Scotland) Act applies.

---

[111] [2003] EWCA Civ 1856, 148 Sol Jo LB 61, [2003] All ER (D) 409 (Dec).

12

Disciplinary, Dismissal and Grievance Procedures

12.1 During the performance of the employment contract the employer may find it necessary, through the appropriate manager, foreman or supervisor who is charged with the necessary responsibility, to exercise some form of disciplinary authority over the employee. This may take one of a number of forms, ranging from counselling, informal warnings, etc, through to final warning or dismissal. The prime objective must be corrective, not punishment. Disciplinary procedures and powers must be exercised in a manner that will enable the employee to retain his position as a valued member of the staff, and not used purely as a matter of form of mechanical exercise. Thus adherence to a well-drafted disciplinary procedure is an essential part of any decision-making process. Equally, there will be occasions when the employee will wish to pursue a grievance over the way he is treated, and a suitable grievance procedure is the obvious channel to be used.

Disciplinary procedures

A. Procedures in operation

12.2 From the employer's point of view, there are likely to be three categories of 'hearing', and it is important to establish from the outset the distinctions. First, there is an informal interview or counselling session, at which matters can be discussed. So long as this session does not result in any form of disciplinary sanction, the worker does not have the right to be accompanied (see para 12.23) and matters are best resolved by the parties concerned. Second, there is the investigatory type of hearing, which is designed to ascertain facts and collate evidence. Again, the employee has no right to be accompanied even though the meeting could lead to disciplinary proceedings (*Skiggs v South West Trains Ltd*[1]). Finally there is the disciplinary hearing itself where certain fundamental principles will apply. The important thing is that employers should not allow the informal interview or investigatory hearing to turn into a disciplinary hearing and, if there is a possibility that this is going to happen, those hearings should be terminated and a formal disciplinary hearing convened. If an allegation is so minor that it is dealt with under the informal misconduct procedure, it would clearly be wrong to dismiss an employee for gross misconduct on the same facts (*Sakar v West London Mental Health Trust*[2]).

Investigations by the employer

12.3 Clearly, no disciplinary action should be taken in advance of proper investigation by the employer. As Megarry VC stated in *John v Rees*[3] (see para 12.22) the paths of the law

---

[1] [2005] IRLR 459.
[2] [2010] IRLR 508, [2010] EWCA Civ 289, CA.
[3] [1970] Ch 345, [1969] 2 All ER 274, [1969] 2 WLR 1294, 113 Sol Jo 487.

are strewn with examples of unanswerable charges which were eventually answered. But there are certain limits on the extent to which an employer may properly make enquiries into an incident, particularly if the charge is a serious one, such as theft, for there may well be an improper interference with the processes of justice (*Tesco (Holdings) Ltd v Hill*[4]). On the other hand, when an allegation is made against an employee, which is disputed, a most careful and conscientious investigation must be carried out, and the investigator must focus no less on evidence which may exculpate the employee, or at least point to his innocence. This is particularly so when the employee is suspended, and has thus been denied an opportunity of being able to contact potentially relevant witnesses (*A v B*[5]).

12.4 Whether an employer should carry out his own investigations after being informed that criminal charges are to be brought against an employee in respect of matters arising out of his employment is a question of circumstances, and the employer has a wide discretion whether to continue or postpone the hearing (*Secretary of State for Justice v Mansfield*[6]).

On the one hand, it is incumbent on an employer to embark on some form of investigation involving at least an interview with the employee, to give him an opportunity to state his position. On the other hand, if the circumstances are so blatant and sufficient to warrant a belief as to the employee's guilt, no further investigation is necessary. Within this spectrum there are many situations where a further consideration of the position should be considered before disciplinary action is taken (*Lovie Ltd v Anderson*[7]). Although an employer cannot be expected to carry out its own independent investigation in order to test the reliability of the information provided by a responsible public authority, it should not take an uncritical view of the allegations. Rather, it should insist on a sufficient degree of formality and specificity about the disclosure before contemplating taking any action against the employee on the basis of it (*A v B*).[8]

12.5 The employer is not obliged to hold a full-scale trial, but there must be a careful examination of all the relevant matters. An investigation should not be conducted with such haste that important evidence is overlooked (*Johnson Matthey Metals v Harding*[9]), neither should it be delayed so long that issues become stale and hazy in the minds of witnesses (*Marley Homecare v Dutton*[10]). It is particularly important to conduct a fair investigation and test the evidence of an accuser where there could be serious consequences to the employee – in *Salford Royal NHS Foundation Trust v Roldan*[11] dismissal could have meant deportation. An employer should also investigate allegations of dishonesty involving breach of trust with care. In Stuart v London City Airport[12] it was unreasonable that the employer did not look into evidence which might have shown that the employee was not dishonest. There is no particular form of procedure to be adopted, as long as the employee is given a fair hearing (*Bentley Engineering Co v Mistry*[13]). If it is necessary to consider an investigation in advance of criminal proceedings, it is still possible to discuss the matter without prejudicing a fair trial (*Harris (Ipswich) Ltd v Harrison*[14]), and a decision may be made on the basis of known facts, even though the employee has been advised to remain silent. If the evidence produced is sufficiently indicative of guilt (in the absence of any explanation) the employer is entitled to take some action. If, however, there are doubts, fairness may require the employer to wait until the criminal proceedings have been concluded (*Harris and Shepherd v Courage (Eastern) Ltd*[15]). The employer has a wide discretion

---

[4] [1977] IRLR 63, EAT.   [5] [2003] IRLR 405, [2003] All ER (D) 184 (May), EAT.
[6] EAT/0539/09/RN.   [7] [1999] IRLR 164, EAT.
[8] [2010] IRLR 844.   [9] [1978] IRLR 248, 13 ITR 407, EAT.
[10] [1981] IRLR 380, EAT.   [11] [2010] IRLR 721, CA, [2010] EWCA Civ 522.
[12] UKEAT/0273/12/BA.   [13] [1979] ICR 47, [1978] IRLR 437, EAT.
[14] [1978] ICR 1256, [1978] IRLR 382, EAT.
[15] [1982] ICR 530, [1982] IRLR 509, CA.

on whether to continue with or postpone disciplinary hearings if the employee's conduct is also being investigated by the police (*Secretary of State for Justice v Mansfield*[16]). The object in holding a full investigation is to confirm suspicions or clear up doubts as to whether or not a particular act of misconduct has occurred (see *British Home Stores v Burchell*[17]). If an employee admits the offence, there is no need for a full investigation, unless some useful information could come to light (*Royal Society for the Protection of Birds v Croucher*[18]).

12.6 When an allegation of an employee's misconduct has been made by an informant, a balance must be maintained between the need to protect the informant and respect his anonymity, and providing a fair hearing to the accused employee. In *Linfood Cash and Carry Ltd v Thomson*,[19] the EAT laid down the following guidelines which could usefully be followed:

(a) the information should be reduced into writing, although it may be necessary to 'doctor' the statement in order to prevent identification;

(b) the statement should contain all the relevant facts, including dates, times, places, etc, the opportunity of the informant to observe clearly and with accuracy, circumstantial evidence, and whether the informant had any reason to fabricate the evidence, whether from a personal grudge or any other reason;

(c) further investigation should then take place to confirm, corroborate or challenge the information;

(d) tactful enquiries should be made about the background of the informant, and to find any other information which would add to or detract from the value of the information given;

(e) if the informant is not prepared to attend the disciplinary hearing, a decision will have to be taken on whether to continue or not;

(f) if it is decided to continue, the person responsible for conducting the hearing should interview the informant, and assess the weight to be given to the information;

(g) the written statement of the informant should be made available to the employee and his representatives;

(h) if there are matters to be put to the informant, the person conducting the hearing should adjourn to make further enquiries;

(i) full and careful notes of the disciplinary hearing should be taken;

(j) evidence from the investigation officer should be prepared in a written form.

12.7 However, such tactics may not always result in the protection of the anonymity of the informant, as an employee who has been dismissed in consequence of information provided in this manner may be able to obtain from the High Court an order compelling his former employer to disclose the identity of the informant, so as to pursue an appropriate remedy, eg defamation and/or malicious falsehood (*P v T Ltd*[20]).

12.8 A distinction must be drawn between the investigatory function and the disciplinary function. If the same person undertakes both, there is usually no problem, but when they are separate and distinct, there is an obligation to give an employee a hearing at both stages. In *Budgen & Co v Thomas*,[21] an employee was dismissed after she had signed a written

[16] [2010] UKEAT/593/09.   [17] [1980] ICR 303n, [1978] IRLR 379, 13 ITR 560, EAT.
[18] [1984] ICR 604, [1984] IRLR 425, EAT.
[19] [1989] ICR 518, [1989] IRLR 235, EAT.
[20] [1997] 4 All ER 200, [1997] 1 WLR 1309, [1977] ICR 887.
[21] [1976] ICR 344, [1976] IRLR 174, EAT.

confession that she had stolen a small sum of money. The matter had been investigated by the security officer, and on the basis of his report, which was sent to the company's head office, the decision to dismiss was taken. This was held to be unfair. She was an 18-year-old girl, diabetic, and subsequently claimed that she was confused at the time she signed the confession, and that it was not true. It could not be said that in view of her personal circumstances the management would have dismissed her had she been given the opportunity to present her case; the person who took the decision to dismiss should at least have given her a hearing.

12.9 A person who is a witness in investigatory proceedings should not act as a judge in disciplinary proceedings, otherwise this could be regarded as a breach of the principles of natural justice. However, there may be occasions when the person who has to take the decision to dismiss is also the person who witnessed the incident, and while this can be acceptable (and indeed inevitable) it is preferable for this dual role to be avoided (*Moyes v Hylton Castle Working Men's Social Club*[22]). Also, a person who is involved in the investigatory stage should not, if possible, be involved in the appeal stage, as this would put him in a situation of being a judge in his own cause, and justice would not be done, as well as not appearing to be done (*Byrne v BOC Ltd*[23]). However, in the case of small employers, this counsel of perfection may not be possible.

12.10 In those cases where witnesses are not part of the employer's organisation, it is not necessary for the employer to carry out a quasi-judicial hearing, with a confrontation and cross-examination of those witnesses (*Ulsterbus Ltd v Henderson*[24]). In *Sainsbury's Supermarkets Ltd v Hitt*,[25] the Court of Appeal confirmed that the band of reasonableness approach applies to the conduct of investigations as much as to other procedural and substantive decisions to dismiss a person from his employment for conduct. Thus provided an employer carries out an appropriate investigation, gives the employee a fair opportunity to explain his conduct, etc, it would be wrong for an employment tribunal to suggest that further investigations should have been carried out for, by doing so, they are substituting their own standards of what was an adequate investigation for the standard that could be objectively expected from a reasonable employer.

12.11 The principle of *res judicata*, namely that a person should not have to face the same allegation twice, applies only to courts and tribunals, not internal procedures *Christou and Ward v London Borough of Haringey*[26] (although this case was on very specific facts).

B. **Types of disciplinary and grievance procedures**

12.12 Basically, disciplinary and grievance procedures should conform to the ACAS Code of Practice Disciplinary and Grievance Procedures in Employment, which should be studied in detail by all levels of management. A failure to follow the Code of Practice will not mean automatically that any action taken will inevitably be unfair (*Lewis Shops Group v Wiggins*[27]) but both sides ignore it at their peril. Employment tribunals should always consider the Code of Practice as a guide when assessing the reasonableness of any action taken, and any relevant provisions should be taken into account when determining the issues before them (*Lock v Cardiff Railway*, see para 17.75).

---

[22] [1986] IRLR 482, EAT.   [23] [1992] IRLR 505, EAT.
[24] [1989] IRLR 251, NICA.
[25] [2001] All ER (D) 344 (Dec), EAT; revsd [2002] EWCA Civ 1588, [2003] ICR 111, [2003] IRLR 23, 146 Sol Jo LB 238, [2002] All ER (D) 259 (Oct).
[26] [2013] EWCA Civ 178.
[27] [1973] ICR 335, [1973] IRLR 205, NIRC.

The revised ACAS Code of Practice makes the following recommendations:

(1) In relation to grievances

    (a) the employee should tell the employer of the grievance

    (b) the employer should hold a meeting with the employee to discuss the grievance

    (c) the employee should be told of the right to be accompanied

    (d) after the meeting, the employer should decide on the appropriate action

    (e) the employer should permit the employee to have a right of appeal.

(2) In relation to discipline and dismissal proceedings

    (a) the employer should first establish the facts of the case

    (b) the employer should then inform the employee of the nature of the problem

    (c) the employer should hold a meeting with the employee to discuss the matter

    (d) the employee should be told of his right to be accompanied

    (e) after the meeting, the employer should decide on the appropriate action to be taken

    (f) the employee should be given the right of appeal.

12.13 If either party unreasonably fails or refuses to follow the provisions of the Code, the employment tribunal may increase or reduce any award made by up to 25%, as appropriate.

12.14 There will also be the normal contractual or non-contractual disciplinary and grievance procedures (many of which will have already been in existence for some time), which are still valid and should still function, provided they meet at least the standards set down by the ACAS Code. They can, however, be more expansive. A failure to follow contractual procedures may constitute a breach of contract by the employer. This may result in (a) the employee seeking an injunction to restrain the employer from taking disciplinary action in breach of the procedure (*Peace v City of Edinburgh Council*[28]), (b) the employee resigning and claiming that he was constructively dismissed (see Chapter 17), or (c) the employee seeking damages at common law, based on the length of time he would have been employed had the appropriate procedure been followed (*Gunton v London Borough of Richmond upon Thames*, see para 3.96). A failure to follow a contractual procedure in relation to a dismissal will render that dismissal unfair (*Polkey v AE Dayton Services Ltd*[29]). If, however, the employer can show that the dismissal would have taken place even if the proper procedure had been followed, then a tribunal can make a 'Polkey' reduction (para 17.218).

C. **Drawing up procedures**

12.15 The responsibility for drawing up disciplinary and grievance procedures is on the employer. Clearly, if he can obtain the co-operation and assistance of any relevant trade union, or of his employees, so much the better, but in the absence of any such co-operation, the employer must act unilaterally. There are practical advantages in having trade union involvement in drawing up procedures, and challenges alleging unfairness are less likely to succeed if agreed procedures are followed.

12.16 The important thing is that the employer does not have to prove that an offence took place, or even satisfy himself beyond all reasonable doubt that the employee committed the act in question. The function of the employer is to act reasonably in coming to

---

[28] [1999] IRLR 417, 1999 SLT 712, OH.   [29] [1987] UKHL 8.

a decision. Thus in *Ferodo Ltd v Barnes*,[30] an employee was dismissed for vandalism. The employment tribunal was not satisfied that the employee was guilty, and therefore held that the dismissal was unfair. This finding was reversed by the EAT. The question was not whether or not the employment tribunal was satisfied that the employee was guilty, but whether they were satisfied that the employer had reasonable grounds for believing that the employee had committed the offence, and had acted reasonably in dismissing for that offence. The employer is not concerned to apply standards of proof which may be relevant in a criminal court. In *Docherty v Reddy*,[31] the employee was dismissed for stealing 50p from the till. The employers took into account that they had suspected him of stealing similar sums on previous occasions, and it was held that they were entitled to have regard to their past suspicions. Clearly, a suspicion of previous theft is hardly evidence which would be admitted in a criminal court, but the issues are different. The employer is having to decide whether or not he wishes to retain the employee, not whether or not he was guilty of a particular offence. Thus the test is, what would a reasonable employer have done on the facts which he knew, taking into account the Code of Practice and current industrial relations practice (*Parkers Bakeries Ltd v Palmer*[32]). The employment tribunal must not act as a court of appeal, nor retry a case, and the fact that in subsequent criminal proceedings an employee is acquitted of a charge against him is irrelevant to the issue of whether or not the employer has acted reasonably (*Davies v GKN Birwelco (Uskside) Ltd*[33]).

12.17 Evidence which is not admissible in criminal proceedings may fairly be considered by an employer in disciplinary proceedings (*Dhaliwal v British Airways Board*[34]) and a confession which would be inadmissible in a criminal court is also properly admissible before a disciplinary board (*Morley's of Brixton Ltd v Minott*[35]).

12.18 If an employee pleaded guilty to a criminal offence in a court of law, or has been found guilty by the court, it is reasonable for an employer to believe that the offence has been committed by the employee. Any other conclusion 'would be ridiculous' (*P v Nottinghamshire County Council*[36]). The fact of conviction might well form an adequate basis for dismissal, although the nature of the offence would be a relevant factor. Thus to dismiss for a trivial offence would not be reasonable (*Secretary of State for Scotland v Campbell*[37]).

D. **Composition of procedural bodies**

12.19 The composition of any disciplinary body will doubtless be determined by each employer in accordance with the size of the firm and the circumstances of each case. The procedure will lay down who can exercise authority, the extent of the authority, and the circumstances when it is exercised. For example, informal warnings may be given at a certain level by supervisors, formal warnings should be given in writing, and signed by someone who has power to issue and act on them, and so on. If an appeal may be made to a disciplinary board, its composition should be specified, with due regard to providing substitutes as appropriate. Otherwise a failure to do this may result in a dismissal being rendered unfair when it may have been fair. Thus in *Westminster City Council v Cabaj*,[38] the employee was dismissed. He was entitled to appeal to an appeal tribunal consisting of three council members. At the actual hearing, only two council members turned up, and they proceeded to hear the appeal, and dismissed it. The employee was not asked if he agreed to the appeal

---

[30] [1976] ICR 439, [1976] IRLR 302, 11 ITR 177, EAT.   [31] [1977] ICR 365, EAT.
[32] [1977] IRLR 215, 12 ITR 111, EAT.   [33] [1976] IRLR 82.
[34] [1985] ICR 513, EAT.   [35] [1982] ICR 444, [1982] IRLR 270, EAT.
[36] [1992] ICR 706, [1992] IRLR 362, CA.   [37] [1992] IRLR 263, EAT.
[38] [1996] ICR 960, [1996] IRLR 399, CA.

being heard by two members. The Court of Appeal held that where there is a failure to comply with a contractually enforceable disciplinary procedure, it was for the employment tribunal to determine whether a consequent dismissal is fair or unfair, and there is no automatic assumption of unfairness. The employment tribunal must decide the issue in accordance with the matters set out in ERA, s 98. But where public institutions are concerned, the persons sitting on the appeal body must have been validly appointed, and there is no power to ratify an invalid appointment (*R v Secretary of State for Education, ex p Prior*[39]). In a case concerning a public institution, when deciding who should sit on the panel regard should be had to the principle that justice must not only be done, but must also be seen to be done, and so care should be taken not only to avoid bias, but also the appearance of bias. *Watson v University of Strathclyde*.[40] A disciplinary panel does not have to be composed entirely of members from outside the employer NHS Trust for it to be independent and impartial. It is sufficient that one of the three members is impartial (*R (Puri) v Bradford Teaching Hospitals NHS Foundation Trust*).[41]

12.20 In *Clark v Civil Aviation Authority*,[42] the EAT gave some broad guidance on how disciplinary proceedings should be conducted. The purpose of the meeting should be explained, those present identified, representation should be arranged, the employee should be informed of the allegations being made, the evidence should be presented in statement form or through witnesses, the employee or his representative should be permitted to ask questions, the employee should be permitted to call witnesses, he or his representative will then explain or argue his case, both sides can then argue on the allegations and any possible consequences, including mitigation, and the employee will finally be asked if there is any further evidence or enquiry which will help his case. The decision will then be reduced to writing (whether or not an earlier oral decision has been given).

12.21 Particular care should be taken when it is proposed to take disciplinary action against shop stewards, and the Code of Practice recommends that it is advisable to discuss the circumstances of the case with a full-time official of the union concerned. However, being a shop steward is not a passport to disciplinary immunity (*Fowler v Cammell Laird (Shipbuilders) Ltd*[43]).

12.22 A disciplinary hearing must be conducted fairly. To achieve this, a number of rules should be observed.

(a) The employee is entitled to know the nature of the charge against him, in sufficient detail to enable him to prepare his case (*Hutchins v British Railways Board*[44]). It is no bad thing to put this in writing, particularly if the employee's command of English is weak, so that he can get someone else to explain to him the nature of the allegations he has to meet (*Sharma v West Yorkshire Passenger Transport Executive*[45]).

In particular, he must not ultimately be disciplined or dismissed because other matters come to light which were not previously notified to him. In *Boyd v Renfrewshire Council*[46] disciplinary proceedings were taken against an employee for disrupting work by taking part in a work-to-rule. At no stage either in the letter calling him to the disciplinary hearing or during the hearing itself was he told that he was liable to dismissal. His subsequent dismissal was held to be unfair. He had not been given an opportunity to put forward matters that were relevant because of fears of harassment by fellow employees, and it was unfair to dismiss him on grounds that

[39] [1994] ICR 877, [1994] ELR 231.   [40] [2011] IRLR 458.
[41] [2011] IRLR 582, [2011] EWHC 970 (Admin).   [42] [1991] IRLR 412, EAT.
[43] [1973] IRLR 72.   [44] [1974] IRLR 303.   [45] [1977] IRLIB.
[46] 2008 SCLR 578, 2008 GWD 20–333.

were significantly more serious than the complaint he expected to face at the disciplinary hearing. Had he realised that he was facing dismissal he would have given a fuller explanation for his conduct in mitigation.

Witness statements should be shown to the person accused (*Louies v Coventry Hood and Seating Co Ltd*[47]) although it is acknowledged that there may be occasions when it is necessary to preserve anonymity (*Linfood Cash and Carry Ltd v Thomson*, see para 12.6). But in *Fuller v Lloyds Bank plc*[48] an employee of the respondents was in a public house on Christmas Eve, and received severe facial injuries from a glass which the claimant held in his hand. The employers took statements from a number of witnesses, but these were not disclosed to the claimant, as a matter of policy. Following a disciplinary hearing, he was dismissed, and claimed his dismissal was unfair. An employment tribunal dismissed his claim, arguing that the claimant knew the nature of the allegations. An appeal to the EAT failed. The procedure adopted was not so defective as to make the overall result unfair. Thus there is no universal requirement of natural justice or general principles of law that in all cases a witness statement must be shown to an employee who has been accused of misconduct. It is only a failure of natural justice if the essence of the case against the employee is contained in the statements, and he has not been otherwise informed of the nature of the case against him (*Hussain v Elonex plc*[49]). There is no rule of law which requires an employer to permit an employee to cross-examine, during a disciplinary hearing, colleagues who have made allegations of misconduct by the employee. The employer must carry out a reasonable investigation into the alleged wrongdoing, not carry out a forensic or quasi-judicial investigation (*Santemera v Express Cargo Forwarding*[50]).

(b) An employee should always be given an opportunity to state his case (*Tesco (Holdings) Ltd v Hill*, see para 12.3) no matter what the circumstances are (as should an office holder, *R (Shoesmith) v OFSTED and others*[51]). He is entitled to plead that he did not do the alleged act, or that he did not intend the construction which has been put on it, or that mitigating circumstances relating to his case should be taken into consideration (*Boyd v Renfrewshire Council*[52]). To dismiss a woman who, because of a pregnancy-related illness, is unable to attend a disciplinary hearing is to cause her to suffer a detriment on grounds of pregnancy, and is therefore direct sex discrimination (*Abbey National plc v Formoso*, see para 4.50). However, it is not essential that the employee should be present in person throughout the hearing, when all the evidence is being given, if his representative is there (*Pirelli General Cable Works v Murray*[53]). The opportunity given to an employee to 'state his case' cannot be underestimated or undervalued. The reason is perhaps obvious; as Sir Robert Megarry said in *John v Rees* (see para 12.3): '...the path of the law is strewn with examples of open and shut cases which, somehow, were not; of unanswerable charges which, in the event, were completely answered; of inexplicable conduct which was fully explained; of fixed and unalterable determinations that, by discussion, suffered a change. Nor are those with any knowledge of human nature who pause to think for a moment likely to underestimate the feelings of resentment of those who find that a decision against them has been made without their being afforded any opportunity to influence the course of events.'

However, in rare cases, where there is no possibility of any explanation of the conduct alleged, or where misconduct is admitted by the employee, it is legally

---

[47] [1990] ICR 54, [1990] IRLR 324, EAT.   [48] [1991] IRLR 336, EAT.
[49] [1999] IRLR 420, CA.   [50] [2003] IRLR 273, [2002] All ER (D) 379 (Nov), EAT.
[51] [2011] IRLR 679, [2011] EWCA Civ 642.   [52] See n 46.   [53] [1979] IRLR 190, EAT.

permissible (although possibly in practice undesirable) to dispense with disciplinary formalities (*Clarke v Trimoco Motor Group Ltd*[54]). Thus in *Sutherland v Sonat Offshore (UK) Inc*[55] the employers had a strict rule forbidding alcohol or drugs while employees were on a drilling unit. The appellant was given a routine drug test, which showed the presence of cannabis in his urine, and the result was confirmed in further tests. He was dismissed without being given a proper chance to state his case, but the EAT upheld a finding of an employment tribunal that his dismissal was nonetheless fair. The requirement for investigation was met by the testing procedures, there was no possibility of an error and there was no way the substance could have been ingested by some other means, eg 'passive smoking'. Thus the employers were entitled to act on the evidence before them without involving the full disciplinary procedure.

(c) He should be permitted the right to be represented or accompanied in accordance with the procedure (*Rank Xerox (UK) Ltd v Goodchild*[56]). There is now a statutory right to be accompanied (see para 12.23).

(d) He should be informed of his right to appeal to a higher level of management, who have not previously been involved in the decision (*S C Brown Communications Ltd v Walker*[57]), or to an independent arbitrator. If he fails or refuses to exercise that right, then he does not contribute to the unfair dismissal, nor does he fail to mitigate his loss (*William Muir (Bond 9) Ltd v Lamb*[58]). As a matter of principle, a person who takes the decision to dismiss should not take any part in the appeal process (*R v Chief Constable of Merseyside Police*[59]), although it has to be conceded that this counsel of perfection cannot be applied to small firms.

E. Right to be accompanied: Employment Relations Act 1999, ss 10–15

12.23 Section 10 of the Employment Relations Act 1999 creates a right for a worker, when invited by his employer to attend a disciplinary or grievance hearing, to make a reasonable request to be accompanied by a single companion, who can be either:

(a) an official of an independent trade union (not necessarily one recognised by the employer); or

(b) a trade union official who has been certified by the trade union as having had experience or having received training in acting as a worker's companion in such hearings (eg a shop steward); or

(c) another of the employer's workers.

The choice of companion does not have to be reasonable, so long as it is someone within the specified categories (*Toal & Anor v GB Oils Ltd*[60]).

12.24 The right to be accompanied is triggered by any hearing which has the characteristic of a disciplinary sanction, however it is described. An investigatory meeting, or one which could only result in a genuine informal warning, will not attract the statutory right to be accompanied. But a requirement to undergo retraining, coaching or counselling is not a disciplinary sanction since it does not contain an element of penalty or punishment (*London Underground Ltd v Ferenc-Batchelor*[61]).

12.25 The companion is entitled to address the hearing in order to put the worker's case, sum up that case, respond to any views expressed at the hearing, and to confer with the

[54] [1993] ICR 237, [1993] IRLR 148, EAT.   [55] EAT 186/93.   [56] [1979] IRLR 185, EAT.
[57] Unreported.   [58] [1985] IRLR 95, EAT.   [59] [2001] IRLR 442.   [60] UKEAT/0569/12/LA.
[61] [2003] ICR 656, [2003] IRLR 252, [2003] All ER (D) 252 (Mar), EAT.

worker during the hearing. He is not entitled to answer questions on behalf of the worker, or address the hearing if the worker does not wish him to do so. Nor can he prevent the worker from explaining his case or prevent any other person from making a contribution to the hearing. However, there is no obligation on any person, whether or not he is a trade union official, to take on the role of companion.

12.26 As a general principle, ERA, s 10 does not confer the right to legal representation at a disciplinary or grievance hearing unless there is a provision in the contract of employment or disciplinary procedure that provides for this, or the employer permits this on an 'ad hoc' basis. The right to be accompanied is confined to being accompanied by an official of a trade union or a fellow worker. However, if the consequences of the disciplinary hearing would have a serious impact upon an employee's working life, or possibly expose him to criminal charges, the courts are leaning to the view he is entitled to have legal representation if he so wishes. This right is based on the European Convention on Human Rights, Art 6(1), which states that every person is entitled to a fair and public hearing, and Art 6(3), which provides that when being faced with a criminal charge, every person has the right to defend himself through legal assistance of his own choosing. In *Kulkarni v Milton Keynes Hospitals NHS Trust*[62] a doctor was charged with professional misconduct in conducting an improper examination of a female patient. As a matter of construction of the trust's procedure it was held that the doctor was entitled to be represented by a lawyer of his professional association, but the view was expressed that if disciplinary proceedings could deprive an employee of the right to practice his profession there could be an implied right to legal representation based on Art 6 of the Convention on Human Rights. Contrast this with the case of *R (Puri) v Bradford Teaching Hospitals NHS Foundation Trust* (see para 12.19), where it was held that Art 6 was not engaged. The difference is that while it would be difficult for Mr Puri to find employment within the NHS, it was not impossible. For Dr Kulkarni, however, it was practically impossible, as he had been found guilty of what amounted to a criminal offence, and still had to complete his training, which could only be done in the NHS. Accordingly there was insufficient link between the dismissal and a denial of the right to practise his profession to engage Art 6.

12.27 Article 6 does not therefore apply where the hearing does not deprive the claimant of the right to practise his profession. It only applies where there is a 'determination of ... civil rights and obligations'. In *R v Governors of X School*,[63] a schoolteacher was subjected to disciplinary action following an allegation of inappropriate behaviour with a young person engaged at the school on a work-experience programme. The school's disciplinary procedure was followed by a hearing before the Independent Safeguarding Authority, which maintains a list of those to be barred from working with children, and which could place the claimant on the 'barred list'. The ISA would exercise its own judgment, and come to its own conclusion. As the school's determination dealt only with his employment, and would not have a 'substantial influence' on the ISA's decision, there was not a sufficient connection between the internal disciplinary proceedings and the ISA proceedings. The Supreme Court found that the former dealt only with his current employment, and was therefore not 'directly decisive' of the issue, and so there was no right to legal representation before the school, although there would be for the ISA hearing.

12.28 Several problems arise from these decisions. The fact that the outcome of disciplinary proceedings could result in the loss of employment does not, per se, warrant legal

---

[62] [2009] EWCA Civ 789, [2010] ICR 101, [2009] IRLR 829, [2009] LS Law Medical 465, (2009) 109 BMLR 133, (2009) *Times*, 6 August.
[63] [2011] IRLR 756, [2011] UKSC 30.

representation (*Kulkarni*). But there are many cases when even a lesser sanction could have an equally disastrous effect on an employee's livelihood or reputation (eg an allegation of sexual misconduct), and when the need for legal representation may be just as important. We may also ask if there is a distinction between the dismissal of an employee and the dismissal of a professional person? Are we to grade employees by their ranking in the food chain in order to see if their status warrants higher standards in disciplinary proceedings, and thus give a professional person the right to legal representation which is denied to others? Finally, cases such as *Kulkarni* and *R v Governors of X School* can only apply to public sector employees who are required to act in a manner which is compatible with the Convention. Would the courts be wiling to extend the right to legal representation to the private sector? It is clear that this topic raises a number of outstanding issues, which no doubt will be the subject of judicial exploration in the coming years.

12.29 If the worker makes a request to be accompanied, but the chosen companion is not available at the time proposed for the hearing, the employer must postpone the hearing to a time proposed by the worker. The alternative time must be reasonable, and within five working days after the date proposed by the employer.

12.30 The employer shall permit a worker to have time off work for the purpose of accompanying another worker, and, when acting in the capacity of a trade union official, this will count as trade union duties for the purpose of TULR(C)A, ss 168–173 and thus the time off work will be with pay.

12.31 The right to be accompanied applies to workers as defined, including agency workers, homeworkers, persons in Crown employment and members of the staff of the House of Lords and House of Commons (s 13). However, persons employed by the Security Services, Secret Intelligence Service and Government Communications Headquarters are excluded from these provisions (s 15).

12.32 A complaint may be made to an employment tribunal (within the usual time limits) that the employer has failed to permit the worker to exercise his rights under s 10, which, if it finds the complaint to be well founded, shall make a compensation award of up to two weeks' pay (s 11).

12.33 A worker has the right not to suffer a detriment because he sought to be accompanied or to accompany another, and any dismissal because of the exercise of the above rights will be automatically unfair. The qualifying period of employment does not apply, and interim relief will be available, as appropriate (s 12).

F. Appeal procedures

12.34 If the initial procedure is flawed in some way a refusal by the employer to permit an employee to exercise the right of appeal to which he is contractually entitled will render a dismissal unfair (*West Midland Co-operative Society v Tipton*[64]). If an employer's decision to dismiss would be fair at the time when the appeal machinery is exhausted, that decision does not become unfair because further information comes to light after the appeal has been dismissed (*Greenall Whitley plc v Carr*[65]).

12.35 Whether an appeal hearing should be a rehearing of all the evidence *de novo*, or a review of all the evidence with an opportunity to make further representations,

---

[64] [1986] AC 536, [1986] 1 All ER 513, [1986] 2 WLR 306, [1986] ICR 192, [1986] IRLR 112, 130 Sol Jo 143, [1986] LS Gaz R 780, [1986] NLJ Rep 163, HL.

[65] [1985] ICR 451, [1985] IRLR 289, EAT.

is a matter of style. At one time it was thought that when an initial decision to dismiss was procedurally flawed, the defect could be cured at the appeal stage, which could be a rehearing or review, as the case may be (see *Whitbread plc v Mills*[66]). However, that approach was disapproved of in *Taylor v OCS Group Ltd* (see para 4.105), where the Court of Appeal stated that the employment tribunal should consider the fairness of the whole of the disciplinary process. If the early stage of the procedure was defective or unfair in some way, the tribunal should examine any subsequent proceedings with particular care. It must then determine whether due to the fairness or unfairness of the procedures adopted, the thoroughness (or lack of it) of the process and the open-mindedness (or not) of the decision-maker, the overall procedure was fair, notwithstanding any deficiencies at the early stage.

12.36 However, it is very important that internal appeals procedures operated by commercial concerns should not be cramped by legal requirements which impose impossible burdens on the way they conduct their affairs. In *Rowe v Radio Rentals*[67] the claimant was alleged to have been guilty of gross misconduct, and was dismissed by the area manager. An appeal was made to the regional manager and at the hearing the area manager outlined the facts of the case and remained present throughout the hearing. It was held that the appeals procedure was perfectly fair, even though it may appear to have offended against the rules of natural justice. It was inevitable that those who take the original decision to dismiss must be in daily contact with their superiors who would be hearing the appeal. Rules about lack of contact cannot be applied in the majority of cases. The EAT quoted with approval Lord Denning in *Ward v Bradford Corpn*: 'We must not force these disciplinary bodies to become entrammelled in the nets of legal procedure. So long as they act fairly and justly, their decision should be supported.'[68]

12.37 If an employee is dismissed, but is given a right to make an appeal in accordance with the company's disciplinary procedure, what is his legal position up to the time the appeal is heard? There are two possibilities.

12.38 First, if he is dismissed (with or without notice) the dismissal takes effect from the effective date of termination, and the fact that an appeal is pending does not alter that date. In *J Sainsbury Ltd v Savage* (see para 20.27) the applicant was dismissed for gross misconduct. On the effective date of termination he did not have the requisite period of continuous employment (26 weeks, as the law then was), but by the time the appeal was heard, more than 28 weeks had elapsed since the commencement of his employment. It was held that he could not pursue a claim for unfair dismissal. Thus using domestic appeal machinery merely suspends the dismissal; if the appeal is rejected, the original decision is confirmed (*Natt v Hillingdon Area Health Authority*[69]).

12.39 Second, if he is dismissed, and placed on full pay pending an internal appeal, there is a suspension which does not terminate the contract, and hence he is still an employee up to the time of the appeal hearing (*Duffy v Northampton Area Health Authority*[70]).

12.40 On the other hand, if a person is dismissed, and then his appeal against dismissal is allowed, his period of employment is to be regarded as being continuous, for it is implicit in the contract that the period between the dismissal and appeal is one of suspension, and the result of the ultimate decision of the appeal process relates back to the date of the purported dismissal (*Howgate v Fane Acoustics*[71]).

---

[66] [1988] ICR 776, [1988] IRLR 501, EAT.   [67] [1982] IRLR 177.
[68] (1971) 70 LGR 27, 115 Sol Jo 606, CA.   [69] Unreported.
[70] Unreported.   [71] [1981] IRLR 161, EAT.

Disciplinary rules

12.41 The actual rules which an employee is expected to observe can be found either in the disciplinary procedure itself, or in the works or staff rules (see Chapter 3) or even a combination of both. At one time it was customary to write them on a prominently displayed notice posted somewhere in the works, but this is not particularly satisfactory nowadays. The important thing is that they must be brought to the employee's attention, whether on an induction course, or in a specially prepared handbook or other suitable method. In *Pitts v Revertex*[72] the employer posted a notice near the canteen on a notice board stating that any employee who absented himself without authority would be guilty of gross misconduct. The applicant was found to be absent, and was dismissed. It was held that if a rule was so important, posting a notice was not sufficient. It should have been communicated individually to each employee. The need to communicate the relevant rules to the employees concerned was stressed once again in *Brooks (W) & Son v Skinner*,[73] where the employers agreed with a trade union that employees who over-indulged themselves at a Christmas party so that they were unable to attend work would be instantly dismissed. This agreement was not communicated to the employees. The applicant was dismissed for failing to turn up for work on the nightshift after a Christmas party, and his dismissal was held to be unfair. He would not have realised that this conduct would attract instant dismissal, and his lack of knowledge of the rule meant that the employers had acted unreasonably.

12.42 The rules should be clear and readily understandable by all affected employers, and should not be confused with extraneous matters. In *Rigden-Murphy v Securicor Ltd*,[74] the claimant was dismissed after being seen to be breaking a company rule concerning the transfer of money from a bank to his vehicle. The rule in question was contained in a manual, which had 'Ten golden rules'. At the end, there was a statement that a failure to comply may lead to instant dismissal. Some of the 'rules' were in fact mere exhortations, such as 'Beware of complacency. Build up the habit of self-discipline'. Other rules had in the past been dealt with by a warning. It was held that the dismissal was unfair. The rules were somewhat ambiguous, in that they contained matters which were unconnected with discipline, and there was no clear line between those rules which attracted dismissal as a punishment, and those which were dealt with (if at all) with lesser severity.

12.43 Employment tribunals had, in the past, been most inconsistent in dealing with rules which contain automatic as opposed to discretionary sanctions. For example, in *Jones v London Co-operative Society*[75] the staff code in a departmental store stated that an incorrect recording of a customer's purchase was a serious offence, 'and the employee *will be* summarily dismissed'. It was held that such a rule was too rigid, for it failed to distinguish between a genuine error and a calculated act. On the other hand, in *Lindsay v Fife Forge*,[76] the works rules stated that employees who left the premises without permission '*may be* subject to instant dismissal' and the employment tribunal held that this did not amount to a clear and specific warning!

12.44 The problems caused by such sophistry can be illustrated by comparing *Dalton v Burton's Gold Medal Biscuits Ltd* (see para 10.53) and *Meridian Ltd v Gomersall*.[77] In the former case, a man of 22 years' service was dismissed for a clocking offence, the works rules stating that such action 'will result in instant dismissal'. The National Industrial Relations Court held the dismissal to be fair. In the latter case, it was stated in the works rules that

---

[72] Unreported.   [73] [1984] IRLR 379.   [74] [1976] IRLR 106.   [75] [1975] IRLR 110.
[76] [1976] IRLR 47.   [77] [1977] ICR 597, [1977] IRLR 425, 12 ITR 323, EAT.

anyone guilty of a clocking offence 'will render themselves liable to instant dismissal'. The EAT upheld a tribunal decision that a dismissal was unfair, because the employee might take the view that to be caught once, even suspected of doing it previously, would not necessarily lead to an instant dismissal!

12.45 The question, in reality, is not the mandatory nature of the sanction, but whether the employer acts reasonably in imposing that sanction, or whether some other equally efficacious sanction could be imposed. It must be wrong to dismiss an employee for minor misconduct no matter how strongly worded is the rule, for the mandatory nature of a disciplinary rule does not exclude the jurisdiction of the employment tribunal to decide whether or not the employer has acted reasonably (*Ladbroke Racing Ltd v Arnott*[78]). On the other hand, automatic penalties fail to permit an employer to take account of mitigating circumstances, the employee's record, general conduct and so forth. The employer should be able to tailor the punishment to the offence, and then to the offender. He should be consistent in his procedures, but can be flexible in his punishments. In *Elliott Bros Ltd v Colverd*[79] the EAT resolved doubts by stating that there is no legal requirement that a rule must indicate that a breach would inevitably lead to a dismissal, and a rule book did not need to indicate a distinction between the possibility and inevitability of dismissal. However the rule is worded, the employer is entitled to look at all the circumstances.

12.46 An employer must be prepared to justify any alleged disparity of treatment between different employees. In *Hadjioannou v Coral Casinos Ltd*[80] the claimant was dismissed for breaking a rule which forbade socialising with members or guests at a gambling club. He argued that in the past other employees had broken the rule and had not been dismissed. In upholding a decision of the employment tribunal that the dismissal was fair, the EAT commented that action taken by the employers in previous cases was only relevant in three circumstances (a) to show that there may be certain categories of misconduct which may be overlooked (or at least not dealt with by the sanction of dismissal), (b) if it leads to the conclusion that the purported reason for the dismissal was not the real or genuine reason, and (c) to show that some lesser penalty would have been more appropriate. The EAT went on to comment that it was of the highest importance that flexibility should be retained, and employers should not be encouraged to think that there was a 'tariff' approach to industrial misconduct (see *Paul v East Surrey District Health Authority*,[81] para 17.131).

12.47 Disparity of treatment is acceptable if culpability is not the same. In *Securicor Ltd v Smith*,[82] the claimant and another employee were security guards, collecting and delivering cash. The employers had strict rules about the way they did their work. Following an incident when the rules were breached, the employers held a disciplinary hearing, and both employees were dismissed. An appeal was made to the area manager, who affirmed the dismissals. Both employees then lodged a further appeal to a special panel set up by the company, and at this level it was decided that as one employee was less blameworthy, he would not be dismissed, but the dismissal of the claimant was confirmed. An employment tribunal held that his dismissal was unfair. They held that the original decision to dismiss both men was reasonable, but the final appeal body acted unreasonably in dismissing one employee but not the other on the ground that the other employee was less blameworthy. The decision was confirmed by the EAT. However, the Court of Appeal reversed the decision. The real question was whether the final appeal panel's decision was so unreasonable that no reasonable employer would have accepted it. Indeed, had the employers refused to accept the decision of the appeal panel not to dismiss the other employee, he would

---

[78] [1979] IRLR 192, EAT; on appeal [1983] IRLR 154, Ct of Sess.   [79] [1979] IRLR 92, EAT.
[80] [1981] IRLR 352, EAT.   [81] [1995] IRLR 305, 30 BMLR 41, CA.   [82] [1989] IRLR 356, CA.

have had an unanswerable case for unfair dismissal in an employment tribunal. The appeal panel, having thoroughly investigated the matter, had distinguished the culpability of the two employees, and their decision was not unreasonable.

12.48 Similarly, disparity of treatment is permitted if disciplinary records are not the same. In *Harrow London Borough v Cunningham*,[83] the claimant and a fellow worker were found to be doing unauthorised work in circumstances which amounted to gross misconduct. The claimant was dismissed, but his fellow worker was given a final warning. The reason for this was that the claimant had already been in receipt of a final warning, whereas his fellow worker had a clean disciplinary record. An employment tribunal held that the dismissal of the claimant was unfair, on the ground that both of them should have been treated equally, but the decision was reversed by the EAT. An employer is entitled to take into account aggravating factors, including an employee's previously poor disciplinary record as compared with the other employee concerned, as well as mitigating circumstances which affect one employee when compared with the other.

12.49 Once an employer lays down a particular rule, a failure to enforce it consistently may weaken any subsequent attempt to do so. In *Frame v McKean & Graham Ltd* (see para 10.91), the claimant was dismissed for doing work on his own account contrary to the working rules for the industry. His dismissal was held to be unfair. The rule had never been enforced in the past, and indeed, such conduct had been condoned. Moreover, he had not taken any work away from the employer, for the customer for whom he worked had severed the relationship with the employer.

12.50 Rules may be of a general nature, eg defining conduct which, by the generality of the law of employment, cannot be tolerated; they may be specific, defining the sort of conduct which *this* employer will not tolerate, and they may be special, dealing with instant circumstances which have not arisen hitherto.

A. General rules

12.51 These are rules which govern conduct which is such that by common consent, disciplinary sanctions will be imposed. Examples which readily spring to mind include theft of the employer's property, theft from fellow employees, serious neglect, wilful damage, dangerous practices, and so on. It is not generally advisable to list all the matters which come under the heading of gross misconduct, for this could mean that an employee would be saved from dismissal who committed an act which was so outrageous that no-one thought it would ever happen (*Gardiner v Newport County Borough Council*[84]). In *Clarkson v Brown, Muff & Co Ltd*,[85] 'gross misconduct' was defined as being 'dishonesty, arson, violence, obscenity, neglect and insubordination'. It was held that this definition did not cover an employee who had been telling lies. Some firms make it clear that the definitions of gross misconduct contained in their rules are examples only, and any list of misdeeds is not intended to be exhaustive!

B. Specific rules

12.52 These rules cover the sort of misconduct which *this employer* will not tolerate under any circumstances. Thus each employer must judge for himself the standards which are to apply, based on his own circumstances. Thus fighting, swearing, lateness, absenteeism, drunkenness, trading, betting, and so forth, may all amount to industrial misconduct

---

[83] [1996] IRLR 256, EAT.   [84] [1974] IRLR 262.   [85] [1974] IRLR 66.

which, in the individual case, attracts disciplinary sanctions. Such rules must be fair and reasonable. In *Turner v Pleasurama Casinos Ltd*,[86] the claimant was an inspector who was employed to observe gaming tables, to ensure that there was no dishonesty by croupiers. He was dismissed for 'neglect of duty' after a complaint that a croupier and a member of the public had been cheating under his nose. The allegation was denied by him, but after a full and proper investigation, the employer found against him. It was held that the dismissal was fair; the gaming world is a hard world, and even the smallest of mistakes could not be tolerated.

12.53 Provided such rules meet the standards of reasonableness, they can generally be enforced. In *Higham v International Stores*,[87] the claimant was given to wearing sandals and clogs, and other casual clothes. He was told that he must comply with the company's requirement to wear proper shoes and socks, and to wear a tie and overall when serving customers. After failing to heed due warnings, he was dismissed for not complying with the rules. It was held that an employer is entitled to insist on a reasonable standard of dress. What was reasonable is always a question of fact, to be determined in each case by all the circumstances. Different standards apply in Bond Street and in Petticoat Lane. In this case, the shop had a middle-class clientele in a conventional town, and the dismissal was thus fair.

C. **Special rules**

12.54 Since the rules cannot conceivably cover every possible situation, an employer must be free to lay down a rule specifically to deal with a matter which has not hitherto arisen. In *Spiller v Wallis Ltd*[88] a company rule stated that employees should not have deep emotional relationships with other members of the staff which might impair their marital status. This rule had been promulgated after an incident where the spouse of an employee had come on to the premises and created an unpleasant scene. The claimant was in fact having a love affair with a senior employee, and she refused to discontinue the relationship. Her dismissal was held to be fair. She was told of the rule, but chose not to comply. NB: Whether such a rule contravenes Art 8 of the European Convention on Human Rights (see para 1.104) is a matter upon which no doubt the tribunals will shortly adjudicate!

12.55 Finally, the interpretation of the rules, and their reasonableness, is a matter for the employment tribunal to determine. In *Palmer v Vauxhall Motors Ltd*,[89] the claimant was dismissed for spending 15 minutes in the club bar after her lunch break. It was alleged that this constituted gross misconduct in accordance with the works rules. It was held that even though the rules were somewhat ambiguous, the employment tribunal was entitled to find that the dismissal was fair. The EAT would only reverse that finding if it could be said that no person instructed in the relevant law could have come to that decision.

Disciplinary powers

12.56 The exercise of disciplinary powers is a corrective function, not punitive. The object is to improve an employee's performance, so that he can remain a valued and useful employee, not to give vent to management frustrations. The choice of the disciplinary sanction must therefore reflect this objective, and should, so far as is possible, be tailored to the individual case, bearing in mind the need to show some form of consistency in like cases. The Code of Practice should be borne in mind at all times.

---

[86] [1976] IRLR 151.   [87] Unreported.   [88] [1973] IRLR 362.   [89] [1977] ICR 24, EAT.

A. Fines and deductions

12.57 It is possible to impose a fine or make a deduction for bad or negligent work, but the principles laid down to prevent unlawful deductions (see para 8.4) must be observed. There must be a specific contractual power, and in respect of persons employed in retail employment the restrictions in ERA, s 18 must be observed. Deductions or payments made in consequence of disciplinary proceedings held under a statutory provision are excluded from the Act (eg police and fire service).

12.58 The Act specifically states that the only remedy for a breach is by way of a complaint to an employment tribunal under s 23, but it is submitted that an unauthorised deduction or payment may still give rise to a complaint of constructive dismissal. Thus, in *Lethaby v Horsman Andrew and Knill Ltd*[90] the employer made a deduction from the employee's wages to cover the loss of the firm's property. This was done in the absence of any contractual authority to make such a deduction, and the employee, who refused to agree to it, resigned. It was held that this constituted repudiatory conduct by the employer of the contract, and as such constituted a dismissal (see Chapter 17).

12.59 The employer's power to fine or make deductions must be contained in the express terms of the contract, and it is now no longer possible to rely on an implied term, or (more likely) a customary term to this effect. This makes a number of current employment practices of dubious validity. For example, some firms make a practice of deducting 15 minutes from the pay of an hourly worker when he is a few minutes late (known as quartering); it is doubtful if the unilateral imposition of such a practice would be upheld in law.

B. Suspension without pay for misconduct

12.60 If there is an express term in the contract which permits the employer to suspend an employee for a specific reason, such as misconduct, the courts will uphold such a term provided the suspension is carried out in strict conformity with the laid down procedure. Sometimes the grounds for suspension, and the procedure to be adopted, will be laid down in the works rules, and the extent to which those rules will form part of the individual contract of employment will be a question of fact in each case. Even so, if an employee is, or ought to be, aware of the practice of a firm, or if there is a custom in the trade or industry or locality, then he will be bound by it. In *Bird v British Celanese Ltd*[91] an employee was suspended for two days in accordance with the firm's practice, and this was held to be a valid exercise of disciplinary power by the employer.

12.61 Alternatively, the grounds for suspension and procedure to be adopted may be contained in a collective agreement, in which case there may be an express or implied incorporation of those terms into the individual contract of employment. In *Tomlinson v London, Midland and Scottish Rly Co*[92] a trade union negotiated with the defendant company an agreement which, inter alia, laid down the procedure for dealing with breaches of discipline, and this was held to have been incorporated into an employee's contract of employment.

12.62 It is clear that the right of suspensory lay-off must be based on a contractual power, which will be either expressed, or implied, or based on custom and practice. The courts and tribunals are quite willing to discover such a power when minor disciplinary matters are concerned, though they appear to require strict proof if there is a major disciplinary matter

---

[90] [1975] IRLR 119.
[91] [1945] KB 336, [1945] 1 All ER 488, 43 LGR 199, 109 JP 170, 114 LJKB 184, 172 LT 260, 61 TLR 316, CA.
[92] [1944] 1 All ER 537, CA.

which can lead to a dismissal. The EAT held that it may not be difficult to draw an inference that a contract contains an implied power to suspend as a disciplinary matter, or to enable an investigation to take place (*Pirie and Hunter v Crawford*[93]). But in the total absence of such a power, it is clear that the employer may not purport to exercise it, for this would virtually enable him to assess unilaterally the damages for an employee's misconduct. It further follows that if an employee is wrongfully suspended without pay, he may recover any lost pay by way of damages. In *Hanley v Pease & Partners*,[94] an employee was suspended for one day without pay, and it was held that he was entitled to the money which had been withheld.

12.63 If an employer lawfully suspends an employee, the legal position at common law appears to be that the employment has been temporarily put in abeyance, with a right for the employee to apply for reinstatement at the end of the suspension period (*Marshall v English Electric Co Ltd*[95]). Presumably there is no break in continuity of employment in these circumstances. If the suspension is wrongful, the employee will be entitled to treat this breach as repudiatory conduct by the employer, and he will be entitled to resign and sue for wrongful or unfair dismissal. In *Davies v Anglo Great Lakes Corpn*[96] an employee was suspended without pay after allowing his trade union membership to lapse, and this was held to be repudiatory conduct by the employer.

12.64 But if an employee decides to resign as a result of wrongful suspension he may find the tribunal somewhat unsympathetic, for he would have to argue that he was entitled to resign by reason of the employer's (wrongful) conduct, which the tribunal may not accept as a valid reason, particularly if the employer had reasonable cause to suspend, and the employee's conduct would otherwise have to be dealt with by a dismissal which would have been fair. It can hardly be right for an employer to be saddled with the burden of compensation if he exercises a lesser disciplinary power than he might have done. Another view which may be taken is that the employee's conduct was such that it 'contributed' to the repudiation by the employer, and hence reduced compensation may be awarded. Thus if the employee's conduct is such as to warrant a dismissal, but the employer suspends him without having the contractual power to do so, an action for unfair dismissal would probably fail because the constructive dismissal would be justified because of the misconduct, while an action for wrongful dismissal is unlikely to meet with any greater success. There have been a number of cases where the tribunals have held that an employee should not have been dismissed for misconduct, but the offence warranted some lesser disciplinary measure, such as suspension, even though the employer had no contractual right to do so. Thus in *Unkles v Milanda Bread Co Ltd*[97] an employee was dismissed for smoking in breach of the company's rules. The tribunal thought that an appropriate penalty might have been a suspension for one month without pay, but there is no evidence in the report to suggest that the employer had the power to do this by virtue of the contract of employment. In seeking to encourage employers to exercise this lesser power, it would be inconsistent for the tribunals to penalise them for doing so.

C. **Precautionary suspension**

12.65 If an employee is suspended as a precautionary measure, and not for disciplinary purposes, the position is somewhat different. In *Jones v British Rail Hovercraft Ltd*[98] the employee was suspended from duty without pay pending the outcome of investigations

---

[93] Unreported.
[94] [1915] 1 KB 698, 79 JP 230, 84 LJKB 532, [1914–15] All ER Rep 984, 112 LT 823.
[95] [1945] 1 All ER 653, 43 LGR 275, 109 JP 145, 89 Sol Jo 315, 173 LT 134, 61 TLR 379, CA.
[96] [1973] IRLR 133.   [97] [1973] IRLR 76.   [98] [1974] IRLR 279.

and proceedings against him which were brought by the police. He claimed that this amounted to a dismissal, but this argument was rejected. The rule book, which was part of his employment conditions, mentioned the distinction between precautionary and punitive suspension, and it was reasonable for the employer to take precautionary steps to protect his interest and his property. That the suspension was without pay could be dealt with by making up his back pay if the proceedings ended in his favour. In *Crawford v Suffolk Mental Health Partnership NHS Trust*[99] the Court of Appeal raised concerns that even where there is a contractual power to suspend an employee, the employer should not do so as an automatic knee-jerk reaction to an allegation of misconduct, as this can be very damaging to the employee.

12.66 The Code of Practice indicates that precautionary suspension pending investigation should be with full pay, and this is probably correct in the absence of any contrary term in the contract. This could give rise to difficulties if the investigation is outside the control of management, for this could possibly go on for weeks or months. It is submitted therefore that precautionary suspension should be with pay if there is to be an internal investigation, but this may not be the rule in the case of external investigations. If this were not so, then the only alternatives available to the employer would be to retain an employee on full pay, or to dismiss him, and it is submitted that suspension without pay may turn out to be a better practice in some cases. In *Conway v Matthew, Wright & Nephew*,[100] the claimant was a night-watchman, and he was charged by the police with maliciously causing damage to the company's property. The company investigated the matter, and dismissed him. Subsequently, all criminal charges against him were dropped. It was argued that the company should have suspended him pending the outcome of criminal proceedings, but it was held that there was no legal obligation to do so, as it could have been many months before such charges were disposed of. The employers were under no obligation to refrain from dismissing him until the guilty conduct was established beyond reasonable doubt in a criminal court.

12.67 However, an employer should beware of using suspension as a knee-jerk reaction to a problem, for there may well be circumstances where such action is in fact not warranted. In *Gogay v Hertfordshire County Council*[101] the claimant was a residential care worker at a children's home. A child made some vague allegations of sexual abuse, which caused the employers to suspend the claimant while investigations were carried out. These con-cluded that there was no truth whatsoever in the allegations and the claimant was offered reinstatement. However, she was unable to return to work because she was suffering from clinical depression brought on by the suspension, and she subsequently brought a claim for loss of earnings and damages for personal injury. It was held that her claim would succeed. The employers should have undertaken further enquiries before deciding to suspend the claimant pending an investigation into an allegation of sexual abuse. Further, the claim-ant could have been transferred for a short time, while the enquiries proceeded, or given a short period of leave. In the circumstances, the employers were in breach of the implied term of trust and confidence.

12.68 There is no reason in principle to prevent a court from granting an injunction to restrain an employer from suspending an employee whilst carrying out an investigation into an alleged wrongdoing. In *Mezey v South West London & St George's Mental NHS Trust (No 1)*[102] (see para 10.17) a consultant psychiatrist was suspended pending disciplinary proceedings. It was held that an injunction against this would be granted. Suspension is not

---

[99] [2012] EWCA Civ 138.   [100] [1977] IRLR 89, EAT.
[101] [2000] IRLR 703, [2001] 1 FCR 455, [2000] Fam Law 883, [2000] All ER (D) 1057, CA.
[102] [2007] EWCA Civ 106. See also *Mezey v South West London & St George's Mental Health NHS Trust (No. 2)* [2010] IRLR 512, [2010] EWCA Civ 293, CA.

a neutral act preserving the employment relationship. It changes the status from work to no work, and inevitably casts a shadow over the employee's competence.

12.69 If there is an express contractual right to suspend with or without pay pending an investigation, this is subject to an implied term that the imposition of the suspension and its continuance would be on reasonable grounds. In *McClory v Post Office* (see paras 3.51 and 10.17) three postmen were involved in a fight with employees from another office, and they were arrested and charged by the police with various offences. The Post Office suspended them on full pay, but without any payment for overtime which they would otherwise have worked. After making various enquiries, they were permitted to return to work some seven months later, and subsequently were acquitted of all the criminal charges. They brought an action for a declaration that their suspension had been in breach of their contracts of employment and they also sought damages for loss of overtime pay which they would have earned but for the suspension.

It was held that there was no breach of the employment contract. There was no duty on an employer to give reasons for the suspension or to give the employee an opportunity to be heard before it was imposed. The court refused to import the rules of natural justice into what is essentially a contractual arrangement between employer and employee. There was an implied term that the employer would exercise the express contractual right to suspend and to continue to suspend, only on reasonable grounds. To hold otherwise would enable an employer to suspend indefinitely. On the facts of the case, the employer had acted reasonably, and that aspect of the claim was dismissed.

The court also dismissed the claim for loss of overtime pay. The employees could not show that they had a right to overtime pay, only an obligation to work overtime when required. There was no duty on the employer to provide overtime on a regular basis, and thus the loss of a chance to work extra hours could not constitute the basis of a legal claim.

12.70 There is no legal requirement to suspend an employee prior to the undertaking of a full investigation, and a failure to do so does not weaken an allegation of gross misconduct. As a general rule, it is unwise to draw any conclusion from the act of or absence of suspension (*East Berkshire Health Authority v Matadeen*[103]). If an employee is absent from work because he is suspended, there is no obligation for him to return to work until the suspension is lifted (*Hassan v Odeon Cinemas*[104]).

D. Warnings

12.71 An employer does not need contractual power to issue warnings, but frequently this will be the subject of a disciplinary code or part of the works rules. These may state the procedural steps (for example, first oral warning, first written warning, final written warning), before further disciplinary action is taken. Strict adherence to these steps is necessary and a failure by the employer to observe them may lead to difficulties in unfair dismissal proceedings. Thus a failure to give a warning in writing as required by the agreed procedure resulted in a dismissal being held to be unfair in *Raymond v Sir Lindsay Parkinson Ltd*.[105]

12.72 Nonetheless, the warning system must be operated sensibly, not merely as a form of mechanical procedure. It is possible to give an employee a final warning for a serious misdemeanour without having first to go through the processes of informal warning, first written warning, etc; equally, the fact that an employee has received a final warning does not mean that the next occasion on which he commits an 'offence' will be visited with an

---

[103] [1992] ICR 723, [1992] IRLR 336, [1992] 29 LS Gaz R 24, EAT.
[104] [1998] ICR 127, EAT.   [105] [1974] IRLR 298.

automatic sanction. Either course could lead to ludicrous results. There is no substitute for a full and fair investigation of all the facts. In *Newalls Insulation Co Ltd v Blakeman*,[106] the claimant was dismissed for being absent on two occasions within 14 days, following a final warning for absenteeism. Prior to this, he had had two verbal warnings. The EAT held that the employment tribunal should look at all the circumstances of the case, and not simply whether it was reasonable to dismiss for two days' absence after the final warning. The issues were, what happened before the final warning was given, how many absences were there, why was he absent, and how did the absences fit in as part of the general picture?

12.73 A warning can deal with specific conduct which is the subject of complaint, and it should also deal with general matters, so that the totality of the employee's conduct can eventually be taken into account. This solves the problem, sometimes raised by management, as to whether or not, having given three warnings for one type of misconduct, it is necessary to give a further three warnings in respect of a different series of offences! Thus in *Donald Cook v Carter*,[107] the claimant received a number of warnings; one for using bad language, and a year later, another one for the same offence. Two months later he was given a final warning for inefficiency, with a threat to demote or dismiss. Three months later he was given another final warning for leaving work before the normal finishing time and he was suspended for five days. He was then guilty of inefficiency, and was dismissed. The employment tribunal held that the dismissal was unfair, in that he should have been given a further final warning, but this was reversed by the EAT. As long as the matter leading to the dismissal was properly investigated and the proper procedure followed, it was not open to the employment tribunal to find that fairness required a further warning being given, or that the employers should have suspended the employee, as they had done so previously.

12.74 This approach was confirmed by the EAT in *Auguste Noel Ltd v Curtis*,[108] where an employee was dismissed for mishandling company property. He had previously received two final written warnings for different offences. An employment tribunal held that the previous warnings were not relevant, but the decision was reversed on appeal. The existence of previous warnings, the dates, numbers, and substance of the complaints were all relevant matters which an employer was entitled to take into account.

12.75 It is for the employer to determine the nature of the disciplinary sanction, and, generally speaking, an employment tribunal should not attempt to assess whether or not a final warning should or should not have been given. However, if there is something to suggest that a final warning was 'manifestly inappropriate' or given without prima facie grounds, then the employment tribunal will scrutinise carefully the employer's decision.

In *Davies v Sandwell Metropolitan Borough Council*[109] the Court of Appeal emphasised that a warning in an unfair dismissal claim can only be challenged if it was issued in bad faith or was manifestly inappropriate (see also *Simmonds v Milford Club*[110]).

12.76 A final warning is a severe penalty which just stops short of a dismissal. It is frequently imposed when a dismissal is a permissible and obvious sanction but, for reasons relating to the particular employee, is not imposed. To issue a final warning in respect of a relatively minor incident of misconduct can be a disproportionate response to the employee's conduct, and may enable the employee to resign and claim constructive dismissal (*Stanley Cole (Wainfleet) Ltd v Sheridan*[111]).

---

[106] [1976] ICR 543, [1976] IRLR 303, EAT.   [107] [1977] IRLR 88, EAT.
[108] [1990] ICR 604, [1990] IRLR 326, EAT.   [109] [2013] EWCA Civ 135.
[110] UKEAT/0323/12/KN.
[111] [2003] ICR 297, [2003] IRLR 52, [2002] All ER (D) 11 (Nov), EAT; aff'd [2003] EWCA Civ 1046, [2003] 4 All ER 1181, [2003] ICR 1449, [2003] IRLR 885, [2003] 38 LS Gaz R 33, [2003] All ER (D) 446 (Jul).

12.77 If a warning is stated to last for a certain length of time, then clearly it will lapse at the end of that time. In *Bevan Ashford v Malin*[112] a letter was handed to the employee on 29 January 1992, stating that a final written warning would remain on his personal file for a period of 12 months from the date of the letter. He was dismissed following his involvement in an incident at work on 29 January 1993. The employment tribunal held that the final written warning had expired at midnight on 28 January 1993, and ought not to have been taken into account when considering the disciplinary action to be taken following the incident which occurred the following day, and the decision was confirmed by the EAT. The general rule is that penal documents should be construed strictly, and also any ambiguity has to be construed against the maker. Thus the final warning had expired the day before the conduct which led to the dismissal occurred, and could not be relied upon as a ground for dismissal.

12.78 The warning should refer to the past conduct which is the subject of complaint, and to future conduct. It should, where possible, state the remedial action to be taken, and should specify the period of time in which such action should be taken. Frequently, a disciplinary procedure will specify the length of time the warning will last, but perhaps a better approach is for the warning itself to state the operative period, for mechanical and automatic approaches to disciplinary problems are not sound policy. A warning can also be suspensive, when it will stay on the employee's record until such time as it is removed, or can be ignored, or resolutive, which will lapse on compliance. The latter can therefore be ignored when its objective has been achieved. In *Duncan v GEC Telecommunications Ltd*[113] an employee failed to send in a medical certificate as required by the company's rules. After being warned, she sent in an appropriate certificate. A few months later she again failed to send in a medical certificate. It was held that the earlier warning had lapsed on her compliance, and therefore her dismissal was unfair.

12.79 A warning may lapse after a certain period of time, but an employer is not to be criticised because he is over-generous and extends the warning period, instead of acting on it. Being over-generous is not the same as being unreasonable (*Kraft Foods Ltd v Fox*[114]). Further, a warning which is itself the subject of a pending appeal may be taken into account by an employer when considering dismissal for subsequent misconduct (*Tower Hamlets Health Authority v Anthony*[115]), and a final written warning which has expired may be taken into account in exceptional circumstances. In *Airbus UK v Webb*[116] the claimant was given a final written warning for misuse of company time, which was to stay on his record for 12 months. One month after the warning expired he, and several colleagues, were caught watching television during company time. The claimant was dismissed, although his colleagues, who had not previously had a final warning, were not. The employment tribunal and the EAT held that an expired warning could never be taken into account for dismissal purposes, but the decision was reversed by the Court of Appeal. Reliance on a final warning was a relevant factor in deciding whether the employer had acted reasonably and, though in most circumstances taking it into account would mean that a dismissal was unfair, this was not inevitably so. Reliance on an expired final warning would be the exception, rather than the rule.

12.80 Tribunals have frequently stressed the need to issue warnings before the power of dismissal is exercised. The warnings should be given by a person in authority, should be clear, incisive and firm. They should make clear the nature of the conduct which will not be tolerated, and spell out in no uncertain terms that the consequence of a failure to heed

[112] [1995] ICR 453, [1995] IRLR 360, EAT.   [113] [1976] IRLR 3.
[114] [1978] ICR 311, [1977] IRLR 431, EAT.   [115] [1989] ICR 656, [1989] IRLR 394, CA.
[116] EAT/0453/06, EAT; [2008] EWCA Civ 49, CA.

the warning will be a dismissal. Formal warnings should be given in writing and this is of particular importance when there are language or communication problems.

12.81 Failure to follow these rules may lead to the tribunal making a finding adverse to the employer. In *Wells v West Ltd*[117] the employers gave a warning to an employee that his 'employment might be in jeopardy'. In holding that this was not a sufficient warning, the tribunal held that those who use circumlocutions will have to bear the burden which they subsequently impose. In *Bendall v Paine and Betteridge*[118] the employee was given a verbal warning that smoking would not be tolerated on the premises. It was held that a failure to give a written, final warning meant that the dismissal was unfair. And in *Rosenthal v Louis Butler Ltd*[119] the employee used some offensive language to her manager. It was held that she ought to have been warned about future conduct, and been given an opportunity to apologise before dismissal was warranted.

12.82 It must be stressed that there is no rule of law which requires warnings to be given in all cases; it is merely a rule of good industrial relations practice. Warnings are matters of substance, not procedure (*James v Waltham Holy Cross UDC*[120]). Whether a warning should have been given will depend on all the circumstances of the case, including its effectiveness, and the alternative course which may have been available or adopted. If a tribunal considers that had a clear warning been given, a dismissal would not have been necessary, then it will conclude that a dismissal without such a warning will be unfair (*Jones v GEC Elliott Automation Ltd*[121]). Conversely, if a warning would have had no effect, then a failure to give one will not by itself render a dismissal unfair (*AJ Dunning & Sons (Shopfitters) Ltd v Jacomb*[122]). There should be no need to give a warning to a highly paid and qualified employee that he will be dismissed if there is dissatisfaction with his work, for he should know this. Nor is there a need to give an educated person in a responsible position a warning that he must co-operate with his head of department (*Farnborough v Governors of Edinburgh College of Art*[123]). Each case must be determined on its own merits.

12.83 If an employee is given a final warning against which he has appealed, there is no rule of law which requires the employer to await the outcome of the appeal before dismissing for another disciplinary offence (*Stein v Associated Dairies*).

E. **Reprimand**

12.84 The same is probably true about a reprimand, which is a mark of displeasure about past conduct and a warning about the future. Tribunals have held that misconduct which is not 'gross' should in some circumstances be punished by a reprimand rather than a dismissal, though to what extent a reprimand constitutes a punishment is somewhat difficult to see. Further, employers could be forgiven for thinking that this area of tribunal law is full of hazardous speculation, for when 'misconduct' becomes 'gross' is a somewhat subjective concept. In *King v Motorway Tyres and Accessories Ltd*[124] a manager told his superior to 'fuck off' in the course of an argument. It was held that this did not amount to gross misconduct sufficient to warrant dismissal, and that in view of his long service and satisfactory record, he should have been 'severely' reprimanded! The precise distinction between a reprimand and a severe reprimand, and whether the latter is equivalent to a final warning, has yet to be decided. It is submitted that a reprimand is an appropriate sanction to be used when taking disciplinary action against management, or staff employees.

[117] [1979] IRLR 269.   [118] [1973] IRLR 44.   [119] [1972] IRLR 39.
[120] [1973] ICR 398, [1978] IRLR 202, 14 KIR 576, 8 ITR 467, NIRC.   [121] [1972] IRLR 111.
[122] [1973] ICR 448, [1973] IRLR 206, 15 KIR 9, 8 ITR 453, NIRC.
[123] [1974] IRLR 245, NIRC.   [124] [1975] IRLR 51.

F. **Demotion**

12.85 An employee whose conduct is such that the employer has lost all confidence in his ability to do the job in question may be demoted, with or without review, and at a lower earning rate if this is appropriate. If there is an express power to do this in the contract or rules, then provided the sanction has been fairly exercised, there should not be any legal problem. In the absence of such a power, a demotion imposed following a disciplinary hearing is not a breach of contract when it is a lesser penalty than the dismissal which could otherwise have been imposed (*MacKay Decorators (Perth) Ltd v Millar*[125]). If the employee refuses to accept the demotion, he can either resign and claim constructive dismissal, or leave it to the employer to dismiss him. If the employer has acted fairly, and with the interests of the employee at heart, such dismissal will be fair. In *Hall v Lodge*,[126] the claimant was promoted from a supervisory post to manage a shop. Following serious stock deficiencies, her appointment was terminated, and she was offered re-engagement as a supervisor at another branch, at a lower salary. This offer was refused, so she was dismissed. It was held that her dismissal was fair. The company had made a mistake in promoting her too soon to a job which was too big for her. Having realised this, they then acted fairly by considering the alternatives which were available, by offering her a post which was within her competence. However, there is no legal requirement that an employer should demote a person who is incompetent (*Bevan Harris Ltd v Gair*[127]).

12.86 But if a demotion on disciplinary grounds is out of all proportion to the offence, the employee may regard the employer as having repudiated the contract, and claim constructive dismissal. In *BBC v Beckett*,[128] the claimant was employed for 14 years as a scenic carpenter. He was negligent in his work on one occasion, and was demoted to the position of building maintenance carpenter, at a lower salary. He resigned and claimed constructive dismissal, a claim which was upheld by the employment tribunal and by the EAT. The punishment was out of all proportion to the offence, given his long period of satisfactory service.

G. **Transfer**

12.87 Similar considerations apply to the transfer of an employee from one department to another, or one job to another. This power, however, would be used in different circumstances. Merely to transfer an incompetent employee from one department to another is to export one's problems from one manager to another. Transfer is best used as a means of overcoming personality clashes, so as to minimise the likelihood of future problems arising, or to place an employee in a job which he can do, rather than leaving him doing work which is beyond his competence. In *High v British Railways Board*,[129] it was held that a disciplinary transfer which resulted in the employee suffering a drop in his earnings did not give rise to a claim for constructive dismissal.

H. **Alternative employment**

12.88 In appropriate cases, it may be unfair to dismiss an employee without considering whether there was any alternative work he could do, notwithstanding that he cannot be permitted to continue in his old job. However, there is no requirement that this should be investigated before the decision to dismiss is taken, as opposed to after the decision has been taken but before the expiry of any period of notice which may be given. To hold

---

[125] EAT 782/98.   [126] Unreported.   [127] [1981] IRLR 520, EAT.
[128] [1983] IRLR 43, EAT.   [129] [1979] IRLR 52, EAT.

otherwise would mean that an employee would be unfairly dismissed notwithstanding that during his notice period alternative employment was found for him and the notice never took effect (*P v Nottinghamshire County Council*, see para 12.18).

I. Other sanctions

12.89 There are a number of other disciplinary powers which may be used on appropriate occasions, and provided these are exercised in accordance with the relevant rules and procedures, these should cause few problems. For example, it may be possible to withdraw privileges for a certain period of time so as to deny to an employee certain non-contractual benefits, or to provide for the loss of so many years' seniority for certain purposes (but this does not affect the operation of the legal rules relating to continuity of employment). An employee who is persistently late in starting work may have flexi-time withdrawn, as an alternative to, or a precondition of, the implementation of other disciplinary action.

J. Non-employment situations

12.90 The disciplinary powers described in paras 12.56 to 12.89 can only apply to acts of employees committed in the course of employment. An employer has no inherent power to discipline for acts which have occurred outside the employment, though if such acts adversely affect the employer's business, he may be justified in dismissing the employee (see Chapter 17). But if an employee is convicted of an offence outside his employment which may have an effect on his job, the employer should consider the employee's long and blameless record, and consider, for example, if some other means of dealing with the situation can be found. In *Jones v R M Douglas Construction Ltd*[130] the employee, who was a plant engineer, was dismissed after being convicted of handling a stolen engine. The tribunal thought that the employer should have given some consideration to demoting him to his original trade of mechanic/fitter. Clearly, such a power cannot be found in the contract of employment, and amounts to a unilateral assessment by the employer of the necessary steps to be taken to protect his interests. A demotion is, as we have seen, equivalent to a dismissal, and one can only assume that if such steps are taken in serious disciplinary cases, the exercise of a lesser disciplinary power short of dismissal will, in cases of grave misconduct outside the employment, also be looked upon more favourably by the tribunals.

12.91 If the employee is convicted of an offence in connection with matters outside his employment, he is still entitled to present his side of the story to his employers, and the latter should not treat the fact of conviction per se as being conclusive without at least giving a chance to the employee to state his version (*Parsons v LCC*[131]).

---

[130] [1975] IRLR 175.   [131] (1893) 9 TLR 619.

13

Continuous Employment

Continuity of employment

13.1 In order to obtain certain statutory rights, it is necessary to show that an employee has been continuously employed for a certain length of time, depending on the right in question. The statutory provisions which provide for continuity of employment are contained in ss 210–219 of the Employment Rights Act 1996, which provide 'a complete definition of what is meant by "continuously employed"' (*Wood v York City Council*[1]), and the Employment Protection (Continuity of Employment) Regulations 1996. Continuity of employment is a statutory concept (*Collinson v BBC*[2]), generally used for two statutory purposes, namely (a) to determine whether an employee has been employed for a particular length of time so as to qualify for a specific statutory right, and (b) to ascertain the employee's length of employment for the purpose of obtaining certain financial benefits (ie a basic award (see para 17.195) and a redundancy payment (see para 18.65). However, for some statutory rights, no period of continuous employment is required.

13.2 There is nothing to prevent an employer from so arranging employment contracts so as to prevent continuity, and thus avoiding liability for unfair dismissal and redundancy payments. If there are legitimate breaks in employment, and re-employment does not become an arrangement by virtue of s 212(3)(c) (see para 13.24), continuity can be defeated (*Booth v USA*, see para 2.137).

13.3 Continuity of employment is a concept which is only of importance in a statutory context. Thus, if an employer and employee make a private agreement to treat a particular period of employment as being continuous, this may create a private right, but cannot be used to enforce any statutory right, unless the statutory rules are also met. In *Secretary of State for Employment v Globe Elastic Thread Co Ltd*,[3] an employee worked for a company for 22 years. He was then transferred to another company, after receiving assurances that his employment would be treated as being continuous. Five years later, he was made redundant, and he sought a redundancy payment based on the combined service. The House of Lords held that he was only entitled to a statutory redundancy pay in respect of the latter five years' employment. The private agreement may have given him a contractual right against the employers, but could not be used for the purpose of enforcing a statutory right.

Similarly, in *Hanson v Fashion Industries (Hartlepool) Ltd*,[4] an employee went on strike. Nine weeks later, she was re-engaged under a contract which stated that her continuous employment was to start afresh. In subsequent litigation to enforce a claim for maternity

[1] [1978] ICR 840, [1978] IRLR 228, 122 Sol Jo 192, CA.   [2] [1998] ICR 669, [1998] IRLR 238, EAT.
[3] [1978] QB 86, [1978] 1 All ER 987, [1977] 3 WLR 293, [1978] ICR 473, [1977] IRLR 233, 12 ITR 402, 121 Sol Jo 407, EAT; aff'd [1979] QB 183, [1978] 3 All ER 954, [1978] 3 WLR 679, [1978] ICR 1041, [1978] IRLR 417, 13 ITR 540, 122 Sol Jo 661, CA; revsd [1980] AC 506, [1979] 2 All ER 1077, [1979] 3 WLR 143, [1979] ICR 706, [1979] IRLR 327, 123 Sol Jo 504, HL.
[4] [1981] ICR 35, [1980] IRLR 393, EAT.

pay, it was held that her continuous employment had not been broken by the strike, for the statutory provisions came into play which preserved her continuity, and a private agreement cannot override those provisions.

Counting and computing continuity (ERA, ss 210–219)

13.4 The counting of a period of continuous employment is done in weeks, but the computation is done in months and years (s 210(3)). This requires some explanation. The rule is that to determine if an employee's employment, whether continuous or successive or broken, can be counted as being continuous is done on a week-by-week basis, because there is a general rule that continuity is broken by a complete week which does not count towards continuity (s 210(4)), unless continuity is preserved by one of the special rules (see below). A week will count, for the purpose of establishing continuity, if it is governed by a contract of employment, irrespective of the number of hours or days worked during the week. But a 'week', for the purpose of determining whether there has been a break in employment, means a complete week from Sunday ending with a Saturday (*Jennings v Salford Community Service Agency*[5]).

13.5 Continuity is not broken unless there is a complete week in which there is no contract of employment. If there is one day in any week which is governed by a contract of employment, it matters not how or why a gap occurred, or what the employee did during that gap. Thus if an employee leaves one employer to work for another employer, but returns within a week of so leaving, continuity is preserved (*Sweeney v J S Henderson (Concessionaires) Ltd*[6]).

13.6 However, the computation of the length of continuous employment is done in months and years. Thus, if an employee commences work on (say) 21 January 2011, he will have completed two years' employment on 20 January 2013, assuming there is no break in his employment of a whole week. Similarly, if he commences employment on (say) 19 August 2013, he will have been continuously employed for three months on 18 November 2013. The terms 'years' and 'months' are to be treated as calendar years and months respectively.

13.7 Thus, in order to establish a period of continuous employment, it is necessary to ascertain the day when the employment commenced, the day when it ceased, whether there were any weeks which break continuity, and whether there were any weeks which do not break continuity, but which do not count towards continuity. Formerly, there were special rules to be observed in respect of part-time workers, who worked less than 16 hours per week, but these restrictions were abolished in 1995, and now part-time workers are to be treated in the same way as full-time workers, irrespective of the number of hours worked each week. Indeed, service prior to the change in 1995 is to be counted (ERA, Sch 2, para 14(1)).

13.8 The first rule to note is that there is a presumption that continuity of employment exists. Thus, once an employee can show the date on which he commenced work, his employment will be presumed to be continuous until the effective date of termination (s 210(5), and see *Nicoll v Nocorrode Ltd*[7]). Thus an employee can change his place of work, his terms of employment, or even his contract of employment, without his continuity being affected, provided he remains employed by the same employer (*Wood v York City Council*[8]) or an associated employer. An agency worker who is supplied to an employer on a temporary

---

[5] [1981] ICR 399, [1981] IRLR 76, EAT.   [6] [1999] IRLR 306, EAT.
[7] [1981] ICR 348, [1981] IRLR 163, (1981) *Times*, 10 February.
[8] [1978] ICR 840, [1978] IRLR 228, 122 Sol Jo 192, CA.

basis, and who is then taken on as a full-time employee, has continuity of employment from the date he commenced his temporary work (*RNLI v Bushaway*, see para 2.162). Continuity exists following a period of absence on maternity, paternity, adoption, parental leave etc.

13.9 Continuity begins on the day the employee starts work under the contract of employment, although if the starting day is in fact a non-working day (eg a holiday or a Sunday) the employment will be continuous from that date, even though he does not actually commence working until a day or two later (*Salvation Army v Dewsbury*). If there are periods which do not count towards continuity, but do not break continuity (see para 13.13) the commencement of the period of employment is advanced by the period in question (s 211(3)). If a written statement of terms and conditions of employment given under ERA, s 1 contains a starting date, that will not be conclusive, if in fact the true starting date was different (*System Floors (UK) Ltd v Daniel*, see para 3.119).

13.10 When a period of continuous employment ends will depend on the statutory right which is being claimed by the employee. For employment rights generally, and unfair dismissal claims in particular, it will be 'the effective date of termination' (see para 20.25). If the claim is for a statutory redundancy payment, the period will end on 'the relevant date', which will normally be the effective date of termination, although there are some variations on this (ERA, ss 136(3), 145(3)(b), 145(5), 145(7), 153). There are also provisions dealing with the termination of employment on the death of the employer and employee (ERA, ss 133(1), 174 and 176(1)).

13.11 The employment must be legal for it to be continuous. Thus any period when the employment is illegal cannot count towards continuity, and will break continuity. Thus, if a person has no legal right to work in the UK (see para 2.113) any time spent so working cannot count towards continuity. If a legal contract becomes tainted with illegality (see para 3.8), continuity will be broken, and will have to start again from when it becomes legal. In *Hyland v J H Barker (North West) Ltd* (see para 3.16), the employee was employed from 1967. For four weeks in 1982 he arranged with his employer that he would receive a tax-free lodging allowance, whereas in fact he returned home every night. Clearly, this arrangement was illegal, being an attempt to defraud the Revenue. Thus, when he was dismissed a year later, it was held that the four-week period had broken the continuity, and that therefore he lacked the necessary qualifying period of employment to bring a claim for unfair dismissal.

13.12 Continuity of employment exists if an employee commences work for a subsidiary or associated employer of the original employer, or if there is a takeover of the business (not just its assets) or on the transfer of an undertaking. Nor is it relevant that the employee's job changed. In *Lord Advocate v De Rosa*[9] the employee was employed by Isaac Barrie (Transport) Ltd for 17 years, when the business was transferred to Isaac Barrie (Contractors) Ltd. There was no interruption in his employment, but he changed his job from transport manager to docks manager. It was held that his redundancy payment was to be calculated by reference to both periods of employment, and the fact that there had been a change in his employer and in his terms and conditions of employment was irrelevant.

Preserving continuity (s 212)

13.13 There is a general principle that if an employee is dismissed, or resigns, or his contract of employment comes to an end in some other lawful manner (frustration, project termination etc), then, if he is subsequently re-engaged, continuity will have been broken

[9] [1974] 2 All ER 849, [1974] 1 WLR 946, [1974] ICR 480, [1974] IRLR 215, 118 Sol Jo 479, HL.

if there is a gap of more than one week between the two employments, and he will have to start again so far as computation is concerned. However, there are a number of rules which enable an employee to preserve continuity, despite the existence of a break between the two periods. Sometimes, the weeks in question may be added into the counting of continuity, although sometimes they are not to be counted, even though they do not break continuity.

13.14 Any week during the whole or part of which an employee's relations with his employer are governed by a contract of employment will count when computing the employee's period of employment (s 212(1)). Thus, if an employee is off work sick, away on a holiday (see *Vernon v Event Management Catering Ltd*[10]) or otherwise absent with permission, the weeks in question will still count, as long as the contract of employment is still in existence. The whole of the period when a person is on ordinary maternity, paternity or adoption leave will count towards continuity so far as statutory rights are concerned.

13.15 Continuity will also be preserved in the following three circumstances (see paras 13.16–13.28) (s 212(2)), provided two conditions are met. First, there must be no contract of employment subsisting (because otherwise there would be no need to rely on these provisions to preserve continuity). Second, the employee must be re-employed during the relevant period. In other words, s 212(2) does not guarantee continuity; it merely preserves it in circumstances when it would otherwise be lost.

A. Incapable of work because of sickness or injury (s 212(3)(a))

13.16 For this rule to apply, the contract of employment must have been terminated (whether by dismissal or frustration or resignation etc). If so, then if the employee is re-employed within 26 weeks, his employment will be deemed to be continuous. In other words, he is entitled to be absent from work for up to 26 weeks after his contract of employment has ended without suffering a break in continuity should he be re-employed. He must, however, have been incapable of work, not merely absent from work (*Scarlett v Godfrey Abbott Group Ltd*[11]). In *Donnelly v Kelvin International Services*[12] the employee resigned from his employment with the respondent because his doctor advised him to obtain lighter work. He obtained employment with another employer, but five weeks later resumed his employment with the respondent. He was subsequently dismissed, and his claim for unfair dismissal could only proceed if he could link the two periods of employment in order to establish the necessary continuity. An employment tribunal dismissed his claim, holding that although he had resigned his employment because of sickness, he was not incapable of work because of that sickness, because he had demonstrated his fitness for work by obtaining other employment. The EAT allowed the employee's appeal, and remitted the claim for reconsideration by another tribunal. The phrase 'incapable of work' did not mean incapable of work of any kind. It referred to the work which the employee was doing prior to the period which interrupted the continuity of employment, and the fact that the employee had taken up other work during the period of interruption did not mean that he had ceased to be capable of the work he was doing by reason of sickness, within the meaning of s 212(3)(a). The proper approach was to look at what happened in the intervening period between the two employments in question. If, for example, the employee took employment of light work, in the hope that he may be able to return to his previous employment in time, this may not interrupt the period of continuity. But if the intervening employment was undertaken as full-time permanent employment, then it was possible to conclude that his absence from the first employment was not because of incapacity for work.

---

[10] 2007, IDS Brief No 835.   [11] [1978] ICR 1106, [1978] IRLR 456, 13 ITR 519, EAT.
[12] [1992] IRLR 496, EAT.

13.17 A different result was reached in *Pearson v Kent County Council*,[13] where the employee decided to resign his employment on 31 May on health grounds. He was offered, and accepted, a less demanding job with his employers, and commenced his new position on 11 June. Four years later he was made redundant, and sought to link the two periods of employment for the purpose of enhancing his claim for statutory redundancy pay. His claim failed. There was no medical reason why he could not have commenced his new job immediately after he left his former position. Thus, he was not incapable of work because of sickness or injury, and because there was a break of more than one week, the two periods of employment could not be linked to form one period of continuous employment.

B. Absent from work on account of a temporary cessation of work (s 212(3)(b))

13.18 Weeks will count when an employee is absent from work (again, without a contract of employment) on account of a temporary cessation of work. This provision was probably designed to deal with those industries where there may be lay-offs, eg the construction industry, but the practical effect has been much wider (see *Fitzgerald v Hall, Russell & Co Ltd*[14]). In particular, it should be noted that a lay-off and a temporary cessation of work are the same thing (*Murray v Murray (t/a Newholme Decorators)*[15]).

13.19 The term 'cessation of work' means that the work which the employee was employed to do must have ceased (*Fitzgerald v Hall Russell & Co Ltd*) or the quantum of work no longer exists. If an employee is 'laid off' because existing work has been redistributed, there has been no cessation of work (*Byrne v Birmingham City Council*[16]). Further, the work which has ceased must be paid work, not voluntary work (*University of Aston in Birmingham v Malik*[17]). Nor is the reason for the cessation relevant; it may be due to short-age of orders, shortage of supplies, cash flow problems etc (*Hunter v Smith's Dock Co Ltd*[18]). There must be an interruption in the availability of work which, but for that interruption, would have been performed by the employee.

13.20 The absence from work must be 'temporary'. This is a question of fact, to be looked at with hindsight, not foresight. Although there is dicta in *Ford v Warwickshire County Council*[19] (see para 13.28) to suggest that 'temporary' means 'lasting only for a relatively short time', this guidance has not always been followed (eg see *Bentley Engineering Co Ltd v Crown*,[20] where a period of absence of two years was held to be temporary!). The whole of the employment history must be examined, and evidence may be adduced as to the expectations of the parties. In *Ford v Warwickshire County Council* the claimant was a teacher who was employed on a sessional basis. Each year she taught for three terms, and when the July term ended, her contract came to an end. Each year she was re-employed in September. This arrangement continued for eight years, and when she was not re-engaged at the commencement of a new session, she sought compensation for unfair dismissal and redundancy. The House of Lords held that the word 'temporary' was used in the sense of being 'transient' so that the absence was for a relatively short time. This was a question of

---

[13] [1992] ICR 20, [1992] IRLR 110, EAT; aff'd [1993] IRLR 165, CA.
[14] [1970] AC 984, [1969] 3 All ER 1140, [1969] 3 WLR 868, [1969] 2 Lloyd's Rep 514, 7 KIR 263, 5 ITR 1, 1970 SC 1, 1970 SLT 37, 113 Sol Jo 899, HL.
[15] EAT 750/93.   [16] 85 LGR 729, [1987] ICR 519, [1987] IRLR 191, CA.
[17] [1984] ICR 492, [1984] LS Gaz R 1438, EAT.
[18] [1968] 2 All ER 81, [1968] 1 WLR 1865, [1968] ITR 198, 112 Sol Jo 963, [1968] 1 Lloyd's Rep 354, DC.
[19] [1982] ICR 520, [1982] IRLR 246, 126 Sol Jo 328, CA; revsd [1983] 2 AC 71, [1983] 1 All ER 753, [1983] 2 WLR 399, 81 LGR 326, [1983] ICR 273, [1983] IRLR 126, 127 Sol Jo 154, HL.
[20] [1976] ICR 225, [1976] IRLR 146, 11 ITR 50, DC.

fact to be determined by the employment tribunal. Thus, successive periods of employment with the same employer will be continuous under s 212(3)(b) if the length of time between those periods is short compared with the length of time the employment has lasted. In such circumstances, the intervals in between can truly be regarded as being temporary. In *Hussain v Acorn Independent College Ltd*,[21] following Ford, a teacher was employed on a temporary contract for one term from April to July to cover another teacher who was off sick. That teacher then resigned, and the claimant was then re-employed in his own right when term started again in September and dismissed in June. In considering whether he had the requisite one year's continuity, the EAT held that a tribunal should look at the reasons for the termination of the first contract. The statute did not require that there be an expectation of further work, nor did it matter what kind of contract was formed either side of the divide. There were two contracts, the interval was short and temporary, and so there was continuity.

13.21 There have been a number of cases where employees have been employed on 'intermittent' contracts, each of varying lengths, and being separated by varying periods of non-employment. The correct approach in such cases is to consider all the relevant circumstances, and in particular to consider the lengths of the periods of absence from work in the context of the employment as a whole (*Sillars v Charrington Fuels Ltd*[22]). Sometimes employment tribunals try to circumvent this enquiry by finding that 'a global contract' exists (see para 2.174), but with mixed success. So far as seasonal workers are concerned, if a greater time is spent out of employment than in, the period of non-employment cannot be regarded as being an absence because of a temporary cessation of work (*Berwick Salmon Fisheries Co Ltd v Rutherford*[23]).

13.22 It will be clear that if an employee resigns, or is dismissed, and subsequently re-employed by the employer (or an associated employer, see para 2.5) he cannot be regarded as being absent from work because of a temporary cessation (*Wessex National Ltd v Long*[24]). If, during the period of absence, the employee takes what he regards as being other permanent employment, then the absence ceases to be because of the temporary cessation of work. But if he takes temporary employment, making it clear that he was seeking to be re-employed by his former employers, continuity will be preserved (*Thompson v Bristol Channel Ship Repairer and Engineers Ltd*[25]).

13.23 If a company goes into liquidation, and an employee who is thus dismissed is then employed by another company in circumstances such that both companies are owned and controlled by the same owner, continuity of employment may be preserved, and any period between the dismissal and re-employment may be treated as a temporary cessation of work (*Da Silva v Composite Mouldings & Design Ltd*[26]). This was illustrated in *Welton v Deluxe Retail (t/a Madhouse)*.[27] The claimant worked at a shop in Sheffield that closed down, and his employment was terminated. During what would have been the next working week, he agreed to accept employment with the same employer in Blackpool. His first working day was the following week. His employment was terminated a few months later and he claimed unfair dismissal. On considering whether his continuity had been broken, the EAT held that the absence was on account of a temporary cessation of work, and there was a contract of employment from when he accepted the offer, notwithstanding that work had

[21] [2011] IRLR 463.
[22] [1988] ICR 505, [1988] IRLR 180, [1988] 16 LS Gaz R 42, EAT; aff'd [1989] ICR 475, [1989] IRLR 152, CA.
[23] [1991] IRLR 203, EAT.   [24] (1978) 13 ITR 413, EAT.
[25] [1969] 1 Lloyd's Rep 407, 6 KIR 510, 4 ITR 262, 113 Sol Jo 382, DC; aff'd [1971] 1 Lloyd's Rep 105, 8 KIR 687, 5 ITR 85, 114 Sol Jo 167, CA.
[26] [2009] ICR 416.   [27] UKEAT/0266/12/ZT.

yet to be performed under it. It also confirmed that an arrangement could not be entered retrospectively so as to confer continuity.

C. Absent by arrangement or custom (s 212(3)(c))

13.24 Continuity is preserved if the employee's absence from work is such that, by arrangement or custom, he is regarded as continuing in the employment of his employer for any purpose. Clearly, if an employee's contract enables such absence, eg sabbatical leave, s 212(3)(c) has no relevance. The section only applies if the contract does not exist, and would cover, for example, an employee who has been seconded from one employer to another, or someone who has been given leave of absence for personal reasons. Indeed, the 'arrangement' need not have been made between the employer and the employee, but can arise from an agreement between the employer and a trade union (*Taylor v Triumph Motors Ltd*[28]). Keeping an employee 'on the books' can be an arrangement for the purpose of continuity within s 212(3)(c), especially if the contract of employment has previously been frustrated (*G F Sharp & Co Ltd v McMillan*[29]).

13.25 The arrangement must have been to preserve continuity for any purpose. In *Lloyds Bank Ltd v Secretary of State for Employment*[30] an employee worked one week on and one week off for five years. She became pregnant, the employers paid her statutory maternity pay, and sought to recover the amount from the Maternity Fund. It was held that her employment was continuous for five years, her absence was by arrangement, and, having rightfully paid her the money, they were entitled to a rebate from the Fund. But in *Letheby & Christopher Ltd v Bond*[31] a casual barmaid took leave over a Christmas period. Although this was by arrangement, there was no arrangement that the absence would preserve continuity, for she worked under a number of separate contracts, and it was not possible to say that any contract of employment would have continued after the cessation of the previous contract. Thus the absence broke her continuity.

13.26 However, the arrangement must have been made before the period of absence ceases (*Murphy v A Birrell & Sons Ltd*[32]). One made after the absence has ceased may give rise to private contractual rights, but cannot affect the statutory position. Thus in *Morris v Walsh Western Electric UK Ltd*[33] the appellant was summarily dismissed. Two months later he was re-employed, and was told by the company's general manager that the intervening period would be treated as being a period of unpaid leave. He subsequently terminated his own employment, and claimed that the two combined periods of employment gave him sufficient continuity to bring a case of constructive dismissal. His claim was dismissed by an employment tribunal and the EAT. The statutory provisions envisage that the arrangement exists when the employee is absent from work, not when he returns to work. A contrary view, expressed in *Ingram v Foxon*,[34] that a retrospective arrangement could preserve continuity, was disapproved.

13.27 The 'arrangement' for the purpose of s 212(3)(c) must be such that there was a mutual recognition by the parties that the employee, although absent from work, nevertheless continues in the employment of the employer. Whether such mutual recognition in fact exists will depend on the circumstances and, in particular, any correspondence between the parties, and what the employee was told before taking the period of absence (*Curr v Marks & Spencer plc*, see para 2.151).

---

[28] [1975] IRLR 369.   [29] [1998] IRLR 632, EAT.
[30] [1979] 2 All ER 573, [1979] 1 WLR 498, [1979] ICR 258, [1979] IRLR 41, 123 Sol Jo 47, EAT.
[31] [1988] ICR 480, EAT.   [32] [1978] IRLR 458, EAT.
[33] [1997] IRLR 562, EAT.   [34] [1984] ICR 685, [1985] IRLR 5, EAT.

13.28 There are few cases dealing with 'custom' in modern employment law generally, let alone with reference to s 212(3)(c). Industry-wide customs (of the kind which would be upheld at law) rarely exist nowadays, as the greater formalisation of contracts of employment and collective agreements takes place. Older cases (eg *Sagar v Ridehalgh*, see para 3.80) are no longer particularly relevant. But in *Gray v Burntisland Shipbuilding Co*[35] a recognised custom in the shipbuilding industry whereby workers laid off when work ran out were recalled when more work became available, was used to establish continuity under the statutory provision. In *Ford v Warwickshire County Council* (see para 13.20) the EAT commented that detailed evidence about customs in certain industries could be usefully given, and, if there was an appropriate custom in the teaching profession, it should be brought to the attention of the employment tribunal for consideration.

Re-employment after unfair dismissal (s 219)

13.29 The Employment Protection (Continuity of Employment) Regulations 1996 (as amended) (made under ERA, s 219) deal with the situation where a person is reinstated or re-engaged in consequence of any of the following events, namely:

(a) a claim made under an approved dismissal agreement (s 110: see para 17.4 (there are no such agreements in force at the present time));

(b) the presentation by the employee of a complaint of dismissal, ie under ERA, or in respect of sex, race, disability or other anti-discrimination provisions;

(c) action taken by a conciliation officer of ACAS under the Employment Tribunals Act 1996, s 18 (see para 20.47);

(d) the making of a compromise agreement authorised by ERA, s 203(3);

(e) as a result of an arbitration award made under an approved ACAS arbitration scheme (see para 1.13);

(f) if the employment has been extended of an employee who would otherwise have retired.

13.30 In any of these circumstances, the employee's continuity of employment is deemed to be preserved, and the period beginning with the date on which the dismissal took effect, and the date when the re-engagement or reinstatement took place, will count in the computation of the employee's period of continuous employment.

13.31 The re-engagement or reinstatement must be 'in consequence of' any of these actions. The mere fact of re-engagement or reinstatement, by itself, for some other reason, will not ensure continuity (*Gardener v National Coal Board*[36]), unless the provisions of ERA, s 212(3)(c) apply, it being recalled that this cannot apply to an arrangement which purports to be retrospective (*Morris v Walsh Western UK Ltd*, para 13.26).

13.32 If an employer gives notice of dismissal, and withdraws it following an appeal during the currency of the notice period, there is no break in continuity (*Brock v Minerva Dental Ltd*[37]). If an employee is dismissed and then reinstated, re-engaged or otherwise re-employed by the employer or a successor or associated employer, the effect of reinstatement etc is to annul the dismissal (Continuity of Employment Regulations 1996 (as amended), and *Roberts v West Coast Trains Ltd*[38]) and the period of prior employment

[35] (1967) 2 ITR 255.   [36] EAT 375/82.   [37] [2007] ICR 917.
[38] [2004] EWCA Civ 900, [2005] ICR 254, [2004] IRLR 788, (2004) 101(28) LSG 33, (2004) *Times*, 25 June.

as well as the period between the dismissal and reinstatement etc will count towards continuity.

Weeks which do not count towards continuity (ss 215–217)

13.33 There are certain circumstances when weeks of absence do not count towards continuity, but do not break continuity. The non-counting weeks are used to advance the starting date of the employment, by seven days for each non-counting week (s 215(2)) (except weeks spent abroad in redundancy cases: see para 13.34). The non-counting weeks arise in the following circumstances.

A. **Periods spent working abroad (s 215(1))**

13.34 A person who works outside Great Britain is generally excluded from employment rights and weeks of employment abroad will not normally count. However, there are circumstances when a period of employment spent outside Great Britain will count in computing continuous employment as if it were employment in Great Britain. Thus, if an employee works outside Great Britain, and his contract is then varied so that he works inside Great Britain, the whole of his period of employment will be continuous for the purpose of establishing a qualifying period of employment rights generally. However, for the purpose of calculating statutory redundancy pay, a week of employment abroad will not count towards continuity (but will not break continuity) if the employee spent the whole or part of the week working abroad, and he was not an employed earner for the purpose of national insurance contributions.

B. **Strikes and lock-outs (s 216)**

13.35 Any week during which, or during part of which, an employee takes part in a strike will not count towards continuity, but will not break continuity. This rule applies whether the strike is official or unofficial. However, the strike must be connected with terms and conditions of employment, and not, for example, a 'political' strike. If an employee is dismissed while on strike, and subsequently re-engaged, the weeks on strike will be deducted from his continuous employment, but continuity is preserved (*Hanson v Fashion Industries (Hartlepool) Ltd*, see para 13.3). The total number of days deducted will be the actual number of days (not the number of working days) falling in the period between the last day when the employee worked and the day when he resumed work (s 216(2)). Thus, non-working days, eg Saturday and Sunday, can be deducted. If, during a strike, an employee takes another job, and is subsequently re-engaged then, if that job was a temporary one, his continuity will be preserved; but if it was a permanent job (eg there is evidence that he so regarded it) he will be treated as if he left his original employment, and continuity will be broken (*Bloomfield v Springfield Hosiery Finishing Co Ltd*[39]).

13.36 Issues sometimes arise as to whether or not the employee is 'taking part' in a strike, or is absent from work during an industrial dispute for some other reason (see *Coates v Modern Methods and Material Ltd*[40]). It is not relevant that the employer 'knows' that the employee took part in the strike, for the test is an objective one (see *Manifold Industries Ltd*

[39] [1972] 1 All ER 609, [1972] 1 WLR 386, [1972] ICR 91, 12 KIR 175, 7 ITR 89, 116 Sol Jo 141, NIRC.
[40] [1983] QB 192, [1982] 3 All ER 946, [1982] 3 WLR 764, [1982] ICR 763, [1982] IRLR 318, 126 Sol Jo 577, CA.

v Sims[41]). Indeed, off-duty employees, and employees who are away from work sick may be regarded as taking part in strike action in appropriate circumstances (see *Bolton Roadways Ltd v Edwards*[42]).

13.37 Similarly, continuity of employment is not lost if the employee is absent from work because of a lock-out (s 216(3)), but there does appear to be a difference, in that if the contract of employment still subsists, s 212(1) (see para 13.14) applies, and days when an employee is locked out will still count towards continuity. This is because s 216(1) only refers to strikes, not to lock-outs. It is only when there is no contract of employment in existence that s 216(3) provides that the number of days falling within the period between the employee's last working day and the day he resumes work are to be deducted from the start of the employee's period of continuous employment.

C. **Military service (s 217)**

13.38 An employee who is obliged to serve as an armed forces reservist may apply under the Reserve Forces (Safeguard of Employment) Act 1985 to be reinstated in his former employment within six months of the termination of the period for which he was called up. Weeks when the employee was called up will not count towards continuity, but continuity will not be broken.

Change of employer (s 218)

13.39 As has been noted, if there has been a transfer of an undertaking within the meaning of the TUPE regulations (see Chapter 9) there is an automatic transfer of the contract of employment from the transferor to the transferee. Curiously enough, the regulations make no mention of continuity of employment being preserved in such circumstances, although there can be little doubt that this will happen, for otherwise the UK would be in serious breach of its obligations to transpose the Acquired Rights Directive into domestic law. It would seem that the provisions of ERA, s 218 are sufficient for this purpose, even though many of the legal decisions on this section were decided prior to the introduction of TUPE.

13.40 There are a number of circumstances to consider.

(a) There is a transfer to which TUPE applies. Regulation 5(1) states that the contract shall have effect as if originally made between the person so employed and the transferee. This clearly preserves the continuity of the employee so transferred (*Royal Ordnance plc v Pilkington*[43]).

(b) There is a transfer to which ERA, s 218(2) applies. This section provides for continuity to be preserved when there is a transfer of a trade, business or undertaking from one employer to another. There must be a recognised and identifiable part of the business transferred, not merely a collection of assets (*Melon v Hector Powe Ltd*[44]). But 218(2) does not depend on there being a transfer of employment under the TUPE regulations (*Oakland v Wellswood (Yorkshire) Ltd*[45]).

(c) Statutory change of employer: here ERA, s 218(3) applies when an Act of Parliament substitutes one employer for another (see *Gale v Northern General Hospital NHS Trust*,[46] where the rule was held not to apply).

---

[41] [1991] ICR 504, [1991] IRLR 242, EAT.   [42] [1987] IRLR 392, EAT.

[43] [1988] ICR 606, [1988] IRLR 466, EAT; revsd [1989] ICR 737, [1989] IRLR 489, CA.

[44] [1980] IRLR 80, Ct of Sess; aff'd [1981] 1 All ER 313, [1981] ICR 43, [1980] IRLR 477, 124 Sol Jo 827, HL.

[45] [2009] EWCA Civ 1094, [2010] BCC 263, [2010] IRLR 82.   [46] [1994] IRLR 292, CA.

(d) Although at common law the death of an employer would normally terminate the contract, ERA, s 218(4) provides that if the employee is kept on by the personal representative or trustee of the deceased employer, continuity will not be broken.

(e) If an employee is employed by two partners, and one of them leaves the partnership (for whatever reason) there is no break in the continuity of employment. Section 218(5) ensures continuity when two partners are succeeded by one of them as sole principal (*Stevens v Bower*[47]).

(f) If an employee is transferred from an employer to an associated employer, the transfer does not break continuity (s 218(6)). However, the two employers must be 'associated' in the legal sense, in accordance with the definition contained in ERA, s 231 (see para 2.5).

(g) If an employee transfers from employment by the governors of a school maintained by a local education authority to employment by that authority, continuity is preserved (ERA, s 218(7)). Employees who transfer from one hospital to another, or from an NHS hospital to one with trust status, will generally have continuity preserved by ERA, s 218(8) (see also National Health Service and Community Care Act 1990, s 6), and certain senior hospital appointees whilst undergoing training, which involves being successively employed by different health authorities, have continuity for a number of employment protection rights specified in ERA (Employment Protection (Continuity of Employment of National Health Service Employees) (Modification) Order 1996). For redundancy payment purposes, if an employee transfers from one local authority to another, or to or from certain specified bodies, continuity is preserved (Redundancy Payments (Continuity of Employment in Local Government etc) (Modification) Order 1999). But a transfer to or from a body not included in Sch 1 to the Order will not give rise to continuity (*Liversidge v London Residuary Body*[48]). Similarly, continuity is preserved on a transfer from one NHS body to another (Redundancy Payments (National Health Service) (Modification) Order 1993).

13.41 In particular, it should be noted that artificial breaks in employment consequent on a transfer are not generally favoured, and s 218, combined with TUPE, are to be given a broad interpretation so as to preserve continuity where possible (*Macer v Abafast Ltd*[49]).

The effect of the continuity rules

13.42 The purpose of establishing continuity of employment is to enable an employee to qualify, by virtue of the length of his employment, for certain statutory rights. In particular, however, additional years of employment which can be saved by the continuity rules are of great value to an employee whose employment ultimately comes to an end for reason of redundancy, for he can then obtain a larger redundancy payment (or an increased basic award if he was unfairly dismissed). Thus, when there is a transfer of a business from one employer to another, if there is no continuity, he can apply for his redundancy payment, and then start again with his new employer; on the other hand, if there is continuity, the new employer takes over the obligations to make a redundancy payment should this prove necessary in the future. In principle, if the employer makes a redundancy payment to the employee, whose contract is then renewed by the same or another employer (eg by virtue of

[47] [2004] ICR 1582, [2004] IRLR 957, CA.
[48] (1989) 87 LGR 399, [1989] ICR 228, [1989] 5 LS Gaz R 41, EAT.
[49] [1990] ICR 234, [1990] IRLR 137, EAT.

the TUPE Regulations, see Chapter 9), continuity of employment is broken for redundancy payment purposes (ERA, s 214). There must be a full payment of redundancy money due, the payment must be in pursuance of a statutory obligation to pay (*Rowan v Machinery Installations (South Wales) Ltd*[50]), not a voluntary payment (*Ross v Delrosa Caterers Ltd*[51]) and must not have been paid by virtue of an employment tribunal decision (*Richards v s and H E Fielding Ltd*[52]). Continuity will also be broken if a redundancy payment has been made by the Secretary of State under the provisions of ERA, ss 166–167 (see para 18.67), provided he is satisfied that the requisite conditions for the payment have been met (*Secretary of State for Trade and Industry v Lassman*[53]).

13.43 Continuity is broken if, having been paid a redundancy payment, the employee is re-employed in circumstances in which the Continuity of Employment Regulations apply, but only for the purpose of calculating service for any future entitlement to a redundancy payment. But the regulations provide that if the employee repays the redundancy payment, continuity is restored (Employment Protection (Continuity of Employment) Regulations 1996, reg 4). See Table 13.1 below.

Continuity table

Table 13.1 Continuity of employment

Statutory right	Continuous employment required
Written particulars (ERA, s 1)	Two months
Guarantee pay (ERA, s 29)	One month
Time off work to look for work or arrange training (ERA, s 52)	Two years
Medical suspension pay (ERA, s 65)	One month
Parental leave (Maternity and Parental Leave etc Regulations, reg 13)	One year
Paternity leave (Paternity and Adoption Leave Regulations 2002, reg 4)	26 weeks
Additional Paternity Leave Regulations 2010, reg 4	26 weeks
Flexible working (Flexible Working (Eligibility, Complaints and Remedies) Regulations 2002, reg 3)	26 weeks
Minimum notice (ERA, s 86)	One month
Written reason for dismissal (ERA, s 92) (with exceptions)	Two years (see note 53)
Unfair dismissal (ERA, s 108) (with exceptions)	Two years (this was previously one year until 6 April 2012)[54]
Redundancy payment (ERA, s 155)	Two years
Statutory maternity pay (Social Security Contributions and Benefits Act 1992, s 164)	26 weeks prior to the 15th week before EWC

(Continued)

[50] [1981] ICR 386, [1981] IRLR 122, EAT.
[51] [1981] ICR 393, EAT.
[52] (1966) 1 KIR 365, 1 ITR 376.
[53] [2000] ICR 1109, [2000] IRLR 411, (2000) *Times*, 5 May, (2000) *Independent*, 4 May.
[54] The Unfair Dismissal and Statement of Reasons for Dismissal (Variation of Qualifying Period) Order 2012 extends this for all employment which begins after 6 April 2012. Employees who began their employment before that date will still be subject to the one-year qualifying period.

(Continued)

Statutory right	Continuous employment required
Statutory adoption pay (Social Security Contributions and Benefits Act 1992, s 171ZL(1))	26 weeks prior to the 15th week before the adoptive parent was matched with the child
Statutory paternity pay (Social Security Contributions and Benefits Act 1992, s 171ZA(1))	26 weeks prior to the 15th week before the EWC or the week when the child's adopter was matched with the child
Fixed term contract becoming permanent employee (Fixed term Employees (Prevention of Less Favourable Treatment) Regulations 2002 reg 8)	Four years
Agency Workers Regulations 2010	12 weeks
Time off for study or training	26 weeks

NB. There is no qualifying period of employment for maternity leave. An employee who does not meet the continuity requirements for SMP, SPP or SAP still qualifies for the right to have the statutory time off work, but without the statutory payment. Other payments, eg maternity allowance, income support etc may be claimed.

14

Normal Working Hours and a Week's Pay

Normal working hours

A. **Employment Rights Act, ss 221–229**

14.1 In order to quantify the amount of money payable to an employee in respect of the violation of certain specific statutory rights, it is necessary to ascertain the employee's weekly pay, which is done by reference to the employee's 'normal working hours'. The Employment Rights Act sets out precise formulae for determining how a week's pay is thus to be calculated and, in certain specific cases, puts a cap on that amount.

B. **Contractual provisions**

14.2 The Act envisages that there are a number of different possibilities when trying to assess an employee's 'normal working hours', and it is therefore necessary to choose the one which is most appropriate in the circumstances, so as to calculate the week's pay. To do this, one must start with a consideration of the contract of employment. Thus, if the contract specifies normal working hours, that will generally be conclusive, and it is immaterial that the employee works more or less than those hours, unless it can be shown that there has been a variation (express or implied) of the contract (*ITT Components (Europe) v Kolah*[1]). If the contract is silent on this matter, the employment tribunal must infer the relevant term from what happens in practice (*Larkin v Cambos Enterprises (Stretford) Ltd*[2]). Thus in *Armstrong Whitworth Rolls Ltd v Mustard* (see para 3.109) the contract of employment required the employee to work 40 hours per week. He was then asked to work for 60 hours per week, in order to ensure 24-hour coverage of the plant. He did this for seven years and, when made redundant, it was held that his contract of employment had been varied, so that he was entitled to a redundancy payment on the basis of a 60-hour week.

14.3 Overtime is generally excluded from normal working hours, unless it is included in the minimum number of hours fixed by the contract. In other words, it must be guaranteed by the employer and obligatory for the employee (*Tarmac Roadstone Holdings Ltd v Peacock*[3]). If the employer is entitled, but not obliged, to call for overtime working, such hours as are worked will not count towards normal working hours, even though the employee is bound to work overtime under the terms of his contract (*Lotus Cars Ltd v Sutcliffe*[4]). In *Bamsey v Albion Engineering and Manufacturing plc* (see para 7.85) the

---

[1] [1977] ICR 740, [1977] IRLR 53, EAT.   [2] [1978] ICR 1247, EAT.
[3] [1973] 2 All ER 485, [1973] 1 WLR 594, [1973] ICR 273, [1973] IRLR 157, 14 KIR 277, 8 ITR 300, 117 Sol Jo 186, CA.
[4] [1982] IRLR 381, CA.

employee worked under a contract that entitled him to a basic working week of 39 hours. In fact, he regularly worked a shift pattern which averaged 60 hours per week. He was paid for his period of annual leave on the basis of a 39-hour week, and he claimed that he should have been paid at the same rate as averaged, with overtime, while at work. His claim failed. The Working Time Regulations incorporated the definition of working hours contained in ERA, s 234 and overtime could only be included in a week's pay if it was obligatory on both sides as contractual obligations.

A week's pay

14.4 It is then necessary to establish how much the employee was paid for those hours. Remuneration, for this purpose, can be quite wide. Clearly, wages or salaries will be included, but also contractual bonuses paid on a regular basis, eg per shift, or per site, or for undertaking additional duties (*A & B Marcusfield v Melhuish*[5]). Commission payments are also included, although a commission paid annually has to be apportioned over the period when the employee actually worked (*J & s Bickley Ltd v Washer*[6]), and consequently averaged over a period of 12 weeks (see para 14.8). Expenses do not count as remuneration if they are a reimbursement of an employee's expenditure, but will count if they represent a profit in the employee's hands (*S and U Stores Ltd v Wilkes*[7]). However, expenses which represent a profit must have been declared to the Revenue, otherwise there is a danger that the contract may be illegal (*Tomlinson v Dick Evans U Drive Ltd*, see para 3.8). Payments in kind (car, accommodation, food etc) will not count (*Skillen v Eastwoods Froy Ltd*[8]), although it should be noted that such benefits may be taken into account when determining any relevant compensation award. Tips and gratuities do not count if they are paid by the customer, not the employer (*Palmanor Ltd v Cedron*[9]), but a service charge which is distributed among employees in a fixed proportion will count as part of a week's pay (*Tsoukka v Potomac Restaurants Ltd*[10]) (but not for the purpose of the national minimum wage, see para 8.41). A lodging allowance is not part of a week's pay, although a deduction from pay in respect of lodging clearly would be. Overtime premiums also do not count (*British Coal Corpn v Cheesbrough*[11]).

14.5 When calculating 'a week's pay' for statutory purposes, it is the gross pay which counts, not net pay (*Secretary of State for Employment v John Woodrow & Sons (Builders) Ltd*[12]). Moreover, the amount must be calculated on the basis that the employer is complying with his legal obligations. Thus, in *Cooner v P S Doal & Sons*,[13] an employee was paid less than that to which he was entitled under a Wages Council order, and it was held that it was pay under the order which counted, not the lower wage actually paid. Although the Wages Councils orders have now ceased to exist, the principle applies to the new minimum wage legislation (*Paggetti v Cobb*[14]).

---

[5] [1977] IRLR 484, EAT.   [6] [1977] ICR 425, 12 ITR 137, EAT.
[7] [1974] 3 All ER 401, [1974] ICR 645, [1974] IRLR 283, [1975] KILR 117, 9 ITR 415, NIRC.
[8] (1966) 2 ITR.   [9] [1978] ICR 1008, [1978] IRLR 303, 13 ITR 450, EAT.
[10] (1968) 3 ITR 259.
[11] [1988] ICR 60, sub nom *National Coal Board v Cheesbrough and Secretary of State for Employment* [1988] IRLR 351, CA; revsd sub nom *British Coal Corpn v Cheesbrough* [1988] ICR 769, [1988] IRLR 351, CA; aff'd [1990] 2 AC 256, [1990] 1 All ER 641, [1990] 2 WLR 407, [1990] ICR 317, [1990] IRLR 148, 134 Sol Jo 661, [1990] 11 LS Gaz R 39, HL.
[12] [1983] ICR 582, [1983] IRLR 11, EAT.
[13] [1988] ICR 495, [1988] IRLR 338, EAT.
[14] [2002] IRLR 861, [2002] All ER (D) 394 (Mar), EAT.

A. Quantifying a week's pay

14.6 Having ascertained an employee's normal weekly hours, and how much he is paid for those hours, we can now work out his week's pay for statutory purposes. The following four circumstances should cover all situations.

Remuneration does not vary (ERA, s 221(2))

14.7 If an employee's remuneration does not vary in normal working hours (whether he be an hourly or weekly paid employee, or is paid for any other period) then the amount of a week's pay is the amount which is payable under the contract of employment. If the employee is paid by the hour, then the week's pay is to be determined as if he worked his full contractual hours in that week.

Remuneration varies with the amount of work (ERA, s 221(3))

14.8 If the amount of remuneration does vary with the amount of work done in the period (eg piece workers) the week's pay is ascertained by finding the average hourly remuneration payable in the 12 weeks ending with the calculation date. If an employee is paid on a commission basis, then it can properly be said that the pay varies with the work done, and hence remuneration should be calculated over 12 weeks, and not at a specific, frozen single week, when the commission is earned, or paid (*May Gurney Ltd v Adshead*[15]). If, in any of those 12 weeks, no remuneration was payable for hours when the employee was actually at work, earlier weeks can be taken into account, so as to bring the number up to 12 (s 223). Only weeks when the employee actually works will count (*Adams v John Wright & Sons (Blackwall) Ltd*[16]). Thus if an employee is paid for work actually done in a week, even if those earnings were abnormally low, the week will count. If an employee is a recent recruit, so that he does not have 12 weeks' employment to take into account, an employment tribunal can determine an amount which fairly represents a week's pay, taking into account the amount already received, the remuneration offered in the contract, the remuneration of comparable employees of the same employer, and remuneration received by comparable employees of other employers (ERA, s 228). Weeks with a previous employer which count towards continuity (see Chapter 13) may be taken into account (ERA, s 229).

Remuneration varies according to the time of work (ERA, s 222)

14.9 If an employee is a shift worker, or works on a rota, so that the hours when he is required to work differ according to the time of the day or the day of the week, with the consequence that his remuneration will correspondingly be different, the week's pay will be the average hourly rate multiplied by the average weekly hours in the period of 12 weeks prior to the calculation date. Again, earlier weeks can be counted, if necessary (see para 14.8).

No normal working hours (ERA, s 224)

14.10 If the employee had no normal working hours, the week's pay is determined by taking the employee's average weekly earnings for the period of 12 weeks prior to the calculation date. If the employee was not paid during any of those weeks, earlier weeks can be included, if necessary, to make up the 12-week period, even if the employee agreed to waive an entitlement to be paid, which otherwise was legally required to be paid (*Secretary of State for Employment v Crane*[17]).

---

[15] EAT/0150/06.
[16] [1972] ICR 463, 7 ITR 191, NIRC.
[17] [1988] IRLR 238, EAT.

B. Capping a week's pay (ERA, s 227)

14.11 In respect of the following claims, there is a limit to the amount of a week's pay which can be calculated (currently £464 per week). These claims are:

(a) basic award for unfair dismissal;

(b) additional award of compensation for unfair dismissal;

(c) statutory redundancy pay;

(d) arrears of pay (up to eight weeks), statutory notice, and holiday pay (up to six weeks) and a basic award, payable on an employer's insolvency (ERA, s 186);

(e) right not to be unjustifiably disciplined by a trade union (TULR(C)A, s 67);

(f) unreasonable exclusion from a trade union (TULR(C)A, s 176);

(g) failure to give employment particulars (Employment Act 2002: see para 3.122);

(h) failure to comply with the Flexible Working (Procedural Requirements) Regulations, see para 6.129);

(i) failure to consult under the Transfer of Undertakings (Protection of Employment) Regulations 2006;

(j) breach of right to be accompanied (Employment Relations Act 1999);

(k) duty to notify employee of retirement date and right to make a request (Employment Equality (Age) Regulations 2006);

(l) breach of time off for study or training provisions.

14.12 It will be noted that guarantee pay (see para 7.2) is limited to £25 per day (ERA, s 31) with a maximum of £125 in any period of three months (five days' pay). Pay for time off work to look for another job (see para 18.38) is limited to two-fifths of a week's pay, not capped (ERA, s 54). In all other instances where a week's pay is used for calculation purposes, it is the actual gross pay which has to be taken into account.

C. The calculation date (ERA, ss 225–226)

14.13 The date on which the calculations are to be made will differ, depending on the nature of the employee's claim. Each statutory right has its own formula. For guarantee pay (s 30), it will generally be the day on which the guarantee payment is payable (unless a new contract or variation has been entered into, in which case it will be the last day when the old contract was in force). The calculation date in respect of a claim for remuneration for time off with pay to look for work (s 52) is the day the employer gave notice of termination for reason of redundancy. For time off work for antenatal care (s 55) the calculation date is the date of the appointment, and for time off work for employee representatives (s 62) and time off work for study or training (s 63A) the calculation date is the date on which time off was taken or should have been permitted. For suspension on medical grounds (s 64) or maternity suspension (s 66), the calculation date is generally the day before the suspension begins. If a request is made for contract variation (s 80F) the calculation date is the date on which the application was made.

14.14 For redundancy payment claims, if contractual notice was given which was greater than the statutory notice which could have been given, the calculation date will be the day on which, counting backwards from the effective date of termination, the statutory notice could have been given. If less than statutory notice was given, the calculation date will be the date that notice expires, and if no notice is given, the date the contract terminated.

For payments due to an employee on the employer's insolvency, the calculation date becomes the 'appropriate date', ie the date on which the employer became insolvent (for holiday pay and arrears of pay). For the basic award, it will be the later of the dates when the employer became insolvent, or the employment was terminated, or the basic award was made, as the case may be. For other payments (ie statutory notice, statutory redundancy pay), the calculation date will be the later of the dates when the employer became insolvent or the employment was terminated (ERA, s 186).

15

Rights in Notice

15.1 One of the features which distinguishes a contract of employment from other contractual situations is that a contract of employment is one of continuous obligation, with, generally speaking, no specified time for its ending. Thus, apart from certain exceptions (eg fixed-term contracts, summary dismissal, retirement age, project termination) if either the employer or employee wishes to terminate the contract, notice of such termination must be given. Whether or not there is a termination is a factual and legal question (see para 17.7), but to be operative, the notice must give a clear indication of the actual date of termination (*Morton Sundour Fabrics Ltd v Shaw*,[1] para 18.8). This chapter will explore the rights and duties of the parties to give and receive lawful notice in the event of a termination, ie if there is a dismissal or resignation.

Notice to be given by the employer

15.2 The period of notice to be given by the employer will first be determined by having regard to the contract of employment, as required by ERA, s 1(4)(e). In theory, this is a matter of negotiation between the employer and employee, although in practice it is the employer who will usually dictate the terms, depending on factors such as the need to harmonise terms with those of other employees in similar positions, the nature of the employment, the seniority of the employee's position, and so on.

15.3 If the contract of employment is silent on this matter, at common law, reasonable notice must be given. Again, what is reasonable will depend on the employee's position, the industry, nature of the work, etc. For example, in *Hill v C A Parsons & Co Ltd* (see paras 10.3, 10.4 and 10.16), the Court of Appeal expressed the view that a senior engineer would have been entitled to between six months' to one year's notice, and there are a number of decisions (dating from the nineteenth century and the earlier part of the twentieth century) which deal with what would be reasonable notice for employees such as head gardeners, domestic servants, journalists, commercial travellers, chorus girls, hairdressers' assistants, and so on. The more senior the status, the more notice an employee is entitled to receive. Thus in *Clark v Fahrenheit 451 (Communications) Ltd*[2] three months' notice was held to be appropriate for a director, bearing in mind his seniority and salary.

15.4 However, irrespective of the contractual terms, by statute, certain minimum periods of notice must be given (see ERA, s 86(1)). These periods are to be determined by the length of the employee's period of employment. Thus, after one month's employment, the employee is entitled to one week's notice, and this will apply until he has been employed for two years. Thereafter, he will be entitled to a week's notice in respect of each year's continual employment, ie two weeks' notice after two year's employment, up to a statutory maximum of 12 weeks' notice in respect of employment which has lasted for 12 years or more. But if contractual notice is for a period which is longer than that to be given by statute, the contractual notice will prevail.

---

[1] (1966) 2 KIR 1, 2 ITR 84, DC.   [2] EAT 591/99.

15.5 If a contract of employment comes to an end because of the operation of the doctrine of frustration (see para 17.59) no statutory or contractual notice can be or need be given (*G F Sharp & Co Ltd v McMillan*[3]).

15.6 Notice to terminate a contract of employment may be given at any time, even before the employment has commenced. Thus in *Sarker v South Tees Acute Hospitals NHS Trust* (see para 3.5), the claimant was offered a post in July, and was due to start work in October. However, the offer was withdrawn in September. The claimant brought a claim for her contractual notice, under the provisions of the Employment Tribunals Extension of Jurisdiction Order (see para 1.40). The EAT held that her contract had been terminated, and she was entitled to her contractual notice.

A. **Giving notice**

15.7 Notice may be given by either side either orally or in writing. In either case, apart from summary dismissal, it will run from the day after it is given (*West v Kneels Ltd*[4]), unless a later date is specified, but it cannot operate unless the recipient has had an opportunity to know of it. Thus, if a letter giving notice to an employee is not received on a particular day (because the employee is not at home, or because of a postal strike etc), it will only operate when the employee has had a reasonable opportunity to read it (see *Brown v Southall and Knight*,[5] para 17.5). If there is a collateral contract (see para 16.8) to the main contract, notice must be given in respect of both of them.

15.8 The general common law rule is that once notice has been given, it cannot be unilaterally withdrawn either by the employer (*Riordan v War Office*[6]) or the employee (*Brennan v C Lindley & Co Ltd*[7]) although it can be withdrawn by mutual agreement between the parties (*Harris and Russell Ltd v Slingsby*[8]). The notice period may also be extended by mutual agreement (*Mowlem Northern Ltd v Watson*[9]). However, modern cases draw a distinction between the deliberate giving of notice (by either party) and a resignation or dismissal given 'in the heat of the moment.' In such circumstances (usually following some form of argument) it is incumbent on the recipient to ascertain whether the other party really meant what he said (*Kwik-Fit (GB) Ltd v Lineham*,[10] and see para 17.51). The validity of an unambiguous notice of dismissal which is given by mistake depended not just on what the employer intended, but also on whether it was reasonable for the employee to take it at face value and treat herself as dismissed in *C F Capital plc v Willoughby*.[11] This applies particularly to notice which is given in the heat of the moment.

15.9 If the employer gives notice to terminate the contract of employment, and during the period of that notice the employee gives a counter-notice that he intends to leave at an earlier date, the employee has still been dismissed for the reason for which the employer's notice was given (ERA, s 95(2); see *Lees v Arthur Greaves Ltd*[12]). However, if the employee resigns during the notice period, rather than giving a counter-notice, he will be regarded as not having been dismissed but as having resigned (*Walker v Cotswold Chine Home*

[3] [1998] IRLR 632, EAT.
[4] [1987] ICR 146, [1986] IRLR 430, [1986] LS Gaz R 2488, EAT.
[5] [1980] ICR 617, [1980] IRLR 130, EAT.
[6] [1959] 3 All ER 552, [1959] 1 WLR 1046, 103 Sol Jo 921; aff'd [1960] 3 All ER 774n, [1961] 1 WLR 210, CA.
[7] [1974] IRLR 153, NIRC.
[8] [1973] 3 All ER 31, [1973] ICR 454, [1973] IRLR 221, 15 KIR 157, 8 ITR 433, NIRC.
[9] [1990] ICR 751, [1990] IRLR 500, EAT.
[10] [1992] ICR 183, [1992] IRLR 156, [1992] 4 LS Gaz R 31, EAT.
[11] [2011] IRLR 985, [2011] EWCA Civ 1115.
[12] [1974] 2 All ER 393, [1974] ICR 501, [1974] IRLR 93, [1975] KIR 37, [1974] ITR 91.

School[13]), unless the employer agrees to him leaving, before the expiry of their notice, in which case it is treated as being a variation of the employer's notice of dismissal (*McAlwane v Boughton Estates*[14]). A resignation does not have to be accepted by the employer, nor can it be withdrawn unilaterally. If an employee gives notice to terminate his employment, and during the notice period the employer releases the employee from serving the full notice period, there is no dismissal by the employer. All that has happened is that the employee is no longer required to attend work (*Tom Findlay & Co Ltd v Devlin*[15]).

15.10 There are special provisions dealing with the counter-notice to be given by an employee because he has been laid off or put on short-time working (see para 18.33). Further, it should be noted that during the notice period, an employee retains those statutory rights relating to time off work (see ERA, ss 50–63 and TULR(C)A, ss 186–190, and see para 15.16).

B. **Taxation of payments**

15.11 The taxation of payments on the termination of employment is now covered by the Income Tax (Earnings and Pensions) Act 2003. The position is somewhat complicated because some such payments are taxable in full, some only partly so, and some not at all. The general principle is that if the payment constitutes 'earnings', such as salary to the date of termination, accrued holiday pay, benefits in kind, etc, full income tax and national insurance contributions must be deducted. Money paid as an inducement to enter into a restrictive covenant is taxable (even if it becomes unenforceable), but not the affirmation of an existing covenant. On the other hand, money paid by way of compensation for breach of contract is generally free of tax up to £30,000.

C. **Pay in lieu of notice**

15.12 In *Delaney v Staples* (see para 8.16), Lord Browne-Wilkinson listed four circumstances when a payment in lieu of notice may be made, with different consequences in each case. These are:

(a) the employer gives the appropriate notice of termination to the employee, but does not require him to work during the notice period. In effect, the employee is on 'garden leave'. Generally, there is no breach of contract in not requiring the employee to work until the termination date (but see para 19.8). Tax and national insurance contributions must be deducted, and restrictive covenants will normally be enforceable;

(b) the contract provides that the employer may terminate the contract, either with notice or summarily on the payment of a sum of money in lieu of notice. Here, two alternative ways are set out whereby the contract may be lawfully terminated. If the employer fails to make the payment, the employee can sue for the money as a debt. If the employer makes the payment, income tax should be deducted;

(c) the employer and employee mutually agree to bring the contract of employment to an end, for an agreed payment. Technically, there is no breach of contract, but even though the payment is not strictly 'earnings', it is taxable in full;

(d) the employer summarily dismisses the employee and makes a payment of money in lieu of notice. This is the most common category of payment in lieu of notice. Since the employer is seeking to extinguish a claim for damages (for breach of contract) the payment is free from tax up to £30,000.

---

[13] (1977) 12 ITR 342, EAT.   [14] [1973] 2 All ER 299, [1973] ICR 470, NIRC.
[15] Employment Appeal Tribunal (Scotland), 9 November 2007.

15.13 It follows that if there is no payment at all made in lieu of notice (or if the payment made is in respect of a lesser period than the full notice period), any subsequent payment must be regarded as damages for breach of contract, the first £30,000 of which will not be liable to income tax.

15.14 Either party may waive his right to receive contractual or statutory notice (ERA, s 86(3)) and, in particular, an employer may decide to give a payment in lieu of the employee working during the notice period. Indeed, if the contract of employment gives the employer an option to make a payment in lieu of notice, the employee has no right to work out his notice, or to be compensated for non-contractual benefits he would have obtained had he worked his notice (*Marshall (Cambridge) Ltd v Hamblin*[16]). But an employer cannot use the device of making a payment in lieu of notice to prevent an employee from achieving his contractual earnings, eg commissions, etc. An employee who is on piecework must be given enough work to enable him to earn his usual earnings, and this rule applies equally during the notice period (*Devonald v Rosser & Sons*, see paras 10.17 and 10.19).

15.15 Additionally, as well as his salary, the employee is entitled to be compensated for the loss of other contractual benefits (car, health insurance, accrued holiday pay etc) for the period had the notice been worked out. Further, it was held by the Court of Appeal in *Abrahams v Performing Right Society*[17] that if a contract states that there is a contractual entitlement to pay in lieu of notice, the full amount due is payable and there is no duty to mitigate against any loss. The duty only arises if the employer is not contractually bound to make the payment in lieu. Thus in *Cerberus Software Ltd v Rowley*[18] the contract of employment provided that the employer could either give six months' notice of termination or make a payment on termination in lieu of notice. The claimant was dismissed without notice and without a payment in lieu. After five weeks, he obtained employment at a higher salary, but nonetheless he claimed damages for wrongful dismissal. The Court of Appeal held that a provision in a contract which enabled the employer to make a payment in lieu of notice gives the employer a choice, and is inconsistent with the employee having a right to insist on such payment being made. Consequently, the employee's remedy was for damages for breach of contract, and the measure of such damages was the amount the employee would have received had the employment continued, subject to the ordinary rules relating to mitigation of damages. *Abraham v Performing Right Society* was distinguished because in that case there was a contractual entitlement to pay in lieu, which was not subject to the duty to mitigate, whereas in *Cerberus* the employer had a choice whether or not to make a payment in lieu. In other words, there is a difference between a claim for contractual entitlement and a claim for liquidated damages. In the latter event, where the claim is for damages for breach of contract, the mitigation rules apply.

D. Rights during the notice period (ERA, ss 88–91)

15.16 During the period of notice, the employee will still have certain statutory rights, contained in ERA, ss 88–91. If the employer gives notice, the employee must have been employed for one month or more to obtain the statutory rights, but he will not have any of these rights if the notice to be given by the employer must be at least one week more than the statutory notice laid down in ERA, s 86(1). Thus in *The Scotts Co (UK) Ltd v Budd* (see para 6.30) the claimant was employed for 17 years, and thus entitled to statutory notice of 12 weeks. He was off work sick for two years, and the employers terminated his

16 [1994] ICR 362, [1994] IRLR 260, EAT.   17 [1995] ICR 1028, [1995] IRLR 486, CA.
18 [2000] ICR 35, [1999] IRLR 690, EAT; revsd sub nom *Rowley v Cerberus Software Ltd* [2001] EWCA Civ 78, [2001] ICR 376, [2001] IRLR 160, [2001] All ER (D) 80 (Jan).

employment, giving him the 13 weeks' notice to which he was entitled under his contract. He claimed that he was entitled to be paid for the weeks of his notice period. His claim was dismissed by the EAT. Section 87(4) of ERA makes it quite clear that the entitlement to be paid during the notice period does not apply if the notice to terminate must be at least one week longer than the statutory period of notice. If an employee has been employed for five years, and is given four weeks' contractual notice, or five weeks' statutory notice, the provisions of ss 88–91 apply. However, if the employee gives notice (after being employed for one month or more) he will be able to enjoy these statutory rights only for the statutory notice period required of an employee, ie one week (s 86(1)), even though he gives a longer period of notice.

15.17 The statutory rights in question are as follows:

(a) Where the employee has normal working hours, he is entitled to be paid for those hours when he is ready and willing to work, but

(i) the employer does not provide work (s 88(1)(a)), or

(ii) he is incapable of work because of sickness or injury (s 88(1)(b)), or

(iii) the employee is absent from work because of pregnancy or childbirth or parental leave, adoption leave or paternity leave (s 88(1)(c)), or

(iv) he is absent from work in accordance with the terms of the contract relating to holidays (s 88(1)(d)).

S/he is entitled to be paid at the average hourly rate, produced by dividing a week's pay by the number of normal working hours. It should be noted that, for the purpose of ss 88–91, a 'week's pay' is not subject to the statutory limit which is applied in unfair dismissal and redundancy claims. Any payment made by the employer by way of sick pay, statutory sick pay, statutory maternity pay, paternity pay, statutory paternity pay, adoption pay, statutory adoption pay, holiday pay etc, can be offset.

(b) If the employee does not have normal working hours, the employer shall pay a week's pay (or average weekly remuneration – calculated over a period of 12 weeks), for each week of the notice period, provided the employee is ready and willing to do work of a reasonable nature and amount in order to earn a week's pay (s 89(1), (2)). S/he is also entitled to be paid for periods when s/he is off work because of sickness or injury, absent through pregnancy or childbirth, or parental leave, adoption leave, parental leave or paternity leave, or absent because of contractual holidays (s 89(3)). Any payments made by the employer can be offset (see (a)).

(c) ERA, s 91 provides that an employer is not required to make payments under ss 88–89 in respect of any period during which the employee is absent from work with leave from the employer granted at the request of the employee, including any period of time off work taken for the purpose of public duties, looking for work or making arrangements for retraining, antenatal care, acting as an occupational pension scheme trustee, or taking part in trade union duties and activities. At first sight this would appear to be strange, but in fact there is no problem. ERA, ss 50–63 and TULR(C)A, ss 168–170 contain their own remedies for such absences from work, and thus the employee must pursue them under the appropriate section, without reference to ERA, ss 89–90.

15.18 Section 91 further provides that no payment is due to an employee under ss 88–89 in the following circumstances:

(a) if the employee gives notice, and then takes part in a strike;

(b) if the employer gives notice, and the employee then takes part in a strike (because he cannot be said to be ready and willing to perform some work);

(c) if, during the notice period, the employee commits an act which amounts to a breach of contract, eg something which amounts to gross misconduct, and the employer dismisses the employee forthwith (s 91).

15.19 The rights contained in ss 88–90 apply when either the employer or employee give notice of termination of the contract. If the employer terminates the contract without notice, then the rights conferred by ss 88–90 shall be taken into account when assessing his liability for breach of contract.

Time off to look for work (ERA, s 52)

15.20 An employee whose employment has been terminated because of redundancy has the right to have time off work (with pay) to look for work or make arrangements for retraining during his notice period. This topic has been dealt with in Chapter 7.

E. Contractual rights during notice

15.21 It is always open to an employer to give lawful notice to terminate the contract, and to require the employee to work during the notice period. If the employee fails or refuses to do so, he will not be entitled to his pay under s 88 (see para 15.17), because he is not able or willing to work. As an alternative, the employer may give lawful notice, but not require the employee to work during the notice period. During this period, the employee will be entitled to all the contractual benefits. For his part, the employee may be restrained from working for a competitor during the notice period, if by doing so the employer would suffer serious harm (*Evening Standard Co Ltd v Henderson*[19]). An employer may require an employee to stay at home during a notice period, even though there is no garden leave clause in the contract, if the employee's conduct exhibits a behaviour that indicates that he does not wish to be bound by the contract of employment. In such circumstances he has forfeited the right to be provided with work (*SG & R Valuation Service v Boudrais*[20]). Any right to work expressed in the contract does not trump a garden leave clause (*Christie v Johnston Carmichael*).[21]

15.22 Otherwise the fact that the employee takes another job during the notice period is not repudiatory conduct by him, in the absence of a garden leave clause (see para 19.8). Further, since the notice money is contractually due to the employee, there is no requirement to mitigate against his loss (*Hutchings v Coinseed Ltd*[22]).

15.23 If, during the notice period, there is a wage increase (eg as a result of negotiations with a trade union) the employee is entitled to be paid that increase. However, if, subsequent to leaving the employment, a wage increase is negotiated which is backdated to a period when the employee was working, it would appear that he has no legal entitlement to that increase (*Leyland Vehicles Ltd v Reston*, see para 3.76). In legal reasoning, the employee has not given 'consideration' for the increase, because he has already worked under his contract, and 'past consideration is no consideration'.

F. Dispensing with notice

15.24 If a contract provides that an employee may be dismissed with immediate effect, he is still entitled to contractual notice or to a payment in lieu of notice (*T & K Home*

---

[19] [1987] ICR 588, [1987] IRLR 64, CA.   [20] [2008] EWHC 1340 (QB); [2008] IRLR 770.
[21] [2010] IRLR 1016.   [22] [1998] IRLR 190, CA.

Improvements Ltd v Skilton[23]). If the employee has a contractual right to pay in lieu of notice, there is no duty to mitigate (*Abrahams v Performing Rights Society*[24]).

15.25 If an employee commits a 'fundamental breach of contract' which warrants summary dismissal (see para 16.9), the employer need not give notice of termination. If the employer commits a fundamental breach of contract entitling the employee to resign and claim constructive dismissal (see para 17.21) the employee need not give notice of termination. Nor need an employer give notice if the contract had already been frustrated, and the fact that the employer keeps an employee 'on the books' when he is unlikely to return to work may be the sort of arrangement contemplated by ERA, s 212(3)(c) (see para 13.24), but no contract of employment will be in existence (*GF Sharp & Co Ltd v McMillan*[25]). If an employee is on a fixed-term contract (ie one with a fixed date of expiry) no notice of termination need be given, and a letter sent to the employee confirming that the contract will expire on a certain date is not a letter of dismissal (*London Underground Ltd v Fitzgerald*[26]). However, notice will be required if the employer wishes to terminate the contract prior to the expiry of the fixed term (*Dixon & Constanti v BBC*[27]), or if the employee wishes to resign before the end of that term, particularly if there is a restrictive covenant in force (*Thomas Marshall (Exports) Ltd v Guinle*[28]).

15.26 If an employee is on a probationary period for a certain length of time, the successful completion of which will result in him being confirmed in his position, this is not a fixed-term contract, and he may be given lawful notice prior to the expiry of the probationary period. The employer is not obliged to employ the employee for the whole of the probationary period (*Dalgleish v Kew House Farm Ltd*, see para 2.98). A training contract may or may not be a fixed-term contract, depending on how it is worded. If it is, it cannot be brought to an end until the period of training has expired, except for gross misconduct.

15.27 A project contract will expire when the project has been completed, and thus no notice need be given (*Ironmonger v Movefield Ltd*[29]). If an employee's contract comes to an end by virtue of a contractual provision relating to retirement age, again, no notice of termination need be given.

G. **Notice and time limits**

15.28 Once notice (by either side) is given, the effective date of termination, for unfair dismissal and redundancy pay purposes, is the date the notice expires, and the time for bringing a complaint before an employment tribunal will run from that date. However, an employer cannot 'short notice' an employee (ie give less notice than the statute requires) so as to prevent the employee from satisfying the qualifying period of employment. Thus if an employee has been employed for one week less than two years, and is dismissed without notice, his effective date of termination is the day he leaves, and, not having a requisite period of two years' continuous employment, he would appear to be unable to lodge a claim for unfair dismissal. However, ERA, s 97(2) provides that the effective date of termination is

---

[23] [2000] ICR 1162, [2000] IRLR 595, 645 IRLB 14, CA.

[24] [1995] ICR 1028, [1995] IRLR 486, (1995) *Times*, 5 June, (1995) *Independent*, 25 May.

[25] [1998] IRLR 632, EAT.   [26] [1997] ICR 271, EAT.

[27] [1978] QB 438, [1978] 2 All ER 465, [1978] 2 WLR 50, [1978] ICR 357, [1977] IRLR 337, 13 ITR 169, 121 Sol Jo 632, EAT; aff'd [1979] QB 546, [1979] 2 All ER 112, [1979] 2 WLR 647, [1979] ICR 281, [1979] IRLR 114, 122 Sol Jo 713, CA.

[28] [1979] Ch 227, [1978] 3 All ER 193, [1978] 3 WLR 116, [1979] FSR 208, [1978] ICR 905, [1978] IRLR 174, 122 Sol Jo 295.

[29] [1988] IRLR 461.

the date on which his statutory notice would have expired. In other words, he is entitled to add to the period of employment the week's notice to which he is entitled by statute. On the other hand, the dismissal will only operate for computation purposes from the date when the statutory notice expires, not from the date when his contractual notice (had it have been given) would have expired. Thus, if the employee has been employed for two weeks less than two years, and is entitled to four weeks' notice, but is dismissed immediately with pay in lieu of notice, his period of continuous employment is two weeks short of the qualifying period. He is only entitled to add on the period of statutory notice, not his potential contractual notice (see *Fox Maintenance Ltd v Jackson*,[30] para 17.4). This provision also applies to constructive dismissal claims (ERA, s 97(4)). However, s 97(2)–(4) only applies for the purpose of determining the qualifying period of employment (s 108(1)), the calculation of the basic award (s 19(1)), and the calculation of a week's pay where this has been increased by the Secretary of State during the statutory notice period (s 227(3)). A similar extension of the period of continuous employment is contained in s 92(7), with respect to written reasons for dismissal. It should be noted that in general the law takes no account of fractions of a day (*Wang v University of Keele*[31]).

15.29 The continuous period of employment is not extended for the purpose of extending the time limit within which a claim for unfair dismissal may be brought. In other words, an unfair dismissal claim must be brought within three months of the effective date of termination (or other period permitted by law), not from when the statutory notice period would have expired. The effective date of termination is the date on which the employment relationship ends, and that date cannot be varied by any subsequent agreement between the parties. However, the notice that determines the effective date of termination can be varied, so that there can be a subsequent agreement that the effective date of termination can be brought forward or pushed backward, and time will start to run from the new date (*Palfrey v Transco plc*[32]). Finally, it may be noted that an employee who has been given notice may commence proceedings for unfair dismissal without waiting for the notice period to expire, or within three months from the effective date of termination (ERA, s 111(3)).

H. Notice pay on insolvency (ERA, ss 182–186)

15.30 If an employer becomes insolvent (eg bankrupt or wound up; see s 183), so that the contract of employment is no longer capable of being performed, then clearly that contract has terminated. In such circumstances, the employee may make an application for his statutory notice to be paid from the National Insurance Fund. If the Secretary of State is satisfied that the employee is so entitled, he will pay out of that Fund the amount of statutory notice set out in s 86 (as well as certain other payments, see para 7.133), although the 'week's pay' for the purpose of this provision, is limited to the statutory maximum as laid down (currently £464 per week). Other contractual benefits cannot be recovered from the Fund. The employee will be under a duty to mitigate against his loss (*Westwood v Secretary of State for Employment*, see para 7.134), and an employee who obtains fresh employment immediately or during what would have been his notice period can only recover in respect of the period of loss, if any (*Secretary of State for Employment v Wilson*, see para 7.134). Any award made by the Secretary of State from the Fund will be based on pay net of income tax.

---

[30] [1978] ICR 110, [1977] IRLR 306, 12 ITR 455, EAT.
[31] [2011] IRLR 542, EAT.
[32] [2004] IRLR 916, EAT.

Notice to be given by the employee

15.31 An employee is required to give due notice of termination, as laid down in his contract of employment. If there is no such term, then, in theory, he should give reasonable notice, depending on his position, the industry, etc. There does not appear to be any legal authority on this point. We are therefore left with the statutory notice period, set out in ERA, s 86(2), which provides that an employee who has been continuously employed for one month or more has to give at least one week's notice.

Employer's remedies

15.32 If the employee fails to give the required notice of termination of his contract, technically the employer has two remedies. The first arises where there is a restrictive covenant prohibiting the employee from working for a competitor etc (see Chapter 19). The employer may be able to obtain an injunction to prevent a breach of this term. However, he will not be able to obtain an order for specific performance of the contract (TULR(C) A, s 236).

15.33 Second, in theory, the employer may sue for damages for breach of contract, although such actions are virtually unknown and the most an employee stands to lose if he fails to give the requisite notice is his reputation, if any, as a responsible employee. But if, for example, in anticipation of an employee commencing work, the employer incurs considerable expenses (eg purchases equipment or machinery, or hires premises, or enters into an abortive advertising campaign), an action for damages against an employee who fails to meet his contractual obligations could well succeed (*Batty v Melillo*; and see *Tullett Prebon Group Ltd v Ghaleb El-Hajjali*,[33] para 3.6).

15.34 An employer may attempt to pre-empt this problem by providing, in the contract of employment, that he may withhold arrears of wages and/or accrued holiday pay if an employee fails to give proper notice or work out that notice in accordance with the contract.

15.35 So far as the withholding of wages is concerned, this would appear to be perfectly legal, but only in so far as the amount withheld is a genuine pre-estimate of the loss, and not a penalty clause (*Dunlop Pneumatic Tyre Co Ltd v New Garage & Motor Co*[34]). Such deduction would not contravene ERA, s 13(1) (see para 8.4) because the deduction would have been authorised by the employee's contract of employment. For example, in *Giraud UK Ltd v Smith*[35] the employee's contract of employment required him to give four weeks' notice of termination. If he failed to give such notice, the employer would be entitled to deduct from his final payment an amount equivalent to the number of days short. When he left his employment without notice, the employers refused to pay him payments due to him, claiming that under the contract they were entitled to deduct a payment equivalent of four weeks' pay. It was held that the clause was not a lawful liquidated damage clause, because it did not represent a genuine pre-estimate of the loss or damage suffered. Essentially, it was a penalty clause, and was unenforceable.

15.36 So far as accrued holiday pay is concerned, the provisions of reg 13 of the Working Time Regulations must be borne in mind (see para 7.54), and any such deduction would not be lawful.

---

[33] [2008] EWHC 1924 (QB), [2008] IRLR 760.
[34] [1915] AC 79, 83 LJKB 1574, [1914–15] All ER Rep 739, 111 LT 862, 30 TLR 625, HL.
[35] [2000] IRLR 763, 668 IDS Brief 7, EAT.

Employee's remedies

15.37 If an employer fails to give notice to the employee, or gives notice which is less than the contractual or statutory notice (whichever is the longer) the employee's remedy is to bring an action either in the ordinary courts or in the employment tribunal, under the Employment Tribunals Extension of Jurisdiction Order (see para 1.40). A court action would be appropriate if the amount claimed by way of damages is in excess of £25,000, because that is the maximum sum which could be awarded by an employment tribunal. Further, an action for breach of contract may be brought in the ordinary courts any time within six years from the breach, whereas a claim in an employment tribunal must be brought within three months beginning with the effective date of termination, or, if there was no such date, within three months from when the employee last worked, or, if it was not reasonably practicable to present the claim in either of those periods, within such further period as the employment tribunal thinks reasonable.

15.38 The claim by the employee is one for breach of contract, the measure of damages being the monies he would have earned had he been given proper notice. If there was an element of discretion in certain payments (eg annual salary increases, bonuses) it must be assumed that the employer would have exercised that discretion in good faith, and thus they form part of the loss suffered (*Clark v BET plc,* see paras 3.2 and 10.22). The claim is subject to the common law rule that the innocent party to a breach of contract must take reasonable steps to mitigate against his loss. Thus, if the employee is dismissed without notice, and the following day he obtained fresh employment on equivalent or improved terms and conditions, then, since he has lost nothing, he is not entitled to anything (*Secretary of State for Employment v Wilson,* para 15.30). In *Hardy v Polk (Leeds) Ltd*[36] the claimant was entitled to eight weeks' contractual notice. She was unfairly dismissed without notice, but started a new job after four weeks. Her employer was not contractually obliged to make a payment in lieu of notice. It was held that as she had partially mitigated against her loss she was only entitled to compensation for four weeks. Further, credit must be given by the employee for any payment received by way of jobseekers' allowance (*Westwood v Secretary of State for Employment,* para 15.30). In other words, the object of the exercise is to place the employee in the same position financially as he would have been had lawful notice been given.

15.39 In certain special circumstances, an employee may be able to obtain an injunction to restrain an employer from terminating the contract of employment without proper notice. Generally speaking, it has to be shown that the trust and confidence which should exist between employer and employee remains (*Hill v C A Parsons Ltd,* see paras 10.16 and 15.3), but an injunction may also be obtained where it can be shown that the employer has failed to operate a contractual disciplinary procedure, particularly where damages would not be an adequate remedy for the manner in which a dismissal without notice was carried out. The modern test to be applied is 'the workability' of the situation (*Robb v London Borough of Hammersmith and Fulham*[37]).

15.40 It should be noted that there is no implied term that an employee will not be unfairly dismissed (eg without going through proper procedures), and thus the only damages which can be awarded at common law are those which relate to contractual notice (*Fosca Services (UK) Ltd v Birkett,* see para 16.21).

---

[36] [2005] ICR 557, EAT.
[37] [1991] ICR 514, [1991] IRLR 72.

16

Wrongful Dismissal

Background

16.1 Under the law which existed prior to 1971 an employer was entitled to dismiss an employee for any reason or no reason at all; the only issues which arose related to whether or not the employee was entitled to a certain period of notice, or whether his conduct was such as to warrant instant (summary) dismissal without notice. There were certain special cases where the right not to be dismissed was enshrined into an employee's contract by virtue of a special 'status' (see para 2.76), and there were other cases where when a dismissal could not be carried out unless the rules of 'natural justice' were observed (see *Ridge v Baldwin*, see para 2.75), or because the approval of some other person or body had to be obtained (eg *Cory Lighterage v Transport and General Workers' Union*, see para 3.19). These matters are now largely of historical interest.

16.2 In 1971 the Industrial Relations Act created the right for many employees not to be unfairly dismissed, and though that Act was repealed, the relevant provisions were substantially re-enacted (with some minor amendments) in the Trade Union and Labour Relations Act 1974, and further changes were made by the Employment Protection Act 1975. All the relevant law was brought together in the Employment Protection (Consolidation) Act 1978, and further amendments were made in subsequent legislation. The Employment Rights Act 1996 (as amended) contains most of the relevant statutory provisions currently in force (see Chapter 17).

16.3 But although the new legal right has largely subsumed the old common law learning, it is still necessary to examine the old law relating to wrongful and summary dismissal, because there may be situations when the common law remedy is more advantageous, or indeed, the only remedy available. In particular, we may note the following circumstances:

(a) the maximum compensatory award for unfair dismissal is £76,574 from April 2014 plus an appropriate basic award. A highly paid employee who is entitled to a long period of notice may be able to obtain substantially higher damages at common law (see *O'Laoire v Jackel International Ltd*,[1] para 16.28);

(b) an employee who lacks the relevant period of continuous employment to qualify for unfair dismissal rights may nonetheless sue for wrongful dismissal either at common law or in the employment tribunal under the provisions of ETEJO (see para 1.40). However, if the employee is summarily dismissed, or given less than the contractual notice, with the result that he lacks the necessary qualifying period of continuous employment to pursue a claim for unfair dismissal, he cannot claim damages for the loss of the opportunity to claim unfair dismissal (*Johnson v Unisys Ltd*, para 16.25);

---

[1] [1990] ICR 197, [1990] IRLR 70, CA.

(c) a fair dismissal may nonetheless be a wrongful dismissal if proper notice has not been given (*Treganowan v Robert Knee & Co Ltd²*);

(d) an application for unfair dismissal is likely to be time barred if it is not brought within three months from the effective date of termination, whereas a common law action for wrongful dismissal may be brought within six years of the breach;

(e) the rules relating to damages are different. In particular, a common law action does not permit a reduction for contributory conduct, and the mitigation rules are not the same;

(f) the dispute may contain a public law element, and not be concerned with strict contractual rights (*R v Secretary of State for the Home Department, ex p Benwell³*);

(g) a dismissal which is in breach of a contractual dismissal procedure may enable an employee to bring a common law action for breach of contract (*Shook v London Borough of Ealing⁴*) or to seek an injunction to restrain the breach (*Irani v Southampton and South West Hampshire Health Authority*, see para 10.4), or seek a declaration as to his legal rights. But the employee's remedies in such circumstances may be limited to damages for the period up to which he would have been employed had the correct procedure been followed (*Gunton v London Borough of Richmond*, see paras 3.96 and 12.14 *and see Edwards v Chesterfield Royal Hospital NHS Foundation Trust*,⁵ where the Supreme Court held that employees may not recover damages in civil courts for loss suffered as a result of a breach of their contract of employment in relation to the manner of their dismissal unless the loss can be said to precede and be independent of the dismissal).

16.4 Since the jurisdiction of the employment tribunals is concurrent in many respects with that possessed by the ordinary courts, an employee will thus opt for whichever cause of action will produce the most advantageous results (see para 1.40).

16.5 If, before his dismissal, an employee acquires a cause of action at common law (whether for breach of contract or breach of the duty to take reasonable care for the employee's health and safety) that cause of action remains unimpaired by the fact that the employee has brought a statutory unfair dismissal claim. Thus a claim for damages for psychiatric injury caused, for example, by a wrongful application for the contractual disciplinary procedure may succeed (*Eastwood v Magnox Electric plc*, see para 11.113), even though there can be no award for psychiatric illness (or injury to feelings) caused by the manner of actual dismissal (*Dunnachie v Kingston upon Hull City Council*, see para 11.113). Damages for injury to feelings, aggravated and exemplary damages may be awarded in detriment cases, as well as race, sex and disability cases, but not in unfair dismissal cases.

Wrongful dismissal

16.6 There are a number of ways in which wrongful dismissal may occur:

(a) the employer terminates the employment without notice, or with less notice than the employee is entitled to receive under the terms of his contract or the statutory provisions (see Chapter 15);

² [1975] IRLR 112; aff'd [1975] ICR 405, [1975] IRLR 247, 10 ITR 121, 119 Sol Jo 490.
³ [1985] QB 554, [1984] 3 All ER 854, [1984] 3 WLR 843, [1984] ICR 723, [1985] IRLR 6, 128 Sol Jo 703.
⁴ [1986] ICR 314, [1986] IRLR 46, EAT.   ⁵ [2011] UKSC 58.

(b) a fixed-term contract is terminated by the employer before the date it was due to expire;

(c) a contract for the completion of a specific task is terminated by the employer before the task has ended;

(d) the employer terminates the employment without carrying out the disciplinary procedure which has been incorporated into the employee's contract (*Gunton v London Borough of Richmond* (see para 16.3));

(e) the employee is selected for redundancy in breach of a selection procedure which has been incorporated into his contract (*Alexander v Standard Telephones and Cables plc*, see paras 3.59, 3.63 and 10.2);

(f) the employer wrongfully repudiates the contract, his actions indicating that he no longer intends to be bound by the contract (*General Billposting Co Ltd v Atkinson*[6]). Where an employment contract is wrongfully repudiated, the contract is terminated only if and when the other party has accepted that repudiation: Geys v Société Générale[7]. (The Supreme Court affirmed the principle in *Gunton v LB Richmond*, see paras 3.96, 12.13, 16.3, 16.6 and 16.30.) The employee 'accepts' the repudiation by resigning, or, if appropriate, keeps the contract alive and sues for whatever remedy is available (*Rigby v Ferodo*, see para 3.102). For example, if the employer has unilaterally reduced the employee's wages, a claim may be made under the appropriate provisions of the Employment Rights Act (see Chapter 8). On the other hand, if the employee delays action, he may be taken to have affirmed the contract, unless the employer has given him time to make a decision (*Bliss v South East Thames Regional Health Authority*[8]). Whether the employer has in fact repudiated the contract is a matter to be determined in the particular circumstances of the case (*General Billposting Co Ltd v Atkinson*). Thus, if the employer fails or refuses to provide work for the employee (see para 10.16) or makes it impossible for the employee to do his work (*Collier v Sunday Referee Publishing Co Ltd*, see para 10.17), or unilaterally attempts to vary the contract of employment, such actions can amount to a breach of contract by the employer which enables the employee to accept by resigning, and claiming wrongful dismissal. This is the common law counterpart of the statutory concept of 'constructive' dismissal, which will be dealt with in Chapter 17;

(g) the contract specifies that a dismissal may only take place in certain specified circumstances, or on specified grounds, and the employer dismisses for some other reason not stated in the contract (*McClelland v Northern Ireland General Health Services Board*, see para 2.76).

16.7 However, if the contract expressly permits the employer to terminate the employment without notice on the payment of a sum of money in lieu of notice, and the employer summarily dismisses the employee, the dismissal is not wrongful, whether or not the employer pays the money in lieu of notice, because he is acting within the strict terms of the contract. In such circumstances, the employee may sue for any outstanding due under the contract, as liquidated damages, and the employee is under no duty to mitigate against his loss (*Abrahams v Performing Right Society*, see para 15.15, and see para 16.9).

---

[6] [1908] 1 Ch 537, 77 LJ Ch 411, [1908–10] All ER Rep 619, 52 Sol Jo 240, 98 LT 482, 24 TLR 285, CA; aff'd [1909] AC 118, 78 LJ Ch 77, [1908–10] All ER Rep 619, 99 LT 943, 25 TLR 178, HL.

[7] [2012] UKSC 63.

[8] [1987] ICR 700, [1985] IRLR 308, CA.

Collateral contracts

16.8 At common law, when an employer terminates the contract of employment, the only remedy for the employee is to claim money for the period of notice to which he is entitled (see para 15.2). However, if the employer promises that the contract will subsist for a certain period of time, this may be a collateral contract to the main contract, and the employee may be able to claim damages for a breach of that collateral contract. In *Gill v Cape Contracts Ltd*[9] the claimant gave up his job in Belfast to go to work for the defendants in the Shetlands. He was told that the work would last for at least six months, but the defendants repudiated the contract before he could start work. It was held that the plaintiff was entitled to damages for a breach of contract by the defendants, who had made representations which had been acted on by the claimant to his detriment. These representations formed a collateral contract to the main contract of employment.

Summary dismissal

16.9 In *Jupiter General Insurance Co v Shroff*[10] the Privy Council stated that summary dismissal was a strong measure, to be justified only in the most exceptional circumstances. Nonetheless, there are a number of well-recognised grounds on which an employer may dismiss an employee summarily; these include gross misconduct, wilful refusal to obey a lawful and reasonable order, gross neglect, dishonesty, and so forth (see eg *Blyth v Scottish Liberal Club*[11]). Whether the conduct in question is serious enough to warrant dismissal is always a question of fact in each case, and the standards to be applied are those of the current *mores*, not those which may have become somewhat outdated. In *Wilson v Racher*, Edmund-Davies LJ said: 'Many of the decisions which are customarily cited in these cases date from the last century and may be wholly out of accord with current social conditions. What would today be regarded as almost an attitude of Czar–serf, which is to be found in some of the older cases where a dismissed employee failed to recover damages, would, I venture to think, be decided differently today. We have by now come to realise that a contract of service imposes upon the parties a duty of mutual respect.'[12] It is thus clear that many of the older decisions on this subject lack authority today, and must be treated with reserve, if not disdain.

16.10 But certain principles remain constant. In *Sinclair v Neighbour*[13] a manager took £15 from a till and left an IOU in its place. He intended to replace the money a few days later. His conduct was regarded as being dishonest and his summary dismissal was upheld. In *Ross v Aquascutum Ltd*[14] the employee was a nightwatchman. He was observed to be absent from the building he was guarding for two hours of each night, and it was held that his conduct constituted a breach of contract so serious as to justify summary dismissal. When considering conduct which results from the interaction of human personalities, it is necessary to apply the standards of ordinary people, not those of the angels. In *Pepper v Webb* (see para 10.58) a gardener was asked to do certain work, but he refused to do so in language which was somewhat vulgar. His summary dismissal was held to be justified, for by refusing to obey a lawful and reasonable order he had broken his contract. Indeed, his conduct had been such as to give rise to a history of complaints for insolence, and the

---

[9] [1985] IRLR 499.   [10] [1937] 3 All ER 67, PC.

[11] [1983] IRLR 245, 1983 SLT 260, Ct of Sess.

[12] [1974] ICR 428, [1974] IRLR 114, 16 KIR 212, CA.

[13] [1967] 2 QB 279, [1966] 3 All ER 988, [1967] 2 WLR 1, 110 Sol Jo 808, CA.

[14] [1973] IRLR 107.

incident which gave rise to his dismissal was merely the last straw. On the other hand, in *Wilson v Racher* (see para 16.9) a gardener swore at his employer using some even choicer obscenities. Although this could have amounted to gross misconduct, the court held that '...it requires very special circumstances to entitle a servant who expresses his feelings in such a grossly improper way to succeed in an action for wrongful dismissal'. On the facts of the case, the special circumstance existed, and these lay in the employer's own conduct which had provoked the outburst.

16.11 The breach of an express term of the contract or of a provision in the works rules may justify summary dismissal, provided it has been brought expressly to the attention of the employee that there is certain conduct which the employer will on no account tolerate. Certain airlines, for example, have a rule that any pilot who takes drugs (other than on medical prescription) or is discovered drunk whether on or off duty will be instantly dismissed. Other employers may specify other conduct which is detrimental to the business and which may warrant summary dismissal. For example, smoking in prohibited areas, unhygienic practices in food premises, breach of safety rules which may lead to hazards or risk of injury to others, all constitute conduct which may, in the special circumstances, warrant dismissal. In *Dunn v AAH Ltd*[15] a director's contract stated that the employee could be summarily dismissed for 'wilful neglect'. The director was also specifically told to report any potential business risk to the parent company, so that the risk could be assessed. The claimant director failed to report that a supplier company was supplying substituted products worth many millions of pounds, which potentially exposed the parent company to legal action. The Court of Appeal upheld the director's summary dismissal. Gross misconduct is a form of repudiatory conduct, for which instant dismissal was not inappropriate.

16.12 An employee is not in breach of his contract of employment merely because he indicates his intention to open a business in competition with his employer. In *Laughton and Hawley v Bapp Industrial Supplies Ltd*[16] the two claimants, who were employed by the respondents, wrote to the company's suppliers stating that they intended to commence trading in the near future, and asked for product lists, prices and terms. When the employers discovered this, the employees were dismissed instantly without notice. The dismissals were held to be wrongful. There was no abuse of their positions as employees, no breach of any covenant in restraint of trade, and no disclosures of trade secrets or confidential information. The employees had not failed to devote their efforts to their employer's business during working hours, and thus their activities did not constitute gross misconduct. But where a managing director formed a new business entity, sought to persuade his employer's major client to transfer business to it, and induced two senior employees to join him in the new venture which was in direct competition with the employer, it was held that this amounted to gross misconduct warranting summary dismissal (*Marshall v Industrial Systems and Control Ltd*[17]). An employee has a duty to his employer to act in good faith and in the employer's best interests. Thus, if he seeks to divert to himself a contract which his employer is seeking to obtain with a third party, this will amount to dishonest conduct which would warrant summary dismissal (*Item Software (UK) Ltd v Fassihi*, see paras 10.94 and 16.24).

16.13 A more difficult problem arises if conduct of the employee is in the nature of neglect, which causes damage to the employer. Should one consider the act itself, which may be of a minor or major nature, or should one consider the consequences, which may be insignificant or serious? In *Savage v British India Steam Navigation Co*[18] it was stated

[15] [2009] EWHC 692 (QB), [2010] IRLR 709, CA.
[16] [1986] ICR 634, [1986] IRLR 245, EAT.
[17] [1992] IRLR 294, EAT.   [18] (1930) 46 TLR 294.

that it was the nature of the act, not the consequences, which was relevant. A failure to observe instructions which resulted in damage was held to be of sufficient seriousness to warrant summary dismissal in *Howe v Gloucester and Severnside Co-operative Society*,[19] but excessive zeal which caused damage did not warrant such drastic measures in *Newlands v Howard & Co Ltd*.[20] Neglect by senior employees who hold responsible positions appears to amount to a greater dereliction of duty than junior staff, and hence more likely to attract instant dismissal. As a general rule, for an employee to be summarily dismissed on the grounds of neglect, the neglect should be something approaching habitual conduct, but a single act of neglect could justify instant dismissal if its consequences are likely to be serious enough (*Taylor v Alidair Ltd*[21]).

16.14 A strike is a breach of contract by the employee, and is thus an act of such a nature as to justify summary dismissal. So too is any other conduct designed to disrupt the employer's business, such as go-slow tactics, work-to-rule, etc. Persistent lateness, drunkenness, fighting, swearing, immorality, skylarking, are all examples of conduct which could attract summary dismissal in particular circumstances. But it must be stressed that although dismissal would not be wrongful at common law, in most cases, the test of 'fairness' will have to be considered for the purpose of unfair dismissal claims, and this will be explored later in Chapter 17.

16.15 A summary dismissal takes effect immediately. Any rights an employee may have, eg for pay in lieu of notice, expenses, etc may be claimed by an action for damages for breach of contract in the ordinary courts (*Octavius Atkinson & Sons Ltd v Morris*[22]) or the employment tribunal (see para 1.40).

Employment law remedies

A. Common law remedies

16.16 Although most of the cases involving employment law are brought in employment tribunals, there has been a small resurgence in recent years of claims seeking the old common law remedies. Thus actions may still be brought for wrongful dismissal (see para 16.6), and also for damages based on a failure by the employer to follow contractual disciplinary procedures, the measure of damages being the loss suffered by the employee as a result of that failure (*Boyo v Lambeth London Borough Council*, see para 3.96). Also, an application may be made for an injunction to restrain an employer from purporting to act in breach of a contractual disciplinary procedure (*Jones v Lee and Guilding*, see para 3.96) and, somewhat rare, an action seeking specific performance of the contract (*Powell v London Borough of Brent*, see para 10.5). These matters were explored in Chapter 10 (and see *Jones v Gwent County Council*, para 10.6).

16.17 If an employer acts unfairly towards an employee in such a way that the employee has acquired a cause of action at common law prior to, and independent of, a subsequent dismissal (whether fair or unfair, or whether constructive or not), the common law action is not barred by the fact that the employee has brought a statutory unfair dismissal claim (*Eastwood v Magnox Electric plc*, para 16.5).

16.18 It must be stressed that an action for wrongful dismissal is different from a claim for unfair dismissal, although there may well be some overlap in certain instances. But, in

[19] [1975] IRLR 17.   [20] [1973] IRLR 9.
[21] [1978] ICR 445, [1978] IRLR 82, (1978) 13 ITR 180, (1977) 121 SJ 758.
[22] [1988] ICR 880, EAT; revsd [1989] ICR 431, [1989] IRLR 158, CA.

particular, it should be noted that the sole issue in a wrongful dismissal action is whether or not the employer has broken the contract of employment. The 'reasonableness' of the employer's conduct is not in issue, nor does 'contributory conduct' by the employee come into the equation. Also, care must be taken to distinguish between payments made by the employer, and awards against an employer made by a court or tribunal. It is with the latter that this chapter is concerned.

16.19 The normal remedy for wrongful dismissal is for the innocent party to bring an action for damages, although sometimes an application for an injunction or a declaration will be made. Also, if the breach of contract consists not in a dismissal, but an alteration in the terms of the contract which is not permitted by the contract, the employee can, at his option, either accept the breach and resign (claiming wrongful constructive dismissal) or refuse to accept the breach, and sue on the contract as it stands, thus seeking to insist that the employer performs the contract (see *Dietman v London Borough of Brent*[23]). The majority of wrongful dismissal claims are brought in the county court or the High Court, although, with the concurrent jurisdiction conferred on employment tribunals by the Extension of Jurisdiction Order, more claims are now being brought under a procedure which is cheaper and comparatively expeditious.

16.20 In rare cases, an employee may seek a public law remedy, by way of judicial review, generally when a private law remedy either does not exist, or would be inadequate in the circumstances (*R v Chief Constable of Merseyside Police, ex p Calveley*[24]).

Damages

16.21 The general principle in contract law (and it must be remembered that employment law is basically concerned with a contract of employment) is that the purpose of damages is to put the innocent party in the position in which he would have been had the contractual obligations been performed, in so far as it is possible to do this by a monetary award. Thus, since an employer may always give notice to terminate the contract, then this will become the starting point for any claim. If the employer terminates the contract without notice, or gives less notice than the contract or the statutory provisions require, then damages will be initially limited to the period of notice that should have been given (*Fosca Services (UK) Ltd v Birkett*, paras 2.98 and 15.40, and see Chapter 15). Similarly, if the contract was for a fixed term, and is prematurely terminated, damages will be the loss suffered by the employee as the result of the employer's action. However, if a fixed-term contract gives the employer the right to terminate before the end of that term, then damages will be limited to the notice period (*British Guiana Credit Corpn v Da Silva*[25]). If the employer is in breach because he has failed to follow a disciplinary procedure which has been incorporated into the contract, damages will be limited to the period of time it would have taken the employer to put the contractual procedure into effect (*Dietman v Brent London Borough Council*, para 16.19). An apprentice who has been wrongfully dismissed may recover damages for the loss of training and work experience he would have gained had the contract not been broken or the diminution of his future prospects (*Dunk v George Waller & Son Ltd*, see para 2.103). Artistes may be able to recover for loss of publicity (*Withers v General Theatre Corpn*[26]), or the loss of enhancing their reputation (*Herbert Clayton & Jack Waller Ltd v Oliver*, see para 10.17).

16.22 Because there may be certain complications arising out of income tax liability and national insurance contributions, the actual computation of the financial loss may present

[23] [1987] IRLR 146, CA.
[24] [1986] QB 424, [1986] 1 All ER 257, [1986] 2 WLR 144, 130 Sol Jo 53, [1986] LS Gaz R 124, CA.
[25] [1965] 1 WLR 248, 109 Sol Jo 30, PC.
[26] [1933] 2 KB 536, 102 LJKB 719, [1933] All ER Rep 385, 149 LT 487, CA.

problems. In principle, an employee is entitled to the net loss suffered (ie after the deduction of tax and national insurance), and whether one should start with the gross salary, less deductions, or the net figure grossed up, will frequently depend on the amounts at stake. It would appear that the latter course is more advantageous if the amount is comparatively large, whereas the former method appears to be appropriate when the length of the notice period is relatively short (*Shove v Downs Surgical plc*[27]).

16.23 Also to be taken into account are commissions, bonuses, gratuities etc, which were contractually due to the employee (*Addis v Gramophone Co Ltd*, see para 10.21), including an enhanced contractual redundancy payment (*Basnett v J & A Jackson Ltd*[28]) but not discretionary payments (*Lavarack v Woods of Colchester Ltd*, see para 10.22). Damages for breach of contract can also include accrued pension rights, because there is no difference between a lost pension and lost pay (*Silvey v Pendragon plc*[29]). Fringe benefits, eg company car (in so far as it was permitted for private use), subsidised mortgages, free lunches, the loss of the right to obtain share options (if there was a contractual right) or options already granted (*Chapman v Aberdeen Construction Group Ltd*[30]), private medical insurance, rent-free accommodation etc, can be quantified and their value claimed. Expenses are not normally allowable, as they represent a reimbursement for expenditure incurred by the employee on behalf of the employer. Indeed, if it can be shown that the expenses were in fact a device to boost the employee's income, and were not genuinely incurred, it may be argued that this was an attempt to avoid paying income tax on the employee's salary, and, as such, the contract was illegal, and did not give rise at all to any cause of action (see para 3.8).

16.24 Also included in the compensation which may be awarded will be the loss of other actual or potential benefits, such as pension rights and/or the employer's potential pension contributions, profit sharing schemes, the lost value of share options (*Micklefield v SAC Technology*[31]), outstanding holiday pay, loss of statutory protection rights (*Stapp v Shaftesbury Society*[32]), loss of the opportunity to claim a redundancy payment (*Basnett v J & A Jackson Ltd*, para 16.23), and so on. An employee's claim for part-payment of wages outstanding at the date of dismissal is not defeated by the fact that the dismissal was for reason of gross misconduct. The Apportionment Act 1870 applies when a contract of employment is terminated during the payment period, unless there is something in the contract of employment to the contrary (*Item Software (UK) Ltd v Fassihi*, see paras 8.10 and 10.94).

16.25 At common law, no damages may be awarded for the manner of dismissal (*Addis v Gramophone Co Ltd*, para 16.23), whether by way of injured feelings, psychiatric illness, loss of reputation or difficulty in finding fresh employment (*Boardman v Copeland Borough Council*[33]). The decision of the House of Lords in *Malik v BCCI* (see para 3.47) is concerned with a complaint relating to a breach of trust and confidence owed by the employer to his employees during the period they were employed, and is not concerned with the actual manner of dismissal (*Johnson v Unisys Ltd*, para 16.3). There can be no claim at common law for damages for psychiatric illness if an employer conducts a campaign designed to deprive an employee of his job by fabricating evidence for the purpose of conducting disciplinary proceedings. *Johnson v Unisys* established that unfairness in the manner of dismissal does not give rise to a common law action, whether it is founded on contract or

[27] [1984] 1 All ER 7, [1984] ICR 532, [1984] IRLR 17, 128 Sol Jo 221.
[28] [1976] ICR 63, [1976] IRLR 154.
[29] [2001] EWCA Civ 784, [2001] IRLR 685.
[30] [1991] IRLR 505, 1993 SLT 1205, Ct of Sess.
[31] [1991] 1 All ER 275, [1990] 1 WLR 1002, [1990] IRLR 218, [1990] 28 LS Gaz R 43.
[32] [1982] IRLR 326, CA.
[33] [2001] EWCA Civ 888, [2001] All ER (D) 99 (Jun).

tort. Such matters must be the subject of employment tribunal proceedings (*Eastwood v Magnox Electrical plc*, paras 16.5 and 16.17). But in *McCabe v Cornwall County Council*,[34] the Court of Appeal appear to have taken a somewhat different view, and permitted a claim to proceed on the basis that there is no automatic bar to such an action just because a dismissal results from the alleged breach of trust and respect.

16.26 Damages for breach of contract at common law are always subject to the rule that the innocent party must take reasonable steps to mitigate against his loss, which, in this context, involves looking for other suitable employment. Any earnings from such employment (or from self-employment) can be deducted from the loss suffered (*Shove v Downs Surgical plc*, para 16.22). The problem here, however, is that the burden of proof is on the employer to show that the employee has failed to take reasonable steps to mitigate his loss (*London and South of England Building Society v Stone*[35]). This he may be able to do, either by reference to matters known to him, or by obtaining some form of discovery from the employee concerning his attempts to seek alternative employment. Whether an employee has taken reasonable steps to mitigate against his loss is a question of fact to be determined by the court, bearing in mind all the circumstances, including the employee's age, mobility, personal commitments, qualifications, experience, and so on. For example, in *Brace v Calder*, the claimant was dismissed from a partnership as a result of a change in the partners, but offered his old job back by the new partners. He refused this offer, and it was held that he had failed to mitigate his loss, and was therefore only entitled to nominal damages. On the other hand, in *Yetton v Eastwoods Froy Ltd*,[36] a managing director was dismissed from his post, but was offered the job of assistant managing director. It was held that his refusal of this job, which was a significant step down, was not unreasonable.

16.27 It is not unusual for a contract of employment of a senior executive to contain a provision that in the event of a wrongful dismissal the employer will make a lump sum payment by way of liquidated damages, which may in fact be in excess of any amount which would be recoverable at common law (sometimes referred to as 'golden parachutes'). In principle, such damages may be unenforceable, since they may amount to being a penalty clause as they fail to taken into account the duty of the employee to mitigate against his loss by seeking alternative employment. In *Murray v Leisureplay plc*[37] the contract provided that in the event of a dismissal, a chief executive would be entitled to one year's gross salary plus certain benefits. The High Court held that this provision was a penalty clause, rather than liquidated damages, and that consequently it was unenforceable. However, the decision was reversed by the Court of Appeal. The clause would only be a penalty if the party seeking to avoid the terms could show that it was 'extravagant and unconscionable' in amount. The clause may have been generous, but it was not unconscionable. A payment may be so extravagant as to be unenforceable because it is 'ultra vires': see *Gibb v Maidstone and Tunbridge Wells NHS Trust*,[38] para 20.52.

16.28 It is unusual, but not impossible, to bring a claim for unfair dismissal as well as an action for wrongful dismissal, although either the court or tribunal can stay one action, pending the outcome of the other (*Carter v Credit Change Ltd*[39]). If one claim does not fully

---

[34] [2002] EWCA Civ 1887, [2003] ICR 501, [2003] IRLR 87, [2003] 09 LS Gaz R 27, [2002] All ER (D) 294 (Dec).

[35] (1981) 261 Estates Gazette 463; revsd [1983] 3 All ER 105, [1983] 1 WLR 1242, 127 Sol Jo 446, [1983] LS Gaz R 3048, 267 Estates Gazette 69, CA.

[36] [1966] 3 All ER 353, [1967] 1 WLR 104, 111 Sol Jo 32.

[37] [2005] EWCA Civ 963, [2005] IRLR 946, CA.

[38] [2010] IRLR 786, [2010] EWCA Civ 678.

[39] [1979] ICR 908, [1979] IRLR 309, EAT; revsd [1980] 1 All ER 252, [1979] ICR 908, [1979] IRLR 361, 123 Sol Jo 604, CA.

resolve the whole matter, the second action may then be resorted to. One would expect there to be a general rule that any award made in one jurisdiction would be deducted from an award stemming from the second claim. Thus, an award made by an employment tribunal will normally identify the various headings of loss in respect of which compensation is to be awarded, and double recovery of any particular loss would not be permitted in subsequent High Court proceedings. However, where the loss is in excess of the statutory compensation award, it may not always be possible to identify the particular heading awarded by the employment tribunal, and therefore there may not be an element of double recovery. Thus, in *O'Laoire v Jackel International* (see para 16.3), an employment tribunal held that the claimant had been unfairly dismissed, and assessed his loss at £100,000. However, they could only award compensation of £8,000, which was the maximum compensation award at that time. The claimant then brought an action in the High Court, and the judge held that the sum of £8,000 had to be deducted from the damages of £100,000. However, the Court of Appeal held that this was wrong. It was clearly not possible for the employment tribunal to assess the maximum compensation award with reference to any particular head of loss, and thus the rule against double recovery did not apply.

16.29 The general principle relating to any award of damages by a court is that they should be paid net of tax (*British Transport Commission v Gourley*[40]). However, the Income Tax (Earnings and Pensions) Act 2003, ss 401–404 provide that damages for wrongful dismissal are not taxable in the hands of the recipient unless they exceed £30,000. Thereafter, tax must be deducted at the employee's highest marginal rate. Thus a court must award a gross sum which, after tax, would leave the employee with a net sum which represents his loss.

Injunction and/or declaration

16.30 An employee who feels that he has been wrongfully dismissed may be able to bring an action for an injunction to restrain a breach of contract, or seek a declaration as to what are his rights under the contract. These are equitable remedies, and therefore will only be granted at the court's discretion. If an application is made for an interlocutory injunction pending the trial of the action, the principles laid down in *American Cyanamid Co v Ethicon* (see para 10.6) will apply, ie (a) has the claimant shown that there is a triable issue, and (b) does the balance of convenience favour the granting of the injunction? In particular, as we have seen (para 10.1), the courts will rarely grant an injunction if the effect is to compel specific performance of the contract. Exceptionally the court will do so in perhaps two circumstances, ie (a) if there is no loss of trust and confidence in the employee (*Powell v London Borough of Brent*, para 16.16) or (b) where the dismissal was in breach of natural justice or of a contractual disciplinary procedure (*Gunton v London Borough of Richmond*, paras 16.3 and 16.6). It must be shown that damages would not be an adequate remedy (*Wadcock v London Borough of Brent*, see para 10.2). A person seeking an injunction must first of all have pursued all internal remedies in so far as they are available (*R v BBC, ex p Lavelle*, see para 2.66).

16.31 Similarly, an employee may seek a declaration as to his contractual rights. This remedy will usually be sought when an employee refuses to accept a decision by an employer which is outside the terms of the contract. For example, in *Stevenson v United Road Transport Union*[41] an employee was dismissed without being given reasons (in breach of the contractual procedure), and a declaration was granted that the dismissal, in breach of

---

[40] [1956] AC 185, [1955] 3 All ER 796, [1956] 2 WLR 41, [1955] 2 Lloyd's Rep 475, 34 ATC 305, 49 R & IT 11, [1955] TR 303, 100 Sol Jo 12, HL.
[41] [1976] 3 All ER 29; aff'd [1977] 2 All ER 941, [1977] ICR 893, CA.

natural justice, was void. A declaration may be sought if an employer unilaterally reduces an employee's wages, or otherwise purports to act in breach of the contract (*Rigby v Ferodo Ltd*, see para 16.6). As with all equitable remedies, the employee must act expeditiously (*Dietman v London Borough of Brent*, paras 16.19 and 16.21).

Suing for breach of contract

16.32 An employee is not bound to accept a breach of contract which falls short of a wrongful constructive dismissal, and may, instead of suffering the breach in silence, sue for the loss suffered, while not accepting the alleged employer repudiation. Thus in *Rigby v Ferodo Ltd* (see para 16.6), the employee recovered damages for loss of wages when the employer unilaterally reduced his earnings; in *Miller v Hamworthy Engineering Ltd* (see paras 3.102 and 10.19) an employee recovered lost pay when put on short-time working without contractual authority; and in *Keir and Williams v Hereford and Worcester County Council*,[42] damages were awarded to employees when an employer withdrew their car allowance. The correct procedure in such cases is for the employer to give lawful termination of the contract (ie by giving the requisite period of notice) and then to offer the employees new contracts with new terms before the notice period expires. A unilateral variation of the contract, by itself, is not a termination and offer of re-engagement under a new contract (*Burdett-Coutts v Hertfordshire County Council*[43]). Thus by lawfully terminating the contract, the employer avoids any liability for wrongful dismissal, although it must be borne in mind that an employee's rights to claim unfair dismissal will be unaffected. Whether the dismissal is in fact fair or unfair will depend on all the circumstances of the case (see Chapter 17).

B. **Public law remedies**

16.33 An application may be made for judicial review, seeking to ensure that a public body carries out its public duties in a manner consistent with the legal requirements. Generally speaking, there are three grounds on which judicial review may be granted: (1) where the public body has acted illegally, ie contrary to the legal rights and duties of the parties; (2) where the public body has acted irrationally, ie where the decision arrived at was so outrageous that no sensible body or person acting responsibly could have reached that decision; and (3) where there has been a procedural impropriety, ie a failure to act with procedural fairness (*Council of Civil Service Unions v Minister for the Civil Service*,[44] per Lord Diplock). Generally speaking, judicial review is a challenge to the way in which a decision is made, rather than the correctness of the conclusion reached.

16.34 Attempts have been made by employees in the public sector to establish legal rights based on such principles, but with mixed success. The claim must be brought within the procedure laid down in the Civil Procedure Rules (judicial review) and the remedy is not generally available if a remedy based on contractual principles would suffice. There must be a further element of a public right or the enforcement of a public duty (*R v East Berkshire Health Authority, ex p Walsh*[45]).

---

[42] [1985] IRLR 505, (1985) 82 LSG 2823, (1985) *Times*, 17 June.

[43] [1984] IRLR 91.

[44] [1984] IRLR 309; revsd [1984] IRLR 353, CA; aff'd sub nom *Council of Civil Service Unions v Minister for the Civil Service* [1985] AC 374, [1984] 3 All ER 935, [1984] 3 WLR 1174, [1985] ICR 14, 128 Sol Jo 837, [1985] LS Gaz R 437, sub nom *R v Secretary of State for Foreign and Commonwealth Affairs, ex p Council of Civil Service Unions* [1985] IRLR 28, HL.

[45] [1985] QB 152, [1984] 3 All ER 425, [1984] 3 WLR 818, [1984] ICR 743, [1984] IRLR 278, 128 Sol Jo 664, [1984] LS Gaz R 2223, CA.

16.35 In *McLaren v Home Office*,[46] Woolf LJ suggested that there are four general principles which apply when an employee of a public body is proposing to proceed by way of judicial review: (1) in relation to personal claims against an employer, an employee of a public body is in the same situation as other employees; (2) however, if there exists some disciplinary or other body established under the Royal prerogative or a statute to which disputes can be referred, judicial review may be the appropriate remedy; (3) if an employee of a public body is adversely affected by a decision of general application, judicial review of that decision may be sought (see *R v Secretary of State, ex p Council of Civil Service Unions*, para 16.33); (4) if disciplinary procedures are of a domestic nature, judicial review will not be sought.

16.36 However, if a person is seeking to enforce a private right which has a public law element, he can pursue his claim through the normal procedure of issuing a writ, and is not required to seek redress by means of judicial review (*Roy v Kensington and Chelsea and Westminster Family Practitioner Committee*[47]). This is of particular importance if the public law issue is raised after the time for applying for judicial review has lapsed (*Doyle v Northumbria Probation Committee*[48]).

16.37 In Scotland, however, for historical reasons, the situation is slightly different. Scots law does not depend on a distinction between public and private law, but the court will accept jurisdiction by way of judicial review to regulate the process by which decisions are taken by a person or body to whom a power has been delegated by statute, agreement or other instrument, in order to ensure that the person or body does not exceed or abuse that power. But there must always be a tripartite relationship between the person or body to whom the power has been delegated, the person or body by whom it has been delegated, and the person for whose benefit the power is to be exercised. Strict contractual rights, such as those which exist between employer and employee, are not amenable to judicial review (*West v Secretary of State for Scotland*[49]), whether they occur in the public or the private sector. Thus where a local authority suspended a senior employee, it was exercising a power derived from the contract of employment, rather than from a statutory grant (*Blair v Lochaber District Council*[50]).

---

[46] [1990] COD 257, CA.

[47] [1989] 1 Med LR 10; on appeal [1990] 1 Med LR 328, CA; aff'd [1992] 1 AC 624, [1992] 1 All ER 705, [1992] 2 WLR 239, [1992] IRLR 233, 8 BMLR 9, [1992] 17 LS Gaz R 48, 136 Sol Jo LB 62, HL.

[48] [1991] 4 All ER 294, [1991] 1 WLR 1340, [1992] ICR 121, [1991] NLJR 855.

[49] [1992] IRLR 399, 1992 SC 385, 1992 SLT 636, 1992 SCLR 504, Ct of Sess.

[50] [1995] IRLR 135, Ct of Sess.

17

Unfair Dismissal

17.1 The statutory provisions relating to unfair dismissal are to be found in ss 94–107 of the Employment Rights Act 1996. The interpretation of those provisions by the courts and tribunals has led to thousands of reported decisions which have laid down guidelines varying from legal ingenuity, through sound common sense, and ending up, on occasions, with cabalistic mystery! But many decisions can only be explained on their own special facts and on a consideration of the actual evidence presented to the tribunal, and it must be borne in mind that employment tribunal decisions are not, in themselves, binding precedents. Sometimes the successful claimant will be awarded a reduced compensation because of his own contributory conduct, and there have been cases where a dismissal though unfair, has resulted in a nil award.

17.2 Nonetheless, the decisions of the reported cases repay detailed study. In the first place, they give guidance to a generalised stream of thought which is rapidly becoming dominant thinking in employment law; guidance on how an employer should act so as to be regarded as being reasonable and fair, guidance on how disciplinary procedures should be operated, and on when an employer may adopt standards which are less than those expected by a perfectionist. Secondly, the decided cases point out the pitfalls into which other employers have fallen, and thus enable a conscientious personnel manager so to direct his policies as to avoid those very traps. Finally, they provide interpretation of the legislative provisions which have a persuasive effect until a higher court has had an opportunity to pronounce on their validity.

17.3 Every employee to whom the Act applies has the right not to be unfairly dismissed, and the remedy for the infringement of that right is by way of a complaint to the employment tribunal, and not otherwise (ERA, s 94). This means that unfair dismissal cases must go to the employment tribunals, whereas a person who wishes to sue in respect of *wrongful dismissal* must bring the action in the ordinary courts in the normal way, or in the employment tribunal as appropriate (see para 16.4).

Exclusions

17.4 The following categories of employees are not protected by the unfair dismissal provisions of ERA:

- (a) any employment as a master or member of the crew of a fishing vessel where the employee is remunerated by a share of the profits;
- (b) merchant seamen may pursue claims for unfair dismissal provided they are employed to work on ships registered in Great Britain (ie excluding Northern Ireland, the Isle of Man and the Channel Islands) unless their employment is wholly outside Great Britain, or they are not ordinarily resident in Great Britain (ERA, s 199(7), (8)). In *Wood v Cunard Line Ltd*,[1] the claimant was engaged in Southampton, and then

---

[1] [1989] ICR 398, [1989] IRLR 431, [1989] LS Gaz R 42, EAT; aff'd [1991] ICR 13, [1990] IRLR 281, CA.

joined a ship which cruised around the Caribbean. It was held that his employment was wholly outside Great Britain.

Under the Employment Protection (Offshore Employment) Order 1976, employees who work in oil rigs and offshore installations in UK territorial waters or areas designated under the Continental Shelf Act 1964 are not excluded from the provisions of the Employment Rights Act 1996;

(c) apart from specific statutory provisions (see para 17.81) any employment where the employee has been continuously employed for less than two years (but see Table 13.1). The period of continuous employment begins with the day on which he is due to start work under the contract not from the date on which he actually commences work (*Salvation Army v Dewsbury, see* para 13.9). If notice of termination is given, the day on which the notice is given must be disregarded (*West v Kneels Ltd,* see para 15.7). As has been noted (see para 15.28), an employee who had been employed for one week less than the then qualifying period of one year, and is dismissed, is entitled to add to his computation the week's statutory notice to which he is entitled (s 97(2)), but not his contractual notice (see *Fox Maintenance Ltd v Jackson*, para 15.28). But if he is dismissed without notice for gross misconduct, he cannot rely on s 97(2) 'To pull him past the post' (*Ahmed v National Car Parks Ltd*[2])!

The fact that the reason for the dismissal is designated as 'gross misconduct' does not preclude the operation of s 97(2), for the employment tribunal can enquire into the facts on their merits, and decide whether in the circumstances the employer was entitled to terminate the contract without notice. If they decide that the employer was not so entitled, s 97(2) comes into operation (*Lanton Leisure Ltd v White and Gibson*[3]).

If a person is dismissed as a result of being suspended from work on medical grounds, s/he is only required to have one month's continuous employment (see ERA, s 64(2), para 7.7).

No qualifying period of employment is required in those cases where the dismissal is automatically unfair (see para 17.81);

(d) any employment covered by a dismissals procedure agreement which has been designated and approved by the Secretary of State. This enables an employer and an independent trade union to create their own dismissals procedure which, provided it conforms with the laid down criteria, may be approved by the Minister, and those employees covered by it are excluded from the provisions of the Act. There are no such agreements currently in force;

(e) an agreement to submit the dispute to arbitration under a scheme prepared by ACAS (see TULR(C)A, s 212A inserted by s 7 of the Employment Rights (Dispute Resolution) Act 1998) (see para 1.13);

(f) employees who work for foreign governments and other international organisations which enjoy diplomatic immunity (eg see *Gadhok v Commonwealth Secretariat*[4]) can only bring appropriate claims if that diplomatic immunity is waived; otherwise the employment tribunals have no jurisdiction (*Mukoro v European Bank for Reconstruction and Development*[5]). However, by the State Immunity Act 1978, a state is not immune in respect of proceedings relating to a contract of employment if (a) the contract was made in the United Kingdom, or (b) the work is to be wholly or partly performed in the United Kingdom. The Act does not apply if at the time of the claim the applicant was a national of the state

---

[2] IDS Brief 149.   [3] [1987] IRLR 119, EAT.
[4] (1977) 12 ITR 440, CA.   [5] [1994] ICR 897, EAT.

concerned, or at the time when the contract was made he was neither a national of the United Kingdom nor habitually resident here, or if the parties have agreed to exclude the provisions of the Act. In *Kücükdeveci v Swedex GmbH & Co KG*[6] and *Aklagaren v Fransson*,[7] however, the ECJ confirmed that where a fundamental principle of EU law is concerned, such as the right to a fair hearing, the UK courts must disapply a provision which stands in its way. This was done in *Benkharbouche v Sudan*,[8] where the State Immunity Act 1978 prevented domestic workers employed by two embassies from bringing claims. The EAT held that its provisions were to be disapplied by the Charter of Fundamental Rights of the European Union in relation to discrimination and working time claims. Further claims of unfair dismissal and the minimum wage were not covered, as they did not derive from EU law. The EAT effectively held that as a result of the Lisbon Treaty, the EU charter was now directly applicable in the UK, and the tribunal was therefore bound to disapply UK law which conflicted with these principles even between private litigants. It is likely that this case will be appealed;

(g) persons who serve as a member of a constabulary maintained by virtue of an enactment, or who have the powers or privileges of a constable (ERA, s 200). This includes members of the British Transport Police (*Spence v British Railways Board*[9]) but not prison officers (Criminal Justice and Public Order Act 1994, s 126);

(h) employees who work abroad (see Territorial Jurisdiction, para 1.30).

What is a dismissal? (ERA, s 95)

17.5 As a general rule, a dismissal is not effective until it has been communicated to the employee (*Widdicombe v Longcombe Software Ltd*[10]), and this long-standing principle was confirmed by the Supreme Court in *Gisda Cyf v Barratt*.[11] Thus if it is sent by post, it will be effective from the time when the employee has actually read the letter, or had a reasonable opportunity to do so. In *Brown v Southall and Knight* (see para 15.7) the employers sent a letter of dismissal to the claimant who, at that date, did not have the requisite period of continuous employment. He was away on holiday when the letter arrived, and thus did not read it until he returned a week later, by which time he had the necessary qualifying period. It was held that he was entitled to pursue his claim for unfair dismissal. Of course, if he deliberately did not open the letter, or went away in order to avoid reading it, he would have been debarred from saying that the notification of the dismissal was not given to him (see also *McMaster v Manchester Airport plc*[12]).

17.6 There are four ways in which a dismissal may take place.

A. **Employer termination**

17.7 Where the contract of employment is terminated by the employer, with or without notice. It follows that (subject to the doctrine of constructive dismissal, discussed at para 17.21) if an employee resigns of his own volition, there is no dismissal. In *Elliott v Waldair (Construction) Ltd*[13] the claimant was engaged as a driver, and mainly drove a heavy lorry. It was decided that this work was too hard for him, and he was instructed to drive a smaller van. This he refused to do because it would reduce his opportunity of overtime earnings,

---

[6] C-555/07.   [7] C-617/10.   [8] UKEAT/0401/12/GE, UKEAT/0020/13/GE.
[9] [2001] ICR 232, [2000] All ER (D) 1956, EAT.   [10] [1998] ICR 710, EAT.
[11] [2010] UKSC 41, SC.   [12] [1998] IRLR 112, 593 IRLB 17, EAT.   [13] [1975] IRLR 104.

and he resigned. It was held that the order to drive a different vehicle at the same hourly rate but with less opportunity to earn overtime could not be said to constitute a dismissal by the employer.

17.8 Equally, a mutually agreed termination does not amount to a dismissal. In *Harvey v Yankee Traveller Restaurant*,[14] the claimant became pregnant, and although her employer made various arrangements to accommodate her, these were not satisfactory. After a discussion with her employer, she agreed to resign. It was held that this could not amount to a dismissal. A warning that a dismissal is being contemplated in the future (eg for reason of impending redundancy etc) is not a dismissal (*Doble v Firestone Tyre and Rubber Co Ltd*[15]).

17.9 The fact that the employer invited the employee to resign may, however, constitute a dismissal, for the alternative may be expressed or implicit in the request. In *Robertson v Securicor Transport Ltd*[16] the claimant had broken a company rule by signing for a container which had not been received. When this was discovered, he was given the alternative of resigning or being dismissed, and he chose the respectable course. It was held that he had been dismissed nonetheless. But although a resignation under duress may be a dismissal (*East Sussex County Council v Walker*[17]), an invitation to resign as an alternative to facing a disciplinary hearing which may result in a dismissal is not, by itself, a dismissal (*Martin v Glynwed Distribution Ltd*[18]). If the choice is put to the employee 'perform your contract or resign' this is not a dismissal, for the employee is making a decision not to carry out the terms of the contract which the employer is legally entitled to expect.

17.10 To falsely inveigle an employee to resign may also amount to a dismissal (*Caledonian Mining Co Ltd v Bassett and Steel*[19]), and informing an employee that he has been taken off the payroll is a dismissal (*Kirklees Metropolitan Council v Radecki*[20]).

17.11 A dismissal can take place even though the employee invites this course of action. In *Thomas v General Industrial Cleaners Ltd*[21] the claimant was in poor health, but did not wish to resign because of fears that he might lose certain benefits. He left the decision to the employers, who accepted the initiative and terminated his employment. The tribunal held that there was a dismissal by the employers.

17.12 A dismissal takes place if an employer unilaterally imposes radically different terms of employment, which are so substantially different as to have the effect of destroying the basis of the old contract. In *Alcan Extrusions v Yates* (see para 3.103) the employers unilaterally made changes in working hours, shift systems, weekend and bank holiday workings, shift premiums etc. The employees agreed to work the new system under protest, reserving their rights to claim unfair dismissal and/or redundancy payments, which they subsequently did. An employment tribunal chairman held that they had been dismissed, and the decision was upheld by the EAT. It was not correct to argue that the imposition of contractual changes can only be characterised as a potentially repudiatory breach, giving the employee an option to resign and claim constructive dismissal. Substantial departures from the original contract constitutes a dismissal in its own right (but see *Bateman v Asda Stores Ltd*, para 3.87).

17.13 A warning of a possible dismissal in the future is not a dismissal. In *Rai v Somerfield Stores Ltd*,[22] the claimant was away from work. He was informed that if he did not return to

---

[14] [1976] IRLR 35.   [15] [1981] IRLR 300, EAT.   [16] [1972] IRLR 70.
[17] (1972) 7 ITR 280, NIRC.
[18] [1983] ICR 511, sub nom *Martin v MBS Fastenings (Glynwed) Distribution Ltd* [1983] IRLR 198, CA.
[19] [1987] ICR 425, [1987] IRLR 165, EAT.
[20] [2009] EWCA Civ 298, [2009] ICR 1244, [2009] IRLR 555.
[21] (3964/72) IDS Supp 21.   [22] [2004] IRLR 124, EAT.

work by 9 April he would be dismissed. He did not turn up at work on that date, but three days earlier, on 6 April, he presented a claim to an employment tribunal of unfair dismissal. It was held that the tribunal had no jurisdiction to hear the complaint. It had been presented three days before the termination of his employment, and was therefore premature. An employee may bring a complaint once notice has been given, even though it has not expired (ERA, s 111(3)), but in this case, he had not been dismissed with or without notice. He had merely been informed of the consequences which may follow if he failed to turn up for work, but dismissal was not inevitable, for the employer could still have unilaterally withdrawn the threat.

17.14 Traditionally, the words used by the employer to denote that a dismissal has taken place are usually quite clear and explicit, but the niceties of social intercourse are not always observed in real life. In *Kendrick v Aerduct Productions*,[23] the employer told an employee to 'fuck off'! Could this be construed as being equivalent to 'you're fired'? Or was it an expression of abuse with no other ulterior implication? If the words used are ambiguous, the employment tribunal must ask themselves, what would a reasonable man understand by the expression in the context of the industry and the surrounding circumstances? In *Futty v D and D Brekkes Ltd*[24] the employee was a fish filleter. During an altercation with the foreman he was told 'if you do not like the job, you can fuck off'. He took this as a dismissal, found another job and claimed compensation. It was held that in the context of the particular trade, the words meant no more than 'if you do not like the work you are doing, you can clock off'. Indeed, had the applicant not received a promise of another job, he would have gone back to work the following day, and hence he had resigned, and had not been dismissed. But there is little doubt that there can be circumstances where telling an employee to 'fuck off' will amount to a dismissal (*a fortiori*, telling him to 'fuck off and piss off', see *King v Webb's Poultry Products (Bradford) Ltd*[25]).

17.15 Equally, if the words used are unambiguous, the employment tribunal must give them their natural and ordinary meaning (*Sothern v Franks Charlesly & Co*[26]).

17.16 A further refinement on this theme was pursued in *Davy v Collins (Builders) Ltd*.[27] During an argument, the employer said to the employee 'if you are not satisfied, you can fuck off'. The employee left and brought a claim for unfair dismissal, which failed. With dialectic ingenuity the tribunal drew a distinction between an employer saying 'I am not satisfied, so you can fuck off', and 'if you are not satisfied, you can fuck off'. In the former case there is likely to be a dismissal; in the latter case, the employer is saying to the employee, 'If you don't like it, you can lump it' and the claimant, not liking it, lumped it!

17.17 It is thus not the actual words which are used which are significant, but the intention behind them, and this must be ascertained from all the surrounding circumstances and the accompanying words as well as the industry, the relationships between the parties, and so on (*J & J Stern v Simpson*[28]). If an employer or his manager, speaking in anger, behaves in a way which he might not do ordinarily, and utters abusive words, the employment tribunal should consider very carefully whether the words amount to a dismissal, or whether they were little more than abuse (*Chesham Shipping Ltd v Rowe*[29]). Events which followed the utterance of the offensive words and preceding the departure of the employee may be taken into account in so far as they throw light on the employer's intentions (*Tanner v DT Kean Ltd*[30]).

---

[23] [1974] IRLR 322.   [24] [1974] IRLR 130.   [25] [1975] IRLR 135.
[26] [1981] IRLR 278, CA.   [27] [1974] IRLR 324.   [28] [1983] IRLR 52, EAT.
[29] [1977] IRLR 391, EAT.   [30] [1978] IRLR 110, EAT.

17.18 Once a dismissal (or resignation) has taken place, it cannot be withdrawn unilaterally (*Harris and Russell Ltd v Slingsby,* see para 15.8), but words used in the heat of the moment, and withdrawn almost immediately may be ignored, for it is vital to good industrial relations that either the employer or the employee should be given the opportunity to recant (*Martin v Yeoman Aggregates Ltd*[31]).

B. Fixed-term contract expires

17.19 Where the employee is employed under a limited-term contract, a dismissal takes place if that term expires without being renewed under the same contract. But a dismissal which takes place in this manner must still be tested for fairness in terms of the reasonableness of the employer's action in not renewing the contract. Thus if there is a genuine need for an employee to have a fixed-term contract (eg of a temporary nature, or for a specific purpose, etc) then it may be reasonable not to renew this after expiry. It is important that employees should not be deprived of their statutory rights by dressing up an ordinary job as a fixed-term contract (*Terry v East Sussex County Council*[32]). Further, when a fixed-term contract expires, an employer may be acting unreasonably if he fails genuinely to consider the employee for employment in some other suitable post (*Labour Party v Oakley*[33]) (see the Fixed-Term Employees (Prevention of Less Favourable Treatment) Regulations 2002, para 2.128).

C. Completion of a limited-term contract

17.20 A limited-term contract is a contract which is not intended to be permanent and which will end either on the expiry of a fixed term, or on the performance of a specific task, or the occurrence of a specific event (or on the failure of an event to occur). If an employee is employed under such a contract which terminates by virtue of the limiting event without being renewed, this will amount to a dismissal under ERA. The effective date of termination is the date on which the termination takes effect.

D. Constructive dismissal

What amounts to constructive dismissal?

17.21 Where the employee himself terminates the contract, with or without notice, in circumstances where he is entitled to terminate it without notice by reason of the employer's conduct: this is known as 'constructive dismissal', for although the employee resigns, it is the employer's conduct which constitutes a repudiation of the contract, and the employee accepts that repudiation by resigning. The employee must clearly indicate that he is treating the contract as having been repudiated by the employer (*Logabax Ltd v Titherley*[34]), and if he fails to do so, by word or by conduct, he is not entitled to claim that he has been constructively dismissed (*Holland v Glendale Industries Ltd*[35]).

17.22 The doctrine of constructive dismissal has had a somewhat chequered history. The real problem was to determine the nature of the conduct of the employer which entitles the employee to resign. Did such conduct have to amount to an actual breach of contract by

---

[31] [1983] ICR 314, [1983] IRLR 49, EAT.

[32] [1977] 1 All ER 567, 75 LGR 111, [1976] ICR 536, [1976] IRLR 332, 12 ITR 265, EAT.

[33] [1987] ICR 178, [1987] IRLR 79, [1987] LS Gaz R 189, EAT; revsd [1988] ICR 403, sub nom *Oakley v Labour Party* [1988] IRLR 34, CA.

[34] [1977] ICR 369, [1977] IRLR 97, 12 ITR 158, EAT.   [35] [1998] ICR 493, EAT.

the employer, or could any unreasonable conduct by the employer be sufficient to entitle an employee to resign? For a long time the latter theory held sway, leading to some of the most bizarre and eccentric decisions in the whole of employment law. This view was firmly disposed of by the Court of Appeal in *Western Excavating (ECC) Ltd v Sharp*,[36] and earlier decisions must be read subject to this case. The facts were that the employee was dismissed for taking unauthorised time off work. He appealed to the internal disciplinary board, which substituted a penalty of five days' suspension without pay. This he accepted, but being short of money, he asked his employers if he could have an advance on his accrued holiday pay. This was refused. He then asked if he could have a loan of £40, but this too was refused. Consequently he resigned (in order to get his holiday pay) and brought a claim for unfair dismissal, alleging that he was forced to resign by virtue of the employer's conduct. His claim was upheld by the employment tribunal; the conduct of the employers was so unreasonable that the employee could not fairly be expected to put up with it, and justified him leaving. On appeal, the EAT was not sure that they would have come to the same decision had they heard the case, but held that the employment tribunal were entitled to come to that decision. This was reversed by the Court of Appeal. The test for constructive dismissal was to be determined by the contract test, ie did the employer's conduct amount to a breach of contract which entitled the employee to resign. The 'unreasonable conduct' theory was dismissed as leading to a finding of constructive dismissal on the most whimsical grounds. Since there had been no breach of contract by the employers in *Sharp's* case (for the employers were under no contractual obligation to make the payments which were requested) there was no dismissal, constructive or otherwise.

17.23 It follows, therefore, that only those cases where the employer's conduct amounts to a significant breach, going to the root of the contract, can be regarded as being authoritative. There must be a fundamental breach of contract by the employer, not merely a failure to act reasonably (*Wadham Stringer Commercials (London) Ltd v Brown*[37]). Thus, if the employer tries to impose a unilateral change in employment terms, such as a change in the job, a significant change in hours (*Simmonds v Dowty Seals Ltd*[38]), a lowering in earnings (*RF Hill Ltd v Mooney*[39]), a significant change in the location of employment (*Courtaulds Northern Spinning Ltd v Sibson*[40]), a demotion, then provided there is no contractual right to do so, such conduct will entitle an employee to resign. But a failure to pay salary on the due date was held not to have been so serious a breach in *Adams v Charles Zub Associates Ltd*.[41] The employer's action did not show an intention not to be bound by the contract. It should be noted that an employer cannot cure a repudiatory breach of contract before an employee decides to resign (*Bournemouth University Higher Education Corporation v Buckland*).[42]

17.24 An employer may cure a breach of contract before it becomes repudiatory. In *Assamoi v Spirit Pub Company*,[43] an employer accepted a worker's grievance, and so the worker no longer had a breach on which to resign.

17.25 It must be borne in mind that although a constructive dismissal may amount to a dismissal in law, whether the dismissal is fair or unfair has still to be determined by the facts of the case, and whether or not the employer has acted reasonably (*Industrial Rubber Products v Gillon*[44]).

---

[36] [1978] QB 761, [1978] 1 All ER 713, [1978] 2 WLR 344, [1978] ICR 221, [1978] IRLR 27, 121 Sol Jo 814, CA.

[37] [1983] IRLR 46, EAT.   [38] [1978] IRLR 211, EAT.   [39] [1981] IRLR 258, EAT.

[40] [1984] ICR 218, [1984] IRLR 43, EAT.   [41] [1978] IRLR 551, EAT.

[42] [2010] EWCA Civ 121, [2010] ICR 908.   [43] UKEAT/0050/11.

[44] [1977] IRLR 389, 13 ITR 100, EAT.

Genuine dispute over contract

17.26 If there is a genuine dispute concerning the nature of the parties' contractual obligations, this does not indicate an intention on the part of the employer to break the contract, and hence this will not be grounds for claiming constructive dismissal. In *Frank Wright & Co Ltd v Punch*[45] the claimant claimed that he was entitled to receive cost of living increases in his salary. The employers disputed that they were contractually obliged to pay, and so he resigned, claiming constructive dismissal. The EAT held that where there was a genuine dispute as to the construction of a contract, or a genuine mistake as to fact or law, the courts would be unwilling to hold that an expression of intent by a party to carry out the contract in accordance with his (possibly erroneous) interpretation amounts to a repudiation of that contract. However, more recently it has been held that what is significant in constructive dismissal cases is the impact of the employer's conduct on the employee, rather than on what the employer intended. The impact has to be assessed objectively (*Parsons v Bristol Street Motors*[46]). It has to be shown that the employer did not intend to be bound by the contract, as properly construed (*Bridgen v Lancashire County Council*[47]).

Employer's breach of an implied term

17.27 More difficult are those cases where the employee claims he is entitled to resign because the employer has broken an implied term of the contract (see para 3.34) because the nature of these terms may sometimes be a matter for speculation and conjecture. In *British Aircraft Corpn v Austin*[48] a failure to investigate a complaint about the inadequacy of protective spectacles was held to be a breach of the employer's implied duty to take reasonable care for the employee's safety, and in *Graham Oxley Tool Steels Ltd v Firth*[49] it was held that there was an implied term that the employer will provide a proper working environment. If no reasonable employer would have expected the employee to work in those conditions, then there is a fundamental breach of the contract of employment (*Dutton & Clark Ltd v Daly*[50]). It will be recalled that there is an implied duty of mutual respect, and therefore any action by or on behalf of the employer which runs contrary to that duty may amount to constructive dismissal. This could be the use of foul and abusive language (*Palmanor Ltd v Cedron,* see para 14.4), making unjustifiable complaints or giving unjustified warnings (*Walker v Josiah Wedgwood*[51]), making statements which destroy or seriously damage the relationship of trust and confidence which must exist between the parties (*Courtaulds Northern Textiles Ltd v Andrew,* see para 2.4), such as ill-founded allegations of theft (*Robinson v Crompton Parkinson Ltd,* see para 3.43), offensive and insensitive conduct by a supervisor (*Hilton International Hotels (UK) Ltd v Protopapa*[52]), and so on.

17.28 There is no implied term in a contract which entitles an employee to facilities for smoking, and if an employer introduces a general rule which has the effect of banning smoking on the premises, this does not operate so as to frustrate the employee's attempt to perform the contract because he cannot comply with the rule. Such a rule has a legitimate purpose, and the fact that it bears hard on a particular individual does not warrant an inference that the employer had repudiated the contract so as to enable the employee to claim he has been constructively dismissed (*Dryden v Greater Glasgow Health Board,* see para 3.90). Indeed, it is more likely that there is an implied term that the employer will provide a safe working environment, and a non-smoker who is forced to work in areas where he would be affected

[45] [1980] IRLR 217, EAT.   [46] Employment Appeal Tribunal, 28 February 2008.
[47] [1987] IRLR 58, CA.   [48] [1978] IRLR 332, EAT.   [49] [1980] IRLR 135, EAT.
[50] [1985] ICR 780, [1985] IRLR 363, EAT.
[51] [1978] ICR 744, [1978] IRLR 105, 13 ITR 271, EAT.   [52] [1990] IRLR 316, EAT.

by the smoking habits of other employees can claim constructive dismissal for a breach of that term (*Waltons & Morse v Dorrington*[53]). For 'no smoking' rules generally, see para 11.87.

17.29 Even if there is an express term in the contract enabling an employer to transfer the employee to another location, there is an implied term that the employer will give reasonable notice of the transfer and, where appropriate, relocation and other allowances will be made, so as to make it feasible for the employee to comply with the contractual obligation to transfer (*United Bank Ltd v Akhtar*, see para 3.24).

17.30 A further problem arises when the employer makes life as difficult or as uncomfortable as possible, in the hope (or expectation) that the hint will be taken, and the employee will resign. No doubt a great deal will depend on the extent of the evidence which shows whether or not the employer is in breach of an express or implied term of the contract. Situations do occur when the parties wish to part company, but the employer is scared to take the initiative for fear of having a claim being brought against him, and the employee is reluctant to resign without at least having an opportunity to collect some financial reward which is available under modern legislative provisions. It is here that the vagaries of the doctrine of constructive dismissal present the greatest menace, for the uncertainties are enormous.

17.31 In *Haseltine Lake & Co v Dowler*[54] the claimant was told that there was no future with the firm for him and that he should seek another job elsewhere. Eventually he found another job, resigned his employment and claimed he had been constructively dismissed.

The EAT rejected his claim. No date had been fixed by the employers for his resignation, and before a contract of employment can terminate, there must be an ascertainable date on which it came to an end. This was not a case of 'resign or you will be dismissed', and therefore there was no repudiation of the contract by the employers.

17.32 Although the 'implied term' theory has effectively replaced the unreasonable conduct test, it can be just as capricious and whimsical in its results. In *FC Gardner Ltd v Beresford* (see paras 3.2 and 3.43) an employee resigned because she had not had a pay increase for two years, whereas other employees had. It was held that although there was no express term of the contract relating to pay increases, in most cases it was possible to imply a term that an employer would not treat an employee capriciously, arbitrarily or inequitably in matters of remuneration. The EAT remitted the case to the employment tribunal to ascertain whether or not in fact the employer had thus treated the employee, and if so, there would be a good claim for constructive dismissal under the test in *Western Excavating (ECC) Ltd v Sharp* (para 17.22).

17.33 But this does not mean that a failure to give an annual pay rise to an employee is a breach of contract, for it is impossible to say that there is an implied term to that effect. The test is whether such failure is arbitrary and capricious. Thus, if the employer can show a good reason, such as inadequate performance by the employee, there is no breach of the duty of mutual trust and confidence (*Murco Petroleum Ltd v Forge*[55]).

17.34 A constructive dismissal situation arises when the employer, without reasonable and proper cause, conducts himself in a manner calculated or likely to destroy or seriously damage the relationship of trust and confidence which must exist between the parties (*Malik v BCCI SA*[56]). A repudiatory breach of contract, once it has happened, cannot be cured by

---

[53] [1997] IRLR 488, EAT.   [54] [1981] ICR 222, [1981] IRLR 25, EAT.
[55] [1987] ICR 282, [1987] IRLR 50, EAT.
[56] [1998] AC 20, [1997] 3 WLR 95, [1997] 3 All ER 1, [1997] ICR 606, [1997] IRLR 462, (1997) 94(25) LSG 33, (1997) 147 NLJ 917, (1997) *Times*, 13 June, (1997) *Independent*, 20 June.

the contract breaker. Thus even though the employer attempts to 'cure' the breach before the employee resigns, there is no room for the argument that what the employer did was within the range of reasonable responses, for to do so would take away the innocent party's option of accepting the breach and resigning in response to it (*Buckland v Bournemouth University*[57]). (However, see *Assamoi v Spirit Pub Company*[58] where an employer was able to cure a breach *before* it became repudiatory, para 17.23.)

17.35 Occasionally, the 'unreasonable conduct' test makes a reappearance in a new disguise. It will be recalled that in constructive dismissal cases, one must look for the breach of contract. There is generally no difficulty in ascertaining the express terms, but legal authorities are clear that the implied terms are discovered by looking at what was 'obvious', so obvious in fact that the parties omitted to insert them (para 3.38). However, in *Pepper and Hope v Daish* (see para 3.48) the EAT took the view that it was possible to imply a term into a contract if it was 'reasonable' to do so! In this case the applicant negotiated a personal hourly wage rate for himself in December 1978. In January 1979 there was a general increase for all hourly workers of 5%, but this was not given to the claimant. He resigned and claimed constructive dismissal. It was held that he could succeed, on the basis that it was reasonable to imply a term into his contract that he would also be given general wage increases. It will be noted that the reasoning in this case is inconsistent with the later decision in *Frank Wright & Co (Holdings) Ltd v Punch* (para 17.26) for there appeared to be a genuine dispute as to the interpretation of the contract.

17.36 Unreasonable conduct by an employer does not, by itself, constitute constructive dismissal. The conduct must be such as to amount to a breach of contract, ie conduct which fundamentally undermines the employment relationship (*Claridge v Daler Rowney Ltd*[59]).

17.37 The EAT returned to orthodoxy in *White v Reflecting Roadstuds Ltd* (see para 3.24). Here, the employee was working in the employer's despatch department but, at his own request, he was transferred to the mixing department, which involved higher pay, but also harder work. After about a year, he requested a move to lighter work, which was not then possible. From then on, his attendance deteriorated, and, after being given a formal warning, he was transferred to the pressing department, which involved a considerable drop in his pay. He then resigned, claiming that the decision to move him to another department constituted a fundamental breach of his contract of employment. In their defence, the company pointed to a flexibility clause in the contract which gave them the right to transfer employees to alternative work if the requirements of operational efficiency so dictate, and also that a willingness of employees to do so was a condition of the contract. An employment tribunal held that the express right to transfer from one department to another was subject to two implied terms, namely (a) that it would be exercised in a reasonable manner, and (b) that the transfer would not result in a unilateral reduction in the employee's pay. On appeal, the EAT reversed the decision on both grounds. On the first point, the EAT stated that to imply a term that a flexibility or mobility clause should be handled reasonably would be to introduce the 'reasonableness' test into constructive dismissal cases by the back door and would fly in the face of the authority of *Western Excavating (ECC) Ltd v Sharp* (paras 17.22 and 17.32). Although a 'capricious' decision would not create any difficulty (*United Bank Ltd v Akhtar*, para 17.29), if there are sufficient grounds for operating the clause, the employers are entitled to reach such decisions. On the second point, it was held that if an employer acts within the contract, the fact that the change results in a unilateral reduction in the employee's pay does not constitute a fundamental breach of the contract (see *Spafax Ltd v Harrison*[60]).

[57] [2010] EWCA Civ 121, [2010] IRLR 445, (2010) *Times*, 3 May.   [58] UKEAT/0050/11.
[59] [2008] ICR 1267, [2008] IRLR 672.   [60] [1980] IRLR 442, CA.

17.38 Also, if the employer is in breach, but the employee does not resign, and subsequently alleges a further breach, the employment tribunal should take into account the whole of the employer's conduct, and not merely the latest incident which led to the resignation (*Lewis v Motorworld Garages Ltd*[61]) If the employee does resign, it has to be in response, at least in part, to the fundamental breach of contract by the employer (*Meikle v Nottinghamshire County Council*[62]), The tribunal does not have to find a *principal* reason otherwise (*Logan v Celyn House Ltd*[63]).

17.39 If an employee resigns, claiming that the employer has broken the implied term of trust and confidence, can the employer counter this by arguing that in fact the employee was in breach of the same term? In *Aberdeen City Council v McNeill*[64] the employee was accused of bullying, sexual harassment and intoxication at work. The disciplinary procedure was invoked, but the employee resigned, claiming that it was being conducted oppressively, and thus in breach of the implied term of trust and confidence. The employers countered this by arguing that in fact it was the employee who was in breach of the term, and thus he had lost the right to claim constructive dismissal, because there was no trust and confidence left for the employer to breach! The EAT held that the claimant's prior breach meant that he was not entitled to terminate his contract on the basis that his employer had breached the same term.

17.40 Lawful conduct by an employer is not capable of constituting a repudiation (*Spafax Ltd v Harrison*, para 17.37). Thus a disciplinary transfer, carried out in accordance with a proper procedure, which results in an employee suffering a drop in his earnings, is not a constructive dismissal (*High v British Railways Board*, see para 12.87). Nor can an employee claim constructive dismissal merely because he is moved away from that part of his job which he enjoys the most on to less interesting work, if he is contractually obliged to do that work (*Peter Carnie & Son Ltd v Paton*[65]). However, a disciplinary sanction which is disproportionate to the offence, even though carried out in accordance with the terms of the contract, can be a constructive dismissal (*BBC v Beckett*, para 12.86).

17.41 If an employer gives lawful notice, this is not a breach of trust and confidence so as to enable an employee to claim constructive dismissal. In *Kerry Foods Ltd v Lynch*[66] the employer wanted an employee to change from five days a week to six days, but the employee refused to do so. His employer then stated that he would be given lawful notice to terminate the contract, and then be re-engaged immediately on the new terms. Before the notice expired, the employee resigned and claimed constructive dismissal. His claim failed. There was no breach of contract by the employer.

17.42 Since the employee is claiming that the employer has broken the contract, he must resign as a result of that breach (*Holland v Glendale Industries*, para 17.21). If he continues to report to work, he may be deemed to have waived the breach, and can hardly bring a claim subsequently based on the employer's repudiation, for 'the law does not allow him to have his cake and eat it' (*Hunt v British Railways Board*[67]). But if he protests about the breach, but stays on until he finds himself another job, he may not necessarily be deemed to have accepted the employer's breach (*Miller v Shanks & McEwan*[68]) provided that he acts reasonably expeditiously (*WE Cox Toner (International) Ltd v Crook*[69]). But a distinction must be drawn between the waiver of a breach and the non-waiver of a continuing breach.

---

[61] [1986] ICR 157, [1985] IRLR 465, CA.   [62] [2005] ICR 1.   [63] UKEAT/0069/12/JOJ.
[64] [2010] IRLR 374.   [65] [1979] IRLR 260, EAT.   [66] [2005] IRLR 680.
[67] [1979] IRLR 379, EAT.   [68] IDS Handbook 12.   [69] [1981] ICR 823, [1981] IRLR 443, EAT.

17.43 If there is a series of breaches which lead the employee to look for another job before handing in his notice, the employment tribunal must consider whether those breaches were the effective cause of a resignation. They do not have to be the sole cause. If the taking of other employment was the consequence of the breaches, then the employee can claim he has been constructively dismissed (*Jones v Sirl & Son (Furnishers) Ltd*[70]). Harassment can also result in a claim for constructive dismissal, on the basis that the mutual trust and confidence that should exist between employer and employee has broken down (*Blackburn with Darwen Borough Council v Stanley*).

17.44 Constructive dismissal may occur in a 'last straw' situation. In *Lewis v Motorworld Garages Ltd* (see para 17.38) it was stated that the breach of the implied obligation of trust and confidence may consist of a series of actions on the part of the employer which cumulatively amount to a breach of the term, even though each individual incident may not do so. The 'last straw' need not itself be a breach of contract by the employer, but it must contribute, however slightly, to the sustained breach of the implied term of trust and respect. An entirely innocent act by the employer cannot be the 'last straw', even if the employee mistakenly interprets it in that light (*Omilaju v Waltham Forest London Borough Council*[71]).

17.45 When considering the 'last straw' argument in a constructive dismissal case, it is important for the employment tribunal to identify the 'last straw' act, and then consider, objectively, whether cumulatively with the earlier acts a breach of the implied term of trust and confidence has occurred (*Wishaw & District Housing Association v Moncrieff*[72]).

17.46 If the employer announces an intention to break the contract at a future date, and the employee does not accept the breach, it is open to the employer to inform the employee that the contract will be performed. The employee will thus lose the right to claim constructive dismissal (*Norwest Holst Group Administration Ltd v Harrison*[73]). On the other hand, if the employee accepts the constructive dismissal, and gives notice to terminate the contract, conduct between the resignation and termination can be taken into account when assessing compensation (*Peterborough Regional College v Gidney*[74]).

Constructive dismissal be fair dismissal

17.47 It must be stressed that the fact that there is constructive dismissal does not necessarily mean that the dismissal is unfair (*Ford v Milthorn Toleman Ltd*[75]), and there have been a number of cases where a constructive dismissal has been held to be a fair dismissal (eg *Savoia v Chiltern Herb Farms Ltd*[76]). Thus if an employer demotes an employee, without contractual authority, this will amount to a constructive dismissal, but if the demotion was brought about by a well-founded suspicion of dishonesty, the dismissal may be fair (*Hilton v Shiner Ltd*, see paras 3.48 and 10.11). Even if it is unfair, compensation may still be reduced for contributory conduct. An employer faced with a constructive dismissal claim should be prepared to fight it on two fronts: (a) he may argue that there was no dismissal, and (b) in the alternative, if there was a dismissal, it was fair because...etc. A failure to adopt this course may result in a finding that there was a (constructive) dismissal, and, if no reason for the dismissal is advanced, it must automatically be unfair (*Derby City Council v Marshall*[77]). Whether an employer's conduct amounts to a constructive dismissal

[70] [1997] IRLR 493, EAT.   [71] [2004] EWCA Civ 1493, [2005] IRLR 35, CA.
[72] UKEATS/0066/08.
[73] [1984] IRLR 419, EAT; aff'd [1985] ICR 668, sub nom *Harrison v Norwest Holst Group Administration Ltd* [1985] IRLR 240, CA.
[74] EAT 1270/97, 1270A/97.   [75] [1980] IRLR 30, CA.
[76] [1981] IRLR 65, EAT; aff'd [1982] IRLR 166, CA.   [77] [1979] ICR 731, [1979] IRLR 261, EAT.

is a question of fact for the employment tribunal to determine (*Woods v W M Car Services (Peterborough) Ltd*[78]).

17.48 A failure to follow a grievance procedure is not, by itself, relevant in a constructive dismissal claim, because it is the conduct of the employer which is in issue (*Tolson v Mixenden Community School*[79]). In *Amnesty International v Ahmed*[80] (see para 4.144) it was held that although an employer's actions constituted unlawful race discrimination, this did not mean that there was a breach of the implied term of trust and respect. The employer had not acted without reasonable or proper cause, and the conduct in question was not calculated to destroy the relationship of trust and confidence that must exist between the parties.

Termination of the contract

17.49 There are a number of ways in which a contract may come to an end, but which do not amount to a dismissal in law.

A. Resignation

17.50 If an employee resigns, then (unless it is a constructive dismissal) he has not been dismissed. If the words used by the employee are clear and unambiguous (eg 'I am leaving, I want my P45') then there are no grounds for the employment tribunal to find that the words have a significance other than their plain meaning (*BG Gale Ltd v Gilbert*[81]). If the words are ambiguous, then the test is, what would a reasonable employer have understood by those words in that context (*Tanner v Kean Ltd*, para 17.17)? If an employee is threatened that if he does not resign he will be dismissed, a consequent resignation will amount to a dismissal, but if his resignation is brought about by other factors, such as an offer of a financial inducement, this is not a dismissal (*Sheffield v Oxford Controls Co Ltd*[82] but see *Sandhu v Jan de Rijk Transport Ltd*,[83] para 17.72).

17.51 Words spoken or action taken by an employee in the heat of the moment or under extreme pressure should not necessarily be taken at face value. The employer should allow a reasonable time to elapse before accepting such an apparent resignation to see whether this was what was really intended. If the employer fails to make a proper investigation, he runs the risk that an employment tribunal may hold that there are special circumstances where the apparent resignation was not really intended by the employee (*Kwik-Fit (GB) Ltd v Lineham*, para 15.8).

17.52 For a resignation to be effective to terminate the contract there must be an ascertainable date (express or implied) on which it will take effect. To say 'I am resigning at some future point in time' is a statement of intention, not a resignation, but to say 'I am resigning' is not ambiguous, for it indicates a present intention (*Sothern v Franks Charlesly & Co*, para 17.15). An employment tribunal is entitled to conclude on the evidence that the words of apparent resignation used by the employee 'in the heat of the moment' should not be accepted at their face value (*Sovereign House Security Services Ltd v Savage*[84]).

---

[78] [1981] ICR 666, [1981] IRLR 347, EAT; aff'd [1982] ICR 693, [1982] IRLR 413, [1982] Com LR 208, CA.
[79] [2003] IRLR 842, [2003] All ER (D) 312 (Oct), EAT.
[80] [2009] ICR 1450, [2009] IRLR 884, (2009) 159 NLJ 1400, (2009) *Times*, 6 October.
[81] [1978] ICR 1149, [1978] IRLR 453, 13 ITR 547, EAT.   [82] [1979] ICR 396, [1979] IRLR 133, EAT.
[83] [2007] EWCA Civ 430, [2007] IRLR 519, (2007) 104(21) LSG 27, (2007) 151 SJLB 672, [2007] ICR 1137.
[84] [1989] IRLR 115, CA.

17.53 If the employee indicates an intention to resign, but in terms which are somewhat equivocal, so that the position is mistakenly construed by the employer as a resignation, although the employee has not in fact resigned, this can be relied upon by the employer for the purpose of supplying an employment tribunal a potentially fair reason for the dismissal (for some other substantial reason, see para 17.149) even though, in error, the employer is seeking to hold the employee to the alleged resignation. What matters are the facts which led to the dismissal/resignation, not the precise label put on it by the employer (*Ely v YKK Fasteners (UK) Ltd*[85]).

17.54 A resignation does not have to be accepted by the employer, nor can it be withdrawn unilaterally. If an employee gives notice to terminate his employment and, during the notice period, the employer releases the employee from serving the full notice period, there is no dismissal by the employer. All that has happened is that the employee is no longer required to attend work (*Tom Findlay & Co Ltd v Devlin*[86]).

17.55 Whether an employee has resigned or was dismissed is a question of fact for the employment tribunal to determine, and their findings cannot be challenged unless their conclusions were such that no reasonable employment tribunal could have reached them (*Martin v Glynwed Distribution Ltd,* para 17.9).

B. Constructive resignation

17.56 If a breach of contract by the employer entitles the employee to resign and claim constructive dismissal, then why should not a breach of contract by the employee entitle the employer to claim that the contract has been terminated by 'constructive resignation'? This view was supported by a number of decisions by the EAT and employment tribunals, but must be discounted in the light of the decision of the Court of Appeal in *London Transport Executive v Clarke* (see para 3.36), and all earlier decisions must be read in the light of this case. The facts were that Clarke wanted to go to Jamaica on extended unpaid leave, but permission was refused by the employers as he had already exhausted his entitlement under the rules. When he asked what would happen if he went without permission he was told that his name would be removed from the books. Nonetheless he went to Jamaica, stayed for seven weeks, and on his return he submitted a medical note, which the employment tribunal viewed 'with some surprise'. While he was away, the employers wrote to his home address, stating that if no reply was received within 14 days, it would be assumed that he did not wish to continue his employment, and eventually his name was removed from the books. When he returned from Jamaica, he applied for his job back, and when this was refused, he claimed he had been unfairly dismissed. For the employers, it was argued that the applicant had 'resigned' but this view was rejected. It is trite law that if a person breaks a contract, the other party has two options; he can either accept the breach, and treat the contract as being at an end, or refuse to do so, and treat the contract as still subsisting. If he accepts the breach, he terminates the contract. Thus Clarke had been dismissed, and had not resigned. However, the Court of Appeal then went on to find that the dismissal, in the circumstances, was fair.

17.57 There is no doubt that this analysis is correct. The reason for the doctrine of constructive dismissal is because there is a statutory provision for it (ERA, s 95(1)(c)). There is no statutory doctrine of constructive resignation. Thus if an employee walks out of his job, or commits any other breach of contract, but nonetheless claims that he is entitled to resume his work, the employer must expressly or impliedly accept the repudiation, and this

---

[85] [1993] IRLR 500, CA.   [86] Employment Appeal Tribunal (Scotland), 9 November 2007.

will constitute a dismissal. He must then satisfy the employment tribunal that in the circumstances, having regard to the equity and substantial merits of the case, he acted reasonably in treating the repudiatory conduct as sufficient reason for dismissing the employee.

C. Implied resignation

17.58 However, it is submitted that there may be circumstances of implied resignation or resignation by conduct. Thus, if an employee disappears, and does not respond to the employer's communications, or if it is discovered that the employee is working for another employer, it may not be difficult to infer that he has resigned his employment. The point was made by Sir John Donaldson in *Harrison v George Wimpey & Co Ltd*. 'Where an employee so conducts himself as to lead a reasonable employer to believe that the employee has terminated the contract, the contract is then terminated.'[87]

D. Frustration of the contract

17.59 If the performance of the contract of employment is rendered impossible by some intervening event, then it will be terminated by frustration, not by dismissal. In *Anyanwu v South Bank Student Union* (see para 4.203) the claimant was a salaried officer of the student union. He was expelled from the university and excluded from its premises, whereupon the student union treated his contract of employment as being at an end. A claim for unlawful discrimination was dismissed by an employment tribunal, and the decision was upheld on appeal. Impossibility of performance meant that the contract ended by frustration. Frustration can only arise where there is no fault by either party, eg where accident or illness prevents the employee (or employer) from performing the contract. Where there is fault by one party, this is repudiatory conduct, not frustration although there is a view that this could be self-induced frustration. It is thus up to the other party to accept the repudiation and terminate the contract, or keep the contract open, as he chooses (*London Transport Executive v Clarke*, para 17.56). Clearly, if the repudiatory conduct was serious (eg being sent to prison) it would be rare for the dismissal to be categorised as being unfair (*Norris v Southampton City Council*[88]).

17.60 There are two situations which commonly occur, and which may give rise to the doctrine of frustration. The first is long-term absence through accident or illness (*Notcutt v Universal Equipment Co (London) Ltd*[89]), the second is imprisonment (*FC Shepherd & Co Ltd v Jerrom*[90]).

17.61 To decide whether or not a contract will terminate by frustration, regard must be had to the length of time the employee is likely to be away from his work, and thus be unable to perform his contract, the need for the employer to obtain a replacement, the length of time he has been employed, his position, and so forth. In cases where the employee is absent for a long time through sickness, all these factors are relevant, and in addition the employer must consider the nature of the illness (or injury), how long it has continued and the prospects for recovery, as well as the terms of the contract, including the provision of sick pay (see *Marshall v Harland and Wolff Ltd*[91]). The mere absence from work, even for a

[87] (1972) 7 ITR 188, NIRC.   [88] [1982] ICR 177, [1982] IRLR 141, EAT.
[89] [1986] 3 All ER 582, [1986] 1 WLR 641, [1986] ICR 414, [1986] IRLR 218, 130 Sol Jo 392, [1986] LS Gaz R 1314, [1986] NLJ Rep 393, CA.
[90] [1985] ICR 552, [1985] IRLR 275, [1985] LS Gaz R 2162, EAT; revsd [1987] QB 301, [1986] 3 All ER 589, [1986] 3 WLR 801, [1986] ICR 802, [1986] IRLR 358, 130 Sol Jo 665, CA.
[91] [1972] 2 All ER 715, [1972] 1 WLR 899, [1972] ICR 101, [1972] IRLR 90, 7 ITR 150, 115 Sol Jo 484, NIRC.

long time, will not automatically constitute frustration. Thus in *Maxwell v Walter Howard Designs Ltd*[92] the claimant was away sick for nearly two years, during which time he sent in regular sick notes. His job, as a cabinet maker, was one which did not need to be filled by a permanent replacement, and so, despite the passage of time, it was held that the contract had not been frustrated.

17.62 But if it is clear that on the medical evidence, the employee is unlikely to return to work for a considerable time, then there must come a point at which the employer is entitled to decide that the employee will not be returning to work, and consequently treat the contract as being frustrated. The problem is, when, exactly, does that point in time come about, and to this question there is no easy answer (see *Scarr v FW Goodyear & Sons Ltd*[93]). In employment cases, the courts and tribunals must guard against too easy an application of the doctrine of frustration, especially when redundancy occurs, or where the true reason for the dismissal is disability (*Williams v Watsons Luxury Coaches Ltd*[94]).

17.63 In *Egg Stores (Stamford Hill) Ltd v Leibovici*,[95] the EAT stated that there may be a long process before it can be said that illness has brought about a frustration of the contract. But if the time arrives when one can say that matters have gone on for so long, and the prospects for future employment are so poor, that it is no longer practical to consider the contract as still subsisting, then frustration will occur. Among the matters to be taken into account to reach this conclusion are (1) the length of the employment, (2) how long it would have been expected to continue, (3) the nature of the job, (4) the nature, length and effect of the illness, (5) the need to appoint a permanent replacement, (6) the risk to the employer of acquiring further obligations in respect of redundancy payments or unfair dismissals, (7) whether wages are still being paid, (8) the acts and statements of the employer in relation to the employee, including his failure to dismiss, and (9) whether in all the circumstances a reasonable employer could be expected to wait for the employee any longer. To this we may add (a) the terms of the contract as to sick pay, and (b) a consideration of the prospects of recovery (*Williams v Watsons Luxury Coaches Ltd*).

17.64 That none of these tests, by themselves, can be conclusive can be seen from the decision in *Hart v AR Marshall & Sons (Bulwell) Ltd*[96] where the claimant became sick in April 1974. In August of that year, the employers engaged a permanent replacement but the claimant continued to send in sick notes. In January 1976 he presented himself for work, but was told there was no job for him, and he was given his cards. He claimed that this constituted unfair dismissal, but the EAT upheld a tribunal finding that the contract had been frustrated. The failure by the employers to act on the absence by dismissing the claimant was not, by itself, evidence that they will continue to regard him as an employee. Otherwise an employer would be in a difficult situation with regard to a sick employee; if he dismissed him prematurely, this might be unfair, if he engaged a temporary replacement, he might have to pay compensation at the end of that contract in order to permit the sick employee to return to work. Nor was the fact that the employee continued to send in sick notes indicative of anything other than that the employee was keeping in touch in case there was a prospect of future employment. The crucial factor appears to be the finding that the claimant occupied a key position, which had to be filled, and thus the contract was frustrated.

17.65 If it is clear that the employee is permanently unfit to do his job, the contract will be frustrated. The fact that the employer keeps the employee 'on the books' may be an

---

[92] [1975] IRLR 77.   [93] [1975] IRLR 166.   [94] [1990] ICR 536, [1990] IRLR 164, EAT.
[95] [1977] ICR 260, [1976] IRLR 376, 11 ITR 289, EAT.
[96] [1978] 2 All ER 413, [1977] 1 WLR 1067, [1977] ICR 539, [1977] IRLR 51, 12 ITR 190, 121 Sol Jo 677, EAT.

arrangement which falls short of a contract of employment, of the sort expressly recognised in ERA, s 212(3)(c) (see para 13.24) as being relevant to the question of continuity of employment when no contract is actually in existence. But if the contract is frustrated the statutory or contractual rights to notice on termination do not apply (*G F Sharp & Co Ltd v McMillan*, see para 15.25).

17.66 Imprisonment, though self-induced, is not strictly speaking repudiatory conduct, for it does not amount to a breach of the contract of employment. But there is an inherent contradiction, because the doctrine of frustration arises when an event occurs without the fault of either party, and a person who had been given a custodial sentence will invariably be at fault. The answer appears to be that the person asserting the frustration (ie the employer) must show that there was no fault on his part, and the person against whom frustration is being asserted (ie the employee) cannot rely on his own misconduct by way of an answer (*FC Shepherd & Co Ltd v Jerrom*, para 17.60).

17.67 Frustration arises by operation of law, not a conscious decision by the parties, and whilst it is not necessary to be able to point to the exact moment in time when the relationship between the parties is dissolved, the burden of proving that the contract has been frustrated lies on the employer. Thus, if an employee is sent to prison, this can be an instantaneously frustrating event or a potentially frustrating event. Accordingly, regard has to be paid to:

(a) when it was commercially necessary for the employer to make a decision about the employee's future;

(b) what a reasonable employer would consider to be the likely length of the employee's absence; and

(c) whether it was reasonable to engage a permanent rather than a temporary replacement (*Chakki v United Yeast Co Ltd*[97]).

E. **Consensual termination**

17.68 A consensual termination arises when the employment is terminated by mutual agreement, and the reason for that agreement is generally irrelevant (*Birch v Liverpool University*[98]). Since there is no dismissal, no statutory rights ensue. If a person is given the option of working part-time or being made redundant, and chooses the latter option, there is a dismissal for reason of redundancy, and it is not a consensual termination (*Lassman v De Vere University Arms Hotel*[99]). Also, a person who volunteers for redundancy has volunteered to be dismissed, and is entitled to a redundancy payment (*Burton Allton and Johnson Ltd v Peck*[100]).

17.69 A mutual agreement whereby the employment will come to an end on the happening of a future event is not a consensual termination. In *Igbo v Johnson Matthey Chemicals Ltd*[101] the claimant wished to take extended leave. She signed a document which stated that she agreed to return to work by a certain date, and that if she failed to do so the contract of employment would automatically terminate. She failed to return to work on the due date, and her employers treated the contract as being at an end. She claimed that she had been unfairly dismissed. The Court of Appeal applied ERA, s 203 which stipulates that any

---

[97] [1982] 2 All ER 446, [1982] ICR 140, EAT.
[98] [1985] ICR 470, [1985] IRLR 165, 129 Sol Jo 245, CA.
[99] [2003] ICR 44, [2002] All ER (D) 83 (Oct), EAT.   [100] [1975] ICR 193, [1975] IRLR 87, DC.
[101] [1986] ICR 82, [1985] IRLR 189, [1985] LS Gaz R 1011, EAT; revsd [1986] ICR 505, [1986] IRLR 215, 130 Sol Jo 524, [1986] LS Gaz R 2089, CA.

provision in an agreement shall be void in so far as it purports to limit the operation of any provision in the Act. The document she signed purported to take away her right to claim that she was unfairly dismissed, and it was therefore void. The Court of Appeal overruled earlier authorities on this topic (including the case of *British Leyland (UK) Ltd v Ashraf*[102]) and remitted the case to the employment tribunal to determine whether her dismissal was fair or unfair.

17.70 However, a mutual agreement to bring a contract of employment to an end, made for good consideration, after the employee had received proper advice, and made without duress, is effective. In *Logan Salton v Durham County Council*,[103] the claimant was due to attend a disciplinary hearing which was to consider a recommendation that he be dismissed. An agreement was then reached whereby, on terms, his employment would come to an end by mutual agreement. He subsequently claimed he had been unfairly dismissed, but his claim failed. The agreement was not void by virtue of ERA, s 203 because it was not a contract of employment, or the variation of a contract of employment. The EAT distinguished this type of situation from that which occurred in *Igbo v Johnson Matthey Chemicals* (see para 17.69).

17.71 The distinction between a resignation and a termination by mutual agreement is that the former is a unilateral act by the employee, whereas the latter requires the consent of both parties, because otherwise there may be a breach of contract by one party. Thus if an employee gives notice, he resigns. If the employer and employee agree that the employee may leave without giving notice, it is a mutual termination (*L Lipton Ltd v Marlborough*[104]).

17.72 However, the question of 'did he jump or was he pushed' must be determined by reference to all the surrounding circumstances. In *Sandhu v Jan de Rijk Transport Ltd* (para 17.50) the employee was called to a meeting with no indication as to its substance. He was told that his contract was to be terminated. The meeting continued, and the employee negotiated agreed terms for his departure. He subsequently claimed he had been unfairly dismissed. Relying on *Sheffield v Oxford Controls Co Ltd* (see para 17.50) the employment tribunal held that the agreement had converted the dismissal into a resignation, but the Court of Appeal reversed that decision. Earlier cases were distinguished because in them the employee had had time to consider the inevitability of the termination, and subsequently negotiate for himself a financial package, whereas in the instant case the employee had not had a full opportunity to consider his position and, in particular, take independent advice as to his rights.

Fair and unfair dismissal (ERA, s 98)

A. Is it fair?

17.73 Once it has been established that a dismissal has taken place, it must then be determined whether or not the dismissal was unfair. Section 98 of the Employment Rights Act 1996 lays down five grounds on which a dismissal is capable of being fair, as follows:

   (a) a reason relating to the capability or qualifications of the employee for performing the work of the kind which he was employed by the employer to do. 'Capability' includes any assessment by reference to skill, aptitude, health or other physical or mental quality, and 'qualifications' means any degree, diploma or other academic, technical or professional qualification relevant to the position which the employee holds;

102 [1978] ICR 979, [1978] IRLR 330, 13 ITR 500, EAT.
103 [1989] IRLR 99, EAT.   104 [1979] IRLR 179, EAT.

(b) a reason which relates to the conduct of the employee;

(c) the redundancy of the employee;

(d) because the employee could not continue to work in the position which he held without contravention (either on his part or on the part of the employer) of a restriction or a duty imposed by or under a statute;

(e) some other substantial reason such as to justify the dismissal of an employee holding the position which he held.

17.74 Whether a particular dismissal based on one or more of these reasons will be fair or unfair will depend on whether in the circumstances of the case (including the size and administrative resources of the employer's undertaking) the employer acted reasonably or unreasonably in treating the reason as a sufficient reason for dismissing the employee, and the question will be determined in accordance with equity and the substantial merits of the case (ERA, s 98(4)). Further, whereas it is for the employee to prove that he was dismissed, it is for the employer to show the reason for the dismissal, and that it was one of the potentially fair reasons. It will then be for the employment tribunal to find, on the basis of the evidence presented, whether or not the employer had acted reasonably in treating that reason as a sufficient ground for dismissal. Thus if he fails to show the reason, or fails to show a reason which is one of those listed in para 17.73, the dismissal is automatically unfair. In *Raynor v Remploy Ltd*[105] a group general manager was dismissed for alleged lack of business judgment and general inefficiency. He had been employed for five years, and the tribunal rejected the company's allegations as spurious. Since there was no evidence of incapability, the dismissal was unfair. In *Castledine v Rothwell Engineering Ltd* (see para 10.40) the tribunal refused to accept the general allegations of incompetence, pointing to the favourable reference given to an employee subsequent to his dismissal. The employer cannot expect to win his case if he fails to give or call evidence on which the tribunal can reach its conclusion on the reason for the dismissal or its reasonableness, and general allegations without such evidence will normally be insufficient. In *Whitaker v Milk Marketing Board*,[106] an artificial inseminator was dismissed for incompetence and misconduct. Although the Board mentioned various farmers who were supposed to be dissatisfied with the service they had received, none was called to give evidence, and the dismissal was held unfair.

Two-stage procedure

17.75 Broadly speaking, there are two stages in the process of determining whether or not a dismissal was fair. The first is the means whereby the decision is reached. This involves going through proper procedures (see Chapter 12) bearing in mind especially the provisions of the Code of Practice (*Lock v Cardiff Railway Co Ltd,* paras 1.16 and 12.12), so that there is a full investigation, a proper hearing, a right to appeal, etc. The second stage is the actual decision taken, bearing in mind the reason for the dismissal, the need to consider mitigating circumstances, consistency and/or flexibility as appropriate, the terms of the contract, the size and nature of the employer's undertaking, and so on. No single factor, by itself, can be conclusive, and each case will turn on its own peculiar facts.

Has the employer acted reasonably?

17.76 Further, the test is 'did the employer act reasonably?' not 'did the employment tribunal agree with what the employer did?' (*Grundy (Teddington) Ltd v Willis*[107]). An employment tribunal is not entitled to substitute its own views for those of the employer (*Foley v*

---

[105] [1973] IRLR 3.   [106] [1973] IRLR 100.
[107] [1976] ICR 323, [1976] IRLR 118, 11 ITR 26.

Post Office[108]). A decision on whether the employer acted reasonably is a question of fact for the employment tribunal to decide (*Iceland Frozen Foods Ltd v Jones*[109]), which can only be challenged if the decision was perverse or based on an incorrect perception of the law.

17.77 In *Anandarajah v Lord Chancellor's Department*,[110] the President of the EAT, Waite J, made a major policy statement about the use of precedents in employment tribunal hearings. Although these are of great practical assistance, they must not be relied upon as being of binding authority, but rather treated as guidelines. He continued:

> Sometimes the judgment in a particular case will be found to express, in helpful and concise language, some concept which is regularly found in this field of enquiry and it becomes of great illustrative value. But reference to such a case can never be a substitute for taking the explicit directions of the statute as a guiding principle.

17.78 To determine whether or not the employer has acted reasonably in dismissing the employee, the current test is 'What would a reasonable employer have done'? There is a band of reasonableness within which one employer might decide to dismiss, whilst another might decide not to do so. If the circumstances of the case are such that a reasonable employer might dismiss, the dismissal will be fair even though not all the employers would take that view (*British Leyland (UK) Ltd v Swift*[111]). The 'band of reasonableness' test was challenged (somewhat belatedly) by the EAT in *Haddon v Van Den Bergh Foods Ltd*,[112] but in *HSBC v Madden*[113] the Court of Appeal disagreed, and reaffirmed the correctness of the 'range of reasonable responses' test as laid down in *Iceland Frozen Foods Ltd v Jones*. Further, the *Burchell* test (para 17.126) applied to the assessment of the fairness of the dismissal under s 98(4), not to establishing the reason for the dismissal under s 98(1)–(3).

17.79 In *Kent County Council v Gilham*[114] the Court of Appeal stressed once again that whether or not an employer acts reasonably is a question of fact for the employment tribunal. That two employment tribunals, considering the same broad issues, had reached opposite conclusions did not indicate that either had misdirected themselves in law. It is endemic in the system that different answers will be given to broadly similar situations, and the decision cannot be challenged just for that reason. But on rare occasions higher courts will interfere if the decision of the employment tribunal is thought to be perverse (*British Railways Board v Jackson*[115]). The 'range of reasonable responses' relates to facts reasonably known by the employer, not to facts found by the employment tribunal, particularly if the facts are in dispute at the tribunal hearing (*London Ambulance Service NHS Trust v Small*[116]).

17.80 The point in time at which the reasonableness of the employer's decision to dismiss is to be tested is when the employment comes to an end, not when the decision is taken, nor when the notice to terminate is given (*Stacey v Babcock Power Ltd*[117]). Thus if an initial decision to dismiss was unfair because of a defect in the disciplinary proceedings, it may be cured if an appeal hearing is properly conducted (see *Clark v Civil Aviation Authority*, para 12.20). The reason for the dismissal is to be assessed both at the time notice of termination was given right through to the actual date of the termination of the contract (*West Kent College v Richardson*[118]). Matters which come to light after the employment has ended are generally irrelevant (*Greenall Whitley plc v Carr*, para 12.34).

[108] [2001] 1 All ER 550, [2000] ICR 1283, [2000] IRLR 827, sub nom *Post Office v Foley* 652 IRLB 7, CA.
[109] [1983] ICR 17, [1982] IRLR 439, EAT.   [110] [1984] IRLR 131, EAT.
[111] [1981] IRLR 91, CA.   [112] [1999] ICR 1150, [1999] IRLR 672, 628 IRLB 3, EAT.
[113] [2001] 1 All ER 550, [2000] ICR 1283, [2000] IRLR 827, 652 IRLB 7, CA.
[114] [1985] ICR 227, sub nom *Gilham v Kent County Council* [1985] IRLR 16, CA.
[115] [1994] IRLR 235, CA.   [116] [2009] EWCA Civ 220, [2009] IRLR 563.
[117] [1986] QB 308, [1986] 2 WLR 207, [1986] ICR 221, [1986] IRLR 3, 130 Sol Jo 71, EAT.
[118] [1999] ICR 511, EAT.

Automatically unfair dismissals

17.81 Certain dismissals are automatically unfair, and no question arises as to whether or not the employer has acted reasonably. Nor is the length of continuous employment relevant, as a claim for automatically unfair dismissal can be brought from day one of employment. These are dismissals connected with:

(a) pregnancy or childbirth, the taking of ordinary or additional or compulsory maternity leave, ordinary or additional adoption leave, parental leave or paternity leave, or time off to look after dependants, declining to sign a workforce agreement for maternity or parental leave purposes, the performance of functions as a workforce representative (ERA, s 99, and Maternity and Parental Leave Regulations 1999);

(b) a health and safety case (ERA, s 100);

(c) a shop or betting worker who refuses to work on Sundays (ERA, s 101);

(d) the exercise of a right under the Working Time Regulations (ERA, s 101A);

(e) performing a function as trustee of an occupational pension fund (ERA, s 102);

(f) performing a function of an employee representative (ERA, s 103);

(g) the making of a protected disclosure (ERA, s 103A);

(h) the assertion of a statutory right (ERA, s 104);

(i) the exercise of a right under the National Minimum Wage Act (ERA, s 104A);

(j) taking action with regard to a tax credit (ERA, s 104B);

(k) membership or non-membership of a trade union (TULR(C)A, s 154);

(l) the taking of protected industrial action (TULR(C)A, s 238A);

(m) doing a wide range of actions in connection with the statutory procedure for recognition or derecognition (TULR(C)A, Sch A1, see para 21.61);

(n) doing acts in connection with rights under the Transnational Information and Consultation of Employees Regulations 1999, Companies (Cross Border Mergers) Regulations 2007, European Cooperative Society (Involvement of Employees) Regulations 2006, European Public Limited Liability (Employee Involvement) (Great Britain) Regulations 2009;

(o) doing acts in connection with an employee's rights under the Part-time Workers (Prevention of Less Favourable Treatment) Regulations 2000 (see para 2.80);

(p) the exercise of rights in connection with an application for flexible working (ERA, s 104C) (see para 6.129);

(q) taken action under the Fixed-Term Employees (Prevention of Less Favourable Treatment) Regulations 2002: see reg 6);

(r) undertaking jury service (see para 6.129);

(s) acted as a companion;

(t) selection for redundancy for any of these reasons (ERA, s 105);

(u) breach of the Employment Relations Act 1999 (Blacklist) Regulations 2010;

(v) breach of the Time off Work for Study and Training provisions (ERA, s 63D).

17.82 In June 2013 section 13 of the Enterprise and Regulatory Reform Act added new ss (4) to the ERA 1996 s 108. This removed the qualifying period for unfair dismissal where the principal reason for dismissal is an employee's political opinions or affiliation, although this is not an automatically unfair dismissal.

B. Reasons for the dismissal

17.83 Although the Act lays down potentially fair reasons for dismissal, it will be convenient to make further sub-divisions, so that in practice a number of potential reasons for fair dismissal appear. This enables a more practical analysis to be made. Bearing this in mind, we can examine the general approach of the courts and tribunals to the problems of dismissals.

Inherent inability

17.84 To dismiss an employee who is not capable of performing his job properly will be fair provided the employer acts reasonably in the circumstances. Thus, faced with the problem of an incompetent worker, what does the reasonable employer do? He enquires into the matter, to find out why the employee cannot do the job adequately. Has he been trained properly, so that he knows how the job should be done? Has he been properly supervised, been given an adequate job description? Does he have proper equipment, sufficient support staff and facilities? In other words, the employer's first task is to find out the reason for the alleged incompetence, and so far as it is possible, do something about it from the employer's point of view.

17.85 For example, in *Davison v Kent Meters Ltd*[119] the claimant was dismissed for assembling nearly 500 components in the wrong sequence. She claimed that she had followed the pattern of work in accordance with the instructions received from her chargehand, but the latter denied having shown her how to assemble the parts, and maintained that she was entirely to blame for the errors. The employment tribunal thought that if the chargehand had not shown her what to do, he should have done so, and the mistakes were therefore hardly her fault! Further, he should have checked on her performance, and supervised her properly. Not surprisingly, the dismissal was held to be unfair.

17.86 A warning should not be given merely for the sake of conforming with a laid down procedure, for this is to treat it as a mechanical system with no real significance. A warning is designed to do a job of work; it should have as its purpose the object of bringing an employee away from the brink of dismissal. It follows, therefore, that if the employee is suffering from an irredeemable incompetence, no amount of warnings will make any difference, and therefore there cannot be a need to issue them (*Sutton and Gates Ltd v Boxall*[120]). In *Littlewoods Organisation Ltd v Egenti*[121] the EAT pointed out that there is a distinction between disciplinary procedures and capability procedures. The former should be applied strictly, whereas this does not need to be so with regard to the latter. To give a warning in capability cases is not a matter of procedure; it is a matter of substance (*AJ Dunning & Sons (Shopfitters) Ltd v Jacomb,* para 12.82). In other words, the question is, would a warning have done any good? Would it have rendered this dismissal unnecessary? If the answer is yes, then the warning should have been given. If the answer is no, then, since no amount of warnings would make any difference, there is no need to give them. Thus in *Lowndes v Specialist Heavy Engineering Ltd* (see para 10.65) the claimant was dismissed after five serious and costly errors. No written warnings were given, and he was not allowed an opportunity to state his case. The dismissal was held to be fair; it would have made no difference had a different procedure been adopted. Nowadays, however, procedural fairness is essential (see para 12.22).

17.87 Finally, the reasonable employer will consider alternatives before he dismisses the employee. Is there some other work which can be offered within the level of competence

---

[119] [1975] IRLR 145.   [120] [1979] ICR 67, [1978] IRLR 486, EAT.
[121] [1976] ICR 516, [1976] IRLR 334, EAT.

of the employee? Would he accept it if it was offered? Would he make a success of it? Clearly, much will depend on the circumstances of the case. In *Bevan Harris Ltd v Gair* (para 12.85), the claimant, who had been employed as a foreman, was dismissed after 11 years' service for poor performance, about which he had been warned on four occasions. The employment tribunal held the dismissal to be unfair, because a reasonable employer would have demoted him rather than resort to dismissal. The decision was reversed by the EAT. The employer had given serious consideration to offering the claimant another job, but had decided against it. The small scale of the business, and the loss of confidence in the employee's abilities, meant that the decision to dismiss fell within the band of reasonableness and, in the circumstances, the dismissal was fair.

Neglectful incompetence

17.88 Here we must consider the employee who could do the job, but is not achieving his potential. The object of the exercise is to bring him up to the standards which he is capable of reaching, and for this purpose, the disciplinary procedure should be invoked, in accordance with the gravity of the matter.

17.89 If an employee is not working as well as he could, then a warning is appropriate; if he is refusing to obey instructions or is being generally uncooperative, then he should be told, firmly and by someone in authority, of the consequences which are likely to ensue. If the tribunal considers that had a clear warning been given a dismissal would not have been necessary (*Winterhalter Gastronom Ltd v Webb*[122]), then it will conclude that a dismissal without such warning having been given will be unfair (*Jones v GEC Elliott Automation Ltd*, para 12.82). An employee with long service is entitled to more consideration, if only because the employers can hardly be heard to say that it took them many years to discover his incompetence, but the fact that the employer has tolerated poor performance in the past is not conclusive, if the employee fails to respond to proper warnings (*Gozdzik v Chlidema Carpet Co*[123]). A newly appointed employee should be given a chance to prove himself, and not be judged on short-term results. Senior staff should have a greater appreciation of what is expected from them, whereas employees not in the managerial range should have greater attention paid to their requirements. If possible, the employer may consider giving the employee further training, should suitable facilities be available, assuming, that is, that the employee would be likely to benefit from such training. If the employee refuses to take advantage of this offer, at least the employer has acted in a reasonable manner, and a consequent dismissal may well be fair (*Coward v John Menzies (Holdings) Ltd*[124]).

17.90 If there is a minor act of neglect, a warning is appropriate, to be followed, as necessary, with a further or final warning. A serious act of neglect might lead to an immediate final warning. But there are some acts of neglect which dare not be repeated, and hence dismissal is not inappropriate. In *Taylor v Alidair Ltd*,[125] an airline pilot landed his aeroplane in a manner which caused some concern among the passengers and crew. After a proper investigation, it was decided that he had been negligent, and was dismissed. This was held to be fair: there are some activities where the degree of skill required is so high, or where the potential consequences of a departure from the highest standards are so serious, that one failure is sufficient to justify dismissal. A warning in such cases is totally inappropriate.

17.91 The law which prevents unfair dismissal must not be used to impede the efficient management of business by compelling employers to retain incompetent employees (*Cook v Thomas Linnell & Sons Ltd*[126]), and once an employer has lost confidence in the employee's

---

[122] [1973] ICR 245, [1973] IRLR 120, 8 ITR 313, NIRC.   [123] IDS Brief 163.
[124] [1977] IRLR 428, EAT.   [125] [1978] ICR 445, [1978] IRLR 82, (1978) 13 ITR 180, (1977) 121 SJ 758.
[126] [1977] ICR 770, [1977] IRLR 132, EAT.

ability to do the job, then it is reasonable to dismiss and offer other employment should this be available. But the employer is not bound to create a vacancy if none exists; he should at least consider the possibility, and consider if the employee would make a success of it (*Brush Electrical Machines v Guest*[127]).

17.92 If an employee is dismissed because of his incapability, the correct test to apply is whether the employer honestly and reasonably held the belief that the employee was not competent, and whether there are reasonable grounds for that belief. It is not necessary for the employer to *prove* that the employee was incompetent (*Alidair Ltd v Taylor*[128]). In other words, the test under s 98(4) is a subjective one. The employment tribunal must consider the employer's state of mind as well as his reasons. But it is sufficient if the employer honestly believes on reasonable grounds that the employee is incompetent.

Long-term sickness

17.93 An employee who is absent from work for a long time because of sickness or ill-health is entitled to sympathetic consideration by the employer, but the employer can only be expected to act within sensible limits. The questions to be asked are (a) how long has the employment lasted, (b) how long had it been expected the employment would continue, (c) what is the nature of the job, (d) what was the nature, effect and length of the illness, (e) what is the need of the employer for the work to be done, and to engage a replacement to do it, (f) are wages continuing to be paid, (g) why had the employer dismissed (or failed to do so), and (h) in all the circumstances, could a reasonable employer have been expected to wait any longer (*Egg Stores (Stamford-Hill) Ltd v Leibovici,* para 17.63, *BS v Dundee City Council*[129])? In other words, the employer is entitled to consider his business needs, as well as the employee's situation. An important point to consider is 'has the time arrived when the employer can no longer reasonably be expected to keep the absent employee's post open for him?' (*Hart v AR Marshall & Sons (Bulwell) Ltd*, para 17.64). Thus if an employee is away for a long time, the employer should not dismiss as an automatic matter, but consider whether it is necessary to dismiss. The employer should make all necessary enquiries, from the employee, from his doctor, and if possible obtain an opinion from the firm's medical advisers (*East Lindsey District Council v Daubney*[130]).

17.94 In all cases where dismissal on the grounds of ill-health is being considered, there is a need for enquiry, consultation, warnings, a search for alternatives etc, before the decision is taken (*A Links & Co Ltd v Rose*[131]). The purpose of consulting with the employee about his health is to weigh up the situation, balancing the need of the employer to get the work done against the employee's need for time in order to recover his health. Without such consultation, the employer may act precipitously, with unfair consequences. But consultation is not demanded by law; if it is clear that the consultation would not have made any difference to the result, a failure to consult does not make a dismissal unfair (*Taylorplan Catering (Scotland) Ltd v McInally*[132]).

17.95 Earlier cases had stated that an employer should warn an employee that unless he returns to work he will be dismissed, but this view is erroneous, for an employee cannot be warned that he has got to be in good health. However, the employer should make all proper and necessary enquiries from the employee, and not act in a precipitous manner. Perhaps

[127] EAT 382/76.
[128] [1977] ICR 446, [1976] IRLR 420, 12 ITR 21, EAT; aff'd [1978] ICR 445, sub nom *Taylor v Alidair Ltd* [1978] IRLR 82, 13 ITR 180, 121 Sol Jo 758, CA.
[129] [2013] CSIH 91.
[130] [1977] ICR 566, [1977] IRLR 181, 12 ITR 359, EAT.
[131] [1991] IRLR 353, Ct of Sess.   [132] [1980] IRLR 53, EAT.

the best way to express the employer's obligation is to say that he should treat the employee with sympathetic consideration, and that he should hold the job open for as long as is possible. In *Coulson v Felixstowe Dock & Rly Co Ltd*[133] the claimant was away from work due to ill-health for considerable periods of time. He could no longer perform his duties, and was put on light clerical work. He was told that if he could not return to his old job, he would be regarded, and was given six months in which to prove his fitness. However, he fell ill again and was dismissed. It was held that the employer had treated the employee with every consideration, but there must come a time when the employer cannot be expected to keep someone on who is not doing his work. The tribunal had to consider fairness to the business as well as to the employee.

17.96 On the other hand, in *Converform (Darwen) Ltd v Bell*,[134] the claimant was a works director who was off work because of a heart attack. He recovered, but the employers refused to permit him to return to work, as they thought there was the risk of another attack. His subsequent dismissal was held to be unfair. A risk of future illness cannot be used as a ground for fair dismissal unless the nature of the employment is such that the risk made it unsafe for the employee to continue in the job.

17.97 A good employer will try to fix a date by which time he must know when the employee expects to be able to give information about the likely date of return to work (*Marder v ITT Distributors Ltd*[135]), but once having explained and discussed the situation with the employee, the employer is entitled to make a decision in the light of the information available (*Spencer v Paragon Wallpapers Ltd*[136]).

17.98 In *Merseyside and North Wales Electricity Board v Taylor*[137] the Divisional Court held that there is no rule of law which requires the employer to create a special job for an employee who is off sick. Nor is there a rule that an employer is obliged to find alternative employment for an employee plagued by ill-health. Each case must be judged on its own facts in the light of the employer's circumstances. It may be that the employer has some light work available of the kind which is within the employee's capacity to do, and the employee should be encouraged to take such a post, even at reduced rates of pay, before dismissal is considered.

17.99 In larger firms it may be possible for the company to place a sick employee in some form of holding department, so that he can recommence employment when fit, but there are certain legal problems about such a course which require further consideration. In *Burton v Boneham & Turner Ltd*,[138] the management placed an employee in such a holding department after several spells of absence through illness. It was held that such conduct amounted in law to a dismissal, although in the circumstances, it was held to be fair. On the other hand, in *Parker v Westland Helicopters Ltd*[139] a sick employee was transferred from the department concerned with sick employees to a holding department, where she had to wait for a suitable vacancy before being employed again. As this was done with her agreement, on the facts it was held that no dismissal had taken place.

17.100 The legal significance of placing employees in a holding department has yet to be fully explored. In *Marshall v Harland & Wolff Ltd* (para 17.61) the NIRC held that such a transfer meant that the employee ceased to be employed in a legal sense, but the employers merely undertook some obligation to provide work if and when possible. If this is so, then the act of placing in the holding department could well be as the result of a frustrating

---

[133] [1975] IRLR 11.   [134] [1981] IRLR 195, EAT.   [135] [1976] IRLR 105.
[136] [1977] ICR 301, [1976] IRLR 373, EAT.
[137] [1975] ICR 185, [1975] IRLR 60, 10 ITR 52, 119 Sol Jo 272.
[138] IDS Supp 15.   [139] IDS Supp 15.

event, and should not amount to a dismissal (*G F Sharp Ltd v McMillan,* para 15.25). On the other hand, it has been suggested (*O'Reilly v Hotpoint Ltd*[140]) that such transfer suspends the contract of employment. If this view is correct, then continuity will doubtless be preserved for redundancy and other purposes for 26 weeks (ERA, s 212(3)(a)), and presumably there is a legal (as opposed to moral) obligation to find an employee work when he recovers. It is clear that the matter should be subject to a defined policy which can be stated in the works/staff rules, so that the legal situation will be determined by the contractual obligations which can be laid down by the parties in accordance with the objective which they seek.

17.101 If an employee is retired (or dismissed) on ill-health grounds, the employment tribunal should not be concerned with whether or not the illness was caused or contributed to by the employer, but should consider whether the employer acted reasonably in dismissing the employee for that illness. The fact that the employer has caused the incapacity that led to the dismissal does not preclude a finding that the dismissal was fair, but in such circumstances the employer can be expected to go the extra mile in finding alternative employment for the employee, or put up with a longer period of sickness absence than would otherwise be reasonable (*McAdie v Royal Bank of Scotland*[141]).

17.102 Employers cannot be expected to go to unreasonable lengths in seeking to accommodate a sick employee, and what is reasonable is largely a question of fact and degree in each case (*Garricks (Caterers) Ltd v Nolan*[142]). There is no absolute rule that an employer must consult with the employee's general practitioner (and indeed, since this could result in a breach of professional confidence, it may not be a profitable exercise), although it may be desirable to do so if the employee gives his consent (see *Tower Hamlets London Borough v Bull*[143]). In the last analysis, the employer must act within the range of reasonable responses, depending on the circumstances (*Rolls Royce Ltd v Walpole*[144]).

17.103 It is also the duty of the employee to keep the employer informed of the nature of the illness, and, where possible, the prognosis for a recovery. In *McGivney v Portman Mansions Management Ltd* the employee went off sick for six months, claiming to be suffering with 'stress'. However, he failed to produce any medical evidence of his condition, despite a number of requests from his employer for access to his medical records. He also refused to attend an appointment with an occupational therapist. His subsequent dismissal was held to be fair. He had failed to cooperate with his employer, and the dismissal was within the range of reasonable responses.

17.104 The Equality Act 2010 (see para 4.1) makes significant changes to the law relating to the dismissal of long-term sick employees, for many sickness/ill-health absences may well come within the definition of a disability within the Act although sickness, per se, is not a disability, and a person who is dismissed solely on account of sickness is not protected by the prohibition against discrimination on grounds of disability (*Chacon Navas v Eurest Colectividades SA*[145]). Thus dismissals on health-related grounds will be affected by the requirements for employers to make reasonable adjustments to cater for employees who are disabled within the meaning of the Act, and dismissal on the ground of long-term sickness will only be justified if no such adjustments are possible, or if the employee rejects

---

[140] (1969) 5 ITR 68, 113 Sol Jo 979, DC.

[141] [2007] EWCA Civ 806, [2007] IRLR 895, (2007) 104(32) LSG 27, (2007) 157 NLJ 1355, (2007) 151 SJLB 1060.

[142] [1980] IRLR 259, EAT.   [143] [2001] All ER (D) 209 (May), EAT.   [144] [1980] IRLR 343, EAT.

[145] [2007] All ER (EC) 59, [2006] ECR I–6467, [2006] 3 CMLR 40, [2007] ICR 1, [2006] IRLR 706, (2006) *Times,* 9 August.

them. A failure to consult a disabled employee about what reasonable adjustments can be made to his working conditions is not, by itself, a failure to make a reasonable adjustment. It is a matter to be taken into account, but it is not conclusive (*Spence v Intype Libra Ltd*[146]).

17.105 An employee who is away from work through illness etc is still within the pool of selection for redundancy, but the usual criteria of consultation etc must be applied (*Hill v General Accident Fire and Life Insurance Co*[147]).

Persistent absenteeism

17.106 The employee who is persistently away from work (whether because of illness or other reasons) for short periods at a time presents a different problem. This employee can be cautioned about his absences; he can be confronted with his record, told that it must improve, and be given a period of time in which an improvement can be monitored. Indeed, the employer should not ignore the powerful medicinal effect of a final warning, and a failure to give one may mean that the employee is unaware that the situation is causing the employer great concern. The effect of such a warning might be to stimulate the employee into seeking proper medical advice in case there is an underlying cause of the continuous minor ailments, it may deter the employee from taking time off when not truly warranted, and it may even lead the employee to look for other work where such absences could be tolerated (*Smith v Royal Alfred Merchant Seamen's Society*[148]).

17.107 The employer should approach the situation with 'sympathy, understanding and compassion'. Factors to be taken into account include: (a) the nature of the illness, (b) the likelihood of it recurring, (c) the length of the various absences and the spells of good health in between, (d) the need of the employer to have that work done by that employee, (e) the impact of the absences on other employees, (f) the adoption and carrying out of the policy, (g) a personal assessment of the ultimate decision, and (h) the fact that the employee is fully aware that his employment will be terminated unless there is an improvement (*Lynock v Cereal Packaging Ltd*[149]).

17.108 At the same time, the employer can hold out a helping hand; he can enquire from the employee the nature of all these minor ailments, offer such medical help as the firm can provide, provide counselling, etc, in those cases where the employment is itself a major contributing factor to the illness, and so on.

17.109 In practice, it is essential to establish the reason for the absences, as this may well determine the appropriate procedural steps to be taken. For example, the employer may have issued a policy statement on alcohol or drug abuse, which may override standard procedures. In most cases, it will be necessary to interview the employee on his return to work, which will assist in establishing the reasons for the absence, assess the likelihood of recurrence, and determine whether the appropriate 'trigger' has been reached under any attendance procedure. If an underlying medical condition is suspected, advice may be given on the need to seek further treatment. Alternative employment may be considered, or flexibility introduced into attendance improvement schemes. In other words, a great deal can be done to resolve the problem, rather than merely consider dismissal as a solution (*Kerrigan v Rover Group Ltd*[150]).

17.110 In *International Sports Ltd v Thomson*[151] the claimant was away from work for about 25% of the time, with a variety of complaints (all of which were covered by medical

[146] Employment Appeal Tribunal, 27 April 2007.
[147] [1998] IRLR 641, 1999 SLT 1157, 1998 SCLR 1030, 609 IRLB 8, OH.
[148] HSIB 9.   [149] [1988] ICR 670, [1988] IRLR 510, EAT.
[150] Unreported.   [151] [1980] IRLR 340, EAT.

certificates) including dizzy spells, anxiety and nerves, bronchitis, virus infection, cystitis, arthralgia of the left knee, dyspepsia and flatulence. She was given a series of warnings, including a final warning, and before deciding to dismiss her, the company consulted their medical adviser. He saw no useful purpose in examining her, as none of the previous illnesses could be verified, there was no common link between them and she was not suffering from any chronic illness. She was then dismissed, and the EAT held that the dismissal was fair. The company had undertaken a fair review of her attendance record, she had been duly warned and given the opportunity to make representations. A further medical investigation would have produced no worthwhile results. There must come a point in time when a reasonable employer is entitled to say 'Enough is enough'.

17.111 It is normal for many firms to have contractual entitlement to a certain amount of sick leave, some of which may be regarded as 'certified' or covered by fit notes (formerly known as sick notes). Certainly, an employee should keep his employer informed by the proper means, and a failure to do so may mean that the employee contributes to his own dismissal and receives reduced compensation. But sick notes, by themselves, can never be conclusive, for there are serious doubts about their factual validity. Thus, if an employer believes that a sick note is phoney, or may not be accurate, then he is entitled to disregard it (*Hutchinson v Enfield Rolling Mills Ltd*[152]). Otherwise a doctor's medical certificate should be taken at its face value unless there is some evidence to the contrary (*Taylor v Merseyside Electrics 2002 Ltd*[153]). In *Mainwaring v Corus UK Ltd*[154] the claimant had been signed off work by his doctor because of back problems. Following an anonymous tip-off from a colleague that the claimant might be malingering, the employers carried out an investigation, and a video was produced showing him to be walking normally, carrying shopping bags etc. When shown the video, the doctor agreed that he would not have certified the claimant as being unfit for work had he known the truth. After a proper procedure the claimant was dismissed. It was held that the dismissal was fair. The reaction of the doctor to the video evidence overrode the initial medical certificate.

17.112 In *Wilkes v Fortes (Sussex) Ltd*[155] the EAT placed particular emphasis on a consideration of the size of the firm in determining whether or not it would be fair to dismiss an employee who is off work intermittently for sickness reasons. In a large firm, the disruption caused by such illnesses may be minimal; it is easy to have a float of overmanning to cover for absent employees. But in a small business, such absences may be extremely serious or even disastrous.

17.113 If a person's health is such that continued employment may well constitute a hazard, either to himself, to other employees, or is likely to cause damage to property, then provided the employer undertakes full consultation with the employee, and obtains expert medical opinion, this is capable of being a fair dismissal (*Spalding v Port of London Authority*[156]), and it is not necessary for the employer to wait until an accident occurs before taking steps to dismiss (*Parsons v Fisons Ltd*[157]). In *Finch v Betabake (Anglia) Ltd*[158] the claimant was an apprentice motor mechanic. The employers received a report from an ophthalmic surgeon that the boy could not continue to work without undue danger to himself and to others. He was therefore dismissed. It was held that the circumstances in which an apprentice could be dismissed were limited, but in the circumstances, the dismissal was fair.

17.114 If the persistent absenteeism is due to factors other than ill-health, then warnings, as appropriate, should be given. It has been suggested that a dismissal because of

---

[152] [1981] IRLR 318, EAT.   [153] EAT/0162/07.   [154] EAT/53/07.   [155] IRRR, EAT.
[156] [1977] HSIB.   [157] Unreported.   [158] [1977] IRLR 470.

an unacceptable level of short-term persistent absenteeism should properly be considered under the heading of 'some other substantial reason' rather than capability or conduct (*Post Office v Wilson*[159]).

17.115 The ACAS Advisory Handbook gave some guidance to employers on how to handle persistent short-term absenteeism. It was stated that:

(a) absences should be investigated promptly, and the employee asked for an explanation;

(b) if there is no medical evidence to support frequent self-certified absences, the employee should be asked to consult with a doctor to establish whether medical treatment is advisable, and/or whether the underlying reason for the absence is work-related;

(c) if, following a full and careful investigation, there appears to be no valid reason (medical or otherwise) for the absences, the matter should be dealt with under the appropriate disciplinary procedure;

(d) if the absences are due to domestic problems, the employer should consider whether an improvement in attendance is likely;

(e) the employee should be told what improvement in attendance is expected, and warned of the likely consequences if this does not happen;

(f) if there is no improvement, the employee's age, length of service, performance, should be considered, as well as the availability of alternative work. These factors must be balanced against the effect of past and future absences on the business.

17.116 Finally, an employer would need to consider whether persistent absenteeism is due to a long-term illness of the kind covered by the Equality Act 2010 (see para 4.80), and hence appropriate consideration should be given to the need to make reasonable adjustments, where possible.

Lack of qualifications

17.117 There have been very few cases concerning the lack of qualifications for the job as a reason for dismissal. In *Blackman v Post Office*[160] a telegraph officer was required to pass an aptitude test, but he failed after a maximum number of attempts. It was held that his dismissal was fair on the ground of lack of qualifications. But there must be a contractual obligation (express or implied) to hold the relevant qualification. In *Litster v M Thom & Sons Ltd*[161] the applicant was employed as a foreman fitter/driver. Government regulations required that special driving licences had to be obtained for drivers of heavy goods vehicles, and the claimant failed the necessary test. Nonetheless he was continued in employment as a fitter. His contract of employment contained no reference to the necessity of having an HGV licence. Following a dispute, he was told that unless he obtained such a licence, he would be dismissed. It was held that since his contract did not require him to hold that particular licence, a dismissal based on his lack of qualifications would be unfair.

17.118 However, it may be permissible to go outside the formal requirements of the contract. In *Tayside Regional Council v McIntosh* (see para 3.30), the employers advertised for a vehicle mechanic, an essential requirement being that the successful applicant should have a driving licence. The claimant was appointed to the job, but his contract of employment made no mention of the need to hold a driving licence. He was subsequently disqualified

---

[159] [2000] IRLR 834, CA.   [160] [1974] ICR 151, [1974] IRLR 46, NIRC.   [161] [1975] IRLR 47.

from driving, and as there was no other suitable employment for him, he was dismissed. The EAT held that he had been fairly dismissed. The nature of the job clearly required the holding of a valid driving licence.

17.119 But even though it can be shown that the employee lacks the necessary qualification for the job, the employer must still act reasonably in treating that reason as a sufficient ground for dismissal. Thus in *Sutcliffe & Eaton Ltd v Pinney*[162] the claimant was dismissed from his job as a trainee hearing aid dispenser after he failed to pass the necessary examinations. It was held that the employers should have applied for an extension of his training period so that he could take the examination again. In other words, as always, the reasonable employer will look around for alternatives to dismissal.

Conduct inside the employment

17.120 Under this heading we can consider all those acts of the employee which occur during the performance of the contract, and which are alleged to have an adverse effect on that contract. Such acts may be sub-divided in accordance with their gravity, ie acts of a trivial nature (minor misconduct), serious matters (major misconduct) and extremely serious matters (gross misconduct). The importance of such a classification lies in the methods which are required to be adopted to solve the problem in question. For acts of minor misconduct, these can usually be dealt with by a warning (informal, then perhaps formal), but it would be wrong to utilise the full weight of a disciplinary sanction in order to deal with a trivial matter. Thus to give an employee a final warning 'if you come in late again you will be dismissed' is bound to lead to trouble at some later stage, for the sanction is out of all proportion to the offence. Such a person could be dealt with, for example, by a short period of suspension. Further, for some acts a single repetition would suffice to warrant dismissal (eg theft) and hence the warning would spell this out. But other acts may have to be monitored over a period of time, (eg lateness, absenteeism), and hence the warning will indicate the period, spell out the improvement required, and state the ultimate sanction. An act of major misconduct could be handled by an immediate final warning, without the need to go through stages in a procedure (ie informal warning, first written warning, etc), for the seriousness of the matter is sufficient to leap over other stages. And an act of gross misconduct, once proven, can lead to instant dismissal without notice, for this amounts to a breach by the employee which in effect repudiates the contract.

17.121 For all acts of misconduct, the employer must show that he gave the matter a prompt and thorough investigation, that he gave the employee an opportunity to state his case, interviewed witnesses and collected evidence so far as it was possible to do so. Allegations of dishonesty involving breach of trust should be investigated with care. In *Stuart v London City Airport*[163] it was unreasonable for the employer not to look into evidence which might have shown that the employee was not dishonest. There are, however, limits to the power of an employer to investigate, and indeed, it may well be improper for him to do so on occasions. This is particularly true when the matter is to the subject of criminal charges or investigation by the police. Thus in *Carr v Alexander Russell Ltd,*[164] the claimant was dismissed when it was learned that the police had found some company property in his possession, and that he was to be charged with theft. It was held that the employers had no duty to carry out any detailed form of enquiry, for it would have been improper of them to do so, and a subsequent trial might have been seriously prejudiced.

17.122 There is no absolute prescription that an employee must be given an opportunity to explain his conduct before he is dismissed, though this course is clearly desirable. In

---

[162] [1977] IRLR 349, EAT.   [163] UKEAT/0273/12/BA.
[164] [1979] ICR 469n, [1976] IRLR 220, Ct of Sess.

Parker v Clifford Dunn Ltd[165] the employers received information from the police that the claimant had admitted stealing from the company. He was therefore dismissed in accordance with the works rules. He did not appeal through the procedure, and made no protestation of innocence. His dismissal was held to be fair; it was reasonable for the employers to rely on the police investigations rather than carry out their own. But the mere fact that the police intend to charge an employee with theft is not conclusive, as they may decide not to proceed with the charge, or the evidence may be too weak to secure a conviction, and so on. Some enquiry may therefore be necessary (*Scottish Special Housing Association v Cooke*[166]).

17.123 The acts which can constitute misconduct inside the employment are too numerous to categorise. Fighting, swearing, trading, drunkenness, betting, horseplay, incompetence, theft, neglect, dangerous or obstructive conduct, clocking offences, breach of safety rules, immorality, refusal to obey orders, breach of hygiene rules, insubordination, unauthorised absenteeism, disloyalty, breach of confidence, taking unlawful drugs, sleeping while on duty, computer hacking or seeking unauthorised access to a computer program, telling lies, unsuitable clothing, dishonesty, taking property without authorisation and lateness, have all, in their turn, been the subject of employment tribunal proceedings. To deal with such conduct, the employer must consider the gravity of the offence, its effect on the employment generally, and the previous history of the employee. In other words, the employer, it is submitted, must take into account the offence, and the offender.

17.124 Although misconduct may be grounds for a dismissal, it must not be used as an excuse for dismissal. The onus is on the employer to show what was the real reason for the dismissal. Thus if he uses the misconduct as a way of getting rid of the employee, this can be evidence of unfairness. On the other hand, if the employer welcomes the opportunity of dismissing the employee for reason of misconduct, his enthusiasm does not make the dismissal unfair. It is the true reason for the dismissal, and the manner in which it is carried out, which will determine the fairness or otherwise of the dismissal (*Associated Society of Locomotive Engineers and Firemen v Brady*[167]). Also, gross misconduct does not mean that dismissal will automatically be within the band of reasonable responses, as it depends on the individual circumstances of the case (*Brito-Babapulle v Ealing Hospital NHS Trust*[168]).

17.125 It is not the function of the employment tribunal to substitute its views and opinions for those of management, but merely to decide if management has acted reasonably. For example, if an employee has committed an act of theft, it is for management to decide what should be done in the circumstances of the case, and provided a fair procedure is adopted, the eventual decision is that of management. In *Trusthouse Forte Hotels Ltd v Murphy*,[169] the claimant was a night porter. He kept a small supply of liquor for hotel guests, but when his stock was checked, there was a deficiency of £10. He admitted taking some of this for his own use, and was dismissed. The employment tribunal found this to be unfair, but the decision was reversed on appeal by the EAT. It would place an unreasonable burden on employers if they could not fairly dismiss employees who had stolen property which had been entrusted to their care. Although management might have been influenced by compassionate grounds, and might have decided not to dismiss an employee who had stolen a small amount of property, a reasonable management may have taken either view. Hence it was not possible to argue that this employer had acted unreasonably.

17.126 Nor need the employers prove that an offence has been committed beyond reasonable doubt, for this would impose on them a higher commitment than would ever be possible to fulfil, and impose a duty which rightfully belongs to a court of trial. The

---

[165] [1979] ICR 463, [1979] IRLR 56, EAT.   [166] [1979] IRLR 264, EAT.
[167] [2006] IRLR 576, EAT.   [168] UKEAT/0358/12/BA.   [169] [1977] IRLR 186, EAT.

employers must genuinely believe that the employee has been guilty of the misconduct in question, they must have reasonable grounds for that belief, and they must have carried out such investigation into the matter as is reasonable in the circumstances (*British Home Stores v Burchell,* see paras 12.5 and 17.78). In *Laurie v Fairburn*[170] the claimant was dismissed because the employers believed that she was stealing from them. The employment tribunal was not convinced that this was so, and held the dismissal to be unfair. This was reversed on appeal; the question is not whether or not the employee was guilty, or would have been found guilty if tried, but whether it was reasonable for the employers to dismiss her, taking into account all the circumstances and facts known to the employers at the time of the dismissal.

17.127 If an employee makes a confession, this is a fact which the employer is entitled to take into consideration when forming his views, and the rules about the non-admissibility of confessions made involuntarily (the Judge's Rules) have no application in such circumstances (*Morley's of Brixton Ltd v Minott,* see para 12.17).

17.128 Where an employee has pleaded guilty to a criminal offence, or been found guilty by the decision of a court or the verdict of a jury, it is reasonable for an employer to believe that the employee committed the offence. Any other conclusion 'would be ridiculous' (*P v Nottinghamshire County Council,* see para 12.18). This is so even if the employee alleges that he pleaded guilty on the advice of his lawyers, in order to avoid a prison sentence (*British Gas plc v McCarrick*[171]).

17.129 The fact that an employee faces criminal charges subsequently, and is acquitted on those charges, is also irrelevant to the issue of the fairness of the dismissal. In *Da Costa v Optolis*[172] the claimant was dismissed from his job as a book-keeper for not keeping proper accounts, and he subsequently faced criminal charges, though these ended in his favour. It was held that the fact the Crown Court had acquitted him did not preclude a finding by the employment tribunal that the dismissal was fair. The issues involved were different. In the Crown Court, it had to be decided whether he was guilty of the charge beyond reasonable doubt, whereas in the employment tribunal, it had to be shown whether the employer had reasonable grounds for dismissing him.

17.130 It must surely be sound policy for the employer to be consistent in his procedure, flexible in his decisions. Thus an employer may take into account the fact that the employee has had a long record of exemplary conduct (*City of Edinburgh District Council v Stephen*[173]), but the importance of such mitigating factors is a matter for the employer's discretion (*AEI Cables Ltd v McLay*[174]). In *Taylor v Parsons Peebles Ltd*[175] the claimant, who had been employed for 20 years without complaint, was dismissed for fighting. The EAT held the dismissal to be unfair. The company's policy had to be considered in the light of a reasonable employer's reaction to the incident. Given that the applicant had 20 years' good conduct, a reasonable employer would not have applied a rigid sanction of automatic dismissal. In failing to take account of mitigating circumstances, the employers had acted unreasonably. In *Hadjioannou v Coral Casinos Ltd* (see para 12.46) it will be recalled that the EAT stressed the need for flexibility in dealing with industrial misconduct, saying that a tariff approach was not correct.

17.131 An employee who admits that his conduct is unacceptable, and accepts advice and help to avoid any repetition may be treated differently from an employee who refuses to accept responsibility for his actions, argues with management, or makes unfounded

---

[170] IDS Brief 109.   [171] [1991] IRLR 305, CA.   [172] [1977] IRLR 178, EAT.
[173] [1977] IRLR 135, EAT.   [174] [1980] IRLR 84, Ct of Sess.   [175] [1981] IRLR 119, EAT.

allegations that his colleagues have conspired to make false accusations against him (*Paul v East Surrey District Health Authority*, see para 12.46).

17.132 If the conduct in question amounts to gross misconduct, then this should be acted upon immediately by management, for a delay may lead the employment tribunal to conclude that the conduct was not so wrongful as to warrant the drastic punishment of instant dismissal, although in rare cases it is proper to dismiss summarily a long time after the event (*Refund Rentals Ltd v McDermott*[176]). Normally, it would be reasonable to suspend pending an investigation, but again, this counsel of perfection cannot always be followed (*Conway v Matthew, Wright & Nephew Ltd*, see para 12.66).

17.133 If the conduct falls under the heading of breach of works rules (eg smoking in prohibited areas, fighting, failing to observe safety precautions, etc) then provided the rule is a reasonable one, has been duly promulgated and brought to the attention of the employees, the tribunals will usually uphold management action (*Richards v Bulpitt & Sons Ltd*[177]), particularly if there has been an act of dishonesty (*British Railways Board v Jackson*, para 17.79). But a minor breach should not be treated as an excuse for dismissal, no matter how strongly worded the rule may be (*Ladbroke Racing Ltd v Arnott*, see para 12.45).

17.134 Before dismissing for gross misconduct, the employer should consider any alternative course of action, for it is not inconsistent with a finding of gross misconduct to offer the employee alternative employment in a different capacity (*Hamilton v Argyll and Clyde Health Board*[178]). Each case must be considered on its merits, taking into account the special facts and mitigating circumstances. If, in the past, an employee has not been dismissed for a similar offence, management should enquire into those circumstances. The dangers of a tariff or consistent approach in cases where there is no true comparability should be avoided (*Procter v British Gypsum Ltd*[179]).

17.135 Equally difficult is conduct by the employee which is strictly within his contractual rights, but which is obstructive in nature. In *Pengilly v North Devon Farmers Ltd* (see para 10.61) it was held that a refusal to work overtime, even though not compulsory within the terms of the employee's contract, warranted a dismissal, as the refusal was contrary to the normal practice, and the employee was trying to put improper pressure on the employer. But in *Burns v Ideal Timber Products*[180] it was held that a refusal to work overtime in order to get the employer to improve working conditions did not amount to improper pressure.

17.136 The conduct of the employee must in some way reflect on the employment relationship. In *Thomson v Alloa Motor Co Ltd*,[181] the applicant was employed as a petrol pump attendant. One day she finished work, and drove off in her car, but collided with a petrol pump, causing substantial damage. She was summarily dismissed, because of the seriousness of the damage and the fact that her employers would have to sue her for compensation. The dismissal was held to be unfair. The accident had no bearing on her ability to do her work, it was an incident unlikely to be repeated, and her employers were undoubtedly covered by insurance.

17.137 While it may not generally be possible to dismiss an employee who is acting within the terms of the contract, it should be possible to call for a variation of that contract, or to terminate it and offer a new one (see Chapter 3). Provided the proper procedure is adopted, a subsequent dismissal may well be for 'some other substantial reason' (see para 17.149).

---

[176] [1977] IRLR 59, EAT.   [177] [1975] IRLR 134.   [178] [1993] IRLR 99, EAT.
[179] [1964] 3 All ER 731, [1965] 1 WLR 1, [1965] RPC 239, 109 Sol Jo 47.
[180] [1975] IRLR 19, 10 ITR 14.   [181] [1983] IRLR 403, EAT.

17.138 Other types of conduct which have been held to warrant dismissal include a refusal to wear the appropriate clothing required for the job (*Atkin v Enfield Hospital Management Committee*[182]), wearing provocative badges contrary to instructions and warnings (*Boychuk v Symons Holdings Ltd*[183]), carrying on sexual relations during business hours (*Newman v Alarmco*[184]), passing on information to a former employee of the firm who is working for a competitor (*Smith v Du Pont (UK) Ltd*[185]), refusing to cut exceptionally long hair after being warned of a safety hazard (*Marsh v Judge International*[186]), breach of works rules (*Palmer v Vauxhall Motors Ltd,* see para 12.55), suspected dishonesty (*Parkers Bakeries Ltd v Palmer,* see para 12.16), breach of safety instructions (*Wilcox v HGS*[187]), fighting (*Parsons & Co Ltd v McLoughlin*[188]), being a drug addict (*Walton v TAC Construction Materials Ltd*[189]), taking drugs contrary to a zero-tolerance drugs policy (*O'Flynn v Airlinks the Airport Coach Co Ltd*[190]), refusal to go on a training course (*Minter v Wellingborough Foundries Ltd*[191]), unauthorised access to a computer (*Denco Ltd v Joinson*[192]), misusing the office computer to access hardcore pornography (*Hillingdon London Borough Council v Thomas*[193]) and so on.

17.139 Every employer is strongly urged to observe the provisions of the ACAS Code of Practice on Disciplinary and Grievance Procedures, and although a breach of the Code will not automatically make a dismissal unfair (*Lewis Shops Group v Wiggins,* see para 12.12), in practice it can be said that the provisions of the Code matter most when the decision to dismiss is at its weakest. Thus it is still possible to dismiss summarily for gross misconduct (*Retarded Children's Aid Society v Day*[194]), but procedural fairness should always be observed, and a failure to follow the Code's recommendations may lead to a finding that the dismissal was unfair, even though the compensation may be reduced because of the employee's contributory conduct.

Conduct outside the employment

17.140 The problem which arises here is, what has it got to do with the employer what an employee does outside his working hours? The answer will depend on a number of factors, including the nature of the employment, the position held by the employee, the nature of the incident and its effect on the employer, on customers, on fellow employees, and so on. If it can be said that the conduct in question has an adverse effect on the employer's business; then a dismissal may be fair. For example, the conduct may be a conviction by a court of law for a criminal offence unconnected with the employment. In *Richardson v City of Bradford Metropolitan Council*[195] the claimant was a senior meat inspector, who was convicted of theft of money from his local rugby club on several occasions. When his employers were informed, he was suspended, but as there were no other suitable vacancies which could be offered to him, he was dismissed. This was held to be fair. The integrity of a public servant who was in a position of trust was of prime importance. In *Bradshaw v Rugby Portland Cement Co Ltd*[196] the claimant was dismissed following a conviction for incest with his own daughter, for which he was placed on probation by the Crown Court. The dismissal was held to be unfair. The offence had no bearing on his work as a quarryman, the firm's

[182] [1975] IRLR 217, 119 Sol Jo 575, CA.   [183] [1977] IRLR 395, EAT.
[184] [1976] IRLR 45.   [185] [1976] IRLR 107.   [186] HSIB 15.
[187] [1975] ICR 333, sub nom *Wilcox v Humphreys and Glasgow Ltd* [1975] IRLR 211, [1975] ITR 103; aff'd sub nom *Wilcox v HGS* [1976] ICR 306, [1976] IRLR 222, 11 ITR 43, CA.
[188] [1978] IRLR 65, EAT.   [189] [1981] IRLR 357, EAT.   [190] [2002] All ER (D) 05 (Jul), EAT.
[191] [1981] IDS Brief 202.
[192] [1992] 1 All ER 463, [1991] 1 WLR 330, [1991] ICR 172, [1991] IRLR 63, EAT.
[193] [2002] All ER (D) 202 (Sep), EAT.
[194] [1978] 1 WLR 763, [1978] ICR 437, [1978] IRLR 128, 122 Sol Jo 385, CA.
[195] [1975] IRLR 296   [196] [1972] IRLR 46.

customers would not have objected to his continued employment, and his relationship with his fellow-employees had not deteriorated to the extent that they objected to working with him. There must have been strong mitigating circumstances for the court to deal with the matter so leniently, and the tribunal did not see any reason to impose a further punishment. Clearly, different considerations would have applied had the applicant been (say) a schoolmaster. In *Gardiner v Newport County Borough Council* (see para 12.51) the claimant was a lecturer at an art college, in charge of a foundation course on which were pupils who were between the ages of 16–18. He was convicted of gross indecency with another man in a public lavatory, and his dismissal by the college was held to be fair. The tribunal held that *Bradshaw*'s case was no authority for saying that a person who receives a moderate punishment from the court is immune from dismissal, for the courts are frequently being reminded in mitigation that whatever punishment they impose is only part of the misfortune which will befall the accused. The employers could not be expected to waive the consequences which the courts had anticipated and possibly allowed for in fixing the penalty. Nor is it relevant that the employer never told the employee of the kind of conduct outside his employment which would warrant dismissal, for an employer cannot possibly specify or anticipate all the possible circumstances which may lead to a dismissal. To hold otherwise would mean that an employee would be safest from dismissal if he committed some act which was more outrageous than anyone ever envisaged.

17.141 If the employee is charged with a criminal offence, then clearly the employer will need to make a decision about whether the employment can continue, in advance of a hearing in the criminal courts. The employee should be interviewed (strictly, this is not part of the disciplinary procedure, because no breach of internal discipline has occurred), and invited to explain the position. If he intends to plead guilty, the employer can then make a decision, depending on the circumstances, nature of employment, position held etc. If the employer considers that valuable customers would be lost if the employment continued, he should first attempt to ascertain the views of those customers, and not just make bland assumptions. If the employee states that he intends to plead not guilty, then ideally he should be suspended until the outcome of the criminal proceedings. Whether this suspension should be with pay or without pay is a matter of style and agreement, taking into account the length of time it will be before the hearing takes place, the circumstances of the employer's business, the seriousness or otherwise of the offence, and so on. If there is a collective agreement or a disciplinary procedure which provides that suspension on full pay will be appropriate where investigations cannot be completed, then that agreement or procedure must be followed (*Securicor Guarding Ltd v R*[197]).

17.142 Thus an employer is entitled to make a judgment based on the criminal conduct of the employee, as to whether or not the conviction has impaired the employee's ability to do the job, and whether there has been a loss of confidence in the employee (*Robson v Brian Mills*[198]). In *Moore v C & A Modes*[199] the claimant was a section leader in a store, where she had been employed for 20 years. It was alleged that she had been caught shoplifting at another store. Her consequent dismissal was held to be fair. No-one should be more alert to the damage caused by shoplifters than such an employee, and it was unreal to expect an employer in the retail trade not to dismiss an employee whom he believed to be stealing from another store. In *Mathewson v R B Wilson Dental Laboratory Ltd*,[200] the claimant was arrested during his lunch break for purchasing a small amount of cannabis. His subsequent dismissal was held to be within the range of reasonable responses which a reasonable employer might take.

---

[197] [1994] IRLR 633, EAT.   [198] [1977] IRLIB.
[199] [1981] IRLR 71, EAT.   [200] [1988] IRLR 512, EAT.

17.143 'Moonlighting', ie the taking of additional employment outside normal working hours, may be grounds for dismissal if this has an adverse effect on the employer's business. It will be recalled (para 10.92) that in *Hivac Ltd v Park Royal Scientific Instruments Ltd* the employees were in breach of their contracts for which they could have been dismissed, although this was prevented at the time by the operation of the Essential Works Order. The court stated that it would be reluctant to impose on the employees a restriction which would hamper their ability to increase their earnings in their spare time, but on the facts they were inflicting great harm on the employer's business. In *Gray v C & P Pembroke Ltd* (see para 10.91) the claimant agreed to not engage in any other business without the written consent of the employer. Contrary to this agreement he took a part-time job with a rival company, and this was held to be a breach of faith for which he could be fairly dismissed. However, in *Nova Plastics Ltd v Froggatt*[201] the claimant was employed as an odd-job man. He was dismissed when it was discovered that he was working for a rival firm. The dismissal was held to be unfair. Having regard to the nature of his work as an odd-job man, he could hardly be contributing very seriously to the competition from the rival firm, and in the circumstances there was no breach of duty towards his own employer merely because he worked for a competitor in his spare time.

17.144 In some circumstances, it may be relevant to consider whether or not the outside activity is compatible with the dignity of the employee holding a particular post; in other circumstances an employer may be entitled to forbid an employee engaging in certain leisure pursuits or additional employment if the result is that the employee is too exhausted to follow his normal occupation. If an employee wishes to stand at a parliamentary or local election, this is of concern to the employer only if the activity spills over into the employment scene. For example, supposing a supervisor, who controls a labour force made up largely of coloured immigrant workers, announces his intention of standing for election as a BNP candidate. It could be argued that the potential disruption likely to be caused to a contented workforce may well justify an employer dismissing the employee concerned, although the possible implications of the religion or belief provisions in the Equality Act 2010 would have to be considered (see para 4.154). In *Pay v Lancashire Probation Service*,[202] the claimant was dismissed from his job as a probation officer when it was discovered that in his spare time he was performing shows at various hedonist and fetish clubs, and also acted as a director of a company which sold bondage and sado-masochistic products. It was held that his dismissal was fair, because his activities were incompatible with his position, and there would be potential damage to the reputation of the employer if those activities became public knowledge. An argument that his rights under the Human Rights Act 1998, Art 8 (right to privacy) and Art 10 (freedom of expression) had been violated was not upheld, because of the justification defences provided by the Convention (see para 1.106).

17.145 The conduct in question must be such as to cause a loss of confidence in the employee. Thus in *Whitlow v Alkanet Construction Ltd*[203] the claimant was asked by the company's executive to do some work on the latter's house. There he met the executive's wife, and love play took place between them in the house, and they had sexual intercourse elsewhere. Although the tribunal recognised that the claimant had been subjected to a temptation which few men would have resisted, his dismissal was held to be fair.

Redundancy

17.146 The commonest ground for a dismissal is for reason of redundancy. This will be considered in Chapter 18.

---

[201] [1982] IRLR 146, EAT.　　　[202] [2004] ICR 187, [2004] IRLR 129, [2003] All ER (D) 468 (Oct), EAT.
[203] [1975] IRLR 321.

Statutory restriction

17.147 An employer cannot be expected to continue to employ an employee if such employment would be contrary to the law. For example, if an employee is employed as a driver, and it is a term (express or implied) of his contract that he should hold a valid driving licence, then clearly, if he loses that licence, the employee is barred from pursuing that occupation by statute (Road Traffic Act 1974, s 84). Additionally, the employer may be guilty of an offence if he permits a disqualified driver to drive. But this does not mean that a dismissal will always be fair in such circumstances. The test is, as always, the reasonableness of the employer's action (*Sutcliffe and Eaton Ltd v Pinney*, para 17.119). He must consider the length of the disqualification, the needs of the business, whether the employee can do his job without driving a motor vehicle, whether alternative arrangements can be made, whether the employee could be given some other work to do until his licence is restored, and so on. In *Mathieson v WJ Noble*[204] the claimant was a salesman who was disqualified from driving. He made arrangements to engage a chauffeuse at his own expense to drive him around during the period of disqualification, but his employers decided to dismiss him. It was held that the employers had acted unreasonably in not giving him a chance to see if the new arrangements were satisfactory. This may be contrasted with *Appleyard v FM Smith (Hull) Ltd*[205] where it was an essential requirement for the mechanics that they should hold valid driving licences so that they could test vehicles which they had repaired. When the claimant lost his licence, the company had given some thought to placing him elsewhere in the business, but this was not practicable in such a small firm, and his dismissal was held to be fair.

17.148 There are a number of other legal restrictions on the employment of certain employees in special circumstances. In *Gills v Wall's Meat Co Ltd*[206] the claimant, who was a Sikh, was involved with dealing with open meat. When he commenced employment he was clean shaven, and did not observe his religion by growing a beard, but after a while he was 'converted back to the paths of righteousness' and grew a beard. To have continued to employ him in this capacity would have involved a breach of the Food Regulations 1970, and so the employers, after offering him alternative employment which he refused, dismissed him. This was held to be fair. (It may be noted that a refusal by a Sikh to wear a safety helmet on a construction site as required by regulations made under the Health and Safety at Work etc Act does not entitle an employer to dismiss him as long as he is wearing his turban, see Employment Act 1989, s 11.)

Some other substantial reason

17.149 It was never intended that these reasons for fair dismissal could constitute an exhaustive catalogue of the circumstances in which the employer would be justified in terminating the services of an employee, and there have been a number of cases where 'some other substantial reason' for the dismissal has been held to be fair. In *Wilson v Underhill House School Ltd*[207] the claimant was a schoolteacher in a school which was in financial difficulties, and which could not pay in full a pay award. All the other teachers except her agreed to take less, but she refused and was dismissed. Her dismissal was held to be fair for some other substantial reason. In *Foot v Eastern Counties Timber Co Ltd*[208] the claimant, who was a valued employee, was dismissed when it was discovered that her husband had started a business which was in competition with the employers. It was held that the company had acted reasonably in dismissing an employee who had access to confidential information

---

[204] [1972] IRLR 76.   [205] [1972] IRLR 19.   [206] HSIB 22.
[207] [1977] IRLR 475, 12 ITR 165, EAT.   [208] [1972] IRLR 83.

at a time when her husband was running a rival business. In *Farr v Hoveringham Gravels Ltd*[209] the company had a rule that employees must live within reasonable travelling distance of the firm, and they dismissed a manager who had moved to live 44 miles away. A person in his position may have to be called out in an emergency, and this would prove to be difficult in view of the distance involved. Hence the dismissal was fair.

17.150 It has to be recognised that frequently the legitimate interests of the employer in making a change in employment terms are irreconcilable with the equally legitimate interests of the employee. Thus a sound good business reason for a particular reorganisation has to be looked at in that context (*St John of God (Care Services) Ltd v Brooks*[210]).

17.151 An employer need not wait until a problem arises before he takes action to protect his commercial interests. In *O'Brien v Prudential Assurance Co*,[211] the claimant applied for a job as a district insurance inspector, but deliberately concealed that he had a history of mental illness. When this came to light, the company obtained further medical reports, on the basis of which he was dismissed. Again, this was to be for some other substantial reason, and in the circumstances fair. As an inspector, he would have to go into people's homes, and the company could not risk the possibility that an unsavoury incident might occur.

17.152 Although an employee is not legally obliged to accept a variation in the terms of his contract, a refusal to do so may amount to a substantial reason for dismissal if it is in the commercial interests of the firm that a variation should be made, and it is a reasonable request to make in the circumstances. In *Muggridge and Slade v East Anglia Plastics Ltd*[212] the employers found it necessary to change the working hours, and fairly dismissed two ladies who refused to accept the change, and in *RS Components v Irwin* (see paras 3.94 and 19.25) the company fairly dismissed a salesman who refused to sign a restrictive covenant. But if an employee refuses to sign a restrictive covenant which is unreasonably wide, this will not be a potentially fair reason for dismissal. Nor is it necessary for the employee to make a counter-proposal; if the employer wants the benefit of a restraint clause, he must make sure that the proposal is a reasonable one (*Forshaw v Archcraft Ltd*[213]). However, a dismissal for refusing new contractual terms may be unfair if there is no immediate need for the variation (*Evans v Elemeta Holdings Ltd*[214]).

17.153 A change in employment terms may well be necessary even though these are to the detriment of the employee, if commercial necessity so dictates, for a contract of employment cannot remain static throughout the whole of its existence. In *Sycamore v H Myer & Co Ltd*[215] the claimant refused to accept a new payment system which would have resulted in his wages being reduced from £130 per week to about £90 per week. The new system was negotiated with the trade union because the old method of payment was clearly defective. All the other employees accepted the change, and it was held that the claimant's dismissal was for some other substantial reason, and fair in the circumstances. The new terms were not ungenerous, and had been negotiated with the trade union concerned. In *Storey v Allied Brewery*,[216] the respondents introduced a rota system of working due to the changing pattern of their trade. The claimant refused to work on Sundays, as she wished to go to church. Her dismissal was held to be fair. The change was necessary in the interests of economy, and to balance and share the workload with all the relevant employees. In *Oliver v Sperry Vickers*,[217] the claimant was dismissed for refusing to accept a change in his job

---

[209] [1972] IRLR 104.   [210] [1992] ICR 715, [1992] IRLR 546, [1992] 29 LS Gaz R 24, EAT.
[211] [1979] IRLR 140, EAT.   [212] [1973] IRLR 163.   [213] [2006] ICR 70, [2005] IRLR 600, EAT.
[214] [1982] ICR 323, [1982] IRLR 143, EAT.   [215] [1976] IRLR 84.
[216] (1976) 84 IRLB 9.   [217] [1975] IRLR 358.

title and job content following a reorganisation of the supervisory structure. He was the only one of 22 employees affected who refused. Although this involved minor additions in his duties, he would have received a higher rate of pay. The dismissal was held to be for some substantial reason, and in the circumstances, fair, for he had no reasonable objection to the change.

17.154 A change in working hours does not give rise to a redundancy, but a dismissal due to a refusal to accept such a change consequent on a reorganisation may be for some other substantial reason (*Barnes v Gilmartin Associates*[218]). In *Martland v Cooperative Insurance Ltd*[219] the employer dismissed employees and offered to re-engage them on new contracts with changes to their terms and conditions of employment. It was held that the employees were dismissed for some other substantial reason and were not entitled to a redundancy payment.

17.155 The test in these cases is whether the offer of new terms is within the range of offers which a reasonable employer would make in the circumstances. The task of weighing the advantages to the employer against the disadvantages to the employee is merely one factor to be taken into account (*Richmond Precision Engineering Ltd v Pearce*, see para 3.107). Whether or not other employees have accepted the proposed changes, and whether a trade union have recommended acceptance of the changes are relevant factors to be taken into account. The imposition of the new terms and conditions does not have to be solely on the ground that the changes are vital for the survival of the business, and other valid reasons may be equally acceptable (*Catamaran Cruisers Ltd v Williams*, see para 3.107).

17.156 If an employee is dismissed because he refuses to carry out an order which is not within his contractual obligations, this may be a factor in deciding whether or not he has been unfairly dismissed, but it is not determinative of the issue. There may be sound organisational reasons for the employer seeking to change working conditions or altering the terms of the contract. If the employee has been given ample warnings of the changes, and ample time to discuss his concerns a dismissal for refusing to accept the changes could well be fair (*Farrant v Woodroffe School*, and see *Bateman v Asda Stores Ltd*, para 3.87).

17.157 A difficult situation arises when an employer knows that a disciplinary offence (eg theft) has been committed, but is unable to identify the actual person responsible. Can he then dismiss all the suspects? In *Parr v Whitbread & Co plc*[220] the claimant was a branch manager of an off-licence. There were three other employees working in the shop. It was discovered that the sum of £4,600 was missing, but the circumstances were such that each of the four employees had an equal opportunity of committing the theft. After carrying out a thorough investigation, all four were dismissed. An employment tribunal held that the dismissal was for some other substantial reason, and fair in the circumstances, and the decision was upheld by the EAT. The following guidance was offered: (1) the act must be one which would justify dismissal if committed by an individual; (2) the employer must carry out a reasonable and thorough investigation; (3) as a result of the investigation, the employer must reasonably believe that one of the employees committed the act; (4) the employers must have acted reasonably in identifying the group of employees one of whom could have committed the act; and (5) as between the members of that group, the employer could not reasonably have identified the actual perpetrator.

17.158 But the employer does not have to dismiss all of the group, if he can show solid and sensible grounds for differentiating between members of the group. In *Frames Snooker Centre v Boyce*,[221] three managers had access to a safe in the employers' premises. After

---

[218] EAT 825/97.   [219] Employment Appeal Tribunal, 10 April 2008.
[220] [1990] ICR 427, [1990] IRLR 39, EAT.   [221] [1992] IRLR 472, EAT.

several burglaries had occurred, the police formed the view that each burglary was an inside job. There was no evidence against any of the managers, but the employer decided to dismiss two of them. He did not dismiss the third, because she was his daughter, and he had faith in her honesty and integrity. An employment tribunal held that the dismissal of the two managers was unfair because of the failure to dismiss all the suspects, but the decision was reversed on appeal. There is no 'all or none' principle in dismissing a group when it is not possible to identify the culprit.

17.159 A breakdown in confidence between an employer and a senior executive, for which the latter was responsible because of an inappropriate style of management, is capable of being some other substantial reason for the dismissal. But if a dismissal is procedurally unfair, it is still open to an employment tribunal to find that there was a 100% chance that a fair procedure would have reached the same result, and compensation may be reduced by that percentage (*Perkin v St George's Healthcare NHS Trust*[222]).

17.160 To dismiss one of two incompatible employees in order to restore harmony among the workforce (*Gorfin v Distressed Gentlefolk's Aid Association*[223]) may be fair provided that steps are taken to investigate the conflict and attempts are made to see whether or not an improvement in the relationship can be effected (*Turner v Vesteric Ltd*[224]). Equally, to dismiss an employee who is unable to obtain a fidelity bond (*Moody v Telefusion Ltd*[225]), can be a substantial reason for dismissal. If an appointment is expressed to be of a temporary nature, pending the return to work of an absent employee, this could also constitute grounds which a tribunal may feel justified a dismissal. In particular, the Employment Rights Act 1996, s 106 provides that in two specific instances the dismissal of a temporary employee will be regarded as a substantial reason. These are where a temporary replacement is taken in because there has been a suspension on medical grounds, or a temporary appointment has been made to replace a woman who is absent on the grounds of pregnancy, childbirth, maternity or adoption. In these cases the replacement must be informed in writing of the temporary nature of the appointment, and that he/she may be dismissed when the absent employee returns to work. However, although such dismissal amounts to a substantial reason, it will be without prejudice to the application of the rule that the tribunal must find that the employer has acted reasonably in treating the reason as sufficient ground for dismissal.

17.161 If an employee indicates that he intends to resign his employment, with the result that the employer engages a replacement in anticipation, the employer is entitled to refuse to accept a late notification that the employee has changed his mind, and his dismissal may be fair for some other substantial reason (*Ely v YKK Fasteners Ltd*, see para 17.53).

17.162 An employment tribunal will not accept any reason advanced by the employer as coming within the definition of another substantial reason. In *Hedger v Davy & Co Ltd*[226] the employer received a request from an employment agency for a reference in respect of the applicant. This was held not to be another substantial reason for the dismissal. And in *Wadley v Eager Electrical Ltd*[227] the claimant was a valued worker who had been employed for 17 years. His wife, who worked at the same firm, was summarily dismissed for theft, and the employers felt that they had lost confidence and trust in the applicant. They also felt that his continued employment would have an adverse effect on customers. His dismissal was held not to be for some other substantial reason. It was unfair to dismiss an employee because some other person in the household was fairly dismissed. But a dismissal

---

[222] [2005] IRLR 934.   [223] [1973] IRLR 290.   [224] [1980] ICR 528, [1981] IRLR 23, EAT.
[225] [1978] IRLR 311, 12 ITR 425, EAT.   [226] [1974] IRLR 138.   [227] [1986] IRLR 93, EAT.

because of third party pressure may amount to some other substantial reason (*Davenport v Taptonholme for the Elderly*[228]). Where a client refuses to have a particular employee working for it, then provided the employer has done everything that he reasonably can to avoid or mitigate the injustice brought about by the stance of the client, but has failed to achieve a satisfactory result, then a subsequent dismissal of the employee will be fair (*Henderson v Connect (South Tyneside) Ltd*[229]).

17.163 It must be remembered that even though a reason is capable of being another substantial reason for the dismissal, the employer must still act reasonably in treating that reason as a sufficient reason for dismissal. To do this, he should have a full investigation of the problem, and explore any alternatives which may be available (*Scott Packing and Warehousing Co v Paterson*[230]). There is no absolute requirement that consultation with the employee should take place, but this is one of the factors to be taken into account in determining if the employer has acted reasonably (*Hollister v National Farmers' Union*, see para 3.107). In *Johnson v Tesco Stores Ltd*[231] the claimant made a false statement on his job application form. He was subsequently employed for 18 months before the falsity came to light, during which time he was perfectly satisfactory. Nonetheless he was dismissed, and this was held to be unfair. In *Debaughn v Star Cinemas (London) Ltd*[232] it was contrary to the company's policy to employ people who had had previous criminal convictions, particularly for violence, and they dismissed a doorman who had been employed satisfactorily for 12 months when it was discovered that he had failed to disclose a previous conviction for assault. This was held to be fair. The distinction between these cases lies in the fact that in the former case, there was no real need to act on the information which had come to light, whereas in the latter case the firm's policy could not admit of exceptions for very sound reasons.

17.164 It is frequently useful for an employer to plead or argue 'some other substantial reason' in addition to another reason advanced, for this enables him to have two bites at the cherry! Thus, to dismiss an employee who has been sent to prison may be regarded as conduct or frustration or some other substantial reason. But whatever the 'label', the employer must always be prepared to show that he had acted reasonably in treating the reason as a sufficient reason for dismissing the employee (*Bouchaala v Trusthouse Forte Hotels Ltd*[233]). SOSR is not a catch-all reason for employers who cannot find a more conventional reason for a dismissal. The reason has to be 'substantial' and also a fair process must be followed in all circumstances, *Leach v The Office of Communications (OFCOM)*.[234]

C. Dismissal for asserting a statutory right (ERA, s 104)

17.165 It will be unfair to dismiss an employee because:

(a) he has brought proceedings against an employer to enforce a relevant statutory right; or

(b) he has alleged that the employer has infringed a right of his which is a relevant statutory right.

17.166 The relevant statutory rights for the purposes of s 104 are as follows:

(a) all the rights contained in ERA for which the remedy for infringement is to make a complaint or reference to an employment tribunal;

---

[228] Unreported.　　[229] [2010] IRLR 466.　　[230] [1978] IRLR 166, EAT.
[231] [1976] IRLR 103.　　[232] Unreported.
[233] [1980] ICR 721, [1980] IRLR 382, EAT.　　[234] [2012] EWCA Civ 959.

(b) the following rights made under TULR(C)A – the right not to have the deduction of unauthorised or excessive trade union subscriptions, or unauthorised payment to the union's political fund, right not to have action taken short of dismissal on the ground of union membership or non-membership, right to have time off work for trade union duties or activities, or as a learning representative;

(c) rights conferred by the Working Time Regulations and the Transfer of Undertakings (Protection of Employment) Regulations 2006.

17.167 It will also be unfair to select a person for redundancy on any of the grounds described (s 105(7)).

17.168 The right will apply irrespective of the employee's length of service, because no qualifying period of continuous employment is required.

17.169 It is immaterial whether or not the employee in fact has the right, or whether or not it has been infringed, as long as the employee makes the claim in good faith. Nor need the employee specify the right, as long as it is made reasonably clear to the employer what the right claimed to have been infringed was. Thus, for example, if an employee were to bring a claim before an employment tribunal alleging that he is entitled to a right contained in the Working Time Regulations, and he is dismissed in consequence, the dismissal would be in breach of s 104, irrespective of whether his claim was justified. Thus if an employee genuinely but mistakenly believes that he has the statutory right in question, or genuinely believes that an infringement of his statutory rights has occurred, a consequent dismissal would be unfair (*Philip Hodges & Co v Crush*[235]). The employee cannot be expected to know the precise legal terminology of the right, or the section number of the statutory provision alleged to have been infringed, and it is sufficient if the employee makes it reasonably clear to the employer what right he is relying on (*Jiminez v Nelabrook Ltd*[236]). It would appear that a mere proposal by the employer that a statutory right may be infringed (eg a proposal to reduce wages in circumstances which would amount to an unlawful deduction contrary to ERA, s 13) is not sufficient (*Mennell v Newell & Wright (Transport Contractors) Ltd*,[237] para 17.170).

17.170 But the employee must be able to identify the right alleged to have been infringed by the employer, and if he cannot show that he ever made an allegation that the employer had been in breach of a statutory duty, then the allegation could not be the cause of his dismissal (*Mennell v Newell & Wright (Transport Contractors) Ltd*).

17.171 The interesting thing about this new right is that the 'dismissal' referred to in s 104 must inevitably include a constructive dismissal. Hence, if an employee feels that he is being deprived of his statutory rights, he can resign and make a claim accordingly.

D. **Other dismissals**

17.172 For dismissals on grounds of trade union membership or non-membership, in closed shop situations, lockouts, strikes, and industrial pressure, see Chapter 21. Dismissal on grounds of sex, race, disability or age are dealt with in Chapter 4, maternity dismissals in Chapter 6, and dismissals in health and safety cases in Chapter 11.

[235] EAT 1061/95.
[236] EAT 614/97.
[237] [1996] ICR 607, [1996] IRLR 384, EAT; revsd [1997] ICR 1039, [1997] IRLR 519, [1997] 33 LS Gaz R 26, CA.

E. **National security**

17.173 As already noted, there is a special procedure to be adopted by employment tribunals when dealing with complaints made by members of the security service which involve issues of national security (see para 2.175).

Written reasons for dismissal (ERA, s 92)

17.174 When an employee is dismissed, either with or without notice, or where a limited-term contract terminates without being renewed, he is entitled to receive, on request, and within 14 days, a written statement of the reasons for his dismissal. This statement is admissible in any proceedings before a tribunal or a court. He will not be so entitled unless he has been continuously employed for one year (except for maternity or adoption reasons, see para 17.182).

A. **Adequacy of the statement**

17.175 The employment tribunal must consider three issues, namely (a) was there a failure to provide written reasons, (b) was the failure unreasonable, and (c) are the particulars of reasons given inadequate or untrue?

17.176 The first issue will be largely a question of fact. The reasons must be contained in a document sent for the purpose of complying with the request. Filling in Form ET3 (respondent's reply to an application to an employment tribunal) is not sufficient compliance (*Rowan v Machinery Installations (South Wales) Ltd,* see para 13.42). Nor is it sufficient compliance to refer to other documents, although the sending of documents which contain those reasons is sufficient compliance with s 92 (*Kent County Council v Gilham,* see para 17.79).

17.177 On the second issue, the test of reasonableness is an objective one, ie the standard of behaviour to be expected from a reasonable employer. Thus in *Daynecourt Insurance Brokers Ltd v Iles*[238] the employers ignored a request for written reasons for dismissal following an instruction from the police not to answer any correspondence or deal with the matter which was the subject of an investigation, and it was held that the failure to comply was reasonable in the circumstances. Equally, if the employer genuinely and reasonably believes that no dismissal had taken place then a failure to provide written reasons would be reasonable (*Broomsgrove v Eagle Alexander Ltd*[239]). The fact that the employee knows of the reason does not render the failure to comply with the request reasonable.

17.178 But s 92 has to be strictly construed. In *Keen v Dymo Ltd*[240] the employers sent the written reasons by second class post, so that these arrived a day outside the 14-day period. This was held to be an unreasonable refusal to supply written reasons.

17.179 Finally, the reason given by the employer must be the true reason for the dismissal, but it does not have to be a reason adequate enough to justify the dismissal. That is a matter for subsequent investigation should the employee pursue his claim for unfair dismissal (*Harvard Securities plc v Younghusband*[241]). To be adequate under s 92, the written statement must be such that anyone reading it can know the essential reasons for the dismissal.

[238] [1978] IRLR 335, EAT. [239] [1981] IRLR 127, EAT.
[240] [1977] IRLR 118. [241] [1990] IRLR 17, EAT.

No particular technicalities are involved, and no particular form required (*Horsley Smith and Sherry Ltd v Dutton*[242]).

17.180 If the employee does not make a request for written reasons, he cannot complain that the reasons which were given were untrue, and an employment tribunal has no power to make an award under s 92 in the absence of any such request (*Catherine Haigh Harlequin Hair Design v Seed*[243]).

17.181 A complaint may be presented to an employment tribunal that the employer has unreasonably failed to provide a written statement, or that the statement which has been given is inadequate or untrue. If the tribunal finds the complaint well founded, it may make a declaration as to what it finds to be the employer's reasons for the dismissal, and must make an award of two weeks' pay (ERA, s 93). This award is not subject to the statutory maximum of (currently) £430 per week. The complaint can only be considered by an employment tribunal if it is presented together with a claim for unfair dismissal (ERA, s 93(3)).

B. Written reasons for dismissal on grounds of maternity or adoption (ERA, s 92(4), (4A))

17.182 A woman is entitled to written reasons for her dismissal if she is dismissed at any time while she is pregnant, or after her childbirth in circumstances in which her ordinary or additional maternity leave period ends by reason of her dismissal. She does not need to have the requisite period of continuous employment, and she must be given the written reasons irrespective of whether or not she makes a request for it. The same rule applies if an employee is dismissed while absent from work during an ordinary or additional adoption leave period.

Interim relief (ERA, ss 128–132)

17.183 If an employee complains that the reason for his dismissal was because he was exercising his rights under s 100(1)(a)–(b) (health and safety), s 101A(1)(d) (representative of the workforce for the purpose of the Working Time Regulations), s 102(1) (trustee of occupational pension schemes), s 103 (employee representative under TULR(C)A or Transfer of Undertakings Regulations), or s 103A (protected disclosure), he may make an application for interim relief. A similar application may be made under the provisions of TULR(C)A, ss 161–166 (dismissal for trade union membership and activities, etc) and TULR(C)A, Sch A1, para 161 (playing a role in proposing or opposing trade union recognition). The procedure and remedies are similar to those outlined at para 21.122.

Remedies for unfair dismissal

A. Reinstatement and re-engagement orders (ERA, s 113)

17.184 If an employment tribunal finds that the employee has been unfairly dismissed, it shall explain to him that it has the power to make an order that he be reinstated or re-engaged, and shall ask him if he wishes the tribunal to make such an order. If he expresses such a wish, the tribunal may make the necessary order.

---

[242] [1977] ICR 594, [1977] IRLR 172, 12 ITR 351, EAT.   [243] [1990] IRLR 175, EAT.

17.185 The requirement for the employment tribunal to explain its powers to award reinstatement or re-engagement is mandatory. However, if there is a failure to do so (and in practice many tribunals do so fail) this will not render any other award made a nullity. The order made without compliance with s 113 will only be set aside if the employee has been prejudiced, or if he has suffered an injustice, in consequence of the failure (*Cowley v Manson Timber Ltd*[244]).

17.186 If the order is for reinstatement, the employer shall treat the employee in all respects as if he had not been dismissed, and the tribunal may specify the amount of arrears in pay which are payable to the employee, and rights and privileges, including seniority and pension rights, which must be restored to him, and the date by which the order must be complied with. If the employee would have benefited from an improvement in his terms and conditions of employment had he not been dismissed, the order shall require him to have those improvements. If the tribunal orders re-engagement, this is an order that the employee be re-engaged by the employer or by his successor, or an associated employer, in employment comparable to that from which he was dismissed, or other suitable employment. The tribunal will specify the terms on which the re-engagement will take place, stating the identity of the employer, the nature of the employment (*Khan v Home Office*[245]), the remuneration, any arrears of pay, any rights or privileges which must be restored to him (including seniority and pension rights) and the date by which the order must be complied with. If in either case the tribunal makes an order in respect of arrears of pay it will take into account (for the purpose of reducing the employer's liability) any sums received by the applicant between the date of dismissal and the date of reinstatement or re-engagement, by way of wages in lieu of notice, *ex gratia* payments, remuneration received from another employer, social security benefits, and any other benefits as the tribunal thinks appropriate.

17.187 It must be stressed that the tribunal has a discretion in making either of these orders. It must first consider whether to make an order for reinstatement, and in doing so, it must take into account three considerations:

(a) whether the claimant wishes to be reinstated;

(b) whether it is practicable for the employer to comply with an order for reinstatement. If there is a loss of mutual trust and confidence between the employer and employee, reinstatement is not practicable (*Central and North West London NHS Foundation Trust v Abimbola*[246]);

(c) where the claimant caused or contributed to some extent to the dismissal, whether it would be just to order his reinstatement.

If the tribunal decides not to make an order, it shall then consider whether to make an order for re-engagement, and if so, on what terms. Again, there are three considerations to take into account:

(a) any wish expressed by the claimant as to the nature of the order;

(b) whether it is practicable for the employer or his successor or an associated employer to comply with the order;

(c) where the claimant has caused or contributed to some extent to the dismissal, whether it would be just to order his re-engagement, and if so, on what terms (see *Boots Co plc v Lees-Collier*[247]).

---

[244] [1994] ICR 252, EAT; aff'd [1995] ICR 367, [1995] IRLR 153, CA.
[245] [2008] EWCA Civ 578.   [246] [2009] UKEAT 0542_08_0304.
[247] [1986] ICR 728, [1986] IRLR 485, EAT.

If a re-engagement order is made, it shall, so far as is reasonably practicable, be on terms which are as favourable as an order for reinstatement, unless the tribunal takes into account the contributory fault of the claimant.

17.188 The main restriction on making reinstatement or re-engagement orders appears to be the practicability of doing so. If a permanent replacement has been engaged in place of the dismissed employee, the tribunal shall not take this into account for the purpose of deciding whether it was practicable for the employer to comply with the order unless the employer shows:

(a) that it was not practicable for him to arrange for the dismissed employee's work to be done without engaging a permanent replacement; or

(b) that he engaged the replacement after the lapse of a reasonable time without having heard from the dismissed employee that he wished to be reinstated or re-engaged, and that when the employer engaged the replacement, it was no longer reasonable for him to arrange for the dismissed employee's work to be done except by a permanent replacement.

17.189 It is also submitted that earlier tribunal decisions on the impracticability of making reinstatement or re-engagement recommendations are still valid. For it should be noted that 'practicable' does not mean 'possible'. Thus the orders are unlikely to be made:

(a) if the dismissal was in a redundancy situation, or if reinstatement would result in redundancies (*Cold Drawn Tubes Ltd v Middleton*[248]);

(b) the claimant is unfit for work (see *Rao v Civil Aviation Authority*[249]); or

(c) if there is some friction or personal animosity either with the employer or with fellow-employees (*Coleman v Magnet Joinery Ltd*[250]); or

(d) if the employer is a small firm, with few staff, reinstatement or re-engagement should only be ordered in exceptional circumstances, as there is a close personal relationship between the parties which may make such an order impracticable (*Enessy Co SA v Minoprio*[251]); or

(e) if there is mistrust between the parties (*Nothman v London Borough of Barnet*[252]); or

(f) if the order is likely to be ineffective (*ILEA v Gravett*[253]); or

(g) if there has been a breakdown in trust or confidence between the employer and employee, eg if the dismissal was for alleged misconduct (*Wood Group Heavy Industrial Turbines Ltd v Crossan*[254]). The existence or absence of mutual trust and confidence are relevant factors to be taken into account when determining the question of the practicability of complying with an order for reinstatement or re-engagement (*Central & NW London NHS Trust v Abimbola*[255]). However, a simple assertion that re-engagement was not practicable because there had been a breakdown of trust and confidence between the employee and his managers as a result of the events that gave rise to the dismissal does not, by itself, prevent an order for re-engagement to be made.

[248] [1992] ICR 318, [1992] IRLR 160, EAT.
[249] [1992] ICR 503, [1992] IRLR 203, EAT; on appeal [1994] ICR 495, [1994] IRLR 240, CA.
[250] [1974] ICR 25, [1973] IRLR 361, 17 KIR 11, 9 ITR 74, NIRC; aff'd [1975] ICR 46, [1974] IRLR 343, [1975] KILR 139, CA.
[251] [1978] IRLR 489, EAT.
[252] [1978] 1 WLR 220, [1978] ICR 336, [1977] IRLR 398, EAT; revsd [1978] 1 All ER 1243, [1978] 1 WLR 220, 76 LGR 617, [1978] ICR 336, [1978] IRLR 489, 13 ITR 125, 121 Sol Jo 813, CA; aff'd [1979] 1 All ER 142, [1979] 1 WLR 67, 77 LGR 89, [1979] ICR 111, [1979] IRLR 35, 123 Sol Jo 64, HL.
[253] [1988] IRLR 497, EAT.   [254] [1998] IRLR 680, EAT.   [255] See n 235.

It may well be that the employee's contact with the managers responsible for his dismissal would be minimal (*Johnson Matthey plc v Watters*[256]); or

(h) if the employee's job has disappeared following a reorganisation (*Thamesdown Borough Council v Turrell*[257]).

17.190 In other words, the practicability of ordering reinstatement or re-engagement must be looked at in a subjective and pragmatic sense, bearing in mind the particular circumstances of the case. The employer is entitled to give a logical and reasonable explanation why there are no vacancies, and to make a commercial judgment about the best interests of the business. An employment tribunal is not entitled to substitute its own views for those of management, provide1d the decision not to re-engage is in the bracket of reasonableness, for the test is whether it is practicable, not whether it is possible (*Port of London v Payne*[258]). In practice, very few reinstatement or re-engagement orders are made, as very few applicants request this remedy.

17.191 If an employee is reinstated or re-engaged following an order to that effect from the employment tribunal, his continuity of employment is preserved, and the period between his dismissal and reinstatement or re-engagement counts towards his continuity (Employment Protection (Continuity of Employment) Regulations 1996). This also applies if reinstatement or re-engagement follows a compromise agreement, or action taken by a conciliation officer, or a claim based on a designated dismissal procedure or following an ACAS sponsored arbitration award.

B. **Compensation (ss 117–127A)**

17.192 If the order for reinstatement or re-engagement is made, but its terms are not fully complied with, the tribunal may make an award of compensation of such amount as it thinks fit, having regard to the loss sustained by the claimant in consequence of the employer's failure to comply with those terms.

17.193 If an order is made, but the claimant is not reinstated or re-engaged at all, then the tribunal will make an award of compensation. This will be under three headings:

(a) basic award

(b) compensatory award

(c) additional award.

17.194 If no order for reinstatement or re-engagement is made, the tribunal will make an award which will consist of a:

(a) basic award

(b) compensatory award.

17.195 *Basic award (i).* In two instances this will amount to two weeks' pay, with a maximum of £464 per week in 2013–14 (these figures change in April each year). The two instances are:

(a) Where an employee's contract is renewed, or he is re-engaged under a new contract, he is not regarded as having been dismissed under his old contract (s 138). If the

[256] EAT/0236/0237/0238/06.   [257] Unreported.
[258] [1993] ICR 30, [1992] IRLR 447, [1992] 31 LS Gaz R 35, EAT; aff'd [1994] ICR ICR 555, [1994] IRLR 9, CA.

terms and conditions of the new contract (including capacity and place in which he is employed) differ from the previous contract, and during the trial period the employer or employee terminates the contract for a reason connected with the dif-. ference, the employee will be treated as having been dismissed on the date on which his previous contract ended. If the reason for that dismissal was redundancy, he will be entitled to a minimum basic award of two weeks' pay (s 121(a)).

(b) Where there is an offer to renew the contract, or an offer of re-engagement under a new contract, and the provisions of the contract as to capacity and place of employment, and other terms and conditions would not differ from the old contract, or, if they do differ, but the offer constitutes an offer of suitable alternative employment, the employee is not entitled to a redundancy payment if he unreasonably refuses that offer (see para 18.28). This also applies if the employee unreasonably terminates the contract during the trial period. Nonetheless, he is entitled to a basic award of two weeks' pay (s 121(b)).

17.196 *Basic award (ii).* Where a dismissal has been held to be unfair because the employee was selected for dismissal because of trade union membership or activities (TULR(C)A, s 152), or because he was designated to carry out health and safety activities or was a health and safety representative (ERA, s 100(1)(a)–(b)), or because he was a workforce representative under the Working Time Regulations (ERA, s 101A(d)), or was a trustee of an occupational pension scheme (ERA, s 102(1)), or an employee representative for consultation purposes (ERA, s 103), or was selected for redundancy for any of these reasons, the minimum basic award shall be (currently) £5,676.

17.197 *Basic award (iii).* The basic award will depend on the number of years the employee has been employed (with a maximum of 20 years' service to count) and his normal week's pay (capped). There is no lower or upper age limit, and the tapering provision which used to apply to employees over the age of 64 was abolished by the Employment Equality (Age) Regulations 2006. There will be a multiplier of one half of a week's pay for each year's service below the age of 21, one week's pay for each year's service between the ages of 22 and 40, and one and a half week's pay for each year's service over the age of 41.

17.198 The amount of the basic award can be reduced in three circumstances (ERA, s 122).

(a) If the employer has made an offer to reinstate the employee, so that in all respects he would be treated as if he had not been dismissed, and the employee unreasonably refuses that offer, the employment tribunal may reduce the basic award by an amount it thinks to be just and equitable. (Note that if the offer is made with different terms and conditions, an unreasonable refusal will not justify reducing the basic award, although it may be relevant to reduce the compensation award, because the employee has failed to mitigate his loss.)

(b) If the employee's conduct prior to the dismissal (or, where notice was given, before notice of dismissal) was such that it would be just and equitable to reduce (or further reduce) the basic award, the employment tribunal may do so. Normally, the conduct in question would have caused or contributed towards the dismissal, but this is not essential so far as the employment tribunal's powers under this section are concerned. Indeed, conduct which only comes to light after the dismissal (which occurred before the dismissal) may be grounds for reducing the basic award, eg if it is subsequently discovered that the employee had set up a rival business during his employment, or had been stealing from his employer. But misconduct during the notice period is not a ground for reducing the basic award, even though it would not be just and equitable to make that award, although it may be grounds for reducing the compensation award.

It is not permissible to make a reduction of the basic award on grounds of contributory conduct if the reason for the dismissal was redundancy, except in those cases where the dismissal was for an inadmissible reason (trade union membership or activities (TULR(C)A, s 157), designated safety representatives (s 100), occupational pension scheme trustee (s 102), and employee representative (ss 101A and 103)), when the minimum basic award of (currently) £5,676 applies (s 120). In such cases, if the employee caused or contributed to the dismissal, there may be a reduction in the amount by which the minimum basic award exceeds the normal basic award (s 122(3)). Thus, assume that the employee was dismissed for one of the inadmissible reasons, and his contribution towards the dismissal is assessed at 50%. Assume also that his normal basic award would have been £1,856 (based on four years' service). Since he is entitled to £5,676 by virtue of s 120, we deduct the former sum from the latter, leaving, £3,820; 50% of this sum is £1,910 which is deducted from £5,676, making a total basic award of £3,766. But if the conduct led to a selection for redundancy for trade union reasons (membership, non-membership or activities) no reduction can be made for contributory conduct (TULR(C)A, s 155), eg if an employee was selected for redundancy because he refused to join a particular trade union.

(c) If an employee was dismissed for reason of redundancy, and was given a redundancy payment, the amount paid by the employer or awarded by a tribunal is to be deducted from the basic award. Normally, this would extinguish the basic award altogether. But the fact that a redundancy payment was made will not extinguish the basic award if the real reason for the dismissal was not in fact redundancy (*Boorman v Allmakes Ltd*[259]).

17.199 The entitlement to a basic award is automatic once a dismissal is held to be unfair, and cannot be reduced on the ground that there has been no financial loss to the claimant (*Cadbury Ltd v Doddington*[260]). It is payable even if no compensation award is made (*British United Shoe Machinery Co Ltd v Clarke*[261]). It cannot be reduced on the ground that the claimant has failed to mitigate against his loss, because there is no provision to this effect (*Lock v Connell Estate Agents*[262]). And it cannot be reduced when an *ex gratia* payment or a severance payment is made, unless it is made clear that the payment is in respect of all compensation an employee is entitled to should the employee subsequently bring a claim in an employment tribunal (*Chelsea Football Club and Athletic Co Ltd v Heath*[263]). There is no requirement to make the same reduction in the basic and compensatory awards on the grounds of contributory conduct (*Optikinetics Ltd v Whooley*[264]).

17.200 When assessing a week's pay for the purpose of the basic and compensation awards, the employment tribunal must not disregard the employer's obligation to pay the national minimum wage, and must base the award on what the employee should have received under the National Minimum Wage Act (see Chapter 8), rather than on what he actually received (*Paggetti v Cobb*, see para 14.5).

C. **Compensatory award (ERA, s 123)**

17.201 This award will be such amount as the employment tribunal considers just and equitable in all the circumstances, having regard to the loss sustained by the claimant in

[259] [1995] ICR 842, [1995] IRLR 553, CA. [260] [1977] ICR 982, EAT.
[261] [1978] ICR 70, [1977] IRLR 297, 12 ITR 473, EAT. [262] [1994] ICR 983, [1994] IRLR 444, EAT.
[263] [1981] ICR 323, [1981] IRLR 73, EAT. [264] [1999] ICR 984, EAT.

consequence of the dismissal, in so far as that loss is attributable to action taken by the employer, including any expenses reasonably incurred by him, and the loss of any benefits which he might reasonably have expected to have had (ERA, s 123(1)). Once an employment tribunal finds blameworthy conduct on the part of the employee which brought about his dismissal, it must reduce the compensation award by some proportion, under the just and equitable rule (*Optikinetics Ltd v Whooley*[265]).

17.202 Under the 'just and equitable rule' the employment tribunal has a wide discretion, even so far as awarding nil compensation in appropriate cases (*W Devis & Sons Ltd v Atkins*[266]). For example, in *Courage Take Home Trade Ltd v Keys,*[267] the claimant accepted a sum in settlement of his claim, but then continued with proceedings for unfair dismissal, because, as the settlement did not involve ACAS, it was not binding. The employment tribunal did not think it was just and equitable to make a compensatory award, and declined to do so. If, after the dismissal, it is discovered that the employee had been guilty of conduct before the dismissal which would have merited dismissal, then it may not be just and equitable to award full or any compensation (*W Devis & Sons Ltd v Atkins,* para 20.94), but post-termination conduct should not be taken into account (*Soros v Davison*[268]). If a redundancy dismissal is unfair because of the lack of consultation, the employment tribunal should assess the likelihood of there being a fair dismissal had there been proper consultation, and make an appropriate award on that basis (*Mining Supplies (Longwall) Ltd v Baker*[269]).

17.203 There is no limit on the amount of a week's pay for the purpose of calculating the financial loss, although there is a statutory maximum limit on the compensatory award. This is (currently) £76,574 or 52 weeks' pay, whichever is less (the latter element was introduced in July 2013). This can be exceeded if an additional award is made: see para 17.239. If the reason for the dismissal was because the employee acted as a health and safety representative (ERA, s 100) or because he made a protected disclosure (ERA, s 103A), or if he was selected for redundancy for either of those reasons, there is no limit on the amount of the compensatory award (s 124(1A)). The employment tribunal must assess the compensatory award judicially, and specify how it is made up, but they can, and do, use a 'broad brush' approach (*Norton Tool Co Ltd v Tewson*[270]). Only financial loss may be taken into account, for the object is to compensate the claimant, not to punish the employer for his wrong behaviour. The manner of dismissal cannot be the subject of a compensatory award, unless there is evidence that this has caused financial loss, eg if it affected the claimant's reputation, making him less attractive to future employers. Thus, unlike awards made in discrimination cases, no award can be made for injured feelings. It follows that if the claimant has lost nothing, eg if he has obtained other employment immediately, no award under this head can be made. The assessment of past losses should not be too difficult, but, when assessing future losses, the employment tribunal must inevitably indulge in a form of speculation. The burden of proof is on the employee to show the past and/or future loss, but this should not prove to be an onerous task in practice (*Adda International Ltd v Curcio*[271]).

[265] [1999] ICR 984.
[266] [1976] 2 All ER 822, [1976] 1 WLR 393, [1976] ICR 196, [1976] IRLR 16, 11 ITR 15, 120 Sol Jo 62; on appeal [1977] AC 931, [1977] 2 All ER 321, [1977] 2 WLR 70, [1977] ICR 377, [1976] IRLR 428, 12 ITR 12, 121 Sol Jo 52, CA; aff'd [1977] AC 931, [1977] 3 All ER 40, [1977] 3 WLR 214, 8 BLR 57, [1977] ICR 662, [1977] IRLR 314, 13 ITR 71, 121 Sol Jo 512, HL.
[267] [1986] ICR 874, [1986] IRLR 427, EAT.   [268] [1994] ICR 590, [1994] IRLR 264, EAT.
[269] [1988] ICR 676, [1988] IRLR 417, EAT.
[270] [1973] 1 All ER 183, [1973] 1 WLR 45, [1972] ICR 501, [1972] IRLR 86, 117 Sol Jo 33, NIRC.
[271] [1976] 3 All ER 620, [1976] ICR 407, [1976] IRLR 425, EAT.

17.204 Generally speaking, there are five headings to consider.

Immediate loss of earnings

17.205 The immediate loss is the loss incurred between the date the employment was terminated and the date when the employment tribunal assess the loss. In some cases, a considerable time may have elapsed between these two dates, while issues of procedure and/ or liability are being argued. Nonetheless, if the employment tribunal feel that the claimant has taken reasonable steps to mitigate his loss, the length of time which may have elapsed is irrelevant (*Gilham v Kent County Council (No 3)*[272]). The claimant's loss is assessed by reference to the net pay he would have received, although bonuses, overtime pay and pay increases can be taken into account, had these been likely (*Mullet v Brush Electrical Machines Ltd*[273]). Tips which form part of normal remuneration (*Palmanor Ltd v Cedron*, see paras 14.4 and 17.27), expenses, to the extent they represent a profit in the hands of the employee (*S & U Stores v Wilkes*, see para 14.4), and the loss of the opportunity to obtain an enhanced redundancy payment (*Lee v IPC Business Press Ltd*[274]) are all part of the loss suffered. The loss of private use of a company car can be valued either by using the annual tables produced by the AA or RAC, or using the Revenue calculations. Free or subsidised accommodation, private medical insurance, subsidised mortgage schemes (*UBAF Bank Ltd v Davis*[275]) and luncheon vouchers are all benefits, the value of which can be calculated.

17.206 If, at the time when the employment tribunal assess the loss, the employee has obtained fresh employment with the same or a lower earnings, those earnings can be offset when assessing the net loss, but compensation does not end merely because an employee has found fresh employment (*Dench v Flynn & Partners*[276]). If, following a dismissal, and employee takes a new job that is temporary, or on probation, and he loses that job within a short time, this can result in further compensation being awarded. Losses do not automatically cease to be attributable to the first employer upon fresh employment being obtained (*Cowen v Rentokil Initial Facility Service (UK) Ltd*[277]).

17.207 A problem may arise if the employee obtains employment which is better paid, because then compensation will be based on his loss during the period of unemployment, but the excess between his old and new salary also falls to be deducted (*Ging v Ellward Lancs Ltd*[278]). However, because this can lead to an unfair result on occasions, the employment tribunal may fall back on the 'just and equitable' principle, and ignore this rule, particularly when there has been a long period of time between the dismissal and the date when compensation is assessed (*Fentiman v Fluid Engineering Products Ltd*[279]). The principles to be adopted in these circumstances were set out by the EAT in *Whelan v Richardson* (para 17.211), where it was held that loss of earnings should be calculated from the date of dismissal up to the date when the applicant obtains higher paid permanent employment. Similarly, credit must be given in respect of earnings from self-employment (*Justfern Ltd v D'Ingerthorpe*[280]).

17.208 Income support and/or jobseekers' allowance is not deducted at this stage, but are subject to the recoupment provisions (see para 17.244). There are conflicting authorities on how invalidity benefit received should be treated (compare *Rubenstein v McGloughlin*[281] and *Puglia v C James & Sons*[282]), but the better view appears to be that it is correct to deduct

[272] [1986] ICR 52, [1986] IRLR 56, EAT. [273] [1977] ICR 829, EAT.
[274] [1984] ICR 306, EAT. [275] [1978] IRLR 442, EAT.
[276] [1998] IRLR 653, CA. [277] Employment Appeal Tribunal, 6 March 2008.
[278] [1991] ICR 222n, 13 ITR 265, EAT. [279] [1991] ICR 570, [1991] IRLR 150, EAT.
[280] [1994] ICR 286, [1994] IRLR 164, EAT. [281] *Times*, 28 December 1995, EAT.
[282] [1996] ICR 301, [1996] IRLR 70, EAT.

the amount of invalidity benefit received from the compensation award (*Chan v London Borough of Hackney*[283]). The same rule applies to incapacity benefit (*Morgans v Alpha Plus Security Ltd*[284]). The fact that a claimant is in receipt of incapacity benefit did not preclude the employment tribunal from awarding compensation for loss of earnings during the same period. Eligibility for incapacity benefit is based on 'deemed' incapacity for work, which does not mean that the claimant is in fact incapable of earning during that period (*Sheffield Forgemasters International Ltd v Fox*[285]). Housing benefit should not be deducted (*Savage v Saxena*[286]). Money received under an early retirement scheme or ill-health retirement scheme is not to be deducted (*Smoker v London Fire and Civil Defence Authority*[287]).

17.209 If an employee is dismissed without notice and without pay in lieu of notice, but nonetheless finds work within what would have been the statutory notice period, he is still entitled to receive compensation for that period, because that is a legal entitlement, not to be deducted from the compensatory award (*TBA Industrial Products Ltd v Locke*[288]). In *FATA Ltd v Addison*[289] it was held that full wages should be paid for what would otherwise have been the notice period, without regard to the principle of mitigation, as this was in accordance with good industrial relations practice. A tribunal cannot make an award greater than the loss suffered by the employee as a consequence of the dismissal so as to result in a bonus payment. Thus if an employee would only be entitled to statutory sick pay during what would have been the notice period, compensation can only be based on sick pay entitlement (*Langley and Carter v Burlo*[290]). But if the employee's notice period would have been particularly long (eg on the premature termination of a fixed-term contract), the additional notice period will not be added to the compensatory award, on the ground that the employee should have mitigated against his loss (*Vaughan v Weighpack Ltd*[291]). If the employee is dismissed without notice but given his proper entitlement in lieu of notice, credit for this sum must be given (*Addison v Babcock FATA Ltd*[292]), although the EAT in Scotland appear to have come to a different conclusion on this point (*Finnie v Top Hat Frozen Foods*[293]).

17.210 *Ex gratia* payments should always be offset, to the extent that these exceed the basic award (*Horizon Holidays Ltd v Grassi*[294]), as should severance payments (*Darr v LRC Products Ltd*[295]). Income tax rebates received by the employee during his period of unemployment should be ignored unless there are substantial sums involved (*MBS Ltd v Calo*[296]).

Future loss

17.211 The employment tribunal must estimate the likely future loss, inevitably by indulging in speculation. They can take into account all the relevant circumstances, eg the age of the applicant and his general employability, his personal circumstances, his health

---

[283] [1997] ICR 1014, EAT.   [284] [2005] ICR 525, EAT.   [285] [2009] ICR 333, [2009] IRLR 192.
[286] [1998] ICR 357, [1998] IRLR 182, EAT.
[287] [1991] 2 AC 502, [1991] 2 WLR 422, [1990] IRLR 271; revsd [1991] IRLR 22, CA; aff'd [1991] 2 AC 502, [1991] 2 All ER 449, [1991] 2 WLR 1052, [1991] ICR 449, [1991] IRLR 271, HL.
[288] [1984] ICR 228, [1984] IRLR 48, EAT.
[289] [1988] QB 280, [1987] 3 WLR 122, [1987] 2 All ER 784, [1987] ICR 805, [1987] IRLR 173, [1987] 1 FTLR 505, (1987) 84 LSG 1409.
[290] [2006] 2 All ER 1104, [2006] ICR 850, [2006] IRLR 460, EAT; aff'd [2006] EWCA Civ 1778, [2007] 2 All ER 462, [1007] ICR 390, [2007] IRLR 145, (2007) 104(2) LSG 30, (2007) 151 SJLB 61, CA.
[291] [1974] ICR 261, [1974] IRLR 105, 16 KIR 233, 9 ITR 226, NIRC.
[292] [1987] ICR 45, [1986] IRLR 388, [1986] LS Gaz R 2568, EAT; revsd [1988] QB 280, [1987] 2 All ER 784, [1987] 3 WLR 122, [1987] ICR 805, 131 Sol Jo 538, [1987] LS Gaz R 1409, sub nom *Babcock FATA Ltd v Addison* [1987] IRLR 173, [1987] 1 FTLR 505, CA.
[293] [1985] ICR 433, [1985] IRLR 365, EAT.   [294] [1987] ICR 851, [1987] IRLR 371, EAT.
[295] [1993] IRLR 257, EAT.   [296] [1983] ICR 459, [1983] IRLR 189, EAT.

(*Fougère v Phoenix Motors*[297]), local employment conditions, the scarcity of jobs in a particular trade, industry, the current economic climate (*MacNeilgae v Arthur Roye Ltd*[298]) and so on. They must form a judgment as to how long it will be before the claimant obtains comparable employment (*Courtaulds Northern Spinning Ltd v Moosa*, see para 17.213). There is no objection, in theory, to consider making an award for the rest of the claimant's working life (see *Morganite Electrical Carbon Ltd v Donne*[299]) although the existence of a maximum award of £76,574 or 52 weeks' pay will inevitably come into play at some point. If a claimant has become self-employed, future loss can be estimated to a point when he establishes an income comparable with that he has lost. As a general rule, the more senior the employee, the longer it may take him to obtain fresh employment, but the whole exercise is speculative. Of course, when assessing future loss, the employment tribunal will already have at its disposal much of the information needed on past losses, and will merely be projecting those losses forward for a period of time. Thus if the employee obtained new employment after the date of dismissal at a higher rate of pay, the employment tribunal should calculate the compensatory award from the date of the dismissal up to the date when the new employment commenced, and not up to the date when the tribunal makes the award (*Whelan v Richardson*, para 17.207, but see *Dench v Flynn & Partners*, para 17.213). In *Wardle v Credit Agricole Corporate and Investment Bank (Calyon)*[300] the Court of Appeal gave guidance as to the correct approach to the duration of loss. It would be rare to award career-long loss. This should be done only in those cases where there was no real prospect of the employee obtaining another job. In most other cases, damages should only be awarded to the time when the employee was likely to obtain an equivalent job, ie that there was a more than 50% chance of obtaining an equivalent salary.

17.212 If the employment tribunal has evidence which would lead to the conclusion that the claimant would have lost his job anyway at some point in time, eg because of the redundancy situation, then that is a factor which should be taken into account when assessing the past and future loss of earnings (*Young's of Gosport Ltd v Kendell*[301]). Equally, a supervening event, eg illness, which arises after the dismissal, and which causes the claimant to be out of work for a long time, is not a loss which is attributable to the action taken by the employer. But if the illness was brought on to some extent by the employer's action, that is a matter which an employment tribunal can take into account, for a certain period of time, at least (*Devine v Designer Flowers Wholesale Florist Sundries Ltd*[302]).

17.213 Since the employment tribunal is projecting the claimant's loss into the future, there is authority for the proposition that the employer should receive a discount of around 2–5% for accelerated payment, although there may be a premium of a similar amount in respect of a delayed payment (*Melia v Magna Kansei Ltd*[303]). It has been suggested that this brings into the calculations a complication which should not be introduced (*Les Ambassadeurs Club v Bainda*[304]). Losses which are too remote from the employer's actions should also be excluded. For example, if the claimant obtained permanent employment, that is a fact which will normally break the chain of causation, so that if he has lost that employment at the time when the employment tribunal is assessing compensation, the subsequent period of unemployment is not a future loss which could have been contemplated (*Courtaulds Northern Spinning Ltd v Moosa*, para 17.211). But this rule is not one of

[297] [1977] 1 All ER 237, [1976] 1 WLR 1281, [1976] ICR 495, [1976] IRLR 259, 11 ITR 181, 120 Sol Jo 603, EAT.

[298] [1976] IRLR 88.   [299] [1988] ICR 18, [1987] IRLR 363, EAT.

[300] [2011] IRLR 604, [2011] EWCA Civ 545.   [301] [1977] ICR 907, [1977] IRLR 433, 12 ITR 269, EAT.

[302] [1993] IRLR 517, EAT.   [303] [2006] ICR 410, [2005] EWCA Civ 1547, CA.

[304] [1982] IRLR 5, EAT.

universal application, for the ultimate duty of the employment tribunal is to make an award which is just and equitable (see *Dench v Flynn & Partners*, para 17.234). There is also an overlap between the question of remoteness and the claimant's duty to mitigate against his loss, which can usually be resolved by the application of the 'just and equitable' principle (*Simrad Ltd v Scott*[305]).

In *Norton Tools Co Ltd v Tewson*, decided in 1972, it was held that only quantifiable pecuniary loss could be compensated for, and non-economic loss was not recoverable. In *Dunnachie v Kingston upon Hull City Council* (see paras 11.113 and 16.5), the Court of Appeal threw doubt on the correctness of that decision, holding that the provision in the Act which provided for compensation to be 'just and equitable in all the circumstances' could include a sum in respect of injury to feelings, pride and self-respect. However, on appeal, the decision in the *Dunnachie* case was reversed by the House of Lords, who held that no award for non-economic loss of that nature may be made under the statutory provisions.

Expenses

17.214 The employment tribunal may award to the claimant any expenses reasonably incurred by him in consequence of the unfair dismissal. This could include money spent seeking fresh employment, eg on travelling to interviews, on buying-selling a home in order to obtain employment in a different area, or on setting up a new business (*Gardiner-Hill v Roland Berger Technics Ltd*[306]). However, legal expenses incurred in the bringing of the employment tribunal proceedings cannot be awarded under this heading, although there is a residue power for the employment tribunal to make an award of costs in appropriate cases (see para 1.22).

Loss of statutory rights

17.215 Since it will take some time before a claimant is employed in a new job long enough to obtain the benefit of a number of statutory rights, (in particular, he will have to wait for a further year before he is protected against a future unfair dismissal), the employment tribunals will usually award a modest sum of £200 by way of compensation for this loss (*S H Muffett Ltd v Head*[307]). Also, in the case of a claimant who had a long period of service with his former employer, it is possible to make an award in respect of the loss of the right to have a long period of statutory notice (*Arthur Guinness Son & Co (Great Britain) Ltd v Green*[308]).

Loss of pension rights

17.216 The loss suffered by a claimant under this heading will sometimes depend on the type of pension scheme, ie final salary scheme or money purchase scheme. The former scheme does not depend on contributions to the fund by the employer and/or employee, whereas the latter schemes are so dependent. So far as the compensatory award is concerned, a claimant may have lost (a) pension rights accruing to him since the dismissal, (b) future pension rights, and (c) the loss of enhancement of accrued pension rights. To assist in resolving and quantifying the loss, reference may be made to the Government's Actuary's Guidelines 'Compensation for loss of pension rights—Employment Tribunals' (see *Greenhoff v Barnsley Metropolitan Borough Council*[309]). If, following a dismissal, an employee chooses to take his pension early, the value of his pension benefits should not be deducted from any compensation award (*Knapton v EEC Card Clothing Ltd*[310]).

---

[305] [1997] IRLR 147, EAT.   [306] [1982] IRLR 498, EAT.
[307] [1987] ICR 1, [1986] IRLR 488, [1986] LS Gaz R 2653, EAT.
[308] [1989] ICR 241, [1989] IRLR 288, EAT.   [309] [2006] ICR 1514.
[310] [2006] ICR 1084, [2006] IRLR 756, EAT.

17.217 When calculating the compensation awarded in respect of an unfair dismissal it is proper to take into account the fact that in any new employment it is almost impossible nowadays in the private sector to find a job that provides membership of a final salary pension scheme as opposed to a money purchase scheme (*Roberts v Aegon UK Corporate Services Ltd*[311]).

D. Reducing the compensatory award (ERA, s 123(4), (6))

The reduction

17.218 In *British Labour Pump Co Ltd v Byrne*[312] it was held that where there was a procedural irregularity in an otherwise fair dismissal, eg a failure to consult in a redundancy situation, but it was shown that carrying out the proper procedure would have made no difference, then a consequent dismissal was nonetheless fair. This 'it makes no difference rule' was overturned in *Polkey v A E Dayton Services Ltd* (see para 12.14), except in those circumstances where the employer can show that carrying out a proper procedure would have been utterly useless or futile. Thus if an employee is caught literally or metaphorically with his hands in the till, it is perfectly possible for a dismissal to be unfair (eg, because the correct procedure has not been followed) but to award nil compensation on the ground that the employee contributed totally towards his dismissal (*Kristapaitis v Thistle Seafood Ltd*[313]).

17.219 However, following from another decision of the House of Lords in *Devis v Atkins*[314] that 'it cannot be just and equitable that a sum should be awarded in compensation where in fact the employee has suffered no injustice by being dismissed' *Polkey* decided that where there has been a failure to follow a fair procedure, the compensation award (but not the basic award) may be reduced, potentially to nil if necessary.

Adjustment of compensation awards (TULR(C)A, s 207A)

17.220 If it appears to the employment tribunal that an employer has unreasonably failed to comply with the ACAS Code on Disciplinary and Grievance Procedures (eg by failing to adopt the appropriate dismissal procedure), the tribunal may, if it considers it is just and equitable to do so, increase any award it makes to the employee by up to 25%.

17.221 Similarly, if the employee has unreasonably failed to comply with the ACAS Code (eg by failing to go through a grievance procedure) the tribunal may, if it considers it is just and equitable to do so, reduce any award it makes in favour of the employee by up to 25%.

17.222 The ACAS Code does not apply to redundancy dismissals or to the non-renewal of fixed-term contracts on their expiry.

17.223 The adjustments for breach of the ACAS Code only applies to cases brought under the 25 jurisdictions listed in Sch 2A of TULR(C)A.

Mitigation of loss

17.224 A dismissed employee is under a duty to mitigate against his loss so far as possible (*Scottish and Newcastle Breweries plc v Halliday*[315]). This means that he should take

[311] [2009] EWCA Civ 932, [2010] ICR 596, [2009] IRLR 1042, (2009) 106(31) LSG 18.
[312] [1979] ICR 347, [1979] IRLR 94, EAT.
[313] Employment Appeal Tribunal (Scotland), 29 October 2009.
[314] [1977] AC 931, [1977] 3 WLR 214, [1977] 3 All ER 40, 8 BLR 57, [1977] ICR 662, [1977] IRLR 314, (1978) 13 ITR 71, (1977) 121 SJ 512.
[315] [1986] ICR 577, [1986] IRLR 291, EAT.

reasonable steps to obtain other employment, taking into account his skills, personal circumstances, health, etc (*Fourgère v Phoenix Motor Co Ltd*). Whether a claimant has taken such reasonable steps is a question of fact in each case (*Gardiner-Hill v Roland Berger Technics Ltd*, para 17.236). Thus, if an employer changes his mind about a dismissal, or recognises that it is unfair, and offers reinstatement or re-engagement on suitable terms which the employee unreasonably refuses, this may indicate that he has not taken reasonable steps to mitigate against his loss, and compensation may be reduced accordingly (*Hepworths Ltd v Comerford*[316]). A failure by an employee to invoke an internal appeals machinery is not a failure to mitigate against the loss (*William Muir (Bond 9) Ltd v Lamb*, see para 12.22), for the rules relating to mitigation apply to conduct after the dismissal (*McAndrew v Prestwick Circuits Ltd*[317]).

17.225 If, after being dismissed, the claimant decides to have a complete change of career, which involves retraining, the employment tribunal may find that such action was reasonable, and the loss of income during the training period may be the subject of compensation. A failure to seek alternative employment in such circumstances is not a failure to mitigate against the loss (*Orthet Ltd v Vince-Cain*[318]).

17.226 The burden of proof lies on the employer to show that the claimant has failed to mitigate against his loss (*Fyfe v Scientific Furnishing Ltd*[319]). An employment tribunal is not bound to consider this heading unless it is raised by the employer, along with some supporting evidence. The employment tribunal should identify the steps taken to mitigate the loss, find the date by which such steps would have produced an alternative income, and then reduce the amount of compensation by the amount of income which would have been earned (*Savage v Saxena*, para 17.208, and see *Hardy v Polk (Leeds) Ltd*, para 15.38).

17.227 So far as mitigation is concerned, the following principles were laid down by the Court of Appeal in *Wilding v British Telecommunications plc*:[320]

(a) it is the duty of the employee to act as a reasonable person unaffected by the prospect of compensation from his former employer;

(b) the onus is on the former employer as the wrongdoer to show that the employee has failed in his duty to mitigate his loss by unreasonably refusing an offer of re-employment;

(c) the test of reasonableness is an objective one based on the totality of the evidence;

(d) in applying that test, the circumstances in which the offer was made or refused, the attitude of the former employer, and all the surrounding circumstances, including the employee's state of mind, should be taken into account;

(e) the court or tribunal should not be too stringent in its expectations of the injured party.

Contributory conduct

17.228 Where an employment tribunal finds that the dismissal was to any extent caused or contributed to by any action of the claimant, it shall reduce the amount of the compensatory award by such proportion as it thinks just and equitable, having regard to that

---

[316] Unreported.

[317] [1988] IRLR 514, EAT; on appeal sub nom *Prestwick Circuits Ltd v McAndrew* [1990] IRLR 191, 1990 SLT 654, Ct of Sess.

[318] [2005] ICR 374, EAT.

[319] [1989] ICR 648, [1989] IRLR 331, EAT.

[320] [2001] All ER (D) 03 (Apr), EAT; aff'd [2002] EWCA Civ 349, [2002] ICR 1079, [2002] IRLR 524, [2002] All ER (D) 278 (Mar).

finding (ERA, s 123(6)). In *Nelson v BBC (No 2)*,[321] the Court of Appeal stated that there are three matters which must be taken into account under this heading. First, the action of the employee must be culpable or blameworthy; second, that action must have caused or contributed towards the dismissal; and, third, it must be just and equitable to reduce the compensatory award by the specified proportion. For example, in *Scottish Co-operative Wholesale Society Ltd v Lloyd*[322] a dismissal was held to be unfair because no specific warnings had been given to the claimant. But he had failed to reply to complaints which had been made against him, failed to obey certain instructions, and failed to achieve a modest sales target. All these factors were held to be conduct which contributed towards the dismissal and were therefore grounds for reducing the compensatory award. A failure to follow works rules, using company property for private purposes, unco-operative conduct, failure to apologise for wrongful acts (eg swearing at a manager), failure to explain unauthorised absences, a refusal to give an explanation for certain conduct, failing to return to work on time after holidays, and so on, have all been held to be grounds for reducing the compensatory award.

17.229 Since the conduct must in some way be blameworthy or culpable, matters which are beyond the employee's control, eg ill health (*Slaughter v C Brewer & Sons Ltd*[323]) ought not to be taken into account. Similarly, an employee who is incompetent or incapable does not contribute to his dismissal, provided he is trying his best (*Kraft Food Ltd v Fox*), although if an employee is lazy, indolent, or does not make an effort to improve or avoid errors, he does so contribute. Further, the conduct in question does not have to be the main reason for the dismissal; it is sufficient (for the purpose of reducing the compensatory award) for it to have played a material part in the dismissal (*Robert Whiting Designs Ltd v Lamb*[324]). A senior employee who is dismissed for serious misconduct must expect to have his compensatory award reduced substantially, for a higher standard of conduct is expected from him (*McPhail v Gibson*[325]).

17.230 It is unlikely that the employment tribunal would reduce the compensatory award in cases of constructive dismissal, but there is no reason in principle why this cannot be done, because the employee's conduct may have played a material part in the events which led to his resignation (*Morrison v Amalgamated Transport and General Workers' Union*[326]). For example, in *Polentarutti v Autokraft Ltd*,[327] the employee machined a number of defective hubcaps. Subsequently, the employer refused to pay him for working overtime, and he resigned, claiming constructive dismissal. Although his dismissal was held to be unfair, the employment tribunal reduced the compensatory award by two-thirds on the ground that his poor workmanship contributed to the dismissal. The EAT dismissed an appeal by the employee, holding that there was a sufficient link between the events in question which justified a reduction in the award. An employee who has been constructively dismissed must give credit for sums earned from other employment during what would otherwise have been the notice period. The Court of Appeal has held that the *Norton Tool* principle does not extend to cases of constructive dismissal (*Stuart Peters Ltd v Bell*[328]).

17.231 If a claimant was dismissed on the ground of his non-membership of a trade union, no reduction can be made in the compensatory award because he refused to join a trade union (see *Transport and General Workers' Union v Howard*.[329]) Nor can a reduction be

---

[321] [1980] ICR 110, [1979] IRLR 346, 123 Sol Jo 552, CA.

[322] [1973] ICR 137, [1973] IRLR 93, 8 ITR 178, NIRC.   [323] [1990] ICR 730, [1990] IRLR 426, EAT.

[324] [1978] ICR 89, EAT.   [325] [1977] ICR 42, [1976] IRLR 254, EAT.

[326] [1989] IRLR 361, NICA.   [327] [1991] ICR 757, [1991] IRLR 457, EAT.

[328] [2009] EWCA Civ 938, [2010] 1 WLR 10, [2010] 1 All ER 775, [2009] ICR 1556, [2009] IRLR 941, (2009) *Times*, 7 October.

[329] [1992] ICR 106, [1992] IRLR 170, EAT.

made if the dismissal was because of his trade union membership or activities (TULR(C)A, s 155). If an employee is dismissed because he took part in a strike, and it is subsequently held that that dismissal was unfair on ground of selective re-engagement (see para 21.101), a reduction for contributory conduct should not be made merely because he took part in the strike. It is only where there was some individual blameworthy conduct additional to or separate from the participation in industrial action that the employment tribunal should consider reducing the compensatory award (*Crosville Wales Ltd v Tracey*[330]).

17.232 Contributory conduct has resulted in some cases with a reduction as high as 80–90%, and for some time there was doubt as to whether it was a proper reduction to make, because there appears to be a logical inconsistency in saying that an employee was treated unfairly, and yet contributed to that extent towards his dismissal. However, in *Maris v Rotherham Corpn*[331] the House of Lords thought that there was no particular problem in finding a dismissal unfair, yet reducing the compensatory award by 100%. Compensation should only be awarded when it is just and equitable to do so, and it cannot be just to award compensation when the employee was totally responsible for his dismissal. Nor is there an inconsistency in finding a dismissal unfair yet not awarding compensation.

17.233 The assessment of the percentage reduction to be taken into account because of contributory conduct is essentially a question of fact, to be determined by the employment tribunal (*Hollier v Plysu Ltd*[332]).

Remoteness of loss

17.234 The tribunal must compensate the employee for the loss caused by the employer's wrongful conduct. That loss does not cease when the employee finds new alternative employment, because it is quite possible for the loss to continue. Thus, if the new employment is at a lower rate of pay, or is of a temporary nature, or entails additional expense by way of travel, relocation etc, these factors can be taken into account when assessing the compensation. In *Dench v Flynn & Partners* (paras 17.206, 17.211 and 17.213), the claimant was unfairly dismissed. She obtained employment with another firm but this only lasted for two months. The Court of Appeal held that the tribunal was wrong to limit the compensation award up to the time when she had obtained the new employment. The question was whether her losses were attributable to her unfair dismissal.

17.235 If an employee decides not to seek other employment, but to make a career change by going on a training course a tribunal may take the view that this is a reasonable course to take, having regard to the employee's age, the state of the employment market, the level of remuneration, the viability of the course, etc. However, there may well come a point in time when the loss suffered by the employee is too remote from the employer's wrongful action. Thus in *Simrad Ltd v Scott* (para 17.213) an electronics technician was unfairly dismissed. She decided to change career and took a course in nursing. Although the tribunal thought that she had acted reasonably in taking up a new career, the EAT held that compensation was not payable from the time she commenced the nursing course, because this was too remote to be attributed to the actions of the employer. However, a contrary conclusion appears to have been reached in *Orthet Ltd v Vince-Cain*, see para 17.225).

---

[330] [1993] IRLR 60, EAT; revsd sub nom *Tracey v Crosville Wales Ltd* [1996] ICR 237, sub nom *Crosville Wales Ltd v Tracey (No 2)* [1996] IRLR 91, CA; aff'd sub nom *Tracey v Crosville Wales Ltd* [1998] AC 167, [1997] 4 All ER 449, [1997] 3 WLR 800, [1997] ICR 862, [1997] 41 LS Gaz R 28, [1997] NLJR 1582, sub nom *Crosville Wales Ltd v Tracey (No 2)* [1997] IRLR 691, HL.

[331] [1974] 2 All ER 776, [1974] ICR 435, [1974] IRLR 147, 16 KIR 466, 9 ITR 288, NIRC.

[332] [1983] IRLR 260, CA.

17.236 In some cases, it may well be reasonable for the employee to become self-employed, and this should not be held against him, when weighed against his employment prospects generally. In *Gardiner-Hill v Roland Berger Technics* (see paras 17.214 and 17.224) a 55-year-old managing director acted reasonably in setting up his own specialised business. Clearly, his initial loss was greater than if he had attempted to obtain immediate employment, but the loss was not too remote, although it could not be expected to go on indefinitely! Expenses reasonably incurred in setting up a new business are not too remote, but again, a sensible limit should be imposed.

E. Order of adjustments to compensation awards

17.237 The tribunal must first ascertain the employee's loss in consequence of the dismissal, insofar as that loss is attributable to the action of the employer. The following adjustments to that amount may be made in the following order, where applicable:

(a) a deduction of any payment made to the employee as compensation for the dismissal (eg a payment in lieu of notice, or an *ex gratia* payment, but not an enhanced redundancy payment) (*Digital Equipment Co Ltd v Clements*[333]);

(b) a deduction of any sum earned by the employee by way of mitigation of the loss, or to reflect the failure by the employee to mitigate against the loss (ERA, s 123(4));

(c) a percentage reduction under the *Polkey* principle, reflecting the fact that the employer would have a fair reason for the dismissal had the relevant contractual disciplinary procedure been followed (*Rao v Civil Aviation Authority*, see para 17.189);

(d) an increase in the compensation because the employer has failed to follow the ACAS Code or a decrease in compensation because the employee has failed to comply with the ACAS Code;

(e) an increase because the employer has failed to provide written particulars of employment (Employment Act 2002, s 38);

(f) a percentage reduction because the employee has contributed to the dismissal (ERA, s 123(6));

(g) the deduction of any enhanced redundancy payment to the extent that it exceeds the basic award (ERA, s 123(7));

(h) a deduction under the recoupment provisions.

17.238 After all these adjustments have been made, the statutory cap of (currently) £76,574 is applied.

F. Additional award (ERA, s 117)

17.239 It will be recalled that if an employer totally ignores a tribunal order to reinstate or re-engage the employee, an additional award can be made. This order should not be made if the employer satisfied the tribunal that it was not practicable to comply with the order, but since the tribunal will have already considered this point when making the order (see para 17.184) it will presumably be open to the employer to adduce new evidence as to why it is not practicable to do so. Otherwise, if re-engagement or reinstatement is ordered and not complied with, and the reason for the dismissal was because of race, sex or disability discrimination, or victimisation for trade union membership, employee representation, pension scheme trustee, breach of working time provisions, or health and safety reasons,

[333] [1996] ICR 829, [1996] IRLR 513, EAT.

there will be an additional award of between 26 and 52 weeks' pay. A week's pay for the purpose of the additional award shall not exceed (currently) £464.

17.240 However, in the case of a highly paid employee, or where proceedings have been considerably delayed, the total of the maximum of the basic, compensatory and additional awards may not be adequate to meet the loss actually suffered and it may be cheaper not to comply with the reinstatement order. In such cases, ERA, s 124(3) enables an employment tribunal to make a compensation award which is at least equal to the amount of pay lost between the date of dismissal and what should have been the date of reinstatement or reengagement, to show their disapproval of the employer's decision (see *Selfridges Ltd v Malik*[334]), at the same time taking into account the employee's conduct and failure to mitigate against his loss (*Mabirizi v National Hospital for Nervous Diseases*[335]).

17.241 Severance payments made may be deducted from the additional award to the extent that the basic and compensatory awards are exceeded (*Darr v LRC Products Ltd*, para 17.210).

G. **Interest on awards**

17.242 By the Employment Tribunals (Interest) Order 1990, interest is payable on all tribunal awards (but not the recoupment element) after 42 days from the date the decision is recorded and sent to the parties. Interest is also payable on awards made by the EAT. Any award by way of costs or expenses is excluded. If on a review or appeal the award is varied, interest accrues on the amount as varied. However, by the Employment Tribunals (Interest on Awards in Discrimination Cases) Regulations 1996, interest on awards made in respect of injury to feelings may be made from the date of the act of discrimination to which the complaint relates.

17.243 The rate of interest is the rate currently prescribed under the Court Funds Rules 1987 and the Act of Sederunt (Interest in Sheriff Court Decrees or Extracts) 1975.

H. **Recoupment of job-seekers' allowance**

17.244 Under the heading of the compensation award, a sum of money is ascertained as the loss suffered, and the tribunal will then deduct from that sum the amount of jobseekers' allowance which the claimant has received. In fact, this amounts to the Government providing a subsidy to the employers, and thus regulations have been passed enabling the Government to recoup this money from the employer (see Employment Protection (Recoupment of Jobseekers' Allowance and Income Support) Regulations 1996). The consequence is that the tribunal must ascertain the prescribed element (which is the gross loss of earnings from the date of dismissal until the date of the hearing), and this may be withheld from the claimant until the Secretary of State has served a notice on the respondent to pay the whole or part of the prescribed element to the Department. When this has been received, the Secretary of State will pay to the claimant the sum due less the jobseekers' allowance he has received. Recoupment only applies in respect of the period for which compensation is assessed (*Hosnan v Al Baca Ltd*[336]).

17.245 Recoupment does not apply when a settlement is reached without a tribunal hearing, because private settlements (with or without the assistance of the conciliation officer) are not within the scope of the regulations.

---

[334] [1998] ICR 268, [1997] IRLR 577, EAT.   [335] [1990] ICR 281, [1990] IRLR 133, EAT.
[336] Unreported.

18

Redundancy

18.1 The basic purpose of the Redundancy Payments Act 1965 was to compensate a long-serving employee for the loss of a right which he has in a job. There may be other benefits or advantages, such as the need to encourage mobility of labour, redistribute economic skills, and assist in the process of rationalisation of resources, but whether such objects are being achieved must be a matter for the economist rather than the lawyer. The compensation paid is in respect of the loss suffered, and is not intended as a benefit to tide the redundant employee over a period of difficulty. Thus if a person is made redundant, he is entitled to his payment even if he obtains employment elsewhere immediately; similarly, he is entitled to claim jobseekers' allowance in addition to his redundancy money.

18.2 The Act has been repealed and replaced by corresponding provisions in the Employment Rights Act 1996, and in this chapter appropriate references will be made to the latter Act. The provisions relating to collective redundancies are to be found in the Trade Union and Labour Relations (Consolidation) Act 1992 as amended.

Provisions of the Employment Rights Act 1996

A. Persons covered by the Act

18.3 The Act applies to 'employees', ie persons who have entered into a contract of service or apprenticeship. In order to qualify generally, the employee must have at least two years' continuous employment with that employer or with another employer where continuity is preserved (see ERA s 218, para 13.39).

18.4 The usual problem arises with the definition of the term 'employee', illustrated, perhaps, by *Challinor v Taylor* (see para 2.29), which shows one of the disadvantages of being self-employed. A partner is not an employee for redundancy purposes (*Burgess v O'Brien*[1]), nor is a clergyman working at a Mission (*Parker v Orr*[2]). A managing director or director of a company who has executive responsibilities may be an employee, in accordance with the principles set out by the Court of Appeal in *Secretary of State for the Department of Business, Enterprise and Regulatory Reform v Neufeld* (see para 2.13). Nor does the appointment of a receiver alter the position, for if he was an employee before that appointment, he can still be one following the appointment. A person may pay a self-employed insurance stamp, and yet be regarded as an employee, for, as we have already seen, this fact is not conclusive evidence as to the true status. The matter is one to be decided in each case on its own special facts.

---

[1] (1966) 1 KIR 99, 1 ITR 164.
[2] (1966) 1 KIR 513.

B. **What is dismissal? (s 136)**

18.5 A dismissal takes place if:

(a) the employer terminates the contract (with or without notice);

(b) a fixed-term contract expires without being renewed;

(c) the employee is employed under a limited-term contract and the contract terminated automatically on the completion of a particular task or upon the occurrence or non-occurrence of a specific event, without the employment being renewed (whether under the same contract or otherwise);

(d) the employee terminates the contract with or without notice in circumstances which are such that he is entitled to do so by reason of the employer's conduct (*Millbrook Furnishing Industries Ltd v McIntosh*[3]); and

(e) the employment is terminated by the death, dissolution, liquidation of the employer, or the appointment of a receiver.

18.6 We have seen in Chapter 3 that a variation of a contract may amount to a new agreement. If the variation is accepted by both sides, then there is no dismissal, and continuity of employment is preserved. But a variation unilaterally imposed by the employer may amount to a dismissal. In *Marriott v Oxford and District Co-operative Society (No 2)* (see para 3.100), a foreman was told that he would be employed at a lower status and at a reduced rate of pay. This was held to be a dismissal. If the employee accepts the changed situation for a short time under protest there will still be a dismissal, though clearly there will come a point when he will be deemed to have accepted the change if he continues in employment. If the express or implied terms of the contract permit a variation, then no dismissal takes place if the employer exercises his rights thereunder. If the contract of employment contains a mobility clause, an employer can choose to exercise it rather than make the employee redundant. As long as the decision is not made arbitrarily or capriciously, an employee cannot insist on being made redundant as an alternative (*Home Office v Evans*[4]). In *McCaffrey v EE Jeavons & Co Ltd*[5] an express term of the contract stated that the employee should work anywhere in the United Kingdom. He was asked to move from Bristol to Reading, but he refused. His subsequent resignation was held not to amount to a dismissal.

18.7 If the employer and employee mutually agree to 'part company' this will not be a dismissal, unless there is a clear intention to this effect. But the fact that a contract specifically states that it can only be determined by mutual consent or with appropriate notice does not mean that if appropriate notice has not been given it must have been determined by mutual consent (*Hellyer Bros v Atkinson*[6]). For example, some employers may call for 'volunteers' to be made redundant, and they will qualify for redundancy payments despite their willingness to be dismissed (*Burton, Allton and Johnson Ltd v Peck,* see para 17.68) but a mutual agreement whereby the employee accepts terms for early retirement does not constitute a dismissal (*Birch and Humber v University of Liverpool,* para 17.68). If an employee is given the option of being transferred to part-time working, or being made redundant, and he chooses the latter option, there is a dismissal for reason of redundancy, and it is not a consensual termination (*Lassman v De Vere University Arms Hotel,* para 17.68).

18.8 If an employee is told that there may be possible redundancies in the future, he may be penalised if he acts precipitously. In *Morton Sundour Fabrics Ltd v Shaw* (para 15.1) a foreman was warned of impending redundancies, and he left the firm to take other

[3] [1981] IRLR 309, EAT.   [4] [2007] EWCA Civ 1089, [2008] ICR 302, [2008] IRLR 59.
[5] (1967) 2 ITR 636, DC.   [6] [1992] IRLR 540, EAT; revsd [1994] IRLR 88, CA.

employment. His initiative went unrewarded, for it was held that as he had not been dismissed, he was not entitled to a redundancy payment (see also *International Computers v Kennedy*[7]).

18.9 As long as the employee is on the books of the firm, he is still employed, even though he is not working or not being paid. In *Marshall v Harland & Wolff Ltd* (paras 17.61 and 17.100) the employee was absent from work for 18 months because of illness. The company then decided to close down the works, and gave him four weeks' notice of dismissal. It was held that he was nonetheless entitled to a redundancy payment, for the employers had not discharged the burden of showing that the contract had come to an end by virtue of frustration through illness.

18.10 An employer may dismiss an employee with appropriate notice. If, during the period of that notice, the employee gives a written counter-notice, stating that he intends to leave before the notice expires, the employee is still regarded as having been dismissed. However, the employer is not bound to accept the counter-notice, and may (again in writing) inform the employee before the end of the counter-notice that he does not accept it, and require him to work until the expiry of the original period of notice. The sanction is that the employer may contest the redundancy payment, and the tribunal has power to reduce it either in whole or in part, as it thinks just and equitable. On the other hand, if there is a mutual agreement that the employee may leave early, this constitutes a variation of the employer's notice, not a consensual termination of the contract (see para 17.68). The employee, therefore, will still be regarded as having been dismissed (*McAlwane v Boughton Estates Ltd*, see para 15.9).

C. Dismissal for reason of redundancy (s 139)

18.11 For a claim to be made, the employee must be dismissed for reason of redundancy. In *Sanders v Ernest A Neale Ltd*[8] employees went on a work-to-rule campaign in protest against management actions. The employers sacked them, and eventually the factory closed down. It was held that they were not entitled to redundancy payments. They were dismissed because they would not give an undertaking to work normally, and the dismissals caused the redundancy, rather than the redundancy bringing about the dismissals (see *Baxter v Limb Group of Companies*,[9] para 21.103). There is a statutory presumption (s 163(2)) that if an employee is dismissed, it is presumed to have been for the reason of redundancy unless the contrary is proved. The burden of proof is on the employer to show the reason, and if none is forthcoming, or if the tribunal does not accept the reason as a genuine one, the statutory presumption will arise. However, if the employer does show a reason other than redundancy, the question may arise as to whether the dismissal was fair or unfair, but there will be no liability to redundancy payments.

18.12 A dismissal shall be for reason of redundancy if it is wholly or mainly attributable to:

(a) the fact that the employer has ceased, or intends to cease, to carry on that business for the purposes for which the employee was employed; or

(b) the employer has ceased or intends to cease to carry on that business in the place where the employee was employed; or

(c) the fact that the requirements of that business for employees to carry out work of a particular kind, or for them to carry out that work in the place where they were so employed, have ceased or diminished or are expected to cease or diminish.

---

[7] [1981] IRLR 28, EAT.   [8] [1974] 3 All ER 327, [1974] ICR 565, [1974] IRLR 236, NIRC.
[9] [1994] IRLR 572, CA.

Cessation of business

18.13 This is a recognisable situation which produces a few legal problems. In *Gemmell v Darngavil Brickworks Ltd*[10] the firm closed down temporarily for a period of 13 weeks so that repairs could be carried out, and the dismissed employees were held to be redundant, as a temporary cessation is within the meaning of the Act. If the part of the business where the employee works is closed down, but the rest of the business (in its corporate sense) carries on, there is still a cessation of the business.

The employer moving his place of business

18.14 Section 139(1)(a)(ii) provides that a dismissal shall be for reason of redundancy if it is due to the fact that the employer has ceased to carry on business in the place where the employee was employed. According to the EAT, this is a factual matter, not a contractual one. In other words, the test to be applied is where, in fact, the employee worked, not where, under his contract, he was required to work. Thus in *Bass Leisure Ltd v Thomas*,[11] the employee worked from the company's depot in Coventry. It was then decided to close the depot, and transfer it to a suburb of Birmingham, some 20 miles away. Her contract stated that the employer reserved the right to transfer her to any other alternative place of work in order to meet the needs of the business. After working from the new depot for a short while, she found that it involved too much travelling, and she resigned, claiming a redundancy payment. The EAT held that the place where she was employed was at Coventry, and that her contractual terms were evidential in defining the place of her employment. However, it was not permissible to take into account those terms which permitted a variation of the place of employment. The EAT also held that earlier decisions, which take into account mobility clauses (eg *United Kingdom Atomic Energy Authority v Claydon*, see para 10.58) were not to be followed. This view has been given the approval of the Court of Appeal in *High Table Ltd v Horst*,[12] where it was stated that the true test is a factual one, to be determined by the circumstances, and the fact that there was a mobility clause in the contract did not mean that 'the place where the employee was employed' extended to every place where he could be employed. If an employee only worked at one location for the purpose of his employer's business, the place where he was employed cannot be extended merely because there was a mobility clause (a contrary view appears to have been taken in *Home Office v Evans*,[13] see para 18.6). If an employee worked in different places, the contract would be helpful in determining the extent of the place where he was employed. However, the test of the suitability of alternative work (see para 18.28) would still need to be met.

18.15 If the employer moves his place of work, whether the move is sufficient to constitute a redundancy situation will be a question of fact, depending on the distance between the old and the new premises, and the resultant inconvenience caused to the employees affected. In *Managers (Holborn) Ltd v Hohne*,[14] the claimant was the manageress of premises in Holborn. The company decided to move its premises to Regent Street, a short distance away. It was held that it could not be said that there was an implied term in her contract that she would only work in Holborn. Both premises were in Central London, and easily accessible. To hold that the employers had broken the contract would mean that it would have been a breach had the employers moved just around the corner, even though the claimant's work or her travel had been completely unaffected.

---

[10] (1967) 2 ITR 20.   [11] [1994] IRLR 104, EAT.
[12] [1998] ICR 409, [1997] IRLR 513, sub nom *Hosdt v High Table Ltd* [1997] 28 LS Gaz R 25, 141 Sol Jo LB 161, CA.
[13] [2007] EWCA Civ 1089, [2008] IRLR 59, [2008] ICR 302.   [14] [1977] IRLR 230, 12 ITR 379, EAT.

Surplus labour

18.16 In this situation the employer requires fewer employees for existing work (*Carry All Motors Ltd v Pennington*[15]), or there is less work for existing employees (*Chapman v Goonvean and Rostowrack China Clay Co*[16]), and consequently some are redundant. The redundancy can arise because the work has been reorganised, thus requiring fewer employees to do the same work, or because of the introduction of labour-saving devices, or a change in the work pattern which requires the same number of employees but a different kind of skill, or one to whom different terms and conditions of employment will apply. But the time of day in which the work is to be performed does not make it 'work of a particular kind' so that if there is a reduction in the need for night workers, who are thus transferred to day working, this does not amount to a redundancy. In *Johnson v Nottinghamshire Combined Police Authority*,[17] clerks were employed from 9.30am to 5.30pm. It was decided to introduce a shift system whereby they would work from 8.00am to 3.00pm and from 1.00pm to 8.00pm in alternate weeks. The clerks refused to do the shift work, and were dismissed. It was held that the change in the hours was to promote greater efficiency, and they were not entitled to redundancy payments (see also *Barnes v Gilmartin Associates*, para 17.154).

18.17 This reasoning was confirmed by the Court of Appeal in *Lesney Products & Co Ltd v Nolan*,[18] where the company reorganised its working hours so that instead of the employees working one long day shift plus overtime, they were required to work two day shifts. Employees were offered work on the double day shift, and those who refused were dismissed. It was held that they were not entitled to redundancy payments. A redundancy only arises if there is a change in the terms and conditions of employment due to the fact that the employer's need for work of a particular kind is ceasing or diminishing. A reorganisation of work which results in reduced earning does not produce a redundancy situation if there is still the need for the same number of employees doing the same overall work, and the only change is that they earn less wages. The law should not inhibit the ability of the employer to reorganise the workforce so as to improve efficiency. The fact that overtime is reduced does not create a redundancy, if the employer's requirements for the work to be done, and the employees to do the work, are the same as before. But if an employee is on a temporary contract, which is not renewed, this can be a redundancy, even though it is known at the time of his appointment that there would be no work for him at the end of the period. ERA, s 136(1)(b) clearly provides that a failure to renew a fixed-term contract is a dismissal for redundancy purposes, and this would be unnecessary if there was no entitlement to a redundancy payment on the expiry of such a contract (*Lee v Nottinghamshire County Council*[19]).

18.18 In *Hindle v Percival Boats Ltd*[20] the claimant was engaged in repairing wooden boats. The amount of work was declining because of the introduction of fibreglass, and it was uneconomical to retain his services, so he was dismissed because 'he was too good and too slow'. Although he was not replaced (a fact which is sometimes used to determine whether or not a redundancy exists) his work was carried out by other employees working overtime.

---

[15] [1980] ICR 806, [1980] IRLR 455, EAT.

[16] [1973] 1 All ER 218, [1972] 1 WLR 1634, [1973] ICR 50, 8 ITR 77, 116 Sol Jo 967, NIRC; aff'd [1973] 2 All ER 1063, [1973] 1 WLR 678, [1973] ICR 310, 14 KIR 382, 9 ITR 379, 117 Sol Jo 416, CA.

[17] [1974] 1 All ER 1082, [1974] 1 WLR 358, [1974] ICR 170, [1974] IRLR 20, 9 ITR 164, 118 Sol Jo 166, CA.

[18] [1977] ICR 235, [1977] IRLR 77, 12 ITR 6, CA.

[19] [1979] ICR 818, [1979] IRLR 294, 123 Sol Jo 404, EAT; revsd 78 LGR 568, [1980] ICR 635, [1980] IRLR 284, CA.

[20] [1969] 1 All ER 836, [1969] 1 WLR 174, 4 ITR 86, 113 Sol Jo 13, CA.

A majority of the Court of Appeal thought that the employers had rebutted the presumption of redundancy. In another leading case (*North Riding Garages Ltd v Butterwick*[21]) the employee was the manager of a repair workshop. New employers took over the business, and introduced new working methods to which the employee could not adapt. He was dismissed for incompetence and inefficiency, and applied for a redundancy payment. It was held that if the new methods had so altered the nature of the work that there was a lessening of the work of a kind he was formerly employed to do, this would amount to redundancy. On the facts, however, the overall requirements of the firm had not changed. It was the inability of the employee to change and adapt to new methods which brought about his dismissal.

18.19 In considering the definition of redundancy, earlier cases appear to have concentrated on the work which the employee actually did (the function test) and the work which the employee was obliged to do under his contract (the contract test); but in *Safeway Stores plc v Burrell*[22] it was stated that both these approaches were wrong, and that it is the statutory definition which must be considered. The true test requires employment tribunals to consider whether there was a diminution or cessation in the employer's requirement for *employees* to carry out work of a particular kind, and not to focus on the work of the individual employee.

18.20 The issue was finally resolved by the House of Lords in *Murray v Foyle Meats Ltd*[23] where it was held that the key word on which tribunals should concentrate is 'attributable'. Thus if a dismissal of an employee was 'attributable' to a diminution of the employer's need for employees, then it is irrelevant to consider either the contractual obligations or the functions which the employee performed. It can therefore still be a redundancy if the employee is dismissed when his own job remains, but the needs of the business for different kinds of employee reduces. In *Contract Bottling v Cave*[24] a group of staff with different roles were put into a pool with the lowest scoring staff dismissed. Those who remained were retrained. There was a diminution in the needs of the employer to carry out work of several kinds, and the dismissals were attributable to this state of affairs, and so a 'bumping' or transferred redundancy situation existed.

D. **Transferred redundancy**

18.21 If an employee is redundant, but, in accordance with a redundancy procedure he is retained in another post because he has seniority, and the holder of that other post is consequently dismissed, can the latter claim that he was redundant? Such transferred or 'bumping redundancy' has been considered in a number of cases, the prevalent view being that such a claim is valid and statutorily correct. Thus in *Elliott Turbomachinery v Bates*,[25] a redundant employee was transferred to the claimant's department, 'bumping' the applicant out of a job. It was held that he was redundant. This line of cases was supported by the EAT in *Safeway Stores Ltd v Burrell*, but another division of the EAT expressed disagreement (*Church v West Lancashire NHS Trust*[26]), where it was stated that a bumped employee was not dismissed for reason of redundancy, but rather because of the application of a procedure which required the dismissal of that employee to complete a reorganisation.

---

[21] [1967] 2 QB 56, [1967] 1 All ER 644, [1967] 2 WLR 571, 2 ITR 229, 111 Sol Jo 72.

[22] [1997] ICR 523, [1997] IRLR 200, 567 IRLB 8, EAT.

[23] [1997] NI 429, NICA; aff'd [2000] 1 AC 51, [1999] 3 All ER 769, [1999] 3 WLR 356, [1999] ICR 827, [1999] IRLR 562, [1999] 31 LS Gaz R 36, 143 Sol Jo LB 214, HL.

[24] UKEAT/0525/12/DM.   [25] [1981] ICR 218, EAT.

[26] [1998] ICR 423, [1998] IRLR 4, 588 IRLB 7, EAT.

18.22 However, in *Murray v Foyle Meats Ltd* (para 18.20) the House of Lords approved *Safeway Stores Ltd v Burrell*, and thus a transferred redundancy is still a redundancy under the Act.

E. Presumption of redundancy

18.23 Section 163(2) of ERA provides that if there is a dismissal, it is presumed to be by reason of redundancy, unless the contrary is proved. Thus if two employees are dismissed, although only one is redundant, they are both entitled to rely on the statutory presumption (*Willcox v Hastings*[27]) in the absence of evidence to the contrary.

F. Renewal or re-engagement (ERA, s 138)

18.24 If the employee's contract of employment is actually renewed, or he is re-engaged under a new contract made before the end of his previous contract, and the renewal or re-engagement takes place immediately on the end of that employment, or within four weeks thereof, he will not be regarded as having been dismissed under the old contract. This does not apply if the new contract differs, as to capacity, place of employment, or other terms and conditions of employment.

18.25 The employee is entitled to have a trial period of four weeks, or such longer period as may be agreed between the parties for the purpose of retraining the employee under that new contract. In the latter case the new agreement must be made before the employee starts to work under the new contract. It must be in writing, specifying the length of the trial period, and the terms and conditions of employment which will apply after the trial period. If before or during the trial period the employee terminates the contract, or the employer does so for a reason connected with the new contract, the employee shall be treated as being dismissed on the date on which his previous contract ended, and for the reason he was dismissed under that contract (*McKindley v William Hill (Scotland) Ltd*[28]). However, in *Hempell v W H Smith & Sons Ltd*[29] the EAT stated that this did not preclude an enquiry under s 98(4) to ascertain whether the dismissal during the trial period was fair or unfair. In other words, even if the employee accepts the job after a trial period, s 138(3) only provides that he has not been dismissed for reason of redundancy; he may (or may not) have been unfairly dismissed from his old job, and he is entitled to have that issue resolved by an employment tribunal (*Jones v Burdett Coutts School*[30]). If before or during the trial period the employee unreasonably terminates the contract, he shall not be entitled to a redundancy payment by reason of his dismissal from the previous contract.

18.26 The statutory right to a trial period of four weeks applies to employees who are dismissed by the employer, or whose fixed-term contracts have expired, and who have been offered renewal or re-engagement under the provisions of s 138. There is no additional common law trial period running alongside s 138 (*Optical Express Ltd v Williams*[31]).

18.27 Since an employee has a statutory right to a trial period, a refusal to offer him one may lead to a finding that his dismissal was unfair (*Elliot v Richard Stump Ltd*[32]). The

[27] [1987] IRLR 298, CA.   [28] [1985] IRLR 492, EAT.
[29] [1986] ICR 365, [1986] IRLR 95, EAT.
[30] [1997] ICR 390, 571 IRLB 9, EAT; revsd [1999] ICR 38, [1998] IRLR 521, [1998] 18 LS Gaz R 32, 142 Sol Jo LB 142, CA.
[31] [2007] IRLR 928, [2008] ICR 1, EAT.
[32] [1987] ICR 579, [1987] IRLR 215, [1987] LS Gaz R 1142, EAT.

statutory trial period of four weeks is four calendar weeks, not four working weeks (*Benton v Sanderson Kayser Ltd*[33]).

G. **Offer of suitable alternative employment (s 141)**

18.28 If the employer makes an offer (whether in writing or not) to the employee to renew the contract of employment, or to re-engage him under a new contract, which is to take effect on the expiry of the old contract or within four weeks thereafter, then:

(a) if the provisions of that new contract as to capacity, place at which employed, and other terms and conditions of employment would not differ from the corresponding terms of the previous contract; or

(b) these terms and conditions do differ, but the offer constitutes an offer of suitable employment,

and in either case the employee unreasonably refuses that offer, then he will not be entitled to a redundancy payment.

18.29 When making an offer of alternative employment to an employee who is potentially redundant, the employer should provide the employee with as much information as is necessary to enable the employee to make an informed choice. In particular, the employee is entitled to know about the financial prospects in the alternative position (*Fisher v Hoopoe Finance Ltd*[34]). It is a question of fact and degree in each case. In *Sheppard v National Coal Board*[35] a redundant carpenter was offered a similar job which would have involved more travelling, less overtime, and the loss of certain fringe benefits. It was held that the additional travel was not excessive, and the loss of overtime did not, by itself, render the employment less suitable. The loss of the fringe benefits was more important, and it was held that the offer was not of suitable employment.

18.30 The suitability of the offer of alternative work must be assessed objectively, whereas to assess whether or not the employee's refusal is unreasonable (whether in relation to the offer to renew the old contract on the same terms or the offer of suitable alternative employment) it is permissible to take into account subjective considerations (*Cambridge & District Co-operative Society Ltd v Ruse*,[36] *Readman v Devon PCT*[37]). Thus the employee's own personal problems which may arise through taking up the offer are relevant factors. Domestic difficulties, inadequate or inconvenient travel facilities, lack of suitable educational facilities for children, loss of friends, have all been matters which have been held to constitute reasonable grounds for refusal of the offer (*Paton Calvert & Co Ltd v Westerside*[38]). The test is whether this employee made a reasonable decision on the basis of the facts that appeared before him, or ought reasonably to have appeared at the time. There is no room for the test of the range of reasonable responses of a reasonable employee (*Hudson v George Harrison Ltd*,[39] *Devon Primary Care Trust v Readman*[40]). An employee does not act unreasonably in refusing to accept alternative employment if he feels he cannot achieve a satisfactory standard in the new post (*Spencer v Gloucestershire County Council*[41]).

18.31 If an offer of alternative employment made to a redundant employee is only marginally suitable, this could impact on the reasonableness of the refusal to accept that offer.

[33] [1988] ICR 313, [1988] IRLR 235, [1988] 8 LS Gaz R 35, EAT; revsd [1989] ICR 136, [1989] IRLR 19, CA.
[34] Unreported.   [35] (1966) 1 KIR 101, 1 ITR 177.   [36] [1993] IRLR 156, EAT.
[37] UKEAT/0116/11/ZT.   [38] [1979] IRLR 108, EAT.   [39] [2003] All ER (D) 381 (Mar), EAT.
[40] [2013] EWCA Civ 1110.   [41] [1985] ICR 223, EAT; rev [1985] IRLR 393, CA.

However, if the new job offer was overwhelmingly suitable, it would be easier for the employer to show that a refusal was unreasonable (*Commission for Healthcare Audit and Inspection v Ward*[42]).

18.32 But a personal whim or fad cannot constitute a reasonable refusal. In *Fuller v Stephanie Bowman (Sales) Ltd*[43] the claimant was a secretary working in Mayfair. The employers decided to move the office to Soho. The claimant rejected the offer of employment at the new premises, for these were above a sex shop, and as she was opposed to 'money for sex' activities, she found the move too distasteful. Her application for a redundancy payment failed. The tribunal pointed out that the commercial exploitation of sex was no less in Mayfair than in Soho (except, perhaps a little more discreet), and if this was the basis of her reasoning, she should move away from London altogether. Her dislike of working near a sex shop was based on a personal fad, and thus it was held that she had unreasonably refused alternative employment.

H. Laying off and short-time working (s 147)

18.33 An employer may find himself in a difficult economic situation which may be envisaged to be of a temporary nature, and he may decide, instead of dismissing his employees, to lay them off temporarily, or to put them on short-time. A lay-off is where there is no work for the employees and no remuneration provided; short-time working is defined as being where less than half the normal week's pay is earned. If the lay-off or short-time has lasted for more than four consecutive weeks, or more than six weeks in any 13, then the employee may give written notice (not more than four weeks after the lay-off or short-time has finished) that he intends to claim a redundancy payment. He must then give the requisite notice to terminate his contract, and will be entitled to be considered redundant. The employer may agree to meet the claim, or refuse to do so and serve a counter-notice within seven days on the ground that he reasonably expects to be able to provide at least 13 weeks' continuous employment without further resort to lay-offs or short-time working. If the claim or counter-notice is not withdrawn, the matter will be determined by the employment tribunal, which will consider whether or not there was a reasonable prospect of full employment for 13 weeks. If the counter-notice is withdrawn by the employer, or the 13 weeks' continuous employment fails to materialise, the employee is entitled to be paid redundancy money.

18.34 If the employer offers work, but the employee refuses the offer because the rate of pay is too low, the employer has still offered to provide the work, and if, had he accepted the work the employee would have earned more than half a week's pay, there is no short-time working (*Spinpress Ltd v Turner*[44]).

18.35 But an employer has no inherent right to lay off workers as he chooses. In the absence of an express right to do so in the contract, such unilateral action can be regarded as a repudiation of the contract, and hence a dismissal. Thus (in theory) at least one week's notice should be given of such intended lay-off (*Johnson v Cross*[45]). But if the employer reserves the right to resort to a lay-off in the contract, the employee cannot treat this as a termination.

18.36 If the employer has a contractual right to lay off for an indefinite period (eg in the building industry) the employee's remedy is under s 148, and he cannot claim that the lay-off was for such an unreasonable length of time as to constitute a constructive dismissal (*Kenneth MacRae & Co Ltd v Dawson*[46]).

---

[42] Employment Appeal Tribunal, 6 March 2008.   [43] [1977] IRLR 87.
[44] [1986] ICR 433, [1986] NLJ Rep 892, EAT.   [45] [1977] ICR 872, EAT.
[46] [1984] IRLR 5, EAT.

18.37 It should be noted that the introduction of short-time working, without any contractual authority to do so, could result in a claim being made for unauthorised deductions from wages, under ERA, s 13 (*International Packaging Corpn (UK) Ltd v Balfour,* see para 8.18).

I. Time off to look for work (ERA, s 52)

18.38 An employee who is dismissed for reason of redundancy shall be entitled, before the expiration of his notice, to be given reasonable time off during his working hours to look for new employment or to make arrangements for retraining. This right, however, only applies to employees who have been continuously employed for more than two years. The redundant employee is entitled to be paid at his appropriate hourly rate, and if the employer unreasonably refuses to allow him to have the time off, or fails to pay him for it, a complaint may be presented to an employment tribunal within three months. An award of up to two-fifths of a week's pay may then be made.

18.39 It is not a prerequisite for time off that the employee should provide the employer with details of interviews or appointments he has made, as he is entitled to go to look for a job without having made any such arrangements. But if an employer thinks that the request for time off is not bona fide, it may be that he does not unreasonably refuse to permit it. The right to time off work and the right to a redundancy payment are independent of each other, so that an employee can claim time off work under s 52 irrespective of his entitlement to a redundancy payment, for example, if the employee has unreasonably refused alternative employment (*Dutton v Hawker Siddeley Aviation Ltd*[47]). The employee must have been given notice of dismissal by reason of redundancy, and had the requisite two years' continuous employment.

Fair/unfair redundancy dismissals

A. Guidelines for good industrial relations practice

18.40 Although a redundancy situation may be grounds for dismissal, in respect of which the employee may be able to obtain a redundancy payment (see para 18.65), it does not follow that such a dismissal will automatically be fair, or that the employer acts reasonably in treating that reason as a sufficient ground for dismissal. In *Williams v Compair Maxam Ltd*[48] the EAT laid down five principles for good current industrial relations practice which should be adopted in appropriate circumstances:

    (a) the employer will give as much warning as possible of impending redundancies so as to enable trade unions and employees to consider alternative solutions and seek alternative employment;

    (b) the employer will consult with the unions as to the best means by which the desired object can be achieved with as little hardship as possible. In particular, the criterion for selection should be agreed, and the actual selection should be made in accordance with that criterion;

    (c) the criterion for selection should not depend solely on the opinion of the person making the selection, but should be one which can be objectively checked;

    (d) the employer must ensure that the selection is made in accordance with that criterion, and will consider any representations made;

    (e) the employer will ascertain whether there is any alternative employment which can be offered.

---

[47] [1978] ICR 1057, [1978] IRLR 390.   [48] [1982] ICR 156, [1982] IRLR 83, EAT.

18.41 However, the principles laid down in *Williams v Compair Maxam Ltd* are guidelines, not rules of law. They refer primarily to the situation found in large companies when a significant number of redundancies are being contemplated. They should be applied with caution in small firms (*Meikle v McPhail*, see para 9.57) or where there is no trade union involved. The principles should not be regarded as a shopping list with a finding of unfairness if one or more points have not been followed (*A Simpson & Son (Motors) v Reid*[49]).

B. Handling redundancies

18.42 The fact that the employer has a redundancy policy is not, by itself, conclusive of anything. The employer must be prepared to justify that policy, and show, in particular, that it is fair and non-discriminatory (*Whiffen v Milham Ford Girls' School*[50]). Whatever method of selection is used for redundancy purposes, it must be fair in general terms and reasonably applied in relation to the employee(s) concerned (*British Aerospace plc v Green*[51]). Bearing this in mind, there are three ways in which redundancies should be handled.

Consideration of alternatives

18.43 Faced with a redundancy situation, the reasonable employer considers whether it is necessary to act on it, or whether there is some other way of dealing with the problem. For example, it may be possible to restrict recruitment, cut down on overtime, introduce work-sharing, introduce short-time working. In *Allwood v William Hill Ltd*[52] the employers closed down 12 betting shops and declared the managers redundant. No warning was given and no alternative employment within the company was offered. It was held that merely because a redundancy situation existed, it did not follow that the employees had to be made redundant. There was a high wastage in the industry, and more effort should have been made to transfer them to other establishments, even on a temporary basis. The employers should also have considered retraining the employees until vacancies arose through wastage or expansion. It may be possible to offer a redundant employee another job which amounts to a demotion, and leave it to him to decide whether or not to accept (*Avonmouth Construction Co Ltd v Shipway*[53]).

18.44 The reasonable employer also takes steps to see if the employee can be absorbed elsewhere in the concern, or with associated companies (*Vokes Ltd v Bear*[54]), but the employer need only take such reasonable steps as are available for this purpose, and though an employment tribunal must scrutinise critically a complaint of unfair redundancy, it should also guard against adopting a standard which is unrealistic, and it should not find a dismissal unfair merely as a means of topping up an inadequate redundancy payment (*British United Shoe Machinery Co Ltd v Clarke*, see para 17.199). If an employer merely states that he decided not to offer a redundant employee alternative work, without advancing any reasons for the decision, he does not discharge the burden of showing that he has acted reasonably (*Thomas and Betts Manufacturing Ltd v Harding*[55]). If the employer has failed to act reasonably in searching round for alternative employment, the employment tribunal must consider whether in fact any loss has accrued to the employee as a result of that failure, or whether in fact it made no difference. In the latter case, there could be a finding that the dismissal was consequently not unfair, or that even if it was unfair, no loss was suffered by the employee, and therefore he is not entitled to any compensation.

[49] [1983] IRLR 401, EAT.
[50] [2001] EWCA Civ 385, [2001] LGR 309, [2001] ICR 1023, [2001] IRLR 468, [2001] All ER (D) 256 (Mar).
[51] [1995] ICR 1006, [1995] IRLR 433, CA.   [52] [1974] IRLR 258.
[53] [1979] IRLR 14, EAT.   [54] [1974] ICR 1, [1973] IRLR 363, 15 KIR 302, 9 ITR 85, NIRC.
[55] [1978] IRLR 213, EAT; aff'd [1980] IRLR 255, CA.

Lack of consultation

18.45 To dismiss without warning or proper consultations, or without considering the recommendations of the Code of Practice relating to redundancies, may also result in a finding that a dismissal is unfair. But a failure to consult with the unions as provided by TULR(C)A, s 188 (see paras 18.69–18.71) does not by itself mean that a dismissal is unfair (*Forman Construction Ltd v Kelly*[56]). At the same time, consultation with trade unions does not preclude consultation with individuals (*Walls Meat Co Ltd v Selby*[57]). If the employer fails to consult with the affected individuals, he must supply a cogent reason why it was not possible to do so (*Holden v Bradville Ltd*[58]).

18.46 The fact that the employer has established a policy not to consult in the event of redundancies being imminent, based on previous experience and the wishes of the work-force in the past, is not, per se, sufficient reason not to consult (*Ferguson v Prestwick Circuits Ltd*[59]), particularly when the criteria for selection are vague and subjective (*Graham v ABF Ltd*[60]). Even a small company is expected to act reasonably. Thus, if redundancy is being proposed, the size of the undertaking may affect the nature or formality of the consultation process, but it does not excuse the lack of consultation (*De Grasse v Stockwell Tools Ltd*[61]).

18.47 In *Mugford v Midland Bank plc*[62] the EAT suggested three propositions for the guidance of employment tribunals: (1) If there is no consultation with trade unions or individuals when redundancies are contemplated, a dismissal will normally be unfair, unless a reasonable employer would have concluded that consultation would be an utterly futile exercise. (2) Consultation with a trade union does not of itself release the employer from an obligation to consult with individuals concerned. (3) It will be a question of fact and degree for the employment tribunal to consider whether such consultations as had taken place were so inadequate as to render a dismissal unfair. The lack of consultation by itself does not automatically lead to a finding of unfairness.

18.48 A mere warning that redundancies are being contemplated, coupled with an indication of the selection procedure, does not satisfy the requirements of a fair procedure. Consultation must be fair and genuine. An opportunity must be given to the affected employees to express their views (*Rowell v Hubbard Group Services*[63]). Thus in *Heron v Citilink-Nottingham*[64] the employers found it necessary to make significant economies, and dismissed the claimant without any warning. The EAT held that his dismissal was unfair. For there to be exceptional circumstances which obviates the need for consultation, it had to be shown that it was necessary to dismiss the applicant when they did, and at no later date. It may well be that had he been consulted, he may have been able to make suggestions as to how the situation could be ameliorated. He may have agreed to accept a more junior post, or work for a lower salary. Unless the employer consults the employee in such circumstances, the latter will have no opportunity to put forward any suggestions.

18.49 It had been suggested that a redundancy dismissal without consultation can only be fair if the employer took a deliberate decision not to consult (see *Robertson v Magnet Ltd (Retail Division)*[65]) but this view was rejected by the Court of Appeal in *Duffy v Yeomans and Partners Ltd*.[66] What matters is whether consultation would have been useless, taking into account the circumstances known to the employer at the time.

[56] [1977] IRLR 468, EAT. [57] [1989] ICR 601, CA. [58] [1985] IRLR 483, EAT.
[59] [1992] IRLR 266, EAT. [60] [1986] IRLR 90, EAT. [61] [1992] IRLR 269, EAT.
[62] [1997] ICR 399, [1997] IRLR 208, EAT. [63] [1995] IRLR 195, EAT.
[64] [1993] IRLR 372, EAT. [65] [1993] IRLR 512, EAT.
[66] [1993] ICR 862, [1993] IRLR 368, EAT; aff'd [1995] ICR 1, [1994] IRLR 642, CA.

18.50 If a dismissal is unfair because of a failure to consult, the employment tribunal must consider whether consultation would have made any difference, or whether the employee would have had a chance of being retained in his employment. If the answer is uncertain, then a percentage assessment should be made to reflect the probability that he would have been retained (*Dunlop Ltd v Farrell*[67]), because the claimant must still show that a loss has resulted from the unfairness, and the employment tribunal must not speculate, guess or indulge in conjecture. The claimant must show a sensible and coherent suggestion as to what was the result of the failure to consult or warn, and what would have happened had there been no such failure. The employer must then refute such suggestions (*Barley v Amey Roadstone Corpn Ltd*[68]). The employment tribunal may then decide that the failure made little or no difference, and reduce compensation to an amount they deem appropriate, to reflect the additional period of time by which the employee's employment would have been extended had consultations taken place (*Mining Supplies (Longwall) Ltd v Baker*, see para 17.202).

Proper selection procedures

18.51 It is the duty of the employment tribunal to examine the employer's procedures for selecting redundancies to ensure that these are fair. Even a selection system which is based on custom and practice in the industry can be challenged if it is unreasonable (*Watling & Co v Richardson*[69]). The tribunal is entitled to know (a) who made the decision to select, (b) what information was taken into account, and (c) upon what criteria the information was assessed (*Bristol Channel Ship Repairers Ltd v O'Keefe*[70]). Otherwise unfair selection for redundancy may also amount to an unfair dismissal. Faced with the decision of choosing which employee(s) shall be made redundant, the employer must engage in a genuine exercise in reaching his choice. The first decision that he should make is who should go in the pool for redundancy. There is no reason why there cannot be a pool of one, as long as choosing to do so is within the range of reasonable responses (*Wrexham GC v Ingham*;[71] *Capita Hartshead Ltd v Byard*[72]).

If there is an established procedure in existence, the employer should follow it; in the absence of such pre-arranged procedure, the general rule in industry for redundancy selection used to be based on the principle of 'Last In First Out' (LIFO), although this appears to be falling out of favour in recent times, being replaced by a more sophisticated system based on skills, flexibility, etc. Length of service as a criterion for redundancy selection is prima facie discriminatory against younger workers, although there is an exception in respect of service-related benefits where the service to be taken into account is five years or less. However, the use by an employer of a length of service criterion within a selection matrix for redundancy is a proportionate means of achieving a legitimate aim of advancing an employment policy that achieved a peaceable process of redundancy selection agreed with the recognised trade unions. Giving credit for length of service in a redundancy selection policy could be considered to be a benefit under reg 32 of the Employment Equality (Age) Regulations (*Rolls Royce plc v Unite*[73]).

18.52 If there is no agreed procedure or customary arrangement, the employer may take into account long service, superior abilities and experience, and the respective hardship caused. In *Selby and Tesse v Plessey Co Ltd*,[74] it was held that a selection based on an effective

---

[67] [1993] ICR 885, EAT.   [68] [1977] ICR 546, [1977] IRLR 299, 11 ITR 283, EAT.

[69] [1978] ICR 1049, [1978] IRLR 255, (1979) 13 ITR 333.

[70] [1977] 2 All ER 258, [1978] ICR 691, [1977] IRLR 13, EAT.

[71] UKEAT/0190/12/RN.   [72] UKEAT/0445/11/RN.

[73] [2009] EWCA Civ 387, [2010] 1 WLR 318, [2010] ICR 1, [2009] IRLR 576, (2009) 106(21) LSG 15, (2009) 153(20) SJLB 38, (2009) *Times*, 27 May.

[74] [1972] IRLR 36.

evaluation system, which was customary in the company, was fair. While having objective criteria is important, it is possible to go too far in the quest for objectivity. In *Mental Health Care (UK) Ltd v Biluan & Anor*,[75] employee capability was assessed entirely on the basis of competency tests, with no account taken of past performance. The employer chose an elaborate and HR-driven method which deprived it of the benefit of input from managers and others who actually knew the staff in question, and which by its very elaborateness could be difficult to apply consistently.

18.53 Adherence to a redundancy agreement made with a trade union is generally sufficient evidence to rebut unfairness (*Taylor v Conveyancer Ltd*[76]) though a failure to consult that union as provided by the agreement may be unfair. However, if the decision has to be made in a hurry for sound reasons, and consultations with the union or employees would result in serious delay, the employer does not act unfairly in failing to consult (*Guy v Delanair (Car Heater) Ltd*[77]). Selection for redundancy will also be unfair if it is discriminatory on grounds of sex, sexual orientation, race, disability, part-time worker, fixed term employee, religion or belief, age etc (see Chapter 4).

18.54 Although the actual selection criteria is for management to determine, it is sound practice to agree this in advance with trade unions. The more vague and subjective the criteria, the greater is the need to consult with affected employees (*Graham v ABF Ltd*[78]). It is the employer's responsibility to set up a fair system of selection, and to administer it fairly. If selection for redundancy is based on proper assessments, it is not for the employment tribunal to engage in a re-assessment exercise (*Eaton Ltd v King*[79]).

18.55 In *Clyde Pipeworks v Foster*,[80] selection for redundancy was based on a points system, which took into account bad time-keeping, workmanship, absenteeism, and merit on conduct. This procedure had been agreed with the unions, but they were not consulted about its implementation. It was held that there was no need to involve the unions in the detailed arrangements for selection for redundancy, provided the method was fair in general terms. But if management were to take into account improper factors (such as a disciplinary warning which should have been expunged from his record) there could be an unfair selection (*Pyle v Cleeson Civil Engineering Ltd*[81]). If jobs are interchangeable between departments, then the basis for selection is between employees of the same description within the whole concern, not on a departmental basis (*Wailes Dove Bitumastic v Woolcocks*[82]).

18.56 If a dismissal for redundancy is generally fair in terms of the procedure adopted and the selection criteria, it does not become unfair because of a failure by the employer to give the affected employees a right of appeal against their dismissal, even though an employee dismissed for gross misconduct would have that right. There is no suggestion in the Code of Practice that there should be a right of appeal against a dismissal for redundancy (*Robinson v Ulster Carpet Mills Ltd*[83]). The advantage of having an appeal machinery is that an original decision to dismiss for redundancy which is unfair can be cured if there is a complete rehearing on appeal (*Lloyd v Taylor Woodrow plc*[84]).

18.57 But if there is an appeal procedure, it must be operated fairly, and not be a mere sham. Thus, if selection for redundancy is based on a points system which had been agreed with union representatives, an employee is still entitled to know how his own marks had been calculated, otherwise he will have no material with which to present his case on appeal (*John Brown Engineering Ltd v Brown*[85]).

[75] UKEAT/0248/12/SM.   [76] [1972] IRLR 37.   [77] [1975] IRLR 73.   [78] [1986] IRLR 90, EAT.
[79] [1995] IRLR 75, EAT; revsd sub nom *King v Eaton Ltd* [1996] IRLR 199, 1997 SLT 654, Ct of Sess.
[80] [1978] IRLR 313, EAT.   [81] IDS Handbook 12.   [82] [1977] ICR 817, 12 ITR 420, EAT.
[83] [1991] IRLR 348, NICA.   [84] [1999] IRLR 782, EAT.   [85] [1997] IRLR 90, EAT.

18.58 To select a woman for dismissal because she is pregnant, or on maternity leave of absence, would be unfair under s 99 (see para 6.52), but if a woman is made redundant because of the operation of a fair selection procedure then the fact that she is or was pregnant is coincidental, and has nothing to do with her selection. Her dismissal would be fair in accordance with the usual criteria (*Brown v Stockton-on-Tees Borough Council*[86]). Equally, a long-term sick employee may still be selected for redundancy, even though this terminates his entitlement to sickness pay under the employer's scheme (*Hill v General Accident Fire and Life Assurance Corpn plc*, see para 17.105). An employer must therefore not assess those who have been off work on parental leave (or sickness leave) on different criteria to those who have not been on leave (*Riezniece v Zemkopības Ministrija*[87]).

18.59 In the last analysis, the test is not whether the employment tribunal agrees with the actual selection made by the employer, but whether the employer acted reasonably. Thus it is not the duty of the employment tribunal to decide who they would have made redundant had they had to make the choice, but to ensure that management acts from genuine motives. In *Grundy (Teddington) Ltd v Willis* (see para 17.76), the choice for making an employee redundant lay between two persons. Management chose one, but the employment tribunal held that this was unfair, in that the other should have been chosen. The EAT reversed this finding; the ultimate decision must remain with management, provided it acts fairly.

18.60 If an employee is given notice of dismissal, for reason of redundancy, and during that notice period new work becomes available, it may be unfair not to rescind the notice and offer further employment to him (*Stacey v Babcock Power Ltd*, see para 17.80). However, if the alternative employment becomes available after the employee's contract of employment has ended, an employer does not act unreasonably in failing to offer that employment to him (*Octavius Atkinson & Sons Ltd v Morris*, see para 16.15).

C. Unfair selection for redundancy (ERA, s 105)

18.61 It is unfair to dismiss a person for redundancy if the reason for his/her selection for dismissal was (a) health and safety reason (s 100), (b) protected or opted-out shop worker (s 101), (c) refusal to comply with a requirement in contravention of the Working Time Regulations (s 101A), (d) acting as a trustee of an occupational pension fund (s 102), (e) acting as an employee representative (s 103), (f) making a protected disclosure (s 103A), (g) asserting a statutory right (s 104), (h) asserting a right under the National Minimum Wage Act (s 104A), (i) taking action to obtain a tax credit (s 104B), (j) taking action under the Transnational Information and Consultation of Employees Regulations 1999, (k) taking action under the Part-time Workers (Prevention of Less Favourable Treatment) Regulation 2000, or the Fixed-Term Employees (Prevention of Less Favourable Treatment) Regulations 2002 or the Employment Equality (Age) Regulations 2006. Unfair selection for trade union membership and activities etc is covered by TULR(C)A, s 153. Unfair selection for redundancy by reason of pregnancy, maternity leave, parental leave, time off to care for dependants, and workforce agreement cases is dealt with in the Maternity and Parental Leave etc Regulations 1999 (see Chapter 6) and there is similar protection for persons who take paternity and adoption leave. Such dismissals will be automatically unfair, and no period of continuous employment is required.

---

[86] [1986] ICR 842, [1986] IRLR 432, (1986) 83 LSG 3746, (1986) 136 NLJ 892, EAT; aff'd [1987] ICR 897, [1987] IRLR 230, CA; rev [1989] AC 20, [1988] 2 WLR 935, [1988] 2 All ER 129, [1988] ICR 410, [1988] IRLR 263, 86 LGR 561, (1988) 85(19) LSG 41, (1988) 138 NLJ Rep 117, (1988) 132 SJ 624, HL.

[87] (Case C-7/12), [2013] WLR (D) 247.

D. Dismissal during the period of notice (s 140)

18.62 If an employee has been given due notice that he will be dismissed for reason of redundancy, and whilst he is working out that notice, he commits an act of misconduct which is sufficiently serious to warrant his instant dismissal without notice, and he is summarily dismissed, the question will arise as to whether or not he is entitled to his redundancy payment. On the assumption that the dismissal was justified (eg because the employee refused to obey a lawful order (*Cairns v Burnside Shoe Repairs Ltd*[88]), or because the employee stole from the employer (*Jarmain v E Pollard & Co Ltd*)[89]), then the employment tribunal shall determine whether it is just and equitable that the employee should receive the whole or part of the redundancy payment, as it thinks fit. In *Lignacite Products Ltd v Krollman*[90] the claimant was given notice of redundancy. He was then found stealing from his employers and summarily dismissed. The employment tribunal reduced his redundancy pay by 40%, and the EAT upheld the decision. It is difficult to reconcile this decision with *Bonner v H Gilbert Ltd.*[91]

18.63 If an employee is given notice of dismissal by reason of redundancy, and during his notice period he takes part in a strike, then although this is conduct which entitles the employer to terminate the contract without notice, the employee is not barred from getting the whole of his redundancy payment (s 143). However, if an employee is on strike, and then is dismissed for reasons of redundancy, his claim will fail. The reason is that s 140 of the Act provides that the employee will not be entitled to a redundancy payment if the employer, being entitled to terminate the contract of employment, terminates it, with or without notice. Since an employee who is on strike is in breach of his contract, the employer is entitled to terminate it. In other words, s 143 deals with the situation when an employee is dismissed for reason of redundancy, and then goes on strike. In *Simmons v Hoover Ltd*[92] employees who were actually on strike were dismissed for reason of redundancy, and it was held that s 140 operated, and s 143 did not operate to save their claim.

Excluded classes of employees

18.64 The following employees are not eligible for, or will not be entitled to, a redundancy payment:

(a) a person employed under a fixed-term contract for two years or more, if before that term expires, he agrees in writing to exclude his rights to make a claim (s 197(3)). This is one of the very few circumstances when an employee can forgo his legal rights (see para 20.47). However, this exclusion only applies to agreements which were made before 10 July 2002;

(b) a miscellaneous class of employees, ie share fishermen, holders of certain public offices (see s 159) employment by a Government of an overseas territory (see s 160). Domestic servants employed in a private household *are* within the scope of the Act, unless the servant is a close relative of the employer (s 161);

(c) an agreement made between an employers' organisation and a trade union may provide exemption from the Act by a ministerial order on an application by both parties thereto, provided the conditions in s 157 are satisfied.

---

[88] (1966) 2 KIR 23, 2 ITR 75.   [89] (1967) 2 ITR 406.
[90] [1979] IRLR 22, EAT.   [91] [1989] IRLR 475, EAT.
[92] [1975] IRLR 263; aff'd [1977] QB 284, [1977] 1 All ER 775, [1976] 3 WLR 901, [1977] ICR 61, [1976] IRLR 266, 10 ITR 234, 120 Sol Jo 540, EAT.

Claims for redundancy payments

18.65 A claim must be made to the employment tribunal within six months from the relevant date, which is the date of the expiry of the notice to terminate the employment, or the date when the contract expires, or the date on which a fixed-term contract comes to an end. The tribunal has a discretion to admit a claim which is outside the time limit if it thinks it would be just and equitable to do so, but no claim can be entertained after 12 months have elapsed. The claim, if admitted or successful, must be met by the employer. The amount of the claim will be determined by the length of time the employee has been employed, his normal week's pay, and his age.

18.66 The calculation of the amount of the redundancy payment will be determined in accordance with the rules on continuous employment (see Chapter 13) normal working hours and a week's pay (see Chapter 14) and age. For each year's continuous employment below the age of 22 (with no lower age limit) an employee is entitled to one half a week's pay; for each year's employment between the ages of 22 and 40, he will be entitled to one week's pay; for each year's employment over (and including) the age of 41, he will be entitled to one and a half weeks' pay. There is no longer an upper or lower age limit, and the tapering provision which used to apply to employees over the age of 64 has been abolished. However, an employee will still have to have been employed for two years or more, and no more than 20 years' employment may be counted when calculating the payment. The maximum week's pay to count is (currently) £464. When making the payment, the employer shall give to the employee a written statement showing how the amount of the payment is calculated, and it is an offence, punishable on summary conviction by a fine not exceeding level 1 on the standard scale, not to do so (s 165). If an employer gives a lump sum to a redundant employee without indicating how it is made up, this may be regarded as an *ex gratia* payment, not intended to be by way of a redundancy payment (*Galloway v Export Packing Services Ltd*[93]).

Payments by the Secretary of State (ERA, ss 166–170)

18.67 If an employee claims that, despite taking all reasonable steps, the employer has failed or refused to make him a redundancy payment, or claims that the employer is insolvent, he may apply to the Secretary of State for a redundancy payment, to be paid out by the Insolvency Service (an executive agency of the Department for Business, Innovation and Skills). An employer will be insolvent if:

(a) he is an individual, and he has been adjudged bankrupt or made a composition or arrangement with creditors, or he has died and his estate falls to be administered under the Insolvency Act 1986 (there are comparable provisions for Scotland); or

(b) if a company, there has been a winding-up order or an administration order made, or a resolution for a voluntary winding up has been passed or a receiver or manager appointed.

18.68 Once the Secretary of State has made the payment due to an employer's insolvency, this will break continuity of employment for those employees who are re-engaged by virtue of the Transfer of Undertakings (Protection of Employment) Regulations 2006 (*Lassman v Secretary of State for Trade and Industry*,[94] and see Chapter 9).

[93] [1975] IRLR 306.
[94] [1999] ICR 416, [1999] IRLR 413, EAT; revsd sub nom *Secretary of State for Trade and Industry v Lassman (Pan Graphics Industries Ltd, in receivership)* [2000] ICR 1109, [2000] IRLR 411, CA.

Consultation on redundancies (TULR(C)A, ss 188–192)

A. EC Directive on Collective Redundancies

18.69 Article 2 of the EC Directive on Collective Redundancies (75/129/EEC) lays down the principle that when an employer is contemplating collective redundancies, he shall consult with employee representatives. Although a Directive is generally enforceable against a state body (see *Foster v British Gas*, para 1.72) this Directive is not so unconditional or sufficiently precise as to be capable of direct enforcement (*Griffin v South West Water Services Ltd*[95]). Requirements for such consultations were provided for in the Employment Protection Act 1975, s 99, and repeated in the Trade Union and Labour Relations (Consolidation) Act 1992, s 188 (as amended by the Trade Union Reform and Employment Rights Act 1993). However, in *EC Commission v United Kingdom* (see para 1.100) infringement proceedings were brought alleging that neither the Transfer of Undertakings Regulations 1981 (see Chapter 9) nor the provisions of TULR(C)A correctly transposed the Directive, because there were no provisions which would require an employer to consult with employee representatives when the employer did not recognise a trade union. The UK Government argued that employee representation was traditionally based on the voluntary recognition by employers of trade unions, and therefore if an employer did not recognise a trade union, there were no 'employee representatives' with whom to consult. Nonetheless, the European Court held that the UK Government was in breach of the Directive. Legislation had to ensure that there was a mechanism whereby employee representatives were designated so as to enable employers to consult with them.

18.70 Section 188 of TULR(C)A was thus amended by the Collective Redundancies and Transfer of Undertakings (Protection of Employment) (Amendment) Regulations 1995, although it was not certain whether these regulations fully implemented the Directive, because although there arose a duty to consult with either trade unions or employee representatives, there was no mechanism by which those representatives could be elected. Thus the Collective Redundancies and Transfer of Undertakings (Protection of Employment) (Amendment) Regulations 1999 were passed to regularise the position. These latter Regulations make provision for the election of employee representatives (by inserting s 188A into TULR(C)A), and other changes).

18.71 However, there is still some doubt as to whether UK law adequately transposes the EC Directive. Section 188 requires consultation to take place when an employer is 'proposing' redundancies, whereas the Directive requires consultation when the employer is 'contemplating' redundancies (see *MSF v Refuge Assurance plc*[96]).

B. Who, and when to consult

18.72 Where an employer is proposing to dismiss as redundant 20 or more employees at one establishment within a period of 90 days or less, he shall consult with the appropriate representatives of any of the employees affected by the proposed dismissals (and not just those whom the employer proposes to make redundant), or may be affected by the measures taken in connection with those dismissals. The appropriate representatives are:

(a) if the employees are of a description in respect of which an independent trade union is recognised (whether or not the affected employees are members of the trade union

---

[95] [1995] IRLR 15.   [96] [2002] ICR 1365, [2002] IRLR 324, [2002] All ER (D) 209 (Feb), EAT.

concerned, see *Northern Ireland Hotel and Catering College v National Association of Teachers in Further and Higher Education*[97]), representatives of that union. Whether a trade union is recognised for the purpose of the consultation provisions is a question of fact (see Chapter 23). In any other case,

(b) either employee representatives who have been appointed or elected by the affected employees for some other purpose, who have authority to receive information or be consulted about proposed dismissals, or employee representatives who have been elected by the affected employees for consultation purposes, in an election which satisfies the requirements set out in s 188A.

If there is no recognised trade union, the employer must consult with either existing representatives or representatives elected for TUPE consultation purposes. If there are no trade union or elected representatives, the employer must invite the employees to elect representatives. If they fail to do so within a reasonable time, the employer must give each affected employee the information he would otherwise have given to the representatives (*Howard v Millrise Ltd*[98]). (Where in a proposed election for employee representatives, the number of candidates precisely matched the number of available places for elected employee representatives, the employer was entitled to treat them as 'elected' without proceeding to a formal ballot (*Phillips v Xtera Communications Ltd*[99]).)

18.73 The employer shall allow the appropriate representatives access to the employees affected, and shall afford those representatives such accommodation and facilities as may be appropriate, and time off work for training (ERA, s 61). An employee who is an employee representative, or a candidate for election as such, has the right not to suffer a detriment on the ground that he has performed any function or activity as such, the right to have time off with pay to perform his functions, and the right not to be unfairly dismissed because he performed any function or activity as such.

18.74 The consultation shall begin in good time, and, in any event, if the employer is proposing to dismiss 100 or more within 90 days or less, consultation shall begin at least 45 days before the dismissals take effect. (This was changed from 90 days in 2013.) If less than 100 (but 20 or more) are to be dismissed within the 90-day period, consultation must begin at least 30 days before the dismissals take effect (see *Junk v Wolfgang Kuhnell*[100]). Employees who volunteer for redundancy are nonetheless dismissed for the purpose of including them in the head count of 20 or 100 respectively which triggers the collective consultation provisions (*Optare Group Ltd v TGWU*[101]). The question of when the obligation on an employer to consult in a collective redundancy situation arises has been referred to the CJEU in *United States of America v Nolan*.[102] The court has been asked to decide whether it is when the employer is proposing, but has not yet made, a strategic business or operational decision that will foreseeably or inevitably lead to collective redundancies or whether it arises only when that decision has actually been made and he is then proposing consequential redundancies?

18.75 Where there is a proposed transfer of undertakings (Chapter 9), section 198A of TULRCA 1992 allows a transferee who is proposing to make 20 or more employees redundant to start consulting about this before the date of the transfer, if the transferor consents.

---

[97] [1995] IRLR 83, NICA.   [98] [2005] ICR 435, EAT.
[99] [2011] IRLR 724.   [100] (C-188/03) IDS Brief 775, ECJ.
[101] [2007] IRLR 931, (2007) 104(30) LSG 34, EAT.   [102] [2010] EWCA Civ 1223, [2011] IRLR 40.

What is an establishment?

18.76 The term 'establishment' is not defined in the Act, and has thus been the subject of interpretation by the tribunals. In *Clarks of Hove Ltd v Bakers' Union*[103] it was held that separate premises can amount to one establishment, if there is no separate accounting, management or trading. In *Barratt Developments (Bradford) Ltd v UCATT*[104] the company, which had its headquarters in Bradford, operated 14 building sites in Lancashire. On each site there was a temporary shed, with a telephone link to the headquarters. It was decided to reduce the labour force, and 24 employees were made redundant, being selected from eight different sites. It was held that all 14 sites were part of one establishment, and as there had been a failure to consult with the trade union, a protective award would be made.

18.77 However, in *Athinaiki Chartopoiia AE v Panagiotidis*[105] the European Court of Justice held that an establishment may consist of a single entity, having a certain degree of permanence and stability, which is assigned to perform one or more given tasks and which has a workforce, technical means and a certain organisational structure allowing for the accomplishment of those tasks. The entity in question need not have any legal, economic, financial, administrative or technical autonomy in order to be regarded as an 'establishment'. In *Rockfon A/S v Specialarbejderforbundet i Danmark* it was held that the term 'establishment' must be understood as meaning the unit to which the workers who are made redundant are assigned to carry out their duties (see para 9.13). It is not necessary for the unit in question to have its own management structure which can carry out a redundancy programme independently.

Where a chain of stores went into administration, the question arose as to which employees should be consulted. The employment tribunal, following the wording in section 188 of the Trade Union and Labour Relations (Consolidation) Act 1992, said that collective redundancy consultation was required for those who worked at the larger shops which employed 20 or more people, but not at the smaller shops which employed fewer than 20 people. If article 1(a)(ii) of the EC Directive (which stated that there should be consultation if at least 20 are being made redundant, whatever the number of workers normally employed at the establishments in question) had been followed, then there should have been collective consultation with all employees, regardless of the number employed at any individual store. It was held by the EAT that the words 'at one establishment' should be deleted from section 188 so that the Directive would be properly implemented, and the words should therefore be disregarded in any collective redundancy involving more than 20 employees. This means that if more than 20 employees in a single business are to be made redundant, their location is irrelevant and there has to be consultation, *USDAW and another v UNITE the Union and others*.[106] The question of what constitutes an 'establishment' for the purposes of redundancy consultation has been referred to the CJEU.

The consultation provisions

18.78 An employer is 'proposing to dismiss' employees as redundant (thus triggering the consultation provisions of the Act) when, 'following a diagnosis of the problem, specific proposals are formulated, with redundancies as one of the available options' (*Hough v Leyland*

---

[103] [1978] 2 All ER 15, [1978] 1 WLR 563, [1977] ICR 838, [1977] IRLR 264, 121 Sol Jo 528, EAT; revsd [1979] 1 All ER 152, [1978] 1 WLR 1207, [1978] ICR 1076, 13 ITR 356, sub nom *Bakers' Union v Clarks of Hove Ltd* [1978] IRLR 366, 122 Sol Jo 643, CA.

[104] [1978] ICR 319, [1977] IRLR 403, 12 ITR 478, EAT.   [105] (C-270/05) [2007] IRLR 284, ECJ.

[106] UKEAT/0547/12/KN UKEAT/0548/12.

DAF Ltd[107]). 'Proposing to dismiss' means 'proposing to give notice of dismissal'. A proposal means something less than an actual decision that dismissals are to be made, and something more than a possibility that they may occur (*Leicestershire County Council v Unison*[108]). Thus where directors of a company were considering the options of either selling the business as a going concern or selling it as a development site, this amounted to a proposal to dismiss the workforce, even though no final decision had been reached on which option they would adopt (*Scotch Premier Meat Ltd v Burns*[109]).

18.79 The actual notice of dismissals can be issued during the consultation period, provided that the dismissals do not take effect until after the consultation period has elapsed. But if an employer issues dismissal notices the day after consultations begin, it may be thought that he does not intend meaningful consultations to take place (*National Union of Teachers v Avon County Council*[110]). Similarly, if the employer does not give the appropriate representatives sufficient time to consider the proposals before they are implemented, meaningful consultation is being denied (*Transport and General Workers' Union v Ledbury Preserves (1928) Ltd*[111]).

18.80 The purpose of consultation is to consult about ways of:

(a) avoiding the dismissals;

(b) reducing the numbers of employees to be dismissed; and

(c) mitigating the consequences of the redundancies (TULR(C)A, s 188(2)).

18.81 Consultation with employee representatives does not mean reaching an agreement, but should be undertaken by the employer with a view to reaching agreement. Thus, the consultation process must be genuine. If a redundancy situation is presented as a *fait accompli*, subsequent consultations may not be a genuine and open-minded review of the decision (*GMB and AEEU v Campbell's UK Ltd*[112]). In *Middlesbrough Borough Council v TGWU*[113] it was held that the consultations on avoiding redundancies had been a sham, because the decision on numbers had already been taken.

18.82 If a workplace is closing down, with the result that employees are made redundant, the employer is obliged to consult with the recognised trade union over the reasons for the closure, because the dismissals and the closure are inextricably linked. Further, the Information and Consultation of Employees Regulations 2004 (see para 23.142) require consultation over economic decisions, and it would be strange if this did not apply at a time when job losses were being considered (*UK Coal Mining Ltd v National Union of Mineworkers*[114]).

18.83 True consultation involves:

(a) consulting with employee representatives when the proposals are still at a formulative stage;

(b) giving adequate information to which those representatives can respond;

(c) giving adequate time for the response; and

(d) a conscientious consideration by the employer of the response (*Rowell v Hubbard Group Services Ltd,* para 18.48);

(e) providing information about the reasons for the dismissals.

---

[107] [1991] ICR 696, [1991] IRLR 194, EAT.   [108] [2005] IRLR 920, EAT.
[109] [2000] IRLR 639, EAT.   [110] (1978) 76 LGR 403, [1978] ICR 626, [1978] IRLR 55, EAT.
[111] [1986] ICR 855, [1986] IRLR 492, EAT.   [112] Unreported.
[113] [2002] IRLR 332, [2001] All ER (D) 79 (May), EAT.
[114] [2008] ICR 163, [2008] IRLR 4, (2007) 151 SJLB 1400, (2007) *Times*, 23 November.

18.84 An employer does not warrant the accuracy of the information provided, and if he consults on the basis of a mistaken understanding of the effect of TUPE on the affected employees, this does not mean that there is a breach of the consultation provisions (*Royal Mail Group Ltd v Communication Workers Union*[115]).

18.85 But consultation does not imply agreement with those representatives, nor the adoption of any proposals made by them (*R v British Coal Corpn, ex p Price*[116]).

A. Disclosures required by the employer

18.86 In such consultations, the employer must disclose (in writing to the appropriate representative):

(a) the reasons for his proposals;

(b) the numbers and descriptions of employees whom it is proposed to dismiss as being redundant;

(c) the total number of employees of that description employed by the employer at that establishment;

(d) the proposed method of selecting the employees who are to be dismissed;

(e) the proposed method of carrying out the dismissals, with due regard to agreed procedure, including the period over which dismissals are to take effect; and

(f) the proposed method for calculating any redundancy payments to be made, other than statutory redundancy pay (s 188(4)).

18.87 Having provided this information, the employer must consider any representations made by the appropriate representatives and reply to them. If he rejects any of those representations, he must state his reasons. It must be stressed that the employer's duty is to consult with the representatives. He does not have to reach any agreement, and the final decision is his. In *Perez v Mercury Display Ltd*[117]the employer consulted with a trade union about a redundancy. The employer wanted selection to take place on the basis of LIFO (in the days before age discrimination legislation), but the union wanted volunteers to be selected. The employer gave to the union his reasons for rejecting the representations, and dismissed the employees on the basis of LIFO. It was held that the employer had complied with his statutory obligations.

B. Special circumstances

18.88 If there are special circumstances which render it not reasonably practicable for the employer to comply with any of the provisions relating to consultation or considering representations, he shall take all such steps as are reasonably practicable in the circumstances. Special circumstances may exist if a company becomes insolvent but insolvency per se is not a special circumstance, for reasonable and prudent management may well foresee such a possibility (*Clarks of Hove Ltd v Bakers' Union*, para 18.76). The sudden appointment of a receiver would be a special circumstance (*FTATU v Lawrence Cabinet*[118]). The loss of a key order (*AUEW v Cooper Plastics*[119]) and the unexpected failure to obtain a renewal of an important contract (*National Union of Public Employees v General Cleaning Contractors*[120]) have also come within this defence. But the fact that the employer genuinely believes that

---

[115] [2009] EWCA Civ 1045, [2010] ICR 83, [2009] IRLR 1046, (2009) 106(41) LSG 20, (2009) *Times*, 16 October.
[116] [1993] ICR 720, [1993] IRLR 104.   [117] [1977] IRLIB.   [118] IDS Brief 96.
[119] IDS Brief 90.   [120] [1976] IRLR 362.

he has not recognised a trade union for the purpose of collective bargaining does not constitute a special circumstance which would render it not reasonably practicable to comply with the obligation to consult (*Joshua Wilson & Bros Ltd v Union of Shop, Distributive and Allied Workers*[121]). Special circumstances may also be said to exist if delicate negotiations are taking place which may be prejudiced if consultations are carried on with the union (*Association of Pattern Makers and Allied Craftsmen v Kirvin Ltd*[122]). A circumstance is likely to be special if it is sudden, as opposed to being gradual or foreseeable with reasonable prudence (*Union of Shop, Distributive and Allied Workers v Leancut Bacon Ltd*[123]). However, even though special circumstances exist, the employer must nonetheless take all such steps as are reasonably practicable to consult. If he fails to take such steps, there is still a breach of s 188(1A), although the special circumstances can operate to mitigate the amount of the protective award (*Shanahan Engineering Ltd v UNITE*[124]).

18.89 The dismissal of employees in order to make the sale of a business more attractive to buyers, or the absence of orders, are not special circumstances within the meaning of the Act (*GMB v Rankin and Harrison*[125]). A failure on the part of a person who controls the employer (eg a multinational corporation in control of a subsidiary) to provide information to the employer also does not constitute a special circumstance (s 193(7)).

18.90 An employer does not fail to consult if he deals only with an accredited shop steward, for there is no requirement that the information should be conveyed to a full-time union official (*General and Municipal Workers' Union v Wailes Dove Bitumastic*[126]). The information shall be given to appropriate representatives, or sent by post to a notified address, or sent by post to the union's head office (s 188(5)).

C. Protective award (TULR(C)A, s 189)

18.91 If the employer fails to consult as required by s 186, a trade union or an employee representative or an employee who has been or may be dismissed as redundant may present a complaint to an industrial tribunal (s 189). It further appears that an employee who has been dismissed for reason of redundancy may be able to bring a complaint that the employer has failed to invite potentially redundant employees to elect appropriate employee representatives as required by s 188. If the employer wishes to plead that it was not reasonably practicable for him to comply with these provisions, he must show that this was so, and that he took all reasonably practicable steps in the circumstances. Otherwise, if the tribunal finds the complaint to be well founded, it will make a declaration to that effect, and may also make a protective award, which is remuneration for a protected period for those employees who were dismissed (or whose dismissal was being proposed) and in respect of whom the employer has failed to comply with the legal requirements. The protected period is such time as the tribunal considers to be just and equitable, having regard to the seriousness of the employer's default, but shall not exceed 90 days.

18.92 A protective award can only be made in favour of those employees in respect of whom the trade union is recognised by the employer (*TGWU v Brauer Coley*[127]). Employees who are not of that description would have to bring their own claims under s 189 of TULR(C)A (failure to consult with appropriate representatives). Also, an individual complainant may only claim a protective award on behalf of himself, and not on behalf of all affected employees (*Independent Insurance Co Ltd v Aspinall*[128]).

[121] [1978] 3 All ER 4, [1978] ICR 614, [1978] IRLR 120, 13 ITR 229, EAT.
[122] [1978] IRLR 318, 13 ITR 446.   [123] [1981] IRLR 295, EAT.
[124] Employment Appeal Tribunal, 22 February 2010.   [125] [1992] IRLR 514, EAT.
[126] [1977] IRLR 45.   [127] [2007] ICR 226, [2007] IRLR 207.

18.93 If a protective award is made, every employee to whom it relates shall be entitled to one week's pay for each week of the protected period, with proportionate reductions in respect of a period which is less than one week. There is no maximum week's pay for the purpose of the protective award, because the statutory cap in ERA, s 227 does not include a protective award. If the employer has already made any payment to the employee in respect of any period falling within the protected period, or by way of damages for breach of contract, this will not reduce the employer's liability to pay remuneration under the protective award, and conversely, any payment made under a protective award will not reduce any liability to pay any sum due in respect of a breach of contract by the employer for that period.

18.94 If an employment tribunal finds that the employer is in default of the consultation provisions, then the making of a declaration to that effect is mandatory, but the amount of the protective award is discretionary. The purpose of the protective award is to provide for a sanction against an employer for being in breach of the statutory consultation provisions, rather than to compensate employees for the loss which they have suffered in consequence of the breach. The maximum period of 90 days' protective award should only be reduced if there were mitigating circumstances justifying a reduction to the extent which the tribunal considers appropriate (*Susie Radin Ltd v GMB*[129]). The presumption in favour of a 90-day protective award applies whether the minimum consultation period is 30 days (because there are 20 or more employees being made redundant) or 90 days (where 100 or more employees are being made redundant (*Evans v Permacell*[130])).

18.95 An award for a failure to consult on redundancies is determined by the seriousness of the employer's default, not his ability to pay. Thus if the employer fails to consult and has become insolvent, a maximum award may still be made, the point being that it will be the Secretary of State who will have to pay (*Smith v Cherry Lewis Ltd*[131]). The protective award is essentially punitive in nature, and the employment tribunal should use the 90-day award as a starting point. However, mitigating factors can be taken into account so as to reduce the award, such as if the employer had taken some genuine steps to provide information or has attempted some form of consultation (*Amicus v GBS Tooling Ltd*[132]).

18.96 As a result of consultations with the appropriate employee representatives, there may well be an agreement that employees will leave the firm before the appropriate period of 90 or 30 days has expired. Whether the agreement has been reached with the employee representatives or employees on an individual basis, it is probably void by virtue of TULR(C)A, s 288, which prevents the contracting out of the various statutory rights. It is clear therefore that the dismissals will take effect before the end of the consultation period, and there will be a breach of the Act. However, on a complaint that the employer has failed to consult within the statutory period, the employment tribunal will make the mandatory declaration, but not a protective award (*Association of Scientific, Technical and Managerial Staffs v Hawker Siddeley Aviation*[133]).

18.97 If, during the protected period, the employee is fairly dismissed for some reason other than redundancy, or if he unreasonably resigns, then his entitlement to the protective award shall cease from the time his contract is terminated. If the employer makes an offer to renew the contract, or to re-engage under a new contract, so that the renewal or re-engagement would take effect before or during the protected period, or the offer constitutes

[128] [2011] IRLR 716.
[129] [2003] All ER (D) 192 (Sep), EAT; aff'd [2004] EWCA Civ 180, [2004] 2 All ER 279, 148 Sol Jo LB 266, [2004] All ER (D) 353 (Feb).
[130] EAT/0350/07.   [131] [2005] IRLR 86, EAT.
[132] [2005] IRLR 683, EAT.   [133] [1977] IRLR 418.

an offer of suitable employment, and the employee unreasonably refuses that offer, then he shall not be entitled to any payment under the protective award in respect of any period during which but for the refusal he would have been employed.

18.98 Once a protective award has been granted, then any individual employee may present a complaint to a tribunal that the employer has failed, in whole or in part, to pay him the remuneration under that award. If the complaint is well founded, the tribunal shall order the employer to make that payment (*Howlett Marine Services Ltd v Bowlam*[134]).

18.99 The fact that the employer has failed to consult in accordance with these provisions is irrelevant to the issue as to whether a particular employee's redundancy is fair or unfair (*Forman Construction Ltd v Kelly*, para 18.45).

18.100 It should be noted that, for the purpose of the consultation provisions only, the definition of redundancy is not the same as the one laid down in ERA, s 139. Under TULR(C)A, s 195, when considering the consultation provisions, references to dismissals for reason of redundancy are references to a dismissal not related to the individual concerned (or for a number of reasons not so related). This wider definition throws out some interesting possibilities. For example, suppose an employer decides to give lawful notice to all his employees, coupled with an offer to re-engage them all on changed terms of employment. Since this 'dismissal' is not related to an individual, it is submitted that prior consultations with employee representatives are required under TULR(C)A, s 195 (*GMB v Man Truck and Bus UK Ltd*[135]).

Notification of mass redundancies to the minister (TULR(C)A, s 193)

18.101 If an employer is proposing to make redundant 100 or more employees at one establishment within 90 days, or 20 or more employees within 30 days, he must notify the Secretary of State of his proposals within 90 or 30 days respectively before any notice of redundancy has been issued. He must also give a copy of this notification to the representatives of any recognised independent trade union and/or to any elected representatives. If there are special circumstances which make compliance not reasonably practicable, he shall take all such steps as are reasonably practicable. But a failure on the part of a person who controls the employer to provide information to the employer does not constitute a special circumstance (s 193(7)).

18.102 An employer who fails to give the required notification to the Secretary of State may be prosecuted in the magistrates' court, and is liable on conviction to a fine not exceeding level 5 on the standard scale (TULR(C)A, s 194(1)).

[134] [2001] ICR 595, [2001] IRLR 201, [2000] All ER (D) 2494, EAT.
[135] [2000] ICR 1101, [2000] IRLR 636, EAT.

19

Duties of Ex-employees

19.1 We have seen (Chapter 10) that during the subsistence of a contract of employment, the relationship between an employer and employee is one of trust, confidence and faith, and any course of conduct which is inconsistent with those obligations may well amount to a breach of contract. In this chapter we shall consider the more limited obligations which apply to an employee who is about to leave his employment (whether voluntarily or otherwise), or who has actually left that employment. The law must strike a delicate balance. On the one hand, an employee has a right to earn his living, and knowledge and skills obtained in his former employment will doubtless enable him to continue to do so; on the other hand, an employer is entitled to limited protection against an employee who may well be seeking to compete. An employer is not entitled to have protection from competition per se; he is entitled to have some limited protection in respect of confidential information, trade secrets, existing customers, and so on.

Employees who are about to leave their employment

19.2 The mere fact that the employee is seeking employment with a competitor is not, by itself, a breach of the duty of fidelity, in the absence of any evidence that the employee is wrongfully seeking to disclose confidential information or trade secrets (*Harris & Russell Ltd v Slingsby*, see paras 15.8 and 17.18). In *Ranson v Customer Systems PLC*[1] Mr Ranson was an employee who was recruited in 2001 straight from university. His contract contained a confidentiality clause, but no post-termination restrictions. He gave notice and during the notice period had discussions with a number of his employer's clients (who were not people he usually dealt with) in relation to obtaining future work for himself. His employer brought an action alleging that he was in breach of his duties as an employee. The Court of Appeal held that his duty did not extend that far, although it would have done had he been a director, as a director owes a wider-ranging duty (see also *Shepherds Investments*, para 19.5).

If an employee steals information from his former employer, however, this gives rise to an equitable duty of confidentiality in respect of trade secrets and confidential information, particularly if the information would give competitors a commercial advantage, and the employer from whom it was stolen suffers a detriment in terms of lost orders etc (*JN Dairies Ltd v Johal Dairies Ltd*[2]). But an employee who is about to leave his employment might attempt to make preparatory steps, either during his working hours, or in his own time, to prepare himself for future employment. He may attempt to solicit customers or suppliers, poach staff, or use information which has been imparted to him in confidence. His status and position as an employee, the nature of the work he is seeking to do, the custom and practice of the industry, etc, may well be relevant factors to be taken into account when determining the rights of his employer.

19.3 If the employee engages in such activities during his working hours, or uses his employer's premises or equipment to do so, then doubtless he will be in breach of his duty

[1] [2012] EWCA Civ 841.   [2] [2010] EWCA Civ 348.

of fidelity. Thus in *Roger Bullivant Ltd v Ellis*[3] a managing director left his employment in order to set up a rival business. He took with him copies of a card index, which listed the names and addresses of all the company's customers. This was held to be a breach of the implied duty of fidelity, and an injunction was granted to restrain him from entering into or fulfilling any contract made with or through any person whose name appeared on the card index. However, this does not necessarily apply if the employee pursues such activities in his own time and uses his own premises or equipment (*Balston Ltd v Headline Filters Ltd*[4]).

19.4 There appears to be a somewhat subtle distinction between a definite intention to compete with the employer and mere preparatory activities. Thus to tender for work already being undertaken by the employer (*Adamson v B & L Cleaning Services Ltd*, see para 10.54) or to rent and equip premises for his own business (*Lancashire Fires Ltd v SA Lyons & Co Ltd*, see para 10.70) or to approach customers with a view to doing business with them (*Wessex Dairies v Smith*, see para 10.93) or to copy out a list of the employer's clients with a view to approaching them after the employment has ceased (*Robb v Green*[5]) are clearly competing activities which will amount to a breach of the duty of faithful service. But an employee who merely indicates, whether by word or deeds, that he intends to compete with his employer at some future point in time is not acting in breach of his implied duty of fidelity (see *Laughton and Hawley v Bapp Industrial Supplies Ltd*, para 16.12).

19.5 As a general principle, an employee's duty of fidelity does not prevent him from competing with a former employer once he has left his employment, and the freedom to do so carries with it the freedom to prepare for future activities that the employee intends to pursue once he has left his employment (*Helmet Integrated Systems Ltd v Tunnard*, see para 10.56). But preparatory activities undertaken by directors or senior employees are more likely to constitute breaches of fidelity and fiduciary duties (*Shepherds Investments Ltd v Walters*;[6] see also *Caterpillar Logistics Services (UK) Ltd v de Crean*[7] and *Ranson v Customer Systems*, para 19.2). In any particular case, it will be necessary to identify the particular duties undertaken by the employee and to ask whether, in all the circumstances, he has placed himself in a position where he must act solely in the interests of his employer (*Nottingham University v Fishel*, see para 10.56).

19.6 If, while still employed, an employee seeks to entice away existing fellow employees, this can amount to a breach of the duty of fidelity, especially if the activities of the employee have gone beyond the mere preparatory stages. But the law on this point is not absolutely clear, and the position of the employee is very relevant. A managing director who seeks to entice away senior staff (*Marshall v Industrial Systems and Control Ltd*, see para 16.12) is more likely to be in breach of his duty of fidelity than a more junior member of staff (*Tithebarn Ltd v Hubbard*[8]).

19.7 An employer must not unreasonably withhold the provision of work where there is work available to be done. But this is subject to the qualification that the employees have not demonstrated in a serious way that they are not ready or willing to work, nor rendered it impossible or reasonably impracticable for the employers to provide work. Thus if an employee is in breach of his contract or other duties, then even though the contract is ongoing the employer is not obliged to provide work. In *SG & R Valuation Services Co v Boudrais*[9] the employee, who possessed confidential information about the employer's business, but had acted in breach of his contractual obligations, resigned his employment.

[3] [1987] FSR 172, [1987] ICR 464, [1987] IRLR 491, EAT.
[4] [1987] FSR 330, [1990] FSR 385.
[5] [1895] 2 QB 1, 59 JP 695, 64 LJQB 593, 44 WR 26, 39 Sol Jo 921, 72 LT 686, 11 TLR 330; aff'd [1895] 2 QB 315, 59 JP 695, 64 LJQB 593, 14 R 580, 44 WR 25, [1895–99] All ER Rep 1053, 39 Sol Jo 653, 73 LT 15, 11 TLR 517, CA.
[6] [2006] EWHC 836 (Ch), [2007] 2 BCLC 202, [2007] IRLR 110, [2007] FSR 15, (2006) 150 SJLB 536.
[7] [2012] EWCA Civ 156.   [8] EAT 532/89.   [9] [2008] EWHC 1340 (QB), [2008] IRLR 770.

The employer sought to enforce the three months' notice period, which had the effect of creating a garden leave situation, even though there was no provision to this effect. It was held that the employee remained in employment during the notice period, and interim relief was granted to prevent him from working for a competitor during that period.

Garden leave

19.8 Because of legal uncertainties which surround the enforcement of post-termination restrictive covenants, some employers seek to obtain some protection from their employees' future competition by inserting a 'garden leave' clause into their contracts. This clause operates when lawful notice of termination is given, either by the employee or employer. During the notice period, the employee is not required to work, but is entitled to his full contractual terms and conditions. For his part, the employee remains bound by the implied duty of fidelity, and cannot work for a competitor, nor disclose trade secrets or confidential information, etc.

19.9 There should be an express contractual term which permits the employer to put the employee on garden leave, and this should set out the rights and obligations of both parties. However, in an unusual case, it was decided that an employer can put an employee on 'garden leave' even where there is no express garden leave clause in their employment contract unless the employee has a 'right to work', or he would become 'de-skilled' by not working (*Christie v Johnston Carmichael*[10]). The garden leave requirement can only be enforced if it is reasonable in terms of the length of time it operates, and if it is intended to protect the employer's genuine interests. During the garden leave period the employer is entitled to have a limited protection against the employee going to work for a competitor, or disclosing confidential information (*Provident Financial Group plc v Hayward*, see para 10.17), and if the employee acts in a manner contrary to the agreement the employer's remedy is for an injunction and/or damages, as appropriate. However, it must be stressed that such remedies are discretionary. And if, contrary to the terms of the garden leave, the employee works for a non-competitor, or discloses information which is not confidential, this will not amount to a breach of the garden leave clause, but he may be in breach of his contract of employment, and the employer may terminate the contract and/or sue for damages.

19.10 But garden leave clauses, like restrictive covenants, are inherently contracts in restraint of trade, and hence will only be enforced by the courts if they are reasonable, ie justified by reference to the legitimate business interests of the employer. Whether or not a court will uphold such a clause is a matter of discretion, to be determined on the facts of each case. On the one hand, there may be little damage to the employee if he is held to the agreement, for he will still be receiving his pay and other contractual entitlements; on the other hand there could well be considerable potential damage to the employer if the employee goes to work immediately for a rival firm (*Euro Brokers Ltd v Rabey*[11]). The employer's legitimate interests have to be balanced against the employee's right to work, especially when it is necessary to practise and exercise his skills and talents (*William Hill Organisation Ltd v Tucker*, see para 10.17). After all, it is to be expected that senior employees will seek employment in the same line of business, and will not take kindly to enforced idleness, even if they are being paid. And employers will sometimes have exaggerated fears as to the damage likely to be caused to their business if the employee takes employment with another firm (*JA Mont (UK) Ltd v Mills*[12]).

[10] [2010] IRLR 1016.   [11] [1995] IRLR 206.   [12] [1993] FSR 577, [1993] IRLR 172, CA.

19.11 A garden leave clause does have one advantage over a post-termination restrictive covenant. If the latter is drafted too widely, it will be void and unenforceable. The covenant must stand or fall on its own terms (but see para 19.48), unless the court can use the 'blue pencil' rule to give it limited validity (see para 19.48). However, when considering a garden leave clause which is too wide in its operation, the courts appear to be quite willing to interpret it and, if necessary, modify it, so as to give effect to its intentions. Thus in *Symbian Ltd v Christensen*[13] the employee's contract, which was terminable on six months' notice, contained a clause which prohibited him from working for anyone during the notice period. The employers learned that he was about to work for a competitor, and applied for an injunction to restrain him from doing so. Clearly, this clause was too wide, for it would have prohibited the employee from working for non-competing employers in non-competing businesses, but the court modified the clause so as to prohibit him from working for the named competitor any time during the six months' notice period.

19.12 Similarly, the court can modify the length of the period of garden leave, and, if necessary, reduce it to a period of time which reflects the realities of the situation (*Provident Financial Group plc v Hayward*). Thus in *GFI Group Inc v Eaglestone*[14] a garden leave period was cut down from 20 weeks to 13 weeks, although in *Euro Brokers Ltd v Rabey* a six-month garden leave period was upheld.

19.13 There is no reason in principle why a garden leave clause cannot be followed by a post-employment restrictive covenant, in effect lengthening the period of time when the employee is prevented from entering into competing employment. The one period cannot be set off against the other. But the existence of a garden leave clause may be a factor to take into account when determining the validity of the restrictive covenant and, if the garden leave clause is exceptionally long, the courts may, on grounds of public policy, refuse to enforce any further protection based on a restrictive covenant (*Credit Suisse Asset Management Ltd v Armstrong*[15]).

Employees who have left their employment

19.14 During his employment, an employee will doubtless come across a considerable amount of information, some of which is likely to be of a confidential nature. Names and addresses of customers and suppliers, prices, production methods, secret processes, etc, are all likely to come his way. Thus when he leaves his employment, he does not leave with an empty mind, yet the disclosure of such information is capable of causing considerable harm to his former employer. The higher the status of the employee, the more likely it is that he will have in his possession confidential information, and therefore the wider the restraint will have to be if it is to afford adequate protection to his former employer. This is particularly true in certain areas of employment where specialised knowledge and connections are involved (*Thomas v Farr plc*[16]). To determine whether particular information falls into the category of information which ought not to be disclosed after the employment has ceased, regard must be had to all the circumstances, and, in particular, to:

(a) the nature of the employment;

(b) the nature of the information;

---

[13] [2001] IRLR 77, CA.   [14] [1994] IRLR 119.
[15] [1996] ICR 882, [1996] IRLR 450, [1996] 23 LS Gaz R 36, 140 Sol Jo LB 140, CA.
[16] [2007] EWCA Civ 118, [2007] ICR 932, [2007] IRLR 419, (2007) 151 SJLB 296.

(c) whether the employer regarded the information as being confidential, and whether the employee was informed of this;

(d) whether the information could easily be isolated from other information which the employee is free to use (*Faccenda Chicken Ltd v Fowler*[17]).

19.15 It appears that there are three classes of information which an employee may acquire during his employment. First, there is information which is trivial or easily available to the public at large. This clearly does not give rise to any implied term of confidentiality. Second, there is information which has been imparted to the employee, or which he learns during the course of his employment for the purpose of his employer's business. During the course of his employment this should not be the subject of unauthorised disclosure, but once the employment has ceased, it remains part of the employee's skill and knowledge, and can be used by him for his own benefit – if necessary in competition with his former employer. The law does not seek to prevent an employee from using his skill and know-how, even though these were obtained during his employment (*Stenhouse Australia Ltd v Phillips*[18]) for to do so would amount to a restraint on competition per se. Thus in *Faccenda Chicken Ltd v Fowler* the employer sought an injunction to restrain two former employees from using their knowledge of sales and price information when they set up a competing business. It was held that this was not confidential information, and the application for an injunction was refused. Finally, there is information which has been imparted in confidence, or which clearly amounts to being a trade secret, such as secret processes, etc. This cannot be disclosed after the employment has ceased, unless there is a public interest in disclosure. A trade secret, as well as being specialised or technical information (such as chemical formulae or specialised processes), must be such that its disclosure would be liable to cause real or significant harm to the employer (*Lansing Linde Ltd v Kerr*[19]). Whether information is to be treated as being confidential, or whether something is a trade secret will clearly depend on the facts of each case (*SBJ Stephenson Ltd v Mandy*[20]), and the mere fact that the employer seeks to regard it as such is by no means conclusive (*Jack Allen (Sales and Service) Ltd v Smith*[21]).

19.16 It will be obvious that the rule against disclosure is easier to state in theory than to enforce in practice, for it is not possible to wipe out from an employee's mind information which he has gained in the course of the employment and which he may properly place at the disposal of his new employer. A distinction must be drawn between trade secrets and confidential information on the one hand, and an employee's skill, knowledge and general familiarity with his former employer's business on the other hand (*Lock International plc v Beswick*[22]). In *Printers and Finishers Ltd v Holloway* (see para 10.70) the claimants sought an injunction against their former works manager restraining him from disclosing certain confidential information which he had obtained during his employment. Some of this information was contained in documents which the defendant had taken with him, and an injunction was granted in respect of these and an enquiry was ordered to ascertain what damage, if any, had flowed from the defendant's breach of duty. So far as confidential matters which were in his memory were concerned, which related to the know-how and general processes of the claimant's business, these were not readily separable from his general knowledge of the whole trade, and it would not be unreasonable for him to recall

[17] [1985] 1 All ER 724, [1985] FSR 105, [1984] ICR 589, [1984] IRLR 61; aff'd [1987] Ch 117, [1986] 1 All ER 617, [1986] 3 WLR 288, [1986] FSR 291, [1986] ICR 297, [1986] IRLR 69, 130 Sol Jo 573, CA.
[18] [1974] AC 391, [1974] 1 All ER 117, [1974] 2 WLR 134, [1974] 1 Lloyd's Rep 1, 117 Sol Jo 875, PC.
[19] [1991] 1 All ER 418, [1991] 1 WLR 251, [1991] ICR 428, [1991] IRLR 80, [1990] NLJR 1458, CA.
[20] [2000] IRLR 233. [21] [1999] IRLR 19, 1999 SLT 820, OH.
[22] [1989] 3 All ER 373, [1989] 1 WLR 1268, [1989] IRLR 481, 133 Sol Jo 1297, [1989] NLJR 644.

particular skills of his former employer's business and use his skills for the benefit of his new employer. Consequently, an injunction relating to these matters was refused.

19.17 It is not necessary that the employer points out to the employee the precise nature or aspects of the production process for which protection as a trade secret is sought (*Lancashire Fires Ltd v SA Lyons & Co Ltd,* see paras 10.70 and 19.4).

19.18 However, if the information obtained, though confidential, relates to a breach of the law or wrongful act by the employer, then there is an entirely different situation, for 'there is no confidence as to the disclosure of an iniquity'. In *Initial Services Ltd v Putterill*[23] the defendant was employed as a manager by the claimants. After leaving his employment he gave information to a newspaper concerning the conduct of the claimants' business, in particular alleging that they had violated the Restrictive Trade Practices Act 1956 by entering into agreements with other laundries which ought to have been registered under that Act, and that they had issued circulars which were misleading to the public. The newspaper proposed to publish an article which would have made detrimental allegations about the claimants' business, and an injunction was sought. It was held that the disclosure would be justified as being in the public interest, and there was no confidence attached thereto.

19.19 If an employee does disclose information relating to the commission of a fraud, crime or act of corruption by his former employer, he can rely on the defence of 'just cause' if the disclosure is made in the public interest. Thus in *Lion Laboratories Ltd v Evans*[24] two ex-employees gave information to a newspaper which showed that there were doubts about the reliability of a breathalyser approved by the Home Office. It was held that the information disclosed was of grave public concern, and would not be restrained (see now para 10.74 for protected disclosures).

19.20 An ex-employee is not in breach of the implied term of confidentiality in disclosing information relating to his former employer's insolvency, because the duty of confidentiality is much more restricted in scope after the employment has ceased than that which is imposed by the general duty of good faith during the employment (*Brookes v Olyslager OMS (UK) Ltd*[25]). Nor can an ex-employee be restrained from disclosing information to regulatory bodies (such as the Financial Services Authority) which have a duty to investigate matters within their remit (*Re a Company's Application*[26]).

19.21 In the absence of an express covenant restricting post-employment activities, there can be no general restriction on an ex-employee canvassing or doing business with customers of his former employer, or competing with him in any way, and there is no implied term prohibiting this (*Wallace Bogan & Co v Cove*[27]). An ex-employee is entitled to make use of the skill and knowledge he has acquired in his previous employment (*United Sterling Corpn v Felton*[28]) and, although he can be restrained by a restrictive covenant not to disclose trade secrets or confidential information, or not to compete with his former employer, such a covenant can only give reasonable protection in limited circumstances (*Herbert Morris Ltd v Saxelby*[29]).

---

[23] [1968] 1 QB 396, [1967] 3 All ER 145, [1967] 3 WLR 1032, 2 KIR 863, 111 Sol Jo 541, CA.
[24] [1985] QB 526, [1984] 2 All ER 417, [1984] 3 WLR 539, 128 Sol Jo 533, CA.
[25] [1988] IRLR 590, 601 IRLB 6, CA.
[26] [1989] Ch 477, [1989] 2 All ER 248, [1989] 3 WLR 265, [1989] ICR 449, [1989] IRLR 477, [1989] BCLC 462, 133 Sol Jo 917.
[27] [1997] IRLR 453, CA.   [28] [1973] FSR 409, [1974] IRLR 314, [1974] RPC 162.
[29] [1915] 2 Ch 57, 84 LJ Ch 521, 59 Sol Jo 412, 112 LT 354, 31 TLR 370, CA; on appeal [1916] 1 AC 688, 85 LJ Ch 210, [1916–17] All ER Rep 305, 60 Sol Jo 305, 114 LT 618, 32 TLR 297, HL.

A. **Springboard injunctions**

19.22 Employees are generally entitled to enter into competition with their former employer in the absence of a valid restrictive covenant, and they are entitled to use the knowledge and expertise that they have acquired during their employment. It is not possible to isolate their accumulated skill and knowledge. However, if an employee deliberately copies information acquired during his employment (eg lists of customers) or other confidential information he can be restrained from using it to his former employer's disadvantage. Further, there is a distinction between a duty of fidelity and the fiduciary duty. A duty of fidelity is implied into every contract of employment, which requires the employee not to do anything contrary to the employer's interests. Additionally, however, directors and others in senior positions have a separate and potentially more onerous fiduciary duty of acting solely and exclusively in the employer's interests. Thus in *Kynixa Ltd v Hynes*[30] a director and senior manager failed to disclose that for a period of two months they had been discussing possible employment prospects with a competitor, and in *Crowson Fabrics Ltd v Rider*[31] two senior employees set up their own company in competition with their former employer. In both cases it was held that the employees were in breach of their fiduciary duty.

19.23 Additionally, the aggrieved employer may apply for a springboard injunction to prevent the former employee from gaining a head start in the new business at the expense of the former employer if there is a serious breach of contract by the latter that could cause serious economic damage to the former employer (*UBS Wealth Management (UK) Ltd v Vestra Wealth LLP*[32]). Indeed, even though there may be the absence of a garden leave clause in their contracts, there may be an implied right to impose one in cases where the employees have so breached their contracts of employment (eg by seeking to take away confidential information and/or fellow employees with them) that they have indicated that they are unwilling to perform their contractual duties (*SG & R Valuation Services Co LLC v Boudrais*, para 19.7).

19.24 Springboard injunctions were originally used to stop an ex-employee from using confidential information, despite the fact that that information was in the public domain and others could be free to use it. However, in *UBS Wealth Management (UK) Ltd v Vestra Wealth LLP* a springboard injunction was used to prevent five former employees and their new employer (Vestra Wealth) from approaching UBS's clients and encouraging more UBS staff to leave in order to work for the defendants, in breach of their own duty of loyalty and fidelity. On the other hand, a springboard injunction was refused in *Utopia (UK) Ltd v Wright*,[33] there being little evidence that the defendants had gained any unfair competitive advantage.

Post-employment restraints

19.25 We have seen that an employer cannot prevent an ex-employee from competing with him, nor using the knowledge, skill and experience gained during the employment. The employer can, however, extract a promise that the ex-employee will not, for a limited period of time, use that knowledge etc to the disadvantage of the employer (*Spafax Ltd v Harrison,* see paras 17.37 and 17.40), provided the restriction is reasonably necessary for the protection of the employer's business. Thus if an employer has a genuine interest to

---

[30] [2008] EWHC 1495 (QB).   [31] [2007] EWHC 2942 (Ch), [2008] IRLR 288, [2008] FSR 17.
[32] [2008] EWHC 1974 (QB), [2008] IRLR 965, (2008) 105(37) LSG 21.   [33] [2007] EWHC 321 (QB).

protect, he can require the employee to sign a covenant, restricting the employee's future activities after the employment comes to an end. Normally, this covenant would be agreed at the commencement of the employment, but this is not essential. In *R S Components Ltd v Irwin*[34] the employer asked a salesman, who was already in employment, to sign a covenant which would have prevented him from soliciting business from the firm's customers for a period of 12 months after leaving the employment. The employee refused to do so, and in consequence was dismissed. It was held that the dismissal was fair for 'some other substantial reason' (see para 17.149).

19.26 There are several limitations on the right of the employer to impose such restraints, for the courts will look with a critical eye on any agreement which has the effect of restraining a person from earning his livelihood in the future. The employer cannot take away the employee's skill, experience and fund of knowledge which he has obtained during the employment, and, in particular, the employer cannot protect himself against competition per se. For example, in *SW Strange Ltd v Mann*[35] the defendant was employed by a firm of bookmakers as a manager. Most of the betting was done by telephone, and hence the defendant had little contact with customers. He agreed that after leaving his employment he would not engage in a similar business within a radius of 12 miles. After leaving his job, he set up as a bookmaker within the prohibited area. It was held that the restriction was void. The purpose of the covenant was not to give legitimate protection to the business interest of the employer, but was a naked attempt to prevent future competition.

19.27 The protection required by the employer must be contained in a restrictive covenant, agreed to by the employee prior to the end of the employment, and is subject to two general limitations. These are (a) the restraint must be designed to protect the legitimate interests of the employer, and (b) it must be reasonable, in terms of the activities prohibited, and in terms of time and area covered by the restraint. The fact that the employee is given a payment to enter into a restrictive covenant is a relevant factor to be taken into account, but it is not conclusive, and the restraint is still required to be justified (*Turner v Commonwealth and British Minerals Ltd*[36]). In addition, a restrictive covenant is not enforceable if the previous employer is no longer carrying on the particular type of work as a result of the departure of the claimant (*Phoenix Partners Group LLP v Asoyag*[37]).

19.28 There are four legitimate interests in respect of which the employer is entitled to limited protection, namely (a) trade secrets and confidential information, (b) existing customers and connections, (c) working for competitors, and (d) enticing existing employees.

A. Trade secrets and confidential information

19.29 If an employer could not ensure that his employees would not pass on information concerning his secret processes, it might restrict the employment relationship to an extent where commercial initiative became impossible. The employer would not be able to trust the employee; furtive attempts would have to be made to disclose some information without disclosing all, industrial espionage would flourish, and employees would attempt to sell secrets by offering themselves on the labour market to the highest bidder. Research and development would be hampered and become unprofitable. So, at least, ran the economic theories of former ages, though with the advent of patent law the modern scene might be somewhat different. Nonetheless, the legal principles remain substantially the same. Thus if a trade secret, or a secret process, exists, the employer is entitled to have his

---

[34] [1974] 1 All ER 41, [1973] ICR 535, [1973] IRLR 239, NIRC.
[35] [1965] 1 All ER 1069, [1965] 1 WLR 629, 109 Sol Jo 352.
[36] [2000] IRLR 114, [1999] All ER (D) 1097, CA.   [37] [2010] EWHC 846 (QB), [2010] IRLR 594.

employee's promise not to divulge that information to a future employer, at least, subject to possible limitations on time and area. In *Forster & Sons Ltd v Suggett*[38] the defendant was a works engineer concerned with a secret process in the glass-making industry. He covenanted that he would not divulge any trade secret or manufacturing process, and would not be employed by a competitor anywhere in the United Kingdom for five years after leaving his employment with the plaintiffs. It was held that the covenant was reasonable and enforceable.

19.30 It is not possible to restrain an employee from disclosing to a future employer a special method of organisation, as opposed to a secret process, for one must draw a distinction between objective knowledge, such as trade secrets and lists of customers, which are part of the employer's property, and subjective knowledge which has been acquired by the employee, such as his general knowledge of the trade or industry, or his organisational ability. In *Herbert Morris Ltd v Saxelby* (para 19.21) an engineer covenanted not to be engaged by a competitor for seven years after leaving his employment. This was held to be void, for it was a restraint on his technical skill and knowledge which he had acquired by his own industry, observation and intelligence, and this could not be taken away from him. On the other hand, in *SBJ Stephenson Ltd v Mandy* (para 19.15), a covenant against the disclosure of any information relating to the company's business affairs which had come into the employee's possession whilst employed by the company was held to be valid. The identity of customers, prices charged, renewal dates, market information and contractual arrangements were objective knowledge capable of being protected. But if an employer wishes to enforce a covenant against the disclosure of confidential information, he must be able to identify a perceived or actual harm from the disclosure which would justify the restraint (*Jack Allen Ltd v Smith*, para 19.15).

19.31 Another example is *Thomas Marshall Ltd v Guinle* (see para 15.25), where the defendant was appointed managing director of the claimant company under a 10-year service contract, which contained clauses against disclosing confidential information relating to the affairs, customers or trade secrets of the company, during his employment or after it ceased. He resigned after five years and set up his own competing business. The court granted an injunction against him from acting in breach of the agreement.

B. Existing customers and connections

19.32 An employer is entitled to have a limited protection against an ex-employee dealing with existing customers, for this is part of the goodwill which has been built up over the years. A covenant can restrict the right to solicit or endeavour to entice away former customers, or to have post-employment dealing with such customers, but it is likely that such clauses should be limited to those customers with whom the ex-employee had some dealings, for otherwise the restraint is likely to be regarded as one designed to prevent competition (*Marley Tile Co Ltd v Johnson*[39]). A clause prohibiting the ex-employee from approaching the employer's customers, or persons with whom the employer had been negotiating or who were in the habit of dealing with the employer may be reasonable, particularly if there is a relationship with potential customers which could be built up over a number of years, and the employee was in a position where he could form a bond with those customers (*International Consulting Services (UK) Ltd v Hart*[40]). In *GW Plowman & Sons Ltd v Ash*,[41] the defendant was employed as a sales representative. He covenanted not to canvass or solicit orders from any person who was a customer of the firm for a period of two years after leaving

---

[38] (1918) 35 TLR 87.   [39] [1982] IRLR 75, CA.   [40] [2000] IRLR 227.
[41] [1964] 2 All ER 10, [1964] 1 WLR 568, 108 Sol Jo 216, CA.

his employment. It was held that the restraint was valid, even though it extended to customers whom the employee did not know or with whom he had no contact during his period of employment. It was argued that the restraint was bad because it could apply to those customers who had ceased to do business with the firm, but the Court of Appeal thought that an employer was entitled not to abandon hope that such customers would return to do business once more. This was reiterated in *Coppage & Anor v Safety Net Security Ltd.*[42]

19.33 On the other hand, if an employee does not come into contact with such customers, then it cannot be argued that he has built up a special relationship with them so as to entitle the employer to extract a covenant restraining the employee from approaching them with a view to taking business away from the employer. A restrictive covenant that prevents an employee from soliciting or accepting business from his former employer's customers will be unenforceable if it extends to customers with whom the employee personally had no dealings (*WRN Ltd v Ayris*[43]). For example, if a firm is engaged mainly in trading in the south of England, and has few customers outside that area, a covenant restraining an employee from working in that type of business anywhere in the UK must of necessity be void, as being wider than legitimately required for the protection of the employer's business (*Dowden and Pook Ltd v Pook*[44]). In *Attwood v Lamont*[45] a tailor's cutter in a department store agreed not to be employed by another firm which competed with his employer. Since it can hardly be said that in his position he had gained the trust and confidence of the customers so that they would follow him if he left the firm, the covenant was void. Again, if the business is such that it is not of a recurring nature, then the employer's interest in the customer ceases on the conclusion of a particular transaction, and he is not entitled to protection against poaching. In *Bowler v Lovegrove*[46] the defendant was a negotiating clerk who worked for a firm of estate agents. He covenanted not to enter into a similar business for one year within a restricted area, but it was held that as the business was of a non-recurring nature, the employer had no interest to protect, and the covenant was void.

19.34 The position held by the employee may be relevant, too. An employer can scarcely claim that he fears competition from an ex-employee if, during the period of employment, he pays him a low wage, for this reflects the regard he has for his services (*M and S Drapers v Reynolds*[47]). Nor is an employer entitled to restrain competition by preventing the ex-employee from approaching persons who are not his customers. In *Gledhow Autoparts v Delaney*[48] the claimants employed the defendant as a commercial traveller. It was agreed that after leaving his employment, the defendant would not seek orders from any firm within the area in which he had previously operated. The restraint was held to be void, for as worded, it would have prevented him from calling on firms who were not then customers of the claimants, and was therefore a covenant designed to restrain competition. Nor can a covenant restrain an ex-employee from dealing with businesses which were not in competition with the employer (*Scully UK Ltd v Lee*[49]).

19.35 Moreover, the personality, temperament and general make-up of an employee is his own possession, and there is thus no proprietary right in an employee's own personality which the employer can keep to himself as part of his own business (*Cantor Fitzgerald (UK) Ltd v Wallace*[50]).

---

[42] [2013] EWCA Civ 972.   [43] [2008] EWHC 1080 (QB), [2008] IRLR 889, (2008) 152(23) SJLB 29.
[44] [1904] 1 KB 45, 73 LJKB 38, 52 WR 97, 48 Sol Jo 50, 89 LT 688, 20 TLR 39, CA.
[45] [1920] 3 KB 571.   [46] [1921] 1 Ch 642, 90 LJ Ch 356, 65 Sol Jo 397, 124 LT 695, 37 TLR 424.
[47] [1956] 3 All ER 814, [1957] 1 WLR 9, 101 Sol Jo 44, CA.
[48] [1965] 3 All ER 288, [1965] 1 WLR 1366, 109 Sol Jo 571, CA.
[49] [1998] IRLR 259, CA.   [50] [1992] IRLR 215.

19.36 The employer's 'connections' are also a legitimate object for protection. Thus an employment agency which supplied temporary staff to business clients was held to be entitled to extract and enforce a restrictive covenant from its own staff who dealt with the temporary staff (the connection) and the clients (*Office Angels Ltd v Rainer-Thomas*[51]).

C. Working for competitors

19.37 We have seen (para 10.1) that the courts will not grant an injunction to compel a person to work for a particular employer, for this would amount to compulsory labour. Thus if an employee agrees that after leaving his employment, he will not work for anyone the courts will rarely enforce such an agreement because the employee will be faced with the alternative of being forced to work for his former employer or starve! But if the latter alternative does not exist, the courts may be more willing to enforce the agreement.

19.38 In *Littlewoods Organisation Ltd v Harris*,[52] the claimants ran a mail order business, their chief rivals being Great Universal Stores (GUS). The defendant worked for the claimants in a senior position, and had access to confidential information about how the business was operated. He agreed that on leaving his employment, he would not work for GUS for a period of 12 months. He then resigned his position in order to take employment with GUS, and the claimants sought an injunction to restrain him. For the defendant it was argued that the covenant was too wide, and therefore void, for, as worded, it would have prevented him from being employed by GUS anywhere in the world, or by one of their companies which was not concerned with mail order. Nonetheless, the restriction was held to be valid by a majority of the Court of Appeal. It was held that where a covenant in restraint of trade was drafted in general terms, which, without alteration could be construed in a sense which was not unreasonably wide in relation to the relevant confidential information or trade secrets for which the covenantee was seeking protection, the court could construe the covenant in that sense, thereby rendering it valid and enforceable. Accordingly, the covenant should not be construed as applying to the whole range of business carried on by GUS throughout the world, but only to the mail order business carried on in the United Kingdom. So construed, it was no wider than was reasonably necessary to protect the confidential information about the mail order side of the claimants' business, and it was thus enforceable. There is little doubt that this case represented a major shift in the judicial approach to the interpretation of restrictive covenants, though it is arguable that the conclusion is warranted on the special facts.

19.39 But the protection taken out by the employer must be in respect of his specific interests, and if it is too wide for this purpose, it will be void. In *Commercial Plastics Ltd v Vincent*,[53] the claimants employed the defendant to work on the production of PVC calendering sheeting for adhesive tape. The defendant agreed not to be employed by a competitor in the PVC calendering field for one year after leaving his employment. This restriction was held to be void. The protection legitimately required by the claimants could only be in respect of their own business, which was the production of adhesive tape. In fact, the covenant covered the whole field of calendering sheeting, and hence was too wide.

19.40 The covenant should only restrict what is necessary to protect the employer. In *Associated Foreign Exchange Ltd v International Foreign Exchange (UK) Ltd*[54] a 12-month non-solicitation restrictive covenant restraining a currency trader was not enforced. The

---

[51] [1991] IRLR 214, CA.   [52] [1978] 1 All ER 1026, [1977] 1 WLR 1472, 121 Sol Jo 727, CA.
[53] [1965] 1 QB 623, [1964] 3 All ER 546, [1964] 3 WLR 820, 108 Sol Jo 599, CA.
[54] [2010] IRLR 964, [2010] EWHC (Ch) 1178.

employee did not hold a senior position, and in the market in which the employer operated, 12 months was longer than reasonably necessary to protect its interests.

D. Enticing existing employees

19.41 A covenant which purports to restrict the right of an employee to solicit or entice other employees to leave the employer's employment and to work for another employer is generally void. Thus in *Hanover Insurance Brokers Ltd v Schapiro*[55] the defendant entered into a restrictive covenant with his employers which provided, inter alia, that for a period of 12 months after leaving his employment he would not '…solicit or entice any employees of the company to the intent or effect that such employee terminates that employment'. When the defendant left his employment, the employers sought an injunction to restrain him from acting in breach of the clause quoted. It was held that an employee has the right to work for any employer who is willing to employ him. Thus employees are not part of the assets of an employer – like stock in trade or goodwill and customers. A restriction which sought to prevent a person from poaching employees – irrespective of their expertise, technical knowledge and/or juniority, and which could also apply to employees who were not in the particular employment when the defendant left, was clearly a restriction against competition, and therefore void (*TSC Europe UK Ltd v Massey*[56]).

19.42 In *Hanover Insurance Brokers Ltd v Schapiro* (above) a non-solicitation clause was held to be unenforceable because it applied to all employees, irrespective of their position or experience, but different considerations may apply if the covenant purports to restrain the poaching of 'an executive' or a person 'in a senior capacity', and, if necessary, the court will identify those who fall within such categories (*Alliance Paper Group plc v Prestwich*[57]). Further, the Court of Appeal has held that an employer has a legitimate interest in maintaining a stable, trained workforce in a highly competitive business (*Ingham v ABC Contract Services Ltd*[58]) which can be protected within the limits of reasonableness by means of a non-solicitation clause (*Dawnay Day Ltd v de Braconier d'Alphen*[59]).

19.43 Employers cannot agree to a restraint among themselves which would not be enforced if it was entered into by their employees. In *Kores Manufacturing Co Ltd v Kolok Manufacturing Co Ltd*[60] two companies, both engaged in the selling of carbon paper, agreed that they would not employ any person who had been employed by the other party for a period of five years after that person had left the other's employment. Had the restraint been imposed by a company on the employees, it would have been void. It was equally void having been made by the employers themselves.

E. Reasonableness of the covenant

19.44 To assess whether or not a covenant in restraint of trade is reasonable, the courts will consider not only the subject-matter of the restraint, but the time and area within which it will operate. If the employer's business is worldwide, a worldwide restraint may be valid (*Nordenfelt v Maxim Nordenfelt Ltd*[61]), but if the employer's business operates in a limited geographical area, a restraint which purports to operate outside that area will not be valid (*Office Angels Ltd v Rainer-Thomas*, para 19.36). A covenant with no geographical limitation

---

[55] [1994] IRLR 82, CA.   [56] [1999] IRLR 22.   [57] [1996] IRLR 25.   [58] Unreported.

[59] [1997] IRLR 285; aff'd [1998] ICR 1068, [1997] IRLR 442, [1997] 26 LS Gaz R 30, 141 Sol Jo LB 129, CA.

[60] [1957] 3 All ER 158, [1957] 1 WLR 1012, [1957] RPC 431, 101 Sol Jo 799, [1957] CLY 1285; aff'd [1959] Ch 108, [1958] 2 All ER 65, [1968] 2 WLR 858, [1958] RPC 200, 1958 SLT 221, [1958] JBL 306, 102 Sol Jo 362, CA.

[61] [1895] 1 QB 151, 64 LJQB 182, 2 Mans 20, 14 R 71, 71 LT 565, 11 TLR 26, CA.

will normally be unenforceable (*Commercial Plastics Ltd v Vincent*), as will a covenant which purports to operate in a densely populated area, which is not reasonably necessary for the protection of the employer's connections (*Office Angels Ltd v Rainer-Thomas*, para 19.36). In *Hollis & Co v Stocks*[62] a covenant which restricted a solicitor from working within a 10-mile radius of Sutton-in-Ashfield in Nottinghamshire was upheld, but in *Mason v Provident Clothing and Supply Co Ltd*[63] a covenant restraining a canvasser from competing with his former employer anywhere within 25 miles from the centre of London was held to be void.

19.45 The time element of a restrictive covenant must also be reasonable. In *Herbert Morris Ltd v Saxelby* (paras 19.21 and 19.30) a seven-year restraint on an engineer was not upheld, although in *Nordenfelt's* case (above) a 25-year restraint was held to be valid. In the latter case, the worldwide nature of the business, and the price paid for the employee's promise were significant factors in upholding the covenant. Time and area may be looked at together to assess the validity of the covenant. In *Fitch v Dewes*[64] a solicitor's clerk was prohibited from entering into the employment of another solicitor within a radius of seven miles of Tamworth Town Hall. Although this was a lifetime restraint, the modest area enabled him to work quite openly outside the geographical limit, and it was held to be valid. On this point see also *Associated Foreign Exchange Ltd v International Foreign Exchange (UK) Ltd.*[65]

19.46 The restriction cannot be worded in a manner which prevents the employee from obtaining non-competing employment (*Commercial Plastics Ltd v Vincent* (para 19.44)). For example, in *Fellowes & Son v Fisher*[66] the defendant was a conveyancing clerk employed by a firm of solicitors in Walthamstow. He agreed that for five years after leaving his employment, he would not (a) be employed or concerned in the legal profession anywhere within the postal districts of Walthamstow and Chingford, or (b) solicit any person who had been a client of the firm whilst he had been with them. After leaving his employment, he commenced work with another firm of solicitors who had offices in Walthamstow. The Court of Appeal refused to grant an injunction to restrain him. A restraint of five years which covered such a thickly populated area was undoubtedly too wide in the circumstances. Further, clause (a), as worded, would have prevented him from being employed as an assistant to a justices' clerk, or in the legal department of the local authority. In *Greer v Sketchley Ltd*,[67] the activities of the company were confined to the Midlands and London area. The employee agreed that after leaving his employment he would not work for any similar business anywhere in the United Kingdom. This was held to be void; the fact that there was a problematical and possible expansion by the company into other areas of the country was too vague to justify such a wide restraint.

19.47 An area restriction will always be considered critically by the courts, since it will frequently amount to a covenant against competition, which would generally be unenforceable. Thus if such a restriction will do little to protect the employer (eg, because most of the orders are placed on the telephone), or if there is no functional connection with the area covered by the restriction and the areas associated with the employee's work, the restraint is likely to be void (*Office Angels Ltd v Rainer-Thomas*, paras 19.36 and 19.44). A covenant that has a time restriction is more likely to be enforceable (*Allen Janes LLP v Johal*[68]).

[62] [2000] IRLR 712, CA.
[63] [1913] AC 724, 82 LJKB 1153, [1911–13] All ER Rep 400, 57 Sol Jo 739, 109 LT 449, 29 TLR 727, HL.
[64] [1921] 2 AC 158, 90 LJ Ch 436, [1921] All ER Rep 13, 65 Sol Jo 626, 125 LT 744, 37 TLR 784, HL.
[65] [2010] EWHC 1178 (Ch), [2010] IRLR 964.
[66] [1976] QB 122, [1975] 2 All ER 829, [1975] 3 WLR 184, 119 Sol Jo 390, CA.
[67] [1979] FSR 197, [1979] IRLR 445, CA.
[68] [2006] EWHC 286 (Ch), [2006] ICR 742, [2006] IRLR 599, Ch.

F. Interpreting a covenant in restraint of trade

19.48 If a covenant is too restrictive, it will be totally void, and the courts will not enforce it or any part of it. They will not normally validate the agreement by altering it, for the test is whether the parties have in fact made a valid agreement, not whether they could have done so, and it must stand or fall on its own merits. Thus in *Wincanton Ltd v Cranny*[69] a non-competition clause prohibiting post-termination involvement 'in any capacity' with a competing firm was held to be void. The court refused to read into the covenant a reasonable coverage (see also *J A Mont Ltd v Mills*, para 19.10). Exceptionally, however, the courts may relax this strict interpretation by use of a device known as 'the blue pencil' rule.

19.49 The court must be satisfied that (a) the unenforceable provision is capable of being removed without the necessity of adding to or modifying the wording of what remains, (b) the remaining terms continue to be supported by adequate consideration, (c) the removal of the unenforceable provision does not so change the character of the contract that it becomes different from that which the parties entered into, and (d) the severance must be consistent with public policy underlying the avoidance of the offending term (*Marshall v NM Financial Management Ltd*;[70] see also *Beckett Investment Management Group Ltd v Hall*[71]).

19.50 If there are terms which are too wide, and others which are valid and reasonable, then the former may be struck out of the agreement altogether. If those terms which thus remain are valid, then they may be enforced. In *T Lucas & Co Ltd v Mitchell*[72] the defendant was employed by the claimants as a sales representative. He agreed that after leaving his employment he would not (a) deal in any goods similar to those which he had previously sold, or (b) solicit orders from or supply any such goods to any customer of the firm within the Manchester area. The first part of the covenant was clearly void, for this was a restraint on competition. The second part was clearly reasonable. Because there were two separate restraints, capable of being enforced separately, the excision of the first was possible without affecting the second.

19.51 Severance is possible if there is no grammatical difficulty in removing the offending words (*Business Seating (Renovations) Ltd v Broad*[73]). If that which remains is reasonable, the covenant will be enforced (*Rex Stewart Jeffries Parker Ginsberg Ltd v Parker*[74]). The courts will prefer an interpretation which gives effect to the parties' intentions, rather than invalidate it by using a literal interpretation (*Turner v Commonwealth and British Minerals Ltd*, see para 19.27).

19.52 If, in the particular circumstances of the case, there is 'a want of accuracy of expression' the court may be prepared to permit an interpretation which would give some sensible meaning to a covenant. Thus in *Business Seating (Renovations) Ltd v Broad*, a clause forbade a sales representative from canvassing, soliciting or endeavouring to take away from the company the business of any client or customers. The nature of 'the business' was not defined, but its meaning could be inferred from the nature of the defendant's employment, and, as a matter of construction, it meant the business carried out by the company.

---

[69] [2000] IRLR 716, CA.

[70] [1995] 4 All ER 785, [1995] 1 WLR 1461, [1995] ICR 1042, [1996] IRLR 20; on appeal [1997] 1 WLR 1527, [1997] ICR 1065, [1997] IRLR 449, CA.

[71] [2007] EWHC 241 (QB), rev [2007] EWCA Civ 613, [2007] IRLR 793, (2007) 151 SJLB 891, [2007] ICR 1539.

[72] [1972] 2 All ER 1035, [1972] 1 WLR 938, 116 Sol Jo 506; revsd [1974] Ch 129, [1972] 3 All ER 689, [1972] 3 WLR 934, 116 Sol Jo 711, CA.   [73] [1989] ICR 729.   [74] [1988] IRLR 483, CA.

19.53 It would appear that the courts are now taking a somewhat more relaxed view when construing a restrictive covenant, by seeking objectively to ascertain the intentions of the parties. Thus in *Hollis & Co v Stocks* (para 19.44) a restrictive covenant contained a clause prohibiting an assistant solicitor from working for a period of 12 months within a 10-mile radius. This clause was clearly too wide, because it would have prevented him from doing any sort of work, but the Court of Appeal upheld an injunction, arguing that it was clear that the clause was designed to prevent him working as a solicitor. The balance of convenience was in favour of granting the injunction, because damages were not an appropriate remedy, and it was not possible for his former employers to quantify the loss.

19.54 There is a tendency in some cases for the courts to attempt to ascertain the true intentions of the parties and give effect to them, even though some redrafting of the covenant is involved (*GFI Group Inc v Eaglestone*, para 19.12), but the principle remains that the court will not rewrite the covenant so that it has a meaning which is different from that which it has when properly construed.

19.55 A restrictive covenant that has been entered into between an employee and a holding company can be enforced, even though it is the subsidiaries that have the interests to protect. The law must take account of the realities of modern business organisation (*Beckett Investment Management Group Ltd v Hall*, para 19.49).

G. **Breach of contract by the employer**

19.56 There is a general rule that a party in breach of contract cannot rely on any of its terms in order to gain an advantage. Thus if an employer wrongfully dismisses an employee, he cannot enforce a restrictive covenant, for the whole of the contract will have been repudiated by him (*General Billposting Co Ltd v Atkinson*, see para 16.6). (Be aware, however, that if the dismissal is an unfair one, as opposed to a wrongful one, it has been held that it does not negate a restraint clause: *Lonmar Global Risks Ltd v West*.[75])

19.57 But in *Campbell v Frisbee* (a case which concerned a contract for services rather than a contract of employment) the High Court held that '...an employee's acceptance of an employer's repudiatory breach cannot displace the employer's established property rights, and these include his right in respect of confidential information'.[76] There is no justification for granting as a windfall to a wrongfully dismissed employee a present of his employer's trade secrets or other secrets or confidences. The wrongful dismissal may arise because of a dismissal without notice, or with insufficient notice, or contrary to a contractual disciplinary procedure (*Dietman v Brent London Borough Council*, see paras 16.19, 16.21 and 16.31), or breach of a fixed-term contract consequence on the dissolution of a partnership (*Briggs v Oates*[77]). It may even arise out of a constructive dismissal (*Cantor Fitzgerald International v Callaghan*, see para 3.35). But if a contract provides that it may be terminated by an employer on giving six months' notice or six months' pay in lieu of notice, an employer who adopts the latter option is not acting in breach of contract (*Rex Stewart Jeffries Parker Ginsberg Ltd v Parker*, para 19.51).

19.58 To avoid this rule, some employers resorted to inserting into the covenant a clause which stated that it was to apply 'howsoever the employment is terminated' or if the contract was terminated 'for whatever reason' etc. Such phrases do not, by themselves,

---

[75] [2011] IRLR 138, QBD.

[76] [2002] EWHC 328 (Ch), [2002] EMLR 656, [2002] All ER (D) 211 (Mar); revsd [2002] EWCA Civ 1374, [2003] ICR 141, [2003] EMLR 76, [2003] IP & T 86, 146 Sol Jo LB 233, [2002] All ER (D) 178 (Oct).

[77] [1991] 1 All ER 407, [1990] ICR 473, [1990] IRLR 472, (1990) 140 NLJ 208 ChD.

render the covenant unenforceable by virtue of being unreasonable. Not every stipulation in a contract falls when there has been a fundamental breach by one side which has been accepted by the innocent party. Thus if an employee is dismissed for reason of misconduct, or he resigns his employment, the restrictive covenant may still be enforced, despite the presence of the above phrases. The fact that the offending term may apply to some circumstances, but not to others, will not invalidate the convenant (*Rock Refrigeration Ltd v Jones*[78]).

19.59 If an employee is dismissed for refusing to sign a restrictive covenant that is too wide, this is still capable of being 'some other substantial reason' for the dismissal (unless the dismissal is in fact a mere ruse to get rid of the employee), but the unreasonableness of the covenant becomes very relevant when determining the fairness of the dismissal. Thus, if it is plainly unreasonable, and not severable, it will be easier for the employment tribunal to conclude that the dismissal was unfair. On the other hand, if the covenant was arguably unreasonable or marginally capable of being severable, the tribunal should consider the employer's approach to the whole issue, including the time given to the employee to consider the proposal and the opportunity for him to obtain legal advice. Even if the covenant is plainly reasonable, the employer must still satisfy the requirements of a reasonable procedure (*Willow Oak Developments Ltd v Silverwood*[79]).

H. Restrictive covenants and transfers

19.60 It will be recalled (see Chapter 9) that if there is a transfer of an undertaking, the contracts of employment of the affected employees will pass automatically from the transferor to the transferee. It therefore follows that if the employee's terms and conditions include a restrictive covenant, then this will bind the employee if he subsequently leaves the transferee's employment. But the covenant needs to be considered in the light of the new situation, otherwise it may be unenforceable (see *Morris Angel & Son Ltd v Hollande*, para 9.31). Equally it is not possible to impose a restrictive covenant on an employee following a transfer, even though the employee agreed to it, if it was introduced by reason of the transfer (*Credit Suisse First Boston (Europe) Ltd v Padiachy*, para 9.36), because the employee is entitled to the terms and conditions which he enjoyed prior to the transfer, and it is irrelevant that he is better off as a result of the variation (*Credit Suisse First Boston (Europe) Ltd v Lister*, para 9.36). However, it does appear that any variation in a contract of employment which takes place unconnected with the transfer may well be valid.

I. Remedies for breach of contract

Injunctive relief

19.61 The prime remedy for the employer if the ex-employee acts in breach of the restrictive covenant is to seek an injunction restraining the breach.

19.62 In considering whether or not to grant an injunction, the court will take account of the 'balance of convenience' in accordance with the principles laid down in *American Cyanamid v Ethicon Ltd* (see paras 10.6 and 16.30). Three questions need to be asked: (a) is there a serious issue to be tried, (b) would damages be an appropriate remedy if the injunction is not granted, and (c) what is the likelihood of the plaintiff succeeding at a full trial? In *Lansing Linde Ltd v Kerr* (para 19.15) it was alleged that the defendant was in breach of a

---

[78] [1997] 1 All ER 1, [1997] ICR 938, [1996] IRLR 675, [1996] 41 LS Gaz R 29, 140 Sol Jo LB 226, CA.

[79] [2006] ICR 55, [2006] IRLR 28, EAT; aff'd [2006] EWCA Civ 660, [2006] ICR 1552, [2006] IRLR 607, (2006) 103(23) LSG 29, CA.

covenant which was designed to prevent him from working for a competitor for a period of 12 months after leaving his employment. The Court of Appeal held that an application for an injunction was rightly refused. The trial of the action would not have taken place until most of the period for which the injunction was sought would have expired. Thus the question was not only whether there was a serious issue to be tried, but also an assessment of the plaintiff's prospect of succeeding at that hearing. The injunction, if granted, would have effectively determined the case in the claimant's favour, and therefore the judge had been correct in considering as an additional factor the strength of the plaintiff's claim.

19.63 Even though an employee is in breach of his covenant, the granting of an injunction to restrain him from working for a competitor is a discretionary remedy, and will only be granted if, on the balance of convenience, it is necessary to do so. In *GFI Group Inc v Eaglestone* (paras 19.12 and 19.54) the defendant was required by his employment contract to give 20 weeks' notice of termination. He, and two other highly paid employees, decided to resign and work for a competitor. The other two employees were only required to give four weeks' notice. The claimant sought an order to restrain the defendant from working in breach of his contract until the end of the 20-week notice period, but the court decided to uphold the restraint only for 13 weeks. The fact that two other employees had already commenced work for the competitor meant that the reality of the situation was that the damage had already been done. It was not necessary for the protection of the claimant's interests to hold the defendant to the full period of 20 weeks.

19.64 If there is a prima facie breach of a covenant not to deal with the employer's former customers, the employer is entitled to an injunction even though the customer has intimated that he will not do further business with the employer (*John Michael Design plc v Cooke*[80]).

Search orders

19.65 In addition (or as an alternative) to obtaining an injunction, the aggrieved employer may seek a search order. This permits the employer to search the employee's premises or home etc, and to remove documents, drawings, records, prototypes or other specified matter. The purpose is to prevent a defendant from destroying, hiding or removing vital evidence, and to enable the claimant to obtain inspection of any relevant matter in the defendant's possession. A refusal to permit the search, and/or the removal, destruction etc of the evidence not only enables the courts to draw an adverse conclusion, but may also amount to a contempt of court (*Anton Piller KG v Manufacturing Processes Ltd*[81]). Before granting the order, the court must be satisfied (a) that there is a strong prima facie case, (b) the actual or potential damage to the plaintiff would be very serious, and (c) that there is clear evidence that the defendant has in his possession incriminating matter, and that there is a real possibility that he would destroy, hide, remove or otherwise dispose of it (*Lock International plc v Beswick*, para 19.16).

19.66 Search orders are not available in Scotland, although there is a separate procedure by way of letters of request, under which a court may grant a commission and a diligence for the recovery of documents relevant to pending litigation.

Damages

19.67 If the employer can show that he has suffered damage as a result of the breach, he may bring an action accordingly. The amount of damages to be awarded will be such as to

---

[80] [1987] 2 All ER 332, [1987] ICR 445, 131 Sol Jo 595, [1987] LS Gaz R 1492, CA.

[81] [1976] Ch 55, [1976] 2 WLR 162, [1976] 1 All ER 779, [1976] FSR 129, [1976] RPC 719, (1975) 120 SJ 63, CA.

put the claimant in the position he would have been in had the contract been performed. Thus in *SBJ Stephenson Ltd v Mandy* (paras 19.15 and 19.30) the defendant signed a restrictive covenant preventing him from disclosing confidential information, engaging in competing activities and soliciting staff of the employer, for a period of 12 months from the end of the termination of his employment. He resigned his position, and subsequently acted in breach of the covenant. The employers were successful in obtaining an injunction, and were subsequently awarded substantial damages in respect of loss of income from former clients and for future loss.

Account of profits

19.68 An action for an account of profits is essentially based on the equitable principle of unjust enrichment, and is normally available only in those cases where there has been a breach of fiduciary duty or breach of the duty of confidence. Damages are assessed on the profits made by the defendant rather than on any proven loss by the claimant. Thus in *Nottingham University v Fishel* (paras 10.56 and 19.5) the defendant, a world-renowned fertility expert, was employed by the university. He carried out outside work for overseas clinics, from which he earned money. He also benefited financially from work performed by junior colleagues under his supervision. It was held that the university was entitled to an account of profits for this breach of fiduciary duty.

Actions against third parties

19.69 An action for inducing a breach of contract may be brought against someone who induces an employee to breach his contract of employment (*Bents Brewery Co Ltd v Hogan,* para 10.69) or to break the terms of a restrictive covenant. As well as obtaining an injunction (*Hivac v Park Royal Scientific Instruments Ltd,* paras 10.92 and 17.143), the injured party may seek damages in tort (*British Industrial Plastics Ltd v Ferguson*[82]).

Training agreements

19.70 An employer may permit an employee to go on a training course (possibly with paid leave of absence) under an agreement whereby the employee agrees to serve the employer for a specified period after completing the course. Clearly, such an agreement can be for the mutual benefit of both parties. The problem arises when the employee fails to serve the employer for the specified period. In *Strathclyde Regional Council v Neil,*[83] the defendant was employed by the claimants as a trainee social worker. She was given paid leave of absence to go on a training course, and signed an agreement to serve the council for two years after completing the course. The agreement also specified that if she left her employment before completing two years' service she would refund to the council a sum of money, proportionate to the unexpired period of the contractual two years. After completing the course, she worked for the council for 15 months, and resigned her employment. It was held that the council could recover a proportion of their expenditure in respect of her salary, course fees, examination fees and book allowance. The terms of the contract were not extravagant or unconscionable.

---

[82] [1938] 4 All ER 504, 56 RPC 271, 82 Sol Jo 970, 160 LT 95, CA; aff'd [1940] 1 All ER 479, 58 RPC 1, 162 LT 313, HL.

[83] [1984] IRLR 11, Sh Ct; aff'd sub nom *Neil v Strathclyde Regional Council* [1984] IRLR 14, 1983 SLT (Sh Ct) 89.

20

Practice and Procedure

Making a claim to an employment tribunal

20.1 An employee who wishes to seek the enforcement of a statutory right, or to obtain a remedy for a breach of that right must present his claim to an employment tribunal within the appropriate time limit. An application for interim relief must be made within seven days of the dismissal, and a claim for a redundancy payment must be made within six months from the relevant date, although the employment tribunal has a discretion to extend the period for a further six months in certain circumstances if it is just and equitable to do so (ERA, s 164). Claims for equal pay must also be presented within six months from the termination of employment, as must a claim based on a dismissal connected with official industrial action (see para 21.104), and a claim against a trade union in respect of unlawful exclusion or expulsion.

20.2 The general rule is that all other claims must be presented within three months of the act complained of. Apart from two exceptions, this rule is mandatory (see paras 20.3 and 20.9). An employment tribunal has no jurisdiction to hear a claim that has been presented out of time. Thus in *Rogers v Bodfari (Transport) Ltd*[1] a claim for unfair dismissal was made out of time, but the employer did not raise an objection. The employment tribunal decided that the dismissal was unfair. At an adjourned hearing to assess compensation, the employers raised the fact that the limitation period had elapsed, and the employment tribunal (reluctantly) dismissed the application on the ground that it had no jurisdiction to hear the claim in the first place. The decision was upheld on appeal. Neither the tribunal nor the parties can waive a jurisdictional provision. To this rule there are two exceptions.

20.3 (a) *Not reasonably practicable.* If it was not reasonably practicable to present the claim within the three months, the claim may be presented within such period as the employment tribunal considers reasonable. If it was reasonably practicable to do so, that will generally be the end of the matter. Otherwise, it is for the employment tribunal to consider whether to exercise its discretion and permit the claim to be admitted within such period as it considers to be reasonable. In *Cambridge & Peterborough Foundation NHS Trust v Crouchman*[2] a claim was admitted outside the three-month limit where the claimant discovered new and crucial information that led him to believe that he had a viable claim.

20.4 In deciding whether or not to allow a claim out of time, the employment tribunal must enquire into the circumstances as to why it was not reasonably practicable to present the claim before the end of the relevant period. 'Practicable' in this connection, means 'feasible' and it is a question of fact for the employment tribunal to determine (*Palmer v Southend-on-Sea Borough Council*[3]). If an employee is reasonably ignorant of the relevant time limits it cannot be said to be reasonably practicable for him to comply with them. The mere fact that there is a pending internal appeal will not by itself allow a claimant to say

---

[1] [1973] ICR 325, [1973] IRLR 172, 14 KIR 532. [2] [2009] ICR 1306.
[3] [1984] 1 WLR 1129, [1984] 1 All ER 945, [1984] ICR 372, [1984] IRLR 119, (1984) 81 LSG 893, (1984) 134 NLJ 148, (1984) 128 SJ 262.

that it was not reasonably practicable to present a claim in time, but the question of the claimant's state of knowledge of the time limit is still relevant. In *John Lewis Partnership v Charman*,[4] the claimant pursued an internal appeal, not realising the time limit for an unfair dismissal claim. The question was whether he should have made proper inquiries, but the EAT, following *Marks & Spencer v Williams-Ryan*,[5] held that it was not reasonable to have expected him to do so until he knew the outcome of the appeal. *Palmer* was distinguished on the basis that in that case the claimant had been represented by a trade union which should have known of the time limit.

20.5 If the time limit expires on a non-working day (eg a Sunday) an application will be out of time if it is presented on the following day (*Swainston v Hetton Victory Club Ltd*[6]). The employment tribunal has a discretion to permit a claim to be submitted out of time, but this will only be permitted in exceptional circumstances (*Walls Meat Co v Khan*[7]).

20.6 If an employee is dismissed on the 14th day of a month, the claim must be presented on or before the 13th day of the third month following. If the effective date of termination is the end of a month, and the month three months afterwards has no corresponding date (ie because it is a shorter month) the three-month period will expire on the last day of the relevant month. Thus if an employee is dismissed on 30 November, the claim must be presented on the 28th of the following February (or 29th, if it is a leap year: see *Pruden v Cunard Ellerman Ltd*[8]). (From April 2014, however, the clock stops when a prospective claimant contacts ACAS for early conciliation to take place, and only starts again when the ACAS 'Early Conciliation certificate' is issued – see para 1.08.)

20.7 If an employee or his representative (eg trade union official or solicitor) are at fault in not presenting the claim in time, it is likely that the employment tribunal will refuse jurisdiction (*Times Newspapers v O'Reagan*[9]) but if an employee is blameless, it may be easier to infer that it was not reasonably practicable to present the claim in time (*Union Cartage Co Ltd v Blunden*[10]). Where the claimant's 'skilled advisor' has got the date wrong because of misleading information from the employer, an extension can be allowed (*Northamptonshire County Council v Entwhistle*[11]). If the employer expressly requests that the claim be delayed so that negotiations can take place with a view to reaching an amicable settlement, then it may not be reasonably practicable to present the claim within the time limits (*Owen v Crown House Engineering Ltd*[12]). Ignorance of one's rights is no excuse for not presenting a claim within the three-month period (*Avon County Council v Haywood-Hicks*[13]) but mistaken advice given by the staff of the employment tribunal may be a ground for extending the time limits (*London International College v Sen*[14]). If a claimant knows of the time limits, or has been advised of them, or if he is capable of looking after his own affairs, it is for the employment tribunal to decide how much weight to place on all the factors that have led to the claim being presented out of time (*Robinson v Post Office*[15]).

20.8 Having submitted that it was not reasonably practicable to comply with the time limits, the claimant must then go on to show that the claim was submitted within such period as the employment tribunal considers reasonable. Thus a claimant must rectify any delay as soon as he becomes aware of it, and there is no particular time scale involved. It is a matter for the employment tribunal to determine as a question of fact. Thus in *James W Cook*

[4] UKEAT/0079/11/ZT.   [5] [2005] ICR 1293.
[6] [1983] 1 All ER 1179, [1983] ICR 341, [1983] IRLR 164, (1983) 127 SJ 171.
[7] [1978] IRLR 499, (1979) ICR 52.   [8] [1993] IRLR 317.   [9] [1977] IRLR 101.
[10] [1977] ICR 420, [1977] IRLR 139.   [11] [2010] IRLR 740, EAT.
[12] [1973] 3 All ER 618, [1973] ICR 511, [1973] IRLR 233, 16 KIR 67, [1973] ITR 539.
[13] [1978] ICR 646, [1978] IRLR 118, (1978) 13 ITR 208.   [14] [1992] IRLR 292.
[15] [2000] IRLR 804.

& Co Ltd v Tipper[16] a claim was allowed to proceed that was presented two weeks after the time limit had expired, because the employment tribunal was satisfied that the claimant had been misled as to the true situation. At the same time, the employment tribunal is entitled to take into account the prejudice that may be caused to the employer by allowing a claim to proceed out of time and balance this against the disadvantage to the claimant (*Baynton v South West Trains Ltd*[17]). If the employer is aware of the facts and the reason for the delay (eg a claimant's ill-health) a delay of months might not be unreasonable (*Whitbread plc v Rees*[18]).

20.9 (b) *Just and equitable.* So far as claims that are based on allegations of discrimination are concerned, the employment tribunal can extend the time limit if it is just and equitable to do so (*British Coal Corpn v Keeble,*[19] and see Equality Act 2010, para 4.218). This test is less stringent than the 'not reasonably practicable' test. Thus in *Department of Constitutional Affairs v Jones*[20] an out-of-time disability discrimination claim was accepted when it was shown that the claimant's delay was in part due to the fact that he was reluctant to admit that his depression was severe enough to amount to a disability.

20.10 If the claimant was not aware of the facts that gave rise to a potential complaint until after the three-month time limit has expired (eg the alleged acts of race or sex discrimination: see *Berry v Ravensbourne National Health Service Trust*[21]) it will be just and equitable to allow the late submission of the claim, provided the claimant acts expeditiously once he is aware of the true state of affairs (*Machine Tool Industry Research Association v Simpson*[22]).

20.11 If the act complained of is a continuing one (eg race or sex or disability discrimination etc), which extends over a period, time will run from the end of the period (*Barclays Bank plc v Kapur*[23]). The date on which the cause of action crystallised will depend on the facts of each case (*Clarke v Hampshire Electro-Plating Co*[24]). If the claimant is ill during the three-month period, attention should be focused on whether the illness falls in the earlier part of the period or in the far more critical weeks leading up to the expiration of the period if the employment tribunal is considering whether to permit the claim outside the three months (*Schutz v Esso Petroleum*[25]).

20.12 In a discrimination case, wrong advice by a legal adviser may be a valid excuse for not complying with the time limits, making it just and equitable to allow the claim to proceed (*Chohan v Derby Law Centre*[26]), and a delay caused by the fact that the claimant was awaiting the outcome of a disciplinary hearing can also be taken into consideration (*Apelogun-Gabriels v London Borough of Lambeth*[27]). When deciding how to exercise its discretion, the employment tribunal may refer to a checklist of factors set out in the Limitation Act 1980, s 33, which is used in personal injury cases, and use them as a guide, although these should not be elevated to the status of a legal requirement. These include (a) the length of and reason for the delay (b) the extent to which the cogency of the evidence would be affected by the delay (c) the extent to which the parties co-operated with requests for information (d) the promptness with which the plaintiff acted once he knew of the facts which gave rise to the cause of action, and (e) the steps which the plaintiff took to obtain prompt advice once he realised that he had a possible cause of action.

[16] [1990] ICR 716, [1990] IRLR 386, (1990) *Times,* 31 May, (1990) *Independent,* 28 May.

[17] [2005] ICR 1730.   [18] EAT/1292–1293/97.   [19] [1997] IRLR 336.

[20] [2007] EWCA Civ 894, [2008] IRLR 128.   [21] [1993] ICR 871.

[22] [1988] ICR 558, [1988] IRLR 212.

[23] [1991] 2 AC 355, [1991] 2 WLR 401, [1991] 1 All ER 646, [1991] ICR 208, [1991] IRLR 136, (1991) *Times,* 25 January, (1991) *Independent,* 6 February, (1991) *Financial Times,* 30 January, (1991) *Guardian,* 31 January, (1991) *Daily Telegraph,* 7 February.

[24] [1992] ICR 312, [1991] IRLR 490, (1991) *Times,* 1 October.   [25] [1999] ICR 1202.

[26] [2004] IRLR 685.   [27] [2001] EWCA Civ 1853, [2002] ICR 713, [2002] IRLR 116.

20.13 All complaints must actually be received (*Secretary of State for Employment v Banks*[28]) by the Central Office of Employment Tribunals (COET) within the appropriate time limits (before midnight: see *Post Office v Moore*[29]), although an application received by a regional office will be valid if presented in time (*Bengey v North Devon District Council*[30]). If the application does not arrive in time because of an abnormal delay in the post, the claimant will have to rely on the escape clause (*Beanstalk Shelving Ltd v Horn*[31]) (although many applications are now submitted electronically). A claim which was presented 88 seconds late was held to be out of time in *Beasley v National Grid*.[32] There is no grey area for complaints that are 'only a bit out of time!' It would be for the claimant to show that it was not reasonably practicable to bring the claim within the appropriate time limit.

20.14 Documents or letters dispatched by first class post are expected to arrive in the ordinary course of events on the second working day after posting; documents and letters sent by second class post are expected to arrive on the fourth working day after posting (*St Basil's Centre Ltd v McCrossan*[33]). If there is a postal strike, appropriate allowances should be made (*Beanstalk Shelving Ltd v Horn*) although alternative means of delivery should be arranged. Working days are Monday to Friday but, technically, bank or public holidays are *dies non* (non-days), and time limits are accordingly extended (*Ford v Stakis Hotels and Inns Ltd*[34]).

20.15 Thus if an application is posted, but arrives one day after the time limits have expired, it is open to the employment tribunal to decide if the claimant could have reasonably expected the application to be delivered in the ordinary course of the post. This is a question of fact for the employment tribunal to determine on the evidence (*St Basil's Centre v McCrossan*[35]). On the post rules generally, see *Consignia plc v Sealy*.[36]

20.16 But if, though posted in time, an application does not appear to have been received by COET, prudence requires that the claimant (or his representative) should make further enquiries, because it should be obvious from the failure to receive an acknowledgment that something is amiss, and therefore confirmation should be sought as to its arrival. It follows that if nothing is done to check the receipt of an application which has in fact never arrived, a fresh application may well be out of time (*Capital Foods Retail Ltd v Corrigan*[37]). Indeed, a solicitor who submits an application on behalf of a client is expected to have a proper system operating which enables him to find out, contemporaneously, whether the conduct of business is taking a normal course, and to check, at or near the time, that replies which should have been received at a given date have in fact been received. Thus in *Camden and Islington Community Services NHS Trust v Kennedy*,[38] the claimant's claim for unfair dismissal had to be presented by 27 December. Her solicitor posted her application on 19 December, but although he expected to receive an acknowledgment by 5 January, he delayed checking with the tribunal office until 30 January, when he was told that it had not been received. He posted another application the following day. It was held that the claim was out of time. Solicitors practising in the field of employment law must be aware of the need to comply strictly with the appropriate time limits, and ensure that they have in place systems which ensure that time limits are complied with.

---

[28] [1983] ICR 48, EAT.   [29] [1981] ICR 623, EAT.
[30] [1977] ICR 15, 11 ITR 211, EAT.   [31] [1980] ICR 273, EAT.
[32] [1980] ICR 273, EAT.   [33] [1992] ICR 140, [1991] IRLR 455, EAT.
[34] [1987] ICR 943, [1988] IRLR 46, [1987] LS Gaz R 2192, EAT.
[35] [1992] ICR 140, [1991] IRLR 455, EAT.
[36] [2002] EWCA Civ 878, [2002] 3 All ER 801, [2002] ICR 1193, [2002] IRLR 624, [2002] All ER (D) 129 (Jun).
[37] [1993] IRLR 430, EAT.   [38] [1996] IRLR 381, EAT.

20.17 If, in error, a claimant names the wrong employer in his application, an employ-ment tribunal may, at the request of the claimant or on its own motion, add any other person to be joined in the proceedings, even though this is done outside the normal time limit for presenting a claim. The employment tribunal may exercise its discretion to join the other party not only when the claimant has misnamed or misdescribed the respondent, but also when he has failed to identify the 'correct' employer (eg where his contract has been transferred by virtue of the Transfer of Undertakings (Protection of Employment) Regulations: see *Drinkwater Sabey Ltd v Burnett*[39]).

20.18 The general power to extend time limits on the ground that it is just and equitable to do so is to be used sparingly. The onus is on the applicant to show good reason, and the initial assumption is that an extension is to be the exception, not the rule (*Robertson v Bexley Community Centre*[40]).

20.19 The statutory time limits go to the employment tribunal's jurisdiction, and if a claim is presented out of time, the tribunal will be unable to hear the claim even though the employer fails to take the point (*Rogers v Bodfari (Transport) Ltd*,[41] para 20.2). But there is no time limit as such when it is proposed to add a new respondent, or substitute another one, to an application which has been lodged in time (*Drinkwater Sabey Ltd v Burnett*, para 20.17). If the claimant's claim is for breach of contract under the Employment Tribunals Extension of Jurisdiction Order, which is out of time, the employer's counterclaim, pre-sented in time, can be proceeded with (*Patel v RCMS Ltd*, see para 1.41).

A. Time limits for enforcing Community rights

20.20 European law (ie the Treaty of Rome or EC directives) does not specify any par-ticular time limits for bringing proceedings when an employee is seeking to enforce a Community right. The general principle to be adopted was laid down in *Fisscher v Voorhuis Hengelo BV* where the European Court held that national rules relating to time limits for bringing such actions were to be applied, providing that they are no less favourable than similar actions of a domestic nature, and do not render the exercise of rights conferred by Community law impossible in practice.

20.21 Thus, in principle, domestic time limits will apply, but the question arises, what are the time limits when it is discovered that UK law does not meet the requirements of EC law? Does time start to run from when the cause of action arose, or from when it is dis-covered that UK law is defective, or from when UK law is brought into line with EC law?

20.22 Part of the answer is to be found by considering the EC law which is being sought to enforce, bearing in mind that employment tribunals are creatures of statute, and may only exercise jurisdiction over matters specified in respective UK legislation. There have been a number of cases where the UK have failed to implement an EC requirement altogether, or failed to implement it fully or properly, and claimants have tried to re-open matters at a later date, arguing that time runs from when the UK should have implemented the article of the Treaty of Rome or Directive, as appropriate, or from when it was discovered that such a right existed. Generally speaking, these arguments will fail. Thus in *Biggs v Somerset County Council* (see paras 1.103 and 20.24) the claimant worked for 14 hours per week as a teacher. She was dismissed in 1976, after having been employed for less than two years. As the law then stood, she had no right to bring a claim for unfair dismissal, but following

[39] [1995] ICR 328, [1995] IRLR 238, EAT.

[40] [2002] All ER (D) 78 (Jul), EAT; revsd [2003] EWCA Civ 576, [2003] IRLR 434, [2003] All ER (D) 151 (Mar).   [41] [1973] ICR 325, [1973] IRLR 172, 14 KIR 532, NIRC.

the decision in *R v Secretary of State for Employment, ex p Equal Opportunities Commission* (decided in 1994, see para 1.102), she immediately brought a claim for unfair dismissal, arguing that the qualifying threshold condition should be disapplied, as being contrary to EC law. The Court of Appeal held that her claim was not brought within the requisite time limit of three months from the date of her dismissal. Although in 1976, when she was dismissed, she would have been unaware of the impact of s 2 of the European Communities Act 1972 or the effect of the decision of the European Court of Justice in *Defrenne v Sabena* (see para 1.72), her mistake was one of law, not of fact. There was no legal impediment to her bringing a claim and arguing that the restriction on part-time workers was indirectly discriminatory. The fact that she (and her advisers) did not fully understand the law at the time was not a ground for re-opening past transactions. The complaint was not presented within the time limit of three months, nor within a reasonable time after the expiry of that limit.

20.23 Similarly, in *Barber v Staffordshire County Council*,[42] the Court of Appeal refused to permit a claimant to bring a new claim based on EU law when an earlier claim had already been dismissed by an employment tribunal. The doctrine of issue estoppel applies.

20.24 However, the decision in *Biggs v Somerset County Council* (para 20.22) does not preclude all retrospective claims which are instituted as a result of a new interpretation of EC law. In *British Coal Corpn v Keeble* (see para 20.9) the EAT expressed the view that the decision in *Biggs* was only applicable to those cases where the claimant had failed to show that it was not reasonably practicable to bring the claim within the appropriate time limits. But, said the EAT, this did not apply to those cases where an extension of time is possible because it is 'just and equitable' to do so. Thus if a person is under a misapprehension of the law (eg due to some earlier legal ruling) a tribunal would still have a discretion to grant an extension of time. This discretion is only available in the areas of sex, race and disability discrimination etc. Thus in *DPP v Marshall*[43] a transsexual made a claim for unlawful discrimination three years after the date when the cause of action arose, but within three months from the date of a decision of the European Court which had decided that gender re-assignment came within the scope of the EC Equal Treatment Directive. The EAT upheld a tribunal's finding that it was just and equitable to permit the claim to be heard on its merits.

B. Effective date of termination (s 97)

20.25 So far as unfair dismissals are concerned, the claim must be presented within three months from the effective date of termination (EDT) of employment. This date can be:

(a) if the employment is terminated with notice, the date on which that notice expires; or

(b) if the employment is terminated without notice, the date on which the termination takes effect; or

(c) in the case of a limited-term contract (ie a fixed-term or a task contract: see para 17.20) which terminated by virtue of the limiting event without being renewed under the same contract, the date on which the termination takes effect.

In other words, the effective date of termination is the actual date when the employment comes to an end (*Alboni v Ind Coope Retail*[44]) and that date cannot be varied by any

---

[42] [1996] 2 All ER 748, [1996] IRLR 209, [1996] 06 LS Gaz R 26, sub nom *Staffordshire County Council v Barber* [1996] ICR 379, CA.   [43] [1998] ICR 518, EAT.   [44] [1998] IRLR 131, CA.

subsequent agreement between the parties. However, the notice that determines the effective date of termination can be varied, so that there can be a subsequent agreement that the
effective date of termination can be brought forward or pushed backward, and time will
start to run from the new date (*Palfrey v Transco plc*, see para 15.29).

20.26 Certain problems have arisen out of this. In *Dixon v Stenor Ltd*[45] Sir John Donaldson
pointed out that there were four situations commonly met. The first is where the employee
is given notice, and works to the end of that notice. The second is where there is a summary
dismissal, and the third is where the employee is given money in lieu of notice. These cases
are fairly straightforward, but the fourth situation presented a problem. This was where the
employee is dismissed with notice, but is not required to work the period of that notice.
In effect, he is on paid garden leave, and his employment does not effectively terminate
until the notice expires, even though he may not be working during that time. If he were to
submit an application during this period, in effect it would be premature. However, ERA,
s 111(3) provides that if a dismissal is with notice, a tribunal may consider a complaint
notwithstanding that it is presented before the effective date of termination of the employment. In other words, an employee may bring a complaint as soon as he receives his notice,
or within three months from the effective date of termination of his employment.

20.27 If an employee is dismissed, and pursues an appeal through the domestic procedures, there are two possibilities. If the procedure provides for an immediate dismissal,
with the possibility of reinstatement should the appeal be successful, the EDT is the date of
dismissal (*J Sainsbury Ltd v Savage*, see paras 4.197 and 12.38). If the procedure provides
for a suspension of the dismissal with the possibility of it being lifted following a successful
appeal, the EDT is the date when the appeal was dismissed should the dismissal be confirmed (*Drage v Governors of Greenford High School*[46]).

20.28 The fact that the employer retains the employee's P45 is irrelevant to the effective
date of termination (*Newham London Borough v Ward*[47]).

20.29 If an employer dismisses an employee without notice, but gives him a payment
in lieu of notice, the effective date of termination is the date of dismissal (ERA, s 97(1)).
Consequently, if on that date the employee does not have the requisite length of continuous employment, he cannot pursue his claim for unfair dismissal, unless, of course, he can
add on his statutory notice 'to pull him past the post' (s 97(2), see para 17.4). If notice of
termination is given orally, the period of notice commences the day after it has been given,
and the effective date of termination is calculated accordingly (*West v Kneels Ltd*, see paras
15.7 and 17.4).

20.30 If an employee is dismissed with notice, he may bring his claim before the notice
period expires, ie before the effective date of termination (ERA, s 111(3)), but a warning of
a possible dismissal in the future is not a dismissal, and hence the presentation of a claim
may be premature (*Rai v Somerfield Stores Ltd*, para 17.13 and see para 18.8).

20.31 The effective date of termination cannot be earlier than the date on which the
employee receives notice of the dismissal. Where an employer notifies an employee of his
summary dismissal by letter sent in the post, the date of dismissal is the date the employee
actually reads the letter, not the date when it is written, posted or delivered (*Gisda Cyf v
Barratt*[48]). In other words, it is the date that she is informed of the dismissal, even if this is

[45] [1973] ICR 157, [1973] IRLR 28, 8 ITR 141, NIRC.
[46] [2000] ICR 899, [2000] IRLR 314, 144 Sol Jo LB 165, [2000] All ER (D) 343, CA.
[47] [1985] IRLR 509, CA.
[48] [2009] EWCA Civ 648, [2009] ICR 1408, [2009] IRLR 934, Supreme Court [2010] UKSC 41.

before she reads the letter (*Robinson v Fairhill Medical Practice*[49]). There is no room for a doctrine of 'presumed or constructive knowledge' of a dismissal (*McMaster v Manchester Airport plc,* para 17.5). Although the parties may agree a prospective date of termination, they cannot agree a retrospective date, because the EDT is dependent on what actually happened, and not what they may have agreed to treat as having happened. In any case, a consensual arrangement to antedate the date of termination would be a provision which purports to limit the operation of the Act, which would be void under s 203(1) (*Fitzgerald v University of Kent at Canterbury*[50]).

20.32 It should be noted that s 97(2) ('pulling him past the post', see para 17.4) will extend the effective date of termination by the requisite statutory notice for the purposes of s 92 (right to have written reasons for dismissal), s 94 (unfair dismissal), s 119(1) (calculation of the basic award) and s 227(3) (increases the maximum allowable week's pay), but not for the purpose of computing the time limit within which a claim must be brought under s 111(2).

20.33 If an employee's claim is based on constructive dismissal, time will run from when the resignation is actually communicated to the employer, whether by written or oral communication or by conduct (*Edwards v Surrey Police*[51]). In so far as the employer's conduct may have resulted in the employee suffering a detriment, the three-month time limit runs from the date of that conduct, not from when the employee decides to treat the repudiatory breach as putting an end to the contract of employment (*Metropolitan Police Comr v Harley*).

20.34 If the employee resigns with notice, he may present his claim before that notice has expired (*Presley v Llanelli Borough Council*[52]), but if he resigns without notice, he can rely on the provisions of s 97(4) to 'pull him past the post' if he lacks the necessary period of continuous employment (see para 15.28).

C. **Restrictions on contracting out (ERA, s 203)**

20.35 Subject to the exceptions noted at para 20.47, an employee cannot voluntarily surrender or contract out of his statutory rights, and any statement or agreement to that effect is void. A private settlement between the parties, even one purporting to be in full and final settlement of all or any outstanding claims, cannot prevent an employee from pursuing the matter further in the employment tribunal, for an employee cannot opt out of his statutory rights.

20.36 Thus in *Council of Engineering Institutions v Maddison*[53] the employee accepted £1,600 in consideration that he would forgo any claim against his former employers. This was held to be unenforceable. The object of the legislation is to prevent hasty and imprudent agreements being entered into by the employee. On the other hand, such an agreement, whilst unenforceable, can be taken account of by the employment tribunal, and if it provides for compensation at a level not less than that which would have been awarded by the tribunal, then the employee will not have suffered any loss, and no further award will be made. Further, it will be recalled that an agreement for a financial settlement as a price for a resignation is not void under the Act (*Sheffield v Oxford Controls Co Ltd,* see paras 17.50

[49] UKEAT/0313/12/JOJ.
[50] [2003] All ER (D) 152 (May), EAT; revsd [2004] EWCA Civ 143, 148 Sol Jo LB 237, [2004] All ER (D) 262 (Feb).
[51] [1999] IRLR 456, EAT. [52] [1979] ICR 419, [1979] IRLR 381, EAT.
[53] [1977] ICR 30, [1976] IRLR 389, 11 ITR 272, EAT.

and 17.72). In practice, if an agreed settlement is reached, it is sound policy to call in the conciliation officer, thus turning the agreement into a binding one.

20.37 The exceptions to the rule are as follows:

(a) Any settlement made under the auspices of the conciliation office from ACAS acting under his statutory powers, whether the settlement is made orally or in writing,
will be binding on the parties (*Gilbert v Kembridge Fibres Ltd*, see para 1.10), and
can be enforced. But the settlement will only apply to the matters contained therein.
Thus if a settlement is made to an unfair dismissal claim made under ERA, this will
not bar a subsequent claim under other legislation, eg Equality Act 2010 etc unless
such claims have been specifically excluded (*Livingstone v Hepworth Refractories
Ltd*[54]). In the absence of precise language, signing a conciliation form does not
necessarily bar a further claim by an employee based on facts of which the employee
was ignorant at the time the agreement was signed (*Bank of Credit and Commerce
International SA v Ali*, see paras 3.47 and 10.12).

Where a counsel, solicitor, CAB adviser or member of a law centre, who has been
named as a representative, holds himself out as having authority to negotiate and
reach a settlement on behalf of a claimant, then, in the absence of any notice to the
contrary, the other party is entitled to assume that the adviser has such authority.
Thus an agreement reached between the adviser and the conciliation officer will be
binding on the claimant whether or not the adviser has actual authority to enter into
it. Thus the ostensible authority of the adviser extends beyond the pleadings and
presentation of the case, but includes all the actual and potential issues which are
known to the parties (*Freeman v Sovereign Chicken Ltd*[55]).

(b) A collective agreement which provides for guaranteed remuneration where all parties have applied to the minister for an order excluding the right to receive guarantee
pay under s 35. About 30 such orders have been made.

(c) A dismissal procedure agreement which provides for remedies at least as effective
as ERA which has been designated by the minister by order on an application by all
the parties. However, such exclusion from statutory rights does not apply to failure
to permit a woman to return to work after childbirth, dismissal for reason of pregnancy or childbirth, dismissal of protected shop or betting workers, dismissal for
asserting a statutory right, and an inadmissible reason for redundancy.

(d) A collective agreement which provides for redundancy payments where all the parties have applied to the minister for an exemption order. A few such orders have
been made under this provision.

(e) A settlement agreement under section 111A of the ERA (known as a compromise
agreement until April 2014), which satisfied the following conditions:

(i) the agreement must be in writing;

(ii) it must relate to particular proceedings;

(iii) the employee must have received advice from a relevant independent adviser as to
the terms of the proposed agreement and its effect. An independent legal adviser
is a qualified lawyer (barrister, solicitor, Fellow of the Institute of Legal Executives,
or advocate), official, employee or member of an independent trade union who
has been certified in writing as being competent and authorised to give advice on
behalf of the trade union, a worker at an advice centre who has been certified in

---

[54] [1992] 3 CMLR 601, [1992] ICR 287, [1992] IRLR 63, [1992] 5 LS Gaz R 31, EAT.
[55] [1991] ICR 853, [1991] IRLR 408, EAT.

writing as being competent to give advice on behalf of the centre, or a person of a description specified in an order made by the Secretary of State;

(iv) the adviser must have a professional indemnity insurance policy or be covered by a contract of insurance;

(v) the agreement must identify the adviser; and

(vi) the agreement must state that the conditions regulating the compromise agreement under the Act are satisfied.

Settlement agreements may be made in respect of all those claims for which the employment tribunal has jurisdiction under the Employment Tribunals Act 1996, s 18(1), which covers most, though not all, of the rights contained in ERA, TULR(C)A (except a failure to consult with a trade union on redundancies), Equality Act, Part-time Workers (Prevention of Less Favourable Treatment) Regulations 2000, Fixed-Term Employees (Prevention of Less Favourable Treatment) Regulations 2002. Settlement agreements are binding in respect of the particular complaints mentioned therein. A further claim may be made (within the appropriate time limits) in respect of matters not within the terms of the agreement (*Lunt v Merseyside TEC Ltd*[56]). Thus the agreement should be drawn up in such a way that all matters which could be the subject of a complaint are effectively covered.

(f) An agreement to submit the dispute to arbitration under a scheme prepared by ACAS, which has been approved by the Secretary of State, under the provisions of TULR(C)A, s 212A (see para 1.13).

20.38 Strictly speaking, a settlement agreement can only settle those disputes which have actually been raised (as a concern, not necessarily as a tribunal claim) at the date of the agreement (*Lunt v Merseyside TEC Ltd*,[57] also see *McWilliam v Glasgow City Council*[58]). Thus very clear language must be used to ensure that a claimant releases claims or rights of which he is unaware or could not have been aware (*Hinton v University of London*[59]).

20.39 One distinction between an ACAS conciliation and a settlement agreement is that the conciliation agreement can be made in full and final settlement of all claims, whether actual or potential, whereas a settlement agreement 'must relate to the particular proceedings'. However, if the applicant (or his adviser) was aware of the possibility of further claims, the signing of a settlement agreement will be binding, because such additional claims would have been in contemplation when the agreement was signed (*Byrnell v British Telecommunications plc*[60]).

20.40 A settlement agreement is subject to the general principles of contract law and would, for example, be unenforceable if it was affected by a mistake or misrepresentation (*Industrious Ltd v Horizon Recruitment Ltd*[61]). In *Crystal Palace v Dowie*[62] a football manager stated that he wanted to leave his job in order to move closer to his family, and a settlement agreement was signed that released him from the liability to make payment of contractual compensation. In fact, he intended to join a neighbouring club. It was held that the club was entitled to damages for misrepresentation.

20.41 A settlement agreement may be the subject of a condition precedent which will nullify the agreement if the condition is not fulfilled prior to the date for payment. In *Collidge v Freeport plc*[63] the chief executive of a company warranted that there were no circumstances

[56] [1999] ICR 17, [1999] IRLR 458, EAT.   [57] [1999] IRLR 458.   [58] UKEATS/0036/10/BI.
[59] [2005] ICR 1260, [2005] EWCA Civ 532, CA.   [60] IDS Brief 774, EAT.
[61] Appeal No. UKEAT/0478/09/JOJ.   [62] [2007] EWHC 1392 (QB); [2007] IRLR 682.
[63] [2008] EWCA Civ 485, [2008] IRLR 697.

of which he was aware that would constitute a repudiatory breach on his part of his contract of employment. Before the employers paid a substantial sum under the agreement, it was discovered that the chief executive had been guilty of serious financial impropriety, and the financial payment was not made. The chief executive sued for the money, but his claim failed. The employers had protected themselves in the event that subsequent investigations showed that the promise was untrue.

20.42 A settlement agreement is a contract connected with employment, and as such it may be enforced in an employment tribunal under the provisions of the Employment Tribunals Extension of Jurisdiction Order 1994 (*Rock-It Cargo Ltd v Green*[64]), and see para 1.40) provided that the claim arises out of or is outstanding on the termination of the employee's employment. An agreement reached after the employee has left the employment may be enforced in the civil courts in the usual way (*Miller Bros & F P Butler Ltd v Johnston*[65]). A settlement agreement can only be made to settle a valid legal claim, and cannot be used for other types of agreements. In *Gibb v Maidstone & Tunbridge Wells NHS Trust*[66] a severance payment of £250,000 was made the subject of a settlement agreement between the chief executive and the trust in order to remove her from office in anticipation of a damaging report which was known to be critical of her leadership. Although the amount agreed upon, which was intended to take into account the public interest, was made with Treasury guidance, the Trust only paid £50,000, and the claimant sued for the balance. The Court of Appeal upheld her claim, holding that, in the circumstances, the payment was not irrational and was not ultra vires. There is an ACAS Code on Settlement Agreements (para 1.08).

20.43 From the available figures, it would appear that more than half of the complaints are settled without a tribunal hearing, though the confidential nature of the work of the conciliation officer is such that we have little knowledge of the terms or circumstances. About 70% of the cases referred to conciliation officers are settled on the basis of some form of monetary payment by the employer. The bulk of the remaining cases are settled because the claimant withdraws the claim, and in a few cases, there will be an agreement for reinstatement or re-engagement. Any communication to the conciliation officer is not admissible in evidence without the consent of the party who communicated it. In *M and W Grazebrook Ltd v Wallens*[67] certain documents, which had been prepared by the personnel manager after the claimant had been dismissed, were shown to the conciliation officer. It was held that the documents were not covered by the privilege, for to find otherwise would enable a party to prevent disclosure of evidence by deliberately communicating it to the conciliation officer. On the other hand, if the documents had been specially prepared for the purpose of showing them to the conciliation officer then no disclosure can be ordered.

20.44 A claim under ERA, s 94 (unfair dismissal) has two objects. First, the claimant will be seeking a finding that he has a statutory remedy and, second, he will be seeking compensation. Both those matters are justiciable before the employment tribunal. Thus, if the employers offer to pay the maximum compensation which would be payable, this does not prevent the claimant from proceeding with his claim in order to obtain a finding that the dismissal is unfair, where the employers are unwilling to concede this (*Telephone Information Services Ltd v Wilkinson*,[68] but see *Nicolson Highlandwear Ltd v Nicolson*, where the EAT came to a different conclusion[69]).

---

[64] [1997] IRLR 581, EAT.
[65] [2002] ICR 744, [2002] IRLR 386, [2002] Emp LR 1088, (2002) *Times*, 18 April.
[66] [2010] EWCA Civ 678.   [67] [1973] 2 All ER 868, [1973] ICR 256, [1973] IRLR 139, 8 ITR 258, NIRC.
[68] [1991] IRLR 148, EAT.   [69] UKEATS/0058/09/BI.

20.45 It has been seen (para 20.35) that an agreement reached whereby an employee agrees to waive his statutory rights is generally void, subject to certain exceptions, and hence the fact that the employee has accepted a sum in settlement (even though this may be in excess of the statutory compensation limits) does not preclude an employment tribunal from hearing the claim (*NRG Victory Reinsurance Ltd v Alexander*[70]), and it is not vexatious or frivolous to pursue such a claim.

Employment tribunal procedure

20.46 The Employment Tribunals (Constitution and Rules of Procedure) Regulations 2013 lay down the procedural rules for claims brought before an employment tribunal. Schedule 1 lays down the general procedural rules, Sch 2 deals with national security issues and Sch 3 deals with equal value claims. The overriding objective of these Rules (set out in Sch 1 rule 2) is to enable employment tribunals to deal with cases fairly and justly, which includes:

(a) ensuring that the parties are on an equal footing;

(b) dealing with cases in ways which are proportionate to the complexity and importance of the issues;

(c) avoiding unnecessary formality and seeking flexibility in the proceedings;

(d) avoiding delay, so far as compatible with proper consideration of the issues; and

(e) saving expense.

To take account of the overriding objective, therefore, it is permissible to take account of the apparent skills and experience of a party or representative and any apparent inequality in such skills and experience, and adjust procedures accordingly. An example of avoiding delay and informality is that hearings can be conducted by electronic communication, including by telephone, so long as the parties and any members of the public can hear what the judge is hearing (Sch 1 rule 46). Tribunals should also encourage parties to use other means of settling their disputes, such as ACAS or mediation.

20.47 Although the procedural rules are detailed and precise, and are, in some respects, strictly construed, they should not be interpreted in such a way as to avoid injustice, or to drive away a possibly meritorious claimant or respondent (*Richardson v U Mole Ltd*[71]). Regard must always be had to the interests of justice. The rules must not be interpreted so as to prevent an employment tribunal from entertaining jurisdiction to hear a claim for which primary legislation has provided an employment right, and a mandatory requirement in the rules must not be taken to the point of denying a claimant access to the tribunal system.

A. **Submitting a claim**

20.48 All claims must be presented to an employment tribunal office on the prescribed form (ET1), the only exceptions being certain claims brought under the National Minimum Wage Act, ss 19, 20, 22; proceedings brought by an employer under ERA, s 11, appeals against the industrial training levy, and appeals against an unlawful notice. A claim must contain the prescribed information, which basically will be the name and address of the claimant and respondent, and details of the claim. It must also include the Early Conciliation certificate issued by ACAS (paras 1.08, 20.06). The Secretary of Tribunals

---

[70] [1992] ICR 675, EAT.   [71] [2005] IRLR 668.

must reject the claim if it does not provide the relevant names and addresses, or if it is not on the prescribed form, or if the tribunal does not have power to consider the claim (eg, because the claimant lacks the necessary qualifying conditions, or because the tribunal has no jurisdiction in the matter). The claim will also be refused if the correct fee is not paid (see para 20.51), or an application for remission of the fee made. The claimant can apply for reconsideration of this rejection within 14 days, on the basis that the rejection was wrong, or the defect has been rectified. If rectified, the claim shall be treated as having been presented the day it was rectified.

20.49 If the Secretary does refuse to accept the claim, he may refer the matter to an employment judge who will decide whether the claim should be accepted. The judge may invite the claimant to a pre-acceptance hearing, before he decides the matter.

20.50 It is the duty of the claimant to state (with as much precision as possible) the nature of the claim, but the employment tribunal will not investigate on its own motion every allegation made but not pursued by a party (*Mensah v East Hertfordshire NHS Trust*[72]). Generally a claimant will be precluded from bringing fresh proceedings in respect of a matter which could and should have been litigated in earlier proceedings (*Divine-Bortey v Brent London Borough Council*[73]).

B. **Tribunal fees**

20.51 Fees were introduced in the employment tribunal in 2013 by the Employment Tribunals and the Employment Appeal Tribunal Fees Order 2013. Claims are divided into two types:

  (a) Type A claims (simpler claims, such as unlawful deduction from wages, holiday pay and redundancy payment claims). The issue fee is £160, and the hearing fee is £230.

  (b) Type B claims (those likely to be more complex and take more time to determine, such as unfair dismissal, discrimination and whistleblowing). The issue fee is £250 and the hearing is £950.

For claims submitted to the EAT, the issue fee is £400 and the hearing fee is £1,200. (There is currently a challenge to the fee regime in the courts.)

Employment tribunals will have the power to order the unsuccessful party to reimburse the successful party. The current remission system that is used in the civil courts, under which fees can be waived if the party cannot afford to pay, is extended to employment tribunals and the EAT.

C. **Employer's response**

20.52 A copy of the claim will be sent to the respondent employer, who must reply on the prescribed response form (ET3) within 28 days of it being sent to him, although an application may be made before the 28 days have elapsed for an extension of time. The response form must also contain the prescribed information, and be presented on time, or it will be rejected. An application can be made for a reconsideration of the rejection on the basis that it was wrong, or that the failure has been rectified. If rectified, the response shall be treated as having been presented the day it was rectified, and the judge has the power to extend time. If a response has been rejected, and there is no application for reconsideration, or

---

[72] [1998] IRLR 531, [1998] All ER (D) 260, CA.
[73] [1998] ICR 886, [1998] IRLR 525, [1998] 22 LS Gaz R 29, 142 Sol Jo LB 152, CA.

if a respondent has an indication he will not contest the claim, an employment judge will decide if he can decide the case on the material before him. If not, a hearing will be fixed before a judge sitting alone.

If a respondent does not receive a copy of the claim form due to errors in the name or address on the ET1, it cannot be said that he has been notified of the claim, and thus he cannot be penalised for failing to respond within the 28-day time limit (*Chowles t/a Granary Pine v West*[74]).

20.53 The 'label' which is attached to the response by the employer is generally irrelevant, as long as the response contains all the relevant information, for the actual legal position is a matter for the tribunal to determine on consideration of the factual evidence. Thus, if an employer submits that the reason for a dismissal was 'redundancy', and the facts are fully investigated by the tribunal, it is open to them to find that the reason was for 'some other substantial reason' (*Hannan v TNT-IPEC (UK) Ltd*[75]). All relevant defences should be pleaded, if necessary in the alternative (*Church v West Lancashire NHS Trust*, see para 18.21).

D. **Initial consideration of claim and response**

20.54 The 2013 regulations add a new 'sift' stage to the Employment Tribunal process (Sch 1 regs 27 and 28). This should be done as soon as possible after the receipt of the response. The employment judge has to look at the papers in the case, and if he considers either that the tribunal has no jurisdiction to consider the claim or response or that it has no reasonable prospect of success, he will dismiss it (or part of it, if the problem is with just part of it), and send a notice asking for written representations within a certain date. If representations are received, he shall either permit the claim or response, or fix a hearing to decide whether to permit it. The employment judge can also make any case management orders at this stage that he sees fit.

E. **Preliminary hearings**

20.55 There are two types of hearing in the employment tribunal – preliminary hearings (an amalgamation of the pre-2013 pre-hearing reviews and case management hearings) and final hearings. At a preliminary hearing the judge can make case management orders, or deal with any other kind of issue. Preliminary hearings, which are generally heard by a judge alone) replaced case management hearings and pre-hearing reviews from 2013. At a preliminary hearing the judge can consider the claim and response, issue case management orders (para 20.54), deal with any preliminary issue, consider whether a claim or response (or part of one) should be struck out, make a deposit order if he considers it necessary, and explore the possibility of settlement. There may be more than one preliminary hearing in a case, and a preliminary hearing can be treated as a final hearing if neither party would be prejudiced by this.

At a preliminary hearing the employment judge may determine interim or preliminary matters, issue directions or, if he considers that the contentions put forward in relation to a matter to be determined by the tribunal have little prospect of success but are nevertheless arguable, he may order that party to pay a deposit not exceeding £1,000 as a condition of being permitted to continue to take part in the proceedings. When considering making a deposit order, the employment judge must first ascertain the ability of the party to comply with the order. If the deposit is not paid within the time limit, the claim or response (or

[74] Employment Appeal Tribunal, 8 January 2009.   [75] [1986] IRLR 165, EAT.

the allegation to which the deposit order is made) may be struck out. If the deposit is paid it shall be refunded in full unless the tribunal makes a costs or preparation time order (see paras 20.106 and 20.110) on the ground that the party has conducted the proceedings unreasonably in persisting in having the matter determined.

20.56 An employment judge may strike out the claim (or defence) if it is considered that the case is so weak that it has no reasonable prospect of success, and ought not to be permitted to proceed to a hearing. Since no evidence is called for at a preliminary hearing, the striking out option will be applicable in those cases where there is no conflict of evidence, or where the evidence presented is self-explanatory, or where the matter has already been litigated. The employment judge may also strike out or amend any claim or response on the ground that it is scandalous, or vexatious, or on the ground that the manner in which the proceedings have been conducted by or on behalf of the claimant or respondent has been scandalous, unreasonable or vexatious. A claim may be struck out where there is intentional and contumelious fault by the claimant, or where there has been inordinate and inexcusable delay such as to give rise to a substantial risk that a fair trial is not possible or where there would be serious prejudice to the respondent (*Rolls Royce plc v Riddle*[76]). A claim or response may also be struck out if there is threatening or abusive conduct or intimidation against a party or witness. However, such action will only be taken if a fair trial is no longer possible (*Force One Utilities v Hatfield*[77]). It is only in exceptional cases that such a course of action should be taken (*Ezsias v N Glamorgan NHS Trust*[78]).

20.57 A restricted reporting order may be made in any case which involves an allegation of sexual misconduct or a disability case in which evidence of a personal nature is likely to be heard. The order will prohibit the publication of any identifying material, ie the names of the parties, until a decision on liability has been reached and entered into the register (*X v Metropolitan Police Comr*[79]). Such order cannot be made to protect the identity of a corporate employer who may be vicariously liable for the acts of its employees, even though its commercial reputation may suffer (*Leicester University v A*[80]). An employment tribunal can also make a 'permanent anonymity order', and anonymise its judgment if the loss of a claimant's anonymity would breach his right to privacy under the Human Rights Act (*A v B*).[81] There is no power, however, to exclude the press or members of the public (*R v Southampton Industrial Tribunal, ex p INS News Group Ltd*[82]). (For restricted reporting orders, see *Tradition Securities SA v Fariad*,[83] 'closed material procedure' where the claimant and his representatives can be excluded, see para 20.74.)

20.58 It is an offence punishable by a fine not exceeding level 5 on the standard scale to act in contravention of any restricted reporting order.

F. Case management

20.59 In the original scheme of things, employment tribunals (formerly known as industrial tribunals) were intended to be a cheap, speedy and informal method of resolving employment disputes. The parties frequently represented themselves, and the employment judge would assist them in presenting their respective cases. However, the growth of employment rights over the years and the tremendous increase in the number of claims made has resulted in more complex legal rules, frequently requiring the use of legal or other

---

[76] [2008] IRLR 873.   [77] [2009] IRLR 45.
[78] EAT/0705/05, EAT/0612/05; aff'd [2007] EWCA Civ 330, [2007] 4 All ER 940, [2007] ICR 1126, [2007] IRLR 603, (2007) 104(12) LSG 34.   [79] [2003] ICR 1031, [2003] IRLR 411, [2003] NLJR 719, EAT.
[80] [1999] ICR 701, [1999] IRLR 352, EAT.   [81] [2010] IRLR 844, EAT.
[82] [1995] IRLR 247.   [83] [2009] IRLR 354.

skilled representatives. In consequence, tribunal procedures became more formal and less flexible. The Employment Tribunals (Constitution and Rules of Procedure) Regulations 2013 contain a number of provisions designed to speed up hearings, concentrate on relevant facts and information, and discourage weak claims.

20.60 The overriding objective of the rules is to enable tribunals to deal with a case justly, including, so far as is practicable, ensuring that the parties are on an equal footing, saving expense, dealing with the case in ways which are proportionate to the complexity of the issues, ensuring that the case is dealt with expeditiously and fairly while avoiding unnecessary formality and seeking flexibility in the proceedings. An employment judge has a general power to manage proceedings in order to achieve these objectives.

20.61 An employment judge has wide powers to issue directions on any matter he considers to be appropriate, whether on his own volition or on an application by either party. Directions may be given as to the manner in which proceedings are to be conducted (witness statements prepared and exchanged, agreed bundles of relevant documents, statement of agreed facts, skeleton arguments etc), requiring additional information, extending time limits, provision of written answers to questions put, disclosure and/or production of documents, staying part of the proceedings, joining other respondents, postponing or adjourning proceedings, conducting a preliminary hearing, permitting an amendment to the claim or response, etc. If a direction is not complied with an employment judge may make an order in respect of costs or preparation time, and may, at a preliminary hearing or final hearing, make an order to strike out the whole or part of the claim or response, as appropriate, but this punitive power should only be exercised if a fair trial is not possible due to the failure to comply. If there is a last-minute compliance, with an acceptable explanation, it is not appropriate to strike out the claim or defence (*National Grid Co plc v Virdee*[84]). However, either party may apply for a review of directions given.

20.62 If a claimant is so unwell as to be able to proceed with the claim, and there is no prospect of being able to do so in the foreseeable future, it is open to an employment tribunal to strike out the claim altogether (*Peixoto v British Telecommunications plc*[85]).

20.63 Either party may apply to a tribunal for an order for further particulars or disclosure of documents, but such orders are not made as a matter of routine, but only if the party requiring the information can show that he will be prejudiced without such information (*White v University of Manchester*[86]). In particular, disclosure of documents will not be ordered to enable a party to indulge in a 'fishing expedition' ie to search for material in order to establish a case (*British Aerospace plc v Green,* see para 18.42; *Aon Ltd v JLT Reinsurance Brokers Ltd*[87]). An employment tribunal cannot order a party to produce 'evidence' or to create documentary evidence which was not in existence, because an order for discovery is limited to those documents which are in being (*Carrington v Helix Lighting Ltd*[88]). The party against whom an order for discovery of documents is made is under a continuing duty to disclose all relevant documents, right up to the conclusion of the hearing (*Scott v Commissioners of Inland Revenue*, para 20.97).

20.64 Documents which are produced in order to comply with an order for discovery may only be used for the purpose of the hearing, and not for any other cause of action. In *Riddick v Thames Water Board Mills Ltd*[89] an employee of the defendants wrote a confidential memorandum about the manner of the claimant's dismissal, which was allegedly

---

[84] [1992] IRLR 555, EAT.   [85] Employment Appeal Tribunal, 22 January 2008.
[86] [1976] ICR 419, [1976] IRLR 218, 11 ITR 143, 120 Sol Jo 503, EAT.
[87] [2010] IRLR 600, [2009] EWHC 3448 (QB).   [88] [1990] IRLR 6, EAT.
[89] [1977] QB 881, [1977] 3 All ER 677, [1977] 3 WLR 63, 121 Sol Jo 274, CA.

defamatory. The claimant got to know about the document as a result of an order for discovery, made during the course of a legal action brought against the employer. The action was settled, but the claimant brought a further action for defamation. It was held that the public interest required that documents which were compulsorily disclosed on discovery should only be used for the purpose of the action in which they were disclosed, and that each party impliedly undertook not to use them for any other ulterior or improper motive.

20.65 In complex cases, such as those alleging race discrimination (*Martins v Marks & Spencer plc*), or disability discrimination (*Goodwin v Patents Office*), or protected disclosure claims (*ALM Medical Services Ltd v Bladon*[90]), or where there are likely to be a large number of witnesses or a large number of documents, or many claimants (eg equal value claims), it is good practice to hold a meeting for preliminary directions, so as to ensure as far as possible that the parties and tribunal can identify the relevant issues to be determined.

20.66 If one party is seeking the disclosure of documents which the other side regards as being of a confidential nature, such as references, confidential assessments on the applicant or other employees, and so forth, the employment judge should himself inspect the document to satisfy himself that discovery is essential in order to dispose fairly of the proceedings. If he does decide that they should be disclosed, the interests of third parties can be protected by 'covering up', substituting names, and, in rare cases, hearing the proceedings in camera (*Science Research Council v Nassé*[91]).

20.67 If privilege is claimed from disclosure, a balance must be held between the public interest in non-disclosure and that of justice in the production of the documents (*Halford v Sharples*[92]). Communications between parties headed 'without prejudice' should be excluded from the evidence submitted, unless the material was such that without them a dishonest case was being presented (*Independent Research Services Ltd v Catterall*[93]).

20.68 Privilege from the disclosure of documents only applies to communications between clients and professional legal advisers, such as solicitors and barristers (*New Victoria Hospital v Ryan*[94]).

20.69 There is no general duty on a party to disclose any documents in his possession or power, in the absence of any formal order to that effect. However, if he voluntarily discloses documents, there is a duty not to be selective in that disclosure, and he must not withhold other documents if there is a risk that the non-disclosure might convey a false or misleading impression as to the nature of any document disclosed (*Birds Eye Walls Ltd v Harrison*[95]).

20.70 Attendance orders, compelling a person to attend as a witness, may also be made in appropriate circumstances. But a tribunal cannot direct that a representative chosen by a party to the proceedings shall not act as such (*Bache v Essex County Council*[96]).

20.71 If there are High Court proceedings between the employer and employee in which there are issues in common with an application for unfair dismissal, the employment judge has a discretion to order that the latter claim be postponed, pending the outcome of the High Court proceedings (*Carter v Credit Change Ltd,* para 16.28). He should take into

---

[90] EAT/709/00, EAT/967/00, EAT; [2001] EWCA Civ 1183, CA, [2002] EWCA Civ 1085, [2002] Emp LR 1054, [2002] ICR 1444, [2002] IRLR 807, CA.

[91] [1978] ICR 777, [1978] IRLR 201, 122 Sol Jo 316, EAT; on appeal [1979] QB 144, [1978] 3 All ER 1196, [1978] 3 WLR 754, [1978] ICR 1124, [1978] IRLR 352, 122 Sol Jo 593, CA; aff'd [1980] AC 1028, [1979] 3 All ER 673, [1979] ICR 921, [1979] IRLR 465, 123 Sol Jo 768, HL.

[92] [1992] ICR 146, EAT; aff'd [1992] 3 All ER 624, [1992] 1 WLR 736, [1992] ICR 583, CA.

[93] [1993] ICR 1, EAT.   [94] [1993] ICR 201, [1993] IRLR 202, [1993] 5 LS Gaz R 41, EAT.

[95] [1985] ICR 278, [1985] IRLR 47, EAT.

[96] [2000] 2 All ER 847, [2000] IRLR 251, [2000] 05 LS Gaz R 33, [2000] NLJR 99, CA.

account the convenience, expedition and cost when exercising his discretion (*First Castle Electronics Ltd v West*[97]). The test to be applied is 'In which court is this action most conveniently and appropriate to be tried, bearing in mind all the surrounding circumstances, including the complexity of the issue, the amount involved, the technicality of the evidence and appropriateness of the procedure?' Thus, where a managing director was alleging a repudiatory breach of contract by the employers which was claimed to be a wrongful and unfair dismissal, the Employment Appeal Tribunal ordered that employment tribunal proceedings should be adjourned until after the hearing of the High Court action (*Bowater plc v Charlwood*[98] and see *GFI Holdings Ltd v Camm*[99]).

G. **The final hearing**

20.72 Proceedings at the actual hearing are reasonably informal, for employment tribunals have the power to conduct them in whatever manner they consider to be most suitable. The parties may represent themselves, or be represented by a solicitor or barrister, or a representative of a trade union or employers' association, or any other person whom they desire to represent them.

20.73 Hearings before an employment tribunal must be held in public (*Storer v British Gas plc*[100]). An employment tribunal may only sit in private if:

(a) it would be against the interests of national security to allow evidence to be given in public;

(b) a person is giving evidence which he could not disclose without contravening a prohibition imposed by an enactment;

(c) the evidence has been communicated to a person in confidence; or

(d) the evidence is information which if disclosed in public, could cause substantial injury to an undertaking of the witness or in which he works for reasons other than its effect on collective bargaining (see rule 29, 1st Schedule).

20.74 However, it is permissible for a tribunal to hear certain evidence in private in order to protect the right to respect for private or family life, as required by Art 8 of the European Convention on Human Rights (*XXX v YYY*[101]). If a private hearing is ordered, this does not preclude the presence of a party's representative (*Fry v Foreign and Commonwealth Office*[102]). In addition, rule 54(2) of Sch 1 to the Employment Tribunals (Constitution and Rules of Procedure) Regulations 2004 provides for the adoption of a 'closed material procedure' whereby a claimant and his representatives may be excluded from part of employment tribunal proceedings on grounds of national security. The Supreme Court has held in *Home Office v Tariq*[103] that this is not incompatible with EU law or the European Convention on Human Rights.

20.75 When dealing with a litigant in person, an additional responsibility falls on the employment judge to clarify exactly what is being alleged, and to ensure from the start of the proceedings that the parties know precisely what the issues are, and what ground is to be covered (*Akintola v Capita Symonds Ltd*[104]). A litigant in person is entitled to generous treatment and some leeway (*Shea v Marcos Fidelio*[105]).

---

[97] [1989] ICR 72, EAT.   [98] [1991] ICR 798, [1991] IRLR 340, EAT.
[99] [2008] All ER (D) 74.
[100] [2000] 2 All ER 440, [2000] 1 WLR 1237, [2000] ICR 603, [2000] IRLR 495, CA.
[101] [2004] EWCA Civ 231, [2004] IRLR 137, [2004] All ER (D) 144 (Feb).   [102] [1997] ICR 512, EAT.
[103] [2011] UKSC 34.   [104] [2010] EWCA Civ 405.   [105] UKEAT/0159/11/JOJ.

20.76 If there is no prior settlement or withdrawal, the employment tribunal will hear the case. A date, time and place for the hearing will be notified to the parties, although applications for adjournments will be considered on appropriate grounds. At the hearing, as a general rule, the burden of proof is on the claimant, and he should therefore give evidence first in order to support his allegations. In discrimination cases, the burden of proof is reversed: see Equality Act 2010, s 135.

20.77 If an employment tribunal is unable to come to a conclusion on a question of fact, they may apply the burden of proof. Thus in *Morris v London Iron and Steel Co Ltd*[106] the tribunal could not decide whether an employee had been dismissed or resigned, and they held that he had not discharged the burden of proof which was on him to show that he was dismissed.

20.78 In unfair dismissal cases, if the dismissal is admitted, the employer will be required to give evidence first, and he must establish:

(a) the reason for the dismissal (or, if there is more than one reason, the principal reason, see *Smith v Glasgow City District Council*[107]), and

(b) that it was a statutory reason.

He should then seek to show that he acted reasonably in the circumstances.

20.79 From a practical point of view, the employer should recognise that there are a number of matters within his knowledge about which the tribunal may wish to learn, and therefore should be prepared to give evidence on these matters. Thus it is not sufficient to show a reason for dismissal; the reasonableness of acting on that reason must also be shown. If an employee is dismissed because of redundancy, an employer should normally lead evidence to show that there was a fair selection system, full consultation with the individual concerned and trade union (if appropriate) and that efforts were made to find alternative employment, even if the applicant does not raise all these matters (*Langston v Cranfield University*[108]). If the dismissal is for incompetence, the employer would need to show all those matters which a reasonable employer should have done before taking the decision to dismiss (see Chapter 17).

20.80 If one party is taken by surprise by the evidence of the other side, it will normally be possible to apply to introduce rebutting evidence, even if it is necessary to apply for an adjournment in order to produce the necessary evidence and/or witnesses. However, unreasonable applications for adjournments may be visited by an award of costs against the offending party although costs cannot be awarded as a pre-condition for resuming a hearing (*Cooper v Weatherwise (Roofing and Walling) Ltd*[109]). An employment tribunal may permit a witness to be recalled for further examination, but should then give the other party an opportunity to make a further rebuttal (*Aberdeen Steak House Group v Ibrahim*[110]).

20.81 If an employment tribunal, on its own volition, takes a point which was not taken by the parties, natural justice requires that the parties should be alerted to the fact, so that they can be given an opportunity to present further evidence on the matter, and/or make further submissions (*Laurie v Holloway*[111]).

20.82 The standard of proof, ie the quantum of evidence which must be given in support of any particular allegation, must be sufficient to establish the balance of probabilities in that party's favour. The informality of tribunal procedure can sometimes mislead the parties

---

[106] [1986] ICR 629, EAT; revsd [1988] QB 493, [1987] 2 All ER 496, [1987] 3 WLR 836, [1987] ICR 855, [1987] IRLR 182, 131 Sol Jo 1040, [1987] LS Gaz R 2274, CA.

[107] [1985] IRLR 79, 1985 SLT 138, Ct of Sess; aff'd [1987] ICR 796, [1987] IRLR 326, 1987 SC (HL) 175, 1987 SLT 605.   [108] [1998] IRLR 172, EAT.   [109] [1993] ICR 81, EAT.

[110] [1988] ICR 550, [1988] IRLR 420, [1988] NLJR 151, EAT.   [111] [1994] ICR 32, EAT.

into thinking that they can escape with a standard of proof which is in fact unacceptable. If the employer, for example, fails to prove the reason or the principal reason for the dismissal (*Smith v Glasgow City District Council*, para 20.78) or fails to show any reason, or gives a reason which the tribunal does not believe, then he will have failed to discharge the burden of proof which is placed on him, and the dismissal will be unfair. Although the tribunals will admit hearsay evidence in the proceedings, the weight which is given to such evidence is a matter for them to decide (*Coral Squash Clubs Ltd v Matthews*[112]) and they will seldom base a decision in favour of an employer on such evidence, particularly if it is controverted by the direct evidence (or denials) of the claimant (*Mawson v Leadgate Engineering Ltd*[113]). The tribunals will give such assistance as they can to a person who is not legally qualified or represented, but it is the duty of the parties to present all the relevant evidence before the tribunals, and applications of adjournments may be made if a party considers it necessary to call someone whose attendance was not thought necessary.

20.83 The evidential requirements in the employment tribunals are not the same as other courts. For example, in *Docherty v Reddy* (para 12.16), the claimant was dismissed for suspected theft. The tribunal permitted the employer to introduce evidence that the claimant had stolen on previous occasions. Such evidence would scarcely have been admissible in the criminal courts, as its probative value would have been exceeded by its prejudicial value, but the EAT held that the evidence was rightly admitted. The issues in the employment tribunals and the criminal courts are different; in this case, the tribunal had to decide if the employer had reasonable grounds for dismissing, and the claimant's previous conduct was a relevant factor to be taken into account.

20.84 Equally, whether a dismissal was fair or unfair can only be determined on the basis of the facts which were known to the employer at the time he dismissed the employee, and subsequent information which comes to light is only relevant if it confirms that reason. Such information cannot be admissible to show a separate and additional reason for dismissal, because when the employer dismissed the employee, he did not know of those facts. This can be illustrated by *W Devis & Sons Ltd v Atkins* (paras 17.202 and 17.219), where the company dismissed a manager for failing to follow company directives. After he had left, it was alleged that facts were discovered which indicated that he had been guilty of gross misconduct, and that he had been taking secret commissions from customers, for which he could have been dismissed summarily. The employment tribunal refused to allow such evidence to be called on the issue of the fairness of the dismissal, and this was upheld on appeal to the House of Lords. It was permissible to adduce evidence which was discovered after the dismissal to prove the fairness of that reason, but not for the purpose of showing that the employers had discovered subsequently another reason which would have enabled them to dismiss fairly. However, if the dismissal is found to be unfair, the subsequent evidence can then be admitted for the purpose of determining the remedies which would be considered by the tribunal.

20.85 If a claimant fails to attend the tribunal hearing, without good cause, the tribunal can dismiss the claim without having to be satisfied that the respondent could establish a good defence (*Roberts v Skelmersdale College*[114]), or adjourn to another date (with or without an order for costs), but if the failure to attend was due to a medical reason, the decision whether to postpone is one within the discretion of the tribunal. Adequate reasons for taking this course of action must be given (*Teinaz v London Borough of Wandsworth*[115]).

---

[112] [1979] ICR 607, [1979] IRLR 390, EAT.   [113] [1972] IRLR 105.

[114] [2002] All ER (D) 145 (Nov), EAT; revsd [2003] EWCA Civ 954, [2003] ICR 1127, [2004] IRLR 69, [2003] All ER (D) 272 (Jun).

[115] [2001] All ER (D) 497 (Nov), EAT; aff'd [2002] EWCA Civ 1040, [2002] ICR 1471, [2002] IRLR 721, [2002] All ER (D) 238 (Jul).

If, having heard the claimant's case, the respondent makes a submission of no case to answer, on the ground that the claim is weak or misconceived, the tribunal should still continue to hear the respondent's evidence, for it is very rare that a submission of no case to answer can succeed (*Logan v Customs and Excise Comrs*[116]). The tribunal should always be prepared to hear evidence from the other side, except perhaps in the most hopeless or frivolous cases (*Hackney London Borough Council v Usher*[117]).

20.86 Otherwise, after considering all the facts, hearing the witnesses, and studying any evidence tendered, the employment tribunal must determine the issue on the basis of the relevant legal requirement. Thus if the issue is whether or not the employer has acted reasonably, this does not mean that the tribunal must agree with the employer's decision, for in many cases more than one course of action is possible, and an employer is not to be criticised because he adopts one in preference to another. It is not the duty of the tribunal to decide if they would have come to the same conclusion as the employer based on the facts which were within the employer's knowledge (*Ferodo v Barnes*, para 12.16), nor should the tribunal substitute their own judgment for that of the employer (*Donn v Greater London Council*, para 2.96), and any temptation to interfere with management prerogatives should be resisted. In *St Anne's Board Mills Co Ltd v Brien*[118] four employees refused to work with another employee, who they considered had been responsible for an accident. The employers investigated the matter, came to the conclusion that that employee was not to blame, and required the four to continue to work with him. They continued to refuse, and were dismissed. After considering the facts, the tribunal decided that the other employee had been responsible for the accident, and hence the four employees had not acted unreasonably in refusing to work with him. The dismissals were therefore unfair. On appeal, it was held that the question before the tribunal was not who was responsible for the accident, but whether the employers had acted reasonably in the circumstances. They had investigated the matter thoroughly and carefully, and come to certain conclusions. They had had the choice of dismissing an employee whom they considered to be blameless, or the four employees who were (in their view, wrongfully) refusing to work with him. In the circumstances, they had not acted unreasonably in dismissing the latter.

20.87 It is the practice of some employment tribunals to give an oral decision immediately the hearing finishes, and then promulgate the decision in writing at a later date. In rare cases it is possible for the employment judge, before such written promulgation, to announce his intention to recall the tribunal in order to reconsider some point of law which he has omitted to notice, or which was not drawn to his attention. While such practice is unusual, there is no legal objection to it (*Hanks v Ace High Productions Ltd*[119]). However, it is not possible for an employment tribunal to depart from their oral decision when it is reduced to writing (*Arthur Guinness Son & Co (Great Britain) Ltd v Green*, para 17.215).

20.88 If, at the end of the oral hearing, both sides agree to put their submissions in writing, the employment tribunal must send a copy of each party's submission to the other party, and give a specified time in which any response is to be made. Such comments should be limited to the correction of factual errors and legal submissions on any new points of law raised (*Barking and Dagenham London Borough Council v Oguoko*[120]).

20.89 After all the evidence has been heard, and representations made, the tribunal will either give an oral judgment or reserve its decision to be given in writing at a later date.

---

116 [2002] All ER (D) 360 (May), EAT; aff'd [2003] EWCA Civ 1968, [2004] ICR 1, [2004] IRLR 63, [2003] 37 LS Gaz R 31, [2003] All ER (D) 388 (Jul).

117 [1997] ICR 705, EAT.   118 [1973] ICR 444, [1973] IRLR 309, NIRC.

119 [1978] ICR 1155, [1979] IRLR 32, 13 ITR 524, EAT.   120 [2000] IRLR 179, EAT.

If an oral decision has been given, written reasons will only be provided if requested by one of the parties at the hearing or within 14 days of the judgment.

20.90 The written reasons should include the following information:

(a) the issues which the tribunal has determined;

(b) details of issues not determined, and the reason why;

(c) any findings of fact relevant to those issues;

(d) a concise statement of the relevant law;

(e) how the relevant findings of fact and applicable law have been applied in order to determine the issues; and

(f) where the judgment includes an award of compensation, a table of how the amount has been calculated.

H. Allegations of bias

20.91 Generally speaking, the tribunal will regulate its own procedure. However, within that parameter, a tribunal must not only act fairly but be seen to act fairly. Thus, an employment judge or member should not adjudicate on a case if s/he has some personal connection with either of the parties, or some knowledge of the facts (over and above those facts which are presented in evidence), or have an interest in the outcome of the case. If a wing member has had contentious dealings with either party to the proceedings, this must be disclosed to the parties, as this would give rise to apparent bias, even though the actual identity of the parties is unknown to the member (*City and County of Swansea v Honey*[121]). In particular they must be careful not to show any animosity against a party or any form of bias, whether against a party to the proceedings or a representative. If there is any possibility of a conflict of interest arising, the employment judge should first seek to ascertain whether there is another employment judge (or tribunal member, as appropriate) who can hear the case. If not, he should give a full explanation (recorded or carefully noted, so as to avoid controversy about what was said), and, if there is a serious objection, as opposed to a fanciful one, give the party affected the option of having the hearing continued, or having it heard by a differently constituted tribunal (*Jones v DAS Legal Expenses Insurance Co Ltd*[122]).

20.92 So far as allegations of bias are concerned, there are two aspects to consider. The first is actual bias, where an employment judge or member may have some pecuniary or proprietary interest in the outcome of the case (see *Locabail Ltd v Bayfield Properties Ltd*[123]). The second is apparent bias, where a fair-minded and informed observer, having considered all the facts, would conclude that there is a real possibility that the tribunal was biased. A comprehensive series of principles to be adopted in all cases where allegations of bias are made was set out by the EAT in *Hamilton v GMB (Northern Region)*.[124]

20.93 There is a difference between a tribunal member being rude and being biased, and the fact that the tribunal member is making facial gestures or his body language indicates a disapproval of the claimant's evidence does not, by itself, indicate that the member's mind has been made up (*Ross v Micro Focus Ltd*[125]).

---

[121] Employment Appeal Tribunal, 7 November 2008.
[122] [2003] EWCA Civ 1071, [2004] IRLR 218, 147 Sol Jo LB 932, [2003] All ER (D) 425 (Jul).
[123] (1999) *Times* 31 March, (1999) *Independent* 19 April.   [124] [2007] IRLR 391.
[125] Employment Appeal Tribunal, 18 November 2009.

20.94 There is a legal adage that justice must not only be done but must be seen to be done. This is also enshrined in Art 6 of the European Convention on Human Rights, which requires that an individual has the right to a fair and public hearing within a reasonable time by an independent and impartial tribunal established by law. Thus if there is a doubt about the impartiality of a member of the employment tribunal, the doubt should be resolved in favour of recusal. Apparent bias, as well as actual bias, is sufficient to disqualify a person from acting in a judicial capacity (*City and County of Swansea v Honey*[126]).

20.95 It can sometimes happen that during the course of the hearing, the tribunal may express a forcefully held opinion as to the merits of the case. This, by itself, does not indicate bias, as such views may well assist the parties in the manner in which they continue to conduct the proceedings. But the tribunal must indicate that the views expressed were only provisional, and that they remain open to persuasion to the opposite view (*Jiminez v Southwark London Borough Council*[127]).

I. Financial remedies

20.96 Monetary awards in respect of proceedings brought before an employment tribunal are subject to the special rules applicable in each case (see Appendix A). In particular, it should be noted that in discrimination claims, there is currently no limit to the amount which may be awarded (although the Government are considering whether to change this), and an award may also be made in respect of injury to feelings. Nor is there a limit to compensation awards in cases of health and safety and protected disclosure dismissals. Special rules are also applicable in claims brought under EU law (eg the Equal Treatment Directive) because 'full compensation' is required, and hence there is a difference in the stages at which percentage reductions are to be made for mitigation, contributory conduct, *ex gratia* payments, etc (see *Ministry of Defence v Hunt*[128]).

20.97 Aggravated damages may be awarded where the injury to the claimant was inflicted by conduct that was high-handed, malicious, insulting or oppressive (*Alexander v Home Office*[129]). This head of damages is separate from any other awarded for injury to feeling (*Scott v Commissioners of Inland Revenue*, para 20.63).

Interest on awards

20.98 An award made by an employment tribunal will attract interest, on a day-to-day basis, at the stipulated rate of interest, from the day after the date of judgment. If the award is paid within 14 days of the order, then no interest is payable. Interest is also not payable on costs awarded, nor on any part of the award which is subject to the recoupment provisions.

20.99 Interest is still payable if the tribunal's decision is subject to appeal or review, but if the amount of the award is subsequently varied, interest is payable on the amount as varied (Employment Tribunals (Interest) Order 1990, as amended in 2013).

20.100 In cases of sex, race and disability discrimination, and in equal pay claims, interest on awards will accrue from the date of the act of discrimination complained of (Employment Tribunals (Interest on Awards in Discrimination Cases) Regulations 1996, as amended in 2013).

---

[126] See n 121.
[127] [2003] EWCA Civ 502, [2003] ICR 1176, [2003] IRLR 477, [2003] 23 LS Gaz R 37, 147 Sol Jo LB 476, [2003] All ER (D) 123 (Apr).
[128] [1996] ICR 554, [1996] IRLR 139, EAT.   [129] [1988] IRLR 190, CA.

J. Reconsideration of judgment

20.101 An application may be made to an employment tribunal within 14 days from the time the decision was sent to the parties, asking for it to reconsider its decision (rule 70) if it is in the interests of justice to do so. This is not an appeal, and there are limited circumstances in which the tribunal will accede to such a request. The main reason stated by the legislation is where the interests of justice require a review. This general power can be illustrated by the case of *Berkeley Garage Ltd v Edmunds*[130] where the employers were told by officers from the Department of Employment that the claimant was bringing his case out of time. Consequently, they did not bother to attend the hearing. The tribunal found that it was not practicable for the claimant to have presented the case earlier, and proceeded to hear the case on its merits. When the employers discovered this, they applied for a review and a rehearing, which the tribunal refused. On appeal this was reversed, for the interests of justice clearly required that the employers be given an opportunity to present their side of the story. Similarly, in *Help the Aged Housing Association (Scotland) Ltd v Vidler*[131] the claimant was awarded £4,700 compensation for unfair dismissal, mainly on the basis that he was 60 years of age, and the tribunal thought that it would be a considerable length of time before he obtained further employment. Within two weeks of the tribunal's decision, he obtained employment. It was held on appeal that the tribunal should have exercised its powers of review and reviewed the compensation in the light of the new situation, for the original assessment was totally wrong. Because the claimant had obtained alternative employment so quickly, this altered the substratum of the tribunal's reasoning in computing the loss likely to be suffered, and hence it was in the interests of justice that there should be a review.

There are other reasons why a judge may reconsider a decision, such as:

(a) if the decision was wrongly made as a result of an error on the part of the tribunal's staff;

(b) if a party did not receive notice of the proceedings (*Hancock v Middleton*);[132]

(c) if the decision was made in the absence of a party entitled to be heard. If an employer fails to reply to a complaint by not returning the appropriate defence within the stated time he may be denied the right to be heard unless he can show some valid reason for this. But if a party is prevented from attending a hearing through illness, then the tribunal should consider whether the absence was for a genuine reason, and if his story is believed, a review should be granted (*Morris v Griffiths*[133]). In addition to seeking a review, the person applying should state in writing his reasons not only for the application, but also for contending that the decision of the employment tribunal was wrong. In *Drakard & Sons Ltd v Wilton*,[134] the employers did not attend a tribunal hearing as they believed that once having made an offer of settlement to the conciliation officer, they would be contacted if any further steps were required. The EAT held that the tribunal should have granted a review. They should have enquired into the circumstances surrounding the failure to attend the hearing;

(d) new evidence comes to light, which could not have been discovered before. For example, if, after the claimant has been awarded compensation for unfair dismissal, new evidence comes to light that he had been defrauding the employer

---

[130] [1975] ICR 228, [1975] IRLR 124, 10 ITR 70, 110 Sol Jo 460, DC.
[131] [1977] IRLR 104, EAT.   [132] [1982] ICR 416, EAT.
[133] [1977] ICR 153, EAT.   [134] [1977] ICR 642, 12 ITR 170, EAT.

during the period of employment, so that it would have been possible to have dismissed him summarily, then this will be taken into account by the tribunal when it reviews the decision, and any previous award of compensation may be altered accordingly (*McGregor v Gibbings Amusements Ltd*[135]). It must be shown that the new evidence which has now become available could not have been presented at the original hearing, and the application should be accompanied by the substance of that new evidence, including, if possible, proofs of witnesses (*Simmons v Medway Welding Ltd*[136]).

20.102 Before refusing an application for reconsideration, the employment tribunal should give the claimant an opportunity to elaborate in writing the grounds which he intends to put forward (*Drakard & Sons Ltd v Wilton*).

20.103 The power to reconsider only applies when the employment tribunal has made a decision. There is no power to review an actual settlement reached during or at the end of proceedings, where the tribunal has not made a finding on liability (*Larkfield of Chepstow Ltd v Milne*[137]).

20.104 An application for reconsideration may be made on the ground that there was an error in the proceedings, but not on the ground that the decision of the employment tribunal discloses an error of law, for that is a matter which must be dealt with on appeal to the EAT (*Trimble v Supertravel Ltd*[138]).

20.105 An employment tribunal may also reconsider its decision on its own motion. On reconsideration, the original decision may be confirmed, varied or revoked. If it is revoked it may be taken again.

K. Costs

20.106 In some circumstances, the tribunal may make an order that one party makes a payment to the other party in respect of costs incurred. Notice must be sent to the party against whom the order may be made to give him an opportunity of arguing why the order should not be made. A costs order may only be made if the other party was represented at the hearing, ie either by a solicitor or barrister or a lay representative, who charged for the service. The amount of costs is in the discretion of the tribunal up to £20,000, and an employment judge can carry out a detailed assessment of costs which exceed £20,000, as is done in the county court. For a costs order to be made, there must be some abuse of process. A representative does not behave improperly, unreasonably or negligently simply by acting for a client whose case is doomed to fail, or failing to advise the claimant that the case has little chance of success (*Mitchells Solicitors v Funkwerk Informations Technologies York Ltd*[139]).

20.107 A costs order must be made in an unfair dismissal case where the claimant has expressed a wish to be reinstated or re-engaged not less than seven days before the hearing, and the hearing has been adjourned or postponed because the respondent has failed, without a special reason, to adduce reasonable evidence as to the availability of a suitable job. A costs order may be made if a preliminary hearing is postponed, or if a party has, in bringing the proceedings, or he or his representative has, in conducting the proceedings, acted vexatiously, abusively, disruptively, or otherwise unreasonably, or the bringing or conducting of the proceedings has been misconceived (ie has no reasonable prospect of success). If a

---

[135] [1975] ITR 64. [136] [1973] ITR 373, NIRC. [137] [1988] ICR 1, [1987] LS Gaz R 2530, EAT.
[138] [1982] ICR 440, [1982] IRLR 451, EAT. [139] [2008] PNLR 29.

claimant has brought proceedings based on evidence which is a lie, it is appropriate for an award of costs to be made against him (*Daleside Nursing Home Ltd v Mathew*[140]). Costs may also be awarded against a party who has not complied with a practice direction.

20.108 If the employer makes an offer to settle the claim prior to the tribunal hearing, which is unreasonably rejected by the claimant, the tribunal is within its rights to exercise a discretion and make an award of costs (*Kopel v Safeway Stores plc*[141]).

20.109 Costs, however, remain the exception rather than the rule in employment tribunals.

L. Preparation time order

20.110 A preparation time order may be made in favour of a party who was not legally represented at a hearing in order to compensate for the time spent on preparatory work directly relating to the proceedings, including time spent by legal or other advisers, but not in respect of time spent at the hearing. An application for a preparation time order must be made within 28 days from the issuing of the judgment. The amount of the order will be determined by the tribunal's assessment of the number of hours spent on preparation time by the party in whose favour the order is to be made, based on the information provided by that party, and the tribunal's own assessment of what it considers to be a reasonable and proportionate amount of time spent on such preparatory work with reference to the complexity of the proceedings and the number of witnesses and documentation required. A preparation time order may not exceed £20,000, and the ability of the party who is to pay must be taken into consideration.

20.111 A preparation time order must be made in unfair dismissal proceedings which have been postponed or adjourned and the claimant has expressed a wish to be reinstated or re-engaged but the respondent has failed, without a special reason, to adduce reasonable evidence as to the availability of a suitable job. An order may be made where a party has, in bringing the proceedings, or he or his representative has in conducting the proceedings, acted vexatiously, abusively, disruptively, or otherwise unreasonably, or the bringing or conducting of the proceedings has been misconceived, in that it has no reasonable prospect of success.

20.112 A tribunal cannot make a preparation time order and a costs order in favour of the same party in the same proceedings. If a deposit has been taken from a party as a condition of the claim going forward, that may be paid in part or full settlement of the costs or preparation time order.

M. Wasted costs order

20.113 A tribunal may make a wasted costs order against a party's representative to disallow or pay (or refund) to his client any wasted costs, which will cover any costs incurred by a party as a result of any improper, unreasonable or negligent act or omission by that representative. However, such an order cannot be made against a representative who is not acting in pursuit of profit with regard to the proceedings. Before making such an order the tribunal must give the representative a reasonable opportunity to make oral or written representations, and take into account his ability to pay.

[140] Employment Appeal Tribunal, 18 February 2009.
[141] [2003] IRLR 753, [2003] All ER (D) 05 (Sep), EAT.

N. **Death of the employer or employee**

20.114 Where the employer dies, certain tribunal proceedings may be defended by the personal representative of the deceased employer (ERA, s 206). The relevant proceedings are those arising out of itemised pay statements, guarantee payments, protection from detriments, time off work (but not occupational pension scheme trustees), suspension from work on medical or maternity grounds, maternity, paternity, adoption and parental leave, written statements of reasons for dismissal, unfair dismissal, redundancy payments and rights on employer's insolvency. The personal representatives will have to perform all the obligations of the deceased, and any rights which accrue after death shall continue to devolve, and any liability which has not so accrued prior to death shall be treated as if it was a liability of the deceased employer immediately before death. For example, if an employer dies before or during a tribunal hearing, at the time of death, no liability has been incurred; once the tribunal makes an award, the liability shall be treated as if it had occurred prior to the death.

20.115 If the business does not carry on after the death of the employer, the employee will be deemed to have been dismissed for reason of redundancy, and will be entitled to the appropriate payment from the personal representatives. If the business does carry on functioning, and the employee continues to be employed by the personal representatives or trustees, there is no termination of employment, and continuity of employment is preserved (ERA, s 218(4)).

20.116 Similarly, where it is the employee who has died, the tribunal proceedings may be instituted or continued by his personal representatives, or, if there is no such person, by any appropriate person appointed by the tribunal. On a claim for unfair dismissal, obviously the reinstatement or re-engagement provisions cannot apply, but the tribunal can nonetheless consider the question of compensation, and this can be enforced accordingly (Employment Tribunals Awards (Enforcement in case of Death) Regulations 1976).

20.117 There are no specific provisions which permit claims for discrimination to be continued after the death of the employee, but apparently such claims may be brought under the provisions of the Law Reform (Miscellaneous Provisions) Act 1934 (see *Lewisham and Guy's Mental Health Trust v Andrews*, para 5.65). The 1934 Act does not apply to Scotland, but this was not necessary because Scottish common law always permitted an executor to pursue claims on behalf of a deceased person, and thus there is no reason why discrimination claims cannot be continued after the death of the claimant (*Executors of Soutar v James Murray & Co (Cupar) Ltd*[142]).

O. **Appeals**

20.118 It has already been noted (see Chapter 1) that the Employment Appeal Tribunal will hear appeals on points of law from employment tribunals, and on points of law from the decisions of the certification officer. An appeal on a point of law from the employment tribunals must be made within 42 days from the date when the document recording the full reasons for the decision was sent to the appellant (*Hammersmith London Borough Council v Ladejobi*),[143] not from the date on which under the normal postal rules they might be deemed to have been received (*Mock v IRC*),[144] although it is possible in exceptional circumstances to apply for an extension of time, but a good reason for the delay must be shown (*Duke v Prospect Training Services Ltd*[145]). From 2013, an appeal fee must also be paid of £400 for issuing the appeal, and £1,200 for a hearing.

---

[142] [2002] IRLR 22, [2002] All ER (D) 45 (Jan).   [143] [1999] ICR 673, EAT.
[144] [1999] IRLR 785, EAT.   [145] [1988] ICR 521, [1989] IRLR 196, EAT.

20.119 It will only be in the most exceptional cases that the EAT will relax the 42-day time limit for bringing an appeal. The principles set out in *United Arab Emirates v Abdelghafar*[146] remain good law, and only in exceptional circumstances will an extension be granted (*Jurkowska v Hlmad Ltd*[147]). Legal aid is available in the EAT, but it should be noted that a delay in obtaining legal aid, or the fact that the assistance of the Equality and Human Rights Commission is being sought for the purpose of pursuing an appeal are not reasons for not adhering to the 42-day time limit. In particular, a Practice Direction issued by the EAT makes it clear that if an application for a review is made to an employment tribunal, this does not prevent the time for appealing from running (although this obviously does not prevent an appeal against the refusal of the tribunal to grant the review), and further, if an employment tribunal makes a finding of liability, but adjourns the question of compensation, the time for appealing runs from the date of the decision, and is not suspended until the final matter of compensation has been dealt with. The EAT will also consider the motives of the appellant, the tactics used, whether the delay was intentional, the length of the delay, the merits of the appeal, and whether there would be any injustice or prejudice to the party who was successful before the employment tribunal (see *Aziz v Bethnal Green City Challenge Co Ltd*[148]).

20.120 Once an appeal to the EAT has been lodged, a preliminary hearing/directions (PHD) will take place. The appellant will be required to satisfy the EAT that it is reasonably arguable that the employment tribunal made an error of law. If so satisfied, the appeal will be allowed to proceed, and the EAT will make any appropriate directions to ensure that the appeal may be determined efficiently and effectively. A special PHD form must be completed, enabling amendment to be made to the notice of appeal, giving time estimates for argument, and, if needed, requesting the employment judge's notes of evidence. If the appeal does not raise an arguable point of law, it will be dismissed at the PHD stage. Only in very limited circumstances will an appellant be permitted to raise a point of law on appeal which was not canvassed before the employment tribunal (*Church v West Lancashire NHS Trust,* paras 18.21 and 20.53).

20.121 As a general rule, an appeal on a point of law cannot be made if the point was not raised before the employment tribunal, or if it was conceded, but, like most aspects of employment law, there are always exceptions to the rule. Thus in *Secretary of State for Health v Rance*[149] the EAT gave guidance on the circumstances in which new points may be taken on appeal. Thus, a new point may be taken for the first time if it would be unjust to allow the other party to get away with a deception or unfair conduct, or if there is a glaring injustice in not permitting an unrepresented party to rely on evidence that could have been given to the employment tribunal, or if it is of particular public importance for a legal point to be decided, and so on. No further factual investigation must be required, and all the relevant material must be before the EAT (see also *Lipscombe v Forestry Commission,*[150] *Bennett v Governing Body of Pennoweth School*[151]).

20.122 An appeal from a decision of an employment tribunal can only hope to succeed if the employment tribunal have misdirected themselves in law, or entertained the wrong issue, or proceeded on a misapprehension or misconstruction of the evidence, or taken matters into account which were irrelevant to the decision, or reached a decision which no reasonable employment tribunal, properly directing themselves in law, could have arrived

---

[146] [1995] ICR 65, [1995] IRLR 243.
[147] [2008] EWCA Civ 231, [2008] CP Rep 27, [2008] ICR 841, [2008] IRLR 430.
[148] [2000] IRLR 111, CA.   [149] [2007] IRLR 665, [2007] Pens LR 313, EAT.
[150] [2007] EWCA Civ 428.   [151] Employment Appeal Tribunal. 22 July 2008.

at. In *Neale v Hereford and Worcester County Council*,[152] May LJ propounded the so-called 'Biggles' test. He stated that the EAT should not interfere with the decision of the employment tribunal (except when they erred on a point of law) unless it was possible to say 'My goodness, that was certainly wrong!' Thus, if there is evidence to support their decision, the EAT will not normally interfere, particularly where the questions of fact and degree are at issue. The task of the EAT is to hear appeals only on points of law (*Spook Erection Ltd v Thackray*[153]). It is not an error of law that the employment tribunal has misunderstood the facts (*British Telecommunications plc v Sheridan*[154]).

20.123 In *Piggott Bros & Co Ltd v Jackson*[155] the Court of Appeal stated that a decision of the employment tribunal can only be characterised as being perverse if it was not a permissible option. The EAT would have to identify a finding of fact which was unsupported by any evidence or a clear self-misdirection of law. However, in *East Berkshire Health Authority v Matadeen* (para 12.70) the EAT held that in addition, 'perversity' was a freestanding basis for interfering with an employment tribunal's decision, if that decision 'was not a permissible option' or was 'a conclusion which offends reason' or 'so outrageous in its defiance of logic or of acceptable standards of industrial relations'. In particular, the EAT thought that the lay members were there to bring their experience and industrial judgment to the application of the law and to the decision to be reached on appeal. They were entitled to use that experience to ensure that employment tribunal decisions did not ignore generally acceptable standards. In *Yeboah v Crofton*[156] the Court of Appeal gave some guidance on whether an appeal based on perversity should be brought.

20.124 The weight to be attached to the evidence is a matter for the employment tribunal, and it is not permissible for the EAT to substitute their own views on this (*Eclipse Blinds Ltd v Wright*[157]). But an employment tribunal must consider whether a dismissal falls within the range of reasonable responses open to a reasonable employer, and not substitute their own judgment. A failure to adopt this approach may result in the decision not being a permissible option (*United Distillers v Conlin*[158]).

20.125 The notice of appeal should state quite precisely what point of law is to be argued. It is not sufficient to make a bald statement that the employment tribunal misdirected itself on a point of law without specifying the error or misdirection to be appealed against. As Phillips J has pointed out, to say that something is an error of law does not, without further explanation, make it so. Indeed, if it turns out that there is in fact no arguable point of law involved in the appeal, the EAT is quite likely to make an award of costs against the unsuccessful party. Further, if no arguable point is disclosed in the notice of appeal, the notice itself can be rejected by the EAT, so that the appeal will never be heard.

20.126 In the Practice Direction issued in 2008 the EAT made clear that copies of the notes taken by the employment judge will only be made available if they are necessary for the purpose of arguing a point of law on appeal. More latitude will be allowed to applicants who were not legally represented at the tribunal hearing (*Webb v Anglian Water Authority*[159]). The facts of the case will be found in the tribunal's decision, and any appeal must be based on the law as applied to those facts. However, it is permissible in argument to refer to the employment judge's notes for the purpose of clarifying any ambiguity in the case. If an appeal is based on the actual conduct of the case by the employment judge, or an

---

[152] [1985] IRLR 281, EAT; revsd [1986] ICR 471, sub nom *Hereford and Worcester County Council v Neale* [1986] IRLR 168, CA.   [153] [1984] IRLR 116, 1983 SLT 630, Ct of Sess.   [154] [1990] IRLR 27, CA.
[155] [1992] ICR 85, [1991] IRLR 309, CA.   [156] [2002] EWCA Civ 794, [2002] IRLR 634, [2002] All ER (D) 512 (May).   [157] [1992] IRLR 133, 1992 SLT 664, Ct of Sess.
[158] [1992] IRLR 503, EAT; *Conlin v United Distillers* [1994] IRLR 169, Ct of Sess.
[159] [1981] ICR 811, 125 Sol Jo 693, [1981] IRLR 494, EAT.

allegation of bias by the employment judge or members (*Facey v Midas Retail Security*[160]), or some evidence contrary to that found by the tribunal, the claimant must first inform the Registrar of the EAT, so that this can be communicated to the respondent, and the views of the employment judge sought. The EAT will not interfere with an award of compensation unless it is more than a trifling matter. If the question of the amount of compensation is alleged to be an error of law, it must be of a substantial nature for the EAT to interfere (*Fougère v Phoenix Motor Co Ltd*, para 17.224).

20.127 The EAT does have power to hear new evidence on appeal, but only if a reasonable explanation is produced as to why the evidence was not put before the employment tribunal (see *Hygia Professional Training v Cutter*[161]). It must be shown that the existence of the new evidence could not have been known or foreseen, and that had it been available at the employment tribunal hearing, it would have had an important influence on either the outcome of the case or the award of compensation (*Photostatic Copiers (Southern) Ltd v Okuda*[162]). The evidence must be credible, and of such a nature that it would have had a decisive effect on the tribunal's decision had they heard it (*Hussein v Mite Security Ltd*[163]). It is also possible to argue a new point of law, not canvassed before the employment tribunal, if the balance of justice so requires (*Russell v Elmdon Freight Terminal Ltd*, para 2.7).

20.128 If the decision of the employment tribunal is defective, because no reference or insufficient reference had been made to a particular aspect of the case, the EAT must not remit the case back to the employment tribunal for further amplification or clarification. The proper course is to allow the appeal and remit the case back for a further hearing (*Reuben v Brent London Borough Council*[164]). However, there is no objection to remitting a matter back to the employment tribunal for fuller reasons or an amplification of the reasons (*Barke v SEETEC Business Technology Centre*[165]) where the ground of appeal is the inadequate reasoning of the original decision (*Burns v Consignia plc (No 2)*[166]). Where the EAT remits a case back to the employment tribunal to consider certain specific issues, the tribunal has no jurisdiction to hear or determine matters outside the scope of those issues. In particular, there is no power to permit one party to amend its case so as to raise issues which were not previously before the employment tribunal (*Aparau v Iceland Frozen Foods Ltd (No 2)*[167]).

20.129 If there is a complaint about the actual conduct of the employment tribunal proceedings (eg that a member is falling asleep) this should be raised with the employment judge at the time, and not after the tribunal has reached its conclusions (*Red Bank Manufacturing Co Ltd v Meadows*[168]), although more serious matters, such as allegations of bias, can be raised at any time (*Peter Simper & Co Ltd v Cooke*[169]). The procedure to be followed in such cases was outlined by the EAT in *Facey v Midas Security* (para 20.126).

20.130 An appeal may be brought on the ground that the promulgation of the decision of the employment tribunal has been delayed for an unconscionable length of time. In *Kwamin v Abbey National plc*[170] it was suggested by the EAT that three and a half months should be the maximum time after the end of a case for the preparation and promulgation

---

[160] [2001] ICR 287, [2000] All ER (D) 1306, EAT.   [161] (2007) 151 SJLB 1297.
[162] [1995] IRLR 11, EAT.   [163] UKEAT/0342/08.
[164] [2000] ICR 102, [2000] IRLR 176, EAT.   [165] [2005] EWCA Civ 578, [2005] WLR (D) 46, CA.
[166] [2004] IRLR 425, [2004] ICR 1103.   [167] [1996] IRLR 119, EAT; revsd [2000] 1 All ER 228, [2000]
IRLR 196, [1999] 45 LS Gaz R 31, CA.   [168] [1992] ICR 204, [1992] IRLR 209, EAT.
[169] [1986] IRLR 19, EAT.   [170] [2004] IRLR 516, EAT.

of all but the most complicated and lengthy judgments. If there is a delay beyond that time, the delay will be regarded as being culpable in the absence of a proper explanation. However, even though there is a delay, there is no automatic presumption that the decision will be set aside. It is for the party impugning the decision to show a material error or omission due to faulty recollection, so as to establish that the decision is unsafe by virtue of the delay.

P. Reviews by the Employment Appeal Tribunal

20.131 The EAT has power to reconsider its own decision on the grounds (a) that the order was wrongly made as a result of an error on the part of the tribunal or its staff, (b) a party did not receive proper notice of the proceedings, and (c) the interests of justice require such review. However, the purpose of a reconsideration is not to allow appeals to be reheard and, in particular, a reconsideration will not be granted if an appeal has been lodged to the Court of Appeal (*Blockleys plc v Miller*[171]).

Q. Vexatious litigants (Employment Tribunals Act 1996, s 33)

20.132 If the EAT is satisfied that any person has habitually and persistently and without reasonable grounds instituted vexatious proceedings or made vexatious applications before an employment tribunal or the EAT, then, on an application by the Attorney-General or the Lord Advocate, the EAT may make a restriction of proceedings order, the effect of which will be to debar that person from instituting proceedings or making applications without leave from the EAT. The hallmark of vexatious proceedings is that it has little or discernible basis in law, with the effect of subjecting the defendant to inconvenience, harassment and expense out of all proportion to any gain likely to accrue to the claimant (*A-G v Wheen*[172]).

R. Further appeals

20.133 An appeal will lie from the EAT to the Court of Appeal (in Scotland the Court of Session). Leave to appeal must be given by the EAT, but if this is refused an application for leave to appeal must be made to the Court of Appeal or the Court of Session. It must be shown that there is a genuine point of law of practical consequence involved (*Campbell v Dunoon and Cowal Housing Association Ltd*[173]).

The jurisdiction of the Court of Appeal is to hear appeals from the Employment Appeal Tribunal, not from the employment tribunal. The question before the Court of Appeal is whether the EAT erred in law in the judgment under appeal (*Balfour Beatty Power Networks Ltd v Wilcox*[174]) and it has emphasised many times that a decision at first instance will not be overturned merely because one of several reasons for that decision turns out to be wrong, as long as the overriding reason for the decision can be identified and upheld (*McLoughlin v Jones*[175]).

A further appeal will lie to the Supreme Court.

---

[171] [1992] ICR 749, [1992] 34 LS Gaz R 39, EAT.
[172] [2000] IRLR 461, [2000] All ER (D) 767, EAT; aff'd [2001] IRLR 91, [2000] All ER (D) 2186, CA.
[173] [1992] IRLR 528, 1992 SLT 1136n, Ct of Sess.
[174] [2006] IRLR 258, EAT; aff'd [2006] EWCA Civ 1240, [2007] IRLR 63, CA.
[175] [2001] EWCA Civ 1743, [2002] QB 1312, [2002] 2 WLR 1279, [2002] PLQR P20, [2002] PNLR 21.

21

Individual Trade Union Rights

21.1 In this chapter we shall consider the rights of an individual in respect of his trade union membership and/or non-membership. These rights exist vis-à-vis a trade union or against an actual or potential employer. The relevant statutory provisions are contained in the Trade Union and Labour Relations (Consolidation) Act 1992 (TULR(C)A), which has been amended by subsequent legislation, and reference will also be made to a number of legal decisions.

Rights vis-à-vis a trade union

A. Right not to be excluded from any trade union (TULR(C)A, s 174)

21.2 An individual cannot be excluded or expelled from any trade union unless:

(a) he does not satisfy an enforceable membership requirement contained in the rules of the union. Enforceable means the restriction of membership solely by reference to employment in a specified trade, industry or profession, or occupational description, or the possession of a specified trade, industrial or professional qualification or work experience;

(b) he does not qualify for membership by reason of the union operating only in a particular part of Great Britain;

(c) the union negotiates with one particular employer (or a number of particular employers who are associated) and the applicant is no longer employed by that employer;

(d) the exclusion or expulsion is entirely attributable to the applicant's conduct, and the conduct is neither 'excluded conduct' nor 'protected conduct'. Conduct is excluded if the individual ceases to be a member of a trade union, or being employed by a particular employer or at a particular place, or is conduct for which an individual may not be disciplined by a union by virtue of s 65 of the Act (see para 21.9). Conduct is protected (see s 174(4A)) if the individual is a member of a political party, or ceased to be a member, but conduct which consists of activities undertaken by an individual as a member of a political party is not protected. This means that although a trade union cannot expel or exclude a person from membership because he is a member of a political party, he can be excluded or expelled because of his activities as a member of that political party.

21.3 In *ASLEF v United Kingdom*[1] a trade union expelled a member because of his membership of the British National Party. A court held that the expulsion was unlawful because of the provisions of s 174(1). However, the union appealed to the European Court of Human Rights, which held that to give associations that promote particular values no control over their membership was contrary to their freedom of association under Art 11 of the Convention. Thus s 174 was amended by the Employment Act 2008, which added s 174(4C) to TULR(C)A. This provides that conduct which consists of an individual being or having

---

[1] [2007] IRLR 361, (2007) 45 EHRR 34, 22 BHRC 140, (2007) *Times*, 9 March.

been a member of a political party is not protected conduct falling within s 174(4A) if the membership of that political party is contrary to (a) the rule of the trade union, or (b) an objective of the trade union. However, an exclusion or expulsion from the trade union is not permitted if the decision to exclude or expel is taken unfairly, or is contrary to the rules of the trade union, or the individual would lose his livelihood or suffer exceptional hardship by reason of his not being a member of the trade union.

21.4 If a person's application for membership of a trade union is neither granted nor rejected within a reasonable period, he shall be treated as having been excluded from the union (s 177).

21.5 The significance of s 174 is two-fold. First, at common law a trade union was entitled to lay down the description of persons who were eligible to join, and could specify any qualification for membership it desired (see *Boulting v Association of Cinematograph, Television and Allied Technicians*[2]), and exclude a person on any ground (see *Faramus v Film Artistes' Association*[3]). The courts did take the view that a rule which operated arbitrarily and unreasonably was void as being against public policy (see *Nagle v Feilden*, para 10.16), but such cases were rare and, generally speaking, a trade union could control its own admissions, and the court had no power to order it to grant membership to any particular individual. Section 174 now overrides the common law in this respect. A trade union may lay down certain requirements for membership, as above, but otherwise must admit any person seeking to join.

21.6 The second significance of the law is that the principles of the Bridlington Agreement, which used to govern inter-union disputes arising from competition for members, and applied to TUC affiliated unions, can no longer be relied upon. Previously, if a trade union commenced recruitment in an area in which another union already had a substantial membership, the TUC could order the interloper to surrender the members gained in the recruitment drive (see *Rothwell v Association of Professional, Executive and Computer Staff and the Trade Union Congress*[4]). This is no longer possible, because the individual has an indefeasible right to join whichever union he pleases, and cannot be expelled as a result of any award made by the TUC Disputes Committee.

21.7 A union may still specify who is entitled to join as a member within the limits specified above, but it is submitted that even these requirements cannot be exercised in an arbitrary and unreasonable manner (see *Nagle v Feilden*[5]). But if an applicant needs a trade union card because an actual or prospective employer operates a 'closed shop' he cannot otherwise be excluded from membership (*Clark v NATSOPA (SOGAT '82)*[6]). In any case, the aggrieved person would have a right against the actual or potential employer under the 'unfair recruitment' provisions (see para 21.28).

21.8 The remedy for a failure to admit or to expel an applicant to or from membership is dealt with at para 21.18.

B. Right not to be unjustifiably disciplined (TULR(C)A, ss 64–65)

21.9 The power of a trade union to take disciplinary action against a member, and the procedural rules which should be followed, is noted in Chapter 22. In addition, a member

---

[2] [1963] 2 QB 606, [1963] 1 All ER 716, [1963] 2 WLR 529, 107 Sol Jo 133, CA.
[3] [1963] 2 QB 527, [1963] 1 All ER 636, CA; on appeal [1964] AC 925, [1964] 1 All ER 25, [1964] 2 WLR 126, 108 Sol Jo 13, HL.   [4] [1976] ICR 211, [1975] IRLR 375.
[5] [1966] 2 QB 633, [1966] 2 WLR 1027, [1966] 1 All ER 689, (1966) 110 SJ 286.
[6] [1986] ICR 12, sub nom *Clark v NATSOPA (SOGAT '82)* [1985] IRLR 494, EAT.

has the right not to be unjustifiably disciplined by the trade union. A member is unjustifiably disciplined if the reason for the disciplinary action was conduct by him which was:

(a) a failure to participate in or support a strike or other industrial action (whether by members of that union or by others) or indicate his opposition to or lack of support for any such strike or other industrial action; or

(b) something required from him by virtue of an obligation imposed by his contract of employment or other agreement made with his employer; or

(c) the making of an assertion that the union, or an official or representative or trustee of the union's property has contravened or is proposing to contravene a requirement of the union's rules or any other agreement or legal provision, or attempts to vindicate any such assertion; or

(d) the encouraging of any person to perform an obligation imposed by virtue of a contract of employment or any other agreement; or

(e) the contravention by him of any requirement imposed by a determination which itself constitutes an infringement of his rights or of the right of any other individual; or

(f) failing to agree to, or withdrawing from, a check-off agreement; or

(g) resigning from a union, becoming a member of another union, or refusing to join any other union; or

(h) working with individuals who are not members of the union or any other union; or

(i) working for an employer who employs individuals who are not members of the union, or who are or are not members of any other union; or

(j) requiring the union to do something which the union is required to do on the requisition of any member; or

(k) an approach to the certification officer for advice or assistance on any matter whatsoever, or involves any other person being asked for advice or assistance with respect to any assertion made under (c) above; or

(l) a proposal to engage in conduct outlined in paras (a) to (k) above, or preparatory conduct (s 65).

But a refusal to accept union policy that members should not take on additional work is not protected, because the policy is not 'other industrial action' (*Knowles v Fire Brigade Union*[7]).

21.10 Discipline, for the purpose of this section, is a determination made under the union's rules by an official of the union, or by a number of persons including an official:

(a) that an individual shall be expelled from the union (or branch or section). In *Transport and General Workers' Union v Webber*,[8] it was held that a recommendation that the claimant be expelled was not a determination for the purpose of s 174. Until an appeal against the recommendation had been heard, he was still a member of the union;

(b) that an individual shall pay any sum to the union (or branch or section) or to any other person whatsoever;

(c) that sums tendered by that individual in respect of any obligation to pay a subscription or other sums to the union (or branch or section) should be treated as unpaid or as paid for a different purpose;

---

[7] [1996] 4 All ER 653, [1997] ICR 595, [1996] IRLR 617, [1996] 34 LS Gaz R 34, 140 Sol Jo LB 206, CA.
[8] [1990] ICR 711, [1990] IRLR 462, [1990] 27 LS Gaz R 40, EAT.

(d) that that individual should be deprived of, or refused access to, benefits, services or facilities which would otherwise be available to him as a member of the union. Suspending a member involves depriving him of benefits which accrue from union membership (*National and Local Government Officers' Association v Killorn*[9]);

(e) that another trade union (or branch or section) should be encouraged or advised not to accept that individual as a member; or

(f) that that individual should be subjected to any other detriment. Naming a person as a 'strike breaker' in a union circular, with the intention of causing him embarrassment is to subject that person to a detriment (*National and Local Government Officers' Association v Killorn*).

21.11 However, a member will not be unjustifiably disciplined if the reason for the disciplinary action was that he made an allegation that the union, an official, a representative or a trustee had contravened the union's rules or an agreement or an enactment or rule of law, and the assertion was false, and the member knew it was false or otherwise acted in bad faith.

21.12 If a complaint relating to an expulsion is brought under s 174, and is declared to be well founded, no further complaint relating to that matter can be brought under s 64 (unjustifiable discipline).

C. **Complaints of unjustifiable discipline (TULR(C)A, ss 66–67)**

21.13 An individual who believes that he has been unjustifiably disciplined by a trade union may present a complaint to an employment tribunal, alleging that his rights have been infringed. The complaint must be presented within three months of the alleged infringement, unless the employment tribunal is satisfied that it was not reasonably practicable to present the complaint earlier, and that any delay in making the complaint was wholly or partially attributable to any reasonable attempts to appeal against the decision or to have it reconsidered or reviewed.

21.14 If the employment tribunal find that the claimant has been unjustifiably disciplined contrary to s 64, they will make a declaration that the complaint is well founded. An application may then be made to an employment tribunal for an award of compensation, and an order that the union repay him any sum he has paid by way of a fine. The application must be made after four weeks but within six months of the declaration.

21.15 The amount of the award shall be such as the employment tribunal considers to be just and equitable in all the circumstances. The applicant is under a duty to mitigate against his loss, and the compensation award may be reduced if the infringement complained of was to any extent caused or contributed to by him. The amount of the award shall not exceed 30 times a week's pay (capped at £464 per week) plus £76,574. If on the date the application for compensation was made, the determination infringing the applicant's right not to be unjustifiably disciplined has not been revoked, or the union has failed to take steps to reverse anything done for the purpose of giving effect to the determination, the amount of compensation shall not be less than £8,669. An award of compensation for injury to feelings may be made (*Massey v UNIFI*[10]).

D. **Right to resign from a trade union (TULR(C)A, s 69)**

21.16 In every contract of membership of a trade union, whether made before or after the passing of the Act, there shall be an implied term conferring a right on the member, on

---

[9] [1991] ICR 1, [1990] IRLR 464, EAT.
[10] [2007] EWCA Civ 800, [2007] IRLR 902, (2007) 151 SJLB 1059, [2008] ICR 62.

giving reasonable notice and complying with any reasonable conditions, to terminate his membership of the union. In *Ashford v Association of Scientific, Technical and Management Staffs*[11] (decided under the provisions of the Industrial Relations Act 1971) the claimant wrote a letter of resignation to the union, which was to take immediate effect. This was not in accordance with the union rules, and subsequently expulsion proceedings were commenced. It was held by the NIRC that as the member had failed to give reasonable notice, he was bound by the union's rules. It was suggested that although it might be reasonable to invite members to state their reasons for resignation, it would not be reasonable to make such a statement a condition of resignation.

E. Right not to be expelled from the union (TULR(C)A, s 174)

21.17 The grounds upon which a person cannot be excluded from trade union membership (see para 21.2) apply equally to the right not to be expelled from a union. However, a person who resigns from the union because of dissatisfaction with the way the union is conducting its affairs cannot bring proceedings under s 174, for there is no such doctrine as 'constructive expulsion' (*McGhee v Transport and General Workers' Union*[12]). If a member ceases to be a member of the union on the happening of an event specified in the rules of the union, he shall be treated as having been expelled from the union (s 177).

F. Remedies for wrongful exclusion or expulsion (TULR(C)A, ss 175–176)

21.18 A person who claims that he has been wrongly excluded or expelled from a trade union may present a complaint to an employment tribunal within six months from the date of the exclusion or expulsion, or, where it was not reasonably practicable to do so, within such further period as the tribunal considers reasonable. The fact that the internal appeal procedure has not been exhausted does not, by itself, render it not reasonably practicable to present the claim earlier (*GMB v Hamm*[13]). If the tribunal find the complaint to be well founded, it shall make a declaration to that effect. If the tribunal find that the exclusion or expulsion was mainly attributable to 'protected conduct' (ie being or ceasing to be a member of a political party), it shall make a second declaration to that effect. A third declaration shall be made if the exclusion or expulsion was attributable to conduct which would have been contrary to the rules of the union.

21.19 If the application is declared to be well founded, and the applicant has been admitted or re-admitted to the union, an award of compensation shall be made which is just and equitable in the circumstances, and may be reduced if the applicant caused or contributed to the exclusion or expulsion. If on the date when the application was made the applicant has not been admitted or re-admitted to the union, the tribunal shall award compensation (see para 21.15), but this minimum award does not apply where either of the above second or third declarations have been made, when the just and equitable rule will apply.

G. Right of access to the courts (TULR(C)A, s 63)

21.20 A member who is seeking a determination or conciliation of a dispute under the union's rules should first pursue his case through the union's internal disputes procedure before seeking recourse to the courts (*White v Kuzych*[14]). But irrespective of any provision in the union's rules, the member has an indefeasible right to apply to the courts any time after six months from when the union first receives his application to have the matter

---

[11] [1973] ICR 296, NIRC.   [12] [1985] ICR 503, [1985] IRLR 198, EAT.   [13] IDS Brief 682.
[14] [1951] AC 585, [1951] 2 All ER 435, 95 Sol Jo 527, [1951] 2 TLR 277, PC.

determined or conciliated. However, if the delay is attributable to the unreasonable conduct of the union member, the court can extend the six-month period (ie to give the union more time to deal with the complaint).

21.21 The right to apply to the court after six months is of course without prejudice to a member's right to apply to the court at any time when, for example, an appeal cannot cure a defect because the action complained against is ultra vires or otherwise contrary to law.

H.　Right to a ballot before industrial action (TULR(C)A, s 62)

21.22 If a trade union calls on members to engage in a strike or other industrial action without the affirmative support of a ballot conducted in accordance with the stringent requirements of the Act, any member may apply to the court for an order seeking to have the authorisation or endorsement of the action withdrawn by the union. If the strike is not called by the specified person, or the Act's requirements relating to the functions of the independent scrutineer are not satisfied, or members have not been given an equal opportunity to vote, or a ballot has been held but a majority have not voted in favour, then the court will make such order as it considers appropriate for requiring the union to take steps for ensuring that there is no further inducement to take part in the action, and that no member engages in conduct after the making of the order by virtue of having been induced before the order to take part or continue to take part in the action.

21.23 The right to apply to the court for an order is thus available to an individual member of the union, whether or not the strike is actionable by anyone else (eg an employer, see para 23.46) and is additional to any right a member may have in respect of any breach which may have occurred of the trade union's rules. The right exists in respect of calls for any strike or other industrial action, whether or not the member is in breach of his contract of employment. Thus secondary action (see para 23.73) is covered.

21.24 A court may grant interlocutory or interim relief by ordering that the authorisation or endorsement of the industrial action is withdrawn, but it cannot order the union to hold a ballot. The right to bring an action under s 62 applies to self-employed persons, as well as to employees (s 62(8)).

21.25 Crown employees (who may not be employed under a contract of employment) are within the provisions of s 62 (see s 62(7)).

I.　Other individual rights

21.26 A member of a trade union has the right to restrain the union from indemnifying unlawful conduct (see para 22.63), to bring an action against the union's trustees in respect of unlawful application of the union's property (see para 22.65), and to bring a complaint about the conduct of the ballot in respect of a political fund (see para 22.67). He has the right to inspect the register of members (see para 22.18) and examine the union's accounts, and can apply to the court if the union has failed to comply with the requirements relating to union elections, election addresses, appointment of a scrutineer, etc. These matters will be considered in Chapter 22.

Rights vis-à-vis an employer

21.27 An individual worker has a number of legal rights against an actual or potential employer, as follows.

A. Access to employment (TULR(C)A, s 137)

21.28 It is unlawful to refuse a person employment:

(a) because he is, or is not, a member of a trade union; or

(b) because he is unwilling to accept a requirement:

    (i) to take steps to become or cease to be, or to remain or not to become, a member of a trade union; or

    (ii) to make payments or suffer deductions in the event of his not being a member of a trade union.

21.29 A person shall be taken to have been refused employment if the person to whom he is applying:

(a) refuses or deliberately omits to entertain and process his application or enquiry; or

(b) causes him to withdraw or cease to pursue his application or enquiry; or

(c) refuses or deliberately omits to offer him employment of that description; or

(d) makes him an offer of such employment the terms of which are such that no reasonable employer who wished to fill the post would offer, and which is not accepted; or

(e) makes him an offer of such employment but withdraws it or causes him not to accept it.

21.30 The law is aimed at preventing any form of discrimination against a worker on the ground of his trade union membership. The employer is quite entitled to refuse to employ someone because of that person's previous trade union activities (eg a well-known militant, see *Birmingham District Council v Beyer*[15]), because the refusal is not based on trade union membership, but disruptive conduct in his previous employment. Whether the employer thus refuses employment because of past trade union membership or past trade union activities is a question of fact for the employment tribunal to determine in accordance with the evidence. However, once the worker has entered employment slightly different considerations may apply (see *Fitzpatrick v British Railways Board*,[16] para 21.85).

21.31 The precise scope of s 137 is not clear. In *Harrison v Kent County Council*[17] the claimant had previously been employed for some 14 years, during which time he was known to be the leader of a long and bitter industrial dispute. He then left the employment, and subsequently applied for an advertised vacancy. He was refused employment. He argued that the refusal was because of his trade union membership, and hence contrary to s 137. The employers argued that he was refused employment because of his unco-operative attitude and anti-management style. His claim failed before the employment tribunal, but this was reversed by the EAT, who held that there was an overlap between trade union membership and activities. If a person was refused employment because of his trade union activities, it was open to an employment tribunal to find that he was refused employment because of his trade union membership. However, it should be noted that the decision in this case was made prior to the House of Lords' decisions in *Associated Newspapers Ltd v Wilson*[18] and *Associated British Ports v Palmer*[19] where it was pointed out that there is a distinction

---

[15] [1978] 1 All ER 910, [1977] IRLR 211, 8 BLR 83, EAT.

[16] [1990] ICR 674, EAT; revsd [1992] ICR 221, [1991] IRLR 376, CA.   [17] [1995] ICR 434, EAT.

[18] [1992] ICR 681, [1992] IRLR 440, [1992] 33 LS Gaz R 35, EAT, [1994] ICR 97, sub nom *Wilson v Associated Newspapers Ltd* [1993] IRLR 336, CA; revsd sub nom *Associated Newspapers Ltd v Wilson* [1995] 2 AC 454, [1995] 2 All ER 100, [1995] 2 WLR 354, [1995] ICR 406, [1995] IRLR 258, [1995] 17 LS Gaz R 48, [1995] NLJR 417, HL.

[19] [1993] ICR 101, [1993] IRLR 63, [1992] 42 LS Gaz R 39, EAT; revsd [1994] ICR 97, [1993] IRLR 336, [1993] 26 LS Gaz R 37, 137 Sol Jo LB 134, CA; revsd [1995] 2 AC 454, [1995] 2 All ER 100, [1995] 2 WLR 354, [1995] ICR 406, [1995] IRLR 258, [1995] 17 LS Gaz R 48, [1995] NLJR 417, HL.

between 'the purpose' and 'the effect' of an act, and thus the decision in *Harrison* must be regarded as being of doubtful authority.

Job advertisements (TULR(C)A, s 137(3))

21.32 Where a job advertisement (including every form of advertisement or notice, whether to the public or not), is published, which indicates (or might reasonably be understood as indicating) that the employment is only open to a person who is, or who is not, a member of a trade union, or make payments or suffer deductions (see para 21.28), then if a person applies for a job, and he is refused employment, it will be conclusively presumed that he was refused employment for that reason. Thus it is clear that all references to trade union membership or non-membership should be eliminated from job advertisements. However, the job advertisement per se is not unlawful (unlike advertisements which seek to discriminate on grounds set out in the Equality Act 2010, see para 4.207), and the only remedy is for an individual who has been refused employment to bring a personal complaint.

Unfair practices (TULR(C)A, s 137(4))

21.33 Where there is an arrangement or practice under which employment is only offered to persons put forward or approved by a trade union, a person who is not a member of the trade union, and who is refused employment because of that arrangement or practice, shall be taken to have been refused employment because he is not a member of the trade union.

Employment agencies (TULR(C)A, s 138)

21.34 The Act covers employment agencies, defined as any person who provides services for the purpose of finding employment for workers or for supplying employers with workers. In so far as the employment agency acts as an agent for an employer, the provisions of s 137 (see para 21.28) apply. In so far as the agency is acting in its own right, the identical provisions apply, and a person who has been refused the services of an employment agency (on grounds on his membership or non-membership of a trade union) will have a right to complain against the agency to an employment tribunal. Advertisements by employment agencies are also covered by identical provisions (s 138(3)).

Exceptions to the Act

21.35 The Act only deals with employment under a contract of service or apprenticeship. Thus it cannot apply to self-employed persons. Further, if a person is being considered for appointment or election to an office in a trade union, then s 137 does not prevent anything done for the purpose of securing the compliance with a condition that he be or become a member of the trade union, even though this would constitute employment. Thus it is not unlawful to insist that a trade union official becomes a member of the union concerned.

21.36 The unfair recruitment provisions do not apply to members of the armed forces, police, share fishermen, employees who work outside Great Britain, seamen registered on ships registered at ports outside Great Britain, or who are not ordinarily resident in Great Britain, and when the minister issues an exemption certificate on the ground of national security.

Remedies under the Act (ss 139–142)

21.37 A person who considers that his rights have been violated under the Act may make a complaint to an employment tribunal within three months from the date of the act complained of, with the usual extension of time if it was not reasonably practicable to present it earlier. If the tribunal uphold the complaint, they must make a declaration to that effect, may award compensation, and may make a recommendation that the respondent takes action to obviate or reduce the effect on the complainant of the conduct which is the subject of the complaint. If the complaint is made against an employment agency and a prospective employer, there are provisions which permit the joinder of both parties, and any award of compensation may be apportioned between them, as the tribunal think just and equitable. It is also possible to join a third party (eg a trade union or shop steward) if the act complained of came about by virtue of industrial pressure.

21.38 The practical effect of legislation is that the pre-entry and post-entry closed shop is no longer lawful in Great Britain.

Trade union blacklists

21.39 Following an investigation by the Information Commissioner into the activities of an organisation called the Consulting Association the Employment Relations Act 1999 (Blacklists) Regulations 2010 were passed. It was found that the Consulting Association was providing a number of companies with a list purporting to appraise the suitability of applicants for employment, with a strong emphasis on the names of trade unionists who were actual or potential 'troublemakers'. The Consulting Association has now ceased to exist, but the Blacklist Regulations are designed to prevent any resurgence of such activities.

21.40 Regulation 3 defines a prohibited list as a list that contains details of members of trade unions or persons who have taken part in the activities of trade unions, and is compiled with a view to being used by employers or employment agencies for the purpose of discrimination in relation to the recruitment or in relation to the treatment of workers.

21.41 Regulation 3 states that no person shall compile, use, sell or supply a prohibited list (there are specific exceptions where it is permissible to draw up or use such lists). If a person is refused employment because a potential employer has relied on information supplied by a person who has contravened reg 3, a right of complaint exists to an employment tribunal. The refusal may come about because the employer has refused or deliberately omitted to entertain or process a job application or enquiry, or caused the job applicant to withdraw the application, or has refused to offer employment, or has made an offer of employment in terms that no reasonable employer would make, or withdraws an offer of employment, etc. It is also unlawful for an employment agency to refuses its services to a person for a reason relating to a blacklist.

21.42 If, in the absence of any other explanation, the employment tribunal find that the employer or employment agency has contravened reg 3, or relied on information supplied in contravention of reg 3, the burden of proof will shift to the employer or employment agency to prove that there was no such contravention.

21.43 A complaint may be made to an employment tribunal before the end of three months beginning with the date of the conduct to which the complaint relates, or such further time as the employment tribunal considers reasonable, having regard, in particular, to when the facts to which the complaint relates came to the attention of the complainant. If the employment tribunal find the complaint well-founded, it shall make a declaration to that effect, and may make an order of compensation, and a recommendation that the respondent takes action for the purpose of obviating or reducing the adverse effect on the complainant.

21.44 A complaint may also be made if a person suffers a detriment for a reason that relates to a prohibited list, and it will be an automatically unfair dismissal if a person is dismissed (or selected for redundancy) because his employer has contravened reg 3 or relied on information supplied by a person in contravention of reg 3. There will be a minimum award of £5,000 (subject to a reduction in the event of contributory conduct) and a maximum of £65,300. Unlike other compensation limits, these are not subject to an annual review.

21.45 A person who has suffered because of an actual or apprehended contravention of reg 3 may, in the alternative, bring a claim for damages in a civil court for breach of statutory duty. Interim relief (an interim order in Scotland) is also available.

B. Inducements relating to union membership or activities (TULR(C)A, s 145A)

21.46 A worker has the right not to have an offer made to him by his employer for the sole or main purpose of inducing the worker:

(a) not to be or seek to become a member of an independent trade union;

(b) not to take part in the activities of an independent trade union at an appropriate time;

(c) to be or become a member of any trade union or of a particular trade union.

Inducements relating to collective bargaining (TULR(C)A, s 145B)

21.47 A worker who is a member of an independent trade union which is recognised by his employer has the right not to have an offer made to him by his employer if:

(a) acceptance of the offer (together with the other workers' acceptance of similar offers) would have the result that the workers' terms of employment will no longer be determined by collective agreement negotiated by or on behalf of the union; and

(b) the employer's sole or main purpose in making the offer is to achieve this result.

21.48 A worker has the right to make a complaint to an employment tribunal on the ground that his employer has made him an offer in contravention of s 145A or 145B. It will be for the employer to show what his sole or main purpose was in making the offer. If the tribunal uphold the complaint, it shall make a declaration to that effect, and also award compensation to the worker of £3,715.

21.49 The purpose of ss 145A and 145B (which were inserted into TULR(C)A by the Employment Relations Act 2004) is to prohibit 'sweetener payments' as an inducement to workers not to belong to trade unions, such payments being held by the European Court of Human Rights to contravene Art 11 of the European Convention (see *Wilson v United Kingdom*, para 1.106).

C. Action short of dismissal (TULR(C)A, s 146, as amended)

21.50 Every worker has the right not to be subjected to any detriment as an individual by any act, or any deliberate failure to act, by his employer, if the act or failure takes place for the purpose of:

(a) preventing or deterring him from being a member of an independent trade union, or penalising him for being so; or

(b) preventing or deterring him from taking part in the activities of an independent trade union at an appropriate time, or penalising him for doing so; or

(c) preventing or deterring him making use of trade union services at an appropriate time, or penalising him for doing so; or

(d) compelling him to become a member of a trade union.

Detriment, for the purpose of this section, is detriment short of dismissal.

21.51 The first matter to be determined is whether the action was taken against the worker 'as an individual'. If action is taken against a trade union this may affect an individual worker, but the action was not necessarily taken against him as an individual. In *F W Farnsworth Ltd v McCoid*,[20] a collective agreement provided that the employer had the right to derecognise a shop steward if his conduct was called into question. The employer notified the union that they intended to derecognise the claimant because his conduct was such that he was not suited to hold the office of shop steward. The claimant claimed that this derecognition constituted a breach of s 146(1). For the employer, it was argued that the action had not been taken against him as an individual, because it only affected his status as a shop steward, not as an employee. The argument was rejected. The Court of Appeal held that the purpose of s 146(1) was to allow an individual (in whatever capacity) to bring a complaint before an employment tribunal. However, it was thought that the employer could still successfully defend the action if they could show that the action taken was not for the purpose of preventing or deterring him from taking part in the activities of an independent trade union, but for the purpose of removing someone from the office of shop steward who was not fit for that role.

21.52 There is no breach of s 146 if the action taken (or omission) had the effect of so doing, if it was not done for that purpose. Thus in *Gallacher v Department of Transport*,[21] the claimant was a civil servant, who spent most of his working time carrying out trade union duties. He put his name forward for promotion to a higher grade, but was turned down because of his lack of management skills. He was told that the only way he could acquire those skills was by taking a line job, and thus reduce the amount of time spent on trade union duties. He complained to an employment tribunal, who found that the advice given to him that he should spend more time gaining management experience was intended to deter him from spending time on trade union duties and activities. However, the EAT allowed the employer's appeal and that decision was upheld by the Court of Appeal. The employer's purpose was to ensure that only employees with sufficient line management experience were promoted. Thus any action taken was not for the purpose of deterring the applicant from exercising his statutory rights.

21.53 The 'appropriate time' for carrying out trade union activities or making use of trade union services means time which is outside his working hours, or at a time within his working hours at which, in accordance with arrangements agreed with or consent given by, his employer, it is permissible for him to take part in those activities. Such consent may be express, and will frequently be implied from the conduct of the parties. However, it would be rare that consent can be implied in the case of a shop steward who is not accredited (*Marley Tile Co Ltd v Shaw*[22]). A worker cannot just engage in trade union activities in working hours when he feels like it. Thus in *Brennan and Ging v Ellward (Lancs) Ltd*[23] the claimants left a site on which they were working to consult their trade union official, despite a warning that if they did so they would be dismissed. Although this may have amounted to trade union activities, it was not within the appropriate time for such activities.

21.54 In *Robb v Leon Motor Services*[24] the claimant was a long distance coach driver. He was appointed shop steward. He was then told that he would have to drive other vehicles, because of all the trouble he was causing, and he claimed that by taking him off better paid and more important work, he was being deterred from carrying out his trade union activities at an appropriate time. It was held that even though this was action taken against him

---

[20] [1998] IRLR 362, EAT; aff'd [1999] ICR 1047, [1999] IRLR 626, [1999] 16 LS Gaz R 35, CA.
[21] [1993] ICR 654, EAT; aff'd [1994] ICR 967, [1994] IRLR 231, CA.
[22] [1978] ICR 828, [1978] IRLR 238, 13 ITR 257, EAT; revsd [1980] ICR 72, [1980] IRLR 25, 123 Sol Jo 803, CA.
[23] [1974] IRLR 153, NIRC.   [24] [1977] IRLR 245; revsd [1978] ICR 506, [1978] IRLR 26, EAT.

short of dismissal, and even though it was done for the purpose of deterring him from taking part in trade union activities, he could not succeed. There was no attempt to stop him from taking part in union activities outside his working hours, and the activities he was engaged in within working hours were not done with any arrangement or with the consent of the employers. Consequently, he was not being deterred from taking part in trade union activity at the appropriate time.

21.55 Whether the activities in question are the activities of an independent trade union is an issue of fact for the employment tribunal to determine (*Marley Tile Co Ltd v Shaw*). There must be some institutional link, with the union or an accredited shop steward being involved. Individual requests or complaints, or group meetings which have no union connection, are outside the statutory protections (*Dixon and Shaw v West Ella Developments Ltd*[25]).

21.56 If there is a requirement (whether contractual or not) that in the event of a failure by the worker to become or remain a member of a trade union, he must make a payment (usually to charity), and a deduction is made from the worker's wages in consequence, this shall be treated as a detriment. Further, where a worker notifies the employer that he has ceased or will cease to be a member of a trade union as from a certain date, the employer will ensure that no amount representing his trade union subscription shall be deducted from the worker's pay (TULR(C)A, s 68, see para 21.79). If the employer fails to comply, the worker may seek a declaration in the county court. The court may make an order to ensure that the employer's actions are not repeated, but for any unlawful past deductions, the worker must seek a remedy in the employment tribunal under the provisions of s 23 of the Employment Rights Act 1996.

21.57 A complaint may be presented to a tribunal that an employer has taken action against a worker in violation of the above rights. The burden of proof is placed on the employer to show the purpose for which the action was taken. Moreover, no account is to be taken of any pressure which may have been exercised on the employer by way of strike or other industrial action (or threats of such), and the tribunal will determine the issue as if no such pressure has been exercised. But if the complaint is on the ground that the employer has taken action against the worker for the purpose of compelling him to be or become a member of a trade union, and the employer or worker claims that the employer was induced to take such action by such pressure, the employer or the worker may, before the hearing of the complaint, require the person who he claimed exercised the pressure to be joined as a party to the proceedings.

21.58 The employment tribunal may then make an award of compensation to the claimant either against the employer or the party who exercised the pressure, or partly against each of them as it thinks just and equitable in the circumstances (TULR(C)A, s 150).

21.59 The complaint must be presented within three months from the date of the last action complained of (see *Adlam v Salisbury and Wells Theological College*[26]), with the usual extension of time in cases where it was not reasonably practicable to present it earlier. If the tribunal upholds the complaint, it may make a compensation award as it considers just and equitable having regard to the claimant's loss, and the infringement of his rights, including any expenses incurred and any benefits he might have received but for that action. There is no limit (in theory) on the amount of compensation which can be awarded. The claimant must mitigate against his loss, and compensation is subject to a reduction on the ground of contributory conduct.

---

[25] [1978] ICR 856, [1978] IRLR 151, 13 ITR 235, EAT.   [26] [1985] ICR 786, EAT.

21.60 The basis of the award is to compensate the worker for any loss suffered, not for the purpose of imposing a fine on the employer. In *Brassington v Cauldon Wholesale Ltd*[27] an employer threatened to close his business down if he was forced to recognise a trade union. The claimant claimed this was action short of dismissal taken against him for the purpose of preventing or deterring him from joining an independent trade union, and with some hesitation, the EAT agreed that this was so and remitted the appeal back to an employment tribunal to assess compensation under TULR(C)A, s 149(2). Thus the infringement of a person's trade union rights will lead to an employment tribunal making a mandatory declaration, and compensation if the employee can show that he has suffered a loss. This could be, for example, stress causing ill-health (*Cheall v Vauxhall Motors Ltd*[28]), injury to feelings as a result of being overlooked for promotion (*Cleveland Ambulance NHS Trust v Blane*[29]), the loss of the benefit of trade union advice or assistance, and so on.

D. Detriment and dismissal in statutory recognition cases (TULR(C)A, Sch A1)

21.61 We shall see (Chapter 23) that Sch A1 inserted into TULR(C)A sets out a statutory procedure whereby a trade union may obtain recognition or suffer derecognition. The Schedule also (in Pt VIII) provides protection for any worker (see para 23.6) against suffering a detriment because he did or did not do any of a wide range of actions in connection with the statutory procedure for recognition or derecognition, including supporting or opposing the application, influencing others to support or oppose the application, voting in a ballot, and so on (see para 156 of the Schedule). However, there will be no protection if what the worker did was unreasonable (query whether a breach of contract by the worker, eg a strike, is unreasonable conduct on his part). A worker may make a complaint to an employment tribunal, which may make a declaration, and may also award compensation to be paid by the employer in respect of the act or omission complained of; the amount shall be such as the tribunal consider to be just and equitable.

21.62 If the detriment amounts to the termination of the worker's contract, but that contract is not a contract of employment, the amount awarded by the tribunal may be the equivalent of the normal basic and compensatory awards which can be made in unfair dismissal cases under ERA, ss 119 and 124(1).

21.63 So far as workers who are employees are concerned, if the detriment amounts to a dismissal, that dismissal shall be regarded as being automatically unfair under ERA, Pt X. It will also be unfair to select an employee for redundancy if the reason was any of the above specified reasons.

21.64 Similar protections are given to employees who are employed under a fixed-term contract, and the normal qualifying periods of employment and the age limits provisions do not apply to any of the rights referred to earlier. Interim relief will also be available, as appropriate.

21.65 Workers who act or omit to act in circumstances which are outside the statutory procedure of Sch A1 must rely on those provisions which protect against detriment or dismissal in respect of trade union activities contained in TULR(C)A, ss 146 and 152 (see paras 21.50 and 21.85). Thus recruiting members, distributing literature, etc, with a view to obtaining recognition outside the statutory procedures, will constitute trade union activities under the existing TULR(C)A provisions, and are thus protected (*Lyon v St James Press Ltd*[30]).

---

[27] [1978] ICR 405, [1977] IRLR 479, EAT.   [28] [1979] IRLR 253.
[29] [1997] ICR 851, [1997] IRLR 332, EAT.   [30] [1976] ICR 413, [1976] IRLR 215, EAT.

E. Time off work for trade union duties (TULR(C)A, s 168)

21.66 An employer shall permit an employee of his who is an official of a recognised independent trade union to take time off work during his working hours, for the purpose of carrying out any duties as such officially concerned with:

(a) negotiations with the employer related to or connected with collective bargaining; or

(b) the performance on behalf of the employees of functions in relation to or in connection with matters falling within collective bargaining which the employer has agreed may be performed by the union; or

(c) the receipt of information from the employer and consultations by the employer concerned with redundancies (see para 18.69) and the transfer of an undertaking (see para 9.75).

21.67 The employer will also permit the employee to have time off work during working hours to undergo training in aspects of industrial relations which is relevant to the carrying out of those duties, and which has been approved by the TUC or by his union.

21.68 Time off work for this purpose is not confined to face-to-face meetings with the employers, but can also include preparatory or co-ordinating meetings in order to discuss forthcoming negotiations, as long as these are in connection with the collective bargaining purposes outlined in s 178 (*London Ambulance Service v Charlton*[31]).

21.69 A trade union official wishing to take time off work for training should show a copy of the syllabus to the employer. In *Menzies v Smith and McLaurin Ltd*[32] the claimant wished to go on a course relating to job security. The union sent a copy of the syllabus to the employers, showing that topics to be covered included import controls, North Sea Oil, EEC policies, and so on. The company decided that all this was not relevant to his trade union duties, but agreed to give him time off work (without pay) for trade union activities. He went on the course and then claimed his pay. It was held that he was not entitled to be paid. The syllabus clearly indicated that the course was not relevant to his duties as a trade union official.

21.70 The amount of time off, the purposes for which, the occasions on which, and any conditions subject to which time off may be taken are those that are reasonable in all the circumstances having regard to the relevant provisions of the code of practice issued by ACAS. The employer shall pay an employee who has taken time off for these purposes in accordance with his usual rate of remuneration. A failure to permit an employee to have time off under this section, or a failure to pay him for time off, may be the subject of a complaint to an employment tribunal by the aggrieved employee. In *Blower v CEGB*[33] the claimant, who was a night shift worker, was a member of a works committee which met during the day. His day shift colleagues were paid for attending, whereas he was not. It was held that he was not entitled to be paid. It was part of his union work that his leisure time would be eaten into; the law only requires time off to be paid for if it is during his normal working hours, not for time spent on trade union duties outside his working hours (see *Hairsine v Kingston upon Hull City Council*[34]).

21.71 Whether it is reasonable to have time off under s 168 is a question of fact for the employment tribunal, and its findings cannot be challenged in the EAT unless it took into account matters which ought not to be taken into account (*Thomas Scott & Sons (Bakers) Ltd v Allen*[35]).

---

[31] [1992] ICR 773, [1992] IRLR 510, EAT.   [32] [1980] IRLR 180, EAT.   [33] Unreported.
[34] [1992] ICR 212, [1992] IRLR 211, EAT.   [35] [1983] IRLR 329, CA.

F. **Time off work for trade union activities (TULR(C)A, s 170)**

21.72 An employer shall permit an employee who is a member of a recognised independent trade union to take time off during the employee's working hours for the purpose of taking part in:

(a) any activities of that trade union; and

(b) any activities in relation to which the employee is acting as a representative of that union. This might include, for example, attendance at a conference as a union delegate, etc, but the activities for which permission is to be granted do not include anything which involved the taking of industrial action, whether or not in contemplation or furtherance of a trade dispute. Nor does the lobbying of Parliament to protest against proposed legislation come within the definition of 'trade union activities', even if the lobby is organised by a trade union, because it is intended to convey political and ideological objections to the proposed legislation, and is not as such a trade union activity (*Luce v London Borough of Bexley*[36]).

21.73 Again, the amount of time off, the purposes, the occasions and the conditions are those that are reasonable in all the circumstances having regard to the relevant provisions in the Code of Practice issued (see *Depledge v Pye Telecommunications Ltd*[37]). When determining the reasonableness of time off to be taken for a particular purpose, the nature, extent and purpose of time off already taken by the employee may be taken into consideration (*Wignall v British Gas Corpn*[38]). It will be noted that the employer does not have to pay an employee for time taken off for trade union activities. A failure to permit time off for these purposes may be the subject of a complaint to an employment tribunal by the aggrieved employee.

G. **Time off work for trade union learning representatives (TULR(C)A, s 168A)**

21.74 An employer shall permit an employee of his who is a member of an independent trade union recognised by the employer, and a learning representative of the trade union, to take time off work during his working hours, with pay, for the purpose of carrying on the following activities in relation to qualifying members of the trade union, ie members of the trade union who are employees of the employer of a description in respect of whom the union is recognised, and in relation to whom it is the function of the union learning representative to act as such.

21.75 The purposes in question are:

(a) any of the following activities –

(i) analysing learning or training needs,

(ii) providing information and advice about learning or training matters,

(iii) arranging learning or training, and

(iv) promoting the value of learning or training;

(b) consulting with the employer about carrying on such activities; and

(c) preparing for any of the above.

21.76 The trade union must give notice in writing to the employer that the employee is a learning representative of the trade union, and that he has undergone (or will be

---

[36] (1990) 88 LGR 909, [1990] ICR 591, [1990] IRLR 422, [1990] 27 LS Gaz R 41, EAT.
[37] [1981] ICR 82, [1980] IRLR 390, EAT.   [38] [1984] ICR 716, [1984] IRLR 493, EAT.

undergoing) sufficient training to enable him to carry on such activities. The training must be sufficient for the above purpose, having regard to any Code of Practice issued by ACAS or the Secretary of State. The amount of time off, the occasions on which, and any conditions subject to which time off may be taken are those that are reasonable having regard to any relevant provision of the Code of Practice.

21.77 An employee may present a complaint to an employment tribunal that his employer has failed to permit him to take time off as required by s 168A which, if the complaint is well founded, shall make a declaration, and may make an award of compensation.

21.78 A trade union member is entitled to reasonable time off work (without pay) for the purpose of having access to the services of his union learning representative. It will be unfair if an employee is dismissed because he brought proceedings to enforce his rights under s 168A.

H. Check-off arrangements (TULR(C)A, s 68)

21.79 If a trade union and an employer have an agreement whereby the employer will deduct the union subscriptions from the worker's wages and pay this direct to the union (ie a check-off agreement) the employer shall ensure that the worker has authorised the deduction in a document which is signed and dated, that the amount of the deduction does not exceed the permitted amount, and that the authorisation is current on the day of the deduction. An authorisation once made will be operative until the worker withdraws it in writing. The permitted amount to be deducted is the amount of the union subscription. It is no longer necessary for the employer to give one month's notice in writing before deducting an increase in the union subscription, but the amount of the deduction will still have to be shown on the regular itemised pay statement, and the worker is free to withdraw from the check-off arrangement at any time (Deregulation (Deduction from Pay of Union Subscriptions) Order 1998).

21.80 The fact that the worker has given his authorisation to the deductions does not give rise to any obligation on the part of the employer to continue to make the deductions (s 68(9)). That is clearly a matter between the employer and the trade union.

21.81 A worker may bring a complaint before an employment tribunal that his employer has made a deduction in contravention of s 68. The complaint must be presented within three months from the date of the last deduction, with the usual extension of time if it was not reasonably practicable to present the claim earlier.

21.82 If the tribunal find the complaint to be well founded, it shall make a declaration to that effect, and also order the employer to pay to the worker the unauthorised deduction (or unauthorised increase in subscription).

I. Deductions for the political fund of the union (s 86)

21.83 If a member of a trade union informs the employer in writing that he is exempt from paying the levy to the political fund of the union, the employer shall ensure that no amount representing the contribution to the political fund is deducted from the employee's wages.

21.84 If a person alleges that his employer has wrongly deducted a political fund contribution, or has refused to deduct union dues, he may make a complaint to an employment tribunal within three months, and the tribunal may make a declaration, order the employer to pay the applicant the amount deducted in contravention of s 87, or make an order requiring the employer to take steps specified in relation to emoluments payable. In the latter case, if there is still a failure to comply, there is an ultimate sanction of two weeks' pay (TULR(C)A, s 87).

J. Dismissal on the ground of trade union membership or non-membership, or trade union activities (TULR(C)A, s 152)

21.85 The dismissal of an employee will be unfair if the reason (or principal reason) was because the employee:

(a) was, or proposed to become, a member of an independent trade union; or

(b) had taken part, or proposed to take part, in the activities of an independent trade union at an appropriate time, or made use of trade union services at an appropriate time, or had failed to accept an offer made in contravention of ss 145A–145B (inducement relating to union membership or collective bargaining, see para 21.46). 'Appropriate time' means time which is outside his working hours, or time within his working hours at which, in accordance with arrangements agreed with or consent given by his employer it is permissible to take part in those activities. 'Working hours' means any time when the employee is required to work. A person is not taking part in trade union activities merely because he is a trade union activist, for one must distinguish between individual and trade union activities (*Chant v Aquaboats Ltd*[39]). Nor do the activities of an unofficial strike committee constitute trade union activities. But enlisting the help of a trade union official to assist in negotiations of terms and conditions of employment may constitute trade union activities (*Discount Tobacco and Confectionery Ltd v Armitage*[40]), (but see *Speciality Care plc v Pachela*[41]). Going on strike does not constitute trade union activities, but leading an official strike will (*Britool Ltd v Roberts*[42]).

If the employee is dismissed because the employer learns of his trade union activities in a previous employment (eg as a trade union activist), it would be inevitable that the employer was dismissing him because of the belief that he would be involved in trade union activities in his current employment, and thus the principal reason for the dismissal would be that the employee proposed to take part in trade union activities, and hence the dismissal is unfair (*Fitzpatrick v British Railways Board*, para 21.30). But if the trade union activist has obtained employment by deceit (eg by changing his name) then a dismissal for that deceit may be fair, and the reason is not because of past or proposed trade union activities (*Birmingham City District Council v Beyer*, para 21.30);

(c) was not a member of any trade union, or a particular trade union, or had refused or proposed to refuse to become or remain a member (*Crosville Motor Services Ltd v Ashfield*[43]). This provision gives general rights to non-unionists not to be dismissed because of their non-membership of a trade union.

A distinction may be drawn between the fact of involvement in trade union activities and the manner of such involvement. Thus if, in the course of such activities, the trade unionist makes statements which are malicious, untruthful or irrelevant to the matter in hand, his manner of conducting those activities may take him outside the protection of s 152 (*Bass Taverns Ltd v Burgess*[44]);

---

[39] [1978] 3 All ER 102, [1978] ICR 643, EAT.   [40] [1990] IRLR 15, [1995] ICR 431, EAT.
[41] [1996] ICR 633, [1996] IRLR 248, EAT.   [42] [1993] IRLR 481, EAT.
[43] [1986] IRLR 475, EAT.   [44] [1995] IRLR 596, CA.

(d) had made use of trade union services at an appropriate time, or had failed to accept an offer which was made in contravention of ss 145A and 145B.

21.86 If a person is dismissed for any of the above reasons, it will be an unfair dismissal, and thus it is not necessary for him to have the normal qualifying period of employment of one year before he can bring his claim (TULR(C)A, s 154, and see *Carrington v Therm-A-Stor Ltd*[45]). Nor does the upper age limit exclusion apply. Taking part in a strike may be trade union activity, but it is not at an appropriate time (see para 21.66).

21.87 It is also an unfair dismissal to select a person for redundancy because of his trade union membership/non-membership, or his trade union activities, or making use of trade union services (TULR(C)A, ss 152(1)–153).

21.88 To select an employee for redundancy because of his trade union membership or non-membership or trade union activities would, of course, be manifestly unfair, but it must be shown that the circumstances constituting the redundancy applied equally to other employees who held positions similar to that employee, and that they were not dismissed. Thus in *O'Dea v ISC Chemical Ltd*,[46] the claimant, who was a senior shop steward, was paid as a technical services operator, although in fact he spent half of his working time working as a packaging operator and the other half on trade union activities. He was dismissed for reason of redundancy, although two other technical service operators were retained. It was held that his dismissal was not unfair. When considering his 'position' account had to be taken of his status as an employee, the nature of his work and his terms and conditions of employment. The claimant could not compare himself with technical service operators because he did not do that job.

21.89 It does not need to be shown that the employer acted maliciously or with a deliberate desire to get rid of a trade union activist. Thus if an employee spends a major part of his working hours on trade union duties, with the result that he is given a poor assessment when redundancy selection procedures are being implemented, 'the reason' for his selection is his trade union activities, carried out at an appropriate time with the consent (albeit reluctantly given) of the employer, and hence his dismissal falls within s 152(1) (*Dundon v GPT Ltd*[47]).

K. Dismissal in connection with industrial action (TULR(C)A, ss 237–239)

21.90 The law on dismissal for taking part in industrial action is somewhat complicated, and needs careful consideration. There are five different situations to consider.

21.91 The first situation arises when the employer conducts a lock-out. Here, the provisions of s 238(1)(a) apply, and if there is a dismissal, the 'no picking and choosing' rule applies.

21.92 The second situation arises when employees, who may be all union members, or some of whom are union members (and some are not), go on strike and the strike has not been authorised or endorsed by the trade union to which they belong. This is an unofficial strike, and the provisions of s 237 apply.

21.93 The third situation arises when none of those who go on strike or take industrial action are members of a trade union. This is not an unofficial industrial action, and clearly it is not official industrial action. Here, a dismissed employee can only complain of unfair dismissal if the 'no picking and choosing' rule has been violated (s 238(2)).

[45] [1982] ICR 8, EAT; revsd [1983] 1 All ER 796, [1983] 1 WLR 138, [1983] ICR 208, sub nom *Therm A Stor Ltd v Atkins* [1983] IRLR 78, 126 Sol Jo 856, CA.
[46] [1996] ICR 222, [1995] IRLR 599, CA.   [47] [1995] IRLR 403, EAT.

21.94 The fourth situation arises when a union authorises or endorses industrial action, but the action is not protected by virtue of s 219 because the balloting provisions have not been complied with, or secondary action, etc is being taken. This is official unprotected industrial action, and the 'no picking and choosing' rules in s 238(2) apply.

21.95 The fifth situation arises when a union calls a protected strike, ie one that is protected by TULR(C)A, s 219 (immunity from actions in tort, see para 23.41), and the union has not lost its immunity through a failure to comply with the legal rules which would lead to such loss, eg it has complied fully with the balloting provisions (see ss 222–235). Here, the provisions of s 238A apply, and dismissed employees enjoy much greater protection.

21.96 There is a further subtle distinction between ss 237–238 and 238A. Sections 237 and 238 are both concerned with a dismissal which takes place *while* an employee was taking part in industrial action, whereas 238A deals with a dismissal *for* taking part in industrial action. In other words, ss 237 and 238 apply whenever an employee is dismissed during the action industrial action, whereas s 238A will apply if the participation in the industrial action was the reason for the dismissal.

These situations can now be examined in more detail.

Dismissal in connection with a lock-out (TULR(C)A, s 238(I)(a))

21.97 A lock-out is the closing of a place of employment, or a suspension of the work, or the refusal by the employer to continue to employ his employees, done with a view to compelling those employees to accept terms and conditions of or affecting employment (ERA, s 235(4)). A lock-out by an employer is not necessarily a breach of contract by him (*Express and Star Ltd v Bunday*[48]). If an employee claims that he has been dismissed by virtue of the lock-out, an employment tribunal is precluded from determining whether or not such dismissal is fair or unfair unless it can be shown that (a) one or more of the relevant employees were not dismissed, or (b) if they were dismissed, they were re-engaged within three months from the date of dismissal, but the applicant was not offered re-engagement. The relevant employees are those who were directly interested in the dispute on the day of the lock-out (*H Campey & Sons Ltd v Bellwood*[49]).

Dismissal of unofficial strikers (TULR(C)A, s 237)

21.98 An employee who is dismissed after taking part in unofficial industrial action has no right to claim unfair dismissal. Further, if there is mass industrial action that causes enormous disruption to an employer's business, and which requires an immediate and firm response, the employer's policy of dismissing all employees who were absent without leave or explanation, but who then tries to sort out the exceptional cases of genuine non-participation by way of an appeal process, amounts to a reasonable response (*Sehmi v Gate Gourmet London Ltd*[50]).

21.99 A strike or other industrial action will be unofficial unless:

(a) he is a member of the trade union, and the strike or other industrial action was authorised or endorsed by his trade union; or

(b) he is not a member of the trade union, but there are others who are taking part in the strike who are members of the trade union by which the strike or other industrial action has been authorised or endorsed.

21.100 In other words, if some or all of the employees who are taking industrial action are members of a trade union, and the union has not authorised or endorsed the industrial

[48] [1987] ICR 58, [1986] IRLR 477, [1986] LS Gaz R 3591, EAT; revsd [1988] ICR 379, [1987] IRLR 422, CA.
[49] [1987] ICR 311, EAT.   [50] [2009] IRLR 807.

action, any employee who is consequently dismissed will have no claim for unfair dismissal, even if others who took part in the industrial action were not dismissed (s 237). If the trade union authorised or endorses the action, but then repudiates it, the action will become unofficial the next working day after the repudiation takes place. What amounts to a repudiation is set out in s 21 (see para 23.82). Thus an employer could dismiss the ringleaders of an unofficial strike without having to worry about the prospect of defending an unfair dismissal claim, subject to the exception in respect of protected reasons (see para 21.112).

Dismissal in connection with industrial action (s 238(1)(b), (2)(b))

21.101 The third situation applies when none of those who are taking industrial action are members of a trade union. This is not official industrial action, because they are not members of a trade union, nor is it unofficial industrial action, presumably because there is no-one to make it official. It is just industrial action. In these circumstances, if an employee is dismissed while taking part in industrial action, the tribunal shall not determine whether the dismissal was fair or unfair, unless it is shown that:

(a) one or more of the relevant employees (ie, those taking part in the industrial action) were not dismissed, or

(b) that any such employee who was dismissed was offered re-engagement within three months of the claimant's dismissal, but that the claimant was not so offered.

There is no requirement that the offer to re-engage must be in writing (*Marsden v Fairey Stainless Ltd*[51]).

21.102 Whether or not an employee is taking part in a strike or other industrial action must be determined as an objective fact. In other words, the test is 'what is the employee doing or omitting to do?' The subjective knowledge of the employer is not relevant (*Manifold Industries v Sims,* para 13.36).

21.103 An employee who is dismissed for taking part in a strike is not entitled to a redundancy payment, even though it can be shown that a subsequent redundancy situation is revealed. In *Baxter v Limb Group of Companies* (para 18.11), dock workers refused to work overtime following a dispute with the employers over bonus payments. They were dismissed, and subsequently the employers discontinued using direct labour and contracted the work out. The dismissed employees argued that the employers had decided to dispense with direct labour, and had manoeuvred the employees into a position where it appeared that they were dismissed for taking part in a strike or other industrial action, whereas the real reason for the dismissal was redundancy. The Court of Appeal dismissed their claim. The industrial action was the reason for the dismissal and for the decision to use contract labour. TULR(C)A, s 238 prohibits an employment tribunal from considering whether a dismissal is fair or unfair if, at the date of dismissal, the employee *was taking part* in a strike or other industrial action. It does not say that the employee was dismissed *because* he was taking part in such action. In other words, if the dismissals caused the redundancy, a redundancy payment cannot be made (*Sanders v Ernest A Neale Ltd,* para 18.11).

21.104 It will be recalled that a strike is a breach of contract by the employee which entitles the employer to dismiss him. Provided the employer dismisses all the strikers, or offers all of them re-engagement after the strike is over within three months, the employment tribunal has no jurisdiction to hear any complaint. This is the 'no picking and choosing' rule (see *McCormick v Horsepower Ltd*[52]). But if an employer is selective in his dismissals

---

[51] [1979] IRLR 103, EAT.
[52] [1980] ICR 278, [1980] IRLR 182, EAT; aff'd [1981] 2 All ER 746, [1981] 1 WLR 993, [1981] ICR 535, [1981] IRLR 217, 125 Sol Jo 375, CA.

or offers of re-engagement, those employees who have been excluded may bring claims in the employment tribunals. To avoid a finding of unfair dismissal, the employer must show that he has acted reasonably in not taking back those strikers who were not offered re-engagement. The question will be determined by the circumstances, having regard to the equity and substantial merits of the case (*Edwards v Cardiff City Council*[53]).

21.105 Further, the employer can re-engage an employee who has been dismissed for striking any time after three months from the time another striker was dismissed without exposing himself to a claim for unfair dismissal from the latter.

21.106 But if the employer (or an associated employer) re-engages a striker by mistake (eg in ignorance of the fact that he had been on strike) this gives the employment tribunal jurisdiction to consider a claim from a striker who has not been offered re-engagement (*Bigham v GKN Kwikform Ltd*[54]).

21.107 The three-month period is in the nature of a 'cooling off' period, designed to enable industrial disputes to be settled on honourable terms. As long as the offer of re-engagement is made within that period, the employment tribunal has no jurisdiction to hear a claim by a person who does not wish to accept that offer (*Highland Fabricators Ltd v McLaughlin*[55]).

21.108 But the employer will lose the protection of s 238 if he seeks to dismiss before the strike has begun or after the strike is over. In *Heath v Longman (Meat Salesmen) Ltd*[56] employees went out on strike, but subsequently decided to return to work. One of them informed the employer that the strike was over, but when they returned to work they were dismissed. The NIRC held that since they had returned to work, they were no longer on strike, and hence the dismissals were unfair. In *Midland Plastics Ltd v Till*,[57] a letter was sent to the company management stating that unless certain demands were met, industrial action would commence at 11am. At 9.30am, the managing director spoke to four employees, who confirmed that they would abide by the decision, and they were immediately dismissed. It was held that the employment tribunal were not precluded by s 238 from entertaining a complaint of unfair dismissal. The threat to take part in a strike was a mere display of power by one side to a dispute which is a substantial feature of industrial relations negotiations. As the dismissals took place before the strike, s 238 did not apply.

21.109 The offer of re-engagement must be made to the striking employee. A general advertising campaign offering employment to those who apply does not amount to an offer of employment to any particular individual. Such a campaign merely makes available the opportunity to be offered employment (*Crosville Wales Ltd v Tracey*, para 17.231).

21.110 If a dismissal is unfair because the employer has re-engaged some of the strikers contrary to TULR(C)A, s 238, compensation is not to be reduced on the ground of contributory conduct merely because the employees who were not re-engaged took part in the strike. There must have been some other sufficiently blameworthy conduct which makes it just and equitable to reduce their compensation, for example if the strikers' leaders were over-hasty or indulged in inflammatory language. The circumstances of each claimant must be examined to see whether *his* compensation should be reduced because of *his* conduct other than the mere fact that he was on strike (*Tracey v Crosville Wales Ltd*).

---

[53] [1979] IRLR 303, EAT.   [54] [1992] ICR 113, [1992] IRLR 4, EAT.
[55] [1985] ICR 183, [1984] IRLR 482, EAT.
[56] [1973] 2 All ER 1228, [1973] ICR 407, [1973] IRLR 214, 14 KIR 569, 8 ITR 427, NIRC.
[57] [1983] ICR 118, [1983] IRLR 9, 126 Sol Jo 707, EAT.

Official unprotected industrial action

21.111 The fourth situation arises where a trade union calls a strike, but loses the protection of s 219 because:

(a) the strike was to enforce trade union membership (s 222); or

(b) because of the dismissal of unofficial strikers (s 223); or

(c) secondary action was taken (s 224); or

(d) the strike was to impose union recognition requirement (s 225); or

(e) the balloting provisions of ss 226–234 were not complied with; or

(f) notice was not given to the employer (s 234A).

In these circumstances the strike is no longer protected under s 238A (see para 21.112), and hence the dismissal of employees on strike falls to be considered under the 'no picking and choosing' rule in s 238(2) (see para 21.101). The action may be official, but it is not protected industrial action.

Protected industrial action (s 238A)

21.112 Finally, protected industrial action is industrial action in respect of which the trade union will be immune from liability in tort by virtue of TULR(C)A, s 219, and has not lost that immunity by virtue of the above matters. Those who take part in such industrial action have the protections conferred by s 238A, which will arise if the date of dismissal is:

(a) within the protected period, which is the basic period of 12 weeks beginning with the first day of protected industrial action, plus any extension period brought about by an employer lock-out; or

(b) after the end of the protected period, but the employee had ceased to take part in the industrial action before the end of that period; or

(c) after the end of the protected period, but the employer had not taken such procedural steps as would have been reasonable for the purposes of ending the dispute. The procedural steps include complying with agreed procedures, resuming negotiations, unreasonably refusing the use of conciliation or mediation services, etc (s 238A(6)).

21.113 Any such dismissal is automatically unfair, and there is no qualifying period of employment or upper age limit which would otherwise defeat a claim. A claim may be presented before the end of six months from the date of dismissal, with the usual extension of time provisions. It will be equally unfair to select an employee for redundancy if the selection was because the employee took part in protected industrial action as defined in the above three categories (ERA, s 105(7C)). The action taken must be an official strike called by a trade union which itself would be protected under TULR(C)A, s 219 (see Chapter 23). If the union repudiates the official action, and thus the strike changes from being official to unofficial, employees are given a day's grace in which to cease their action, ie if they continue to be on strike beyond the next working day after the day on which the repudiation took place, they will lose their protection of s 238A.

21.114 To determine whether the employer has taken reasonable steps to resolve the dispute, regard shall be had to:

(a) whether the employer or the union have complied with procedures established by any collective agreement or other agreement;

(b) whether the employer or the union offered or agreed to commence or resume negotiations after the start of the protected industrial action;

(c) whether the employer or the union unreasonably refused, after the start of the protected industrial action, a request for conciliation services to be used;

(d) whether the employer or the union unreasonably refused, after the start of the protected industrial action, a request that mediation services be used.

21.115 In determining whether the employer has taken those steps, no regard shall be
had to the merits of the dispute. If there is a dismissal contrary to s 238A, an employment
tribunal cannot make an order for reinstatement or re-engagement until after the conclusion of the protected industrial action. Additional powers are given to tribunals to carry out
pre-hearing reviews and to adjourn proceedings if they become aware that legal actions are
being brought challenging the legitimacy of the industrial action in question.

Exceptions in certain cases (ss 237–238)

21.116 The general principle is that an employee has no right to claim unfair dismissal
if at the time of the dismissal he was taking part in an unofficial strike or other unofficial
industrial action (s 237). However, this does not apply if the reason for the dismissal (or
selection for redundancy) was a protected reason, ie a reason which violates an employee's
rights with respect to pregnancy, maternity or parental leave, health and safety, working
time, employee representative, jury service, dependants, protected disclosure or flexible
working (s 237(1A)).

21.117 Similarly, if an employee believes that he was unable to claim that he was unfairly
dismissed because at the date of the dismissal the employer did not act in violation of the
'picking and choosing' rule, then again, the employee's rights will revive if the reason for the
dismissal was for one of the above reasons.

L. Dismissal due to industrial pressure (ERA, s 107)

21.118 If an employer is forced to dismiss an employee because of actual, or the threat of,
industrial pressure by other employees, this may amount to an unfair dismissal. The reason
is that ERA, s 107 provides that for the purpose of determining whether the employer has
a statutory reason for dismissing, or whether the employer acted reasonably in dismissing,
no account shall be taken of any industrial pressure (ie strike or other industrial action)
which was put on the employer, and the question must be determined as if no such pressure had been exercised. In *Hazell Offsets v Luckett*,[58] the claimant was dismissed from his
managerial post after trade union representatives had indicated that they would not co-
operate with him. Clearly, the principal reason for the dismissal was the industrial pressure,
but this could not be advanced as a reason. Since there was no other reason, the dismissal
was unfair. The tribunal thought that this did not seem right, nor fair, but it was clearly
what Parliament had decided. But if the employee was partly responsible for the threat of
industrial action, this could amount to contributory conduct so as to warrant a reduction
in the compensation awarded. Thus if the industrial pressure is exercised because of some
personal animosity, and the employee is unco-operative in a difficult situation, and, for
example, refuses to move to another job, he may well have contributed to his dismissal
(*Ford Motor Co Ltd v Hudson*[59]).

21.119 However, if on a claim for unfair dismissal the employer or the claimant claims that
the employer was induced to dismiss the claimant because of pressure which a trade union
or other person exercised on him by way of calling, organising, procuring or financing a

---

[58] [1977] IRLR 430, EAT.
[59] [1978] 3 All ER 23, [1978] ICR 482, [1978] IRLR 66, EAT.

strike, or threatening to do so, and the pressure was exercised because the claimant was not a member of any trade union or a particular trade union, then the employer or the claimant may, before the hearing of the complaint, join that person as a party to the proceedings before the employment tribunal. If the latter decides to make an award of compensation in favour of the claimant, but also finds that the employer was induced to dismiss him because of the pressure, the tribunal may make an award against that person instead of the employer, or partly against that person and partly against the employer. The amount shall be such as the tribunal consider to be just and equitable in all the circumstances (TULR(C) A, s 160).

M. Selection for dismissal on grounds of redundancy (TULR(C)A, s 153)

21.120 We have seen that to select a person for dismissal on grounds of redundancy will be unfair if the reason for the selection was his membership or non-membership of a trade union. No qualifying period of continuous employment is required.

N. Compensations for dismissals (TULR(C)A, ss 155–158)

21.121 In respect of compensation for dismissals for trade union membership or non-membership, there are rules relating to a minimum basic award, an additional award, as well as the usual compensation award (see Chapter 17).

O. Interim relief for dismissed trade unionists or non-unionists (TULR(C) A, ss 161–166)

21.122 If an employee considers that he was unfairly dismissed because he was, or proposed to become a member of an independent trade union, or had taken or proposed to take part in the activities of that union, or he was not a member of a trade union, he may present a complaint to an employment tribunal asking for an order that he be reinstated or re-engaged by the employer or, if this cannot be agreed upon, that he be suspended on full pay pending a settlement or a determination of the complaint. The employee must present the complaint before the end of seven days from the effective date of the termination of his employment, and must, if he is claiming he was dismissed because of his trade union membership or activities, accompany his complaint with a certificate signed by an authorised official of the trade union concerned, stating that the employee was or had proposed to become a member, and that there were reasonable grounds for believing that the reason for the dismissal was the one alleged in the complaint. The signature of a trade union official is prima facie evidence that he is duly authorised to sign the certificate, but if this is challenged, the onus is on the employee to show that the official had actual or implied authority to sign it (*Sulemany v Habib Bank Ltd*[60]).

21.123 The tribunal will give the employer seven days' notice before the hearing, but shall thereupon hear the complaint as soon as is practicable. If the tribunal comes to the conclusion that it is likely that it would uphold a complaint of unfair dismissal on one of the above grounds, it shall announce this preliminary finding and explain to the parties its powers. It will then ask the employer if he is willing to reinstate the employee, or re-engage him on terms and conditions which are no less favourable than he formerly enjoyed, pending the determination or settlement of the complaint. If the employer is willing to re-engage the employee in another job, and specifies the terms and conditions, the tribunal will ask the employee if he is willing to accept, and if so, an order to that effect will be made.

[60] [1983] ICR 60, EAT.

If the employee is unwilling to accept the job on those terms and conditions, then, if his refusal is reasonable, the tribunal will make an order for the continuation of his contract of employment, but if his refusal is regarded as being unreasonable, no order will be made. If the employer fails to attend the hearing, or states that he is unwilling to reinstate or re-engage the employee, the tribunal will make an order for the continuation of the employee's contract of employment.

21.124 The effect of an order for continuation of the contract of employment is that if the employment has ceased, it will continue in force, or if it has not yet ceased, it will continue when it does so cease, until, in either case, the determination or settlement of the complaint, for the purposes of pay, seniority, pension rights, and other similar rights, and for determining for any purpose the period for which the employee has been continuously employed. The tribunal will also specify the pay due to the employee from the time of dismissal until the complaint is finally settled, but it will take into account any lump sum received in lieu of wages. At any time after making the order and before the determination by the tribunal, the employer or the employee may apply for a revocation or variation of the order on the ground that there has been a relevant change in circumstances. Also, the employee may apply to the tribunal on the ground that the employer has not complied with the terms of the order. If his complaint is that the employer has not paid the amount specified, the tribunal will determine the amount due, and make it as a separate award for any other sum it gives by way of compensation. If the complaint relates to any other breach by the employer, then it shall make an award of compensation as it thinks just and equitable having regard to the loss suffered by the complainant.

21.125 An order for continuation of employment merely preserves the employee's rights; the employer does not have to permit him to come back to work, or to allow him on the premises.

21.126 On an application for interim relief, the employment tribunal must decide if the claimant can establish that he has a good chance of succeeding at a full hearing. This is a higher degree of certainty than a mere reasonable chance of success. 'Likely' means more than 'probable', and probable itself suggests more than an even chance (*Taplin v C Shippam Ltd*[61]).

21.127 It will be extremely rare that an employer will admit that a person was dismissed because he engaged in trade union activity, and doubtless some other reason will be advanced. In *Forsyth v Fry's Metals Ltd*[62] the tribunal considered the evidence under four headings: (a) the extent of the alleged behaviour, (b) the extent of the employer's dissatisfaction with the employee, (c) the coincidence in time between the alleged behaviour and the initial steps taken towards dismissal, and (d) the coincidence in time between the behaviour and the actual dismissal. In this case, the claimant was dismissed for alleged poor work performance. There was little direct evidence of this; on the other hand he had been instrumental in persuading most of the employees to join a trade union, and had been elected shop steward. On the facts, there was a likelihood that he would succeed in establishing his claim, and interim relief was granted.

21.128 On an application for interim relief, it is possible to join a person who is exercising pressure to bring about the dismissal (see TULR(C)A, s 160), and such a person shall be given notice of the time, date and place of the hearing as soon as reasonably practicable (s 162(3)).

---

[61] [1978] ICR 1068, EAT.   [62] [1977] IRLR 243.

22

The Law Relating to Trade Unions

22.1 In this chapter we shall concentrate on the law as it affects the running of a trade union. All the relevant law is consolidated by the Trade Union and Labour Relations (Consolidation) Act 1992, as amended. In so far as earlier reported decisions were based on provisions in earlier (now replaced) legislation, references to the relevant statutory provisions have, for the sake of convenience, been transposed to the corresponding provisions of the 1992 Act.

What constitutes a trade union?

A. Definition of a trade union (TULR(C)A, s 1)

22.2 A trade union is an organisation (whether permanent or temporary) which either:

- (a) consists wholly or mainly of workers of one or more descriptions and whose principal purposes include the regulation of relations between workers and employers or employers' associations; or
- (b) consists wholly or mainly of:
    - (i) constituent or affiliated organisations which have those purposes; or
    - (ii) representatives of such constituent or affiliated organisations, and in either case whose principal purposes include the regulation of relations between workers and employers or workers' and employers' associations, or include the regulation of relations between the constituent or affiliated organisations.

This definition discloses two functional bodies:

- (a) a single trade union; and
- (b) confederated organisations, such as the Trades Union Congress.

22.3 Whether or not a trade union has a 'legal personality' of its own was always a matter of some controversy. Section 10 provides that a trade union shall not be a body corporate, but shall nonetheless be capable of making contracts, suing and being sued in its own name, and capable of being prosecuted for any offences committed in its name. As, however, it has no 'legal' existence, property must be held by its trustees, and any judgment, order or award shall be enforced against the property held by the trustees. This does not apply to those organisations which were on the special register created by the Industrial Relations Act 1971 (see TULR(C)A, s 117) for these were professional organisations which engaged in collective bargaining on behalf of their members, and their legal personality stemmed from their charter of incorporation, or by virtue of incorporation under the Companies Acts. Such legal personality is to continue (about 12 such professional bodies are on the special register), but other than these, any registration by a trade union under the Companies Acts, or as a friendly society or an industrial and provident society, is void.

22.4 Between 1901 and 1971, a series of legal decisions had laid down that a trade union had some form of quasi-legal personality, but this status has been clearly removed by s 10.

In *Electrical, Electronic Telecommunications and Plumbing Union v Times Newspapers*,[1] it was held that a trade union, not having a legal personality, could not therefore sue for libel in respect of its reputation, for s 10 states that a trade union shall not be 'or treated as if it were', a body corporate, and hence the claimant trade union did not have the personality which could be protected by an action for defamation.

B. Listing of trade unions (TULR(C)A, s 2)

22.5 The certification officer (a post created in 1975 by the Employment Protection Act – see Chapter 1) has taken over and maintains a list of trade union organisations which were formerly held by the Registrar of Friendly Societies (s 257). On this list there will be organisations which were registered under the pre-1971 law (or formed as a result of an amalgamation of two or more bodies which were registered), all organisations registered under the Industrial Relations Act 1971, and all TUC affiliated trade unions. Any organisation (including employers' associations) which is not listed may apply for inclusion, submitting the appropriate fee, a copy of its rules, a list of officers, the address of its head office, and details of its name. The certification officer will refuse to enter on the list any organisation the name of which is the same as a previously registered or listed organisation, or a name which so closely resembles any such organisation as to be likely to deceive the public. If it appears to the certification officer that an organisation whose name is on the list is not a trade union he may remove it from the list, but not without giving notice of his intention to do so, and considering any representations which may be made. An organisation which is aggrieved by the decision of the certification officer to refuse to enter it on the list, or a decision to remove it from the list, may appeal either on a question of law or of fact, to the Employment Appeal Tribunal. Copies of the list shall be available for public inspection.

22.6 There are certain advantages of being a 'listed' trade union. First, it is evidence (but not conclusive evidence) that the body concerned satisfied the statutory definition. Second, there are procedural advantages in connection with the passing of property consequent on the change of trustees. Third, and perhaps the most significant of all, only a listed trade union can apply for a certificate of independence.

C. Certification of trade unions (TULR(C)A, s 6)

22.7 Any trade union which is on the list may apply to the certification officer for a certificate that it is an independent trade union. A union is independent if:

(a) it is not under the domination or control of an employer or groups of employers or an employers' association; and

(b) it is not liable to interference by an employer or any such group or association arising out of the provision of financial or material support or by any other means whatsoever tending towards such control (s 5).

If, after making enquiries the certification officer decides that the union is independent he will issue a certificate accordingly; otherwise he will refuse to do so, but must give reasons for his refusal. Even if he grants the certificate, he may withdraw it if he is of the opinion that the union is no longer independent, but he must notify the trade union concerned of his intention, and may take into account any relevant information supplied by any person. An appeal will lie on a point of law or fact to the Employment Appeal Tribunal against the decision of the certification officer to refuse to grant, or to withdraw, a certificate.

---

[1] [1980] QB 585, [1980] 1 All ER 1097, [1980] 3 WLR 98, 124 Sol Jo 31.

22.8 Only a trade union aggrieved by the decision not to grant a certificate may appeal. There is no general right of appeal by anyone who is aggrieved. In *General and Municipal Workers Union v Certification Officer*,[2] a trade union objected to a decision of the Certification Officer to grant a certificate to another organisation, but it was held that the trade union had no right to appeal against that decision.

22.9 Once granted, the certificate is conclusive evidence of the independence of the trade union, and in any proceedings before any court, the Employment Appeal Tribunal, the Central Arbitration Committee, or an employment tribunal, where the independence of the trade union is in issue and there is no certificate in force and no refusal, withdrawal or cancellation recorded, the proceedings shall be stayed until a certificate has been issued or refused by the certification officer.

22.10 To understand the arguments about certification, it is necessary to make a short excursus into industrial relations. Some years ago there was an expansion of unionisation, particular among the so-called 'white collar' workers and management. A considerable number of staff associations sprang up in order to exercise the sort of industrial pressure hitherto reserved for the blue collar workers. These staff associations are looked upon as not being 'proper' trade unions, and are sometimes referred to in a derogatory tone as being 'sweetheart unions' or 'house unions'. The test of independence for certification purposes is to permit through the net those unions which can demonstrate that they are truly independent, and not just the tame adjuncts of management. A considerable number of such staff associations have applied for and obtained certificates of independence; many have not bothered, on the ground that they can obtain by negotiation all the advantages which certification confers. Those that have succeeded in obtaining a certificate are criticised for bringing about a proliferation of trade unions (at a time when a reduction in the number of unions is thought to be desirable) and for not joining in with the existing established (ie TUC) trade unions.

22.11 The first case to be challenged under this branch of the law was *Blue Circle Staff Association v Certification Officer*.[3] In 1971 the staff association was formed for salaried staff at the instigation of higher management. Subsequently, changes were made to the association's constitution and an application was made for certification. It was held by the EAT that the certification officer was right in his refusal to grant a certificate. The association had not yet attained the freedom from domination by the employer under which it had lived since its formation. There is a heavy burden to show that it had shaken off such paternal control.

22.12 A different view of the realities of the scene was taken in *Association of HSD (Hatfield) Employees v Certification Officer*,[4] where the association was formed with the active encouragement of the employers, who shared the opposition of the association to proposals for nationalisation. After the decision to nationalise was taken, the new head of the industry visited the factory, and was met by a hostile demonstration organised by the association. A subsequent application for a certificate of independence was refused by the certification officer, and the association appealed to the EAT. It was held that the certificate should be granted. Under s 5(a) the organisation must show that it is not under the domination or control of the employer. This involves an examination of the factual situation, including finance, the extent (if any) of employer assistance or interference, the history, rules, organisation, membership base and general attitude. Under s 5(b) there is inevitably a degree of speculation, but the certification officer ought not to be unduly

---

[2] [1977] 1 All ER 771, [1977] ICR 183, 120 Sol Jo 736, EAT.
[3] [1977] 2 All ER 145, [1977] 1 WLR 239, [1977] ICR 224, [1977] IRLR 20, 121 Sol Jo 52, EAT.
[4] [1978] ICR 21, [1977] IRLR 261, EAT.

anxious about future possibilities as he always has the power to revoke the certificate if he thinks he should do so. On the facts of the case, the EAT was clearly impressed by the hostile demonstration, and held that as the association had demonstrated that it was 'fiercely independent of management' a certificate should be granted.

22.13 The fact that an association is company-based is not fatal to the association's independence, for there are many trade unions in industry which negotiate with a single employer (eg the Post Office, or civil service unions). Nor is the fact that the employer makes facilities available to a trade union destructive of its independence, for this may be seen as good industrial relations practice, and is in accordance with the Code of Practice on Time Off for Trade Union Duties and Activities. In *Squibb UK Staff Association v Certification Officer*,[5] a certificate of independence was refused because of fears of vulnerability to employer interference. This was based largely on the extensive facilities which were provided by the employer, which included time off with pay for the officials of the association when performing their duties, free use of office accommodation and rooms for meetings, the provision of free stationery, free use of the employer's telephone, photocopying and internal mailing system, and a free check-off system. In view of the obvious limited resources of the association, and its narrow membership base, the certification officer thought that it would be very difficult to function effectively if these were withdrawn by the employer. The EAT held that nonetheless the certificate should be granted, but this decision was reversed by the Court of Appeal, and the original ruling of the certification officer was confirmed. The test of 'liability to interference' by the employer, which would be fatal to the association's independence, meant vulnerable to, or at risk of, interference. The degree of the likelihood of the risk was irrelevant as long as it was not insignificant.

22.14 If the continued existence of the staff association is dependent on the approval of the employer, then it is 'liable to interference' and hence cannot be an independent trade union (*Government Communications Staff Federation v Certification Officer*[6]).

22.15 The purpose of the organisation is important too – if its primary aim is merely to help provide representation at disciplinary and grievance hearings then it is not a trade union as it does not have as its principal purpose the regulation of relations between workers and employers (*Akinosun (on behalf of General & Health Workers Union) v The Certification Officer*[7]).

Advantages of certification

22.16 There are a number of advantages in having a certificate of independence, which benefit the union, its officials (including shop stewards) and members, as follows:

(a) a member is entitled not to suffer a detriment (TULR(C)A, s 146(1)) or to be dismissed (s 152(1)) on grounds of trade union membership or activities, or making use of trade union services (s 152(1)). Interim relief is also available (s 161);

(b) an independent trade union may negotiate a dismissal procedure agreement which will replace individual statutory rights (ERA, s 110);

(c) an independent trade union may negotiate away the right of employees to strike (TULR(C)A, s 180);

(d) an independent trade union may negotiate a collective agreement modifying or derogating from rights contained in the Working Time Regulations, the Fixed-Term

---

[5] [1978] ICR 115, [1977] IRLR 355, EAT; revsd [1979] 2 All ER 452, [1979] 1 WLR 523, [1979] ICR 235, [1979] IRLR 75, 123 Sol Jo 352, CA.

[6] [1993] ICR 163, [1993] IRLR 260, [1993] 5 LS Gaz R 41, EAT.   [7] UKEAT/0180/13/RN.

Employees (Prevention of Less Favourable Treatment) Regulations 2002, and replace the statutory default scheme on parental leave under the Maternity and Parental Leave etc Regulations 1999;

(e) an official or member of an independent trade union can act as an independent adviser for the purpose of compromise agreements (ERA, s 203(3A));

(f) an independent trade union will be able to receive money from the Secretary of State under the trade union modernisation scheme.

22.17 If the independent trade union is recognised by the employer for collective bargaining purposes, then:

(a) it has the right to receive information for collective bargaining purposes (TULR(C)A, s 181);

(b) it has the right to be consulted on redundancies (TULR(C)A, s 188) and proposed transfers (Transfer of Undertakings (Protection of Employment) Regulations 2006);

(c) an official of the union is entitled to paid time off work for trade union duties, and unpaid time off work for trade union activities and to act as a union learning representative (TULR(C)A, ss 168–170);

(d) the union can appoint safety representatives under the Health and Safety at Work Act 1974, s 2;

(e) representatives of an independent trade union can act as employee representatives for the purpose of the Transnational Information and Consultation of Employees Regulations 1999, European Public Limited-Liability (Employee Involvement) (Great Britain) Regulations 2009, Companies (Cross-Border Mergers) Regulations 2007;

(f) the union is entitled to receive information from an employer concerning occupational pension schemes (Pension Schemes Act 1993);

(g) the union will be entitled to receive information on recent and probable development of the undertaking's activities under the Information and Consultation Regulations (see para 23.142).

D. Register of members (s 24)

22.18 A trade union shall maintain a register of the names and addresses of its members. The register shall be accurate, up to date, and may be kept by means of a computer.

22.19 A member is entitled to know whether there is an entry in the register relating to him, and be supplied with a copy of that entry. The person who has been appointed as an independent scrutineer for election purposes must also be permitted to inspect the register and be provided with an up-to-date copy of it (see para 22.50).

Confidentiality of the register of members (s 24A)

22.20 A trade union shall impose a duty of confidentiality on the independent scrutineer who has been appointed to oversee any ballot held on an election for office, political resolution or resolution to approve an instrument of amalgamation or transfer. The scrutineer or independent person must not disclose any name or address on the register (except in permitted circumstances), and must take all reasonable steps to ensure that no such disclosure takes place. Disclosure will be permitted (a) when the member consents, (b) where required for the purposes of the discharge of functions by the certification officer or of the scrutineer under the terms of his appointment, or (c) where required for the purpose of investigating crime or of criminal proceedings.

Remedies (ss 25-26)

22.21 A member of a trade union who claims that the union has failed to comply with ss 24 or 24A may apply to the certification officer for a declaration to that effect (s 25), or, in the alternative, to the court (s 26). The certification officer can make an enforcement order requiring the union to remedy the breach and/or abstain from acts which might lead to a future recurrence of the same breach. Any member of the union (who was a member at the time of the declared failure) may apply to the court to force the union to comply with the order. An appeal against the decision of the certification officer may be made to the EAT.

Membership of a trade union

22.22 In principle, it is for the trade union to lay down the description of persons who are eligible to join, and this will usually be laid down in the union's rules (*Boulting v Association of Cinematograph, Television and Allied Technicians*, para 21.5). It follows that it cannot accept for membership someone who is not within the prescribed class, and cannot create a category of membership not provided for in the rules (*Martin v Scottish Transport and General Workers' Union*[8]). The rules may also specify a class of person who is not eligible to join (*Faramus v Film Artistes' Association*, para 21.5). However, a trade union cannot exclude a person from membership on arbitrary and unreasonable grounds (*Nagle v Feilden*, paras 10.16, 21.5 and 21.7), nor can it discriminate against someone on the grounds set out in the Equality Act 2010 (although positive action is permitted in certain respects in section 158 of that Act).

22.23 However, notwithstanding anything contained in the union's rules, a person cannot be excluded (or expelled) from a trade union unless this is permitted by the provisions of TULR(C)A, s 174 (see para 21.2), and a person who is so excluded or expelled has the right to bring a complaint before an industrial tribunal or the EAT as appropriate.

22.24 There is no statutory definition of who is a 'member' of a trade union, and the term has to be looked at in its context. Thus, if a trade union has a class of 'limited members', who have restricted rights, precisely defined in the union's rules, then they may not be 'members' for the purpose of voting in certain elections (eg on a proposal for the transfer of engagements, see *National Union of Mineworkers (Yorkshire Area) v Millward*[9]).

Rules of a trade union

22.25 At common law, a trade union was tainted with illegality because its rules and/or objects were in 'restraint of trade'. In the nineteenth century this led to certain problems; the trade unionists were prosecuted for criminal conspiracy, and the rules of the unions were generally unenforceable. The effect of the doctrine against restraint of trade on trade unions, was nullified by the 1871 Trade Union Act (see now TULR(C)A, s 11), which provides that the purposes of a trade union or an employers' association shall not, by reason of being in restraint of trade, make any member liable for criminal conspiracy, or make any agreement or trust void or voidable, nor shall the rules be unlawful or unenforceable by virtue of their being in restraint of trade (see *Goring v British Actors Equity Association*[10]). This also applies to incorporated employers' associations and special register bodies in so far as the purposes or rules relate to the regulation of relations between employers or employers' organisations and workers. It should be noted that Art 11 of the European Convention on

---

[8] [1952] 1 All ER 691, 96 Sol Jo 212, [1952] 1 TLR 677, 1952 SLT 224, HL.
[9] [1995] ICR 482, [1995] IRLR 411, EAT.   [10] [1987] IRLR 122.

Human Rights guarantees the right to freedom of association. Since the Convention now applies in the United Kingdom by virtue of the Human Rights Act 1998 (see para 1.104) it is arguable that the common law doctrine that trade unions are unlawful organisations (by virtue of having objects which are in restraint of trade) is no longer good law.

22.26 As long as a trade union complies with the various statutory requirements, there are no general restrictions on the rules which it may adopt. But the rules constitute a contract between the union and its members, and must be strictly observed.

A. **Disciplinary action**

22.27 If the trade union wishes to take disciplinary action, by way of fines or forfeitures, or wishes to expel a member, such powers must be contained in the rules, otherwise they cannot be exercised. In *Spring v National Amalgamated Stevedores and Dockers' Society*[11] the plaintiff was enrolled as a member of the defendant union contrary to the Bridlington Agreement, which was designed to prevent poaching of members among TUC affiliated unions. The TUC ordered the union to expel the members, which it did, but the expulsion was held to be void when it was discovered that the union rules contained no power of expulsion.

22.28 However, it is possible for the court to imply into the union's rules a power to discipline a member, although since such a power is penal and could involve serious consequences which would affect the reputation and livelihood of the member, an implied disciplinary power would only arise when there are compelling circumstances to justify it. In *McVitae v UNISON*[12] the claimant was a member of the National and Local Government Officers' Association (NALGO). Various complaints of intimidation, oppressive and sexist conduct were made against him and disciplinary proceedings were arranged. However, before they could take place, NALGO amalgamated with two other unions, to form Unison, and, following an investigation into the original complaints, Unison decided to re-institute the disciplinary proceedings. The claimant sought an injunction to prevent Unison from taking disciplinary action against him in respect of conduct which occurred prior to the union coming into existence.

There was no power in the instrument of amalgamation or the rules of the new union to discipline members in respect of conduct which occurred before its inception, but in the circumstances of the case, the court was prepared to imply such a power. The conduct in question was contrary to the rules of NALGO and Unison, and it could not have been intended that there should be a complete amnesty for conduct which occurred before the new union was created out of the amalgamation of the three unions.

22.29 If the rules specify the grounds on which disciplinary action may be taken, then the union must adhere to these grounds, and not proceed on others. Moreover, the courts have in the past exercised the power to interpret the rules of the union in accordance with the courts' understanding of the rules, not the union's. In *Lee v Showmen's Guild*,[13] the claimant was expelled from the defendant guild for violating a rule designed to prevent 'unfair competition'. It was held that since the guild had misconstrued the meaning of this term, the court could substitute its own interpretation, and the expulsion was declared void. The interpretative power is particularly important in those cases where the rules are somewhat vague (eg 'conduct detrimental to the union' in *Kelly v National Society of Operative Printers' Assistants*[14]), although the legitimate interests of the union will be upheld. In *Evans v National Union of Printing, Bookbinding and Paperworkers*,[15] the rules provided that a member who

---

[11] [1956] 2 All ER 221, [1956] 1 WLR 585, [1956] 1 Lloyd's Rep 331, 100 Sol Jo 401.
[12] [1996] IRLR 33.   [13] [1952] 2 QB 329, [1952] 1 All ER 1175, 96 Sol Jo 296, [1952] 1 TLR 1115, CA.
[14] (1915) 84 LJKB 2236, 59 Sol Jo 716, 113 LT 1055, 31 TLR 632, CA.   [15] [1938] 4 All ER 51.

acted contrary to the interests of the union might be expelled. The claimant absented himself from work on several occasions, contrary to an agreement between the union and the employers. As a result of such conduct, he was expelled. It was held that the expulsion was valid, for it was designed to uphold the success of the collective bargaining arrangements.

22.30 If the union rules provide for a procedure to be adopted in disciplinary cases, then that procedure must be strictly adhered to, and the smallest irregularity will be as fatal as the greatest. The rules cannot be so framed as to oust the jurisdiction of the courts by declaring that the decision of the union shall be final and binding (*Chapple v Electrical Trades Union*[16]), and if there is an appeal procedure which is denied to the aggrieved member, the expulsion will be invalid (*Braithwaite v Electrical Electronics and Telecommunications Union*[17]). If the expulsion is void because of lack of authority or some other reason, then, as the appeal procedure cannot cure the defect, the aggrieved member may apply to the courts nonetheless, without exhausting the internal machinery. In *Porter v National Union of Journalists*,[18] the union called a strike of provincial journalists without holding a ballot as required by its rules. An injunction was granted to restrain the union from taking disciplinary action against those members who refused to comply with the instruction, for the strike call was unconstitutional.

22.31 Although the statutory requirements that a trade union must act in accordance with the rules of natural justice have been repealed, it is submitted that the common law position remains unchanged. This means that a trade union, in the exercise of what is essentially a quasi-judicial function, cannot expel a member without giving him a hearing, notifying him of the charges against him, and giving him an opportunity to rebut them (*Lawlor v Union of Post Office Workers*[19]). It also means that the officials of the union should avoid being placed in the position of being prosecutor, judge and jury. In *Taylor v National Union of Seamen*,[20] the general secretary of the union dismissed the claimant for insubordination. When the claimant appealed to the executive council, the general secretary was the chairman of the meeting, and after the claimant had withdrawn, the meeting was treated to a long statement of matters which were not the subject of the charge, but which were prejudicial to him, and he had no opportunity of rebutting. It was held that the hearing of the appeal offended against the rules of natural justice.

22.32 However, the withdrawal of a privilege, granted outside the rules is not disciplinary action. In *Hudson v GMB*,[21] a federated trade union nominated the claimant to attend a regional conference of the Labour Party. It was then alleged that she was a member of 'Militant', an organisation proscribed by the Labour Party, and so her nomination was withdrawn. She claimed that this was disciplinary action in violation of the rules of the union, as she had not been allowed to state her case. Further, she claimed that her nomination was a privilege which could not be withdrawn without proceedings taken in accordance with the principles of natural justice. Her claim failed. The withdrawal of the nomination was not a disciplinary measure relating to an office within the union's rules. Nor was the nomination made in respect of any permanent position which would involve a financial advantage. The union had no rules concerning such delegates, and the nomination could therefore be withdrawn at will.

22.33 A member who has been wrongfully expelled may apply for a declaration that he is still a member, an injunction restraining the union and its officials from acting on the

---

[16] [1961] 3 All ER 612, [1961] 1 WLR 1290, 105 Sol Jo 723.
[17] [1969] 2 All ER 859, 6 KIR 169, 113 Sol Jo 305, CA.   [18] [1979] IRLR 404, CA; aff'd [1980] IRLR 404, HL.
[19] [1965] Ch 712, [1965] 1 All ER 353, [1965] 2 WLR 579.
[20] [1967] 1 All ER 767, [1967] 1 WLR 532, [1966] 2 Lloyd's Rep 504, 111 Sol Jo 192.   [21] [1990] IRLR 67.

purported expulsion, and damages for wrongful expulsion. In *Bonsor v Musicians' Union*,[22] the appellant was expelled by the branch secretary, when this power could only be exercised by the branch committee. In consequence, he could not get work, and was reduced to earning a living by scraping rust off Brighton Pier. It was held that as the expulsion was void, he could recover damages for wrongful expulsion.

22.34 In addition (as already indicated) whatever the rules may or may not state, a member of a trade union has a statutory right not to be unjustifiably disciplined (see para 21.8) or expelled from a trade union (see para 21.2) unless the discipline or expulsion is not prohibited by the statute, and may seek an appropriate remedy before an employment tribunal.

B. Conduct of union affairs

22.35 Membership of a trade union confers certain rights and privileges on the members, and they are entitled to damages if these are not forthcoming. If the rules provide that members shall be entitled to legal advice, then a union which fails to provide that advice, or negligently provides incorrect advice, may be sued for the loss which flows from that breach. The tremendous increase in the statutory rights of employees is bound to throw an additional burden on trade union officials, who now need to be as familiar with those rights as management. Thus it is submitted that if a trade union fails to apply for a protective award in appropriate circumstances, or negligently delays the presentation of a claim to an employment tribunal so that it becomes out of time, the aggrieved member will have a right of action against that union for damages. No breach of contract arises if the member fails to show that his action had a reasonable prospect of success (*Buckley v National Union of General and Municipal Workers*[23]), and in any case the union can fulfil the duty to use ordinary care and skill by handing over a potential claim to a firm of competent solicitors (*Friend v Institution of Professional Managers and Specialists*[24]).

22.36 In the conduct of union affairs, the officials can only act within the confines of the rules. Thus in *Weakley v Amalgamated Union of Engineering Workers*[25] the president of the union exercised a casting vote on a motion when the committee was equally divided. An injunction was granted restraining the union from acting on the motion, for, on a true construction of the rules, the president was not entitled to exercise a casting vote. But the officials may have implied power to do certain things which are in the interests of the union. In *Hill v Archbold*,[26] two union officials brought an action in respect of matters which arose out of their employment. The actions were dismissed, but the union sought to pay the legal costs on behalf of the officials, though there was no provision in the rules for such expenditure. It was held that the union had implied power to do so, for the matter was incidental to their work as officials of the union.

22.37 A trade union which pays out strike pay which is not authorised by the rules (*Taylor v National Union of Mineworkers (Derbyshire Area)*[27]) or imposes a levy for a purpose which is ultra vires (*Hopkins v National Union of Seamen*[28]) can be restrained from so doing by an injunction. However, allegations of electoral irregularities can be pursued under the provisions of s 54 (see para 22.55).

---

[22] [1954] Ch 479, [1954] 1 All ER 822, 98 Sol Jo 248, CA; revsd [1956] AC 104, [1955] 3 All ER 518, [1955] 3 WLR 788, 99 Sol Jo 814, HL.

[23] [1967] 3 All ER 767, 112 Sol Jo 292.   [24] [1999] IRLR 173.   [25] (1975) 125 NLJ 621.

[26] [1967] 2 QB 418, [1967] 1 All ER 1038, [1967] 2 WLR 1180, 111 Sol Jo 193; aff'd [1968] 1 QB 686, [1967] 3 All ER 110, [1967] 3 WLR 1218, 111 Sol Jo 543, CA.

[27] [1984] IRLR 440.   [28] [1985] ICR 268, [1985] IRLR 157.

22.38 A problem arises when a trade union takes action that benefits a majority of its members, but the end result is a detriment to a minority. In *GMB v Allen*[29] the union encouraged its members to agree to the settlement of an equal pay claim against a local authority, based on its policy to promote single status pay, preservation of jobs, and pay protection for those losing out. However, the end result was to seriously undervalue the claims of a number of women. The latter brought claims against the union alleging sex discrimination, claims that were upheld by the Court of Appeal. It was held that the striking of a deal by a trade union with a local authority, which established a single status common pay and grading structure, was indirectly discriminatory of women, since it applied a provision, criterion or practice that applied equally to men but was detrimental to a large number of women. Although the deal attempted to achieve compensation for some union members for past inequality as well as providing ongoing pay and employment protection for all members, which were legitimate aims, the means adopted by the union included mis-selling and manipulation, and were not therefore proportionate to the union's legitimate aim of achieving single status with a minimum of losers.

C. **Copy of the rules (s 27)**

22.39 A trade union shall supply, at the request of any person, a copy of its rules, either free or on payment of a reasonable charge.

Executive committee (TULR(C)A, s 46)

22.40 Every member of the principal executive committee of a trade union (including those members who are members by virtue of holding an office) shall be elected by a ballot at least every five years. A person who holds his membership of the principal executive committee as a result of an election may continue as a member or official for such period as may be necessary (not exceeding six months) to give effect to an election result. In such a ballot, every member of the union shall be entitled to vote, except:

(a) those members who as a class are excluded by the rules from voting;

(b) members not in employment;

(c) members in arrears; and

(d) members who are students, trainees, apprentices or new members.

If the rules permit, it is possible to have voting restricted to special classes of membership, determined by reference to:

(a) trade or occupation;

(b) geographical area;

(c) separate sections of the union; or

(d) any combination of these.

Voting at an election must be made by the marking of a ballot paper by the person voting, and every person entitled to vote (a) must be allowed to do so without interference or constraint imposed by the union or any of its members, officials or employees, and (b) so far as is reasonably practicable, be able to do so without incurring any direct cost. So far as is reasonably practicable, voting papers must be sent to voters by post, containing or

---

[29] [2007] IRLR 752, (2007) 104(33) LSG 26, (2007) 151 SJLB 1129, EAT.

accompanied by a list of candidates, and the voter must be given a convenient opportunity to vote by post. So far as is reasonably practicable, voting shall be in secret, and the result shall be determined by the counting of the number of votes cast for each candidate (with or without the transferable vote) and votes shall be fairly and accurately counted.

22.41 These provisions do not apply to trade unions which consist of representatives of constituent or affiliated organisations, merchant seamen who are ordinarily resident outside the United Kingdom, newly formed trade unions, or to members of the principal executive committee who are near retirement.

22.42 The president and general secretary (or persons who hold equivalent positions) shall be deemed to be members of the principal executive committee (and hence subject to the balloting provisions) as will be any other persons, notwithstanding anything in the rules of the union, if they are permitted to attend and speak at the meeting of that committee, other than for the purpose of providing the committee with factual information or technical or professional advice.

22.43 However, a person who is the president or general secretary of the union, and who is neither a voting member of the principal executive committee, nor an employee of the union, is not required to be elected in the above manner if he holds his office for a period of less than 13 months. Nor does the president need to be re-elected if he has been elected within the previous five years to the post of general secretary or member of the executive.

22.44 Elections for the members of the principal executive committee shall be by means of postal ballot, but there is no need to hold a ballot if the election is uncontested. If voting is done by means of a transferable vote system, and the same number of votes are cast for the final candidates, there is an implied term in the union's rules that the candidate with the most first-choice votes shall be declared the winner, especially if this method has been used as a tie-breaker in the past (*AB v CD*[30]).

A. **Election of candidates (TULR(C)A, s 47)**

22.45 No member of a trade union may be unreasonably excluded from standing as a candidate for election to any position unless he belongs to a class of which all members are excluded by the rules of the union. The rules of the union may give the executive committee of the union a discretion to decide certain prescribed qualifications for a union post, but not having the confidence of the executive committee is not a qualification (*Ecclestone v National Union of Journalists*[31]). No candidate shall be required to be a member of any political party.

If there is a tie between two candidates in a union election, and there is no express mechanism for resolving the tie, a tie-breaker must be implied into the union's rules (*AB v CD*).

B. **Election addresses (TULR(C)A, s 48)**

22.46 Every candidate in an election for the principal executive committee must be provided with an opportunity of preparing an election address, in his own words, and submitting it to the union to be distributed to those who are entitled to vote. Such election addresses are to be sent out with the voting paper, and the candidates are not required to bear any expense for the production of these copies. The election address shall be sent out without any modification except at the request of or with the consent of the candidate, or where the modification is necessarily incidental to the method adopted for the production

---

[30] [2001] IRLR 808, [2001] All ER (D) 354 (May).   [31] [1999] IRLR 166.

of the copy. The same method of production is to be used for the election addresses of all candidates. A trade union may determine that election addresses may not exceed a certain length (but must permit a minimum of 100 words), and may incorporate only such photographs or other matter as the union may determine. So far as is reasonably practicable, the union must ensure that the same facilities and restrictions with respect to the preparation, submission, length and modifications, and the incorporation of photographs or other matter not in words are provided or applied equally to each of the candidates.

22.47 No person other than the candidate himself shall be subject to any criminal or civil liability in respect of the publication of a candidate's election address made under s 48.

C. Independent scrutineer (ss 49, 75, 100A, 226B)

22.48 Before an election is held for positions in the principal executive committee, or a ballot is held on the approval of a political fund, or approving an instrument of amalgamation or transfer, or a ballot on the holding of industrial action, the trade union must appoint a qualified independent person as a scrutineer, who will carry out his functions without interference. A person will be eligible for such appointment if he satisfies the conditions laid down in the Trade Union Ballots and Elections (Independent Scrutineers' Qualifications) Order 1988–2010.

22.49 However, a scrutineer need not be appointed if there is a ballot on the holding of industrial action, and the number of members entitled to vote does not exceed 50 (s 226C).

22.50 The union will supply the scrutineer with a copy of the register of members, which he will inspect as appropriate, and in particular if requested to do so by a member or candidate who suspects that it was not accurate or up to date. The name of the independent scrutineer must be sent to every member of the union by notice, or communicated to members in the same manner as when matters of general interest are brought to their attention. His name must also appear on any ballot paper.

22.51 The storage, distribution and counting of ballot papers must be undertaken by an independent person, who may be the scrutineer or other person whose competence and independence is not in doubt (s 51A). The scrutineer must supervise the production and distribution of all voting papers, which are to be returned to him by those voting. He will retain them for one year after the announcement of the result of the election or ballot or, if the result is challenged before the certification officer or a court, until disposal is authorised.

22.52 As soon as is reasonably practicable after the last date for the return of the voting papers, the scrutineer shall make a report to the union, stating:

(a) the number of voting papers distributed;

(b) the number of voting papers returned to him;

(c) the number of valid votes cast in the election for each candidate, or, in a ballot, for each proposition;

(d) the number of invalid or spoiled votes returned; and

(e) the name of the person (if any) appointed as an independent person to count the votes.

22.53 The report will also state if he is satisfied that there was no contravention of any requirement imposed by law, that the arrangements for the ballot or election (including any security arrangements) minimised the risk of any unfairness or malpractice, and that he was able to carry out his functions without interference or anyone calling his independence into question. He will also state if he has inspected the register of members, and whether any such inspection has revealed any matter which should be brought to the attention of the union in order to ensure that it is accurate and up to date (s 52).

22.54 Within three months of receiving the scrutineer's report on an election (s 52(4)), on a political fund resolution (s 78(4)), or on an amalgamation or transfer resolution (s 100E(6)), the trade union shall send a copy to every member to whom it is reasonably practicable to send such a copy, or take all such steps for notifying the contents of the report to members of the union as it is the practice for the union to take when matters of general interest need to be brought to the members' attention. So far as ballots on industrial action are concerned, any person entitled to vote in the ballot, and the employer of any such person, is entitled to be supplied with a copy of the scrutineer's report on request. This may be supplied free of charge or on the payment of a reasonable fee.

D. Remedies (s 54)

22.55 Any member may apply to the High Court (or Court of Session) or the certification officer (but not both) for a declaration that the trade union has failed to comply with any requirement of the Act relating to secret ballots for trade union elections or relating to election addresses or to scrutineers. The court may make an enforcement order specifying the action which the trade union shall take in consequence of its failure to comply with the Act (s 56). The certification officer may grant the declaration, and, if necessary, make an enforcement order requiring the union to hold a fresh election (s 55). An appeal from the order of the Certification Officer may be made to the EAT.

Accounts, records, etc (TULR(C)A, s 28)

22.56 Every trade union and employers' association shall keep proper records, and establish a satisfactory system of control over its cash holdings, receipts and remittances. An annual return must be sent to the certification officer, with accounts duly audited. There are provisions in ss 32–42 detailing the matters which must be contained in the annual return including the salaries paid to, and the benefits provided for, the president, general secretary and members of the executive committee, together with the qualifications, appointment, functions, and removal of auditors, and for the control over members' superannuation schemes. Any person who refuses or wilfully neglects to perform a duty imposed by these provisions, or who alters a document required for those purposes, shall be guilty of an offence, punishable by a fine of up to level 3 and 5 on the standard scale respectively.

22.57 An annual statement must be sent to all members of the union (or otherwise communicated to them) giving details of the union's income and expenditure, salaries paid to the president, general secretary and executive members, and the income and expenditure of the political fund. The statement will also include prescribed information on the remedies to members who are concerned about any irregularities in the conduct of the union's affairs (s 32A).

A. Right to inspect accounts (ss 29–31)

22.58 A trade union shall keep its accounting records available for inspection for six years from 1 January following the end of the period to which those records relate.

22.59 Any member of a trade union may request to be permitted access to those records in respect of any period when he was a member. Such access shall be permitted within 28 days of the request and, unless otherwise agreed, at a reasonable hour and at the place where the records are normally kept. The member is entitled to take an accountant with him, and to take, or be supplied with, such copies or extracts from those records as he may require. The trade union may make a charge in respect of reasonable administrative expenses incurred (s 30).

22.60 If the trade union fails to comply with the member's request for access to the accounting records, the member may apply to the court or the certification officer (but not both), who may make such order as is considered appropriate for ensuring that that person:

(a) is allowed to inspect the records;

(b) is allowed to be accompanied by an accountant; and

(c) is allowed to take, or is supplied with, such copies of or extracts from those records as he may require (s 31).

22.61 The certification officer has the power to require the production of documents, take copies etc and appoint an inspector to investigate the financial affairs of the union, if he suspects that the financial affairs of the union have been conducted in a fraudulent manner, or a person managing its affairs has been guilty of fraud, or the union has failed to comply with a provision of the Act or its own rules with relation to the conduct of its financial affairs (TULR(C)A, s 37B). The inspector has wide powers of investigation, and will report back to the certification officer.

Offences (ss 45–45C)

22.62 If a trade union refuses to supply a copy of its rules (s 27), fails to keep accounting records (s 28), fails to keep records available for inspection (s 29), fails to give members access to the accounts (s 30), fails to make an annual return (s 32), make an annual statement to members (s 32A), breaches the auditing requirements (ss 33–37), or breaches the requirements relating to members' superannuation schemes (ss 38–42), it commits an offence. The offence will also be committed by every officer who is bound by the rules to discharge any of those duties, or, if there is no such officer, every member of the management committee. It will be a defence for the officer or member of the management committee to prove that he had reasonable cause to believe that some other competent person was authorised to discharge that duty. It is also an offence wilfully to alter a document, fail to produce a document, destroy, mutilate or falsify a document relating to the financial affairs of the union, or fraudulently alter or delete anything in such document, or to make a false statement. The offences may be punishable by a fine or, in some circumstances, up to six months' imprisonment. A person who has been convicted under these provisions shall not hold office as a member of the executive, president or general secretary for a period of five or ten years, depending on the offence.

A. Indemnifying unlawful conduct (s 15)

22.63 It is unlawful for any property of a trade union to be applied towards the payment for any individual, or towards the provision of anything for indemnifying an individual, in respect of any penalty which has been imposed on him for a relevant offence, or for contempt of court. A 'relevant offence' is any offence other than one which has been designated as an offence by the Secretary of State in relation to which s 15 does not apply.

22.64 If property has been so applied in contravention of this section, the equal amount of any payment is recoverable from the individual concerned by the trade union, and in the case of property, the individual shall be liable to account for its value. If the trade union unreasonably fails to make a claim against the individual, any member may apply to the court for authorisation to bring or continue proceedings on the union's behalf and at the union's expense.

B. Remedies against trustees (s 16)

22.65 If a member of a trade union considers that the trustees of the union's property are carrying out their functions so as to permit an unlawful application of the union's property, or are complying with an unlawful direction which has been given to them under the union's rules, he may apply to the court for an order. If the court is satisfied that the application is well founded, it may make such orders as it deems appropriate, including:

(a) requiring the trustees of the union to take all such steps as may be specified for the purpose of protecting or recovering the union's property;

(b) appointing a receiver (or judicial factor) of/on the union's property;

(c) the removal of one or more trustees.

22.66 Should the trustees act in contravention of the court's order, the court may remove all the trustees except those who can satisfy the court that there is good reason to allow them to remain a trustee.

Political fund and political objects (TULR(C)A, ss 71–74)

22.67 The Act lays down the necessary requirements before a trade union can have a political fund and pursue political objects. A resolution to establish a political fund must be passed at least every ten years by a ballot of all the union's members, and if approved, a separate political fund may be created. The ballot must be by the use of a voting paper, and every person entitled to vote must be allowed to do so without interference from or constraint imposed by the trade union or any of its members, officials or employees. The member must be able to vote without incurring any direct cost.

22.68 So far as is reasonably practicable, every person who is entitled to vote on a ballot concerning the establishment of a political fund must have the voting papers sent to him at his home or postal address, and be given a convenient opportunity to vote by post. The voting must be in secret, and the votes fairly and accurately counted (s 77).

22.69 If the political fund is established, no property of the trade union shall be added to that fund other than sums representing contributions made to the fund by the members or any other person and property accruing to the fund in the course of administering its assets. No liability of the political fund shall be met out of any other fund of the trade union. If there is no resolution in force establishing the political fund, no property shall be added to an existing fund (other than that which accrues in the course of administering the fund) and no union rule shall require any member to contribute towards the fund. The union may transfer the whole or part of the assets of an existing fund to such other fund of the trade union as it thinks fit. Where a resolution is passed rescinding an existing fund, the trade union may use the fund for a period of six months, but not so as to put the fund in deficit.

22.70 If a resolution to have a political fund ceases to have effect, the union shall take such steps to ensure that the collection of contributions to the fund is discontinued as soon as is reasonably practicable, and any contribution collected after the resolution ceases to have effect may be paid to any other fund of the trade union. If the trade union continues to collect contributions these are refundable at the members' request.

22.71 Any member of a trade union who wishes to contract out of a political fund must be free to do so, and if he does, he shall not in consequence be excluded from any benefit or disqualified from holding any office other than a position connected with the management of the political fund. Contributing towards the fund must not be a condition of membership.

22.72 The TUC has issued a 'Statement of Guidance' on political funds. It advises trade unions to draw up 'information sheets' about their political funds, and inform members why it has a fund, make clear members' legal rights to opt out, state the current amount of the levy, and provide information on how members may contract out.

22.73 The political fund may be used for the following purposes:

(a) any contribution to the funds of, or the payment of any expense incurred by, a political party;

(b) the provision of any services or property for the use by or on behalf of a political party;

(c) the registration of electors, the candidature of any person, the selection of any candidate, or the holding of a ballot by the union in connection with any election to a political office;

(d) the maintenance of any holder of a political office;

(e) the holding of any conference or meetings by or on behalf of a political party, or any other meetings the main purpose of which is the transaction of business in connection with a political party;

(f) the production, publication or distribution of any literature, document, film, sound recording or advertisement the main purpose of which is to persuade people to vote for a political party or candidate or not to vote for it or him.

22.74 An allegation that a trade union has broken a rule as to the use to which the political fund may be put may be the subject of an investigation by the certification officer. In *Richards v National Union of Mineworkers*[32] a complaint was made that the union had spent money from the general fund sending members on a lobby of Parliament organised by the Labour Party, and had also paid money to a trade union consortium which was developing Labour Party headquarters. It was held by the certification officer that such expenditure was in furtherance of political objects, and he ordered that the money should come from the political funds of the union, not the general funds.

22.75 A member who claims that the union has applied its funds in breach of s 71 may apply to the certification officer for a declaration. After making the necessary enquiries, the certification officer may grant the declaration, specifying the amount of funds applied in breach of s 71 and any remedial action to be taken, and specify any steps to be taken to ensure that the same or similar breach does not take place in the future (s 72A).

A. Complaints over political fund ballots (TULR(C)A, ss 79–81)

22.76 A member of a trade union who complains that a ballot on the political fund was taken otherwise than in accordance with the rules approved by the certification officer, or

---

[32] [1981] IRLR 247.

that there has been a failure to comply with those rules, may apply to the certification officer or to the court (but not both) for a declaration. The application must be made within one year from the date when the result of the ballot was announced.

22.77 The court may make an enforcement order, specifying the action which the trade union shall take in consequence of its failure to comply with the Act.

Breach of union rules (ss 108A–108B)

22.78 A member of the union who claims that there has been a breach of other rules of the union may apply to the certification officer for a declaration. The rules in question are:

(a) the appointment or election of a person to, or the removal of a person from, any office;

(b) disciplinary proceedings by the union (including expulsion);

(c) the balloting of members on any issue other than industrial action;

(d) the constitution or proceedings of any executive committee or of any decision-making meeting;

(e) such other matters as may be specified in an order made by the Secretary of State.

22.79 The application must be made within six months from the day when the breach occurred, or, if an internal complaints procedure was invoked, six months from when it was concluded. The certification officer is not entitled to consider a complaint about the discipline or dismissal of an employee of the union, as these are matters capable of being dealt with under the general law on individual employment rights.

22.80 The certification officer may refuse to consider the complaint unless reasonable steps were taken to resolve the issue by use of the internal complaints procedure, but if he hears the complaint he may make a declaration, and, if appropriate, an enforcement order, requiring the union to remedy the breach, or abstain from specified acts. An appeal from any proceedings under this section will lie to the EAT on a point of law.

Amalgamation and transfers (ss 97–105)

22.81 Two or more trade unions may decide to amalgamate into one union, or a union may wish to transfer its engagements to another union. In both cases, the instrument of amalgamation or transfer must first be submitted to the certification officer for approval, and then voted upon by the members of the amalgamating unions or transferor union, as the case may be. The union must give the members a notice in writing, which either sets out the instrument of amalgamation or transfer, or gives an account of it so as to enable the member to form a reasonable judgment of its main effects. Section 100 of the Act provides that the instrument may be approved by a simple majority of votes recorded, unless the rules of the union specifically exclude this provision, in which case some other specified proportion of members will be required to approve.

22.82 An independent scrutineer must be appointed, who will supervise the production and distribution of the voting papers, inspect the register of members, and generally report to the union after the ballot has been concluded. Voting in the ballot shall be accorded equally to all members of the union, the ballot papers will be numbered consecutively, and sent to members' homes or postal address. The notice sent to members shall not contain any statement making a recommendation or expressing an opinion about the proposed transfer or amalgamation. A copy of the scrutineer's report must be sent to every member or otherwise suitably published.

22.83 A complaint about the procedure relating to an amalgamation or transfer may be made to the certification officer, who may make a declaration, and an order specifying the steps to be taken before he will entertain the application (s 103).

Employers' associations

A. Definition of employers' association (TULR(C)A, s 122)

22.84 An employers' association is defined as an organisation which either:

(a) consists wholly or mainly of employers or individual proprietors, and whose principal purposes include the regulation of relations between employers and workers or trade unions; or

(b) consists wholly or mainly of constituent or affiliated organisations with those purposes or representatives of such constituents or affiliated organisations, whose principal objects include the regulation of relations between employers and workers or between the constituent or affiliated organisations.

22.85 An employers' association may be incorporated under the Companies Acts, or may be an unincorporated association. In the latter case it shall nonetheless be capable of making contracts, or suing and being sued in its own name, and of being prosecuted in its own name. Its property, however, will have to be held by trustees, and any judgment, award or order would have to be enforced against that property. A trade association, which is largely concerned with the business interests of employers, is not an employers' association within the statutory definition, but if it did have as one of its purposes collective bargaining objectives, or if it regulated the relations between organisations which have such objectives, it could be an employers' association. This is because the Act requires the principal objects of an employers' association to 'include' the statutory objects, not that the principal objects 'shall be' the statutory objects.

B. Listing of employers' associations (TULR(C)A, s 123)

22.86 The Act permits the employers' associations to be entered on the appropriate list, but there are few advantages of doing so. Many employers' associations are incorporated under the Companies Act, and therefore do not require trustees to hold property. They do not have provident funds, and do not require certificates of independence. Not surprisingly, less than half of employers' associations have bothered to become listed.

23

Law Relating to Industrial Relations

Trade union recognition

23.1 Since 1871, when trade unions were legalised by the Trade Union Act of that year, the history of industrial relations in the United Kingdom has been somewhat turbulent. This is partly due to conflicting ideologies, sometimes of a political nature, but mainly due to a conflict between those who favour individual as opposed to collective bargaining arrangements. A consideration of the extent to which the law should play a role in the control of industrial relations, and the precise nature of that law, has always been a subject for political controversy. Various governments of differing political persuasions have made their impact throughout the years, but, mainly due to the reforms pushed through in the Thatcher era, trade unions have now achieved a respectability and a role recognised by employers and confirmed by law. The whole story, though interesting from a legal and philosophical point of view, need not detain us in this book, but history has left its mark, and it is not possible to understand the present legal position without some reference to the previous law on this topic, though it is intended to keep such excursus to a minimum. In particular, it will be necessary to examine certain common law rules which, though they may now be only of historical importance, have shaped the legislative provisions.

23.2 Freedom of association, ie the right of an individual to join a trade union, is guaranteed by the European Convention on Human Rights and is now accepted in the United Kingdom as axiomatic. However, the right of a trade union to bargain and/or negotiate on behalf of its members is initially dependent on the willing co-operation of employers. Thus an employer may refuse to recognise a trade union, may recognise it for some purposes only (eg representation) or for all purposes (eg negotiations). Whether an employer recognises a trade union, and the extent of that recognition, are questions of fact; there need not be a formal agreement to confirm this (see para 23.4). Once recognition has been granted, various legal consequences will flow, including the right to receive information for collective bargaining purposes (para 23.15), the right to be consulted on redundancies (Chapter 18) and on transfers of the undertaking (Chapter 9) etc. Members of independent trade unions which are recognised by the employer are entitled to certain benefits, including time off work for union duties and activities, and have various protections from dismissal and detriment (Chapter 21).

23.3 One of the reasons for industrial unrest in the past was the reluctance of some employers to recognise a trade union for any purpose, for whatever reason. An attempt to force employers to recognise a trade union was made in the Employment Protection Act 1975, but this was not a success, and the provisions were subsequently repealed.

A. **Voluntary recognition**

23.4 Employment tribunals appear to operate under the general rule that it is for the trade union to show that there is some formal agreement (not necessarily in writing) that it is recognised for collective bargaining purposes (*T&GWU v Dyer*[1]). The mere fact that there are employees who are trade union members, and that one of them negotiates, but without specific trade union authority, will not constitute recognition (*AUEW v Sefton Engineering*[2]). A history of consultation between an employer and a trade union was not sufficient to show that the trade union had been recognised for the purposes of collective bargaining. There must be clear evidence that a trade union has been recognised by an employer for collective bargaining purposes within the meaning of s 178 of TULR(C)A (*Working Links v Public and Commercial Services Union*[3]). Negotiations which may lead to recognition do not themselves constitute recognition (*T&GWU v Stanhope Engineering*[4]). Nor can recognition be inferred for the purpose of collective bargaining if a full-time union official represents an individual in a disciplinary proceeding (*T&GWU v Courtenham Products*[5]). The fact that an employer is a member of an association which negotiates with a trade union does not mean that the individual employer recognises the union (*NUGSAT v Albury Bros Ltd*[6]). Nor does recognition by a former employer by itself constitute recognition by a successor (*UCATT v Burrage*[7]). In *NUTGW v Charles Ingram & Co Ltd*[8] five propositions were established: (1) recognition is a mixed question of law and fact; (2) recognition requires mutuality; (3) there must be an express or implied agreement for recognition; (4) if the agreement was implied, there must be clear and unequivocal acts or conduct, usually over a period of time; (5) there may be partial recognition, for some, but not all purposes. Recognition for representation purposes only is not the same thing as recognition for negotiating purposes (*USDAW v Sketchley Ltd*[9]).

B. **Statutory recognition (TULR(C)A, Sch A1)**

23.5 The Employment Relations Act 1999 lays down a new complex statutory procedure for recognition and derecognition of trade unions, which can be found in TULR(C)A, Sch A1. The detailed provisions, including time limits and balloting procedures can be found in some 172 paragraphs of the Schedule (as amended), which additionally deal with semi-voluntary recognition, derecognition procedures, and protection of workers from detriments or dismissal on grounds relating to trade union membership or non-membership. However, the provisions do not apply where an employer employs fewer than 21 workers.

23.6 Schedule A1 is divided into nine parts, as follows:

Part I: statutory recognition;

Part II: voluntary recognition following a request for statutory recognition;

Part III: changes affecting the bargaining unit;

Part IV: derecognition, general;

Part V: automatic derecognition;

Part VI: derecognition of non-independent trade union;

Part VII: derecognition when a trade union loses its certificate of independence;

Part VIII: detriment and dismissal;

Part IX: general matters.

---

[1] [1977] IRLR 93, 12 ITR 113, EAT.   [2] [1976] IRLR 318.
[3] UKEAT/0305/12/RN.   [4] IRLR (LIB (121)).
[5] [1977] IRLR 8.
[6] [1978] ICR 62, [1977] IRLR 173, 12 ITR 413, EAT; aff'd [1979] ICR 84, [1978] IRLR 504, 122 Sol Jo 662, CA.
[7] [1978] ICR 314, EAT.
[8] [1978] 1 All ER 1271, [1977] ICR 530, [1977] IRLR 147, 12 ITR 285, EAT.
[9] [1981] ICR 644, [1981] IRLR 291, EAT.

23.7 An independent trade union can apply to the Central Arbitration Committee (CAC) for a declaration requiring the employer to recognise it for collective bargaining purposes in respect of workers in a particular bargaining unit. CAC will grant the declaration if a majority of workers in the bargaining unit already belong to the trade union, or where the union obtains the support of a majority of those voting in a secret ballot, which consists of at least 40% of those entitled to vote. The employer and the union should then agree to a method of collective bargaining, although if they fail to do so, an application may be made by either party to CAC, who will impose one. Recognition, thus obtained, will last for a minimum of three years, and cannot be ended unilaterally by the employer even after the end of that time, unless the derecognition procedure has been followed (Pt I, paras 1–51). The manner in which collective bargaining is to be conducted is set out in the Trade Union Recognition (Method of Collective Bargaining) Order 2000, which is legally binding, and can be enforced by an order for specific performance.

23.8 An alternative method is an agreement for recognition, which will arise when the union makes an application to CAC for recognition, but then abandons it because the employer agrees voluntarily to recognise the union. Nonetheless, either side may still request CAC to impose a method of collective bargaining. An agreement for recognition will last for three years, but does not require the derecognition procedure to be followed to terminate it (Pt II, paras 52–63).

23.9 It should be noted that neither of the two procedures in paras 23.7 and 23.8 in any way affects existing voluntary collective bargaining arrangements, which will no doubt continue without the necessity of being underpinned by a statutory procedure. Indeed, if there is a collective agreement in force a statutory claim for recognition cannot succeed (TULR(C)A, Sch A1, para 35, see *R(NUJ) v CAC*[10]).

23.10 It is the task of CAC to determine the appropriateness of the bargaining unit. The employer has the right to make representations on such matters and, indeed, frame objections to the union's proposals. But as long as CAC takes such arguments into account, their function is to determine the appropriateness of the union's original proposals, and not to shop around seeking an alternative (*R (Kwik-Fit (GB) Ltd) v Central Arbitration Committee*[11]).

23.11 If, for whatever reason, the original bargaining unit is no longer considered to be appropriate, either side may apply to CAC to select a new bargaining unit. There are provisions which are designed to ensure that the new unit does not overlap with an existing bargaining unit (including balloting if necessary), and CAC can make arrangements for workers who consequently fall outside the original unit into a residual unit (Pt III, paras 64–95).

23.12 An employer may derecognise the union if the number of workers falls below 21, or if an application is made to CAC (by the employer or by the workers) for a secret ballot to be held, at any time after three years from a CAC declaration. There is a further procedure for the workforce to apply for the derecognition of a non-independent trade union (which had achieved voluntary recognition), and for dealing with the situation which arises if a trade union loses its independent status (Pts 4, 5, 6, 7, paras 96–155).

C. **Employers' training policies (TULR(C)A, s 70B)**

23.13 If a trade union has obtained recognition for collective bargaining purposes under Sch A1, and CAC has imposed a method of collective bargaining (and the parties have

---

[10] [2005] IRLR 28.
[11] [2002] EWHC 277 (Admin), [2002] All ER (D) 111 (Feb); revsd [2002] EWCA Civ 512, [2002] ICR 1212, [2002] IRLR 395, [2002] All ER (D) 272 (Mar).

not agreed that the imposed method should not be legally binding) a trade union will be entitled to be consulted about the employer's policy on training for workers within the bargaining unit, the plans for training those workers during the following six months, and to receive information about training provided since the previous meeting. Two weeks before a meeting is held for this purpose, the employer must provide the union with whatever information is required to ensure that the union's representative can participate meaningfully in the meeting, and which it would be in accordance with good industrial relations practice for the employer to disclose. The employer shall take account of any written representations made by the union within four weeks from the date of the meeting. If the employer fails to comply with s 70B, the trade union may present a complaint to an employment tribunal, which may make a declaration, and award compensation of up to two weeks' pay to each person who was a member of the bargaining unit.

Collective bargaining (TULR(C)A, Sch A1, para 94)

23.14 The existing definition of collective bargaining refers to negotiations between a trade union and an employer on a wide variety of matters, including terms and conditions of employment, termination and suspension of employment, allocation of work, discipline and physical conditions of work (TULR(C)A, s 178). However, for the purposes of Sch A1, the definition is more restrictive, with the following result:

(a) So far as existing voluntary arrangements are concerned, collective bargaining refers to those matters listed in TULR(C)A, s 178.

(b) Where statutory recognition is awarded under Pt I of Sch A1, collective bargaining refers to the three core issues of pay, hours and holidays.

(c) If the parties agree matters as the subject of collective bargaining (eg if there is an agreement for recognition under Pt II, or an agreement to change the agenda in relation to a new unit under Pt III), the matters referred to in the agreement.

(d) If there is a new unit, or a residual unit under Pt III (with certain exceptions, see para 94(2)), collective bargaining means negotiations on the matters which were the subject of collective bargaining in the corresponding or parent unit.

A. Disclosure of information (TULR(C)A, s 181)

23.15 For the purpose of all stages of collective bargaining it shall be the duty of the employer, on request, to disclose to representatives of a recognised independent trade union all such information relating to his undertaking as is in his possession, and is information without which the representatives would to a material extent be impeded in carrying on such bargaining, and is information which it would be in accordance with good industrial relations practice that he should disclose. In one of its earliest findings, the CAC held that the test of 'materially impeded' meant that the information should be both relevant and important (*Institute of Journalists v Daily Telegraph*[12]). The employer need only make the disclosure to unions which are recognised by him. In determining what is good industrial relations practice, regard will be had to any Code of Practice issued by ACAS. If the trade union representatives so request the employer will disclose or confirm the information in writing, but he need not disclose:

(a) information the disclosure of which would be contrary to the national interest;

(b) any information which he could not disclose without breaking the law;

[12] IDS Supp 22.

(c) information which he received in confidence;

(d) information relating to an individual, unless he has consented to the disclosure;

(e) information the disclosure of which would cause substantial injury to the employer's business for reasons other than its effect on collective bargaining;

(f) information obtained by the employer for the purpose of bringing or defending any legal proceedings.

23.16 The employer is not bound to produce, or allow the inspection of, any document, or to compile information where this would involve an amount of work or expenditure out of all reasonable proportion to its value in the conduct of collective bargaining.

23.17 If an independent trade union wishes to make a complaint that an employer has failed to disclose information which he is required to produce, it may report the matter to the CAC. If that body thinks that the complaint can be settled by conciliation it will refer the matter to ACAS, which will try to promote a settlement. If this does not prove possible, or if the complaint is not so referred, the committee will hear and determine the complaint. If it finds the complaint is wholly or partly well founded, it will issue a declaration, stating:

(a) the information in respect of which the complaint is well founded;

(b) the date on which the employer refused or failed to disclose the information; and

(c) a period (being more than one week from the date of the declaration) within which the employer ought to disclose the information. If, at the end of that period, the employer still fails to disclose, a further complaint may be made by the trade union.

23.18 The complaint may be accompanied by a claim relating to the terms and conditions of the employees, and if the employer still persists in his refusal, the committee may make an award that in respect of the employees of any description specified in the claim, the employer shall observe the terms and conditions demanded, or other terms and conditions which the committee considers to be appropriate. These will form part of the contracts of employment of those employees from a date specified in the award, until varied or superseded by a further award or a subsequent collective agreement, or an express or implied agreement made between the employer and the employees which is an improvement on the award. As a general rule, CAC would consider the likely loss which flows from the failure to give the union the relevant information, and make an award accordingly.

B. Legal liabilities and legal proceedings

23.19 At common law it is impossible for a trade union to engage in any effective industrial relations activity without falling foul of some well-established legal rule. An understanding of those liabilities is necessary in order to understand and appreciate the statutory protections which have been developed over the years.

Inducing or procuring a breach of contract

23.20 It is a tort (civil wrong) for a person to induce another to break a contract to which the other is a party, or to procure a breach of that contract. In *Lumley v Gye*,[13] an opera singer contracted to sing at a theatre owned by the claimant. The defendant induced her to break that contract and sing for him instead. Clearly, the singer was liable for her own breach of contract, but it was held that the claimant could successfully sue the defendant

---

[13] (1853) 2 E & B 216, 22 LJQB 463, 17 Jur 827, 1 WR 432, [1843–60] All ER Rep 208.

for inducing her to break the contract. In terms of industrial relations, the tort is peculiarly appropriate (see, for example, the county court decision in *Falconer v ASLEF and NUR*[14]). An employer has a contract (of employment) with an employee. If a trade union official calls upon that employee to strike, the employee is breaking the contract (for which he can be dismissed – but see Chapter 21) but the union official (and possibly the union also) could be held liable for inducing a breach of that contract. Equally, if a trade union was to call for a secondary boycott, it may be furthering strike action, but it is also inducing (or procuring) a breach of a commercial contract. In *Torquay Hotel Co Ltd v Cousins*,[15] a trade union was in dispute with a hotel. A union official informed a company which was supplying oil to the hotel of the existence of the dispute, and instructed its members not to deliver oil supplies. It was held that an injunction would lie restraining the union officials from causing any fuel supplier to breach its contract to supply oil.

23.21 If a shop steward has express or implied authority to act on behalf of a trade union, then the union may be responsible for his actions unless it can shelter behind some legal protection (*Heatons Transport (St Helens) Ltd v Transport and General Workers' Union*, see para 3.82). But a union cannot be responsible for activities of unofficial committees of shop stewards, particularly when they are pursuing policies which are contrary to those of the union, and where union officials are trying to solve problems through machinery for negotiation and conciliation, while the shop stewards are taking militant industrial action (*General Aviation Services (UK) Ltd v Transport and General Workers' Union*[16]). However, in such a situation, the union must repudiate the activities in question (see para 23.82) if it wishes to retain its immunities.

23.22 For the tort of inducing or procuring or otherwise wrongfully interfering with contractual rights to be made out, five conditions must be satisfied: (1) it must be shown that the defendant persuaded or procured or induced a third party to break its contract with the claimant; (2) when the defendant so acted he had knowledge of the existence of the contract, if not its precise terms; (3) it must be shown that the defendant intended to persuade, induce or procure a breach of that contract because it is an essential prerequisite for establishing the tort of inducing a breach of contract that the alleged wrongdoer deliberately and specifically intended to induce the breach. A mere careless or negligent inducement will not suffice (*Mainstream Properties Ltd v Young*[17]); (4) the claimant must show more than nominal damage; (5) if the defendant puts forward the defence of justification, the claimant has to rebut that defence (*Timeplan Education Group Ltd v National Union of Teachers*[18]).

Conspiracy

23.23 A conspiracy is a combination of two or more persons to do an unlawful act, or a lawful act by unlawful means. Such acts could lead to a prosecution for criminal conspiracy (ie where the conspirators combine in order to pursue criminal objects) or an action for civil conspiracy where the alleged act constitutes a tort. Since trade unions are by necessity combinations, it is not surprising that they are particularly vulnerable to this form of legal constraint. For example, in *Quinn v Leathem*,[19] Leathem was a butcher who employed non-union

[14] [1986] IRLR 331, [1986] BTLC 258.
[15] [1969] 2 Ch 106, [1968] 3 All ER 43, [1968] 3 WLR 540, 4 KIR 635, 112 Sol Jo 688; aff'd [1969] 2 Ch 106, [1969] 1 All ER 522, [1969] 2 WLR 289, 6 KIR 15, 113 Sol Jo 52, CA.
[16] [1974] ICR 35, [1973] IRLR 355, NIRC; revsd [1975] ICR 276, 119 Sol Jo 589, CA; on appeal [1985] ICR 615, [1976] IRLR 224, HL.
[17] [2005] EWCA Civ 861, [2005] IRLR 964, (2005) 102(30) LSG 31.
[18] [1997] IRLR 457, CA.
[19] [1901] AC 495, 65 JP 708, 70 LJPC 76, 50 WR 139, [1900–3] All ER Rep 1, 85 LT 289, 17 TLR 749, [1901] 2 IR 705, HL.

labour. The union called upon him to dismiss them, but he refused to do so. Instead, he offered to pay the men's arrears of subscriptions if they were admitted into the union. This offer was rejected by the union officials, who wanted to teach the non-unionists a lesson 'and make them walk the streets for 12 months'. Munce supplied meat to Leathem, and the union threatened to call a strike of Munce's men unless supplies of meat to Leathem were cut off, and Munce complied with this request. It was held that the union officials had conspired together to cause harm to Leathem without lawful jurisdiction. Their legitimate trade union objectives could have been achieved by accepting Leathem's offer and admitting the men to member-ship, but in fact their subsequent conduct had been motivated by vindictiveness.

23.24 But the mere fact that an act causes harm does not, by itself, amount to a conspiracy. Clearly, a strike causes harm to an employer, but if the object is a legitimate one, eg obtain-ing higher wages, no actionable conspiracy exists (*Crofter Hand Woven Harris Tweed Co v Veitch*[20]). In *Scala Ballroom (Wolverhampton) Ltd v Ratcliffe*,[21] the claimants operated a colour bar at their dance hall. Officials of the Musicians' Union placed a boycott on the premises in protest. It was held that this was not a conspiracy to injure, for the combination was a legitimate furtherance of the union's interests.

Intimidation

23.25 This 'obscure and unfamiliar' tort was resurrected from oblivion in the controver-sial case of *Rookes v Barnard* (see para 3.79), where a shop steward threatened to call a strike at Heathrow Airport unless the claimant, a non-unionist, was dismissed. This 'threat' constituted a breach of contract, which was held to be an unlawful act (ie in the same way that a threat to commit an act of violence would be unlawful) and the defendants were held liable for intimidation.

Other tort liabilities

23.26 There are a number of other possible headings of legal liabilities which trade unions may run up against, including such headings as unlawful interference with trade busi-ness or employment, interference with future contracts, and so forth. Such torts are to be found in judicial hints rather than actuality, and the fear was of their emergence rather than their existence. With the increased statutory control over the conduct of trade unions, it is unlikely that these obscure torts will be revived.

23.27 But if there are unlawful acts committed by a trade union, an injured party may apply for an injunction to restrain the commission of such acts, and sue for damages in respect of any loss suffered, including, if necessary, exemplary damages (*Messenger Newspapers Group Ltd v National Graphical Association*[22]). A trade union can only defend itself if it can rely on the statutory protections.

Statutory protections

23.28 It is clear from paras 23.20 to 23.27 that if trade unions are to carry out their legiti-mate functions in industrial relations, they require protection from these headings of com-mon law liability, and arguably against judicial ingenuity in developing new case law which would restrict their activities. This has been the object of statute law since 1906; it was a process which was carried on by the Industrial Relations Act 1971, and has been continued in TULR(C)A. But the statutory immunities are not a licence to do anything; they only

[20] [1942] AC 435, [1942] 1 All ER 142, 111 LJPC 17, 166 LT 172, 58 TLR 125, HL.
[21] [1958] 3 All ER 220, [1958] 1 WLR 1057, 102 Sol Jo 758, CA.
[22] [1984] IRLR 397; aff'd [1984] 1 All ER 293, [1984] ICR 345, 134 NLJ 257, CA.

provide a protective cover for trade unions when legitimate objectives are being pursued. These objectives are limited to acts done in furtherance or contemplation of a trade dispute, and it is to the wide meaning of this phrase that we must now turn.

A. 'Trade dispute' (TULR(C)A, s 244)

23.29 A trade dispute means a dispute between workers and their employers which relates wholly or mainly to one or more of the following:

(a) terms and conditions of employment, or the physical conditions in which any workers are required to work;

(b) the engagement or non-engagement or termination or suspension of employment or the duties of employment, of one or more workers;

(c) the allocation of work or the duties of employment between workers or groups of workers;

(d) matters of discipline;

(e) membership or non-membership of a trade union on the part of a worker;

(f) facilities for officials of trade unions;

(g) machinery for negotiations or consultation, and other matters relating to the foregoing (ie (a)–(f) above), including recognition by employers or employers' associations of the right of a trade union to represent workers in any such negotiations or consultations or in the carrying out of such procedures.

23.30 The important change made by the Employment Act 1982 is that the dispute must relate 'wholly or mainly' to these matters. In *Mercury Communications Ltd v Scott-Garner*,[23] the claimants were granted a licence by the Government to run a telecommunications system (the 'liberalisation' agreement), which effectively broke the Post Office monopoly. The Government also proposed to privatise British Telecommunications. The Post Office Engineering Union opposed both the liberalisation and privatisation of the work, and gave instructions to its members not to do work which would enable the plaintiffs to connect to the British Telecommunications network. The claimants applied for an injunction to restrain the union from inducing a breach of contractual relations between themselves and British Telecommunications. The Court of Appeal granted the injunction. It was unlikely that the union would be able to establish at the trial that there was a trade dispute within the statutory definition. There was little evidence to support the union's contention that there was a dispute about the risk of loss of jobs. The reality was that the union was waging a campaign against the political decisions to liberalise and privatise the industry. But in *UNISON v Westminster County Council*[24] a dispute between a local authority and employees about the proposed privatisation and contracting out of certain advisory services was held to be a dispute about terms and conditions of employment, and not a dispute about public policy. Similarly, a dispute about the reasonableness of an instruction from an employer can be a dispute about terms and conditions of employment within the meaning of s 244(1)(a) (*P v National Association of Schoolmasters/Union of Women Teachers*[25]).

---

[23] [1984] Ch 37, [1984] 1 All ER 179, [1983] 3 WLR 914, [1984] ICR 74, [1983] IRLR 485; revsd [1984] Ch 37, [1984] 1 All ER 179, [1983] 3 WLR 914, [1984] ICR 74, [1983] IRLR 494, 127 Sol Jo 764, CA.

[24] [2001] EWCA Civ 443, [2001] LGR 378, [2001] ICR 1046, [2001] IRLR 524, [2001] 20 LS Gaz R 41, [2001] All ER (D) 250 (Mar).

[25] [2001] EWCA Civ 652, [2001] ICR 1241, [2001] IRLR 532, [2001] ELR 607, [2003] NLJR 350, [2001] All ER (D) 107 (May); aff'd [2003] UKHL 8, [2003] 2 AC 663, [2003] 1 All ER 993, [2003] 2 WLR 545, [2003] ICR 386, [2003] IRLR 307, [2003] ELR 357, [2003] NLJR 350, [2003] All ER (D) 384 (Feb).

23.31 In addition, there are three other circumstances to consider. First, a trade dispute will exist between a minister of the Crown and a group of workers notwithstanding that the minister is not the employer of those workers, if the dispute relates to matters which have been referred for consideration to a joint body on which that minister is bound by statute to be represented, and which cannot be settled without the minister exercising a power.

23.32 For example, in *Wandsworth London Borough Council v National Association of Schoolmasters Union of Women Teachers*,[26] the defendants wished to ballot their members to protest against the excessive workload caused by the assessment requirements of the national curriculum, which had been imposed by the Government. A local authority sought an injunction against the unions, arguing that the dispute was not about terms and conditions of employment, but about the very idea of the national assessment, and this was a matter which could only be resolved by the Secretary of State exercising a power conferred by statute. It was held that the dispute was wholly or mainly about the workload imposed on teachers and, therefore, since it was about the terms and conditions of employment, the statutory protection (see para 23.34) applied, and the application for an injunction was refused.

23.33 Second, there is a trade dispute even though it relates to matters occurring outside the United Kingdom as long as the persons who are taking action are likely to be affected in respect of one or more of the matters mentioned at para 23.29. The third situation is more curious. In *Cory Lighterage Ltd v Transport and General Workers' Union* (see paras 3.19 and 16.1), a lighterman named Shute decided to leave the union, and the employers were informed that none of the crew would sail if he did not pay his union dues. The employers had no quarrel with the union, for they accepted the principle of 100% unionisation, but they could not dismiss Shute under the Dock Workers Employment Scheme, so they sent him home on full pay. It was held that as there was no dispute between the employers and the union, the statutory protections did not apply. The employers did not resist the demands of the union, but rather acceded to them by taking Shute off the lighter. In line with the policy of giving the widest possible protection to trade unions in all actual and potential conflict situations, TULR(C)A, s 244(4) provides that an act, threat or demand done or made by one party or organisation against another which, if resisted, would have led to a trade dispute with that other, shall, notwithstanding that because that other submits to the act or threat or accedes to the demand no dispute arises, be treated as done or made in contemplation or furtherance of a trade dispute.

23.34 There is no trade dispute if a strike is called about the terms and conditions of employment of employees of a third party who have never been employed by the employer with whom the union is in dispute, nor is there a trade dispute if it concerns the employment of the employees with a future unidentified employer. In *University College London Hospitals NHS Trust v UNISON*[27] the claimant entered into a contract with a consortium for the latter to build and run a new hospital. The union was opposed to the scheme, and sought to persuade the claimant to enter into a contractual agreement with the consortium whereby the terms and conditions of staff who were transferred to the new hospital would receive equivalent terms and conditions of employment to those who were not transferred. When the claimant refused to accede to the demand, the union called a strike, which was approved in a ballot of members. An injunction to restrain the strike was confirmed by the Court of Appeal. The dispute was about the terms and conditions which would apply to another employer, and in respect of employees who may at some future

26 92 LGR 91, [1994] ICR 81, [1993] IRLR 344, [1994] ELR 170, [1993] NLJR 655n, CA.
27 [1999] ICR 204, [1999] IRLR 31, [1998] 41 LS Gaz R 45, 142 Sol Jo LB 270, [1998] All ER (D) 450, CA.

stage be employed by that other employer. The dispute was not between 'workers and their employer', because, at this stage, neither the future employer nor the workers employed by him could be identified.

23.35 But a strike called for political reasons is not a trade dispute. In *BBC v Hearn*,[28] the Association of Broadcasting Staff threatened to stop a transmission of the Cup Final by satellite to South Africa, in protest of the alleged racist policies of the Government of that country. This would also have affected a number of other countries throughout the world. The Court of Appeal held that there was no trade dispute, and granted an injunction restraining the union from telling its members to break their contracts of employment, and from inducing the BBC to break its contracts with other countries. In *Express Newspapers v Keys*,[29] three trade unions instructed their members to strike in response to a call sent out by the TUC for a one-day national stoppage in protest against Government policies. It was held that this was a political strike, not in connection with a trade dispute, and injunctions were granted restraining the unions from inducing or procuring breaches of contract between the claimants and their employees.

23.36 In *Examite Ltd v Whittaker*,[30] a trade union called a strike against a firm called Baldwins Industrial Services, with the result that the company's business came to a standstill. A new company called Examite was formed, with two shares being issued, and it took over the business of Baldwins and engaged some of its former employees. The union continued the strike against the new company, as it was considered to be a sham, and the company sought an injunction to restrain the union officials from intimidating the employees and to restrain them from procuring a breach of contract. It was held that a trade dispute existed between the union and Examite. There was sufficient evidence to show that the company had been formed to take over the business formerly carried on by Baldwins. The 'hat' worn by the employer was irrelevant. The truth was that the new company was carried on by the same people who ran the old one, and the legal form it took was irrelevant.

B. 'In contemplation of'

23.37 Having obtained the formula for a trade dispute, for an act to come within the statutory protection, it must be in contemplation of that dispute. The act may be so done if it is committed before the dispute arises, but is imminent. However, the dispute must be more than a mere possibility. In *Bents Brewery Co Ltd v Hogan* (see paras 10.69 and 19.69) managers of a brewery were asked by a trade union official to obtain information about the firm's salaries, sales, etc. In providing this, the managers were in breach of their contract not to disclose confidential information to unauthorised persons (see Chapter 10). The union official was clearly inducing a breach of that contract, and it was held that his action was not in contemplation of a trade dispute, even though one may well have arisen at some future date. His actions may have been preparatory to the dispute, but were not in contemplation of one.

C. 'In furtherance of'

23.38 The act committed must also be in furtherance of the trade dispute, and not in furtherance of some other issue. In *Conway v Wade*[31] a union official informed employers

[28] [1978] 1 All ER 111, [1997] 1 WLR 1004, [1977] ICR 685, [1977] IRLR 273, 121 Sol Jo 374, CA.
[29] [1980] IRLR 247.
[30] [1977] IRLR 312, CA.
[31] (1908) 24 TLR 604; on appeal [1908] 2 KB 844, 78 LJKB 14, 52 Sol Jo 748, 99 LT 634, 24 TLR 874, CA; revsd [1909] AC 506, 78 LJKB 1025, [1908–10] All ER Rep 344, 53 Sol Jo 754, 101 LT 248, 25 TLR 779, HL.

that unless a worker was dismissed there would be a strike. This was untrue, and the union official's actions were prompted by his desire to get the worker to pay a fine which was due to the union. It was held that although a trade dispute existed, the act was not done in furtherance of that dispute, but for some other motive. A more difficult problem arises when there is more than one motive for the acts in question, and some of the pre-1971 cases, which were decided on a much narrower definition of the term 'trade dispute' must now be viewed with greater care. For example, in *Huntley v Thornton*[32] the claimant was recommended for expulsion by the branch committee of a trade union, but this was not upheld by the national executive. Nonetheless, the local officials regarded him as being expelled, and took steps to ensure that he did not obtain employment. The judge thought that there was no trade dispute, but such conduct would nowadays clearly be covered by the new, wider definition. More interesting was the finding that some of the officials were not acting in furtherance of a trade dispute, but in furtherance of a personal grudge, and their actions were in the nature of a vendetta. In other words, if protection is sought for acts done in furtherance of a trade dispute, the predominant motive must be the advancement of legitimate objects, and trade unionists cannot use the cover of the statutory protection to pursue improper aims.

23.39 But not every action which flows from a trade dispute is necessarily in furtherance of that dispute. In *Beaverbrook Newspapers Ltd v Keys*,[33] a trade dispute existed between the *Daily Mirror* newspaper and a trade union, which resulted in a complete stoppage of production. The *Daily Express* decided to print more copies to cater for the increase in demand, but the general secretary of the printing union told his members not to handle the additional copies. The claimants applied for an injunction to restrain the union from inducing their employees to break their contracts of employment. It was held that the injunction would be granted. There was no trade dispute between the members of the defendant's union and the claimants, and the action would not further the dispute between the *Daily Mirror* and its employees.

23.40 Armed with the 'golden formula', we can now consider those statutory protections, and consider when the immunities will be lost.

Statutory protection and loss of immunities

A. The provisions of TULR(C)A, s 219

23.41 Subsection (1) provides that an act done by a person in contemplation or furtherance of a trade dispute shall not be actionable in tort on the ground only (a) that it induces another person to break a contract or interferes or induces any other person to interfere with its performance; or (b) that it consists of his threatening that a contract (whether one to which he is party or not) will be broken or its performance interfered with, or that he will induce another person to break a contract or to interfere with its performance.

23.42 This subsection does three things. First, it gives immunity against legal action to anyone who calls a strike or other industrial action and thus induces a breach of contract (of employment) by the strikers, or a breach of a commercial contract by any other person. It also covers any inducement which interferes with the performance of a contract. A strike includes any refusal to work for specified periods when workers would normally work, provided it is concerted, ie mutually planned. It does not have to be a total stoppage

---

[32] [1957] 1 All ER 234, [1957] 1 WLR 321, 101 Sol Jo 171.
[33] [1978] ICR 582, [1978] IRLR 34, CA.

(*Connex South Eastern Rly v National Union of Rail, Maritime and Transport Workers*[34]). Whether an overtime ban is 'other industrial action' is a question of fact for the employment tribunal to determine (*Naylor v Orton & Smith Ltd*[35]). Second, the subsection provides immunity where a threat of strike or other industrial action is made, whether this is done by the actual strikers or some other person, eg a trade union official. Thus, the threat to call a strike – the unlawful act in *Rookes v Barnard* (paras 3.79 and 23.25) – is no longer actionable. Third, it protects those who threaten to induce a breach of contract or to interfere with its performance.

23.43 Section 219(2) provides that an agreement or combination of two or more persons to do or procure the doing of an act in contemplation or furtherance of a trade dispute shall not be actionable in tort if the act is one which, if done without such agreement or combination, would not be so actionable. This subsection is designed to nullify the law of conspiracy as applied to trade disputes (see para 23.23). If an act in contemplation or furtherance of a trade dispute would be actionable if done by one person, then a civil conspiracy would be committed if a group of persons did it. For example, if strikes commit a trespass by engaging in a sit-in, or commit a nuisance, or libel someone by picketing with defamatory placards, such conduct would be actionable if done by one person, and therefore no statutory protection exists.

23.44 Thus, in *News Group Newspapers Ltd v Society of Graphical and Allied Trades 1982*[36] the defendants were responsible for organising mass picketing at the claimant's premises at Wapping. This was held to be a public nuisance, intimidation and an interference with commercial contracts, and injunctive relief was granted. But if the act was lawful if done by one person, it does not become an actionable conspiracy merely because a group of persons do it. Thus it is not unlawful for one person to threaten to strike or to go on strike. It therefore cannot be a conspiracy if more than one person does so. It is unlawful for one person to use violence; it will be a conspiracy for a group of persons to agree to use violence or actually to use it in a strike situation, and civil, as well as potential criminal liability, may arise.

23.45 However, it was suggested in *Meade v Haringey London Borough Council*[37] that the immunity of a trade union from actions in tort based on conspiracy may not apply if there is an inducement to break a duty laid down by statute. Thus, if a local authority is forced to close a school (which it is under a statutory duty to keep open) because of trade union pressure, the union officials may be liable for inducing a breach of statutory duty and will not be protected by TULR(C)A. But if the statutory duty can be re-arranged so that it can still be carried out, injunctive relief will not be granted (*Barretts & Baird (Wholesale) Ltd v Institution of Professional Civil Servants*[38]). Also, if there is no statutory obligation to break, a trade union cannot be liable for inducing an alleged breach (*Associated British Ports v Transport and General Workers' Union*[39]).

B. **Loss of immunities**

23.46 In recent years, the tactics adopted by trade unions in industrial disputes have not always attracted universal approval, and Parliament has intervened to place restrictions on certain types of activities, by limiting the immunity conferred by TULR(C)A, s 219. The

---

[34] [1999] IRLR 249, CA.   [35] [1983] ICR 665, [1983] IRLR 233, EAT.

[36] [1986] ICR 716, [1986] IRLR 227, 130 Sol Jo 407, [1986] LS Gaz R 1726, CA.

[37] [1979] 2 All ER 1016, [1979] 1 WLR 637, 77 LGR 577, [1979] ICR 494, 123 Sol Jo 216, CA.

[38] [1987] IRLR 3, [1988] NLJR 357.

[39] [1989] IRLR 291; on appeal [1989] 3 All ER 796, [1989] 1 WLR 939, [1989] ICR 557, [1989] IRLR 305, CA; revsd [1989] 3 All ER 822, [1989] 1 WLR 939, [1989] ICR 557, [1989] IRLR 399, HL.

objects are twofold: first, to ensure greater democracy in trade unions by requiring secret ballots to be held before strikes or other industrial action are called, so as to negate decisions made at mass meetings by show of hands, or calls for action which may be unsupported by the rank and file; second, to prevent unnecessary hardship caused by industrial action to third parties who are in no way involved with or connected with the dispute. The primary purpose is to regulate official trade union action; unofficial action, though covered by the law, is seldom the subject of court proceedings (but see para 23.72).

Consequently, the immunity provided by TULR(C)A, s 219 will be lost unless the following legal hurdles can be surmounted.

Secret ballots before industrial action (TULR(C)A, ss 226–234A)

23.47 There is no legal requirement which insists that a ballot be called by the union before industrial action can be taken. However, a failure to do so will have the following legal consequences:

(a) industrial action which is authorised or endorsed by the union will not have the statutory immunity under s 219 from actions in tort, and an employer affected by the strike will be able to obtain an injunction and sue for damages;

(b) members of the trade union will be able to apply to the court for an order restraining the union from calling for strike action (TULR(C)A, s 62, see Chapter 21);

(c) any member of the public who suffers a reduction or delay in the quality or supply of goods or services may apply to the court for an injunction to restrain the strike (s 235A);

(d) employees who go on strike will not have the protection afforded by s 238A (para 21.112) although they will have the protection contained in s 238(1)(b) (para 21.101).

23.48 The balloting provisions contained in TULR(C)A, ss 226–235 have been amended by the Employment Relations Act 2004, and a Code of Practice on Industrial Action Ballots and Notice to Employers has been issued. The requirements apply only to official industrial action. It should be noted that for the purpose of the balloting provisions (as with secondary action, see para 23.73) any reference to a contract of employment also includes a contract under which a person personally does work or performs services for another. Thus self-employed workers who are union members are covered by the statutory provisions.

23.49 An act done by a trade union to induce a person to take part in industrial action will not be protected unless the industrial action has the support of a ballot, and the other detailed requirements of TULR(C)A are satisfied (s 226). These are that, not later than seven days before the opening day of the ballot, the union must take reasonable steps to notify the employer of persons who are entitled to vote:

(a) that a ballot is to be held;

(b) the date of the opening day of the ballot;

(c) a list of the categories of employee to which the employees concerned belong, a list of the workplaces of the employees concerned, the total number of employees, together with the figures of the total number of employees concerned, the number of employees in each category, and the number of employees concerned who work at each workplace. The list and figures supplied must be as accurate as is reasonably practicable in the light of the information which the union possesses (s 226A(3A)).

23.50 As an alternative, if there is a union subscription arrangement in force (see para 21.79) the union may send the list and figures containing the information (s 226A(2)(c) (ii)). In either case, there is no need to name the actual employees who are to be balloted.

23.51 A sample voting paper is to be sent to the employer at least three days before the opening day of the ballot. If the employees concerned are not all to be sent the same voting paper, a sample of each form of voting paper which is sent to any of them. Before the ballot is held, the union must appoint a scrutineer (see para 22.48), unless the number of those to be balloted is fewer than 50.

23.52 All those members of the trade union whom it is reasonable to believe (at the time of the ballot, see *London Underground Ltd v National Union of Rail Maritime and Transport Workers*[40]) will be induced by the union to take part in the industrial action must be balloted, and no other person (s 227(1)). A union's policy of not balloting members who are in arrears of subscriptions does not satisfy s 227(1) because such persons might nonetheless be induced to take part in strike action as a gesture of solidarity, and therefore were entitled to vote on the matter (*National Union of Rail, Maritime and Transport Workers v Midland Mainline Ltd*[41]). It is for the union to ensure that it has up-to-date information on the addresses of its members and their current job classifications. But if the union acquires new members, or if existing members transfer from employments which are not in dispute into the area of a dispute, immunity will not be lost, because it would hardly be reasonable for the union to believe that they would be induced to take part in the industrial action (s 232A). Section 232B provides that if there is a failure to comply with s 227(1), and the failure is accidental and on a scale which is unlikely to affect the result of the ballot, the failure must be disregarded. In *British Airways plc v Unite (No. 1)*[42] the union included in its ballot employees who had accepted voluntary redundancy, and who would not be employed by the time the strike action was due to start. An injunction to restrain the union from acting on the ballot was granted because although the court accepted that the failure to comply with s 227(1) was unintentional, it was not accidental.

23.53 So far as is reasonably practicable, a voting paper must be sent to the home address of the member, and he must be given a reasonable opportunity to vote by post (s 230(2)). If a member is denied the opportunity to vote, and is subsequently induced to take part in the industrial action, the trade union will lose its statutory immunity (s 232A), but the inadvertent failure to supply a ballot paper to union members will be disregarded for all purposes if the failure was accidental and not likely to affect the result of the ballot (s 232B). An inadvertent mistake which leads a member not to be accorded an opportunity to vote in a ballot does not mean that the union loses its immunity for failing to follow the correct balloting procedure. If the failure was accidental, and not likely to affect the result, it can be disregarded. Inadvertently failing to give a member the opportunity to vote is not the same thing as denying him an entitlement to vote (*P v National Association of Schoolmasters/ Union of Women Teachers*, para 23.30).

Separate workplace ballots (TULR(C)A, ss 228–228A)

23.54 The general rule about balloting is that a separate ballot shall be held for each workplace (s 228(3)), and industrial action will not be protected unless a majority of workers at that workplace voted in favour (s 226(3)). A person's workplace is a single set of premises (if that is where he works) or premises with which the person's employment has the closest connection (s 228, and see *InterCity West Coast Ltd v National Union of Rail Maritime and Transport Workers*[43]). This requirement does not apply where the union reasonably believes that all the members who are entitled to vote have the same workplace (s 228(2)).

---

[40] [1996] ICR 170, CA.
[41] [2001] EWCA Civ 1206, [2001] IRLR 813, [2001] 38 LS Gaz R 37, [2001] All ER (D) 352, (Jul).
[42] [2010] IRLR 423, [2009] EWHC 3541 (QB).
[43] [1996] IRLR 583, CA.

23.55 If the union wishes to call an aggregate ballot of a genuine bargaining unit (instead of separate ballots), certain conditions must be satisfied. The entitlement to vote must be limited to all members of the union who, according to the union's reasonable belief, have an occupation of a particular kind, and are employed by a particular employer or any number of employers with whom the union is in dispute. There must be at least one of its members at each of the workplaces directly affected by the dispute, or the union must be balloting members of a particular occupational category who are employed by a particular employer or by a group of employers, or balloting all of its members who are so employed (s 228A).

Ballots for overseas members (TULR(C)A, s 232)

23.56 Generally, a trade union can elect whether or not to ballot overseas members (ie a person who is not a merchant seaman or offshore worker), who is outside Great Britain during the period of the ballot (s 232(3)) (Great Britain means England, Scotland and Wales). However, if the ballot relates to industrial action involving Great Britain and Northern Ireland, or if a member is temporarily seconded to Northern Ireland, members in both countries must be balloted. If a trade union reasonably believes that a merchant seaman will be at sea or a place outside Great Britain at the time of the ballot, then, if it is reasonably practicable, he is entitled to have a voting paper made available while on ship or at the place where the ship is.

Voting requirements (TULR(C)A, ss 229–231A)

23.57 Voting must be by means of marking a voting paper. This must state the name of the independent scrutineer, specify the address to which and the date by which it is to be returned, and be given one of a series of consecutive numbers, and marked with that number. The voting paper must contain the question (however framed) which requires the member to answer 'Yes' or 'No' whether he is prepared to take part in (or continue to take part in) a strike. A similar question must be posed if the issue is industrial action short of a strike, and for this purpose an overtime ban and a call-out ban will constitute industrial action short of a strike (*Connex South Eastern Ltd v National Union of Rail Maritime and Transport Workers*, para 23.42, being thus overruled). The requisite majority must be on each of the relevant questions, not the combined voting figures on both ballots (if two questions are being posed) (*West Midlands Travel Ltd v Transport and General Workers' Union*[44]). After all, a member might be willing to take part in industrial action short of a strike, but not a strike, and vice versa (*Post Office v Union of Communication Workers*[45]).

23.58 The question on the ballot paper must relate to a trade dispute (within the statutory definition) and not to matters in respect of which no statutory immunity applies (*London University Ltd v National Union of Railwaymen*[46]).

23.59 The voting paper must also specify who, in the event of the vote being in favour of industrial action, is authorised to call upon members to take the industrial action. It is not necessary to name the individual in question, but he must be a person duly authorised either by the rules of the union, or the principal executive committee, or president or general secretary, or any other committee or official of the union (including shop stewards) (s 229(3), s 230(2)).

23.60 The ballot paper must contain the following statement: 'If you take part in a strike or other industrial action, you may be in breach of your contract of employment. However, if you are dismissed for taking part in a strike or other industrial action which is called

44 [1994] ICR 978, [1994] IRLR 578, CA.
45 [1990] 3 All ER 199, [1990] 1 WLR 981, [1990] ICR 258, [1990] IRLR 143, CA.
46 Unreported.

officially and is otherwise lawful, the dismissal will be unfair if it takes place fewer than 12 weeks after you started to take part in the action, and depending on the circumstances may be unfair if it takes place later.' There must be no further comment or qualification on this statement.

23.61 Every person who is entitled to vote must be allowed to do so without interference from, or constraint imposed by the union, or any of its members, officials or employees, and without direct cost. So far as is reasonably practicable, he must have the voting paper sent to his home address or other address as may be requested, and be given a convenient opportunity to vote by post (s 230(2)). The ballot shall be so conducted as to ensure that, so far as is reasonably practicable, voting is done in secret. The votes must be fairly and accurately counted, but accidental inaccuracies, which could not affect the result of the ballot, may be disregarded.

23.62 As soon as is reasonably practicable after the holding of the ballot, the trade union shall inform all persons entitled to vote of the number of:

(a) votes cast;

(b) individuals answering 'yes';

(c) individuals answering 'no'; and

(d) spoilt papers.

23.63 In *British Airways plc v Unite (No. 2)*[47] the trade union posted the results of a strike ballot on its website, distributed hard copy leaflets to members in crew centres, left the result in news-stands, made an announcement at a press conference, issued a press release, and sent e-mails and text messages to members who had signed up for these services. Not all the information was in the statutory form (eg percentage results were given, as opposed to the actual numbers). The employers obtained an interim injunction restraining the strike, but this was discharged by the Court of Appeal. Section 231 did not require that every member should receive an individual report of the full results, but rather that it be put where members can access it if they want to.

23.64 The union will also ensure that every relevant employer receives this information (s 231A), ie every employer who it is reasonable for the union to believe was the employer of any persons entitled to vote. A failure to do so would make subsequent industrial action unlawful.

23.65 A scrutineer's report will also be prepared, stating whether there were grounds for believing that the statutory grounds for holding the ballot were contravened, that the arrangements with respect to the production, storage, distribution, return or handling of the voting papers, and the arrangements for the counting of the votes, including all security arrangements, were such as to minimise the risk of unfairness or malpractice, and that he was able to carry out his functions without interference from the trade union, or any of its members, officials or employees.

Effectiveness of the ballot (TULR(C)A, ss 233–234)

23.66 A ballot will not be effective in so far as it relates to a call for a strike or other industrial action before the date of the ballot, or any such call after the ballot ceases to be effective (s 233(3)). In other words, industrial action cannot be subsequently validated by a ballot. But this does not require a union to adopt a neutral stance on the matter, and urging members to vote in favour of strike action is not the same thing as calling them

---

[47] [2010] EWCA Civ 669.

to strike (*Newham London Borough Council v National and Local Government Officers' Association*[48]).

23.67 A ballot will also cease to be effective after the end of four weeks, or such longer period not exceeding eight weeks, from the date of the ballot, as may be agreed between the employer and the trade union. Industrial action which takes place after that time will not be supported by a ballot (*RJB Mining (UK) Ltd v National Union of Mineworkers*[49]). If, during the four or eight-week period, industrial action is prohibited by a court order (eg on an application for a temporary injunction), and the order is subsequently discharged, or it lapses, the trade union may request the court to order that the period during which the prohibition took effect shall not count towards the four or eight-week period. Once industrial action has started, it may continue indefinitely if necessary, and if at any time it is suspended (eg to enable negotiations to take place), a new ballot will not be required if the resumption of industrial action was part of the original dispute (*Monsanto plc v Transport and General Workers' Union*[50]), although if there is a fresh dispute a new ballot will be required (*Post Office v Union of Communication Workers*, para 23.57).

Notice of industrial action (TULR(C)A, s 234A)

23.68 An act done by a trade union to induce a person to take part in industrial action shall not be prevented from being actionable in tort by s 219 unless the union takes such steps as are reasonably necessary to ensure that the employer receives a relevant notice of the industrial action within the appropriate period, ie the period beginning with the day when the union informed the employer of the result of the ballot, and ending with the seventh day before the day specified in the notice for industrial action to commence. The notice must be in writing, and must contain a list of the categories of employee to which the affected employees belong, a list of the workplaces, the total number of affected employees, and the number of affected employees who work at each workplace or a list of employees in respect of whom a union subscription arrangement (see para 21.79) is in force (s 234A(3)(a)(ii)). The 'affected employees' are those employees of the employer who the union reasonably believes will be induced by the union to take part in the industrial action, but there is no need for the union to identify by name the employees concerned. The notice must state whether the industrial action is to be continuous or discontinuous, and if continuous, the date when it will commence, and if discontinuous, the dates when the action will take place.

23.69 In *Metrobus Ltd v Unite*[51] an injunction was upheld on a trade union restraining industrial action. The union had failed to notify the employer of the numbers and categories of employee involved in the action (contrary to s 226A), had failed to notify the employer of the outcome of the ballot as soon as was reasonably practicable (contrary to s 231A) and had failed to provide the employer with figures that were as accurate as reasonably practicable (contrary to s 234A). Minor failures relating to the provision of information about the results to union members, however, should not undermine the entire ballot process (*British Airways plc v Unite the Union (No. 2)*[52]). In maintaining the records, a union is only obliged, as far as is reasonable, to ensure that the records are accurate, but it is not reasonable to expect them to be perfectly accurate. Statutory requirements imposed on trade unions regarding ballots of members and notices to employers before calling a strike should be given a reasonably relaxed, practical, interpretation (*National Union of*

---

[48] [1993] ICR 189, [1993] IRLR 83, CA.
[49] [1997] IRLR 621.
[50] [1987] 1 All ER 358, [1987] 1 WLR 617, [1987] ICR 269, [1986] IRLR 406, 131 Sol Jo 690, [1987] LS Gaz R 1572, [1986] NLJ Rep 917, CA.
[51] [2009] EWCA Civ 829, [2010] ICR 173, [2009] IRLR 851.
[52] [2010] IRLR 809, [2010] EWCA Civ 669.

Rail, Maritime & Transport Workers v Serco Ltd[53]). (In the case of *RMT v UK*, formerly *EDF Energy Powerlink v UK*[54] it was suggested that the balloting requirements are in contravention of Article 11 of the European Convention, but the case was dismissed by the European Court of Human Rights on the specific facts of the case.)

23.70 Technically, if the union suspended industrial action (to enable negotiations to take place) a further seven days' notice would be required before the action could be resumed. However, s 234A(7B) now provides that if the union agrees with the employer that it will cease to authorise industrial action from a specified date (the suspension date) but that it may be again authorised with effect from a date not earlier than a specified date (the resumption date), then if the action is suspended, it may be resumed without the necessary notice being required.

Industrial action to enforce a closed shop (TULR(C)A, s 222)

23.71 Section 219 shall not provide an immunity in tort for acts done in furtherance or contemplation of a trade dispute if the reason for the act is that the employer is employing or proposes to employ a person who is not a member of a trade union or of a particular trade union. Immunity is also removed if the action is designed to put pressure on an employer into treating persons less favourably on grounds of their non-membership of a trade union.

Industrial action in support of unofficial strikers (TULR(C)A, s 223)

23.72 We have noted that if a person goes on unofficial strike, and is dismissed, he has no right to claim that he has been unfairly dismissed (see para 21.90). Section 223 provides that s 219 will not prevent an act from being actionable in tort, if the reason for the action was that an employer had lawfully dismissed unofficial strikers.

Secondary action (TULR(C)A, s 224)

23.73 The immunities conferred by s 219 will only apply when a trade union takes industrial action (supported by the appropriate ballot) vis-à-vis an employer with whom there is a trade dispute. In recent years, it became an increasingly popular technique to strengthen the effectiveness of such action by extending it to employers who were not themselves parties to the dispute, in the hope that pressure (direct or indirect) would be thereby exerted on the employer with whom there was a dispute. This is known as secondary action (see, eg *Duport Steels Ltd v Sirs*[55]).

23.74 Secondary action is defined as when a person:

(a) induces another to break a contract of employment; or

(b) interferes or induces another to interfere with its performance; or

(c) threatens that a contract of employment under which he or another is employed will be broken, or its performance interfered with; or

(d) threatens that he will induce another to break a contract of employment, or to interfere with its performance;

and the employer under the contract of employment is not the employer party to the dispute (s 224(2)).

---

[53] The joined cases *National Union of Rail, Maritime & Transport Workers (RMT) v Serco Ltd t/a Serco Docklands* and *Associated Society of Locomotive Engineers & Firemen v London & Birmingham Railway Ltd t/a London Midland* [2011] IRLR 399, [2011] EWCA Civ 226.

[54] (Application 31045/10) [2010] IRLR 114.

[55] [1980] IRLR 112, CA; revsd [1980] 1 All ER 529, [1980] 1 WLR 142, [1980] ICR 161, [1980] IRLR 116, 124 Sol Jo 133, HL.

23.75 In these circumstances, nothing in s 219 shall prevent an act from being action-able in tort where one of the facts relied upon for the purpose of establishing such liability amounts to secondary action which is not lawful picketing.

23.76 The current definition of secondary action is wider than the original definition con-tained in the Employment Act 1980, and thus there are greater pitfalls for those who engage in such action. Secondary action must result in a breach of a contract of employment, whether or not there is a breach of a commercial contract. Further, the present definition extends the meaning of contract of employment to include the contract of a self-employed person who contracts personally to do work or perform services for another, thus clos-ing a loophole revealed in *Shipping Co Uniform Inc v International Transport Workers' Federation*[56] (see TULR(C)A, s 224(6)).

23.77 The only type of secondary action which now remains lawful is peaceful picket-ing, as laid down in TULR(C)A, s 220 (see para 23.105), ie by workers who are (or were) employed by the employer who is a party to the dispute, and by a trade union official whose attendance is lawful by virtue of s 220(4) of the Act. Secondary picketing (ie at the gate of an employer who is a customer or supplier to the employer who is a party to the dispute) is not lawful.

Pressure to impose union recognition requirement (s 225)

23.78 An act will not be protected by s 219 if it constitutes an inducement of a person to incorporate into a contract a term requiring a party to a contract for goods or services to recognise a trade union for the purpose of negotiating on behalf of workers employed by him, or to negotiate or consult with an official of a trade union (such a contract term would be void by reason of s 186, see para 23.120). Nor will an act be protected if it interferes with the supply of goods or services, by inducing another person to break a contract of employ-ment, the reason being that the supplier does not recognise or negotiate or consult with a trade union (see para 23.117).

C. Immunity of trade unions (TULR(C)A, s 20)

23.79 Section 14 of TULRA 1974 (which re-enacted provisions dating from the Trade Disputes Act 1906) conferred total legal immunity on trade unions in respect of most actions in tort. This immunity was repealed by the Employment Act 1982, and nowadays a trade union will be liable in tort if the protection of TULR(C)A, s 219 is not available. However, a trade union cannot be responsible for everything which is done in its name by its members, shop stewards or officers, but only for those actions which have been author-ised or endorsed.

23.80 A trade union will only be liable for inducing breaches of contract, or threatening that a contract will be broken, or for actions for conspiracy, if the act in question is author-ised or endorsed by the union. An act shall be taken to have been endorsed or authorised by the trade union if it was done or authorised or endorsed by:

    (a) any person empowered by the rules to do, authorise or endorse the act; or

    (b) the principal executive committee or the president or general secretary of the union; or

    (c) by any other committee of the union, or any other official of the union (whether employed by the union or not).

---

[56] [1985] 1 Lloyd's Rep 173, [1985] ICR 245, [1985] IRLR 71.

23.81 Thus, under the current law, a trade union may be held to be legally liable not only for the acts of its full-time officials, but also for its shop stewards if they are authorised to do an act. Further, the liability arises for the acts of any committee (set up in accordance with the union's rules) and also for the acts of any group of members of which a shop steward was a member, and the purpose of which included the organising or co-ordinating of industrial action (TULR(C)A, s 20(4)). This is so notwithstanding anything in the rules of the union, or any contract or rule of law subject to the repudiation provisions, see para 23.82.

23.82 However, the union will not be liable if the act was repudiated by the principal executive committee or president or general secretary as soon as was reasonably practicable. Written notice must be given to the committee or official in question, without delay, and the union must do its best to give written notice of the fact and date of repudiation, without delay, to every member whom the union believes is taking part in the industrial action, and to the employer of every such member (s 21).

23.83 The written notice must be in the following form: 'Your union has repudiated the call (or calls) for industrial action to which this notice relates and will give no support to unofficial industrial action taken in response to it (or them). If you are dismissed while taking industrial action, you will have no right to complain of unfair dismissal.'

23.84 The repudiation will not be effective if the principal executive, president or general secretary behave in a manner inconsistent with the repudiation (see *Richard Read (Transport) Ltd v National Union of Mineworkers (South Wales Area)*[57]). If, within three months of the purported repudiation, a person who is a party to a commercial contract which has been interfered with by the unofficial industrial action so requests, the union must confirm the repudiation in writing.

D. **The effect of the Act**

23.85 If a trade union calls for a strike or other industrial action in violation of the balloting provisions of the Act, or for a reason which is not permitted by the Act, it can be sued, and will not have the immunity conferred by s 219. An application may be made by an aggrieved person to the court for an injunction (*Solihull Metropolitan Borough Council v National Union of Teachers*[58]) and a failure to comply constitutes contempt of court, which would lead to a fine or imprisonment being imposed (*Express and Star Ltd v National Graphical Association*[59]) or sequestration of property (*Kent Free Press v National Geographical Association*[60]). Additionally, an action for damages could be brought against the trade union, subject to the limits on the amount which can be awarded, depending on the size of the trade union.

Amount of damages (TULR(C)A, s 22)

23.86 If a trade union is sued successfully in tort, there are limits to the amount of damages which may be awarded. These limits are dependent on the size of the union's membership and are as follows:

fewer than 5,000 members, the limit is £10,000

5,000 or more, but less than 25,000, the limit is £50,000

---

[57] [1985] IRLR 67.   [58] [1985] IRLR 211.
[59] [1985] IRLR 455; aff'd [1986] ICR 589, [1986] IRLR 222, [1986] LS Gaz R 2083, CA.
[60] [1987] IRLR 267.

25,000 or more, but less than 100,000, the limit is £125,000

100,000 or more, the limit is £250,000.

23.87 These limits are applicable in each claim brought against the union, and are not global limits on each incident. Thus, if a trade union calls a strike in circumstances where it lacks legal immunity under s 219, each employee who has suffered damage may sue the union for the maximum sum, depending on the number of members it has. In addition, interest may be added to the award (*Boxfoldia Ltd v National Graphical Association*[61]). For example, in *Willerby Holiday Homes Ltd v Union of Construction, Allied Trades and Technicians,*[62] a trade union called a strike despite the fact that the pre-ballot notice did not conform to s 226A, the actual ballot did not conform to s 227(1), and the notice of strike action did not conform to s 234A. An award of damages amounting to £130,000 was made.

23.88 The limits do not apply to any action in tort in respect of personal injury caused by negligence, nuisance or breach of statutory duty, nor to any breach of duty in connection with the ownership, occupation, possession, control or use of property.

23.89 If damages, costs or expenses are awarded against a trade union, these cannot be enforced against the 'protected property' ie property which belongs to trustees other than in their capacity as trustees of the union, property owned by members in association with other members (ie common property), the property of an official who is not a member or trustee, political funds and provident benefit funds.

Injunctions and interdicts (TULR(C)A, s 221)

23.90 An injunction without notice is an application for a temporary injunction to restrain the commission of some act. It is usually made in great haste, and thus only the party applying will have the time and opportunity to argue the case and be represented. Section 221 states that the court shall not grant such an application if the party against whom the injunction is sought claims, or the court thinks he might claim, that the act was done in contemplation or furtherance of a trade dispute, unless all reasonable steps have been taken to give that person notice of the hearing and an opportunity has been given for that party to be heard.

23.91 If an application is made for an interlocutory injunction (ie restraining an act until the matter comes to trial), and the party against whom the injunction is sought claims that he acted in contemplation or furtherance of a trade dispute, the court shall, in exercising its discretion whether or not to grant the injunction, assess the likelihood of success of any defence which may be raised that the act complained of will be protected by the statutory immunities (s 221(2)). For the procedure in Scotland, see *NWL Ltd v Nelson and Laughton.*[63]

A. **Injunctive relief (TULR(C)A, s 20(6))**

23.92 If a trade union is responsible for official or unofficial strike action under the provisions of s 20 then in any court proceedings arising out of the act in question, the court

---

[61] [1988] ICR 752, [1988] IRLR 383.

[62] [2003] EWHC 2608 (QB), [2003] All ER (D) 93 (Nov).

[63] [1979] 2 Lloyd's Rep 317, [1979] ICR 755, [1979] IRLR 321, 123 Sol Jo 488, CA; aff'd [1979] 3 All ER 614, [1979] 1 WLR 1294, [1980] 1 Lloyd's Rep 1, [1979] ICR 867, [1979] IRLR 478, 123 Sol Jo 751, HL.

may grant an injunction requiring the trade union to take such steps as the court thinks appropriate for ensuring:

(a) that there is no, or no further, inducement of persons to take part in industrial action; and

(b) that no person engage in any conduct after the granting of the injunction because he was induced to take part in industrial action before the injunction was granted.

23.93 This appears to give the court power to order a trade union to take disciplinary action against those who continue to induce or take part in industrial action after it has been repudiated by the union. However, no court shall make an order of specific performance or grant an injunction if the effect is to compel an employee to work or attend any place for the doing of any work (s 236).

23.94 A failure by a trade union (or any other person) to observe the terms of an injunction amounts to contempt of court, in respect of which a fine and/or imprisonment or sequestration of property may be ordered (*Kent Free Press v National Geographical Association*, para 23.85).

B. Industrial action affecting an individual (s 235A)

23.95 Any individual, who claims that industrial action has been called by a trade union which is actionable in tort or which has not been supported by a ballot under s 226, and the effect of which is to prevent or delay the supply of goods or services, or reduce their quality, may make an application to the High Court or Court of Session. It is immaterial that the individual in question is entitled to be supplied with the goods or services in question. If the court is satisfied that the claim is well founded, it shall make such order as it considers appropriate for requiring the union to take steps for ensuring that no further act is done by him to induce any person to take part in the industrial action, and that no person engages in any conduct before the making of the order because he has been induced before the making of the order to take part in industrial action. This section also applies to Crown employment even though no contract of employment may exist.

23.96 The situation may sometimes arise where a trade union calls for industrial action which would otherwise be actionable in tort because the various statutory provisions have not been complied with, but (for whatever reason) the employer (or union members) are unwilling to seek to restrain the industrial action. In such circumstances, any individual, whether affected by the industrial action or not, can bring an application to the court, seeking an appropriate order.

C. Industrial action and European law

23.97 There may be circumstances when the right to strike is restricted by EC law. Article 43 of the Treaty of Rome provides that there shall be no restriction on companies of one member state establishing undertakings in the territory of another member state. In *International Transport Workers' Federation v Viking Line*[64] the issue arose as to whether collective action taken by a trade union aimed at preventing a ferry operator from registering one of its vessels in a foreign country in order to reduce labour costs constituted a restriction on the company's right to freedom of establishment. The Treaty provides that any such restriction might be justified by an overriding reason of public interest, provided

---

[64] (C-438/05) [2008] All ER (EC) 127, [2008] IRLR 143, [2008] 1 CMLR 51, ECJ.

it does not go beyond what is necessary to achieve that objective. In this case, a Finnish ship that sailed around the Baltic was running at a loss because of competition from Estonian ships operating on the same route. The owners sought to reflag the ship by registering her in Estonia, with the aim of benefiting from lower labour costs. This move was opposed by the trade unions concerned, and strike action was threatened. The owners sought a declaration that the action violated their right to freedom of establishment under Art 43. The European Court held that the collective action constituted a restriction within the meaning of Art 43, which could be justified by an overriding reason of public interest, such as the protection of workers, provided that the restriction was suitable for the attainment of that legitimate objective and did not go beyond what was necessary to achieve that objective. The case was referred back to the Court of Appeal for it to find on complex questions of 'suitability', 'necessity', ' proportionality' and whether the union had other means at its disposal that were less restrictive of freedom of establishment than the industrial action.

23.98 It is thought that the decision of the European Court of Human Rights in *Demir v Turkey* (see Chapter 1) does not sit easily with the decision in the European Court of Justice in *International Transport Workers' Federation v Viking Line*,[65] which requires trade unions to justify the proportionality of their actions. The *Demir* case appears to reverse this burden of proof, by ruling that the right to strike may only be limited in strictly defined circumstances.

Legal effect of collective agreements (TULR(C)A, ss 178–179)

23.99 A collective agreement is any agreement or arrangement made by or on behalf of a trade union on the one part, and one or more employers or employers' associations on the other part, relating to one or more of the matters contained in the definition of a trade dispute (see para 23.29). In essence, a collective agreement performs two functions. First, it lays down the guiding procedures which will govern the relationship between the signatory parties, by providing, for example, for the constitution of any joint body, or the procedure to be adopted in the event of a dispute or disagreement. Second, it will lay down patterns of terms and conditions of employment which are to cover union members, and possibly others as well, and which are to be observed by all federated and some assenting non-federated firms. Such terms and conditions are usually the minimum, not the maximum rate, so if national bargaining results in a particular award, this may frequently be supplemented at a local level by a further bout of negotiations.

23.100 So far as legal enforceability of these agreements is concerned, s 179 provides that any agreement shall be conclusively presumed not to have been intended by the parties to be a legally enforceable contract, unless the agreement is in writing, and contains a provision stating that the parties do intend the agreement to be legally binding (*Universe Tankships Inc of Monrovia v International Transport Workers' Federation*, see para 3.19). It is possible for the parties to state expressly that only part of the agreement is intended to be legally binding, and part not, in which case the parties' intentions will be given effect to, though it is possible to look at a non-legally binding part for the purpose of interpreting a part which is legally binding.

23.101 There must be an express statement to the effect that the parties intend the collective agreement to be legally enforceable (*Prison Service v Bewley*, see para 7.97). If the agreement states that the parties intend to be bound by it, this may indicate that it is intended

---

[65] [2008] All ER (EC) 127, [2007] ECR I–10779, [2008] 1 CMLR 51, [2008] CEC 332, [2008] ICR 741, [2008] IRLR 143, (2007) *Times*, 14 December.

to be binding in honour only, which would not satisfy the provisions of TULR(C)A, s 179 (*National Coal Board v National Union of Mineworkers,* see para 3.59).

23.102 The extent to which, and the circumstances in which, the terms of a collective agreement can be incorporated into the contract of employment of an individual employee have already been examined in Chapter 3. Section 180 lays down one further important rule. If a collective agreement, whether legally binding or not, contains a clause prohibiting or restricting the right of workers to engage in a strike or other industrial action, this particular clause shall not be incorporated into the individual contract of employment of any worker, unless the collective agreement:

(a) is in writing;

(b) contains a provision expressly stating that such term shall be or may be incorporated into such contract;

(c) is reasonably accessible at the place of work of such a worker, and is available for him to consult during working hours; and

(d) is one made by an independent trade union.

It should have been noted that this rule applies notwithstanding any agreement to the contrary, whether contained in a collective agreement or an individual contract of employment.

23.103 Thus, if a collective agreement provides that 'the union will not call a strike until the disputes procedure is exhausted', a breach of this clause would be governed by the law relating to the legal effect of the agreement, as mentioned at para 23.100. If the collective agreement states: 'The employees will not go on strike until the disputes procedure is exhausted', then this clause will only form part of the individual contract of employment if the conditions are fulfilled. The matter, however, is not really important, for a strike is likely to be a breach of most individuals' contracts of employment (whether or not it is in breach of the terms of a collective agreement) as it is a breach of the duty of faithful service (see Chapter 10) and a breach of contract of such importance that a striker may be dismissed.

23.104 However, if CAC grants a declaration imposing a statutory collective bargaining framework (see para 23.7) the procedure to be followed is legally binding, and can be enforced by specific performance (Trade Union Recognition (Method of Collective Bargaining) Order 2000).

Peaceful picketing (TULR(C)A, s 220)

23.105 It shall be lawful for a person in contemplation or furtherance of a trade dispute to attend:

(a) at or near his own place of work; or

(b) if he is an official of a trade union, at or near the place of work of a member of that union whom he is accompanying and whom he represents;

for the purpose only of peacefully obtaining or communicating information, or peacefully persuading any person to work or to abstain from working. If a person works at more than one place, or at a place where it is impracticable to picket because of its location, his place of work shall be any premises from which he works, or from which his work is administered. A person whose employment has been terminated because of a trade dispute is allowed to picket at his former place of work.

23.106 A trade union official who has been elected or appointed to represent some of the members shall be regarded as representing only those members. Otherwise, a union official shall be regarded as representing all its members (s 220(4)). The purpose of this provision is to draw a distinction between officials who are shop stewards and full-time officials.

23.107 An employee's 'place of work' means his principal place of work or base. It does not refer to premises which, during his work, he may visit from time to time (*Union Traffic Ltd v Transport and General Workers' Union*[66]).

23.108 Whether the picketing has taken place at or near the place of work is a question of fact and degree. In *Rayware Ltd v Transport and General Workers' Union*,[67] pickets stood at the entrance of a private estate, about three-tenths of a mile from the employers' premises. An application by the employers for an injunction to restrain unlawful picketing failed. The pickets could not get any nearer to their place of work without trespassing, and thus they were picketing lawfully near their place of work.

23.109 Section 220 only makes lawful the acts in para 23.105. If something else is done, the section provides no protection. Thus in *Piddington v Bates*,[68] a policeman wished to restrict the number of pickets who were outside a factory. When a striker tried to join the picket line, he was arrested, and charged with obstructing the policeman in the course of his duty. A conviction was upheld, for the policeman had acted on reasonable grounds that a breach of the peace might have occurred. In *Tynan v Balmer*,[69] a group of pickets walked in a circle at the entrance of a factory in order to prevent traffic from entering and this was held to be an obstruction of the highway and a nuisance.

23.110 Nor do pickets have the power to stop vehicles, for traffic control is a matter for the police. In *Broome v DPP*[70] a trade union official stood in front of a lorry and attempted to persuade the driver not to deliver goods to a factory where a dispute was on. The police told him to get out of the way, but he refused, and he was arrested and charged with obstructing the highway, an offence under the Highways Act 1959. It was held that he was guilty of the offence. Views were expressed in *Broome's* case that the law gave no right to pickets to stop persons or vehicles, for that would indicate that those persons were under a duty to stop and listen. The purpose of the statute was to make attendance at a picket line lawful, and then only for the statutory purposes of peacefully communicating information, etc.

23.111 Mass picketing can also amount to the tort of public nuisance (unreasonable obstruction of the highway), private nuisance (interference with access to the highway) and intimidation (see *News Group Newspapers Ltd v Society of Graphical and Allied Trades 1982*, para 23.44). Thus under the new law, 'flying pickets' and mass demonstrations are clearly unlawful, the former because they will not normally be picketing at their own place of work, the latter because it is unlikely that it is for the purpose of peacefully persuading. In *Thomas v National Union of Mineworkers (South Wales Area)*,[71] it was held that mass picketing constituted a common law nuisance (as well as an offence under TULR(C)A, s 241(1)), for all citizens had the right to use the highway without harassment or unreasonable interference. Accordingly, injunctions were granted against various trade union

[66] [1989] ICR 98, [1989] IRLR 127, CA.
[67] [1989] 3 All ER 583, [1989] 1 WLR 675, [1989] ICR 457, [1989] IRLR 134, [1989] 29 LS Gaz R 44, CA.
[68] [1960] 3 All ER 660, [1961] 1 WLR 162, 105 Sol Jo 110, DC.
[69] [1967] 1 QB 91, [1966] 2 All ER 133, [1966] 2 WLR 1181, 110 Sol Jo 129, DC.
[70] [1974] AC 587, [1974] 1 All ER 314, [1974] 2 WLR 58, [1974] ICR 84, [1974] IRLR 26, [1974] Crim LR 311, 118 Sol Jo 50, HL.
[71] [1986] Ch 20, [1985] 2 All ER 1, [1985] 2 WLR 1081, [1985] ICR 886, [1985] IRLR 136, 129 Sol Jo 416, [1985] LS Gaz R 1938.

officials to prevent them from organising, encouraging, etc, members of the union congregating at coal mines, other than for the statutory purpose of peacefully communicating information, numbers in such cases being restricted to six.

23.112 Section 219(3) of TULR(C)A now provides that if an act is done in the course of picketing which is not lawful then s 219 will not provide a defence to any action which may be brought. Thus, if a picket induces workers to break their contracts of employment, and he is picketing at some place other than his own place of work, he can be sued in tort, and the statutory immunity of s 219 will not be available to him. Thus, unlawful picketing may now attract civil, as well as criminal liabilities. A Code of Practice on picketing has been approved by Parliament laying down the parameters for peaceful picketing.

23.113 If a tort is committed by picketing, s 220 will provide a trade union with legal protection provided the picketing is lawful within that section. But if no tort has been committed, the statutory rules are basically irrelevant. Thus, in *Middlebrook Mushrooms Ltd v Transport and General Workers' Union*,[72] the employers were mushroom producers, employing some 300 workers. They wished to introduce certain cost-saving measures, but these were not agreed to, and the union called a strike. The employer then dismissed all those employees who went on strike.

The union then urged its members to attend at supermarkets which were supplied with the mushrooms by the employers, and hand out leaflets to members of the public, asking them not to buy the employers' mushrooms. The employers brought an action for an interlocutory injunction restraining the union and its officials from organising the 'pickets' outside the supermarkets. The judge held that there was a direct interference with the contracts between the employers and the supermarkets, and granted the injunction.

However, the Court of Appeal reversed the decision. There was nothing in the leaflets which were handed out to members of the public which was aimed at the managers of the supermarket who placed orders with the employers. Thus the union was not seeking to persuade a party to the contract (ie the employers and the supermarkets) but members of the public, who, of course, had no contractual relations with the employers. It may well be that the managers of the supermarket might react to the reaction of the public (not to the picketing), but this, at most, would amount to an indirect inducement not to enter into future contracts, and, as no unlawful means had been used, the application for an injunction was dismissed.

23.114 If the industrial action is unofficial, and a trade union representative is routinely present when picketing is taking place, it will be presumed that he had sufficient knowledge of the unlawful element of the picketing to have endorsed those actions, and possibly to have, in practice, organised the unlawful activity which the union has not repudiated (*Gate Gourmet London Ltd v TGWU*[73]).

A. Sit-in

23.115 Workers who engage in a sit-in or work-in are in breach of their contractual licence to remain on the employers' premises (*City and Hackney Health Authority v National Union of Public Employees*[74]), and as such, if they refuse to leave after being given reasonable notice to do so are committing the tort of trespass and interfering with business by unlawful means (*Norbrook Laboratories Ltd v King*[75]). It is possible to obtain an injunction against

---

[72] [1993] ICR 612, [1993] IRLR 232, CA.
[73] [2005] EWHC 1889 (QB), [2005] IRLR 881.   [74] [1985] IRLR 252, CA.
[75] [1982] IRLR 456, [1982] 2 NIJB; aff'd [1984] IRLR 200, [1983] 14 NIJB, NIRC.

those involved, and also an employer may use the special expedited procedure to obtain possession of the property (see Ord 113 of the Rules of the Supreme Court).

23.116 If a trade union called for or authorised the sit-in or work-in, it would not be protected by the immunity conferred by s 219, even if a ballot was held, because the immunity in respect of interference with business by unlawful means was removed with the repeal of earlier legislation.

Union recognition

A. Union or non-union members only contracts (TULR(C)A, s 144)

23.117 Any term or condition in a contract for the supply of goods or services shall be void in so far as it purports to require that the whole or part of the work shall be done by persons who are not members of a trade union (or a particular trade union), or who are members of a trade union (or a particular trade union).

23.118 It will be a tort of breach of statutory duty if, on the grounds of union membership or non-membership, a person:

(a) fails to include a particular person's name on a list of approved suppliers of goods or services;

(b) terminates a contract for the supply of goods or services;

(c) excludes a person from tendering for the supply of goods or services;

(d) fails to permit a person to submit a tender; or

(e) otherwise determines not to enter into a contract for the supply of goods or services.

23.119 Thus any person who suffers damage through the failure or refusal of another to enter into a contract with him for the supply of goods or services on the grounds of union membership or non-membership may sue for breach of statutory duty, and will be able to recover damages (subject to any general defences which may exist to such an action). Further, if there is pressure from any person to induce another to incorporate into a contract to which that other is a party any term or condition which would be void by the provisions in para 23.118 then s 219 shall not be a defence. Nor will s 219 be a defence if a person induces or threatens to induce another person to break a duty imposed by s 144. Thus if trade unionists threaten to strike unless an employer enters into a union labour only contract, or unless he removes non-union sub-contractors from a site, such acts will be actionable despite the general immunity of s 219 (see s 222(3)).

B. Prohibition on union recognition requirements (TULR(C)A, s 186)

23.120 Any term or condition of a contract for the supply of goods or services shall be void in so far as it purports to require any party to the contract:

(a) to recognise one or more trade unions; or

(b) to negotiate or consult with any official of a trade union.

C. Refusal to deal on union exclusion grounds (TULR(C)A, s 187)

23.121 If a person maintains a list of approved suppliers of goods or services, or list of persons from whom tenders may be invited, and fails to include on that list a person who does not recognise trade unions, or terminates a contract for the supply of goods or services on that ground, or does other acts which prevent a person from being able to enter into a contract for the supply of goods or services because he does not recognise trade unions, such action will amount to a breach of statutory duty, and is actionable accordingly (subject to any relevant defences) by the person against whom the action was taken or by any other person adversely affected.

23.122 An act will not be protected by s 219 if it consists of inducing a person to impose a union recognition requirement contrary to ss 186–187 (see s 225).

Criminal liabilities

23.123 Members of the armed forces and policemen have no right to strike, and it is unlawful to induce a member of the prison service to strike or commit a breach of discipline, which effectively prevents them from taking part in an official strike (Criminal Justice and Public Order Act 1994, s 127). Merchant seaman may lawfully terminate their contracts and give 48 hours' notice of strike action provided their ship is in a safe berth in the United Kingdom. Industrial action by post office workers may involve criminal liability (see *Gouriet v Union of Post Office Workers*[76]) and there are restrictions on aliens who promote industrial action.

23.124 Sections 240–241 of TULR(C)A enact two provisions which may be relevant in trade disputes generally. The first is contained in s 240 of the Act, which provides that where any person wilfully and maliciously breaks a contract of service of hiring, knowing or having reasonable cause to believe that the probable consequences of his doing so, either alone or in combination with others, will be to endanger human life, or cause serious bodily injury, or to expose valuable property whether real or personal to destruction or serious injury, he shall, on conviction, be liable to a fine or to imprisonment for a term not exceeding three months.

23.125 The second provision is contained in s 241 of the Act. This states that every person who, with a view to compelling any person to abstain from doing an act which he has a legal right to do:

(a) uses violence to or intimidates such other person or his wife or children, or injures his property; or

(b) persistently follows such other persons from place to place; or

(c) hides any tools, clothes or other property owned or used by such other person, or deprives him of or hinders him in the use thereof; or

(d) watches or besets the house or other place where such person resides, or works, or carries on business, or happens to be, or the approach to such house or place; or

(e) follows such other person with two or more other persons in a disorderly manner along any street or road,

then he shall be liable to a fine not exceeding level 5 on the standard scale or a term of imprisonment not exceeding six months, or both.

23.126 Section 241 was considered in the case of *Galt v Philp*,[77] where workers engaged in a 'sit-in', during which they locked and barricaded laboratories, thus preventing other employees from entering the rooms. This was held to be 'besetting' within the meaning of s 241(1)(a) and the individuals concerned were found guilty of an offence under the Act.

---

[76] [1977] QB 729, [1977] 1 All ER 696, [1977] 2 WLR 310, 121 Sol Jo 103, CA; revsd [1978] AC 435, [1977] 3 All ER 70, [1977] 3 WLR 300, 141 JP 552, 121 Sol Jo 543, HL.

[77] [1984] IRLR 156, 1984 SLT 28.

23.127 It must be remembered that TULR(C)A, s 219 only protects a person from civil liability, and does not give any immunity in respect of criminal acts.

A. **Public Order Act 1986**

23.128 This Act abolished the common law offences of riot, rout, unlawful assembly and affray, and repealed the provisions of the Public Order Act 1936, relating to threatening behaviour likely to provoke a breach of the peace. A number of statutory criminal offences have been introduced by the new Act, which may be invoked when the conduct of industrial disputes gets out of hand. These are:

(a) *Riot* (s 1). This is where 12 or more people use or threaten to use violence for a common purpose which would cause a person of reasonable firmness to fear for his personal safety.

(b) *Violent disorder* (s 2). This has the same elements as *riot*, except that it applies when three or more persons are taking part.

(c) *Affray* (s 3). This also has the same elements as *riot*, except that only one person need be involved, and threats, by themselves, would not be sufficient.

(d) *Fear or provocation of violence* (s 4). It is an offence to use threatening, abusive or insulting words or behaviour or to distribute or display any visual representation which is threatening, abusive or insulting, where the act is intended or likely to make a person fear immediate violence, or to provoke immediate violence.

(e) *Harassment, alarm or distress* (s 5). This has almost the same elements as *fear or provocation of violence*, but the accused may defend himself by arguing that he had no reason to believe that a person alarmed was within his hearing or sight, or that his conduct was reasonable.

23.129 The Act also lays down rules for marches, processions, demonstrations and public assemblies.

B. **Intentional harassment**

23.130 The Criminal Justice and Public Order Act 1994, s 154 creates the criminal offence of intentional harassment. This is committed if a person, with intent to cause another person harassment, alarm or distress:

(a) uses threatening, abusive or insulting behaviour, or disorderly behaviour;

(b) displays any writing, sign or visible representation which is threatening, abusive or insulting

so that the other person feels harassment, alarm or distress.

23.131 This offence could be committed in a number of employment situations, including verbal or written abuse etc to those who cross picket lines, and harassment on grounds of race, sex, sexual orientation, disabilities, religion, and so on.

European Works Councils

23.132 The Transnational Information and Consultation of Employees Regulations 1999 came into force in January 2000, and implemented the European Works Council Directive 94/45/EC. The regulations were amended as from June 2011 by the Transnational

Information and Consultation of Employees (Amendment) Regulations 2010 (SI 2010/1088) which gave effect to Directive 2009/38/EC. There is also Government guidance produced by BIS which, although not legally binding, can be taken into account by tribunals.

23.133 The regulations apply to undertakings and groups of undertakings with at least 1,000 employees in the European Economic Area (ie, the 15 member states of the EU and Norway, Liechtenstein and Iceland), and at least 150 employees in each of two or more states. Employee numbers are calculated by adding together the number of employees in each month in a two-year period, and dividing the total by 24 (reg 6). An employee (or employee representative) may request information from the management for the purpose of determining whether the establishment or undertaking is part of a European-scale undertaking, and if there is a failure to supply the information, a complaint may be made to the Central Arbitration Committee, which can order the disclosure of the relevant information (reg 8), or, if it considers the matter to be beyond doubt, declare that the undertaking is a Community-scale organisation, ie within the scope of the regulations.

23.134 If there is a valid request by employees or their representatives (see reg 9) management shall set up a special negotiating body, charged with the task of determining the scope, composition, functions, and term of office of a European Works Council, or, as an alternative, the arrangements for an information and consultation procedure (regs 11–17). The members of the special negotiating body must be elected by ballot, organised by management, and an employee or employee representative may complain to CAC if there is dissatisfaction with the balloting plans. CAC can require that the ballot arrangements be modified so as to reflect the interests of UK employees. However, if there is already in existence a consultative committee which has been elected by ballot and represents all UK employees, that committee may nominate its own members to be members of the special negotiating body.

23.135 Negotiations between management and the special negotiating body must be carried out in a spirit of co-operation, with a view to reaching agreement, either by establishing a European Works Council or an information and consultation procedure. If necessary, one or more experts may be engaged to assist. If a Works Council is established, the agreement will determine the undertakings covered, the composition of the Works Council, its functions, venue, frequency and duration of meetings, financial and material resources to be allocated, and the duration of the agreement and procedure for renegotiation. If an information and consultation procedure is adopted, the agreement will specify a method by which the representatives are to meet to discuss the information conveyed to them, which must in particular relate to transnational questions which significantly affect the interests of the employees (reg 17).

23.136 If management fails to establish a European Works Council or an information and consultation procedure, or if the terms of the agreement are not complied with by management, a complaint may be made to the EAT, which can make an order specifying the steps which central management shall take, with the ultimate sanction of a penalty notice (up to £100,000) if there is a failure to take the required steps.

23.137 A person who is or was a member of the European Works Council or information and consultation representative (or an expert who was assisting) shall not disclose any information or document which has been in his possession by virtue of his position as such, which central management has entrusted to him on terms requiring it to be held in confidence. A breach of this duty is actionable, although not in respect of a protected disclosure (see para 10.74). Disputes as to whether it was reasonable for management to impose a requirement of confidentiality, as well as complaints that management have improperly withheld information which ought to be disclosed, may be referred for settlement to CAC.

A. Time off work for members of a European Works Council (regs 25–27)

23.138 An employee who is:

    (a) a member of a special negotiating body;

    (b) a member of a European Works Council;

    (c) an information and consultation representative; or

    (d) a candidate for election as a member or representative

is entitled to take reasonable time off work, with pay (at the appropriate hourly rate), during working hours, in order to perform his functions as a member, representative or candidate, or for training which is necessary for the exercise of his duties. He may bring a claim to an employment tribunal, that:

    (a) his employer has unreasonably refused to permit him to take time off work; or

    (b) has failed to pay him for taking time off work.

The complaint must be made within the usual time limit of three months (with the usual extension if it was not reasonably practicable to present it earlier). If the complaint is well founded, the tribunal will make a declaration, and order the employer to pay the amount to which the employee was entitled, or would have been had he taken the time off work.

B. Protection from detriment and dismissal (regs 28–33)

23.139 An employee who is:

    (a) a member of a special negotiating body;

    (b) a member of a European Works Council;

    (c) an information and consultation representative; or

    (d) a candidate for election as a member or representative

has the right not to be subjected to any detriment by an act or deliberate failure to act, or to be dismissed, on the ground that the employee performed any functions or activities as a member, representative or candidate, or made a request for time off work or for pay for time off work to perform those functions or activities.

23.140 Any employee (whether or not he is one of the categories in para 23.139) has the right not to be subjected to any detriment, or to be dismissed because:

    (a) he took proceedings before an employment tribunal to enforce a right or secure an entitlement under the regulations;

    (b) exercised an entitlement to complain to an appeal tribunal or CAC;

    (c) requested information from management to ascertain whether the establishment is part of a Community-scale undertaking (see reg 7);

    (d) acted with a view of securing that a special negotiating body, or European Works Council or an information and consultation procedure, did or did not come into existence;

    (e) indicated that he supported or did not support any of those institutions;

(f) stood as a candidate for membership of a special negotiating body, or European Works Council or as an information and consultation representative;

(g) influenced the way in which votes were to be cast by other employees in a ballot under the regulations;

(h) voted in such ballot;

(i) expressed doubts as to whether the ballot was properly conducted; or

(j) proposed to do or declined to do any of the things mentioned in paras (d)–(i) above.

23.141 A complaint may be made to an employment tribunal by a person who alleges that he has suffered a detriment or been dismissed on any of the above grounds. The complaint must be made within the usual time limits. If the complaint relates to a detriment, and is well founded, the tribunal will make a declaration, and may award compensation, as it thinks just and equitable. If the complaint relates to a dismissal, reinstatement or re-engagement can be ordered, or the usual basic and compensation awards will be made (see Chapter 20).

C. Information and Consultation of Employees Regulations 2004

23.142 These regulations give effect to EC Directive 2002/14/EC and are designed to create a framework for informing and consulting with employees. They apply to all undertakings with more than 50 employees. However, they only apply to undertakings which have a registered office or a principal place of business in Great Britain.

23.143 An 'undertaking' is a public or private undertaking which carries out an economic activity, whether or not operating for gain (see reg 2). This can be an incorporated legal entity, or an unincorporated body such as a partnership, co-operative, charity, mutual society, building society, etc. An undertaking does not include a group of companies, and therefore each company within a group must make its own arrangements. However, certain parts of the public sector will not come within the scope of the regulations, although a Cabinet Office Code of Practice will apply to such bodies, and local authorities will be encouraged to adopt similar arrangements.

23.144 To determine how many employees are employed in the undertaking, an average is taken in respect of the previous 12 months. The monthly total of number of employees employed in each calendar month is added together, and that total is divided by 12. Part-time employees can be counted provided they work for a certain number of hours (see reg 4(3)).

D. Pre-existing agreements (regs 8–9)

23.145 Many undertakings will already have a pre-existing agreement, which has been voluntarily negotiated outside of, or prior to, the regulations. If so, there is no requirement to enter into a new arrangement unless at least 40% of existing employees make a request, and this request is endorsed by a majority of those voting and 40% of those eligible to vote in a ballot. To be a valid pre-existing agreement, certain conditions must be met:

(a) The pre-existing agreement must be in writing. Thus, existing informal or customary arrangements will have to be formalised.

(b) All employees in the undertaking must be covered. This requirement may cause difficulties in practice, either in respect of members of senior management who are outside formal arrangements, or parts of the workforce not covered by a formal collective agreement.

(c) It must set out the manner in which the employer will give information to the employees or their representatives. This is the 'what', 'where' and 'how' requirement, which must be satisfied.

(d) It must have been approved by the employees. There can be an express approval, or an approval given by representatives of an independent trade union or other appropriate representatives.

E. Negotiated agreements (reg 7)

23.146 In the absence of any such pre-existing agreements, there is no obligation on an employer to do anything. However, the statutory procedure may be triggered by a request from 10% of the employees to commence negotiations about the establishment of an information and consultation procedure. (If 10% would amount to fewer than 15 employees, or more than 2,500 employees, a valid request occurs if there is a request by 15 or 2,500 employees respectively.) Employees (or their representatives) may request data from the employer to determine the number of employees employed so as to ascertain whether or not the regulations apply. There are certain formalities to be observed when making the request.

23.147 The employer may, at this stage, seek a declaration from CAC that the request is not valid (eg because it lacks the relevant support from the employees, or because there is an insufficient number of employees employed in the undertaking, etc). If this is upheld by CAC, that will be the end of the matter, although there is nothing to prevent a further request being made once any apparent defect in the earlier request has been remedied. A request will not be valid if it is made within three years of a previous agreement having been made, or the standard provisions (see para 23.151) are deemed to apply.

23.148 Otherwise, the employer must enter into negotiations to reach a negotiated agreement. The regulations provide for the election or appointment of negotiating representatives, ensuring that they represent all the employees. Both parties should 'work in a spirit of cooperation and with due regard for the reciprocal rights and obligations, taking into account the interests of both the undertaking and the employees' (reg 21). Negotiations for an agreement should not last more than six months, although there is a certain flexibility with regard to the timetable. There may be a single agreement covering all the employees, but there may be separate consultation arrangements for different parts of the undertaking, because parts of an undertaking may have little in common with other sectors and have different activities. The agreement will provide for the appointment or election of information and consultation representatives. It must be signed on behalf of the employer and by all the negotiating representatives, or signed by a majority of them and either approved in writing by 50% of the employees or approved in a ballot of all the affected employees.

23.149 The agreement may provide that consultation will take place through representatives or provide for information and consultation to be provided or undertaken directly with the employees. A Guidance Note issued by the DTI makes certain suggestions about the contents of the agreement, but the employer and employee representatives are free to agree different arrangements about the coverage of the agreement, the methods chosen for providing information and consultation arrangements, the frequency with which information is provided, the subject-matter to be covered, and the methods adopted for the exchange of views and opinions. Statutory consultation requirements such as handling redundancies, TUPE transfers, health and safety consultations, etc may be included or excluded in the agreement, although if they are excluded they must still be observed in the usual manner. The agreement should consider how confidential information is to be handled, the resolution of disputes, and the circumstances in which the agreement can be reviewed, revised or terminated.

23.150 It must be stressed that consultation is not collective bargaining. It is about the exchange of views and the establishment of a dialogue with the workforce. However, where the Standard Information and Consultation Provisions apply (see para 23.151), consultation about changing work organisation or contractual relations must be conducted with a view to reaching agreement, although employers will still be free to make the final decisions if there is disagreement within the consultation arrangements.

F. Statutory default provisions (reg 18)

23.151 If the employer fails to initiate negotiations following a valid employee request, or if they fail to reach a negotiated agreement, the Standard Information and Consultation Provisions (SICP) will come into effect. The employer must hold a ballot, under the supervision of a ballot supervisor, to ensure the election of the relevant number of information and consultation representatives (one representative for each 50 employees, subject to a maximum of 50 representatives). Thereafter, there are specific issues in respect of which the employer is to provide information and on which to consult with the representatives so elected. These are:

(a) the recent and probable development of the undertaking's activities and economic situation;

(b) the situation, structure and probable development of employment within the undertaking and any anticipatory measures envisaged, in particular where there is a threat to employment within the undertaking;

(c) decisions which are likely to lead to substantial changes in work organisation or in contractual relations, including business transfers and collective redundancies.

23.152 The information provided must be given at such time, in such fashion and with such content as to enable the representatives to conduct an adequate study, and to prepare for consultation.

23.153 There is a general requirement that if the employer provides information or documents in confidence, the recipient must not breach that confidence, unless he reasonably believes that the disclosure would be protected by virtue of ERA, s 43A (see Chapter 10). Additionally, the employer may withhold information the disclosure of which would seriously harm the functioning of, or would be prejudicial to, the undertaking. A representative who disputes that the information is confidential, or that disclosure would be harmful or prejudicial may apply to CAC for a ruling.

23.154 An employee who is a negotiating representative or a SICP representative has the usual right to have time off work (with pay) to perform his duties as such. He will have the statutory protection against dismissal or detriment because he performed his functions as such or exercised his right to have time off work to do so. However, a dismissal will not be automatically unfair if the reason was that he disclosed information or documents in breach of his duty of confidentiality, unless he reasonably believed that the disclosure was a protected disclosure (see Chapter 10). An individual employee also has protection against dismissal or detriment if he took action to enforce his rights under the regulations (eg, by acting to secure a negotiated agreement, etc).

23.155 There is no such statutory protection for employees or representatives who have a pre-existing agreement, as these fall outside the scope of the regulations. Such rights as they have will be determined within the existing legal provisions (see especially Chapter 17).

G. **Enforcement (reg 22)**

23.156 Most of the rights contained in the regulations may be enforced by way of a complaint to the Central Arbitration Committee (CAC) (rights in respect of time off work, detriment and dismissal may be enforced in the employment tribunal). There are some 14 types of complaints which can be made, ranging from a breach of the employer's obligation to provide information on the numbers of employees employed, through to a declaration as to whether the disclosure of certain information is covered by the confidence provisions. In most cases, CAC will issue a declaration, which will have effect as if made by the High Court (or Court of Session). There is a right of appeal to the EAT.

23.157 If the employer fails to hold a ballot for the election of SICP representatives, or if he fails to comply with the terms of a negotiated agreement or the SICP, and CAC finds the complaint well founded, the applicant may apply to EAT for a penalty notice. Unless the EAT is satisfied that the failure was beyond the employer's control, or there was some other reasonable excuse, EAT may set a penalty of up to £75,000, depending on its gravity or other factors, including the reason for the failure, etc (see *Amicus v Macmillan Publishers Ltd*[78]).

23.158 The Department for Business, Innovation and Skills has issued Guidance Notes to the regulations. ACAS has issued 'Good practice advice'. CAC has issued 'A Guide for Employers and Employees to the role of the Central Arbitration Committee (CAC)'.

---

[78] [2007] IRLR 885, (2007) 151 SJLB 1058, EAT.

Appendices

Appendix A
Monetary awards (as at 1 February 2014)

Appendix B
Statutory Redundancy Pay Calculation Table

Appendix A
Monetary awards (as at 1 February 2014)

Statutory reference	Statutory right	Maximum rate	Maximum award
1. ERA s 12(4)	Itemised pay statement	None	Un-notified deduction for 13 weeks prior to application to an employment tribunal
2. ERA s 31(1)	Guarantee pay	£25 per day	£125 in any period of three months
3. ERA, s 69(1)	Medical suspension pay	None	26 weeks' pay
4. TULR(C)A 1992 s 149(2)	Action short of dismissal	None	Just and equitable
5. TULR(C)A 1992 s 172(2)	Time off work	None	Just and equitable (refusal to allow) or normal pay or average hourly earnings (failure to pay)
6. ERA s 54(3)	Time off to look for work or arrange for retraining	None	Two-fifths of a week's pay
7. ERA s 93(2)	Written reasons for dismissal	None	Two weeks' pay
8. ERA ss 118–124	Unfair dismissal	£464 per week	Basic award £13,920 Compensatory award £76,574 Additional award £12.064–£24,128 (26 to 52 weeks' pay)
9. TULR(C)A 1992 s 158(1) and (2)	Unfair dismissal for trade union membership or non-membership		**(a)** Re-instatement/ re-engagement not sought
		£464 per week	**(i)** Basic award £13,920 (minimum £5,676) **(ii)** Compensatory award £76,574
		£464 per week	**(b)** Re-instatement/ re-engagement sought, but IT makes no order **(i)** Basic award £13,920 (minimum £5,676) **(ii)** Compensatory award £76,574
			(c) Re-instatement/ re-engagement ordered but not complied with

Statutory reference	Statutory right	Maximum rate	Maximum award
		£464 per week	**(i)** Basic award £13,920 (minimum £5,676)
			(ii) Compensatory award £76,574
		£464 per week	**(iii)** Additional award £12,064–£24,128 (26 to 52 weeks' pay)
			(d) Re-instatement/ re-engagement ordered and complied with Compensation award – loss made good
10. ERA s 162	Redundancy pay	£464 per week	£13,920
11. ERA s 184	Rights on employer's insolvency	£464 per week	Arrears of pay £3,712 (8 weeks' pay maximum)
		£464 per week	Statutory notice £5,568 (12 weeks' pay maximum)
		£464 per week	Holiday pay £2,784 (6 weeks' pay maximum)
		£464 per week	Basic award £13,920
12. Equality Act	Protected characteristic	None	Just and equitable
13. TULR(C)A 1992 s 67(8)	Right not to be unjustifiably disciplined	£464 per week	£90,494 (30 weeks' pay plus amount of compensatory award)
14. TULR(C)A 1992 s 176(6)	Unreasonable expulsion/ exclusion from trade union membership	£464 per week	£90,494 (30 weeks' pay plus amount of compensatory award)
15. TULR(C)A 1992 s 189(4)	Protective award	None	Up to 90 days' pay
16. ET Extension of Jurisdiction Order 1994	Breach of contract	None	£25,000
17. TULR(C)A s 140(4)	Refusal to employ on TU grounds		£76,574
18. TULR(C)A s 70C	Consultation with union on training	£464	£928 (2 weeks' pay)
19. ERelA s 11(2)	Right to be accompanied	£464	£928 (2 weeks' pay)

Appendix B
Statutory Redundancy Pay Calculation Table

The redundancy payment due to each employee under the statutory redundancy payment scheme depends on his or her age and length of service (up to 20 years). This determines the number of weeks' pay due. The maximum week's pay to count is currently £464.

| | Service (years) | | | | | | | | | | | | | | | | | | |
Age	2	3	4	5	6	7	8	9	10	11	12	13	14	15	16	17	18	19	20
17*	1																		
18	1	1½																	
19	1	1½	2																
20	1	1½	2	2½	-														
21	1	1½	2	2½	3	-													
22	1	1½	2	2½	3	3½	-												
23	1½	2	2½	3	3½	4	4½	-											
24	2	2½	3	3½	4	4½	5	5½	-										
25	2	3	3½	4	4½	5	5½	6	6½	-									
26	2	3	4	4½	5	5½	6	6½	7	7½	-								
27	2	3	4	5	5½	6	6½	7	7½	8	8½	-							
28	2	3	4	5	6	6½	7	7½	8	8½	9	9½	-						
29	2	3	4	5	6	7	7½	8	8½	9	9½	10	10½	-					
30	2	3	4	5	6	7	8	8½	9	9½	10	10½	11	11½	-				
31	2	3	4	5	6	7	8	9	9½	10	10½	11	11½	12	12½	-			
32	2	3	4	5	6	7	8	9	10	10½	11	11½	12	12½	13	13½	-		
33	2	3	4	5	6	7	8	9	10	11	11½	12	12½	13	13½	14	14½	-	
34	2	3	4	5	6	7	8	9	10	11	12	12½	13	13½	14	14½	15	15½	-
35	2	3	4	5	6	7	8	9	10	11	12	13	13½	14	14½	15	15½	16	16½
36	2	3	4	5	6	7	8	9	10	11	12	13	14	14½	15	15½	16	16½	17
37	2	3	4	5	6	7	8	9	10	11	12	13	14	15	15½	16	16½	17	17½
38	2			5	6	7	8	9	10	11	12	13	14	15	16	16½	17	17½	18
39	2	3	4	5	6	7	8	9	10	11	12	13	14	15	16	17	17½	18	18½
40	2	3	4	5	6	7	8	9	10	11	12	13	14	15	16	17	18	18½	19
41	2	3	4	5	6	7	8	9	10	11	12	13	14	15	16	17	18	19	19½
42	2½	3½	4½	5½	6½	7½	8½	9½	10½	11½	12½	13½	14½	15½	16½	17½	18½	19½	20½
43	3	4	5	6	7	8	9	10	11	12	13	14	15	16	17	18	19	20	21
44	3	4½	5½	6½	7½	8½	9½	10½	11½	12½	13½	14½	15½	16½	17½	18½	19½	20½	21½

Age	Service (years)																		
	2	3	4	5	6	7	8	9	10	11	12	13	14	15	16	17	18	19	20
45	3	4½	6	7	8	9	10	11	12	13	14	15	16	17	18	19	20	21	22
46	3	4½	6	7½	8½	9½	10½	11½	12½	13½	14½	15½	16½	17½	18½	19½	20½	21½	22½
47	3	4½	6	7½	9	10	11	12	13	14	15	16	17	18	19	20	21	22	23
48	3	4½	6	7½	9	10½	11½	12½	13½	14½	15½	16½	17½	18½	19½	20½	21½	22½	23½
49	3	4½	6	7½	9	10½	12	13	14	15	16	17	18	19	20	21	22	23	24
50	3	4½	6	7½	9	10½	12	13½	14½	15½	16½	17½	18½	19½	20½	21½	22½	23½	24½
51	3	4½	6	7½	9	10½	12	13½	15	16	17	18	19	20	21	22	23	24	25
52	3	4½	6	7½	9	10½	12	13½	15	16½	17½	18½	19½	20½	21½	22½	23½	24½	25½
53	3	4½	6	7½	9	10½	12	13½	15	16½	18	19	20	21	22	23	24	25	26
54	3	4½	6	7½	9	10½	12	13½	15	16½	18	19½	20½	21½	22½	23½	24½	25½	26½
55	3	4½	6	7½	9	10½	12	13½	15	16½	18	19½	21	22	23	24	25	26	27
56	3	4½	6	7½	9	10½	12	13½	15	16½	18	19½	21	22½	23½	24½	25½	26½	27½
57	3	4½	6	7½	9	10½	12	13½	15	16½	18	19½	21	22½	24	25	26	27	28
58	3	4½	6	7½	9	10½	12	13½	15	16½	18	19½	21	22½	24	25½	26½	27½	28½
59	3	4½	6	7½	9	10½	12	13½	15	16½	18	19½	21	22½	24	25½	27	28	29
60	3	4½	6	7½	9	10½	12	13½	15	16½	18	19½	21	22½	24	25½	27	28½	29½
61+	3	4v½	6	7½	9	10½	12	13½	15	16½	18	19½	21	22½	24	25½	27	28½	30

Index

A

abroad, working 2.119–113, 3.113, 10.34, 13.34
absence 4.132, 6.28–37, 6.85–92, 7.52, 10.100, 12.65–70, 13.16–23, 17.206–216
  long-term 7.53, 17.61
  periods of 2.87, 2.167, 6.38–43, 7.121–127, 10.24, 13.8, 13.18–23
absenteeism 12.52, 12.72, 17.120, 18.55
  persistent 17.106–116
absolute discharges 4.241, 4.245
abuse 1.22, 1.91, 4.59, 10.100, 10.115, 16.12, 16.37, 17.17
  sexual 4.83, 12.67
ACAS, see Advisory, Conciliation and Arbitration Service
access to medical reports 7.128–132
accidents 2.145–148, 7.86, 7.95, 9.30, 11.12–18, 17.60, 20.85
  notifiable 10.47
accommodation 2.67, 4.184, 7.23, 8.17, 8.40, 9.77, 11.81, 14.4
account of profits 10.57, 19.68
accountants 4.208, 4.247, 22.60
accrued holiday pay 3.112, 3.125, 7.79–89, 7.133, 8.4, 8.13–15, 15.11, 15.34
accrued pension rights 6.32, 16.23, 17.216
acquired rights, Directive 1.79, 9.2, 13.39
additional adoption leave 6.1, 6.21, 6.39, 6.55, 6.67–81, 6.95, 17.81, 17.182
additional awards 17.241
additional maternity leave (AML) 4.134, 6.1, 6.19–22, 6.32–55, 6.70, 6.89, 6.98, 17.182
additional paternity leave 1.28, 6.103–121, 13.43
  adoptions from overseas 6.111–121
  eligibility 6.104–110
additional responsibilities 1.48, 3.83, 5.30, 20.75
adjournments 20.76–83
adjustments, reasonable 4.102, 7.53, 11.119, 17.102, 17.116

administration orders 7.134, 18.67
administrative functions 1.18, 9.23–29
administrators 9.50–53, 9.59
adopters 6.79, 6.95–121, 6.131, 13.43
adoption
  leave 2.78, 2.102, 6.21, 6.39, 6.55, 6.67–81, 6.111–121, 15.17
    additional 6.1, 6.21, 6.39, 6.55, 6.67–92, 6.65, 17.81, 17.182
    ordinary 6.1, 6.21–31, 6.67–81
    reasonable contact during 6.73
    return to work after 6.75–77
    work during 6.74
  remedies 6.78
  statutory adoption pay (SAP) 2.91, 6.79–81, 6.107, 6.117, 13.43, 15.17
adoptive parents 6.72, 6.84–86, 6.138, 3.43
adult workers 4.259, 7.70, 7.99
advertisements 3.30, 4.16, 4.46, 4.207–208, 4.219, 20.23, 20.37, 21.32
  discriminatory 4.205–206
Advisory, Conciliation and Arbitration Service (ACAS) 1.1–17, 1.45, 1.58, 20.47–48, 21.70, 21.76, 23.15–17
  advice 1.4
  arbitration 1.13
  Code 12.14, 17.221, 17.237
  codes of practice 1.15–17
  conciliation 1.5–12
  enquiries 1.14
  function 1.1–17
  staff 1.1
age 1.93, 2.106–111, 4.62–74, 4.244–247, 6.85, 17.197, 18.52–60, 18.66
  child-bearing 4.50, 6.10–14, 11.80
  discrimination 4.64, 4.73, 4.208, 18.87

retirement 3.63, 4.28, 4.67, 15.1, 15.27
agency workers 1.96, 2.130, 2.152–173, 7.31, 7.49, 8.37, 9.9; see also temporary workers
  Agency Workers Regulations 2010 2.163–173
  Directive 1.96
  employment agencies and employment businesses distinguished 2.152
  status 2.153–162
aggravated damages 4.231, 20.97
aggrieved employees 7.6, 21.70
agricultural workers 7.98, 8.39
alternative employment 6.15–16, 7.3–6, 12.88, 17.96–105, 17.115, 17.134, 18.28–32, 18.40
  and disciplinary procedures 12.88
  suitable 4.104, 6.39–43, 17.98, 17.119, 17.140, 17.186, 17.195, 18.28–32
  unreasonable refusal 18.33–37
alternative work, see alternative employment
amalgamation 22.5, 22.28, 22.54, 22.81–83
  instruments of 22.20, 22.28, 22.48, 22.81
AML, see additional maternity leave
animosity, personal 17.189, 21.118
annual leave 2.152, 2.165, 6.29, 7.103, 14.3
  entitlement 7.73–89
annual statements 22.57–62
anonymity 12.7, 12.22, 20.57
antenatal care 2.71, 4.130, 7.133, 14.13, 15.17
  time off for 6.3–8
anti-discrimination laws, see discrimination
anti-discrimination
  provisions 4.4, 4.66, 4.73, 4.124–127, 4.138, 4.148–151, 4.207–208, 4.217
anxiety 4.92, 10.116, 11.104, 17.110

apparent or ostensible
authority 3.60, 3.102, 20.37
appeal hearings 6.136, 12.34–40,
17.79
appeals 1.13–29, 11.15–24,
12.34–40, 17.64–80,
17.228–233, 19.32–55,
20.118–130
internal 9.34, 12.36, 20.4
applicants 2.50, 4.46–52, 4.67,
4.107–127, 4.148–159,
12.34–40, 21.4, 21.15
apprenticeship 2.28, 2.103–105,
2.130, 2.152, 3.1, 8.39, 8.61, 9.5
contracts of 2.103, 2.130,
5.3, 8.39
appropriate action 4.236, 11.66,
12.15–16
appropriate comparators 4.29–30
appropriate representatives 9.52,
9.76–78, 18.69, 18.80–85,
23.149
arbitration 4.211, 7.6, 13.29,
17.41, 20.37
Advisory, Conciliation and
Arbitration Service 1.1–17
armed forces 1.105, 2.21, 2.71,
2.94, 7.56, 7.98, 7.121–127
reserves 7.121–127
arrears 5.14, 5.63, 8.47, 9.48,
14.11–14, 17.186, 23.23,
23.52
assets 9.8–9, 9.25, 9.35, 9.54–55,
13.12, 13.40, 19.41–43,
22.67–70
transfer of 9.8–13, 9.30–35
associated employers 2.5–9, 5.6,
6.45, 13.8, 13.22, 13.32, 13.40,
17.187
associative discrimination 4.16,
4.46, 4.64, 4.124, 4.140
asylum seekers 2.115, 3.11
attachment of earnings
orders 2.61, 8.5
attendance 1.29, 2.110, 4.246,
20.70, 20.85, 23.77, 23.110
orders 1.29, 4.246, 20.70
audits 5.57, 10.30
auxiliary aids 4.112
award of costs 1.29, 17.214,
20.80, 20.109, 20.125

B
babies 6.103
backdating of awards, equal
pay 5.66
backdating of collective
agreements 3.76
bad faith 1.10, 4.39, 10.82,
11.65, 12.75, 21.11

balance of convenience 10.4,
16.30, 19.62
balance of probabilities 5.4,
11.97, 20.82
ballot papers 22.40, 22.51–52,
22.82, 23.53–55
ballots 21.22–25, 21.94, 22.40–
54, 22.68–83, 23.32, 23.47–67,
23.134, 23.142–158
effectiveness 23.66–67
for overseas members 22.56
political fund 22.76
separate workplace
23.54–55
voting requirements
23.57–65
band of reasonableness
test 17.78, 17.87
bank holidays 2.90, 17.12
bankruptcy 7.133
bargaining, see collective
bargaining
barristers 1.22, 4.216, 4.247,
8.39, 20.37, 20.68, 20.72,
20.106
basic awards 7.107, 14.14, 15.28,
17.195–200, 17.210, 17.219,
17.237
basic working conditions 1.96,
2.164–173
benefits 1.80, 2.133, 3.11, 3.40,
4.67–68, 6.20–37, 9.33–43,
10.86–90
contractual 3.40, 6.70,
9.39–43, 10.23, 15.15,
15.21–23, 15.30
financial 2.107, 13.1
fringe 5.17, 16.23, 18.29
invalidity 17.208
non-contractual 6.29, 12.89,
15.15
service-related 4.68, 18.52
social security 1.72, 6.86,
7.134, 17.186
best interests 10.54, 16.12,
17.190
betting workers 2.61, 7.110,
20.37
bias 12.19, 20.91–95, 20.129
blameworthy conduct 3.91,
17.201, 17.229, 21.110
bonus payments 10.23, 17.209,
21.103
bonus schemes 3.64, 3.88, 8.33,
10.21–24
breach of contract 10.49–57,
15.12–15, 15.19–27, 16.6–8,
16.16–32, 17.21–22, 17.34–46,
23.20–28

repudiatory 3.35, 6.10, 17.12,
17.23, 17.34, 20.33, 20.41,
20.71
suing for 16.32
breastfeeding 6.9–14
bribery 10.66–68, 10.95
broadly similar work 2.85,
2.132, 2.164, 5.13, 5.25
bullying 10.109–117, 17.39
definition 10.109–117
bundles 20.63–71
burden of proof 4.184, 4.189,
4.205, 5.4, 11.97–98, 20.82,
21.42, 21.57
Directive 1.92
equal pay 5.59
equality in
employment 4.222–225
health and safety 11.97–98
bus drivers 8.25, 11.150
business consultants 2.16
business efficacy 3.39, 3.46

C
CAC, see Central Arbitration
Committee
cancer 4.84, 11.110
candidates 1.107, 4.103–111,
9.81, 18.72, 22.48–54, 22.73,
23.139–140
capability 2.67, 2.96, 4.89–94,
10.13, 17.73, 17.84–87,
17.117–119, 18.52
care, duty of 9.72, 10.38, 11.102,
11.106
carers 4.116, 4.247, 4.250, 6.131,
8.44
case management 1.29, 5.39,
20.59–90
hearings 20.55–58
orders 20.55
cash 3.18, 5.2, 5.40, 8.29, 9.45,
12.8, 12.22, 12.47
shortages 8.29–30
casting vote 22.36
casual workers 2.174
Central Arbitration Committee
(CAC) 1.2, 1.13, 1.16, 1.19,
1.21, 1.57, 2.68, 23.8–13,
23.17, 23.134, 23.138, 23.147,
23.153, 23.156, 23.158
certificates of
independence 1.18, 22.7–15,
22.86, 23.6
certification of trade
unions 22.7–15
Certification Officer 1.2, 1.18,
20.118, 21.9, 21.85, 22.7–17,
22.76
cessation of work 13.19

characteristics, protected, see protected characteristics
check-off arrangements 21.79–82
child-bearing age 4.50, 6.10–14, 11.80
child-care responsibilities 4.173, 5.29, 6.3–8
childbearing age 6.10–14
childbirth 4.256, 5.21, 6.2, 6.19–37, 6.53, 15.17, 20.37
children 1.97, 2.106–111, 4.24, 4.64, 6.1–2, 6.50–55, 6.67–137, 11.114–124
  and contracts of employment 2.110–111
Christmas shopping 7.119
civil courts 1.39, 4.217, 16.3, 20.42, 20.57, 21.45
civil liability 10.110, 11.5, 11.31, 11.72, 11.103, 11.114, 11.137, 11.139, 22.47
civil partnerships 2.102, 4.10, 4.18, 4.32, 4.123–127, 4.157, 4.163, 6.112, 6.114, 6.131
civil proceedings 1.58, 6.10, 10.111, 11.31, 11.90
civil service 4.147, 16.33–37, 22.13
clear warnings 12.82, 17.89
clocking offences 12.44, 17.123
closed shops 10.3, 17.172, 21.7, 21.38, 23.71
codes of practice 1.15, 1.49, 1.58–59, 3.21, 10.47, 12.12, 12.16, 12.21, 21.73, 21.76
  health and safety 11.89–91
collateral contracts 3.5, 15.7
  and wrongful dismissal 16.8
collective action 23.95–98
collective agreements 3.57–79, 3.105, 3.110–111, 3.113, 7.6, 7.55, 7.64, 7.72, 7.75, 9.37, 9.68, 9.73, 23.99–104
  backdating 3.76
  changing terms of 3.71–73
  conflicting 3.77
  and contractual terms 3.57–79
  determination of terms to be incorporated into individual contract of employment 3.78–79
  express incorporation 3.57–66
  implied incorporation 3.67–70
  legal effect 23.103
  and non-unionists 3.74–75
  and transfer of undertakings 9.73

collective bargaining 1.15, 1.19, 1.107, 2.8, 21.66, 21.85, 22.17, 22.85, 23.2, 23.4, 23.6, 23.7, 23.9, 23.13–16, 23.102
  disclosure of information 23.15–18
  legal liabilities and legal proceedings 23.19–36
  purposes 1.18, 2.8, 2.70, 22.16, 23.2, 23.4, 23.7
collective consultation, see consultation
collective facilities 2.166, 2.170
collective redundancies 1.78, 9.2, 9.4, 18.2, 18.69–75, 23.151
  Directive 1.78, 18.69–71
  notification to minister 18.101–102
  who and when to consult 18.72–85
colour 2.7, 4.140, 23.24; see also race discrimination
common law 2.148, 2.153, 10.19–20, 11.99, 11.103, 11.114, 15.40, 16.3, 16.5, 16.6, 16.16–20, 16.25–27, 22.25, 22.31
  actions 4.60, 16.3, 16.14, 16.25
  duties 11.35, 11.103, 11.121, 11.130
company directors, see directors
comparators 4.17, 4.28–30, 4.43, 4.100, 5.8, 5.10–14, 5.20, 5.35, 5.40–41, 5.52, 5.64
  hypothetical 2.132, 4.169
compensation 10.83, 10.86–90, 16.28, 17.192–213, 17.234–243, 20.96–105, 21.15, 21.19, 21.58, 21.60, 21.118, 21.121, 21.124
  amount of 9.71, 10.57, 17.228, 20.126, 21.15, 21.59
  awards 6.136, 10.82, 10.86–90, 17.192–203, 20.126, 21.14–15, 21.19, 21.58–60, 21.121, 21.124
  reduced 12.64, 17.1, 17.111
  for unfair dismissal 7.192–200
compensatory periods of rest 7.96, 7.99
competition 10.54, 10.92, 16.12, 17.143, 17.149, 19.9, 19.15, 19.25–36, 19.41, 19.44–53; see also non-competition clauses
competitive tendering 9.15, 9.26, 9.60

competitors 10.91, 17.140, 17.143, 19.2, 19.10–11, 19.25–36, 19.63
  working for 19.37–40
compliance 1.6–7, 2.126, 10.46, 10.58, 12.78, 17.176. 17.185
compromise agreements 1.13, 2.8, 13.29, 17.191, 20.37, 22.16
compulsory insurance 10.24, 11.88, 11.123
compulsory maternity leave 4.135, 6.19–20, 6.29, 10.24, 11.81
compulsory retirement 4.63
computers 18.8
conciliation 1.1–12, 1.58, 3.110, 4.211, 20.6, 20.37, 20.39, 20.43, 20.48, 21.112, 21.114, 23.17, 23.21
  Advisory, Conciliation and Arbitration Service 1.1–17
  early 1.8, 20.6, 20.48
  officers 1.9–10, 4.211, 13.29, 17.191, 17.245, 20.36, 20.43, 20.101
conduct
  employees 12.6, 12.62, 12.73–76, 15.18, 17.198, 17.229, 17.240
  employers 16.18–20, 17.22–25, 17.38–42, 18.5, 20.33
  giving rise to separate proceedings 4.209
  inside the employment 17.120–19
  outside the employment 17.140–145
  prohibited 4.5–7, 4.44, 4.61, 4.129, 4.235, 10.113
confessions 12.8, 12.17, 17.127
confidence 5.8, 10.3, 10.10, 10.12, 10.69, 17.27, 17.34, 17.43, 17.48, 17.187, 17.189, 19.16, 23.153, 23.156; see also mutual trust and confidence
  duty of 10.55, 19.68
confidential information 6.70, 6.88, 10.25, 10.69–73, 19.2, 19.7, 19.14, 19.28–31, 19.38, 19.57, 19.67
confidentiality 5.55, 10.81, 10.96, 19.2, 19.15–20, 22.20, 23.137, 23.154
  clauses 5.55, 19.2
  duty of 10.25–31, 10.81, 19.18, 22.20, 23.153
confinement 6.22, 6.60, 6.65, 6.90, 7.50
conflicts of interest 1.22, 1.107, 20.91

congregation 4.18, 4.142
consensual termination
    17.68–72, 18.7, 18.10
consent 1.9, 1.13, 3.93,
    3.99–102, 4.114, 7.119, 7.127,
    7.130, 8.8–12, 8.23, 11.89,
    11.92, 21.53–54
    mutual 18.7
    written 1.25, 8.8–12, 10.91,
        17.43
consideration 15.23, 20.36
consistency 1.54, 12.56, 17.75
conspiracy 22.25, 23.23–24,
    23.43, 23.80
    criminal 22.25, 23.23–24
constables, see police, officers
constructive dismissal 6.16,
    10.14–15, 12.58, 12.64, 12.76,
    12.85–87, 13.26, 15.25, 15.28,
    16.6, 16.19, 16.32, 17.7, 17.12,
    17.21–28, 17.30, 17.32, 17.34–
    37, 17.39–41, 17.43–48, 17.50,
    17.56–57, 17.171, 17.230,
    18.36, 19.57, 20.33
    definition 17.21–25
    and employer breach of
        implied term 17.27–46
    and genuine dispute over
        contract 17.26
    may be fair 17.47–48
    wrongful 6.19, 16.32
constructive resignation 3.36,
    17.56–57
consultants 2.59, 10.4
    business 2.16
consultation 1.19–23, 1.28,
    1.51, 11.40, 11.43, 11.45–48,
    17.94, 17.102, 18.45–50,
    18.69–75, 23.132, 23.134–140,
    23.142–150
    full 9.57, 17.113, 20.79
    periods 9.4, 18.79, 18.94
    provisions 9.21, 9.78, 18.72,
        18.74, 18.78–85, 18.94,
        18.99, 23.150
contempt of court 11.27, 19.65,
    22.63, 23.94
continuity of employment 1.13,
    2.114, 2.137, 2.151, 2.162,
    12.63, 13.1–15, 17.191
    and absence by arrangement
        or custom 13.24–28
    and absence from work on
        account of a temporary
        cessation of work
        13.18–23
    breaking of 2.8, 2.114, 2.122,
        6.71, 13.4–12, 13.33–37,
        18.68
    and change of
        employer 13.39–41

counting and
    computing 13.4–12
    effect of rules 13.42–43
    and incapability for work
        because of sickness or
        injury 13.16–17
    and military service 13.38
    and periods spent working
        abroad 13.34
    preserving 13.13–28
    and re-employment after
        unfair dismissal 13.29–32
    and strikes and lock-
        outs 13.35–37
    weeks not counting
        towards 13.33–38
continuous employment 6.18,
    6.88, 6.104, 6.112, 13.1–28,
    18.33, 18.38–39, 18.61, 18.66,
    20.29, 20.34, 21.120; see also
    continuity of employment
    period of 7.112–113, 7.115,
        7.118, 13.1, 13.3–4, 13.7–
        17, 13.30, 13.32, 13.37–38,
        15.28–31, 17.5, 17.186
continuous service, see
    continuous employment
contracting out 9.14, 9.25,
    20.35–45, 23.30
    restrictions on 4.211,
        20.35–45
contractors 2.43, 2.56, 2.58–60,
    2.146, 8.15, 9.25–16,
    11.34–35, 11.49, 17.169–170
contracts
    collateral 3.5, 15.7, 15.7
    global 2.174, 13.21
    illegal 2.114, 3.8, 3.11, 4.195
    contracts for services 2.14, 2.36,
        2.52, 2.57, 2.159, 2.161, 9.5,
        19.57
    contracts of employment 7.108,
        9.30–35, 10.1–117, 12.90,
        13.4–5, 13.8–9, 13.13–19,
        13.24–25, 13.37, 15.1–9,
        15.12, 15.14–15, 15.21, 15.25,
        15.30–31, 15.34–35, 15.39,
        16.3, 16.6. 16.8, 16.12. 16.21,
        16.24, 16.27, 16.37, 17.4,
        17.65–66, 17.69–70, 23.74,
        23.76, 23.78, 23.95
    constructive dismissal, see
        constructive dismissal
    disciplinary and grievance
        procedures 3.95–97
    formation 3.1–128
    and holidays 3.125
    implied terms, see implied
        terms
    itemised pay
        statements 3.123–124

nature 2.1–178
    and occupational pension
        schemes 3.126–128
    parties 2.1–35, 2.62–173
    performance 10.1–117
    personal nature 10.1–7
    redundancy, see redundancy
    terms and conditions 3.19–94;
        see also contractual terms
    and transfer of
        undertakings 9.30–35
    unfair dismissal, see unfair
        dismissal
    written particulars 3.112–122
    wrongful dismissal, see
        wrongful dismissal
    and young persons 2.108–9
contracts of service 2.13, 2.21–
    23, 2.25, 2.36, 2.52, 2.57, 2.65.
    2.99, 2.144, 4.191, 6.57; see
    also contracts of employment
contractual arrangements 2.17,
    2.146, 8.27, 12.69, 12.71, 19.30
contractual benefits 3.40, 3.42,
    6.28, 6.70, 9.39, 10.23, 15.14–
    15, 15.21, 15.30
contractual changes 17.12
contractual disciplinary
    procedures 11.113, 15.39, 16.5,
    16.16, 16.30, 17.237, 19.57
contractual duties 2.123, 3.50,
    3.52, 8.23, 19.23
contractual entitlements 1.38,
    3.125, 15.15, 17.111, 19.10
contractual obligations 3.17,
    3.21, 3.29, 3.24, 3.42, 3.50,
    3.85, 3.98, 5.26, 17.23, 17.26,
    17.29, 17.40, 17.100, 17.117,
    17.156, 18.20
    strict 3.2, 3.19, 3.42
contractual relationship
    2.51, 3.39
contractual remuneration 6.47,
    6.63, 6.80, 7.4
contractual rights, strict 3.2,
    16.3, 16.37
contractual terms 2.20, 2.23,
    2.43, 2.132–140, 3.12,
    3.19–56, 5.5–21, 6.15–17,
    6.21, 6.28–31, 8.10, 8.19, 8.44,
    9.4. 9.7. 9.12, 9.26, 9.37–38,
    17.186–187
    and collective
        agreements 3.57–79
    custom as source of 3.80–85
    equality of 5.5–14; see also
        equality
    express incorporation
        of collective
        agreements 3.57–66
    implied, see implied terms

implied incorporation
of collective
agreements 3.67–70
interpretation 3.24–27
new 3.71–73, 3.104–107,
9.7, 9.45, 16.32, 17.41,
17.152–156
statutory 3.56, 3.121, 9.37
unenforceable 4.210–212
variation 3.100–111
contributory fault 17.187
contributory negligence 11.114,
11.147–148
control 2.7–8, 2.11–13, 2.37–40,
2.53–54, 7.7–9, 11.33–35,
22.7, 22.11–12
degree of 2.37–38, 2.54
test 2.36–37
convenience, balance of 10.4,
16.30, 19.62
Convention rights 1.106, 1.107,
4.157
convictions 2.115, 4.163, 4.189,
4.238, 4.241–243, 2,247,
11.96, 17.163,; see also ex-
offenders
religious 4.163, 4.189
corporate manslaughter
11.99–102
correspondence 1.107, 10.43,
10.45, 13.27, 17.177
costs 1.22, 2.34, 8.5, 11.14,
11.22, 11.29, 20.55, 20.61,
20.80, 20.85, 20.98, 20.106–
109, 23.89
award of 1.29, 17.213–217,
20.80, 20.107–108,
20.125–127
direct 7.37, 22.40, 22.67,
23.61
labour 23.97
orders 1.22, 20.106–107,
20.112
COT3 1.13
counsel of perfection 12.9,
12.22, 17.132
counterclaims 1.41–42, 5.58,
8.3, 20.19
county courts 1.43, 2.115, 4.210,
4.226–227, 4.236, 8.23, 8.33,
8.46, 8.54
Court of Appeal 2.155, 2.159,
2.161, 5.25, 5.27, 5.34, 11.105,
11.107, 11.125, 17.69, 17.72,
17.78–79, 17.227–228, 18.14,
18.17–18, 19.32, 19.38, 20.131
Court of Justice of the European
Union 1.68, 1.70–71, 1.74,
1.99–103, 4.62, 6.50, 7.87,
7.104, 7.106, 9.3, 9.5, 9.13
decisions 1.101–103

Court of Session 1.20, 1.23,
2.67, 3.63, 9.10, 9.60, 20.133,
22.55, 23.95
covenants 9.31, 9.36, 10.54,
15.11–12, 15.25, 15.32, 19.8,
19.10–11, 19.13, 19.21–22,
19.25–27, 19.29, 19.30, 19.32–
36, 19.38–65, 19.69
account of profits 19.68
actions against third
parties 19.69
and breach of contract by
employer 19.69
damages 19.67
injunctive relief 19.61–64
interpretation 19.48–55
reasonableness 19.44–47
remedies for breach 19.61–64
search orders 19.65–66
and transfers 19.65–66
criminal charges 1.107, 12.4,
12.26, 12.68–69, 17.121, 17.129
criminal convictions, see
convictions
criminal courts 12.16–17, 12.66,
17.141, 20.83
criminal liability 10.111, 11.93,
22.44, 23.123
criminal offences 7.109, 7.124–
125, 10.68, 10.76, 10.23–24,
10.31, 17.128, 17.140–141,
23.128, 23.130
criminal proceedings 1.107,
3.15, 10.17, 10.96, 11.23,
11.90, 11.97, 12.5, 12.16
criminal record
certificates 4.250–253
enhanced 4.251–253
criminal records 3.4, 4.248; see
also convictions
criminal sanctions 11.5
cross-examination 12.10
Crown Courts 7.102, 11.27,
11.96, 17.129, 17.140
Crown employees 2.68–70,
2.175, 11.95, 21.25
Crown employment 2.23, 2.94,
4.193, 4.250, 12.31, 23.95
Crown immunity 11.25
Crown notices 1.106, 11.25
culpability 11.47
custody 1.18, 4.245–246, 8.12,
10.100, 11.102
legal 6.61, 6.64, 6.66, 6.80,
7.50
youth 4.245
custom and practice 2.84, 3.41,
3.69–70, 3.80, 3.82–83, 3.85,
3.110, 10.99, 12.62, 18.51, 19.2
custom as source of contractual
terms 3.80–85

customers 7.119, 12.53, 17.140–
141, 19.1, 19.21–22, 19.25–26,
19.28, 19.30–36, 19.41, 19.52,
19.64, 20.84
existing 19.1, 19.28, 19.32–36
former 10.91, 19.32, 19.64

D
daily rest 7.70, 7.94, 7.96–97,
7.103
damages 9.39, 9.67, 10.2, 10.4,
10.10, 10.12, 11.103–108,
11.113, 11.129, 11.131–132,
11.136–138, 15.12–13, 15.15,
15.33, 15.37–40, 16.3, 16.5,
16.7–9, 16.10, 16.15,-16,
16.19, 16.21–90, 19.53, 19.62,
19.67, 23.85–89
against trade unions
23.86–89
aggravated 4.231, 20.97
amount of 11.123, 11.131,
11.147, 19.67, 23.85–89
covenants 19.62–64, 19.67,
19.69
exemplary 16.5, 23.27
liquidated 3.6, 15.15, 16.17,
16.27
nominal 16.26, 23.22
for wrongful dismissal 16.19,
16.21–29
danger
imminent 11.17, 11.26,
11.139
physical 4.95, 11.119
dangerous or obstructive
conduct 17.123
data protection 1.107, 10.26–17,
10.47
death 4.215, 5.65, 6.61, 6.95,
6.122, 6.124, 11.93, 11.99–
101, 11.127, 20.114–117
deceit 10.39, 21.85
declarations 6.114–115, 6.128,
7.107–108, 16.30–31, 21.14,
21.18–19, 21.37, 21.43, 21.48,
21.56, 21.60, 22.75–76, 22.78,
22.80, 22.83, 23.7, 23.12–13,
23.17, 23.97, 23.138, 23.141,
23.147, 23.156
mandatory 18.96, 21.60
deductions 3.123–124, 7.89,
8.2–34, 12.57–59, 15.35–36,
17.237, 21.28, 21.32,
21.56, 21.79–84
definition 8.18–22
excepted 8.23
lawful 6.62, 8.18, 8.23
unlawful 2.73, 3.69, 3.72,
3.87, 3.89, 8.3, 8.14–15,
8.18, 8.20–23, 8.32–33, 8.46

defamation 10.38, 12.7, 20.64, 22.4

default retirement age 4.67

defences 11.71, 11.31, 11.140–150, 17.146, 20.53, 20.56, 20.101, 23.119, 23.121
  justification 4.25, 4.65, 4.73, 4.172, 17.144, 23.22

delay 3.35, 20.7–9, 20.12–13, 20.6, 20.13, 20.16, 20.46, 20.56, 20.118–119, 20.130, 21.20, 22.35, 23.82, 23.95

deliberate failure to act 2.88, 2.132, 2.171, 21.50, 23.139

democratic society 1.107, 4.155, 10.43

demotion 3.108, 5.49, 10.61, 12.85–86, 12.90, 17.23, 17.47, 18.43

dependants 1.80, 1.88, 1.97, 6.1, 6.122–128, 17.81, 21.116
  leave, see time off, for dependants

deposit orders 20.55

derecognition 1.59, 17.81, 21.51, 21.61, 23.5–8, 23.12

detriment 4.37, 4.41, 4.48, 4.50–52, 4.73, 4.100, 6.109, 6.121, 6.128, 7.116, 7.120, 10.69, 10.74–75, 10.80, 10.84, 11.63–65, 21.44, 21.50, 21.56, 21.61–65, 23.139–141
  post-employment 7.139

detrimental treatment 7.112, 10.84

dignity 1.48, 4.32, 4.36, 4.59, 4.155, 4.188, 17.144

diplomatic immunities 1.107, 17.4

direct costs 7.37, 22.40, 22.67, 23.61

direct discrimination 4.12, 4.15–22, 4.62–64, 4.121, 4.124–127, 4.142–147, 4.16, 4.167–170, 5.49, 5.52
  motive for 4.19–22
  sex 4.166–176, 12.22

direct effect 1.73–74, 5.1, 7.88

direct sex discrimination 12.22

Directives 1.73–98
  acquired rights 1.79, 9.2, 13.39
  agency workers 1.96
  burden of proof 1.92
  collective redundancies 1.78, 18.69–75
  employers' insolvency 1.83
  equal treatment 1.80–81, 4.42, 4.63, 4.128, 4.132, 4.255, 6.50–51, 20.96

  between persons irrespective of racial or ethnic origins 1.94
  in employment and occupation 1.93
  in occupational social security schemes 1.81
  for self-employed 1.82
  in social security matters 1.80
  European Works Councils 1.86, 23.132–137
  fixed-term workers 1.73, 1.91, 2.80
  information and consultation 1.91
  parental leave 1.88. 1.97
  posted workers 1.90, 2.118
  proof of employment relationship 1.84
  protection of young people at work 1.87
  working time 1.85

directors 2.10–15, 10.21, 10.33, 10.56, 10.61, 10.96, 11.37, 18.79, 19.2–3, 19.5–6, 19.22
  managing 2.13, 2.16, 2.19, 9.31, 9.60, 16.12, 16.26, 17.236, 18.4, 19.3, 19.6

disability 1.22, 1.48–49, 1.57, 1.93, 4.75–118, 4.235, 17.104, 20.9, 20.11, 20.24
  discrimination 1.22, 4.78–122, 11.119, 20.9, 20.11, 20.24, 20.65, 20.100

disabled persons 1.100, 4.18, 4.79, 4.99–100, 4.104–106, 4.112, 4.194, 4.223

disciplinary action 10.36, 10.42, 10.65, 12.3–5, 12.12,12.14, 12.21, 12.77–78, 21.9–11, 22.27–34

disciplinary hearings 10.6, 12.2, 12.4–11, 12.22–29, 12.35, 12.47, 12.85

disciplinary powers 12.56–89
  alternative employment 12.88
  demotion 3.108, 5.49, 10.61, 12.85–86, 12.90, 17.23, 17.47, 18.43
  fines and deductions 12.57–59
  precautionary suspension 12.65–70
  reprimands 12.84
  suspension without pay for misconduct 12.60–64
  transfer 12.87
  warnings 12.71–83

disciplinary procedures 3.95–97, 9.57, 12.2–50, 16.19, 16.21,

16.30–32, 16.34–36, 17.86, 17.88, 17.139, 17.141, 17.155, 22.27–34
  in action 12.2–11
  appeal procedures 12.34–40
  composition of procedural bodies 12.19–22
  drawing up of 12.15–18
  right to be accompanied 12.23–33
  types 12.12–14

disciplinary records 12.48

disciplinary rules 3.114–115, 12.41–50
  general 12.51
  special 12.50
  specific 12.52–53

disciplinary sanctions 12.2, 12.24, 12.51–52, 12.56, 12.75, 17.40, 17.120

disciplinary transfers 12.87

disclosure 10.70, 10.73–85, 10.94–97, 19.14–19, 19.30, 20.61, 20.63, 20.65–69, 23.15–18, 23.133, 23.137, 23.153–154, 23.156
  protected 2.24, 10.74–75, 10.80–85, 17.183, 17.203, 20.65, 20.96, 21.116, 23.137, 23.153–154
  unauthorised 4.252, 10.70, 19.15

discounts 8.17, 8.27, 8.50, 17.213

discovery 4.225, 4.242, 11.53, 11.56, 16.26, 20.63–64, 20.66

discretion 1.29, 1.74, 10.21–24, 15.38, 20.1, 20.3, 20.5, 20.12, 20.17, 20.24, 20.71, 20.85, 20.106, 20.108
  wide 1.29, 1.74, 12.4, 17.202

discretionary payments 16.23

discrimination 1.76–77, 1.80–82, 1.91–94, 1.103, 1.107, 2.61, 2.67, 2.71, 2.74, 2.81, 2.86, 2.90, 2.99, 4.1, 4.4–5, 4.8, 4.12–13, 4.15–259, 5.45, 5.47–52
  acts of 4.136, 4.159, 4.198, 4.219, 17.242, 20.100
  age 4.67, 4.73, 4.208, 18.87
  anti-discrimination provisions 4.4–5, 4.66, 4.73, 4.121, 4.125, 4.138, 4.151, 4.192, 4.195, 4.207–208
  associative 4.16, 4.18, 4.46, 4.62, 4.64, 4.100, 4.126, 4.143
  direct 4.12, 4.15–22, 4.82, 4.121, 4.124–127, 4.142–147, 4.160, 4.205, 5.49, 5.52

disability, see disability,
discrimination
indirect 1.92, 1.94, 4.23–27,
4.65–66, 4.121, 4.125,
4.131, 4.138, 4.161–165,
4.171–176, 4.181, 4.186–
187, 4.201
instructing, causing or
inducing 4.201–202
non-discrimination 1.37,
1.73, 1.91, 2.128, 4.144,
4.217, 4.235, 4.239
perceptive 4.16
positive, see positive action
race, see race, discrimination
religious, see religious
discrimination
sex, see sex, discrimination
sexual orientation, see sexual
orientation
unlawful 1.49, 2.102, 3.11,
4.22, 4.143, 4.175, 4.201,
4.223, 10.37
discriminators 4.19, 4.136,
4.142, 4.146, 4.160, 4.168,
4.200, 4.221, 4.230, 4.237
alleged 4.31, 4.100, 4.237
characteristics 4.31
discriminatory
advertisements 4.205–206
disfigurements 4.76, 4.89
dishonesty 3.14, 4.243, 12.5,
12.51–52, 16.9–10, 16.12, 17.47,
17.121, 17.123, 17.133, 17.138
disloyalty, see loyalty
dismissal 6.33, 6.37–38, 6.40,
6.45–46, 6.49–55, 6.64, 9.48,
9.50–51, 9.54–55, 12.1–91,
15.38–40, 18.5–23, 18.33,
18.35–36, 18.38–41, 20.16,
20.22–23, 20.25–34, 20.37,
20.43–44, 20.51, 20.53–54,
20.64, 20.71, 21.85–110; see
also redundancy
for asserting a statutory
right 17.165–171
and completion of limited-
term contract 17.20
in connection with industrial
action 21.90–117
consequent 12.19, 17.89,
17.142, 17.169, 17.218
constructive, see constructive
dismissal
date of 8.10, 17.186, 17.205,
17.211, 17.240, 17.244,
20.25–32, 21.97, 21.112–
113, 21.117
definition 7.5–20, 18.5–10
due to industrial
pressure 21.118–119

as employer
termination 17.7–18
and expiry of fixed
term 2.142, 17.19
fair 10.53–54, 17.47–48,
17.83–87, 17.96, 17.99,
17.101, 17.103, 17.110–113,
17.202. 17.218–219
on the ground of trade
union membership,
non-membership,
or trade union
activities 21.85–89
instant 12.41–45, 12.50,
16.11–13, 17.120, 17.132,
18.62
letters of 15.25, 17.5
principal reason for 6.128,
10.83, 17.82, 20.82, 21.85,
21.118
by reason of statutory
restriction 17.147–148
redundancy 9.57, 17.202–
203, 17.218, 17.222,
18.38–60
sufficient reason for 9.54,
9.57
and termination of contract
distinguished 17.49–70
on transfers 9.54–55
unfair, see unfair dismissal
written reasons for 17.174–
182
wrongful, see wrongful
dismissal
dismissed employees 9.59–60,
10.22, 16.9, 16.12, 17.244,
18.13, 21.90–110
disputes procedures 10.4, 21.10,
23.149
distress 2.30, 10.27, 10.110,
23.128, 23.130
diversity 1.48–50, 4.109
doctors 2.39, 3.39 7.53, 7.91,
7.95, 7.129–132, 12.6, 12.26,
17.94, 17.111, 17.115
domestic servants 2.112, 7.92,
9.2, 15.3, 18.64
domestic workers 1.107, 11.2,
17.4
double recovery 16.28
dress codes 3.92, 4.21, 4.161,
4.181
drinking water 11.35, 11.81
drivers 2.29, 2.43, 2.145–146,
10.34, 10.104, 10.106, 11.122,
11.138, 11.50
drugs 10.31, 12.22, 16.11,
17.123, 17.138
drunkenness 12.52, 16.14,
17.123

dual discrimination 4.12, 4.181
duress 17.9, 17.70
economic 1.11
duties 7.133–134, 10.8–20,
10.25–34, 11.32–62, 11.89–91,
11.134–115, 19.1–70
of care 9.72, 10.36, 10.38,
11.99, 11.102, 11.105,
11.138
common law 11.35, 11.103,
11.119, 11.130
of confidentiality 10.25–31
contractual 2.123, 2.126,
3.34, 3.37, 3.50,-52, 8.23,
19.23
of disclosure 10.94–97
employees 2.143–151, 9.12–
13, 10.51–64, 10.88–90,
11.60–69, 11.137–148
implied, see implied
duties/obligations,
employees
employers 2.56, 3.49–53,
6.46–47, 6.83, 10.48–49,
10.63, 11.103–110,
11.125–129
implied, see implied duties/
obligations, employers
to ensure employee's
safety 10.48
of faithful service 10.49–57,
10.76, 23.128
implied, see implied duties/
obligations
to indemnify 10.32–33
injuries at work, see injuries
at work
to insure 10.34
legal 10.10, 10.17, 10.35–36,
10.73, 11.114, 11.128,
11.137
to obey lawful and reasonable
orders 10.58–64
to pay wages or other
remuneration when there
is no work 10.18–29
to provide work 10.16–17
public 16.34,2.125, 7.13–19,
15.17, 16.33–37
statutory 7.109, 11.13,
11.17, 11.21, 11.27,
11.29, 11.103, 11.113,
11.130–139, 11.143–144,
11.148, 11.150–151, 23.43,
23.88, 23.118–119,
23.121
trade union 1.30, 7.15, 7.42,
7.133, 12.30, 21.52, 21.66–
71, 21.89
to unborn children 11.114
to use skill and care 10.65

E

e-mails 1.107, 10.30, 10.42, 10.54, 23.63

early conciliation 1.8, 20.6, 20.48

early retirement 4.66–67, 9.42, 17.208, 18.7

earnings 2.61, 2.64, 6.57, 6.59, 6.62, 6.65, 6.79–80, 6.101–102, 6.105, 8.5, 10.17, 15.11–12, 15.14, 16.26, 16.29, 16.32, 17.205–213; see also wages

  attachment of earnings orders 2.61, 8.5

  hourly 7.22, 11.41

  loss of 3.11, 5.17, 10.38, 12.67, 17.205–213

EAT, see Employment Appeal Tribunal

economic, technical or organisational reasons 3.105, 9.34, 9.44, 9.54, 9.56–57

economic loss 10.34, 10.38

economic reasons 6.45, 9.59

economic well-being 1.107, 3.40, 10.43

education 2.67, 2.110–111, 2.128, 2.130, 4.1, 4.7, 7.14, 7.26, 11.148, 12.19

effective date of termination 12.38, 13.8, 13.10, 14.13–14, 15.25, 15.28–29, 15.37, 16.3, 16.6, 20.6, 20.22, 20.25–34

effectiveness 1.39–40, 1.49, 2.71, 7.29, 7.33, 7.35, 10.48, 11.40, 22.66–67, 23.73

EHRC, see Equality and Human Rights Commission

elected representatives 11.46, 18.72, 18.101

election addresses 22.46–47

elections 9.78, 9.81, 11.66, 17.144, 18.72–73, 22.19–20, 22.24, 22.40–41, 22.47, 22.73, 22.78, 23.138, 23.148, 23.151, 23.157

employee liability information 9.68–69

employee representatives 2.73–74, 2.77, 7.139, 9.52, 9.57, 9.77–78, 9.80, 11.25, 11.42–48, 18.69–70, 18.72–73, 18.79, 18.81, 18.83, 18.85, 18.90–92, 18.96, 18.100–101

  election 9.78, 9.81, 18.70, 18.72–73

  time off for 7.23

employee shareholders 2.31–35

employee status 2.155

employees 2.56, 2.58–95, 3.21–85, 9.11–85, 11.20–48, 17.132–162, 18.52–19.67, 21.86–117, 23.141–155; workers

  about to leave 19.1–7

  conduct 12.5–6, 16.32, 12.73, 17.76, 15.18, 15.21–22, 15.26, 17.198, 17.228, 17.240

  and confidential information 10.69–73

  Crown 2.68–70, 2.175, 11.95, 21.25

  dismissed 9.59, 10.22, 16.9–15, 17.156, 17.188, 17.224, 18.13–14, 18.16–18, 21.86–89

  duties 2.142, 9.12, 11.56, 11.58, 11.60–62, 11.137–140

    of disclosure 10.94–97

    of faithful service 10.49–57, 10.66, 19.4, 23.103

    implied 10.49–57

    to obey lawful and reasonable orders 10.58–64

    to use skill and care 10.65

  enticement of 19.41–43

  fellow 4.56, 6.133, 10.53, 10.104, 11.66, 11.129, 12.22, 12.26, 17.140, 17.189

  fixed-term 2.128–142

  foreign 2.113–117

  former 5.11, 10.12, 10.37, 17.138, 17.215, 19.15–16, 23.36

  full-time 2.88, 2.162, 5.18–20, 13.8

  Health Service 2.72

  incompetent 12.85, 17.88–92

  individual 3.39, 3.59, 3.65, 3.71, 3.94, 3.97, 3.111, 23.102

  moonlighting 10.91–93

  part-time 1.89, 2.61, 2.66, 2.80–95, 5.18–20, 7.73–76, 7.85, 13.7, 18.52

  as parties to contracts of employment 2.36

  patents, inventions and copyright 10.86–90

  peripatetic 1.32

  permanent 2.79, 2.128, 2.131–132, 2.137, 2.139, 6.22, 13.43

  probationary 2.96–98

  public interest disclosures 10.74–85

redundant 7.42, 18.1–2, 18.21–22, 18.28–32, 18.38–39, 18.65–66, 18.89–90

seconded 2.143–151, 4.29, 4.150

secret bribes and commissions 10.66–68

and self-employed persons distinguished 2.36–61

  contracts of service 2.36–55

  health and safety implications 2.60

  importance of distinction 2.56–59

  liability implications 2.59

  statutory rights 2.61

  tax implications 2.58

senior 3.40, 10.56, 10.96, 11.125, 12.54, 15.3, 16.12–13, 16.37, 19.5–6, 19.10

with special legal status 2.76–77

temporary 2.78–79, 6.3, 6.43, 7.11, 17.160

transferred 9.22, 9.33–36, 9.56–84

who have left 19.14–21

employer termination 17.7–18

employers 3.11–27, 3.39–73, 3.100–111, 10.11–40, 11.123–129, 11.134–139, 17.110–145, 22.84–86

  actions 1.107, 3.104, 16.21, 17.19, 17.23, 17.27, 17.48, 17.51, 17.147, 17.212–213, 21.56

  associated 2.5–9, 5.6, 6.45, 13.8, 13.12, 13.22, 13.40, 17.186–187

  business 7.2, 7.15–16, 7.21, 7.27, 7.29, 7.33, 10.25, 10.32, 10.47, 10.49, 10.53, 10.66, 10.69–70, 10.91, 17.140–141, 17.143, 19.44

  conduct 16.18, 16.25, 17.21–23, 17.26, 17.38–40, 18.5, 20.33

  decisions 4.218–220, 6.133, 6.136, 12.34–40, 12.74–75, 12.77, 12.79, 17.76, 17.79–80, 17.240, 17.242, 20.86–89

  duty of confidentiality 10.25–31

  duty to ensure employee's safety 10.48

  duty to indemnify 10.32–33

  duty to insure 10.34

duty to pay wages or other remuneration when there is no work 10.18–20
duty to provide work 10.16–17
former 7.134, 17.215, 17.227, 19.1, 19.4–5, 19.14–17, 19.19–24, 19.37, 19.44, 19.55, 19.64
implied duty of trust and confidence 10.10–15
and injuries at work, see injuries at work
negligence 11.103, 11.105, 11.127, 11.130–131, 11.145–151
new 9.39, 9.50, 9.79, 10.55, 13.42, 18.18, 19.16, 19.23–24
as parties to contracts of employment 2.47–48
payment of bonuses, etc. 10.21–24
premises 2.126, 3.51, 4.58, 7.32, 11.1–2, 11.9, 11.66, 19.3
previous 3.112, 6.83, 7.47, 9.32, 10.35, 10.74, 14.8, 19.27
prospective 10.12, 10.35, 10.38–39, 10.55, 21.7, 21.37
prudent 11.108–109, 11.112
reasonable 10.21–22, 11.63, 11.66, 11.98, 11.105, 11.108, 11.141, 12.10, 17.58, 17.84, 17.87, 18.43–44, 18.47
references 10.35–40
response 20.52–53
and right to privacy 10.41–47
temporary 2.148, 10.108
vicarious liability 10.102–108
employers' associations 1.4, 1.18, 1.51, 11.37, 22.2, 22.5, 22.7, 22.84–86, 23.29
definition 22.84–85
listing 22.86
employment agencies 2.152–173, 17.162, 19.36, 21.34, 21.37, 21.40–42
and employment businesses distinguished 2.152
employment and support allowance 7.48–49
Employment Appeal Tribunal (EAT) 1.18, 1.20–23, 1.107, 4.21, 4.26, 4.115, 4.141, 20.90–109, 22.5, 22.7, 22.9
appeals from 20.133
reviews by 20.131

employment businesses 2.152–157
and employment agencies distinguished 2.152
employment contracts, see contracts of employment
employment judges 1.22, 1.25–27, 2.13, 20.49, 20.52, 20.54–56, 20.59–61, 20.66, 20.71, 20.75, 20.87, 20.91–92, 20.106, 20.120, 20.126, 20.129
employment law 2.10, 2.12, 2.24, 2.27, 2.44, 2.73, 2.76, 2.131, 16.16–20, 17,2 17.21
institutions of 1.1–107
employment legislation 2.125, 2.150, 2.152–153; see also employment statutes
employment protection, suspension on medical grounds 1.25, 7.7–12, 7.134, 14.13, 17.160
employment protection 7.1–139
guarantee payments 1.25, 2.133, 7.2–6, 14.12–13, 20.114
time off 7.13–42
employment relationships 1.83, 2.37, 2.47–48, 2.63, 2.152, 2.155–157, 2.160, 10.9, 10.25, 10.49
employment rights 1.25, 1.28, 1.31, 1.38, 1.43, 1.84, 1.90, 2.12, 2.24, 2.32, 2.67–68, 2.71, 2.114, 2.117–118, 2.136–140, 4.211, 4.214, 17.1, 17.4
employment status 2.51, 2.67, 5.20
employment terms, see contractual terms
employment tribunals 1.7–47, 4.209, 4.211–212, 4.217–220, 4.222, 4.229, 4.233–236, 4.239, 4.243, 17.190–194, 17.198–216, 17.220–221, 17.225–245, 18.32–33, 1.38, 18.44, 18.47, 18.50–51, 18.54, 18.59, 18.62, 18.65, 20.1–24, 20.37–38, 20.42–95, 526–113, 21.30–34, 21.37, 21.41–43, 21.48, 21.50, 21.52, 21.55–62, 21.70–71, 21.73, 21.77, 21.81–82, 21.84, 21.97
allegations of bias 20.91–95
appeals 20.118–130
case management 20.59–71
claims for breach of contract 1.40–44
claims submission 20.81, 20.85, 20.88
composition 1.25

constitutional basis 1.24
costs 20.106–109
death of employer or employee 20.114–117
employer's response 20.52–53
fees 20.51
final hearings 20.55, 20.61, 20.72–90
financial remedies 20.96–100
initial consideration of claim and response 20.54
jurisdiction 1.21, 1.28, 20.19, 20.22, 20.106–107
territorial 1.30-38
legal aid 1.39
making claims to 20.1-45
and mediation 1.45
preliminary hearings 20.55-58
preparation time orders 20.55, 20.110-112
procedure 1.29, 20.46-133
reconsideration of judgment 20.101-105
reviews by Employment Appeal Tribunal 20.131
vexatious litigants 20.132
wasted costs orders 20.113
enforceability 3.66, 23.100-101, 23.104
enforcement 1.53-54, 1.68, 4.235-240, 7.99-109, 8.46-56, 11.1, 11.5, 11.9, 22.55, 22.77, 22.80, 23.156-158
equality 4.235-240
Information and Consultation of Employees Regulations 23.158
national minimum wage 8.44-51, 8.57, 8.60-61
officers 7.99, 7.102, 8.49, 8.51, 11.9
orders 22.65, 22.55, 22.77-78, 22.80
powers 1.51, 1.54, 4.235-236, 11.26-28
Working Time Regulations 7.102, 11.138, 14.3
engagements 2.17, 2.41, 2.43, 2.51, 2.54, 2.79, 2.106, 2.155, 3.116, 22.81, 23.29, 23.36
enhanced criminal record certificates 4.251-253
enhanced criminal records 3.4, 4.251-253
enhanced redundancy payments 3.71, 3.80, 3.85, 3.88, 4.69-74, 9.42, 17.205, 17.237

enquiries 1.50, 1.54, 2.14–16, 4.213, 12.3, 12.6, 12.67, 12.69, 17.121–122, 21.29, 21.41, 22.75
    Advisory, Conciliation and Arbitration Service 1.13
    necessary 4.244, 17.93, 22.75
environment, hostile degrading, humiliating or offensive 4.32, 4.59, 4.185
environmental health officers 11.9
equal pay 1.64, 1.72, 1.76, 2.8, 2.71, 4.6, 4.8, 4.18, 4.41, 5.1–66
    audit 5.57
    backdating of awards 5.66
    burden of proof 5.59
    death of claimant 5.65
    discussions about pay 5.55
    equal work 1.72, 5.1, 5.11, 5.22–42, 5.52
    equality of terms 5.5–14
    gender pay gap information 5.56
    jurisdiction 5.58
    material factor defence 5.43–51
    maternity equality clauses 5.21, 5.53
    pay structure 5.54
    remedies 5.63–64
    sex discrimination in relation to contractual pay 5.52
    sex equality clauses 5.15–21, 5.43
    time limits 5.60–62
equal treatment 1.77, 1.80–82, 2.167–168, 4.41–42, 4.45 4.48, 4.57, 4.128, 4.132, 4.256, 4.56–57, 6.51–55; see also discrimination; equality
    Directive 1.98, 1.103, 4.42, 4.63, 4.128, 4.132, 4.255, 6.50–51, 20.24
    in occupational social security schemes, Directive 1.81
    for self-employed, Directive 1.82
    in social security matters, Directive 1.80
equal value 1.76, 5.1, 5.10, 5.13, 5.22, 5.31–32, 5.44, 5.36–42, 20.46, 20.65
    claims 5.9–12, 5.14, 5.38–42, 5.64, 5.66, 20.45–50, 20.65
equal work 1.72, 5.1, 5.11, 5.22–29, 5.52
equalisation 1.80
equality 1.28, 1.35, 1.37, 1.48–50, 1.93–94, 2.68, 2.71,

2.74, 2.81, 4.1–259, 5.5–21, 5.52–54, 5.56–57, 10.109, 10.113–114; see also equal pay; equal treatment
    access to criminal records 4.248
    adult workers 4.259
    aiding contraventions 4.203
    application of Equality Act 4.191–193
    burden of proof 4.222–225
    clauses 3.56, 4.45, 4.48, 4.239, 5.10, 5.15–21, 5.29, 5.43, 5.52–53
    common provisions 4.190–193
    conduct giving rise to separate proceedings 4.209
    death of claimant 4.215
    discriminatory advertisements 4.205–206
    employment of women 4.255–257
    employment of young persons 4.258
    enforcement by Equality and Human Rights Commission 4.235–240
    illegal contracts 4.195
    instructing, causing or inducing discrimination 4.201–202
    interest on awards 4.233–234
    job advertisements 4.207–208
    jurisdiction 4.217
    lawful discrimination 4.194
    liability of employers 4.198–200
    and national security 4.213–214
    occupational requirement exception 4.163–165
    positive action 4.204
    prohibited conduct 4.12–43
    rehabilitated persons 4.241–247
    relationships that have ended 4.196–197
    remedies 4.227–232
    repeals and revocations 4.8
    restriction on contracting out 4.211
    time limits 4.218–221
    transfer of proceedings 4.226
    unenforceable terms 4.210
    unfair recruitment 4.254
    void and unenforceable terms 4.212
Equality and Human Rights Commission (EHRC)

1.48–50, 1.58, 4.16, 4.157, 4.202, 4.206, 4.235
equipment 2.46, 2.49, 2.53–56, 10.93, 11.51–52, 11.54, 11.62, 11.66, 11.78–80, 11.82–84, 11.109–110, 11.123–124, 11.126, 11.128, 11.130, 11.133, 11.138, 11.149–150
    fairground 11.7, 11.51
    work 2.109, 11.78, 11.82, 11.133, 11.149–150
error of law 1.74, 20.104, 20.120, 20.122, 20.125–126
establishments 4.192, 5.6–8, 18.43, 18.72, 18.76–77, 18.86, 18.101, 23.133
ethnic groups 4.140
ethnic minorities 1.25, 4.198
ethnic origins 1.94
European Convention on Human Rights 1.39, 2.67, 4.155, 10.43, 12.54, 20.74, 20.94, 23.2
European Court of Human Rights 1.104–197, 4.30, 4.157, 10.45, 21.3, 21.49, 23.69, 23.98
European Court of Justice, see European Union, Court of Justice of the European Union
European Parliament 1.64, 1.69
European Union 1.61–103, 5.1, 7.87, 17.4
    Commission 1.64, 1.67–68, 1.101
    Council of Ministers 1.66
    Court of Justice of the European Union 1.70, 1.74, 1.99, 1.101–103, 4.63, 6.50, 7.106, 9.5, 18.77
    European Parliament 1.64, 1.69
    expansion 1.65
    impact on employment law 1.61
    institutions 1.66–70
    law 1.71–103
        Directives, see Directives
        health and safety 11.73, 11.76–86
        Recommendations 1.99–100
        time limits for enforcing Community rights 20.20–24
        Treaty articles 1.72
    Treaty of Lisbon 1.63–64
    Treaty of Rome 1.62
European Works Councils 1.86, 23.132–137

prevention from detriment and dismissal for members 23.139–141
time off for members 23.138
evidence 4.73, 4.82, 4.87, 4.225, 4.238, 12.3, 12.5–6, 12.17, 12.20, 12.22, 12.35, 17.74, 20.56–58, 20.63, 20.67, 20.72–72, 20.76, 20.78–86, 20.89, 20.91, 20.93, 20.120–124, 20.126–127, 20.130, 21.123, 21.127, 22.6
medical 4.82, 17.62, 17.103, 17.115
sufficient 3.81, 4.29, 18.53, 23.36
EWCs, see European Works Councils
ex-employees, duties 19.1–70
ex gratia payments 17.186, 17.199, 17.210, 17.237, 18.66, 20.96
excepted deductions 8.23
excepted payments 8.23
excluded conduct 21.2
exclusions 6.22, 6.29, 7.90–98, 8.23, 8.35, 8.44, 21.2–8, 21.18–19
executive committees 22.40–44, 22.78, 23.59, 23.80, 23.82
principal 22.40–44, 22.46, 22.48, 23.59, 23.80, 23.82
exemplary damages 16.5, 23.27
exemptions 11.71, 18.64
expatriate employees 1.32
experts 3.6, 3.40, 3.45, 5.37, 5.39–40, 23.135, 23.137
express incorporation of collective agreements 3.57–66
express terms 3.28–37, 3.108, 10.9, 10.18, 10.58, 10.61, 12.59–62, 17.35
expulsion 20.1, 21.2–3, 21.16, 22.7, 22.29, 22.29
extension of time 1.29, 1.40, 7.107, 20.24, 20.52, 21.37, 21.59, 21.81

F

factories 3.91, 3.93, 4.256, 6.20, 11.17, 11.21, 11.70, 11.78, 11.141, 23.109–110
failure to act, deliberate 2.88, 2.132, 2.171, 21.50, 23.139
failure to mitigate 17.224–225, 17.240
fair and public hearing 1.107, 12.26, 20.94
fair dismissal 10.53, 16.3, 17.47–48, 17.202, 17.218

and unfair dismissal distinguished 17.73–173
fair hearing 1.22, 1.107, 12.5, 7.4
fair investigation 12.5, 12.72
fair procedures 9.55, 17.125, 17.159, 17.219, 18.48
fair reasons 4.67, 17.53, 17.74, 17.82, 17.152, 17.237
fair trial 1.107, 337, 20.56, 20.61
fairground equipment 11.7, 11.51
fairness 3.26, 3.34, 3.36, 12.35, 17.78, 17.86, 17.95, 17.124, 17.129, 17.139, 20.84; see also unfairness
procedural 16.33, 17.86, 17.139
faithful service, duty of 10.49–57, 10.66, 19.4, 23.103
false statements 17.163, 22.62
family friendly rights 6.1–138; see also adoption; flexible working; maternity rights; parental leave; paternity rights; time off for dependants
fathers 6.84, 6.90, 6.93–94, 6.96, 6.103–109
fault 10.37, 10.19, 10.100–101, 11.123, 11.135, 11.144–148, 17.59, 17.66
fees 1.2, 2.11, 2.54, 2.152, 2.165, 8.8, 8.13, 19.70, 20.48, 20.51
fellow employees 4.56, 6.133, 10.53, 10.104, 11.129, 11.149, 12.48, 12.51
females, see women
fidelity, duty of 10.49, 10.53–56, 10.91, 10.93, 19.2–8, 19.22
implied 9.3–4, 9.8
fiduciary duties 10.56, 19.5, 19.22, 19.68
final hearings 20.44, 20.61, 20.72–90
final warnings 12.1, 12.48, 12.72–73, 12.75–77, 12.79, 12.81, 12.83–84, 17.90, 17.106, 17.110, 17.120
written 12.71–72, 12.74, 12.77, 12.79, 12.81
financial benefits 2.107, 13.1
financial loss 7.120, 8.32, 16.21, 17.199, 17.201
fines 8.2, 8.5. 11.104, 12.57–59, 22.27
fixed deductions, standing statements of 3.123
fixed-term contracts 2.80, 2.85, 2.127–142, 6.51, 15.25–26, 16.6, 17.19–20.17.31, 17.209, 18.64–65, 19.57
continuity rules 2.141

expiry of fixed term 2.142, 17.19
four-year rule and other rights 2.136–140
terms not less favourable 2.132–135
fixed-term employees 2.127–135
Fixed-Term Workers Directive 1.73, 1.91, 2.128
flexibility 3.59, 3.63, 3.98–99, 3.109, 6.87, 6.90, 6.129–138, 17.37, 17.109, 20.46, 20.59–60
clauses 3.99, 17.37
flexible working 1.13, 1.28, 2.32, 2.61, 6.129–138, 7.33, 13.43, 14.11
application for 6.131–137
force majeure 1.97, 9.78
foreign employees 2.113–117
foremen 2.43, 2.148, 10.54, 10.60, 11.109, 11.144, 12.1, 17.14, 17.87, 17.117, 18.6, 18.8
foreseeability 10.107–108, 11.132, 11.149
forfeitures 8.5, 8.8, 22.27
formal warnings 12.19, 12.80, 17.37
formalities 1.107, 12.4, 12.22, 18.46, 20.46, 20.60, 23.146
formality 12.4, 18.46, 20.46, 20.60
former employees 5.11, 10.12, 10.37, 17.138, 19.15, 19.22–24, 22.36
former employers 7.134, 7.139, 10.37, 17.227, 19.2, 19.5, 19.14, 19.44, 19.53
four-year rule 2.136–140
France 1.62
Francovich style claims 1.28, 1.74
fraud 3.14–15, 10.94, 10.96, 19.19, 22.61–62
freedom not to assemble or associate 1.107
freedom of assembly 1.107
freedom of association 1.107, 21.2, 22.25, 23.2
freedom of establishment 23.97
freedom of expression 1.107, 10.83, 17.144
freedom of religion 1.107, 2.67
freedom of speech 1.107
freedom of thought, conscience and religion 1.107
fresh employment 3.47, 15.30, 15.38, 16.25, 17.206, 17.211, 17.214
fringe benefits 5.17, 16.23, 16.29

frustration 13.13, 13.16, 15.5,
    17.59–67
full-time employees 2.88–91,
    2.95, 2.162, 5.18–20, 5.29,
    13.8, 13.16
full-time workers 2.84–85.
    2.87–95, 7.76, 13.7–8
    comparable 2.80, 2.85
functions 1.2–2, 1–9, 1.18, 1.48,
    11.40–41, 11.47–48, 11.63,
    17.81, 22.48, 23.134–135,
    23.139
    administrative 1.18, 9.23,
        9.28
fundamental principles 12.2
fundamental rights 1.63, 1.107,
    4.155, 17.4
funds 1.18, 11.125, 17.243, 22.86

G

garden leave 8.16, 10.17, 15.12,
    15.21–22, 19.7–13, 19.23,
    20.26
    clauses 15.21–22, 19.8–11,
        9.13, 19.23
gender 4.10, 4.12, 4.32,
    4.119–122, 4.235, 5.20, 5.32,
    5.48, 5.56, 20.24
gender pay gap
    information 5.56
gender reassignment 4.10, 4.12,
    4.32, 4.119–121, 4.235
general powers 2.44, 20.18,
    20.60, 20.101
general secretaries 22.31,
    22.42–43, 22.56–57, 22.62,
    23.39, 23.80, 23.82, 23.84
genuinely self-employed
    persons 2.83, 2.163
Germany 1.62, 1.74, 10.83
gifts 6.33, 6.88, 10.66
global contracts 2.174, 13.21
golden formula 23.40
good faith 2.47, 6.70, 6.88,
    10.22, 10.62, 10.82, 15.38,
    16.12, 17.169
good industrial relations
    practice 12.82, 17.209,
    18.40–41, 22.13
goodwill 9.9, 19.32, 19.41
government role 1.57
gratuities 8.17, 14.4, 16.23
gravity 10.111, 11.105, 17.88,
    17.120, 17.123, 23.157
grievance hearings 12.26, 22.15
grievance procedures 1.13,
    1.15, 2.53, 2.67, 3.95–97,
    6.33, 6.70, 6.88, 12.1–91,
    17.220–221
    drawing up of 12.15–18
    types 12.12–14

grievances 3.97, 3.115, 4.145,
    4.230, 9.68, 10.15, 12.1–91
gross misconduct 7.80, 8.10,
    8.15, 9.34, 10.94, 12.2, 12.36,
    12.38, 12.41, 12.48, 12.51,
    12.55, 17.124, 17.132, 17.134,
    17.139
gross wages 8.26–27, 9.21
grudges, personal 12.6, 23.39
guarantee payments 1.25, 2.133,
    7.2–6, 10.20, 14.13, 20.114

H

hair 2.7, 3.92, 4.21, 4.97, 17.138,
    17.180
    long 3.92, 4.194, 17.138
harassment 4.32–36, 4.44,
    4.121, 4.138, 4.182, 4.186,
    4.188, 4.196–198, 10.109–117,
    23.128
    intentional 23.130–131
    sexual 1.100, 2.144, 4.35–36,
        4.50, 10.109, 17.39
    tort 4.60, 10.105
hardship 2.6, 18.40, 18.52, 23.46
harm 10.70, 10.102, 11.105–196,
    11.129, 11.138, 15.21, 17.143,
    19.14–15, 19.30, 23.23
    serious 7.131, 15.21
hazardous substances 11.88
hazards 7.64, 11.25, 11.37,
    11.40, 11.42, 11.47, 11.49,
    11.70, 11.82, 11.88, 11.117,
    11.135, 11.149
    potential 11.25, 11.40
    special 7.64, 7.99, 11.37
health, mental 7.129, 7.131,
    10.116, 11.104–105
health and safety 1.51–54, 2.60,
    2.73, 2.151–153, 2.172, 3.115,
    4.18, 4.50, 4.102, 7.97–109,
    11.1–151
    background to Health and
        Safety at Work Act 11.1–8
    burden of proof 11.97–98
    codes of practice 11.89–91
    compensation for injuries at
        work 2.50, 2.140, 10.34,
        10.48, 11.103–113, 12.32
    corporate
        manslaughter 11.99–102
    court enforcement
        powers 11.27–28
    Crown notices 1.106, 11.25
    duty to ensure employee's
        safety 10.48
    enforcement of Health and
        Safety at Work Act
        11.9–30
    impact of European
        law 11.77–88

improvement notices 1.21,
    7.102, 11.10–11, 11.13,
    11.15–21, 11.23–26
information 11.40, 11.42,
    11.46–49, 11.51, 11.55,
    11.79–80, 11.82, 11.84
injuries at work, see injuries
    at work
mental health 7.129, 7.131,
    10.116, 11.104–105
power to deal with imminent
    danger 11.26
powers of inspectors
    11.10–30
prohibition notices 1.21,
    11.5, 11.10, 11.12–24, 11.95
regulations 11.70–76
statutory duties 11.31–69
Health and Safety at Work, etc
    Act 1974 11.1–8
Health and Safety
    Executive 1.51–54, 6.14, 7.99,
    11.9, 11.40, 11.76
Health and Work Advisory and
    Assessment Service 1.55
health assessments 7.62–64,
    7.69, 7.92, 7.99
health authorities 2.44, 5.4, 5.64,
    7.14, 12.46, 12.70, 13.40
health records 10.26
Health Service employees 2.72
health surveillance 11.79–80,
    11.136, 11.139
heat of the moment 15.8, 17.18,
    17.51–52
High Court 1.20, 1.44, 1.74,
    5.62, 7.108, 10.55, 16.19,
    16.27–29, 19.57, 20.71
highly skilled migrants 2.113
HM Revenue and Customs
    (HMRC) 2.46, 4.117, 7.51,
    7.86, 7.88, 8.17, 8.41, 8.49–51
HMRC, see HM Revenue and
    Customs
holiday pay 2.18, 2.25, 2.159,
    3.112, 7.73–89, 7.133, 8.4,
    8.13–15, 8.22, 15.11, 15.15,
    15.17
    accrued 3.52, 3.112, 3.125,
        7.79, 7.85, 7.133, 8.4,
        8.14–15, 15.11, 15.15,
        15.34, 15.36, 17.22
holidays 1.25, 1.37, 1.43, 1.73,
    1.85, 1.96, 2.12–13, 2.15, 2.18,
    2.25, 2.41, 2.159, 2.161, 3.23,
    3.112, 3.125, 7.73–89, 15.17;
    see also working time
    and contracts of
        employment 3.125
    entitlements 2.91, 2.95, 5.17,
        6.29, 7.78, 7.84

home address 17.56, 23.53, 23.61

homeworkers 8.37, 12.31

homosexuals 1.105, 5.59, 4.157–158, 4.185, 4.187–188; see also gay people; sexual orientation discrimination

honoraria 2.62

horseplay 11.29, 17.123

hospitals 2.59, 2.159, 3.5, 7.91, 7.95, 9.26, 12.19, 12.26

hostile, degrading, humiliating or offensive environment 4.32, 4.59, 4.188

hotels 2.46, 9.57, 17.27, 17.68, 17.164, 20.14, 23.22

hourly rates 1.56, 2.95, 2.126, 11.14, 14.7–9, 17.7, 17.35, 18.38
   appropriate 6.5, 7.28, 18.38, 23.138

hours 2.11–12, 2.15–16, 5.18–19, 5.23, 5.28–29, 5.41, 5.45, 6.3, 6.6–7, 6.12, 6.17, 7.4, 7.13–14, 7.18, 7.20, 7.26, 7.28, 7.53, 7.58–72, 7.85, 8.35–45, 14.1–14; see also working time
   normal working 2.161, 5.18, 7.4, 7.28, 7.53, 7.63, 7.65, 7.99, 14.1–14, 15.17

hours of work, see working hours

House of Lords 1.23, 1.32, 1.60, 1.103, 2.67, 2.69, 2.86, 2.94, 3.39, 17.213, 18.20, 18.22

house unions 22.10

HSE, see Health and Safety Executive

human rights 1.48–55, 1.104–107, 4.155–157, 10.43–45, 12,26, 12.54, 20.74, 22.25

Human Rights Act 1.13, 1.104–107, 2.177, 10.44, 17.144, 20.57, 22.27

hypothetical comparators 2.132, 4.169

I

identity 9.6–9, 9.21, 9.25, 6.64, 9.68, 10.25, 10.72, 10.81, 12.7, 17.186, 19.30

ignorance 20.7, 21.106

ill-health 3.40, 11.104, 17.94, 17.98, 17.101, 17.104, 17.114, 17.229, 20.8, 21.60
   retirement schemes 3.40, 17.208

illegal contracts 2.144, 3.8, 3.11, 4.195

illegality 2.144, 3.8, 3.11, 4.195, 13.11, 22.25

illnesses 4.83–84, 4.88, 4.94, 4.132, 4.132, 4.136–137, 4.231, 6.126, 7.53, 7.83, 7.86, 10.116, 11.104, 17.212; see also health and safety
   psychiatric 4.231, 11.104–105, 11.113, 11.136, 16.5, 16.25

immigrants 4.205

immigration
   conditions 3.9
   control 2.113, 2.115
   rules 2.110, 3.11, 3.16

imminent danger 11.17, 11.26, 11.139

immorality 16.14, 17.123

immunities 1.107, 17.4, 21.95, 21.112, 23.28, 23.41, 23.71, 23.73, 23.79–84, 23.112, 23.116, 23.119, 23.127
   loss of 23.40–46
   statutory 23.28, 23.47, 23.53, 23.58, 23.91, 23.112

impairments 4.76, 4.80–98

impartiality 1.107, 11.113, 20.94

impending redundancies 3.63, 17.8, 18.8, 18.40

implied agreement 3.19, 3.23, 23.5, 23.18

implied authority 3.60, 21.122, 23.21

implied duties/obligations 2.47, 10.8–15, 10.21, 17.27–46
   employees 10.49–64
   employers 10.8–48
   of trust 3.48, 6.33, 6.70, 6.88, 10.10–15, 10.35, 10.49, 12.67

implied incorporation 3.57, 3.67–70, 3.75, 12.61
   of collective agreements 3.67–70

implied powers 12.62, 23.36

implied resignation 17.58

implied terms 3.22–24. 3.32, 3.38–55, 3.66–70, 10.8–15, 10.17–22, 10.25, 10.48–57, 12.69, 14,2, 17.27–46
   employer breach of 17.27–46
   theory 3.38–39, 3.48, 10.49, 17.32
   of trust 3.2, 3.22, 3.48, 3.87, 4.35, 10.10–15, 17.39, 17.41, 17.43–45, 17.48

imprisonment 2.115, 4.241, 4.245–246, 7.102, 11.27, 11.96, 17.60, 17.66, 22.62, 23.85, 23.94

improper motives 10.38, 10.82, 20.64

improper pressure 10.61, 17.135

improvement notices 1.21, 7.102, 11.11

in vitro fertilisation 4.128, 6.4

inadmissible reasons 11.69, 17.97, 17.198, 20.37

incapacity 3.112, 5.60, 7.46–58, 7.50, 13.16, 17.101
   benefit 3.112, 17.208

incentives 3.64, 3.107, 10.21–22, 11.103

income 2.47–48, 2.56, 2.58, 3.8, 3.12, 15.11–13, 16.22, 17.205–213, 17.225, 22.57

income tax 2.46, 2.51, 2.56, 2.58, 2.174, 3.12, 6.57, 8.5, 15.11–14, 15.30

incompetence 10.49, 10.65, 17.74, 17.84, 17.86, 17.88–92, 20.79
   neglectful 17.88–92

inconvenience 11.74, 11.111, 11.135, 18.15, 20.132

incorporation 3.57–58, 3.63, 3.67, 3.70, 3.74–75, 3.78–79, 3.95, 12.61, 22.3, 22.25, 22.46

increments 5.44–45, 5.64, 6.21, 6.34, 6.38, 6.71

independence 1.2, 1.18, 1.107, 2.67, 22.6–7, 22.9–10, 22.12–14, 12.16–17, 12.19–20, 22.48–54, 23.6–7, 23.12
   certificates of 1.18, 22.6–18, 22.86, 23.6

independent contractors 2.52, 2.56, 2.58–60, 10.103

independent experts 5.37

independent scrutineers 21.22, 22.19–20, 22.48–54, 22.82, 23.57

independent trade unions 9.74, 9.77, 9.81, 21.46–47, 21.50–52, 21.55, 21.60, 21.66, 21.72, 21.74, 21.85, 21.122, 22.7, 22.14, 22.16–18, 23.2, 23.6–7, 23.12, 23.15, 23.17, 23.102, 23.145

indirect discrimination 1.92, 4.23–27, 4.65–66, 4.121, 4.125, 4.131, 4.138, 4.161–165, 4.181, 4.186
   definition 4.65
   justification 4.172
   sex 4.171–176

indirect sex discrimination 4.171–176, 5.45

individual contracts of employment 1.76, 3.55, 3.57–58, 3.61–71, 3.78–79, 6.90, 8.19, 12.60, 23.102–103; see also contracts of employment

individual trade union
rights 21.1–128
access to employment
21.28–31
action short of
dismissal 21.50–60
check-off arrangements
21.79–82
compensations for
dismissals 21.121
complaints of unjustifiable
discipline 21.13–15
deductions for union political
funds 21.83–84
detriment and dismissal
in statutory recognition
cases 21.61–65
dismissal due to industrial
pressure 2.118–119
dismissal in connection
with industrial
action 21.90–110
dismissal on the ground of
trade union membership,
non-membership, or trade
union activities 21.85–89
inducements relating to
union membership or
activities 21.46
interim relief for dismissed
trade unionists or non-
unionists 21.122–128
remedies for wrongful
exclusion or
expulsion 21.18
right not to be excluded from
any trade union 21.2
right not to be expelled from
union 21.17
right not to be unjustifiably
disciplined 21.9–12
right of access to
courts 21.20–21
right to a ballot before
industrial action
21.22–25
right to resign from trade
union 21.16
selection for dismissal
on grounds of
redundancy 21.120
time off for trade union
activities 21.72–73
time off for trade union
duties 21.66–71
time off for trade
union learning
representatives 21.74–78
vis-à-vis employers 21.27–45
vis-à-vis trade unions
21.2–26

industrial action 1.107, 21.9,
21.22–25, 22.48–54, 23.42,
23.46–65, 23.85, 23.93, 23.95–
98, 23.123; see also picketing;
sit-ins; strikes
affecting an individual 23.93
dismissal in connection
with 21.90–96
to enforce closed shop 23.71
and European Law 23.97–98
notice of 23.68–79
protected 17.81, 21.111–115
right to a ballot before
21.22–25
secondary action 2.22,
21.23, 21.94, 21.111, 23.48,
23.73–77
secret ballots before 23.47–56
in support of unofficial
strikers 23.72
industrial disputes 13.36, 21.31,
21.107, 23.43, 23.46, 23.128
industrial injuries 2.39, 2.60
industrial misconduct 12.46,
12.52, 17.130
industrial pressure 17.172,
21.37, 21.118–119
dismissal due to 21.118–119
industrial relations 1.1, 1.4,
1.14–15, 1.19–20, 3.57,
10.3, 10.16, 10.60, 12.16,
12.44, 17.209, 23.1–158; see
also collective bargaining;
consultation; industrial action
good industrial relations
practice 12.82, 17.209,
18.40–41, 23.13
industrial training boards
1.46–47
industrial training levy 1.47,
2.11, 20.48
industrial tribunals 1.28,
18.91, 20.55, 22.23; see also
employment tribunals
inequality 3.2, 5.4, 5.47, 20.46,
22.38; see also discrimination
inferences 2.89, 2.139, 3.55,
3.63, 3.90, 4.30, 4.169,
4.224–225
informal interviews 12.2
informal warnings 12.1, 12.19,
12.24, 12.72, 17.120
informality 20.46, 20.82
information 2.169, 9.68–69,
10.25–17, 10.31, 10.36,
10.45, 10.48, 10.69–73, 11.40,
11.42, 11.46, 11.48–49,
11.51, 23.13, 23.15–18,
23.132–140, 23.142–144;
see also confidentiality; data
protection; privacy

confidential 6.70, 6.88,
10.25–31, 10.69–73,
19.1–2, 19.8, 19.57, 19.67
factual 11.90, 22.42
gender pay gap 5.56
health and safety 11.40,
11.79, 11.82
prescribed 20.48, 20.52, 22.57
relevant 2.169–170, 11.57,
20.53, 22.7, 23.18
Information and Consultation of
Employees Regulations 1.19,
1.21, 1.28, 1.86, 1.95, 7.24,
17.81, 18.61, 18.82, 22.17,
23.123, 23.142–144
enforcement 23.156–158
negotiated
agreements 23.146–150
negotiating
representatives 23.146–
150
pre-existing
agreements 23.145
statutory default
provisions 23.151–155
Information
Commissioner 10.26–27,
10.47, 21.39
inherent inability 17.84–87
injunctions 10.6–7, 15.32, 15.39,
16.3, 19.3, 19.9, 19.53, 19.61–
65, 19.67, 19.69, 23.20, 23.27,
23.85, 23.90–91–94
interim 10.25, 23.63
interlocutory 3.3, 3.63, 10.6,
16.30, 23.91
springboard 19.22–24
temporary 23.67, 23.90
injuries at work 2.39, 2.59, 2.60,
2.106, 10.48, 11.88,
11.103–127, 12.22
breach of statutory
duty 11.130
contributory
negligence 11.147–148
defences to action for
personal injuries
11.140–146
denial of negligence
11.141–143
duty to unborn
children 11.114
extent of duty 11.103–113
limitation of actions 11.151
new intervening act 11.149
personal, see personal injuries
personal nature of
duty 11.115–120
psychiatric 4.230–231,
11.104–1–5, 11.110,
11.113, 11.136, 16.5, 16.25

risk of injury 11.83–86,
11.98, 11.100, 11.104–106,
11.135–141, 11.150, 16.11
sole fault of
employee 11.144–146
threefold nature of
duty 11.121–128
injustice 17.163, 17.185, 17.219,
20.47, 20.119, 20.121
inland waterways 7.54, 17.56,
7.91, 7.100
innocent parties 3.18, 15.38,
16.19, 16.21, 19.58
innovation 1.57, 8.36, 18.67,
23.158
insolvency 1.25, 1.74, 2.68,
7.133–138, 9.48–53, 14.11,
14.14, 20.114
Directive 1.83
notice pay on 15.30
proceedings, permitted
variations 9.52–53
and transfer of
undertakings 9.48–51
Insolvency Service 7.134, 18.67
inspections 6.23, 11.5, 11.37,
11.40, 11.42, 11.48, 11.65,
22.5, 22.53, 22.58, 22.62, 23.16
inspectors 7.99–101, 8.57, 11.5,
11.10–30, 11.40, 11.47,
11.93–94, 12.52, 22.61
instant dismissal 12.41–44,
16.11, 16.13, 17.120, 17.132,
18.62
institutions 7.95, 12.19, 20.36,
23.140
of employment law 1.1–107
EU 1.66–70, 1.74
instructing, causing or inducing
discrimination 4.201–202
instructions 3.15, 3.19, 3.23,
3.86, 3.90–91, 10.58, 10.60–
61, 10.63, 10.104, 10.106,
11.80, 11.82, 11.125, 11.128
safety 11.59, 17.138
instruments of
amalgamation 22.20, 22.28,
22.48, 22.81
insubordination 12.51, 17.123,
22.31
insurance 2.15, 2.18, 2.29, 2.36,
2.91, 17.136, 20.37
companies 2.153, 11.141
compulsory 10.34, 11.88,
11.123
personal accident 2.123, 3.52
intention 2.67, 3.7, 4.229, 4.239,
17.23, 17.26, 17.46, 19.51,
19.53–54, 22.5, 22.7
of Parliament 7.108, 11.138
true 2.156, 19.54

intentional harassment
23.130–131
interceptions 1.107, 10.45–47
interdicts 4.237, 23.90–91; see
also injunctions
interest on awards 4.233–234,
17.242–243, 20.98–100
equality in
employment 4.233–234
interests of national security, see
national security
interference 1.107, 22.7, 22.40,
22.48, 22.53, 22.67, 23.26,
23.44, 23.61, 23.65, 23.111,
23.113, 23.116
interim injunctions 10.25, 23.63
interim relief 1.25, 1.71, 11.69,
17.183, 21.45, 21.64, 21.122–
128, 21.16
for dismissed trade unionists
or non-unionists
21.122–128
unfair dismissal 17.184–191
interlocutory injunctions 3.3,
3.63, 10.6, 16.30, 23.91, 23.113
internal appeals 9.34, 12.36,
12.39, 20.4
internet 1.107, 10.42
interviews 3.1, 4.46, 4.198,
4.208, 10.28, 12.2, 12.4,
12.6, 17.109, 17.121, 17.141,
17.214. 18.39
intimidation 4.32, 10.115, 20.56,
22.28, 23.25, 23.36, 23.44,
23.111, 23.125
invalidity 1.80, 9.42
benefit 17.208
inventions 10.86–90
investigation
fair 12.5, 12.72
full 10.15, 12.5, 12.70, 17.75,
17.163
proper 10.37, 12.3, 12.52,
17.51, 17.90
wide powers of 1.18, 22.61
Italy 1.62, 1.74
itemised pay statements 2.61,
2.73, 3.123–124, 20.114, 21.79

J
Japan 4.150
job advertisements, see
advertisements
job applicants, see applicants
job descriptions 3.23, 3.98–99,
10.13, 17.84
job evaluation 5.31–35, 5.37–28,
5.47, 5.66
jobseekers' allowance 15.38,
17.208, 17.244, 18.1
joint and several liability 4.200

jokes 11.129
judicial mediation 1.45
judicial review 8.23, 16.20.
16.33–37
juries 11.96, 11.100, 17.128,
22.31
jurisdiction 1.21, 1.25, 1.28,
1.30–33, 1.35–36, 1.38,
1.40, 4.206–209, 4.217,
4.219–220, 4.226, 8.23, 20.2,
20.7, 20.19, 20.47–48, 20.54,
21.104, 21.107
concurrent 16.19
employment tribunals, see
employment tribunals,
jurisdiction
equal pay 5.57
equality in employment 4.217
territorial 1.30–38. 4.192.
4.219–220, 17.4
jury service 2.167, 17.81, 21.116
just and equitable
principle 17.207, 17.213
justice 12.3, 12.9, 12.19, 12.22,
16.30–31, 20.94–101,
20.127–130, 22.30–32
natural 2.75, 12.9, 12.22,
12.36, 12.69, 16.1,
16.30–31, 22.31–32
justification 4.25, 4.67, 4.73,
4.172, 5.45, 5.48, 11.105,
19.57, 23.20–22
defence of 4.25, 4.73, 4.172,
23.20–22
objective 2.95, 2.134, 2.136,
4.67, 5.45, 5.49

L
labour costs 23.97
lack of qualifications 17.117–
119
last-in-first-out (LIFO) 3.59,
3.63, 18.51, 18.87
lateness 12.52, 17.120, 17.123
persistent 10.49, 16.14
lawful and reasonable orders,
duty to obey 10.58–64
lawfulness 1.85, 1.107, 3.26,
10.63
lay-offs 10.29, 13.18–19,
18.33–37; see also
redundancy
legal aid 1.39, 20.119
legal costs 23.36
legal custody 6.61, 6.64, 6.80,
7.50
legal duties/obligations 10.8–20,
10.35–36, 10.76, 11.114,
11.128, 11.130, 11.137
legal representation 1.13, 1.107,
4.237, 12.26, 12.28

legal requirements 7.15, 7.19, 11.19, 11.21, 11.23, 11.39, 11.90, 11.97, 12.36, 12.45, 12.70, 12.85, 12.88
legal status 2.12–13, 2.51–53, 2.74–77
legitimacy 21.115
legitimate interests 10.42, 17.150, 19.10, 19.27–28, 19.42, 22.29
length of service 3.63, 4.68–73, 4.175, 5.44, 6.16–22, 6.30–35, 7.124, 18.51
lesbians 1.105, 4.185; see also sexual orientation discrimination
less favourable treatment 1.28, 1.89, 1.91, 2.80–81, 2.85, 2.89, 2.93, 2.95, 2.133, 2.139–140, 4.16–19, 18.61, 20.37
letters 3.1, 4.41, 10.60, 19.66, 20.14
  of appointment 3.64
  of dismissal 15.25, 17.5
  warning 10.60
liability 2.145–148, 9.22, 9.30–31, 9.33, 9.60, 9.65, 9.70–72, 10.102–108, 10.112, 10.116, 11.103–105, 11.123–150, 20.114
  civil 10.110, 11.5, 11.31, 11.72, 11.110, 22.47
  contractual 7.4, 7.52, 8.26–27
  joint and several 4.200
  vicarious 2.56, 2.147, 2.153, 4.56, 10.84, 10.102–108, 10.112
libel 22.4, 23.43
LIFO, see last-in-first-out
lifting 1.105, 6.12, 11.88
like work 5.22–30
likelihood of recurrence 4.87, 17.107
limitation of actions 11.151
limited protection 19.1, 19.9, 19.27–28
limited-term contracts 17.19–20, 18.5–6, 20.25
  completion 17.20
liquidated damages 3.6, 15.15, 16.7, 16.27
liquidation 2.12–13, 7.135–134, 9.35, 9.48, 9.53, 13.23, 18.5
loans 2.12–13, 8.8, 8.17, 8.40, 17.22
local authorities 1.52, 1.54, 2.44, 2.110, 4.19, 4.157, 7.14, 7.19, 22.38, 23.30, 23.32
location 1.13, 2.132, 3.108, 9.13, 17.23, 17.29, 18.13–15
  theory 9.13

lock-outs 13.35–37, 21.91, 21.97
lodging allowances 3.44, 10.32, 14.4
long hair 3.92, 4.149, 17.138
long hours 7.109
long-term absence 7.53, 17.61
long-term adverse effect, substantial and 4.78, 4.81, 4.86–98
long-term sickness 1.55, 3.89, 6.48, 17.93–105, 18.58
lorry drivers 7.3, 11.144
loss of earnings 3.11, 5.17, 10.37, 12.67, 17.205–213
loss of reputation 10.17, 16.25
Low Pay Commission 1.56, 8.35
loyalty 4.68, 17.123, 19.24
lump sums 8.40, 10.94, 16.27, 18.66
lunch breaks 12.55, 17.142
luncheon vouchers 8.17, 17.205

M

machinery 2.145, 2.148, 4.255, 11.80, 11.82, 11.122, 15.33
magistrates 2.62, 7.102, 11.27, 11.96, 18.102
male comparators, see comparators
malingering 10.30, 17.111
management committees 2.4, 22.62
managing directors 2.13, 2.16, 2.19, 9.31, 9.59, 16.12, 16.26, 17.236, 18.4, 19.6
mandatory declarations 18.96, 21.60
manufacturers 11.4, 11.51, 11.53, 11.55–57, 11.59, 11.110, 11.123–124
marital status 4.174, 4.181, 12.54
marriage 4.10, 4.16, 4.18, 4.32, 4.54, 4.123–127, 4.163, 4.181, 4.187
married women 4.124, 4.126, 7.49
mass redundancies, see collective redundancies
material factor defence 5.43–51
maternity 2.71, 2.73, 2.78, 4.128–139, 5.53, 6.1, 6.66–89, 17.172, 17.182
maternity allowance 6.17, 6.65–66, 6.103, 6.107, 7.50, 13.43
maternity equality clauses 5.21, 5.52–53
maternity grounds 1.28, 2.71, 2.73, 4.130, 6.9–18, 6.46–55, 7.12, 7.134, 20.114

maternity leave 1.25, 2.71, 4.130, 4.134–136, 5.53, 6.19–50, 6.53, 6.55, 6.86, 6.88–89, 6.98, 10.24, 18.58, 18.61
  additional 4.134, 6.1, 6.19–22, 6.24, 6.32–34, 6.39, 6.47–48, 6.50, 6.70, 6.88–89, 6.98, 17.182
  compulsory 4.135, 6.19–20, 6.29, 10.24, 17.81
  ordinary 6.19–23, 6.32, 6.38–43, 6.89
maternity pay 6.17–18, 6.56–64, 6.79–81, 7.49–52, 7.134
maternity rights 6.1–66, 9.36
  maternity allowance 6.19, 6.65–66, 6.103, 6.107, 7.49, 13.43
  maternity leave, see maternity leave
  remedies 6.50–55
  risk assessment and suspension on maternity grounds 6.9–18
  statutory maternity pay (SMP) 6.19, 6.56, 6.64, 6.81, 7.50, 7.134, 13.43
  time off work for antenatal care 6.3–5
maternity suspension pay 6.17–18, 8.13
maximum awards 1.40, 9.84, 17.211, 18.93–95
maximum weekly working time 7.58–89
meal breaks 2.43, 5.40
mediation 1.45, 20.46
  and employment tribunals 1.45
  judicial 1.45
  services 21.112–117
medical advisers 4.82, 7.128–132, 17.110–113
medical certificates 6.60, 12.78
medical evidence 4.83–88. 17.62, 17.103
medical grounds 2.78, 6.18, 7.7–12, 7.134, 14.13, 17.4, 17.160
medical practitioners 4.247, 6.3, 6.13, 7.129
medical reports, access to 7.128–132
medical suspension 1.25, 2.61, 2.133, 7.7–12, 7.133–134, 14.13, 17.160
medical treatment 4.91, 17.115
mental health 7.129, 10.116, 11.104–105
merchant seamen, see seamen

military service 7.121–127
  and continuity of
    employment 13.38–41
minimum awards 21.19, 21.37,
  21.44
minimum standards 2.152, 7.1,
  7.26
minimum wage, national, see
  national minimum wage
ministers 1.64, 1.66–68,
  1.71–73, 1.98, 2.68, 5.56,
  11.74–75, 20.37, 23.31
ministers of religion 2.67
minors and contracts of
  employment 2.103–111
misconduct 8.4, 8.11, 8.15,
  10.94–96, 12.2, 12.22,
  12.26–84, 16.9–15,
  17.120–145
  gross 7.80, 8.4, 8.10, 8.15,
    12.36, 12.51, 12.55,
    16.9–12, 17.120–122,
    17.124, 17.132, 17.134,
    17.139
  industrial 12.49, 17.126
  sexual 1.22, 1.107, 12.28,
    20.57
misrepresentation 3.7, 3.12,
  20.40
misstatements, negligent 10.38–
  39
mitigating circumstances 9.83,
  12.22, 12.45–46, 12.48, 12.58,
  17.75, 17.130, 17.134, 17.140,
  18.94–95
mitigation 3.5, 8.3, 12.22, 15.15,
  17.140, 17.209, 17.224–227,
  17.237
mobile workers 7.54–56, 7.91,
  7.93–100
mobility 3.2, 3.24–25, 3.44,
  3.104–105, 5.95, 4.98, 18.6,
  18.14
  clauses 3.2, 3.21–26,
    3.104–106, 17.35–37, 18.6,
    18.14
monetary awards 16.21, 20.96–
  100, 16.21
money purchase
  schemes 17.216–217
monitoring 1.49, 1.107, 4.109,
  10.30, 10.41, 10.47
moonlighting 10.91, 17.143–145
morals 1.107, 10.43
mothers 2.41, 4.18, 6.9–10, 6.84,
  6.93–94, 6.104, 6.107, 6.109,
  6.111–115, 6.131, 11.139; see
  also maternity
motives 1.25, 4.19–27,
  4.142–151, 4.168, 10.82,
  18.58–61, 23.38

improper 10.38, 10.82, 20.64
  ulterior 1.25, 10.62
mutual agreement 1.45,
  2.128–131, 2.142, 3.61–78,
  3.109–111, 15.8, 17.69–71,
  18.7, 18.10
mutual trust and
  confidence 3.53, 17.33–34,
  17.43–45, 17.187, 17.189
mutuality of obligation 2.2,
  2.40–48, 2.174

N
national agreements 3.44, 3.61,
  3.67, 3.77, 3.109
national courts 1.70, 1.72, 1.74,
  1.99, 1.101, 4.62, 9.5, 9.8
National Health Service 2.72,
  7.14, 13.40
national insurance 2.12, 2.29,
  2.31, 2.37, 2.39, 2.43, 2.51–53,
  2.58, 2.155, 2.174, 6.56–63,
  6.81
  contributions 2.11, 2.36, 2.43,
    2.46–53, 2.56, 2.155, 2.174,
    6.56–57, 6.59, 6.62, 6.79,
    6.81, 7.44–45, 7.48–49,
    7.134–138, 15.11
National Insurance Fund 2.18,
  2.155, 7.134, 9.48, 15.30
National Joint Councils 3.61–
  62, 9.37
national minimum wage 1.25,
  1.28, 1.56, 2.8, 2.125–126, 3.9,
  3.56, 8.35–62, 17.200
  calculation of hourly
    rate 8.40–45
  coverage 8.37–40
  enforcement
    by state 8.48–62
    by worker 8.46–48
national origins 4.140–147
national security 1.106–107,
  2.175–178, 4.74, 4.110,
  4.213–214, 10.43, 17.173, 20.73
  and equality in
    employment 4.213–214
nationality 2.114–117, 4.140–
  143
natural justice 2.75, 12.9, 12.22,
  12.36, 12.69, 16.1, 16.30–32,
  22.31–32
necessary enquiries 4.244,
  17.93, 22.75
necessity 1.74, 2.159, 6.124,
  17.117, 19.33, 19.49, 23.9,
  23.97
neglect 2.115, 8.57–58, 10.65,
  11.92–93, 12.51, 17.90,
  17.123
  wilful 10.49, 16.11

neglectful incompetence
  17.88–92
negligence 2.145–148, 2.153,
  11.91, 11.105, 11.109, 11.114,
  11.122–123, 11.125, 11.127–
  128, 11.130–132, 11.137–138,
  11.141–151
  contributory 11.114, 11.147–
    148
  denial of 11.141–143
  employers 11.103, 11.105,
    11.126–128, 11.130–133,
    11.145–148, 11.150
negligent driving 10.33,
  10.104–106
negligent misstatements
  10.38–39
negotiating bodies 3.61, 3.74,
  23.134, 23.138, 23.140
negotiating
  representatives 23.148,
  23.151–155
negotiation 3.1–6, 3.69, 3.71,
  21.68, 23.2, 23.4, 23.14, 23.29,
  23.70, 23.146–147; see also
  collective bargaining
new employers 9.39–41, 9.49–
  51, 9.79, 10.55–57, 13.40–41,
  18.18, 19.15–24
night shifts 2.126, 4.24, 4.98,
  5.26, 5.28, 8.18,21.70
night work 1.96, 2.165, 3.93,
  4.257, 5.45, 6.12, 7.63, 7.92,
  7.94, 7.96, 7.99
  Working Time
    Regulations 7.57–78
no picking and choosing
  rule 21.91, 21.104, 21.111
no show clauses 3.6
noise 11.35, 11.88, 11.110,
  11.128
nominal damages 16.26, 23.22
non-competition clauses 9.36,
  19.48
non-contractual benefits 6.28,
  12.89, 15.14–15
non-disclosure, see disclosure
non-discrimination 1.36–37,
  1.93–94, 2.128, 4.143–144,
  4.235, 4.239
non-employees 10.104, 11.49
non-employment 4.157, 4.177–
  178, 12.90, 13.21–23
non-independent trade
  unions 23.6, 23.12
non-mobile workers 7.56, 7.91
non-renewal 2.133, 2.138–141,
  4.49, 6.51, 17.222
non-smokers 11.81, 17.28
non-solicitation clauses
  19.42

non-unionists 3.74–75, 21.85, 21.122–128, 23.23, 23.117–118
and collective agreements 3.74–79
normal day-to-day activities 4.76, 4.80–90, 4.95–98
normal practice 3.81, 10.35, 17.135
normal working hours 5.18, 7.4, 7.28, 7.62–63, 7.65–66, 7.99, 14.1–10, 15.17
notice 15.1–10, 15.12–16, 15.21–25, 15.32, 15.37–39
to be given by employee 15.31
to be given by employer 15.2–10, 15.12
contractual rights during 15.21–23
dispensing with 15.24–27
employee's remedies 15.37–40
employer's remedies 15.32–35
giving of notice 15.7–10
pay in lieu of 15.12–15
pay on insolvency 15.30
rights during notice period 15.16–19
taxation of payments 15.11
and time limits 15.28–29
notifiable accidents 11.42, 11.48
notifications 6.25–26, 8.8, 9.69, 17.5, 18.101–102
nuisance 11.151, 23.43–44, 23.88, 23.111
public 23.44, 23.111
nurses 2.39, 2.126, 4.21, 4.179, 4.220, 4.247, 5.8, 11.109

O
objective justification 2.95, 2.134, 2.136, 4.67, 5.45, 5.49
objects 3.3, 3.17, 7.114, 9.63–64, 17.88, 20.36, 22.25, 23.24
legitimate 19.36, 23.38
political 1.18, 22.67, 22.74
obligations 1.74, 2.41–43, 2.46, 2.48, 2.54, 2.174, 3.17, 3.25, 3.48–51, 9.33–34, 9.40, 10.8–9, 10.13, 10.17–23, 10.49–51, 10.53; see also duties
employers 2.58, 3.48, 3.51–52, 6.45–48, 6.88–89, 10.48, 10.63, 10.65, 11.103–106, 11.125–128
implied 2.47, 10.49–50
mutuality of obligation 2.2, 2.40, 2.42–43, 2.45–47, 2.53, 2.174

statutory 3.51, 13.43, 18.87, 23.45
occupational health services 1.55
occupational pensions 1.77, 1.81, 3.126–128, 4.7, 4.216, 7.133, 9.41, 17.183
scheme trustees 7.139, 15.17, 17.183, 17.198, 20.114
time off for 7.20–22
occupational requirements 4.53–54, 4.63–67, 4.122, 4.139, 4.152–153, 4.163, 4.183–184, 4.189
sex 4.177–179, 4.181, 4.185
sexual orientation 4.185–189
occupational social security schemes 1.81
occupations 4.242–244, 4.246–247, 7.121–127, 8.35, 11.105, 17.147–148, 23.88
offensive language 4.22, 4.223, 12.81
office holders 2.27, 2.58, 2.62–67, 4.216, 6.57
official industrial action 20.1, 21.85–96, 21.100–115, 23.47, 23.123
unprotected 21.98–99, 21.111
officials 22.16, 22.31, 22.33, 22.35–36, 22.40, 22.67, 23.23.25, 23.38, 23.65, 23.106
full-time 23.81, 23.106
offsetting 6.62, 6.80, 7.84, 15.17, 17.206, 17.210
offshore employment 1.28, 2.124–125, 4.193, 8.38, 17.4, 23.56
offshore installations 11.3, 11.88, 17.4
omission 3.55, 9.30, 11.60, 11.151, 20.113, 20.130, 21.52, 21.61
deliberate 4.118, 4.221
OML, see ordinary maternity leave
on-call time 7.60
one-off business tasks 9.19
open justice 2.178
opt-out 1.63
opted-out shop workers 7.111, 7.113–117, 18.61
ordinary adoption leave 6.1, 6.21, 6.67–72, 6.75
ordinary courts 3.121, 5.62, 8.23, 15.37, 16.3–4, 16.15, 17.1
ordinary maternity leave (OML) 6.19–23, 6.25–26, 6.28–32, 6.38–39, 6.86–89
organisational reasons 3.105, 9.43–45, 9.54, 9.56–59

organisational test 2.39
organised groupings
of employees 9.7, 9.12–22, 9.30
of resources 9.6, 9.30, 9.68
organised religions 4.54, 4.136, 4.164, 4.189
ostensible authority, see apparent or ostensible authority
output work 8.43
outsourcing 9.14–22
overpayment 7.85, 8.23, 10.57
overriding reason of public interest 23.97
overtime 3.28, 3.45, 3.51, 3.62, 5.18, 10.63, 12.69, 14.3, 18.17–18
amount of 3.61–62, 7.108
bans 3.62, 23.42, 23.57
loss of 12.69. 18.29
premiums 2.91, 14.4
overwork 11.104, 11.108, 11.136

P
package approach 2.134, 5.16
parent companies 9.11, 16.11
parental leave 1.88, 6.1, 6.8, 6.19–21, 6.46–50, 6.78, 6.84–99, 15.7, 17.81, 18.58
Directives 1.88, 1.97
period of 6.36, 6.82, 6.85, 6.91
shared 6.103, 6.138
parental responsibility 6.82, 6.84
parents 2.110, 6.72, 6.84, 6.103, 6.129–138, 11.114
adoptive 6.72, 6.84–92, 6.138, 13.43
part-payment of wages 8.10, 16.24
part-time work, Directive 1.89
part-time work/workers 1.89, 2.62–66, 2.80–95, 5.18–21, 7.73–74, 7.85, 13.7, 18.53, 18.61
particulars of employment, written, see written particulars of employment
partners 2.17–18, 6.93–111, 6.131, 13.40, 16.26, 18.4
civil 2.102, 4.16–18, 4.54, 4.126, 4.163, 6.104, 6.112, 6.114, 6.117, 6.131
partnerships 2.4, 2.17–18, 4.126, 9.25, 13.40, 16.26, 19.57, 23.143
passengers 7.95, 10.104, 11.150, 17.90
passive smoking 12.22
past convictions, see convictions

patents 10.86–90; see also inventions
paternity leave 1.28, 1.97, 2.167, 6.1, 6.86–121, 6.130, 13.43, 15.17
  additional 1.28, 6.103, 6.111, 6.118, 6.120–121, 13.43
paternity pay 6.101–103, 6.105, 13.43
pattern of work 7.19, 7.68, 7.91
pay, see also wages; remuneration; salaries
  definition 5.2
  discussions about 5.55
  in lieu of notice 15.12–15
pay discrimination, see equal pay
pay statements, itemised 2.61, 2.73, 3.123–124, 20.114, 21.79
pay structures 3.87, 5.5–14, 5.54
payroll 1.47, 17.10
peaceable process of redundancy selection 4.72, 18.51
peaceful picketing 23.105–114
penalties 2.115, 8.50, 8.57, 11.87, 11.92–96, 16.26–29, 17.23–25, 23.157
  health and safety 11.92–96
penalty clauses 3.6, 15.35
pension rights 6.44, 6.71, 9.3, 16.24, 17.186, 17.216
  accrued 16.23, 17.216
pension schemes 1.28, 1.77, 3.28, 3.31, 3.39, 3.112, 3.116, 3.126–128, 10.94
pensions 1.57, 1.80, 2.66, 2.133, 3.39, 3.112, 6.38, 6.44
  money purchase
    schemes 17.216–217
  occupational, see occupational pensions
perceptive discrimination 4.16
perfection, counsel of 12.9, 12.22, 17.132
performance 2.110, 3.17, 7.15–33, 17.59, 17.81–91, 17.115–120, 23.41–42, 23.74
  contracts of
    employment 10.1–117
  poor 4.230, 10.21, 17.89–91
peripatetic employees 1.32
permanent employees 2.79, 2.128, 2.131–141, 6.22, 13.43
permanent employment 2.132, 2.163, 13.20, 17.207
permanent health insurance schemes 3.31, 3.40, 9.39
permanent replacement 17.63–64, 17.188
permission 2.115–116, 4.248, 7.128, 13.14, 17.56, 21.72

persistent absenteeism 17.106–116
persistent lateness 10.49, 16.14
personal animosity 17.189, 21.118
personal circumstances 12.8, 17.211, 17.227
personal connection 1.22, 20.91
personal data 10.26; see also data protection
personal grudges 12.6, 23.38
personal injuries 1.42, 3.33, 11.123, 11.145–150, 12.67, 23.88; see also injuries at work
  defences to action
    for 11.140–150
  risk of serious 11.12, 11.17
personal nature 10.1–7, 10.41, 20.57
personal protective equipment (PPE) 11.62, 11.78, 11.83–84, 11.138
personal representatives 4.215, 5.65, 20.115–116
personal service 2.2, 2.54, 4.153, 4.191
personality 18.87, 19.35
  corporate 9.11, 9.28
  legal 22.3–4
philosophical belief 4.155, 4.159
physical, biological or chemical agents 2.109, 6.10–11
physical danger 4.95, 11.119
physical features of the work-place 4.106, 4.112, 4.116
physical or mental impairment 4.80–98
picketing 1.59, 1.107, 7.3, 23.43–44, 23.75, 23.114
  mass 23.111
  peaceful 23.77, 23.105–114
  unlawful 23.108, 23.111–112
piecework 10.19–20, 15.14
pit deputies 7.108
plant agreements 3.57, 3.61–62
poaching 19.33, 19.41–42, 22.27
police 2.73–75, 2.94, 2.99, 4.38, 4.116–117, 4.250, 11.104, 12.66–69, 17.121–122
  authorities 2.73–75, 2.101, 7.14
  cadets 2.73–75, 2.94, 2.99
  officers 2.73–75, 2.99, 4.38, 4.98, 4.247, 23.106
policy statements 3.21, 3.80, 17.77, 17.109
political funds 1.25, 2.68, 17.166, 21.26, 21.83–84, 22.48, 22.54, 22.67–74, 23.89
  ballots 22.73, 22.76
political objects 1.18, 22.67–75

political office 22.73
political parties 4.154, 21.2–3, 21.18, 22.45, 22.73
political strikes 13.35–36, 23.35–36
poor performance 4.230, 10.21, 17.87,
positive action 4.48, 4.74, 4.112, 4.170, 4.204, 22.21
post-employment
  detriment 7.139
postal address 22.68, 22.82
postal strikes 15.7, 20.14
posted workers 1.90, 2.118
potential hazards 11.25, 11.40, 11.42, 11.49
potentially fair reasons for dismissal 17.83–86
PPE, see personal protective equipment
practicability 11.23, 11.105, 17.188, 17.190
practice
  codes of 1.15, 1.17, 1.58–59, 3.21, 10.47, 11.89–91, 12.12, 12.21, 21.73, 21.76
  normal 3.80–82, 10.35, 17.135
pre-hearing reviews 1.29, 20.55, 21.115
precautionary
  suspension 12.65–70
precautions 11.32, 11.88, 11.111, 11.115–120, 11.12, 11.134–135
  safety 2.60, 11.36–37, 11.98, 11.113, 11.115, 11.126–128, 17.133
precedence 3.77
precedents 1.13, 17.1, 17.77
preferential debts 7.133–134
pregnancy 4.10, 4.12, 4.18, 4.45, 4.50, 4.128, 4.132–138, 5.17, 5.21, 6.1–10, 6.20–29, 6.45–55, 12.22
pregnancy-related illness 4.50, 4.132, 4.137, 12.22
pregnant women 2.77, 4.18, 4.128–138, 6.8–18, 6.50–55
prejudice 1.49, 2.78, 4.38, 17.160, 20.8, 20.119, 21.21
preliminary hearings 1.45, 20.55–58, 20.101
premises 4.112, 4.114, 11.2, 11.9, 11.30, 11.35, 11.49, 11.55, 11.87, 18.14–15, 23.105–114
  employer's 2.126, 3.51, 4.58, 7.32, 11.49, 11.66
premium payments 8.40, 10.17

preparation time orders 20.55, 20.110–112
preparatory activities 10.56, 19.4–5
preparatory work 1.66, 20.110
prescribed form 7.113, 20.48, 20.52
prescribed information 20.48, 20.52, 20.57
prescribed rates 6.62, 6.66, 6.80, 6.102, 7.120
pressure 10.2, 21.118–119, 21.57–58, 23.71, 23.119
  to impose union recognition requirement 23.78
  improper 10.61, 17.135
  industrial 17.172, 21.37, 21.118–119, 22.10
previous employers 3.112, 7.47, 9.33, 10.35–36, 10.74, 14.8, 19.29
principal executive committees 22.40–44, 23.59, 23.82, 23.84
principal purpose 8.17, 22.2, 22.16, 22.85
principal reason for dismissal 6.128, 10.83, 17.82, 20.83–84, 21.85–89, 21.118–119
prison 4.246, 7.l14, 7.95, 17.59, 17.67, 17.164
prison staff 2.73, 4.250, 17.4
privacy 1.107, 4.184, 10.26, 10.30, 10.41–47, 20.57
private agreements 13.3
private households 2.112, 7.92, 18.64
private life 1.107, 10.41–47
private use 6.28, 10.42, 16.23, 17.205
privileges 2.62, 2.73–75, 3.91, 12.84, 17.186, 20.43, 20.67–68, 22.32, 22.35
pro rata basis 2.91, 3.52, 7.85, 10.100
probation officers 4.247, 4.250, 17.144
probationary employees 2.96–98
probationary periods 2.97–98, 10.13, 15.26
procedural fairness 16.32, 17.86, 17.179
productivity 5.45, 11.74
professional
  organisations 10.53, 22.3
profit-sharing schemes 2.17, 2.165
profitability 5.45, 9.56, 10.70
profits 2.17, 2.49, 2.53, 2.58, 10.93, 14.4, 16.24, 19.68

prohibited conduct 4.5–6, 4.9–14, 4.61, 4.131, 4.235, 10.113
prohibition notices 1.21, 11.12–24, 11.95
project termination 13.13, 15.1
promises 3.20, 16.8, 17.14, 19.25, 19.29, 19.45, 20.41
promotion 4.38, 4.48, 4.65, 4.165, 4.170, 4.204, 10.5, 21.52, 21.60
proof, burden of 1.92, 4.184, 4.189, 4.205, 4.222–225, 5.4, 11.97–98, 20.76–77, 20.82
proof of employment relationship, Directive 1.84
property 3.33, 10.49, 12.65, 17.121, 17.123, 17.125, 22.3, 22.63, 22.74, 22.85, 23.89
  employees 3.33–37, 3.48–53
  employers 10.49, 10.65, 12.51, 19.30
  sequestration of 23.85, 23.94
proportionality 3.37, 4.73, 4.173, 23.97–98
proportionate means of achieving a legitimate aim 4.24, 4.53–72, 4.102, 4.109, 4.122, 4.152, 4.161–172, 4.183–189
prosecution 2.153, 11.5, 11.14, 11.25, 11.97–101, 23.23
prospective employers 10.12, 10.35, 10.38, 10.55, 21.7, 21.41
protected characteristics 4.5, 4.10–66, 4.124, 4.126–127, 4.136, 4.139, 4.177, 4.188–194, 4.204, 4.223–225, 10.108
protected conduct 21.2–3, 21.18
protected disclosure 2.24, 2.175–177, 10.74–85, 17.181, 17.203, 19.19, 20.65–69, 20.96, 23.133, 23.137, 23.154–144
protected industrial action 17.81, 21.111–115
protected period 4.128–139, 18.91–97, 21.112
protected shop workers 7.111
protection of wages 3.76, 8.1–62
  contractual
    authorisation 8.6–7
  statutory deduction 8.5
  written consent 8.8–12
protective awards 1.25, 7.133–134, 8.13, 9.31, 18.76, 18.91–100, 22.35
protective equipment, personal 11.62, 11.78–84, 11.137–138
protest, under 3.100, 3.106, 17.9, 18.6

prudent employers 11.108, 11.112
psychiatric illness 4.231, 11.104–105, 11.113, 11.136, 16.5, 16.25
psychiatric injury 4.230, 11.105, 11.108, 11.113, 16.4
public administration, transfers within 9.23
public authorities 1.73, 1.78, 1.106–107, 9.28, 10.43
public bodies 1.107, 3.61, 4.147, 8.23, 16.33–37
public domain 10.25, 10.72, 19.24
public duties 16.33, 15.17, 16.33
  time off for 2.69, 2.73, 2.126, 7.13–19
public holidays 3.112, 3.125, 7.73–74, 20.14
public interest 10.72, 10.79–80, 11.25, 19.15–18, 20.42–44, 20.67
  disclosure 2.64, 10.74–85
  overriding reason of 23.97–98
public interest disclosures, see whistleblowing
public nuisance 23.44, 23.111
public policy 3.8, 3.15, 10.16, 19.13, 19.49, 21.5, 23.30
public safety 1.107, 10.43
public sector 1.37, 1.107, 2.6, 4.7, 9.23, 9.41, 16.34, 23.143
publicity 10.17, 11.25, 16.20
punishment 1.39, 4.245, 4.247, 12.1–91, 17.132, 17.240
punitive suspension 12.65

Q
qualifications 2.85, 2.132, 2.164, 4.204, 7.33, 7.37, 17.73, 22.45, 22.56
  lack of 17.117–119
  professional 17.73, 21.2
qualified majority voting 1.62, 1.85, 11.77
qualifying periods of employment 7.63, 7.107, 8.35, 8.48, 13.9–10, 15.18–29, 21.86, 21.113

R
race 1.49, 1.57, 4.10, 4.17, 4.140–141, 4.205, 4.219–220, 4.223, 20.11, 20.24
  discrimination 1.25, 2.114–117, 3.8–9, 4.38, 4.57, 4.228–231, 9.33
  relations 1.25, 2.71, 4.148–151
racial groups 4.22–28, 4.140–153, 4.223

racism 4,22, 4.155, 4.223
re-employment 13.2, 13.23,
  17.225
  after unfair dismissal 13.29–
    33
re-engagement 13.29–32,
  17.184–195, 17.224, 17.231,
  17.239, 18.24, 21.97–110
  orders 8.13, 17.184–191
reasonable adjustments 4.102–
  118, 7.53, 11.119, 17.104,
  17.116
reasonable amount of
  work 2.174, 10.17
reasonable belief 10.77, 11.66,
  23.56
reasonable care 2.60, 3.39, 10.36
reasonable cause 6.134, 7.120,
  11.10
reasonable contact 6.35, 7.6.73
reasonable employers 3.48,
  3.107, 10.21–22, 11.63, 11.66,
  11.98, 11.105, 11.141, 12.10,
  12.16, 12.47, 17.27, 17.50,
  17.58, 17.63, 17.67, 17.78,
  17.84, 17.87, 17.93,17.110,
  17.119, 17.130, 17.142, 17.155,
  17.177, 18.43–44, 18.47,
  20.79, 20.124, 21.29, 21.41
reasonable prospect of
  success 20.55–56, 20.106–
  107, 20.111
reasonable steps 3.39–40, 4.112,
  7.99, 11.105, 11.110, 11.126–
  127, 16.26, 17.224
reasonableness 3.92, 3.104, 12.10,
  12.53, 12.55, 17.19, 17.74–80,
  17.89, 19.42, 19.44–47
  band of 17.78, 17.87
  covenants 19.44–47
  test of 3.92, 17.37, 17.177,
    17, 277
reasonably competent fellow
  employees 11.129
receivers 7.134, 9.11, 18.4–5,
  18.67, 22.65
receivership 7.134, 9.11
recognition 1.107, 3.58, 3.78,
  9.73–74, 11.107, 17.81, 21.61–
  65, 23.1–15
  mutual 13.27
  statutory 2.9, 23.6, 23.14
  trade unions 1.5, 1.19, 9.74,
    23.1–3, 23.78–84
  voluntary 18.69, 23.4–12
Recommendations (EU)
  1.99–100
reconsideration of
  judgments 20.101–105
recoupment 17.208, 17.237,
  17.244–245

SMP, SPP and SAP 6.81
recovery 1.40, 10.96, 17.61,
  17.100
  double 16.28
recruitment 4.63, 4.105, 4.170,
  4.204, 10.13, 10.28, 21.6, 21.40
  unfair 4.254, 21.7, 21.36
recurrence 4.85, 4.92
  likelihood of 4.87, 17.107
reduced compensation 12.64,
  17.1, 17.111
redundancy 3.59–63, 3.71, 3.88,
  4.66–73, 6.39–55, 9.44–67,
  13.42–43, 17.195–205,
  18.1–102
  claims for redundancy
    payments 18.65–66
  collective 1.78, 9.2–4, 18.2,
    18.69–71, 23.151
  consultation on
    redundancies 18.69–100
  definition 2.8, 18.19, 18.100
  dismissal 9.57, 17.203,
    17.218, 17.222, 18.40–41,
    18.45–50
  dismissal during period of
    notice 18.62–63
  dismissal for reason
    of 18.11–20
  Employment Rights Act
    1996 18.3–37
    definition of
      dismissal 18.12–15
    persons covered 18.3
  excluded classes of
    employees 18.64
  fair/unfair redundancy
    dismissals 18.40–63
  guidelines for good industrial
    relations practice 18.40
  handling
    redundancies 18.42–60
  impending 3.63, 18.5–6,
    18.38–40
  laying off and short-time
    working 18.33–39
  and offer of suitable
    alternative
    employment 18.28–31
  pay, statutory 13.3, 13.10,
    13.17, 13.34, 14.11–14,
    18.86
  payments 3.103, 3.110, 6.40,
    6.45, 9.62–63, 13.1, 13.3,
    13.40–43, 17.195, 17.198,
    18.7–39, 18.62–67
    enhanced 3.71, 3.80, 3.85,
      4.69–73, 9.42, 17.205,
      17.237
  payments by Secretary of
    State 18.67–68

peaceable process of
  redundancy selection 4.72,
  18.51
presumption of 18.23
protective awards 18.91–100
and renewal or re-
  engagement 18.24–30
selection 2.91, 3.63, 4.68,
  4.71–72, 4.174–176,
  18.51–61
  peaceable process of 4.72,
    18.51
time off to look for
  work 18.38–39
unfair selection 18.50–61
redundant employees 7.42,
  18.1–4, 18.18–20, 18.38–42,
  18.65–66, 18.89–91
reference periods 7.59–60
references 10.35–40
refusal to deal on union
  exclusion grounds 23.121–
  122
register of members 1.18,
  22.18–24, 22.50–53, 22.82
registered blind 4.84
registered medical
  practitioners 6.3, 6.13, 6.23
registered midwives 6.3, 6.13,
  6.23
rehabilitated persons 4.241–247
rehabilitation period 4.241,
  4.245–246
reinstatement 7.121–125, 8.13,
  9.34, 10.2, 11.67, 12.63, 12.67,
  13.29–32, 13.38, 17.184–194,
  17.198, 17.224, 17.239–240,
  20.27, 20.43, 20.107, 20.111,
  20.116, 21.115, 21.122–123,
  23.141
  committees 7.127
  date of 17.186, 17.240
relationship of trust and
  confidence 10.117, 17.27,
  17.34, 17.48
relevant information 2.169–170,
  3.4, 5.60, 6.11, 11.57, 20.53,
  22.7, 23.18, 23.133
relevant transfers 9.9, 9.14, 9.23,
  9.25, 9.30, 9.52, 9.54, 9.69–70,
  9.75, 9.85
religion 1.93, 1.107, 2.67, 4.8,
  4.10, 4.30, 4.54, 4.127, 4.136,
  4.142, 4.154–165, 4.189,
  4.194, 17.144, 17.148, 18.53,
  23.131
  ministers of 2.67
  organised 4.54, 4.127, 4.163–
    164, 4.189
religious beliefs 1.107, 3.93,
  4.155, 4.158–160

religious communities 7.93, 8.38
religious discrimination 4.158
relocation 17.29, 17.234
remedies 4.213, 15.32–40, 15.3,
  16.16–20, 16.30–31, 16.33–37,
  17.184–191, 22.55, 22.65–66
  adoption leave 6.78
  against trade union
    trustees 22.65–66
  covenants 19.58–60
  equal pay 5.63–64
  equality in
    employment 4.227–232
  maternity rights 6.50–55
  notice 15.32–40
  trade union executive
    committee elections 22.55
  unfair dismissal 17.184–191
  wrongful dismissal 16.16–20
  wrongful exclusion or
    expulsion from trade
    union 21.18–19
remuneration 2.58, 2.63–64,
  2.67, 2.94, 2.120, 2.152, 3.7,
  3.13, 3.20, 3.35, 6.17, 6.21,
  6.28–30, 6.47, 7.4, 7.7–8,
  7.22, 7.133–134, 8.35, 8.40,
  8.45, 14.4, 14.7–12; see also
  salaries; wages
  contractual 6.47, 6.62, 6.80,
    7.4
renewal 2.133, 2.136, 10.54,
  18.24–27, 18.88, 18.97
reorganisations 3.26, 3.104,
  9.23, 10.17, 17.150, 17.153,
  17.189, 18.16–17
repayments 8.8, 8.40
replacement 2.44, 2.53, 4.191,
  6.53, 7.123, 17.61, 17.63–64,
  17.67, 17.73, 17.160,-161,
  17.188
  permanent 17.161, 17.63–64,
    17.188
  temporary 6.53, 17.64, 17.67,
    17.160
representations 4.237–239,
  11.40, 11.47, 12.20, 12.26–28,
  12.35, 16.8, 18.69, 18.87–88,
  20.54, 20.89, 20.113, 22.5
  written 4.238–239, 20.54,
    20.113, 23.14
representatives 9.52, 9.57, 9.75–
  78, 9.80–82, 11.30, 11.37–48,
  18.69–73, 18.79, 18.81, 18.83,
  18.85–92, 18.96, 18.100–101,
  19.32, 23.145–146, 23.148–
  149, 23.151–155, 23.157
  appropriate 9.52, 9.75–78,
    9.80, 18.72–73, 18.79,
    18.86–88, 18.90, 18.92,
    23.146

elected 11.46, 18.72, 18.101
employee, see employee
  representatives
  negotiating 23.148, 23.154
  personal 4.215, 5.65, 13.40,
    20.114
  safety 2.74, 2.77, 11.38–48,
    11.63, 11.65–66, 11.68–69,
    17.196, 17.198, 17.203,
    22.17
  trade union 11.37, 21.118,
    23.15, 23.114
  trade union learning 21.74–
    78
reprimands 12.84
repudiation 3.100, 3.102, 9.65,
  10.17, 12.64, 16.6, 16.32,
  17.21, 17.26, 17.31, 17.40,
  17.41, 17.57, 17.59, 18.35,
  21.100, 21.113, 23.81–82,
  23.84
repudiatory breach of
  contract 6.10, 9.65, 10.62,
  17.23, 17.34, 20.71
reputation 1.107, 3.47, 10.11,
  10.17, 12.28, 15.33, 16.21,
  16.25, 17.144, 17.203, 20.57,
  22.4, 22.28
  loss of 10.17, 16.25
rescue culture 9.49, 9.52
reserve forces 7.121, 7.127,
  13.38
resignation 15.8–9, 17.9, 17.18,
  17.31, 17.38, 17.43, 17.45,
  17.50–58, 17.71–72, 18.6,
  20.33, 20.36, 21.16
  constructive 3.36, 17.56–57
  implied 17.58
responsibilities 1.48–49, 1.57,
  1.67–68, 2.1, 2.49, 2.54, 2.60,
  2.101, 5.7, 5.27, 6.84, 6.93–96,
  6.112, 6.114–115, 6.117,
  11.9–10
  additional 1.48, 3.83, 5.30,
    5.45, 20.75
rest breaks 1.95, 2.165, 6.12,
  7.68, 7.72, 7.94, 7.96–97, 7.99,
  7.103
rest periods 1.85, 2.165, 7.66,
  7.70–71, 7.94, 7.96–97, 7.103
restitution 8.23, 10.94
restraint clauses 17.152, 19.56
restraint of trade 1.42, 16.12,
  19.10, 19.38, 19.44, 19.48–55,
  22.25
restrictive covenants, see
  covenants
retail employment 8.24–30,
  12.57
retail workers, see shop workers
retainers 2.126, 8.14

retirement 3.40, 4.28, 4.63,
  4.65–67, 8.17, 8.40, 9.32,
  9.42, 10.15, 13.29, 14.11, 15.1,
  15.27, 17.208, 18.7; see also
  pensions
  age 4.67, 15.1, 15.27
  compulsory 4.63, 4.67
  early 4.66–67, 9.42, 17.208,
    18.7
retraining 3.41, 12.24, 15.17,
  15.20, 17.225, 18.25, 18.38,
  18.43
review, judicial 8.23, 16.20,
  16.33–37
right to privacy 1.107, 10.30,
  10.41–47, 17.144, 20.57
  and employers 10.41–47
rights, human, see human rights
rights and freedoms of
  others 1.107, 10.43
rights in notice, see notice
risk assessments 2.109, 4.50,
  4.130, 6.9–18, 7.64, 11.79–80,
  11.98, 11.136, 11.139
risk of injury 11.85, 11.98,
  11.135, 11.150, 16.11
rival businesses 4.20, 10.1,
  10.70, 10.91, 17.143, 17.149,
  17.198, 19.3, 19.10
rotas 2.53, 14.9, 17.153
rule of law 1.65, 3.57, 3.77,
  11.25, 12.22, 12.82–83, 17.98,
  18.41, 21.11, 23.81

S
safe plant and
  appliances 11.122–124
safe system of work 11.35,
  11.125–128
safety 1.51–54, 1.107, 2.60–61,
  2.73–74, 2.77, 2.100, 2.109,
  4.102–103, 4.149, 6.9–10,
  6.13–14, 6.16, 6.20, 10.116–
  117, 11.1–151; see also health
  and safety
  committees 11.38–48, 11.63,
    11.69
  precautions 2.60, 11.37,
    11.60, 11.98, 11.110,
    11.115, 11.126–128,
    17.133
  public 1.107, 10.43
  representatives 1.28, 2.74,
    2.77, 2.172, 11.38–48,
    11.63, 11.65–66, 11.68–69,
    17.196, 17.198, 22.17
salaried partners 2.17
salaries 2.11, 2.16, 2.62,
  2.64, 3.28, 3.35, 3.37, 3.61,
  2.102, 3.123, 10.15, 10.17,
  12.85, 17.23, 17.26, 17.207,

17.211, 17.216–217; see also remuneration; wages
salesmen 9.65, 10.68, 17.147, 17.152, 19.24
sanctions 1.107, 6.133, 11.74, 12.2, 12.45–46, 12.49, 12.85, 12.89, 17.120, 17.130, 18.10, 18.94
  disciplinary 12.2, 12.24, 12.51–52, 12.56, 12.75, 17.40, 17.120
  ultimate 1.107, 17.120, 21.84, 23.136
sanitary conveniences 11.81
SAP, see statutory adoption pay
Scotland 1.20, 1.23, 1.25, 1.39–40, 2.110, 5.62, 5.66, 7.110, 7.119, 8.7–8, 8.14, 11.87, 11.94, 11.99, 11.101, 11.151
scrutineers, independent 21.22, 22.19–20, 22.48–54, 22.82, 23.57
seamen 3.1, 3.124, 17.4, 21.36, 22.31, 22.37, 22.41
search orders 19.65–66
second class post 17.178, 20.14
secondary action 2.22–23, 21.94, 21.111, 23.48, 23.73–77
seconded employees 2.143–151, 4.150
secondment 2.143–47,
  liability if seconded employee injures himself 2.148
  liability if seconded employee injures third party 2.145–147
  status of seconded worker during and after employment 2.149–151
secret ballots 22.55, 23.7, 23.12, 23.46–53
secret bribes and commissions 10.66–68
secret processes 19.14–15, 19.29–30
secrets 19.28–32, 19.57
security guards 3.94, 4.243, 7.95, 12.47
security services 2.175, 2.178, 9.46, 12.31, 17.52, 17.173
segregation 4.18, 4.142
selection 3.59, 3.63–64, 4.71, 6.45, 6.50, 6.52, 7.107, 9.58, 10.5, 10.13, 10.27, 10.36, 18.40, 18.42, 18.46, 18.48, 18.51–61
  matrices 4.72, 18.51
  procedures 4.198, 9.57, 16.6, 18.48, 18.51–60
  unfair 18.50–51, 18.53, 18.55–56, 18.58–61

self-certification of illness 7.53
self-employed persons/ workers 2.4, 2.25–26, 2.29, 2.36–61, 7.55, 7.74, 21.24, 21.35; see also employees, and self-employed persons distinguished
self-employment 1.82, 16.26, 17.207, 17.211
senior employees 3.40, 10.56, 10.96, 11.125, 12.54, 16.12–13, 16.37, 19.5, 19.10, 19.22
senior managers 10.96, 11.99, 19.22, 23.145
seniority 6.21, 6.34, 6.38, 6.44, 6.71, 6.75, 12.89, 15.2–3, 17.186, 18.21, 21.124
separate workplace ballots 23.54–55
sequestration of property 23.85, 23.94
serious injuries 11.128, 11.149, 23.142
service provision changes 9.4, 9.14–16
  one-off business tasks 9.19
  organised groupings 9.17–18
  outsourcing 9.14, 9.21–22
  procurement/supply of goods for client's use 9.20
service-related benefits 4.71, 18.51
settlement agreements 1.15, 20.37–42
settlements 5.24, 17.245
severance payments 2.91, 5.17, 5.19, 17.199, 17.210, 17.241, 20.42
sex 1.76–77, 1.80, 1.92, 2.81, 4.18–22, 4.24, 4.28, 4.30, 4.32, 4.34–36, 4.119, 4.122–124, 4.126, 4.163, 4.166–189, 5.45–47, 5.49, 5.54, 6.94–95, 6.111
  discrimination 1.92–93, 2.67, 2.71, 2.81, 2.131, 2.144, 4.8, 4.20, 5.10, 5.34, 5.47, 5.52, 5.66, 6.41–42, 6.45, 6.51, 10.45
  direct 4.167–170, 12.22
  in employment 4.177–182
  indirect 4.171–176, 5.45, 5.47
  in relation to contractual pay 5.52
  and equality in employment 4.163–165
  protected characteristic 4.160–161, 4.167, 4.171, 4.177, 4.182
sexual abuse 4.83, 12.67

sexual harassment 1.100, 2.144, 4.12, 4.32–36, 4.50, 4.53, 10.109–117, 17.39
sexual misconduct 1.22, 1.107, 12.28, 20.57
sexual orientation 1.49, 1.93, 1.105, 1.107, 4.8, 4.10, 4.59, 4.163, 4.185–189
  occupational requirements 4.189
share fishermen 2.27, 3.124, 6.84, 8.38, 18.64, 21.36
share fisherwomen 6.3, 6.22
share option schemes 3.21, 9.40
shared parental leave 6.103, 6.138
sheriff's courts 2.115, 4.210, 4.226–227, 4.235, 4.238, 8.54
shift workers 7.98–99, 14.9, 21.70
shifts 2.126, 7.63, 8.14, 8.18, 8.40, 8.43, 14.3
  night 2.126, 7.63–65, 7.69, 8.18, 21.70
ships 1.35, 7.91, 17.4, 21.36, 23.97, 23.123
shop stewards 12.21, 12.23, 18.90, 21.37, 21.51, 21.53–55, 21.88, 21.127, 22.16, 23.21, 23.25, 23.59, 23.79, 23.81, 23.106
shop workers 7.110–118, 8.25
  opted-out 7.111, 7.113–117, 18.61
  protected 7.111–112, 7.114
shops 2.38, 2.68, 7.110–119, 12.53, 12.85, 13.23, 18.43, 18.77
short-time working 4.50, 7.85, 8.19, 10.20, 15.10, 16.32, 18.33–37, 18.43
sick notes 17.61, 17.64, 17.111
sick pay 2.41, 2.46, 2.53–54, 2.60, 2.91, 2.95, 2.159, 2.161, 2.165, 3.28, 3.46, 3.82, 3.84, 3.112, 3.116, 7.43–53, 7.133
  statutory, see statutory sick pay
sickness 3.28, 3.31–32, 3.38, 3.89, 3.112–113, 3.120, 7.43, 7.50, 13.16–17, 15.17, 17.61, 17.93–105, 18.58
  long-term 1.55, 3.31, 3.89, 17.93–105, 18.58
sift stage 1.45, 20.54
Sikhs 4.30, 4.140. 4.149, 17.148
sit-ins 10.49, 23.43, 23.115–116
skill and care, duty to use 10.65
skills 2.85, 2.101, 2.105, 2.164, 3.6, 3.41, 3.59, 3.63, 5.32, 5.36, 5.44, 5.46, 10.17, 10.65, 10.70, 10.86, 19.15–16. 19.21–22, 19.25–36, 19.30

smoking 3.90, 11.87, 12.22,
12.64, 12.81, 16.11, 17.28,
17.133
SMP, see statutory maternity pay
social security benefits 1.73,
6.86, 7.135, 17.186
social workers 4.247, 4.250,
19.70
solicitors 1.22, 1.25, 19.44–46,
19.53, 20.7, 20.16, 20.36,
20.68, 20.72, 20.106
some other substantial reason
(SOSR) 2.78, 2.175, 3.94,
3.104, 4.67, 6.53, 17.53,
17.114, 17.137, 17.149–164
SOSR, see some other
substantial reason
special circumstances 9.69, 9.76,
9.83, 10.3, 10.17, 15.39, 16.11,
17.51, 17.148, 18.88–90
special facts 5.41, 17.1, 17.134,
18.4, 19.38
special protection 2.76–77,
2.109, 4.136, 4.194
special register 22.3, 22.25
special risks 2.123, 3.52, 10.34,
11.145
special treatment 4.18, 4.131,
4.133, 4.194, 5.21
spouses 1.80, 3.127, 6.111,
6.126, 12.54
SPP, see statutory paternity pay
springboard injunctions
19.22–24
SSP, see statutory sick pay
staff associations 22.10–14
staff rules, see works rules
standard of proof 20.82; see also
burden of proof
standing statements of fixed
deductions 3.123
statements
annual 22.57, 22.62
false 17.163, 22.62
itemised pay 2.61, 2.73,
3.123–124, 20.114, 21.79
written 2.89, 2.92, 2.120,
2.136, 2.139, 3.63, 3.81,
11.36–37, 12.6, 17.174,
17.179
statistical evidence 5.10
status 1.77, 1.80, 2.11, 2.23,
2.31, 2.51, 2.53, 2.67, 2.76–77,
2.82, 2.91, 2.101, 4.174, 4.181,
5.20, 7.55, 7.114, 7.117, 8.37,
23.38
legal 2.11, 2.53, 2.76–77
marital 4.174, 4.181, 12.54
statutory adoption pay
(SAP) 2.91, 6.70, 6.79–81,
6.103, 6.117

statutory duties 3.52, 11.13,
11.17, 11.21, 11.27, 11.29,
11.31–33, 11.103, 11.130–139,
23.45, 23.88, 23.118–119,
23.121
statutory employment
rights 1.38, 6.34
statutory immunities 23.28,
23.47, 23.53, 23.58, 23.91,
23.112
statutory maternity pay
(SMP) 6.19, 6.56–65, 6.74,
6.109, 7.133–134, 13.25, 15.17
statutory obligations, see
statutory duties
statutory paternity pay
(SPP) 6.101–103, 6.105,
13.43, 15.17
statutory recognition 2.9,
21.61–65, 23.5–12
statutory redundancy pay 13.3,
13.10, 13.17, 13.34, 14.11,
14.14, 18.86
statutory rights 2.61, 3.16, 3.25,
13.3, 13.10, 13.14, 13.42–43,
15.10, 15.16–17, 17.169–171,
17.215, 20.35, 20.37
dismissal for
asserting 17.165–171
and transfer of
undertakings 9.36
statutory sick pay (SSP) 2.54,
2.91, 2.133, 6.80, 7.43–53,
7.133, 8.13, 15.17
enforcement 7.51–52
exclusions from
entitlement 7.50
qualifying conditions 7.47–
49
self-certification of
illness 7.53
statutory terms 3.56, 3.121, 9.37
stock 17.125, 19.41
deficiencies 8.26–27, 8.29,
8.31, 12.35, 12.85
stress 4.94, 11.104–108, 11.120,
11.136, 21.60
work-related 6.12, 7.109,
11.105–108
strict liability 11.130
strike pay 22.37
strikes 13.35–37, 15.7, 15.18,
18.63, 19.1, 20.14, 20.56,
20.61–62, 21.9, 21.11,
21.22–23, 21.57, 21.61,
21.85–86, 21.92–93, 21.95,
21.98–111, 21.113, 21.116,
21.118–119, 23.20, 23.23–25,
23.34–36. 23.38, 23.42–44,
23.46–48, 23.52, 23.57, 23.60,
23.63, 23.66, 23.69, 23.72,

23.85, 23.87, 23.91, 23.97–98,
23.102–103, 23.109, 23.113,
23.119, 23.123–127
criminal liabilities
23.123–127
political 13.35, 23.36
postal 15.7, 20.14
unofficial 21.92–83, 21.98–
100, 21.111, 21.113, 21.116,
23.72, 23.92
study or training 1.28, 2.32,
7.26–39, 13.43, 17.81
time off for 1.28, 2.32, 7.26–
39, 17.81
sub-contractors 2.60, 10.103,
11.35, 23.119
subjective knowledge 19.30,
21.102
subsidiaries 9.11–12, 18.89,
19.55
substantial and long-term
adverse effect 4.80–81,
4.86–94
substantial reason, some
other 2.78, 2.175, 3.94, 3.104,
4.67, 6.53, 7.11, 10.63, 11.119,
17.53, 17.73, 17.114, 17.137,
17.149–164
substitutes 2.43–44, 2.48, 2.156,
3.71, 3.86, 4.191, 4.239,
17.76–77, 17.125, 20.124,
22.29
succession of contracts 2.40,
2.42, 2.136
successors 1.9, 5.12, 6.45, 6.76,
13.32, 17.186–187, 23.4
sufficient evidence 3.81, 4.29,
18.53, 23.36
sufficient reason for
dismissal 9.54, 9.57
suitability 2.96–97, 4.109, 4.247,
11.84, 18.14, 18.30, 21.39,
23.97
suitable alternative
employment 4.102–103,
6.15–16, 17.99, 17.118,
17.140, 17.186, 17.195,
18.28–32
summary dismissal 10.57,
15.1, 15.7, 15.25, 16.1, 16.3,
16.9–15
wrongful dismissal 16.6–7
Sundays 1.107, 2.68, 4.156, 5.28,
7.110–118, 7.139, 13.3, 13.9,
13.35, 17.81
supervision 1.18, 2.161, 2.164,
3.104, 4.119, 4.245, 5.23, 7.23,
11.34, 11.37, 11.125
supervisors 3.104, 5.23, 11.37,
12.1, 12.19, 12.85, 17.27,
17.144

suppliers 10.41, 10.68, 11.4, 11.53, 11.57, 16.12, 19.2, 19.14, 23.118, 23.121
Supreme Court 1.23, 1.32, 1.60, 2.66–67, 2.156, 5.8, 5.62, 9.50, 16.3
suspension 2.61, 2.71, 6.9–14, 7.7–12
  maternity suspension pay 6.17–18, 8.13
  medical 1.25, 2.61, 2.133, 7.7–12, 7.133–134, 8.13, 13.43, 14,13, 17.160
  period 7.7, 12.63
  precautionary 12.65–70
  without pay for misconduct 12.60–64
swearing 12.52, 16.14, 17.123, 17.228
Sweden 1.62
sweetheart unions 22.10

T

tapering provision 17.197, 18.66
tariff approach 12.46, 17.130
tax credits 7.139, 17.81, 18.61
taxes 2.11–12. 2.15, 2.29, 2.31, 2.36, 2.46, 2.41–55, 2.58, 3.12–13, 3.18, 15.11, 16.22–23, 16.29
teachers 1.32, 1.103, 1.107, 2.127–128, 3.29, 3.96, 13.20, 18.72, 23.22, 23.31–32
telephone 2.126, 6.35, 6.70, 8.43, 10.41, 19.26, 19.47, 20.46
  calls 1.107, 2.126, 8.11, 10.30, 10.41
television watching 2.126, 12.79
temporary cessations 13.18–23, 18.13
temporary contracts 2.155, 13.20, 18.17
temporary employees 2.78–79, 6.3, 7.11, 17.160
temporary employers 2.148, 10.108
temporary injunctions 23.67, 23.90
temporary replacement 6.53, 17.64, 17.67, 17.160
temporary work agencies 2.162–173
temporary workers 2.78–79, 2.113, 2.152–173; see also agency workers; fixed-term workers/employees
tendering, competitive 9.15, 9.26, 9.60

termination
  date of 5.19, 15.11, 20.31
  effective 12.38, 13.8, 13.10, 14.14, 15.28–29, 15.37, 16.3, 20.6, 20.25–34
  and dismissal distinguished 17.46, 17.49–58
terms, see contractual terms
territorial jurisdiction 1.30–38, 4.192, 4.217, 17.4
  employment tribunals 1.30–38
territorial waters 2.124, 11.3, 17.4
theft 2.103, 3.43, 3.94, 8.23, 10.49, 10.104, 12.51, 17.120–123, 17.125, 17.140, 17.157, 17.162, 20.83
third parties 2.145–147, 10.71, 10.102, 10.113, 11.123, 23.22, 12.34, 23.46
threats 21.57, 21.108, 21.118, 23.25, 23.33, 23.42, 23.128, 23.130
tie-breakers 22.44–45
time limits 1.8, 1.13, 3.39, 5.60–62, 11.18, 11.27, 20.1–25, 23.138–141
  for enforcing Community rights 20.20–24
  equal pay 5.62
  equality in employment 4.220
  and notice 15.28–31
time off 2.67–73, 6.122–128, 7.13–32, 7.133–134, 14.13, 18.38–39, 21.66–78, 23.138; see also working time
  for antenatal care 6.3–8
  for dependants 6.122–128
  for employee representatives 7.23
  employment protection 7.13–42
  for members of a European Works Council 23.138
  for occupational pensions scheme trustees 7.20–22
  for public duties 2.69–73, 2.124–126, 7.13–19
  for study or training 1.28, 7.16–39, 13.43, 14.11
  young persons 7.26–28
  for trade union activities 21.72–73
  for trade union duties 21.66–71
  for trade union learning representatives 21.74–78
tobacco smoke 11.81, 11.87

tort 2.70, 10.105, 10.110, 11.131, 21.95. 23.20, 23.22, 23.25, 23.26–27, 23.41, 23.43, 23.45, 23.47, 23.68–94, 23.111–116
  of harassment 4.60, 10.110
trade disputes 1.5–13, 7.3, 23.29–45, 23.55, 23.58–78, 23.71–80, 23.90–91, 23.97–103; see also industrial action
  definition 23.29, 23.58
trade secrets 10.70, 16.12, 19.2, 19.8, 19.15, 19.29–31, 19.38, 19.57
trade union activities 21.30, 21.40, 21.51, 21.72, 21.85–89, 21.127, 22.18
trade union duties 1.30, 7.15, 7.42, 7.133–134, 12.30, 17.198, 21.52–54, 21.69–70, 21.87–88
trade union learning representatives 21.74–78, 22.17
trade union representatives 11.38, 18.57, 21.118, 23.13, 23.15
trade unions 1.18, 1.25, 3.57–85, 9.74–10.3, 12.23–30, 18.40–55, 18.69–92, 21.1–101, 21.111–23.122
  accounts and records 22.56–62
  amalgamations and transfers 22.81–83
  amount of damages against 23.86–89
  annual statements 22.62, 22.56–62
  breach of union rules 22.78–80
  certification 22.7–17
  Certification Officer 1.2, 1.18–21, 20.118, 21.9, 22.5, 22.7.21, 22.51–61, 22.74–83
  closed shops 17.172, 21.7, 21.38, 23.71
  conduct of union affairs 22.35–38
  conspiracy 22.25, 22.23–24, 23.44–45, 23.80
  deductions for union political funds 21.83–84
  definition 22.2–4
  disciplinary action 22.27–34
  executive committees 22.40–54, 22.78, 23.59, 23.80
  election addresses 22.46–47
  election of candidates 22.45

trade unions (*cont.*)
    independent
        scrutineers 22.48–54
    remedies 22.55
    general secretaries 22.31,
        22.42–44, 22.56–57, 22.63,
        23.34, 23.59, 23.80, 23.82
    immunity 23.79–84
    indemnification of unlawful
        conduct 22.63–64
    independent 9.74, 9.77,
        21.46–50
    inducements relating to
        union membership or
        activities 21.46
    inducing or procuring a breach
        of contract 23.20–22
    industrial action, see
        industrial action
    listing 22.5–6
    members, definition
        22.22–24
    membership 17.172, 17.196,
        17.198, 21.1–8, 21.16–17,
        21.30–32, 21.85, 21.88,
        21.93, 21.119, 22.35, 22.40
    non-independent 23.6–12
    non-membership 17.172,
        17.198, 21.32, 21.85,
        21.119–120, 23.5, 23.29,
        23.117–119
    offences 22.62–66
    political fund and political
        objects 22.67, 22.76
    recognition 1.5, 1.19, 17.183,
        21.111, 23.1–15, 23.78,
        23.120–121
        and employer training
            policies 23.13
        prohibition on
            union recognition
            requirements
            23.120–122
        statutory 23.5–12
        and transfer of
            undertakings 9.73–80
        voluntary 23.4
    register of members 23.4
    remedies against
        trustees 22.18–24
    remedies for wrongful
        exclusion or
        expulsion 22.65–66
    right not to be excluded
        from 21.18–19
    right not to be expelled
        from 21.17
    right to a ballot before
        industrial action 21.22–2.5
    right to resign from 21.16
    rights vis-à-vis 21.2–27

rules 21.9–18, 22.25–44,
    22.78–80, 23.81
shop stewards 12.21, 12.23,
    21.51, 21.53, 23.21, 21.23–
    25, 23.79, 23.81
statutory protections 23.28–85
    'in contemplation
        of' 23.37
    'in furtherance of' 23.38
subscriptions 3.74, 6.62, 8.23,
    21.56, 21.79
supply of copies of
    rules 22.39
sweetheart/house
    unions 22.10
trainees 2.99, 11.2, 19.70, 22.40
training 1.52, 2.91, 2.95, 2.99,
    2.101, 7.20–39, 11.34, 11.37,
    11.40–41, 11.80, 11.82, 13.40,
    13.43, 21.67, 21.69–78, 23.13
    agreements 19.70
    study or 1.28, 2.32, 7.26–39,
        13.43, 14.13
    vocational 1.71, 1.100
transfer of assets 9.8–13
transfer of undertakings 1.28,
    1.76–81, 2.143–151, 9.1–85
    and collective
        agreements 9.73
    consultation on
        transfers 9.75–80
    and contracts of
        employment 9.30–35
    and covenants 19.60
    coverage of regulations 9.5–7
    dismissal on transfers 9.54–
        62
    effect of transfer 9.30–53
    election of employee
        representatives 9.81
    employee liability
        information 9.68–69
        remedy for failure to
            notify 9.70–72
    employees who work outside
        the United Kingdom 9.24
    failure to inform or
        consult 9.82–85
    and insolvency rights 9.48–
        51
    mechanics of transfer
        9.25–29
    permitted variations
        in insolvency
        proceedings 9.52–53
    refusal of transfer 9.63–67
    relevant transfers 9.8–9,
        9.14, 9.25–29, 9.52, 9.54,
        9.69–70, 9.75, 9.84–85
    service provision
        change 9.14–22

and statutory rights 9.36
and trade unions
    recognition 9.74
transfer of an undertaking or
    business 9.8–10
transfer of part of a
    business 9.11–13
transfers within public
    administration 9.28
and variation of contracts of
    employment 9.44–47
transferees 1.79, 5.61, 9.2, 9.4,
    9.11, 9.19. 9.84, 13.40, 18.57
transferors 1.79, 5.61, 9.2, 9.4,
    9.8, 9.11–75, 9.84, 13.39,
    18.75
transferred employees 9.21–23,
    9.36–43, 9.56–57, 9.66,
    9.73–76
transferred redundancy 18.21–22
transport 4.1, 4.7, 11.88
transsexuals 1.77, 4.54, 4.122,
    4.163, 20.24; see also gender
    reassignment
trial periods 17.195, 18.25,
    18.27
tribunal hearings 17.76–79,
    17.244–245, 20.43–44,
    20.84–85, 20.102, 20.110–113,
    20.116, 20.125–126
tribunals, employment, see
    employment tribunals
trust 3.2, 3.24, 3.43, 3.48, 3.53,
    3.72, 16.25, 16.30, 17.189
    implied duties/obligations
        of 3.48, 6.33, 6.70, 10.10–
        15, 17.39, 17.44–45
    implied term of 3.2, 3.22,
        3.49, 3.87, 4.35, 17.39,
        17.44–45, 10.10–15,
        17.48
    mutual 3.53, 17.33–34, 17.43,
        17.187, 17.189
    relationship of 10.117, 17.27,
        17.34, 17.48
trustees 3.126, 7.20–22, 15.17,
    17.183, 17.198, 20.114, 22.3,
    22.65–66, 22.85–86, 23.89
    occupational pension
        schemes 7.20–22, 15.18,
        17.81, 17.183, 17.196,
        17.198, 18.61, 20.114
truth 4.241, 4.241, 11.10,
    17.111, 23.36

U
ulterior motives 1.23, 10.62
ultimate sanction 1.107, 17.120,
    21.84, 23.136
ultra vires 3.10, 16.27, 20.42,
    21.21

unauthorised deductions from
  wages 1.25, 18.37
unborn children, duty to 11.114
underpayment 8.47–62
unemployment 1.80, 4.63,
  17.205–213
unenforceable terms 4.212
unexpected loss of a major
  order 9.45, 9.61
unfair dismissal 2.67–75,
  13.9–23, 15.25–29, 16.1–7,
  17.1–243, 20.13–37, 10.101–
  117, 21.86–110
  automatic 2.92, 7.25, 7.115
  claims 12.73–74, 13.10,
    15.29, 16.18, 17.5, 20.4–12,
    20.37
  compensation 17.192–200
  compensatory
    awards 17.201–223
    additional awards 17.239
    interest on 17.242
    order of adjustments
      to 17.237
    recoupment of job-seekers'
      allowance 17.244
    reduction 17.224–237
  and constructive dismissal
    distinguished 17.44,
    17.47–48
  definition of dismissal 17.5
  exclusions from ERA
    protection 17.4
  and fair dismissal
    distinguished 17.73–174
  fairness 17.73–81
  interim relief 17.183
  re-employment after 13.29
  reasons for dismissal 17.83–
    164
  reinstatement and
    re-engagement
    orders 17.184–191
  remedies 17.184–241
  termination of contract
    and dismissal
    distinguished 17.49–72
unfair recruitment 4.245, 21.7,
  21.36
unfair selection for
  redundancy 18.51, 18.55,
  18.61
unfairness 3.34, 9.57, 12.15,
  12.19, 12.35, 16.25, 17.124,
  18.41, 18.47, 18.50, 18.53; see
  also fairness
unfavourable treatment 4.17,
  4.100, 4.134, 4.136, 4.177
unforeseeable
  circumstances 7.95, 11.33
uniforms 2.43, 4.21, 4.30, 4.157

unilateral variation 3.94, 3.100,
  16.32
unions, see trade unions
United States 2.137, 18.74
unlawful acts 1.50, 3.17, 4.107,
  4.198, 4.235–237, 10.33,
  23.23, 23.25, 23.42
unlawful deductions 2.73,
  3.65, 3.69, 3.72, 3.87, 7.89,
  8.3, 8.14–15, 8.18, 8.20–23,
  8.32–33, 8.46, 10.101
unlawful discrimination 1.49,
  2.102, 3.11, 4.22, 4.143, 4.175,
  4.201, 4.223, 4.239
unlawful picketing 23.108,
  23.112
unmeasured work 8.43–44
unofficial industrial
  action 21.93, 21.98, 21.101,
  21.116, 23.83–84

V

vacancies 1.96, 2.135, 2.166,
  4.219, 6.40, 6.45–46, 17.91,
  17.99, 17.140, 17.190
variation 6.133, 7.38, 9.44–47,
  9.52–53, 14.2, 18.6, 18.10,
  18.14, 19.60
  agreed 7.38, 9.58
  of contractual terms 3.98,
    3.100–111
  permitted 9.52–53
  unilateral 3.94, 3.100, 16.32
verbal warnings 12.72, 12.81
vexatious litigation 1.18, 1.22,
  20.45, 20.56, 20.107, 20.132
vibration 11.118, 11.120
vicarious liability 2.56, 2.147,
  2.153, 4.56, 10.84, 10.102–
  108, 10.112, 10.114
victimisation 2.175, 4.12,
  4.37–43, 4.41–53, 4.66, 4.101,
  4.121, 4.125, 4.138, 4.151,
  4.162, 4.182, 4.186, 5.55,
  7.106, 10.37, 10.112
violence 11.120, 12.51, 17.163,
  23.25, 23.44, 23.125, 23.128
volcano effect 10.98–101
voluntary recognition 18.69,
  23.4
voluntary workers 8.38
votes 1.25, 1.69, 1.85, 2.7, 2.10,
  22.40, 22.44, 22.46, 22.49,
  22.52, 22.54, 22.67–68, 22.73,
  22.81, 23.7, 23.49, 23.52–55,
  23.59, 23.61–63, 23.64–66,
  23.140
voting 2.10, 22.24, 22.40,
  22.44–54, 22.67–68, 22.82,
  23.7, 23.51, 23.53, 23.56–65,
  23.145

papers 22.40, 22.46, 22.51–
  51, 22.67–68, 22.82, 23.51,
  23.53, 23.56–57, 23.59,
  23.61, 23.65
qualified majority 1.62, 1.18,
  11.117
vulnerable adults 3.4, 4.251

W

wages 2.152, 2.155, 2.159, 2.161,
  3.9, 3.18, 3.56, 3.60–62, 3.65,
  3.102, 3.123, 8.1–62, 10.17–
  20, 16.31–32; see also pay;
  remuneration; salaries
  complaints to employment
    tribunals 8.31–34
  deductions and payments in
    retail employment
    8.24–30
  definition 8.13–17
  excepted deductions and
    excepted payments 8.23
  gross 8.21, 8.26
  holiday pay 9.48, 20.51
  minimum, see national
    minimum wage
waivers 2.138, 15.14, 17.42,
  17.140, 20.2, 20.45
warning letters 10.60
warnings 11.128–129, 12.1,
  12.19, 12.24, 12.42–43, 12.48,
  12.53, 12.71–83, 17.8, 17.13,
  17.27, 17.37, 17.86, 17.89–90,
  17.94, 17.106, 17.110, 17.114,
  17.120, 18.43, 18.45, 18.48
  clear 12.82, 17.89,
  formal 12.1, 12.19, 12.24,
    12.72, 12.80, 17.37
  informal 12.1, 12.19, 12.24,
    12.72, 17.120
  verbal 12.72, 12.81
  written
    final 12.71, 12.74, 12.77,
      12.79
    first 12.71–72, 17.120
washing facilities 11.18
wasted costs orders 1.22,
  20.113
weekly rest 7.65, 7.94–105
weekly working time,
  maximum 7.58–64
week's pay 4.70, 7.8, 14.2, 14.4–
  14, 15.16–17, 17.295–203,
  18.33–37, 18.65–66
  calculation date 14.13–14
  capping 14.11–12
  quantification 14.6–10
welfare 4.152–164, 10.112–117,
  11.1–151
well-being, economic 1.107,
  3.40, 10.43

whistleblowing 10.37, 10.72–84, 20.51
witnesses 1.25, 1.27, 12.20, 12.22, 20.56, 20.73
women 4.18–24, 4.41–51, 4.124, 4.140, 4.163–188, 4.255–259, 5.1–4, 5.10–35, 6.1–66; see also equal pay; maternity; pregnancy; sex discrimination
pregnant 2.77, 4.18, 4.128–136, 6.9–16, 6.50–55, 7.50
work equipment 2.109, 11.82, 11.133
work experience 2.110–111, 2.130, 8.38, 16.21, 21.2
work-ins 23.115–16
work of equal value, see equal value
work organisation 23.150
work rated as equivalent 5.31–42
work-related stress 6.12, 7.109, 11.105–106
work-to-rule 3.90, 10.49, 12.22, 16.14, 18.11
worker status 8.37
workers 2.19–54, 2.77–95, 2.152–158, 7.54–118, 8.1–62, 10.74–85, 12.23–33, 21.28–60; see also employees
as parties to contracts of employment 2.21
workforce agreements 6.90, 7.58, 7.64, 7.72, 7.75, 7.85, 17.81
working abroad 2.119–123, 2.150, 3.52, 3.112, 10.34
and continuity of employment 13.33–34
working conditions 1.62, 1.77, 6.10, 6.12, 9.65–66, 17.104, 17.135, 17.156
basic 1.96, 2.164, 2.170
working days 7.4, 7.65–66, 7.85, 12.29, 13.23, 13.35, 13.37, 20.14, 21.100, 21.113
working hours 1.96–97, 4.257, 6.3, 6.6–7, 6.12, 6.17, 7.13–14, 7.18, 7.20, 7.28, 21.53–54,

21.66–67, 21.70, 21.72, 21.74, 21.85, 21.89
normal 5.18, 6.17, 7.4, 7.28, 7.63, 7.65, 14.1–3, 17.143
working rule agreement 3.61, 3.110
working time 1.85, 2.47, 2.108–109, 4.257, 5.18, 7.54–57, 7.88–89, 7.91–94, 7.97, 7.99, 7.102, 7.104, 7.106, 17.166, 17.169, 17.183
Directive 1.85
maximum weekly 7.58–61
night work 2.165
Working Time Regulations 1.85, 1.87, 2.24–24, 2.47, 2.61, 2.108–109, 3.52, 3.125, 4.258–259, 6.33, 7.54–109, 17.166, 17.183
annual leave entitlement 7.73–89
daily rest 7.70
enforcement 7.99–109
exclusions 7.90–98
maximum weekly working time 7.58–61
night work 7.63–67
pattern of work 7.68
records 7.69
rest breaks 7.72
weekly rest periods 7.71
young workers 7.62
workless days 7.2–6
workload 11.108, 17.153, 22.32
workmanship 17.230, 18.55
workplaces 11.39–51, 11.34, 11.63, 11.65, 1.80–81, 11.87, 11.132
works rules 3.23, 3.90–94, 12.41–42, 12.51–55, 12.71–83, 17.102, 17.132–139
as contractual terms 3.90–94
written consent 1.25, 8.8–12, 10.91
written contracts 2.2, 2,12, 2.41, 2.47, 2.53, 3.116, 7.75
written particulars of employment 2.70, 2.73, 3.61,

3.67–68, 3.112–122, 13.43, 17.239
written reasons for dismissal 17.174
adequacy of statement 17.175–181
on grounds of maternity or adoption 17.182
written representations 4.129, 20.54, 20.113, 23.13
written statements 2.89, 2.136–139, 2.170, 3.52, 3.63, 3.112–124, 11.36–37, 17.175–181
written warnings
final 12.72–83
first 12.71, 17.120
wrongful acts 2.56, 4.230, 10.32, 10.53, 10.82, 10.103–104, 10.107, 17.228
wrongful dismissal 1.44, 2.75, 3.96, 12.64, 15.15, 16.1–37, 19.56
background 16.1–5
damages for 16.21–29
definition 16.6
injunction and/or declaration 16.30–31
remedies 16.16–37
common law 16.16–32
public law 16.33–37
suing for breach of contract 16.32

Y

young children 4.24
young persons 2.108–111, 4.208, 4.258, 7.26–28, 11.80, 11.116, 12.27
and contracts of employment 2.108–110
time off for study or training 7.29–33
young workers 2.108, 4.258, 7.54, 7.92, 7.98–103
Working Time Regulations 7.61
youth custody 4.245